FUSHIGI YÛGI

STORY & ART BY
YUU WATASE

FUSHIGI YÛGI
Volume 6
VIZBIG Edition

Story and Art by **YUU WATASE**

© 1992 Yuu WATASE/Shogakukan
All rights reserved.
Original Japanese edition "FUSHIGI YÛGI"
published by SHOGAKUKAN Inc.

English Adaptation **Yuji Oniki** & **William Flanagan**
Touch-up Art & Lettering **Bill Spicer**
VIZBIG Edition Touch-up Art & Lettering **Freeman Wong**
VIZBIG Edition Design **Hidemi Sahara**
Shôjo Edition Editor **Frances E. Wall**
VIZBIG Edition Editor **Nancy Thistlethwaite**

VP, Production **Alvin Lu**
VP, Sales & Product Marketing **Gonzalo Ferreyra**
VP, Creative **Linda Espinosa**
Publisher **Hyoe Narita**

Printed in China

Published by VIZ Media, LLC
P.O. Box 77010
San Francisco, CA 94107

10 9 8 7 6 5 4 3 2 1
First printing, June 2010

www.viz.com

FUSHIGI YÛGI

THE MYSTERIOUS PLAY

VOLUME 16
ASSASSIN

VOLUME 17
DEMON

VOLUME 18
BRIDE

STORY & ART BY
YUU WATASE

SHOJO BEAT MANGA · VIZBIG EDITION

CONTENTS

VOLUME 18: BRIDE

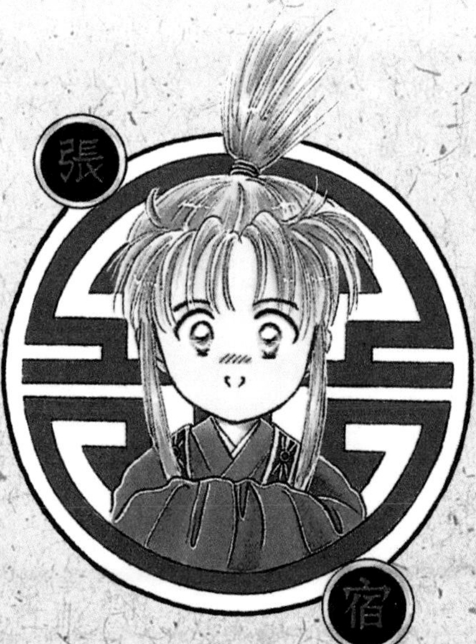

張
宿

CAST OF CHARACTERS

ANCIENT CHINA

SUZAKU CELESTIAL WARRIORS

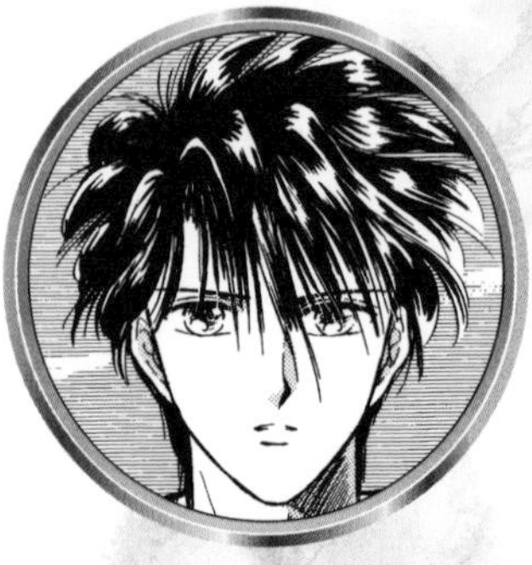

Tamahome

Tamahome is obsessed with money, but he loves Miaka deeply.

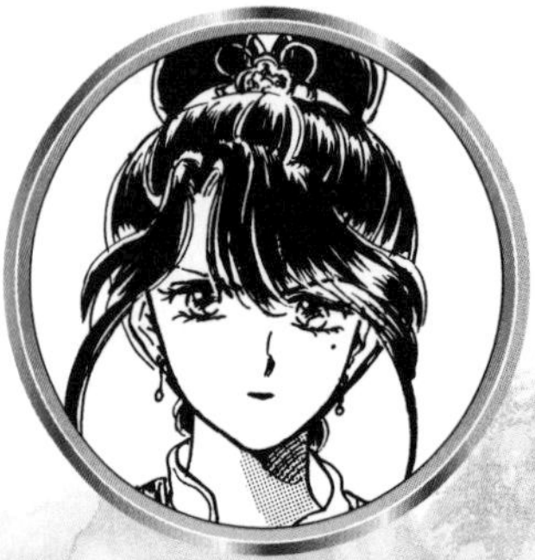

Nuriko

Nuriko is besotted with the emperor and has superhuman strength.

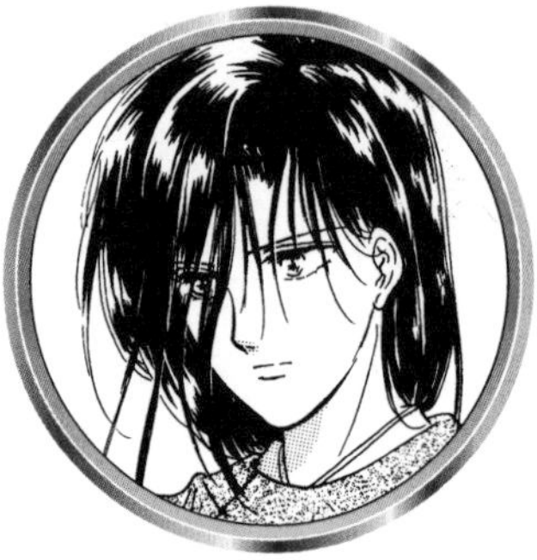

Hotohori

Hotohori is the emperor of Hong-Nan.

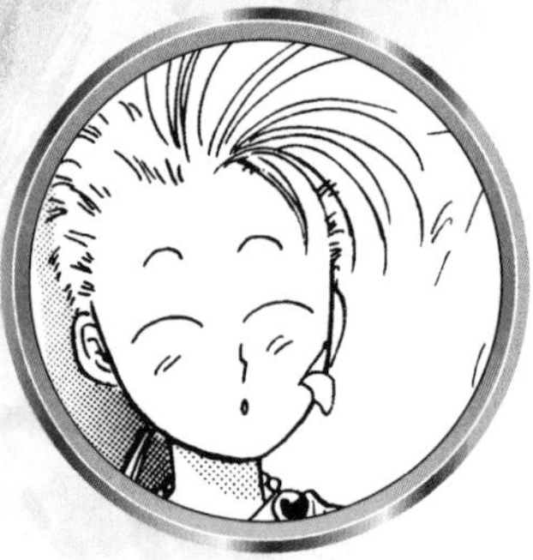

Chichiri

Chichiri can appear and disappear at will.

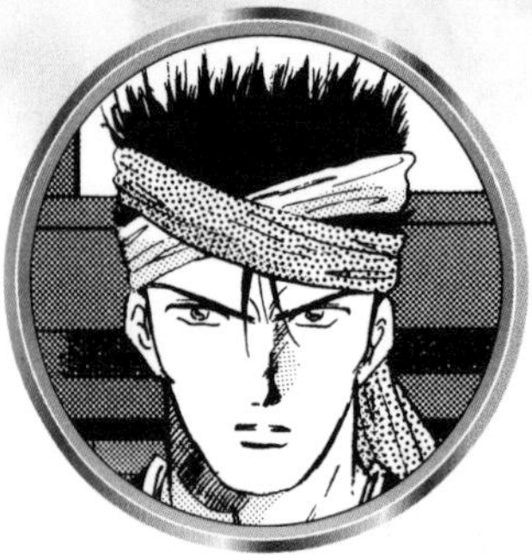

Mitsukake

Mitsukake is a former recluse who practices medicine.

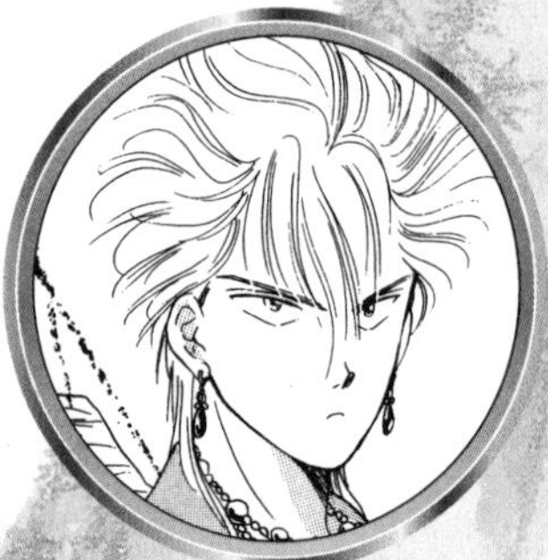

Tasuki

Tasuki is the leader of a gang of mountain bandits.

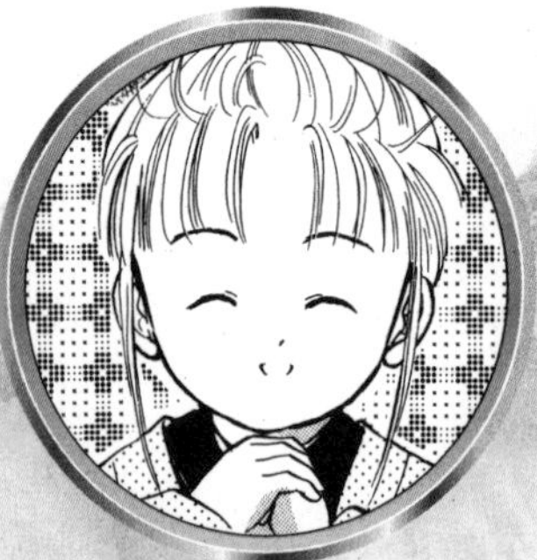

Chiriko

Chiriko is a 13-year-old boy who is studying to become a government minister.

Seiryu Celestial Warriors

Nakago
Nakago is a strong warrior from Qu-Dong who commands the other Seiryu Celestial Warriors.

Suboshi
Suboshi is the twin brother of Amiboshi. He cares for Yui.

Amiboshi
Amiboshi pretended to be a Suzaku Celestial Warrior.

Miboshi
Miboshi is the abbot of an ancient monastery.

Soi
Soi can attack using lightning.

Ashitare
Ashitare is a wolf-like beast.

Tomo
Tomo has the power to enshroud his enemies in illusions.

PRESENT-DAY JAPAN

Yui
Yui is Miaka's best friend. She gets better grades than Miaka.

Miaka
Miaka is a chipper junior high student who is studying for high school entrance exams. She loves food.

Miaka's Mom
She's a divorced single mom who wants Miaka to get into Jonan, a prestigious high school.

Tetsuya
Tetsuya is a friend of Keisuke's who is helping him research *The Universe of the Four Gods*.

Keisuke
Keisuke is Miaka's brother. He knows Miaka is under a lot of pressure from their mother.

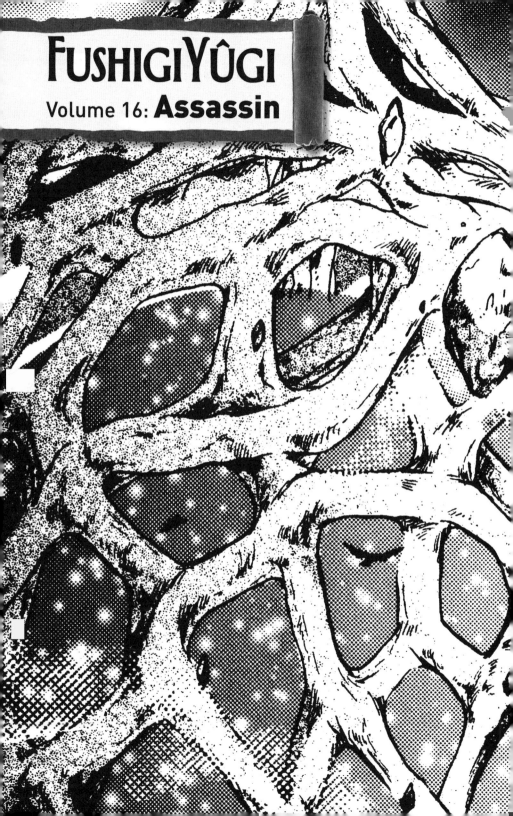

FUSHIGI YÛGI
Volume 16: Assassin

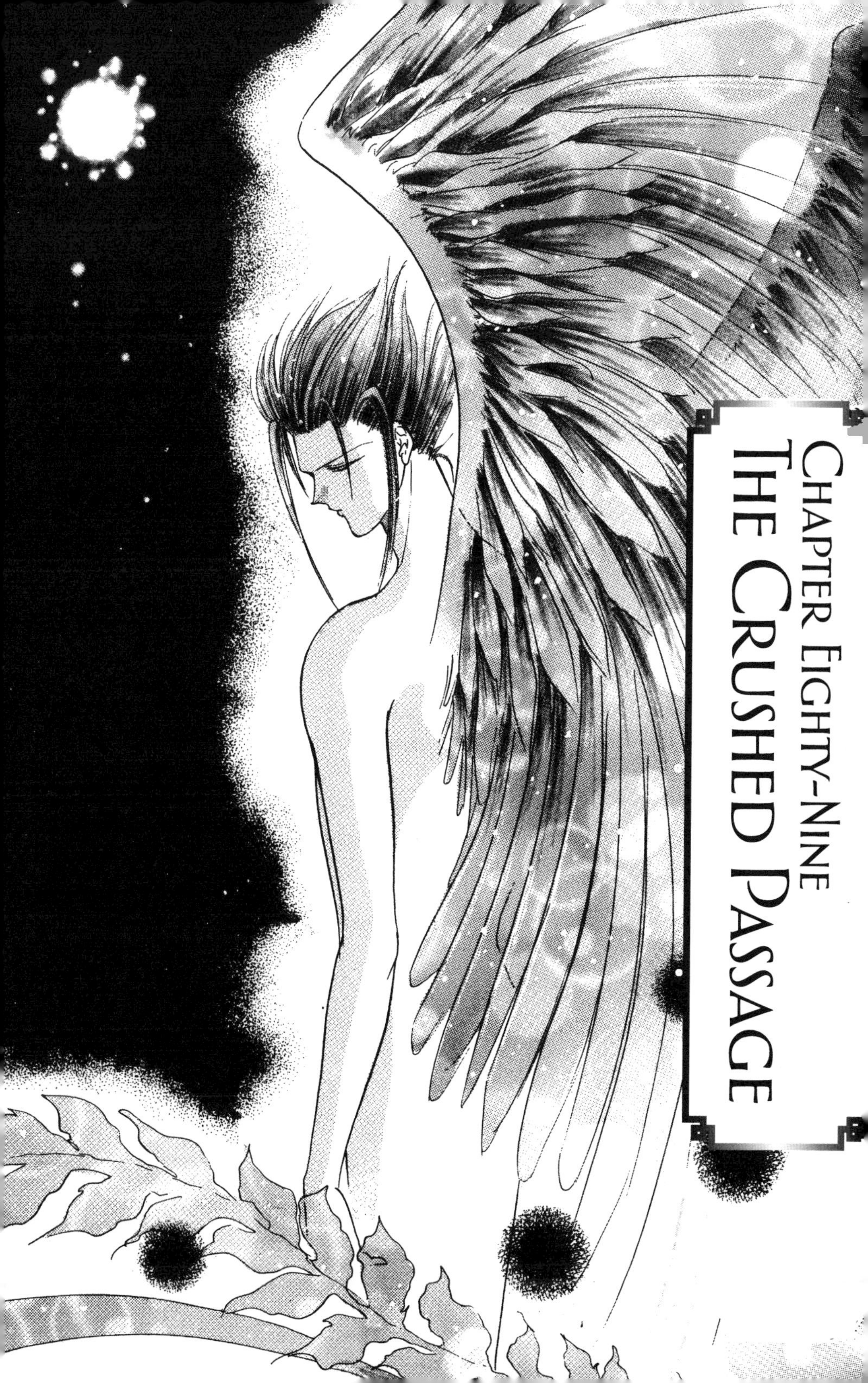
Chapter Eighty-Nine
The Crushed Passage

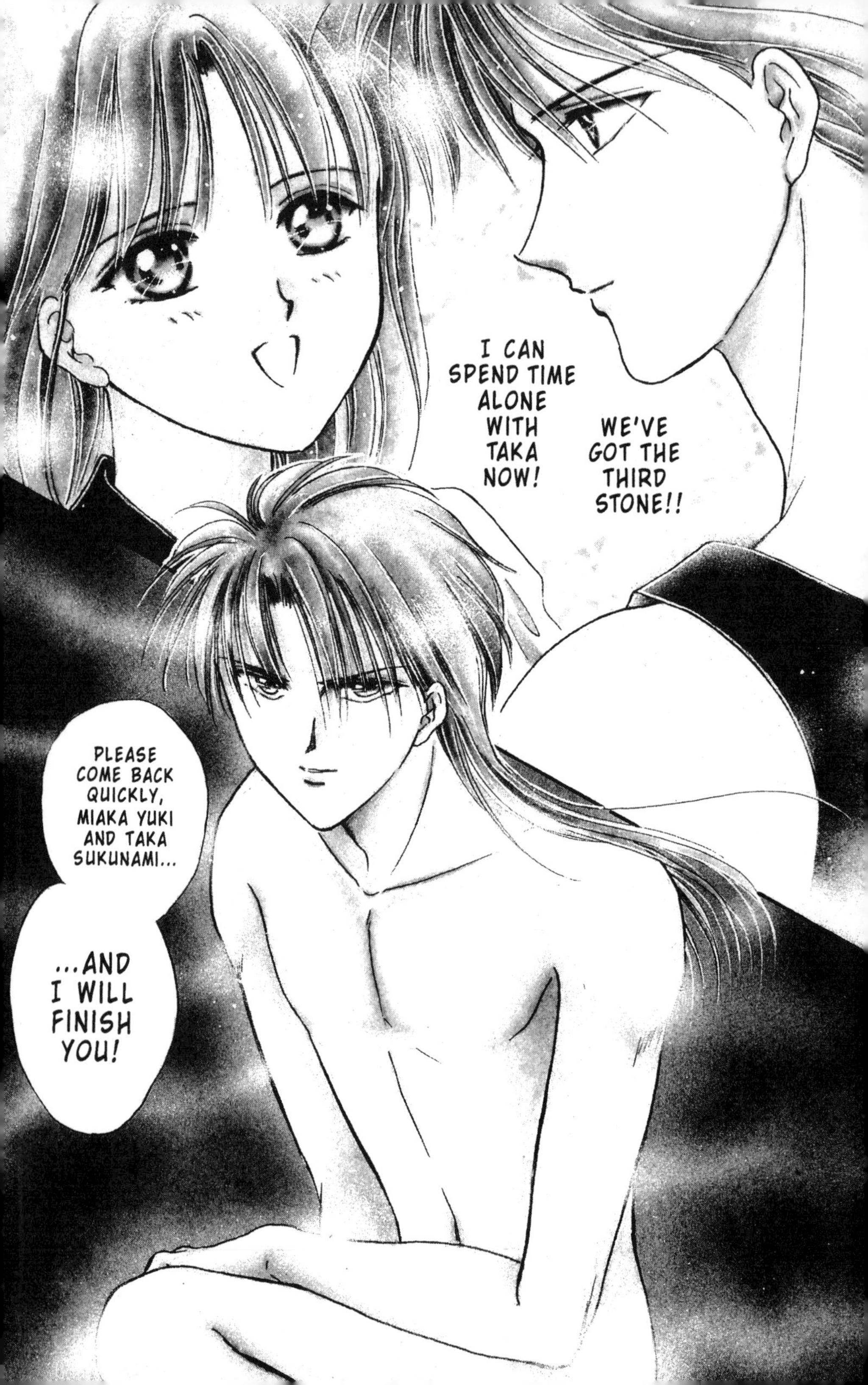
WE'VE GOT THE THIRD STONE!!
I CAN SPEND TIME ALONE WITH TAKA NOW!
PLEASE COME BACK QUICKLY, MIAKA YUKI AND TAKA SUKUNAMI...
...AND I WILL FINISH YOU!

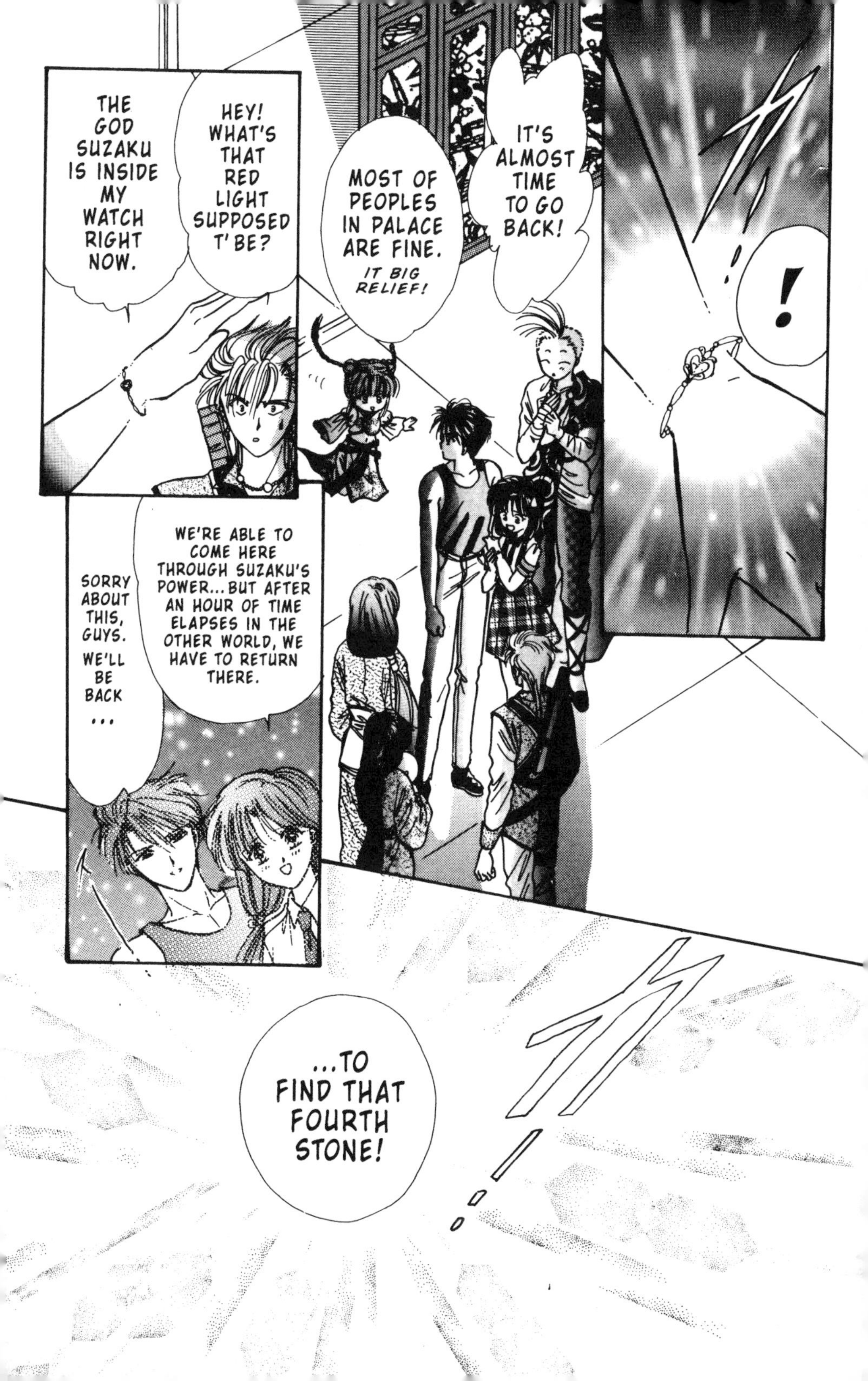
!
IT'S ALMOST TIME TO GO BACK!
MOST OF PEOPLES IN PALACE ARE FINE.
IT BIG RELIEF!
HEY! WHAT'S THAT RED LIGHT SUPPOSED T'BE?
THE GOD SUZAKU IS INSIDE MY WATCH RIGHT NOW.
WE'RE ABLE TO COME HERE THROUGH SUZAKU'S POWER...BUT AFTER AN HOUR OF TIME ELAPSES IN THE OTHER WORLD, WE HAVE TO RETURN THERE.
SORRY ABOUT THIS, GUYS.
WE'LL BE BACK ...
...TO FIND THAT FOURTH STONE!

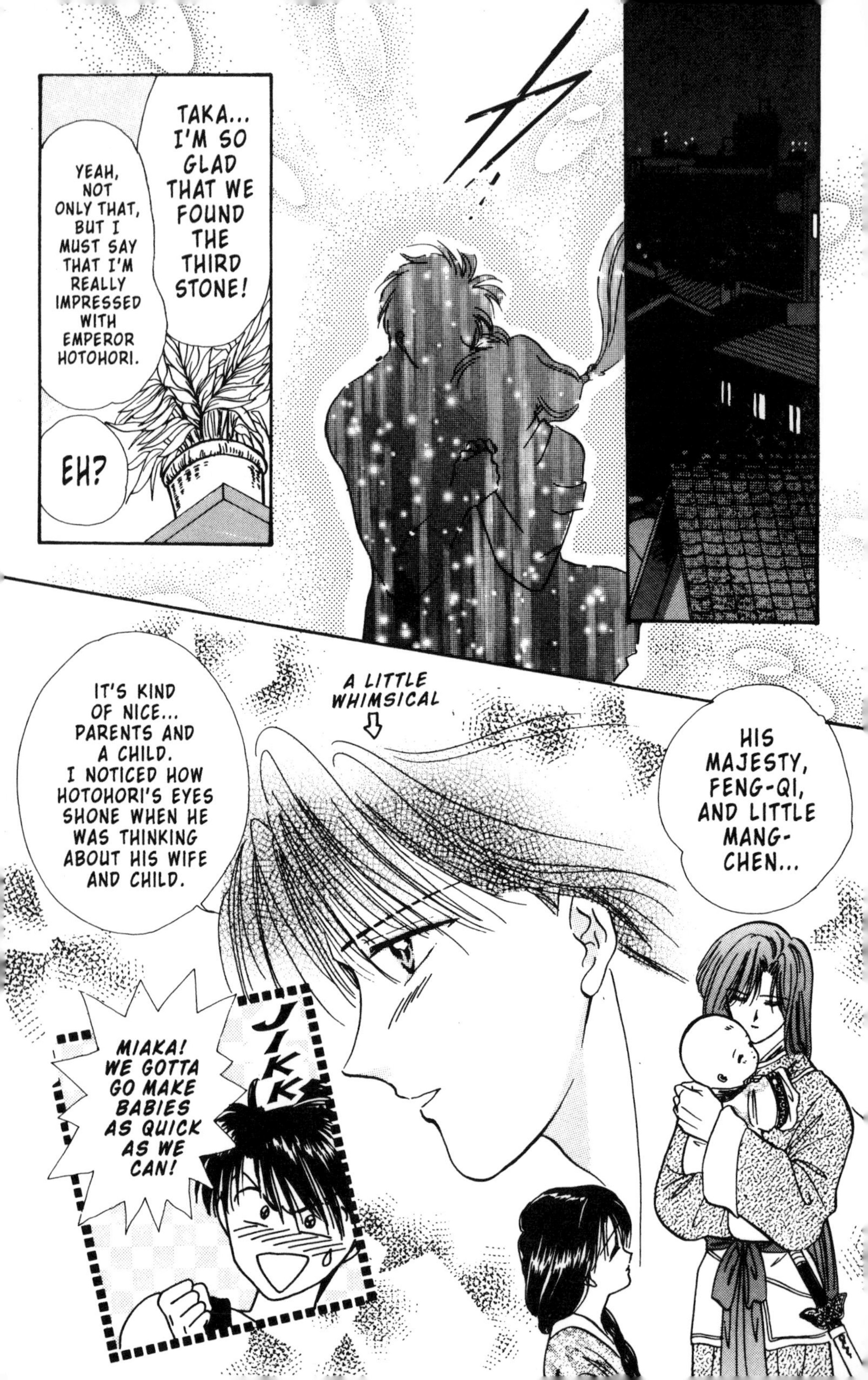
TAKA... I'M SO GLAD THAT WE FOUND THE THIRD STONE!
YEAH, NOT ONLY THAT, BUT I MUST SAY THAT I'M REALLY IMPRESSED WITH EMPEROR HOTOHORI.
EH?
HIS MAJESTY, FENG-QI, AND LITTLE MANG-CHEN...
A LITTLE WHIMSICAL
IT'S KIND OF NICE... PARENTS AND A CHILD. I NOTICED HOW HOTOHORI'S EYES SHONE WHEN HE WAS THINKING ABOUT HIS WIFE AND CHILD.
JIKK
MIAKA! WE GOTTA GO MAKE BABIES AS QUICK AS WE CAN!

I was so surprised that we're already on volume 16! Yay! That's normal for shonen manga, but for shojo manga, it's like...whoa! Yay! *Ha!* What am I talking about?! Hello everybody, this is Watase. In the background, the soundtrack for Miaka and the Seven Warriors is playing. But this isn't a CD. It's a tape where we've put a whole bunch of music from a variety of sources recorded off of CD. I'm lonely for my TV! By the way, have you picked up all nine of the "Character Vocal Collection" CDs yet? Watase loves them all!! The lyrics are great...the music is wonderful! Everything about them! ☺

Now, to continue the story about the Taiwan signing... It ended without incident. (Oh, yeah! I received quite a lot of hand-arranged bouquets!) There were some other things that made for fond memories too.
I was invited to the home of Mr. Xie, a movie director. The interior design of his home was amazing! It was such a clever use of limited space! He lives in an old, traditional Chinese home, and I learned so much! I also got some tea out of the deal! ☺ The president of Daran Publishing was kind enough to give me a seal that he received from Mr. Xie. I was shocked! It's a seal that was made by an artisan named Yù from the Ch'ing (Manchu) dynasty, and usually only serious collectors of cultural objects own stuff like it! It's really valuable! ☺ So right now I'm keeping it very safe! Oh, also Daran Publishing took me to their offices to see how they do things. Everybody was smiling, and I really felt at home!

I got several soundtracks from the animation company! ♪ I also received six famous Taiwanese CDs!

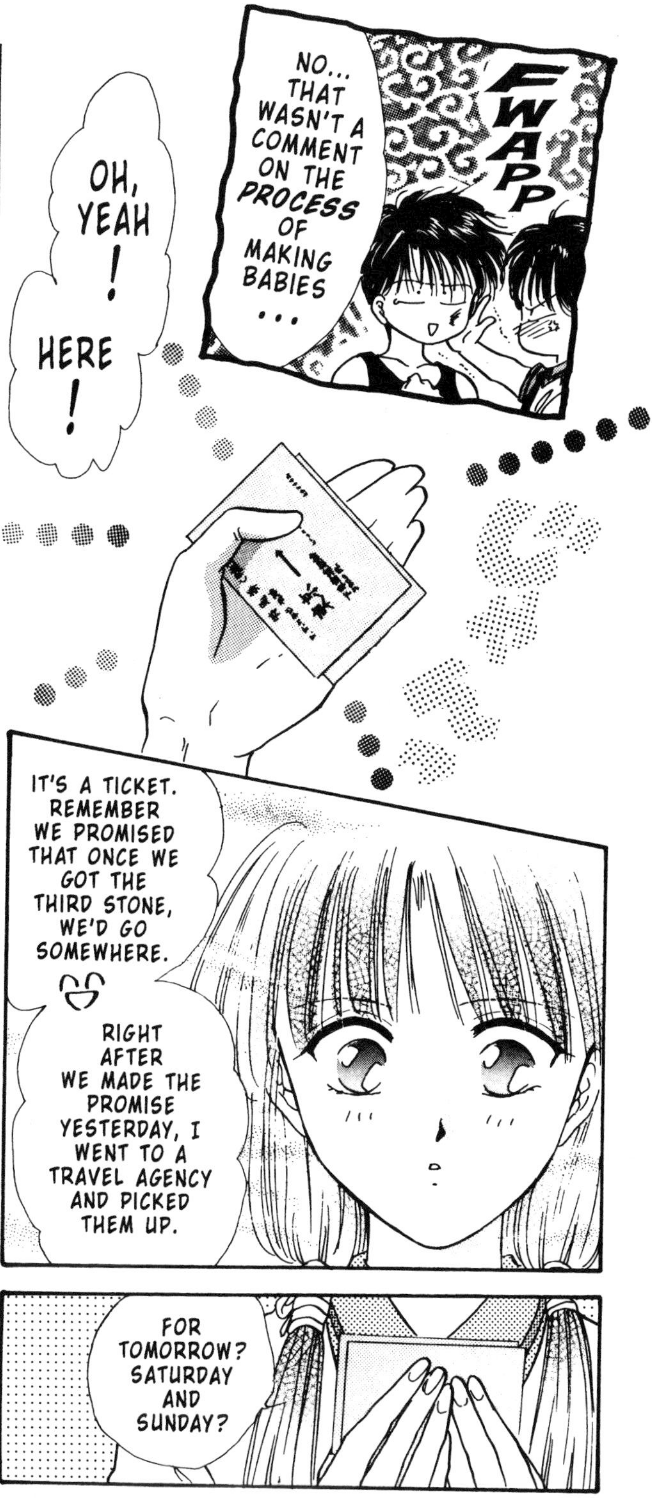
FWAPP
NO... THAT WASN'T A COMMENT ON THE PROCESS OF MAKING BABIES...
OH, YEAH! HERE!
IT'S A TICKET. REMEMBER WE PROMISED THAT ONCE WE GOT THE THIRD STONE, WE'D GO SOMEWHERE.
RIGHT AFTER WE MADE THE PROMISE YESTERDAY, I WENT TO A TRAVEL AGENCY AND PICKED THEM UP.
FOR TOMORROW? SATURDAY AND SUNDAY?

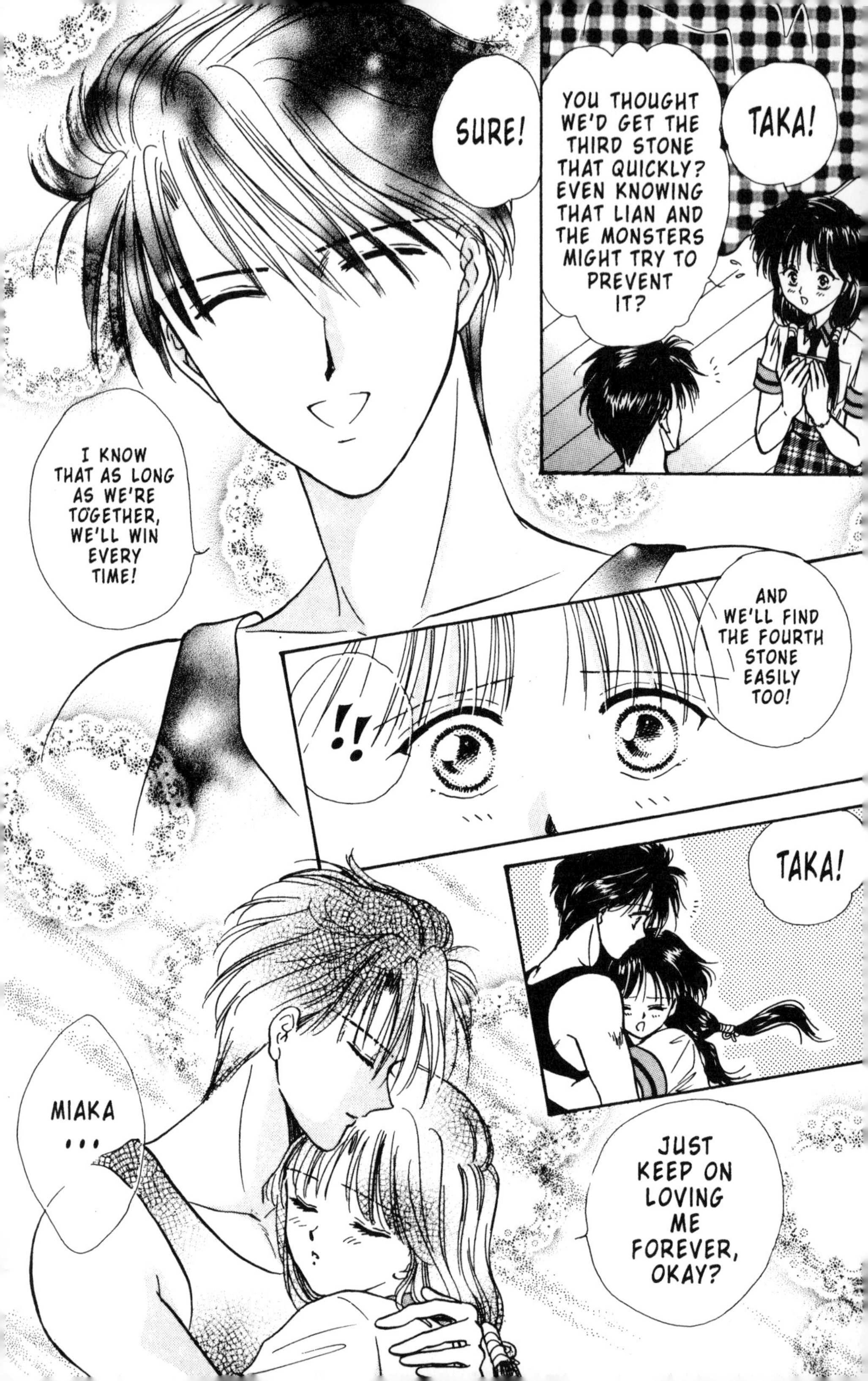
TAKA!
YOU THOUGHT WE'D GET THE THIRD STONE THAT QUICKLY? EVEN KNOWING THAT LIAN AND THE MONSTERS MIGHT TRY TO PREVENT IT?
SURE!
I KNOW THAT AS LONG AS WE'RE TOGETHER, WE'LL WIN EVERY TIME!
AND WE'LL FIND THE FOURTH STONE EASILY TOO!
!!
TAKA!
JUST KEEP ON LOVING ME FOREVER, OKAY?
MIAKA ...

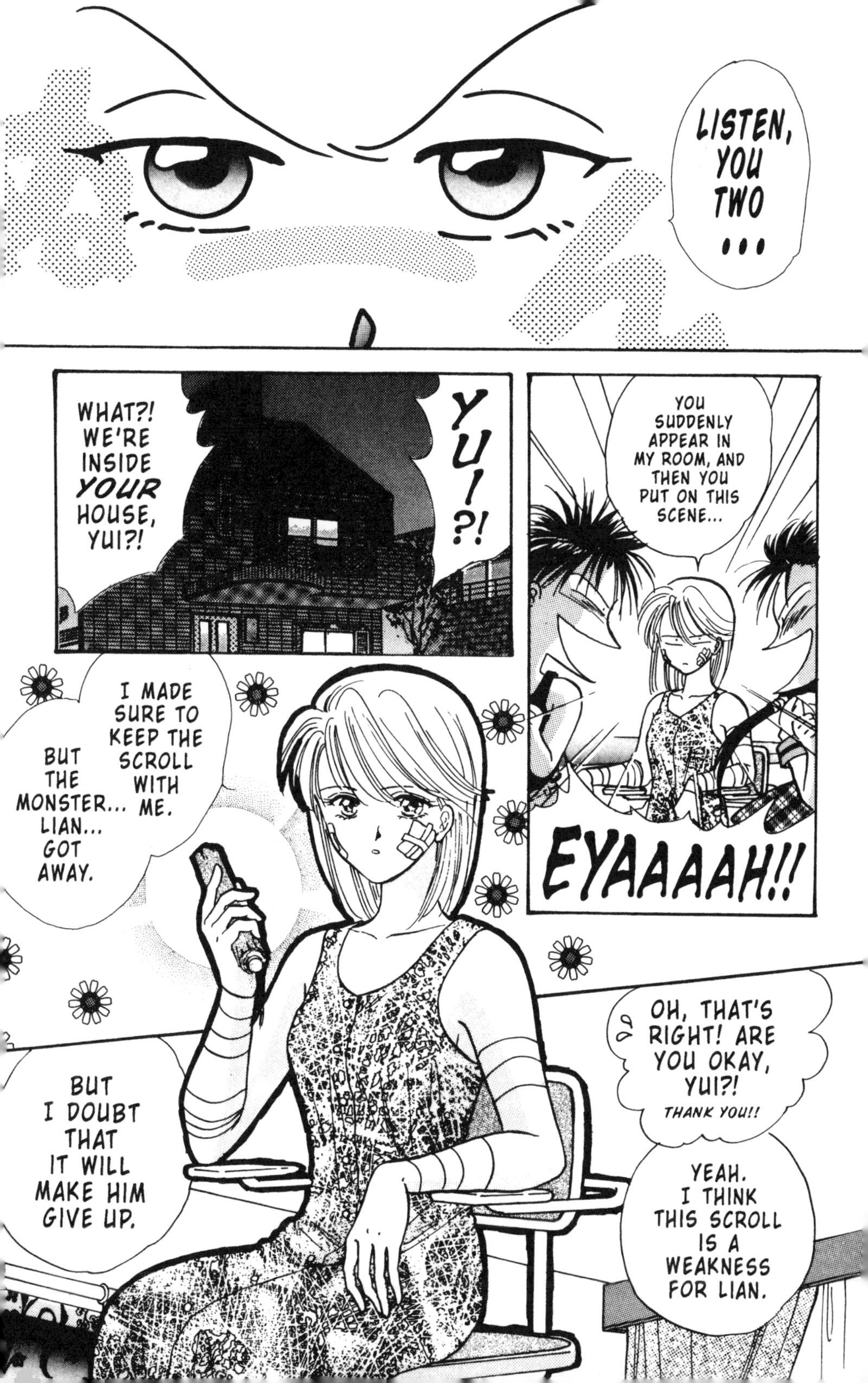
LISTEN, YOU TWO...
YOU SUDDENLY APPEAR IN MY ROOM, AND THEN YOU PUT ON THIS SCENE...
EYAAAAH!!
YUI?!
WHAT?! WE'RE INSIDE YOUR HOUSE, YUI?!
OH, THAT'S RIGHT! ARE YOU OKAY, YUI?!
THANK YOU!!
YEAH. I THINK THIS SCROLL IS A WEAKNESS FOR LIAN.
I MADE SURE TO KEEP THE SCROLL WITH ME.
BUT THE MONSTER... LIAN... GOT AWAY.
BUT I DOUBT THAT IT WILL MAKE HIM GIVE UP.

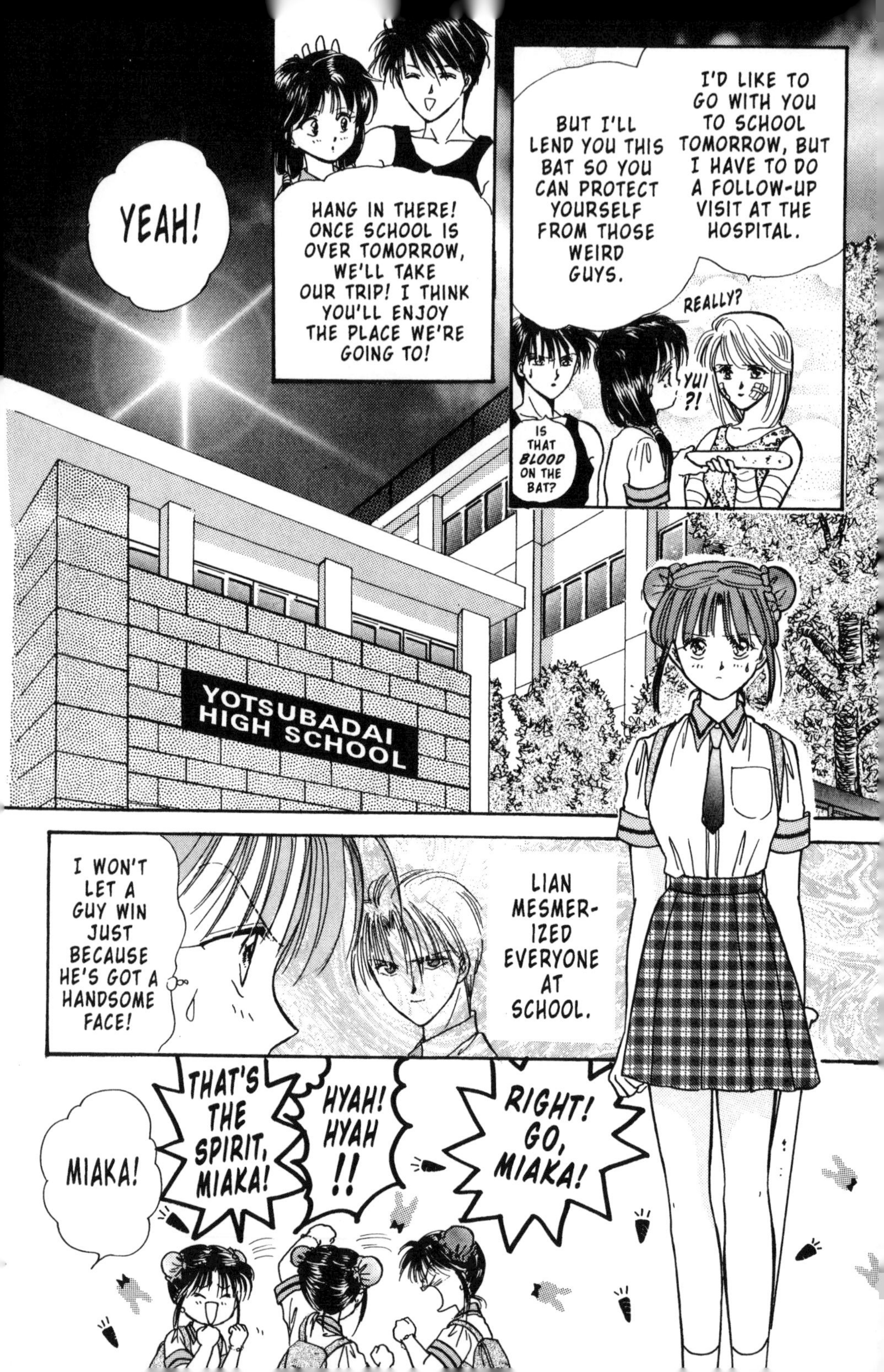
I'D LIKE TO GO WITH YOU TO SCHOOL TOMORROW, BUT I HAVE TO DO A FOLLOW-UP VISIT AT THE HOSPITAL.
BUT I'LL LEND YOU THIS BAT SO YOU CAN PROTECT YOURSELF FROM THOSE WEIRD GUYS.
REALLY?
YUI ?!
IS THAT *BLOOD* ON THE BAT?
HANG IN THERE! ONCE SCHOOL IS OVER TOMORROW, WE'LL TAKE OUR TRIP! I THINK YOU'LL ENJOY THE PLACE WE'RE GOING TO!
YEAH!
YOTSUBADAI HIGH SCHOOL
LIAN MESMER-IZED EVERYONE AT SCHOOL.
I WON'T LET A GUY WIN JUST BECAUSE HE'S GOT A HANDSOME FACE!
RIGHT! GO, MIAKA!
HYAH! HYAH !!
THAT'S THE SPIRIT, MIAKA!
MIAKA!

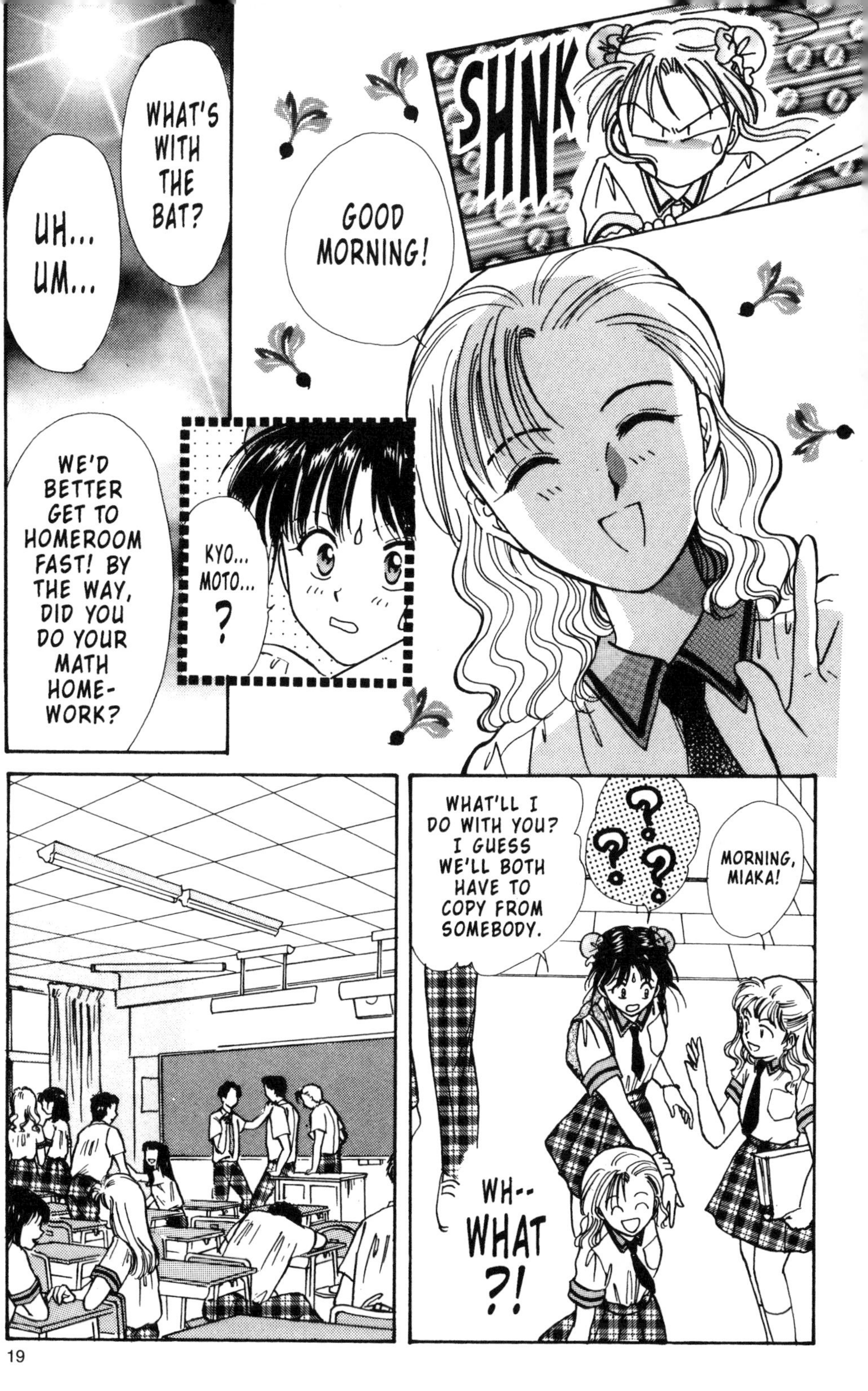
SHNK
GOOD MORNING!
KYO... MOTO... ?
WHAT'S WITH THE BAT?
UH... UM...
WE'D BETTER GET TO HOMEROOM FAST! BY THE WAY, DID YOU DO YOUR MATH HOME-WORK?
MORNING, MIAKA!
WHAT'LL I DO WITH YOU? I GUESS WE'LL BOTH HAVE TO COPY FROM SOMEBODY.
WH-- WHAT ?!

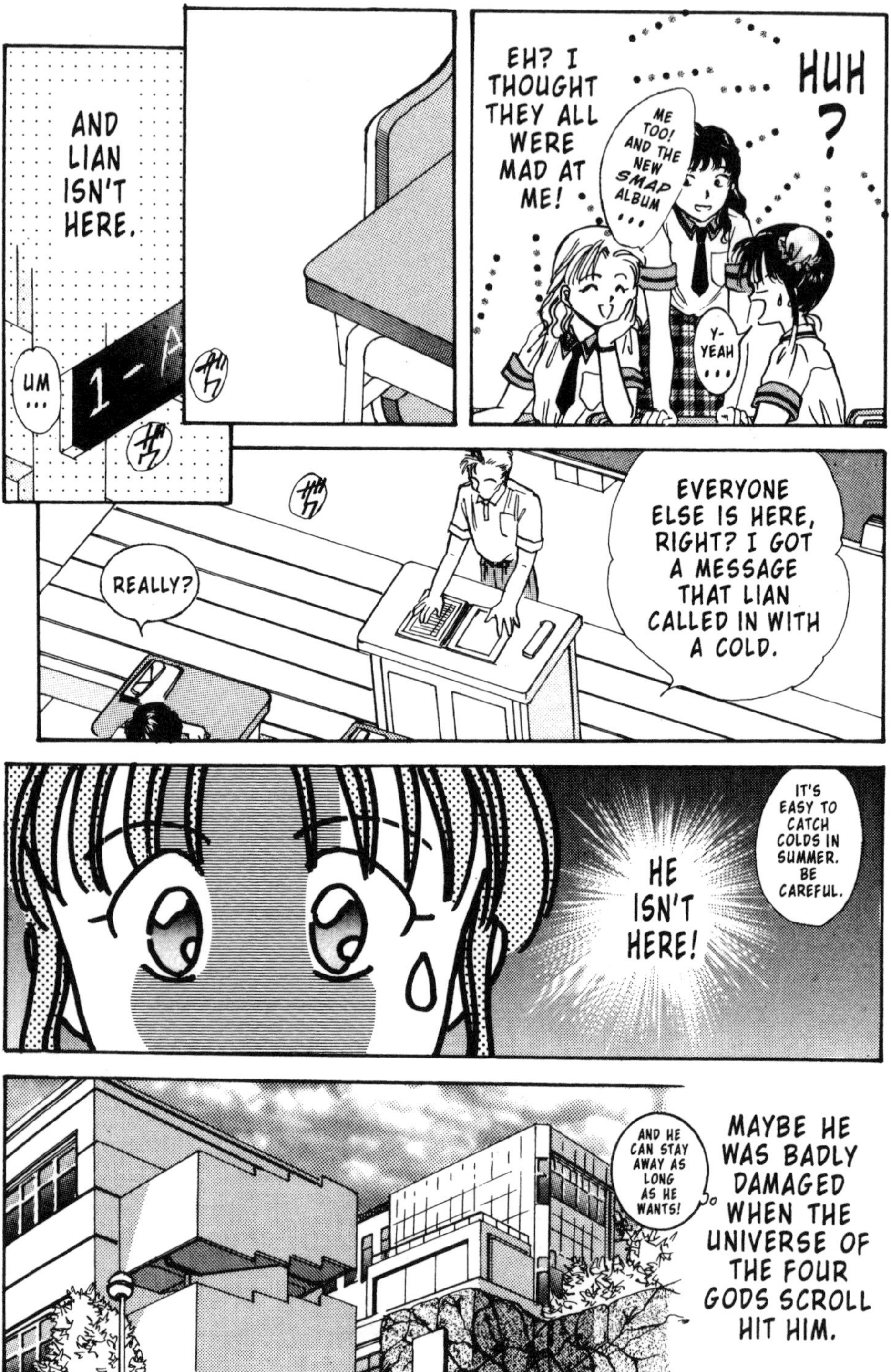
HUH ?
EH? I THOUGHT THEY ALL WERE MAD AT ME!
ME TOO! AND THE NEW SMAP ALBUM...
Y-YEAH...
AND LIAN ISN'T HERE.
UM...
EVERYONE ELSE IS HERE, RIGHT? I GOT A MESSAGE THAT LIAN CALLED IN WITH A COLD.
REALLY?
IT'S EASY TO CATCH COLDS IN SUMMER. BE CAREFUL.
HE ISN'T HERE!
MAYBE HE WAS BADLY DAMAGED WHEN THE UNIVERSE OF THE FOUR GODS SCROLL HIT HIM.
AND HE CAN STAY AWAY AS LONG AS HE WANTS!

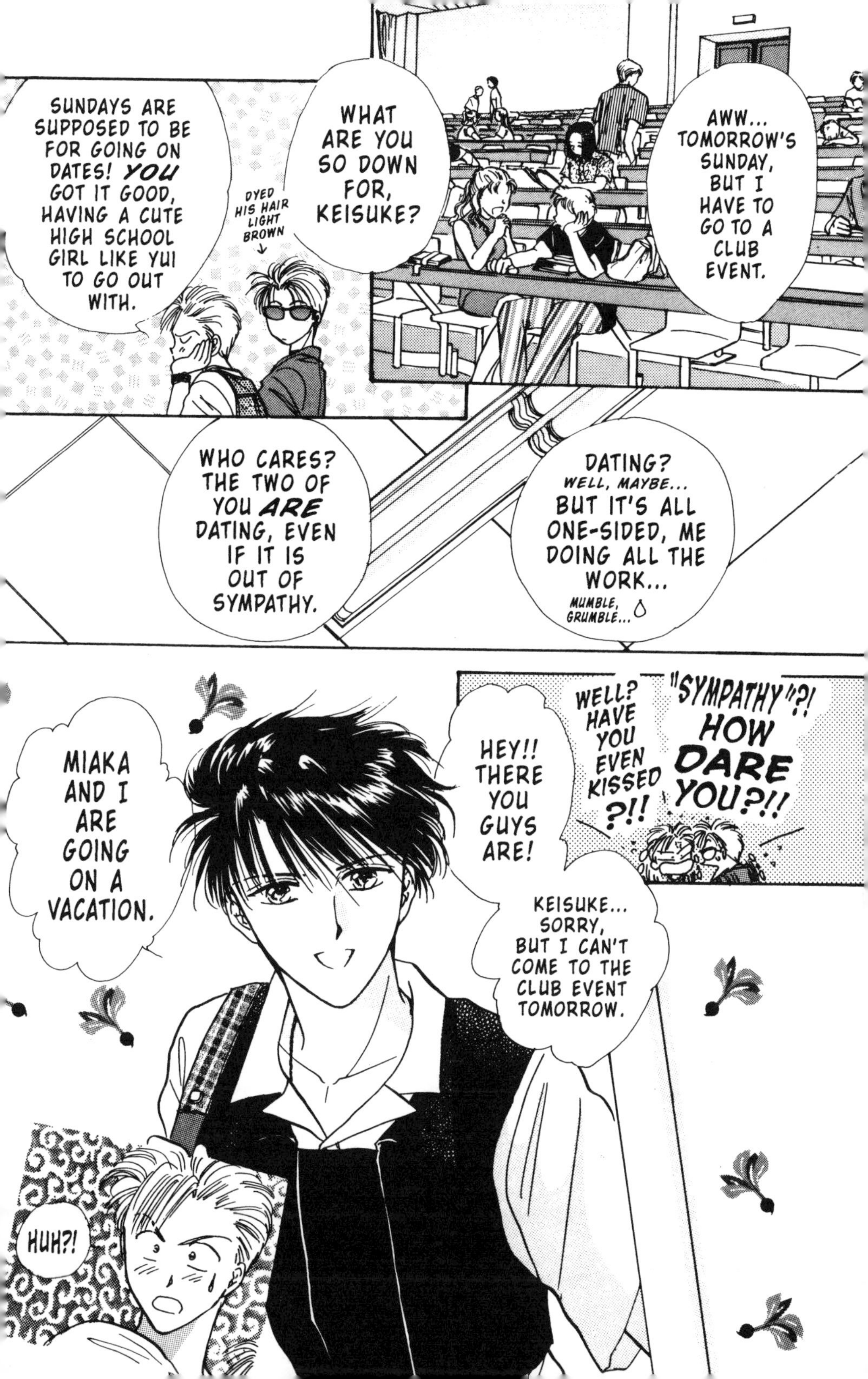
AWW... TOMORROW'S SUNDAY, BUT I HAVE TO GO TO A CLUB EVENT.
WHAT ARE YOU SO DOWN FOR, KEISUKE?
SUNDAYS ARE SUPPOSED TO BE FOR GOING ON DATES! ***YOU*** GOT IT GOOD, HAVING A CUTE HIGH SCHOOL GIRL LIKE YUI TO GO OUT WITH.
DYED HIS HAIR LIGHT BROWN
DATING? *WELL, MAYBE...* BUT IT'S ALL ONE-SIDED, ME DOING ALL THE WORK...
MUMBLE, GRUMBLE...
WHO CARES? THE TWO OF YOU ***ARE*** DATING, EVEN IF IT IS OUT OF SYMPATHY.
"SYMPATHY"?! HOW DARE YOU?!!
WELL? HAVE YOU EVEN KISSED?!!
HEY!! THERE YOU GUYS ARE!
KEISUKE... SORRY, BUT I CAN'T COME TO THE CLUB EVENT TOMORROW.
MIAKA AND I ARE GOING ON A VACATION.
HUH?!

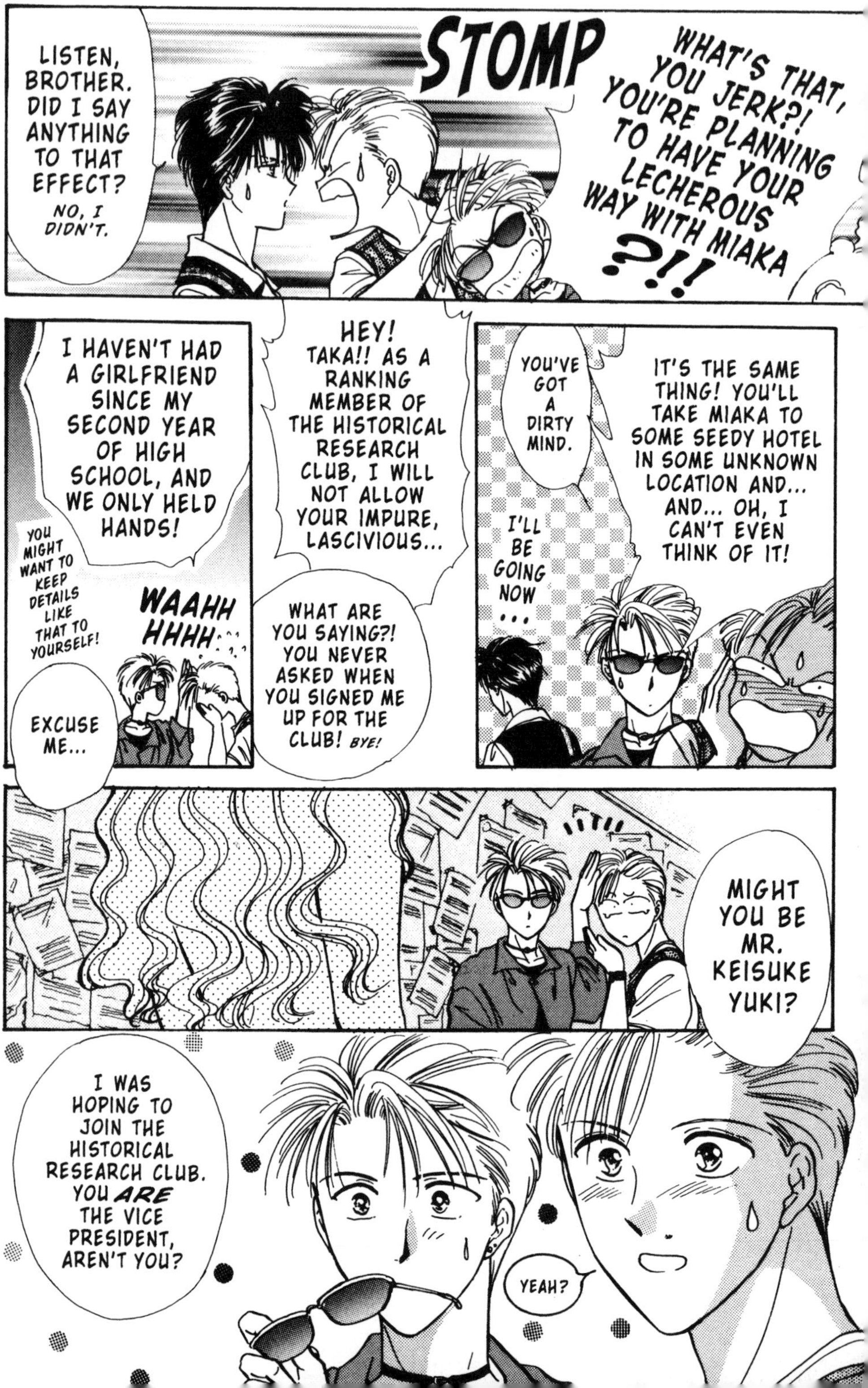
WHAT'S THAT, YOU JERK?! YOU'RE PLANNING TO HAVE YOUR LECHEROUS WAY WITH MIAKA ?!!
STOMP
LISTEN, BROTHER. DID I SAY ANYTHING TO THAT EFFECT?
NO, I DIDN'T.
IT'S THE SAME THING! YOU'LL TAKE MIAKA TO SOME SEEDY HOTEL IN SOME UNKNOWN LOCATION AND... AND... OH, I CAN'T EVEN THINK OF IT!
YOU'VE GOT A DIRTY MIND.
I'LL BE GOING NOW...
HEY! TAKA!! AS A RANKING MEMBER OF THE HISTORICAL RESEARCH CLUB, I WILL NOT ALLOW YOUR IMPURE, LASCIVIOUS...
WHAT ARE YOU SAYING?! YOU NEVER ASKED WHEN YOU SIGNED ME UP FOR THE CLUB! BYE!
I HAVEN'T HAD A GIRLFRIEND SINCE MY SECOND YEAR OF HIGH SCHOOL, AND WE ONLY HELD HANDS!
YOU MIGHT WANT TO KEEP DETAILS LIKE THAT TO YOURSELF!
WAAHH HHHH
EXCUSE ME...
MIGHT YOU BE MR. KEISUKE YUKI?
YEAH?
I WAS HOPING TO JOIN THE HISTORICAL RESEARCH CLUB. YOU ARE THE VICE PRESIDENT, AREN'T YOU?

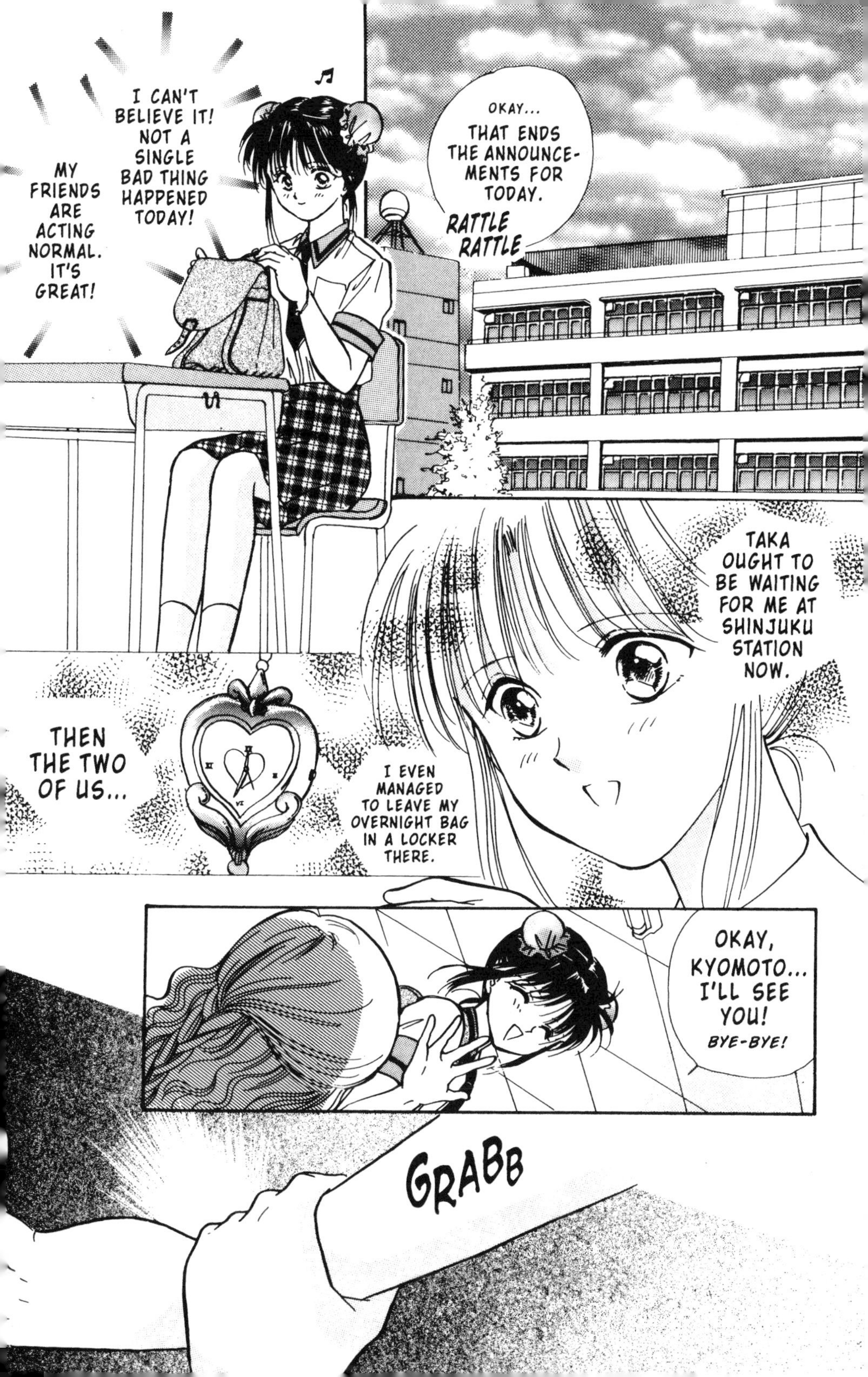
OKAY... THAT ENDS THE ANNOUNCEMENTS FOR TODAY.
RATTLE RATTLE
I CAN'T BELIEVE IT! NOT A SINGLE BAD THING HAPPENED TODAY!
MY FRIENDS ARE ACTING NORMAL. IT'S GREAT!
TAKA OUGHT TO BE WAITING FOR ME AT SHINJUKU STATION NOW.
I EVEN MANAGED TO LEAVE MY OVERNIGHT BAG IN A LOCKER THERE.
THEN THE TWO OF US...
OKAY, KYOMOTO... I'LL SEE YOU!
BYE-BYE!
GRABB

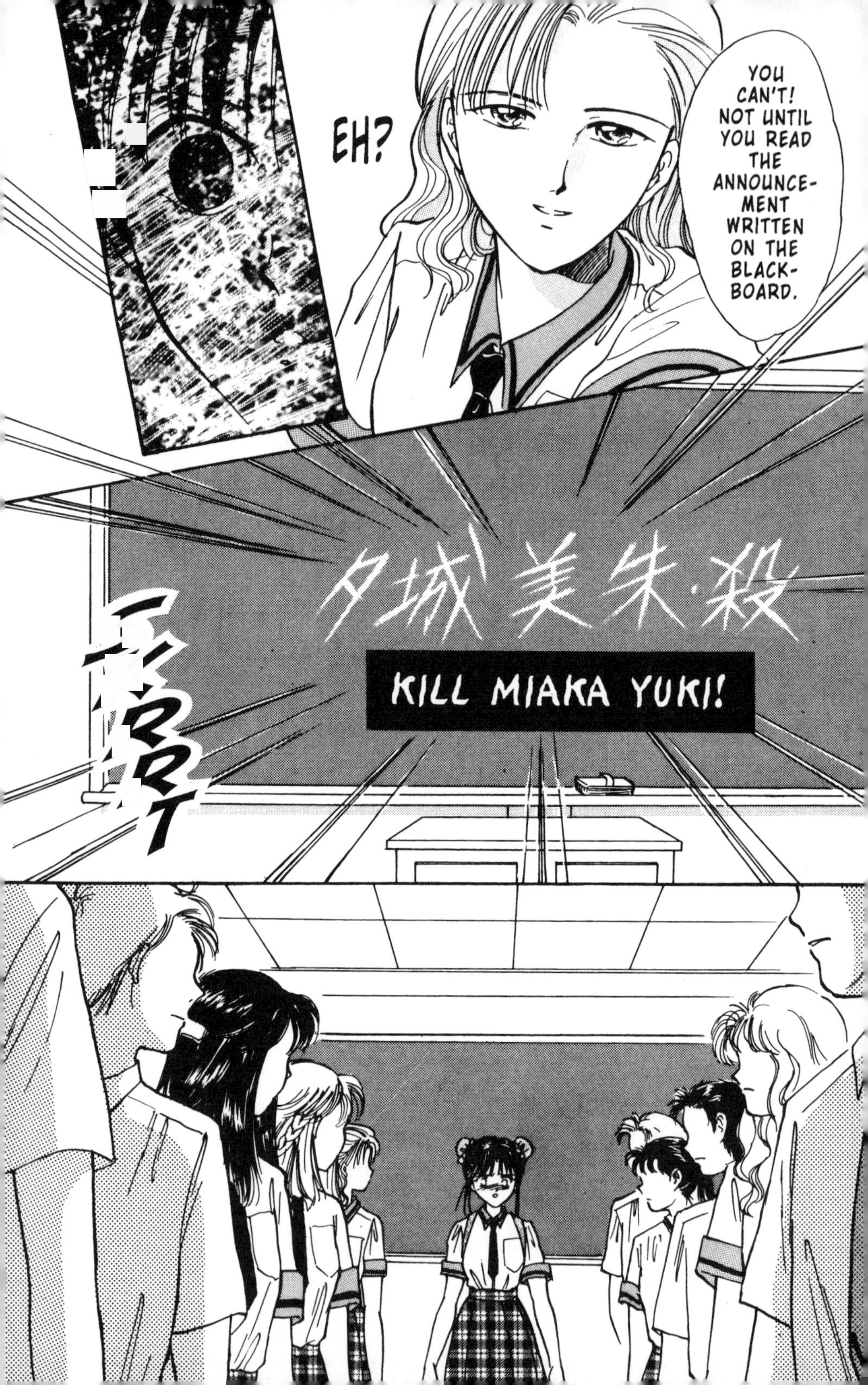

YOU CAN'T! NOT UNTIL YOU READ THE ANNOUNCEMENT WRITTEN ON THE BLACKBOARD.
EH?
夕城美朱·殺
KILL MIAKA YUKI!

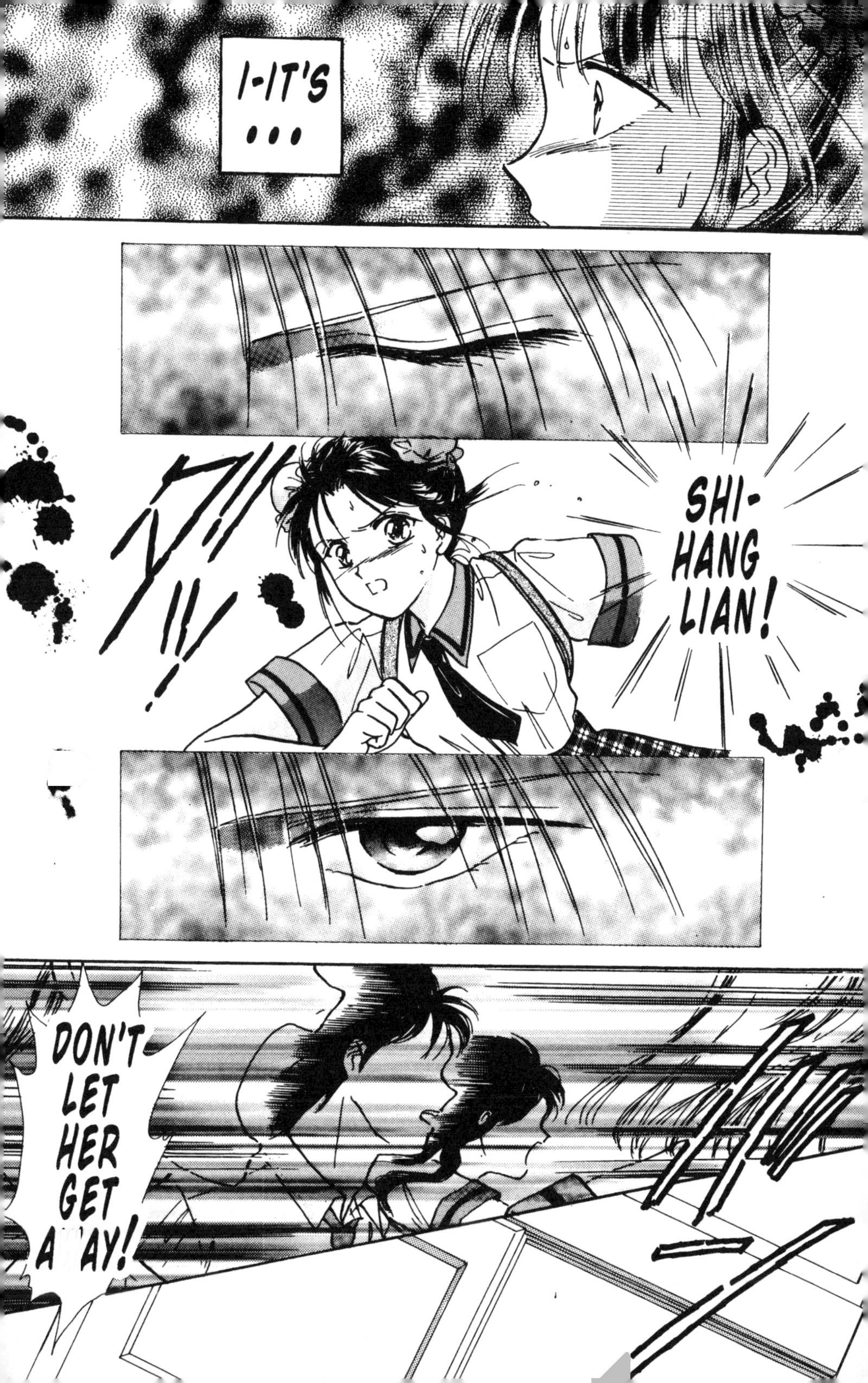
I-IT'S...
SHI-HANG LIAN!
DON'T LET HER GET A AY!

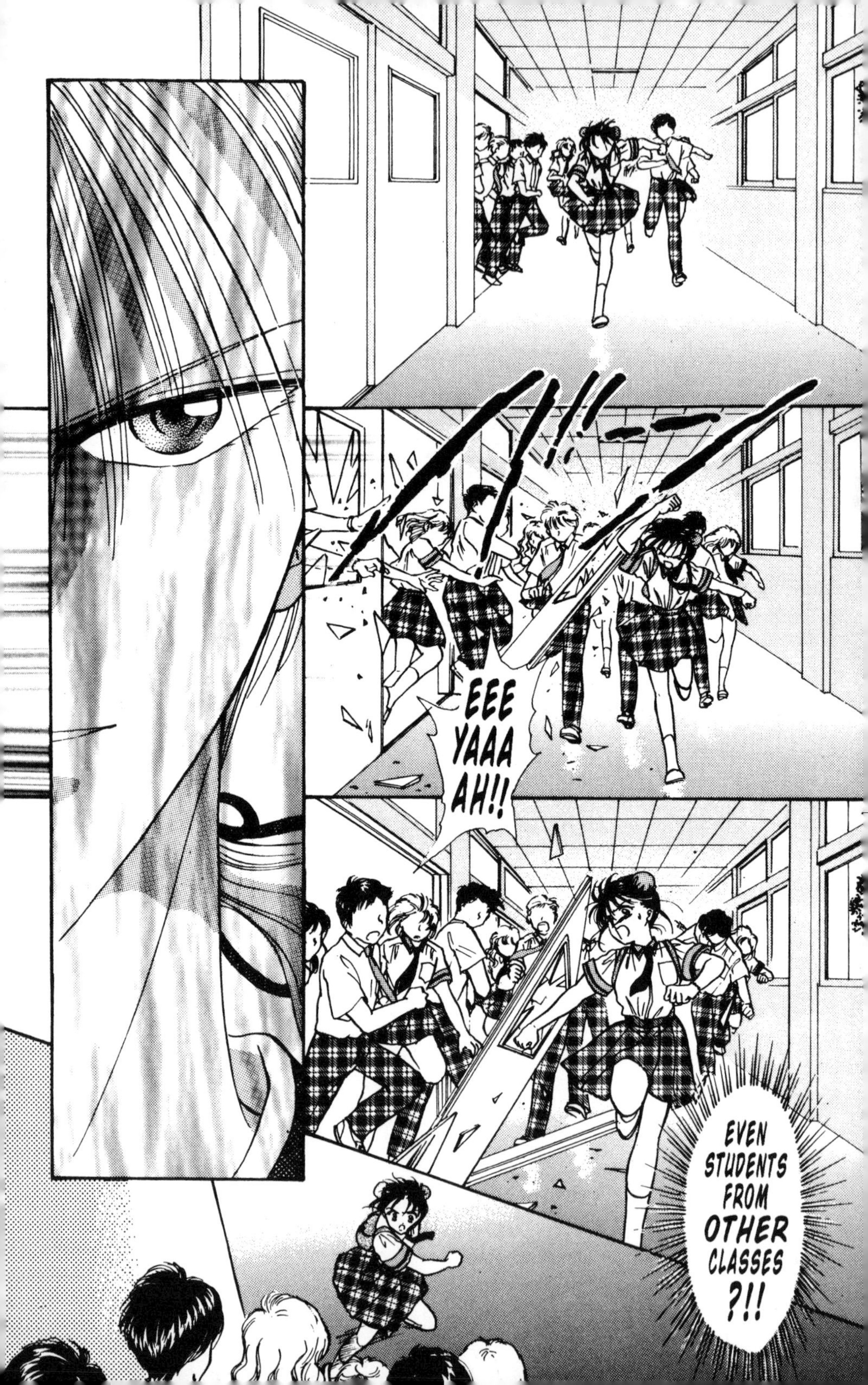
EEE YAAA AH!!
EVEN STUDENTS FROM OTHER CLASSES ?!!

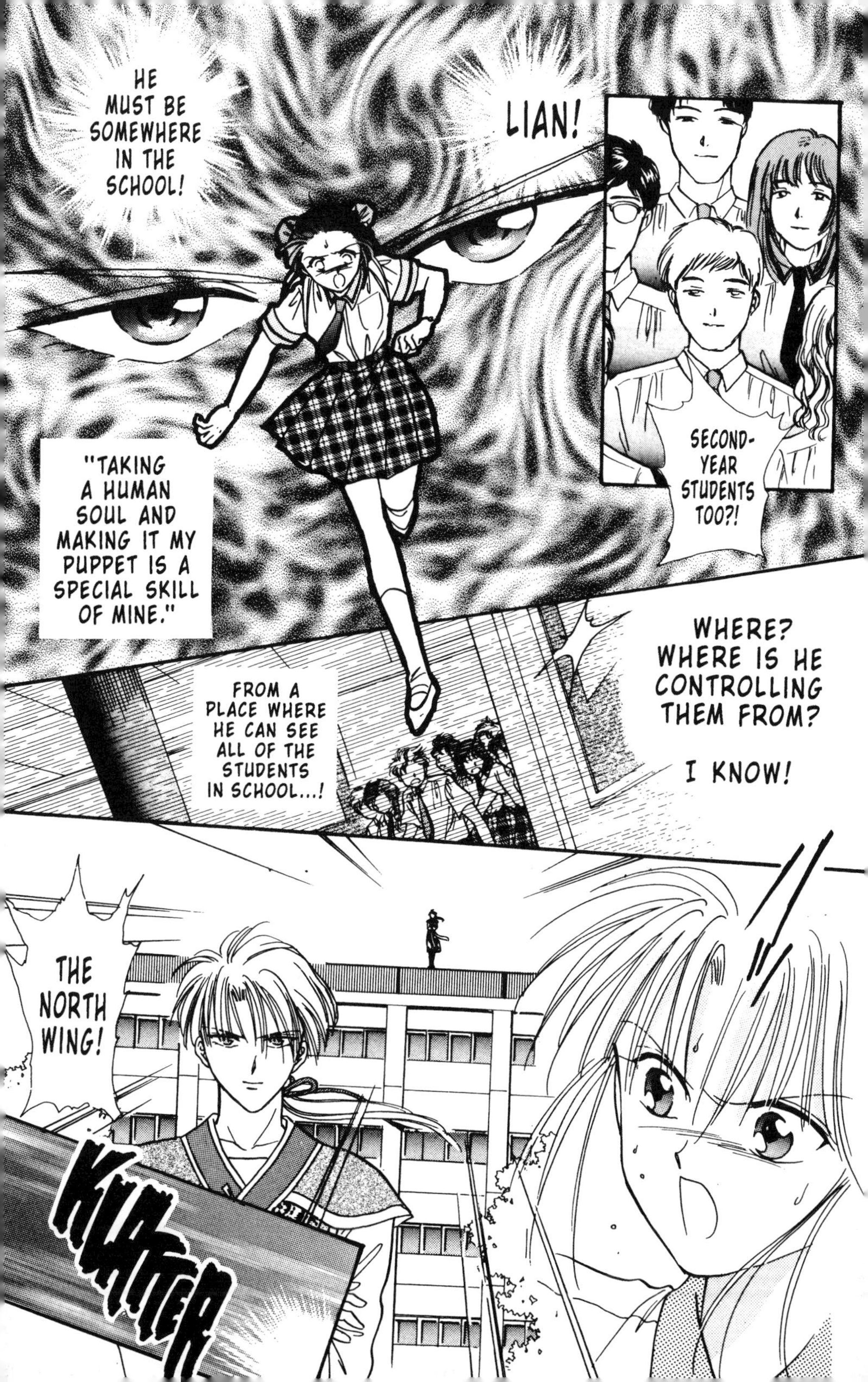
SECOND-YEAR STUDENTS TOO?!
LIAN!
HE MUST BE SOMEWHERE IN THE SCHOOL!
"TAKING A HUMAN SOUL AND MAKING IT MY PUPPET IS A SPECIAL SKILL OF MINE."
WHERE? WHERE IS HE CONTROLLING THEM FROM?
I KNOW!
FROM A PLACE WHERE HE CAN SEE ALL OF THE STUDENTS IN SCHOOL...!
THE NORTH WING!
KLATTER

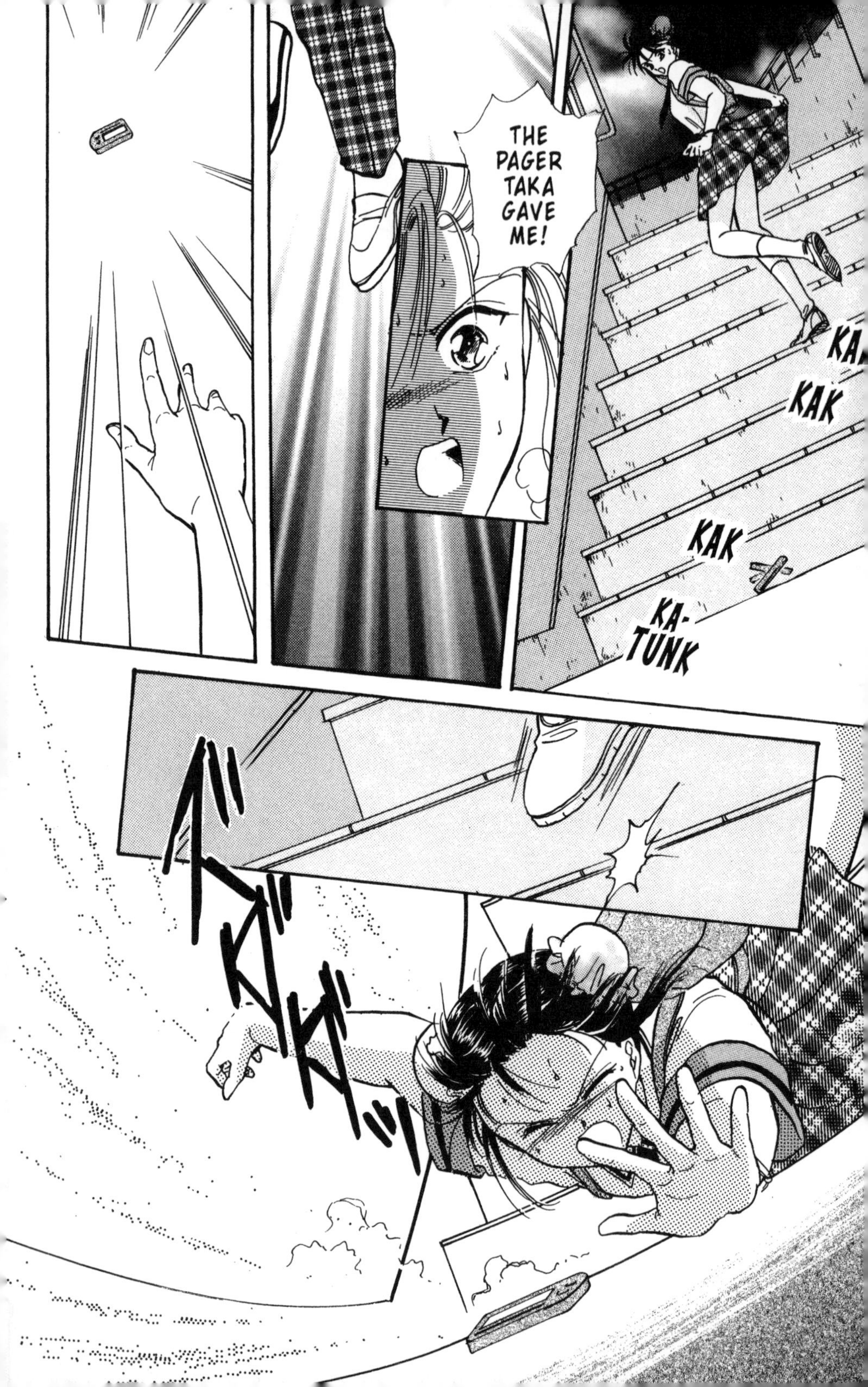
KA
KAK
KAK
KA-TUNK
THE PAGER TAKA GAVE ME!

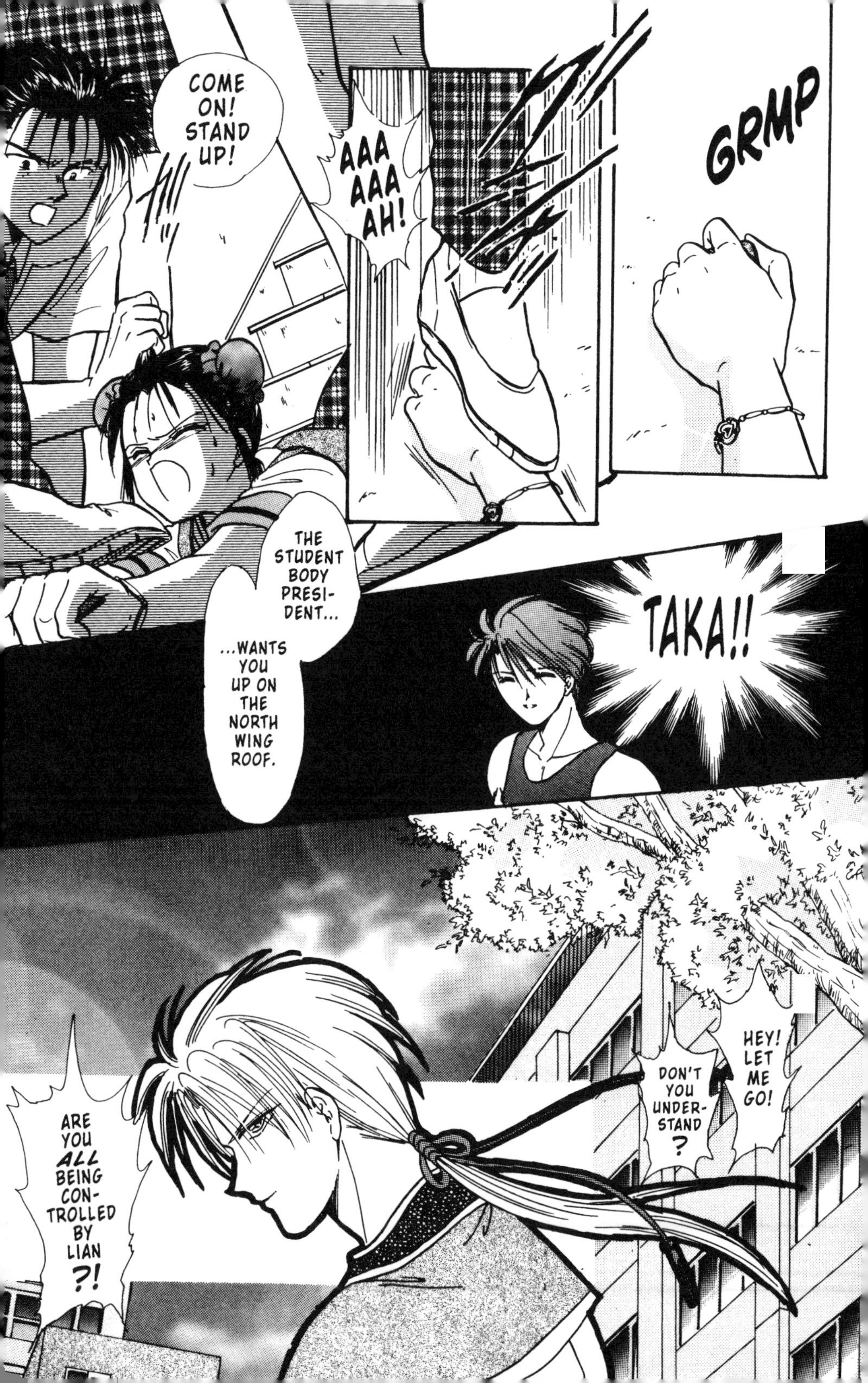
GRMP
AAA AAA AH!
COME ON! STAND UP!
TAKA!!
THE STUDENT BODY PRESIDENT...
...WANTS YOU UP ON THE NORTH WING ROOF.
HEY! LET ME GO!
DON'T YOU UNDERSTAND?
ARE YOU ALL BEING CONTROLLED BY LIAN?!

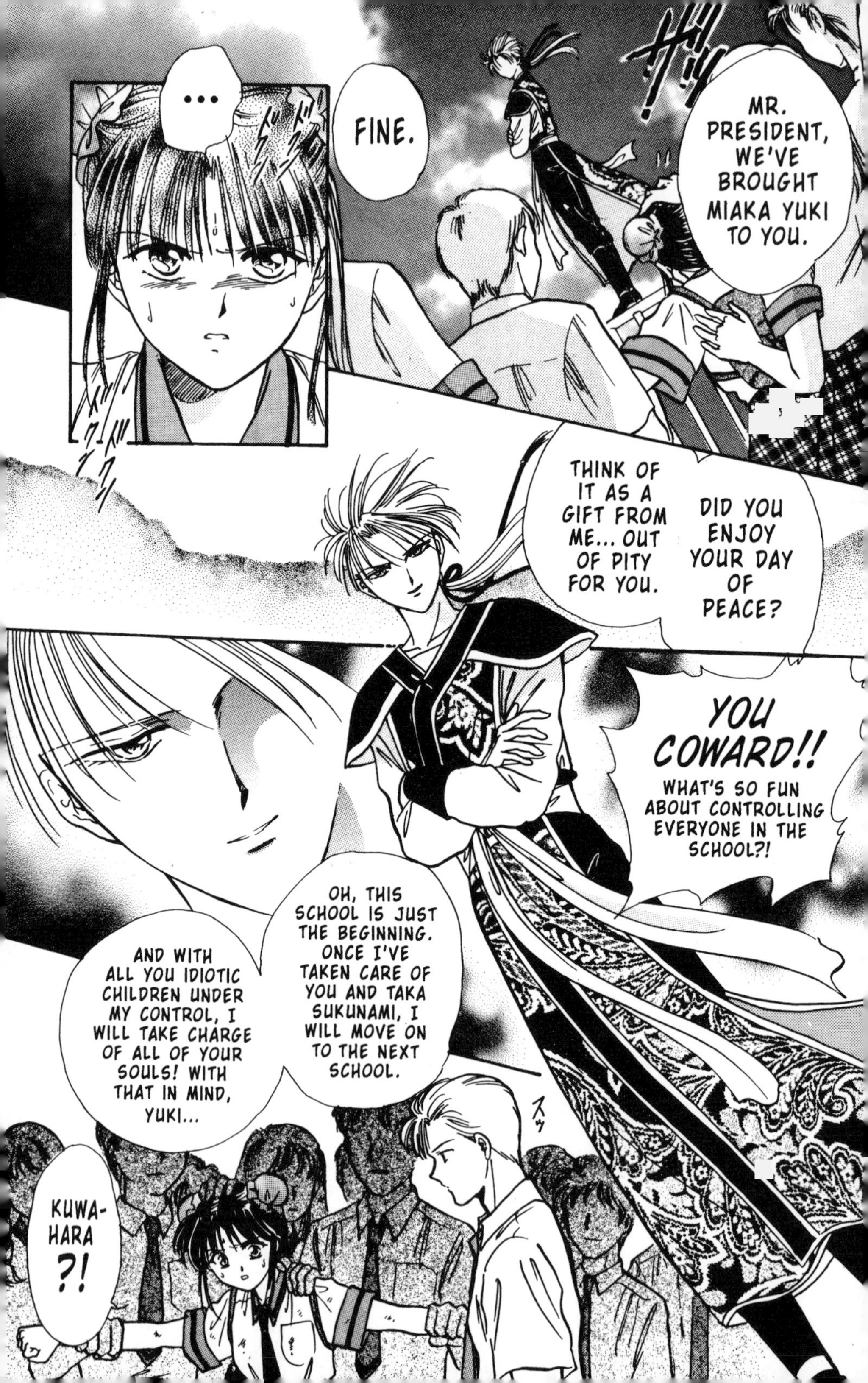
MR. PRESIDENT, WE'VE BROUGHT MIAKA YUKI TO YOU.
FINE.
...
DID YOU ENJOY YOUR DAY OF PEACE?
THINK OF IT AS A GIFT FROM ME... OUT OF PITY FOR YOU.
YOU COWARD!!
WHAT'S SO FUN ABOUT CONTROLLING EVERYONE IN THE SCHOOL?!
OH, THIS SCHOOL IS JUST THE BEGINNING. ONCE I'VE TAKEN CARE OF YOU AND TAKA SUKUNAMI, I WILL MOVE ON TO THE NEXT SCHOOL.
AND WITH ALL YOU IDIOTIC CHILDREN UNDER MY CONTROL, I WILL TAKE CHARGE OF ALL OF YOUR SOULS! WITH THAT IN MIND, YUKI...
KUWA-HARA ?!

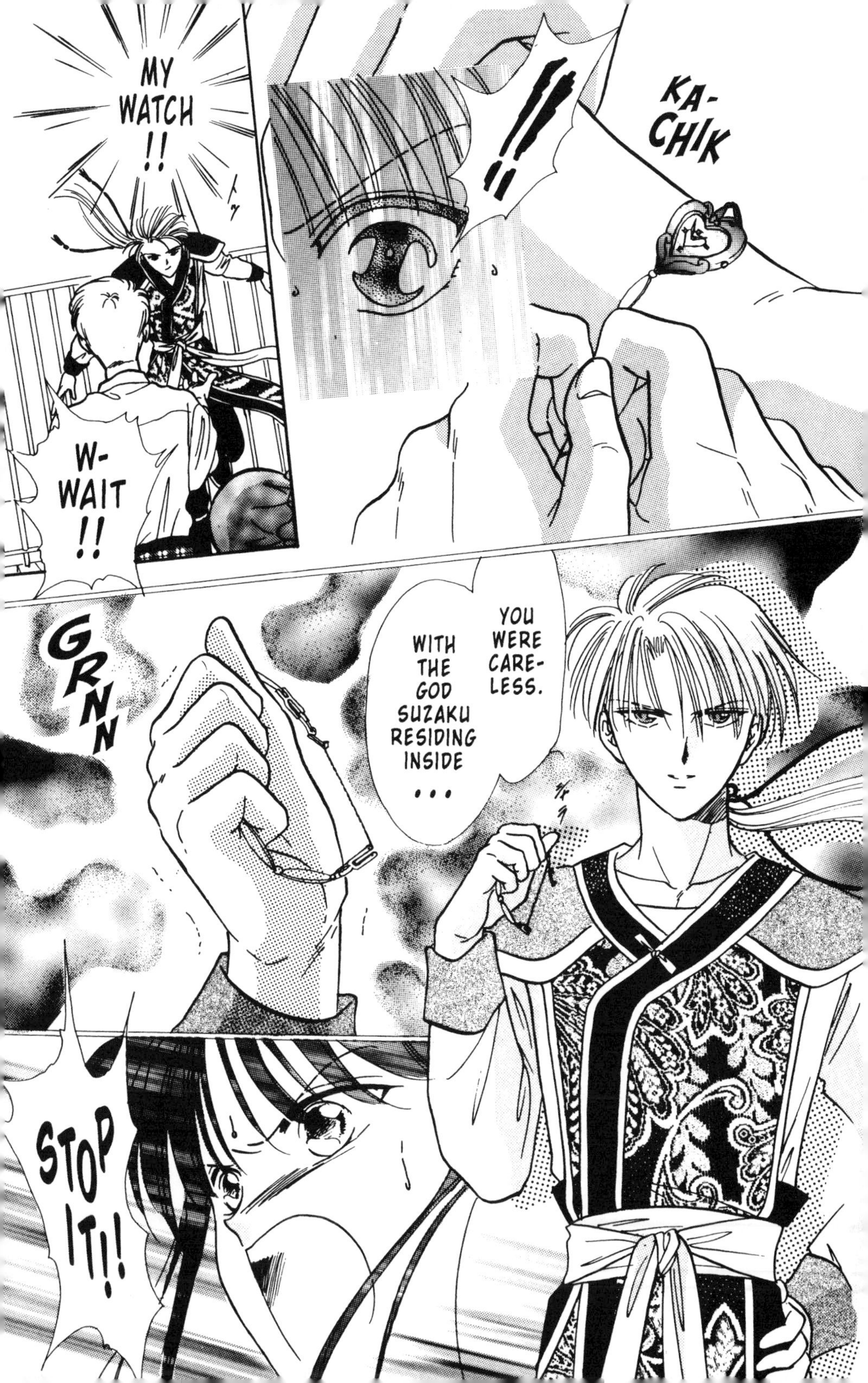
KA-CHIK
!!
MY WATCH!!
W-WAIT!!
YOU WERE CARELESS.
WITH THE GOD SUZAKU RESIDING INSIDE...
GRNN
STOP IT!!

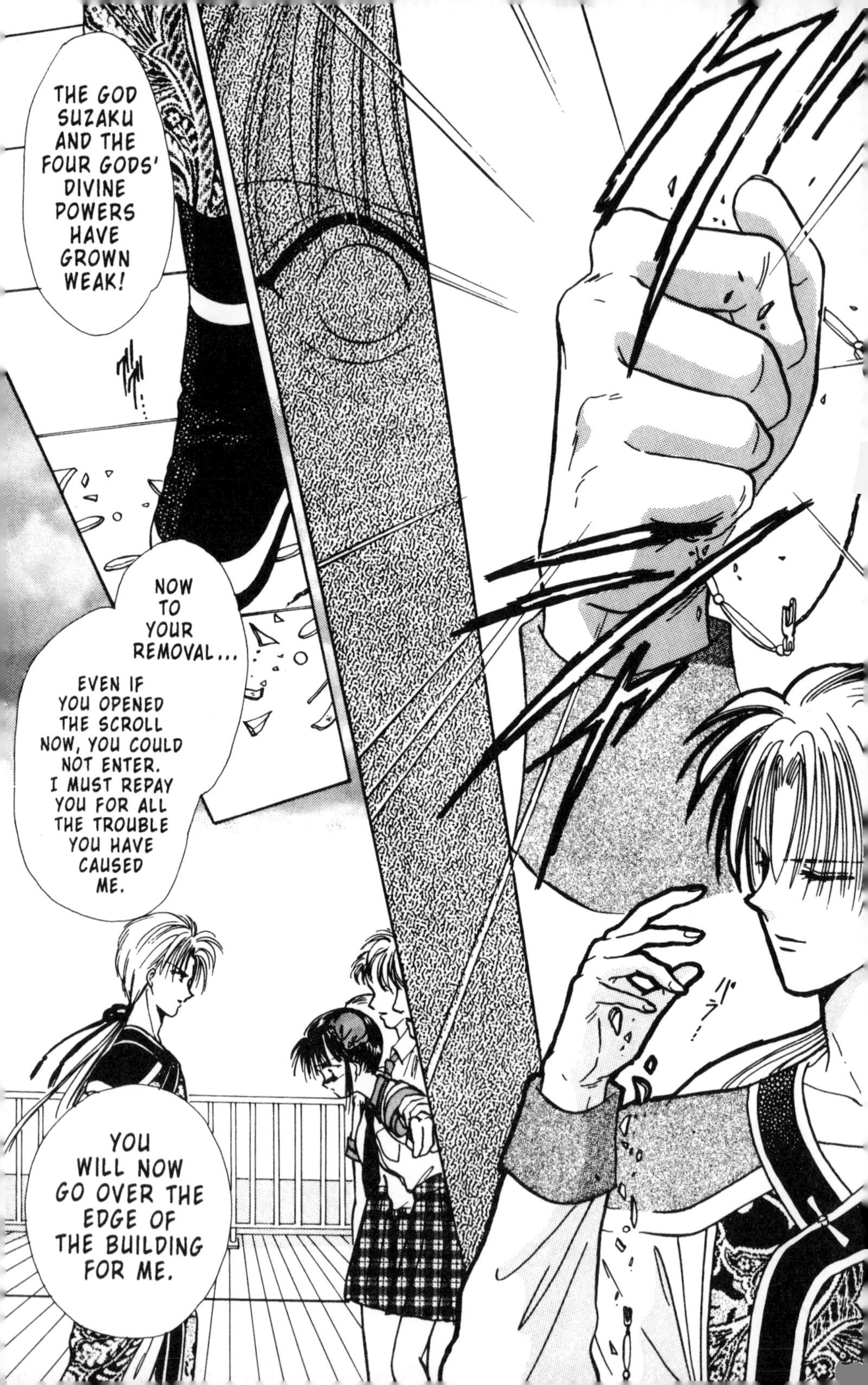
THE GOD SUZAKU AND THE FOUR GODS' DIVINE POWERS HAVE GROWN WEAK!
NOW TO YOUR REMOVAL...
EVEN IF YOU OPENED THE SCROLL NOW, YOU COULD NOT ENTER. I MUST REPAY YOU FOR ALL THE TROUBLE YOU HAVE CAUSED ME.
YOU WILL NOW GO OVER THE EDGE OF THE BUILDING FOR ME.

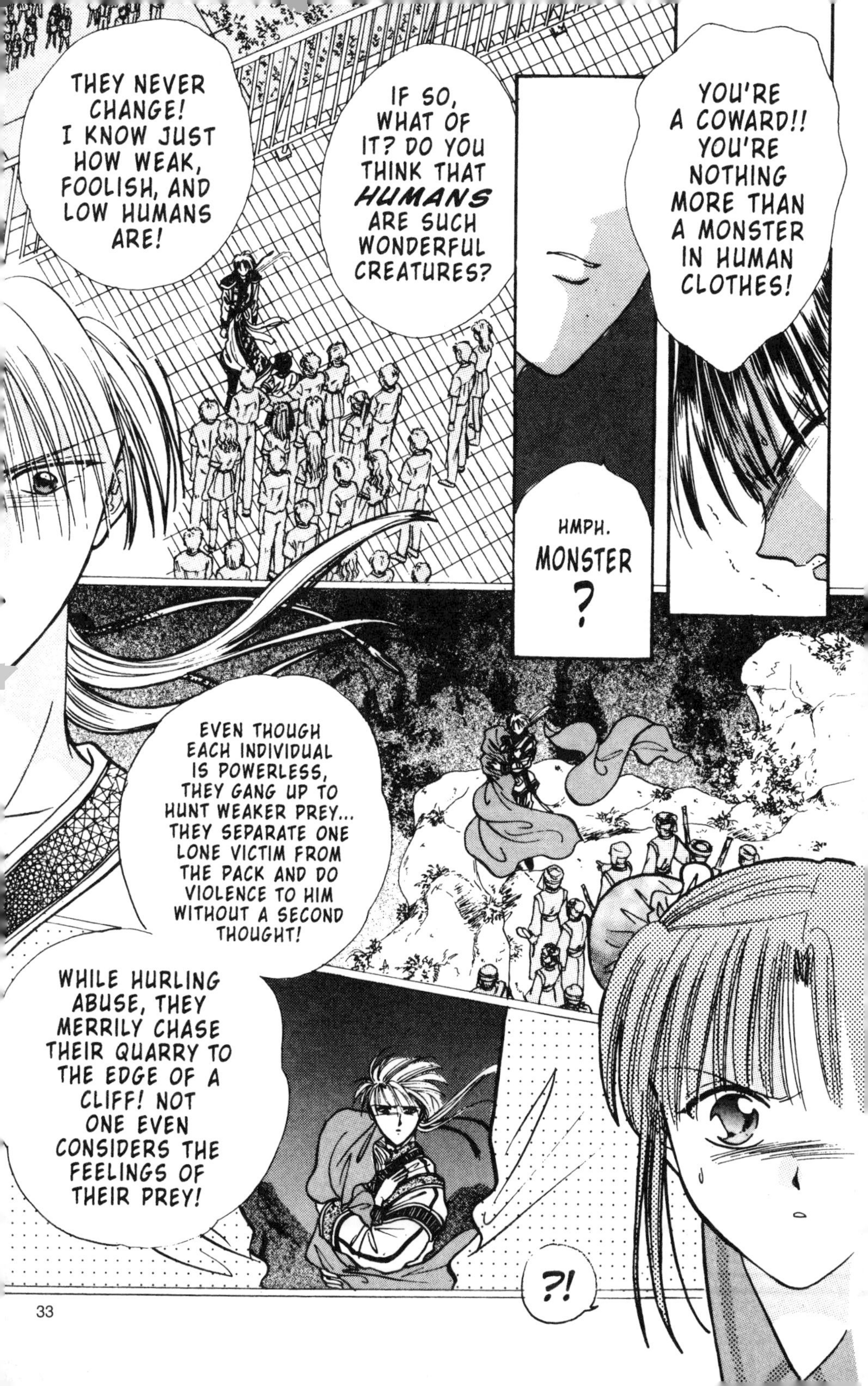
YOU'RE A COWARD!! YOU'RE NOTHING MORE THAN A MONSTER IN HUMAN CLOTHES!
HMPH. MONSTER ?
IF SO, WHAT OF IT? DO YOU THINK THAT *HUMANS* ARE SUCH WONDERFUL CREATURES?
THEY NEVER CHANGE! I KNOW JUST HOW WEAK, FOOLISH, AND LOW HUMANS ARE!
EVEN THOUGH EACH INDIVIDUAL IS POWERLESS, THEY GANG UP TO HUNT WEAKER PREY... THEY SEPARATE ONE LONE VICTIM FROM THE PACK AND DO VIOLENCE TO HIM WITHOUT A SECOND THOUGHT!
WHILE HURLING ABUSE, THEY MERRILY CHASE THEIR QUARRY TO THE EDGE OF A CLIFF! NOT ONE EVEN CONSIDERS THE FEELINGS OF THEIR PREY!
?!

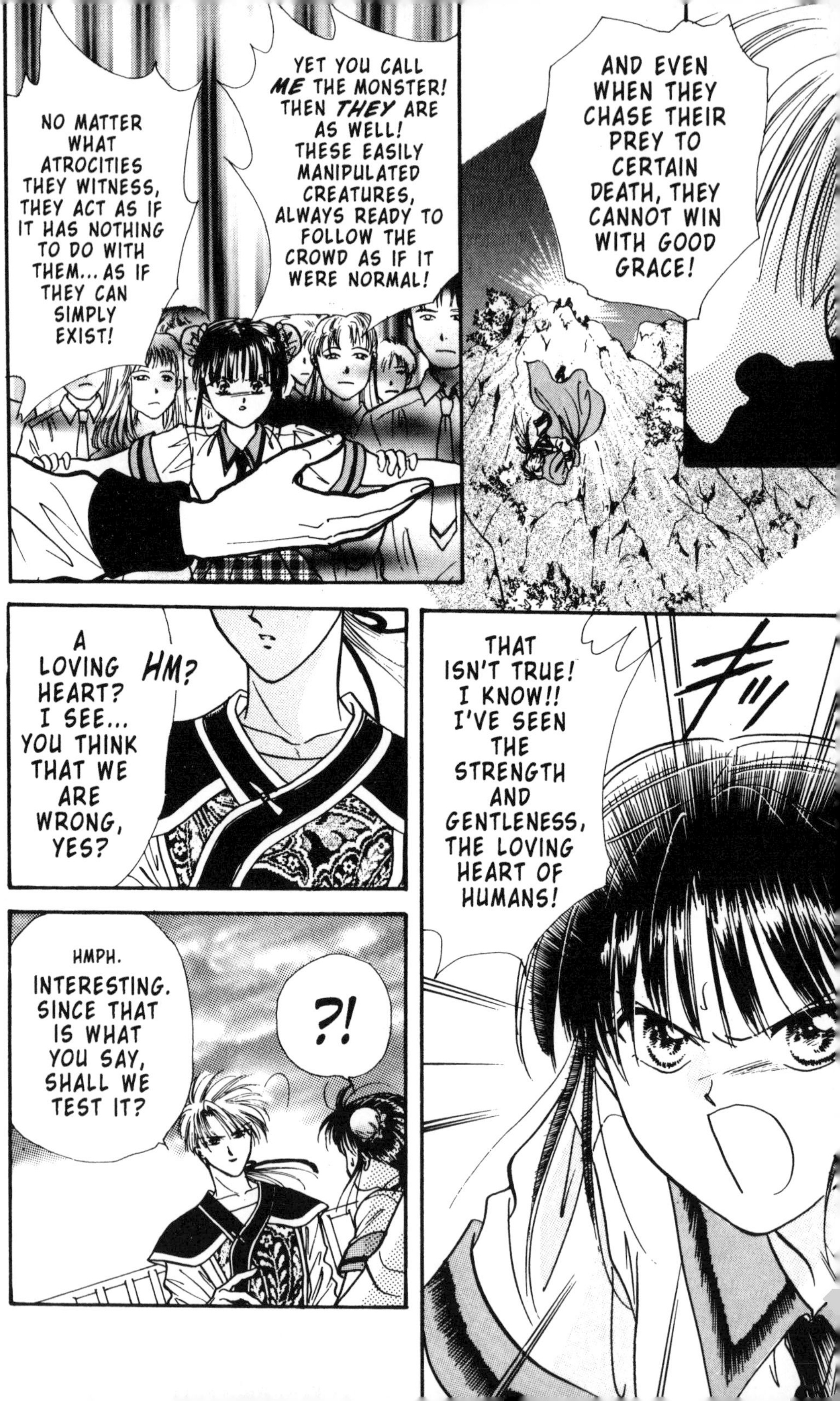
AND EVEN WHEN THEY CHASE THEIR PREY TO CERTAIN DEATH, THEY CANNOT WIN WITH GOOD GRACE!
YET YOU CALL *ME* THE MONSTER! THEN *THEY* ARE AS WELL! THESE EASILY MANIPULATED CREATURES, ALWAYS READY TO FOLLOW THE CROWD AS IF IT WERE NORMAL!
NO MATTER WHAT ATROCITIES THEY WITNESS, THEY ACT AS IF IT HAS NOTHING TO DO WITH THEM... AS IF THEY CAN SIMPLY EXIST!
キッ
THAT ISN'T TRUE! I KNOW!! I'VE SEEN THE STRENGTH AND GENTLENESS, THE LOVING HEART OF HUMANS!
HM?
A LOVING HEART? I SEE... YOU THINK THAT WE ARE WRONG, YES?
HMPH. INTERESTING. SINCE THAT IS WHAT YOU SAY, SHALL WE TEST IT?
?!

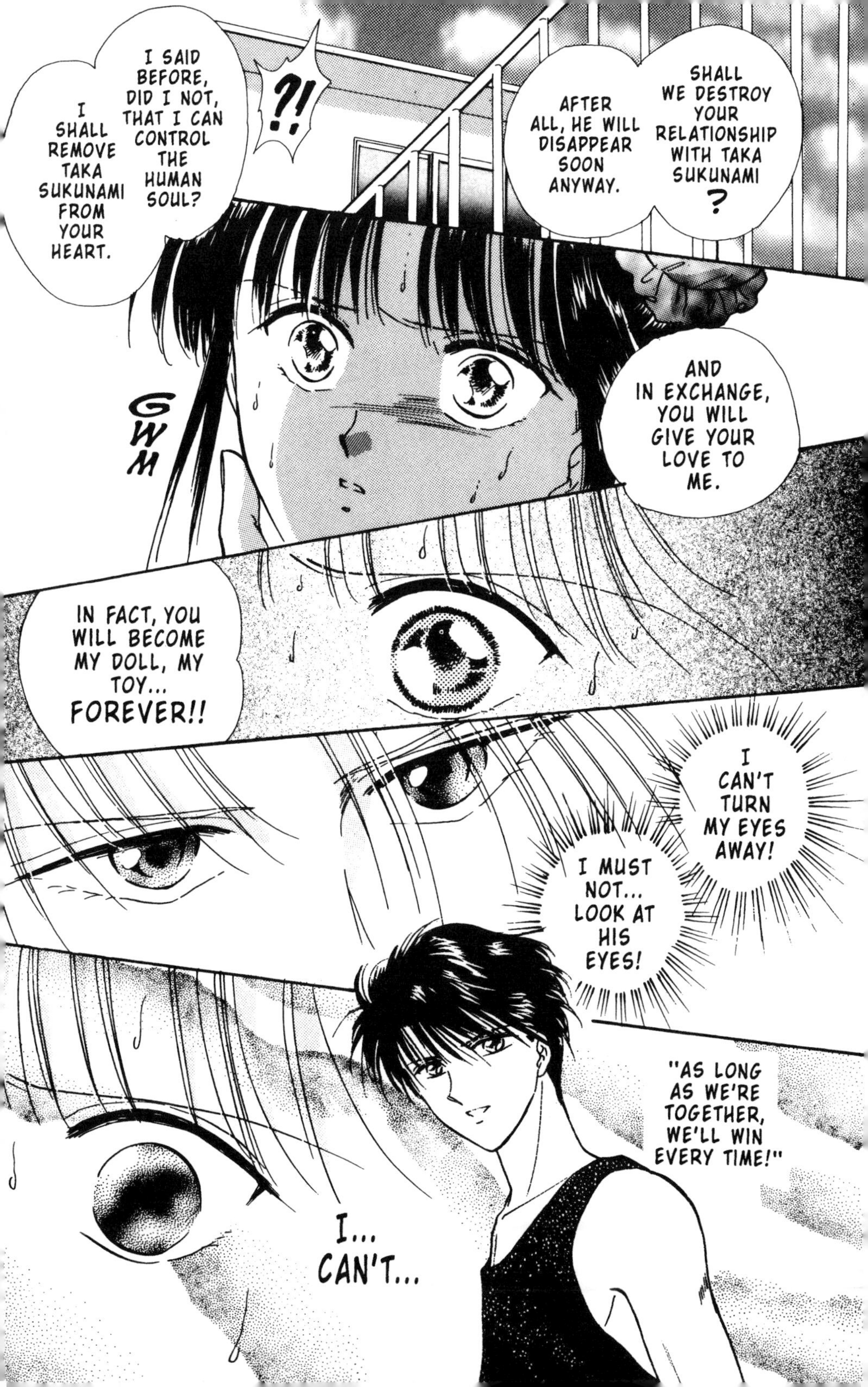
SHALL WE DESTROY YOUR RELATIONSHIP WITH TAKA SUKUNAMI?
AFTER ALL, HE WILL DISAPPEAR SOON ANYWAY.
?!
I SAID BEFORE, DID I NOT, THAT I CAN CONTROL THE HUMAN SOUL?
I SHALL REMOVE TAKA SUKUNAMI FROM YOUR HEART.
AND IN EXCHANGE, YOU WILL GIVE YOUR LOVE TO ME.
GWM
IN FACT, YOU WILL BECOME MY DOLL, MY TOY... FOREVER!!
I CAN'T TURN MY EYES AWAY!
I MUST NOT... LOOK AT HIS EYES!
"AS LONG AS WE'RE TOGETHER, WE'LL WIN EVERY TIME!"
I... CAN'T...

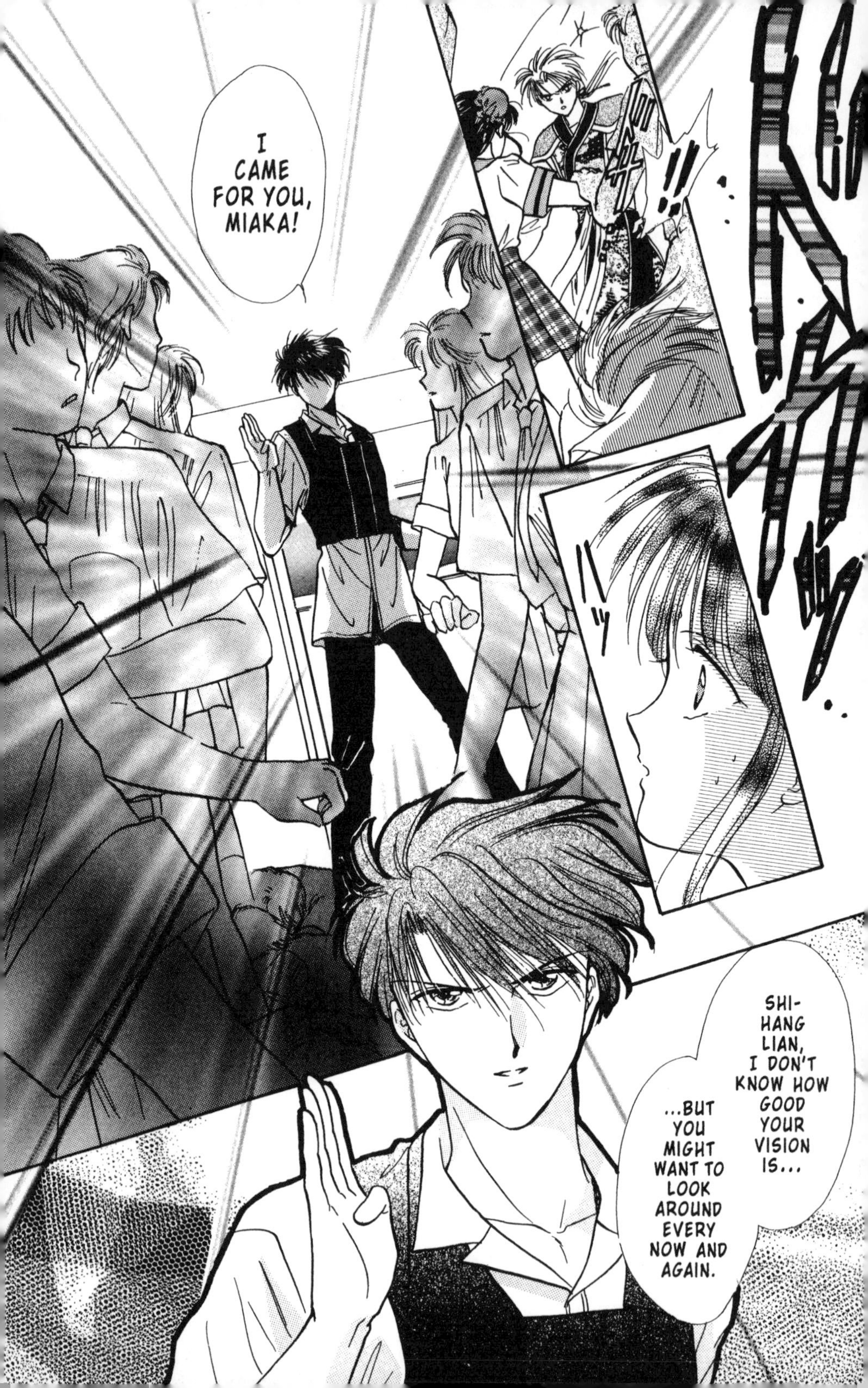
I CAME FOR YOU, MIAKA!
SHI-HANG LIAN, I DON'T KNOW HOW GOOD YOUR VISION IS...
...BUT YOU MIGHT WANT TO LOOK AROUND EVERY NOW AND AGAIN.

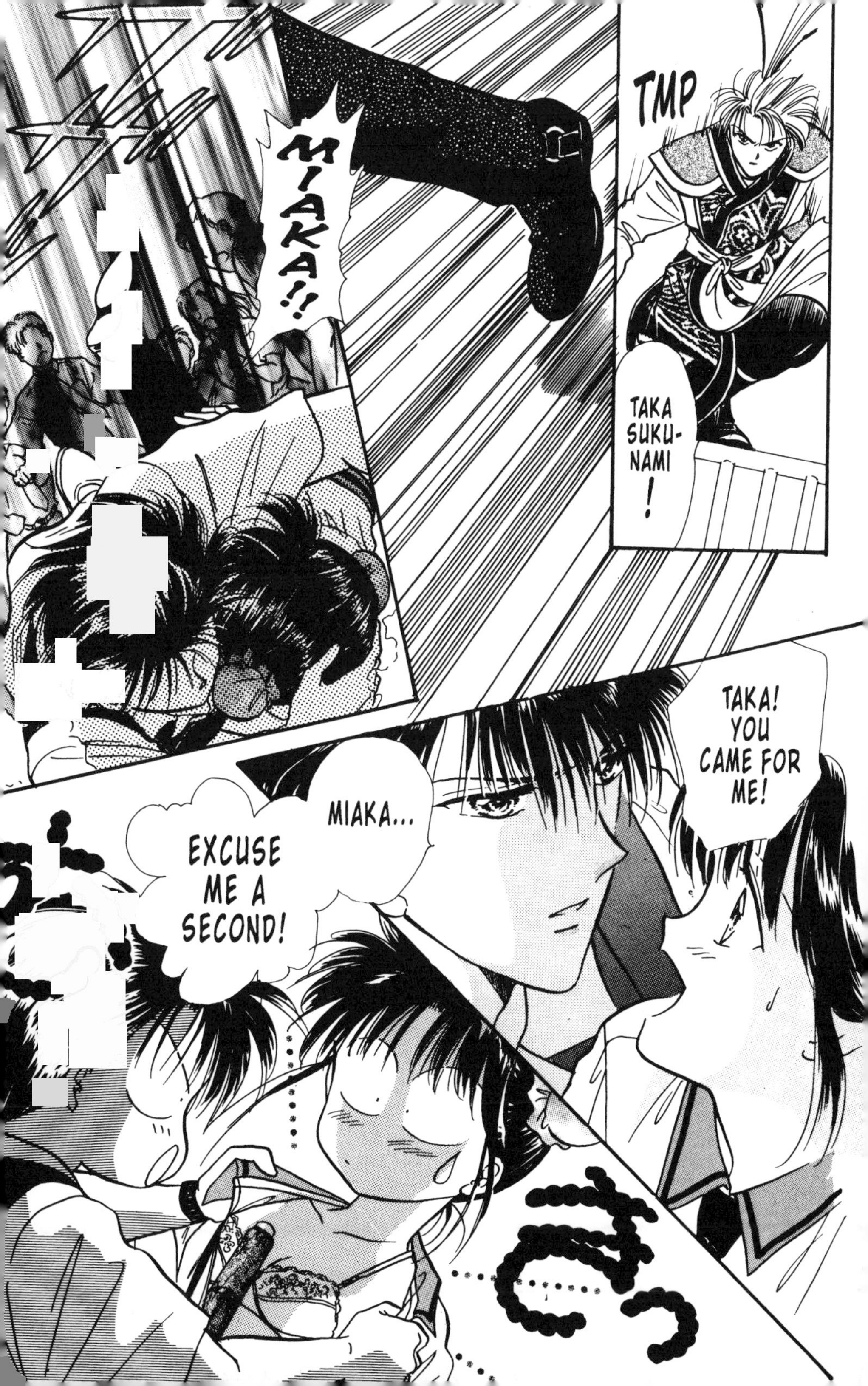
TMP
TAKA SUKU-NAMI !
MIAKA!!
TAKA! YOU CAME FOR ME!
MIAKA...
EXCUSE ME A SECOND!

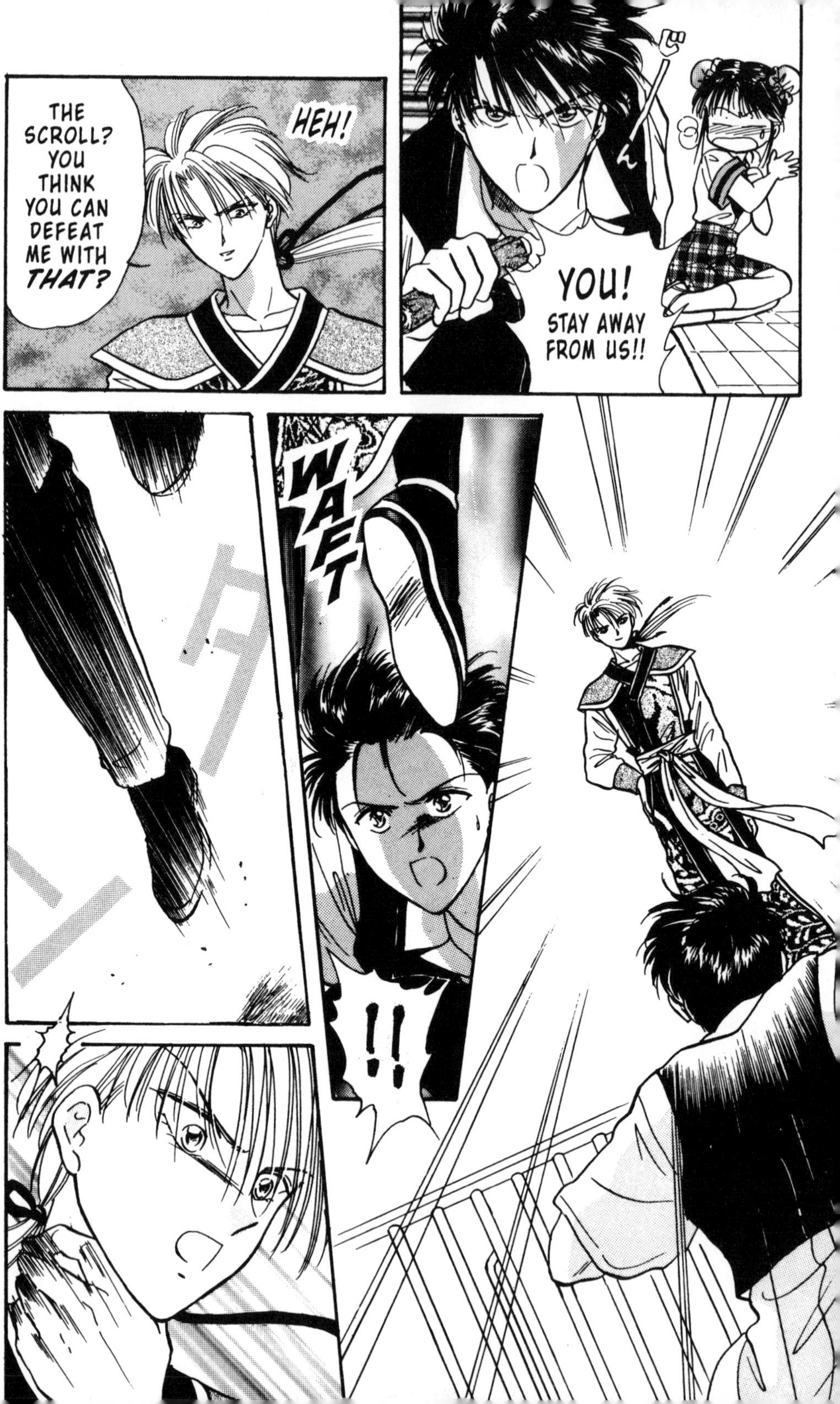
YOU!
STAY AWAY FROM US!!
THE SCROLL? YOU THINK YOU CAN DEFEAT ME WITH *THAT?*
HEH!
WAFT
!!

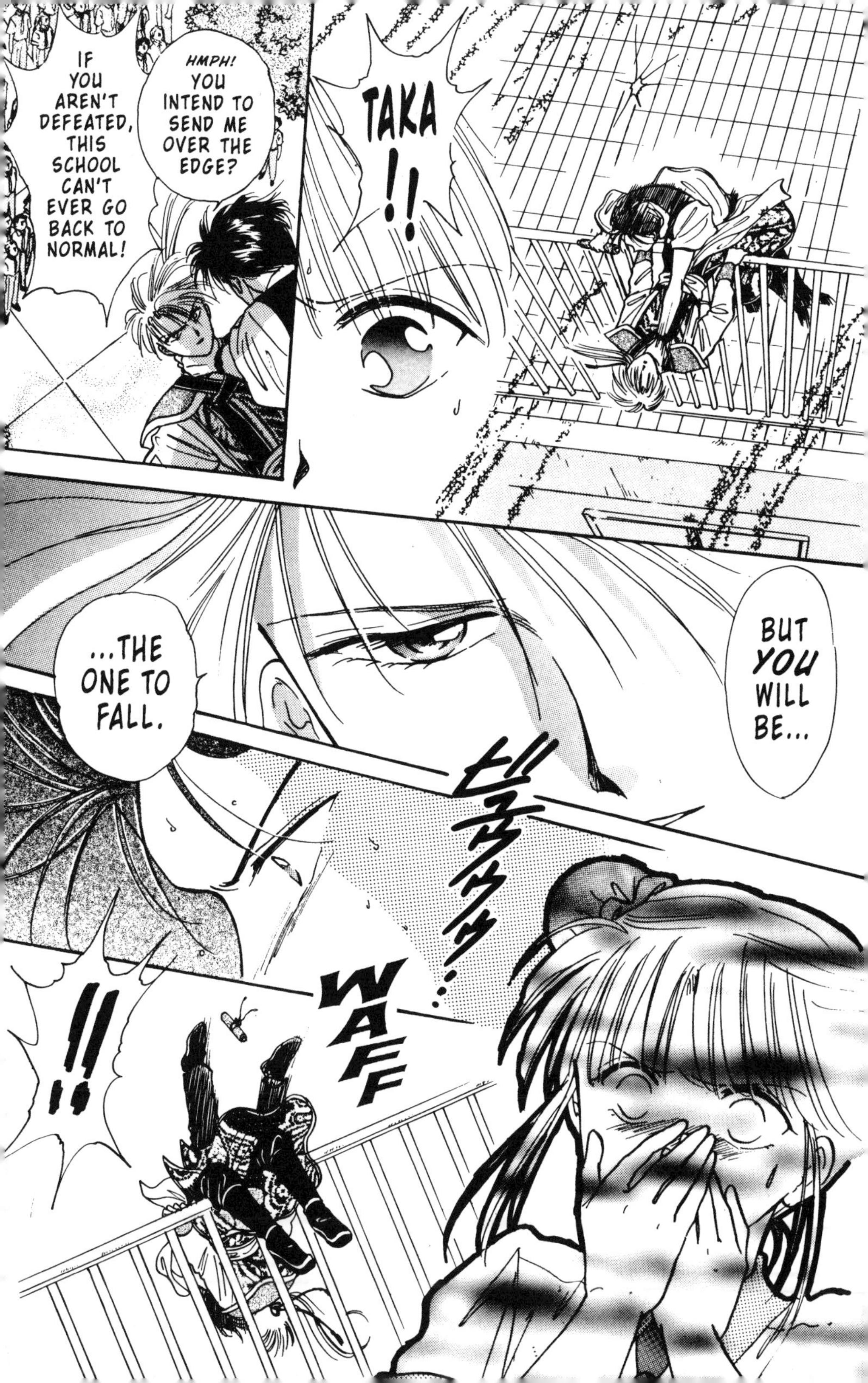
TAKA!!
HMPH! YOU INTEND TO SEND ME OVER THE EDGE?
IF YOU AREN'T DEFEATED, THIS SCHOOL CAN'T EVER GO BACK TO NORMAL!
BUT YOU WILL BE...
...THE ONE TO FALL.
WAFF
!!

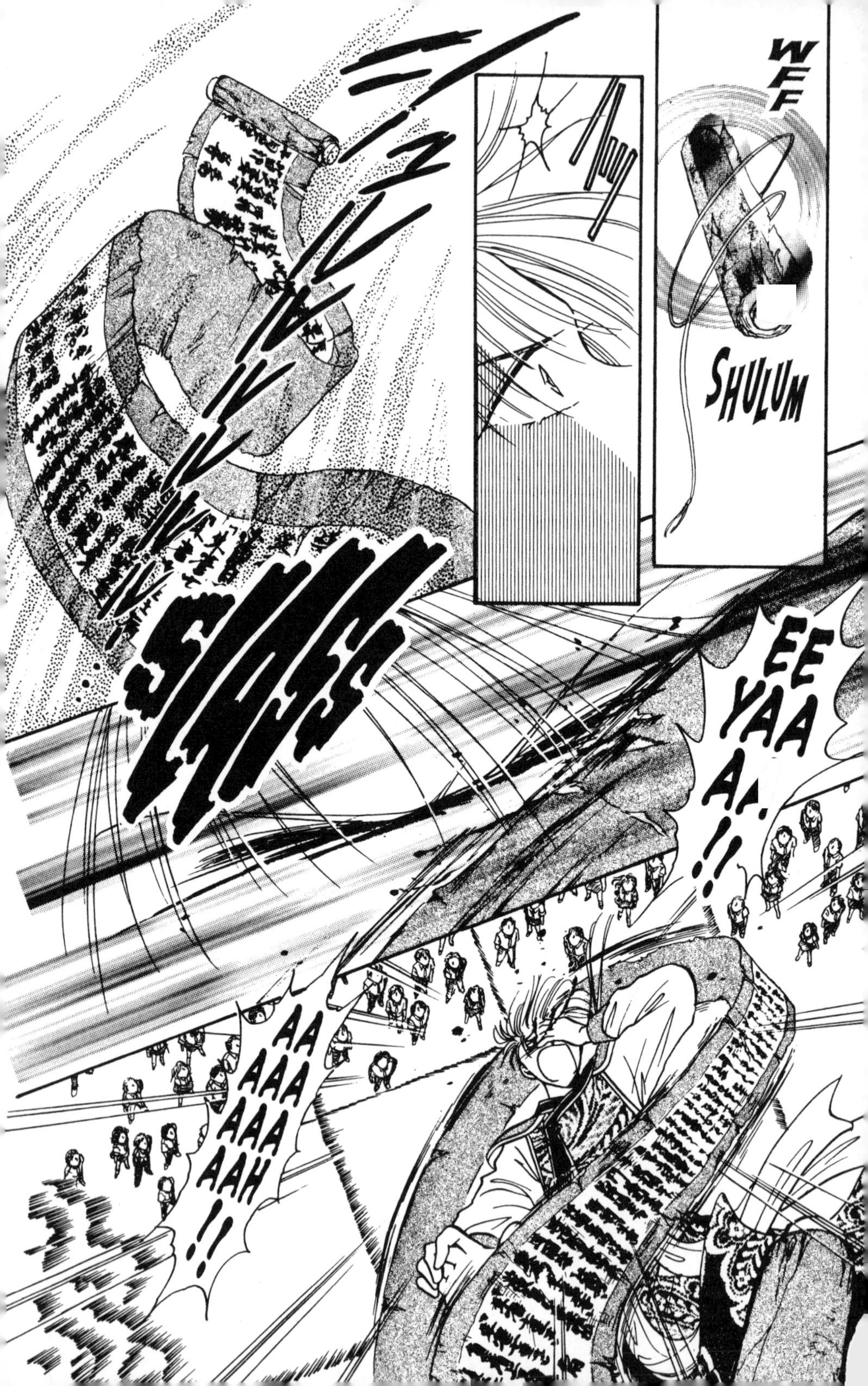
WEFF
SHULUM
EE YAAA A..!!!
AAAAAAAAAAAAAAH!!

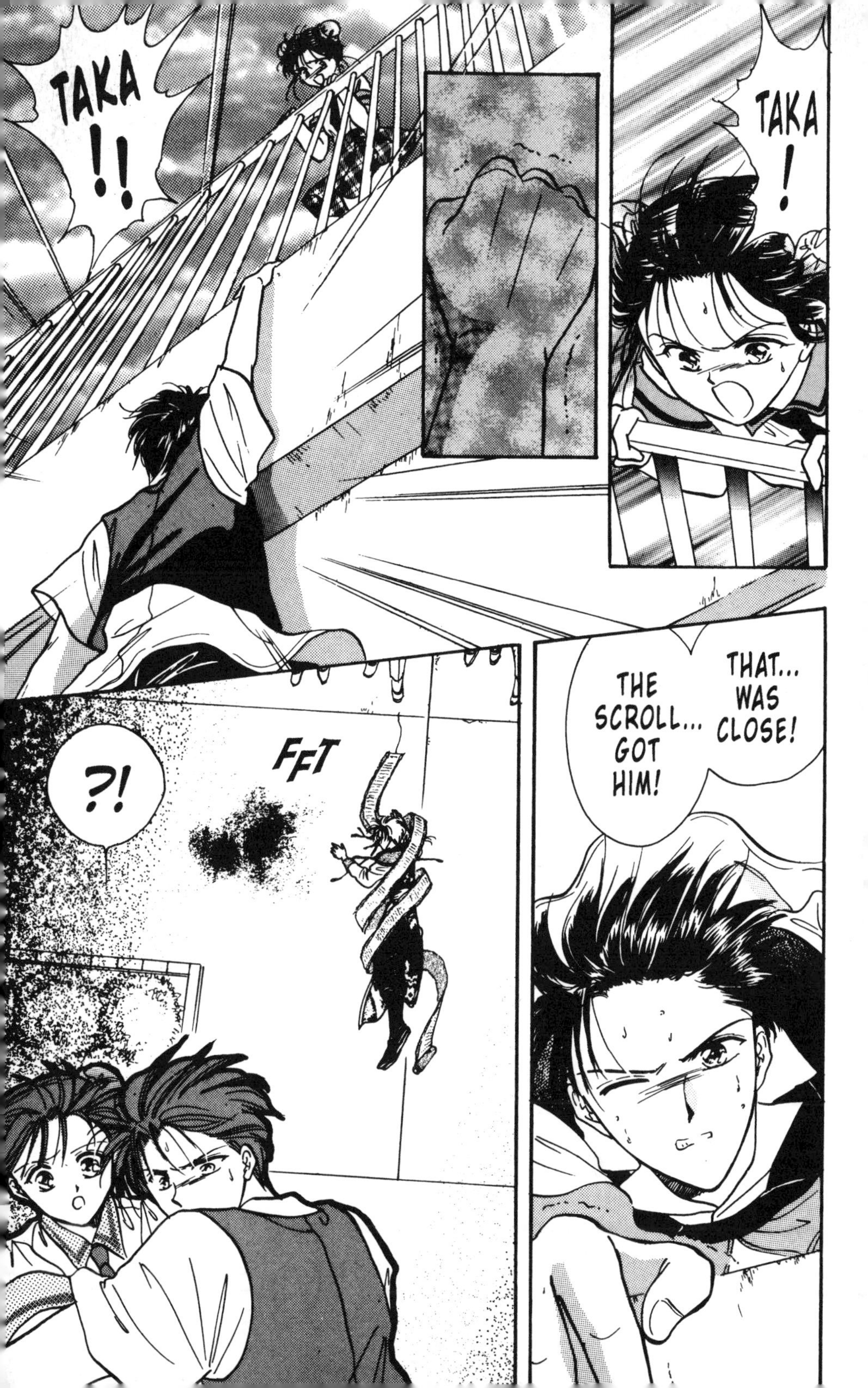
TAKA!
TAKA!!
THAT... WAS CLOSE!
THE SCROLL... GOT HIM!
FFT
?!

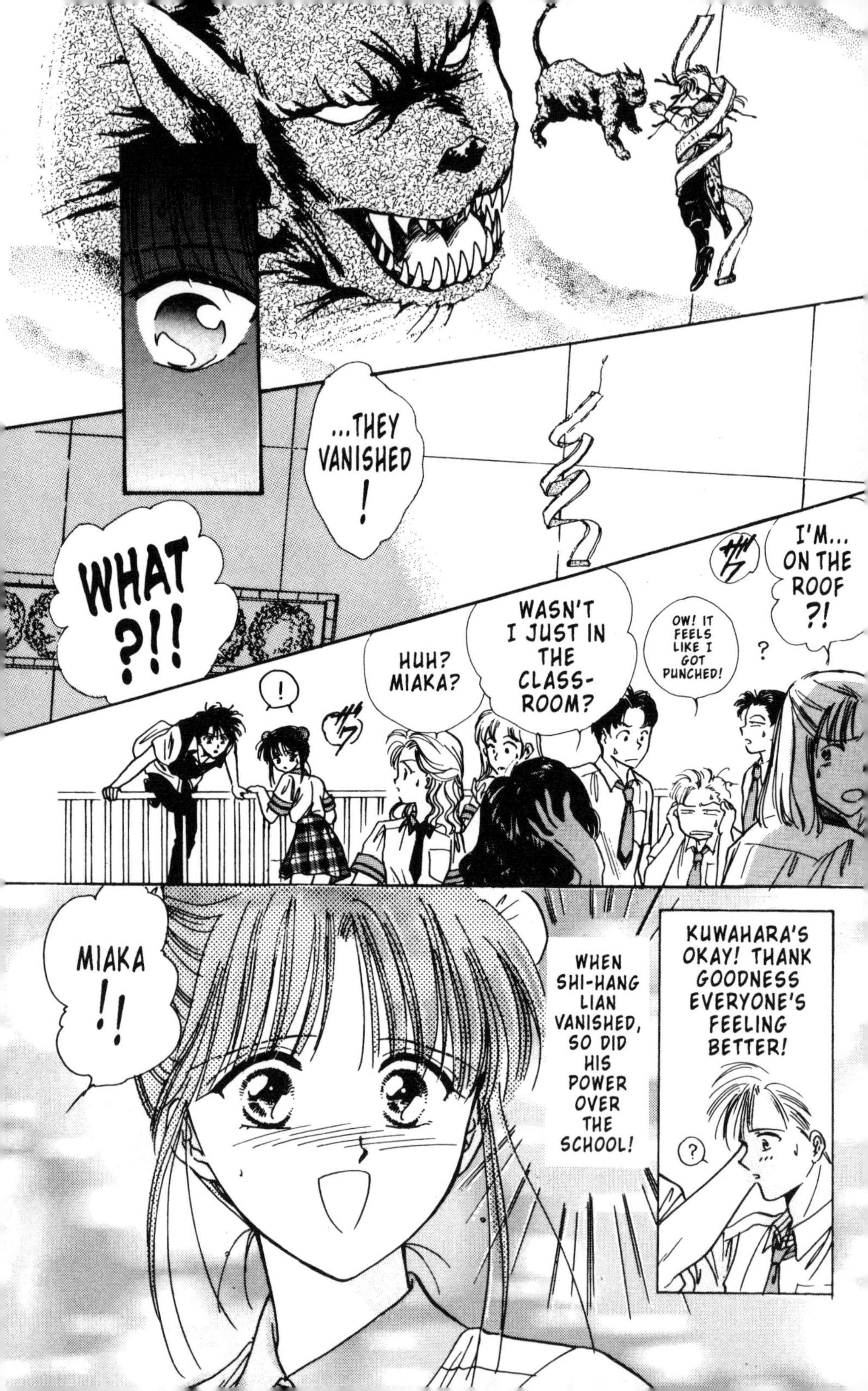
...THEY VANISHED!
WHAT?!!
I'M... ON THE ROOF?!
?
OW! IT FEELS LIKE I GOT PUNCHED!
WASN'T I JUST IN THE CLASSROOM?
HUH? MIAKA?
!
KUWAHARA'S OKAY! THANK GOODNESS EVERYONE'S FEELING BETTER!
?
WHEN SHI-HANG LIAN VANISHED, SO DID HIS POWER OVER THE SCHOOL!
MIAKA!!

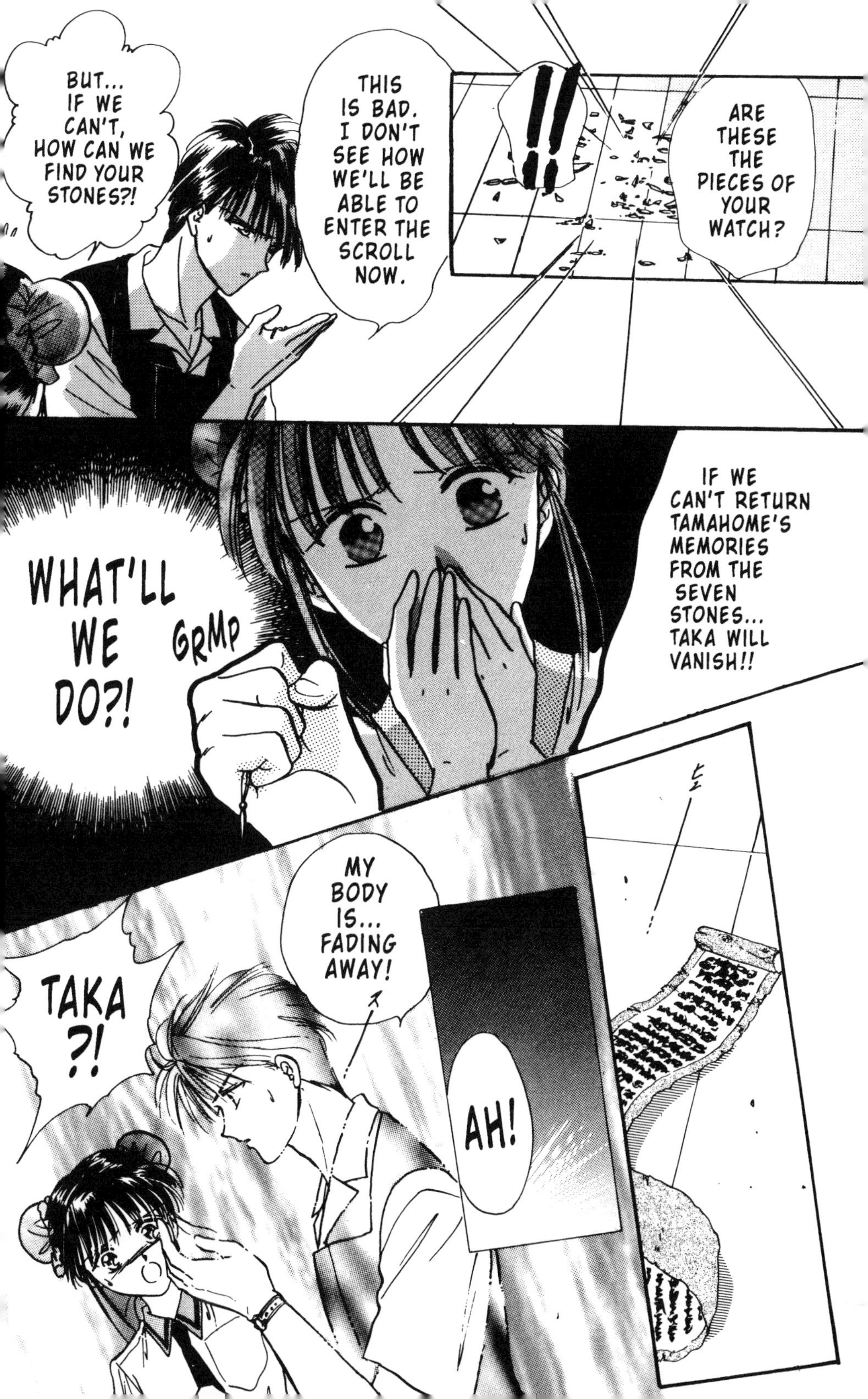
!!
ARE THESE THE PIECES OF YOUR WATCH?
THIS IS BAD. I DON'T SEE HOW WE'LL BE ABLE TO ENTER THE SCROLL NOW.
BUT... IF WE CAN'T, HOW CAN WE FIND YOUR STONES?!
IF WE CAN'T RETURN TAMAHOME'S MEMORIES FROM THE SEVEN STONES... TAKA WILL VANISH!!
WHAT'LL WE DO?!
GRMP
AH!
MY BODY IS... FADING AWAY!
TAKA?!

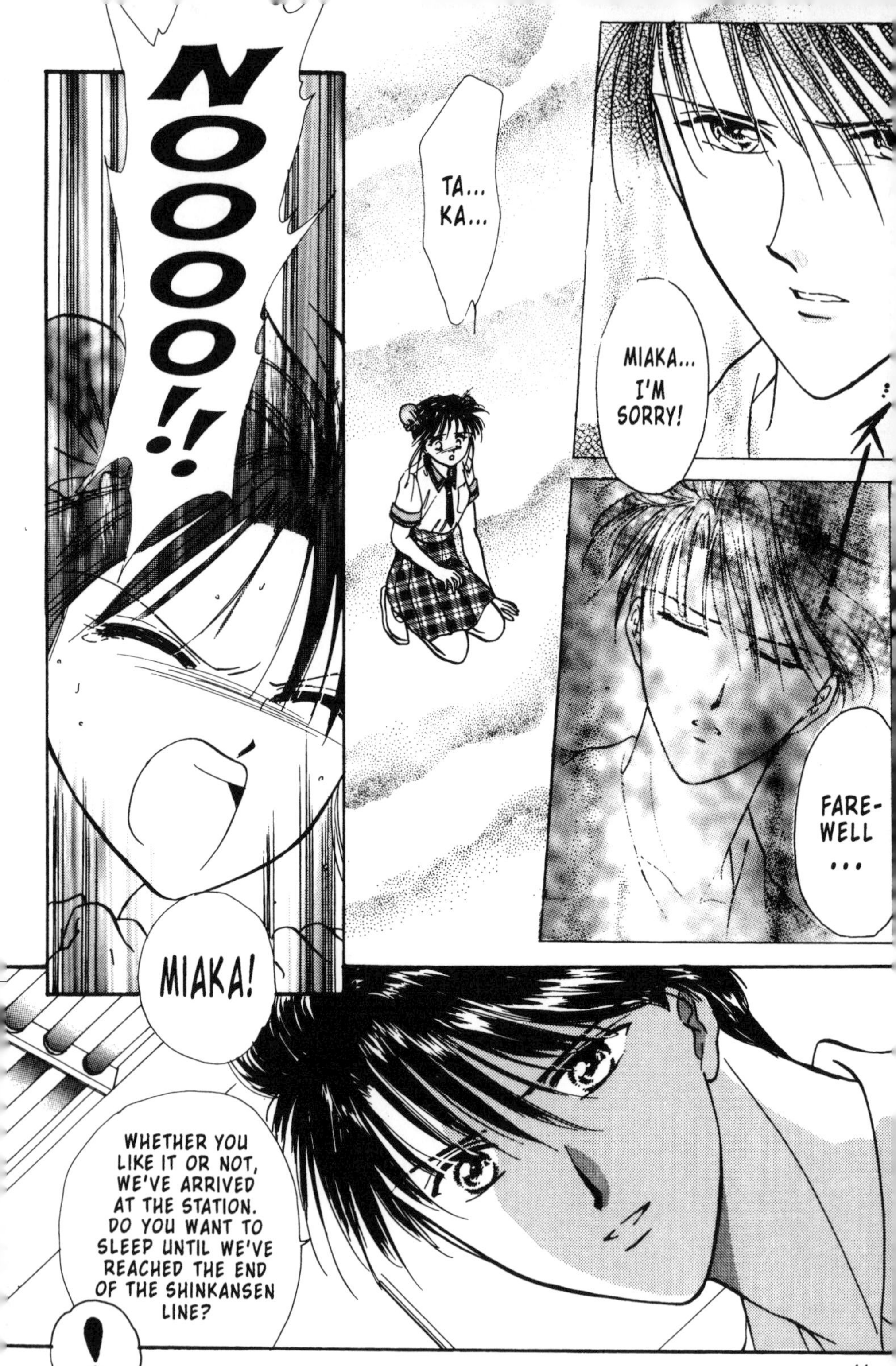
MIAKA... I'M SORRY!
FARE-WELL...
TA... KA...
NOOOOO!!
MIAKA!
WHETHER YOU LIKE IT OR NOT, WE'VE ARRIVED AT THE STATION. DO YOU WANT TO SLEEP UNTIL WE'VE REACHED THE END OF THE SHINKANSEN LINE?
!

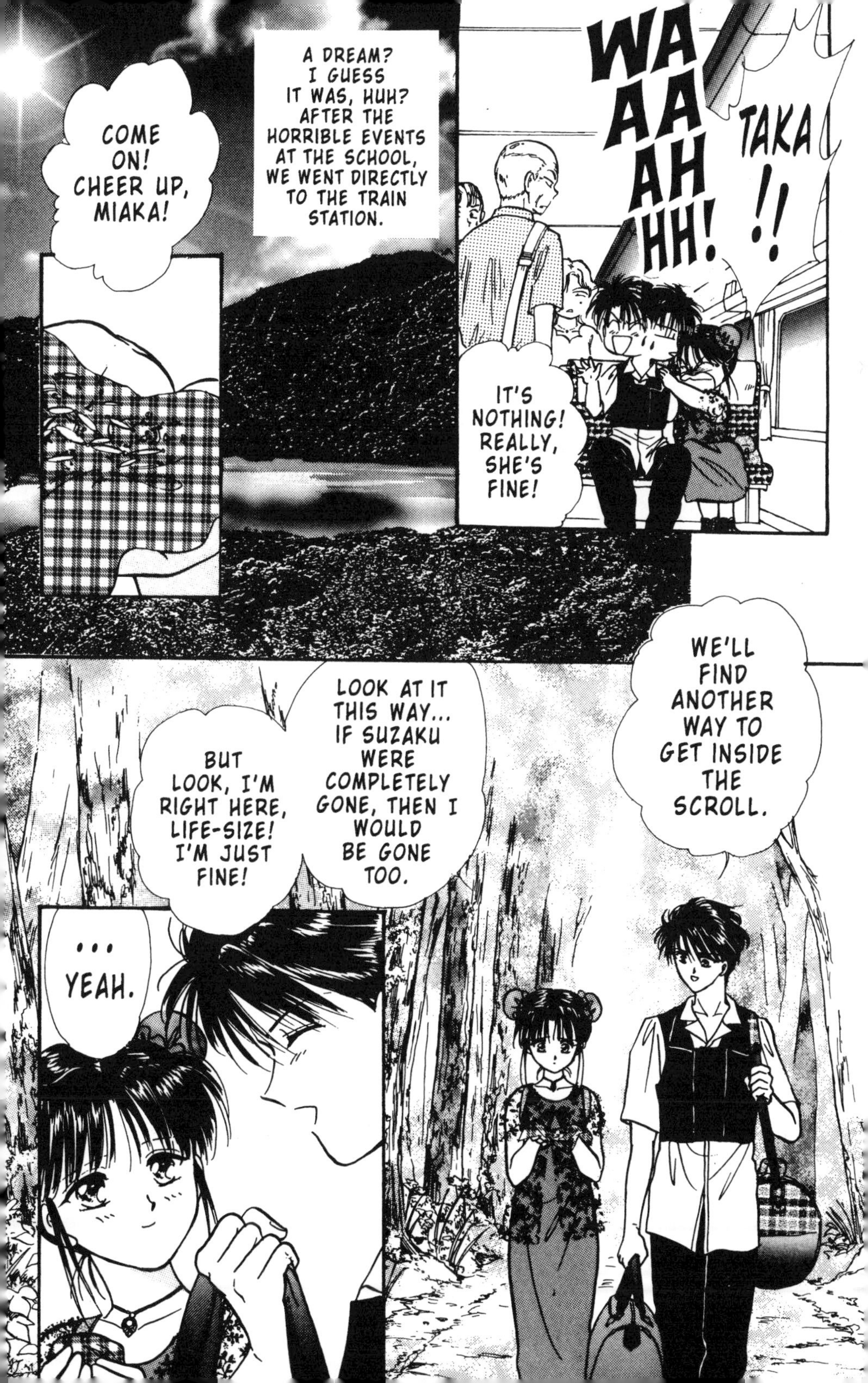
WAAAAHH!
TAKA!!
IT'S NOTHING! REALLY, SHE'S FINE!
A DREAM? I GUESS IT WAS, HUH? AFTER THE HORRIBLE EVENTS AT THE SCHOOL, WE WENT DIRECTLY TO THE TRAIN STATION.
COME ON! CHEER UP, MIAKA!
WE'LL FIND ANOTHER WAY TO GET INSIDE THE SCROLL.
LOOK AT IT THIS WAY... IF SUZAKU WERE COMPLETELY GONE, THEN I WOULD BE GONE TOO.
BUT LOOK, I'M RIGHT HERE, LIFE-SIZE! I'M JUST FINE!
... YEAH.

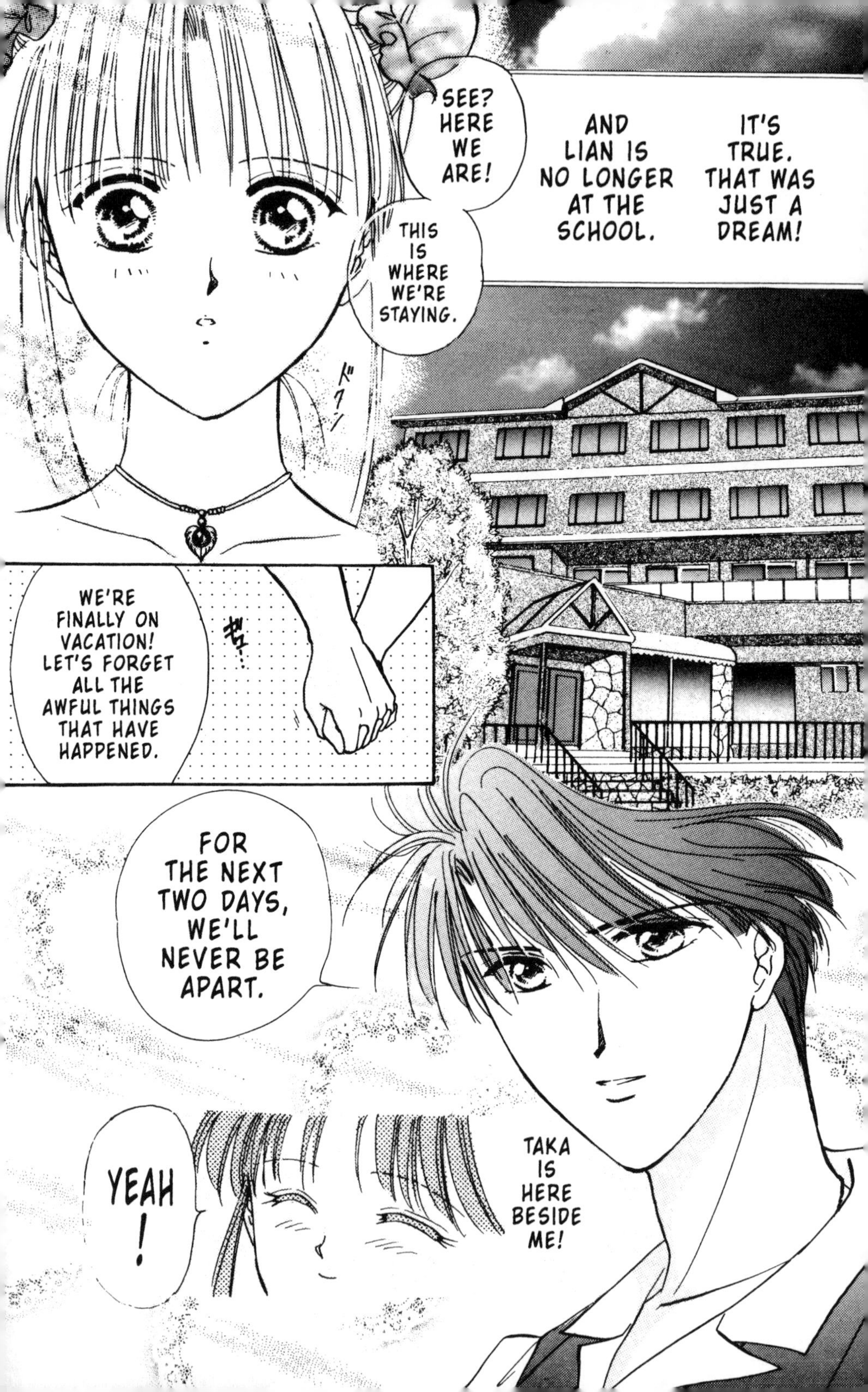
IT'S TRUE. THAT WAS JUST A DREAM!
AND LIAN IS NO LONGER AT THE SCHOOL.
SEE? HERE WE ARE!
THIS IS WHERE WE'RE STAYING.
ドクン
WE'RE FINALLY ON VACATION! LET'S FORGET ALL THE AWFUL THINGS THAT HAVE HAPPENED.
FOR THE NEXT TWO DAYS, WE'LL NEVER BE APART.
TAKA IS HERE BESIDE ME!
YEAH!

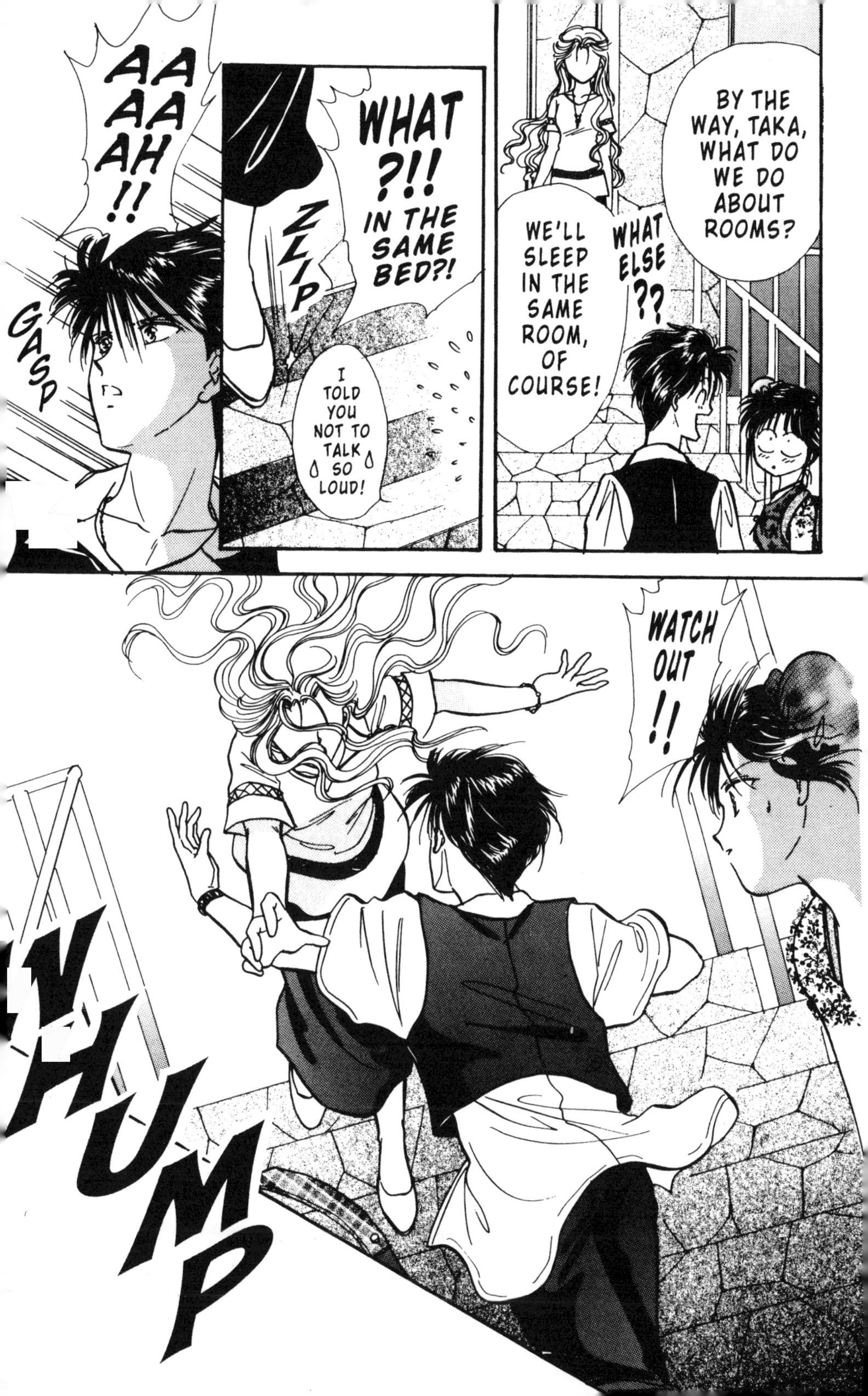
BY THE WAY, TAKA, WHAT DO WE DO ABOUT ROOMS?
WHAT ELSE??
WE'LL SLEEP IN THE SAME ROOM, OF COURSE!
WHAT?!! IN THE SAME BED?!
ZLIP
I TOLD YOU NOT TO TALK SO LOUD!
AAAAH!!
GASP
WATCH OUT!!
HUMP

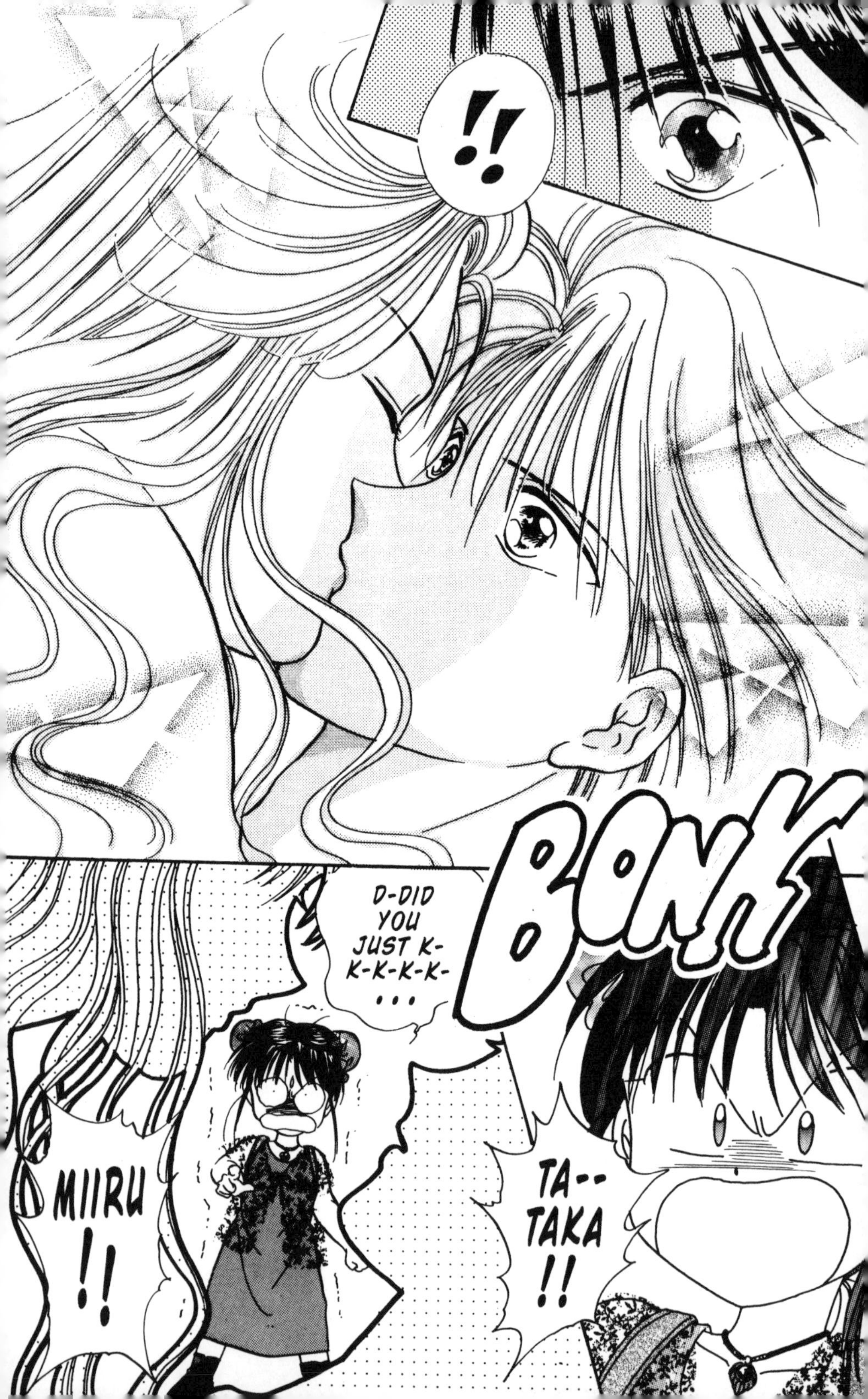
!!
BONK
D-DID YOU JUST K-K-K-K-K-...
TA-- TAKA!!
MIIRU!!

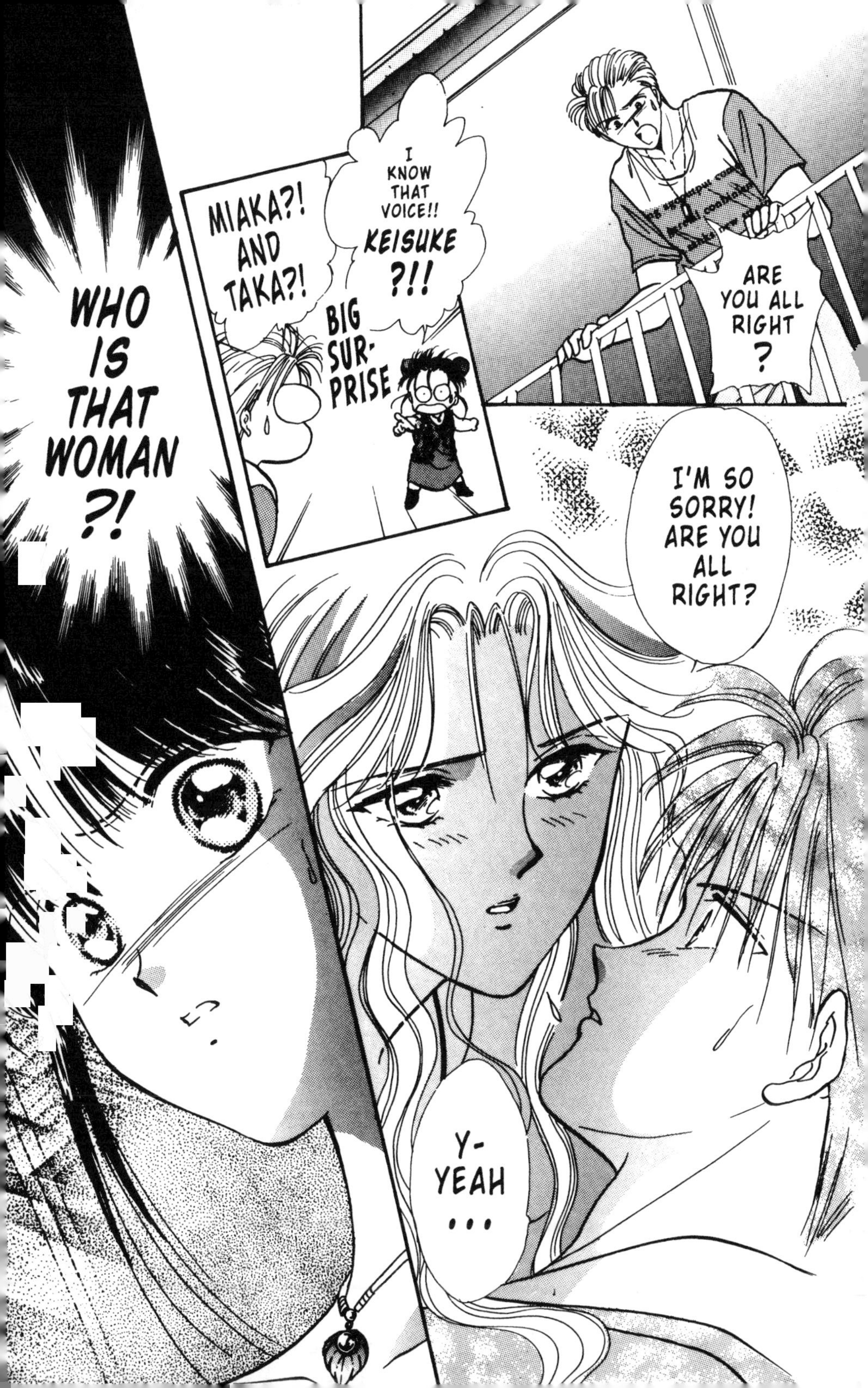

ARE YOU ALL RIGHT ?
I KNOW THAT VOICE!! KEISUKE ?!!
MIAKA?! AND TAKA?!
BIG SUR-PRISE
I'M SO SORRY! ARE YOU ALL RIGHT?
Y-YEAH ...
WHO IS THAT WOMAN ?!

I don't know what I'm talking about, but I'll talk anyway! If you don't like it, just skip to the next page!

There's a book out that has info on both the anime and manga of FUSHIGI YŪGI! They probably shouldn't have done it. I drew new illustrations of Miaka and each of the Seven Celestial Warriors for it! ☺ It also gives you a look at a voicing session and includes interviews with the voice actors and has a whole lot of other stuff, so be sure to check it out! Speaking of the voice actors, I recently attended a recording session and had the privilege of meeting them all face-to-face! Nakago (Mr. Furusawa) and Miaka (Ms. Araki) were at the same meeting I was in, and hearing their voices, I'd say, "Whoa! Huh?" ☺ While we were at dinner (Chinese food), my editor leaned over to me and said that behind us, Nuriko (Ms. Sakamoto) was talking! What was really interesting was when we were playing Bingo... Hotohori (Mr. Koyasu) was the master of ceremonies, but he turned to Mr. Midorikawa, who had been eating the whole time, and said, "Tamahome! Curb your gluttony," warning him in a very imperial voice. Mr. Seki would call out in Chichiri's voice (you know, like when he says "daaa!"), "I'm rich! No da!" or, "Bingo! No da!" Maybe it was because, from where I was seated, I couldn't see the voice actors, but listening to them all chatting in character during their meal made me feel...kind of weird. (?) ☺ At the end, mad-fan Watase had some signboards prepared (but not enough for everybody)! I couldn't get everyone's signatures, but most were kind enough to sign them for me. A large number of them also added personal comments, which made me very happy! I laughed when Mr. Ueda, who plays the twins, signed it "Big Brother!!" Mr. Koyasu and Mr. Midorikawa both signed for me in hiragana script even though they usually don't sign it this way, so it's especially valuable! Woo-hoo!

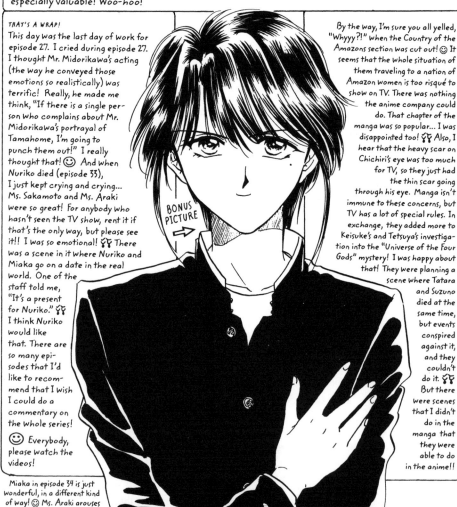

THAT'S A WRAP!
This day was the last day of work for episode 27. I cried during episode 27. I thought Mr. Midorikawa's acting (the way he conveyed those emotions so realistically) was terrific! Really, he made me think, "If there is a single person who complains about Mr. Midorikawa's portrayal of Tamahome, I'm going to punch them out!" I really thought that! ☺ And when Nuriko died (episode 33), I just kept crying and crying... Ms. Sakamoto and Ms. Araki were so great! For anybody who hasn't seen the TV show, rent it if that's the only way, but please see it!! I was so emotional! There was a scene in it where Nuriko and Miaka go on a date in the real world. One of the staff told me, "It's a present for Nuriko." I think Nuriko would like that. There are so many episodes that I'd like to recommend that I wish I could do a commentary on the whole series! ☺ Everybody, please watch the videos!

BONUS PICTURE

By the way, I'm sure you all yelled, "Whyyy?!" when the Country of the Amazons section was cut out! ☺ It seems that the whole situation of them traveling to a nation of Amazon women is too risqué to show on TV. There was nothing the anime company could do. That chapter of the manga was so popular... I was disappointed too! Also, I hear that the heavy scar on Chichiri's eye was too much for TV, so they just had the thin scar going through his eye. Manga isn't immune to these concerns, but TV has a lot of special rules. In exchange, they added more to Keisuke's and Tetsuya's investigation into the "Universe of the Four Gods" mystery! I was happy about that! They were planning a scene where Tatara and Suzuno died at the same time, but events conspired against it, and they couldn't do it. But there were scenes that I didn't do in the manga that they were able to do in the anime!!

Miaka in episode 34 is just wonderful, in a different kind of way! ☺ Ms. Araki arouses my curiosity! ☺

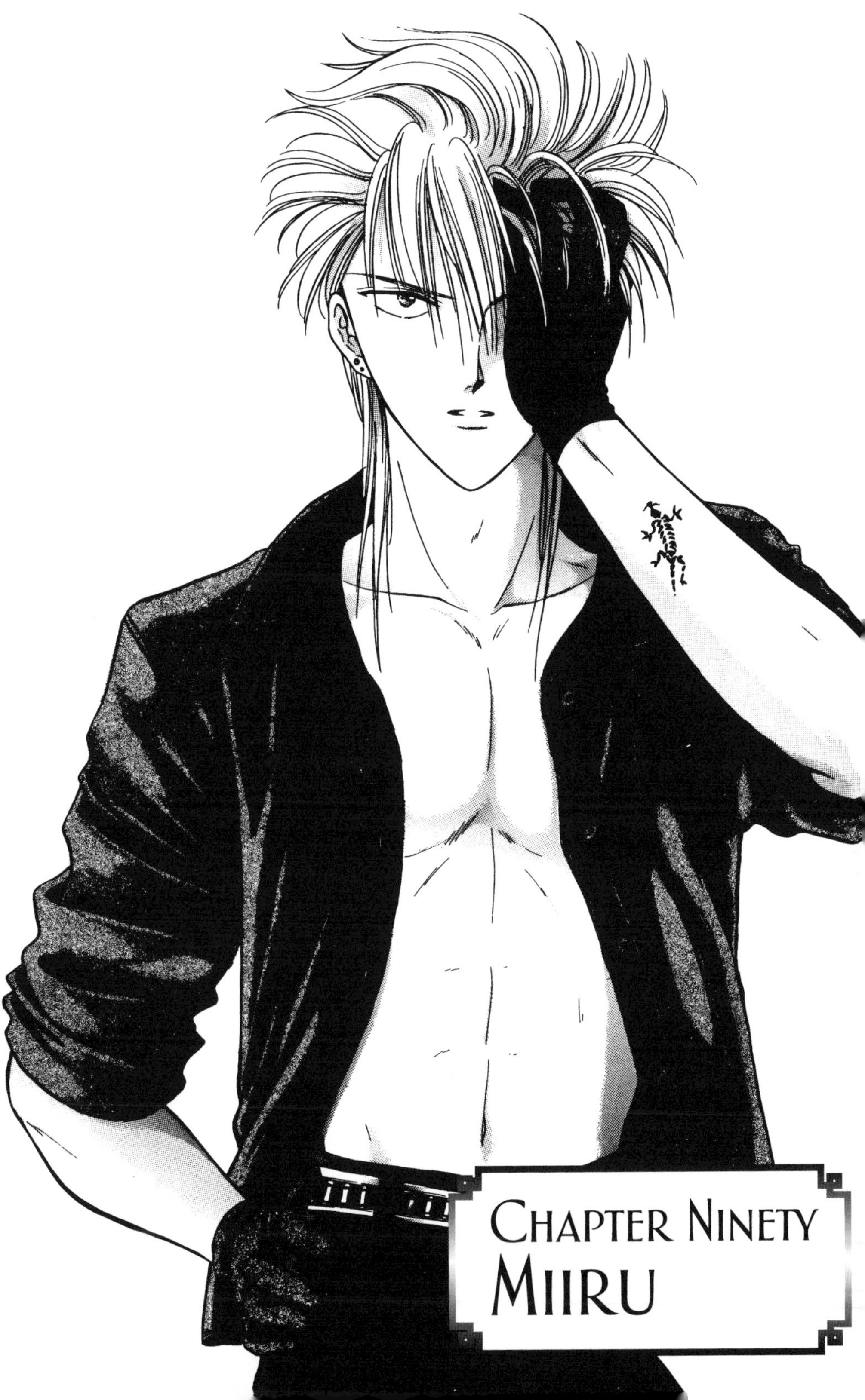
CHAPTER NINETY
MIIRU

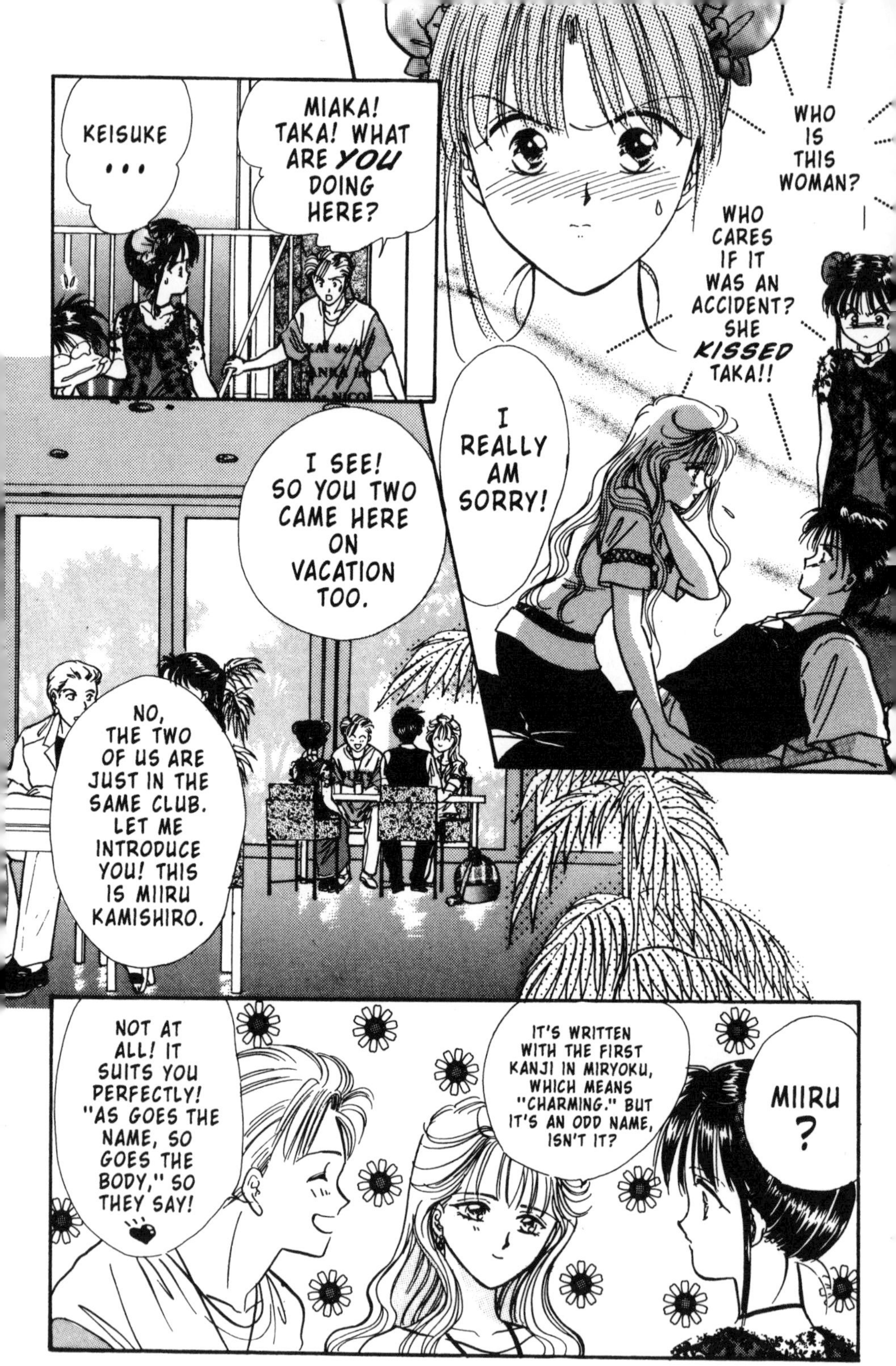
WHO IS THIS WOMAN?
WHO CARES IF IT WAS AN ACCIDENT? SHE *KISSED* TAKA!!
I REALLY AM SORRY!
MIAKA! TAKA! WHAT ARE *YOU* DOING HERE?
KEISUKE ...
I SEE! SO YOU TWO CAME HERE ON VACATION TOO.
NO, THE TWO OF US ARE JUST IN THE SAME CLUB. LET ME INTRODUCE YOU! THIS IS MIIRU KAMISHIRO.
MIIRU ?
IT'S WRITTEN WITH THE FIRST KANJI IN MIRYOKU, WHICH MEANS "CHARMING." BUT IT'S AN ODD NAME, ISN'T IT?
NOT AT ALL! IT SUITS YOU PERFECTLY! "AS GOES THE NAME, SO GOES THE BODY," SO THEY SAY!

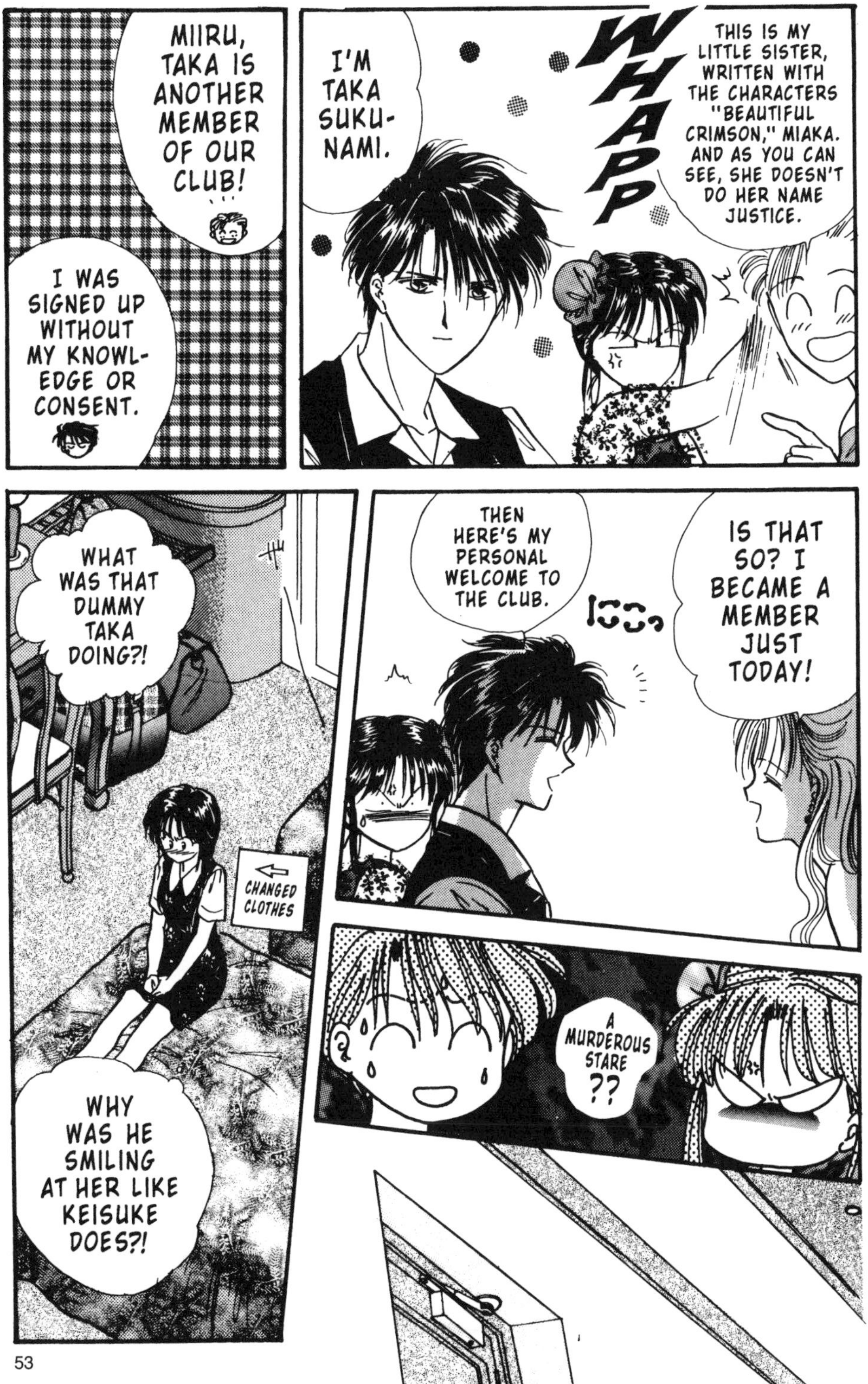
THIS IS MY LITTLE SISTER, WRITTEN WITH THE CHARACTERS "BEAUTIFUL CRIMSON," MIAKA. AND AS YOU CAN SEE, SHE DOESN'T DO HER NAME JUSTICE.
WHAPP
I'M TAKA SUKU-NAMI.
MIIRU, TAKA IS ANOTHER MEMBER OF OUR CLUB!
I WAS SIGNED UP WITHOUT MY KNOWL-EDGE OR CONSENT.
IS THAT SO? I BECAME A MEMBER JUST TODAY!
THEN HERE'S MY PERSONAL WELCOME TO THE CLUB.
にこっ
A MURDEROUS STARE ??
WHAT WAS THAT DUMMY TAKA DOING?!
CHANGED CLOTHES
WHY WAS HE SMILING AT HER LIKE KEISUKE DOES?!

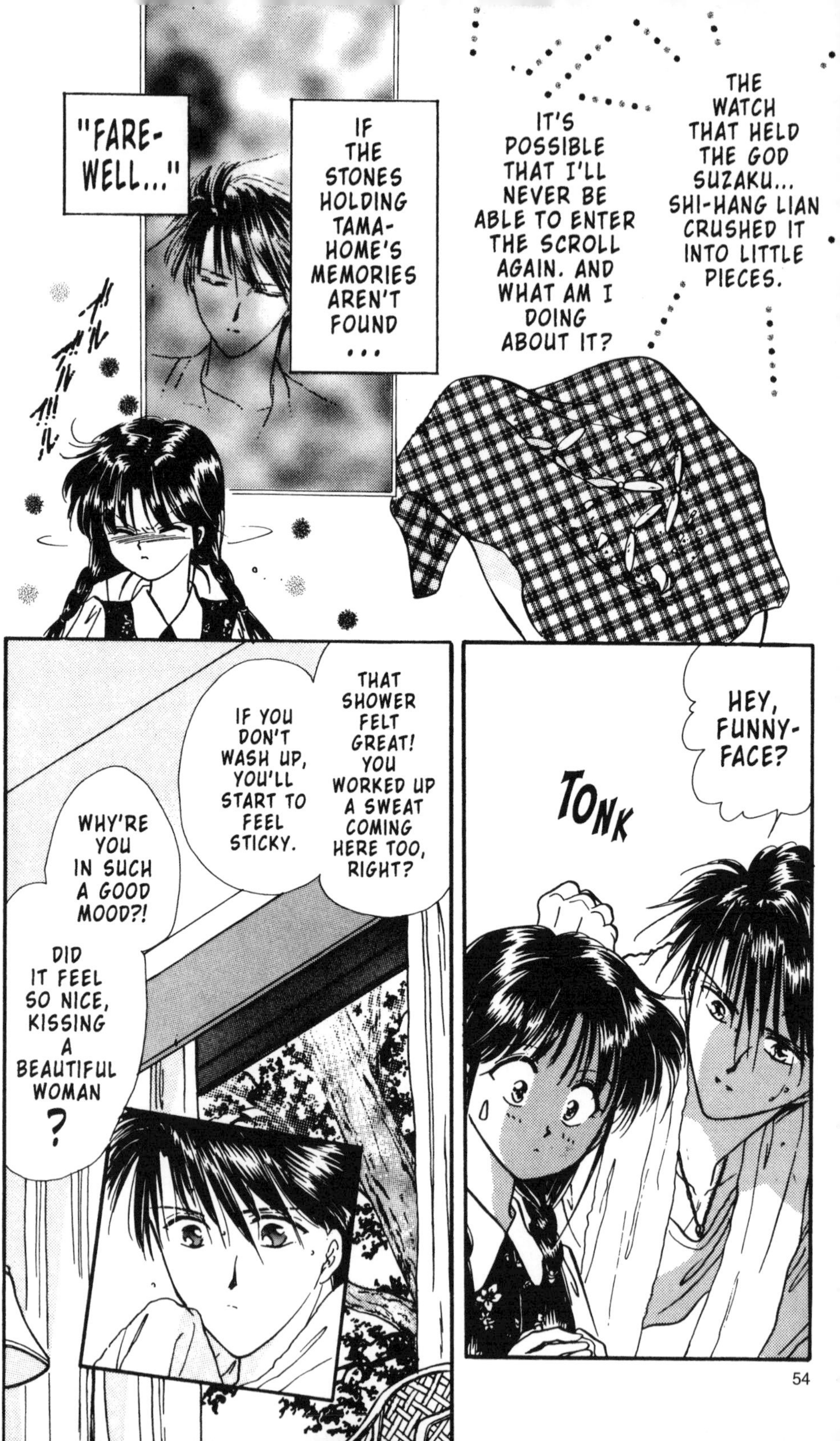
THE WATCH THAT HELD THE GOD SUZAKU... SHI-HANG LIAN CRUSHED IT INTO LITTLE PIECES.
IT'S POSSIBLE THAT I'LL NEVER BE ABLE TO ENTER THE SCROLL AGAIN. AND WHAT AM I DOING ABOUT IT?
IF THE STONES HOLDING TAMAHOME'S MEMORIES AREN'T FOUND...
"FAREWELL..."
HEY, FUNNY-FACE?
TONK
THAT SHOWER FELT GREAT! YOU WORKED UP A SWEAT COMING HERE TOO, RIGHT?
IF YOU DON'T WASH UP, YOU'LL START TO FEEL STICKY.
WHY'RE YOU IN SUCH A GOOD MOOD?!
DID IT FEEL SO NICE, KISSING A BEAUTIFUL WOMAN?

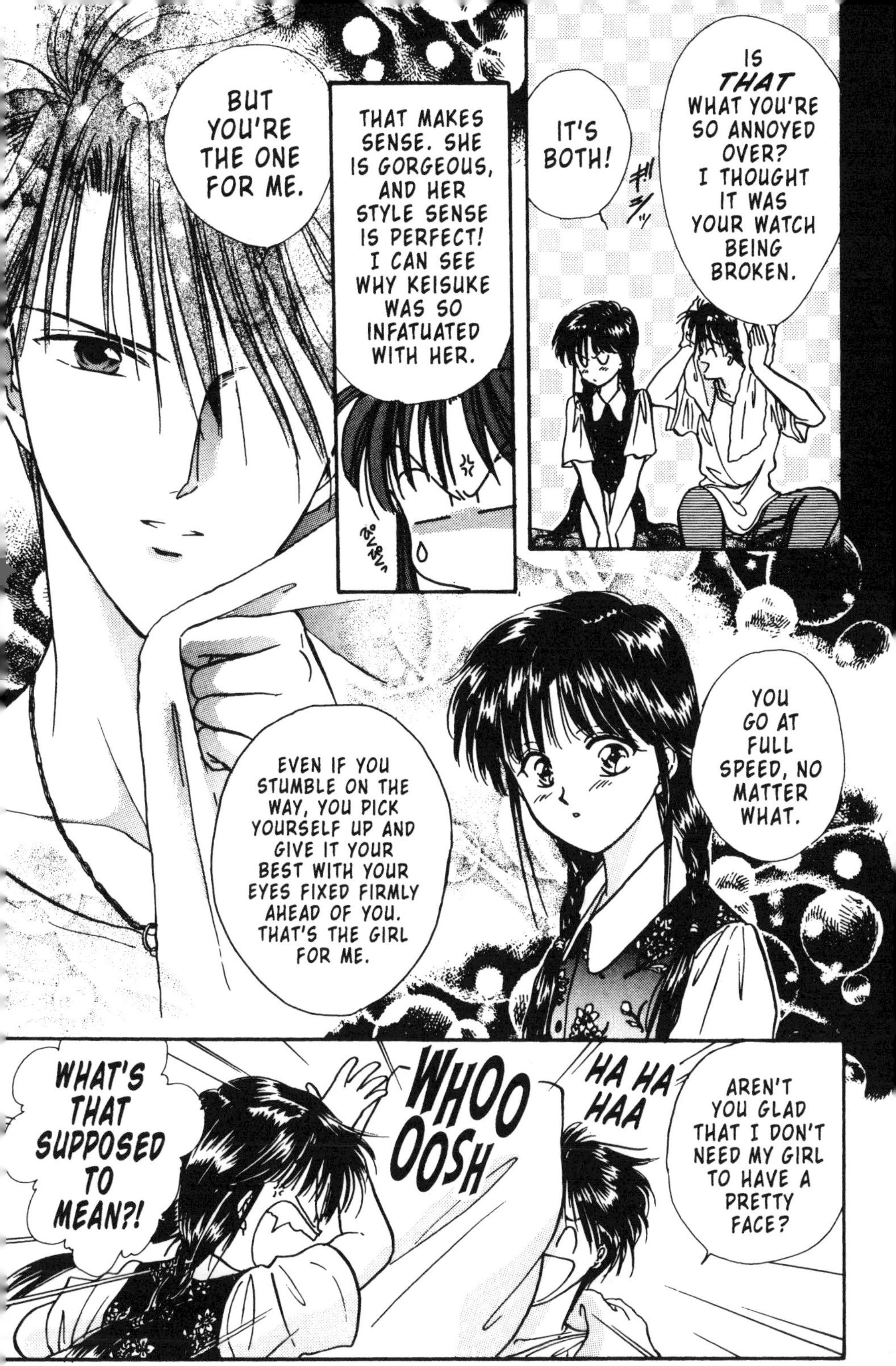
IS *THAT* WHAT YOU'RE SO ANNOYED OVER? I THOUGHT IT WAS YOUR WATCH BEING BROKEN.
IT'S BOTH!
THAT MAKES SENSE. SHE IS GORGEOUS, AND HER STYLE SENSE IS PERFECT! I CAN SEE WHY KEISUKE WAS SO INFATUATED WITH HER.
BUT YOU'RE THE ONE FOR ME.
YOU GO AT FULL SPEED, NO MATTER WHAT.
EVEN IF YOU STUMBLE ON THE WAY, YOU PICK YOURSELF UP AND GIVE IT YOUR BEST WITH YOUR EYES FIXED FIRMLY AHEAD OF YOU. THAT'S THE GIRL FOR ME.
AREN'T YOU GLAD THAT I DON'T NEED MY GIRL TO HAVE A PRETTY FACE?
HA HA HAA
WHOOOOSH
WHAT'S THAT SUPPOSED TO MEAN?!

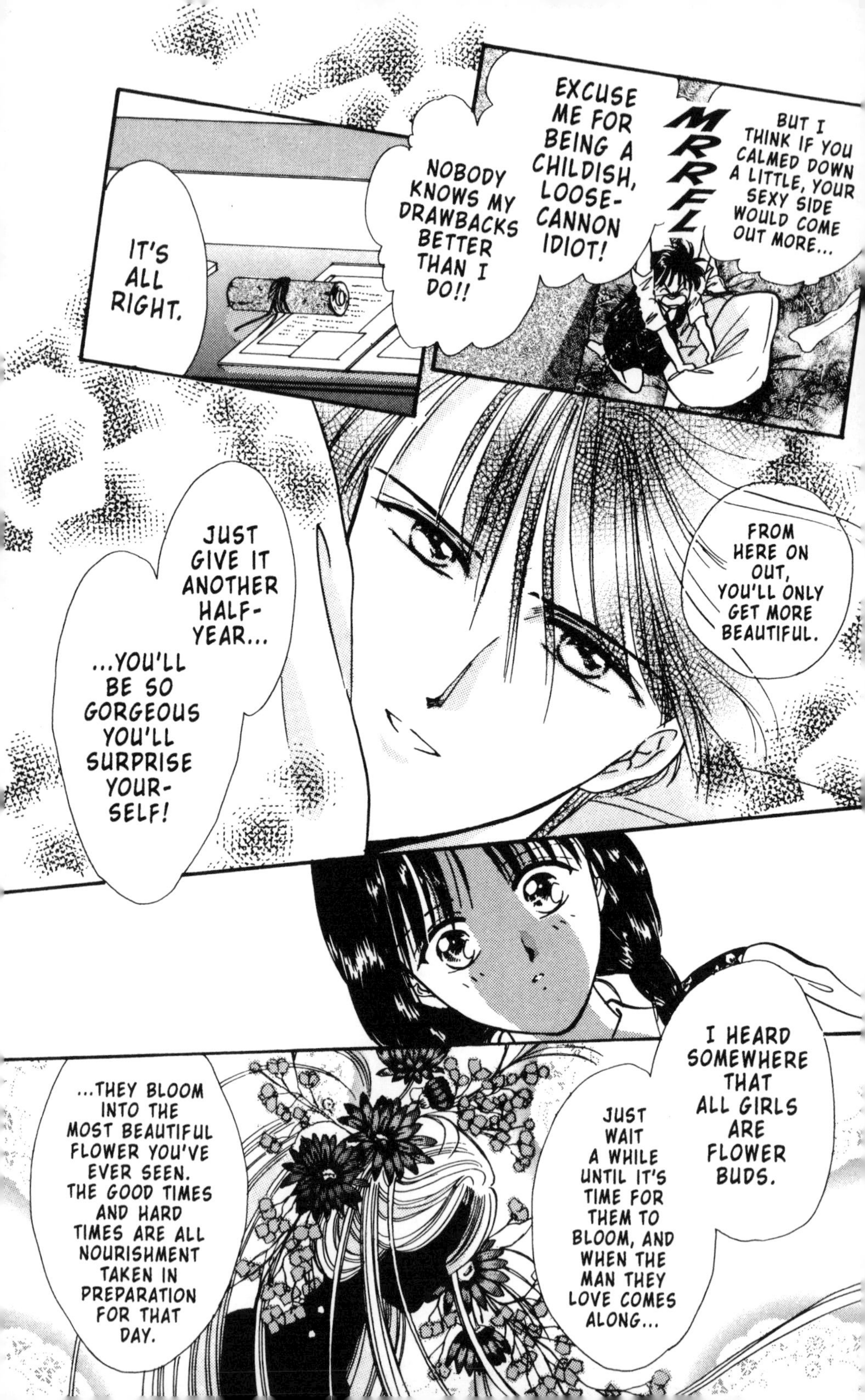
BUT I THINK IF YOU CALMED DOWN A LITTLE, YOUR SEXY SIDE WOULD COME OUT MORE...
MRRFL
EXCUSE ME FOR BEING A CHILDISH, LOOSE-CANNON IDIOT!
NOBODY KNOWS MY DRAWBACKS BETTER THAN I DO!!
IT'S ALL RIGHT.
FROM HERE ON OUT, YOU'LL ONLY GET MORE BEAUTIFUL.
JUST GIVE IT ANOTHER HALF-YEAR...
...YOU'LL BE SO GORGEOUS YOU'LL SURPRISE YOURSELF!
I HEARD SOMEWHERE THAT ALL GIRLS ARE FLOWER BUDS.
JUST WAIT A WHILE UNTIL IT'S TIME FOR THEM TO BLOOM, AND WHEN THE MAN THEY LOVE COMES ALONG...
...THEY BLOOM INTO THE MOST BEAUTIFUL FLOWER YOU'VE EVER SEEN. THE GOOD TIMES AND HARD TIMES ARE ALL NOURISHMENT TAKEN IN PREPARATION FOR THAT DAY.

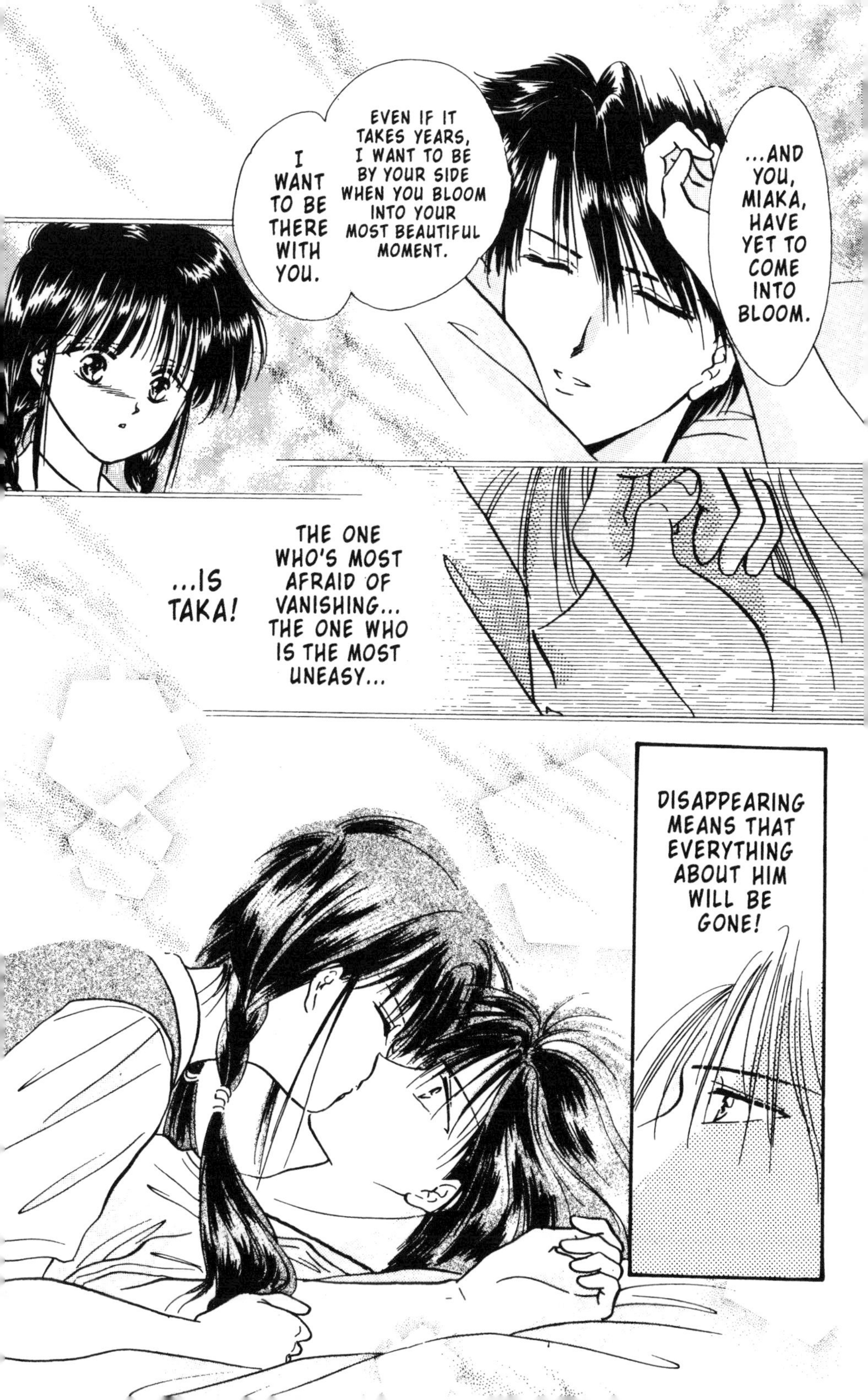
...AND YOU, MIAKA, HAVE YET TO COME INTO BLOOM.
EVEN IF IT TAKES YEARS, I WANT TO BE BY YOUR SIDE WHEN YOU BLOOM INTO YOUR MOST BEAUTIFUL MOMENT.
I WANT TO BE THERE WITH YOU.
THE ONE WHO'S MOST AFRAID OF VANISHING... THE ONE WHO IS THE MOST UNEASY...
...IS TAKA!
DISAPPEARING MEANS THAT EVERYTHING ABOUT HIM WILL BE GONE!

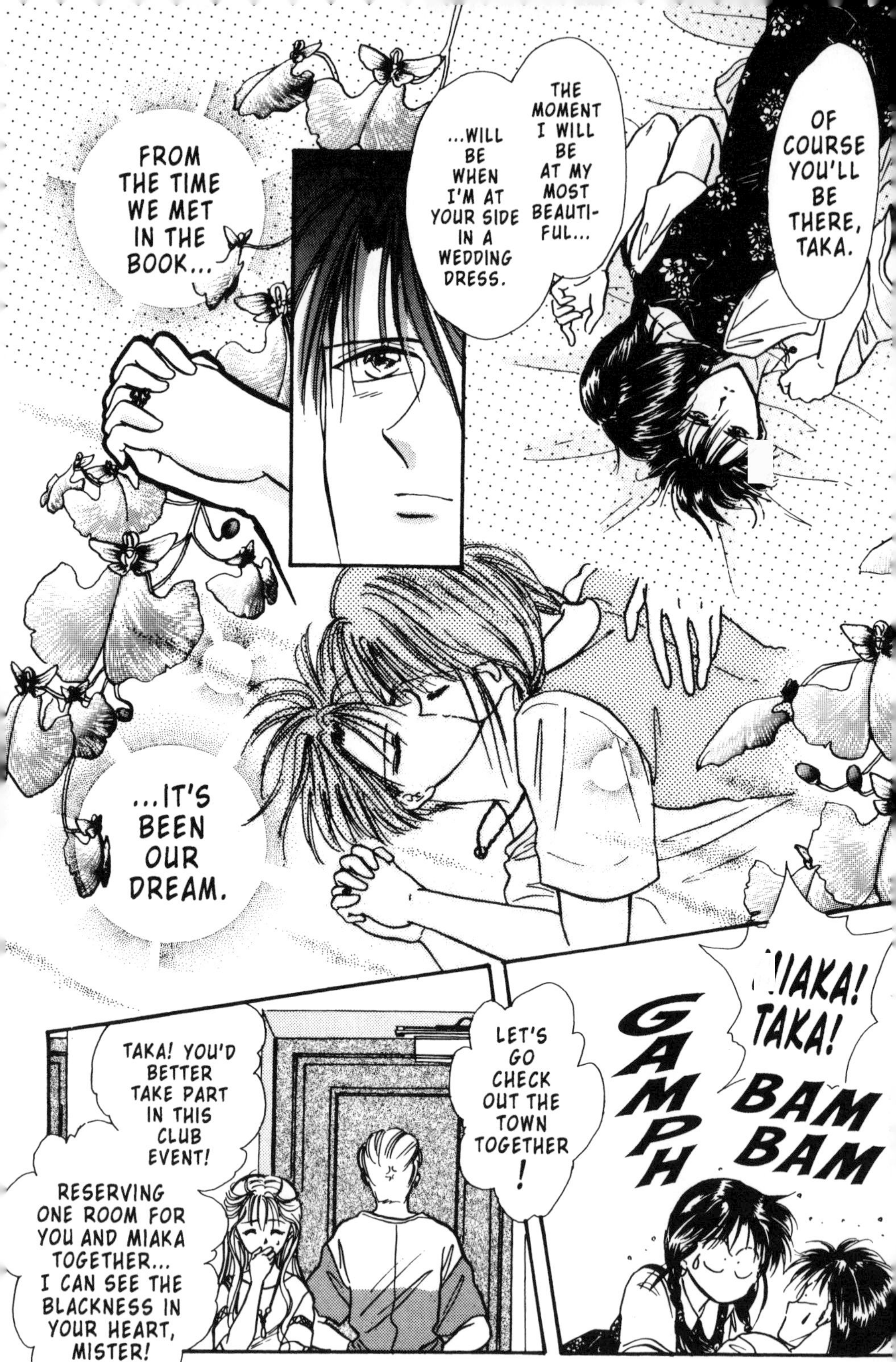
OF COURSE YOU'LL BE THERE, TAKA.
THE MOMENT I WILL BE AT MY MOST BEAUTI-FUL...
...WILL BE WHEN I'M AT YOUR SIDE IN A WEDDING DRESS.
FROM THE TIME WE MET IN THE BOOK...
...IT'S BEEN OUR DREAM.
IAKA! TAKA!
BAM BAM
GAMPH
LET'S GO CHECK OUT THE TOWN TOGETHER!
TAKA! YOU'D BETTER TAKE PART IN THIS CLUB EVENT!
RESERVING ONE ROOM FOR YOU AND MIAKA TOGETHER... I CAN SEE THE BLACKNESS IN YOUR HEART, MISTER!

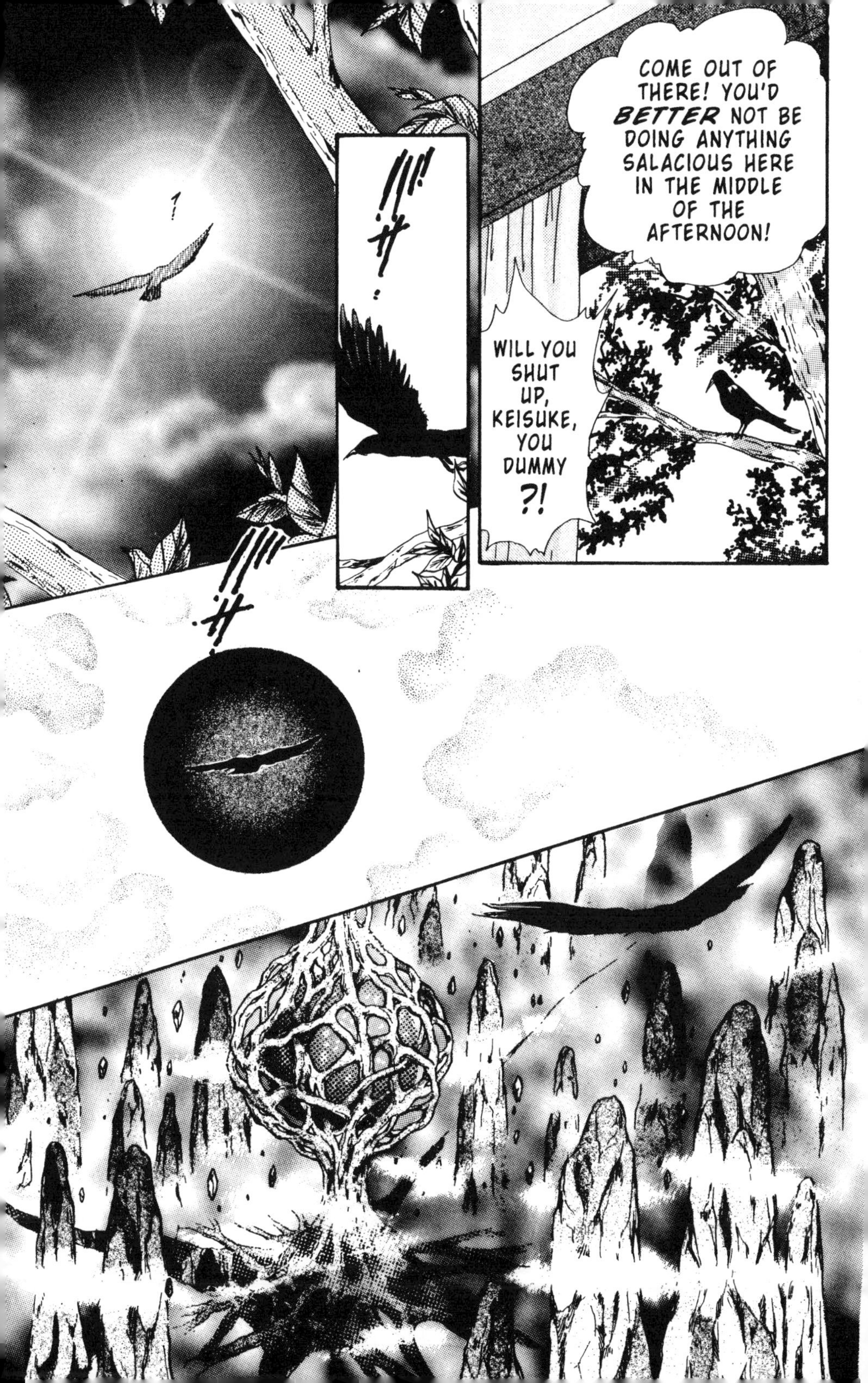
COME OUT OF THERE! YOU'D BETTER NOT BE DOING ANYTHING SALACIOUS HERE IN THE MIDDLE OF THE AFTERNOON!
WILL YOU SHUT UP, KEISUKE, YOU DUMMY ?!
?

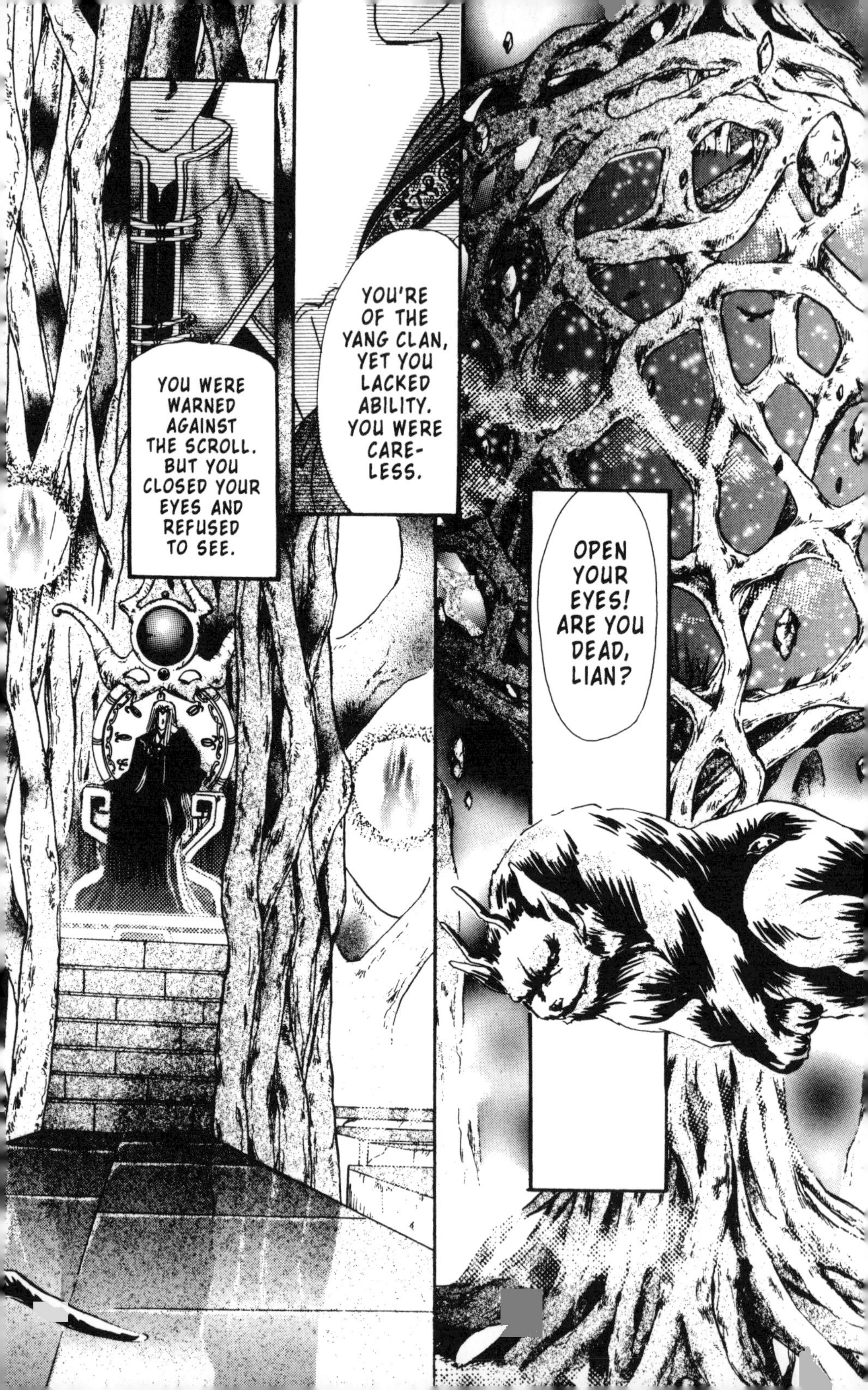
YOU'RE OF THE YANG CLAN, YET YOU LACKED ABILITY. YOU WERE CARE-LESS.
YOU WERE WARNED AGAINST THE SCROLL. BUT YOU CLOSED YOUR EYES AND REFUSED TO SEE.
OPEN YOUR EYES! ARE YOU DEAD, LIAN?

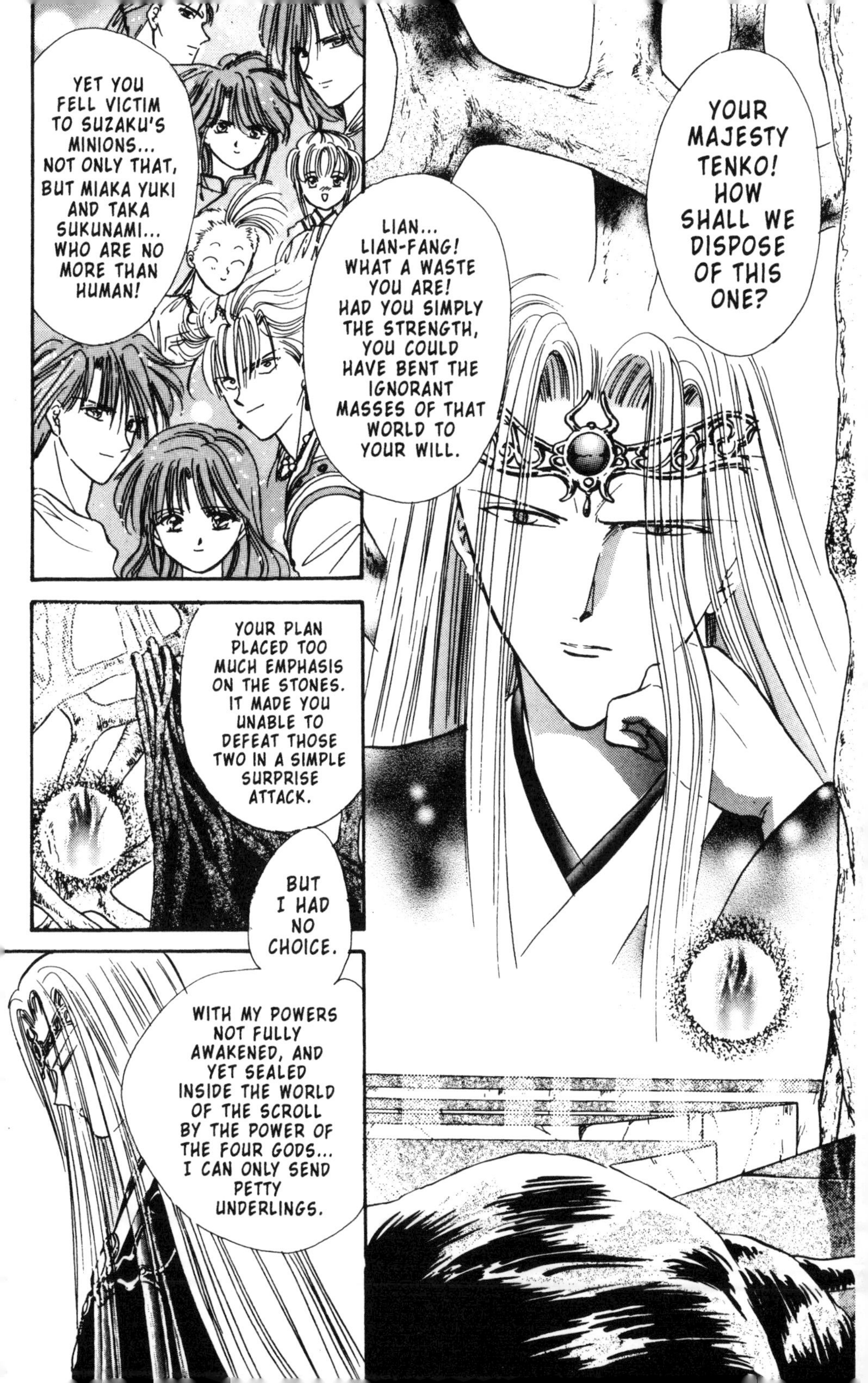
YOUR MAJESTY TENKO! HOW SHALL WE DISPOSE OF THIS ONE?
LIAN... LIAN-FANG! WHAT A WASTE YOU ARE! HAD YOU SIMPLY THE STRENGTH, YOU COULD HAVE BENT THE IGNORANT MASSES OF THAT WORLD TO YOUR WILL.
YET YOU FELL VICTIM TO SUZAKU'S MINIONS... NOT ONLY THAT, BUT MIAKA YUKI AND TAKA SUKUNAMI... WHO ARE NO MORE THAN HUMAN!
YOUR PLAN PLACED TOO MUCH EMPHASIS ON THE STONES. IT MADE YOU UNABLE TO DEFEAT THOSE TWO IN A SIMPLE SURPRISE ATTACK.
BUT I HAD NO CHOICE.
WITH MY POWERS NOT FULLY AWAKENED, AND YET SEALED INSIDE THE WORLD OF THE SCROLL BY THE POWER OF THE FOUR GODS... I CAN ONLY SEND PETTY UNDERLINGS.

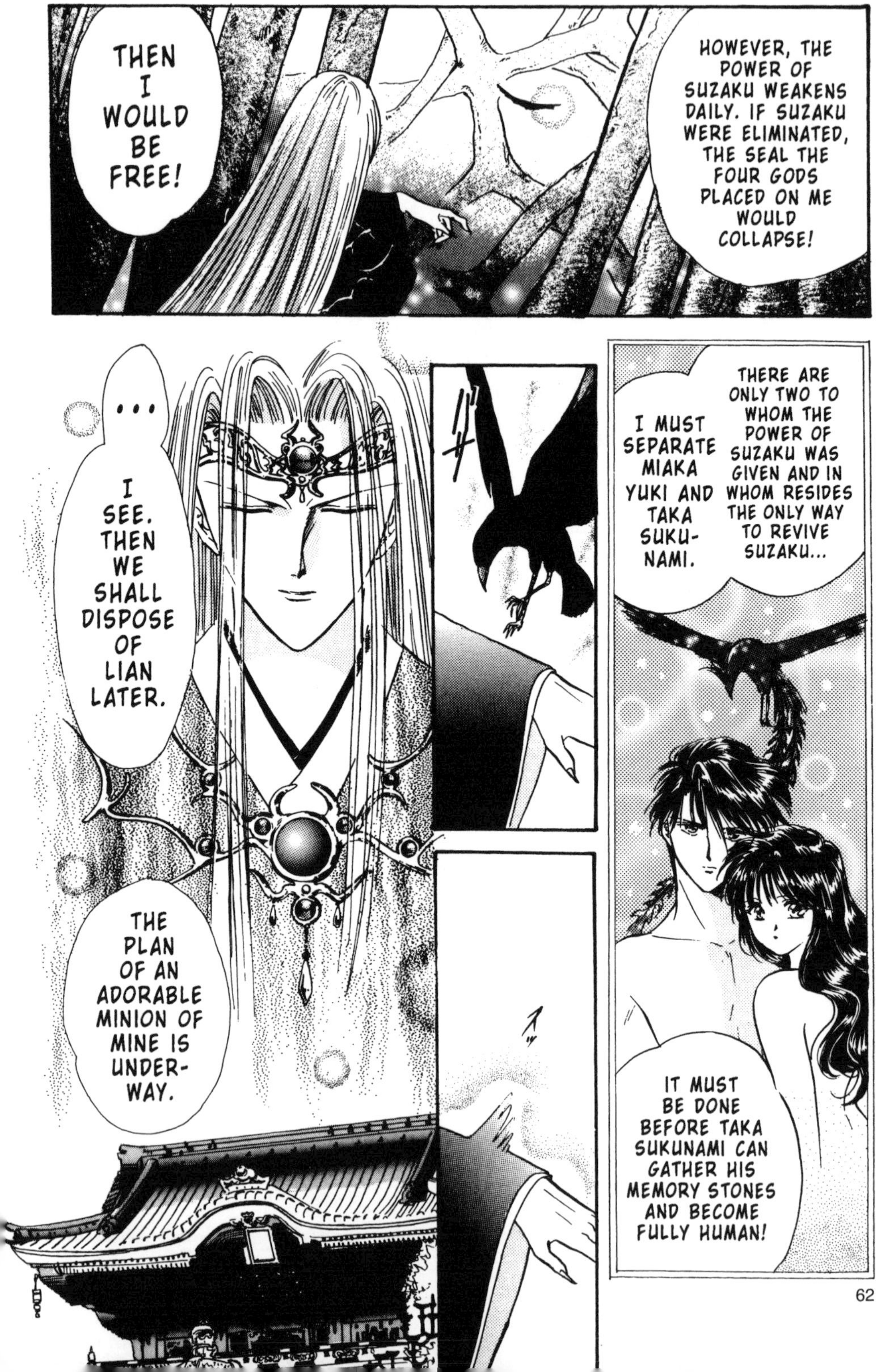
HOWEVER, THE POWER OF SUZAKU WEAKENS DAILY. IF SUZAKU WERE ELIMINATED, THE SEAL THE FOUR GODS PLACED ON ME WOULD COLLAPSE!
THEN I WOULD BE FREE!
THERE ARE ONLY TWO TO WHOM THE POWER OF SUZAKU WAS GIVEN AND IN WHOM RESIDES THE ONLY WAY TO REVIVE SUZAKU...
I MUST SEPARATE MIAKA YUKI AND TAKA SUKU-NAMI.
IT MUST BE DONE BEFORE TAKA SUKUNAMI CAN GATHER HIS MEMORY STONES AND BECOME FULLY HUMAN!
...
I SEE. THEN WE SHALL DISPOSE OF LIAN LATER.
THE PLAN OF AN ADORABLE MINION OF MINE IS UNDER-WAY.

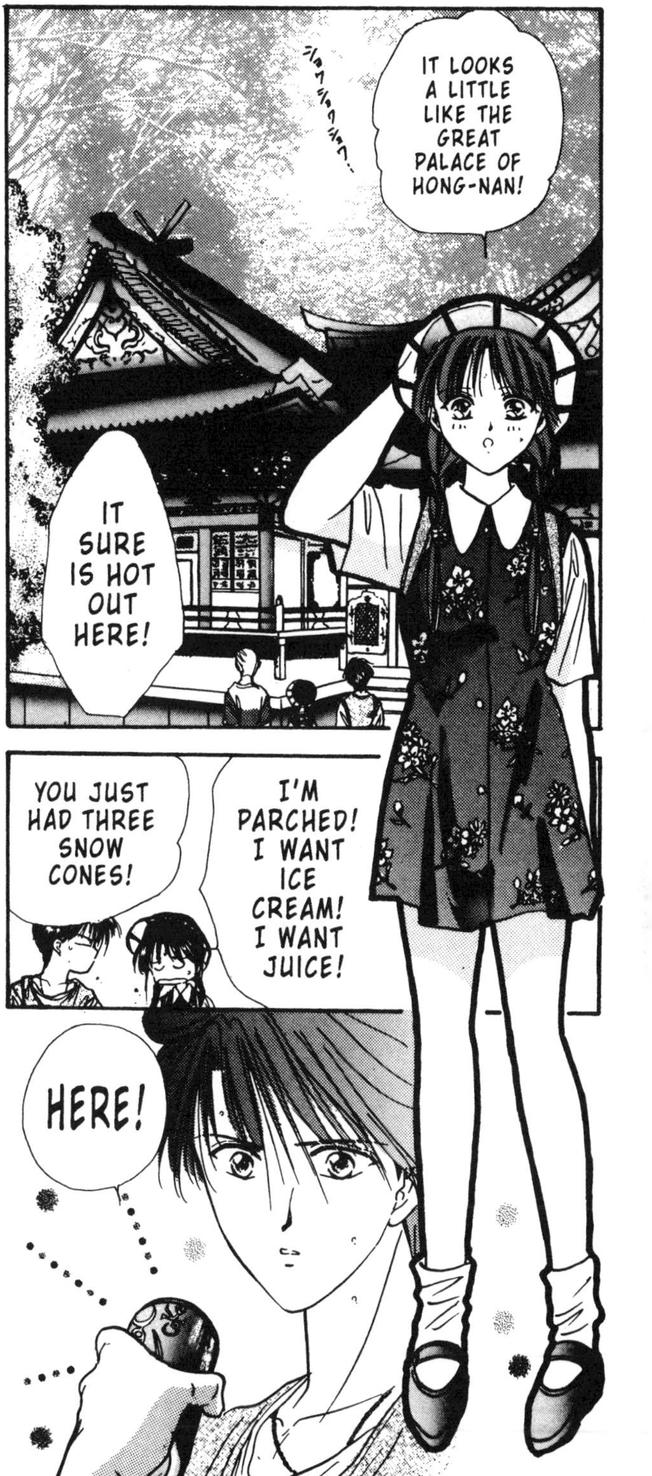
IT LOOKS A LITTLE LIKE THE GREAT PALACE OF HONG-NAN!
IT SURE IS HOT OUT HERE!
I'M PARCHED! I WANT ICE CREAM! I WANT JUICE!
YOU JUST HAD THREE SNOW CONES!
HERE!

So... I received a present through the president of Daran Publishing, and it was a Ming Dynasty (Did I say Ch'ing before? I know nothing!!) woman's jeweled seal that's a real treasure! (By the way, the president is a collector of rare treasures.) And he's got two jeweled necklaces!

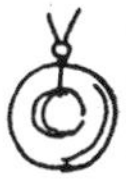

This is one type. The other is in the shape of a dragon.

▷ This one is definitely Ch'ing Dynasty. The jewel that's attached is a stone from the Pamirs region of India.
The dragon is from the Sung Dynasty. (Hong-Nan is based on this time.) The one above is Ming Dynasty. I hope I got the period right!
The most amazing thing I received was a loose jewel (not set into a necklace) from between two and three thousand years ago! Two to three thousand years old! Isn't it...just...***incredible?*** I received other things, but this one was the most amazing. By the way, in China (...this is Taiwan...it's complicated) people keep their heirlooms close. When I was eating, I saw a waitress was wearing a seal on her bracelet. (Seals are very valuable items.) And to give me quite a number of such precious items... I'm really honored by their consideration!
One other thing: I was treated to the best tea in Taiwan by Daran Publishing's president! I even got some of the tea to take home! ☺ I wonder if it is proper to accept so many gifts! ☺
I want to thank all the people who were with me the whole time, Mr. Wong (he speaks Japanese perfectly!) and Mr. Zou...and Ms. Tomoko Takagishi from MSC, etc., etc. Thank you for everything you've done for me!
(And sorry I was so out of it!)

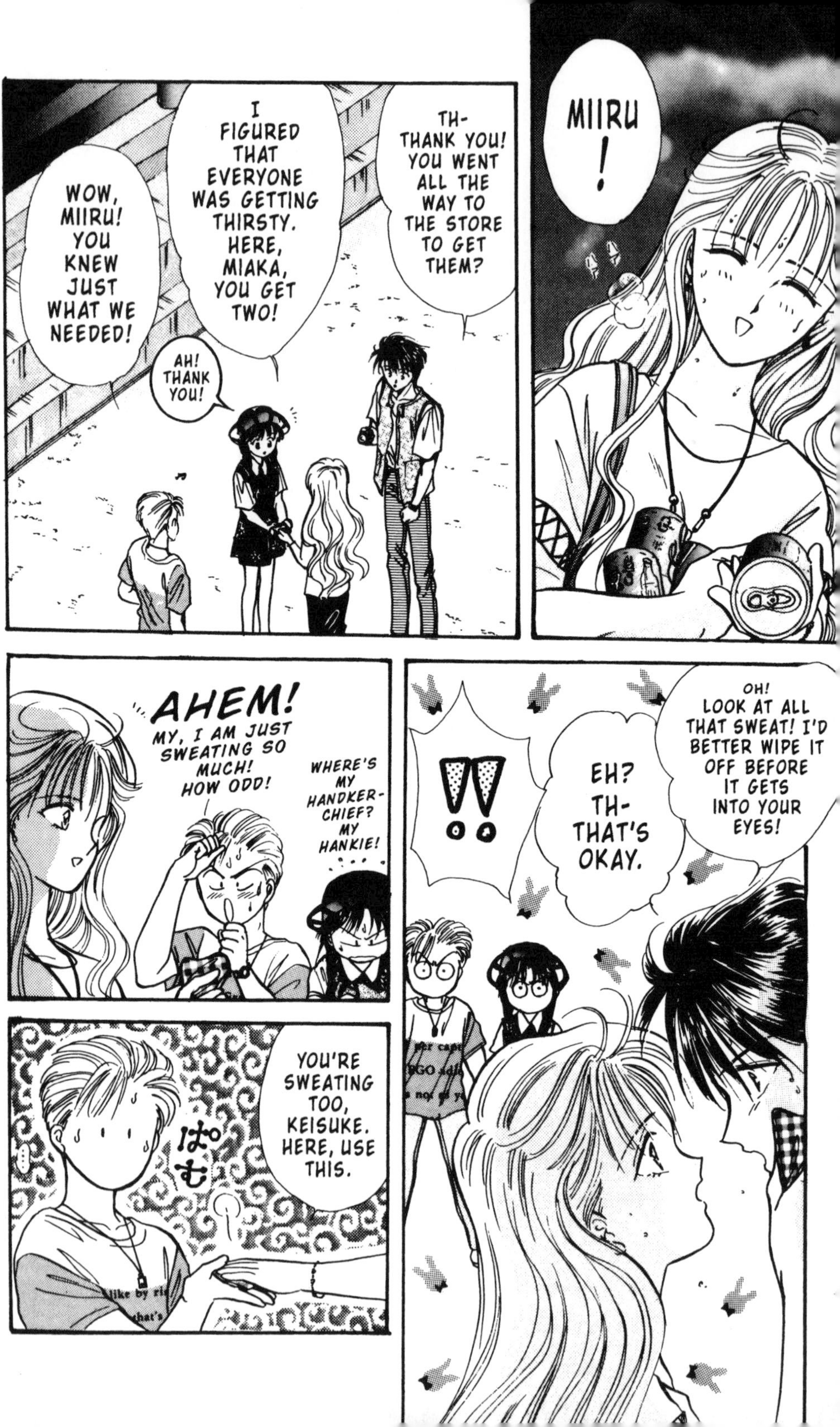
MIIRU!
TH-THANK YOU! YOU WENT ALL THE WAY TO THE STORE TO GET THEM?
I FIGURED THAT EVERYONE WAS GETTING THIRSTY. HERE, MIAKA, YOU GET TWO!
WOW, MIIRU! YOU KNEW JUST WHAT WE NEEDED!
AH! THANK YOU!
OH! LOOK AT ALL THAT SWEAT! I'D BETTER WIPE IT OFF BEFORE IT GETS INTO YOUR EYES!
EH? TH-THAT'S OKAY.
!!
WHERE'S MY HANDKERCHIEF? MY HANKIE!
AHEM!
MY, I AM JUST SWEATING SO MUCH! HOW ODD!
YOU'RE SWEATING TOO, KEISUKE. HERE, USE THIS.
ぱむ
...

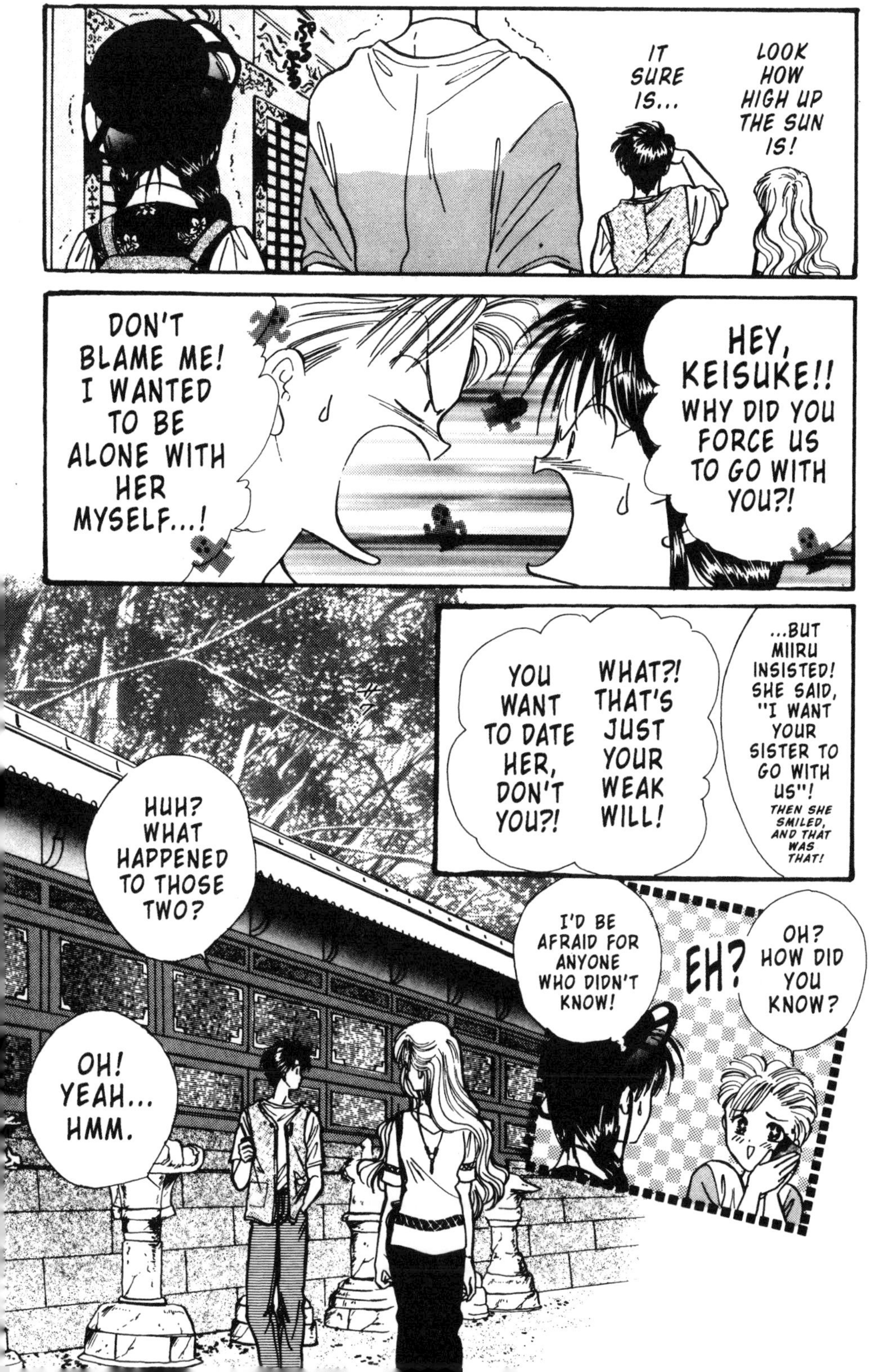
LOOK HOW HIGH UP THE SUN IS!
IT SURE IS...
HEY, KEISUKE!! WHY DID YOU FORCE US TO GO WITH YOU?!
DON'T BLAME ME! I WANTED TO BE ALONE WITH HER MYSELF...!
...BUT MIIRU INSISTED! SHE SAID, "I WANT YOUR SISTER TO GO WITH US"! THEN SHE SMILED, AND THAT WAS THAT!
WHAT?! THAT'S JUST YOUR WEAK WILL!
YOU WANT TO DATE HER, DON'T YOU?!
OH? HOW DID YOU KNOW?
EH?
I'D BE AFRAID FOR ANYONE WHO DIDN'T KNOW!
HUH? WHAT HAPPENED TO THOSE TWO?
OH! YEAH... HMM.

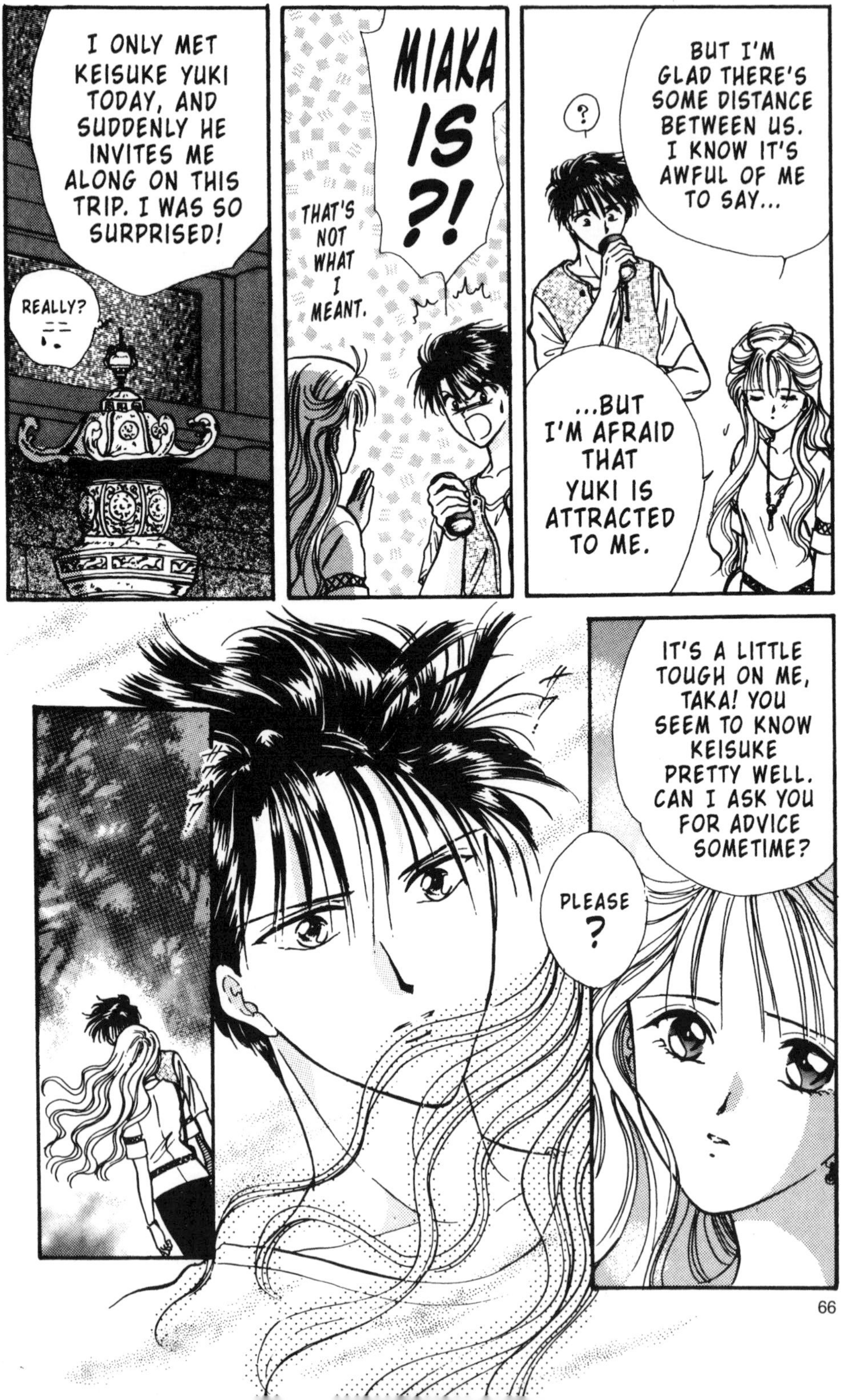
?
BUT I'M GLAD THERE'S SOME DISTANCE BETWEEN US. I KNOW IT'S AWFUL OF ME TO SAY...
...BUT I'M AFRAID THAT YUKI IS ATTRACTED TO ME.
MIAKA IS ?!
THAT'S NOT WHAT I MEANT.
I ONLY MET KEISUKE YUKI TODAY, AND SUDDENLY HE INVITES ME ALONG ON THIS TRIP. I WAS SO SURPRISED!
REALLY?
IT'S A LITTLE TOUGH ON ME, TAKA! YOU SEEM TO KNOW KEISUKE PRETTY WELL. CAN I ASK YOU FOR ADVICE SOMETIME?
PLEASE ?

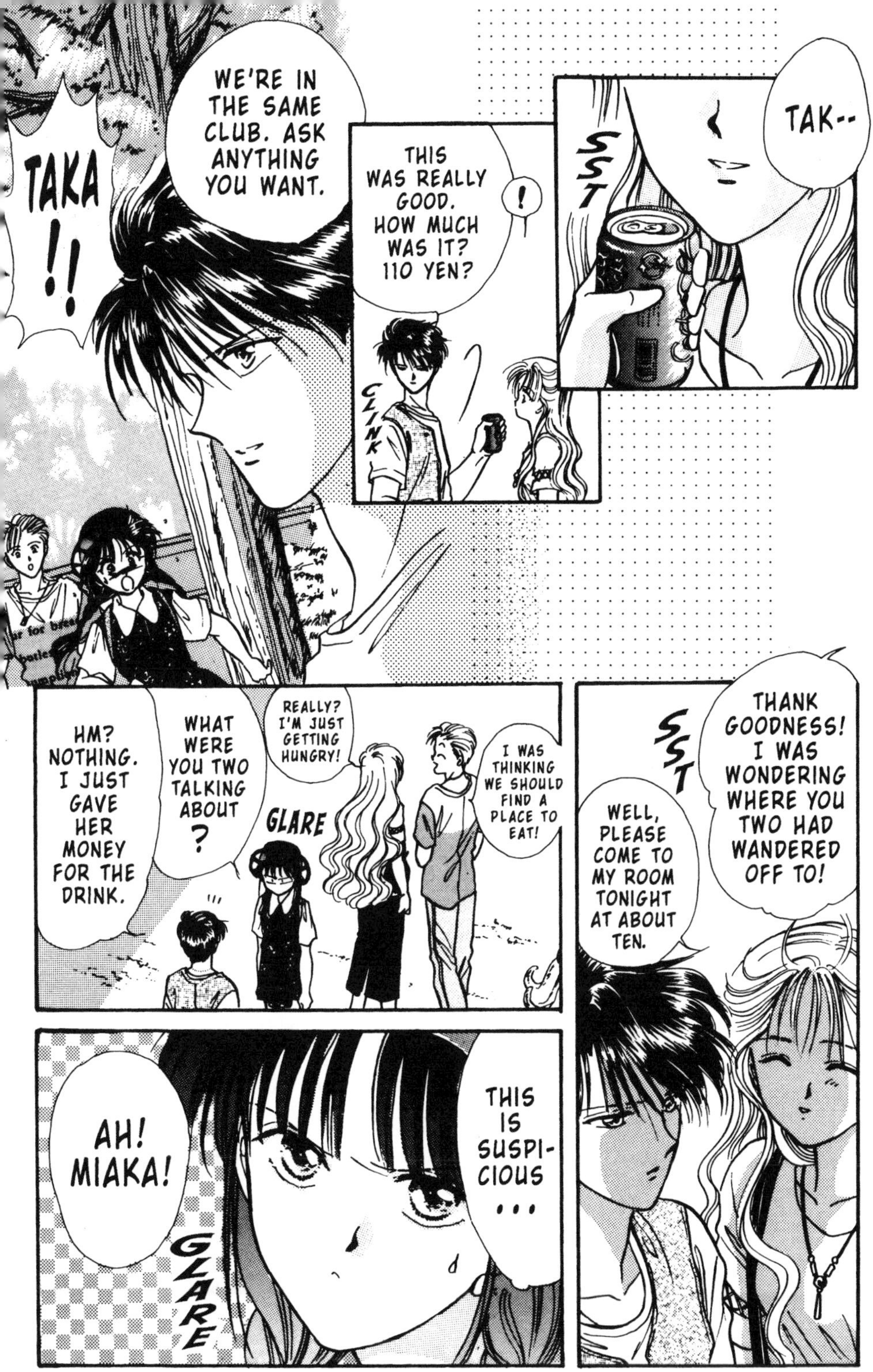
TAK--
SST
THIS WAS REALLY GOOD. HOW MUCH WAS IT? 110 YEN?
!
CLINK
WE'RE IN THE SAME CLUB. ASK ANYTHING YOU WANT.
TAKA!!
THANK GOODNESS! I WAS WONDERING WHERE YOU TWO HAD WANDERED OFF TO!
SST
WELL, PLEASE COME TO MY ROOM TONIGHT AT ABOUT TEN.
I WAS THINKING WE SHOULD FIND A PLACE TO EAT!
REALLY? I'M JUST GETTING HUNGRY!
WHAT WERE YOU TWO TALKING ABOUT?
GLARE
HM? NOTHING. I JUST GAVE HER MONEY FOR THE DRINK.
THIS IS SUSPICIOUS...
AH! MIAKA!
GLARE

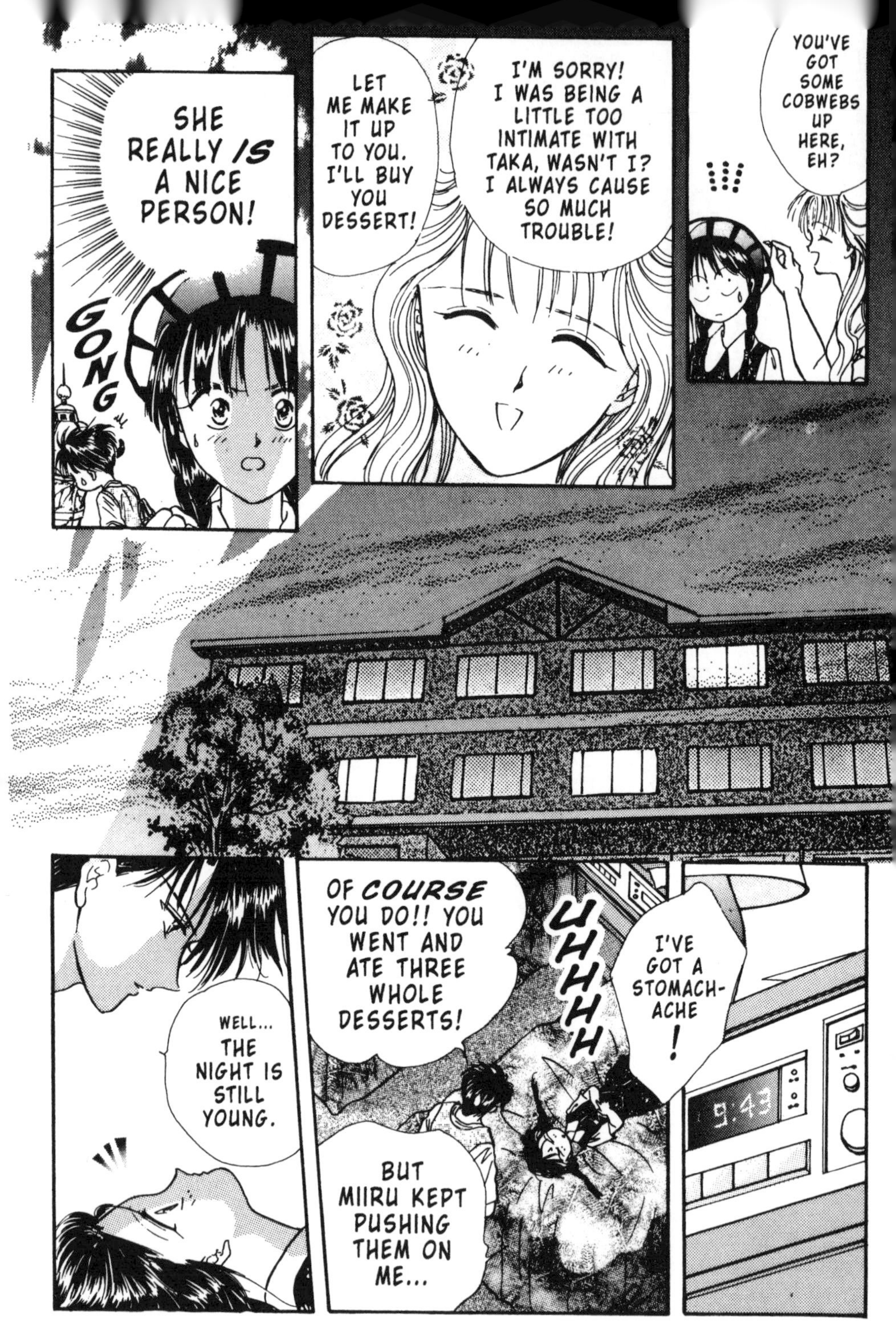
YOU'VE GOT SOME COBWEBS UP HERE, EH?
I'M SORRY! I WAS BEING A LITTLE TOO INTIMATE WITH TAKA, WASN'T I? I ALWAYS CAUSE SO MUCH TROUBLE!
LET ME MAKE IT UP TO YOU. I'LL BUY YOU DESSERT!
SHE REALLY IS A NICE PERSON!
GONG
I'VE GOT A STOMACH-ACHE!
9:43
UHHHH
OF COURSE YOU DO!! YOU WENT AND ATE THREE WHOLE DESSERTS!
BUT MIIRU KEPT PUSHING THEM ON ME...
WELL... THE NIGHT IS STILL YOUNG.

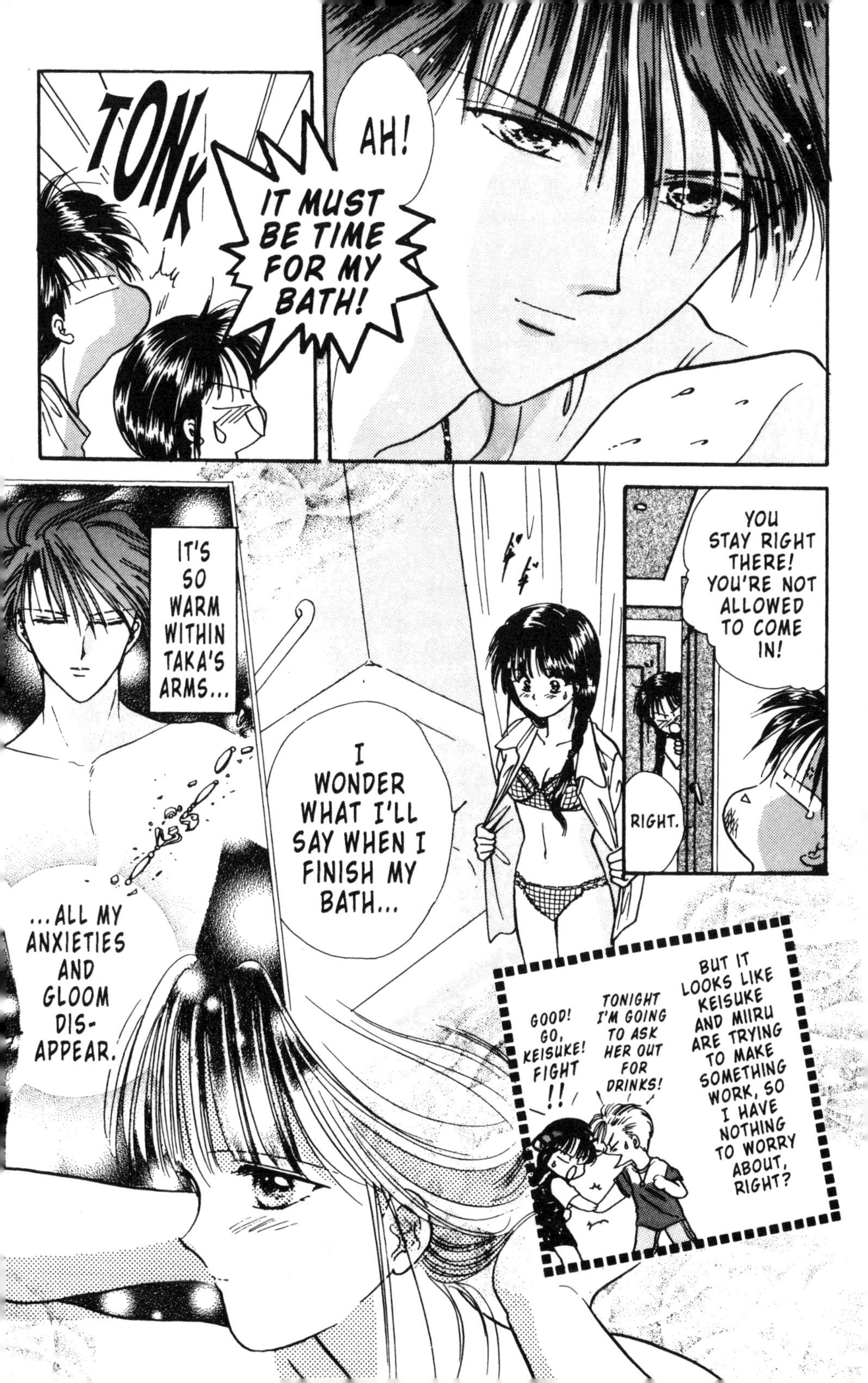
AH!
IT MUST BE TIME FOR MY BATH!
TONK
YOU STAY RIGHT THERE! YOU'RE NOT ALLOWED TO COME IN!
RIGHT.
I WONDER WHAT I'LL SAY WHEN I FINISH MY BATH...
IT'S SO WARM WITHIN TAKA'S ARMS...
...ALL MY ANXIETIES AND GLOOM DIS-APPEAR.
BUT IT LOOKS LIKE KEISUKE AND MIIRU ARE TRYING TO MAKE SOMETHING WORK, SO I HAVE NOTHING TO WORRY ABOUT, RIGHT?
TONIGHT I'M GOING TO ASK HER OUT FOR DRINKS!
GOOD! GO, KEISUKE! FIGHT!!

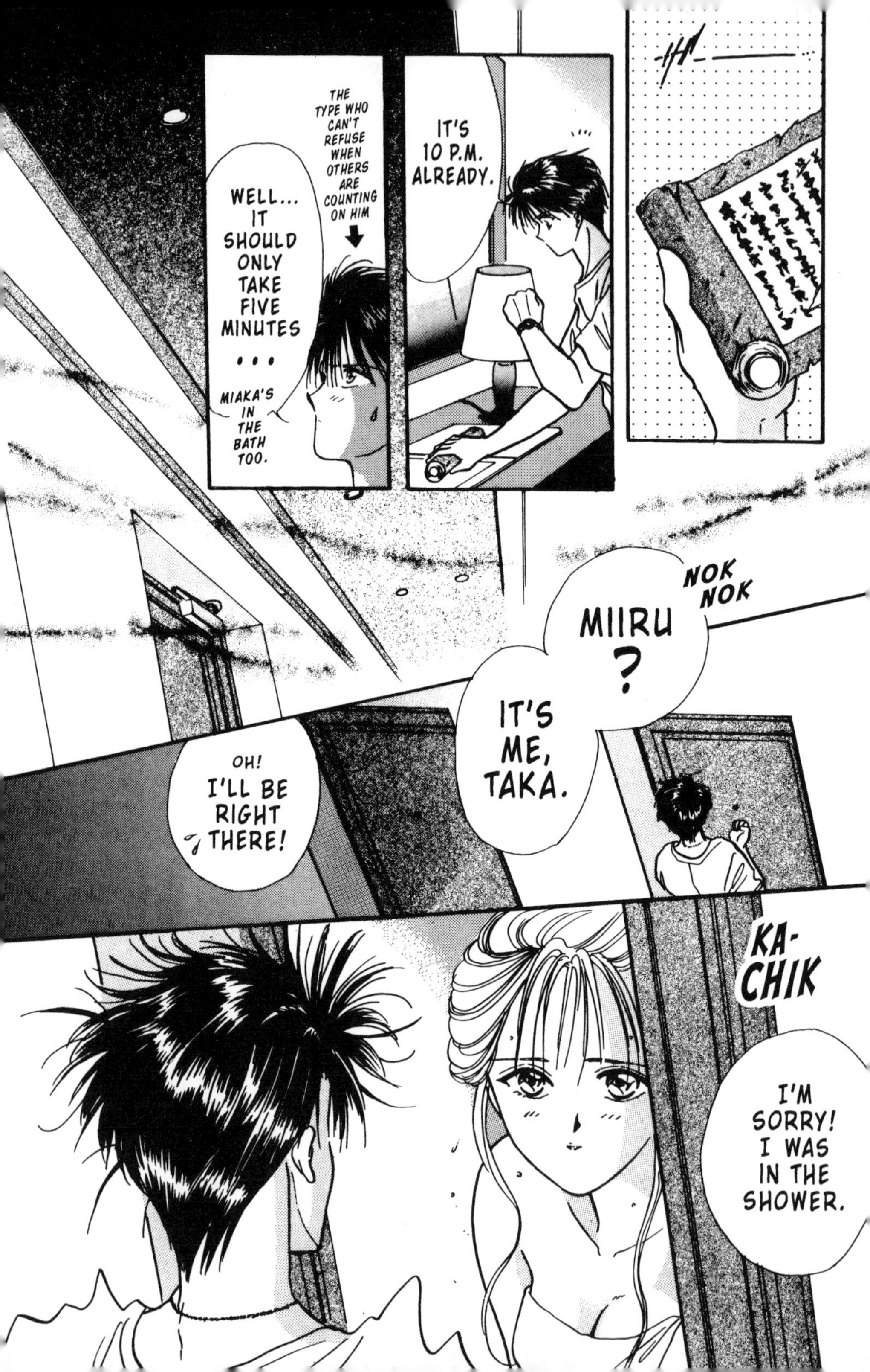
IT'S 10 P.M. ALREADY.
THE TYPE WHO CAN'T REFUSE WHEN OTHERS ARE COUNTING ON HIM
WELL... IT SHOULD ONLY TAKE FIVE MINUTES...
MIAKA'S IN THE BATH TOO.
NOK NOK
MIIRU?
IT'S ME, TAKA.
OH! I'LL BE RIGHT THERE!
KA-CHIK
I'M SORRY! I WAS IN THE SHOWER.

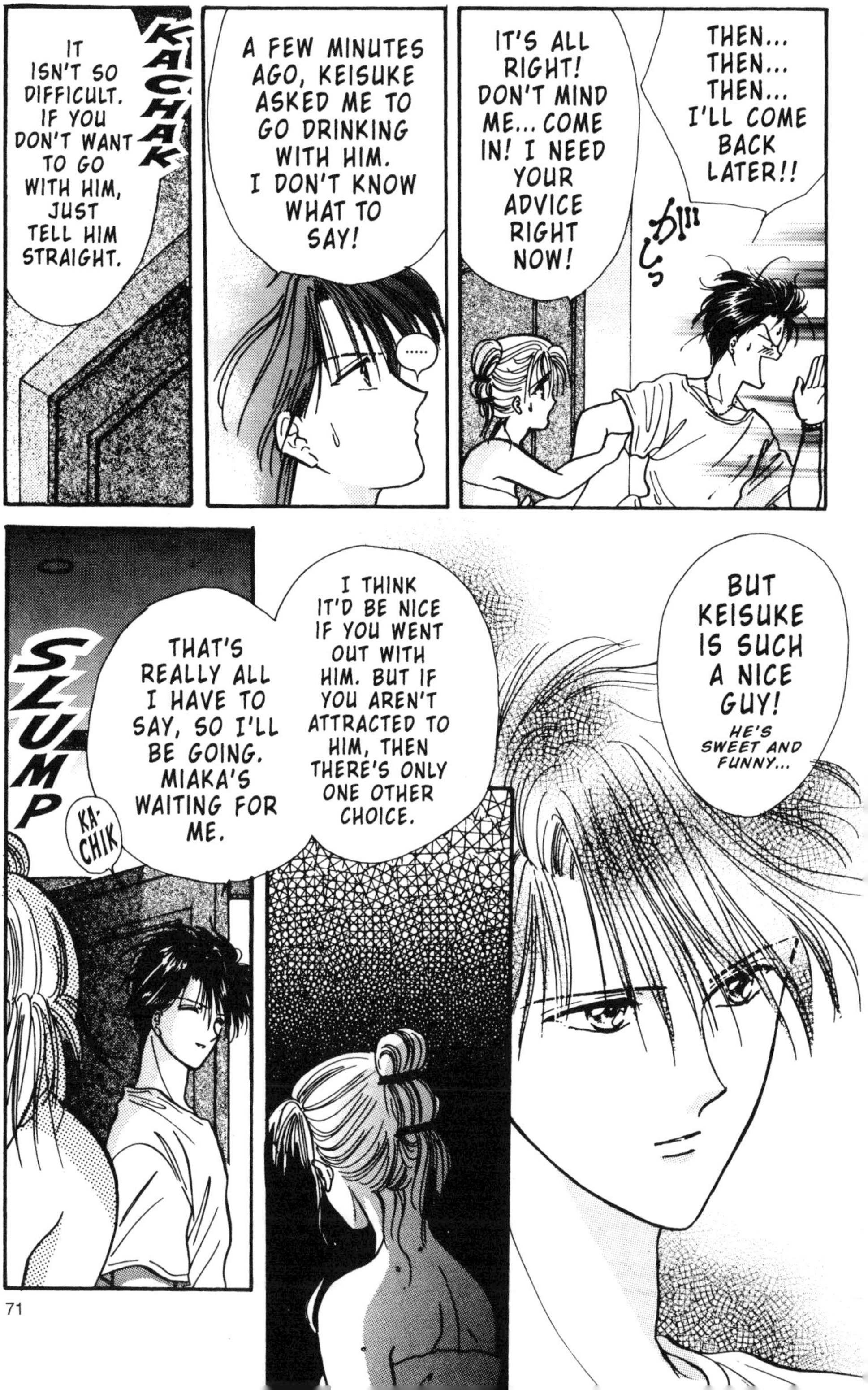
THEN... THEN... THEN... I'LL COME BACK LATER!!
IT'S ALL RIGHT! DON'T MIND ME... COME IN! I NEED YOUR ADVICE RIGHT NOW!
A FEW MINUTES AGO, KEISUKE ASKED ME TO GO DRINKING WITH HIM. I DON'T KNOW WHAT TO SAY!
.....
KACHAK
IT ISN'T SO DIFFICULT. IF YOU DON'T WANT TO GO WITH HIM, JUST TELL HIM STRAIGHT.
BUT KEISUKE IS SUCH A NICE GUY!
HE'S SWEET AND FUNNY...
I THINK IT'D BE NICE IF YOU WENT OUT WITH HIM. BUT IF YOU AREN'T ATTRACTED TO HIM, THEN THERE'S ONLY ONE OTHER CHOICE.
THAT'S REALLY ALL I HAVE TO SAY, SO I'LL BE GOING. MIAKA'S WAITING FOR ME.
SLUMP
KA-CHIK

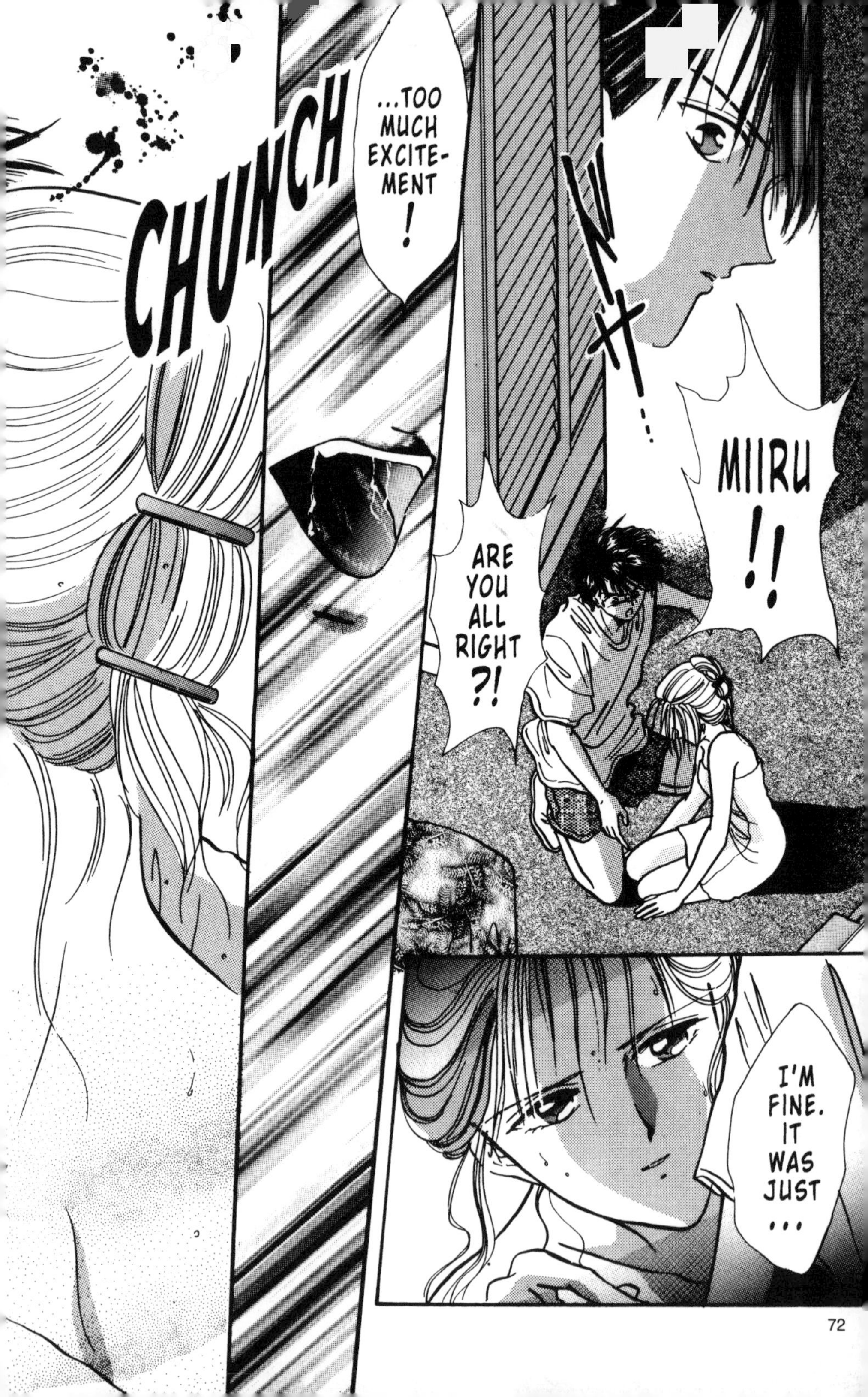
MIIRU!!
ARE YOU ALL RIGHT?!
I'M FINE. IT WAS JUST...
...TOO MUCH EXCITEMENT!
CHUNCH

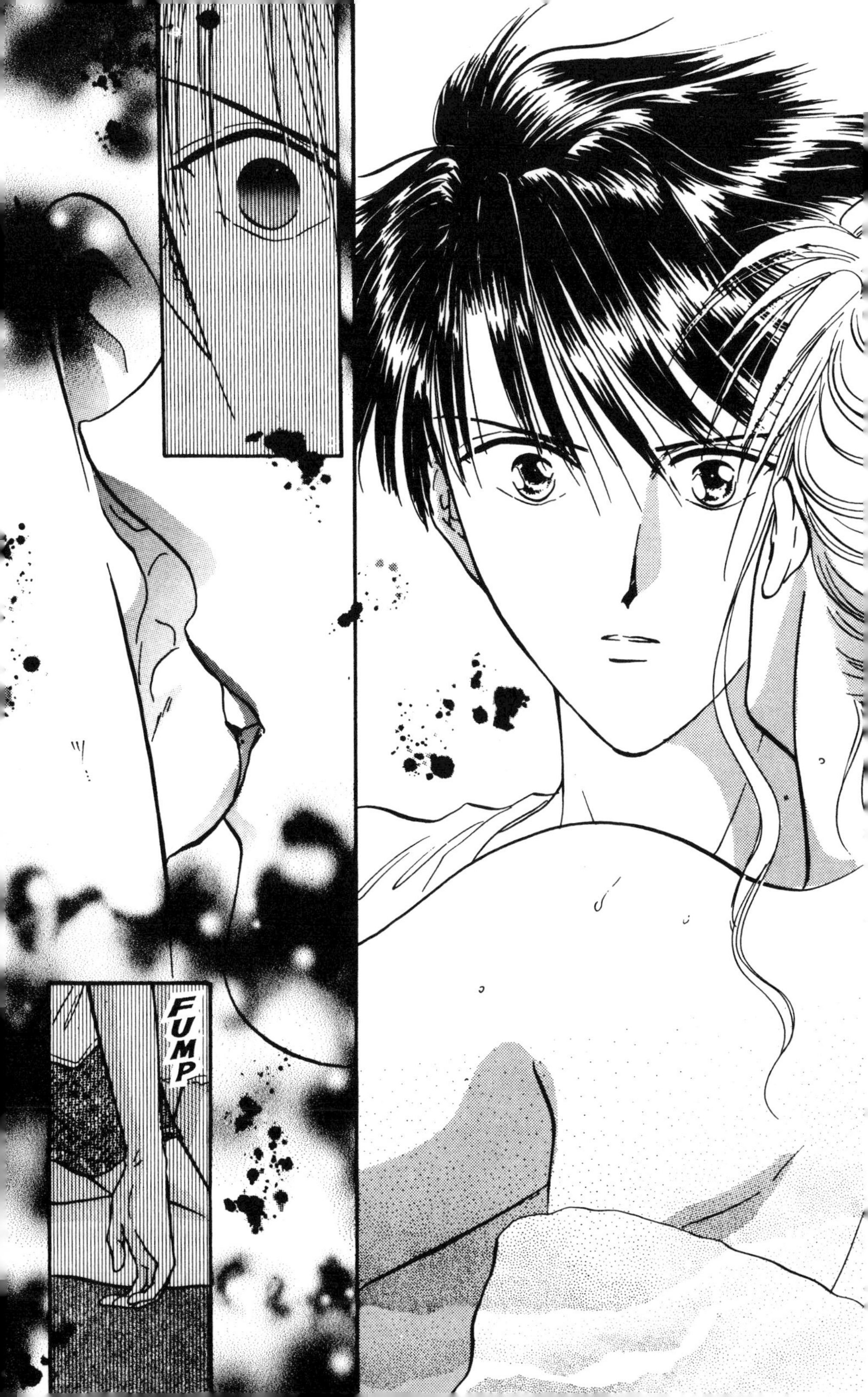
FUMP

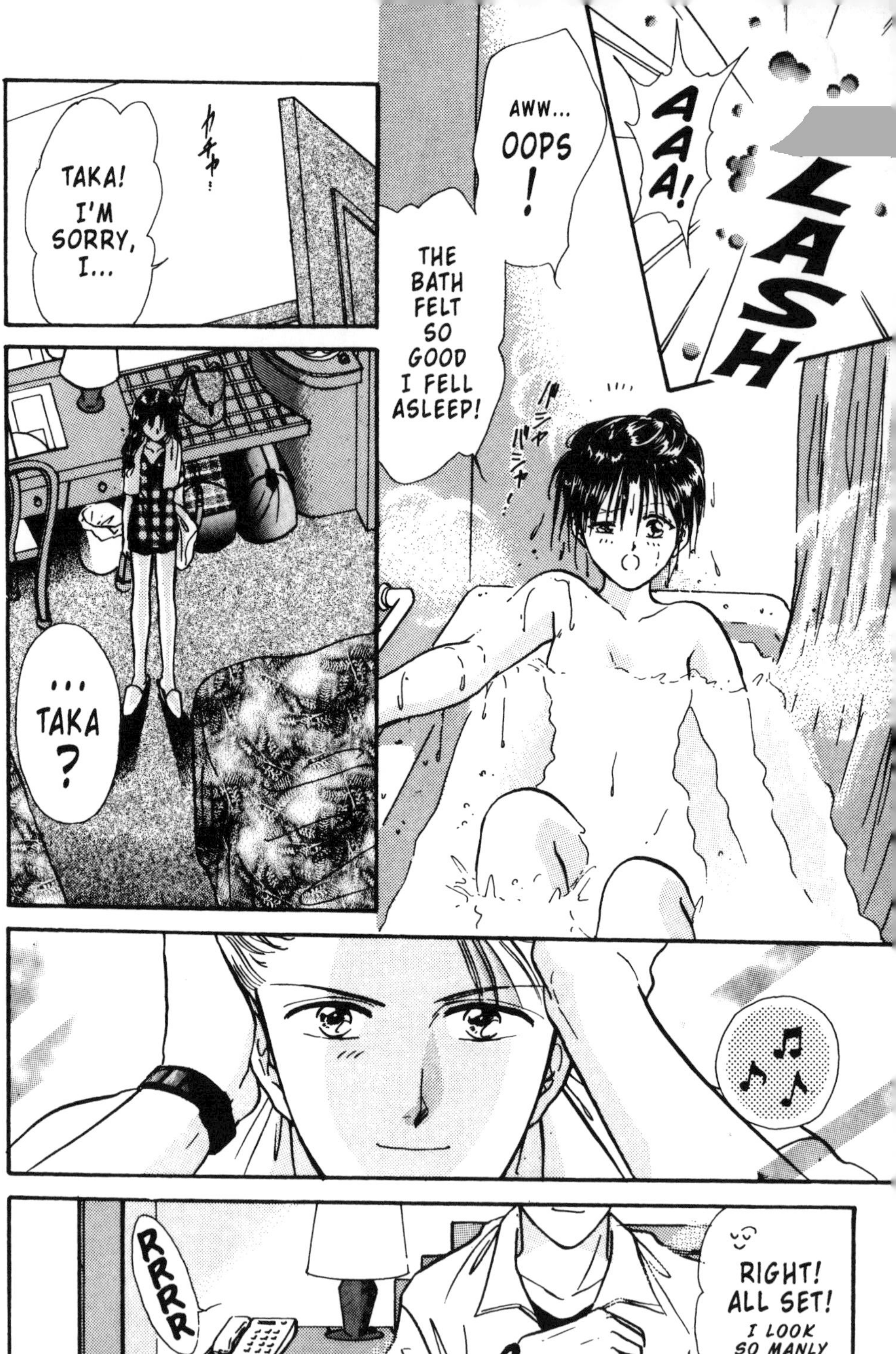
AAAA!
LASH
AWW... OOPS!
THE BATH FELT SO GOOD I FELL ASLEEP!
バシャ バシャ
カチャ…
TAKA! I'M SORRY, I...
...TAKA?
RIGHT! ALL SET! I LOOK SO MANLY LIKE THIS!
RRRR

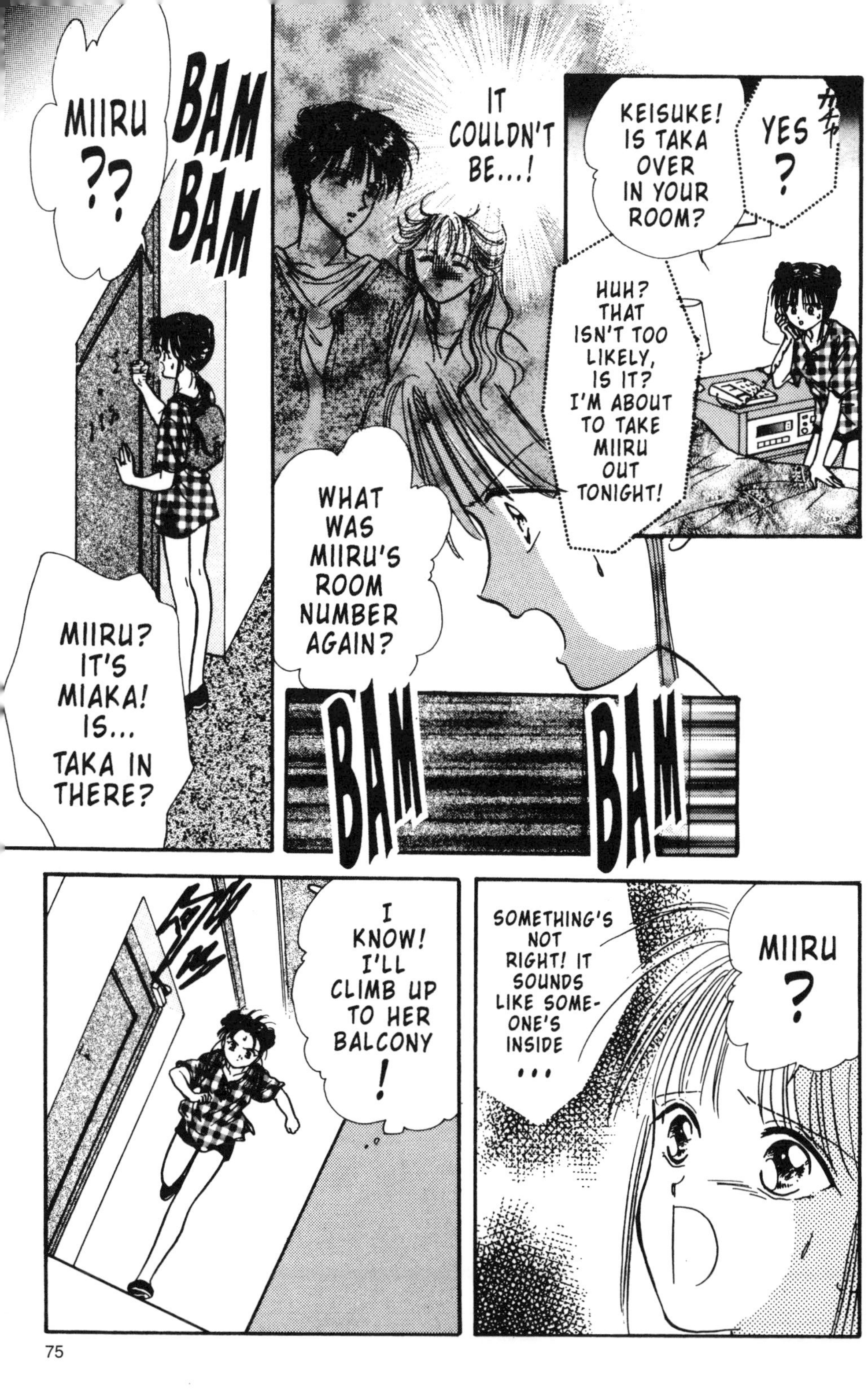
YES?
KEISUKE! IS TAKA OVER IN YOUR ROOM?
HUH? THAT ISN'T TOO LIKELY, IS IT? I'M ABOUT TO TAKE MIIRU OUT TONIGHT!
IT COULDN'T BE...!
WHAT WAS MIIRU'S ROOM NUMBER AGAIN?
BAM
BAM
MIIRU??
BAM BAM
MIIRU? IT'S MIAKA! IS... TAKA IN THERE?
MIIRU?
SOMETHING'S NOT RIGHT! IT SOUNDS LIKE SOME-ONE'S INSIDE...
I KNOW! I'LL CLIMB UP TO HER BALCONY!

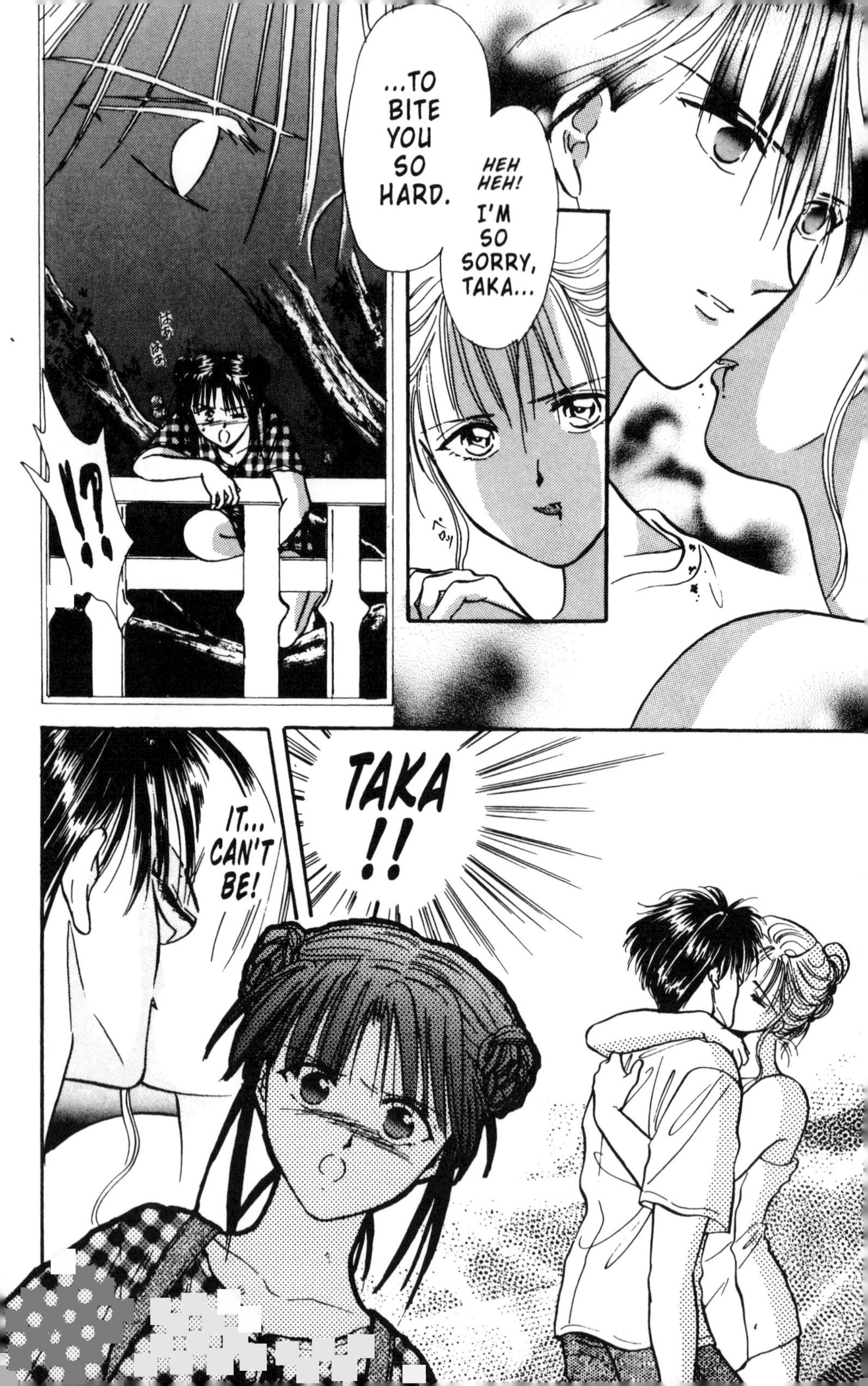
HEH HEH! I'M SO SORRY, TAKA...
...TO BITE YOU SO HARD.
!?
TAKA !!
IT... CAN'T BE!

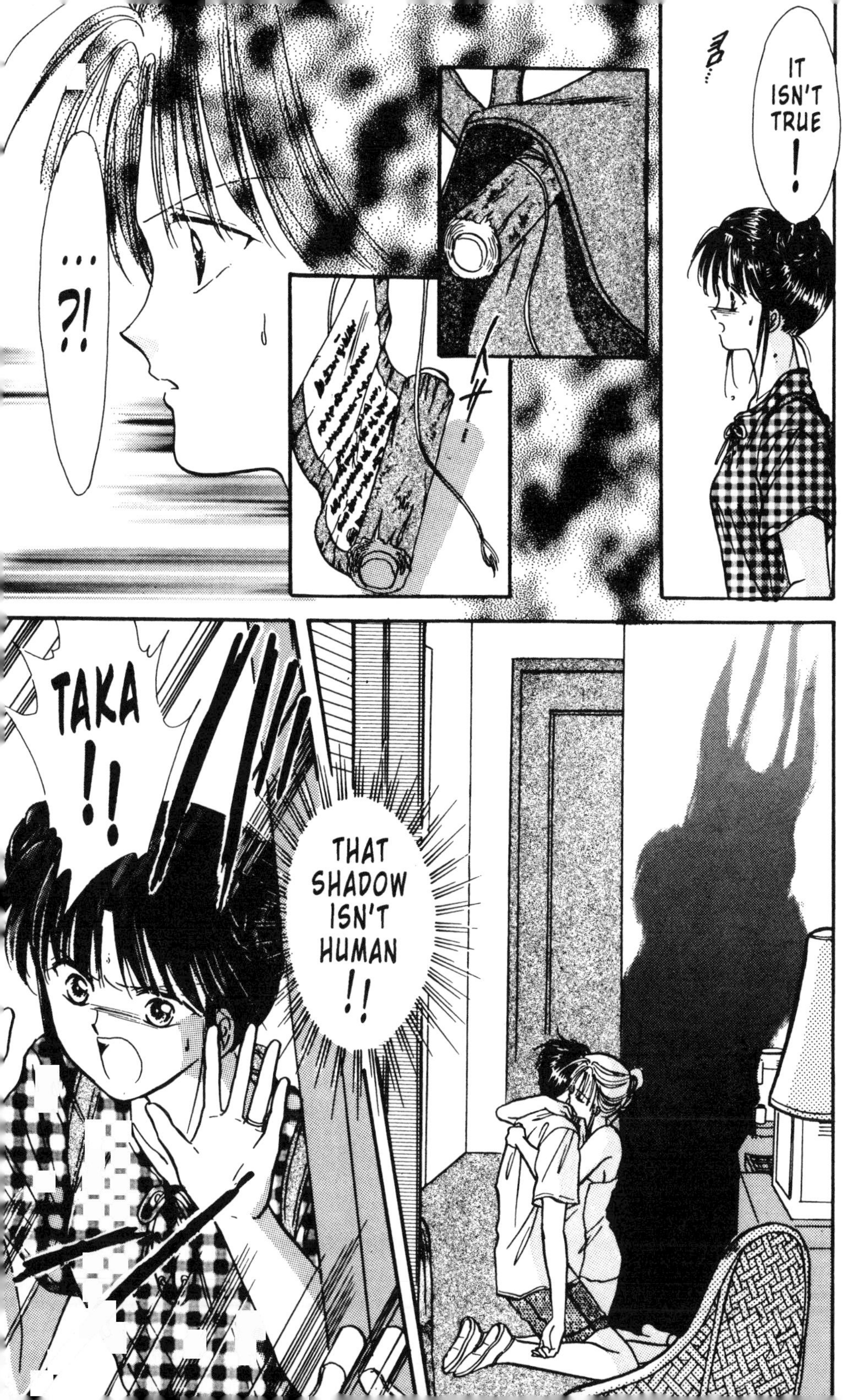
IT ISN'T TRUE!
...?!
THAT SHADOW ISN'T HUMAN!!
TAKA!!

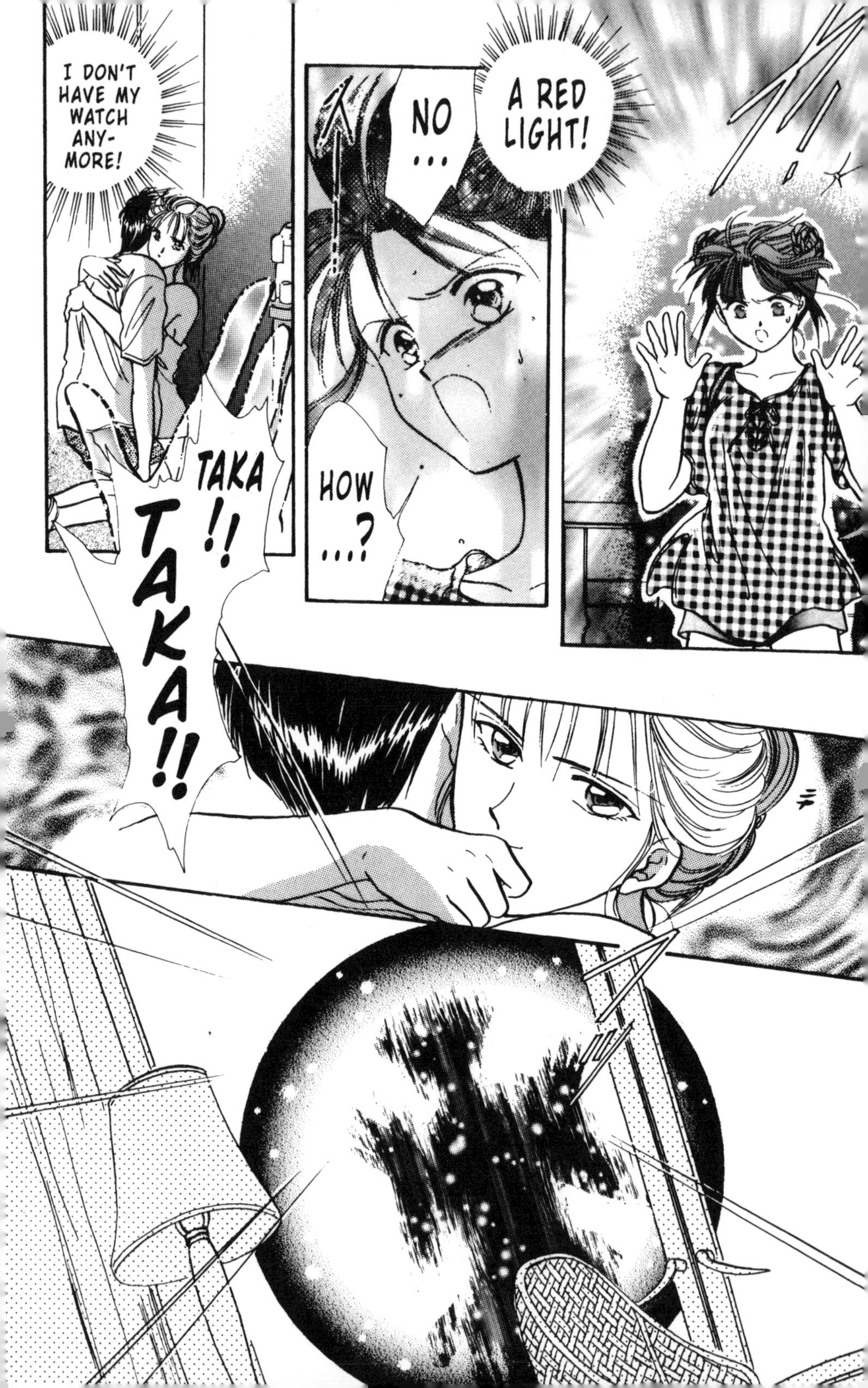
A RED LIGHT!
NO ...
HOW ...?
I DON'T HAVE MY WATCH ANYMORE!
TAKA!!
TAKA!!

Chapter Ninety-One
The Mystic Fang

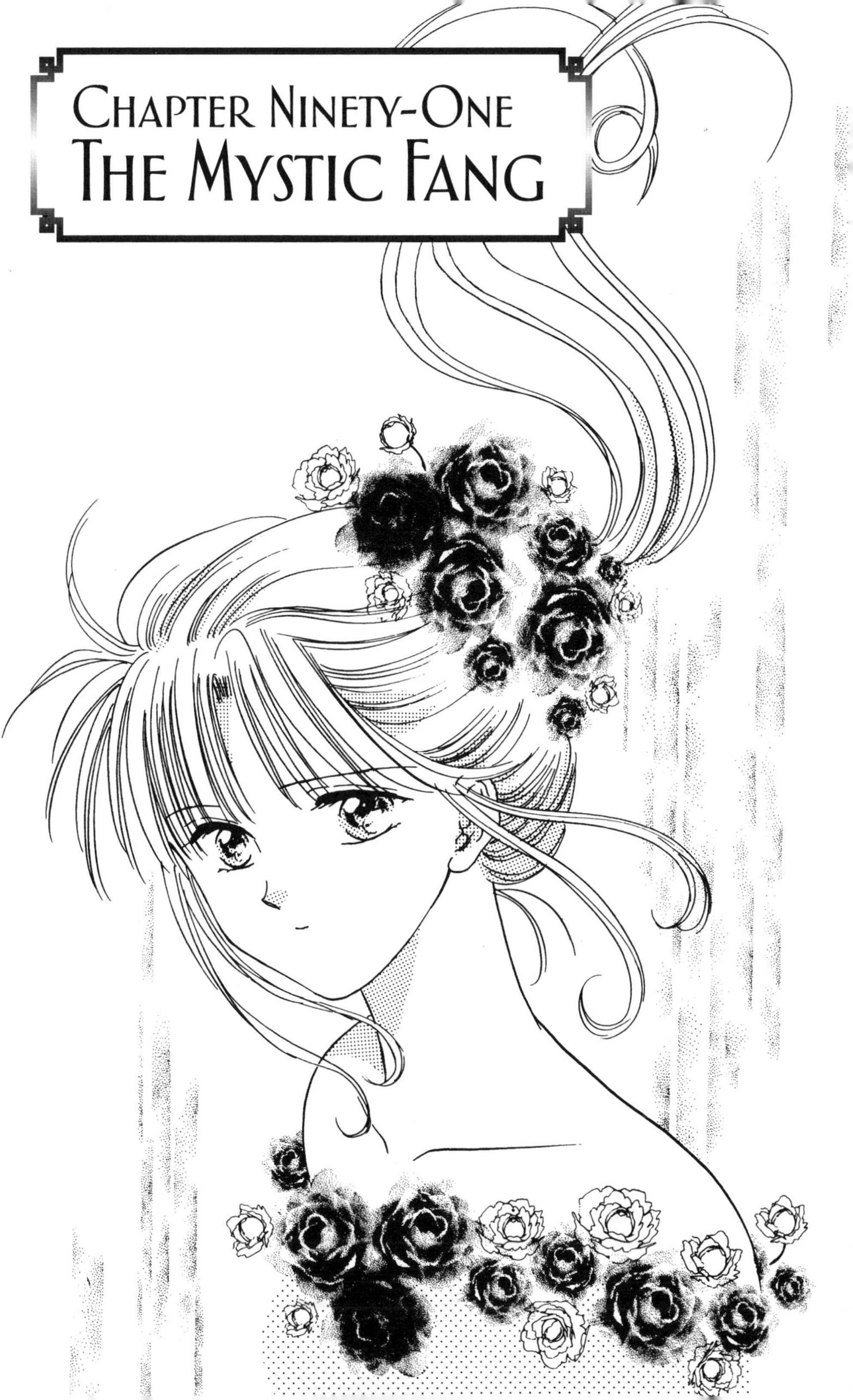

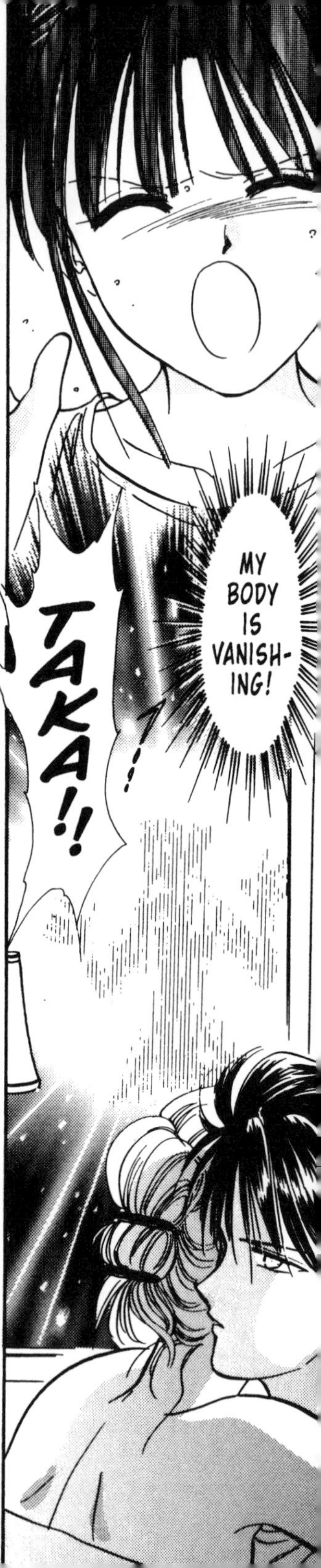
MY BODY IS VANISHING!
TAKA!!

THE TEMPLE BELL THAT SOUNDS THE TIME

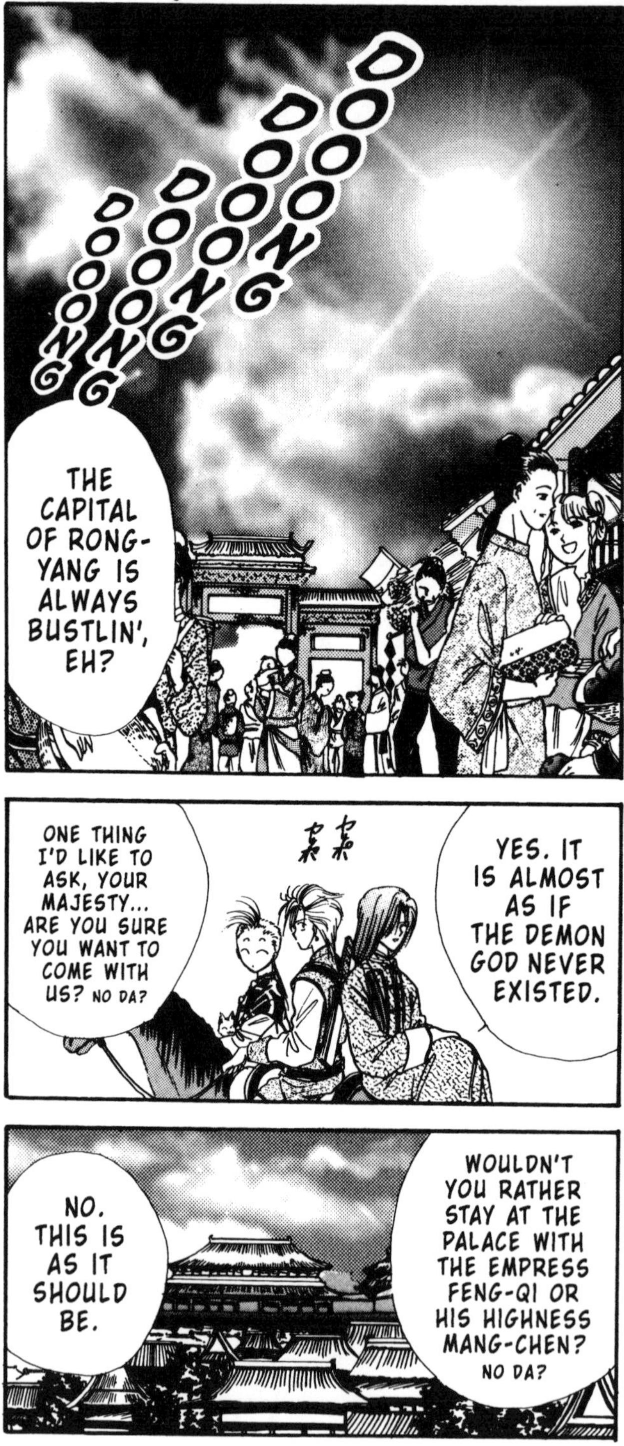
DOOOONG DOOOONG DOOOONG DOOOONG
THE CAPITAL OF RONG-YANG IS ALWAYS BUSTLIN', EH?
YES. IT IS ALMOST AS IF THE DEMON GOD NEVER EXISTED.
ONE THING I'D LIKE TO ASK, YOUR MAJESTY... ARE YOU SURE YOU WANT TO COME WITH US? NO DA?
WOULDN'T YOU RATHER STAY AT THE PALACE WITH THE EMPRESS FENG-QI OR HIS HIGHNESS MANG-CHEN? NO DA?
NO. THIS IS AS IT SHOULD BE.

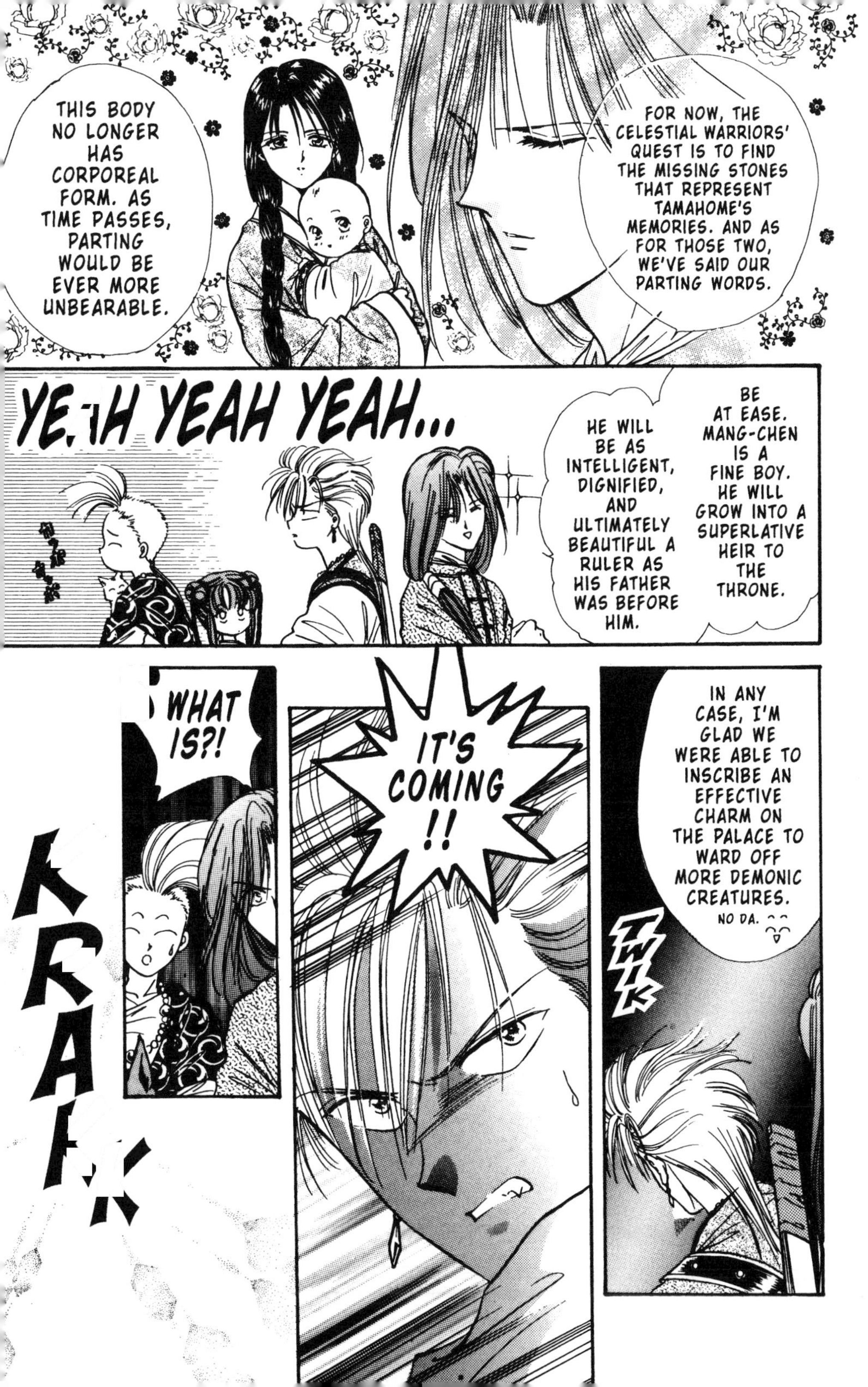
FOR NOW, THE CELESTIAL WARRIORS' QUEST IS TO FIND THE MISSING STONES THAT REPRESENT TAMAHOME'S MEMORIES. AND AS FOR THOSE TWO, WE'VE SAID OUR PARTING WORDS.
THIS BODY NO LONGER HAS CORPOREAL FORM. AS TIME PASSES, PARTING WOULD BE EVER MORE UNBEARABLE.
BE AT EASE. MANG-CHEN IS A FINE BOY. HE WILL GROW INTO A SUPERLATIVE HEIR TO THE THRONE.
HE WILL BE AS INTELLIGENT, DIGNIFIED, AND ULTIMATELY BEAUTIFUL A RULER AS HIS FATHER WAS BEFORE HIM.
YEAH YEAH YEAH...
IN ANY CASE, I'M GLAD WE WERE ABLE TO INSCRIBE AN EFFECTIVE CHARM ON THE PALACE TO WARD OFF MORE DEMONIC CREATURES.
NO DA.
TWIK
IT'S COMING!!
WHAT IS?!

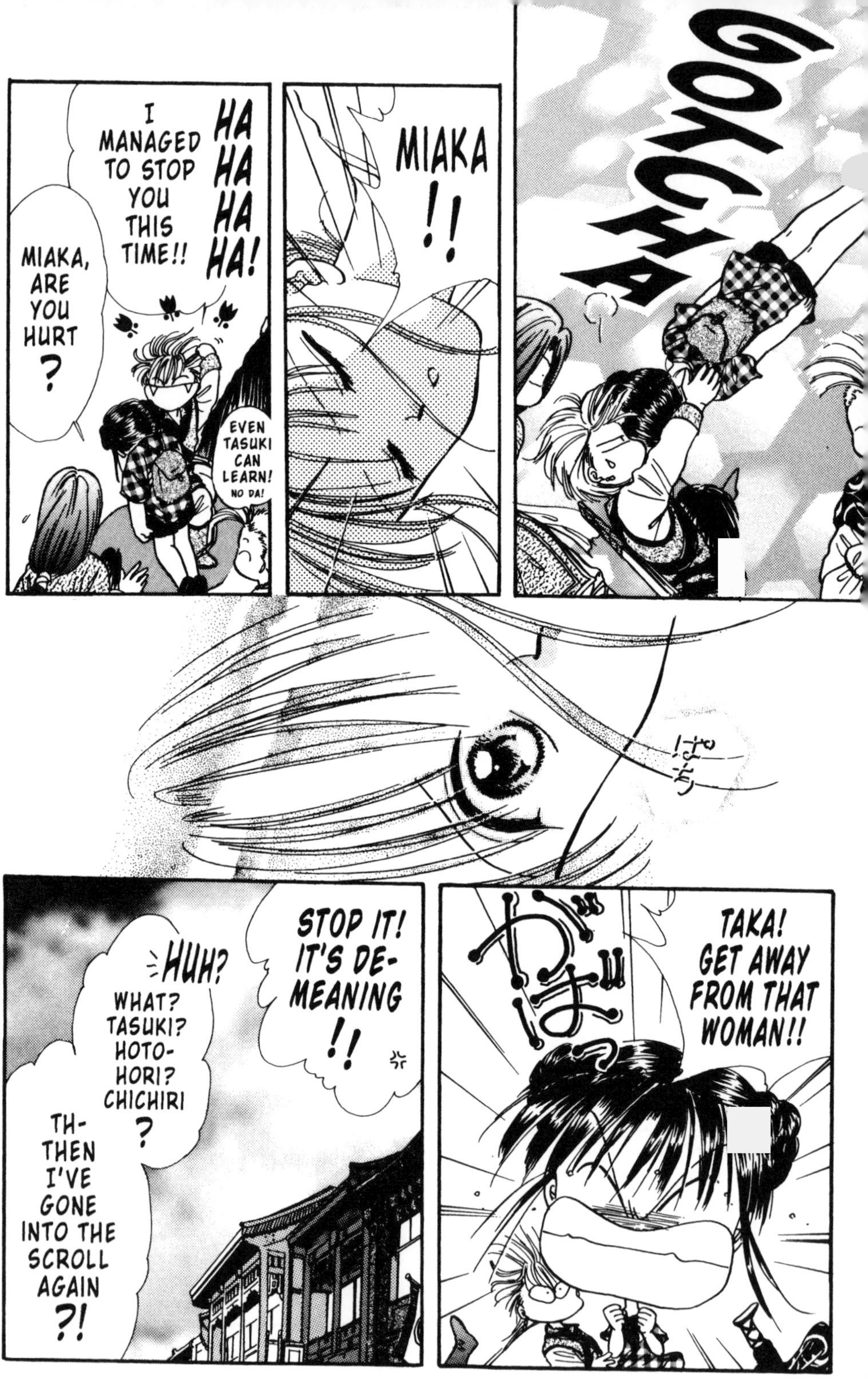
GOTCHA
MIAKA!!
HA HA HA HA!
I MANAGED TO STOP YOU THIS TIME!!
MIAKA, ARE YOU HURT?
EVEN TASUKI CAN LEARN! NO DA!
TAKA! GET AWAY FROM THAT WOMAN!!
STOP IT! IT'S DE-MEANING!!
HUH?
WHAT? TASUKI? HOTO-HORI? CHICHIRI?
TH-THEN I'VE GONE INTO THE SCROLL AGAIN?!

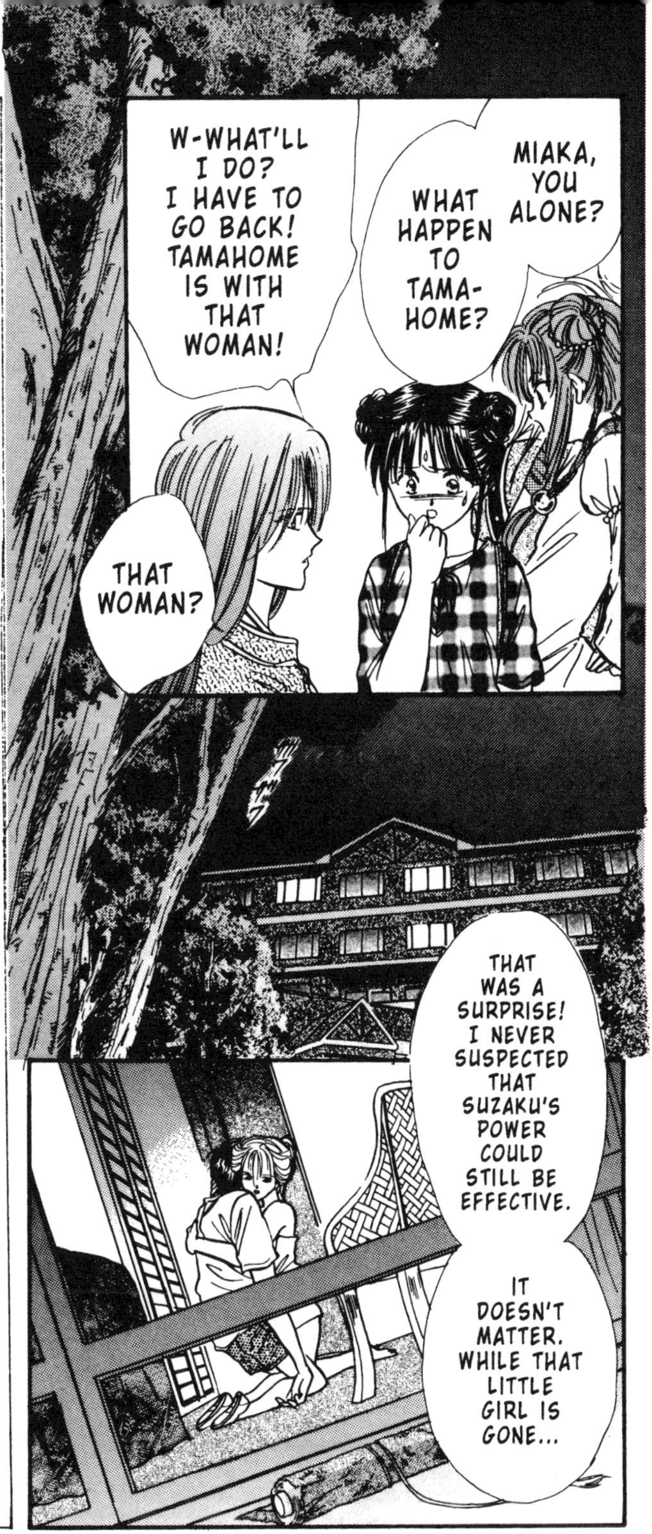
MIAKA, YOU ALONE?
WHAT HAPPEN TO TAMA-HOME?
W-WHAT'LL I DO? I HAVE TO GO BACK! TAMAHOME IS WITH THAT WOMAN!
THAT WOMAN?
THAT WAS A SURPRISE! I NEVER SUSPECTED THAT SUZAKU'S POWER COULD STILL BE EFFECTIVE.
IT DOESN'T MATTER. WHILE THAT LITTLE GIRL IS GONE...

While I was in Taiwan, I was taken to a whole bunch of places! One was the Old Capital Museum (was that the name?)... *I forget.* Because everything there was the real thing! ☺ I learned a lot! Also there was a village that looked like it was out of a movie! (It was incredible! An ancient Chinese village brought intact into modern times! I thought I was caught in a time warp!)
Oh, yeah! The president of the publishing company took me to a massage center! Some of it hurt so much I cried out! ☺ And it went constantly for three hours! I could hear the cracking of bones, but by the end, it was like I had grown wings! (I felt so light!)
The market at night was a real Taiwan hot spot... or I should say it was crowded, crowded, crowded!! Even though it was 10 p.m., children were all over. It was like a night fair! And it happens every night! *I'm so jealous!* The feeling was like Sennichi-mae in Namba, Osaka (a big shopping promenade), but more impressive! (It really is amazing!) And the restaurants were so delicious! (My constitution was in better condition than it is in Japan.) I received some manga from some Taiwanese artists, but I had nothing to give back to them, so I handed them telephone cards.
I signed all sorts of things everywhere! ☺ But I still wonder why they were so enthusiastic after receiving only that. I had heard once that the Taiwanese manga scene grew out of the Japanese manga scene, so Japanese manga artists are treated like gods. Maybe it was true once, but now the Taiwanese artists are so accomplished! And the artwork I got from the readers was beautiful too! If Japan doesn't pay attention, it could fall behind in manga. ☺ I still find it astonishing that manga can cross national and cultural barriers. I don't just mean the language barriers, but that there is no border that can hold back manga! That's what this trip taught me! I'll fondly remember this trip for the rest of my life! And to the people of Taiwan, thank you for letting me know that manga is a worldwide culture! *I'll come back soon!*
☺

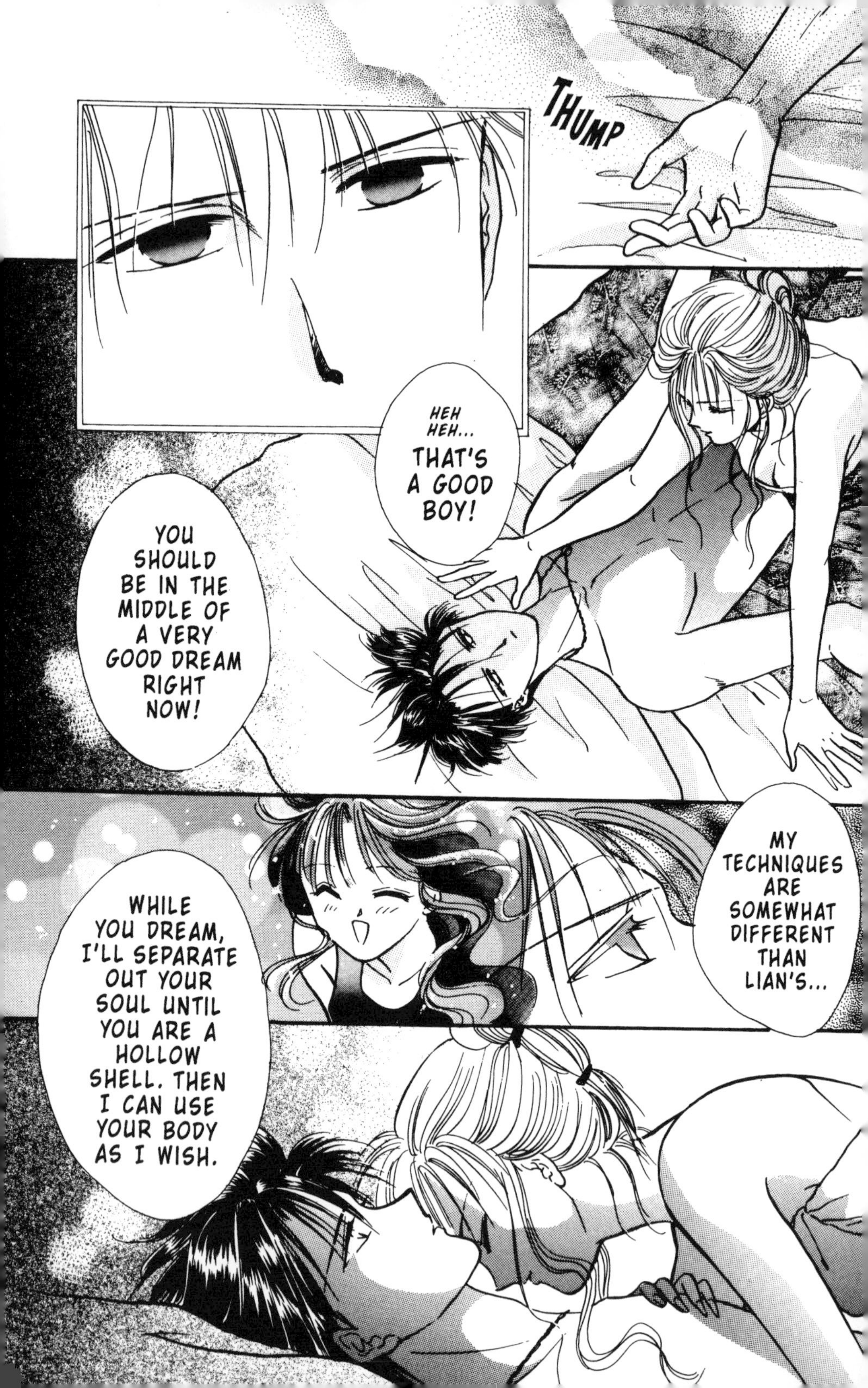
THUMP
HEH HEH... THAT'S A GOOD BOY!
YOU SHOULD BE IN THE MIDDLE OF A VERY GOOD DREAM RIGHT NOW!
MY TECHNIQUES ARE SOMEWHAT DIFFERENT THAN LIAN'S...
WHILE YOU DREAM, I'LL SEPARATE OUT YOUR SOUL UNTIL YOU ARE A HOLLOW SHELL. THEN I CAN USE YOUR BODY AS I WISH.

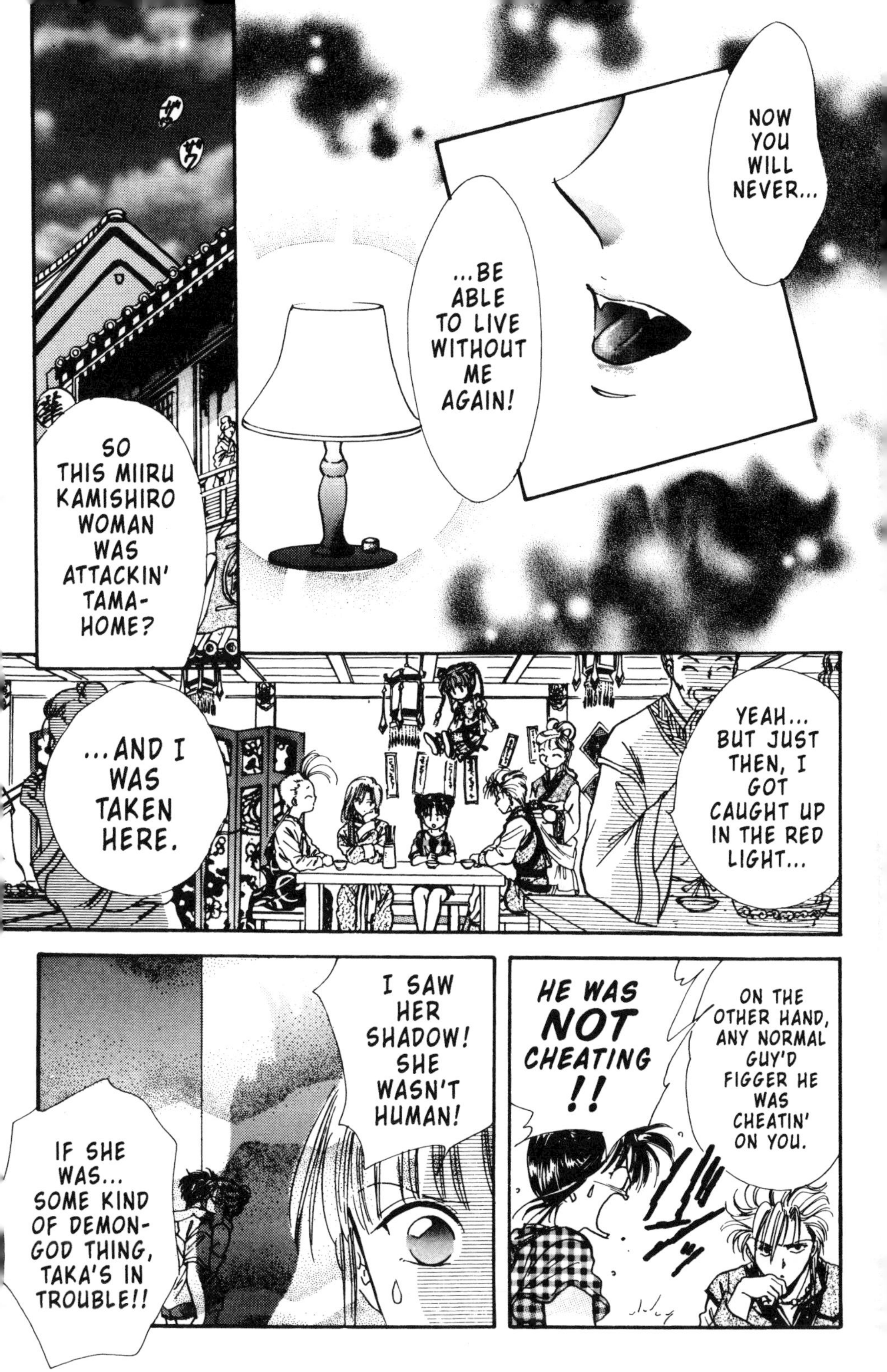
NOW YOU WILL NEVER...
...BE ABLE TO LIVE WITHOUT ME AGAIN!
SO THIS MIIRU KAMISHIRO WOMAN WAS ATTACKIN' TAMA-HOME?
YEAH... BUT JUST THEN, I GOT CAUGHT UP IN THE RED LIGHT...
...AND I WAS TAKEN HERE.
ON THE OTHER HAND, ANY NORMAL GUY'D FIGGER HE WAS CHEATIN' ON YOU.
HE WAS NOT CHEATING!!
I SAW HER SHADOW! SHE WASN'T HUMAN!
IF SHE WAS... SOME KIND OF DEMON-GOD THING, TAKA'S IN TROUBLE!!

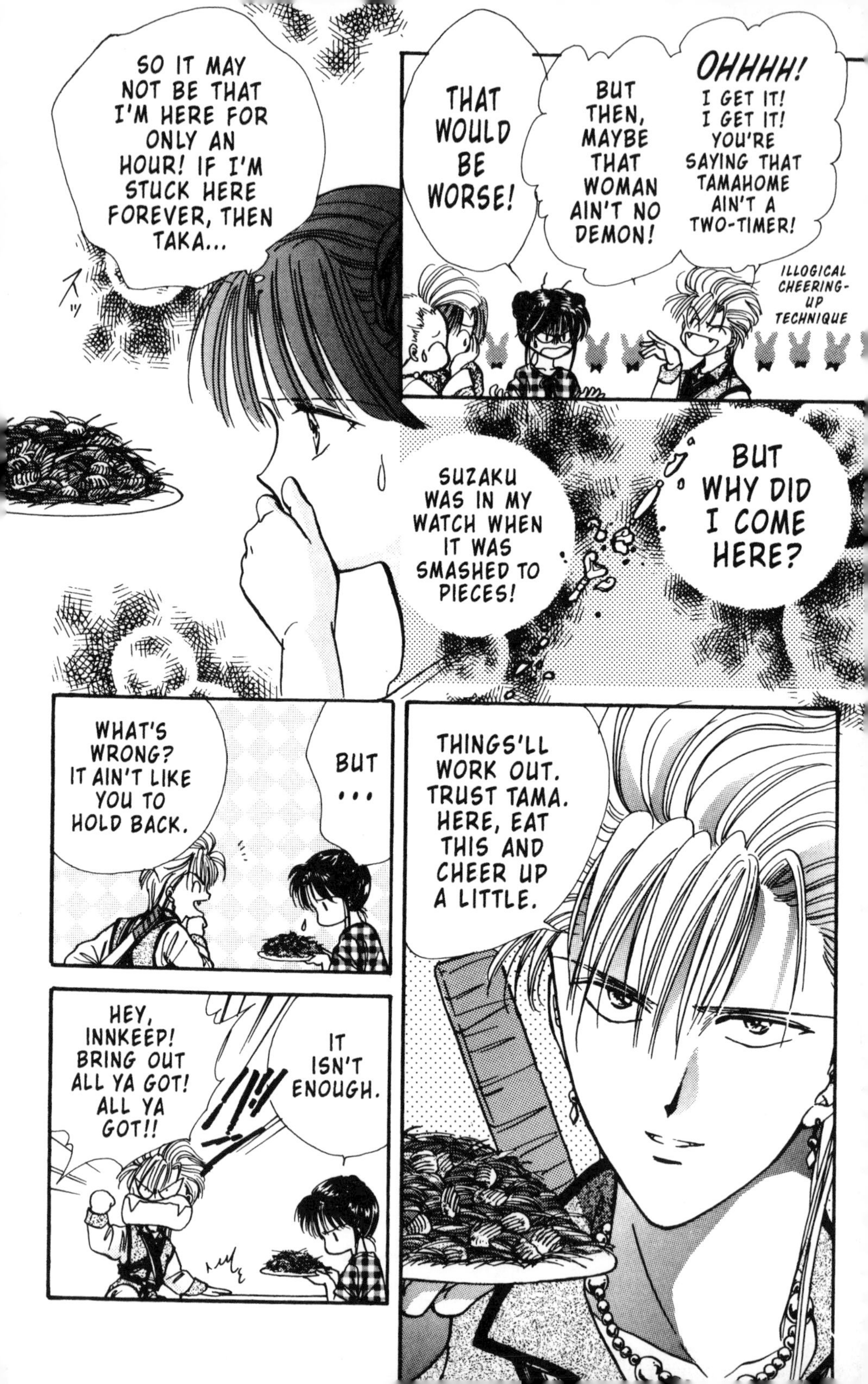
OHHHH! I GET IT! I GET IT! YOU'RE SAYING THAT TAMAHOME AIN'T A TWO-TIMER!
BUT THEN, MAYBE THAT WOMAN AIN'T NO DEMON!
THAT WOULD BE WORSE!
ILLOGICAL CHEERING-UP TECHNIQUE
BUT WHY DID I COME HERE?
SUZAKU WAS IN MY WATCH WHEN IT WAS SMASHED TO PIECES!
SO IT MAY NOT BE THAT I'M HERE FOR ONLY AN HOUR! IF I'M STUCK HERE FOREVER, THEN TAKA...
THINGS'LL WORK OUT. TRUST TAMA. HERE, EAT THIS AND CHEER UP A LITTLE.
BUT...
WHAT'S WRONG? IT AIN'T LIKE YOU TO HOLD BACK.
IT ISN'T ENOUGH.
HEY, INNKEEP! BRING OUT ALL YA GOT! ALL YA GOT!!

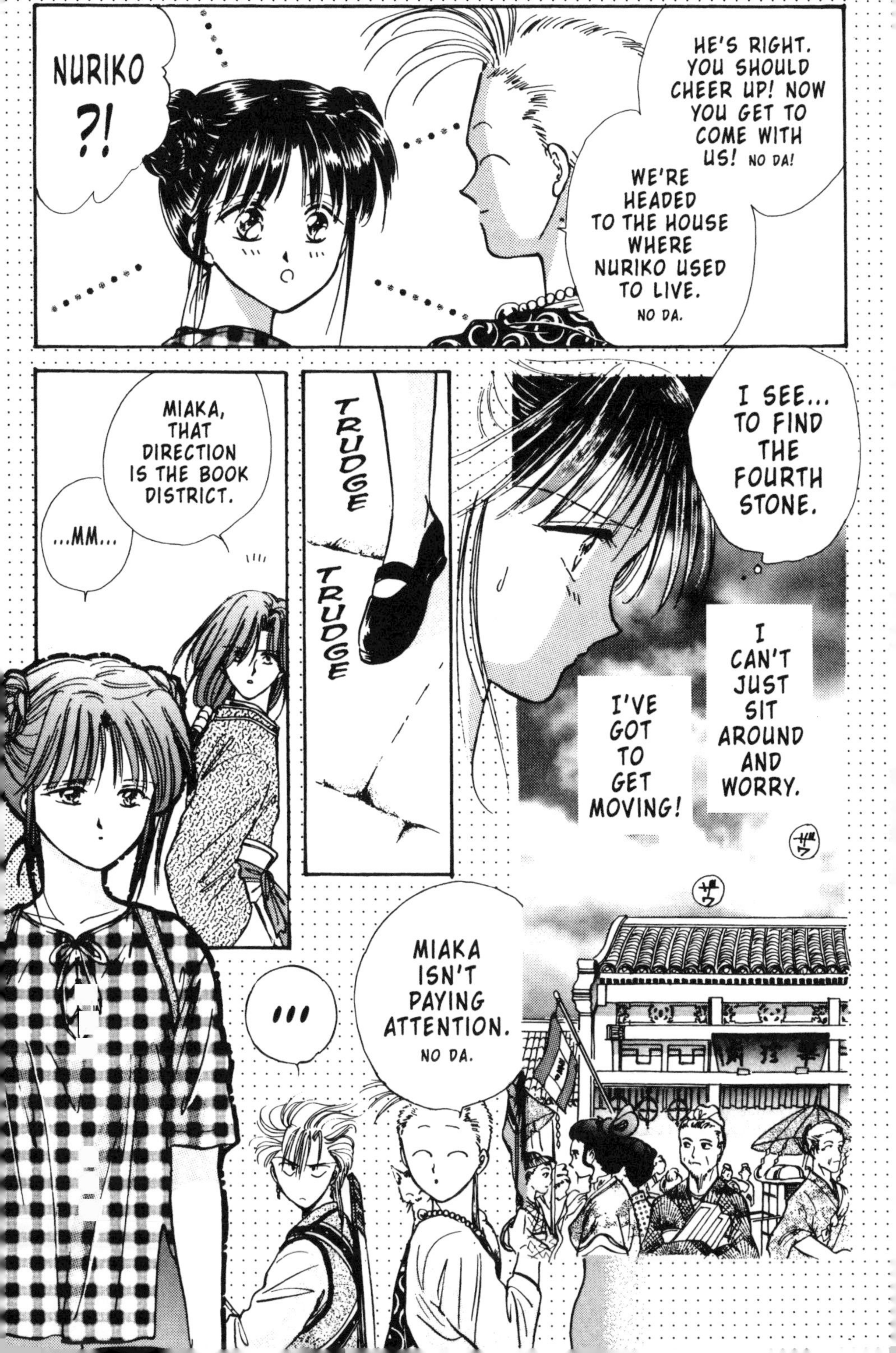
HE'S RIGHT. YOU SHOULD CHEER UP! NOW YOU GET TO COME WITH US! NO DA!
WE'RE HEADED TO THE HOUSE WHERE NURIKO USED TO LIVE. NO DA.
NURIKO ?!
I SEE... TO FIND THE FOURTH STONE.
I CAN'T JUST SIT AROUND AND WORRY.
I'VE GOT TO GET MOVING!
TRUDGE
TRUDGE
MIAKA, THAT DIRECTION IS THE BOOK DISTRICT.
...MM...
MIAKA ISN'T PAYING ATTENTION. NO DA.
...

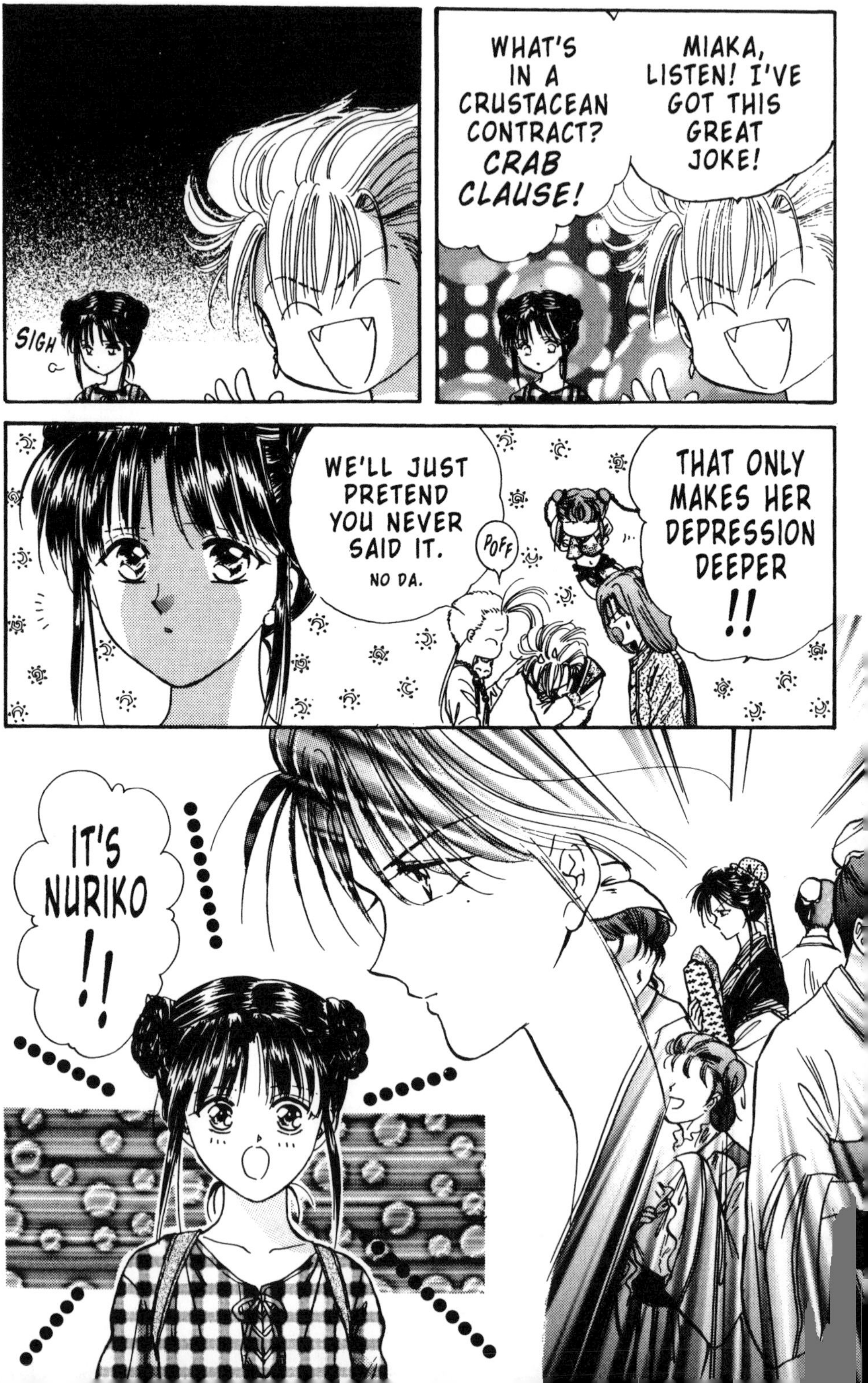
MIAKA, LISTEN! I'VE GOT THIS GREAT JOKE!
WHAT'S IN A CRUSTACEAN CONTRACT? CRAB CLAUSE!
SIGH
THAT ONLY MAKES HER DEPRESSION DEEPER!!
POFF
WE'LL JUST PRETEND YOU NEVER SAID IT.
NO DA.
IT'S NURIKO!!

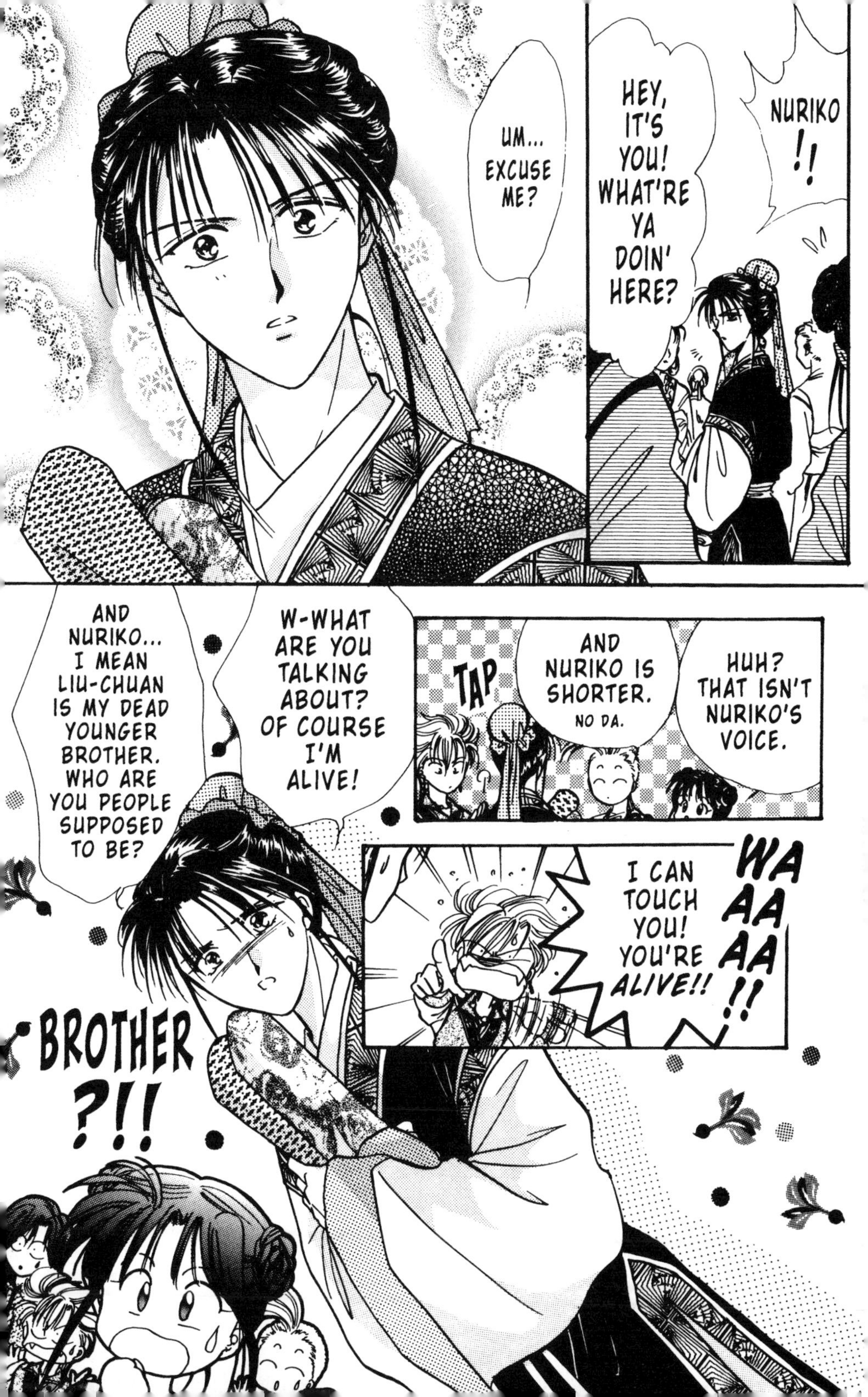
NURIKO!!
HEY, IT'S YOU! WHAT'RE YA DOIN' HERE?
UM... EXCUSE ME?
HUH? THAT ISN'T NURIKO'S VOICE.
AND NURIKO IS SHORTER. NO DA.
TAP
WAAAAA!!
I CAN TOUCH YOU! YOU'RE ALIVE!!
W-WHAT ARE YOU TALKING ABOUT? OF COURSE I'M ALIVE!
AND NURIKO... I MEAN LIU-CHUAN IS MY DEAD YOUNGER BROTHER. WHO ARE YOU PEOPLE SUPPOSED TO BE?
BROTHER?!!

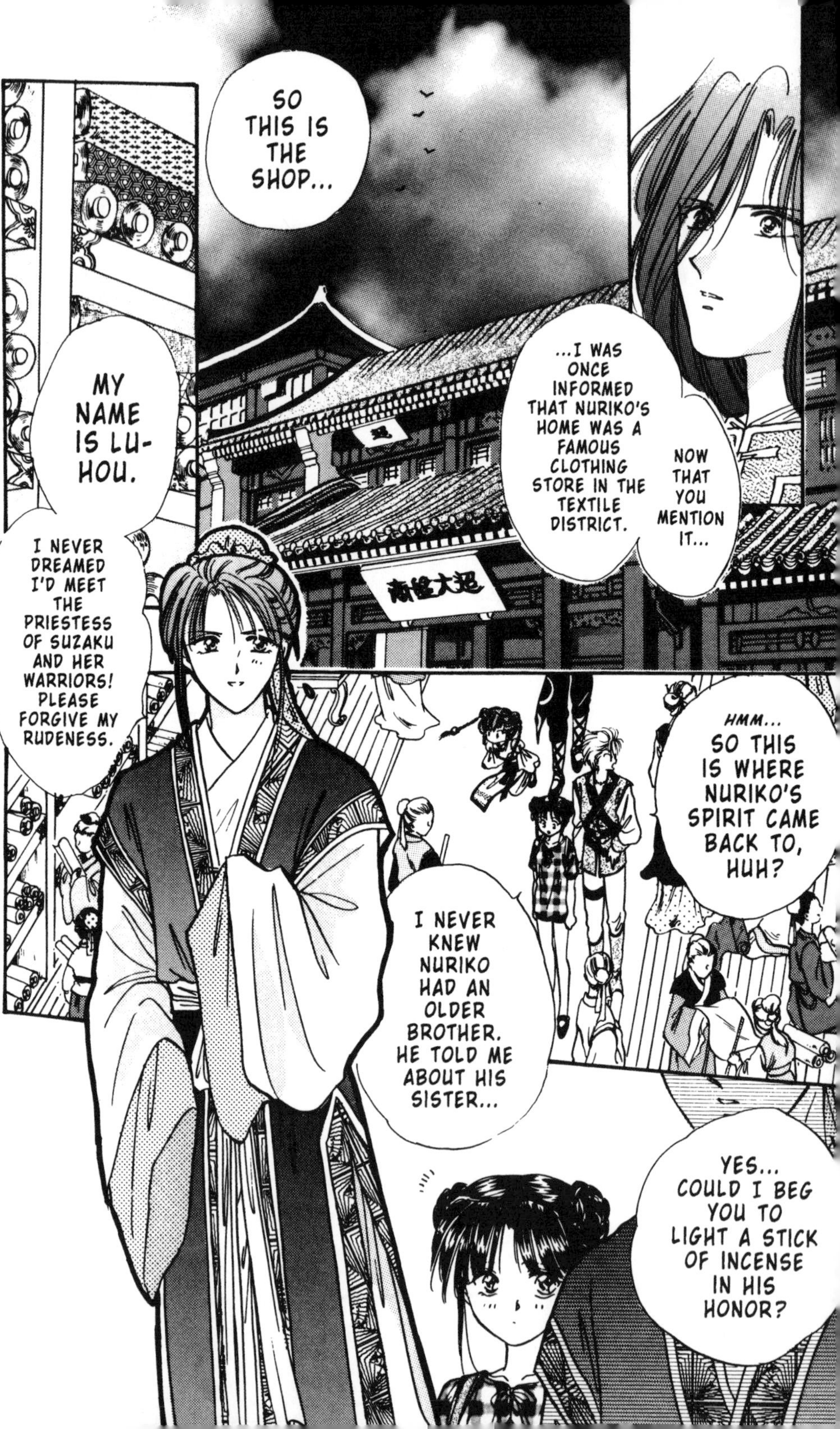
SO THIS IS THE SHOP...
NOW THAT YOU MENTION IT...
...I WAS ONCE INFORMED THAT NURIKO'S HOME WAS A FAMOUS CLOTHING STORE IN THE TEXTILE DISTRICT.
HMM... SO THIS IS WHERE NURIKO'S SPIRIT CAME BACK TO, HUH?
MY NAME IS LU-HOU.
I NEVER DREAMED I'D MEET THE PRIESTESS OF SUZAKU AND HER WARRIORS! PLEASE FORGIVE MY RUDENESS.
I NEVER KNEW NURIKO HAD AN OLDER BROTHER. HE TOLD ME ABOUT HIS SISTER...
YES... COULD I BEG YOU TO LIGHT A STICK OF INCENSE IN HIS HONOR?

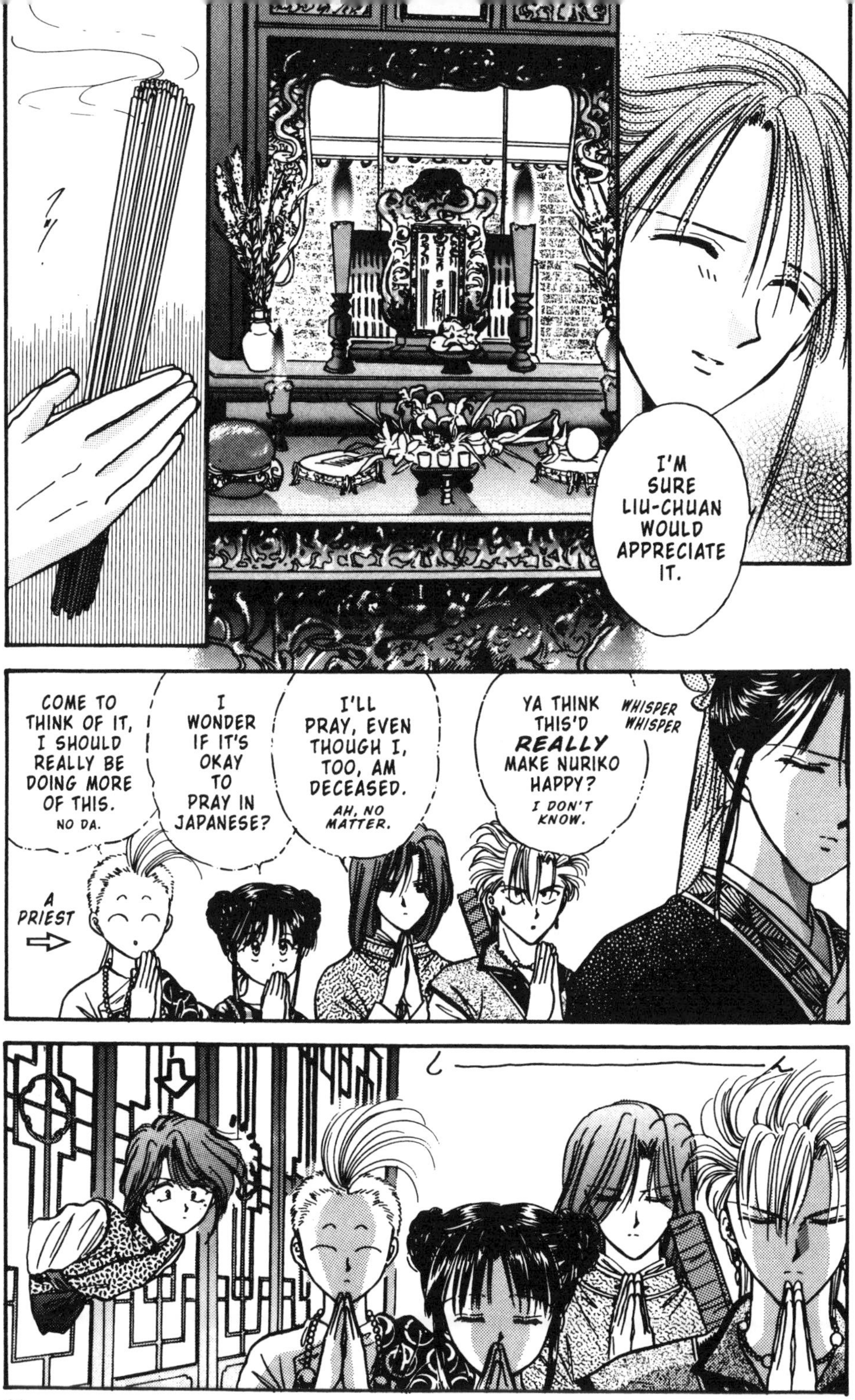

I'M SURE LIU-CHUAN WOULD APPRECIATE IT.
WHISPER WHISPER
YA THINK THIS'D REALLY MAKE NURIKO HAPPY?
I DON'T KNOW.
I'LL PRAY, EVEN THOUGH I, TOO, AM DECEASED.
AH, NO MATTER.
I WONDER IF IT'S OKAY TO PRAY IN JAPANESE?
COME TO THINK OF IT, I SHOULD REALLY BE DOING MORE OF THIS.
NO DA.
A PRIEST

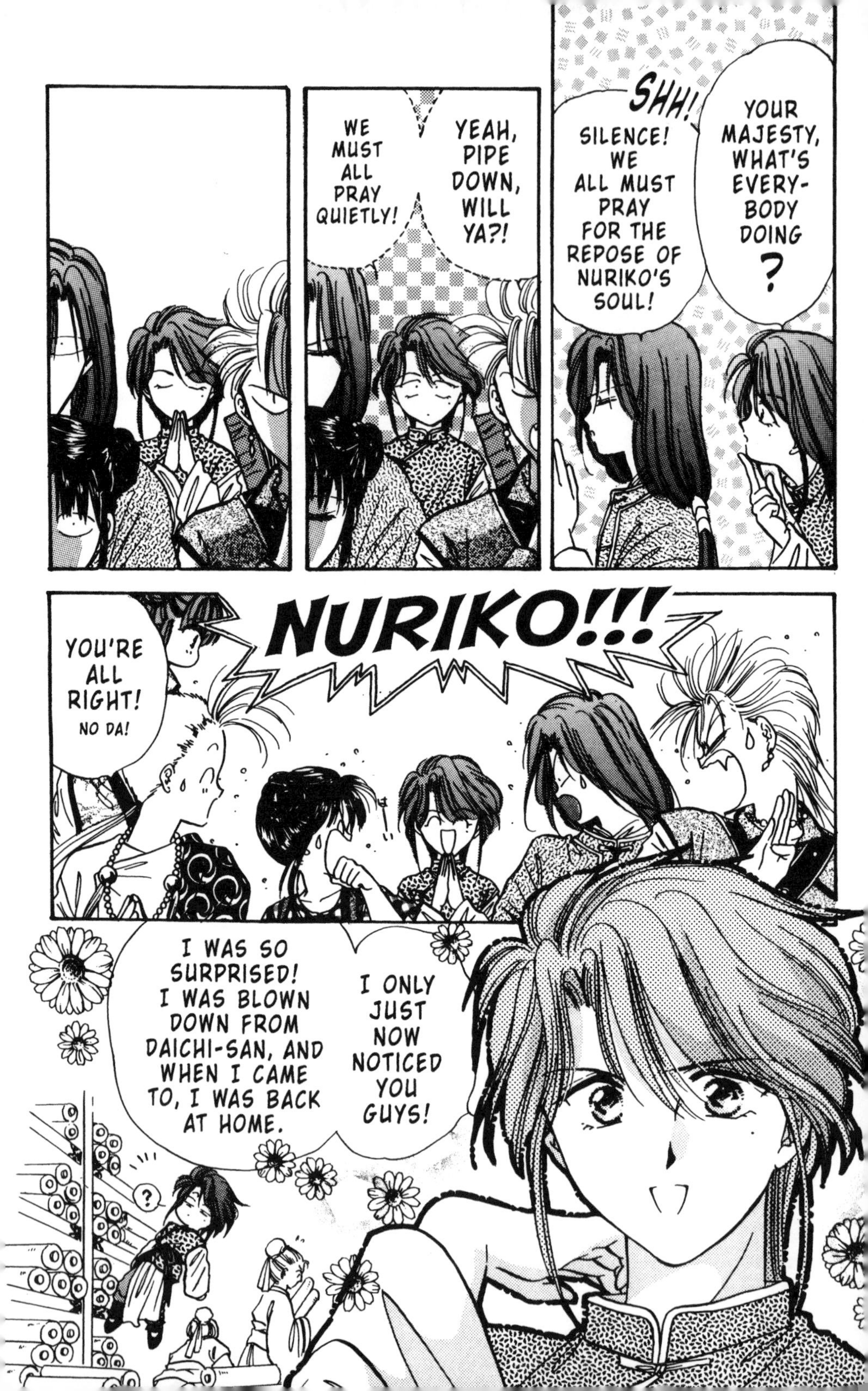
YOUR MAJESTY, WHAT'S EVERYBODY DOING?
SHH!
SILENCE! WE ALL MUST PRAY FOR THE REPOSE OF NURIKO'S SOUL!
YEAH, PIPE DOWN, WILL YA?!
WE MUST ALL PRAY QUIETLY!
NURIKO!!!
YOU'RE ALL RIGHT! NO DA!
I WAS SO SURPRISED! I WAS BLOWN DOWN FROM DAICHI-SAN, AND WHEN I CAME TO, I WAS BACK AT HOME.
I ONLY JUST NOW NOTICED YOU GUYS!
?

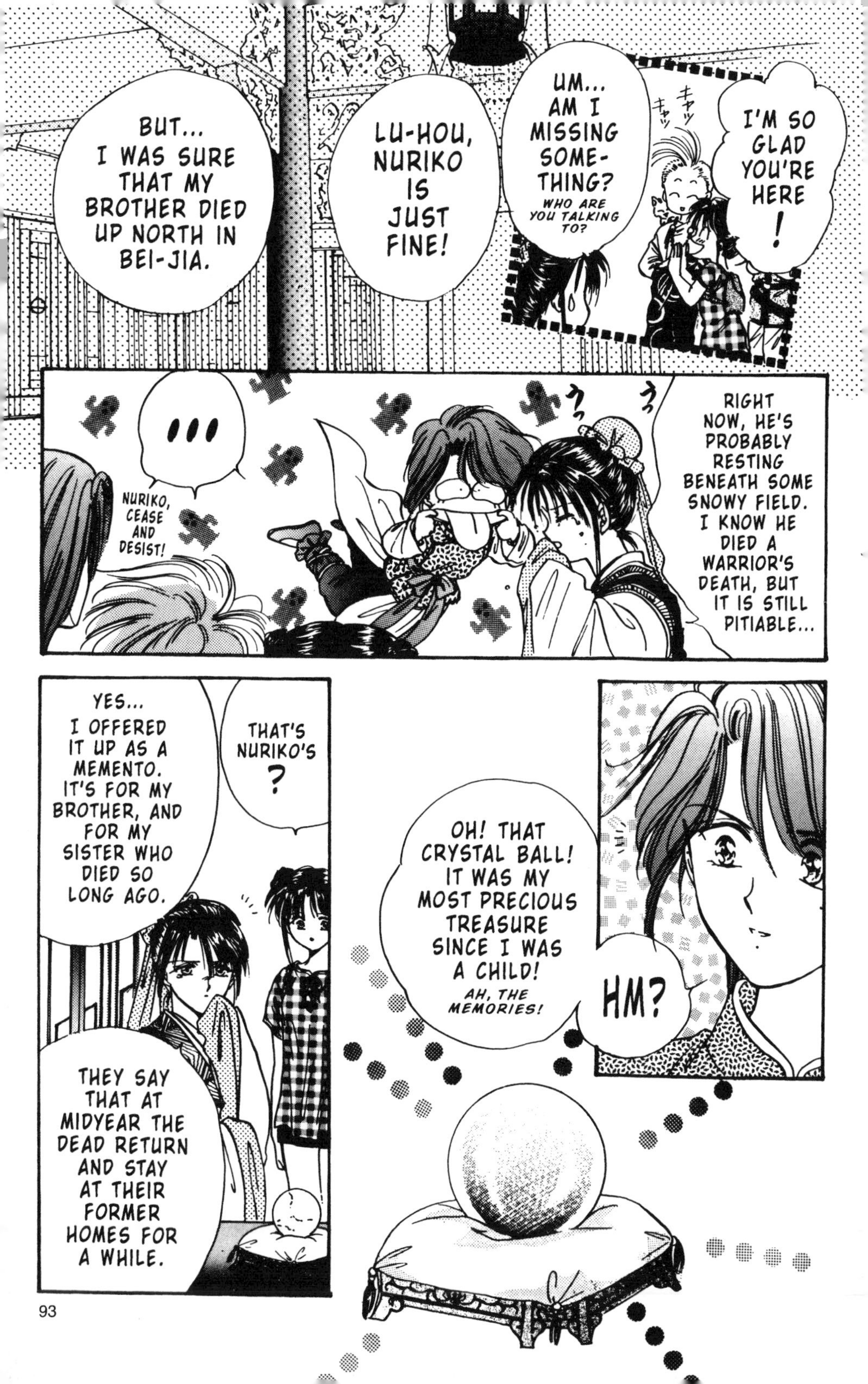
I'M SO GLAD YOU'RE HERE!
キャッ キャッ
UM... AM I MISSING SOME-THING?
WHO ARE YOU TALKING TO?
LU-HOU, NURIKO IS JUST FINE!
BUT... I WAS SURE THAT MY BROTHER DIED UP NORTH IN BEI-JIA.
RIGHT NOW, HE'S PROBABLY RESTING BENEATH SOME SNOWY FIELD. I KNOW HE DIED A WARRIOR'S DEATH, BUT IT IS STILL PITIABLE...
...
NURIKO, CEASE AND DESIST!
HM?
OH! THAT CRYSTAL BALL! IT WAS MY MOST PRECIOUS TREASURE SINCE I WAS A CHILD!
AH, THE MEMORIES!
THAT'S NURIKO'S?
YES... I OFFERED IT UP AS A MEMENTO. IT'S FOR MY BROTHER, AND FOR MY SISTER WHO DIED SO LONG AGO.
THEY SAY THAT AT MIDYEAR THE DEAD RETURN AND STAY AT THEIR FORMER HOMES FOR A WHILE.

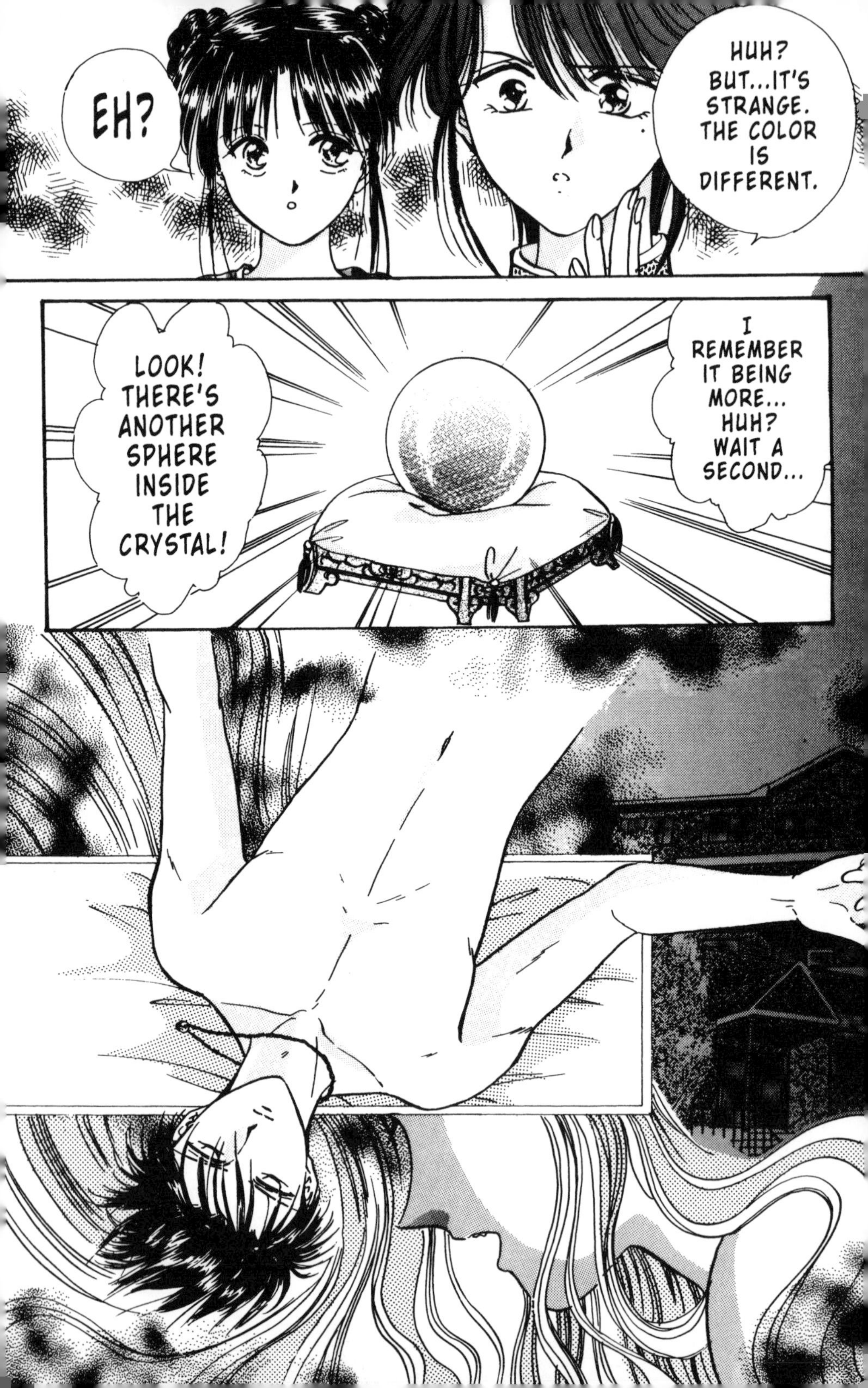
HUH? BUT...IT'S STRANGE. THE COLOR IS DIFFERENT.
EH?
I REMEMBER IT BEING MORE... HUH? WAIT A SECOND...
LOOK! THERE'S ANOTHER SPHERE INSIDE THE CRYSTAL!

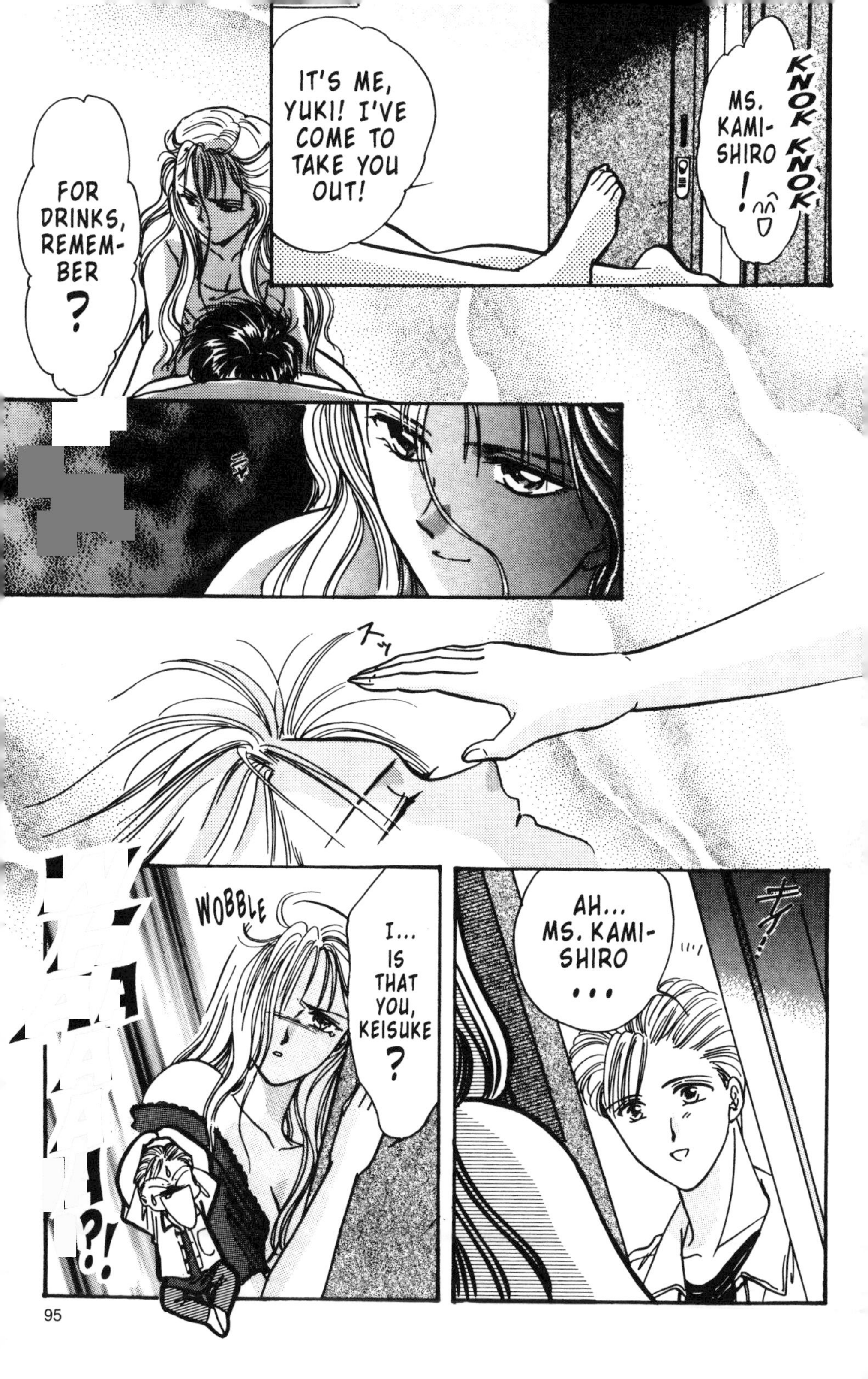
KNOK KNOK
MS. KAMI-SHIRO!
IT'S ME, YUKI! I'VE COME TO TAKE YOU OUT!
FOR DRINKS, REMEMBER?
AH... MS. KAMI-SHIRO ...
WOBBLE
I... IS THAT YOU, KEISUKE?

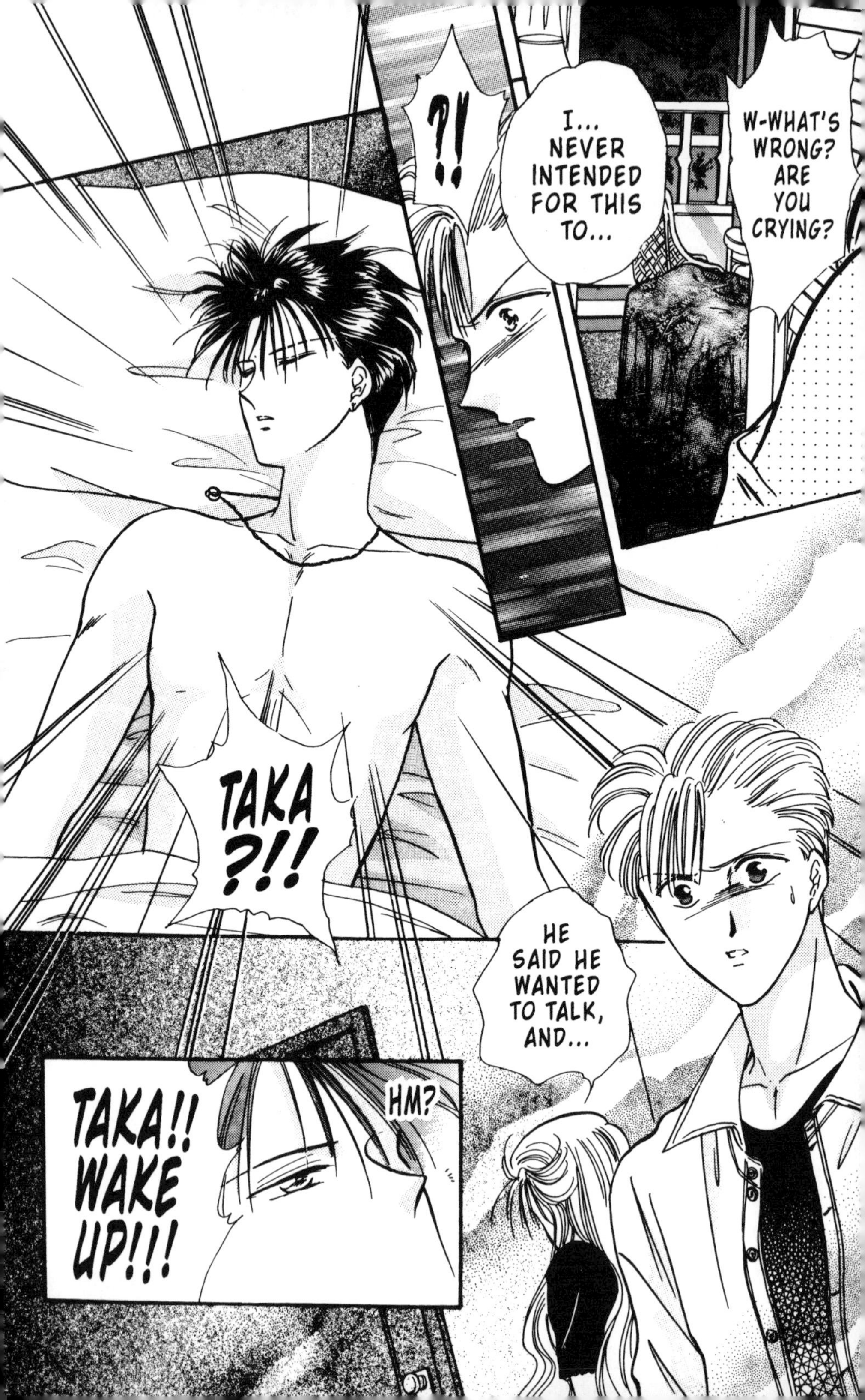
W-WHAT'S WRONG? ARE YOU CRYING?
I... NEVER INTENDED FOR THIS TO...
?!
HE SAID HE WANTED TO TALK, AND...
TAKA ?!!
TAKA!! WAKE UP!!!
HM?

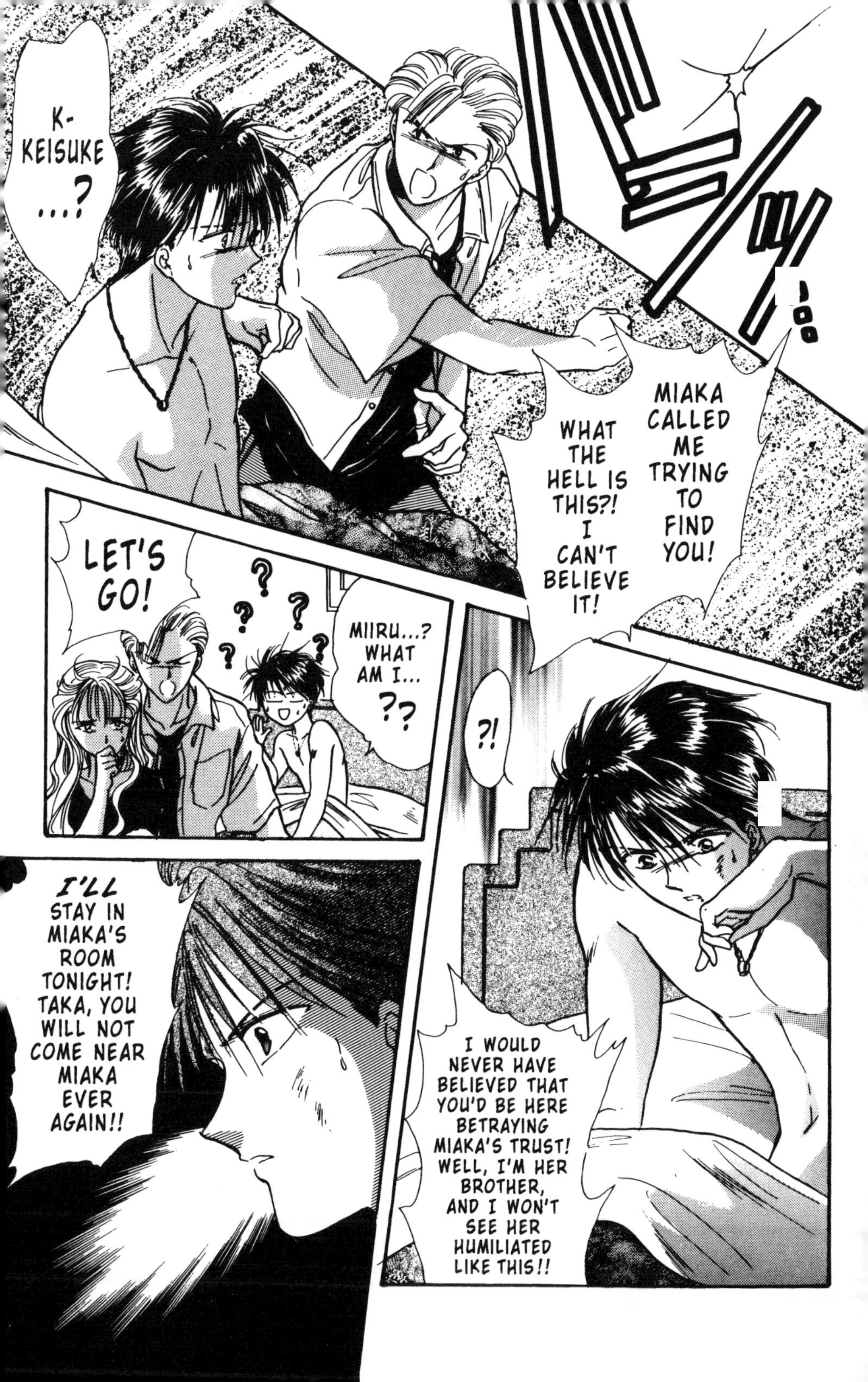
MIAKA CALLED ME TRYING TO FIND YOU!
WHAT THE HELL IS THIS?! I CAN'T BELIEVE IT!
K-KEISUKE ...?
?!
I WOULD NEVER HAVE BELIEVED THAT YOU'D BE HERE BETRAYING MIAKA'S TRUST! WELL, I'M HER BROTHER, AND I WON'T SEE HER HUMILIATED LIKE THIS!!
LET'S GO!
MIIRU...? WHAT AM I... ??
I'LL STAY IN MIAKA'S ROOM TONIGHT! TAKA, YOU WILL NOT COME NEAR MIAKA EVER AGAIN!!

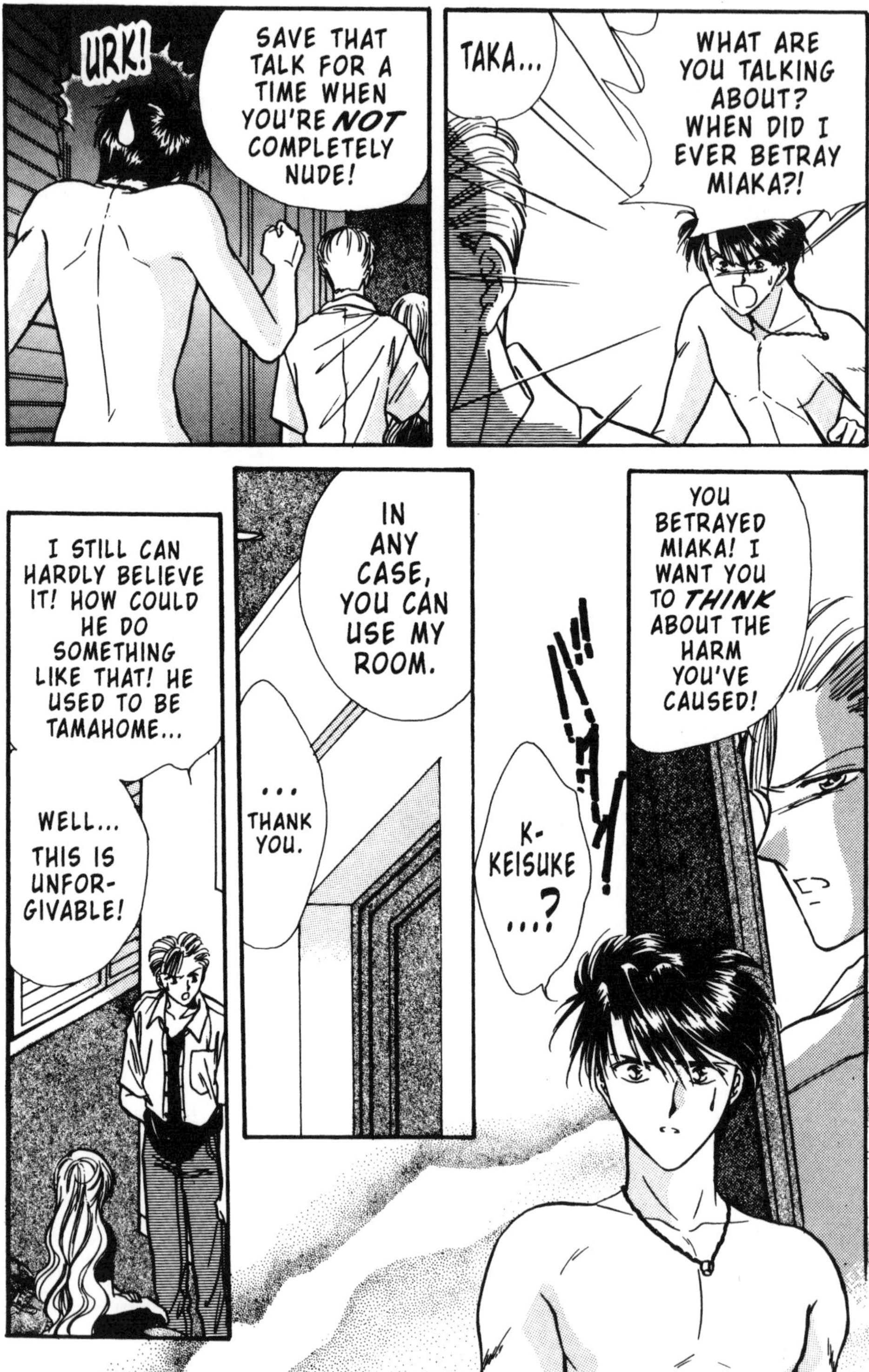
WHAT ARE YOU TALKING ABOUT? WHEN DID I EVER BETRAY MIAKA?!
TAKA...
SAVE THAT TALK FOR A TIME WHEN YOU'RE ***NOT*** COMPLETELY NUDE!
URK!
YOU BETRAYED MIAKA! I WANT YOU TO ***THINK*** ABOUT THE HARM YOU'VE CAUSED!
K-KEISUKE ...?
IN ANY CASE, YOU CAN USE MY ROOM.
... THANK YOU.
I STILL CAN HARDLY BELIEVE IT! HOW COULD HE DO SOMETHING LIKE THAT! HE USED TO BE TAMAHOME...
WELL... THIS IS UNFORGIVABLE!

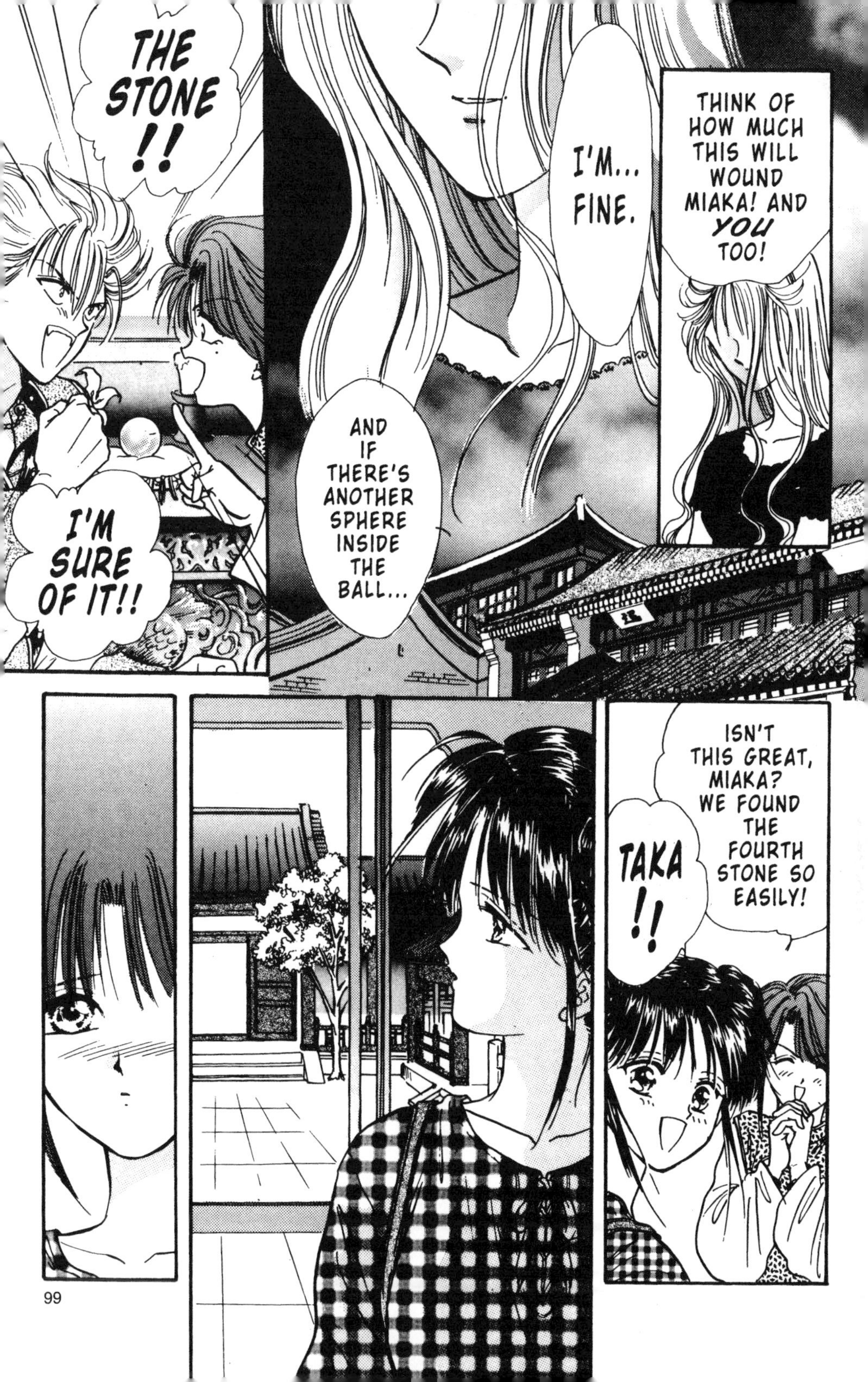
THINK OF HOW MUCH THIS WILL WOUND MIAKA! AND YOU TOO!
I'M... FINE.
AND IF THERE'S ANOTHER SPHERE INSIDE THE BALL...
THE STONE!!
I'M SURE OF IT!!
ISN'T THIS GREAT, MIAKA? WE FOUND THE FOURTH STONE SO EASILY!
TAKA!!

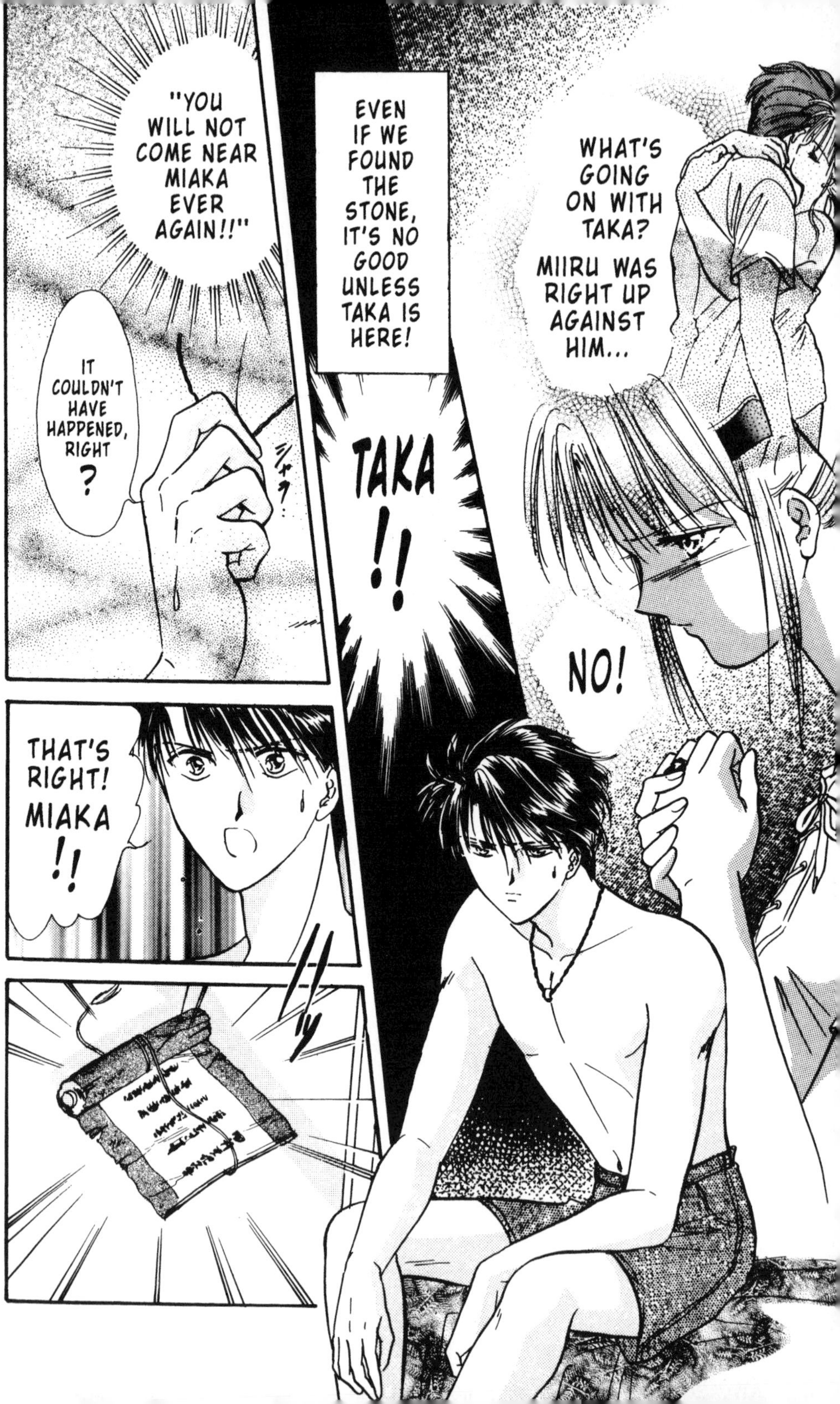
WHAT'S GOING ON WITH TAKA?
MIIRU WAS RIGHT UP AGAINST HIM...
NO!
EVEN IF WE FOUND THE STONE, IT'S NO GOOD UNLESS TAKA IS HERE!
TAKA!!
"YOU WILL NOT COME NEAR MIAKA EVER AGAIN!!"
IT COULDN'T HAVE HAPPENED, RIGHT?
THAT'S RIGHT! MIAKA!!

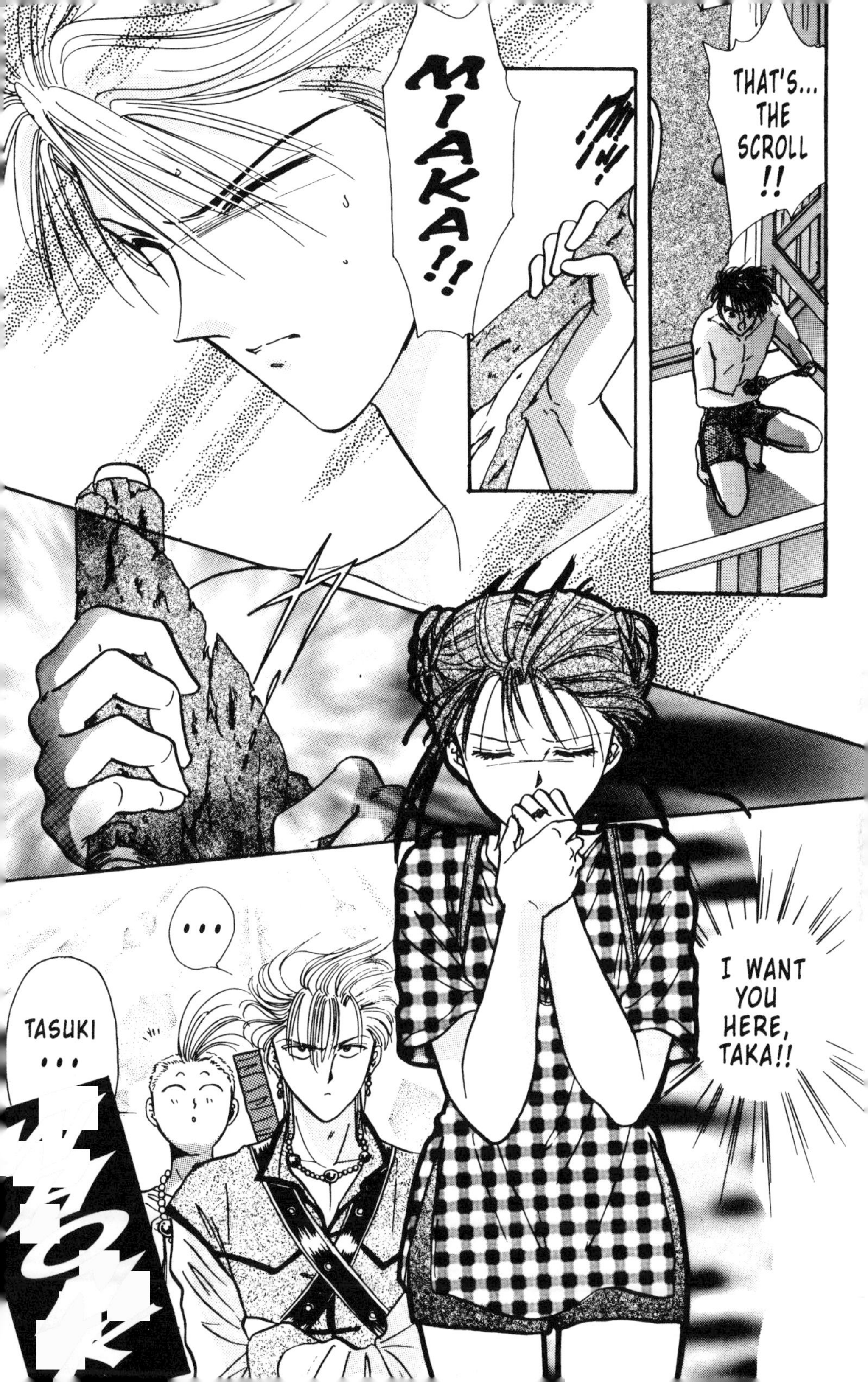
THAT'S... THE SCROLL!!
MIAKA!!
I WANT YOU HERE, TAKA!!
...
TASUKI ...

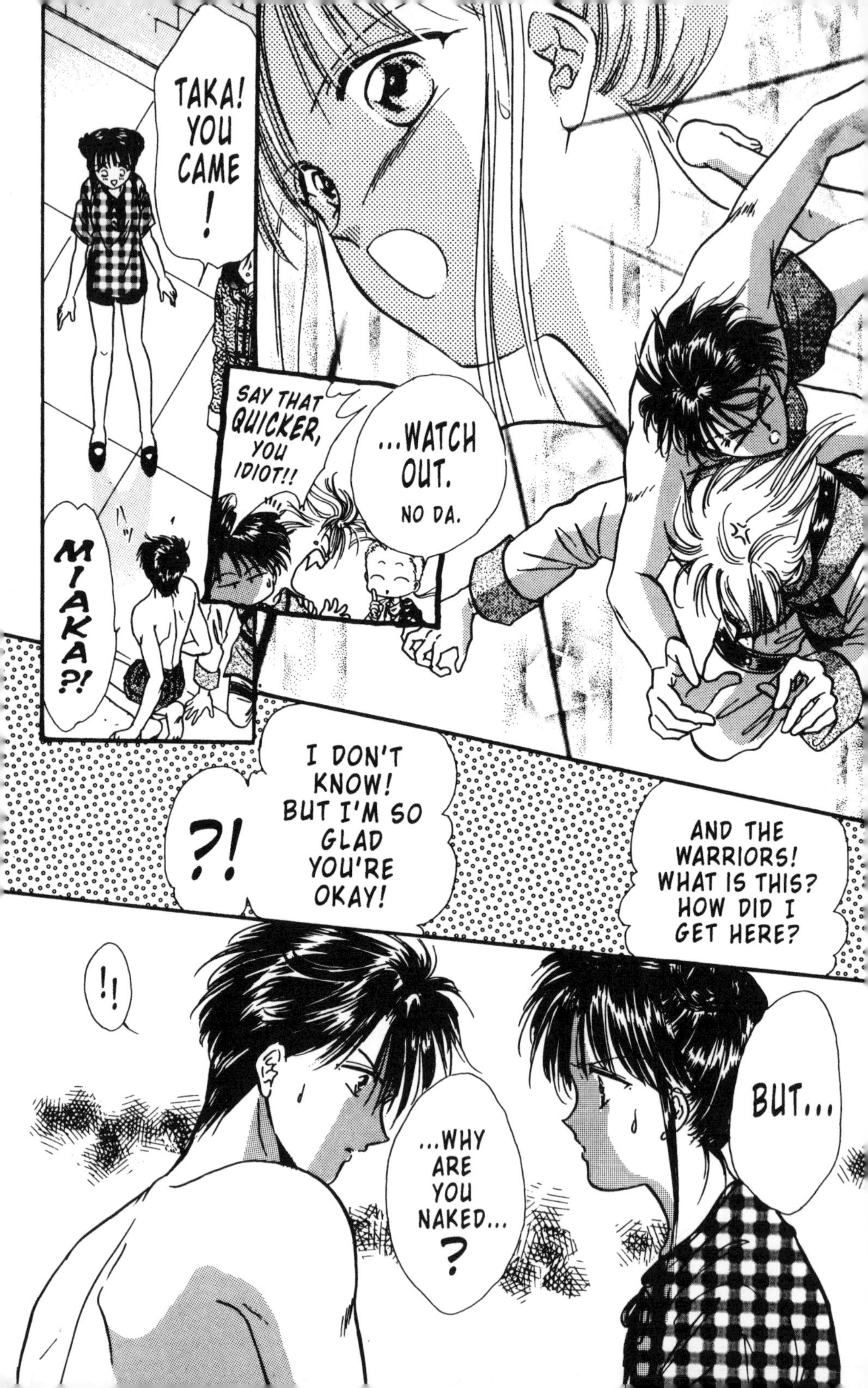
...WATCH OUT. NO DA.
SAY THAT QUICKER, YOU IDIOT!!
TAKA! YOU CAME!
MIAKA?!
AND THE WARRIORS! WHAT IS THIS? HOW DID I GET HERE?
I DON'T KNOW! BUT I'M SO GLAD YOU'RE OKAY!
?!
BUT...
...WHY ARE YOU NAKED...?
!!

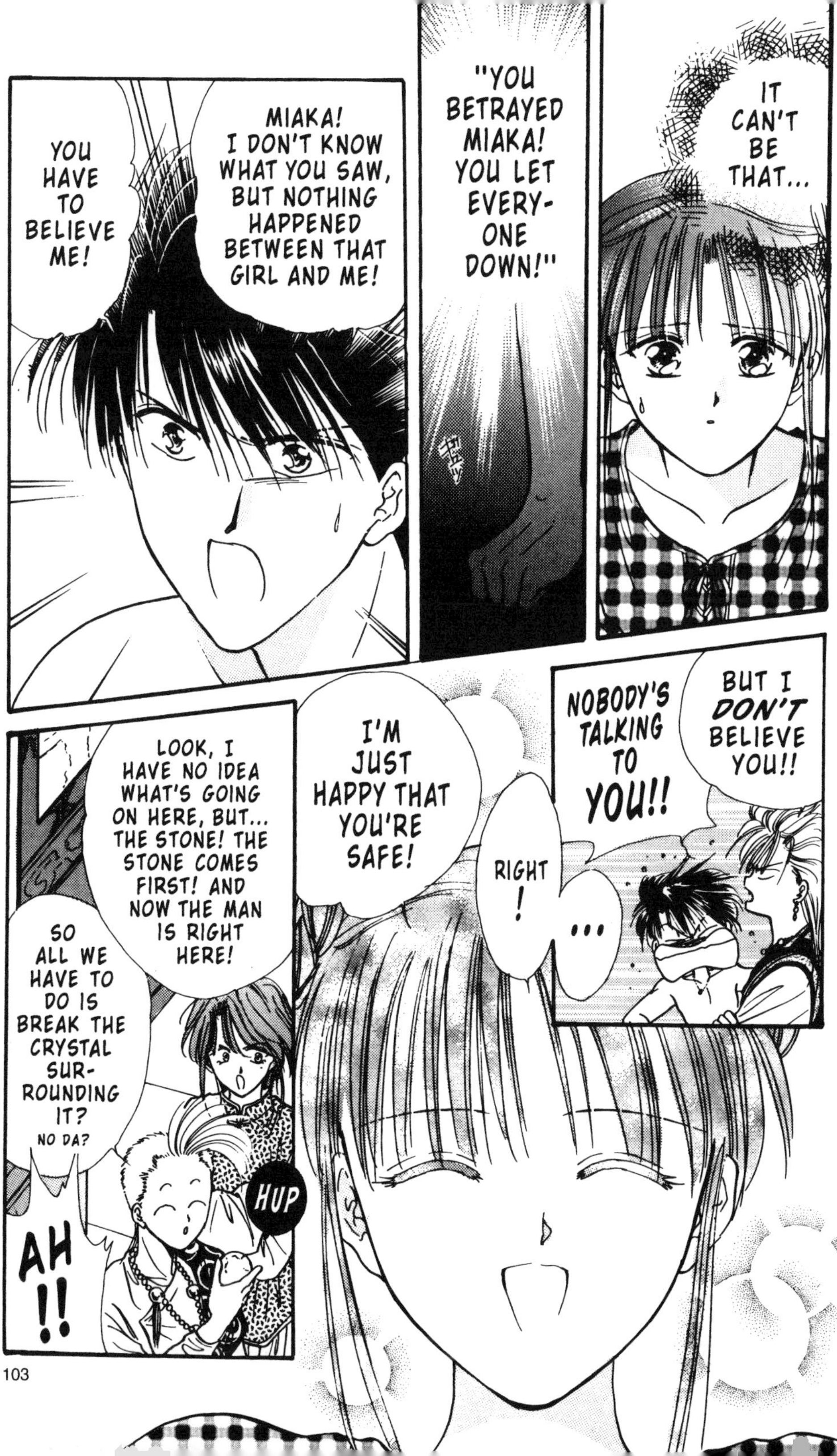
IT CAN'T BE THAT...
"YOU BETRAYED MIAKA! YOU LET EVERY-ONE DOWN!"
MIAKA! I DON'T KNOW WHAT YOU SAW, BUT NOTHING HAPPENED BETWEEN THAT GIRL AND ME!
YOU HAVE TO BELIEVE ME!
BUT I *DON'T* BELIEVE YOU!!
NOBODY'S TALKING TO YOU!!
...
RIGHT!
I'M JUST HAPPY THAT YOU'RE SAFE!
LOOK, I HAVE NO IDEA WHAT'S GOING ON HERE, BUT... THE STONE! THE STONE COMES FIRST! AND NOW THE MAN IS RIGHT HERE!
SO ALL WE HAVE TO DO IS BREAK THE CRYSTAL SUR-ROUNDING IT? NO DA?
HUP
AH!!

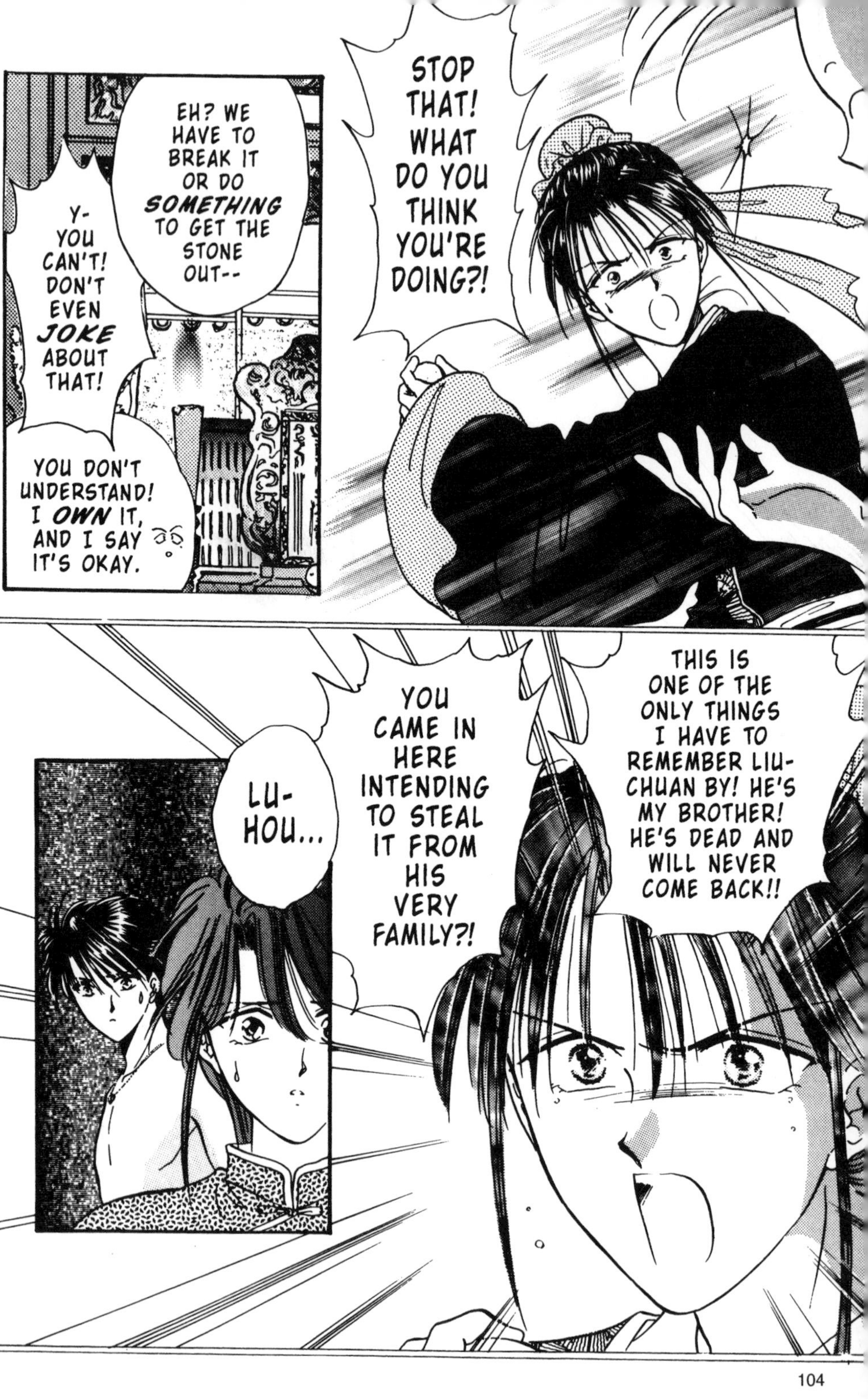
STOP THAT! WHAT DO YOU THINK YOU'RE DOING?!
EH? WE HAVE TO BREAK IT OR DO *SOMETHING* TO GET THE STONE OUT--
Y-YOU CAN'T! DON'T EVEN *JOKE* ABOUT THAT!
YOU DON'T UNDERSTAND! I *OWN* IT, AND I SAY IT'S OKAY.
THIS IS ONE OF THE ONLY THINGS I HAVE TO REMEMBER LIU-CHUAN BY! HE'S MY BROTHER! HE'S DEAD AND WILL NEVER COME BACK!!
YOU CAME IN HERE INTENDING TO STEAL IT FROM HIS VERY FAMILY?!
LU-HOU...

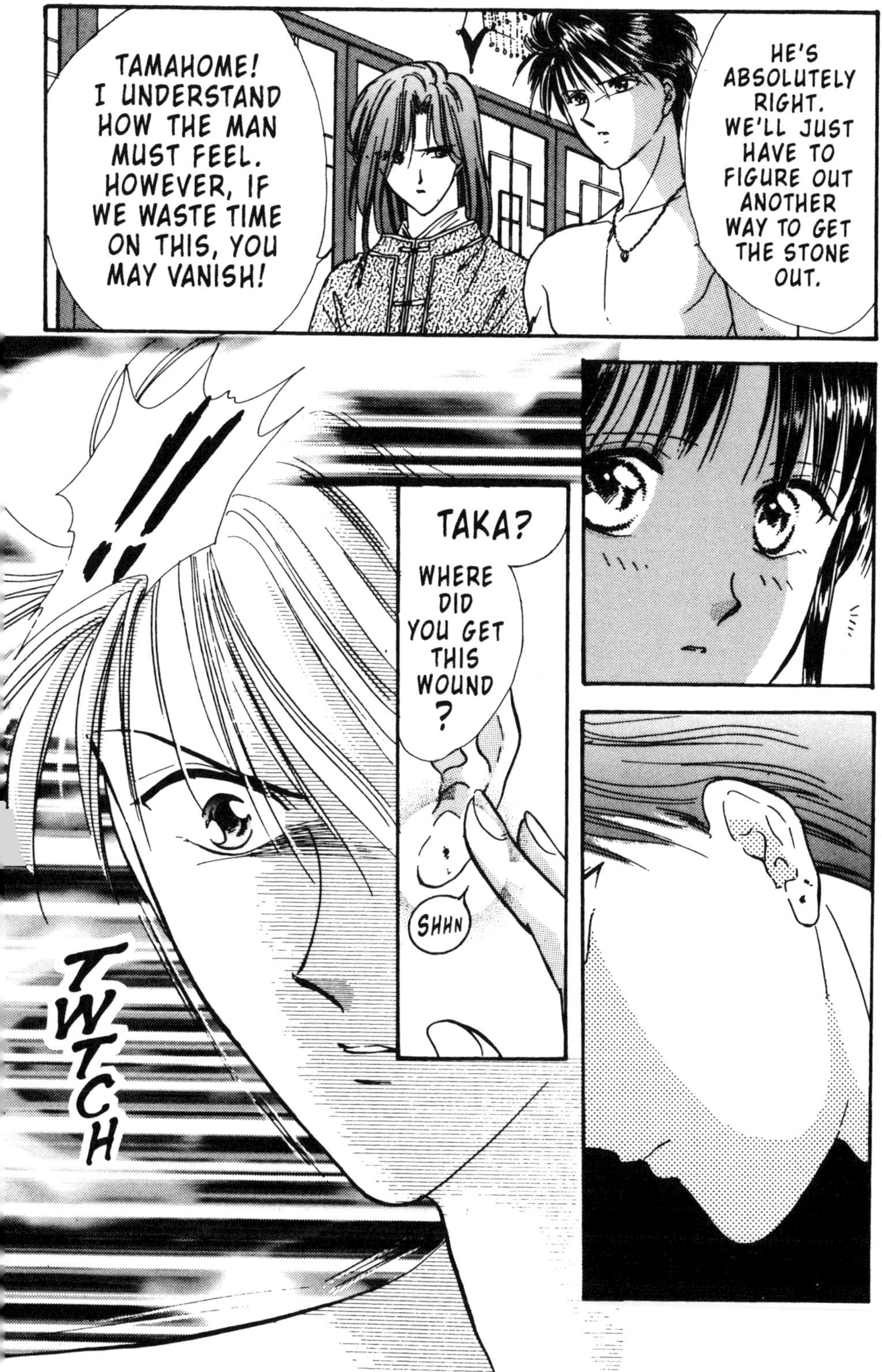
HE'S ABSOLUTELY RIGHT. WE'LL JUST HAVE TO FIGURE OUT ANOTHER WAY TO GET THE STONE OUT.
TAMAHOME! I UNDERSTAND HOW THE MAN MUST FEEL. HOWEVER, IF WE WASTE TIME ON THIS, YOU MAY VANISH!
TAKA?
WHERE DID YOU GET THIS WOUND?
SHHN
TWTCH

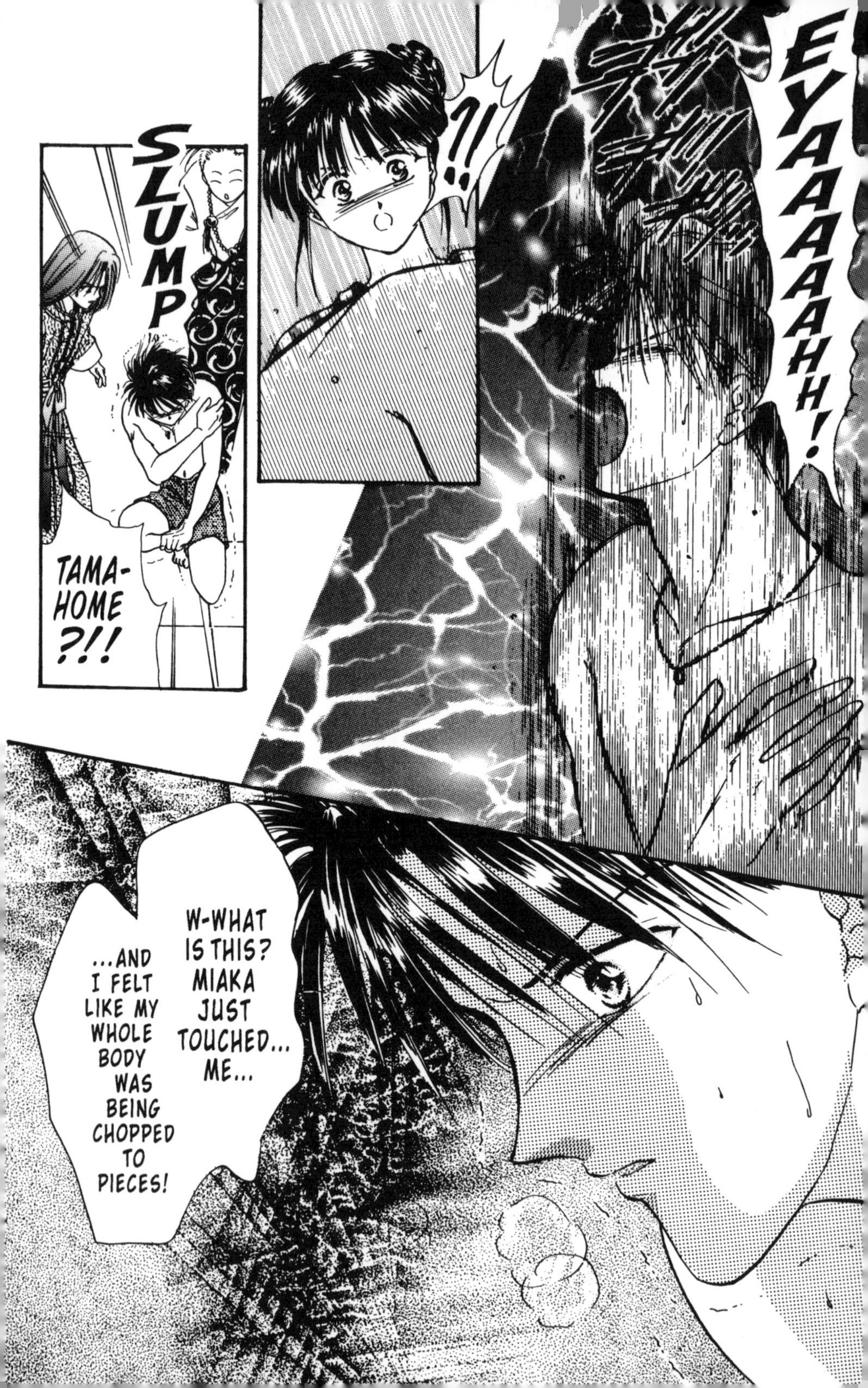
EYAAAAAHH!
?!!
SLUMP
TAMA-HOME ?!!
W-WHAT IS THIS? MIAKA JUST TOUCHED... ME...
...AND I FELT LIKE MY WHOLE BODY WAS BEING CHOPPED TO PIECES!

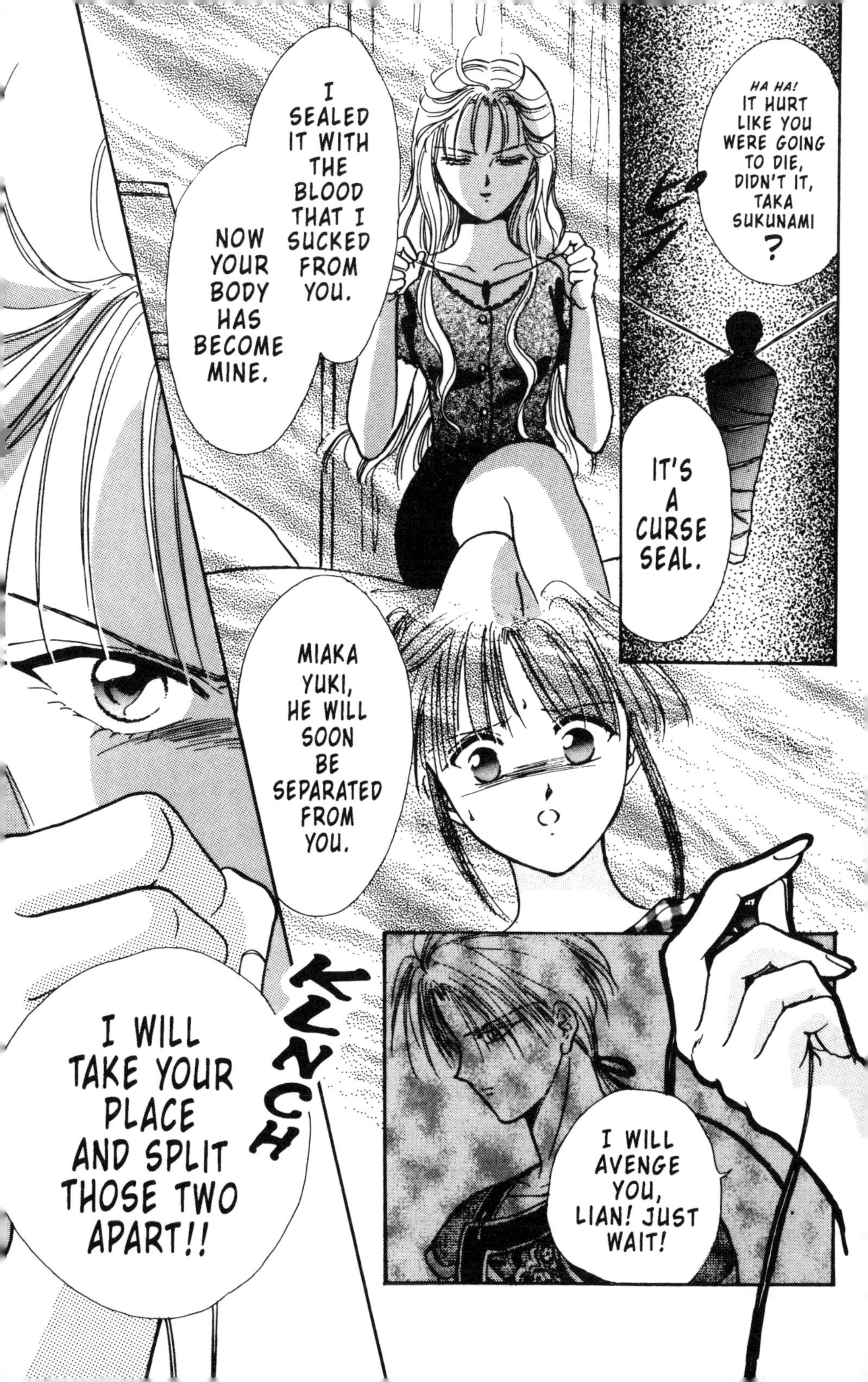
HA HA! IT HURT LIKE YOU WERE GOING TO DIE, DIDN'T IT, TAKA SUKUNAMI?
IT'S A CURSE SEAL.
I SEALED IT WITH THE BLOOD THAT I SUCKED FROM YOU.
NOW YOUR BODY HAS BECOME MINE.
MIAKA YUKI, HE WILL SOON BE SEPARATED FROM YOU.
I WILL AVENGE YOU, LIAN! JUST WAIT!
KUNCH
I WILL TAKE YOUR PLACE AND SPLIT THOSE TWO APART!!

Chapter Ninety-Two
The Broken Plan

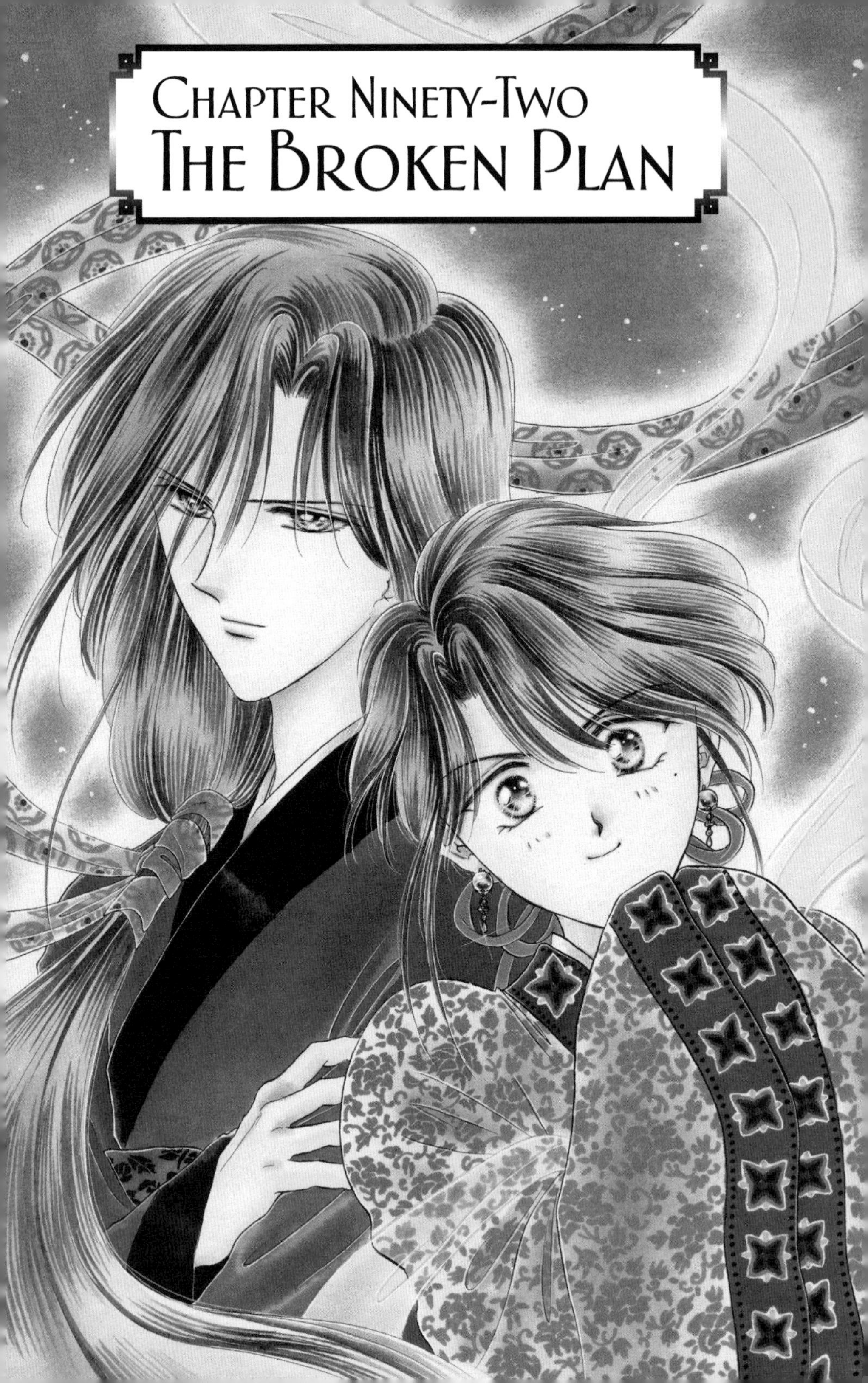

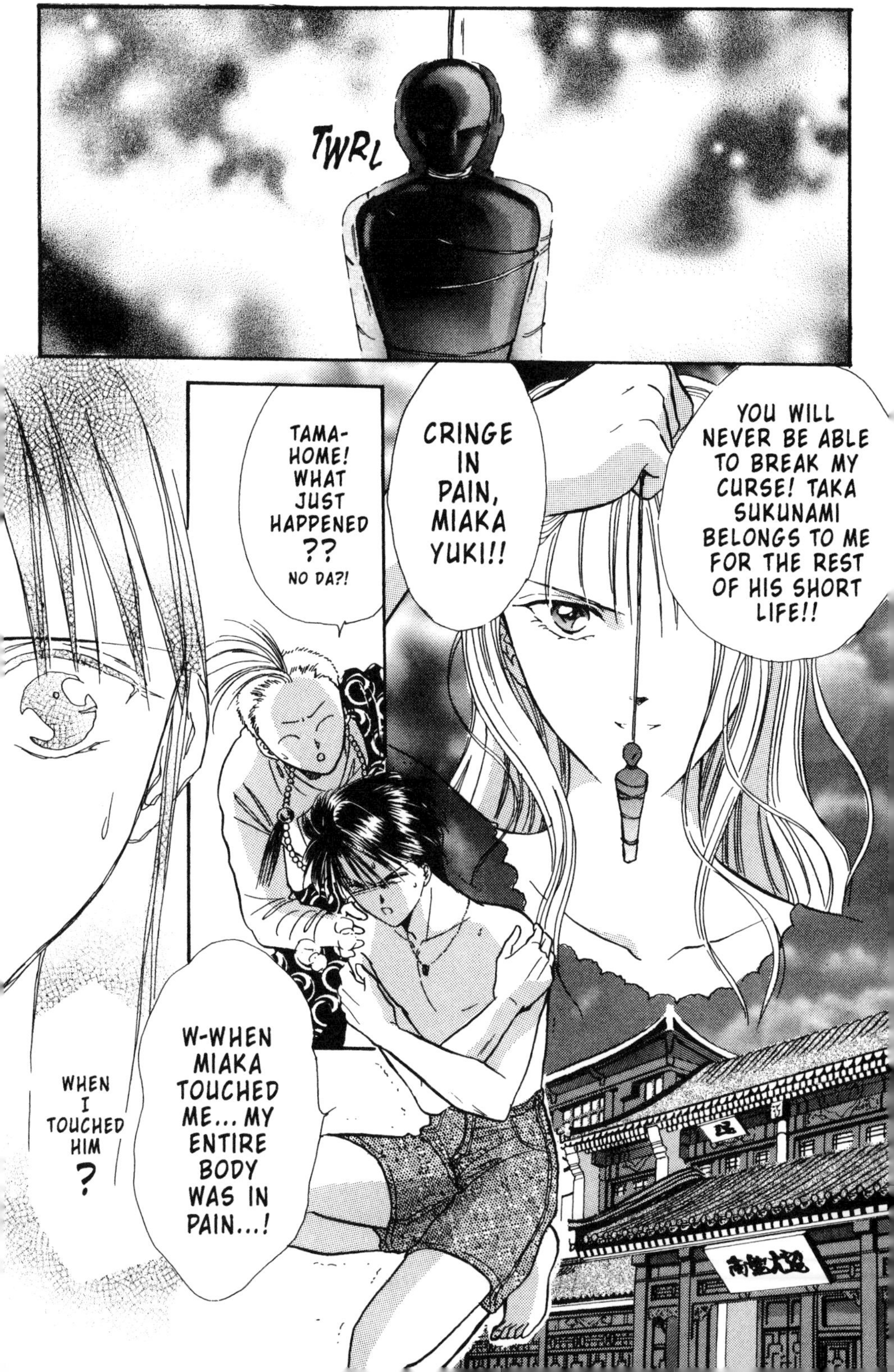
TWRL
YOU WILL NEVER BE ABLE TO BREAK MY CURSE! TAKA SUKUNAMI BELONGS TO ME FOR THE REST OF HIS SHORT LIFE!!
CRINGE IN PAIN, MIAKA YUKI!!
TAMA-HOME! WHAT JUST HAPPENED?? NO DA?!
W-WHEN MIAKA TOUCHED ME... MY ENTIRE BODY WAS IN PAIN...!
WHEN I TOUCHED HIM?

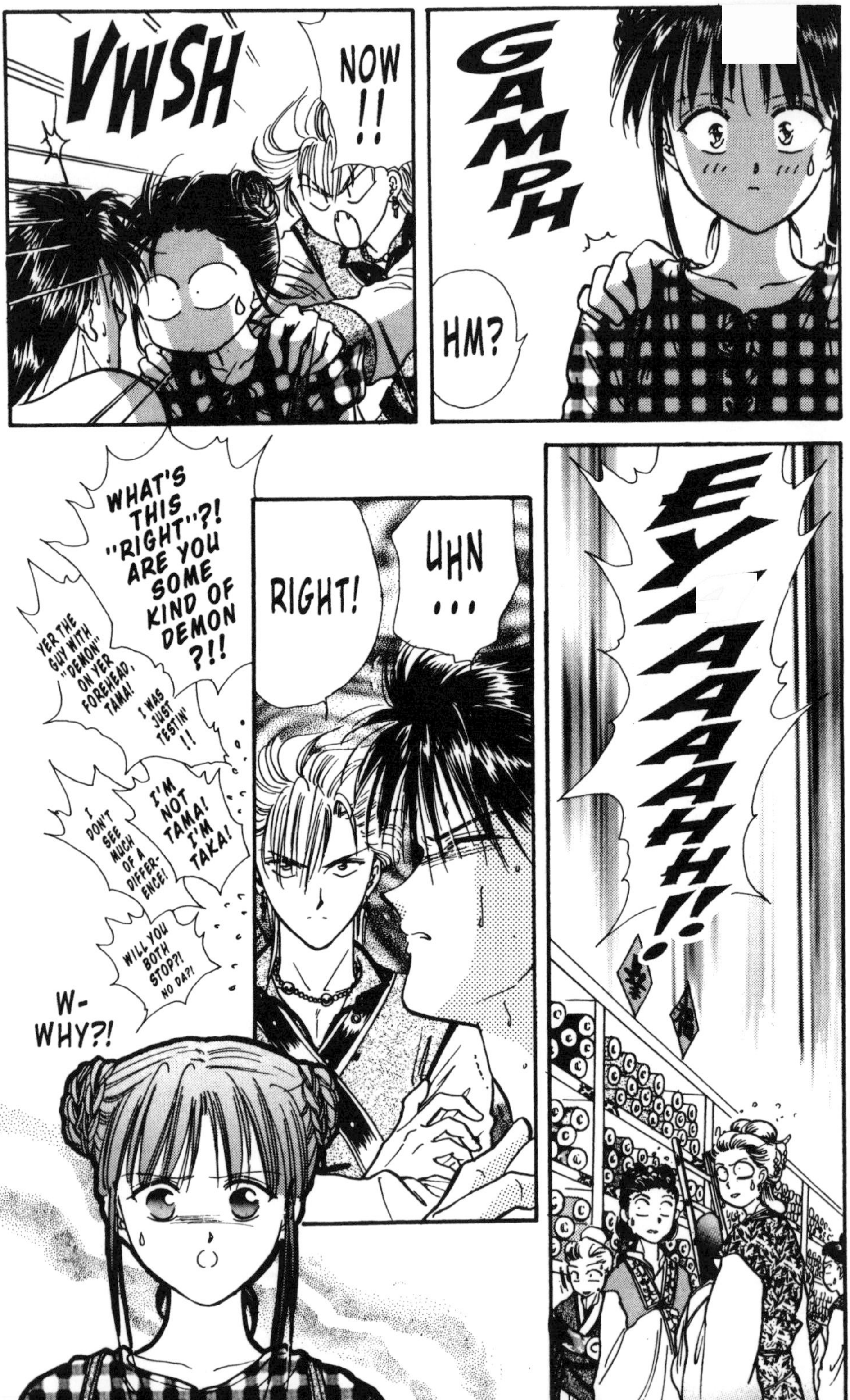
GAMPH
HM?
VWSH
NOW!!
EYAAAAHH!!
UHN...
RIGHT!
WHAT'S THIS "RIGHT"?! ARE YOU SOME KIND OF DEMON?!!
YER THE GUY WITH "DEMON" ON YER FOREHEAD, TAMA!
I WAS JUST TESTIN'!!
I'M NOT TAMA! I'M TAKA!
I DON'T SEE MUCH OF A DIFFERENCE!
WILL YOU BOTH STOP?! NO DA?!
W-WHY?!

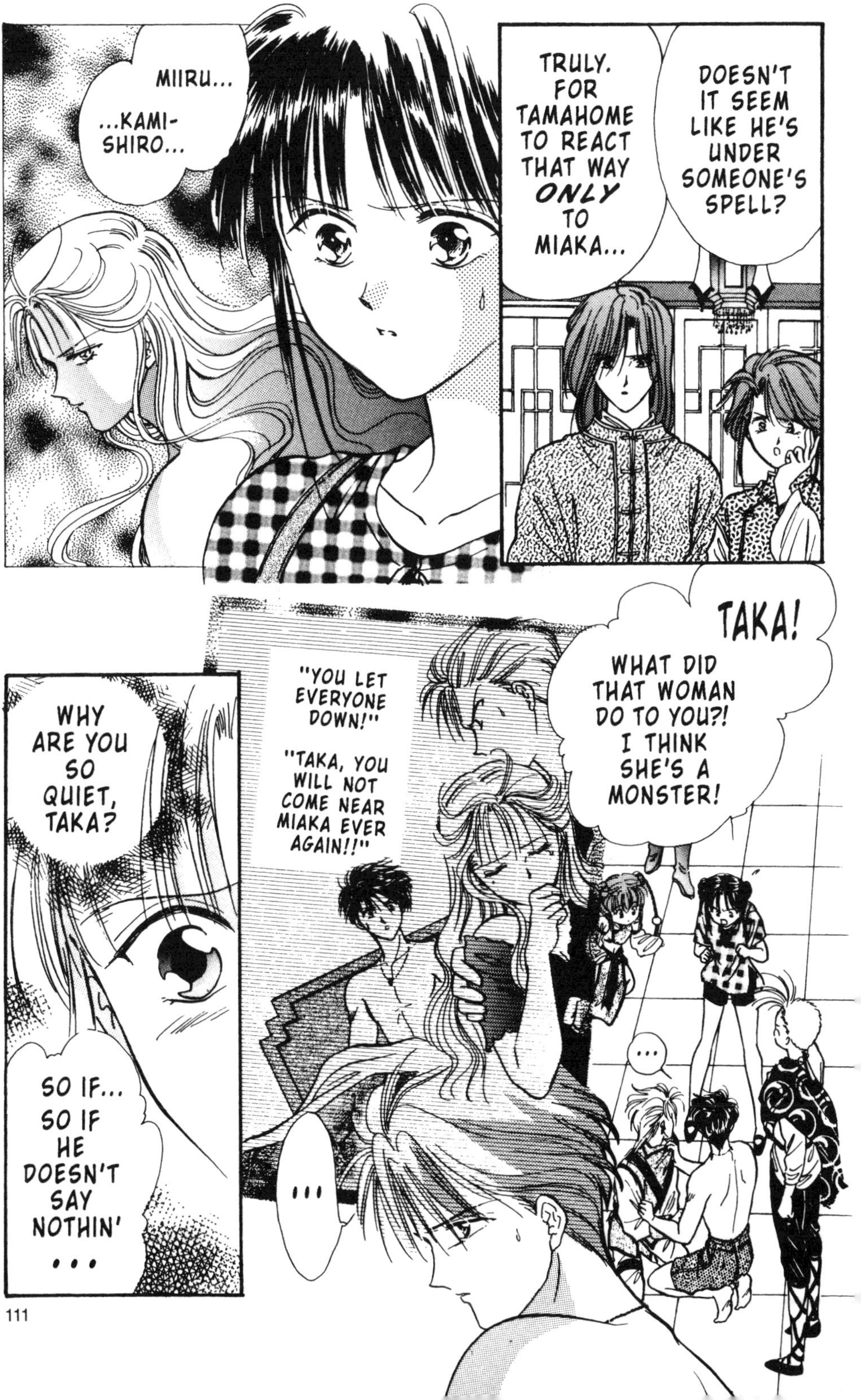
DOESN'T IT SEEM LIKE HE'S UNDER SOMEONE'S SPELL?
TRULY. FOR TAMAHOME TO REACT THAT WAY *ONLY* TO MIAKA...
MIIRU...
...KAMI-SHIRO...
TAKA!
WHAT DID THAT WOMAN DO TO YOU?! I THINK SHE'S A MONSTER!
"YOU LET EVERYONE DOWN!"
"TAKA, YOU WILL NOT COME NEAR MIAKA EVER AGAIN!!"
...
...
WHY ARE YOU SO QUIET, TAKA?
SO IF... SO IF HE DOESN'T SAY NOTHIN' ...

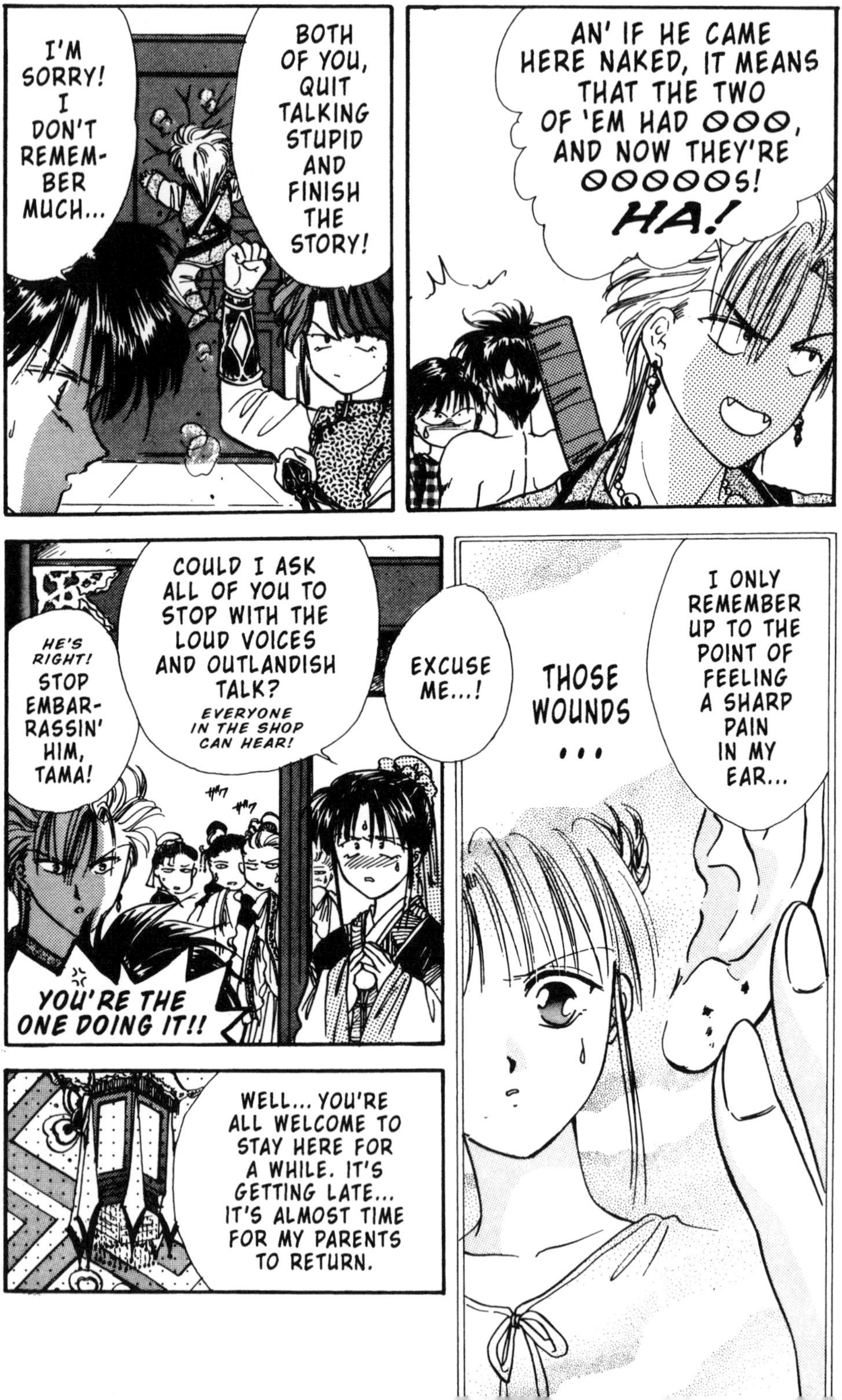
AN' IF HE CAME HERE NAKED, IT MEANS THAT THE TWO OF 'EM HAD ⊘⊘⊘, AND NOW THEY'RE ⊘⊘⊘⊘⊘S! HA!
BOTH OF YOU, QUIT TALKING STUPID AND FINISH THE STORY!
I'M SORRY! I DON'T REMEMBER MUCH...
I ONLY REMEMBER UP TO THE POINT OF FEELING A SHARP PAIN IN MY EAR...
THOSE WOUNDS...
EXCUSE ME...!
COULD I ASK ALL OF YOU TO STOP WITH THE LOUD VOICES AND OUTLANDISH TALK?
EVERYONE IN THE SHOP CAN HEAR!
HE'S RIGHT! STOP EMBARRASSIN' HIM, TAMA!
YOU'RE THE ONE DOING IT!!
WELL... YOU'RE ALL WELCOME TO STAY HERE FOR A WHILE. IT'S GETTING LATE... IT'S ALMOST TIME FOR MY PARENTS TO RETURN.

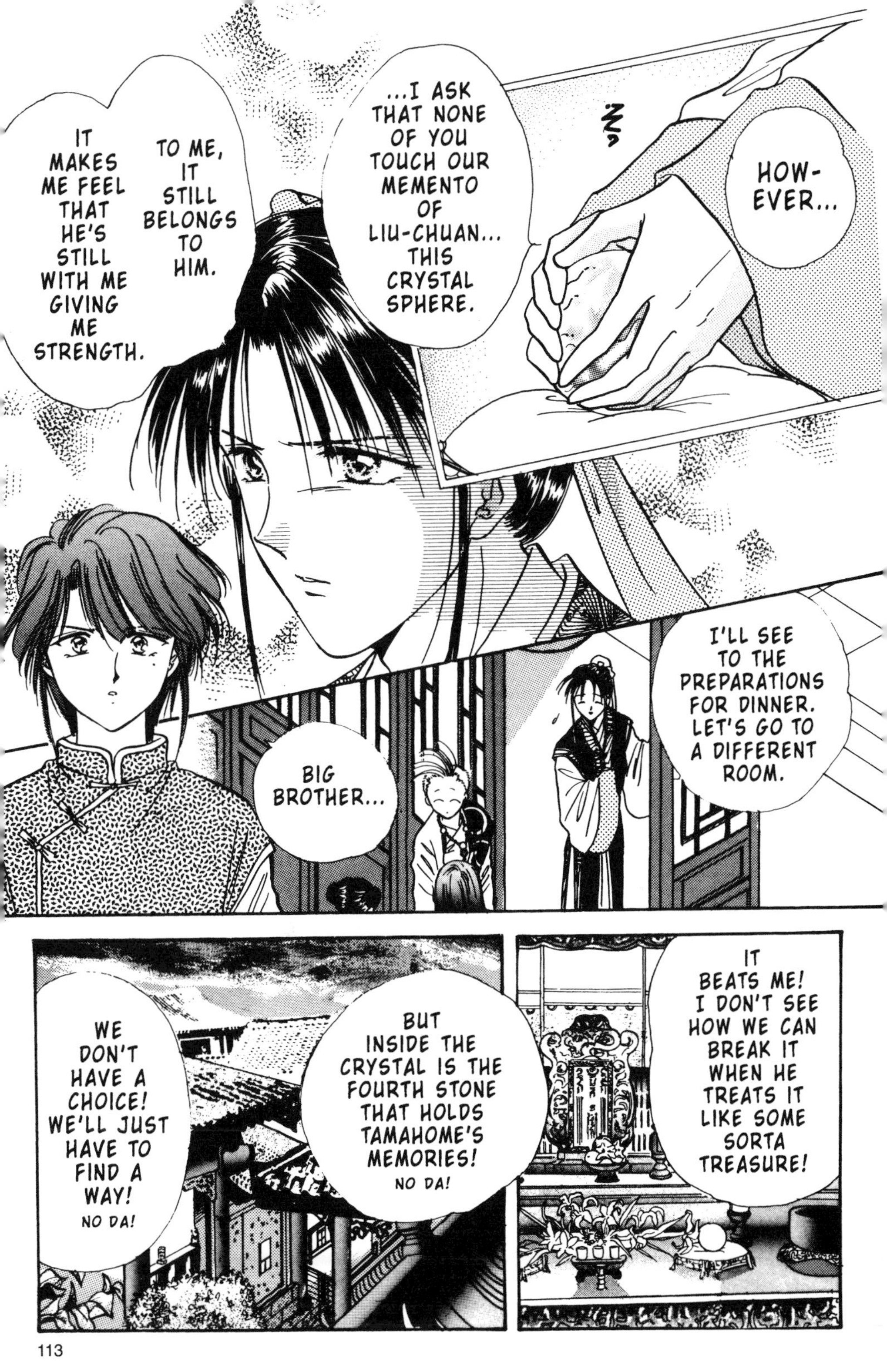
HOW-EVER...
...I ASK THAT NONE OF YOU TOUCH OUR MEMENTO OF LIU-CHUAN... THIS CRYSTAL SPHERE.
TO ME, IT STILL BELONGS TO HIM.
IT MAKES ME FEEL THAT HE'S STILL WITH ME GIVING ME STRENGTH.
I'LL SEE TO THE PREPARATIONS FOR DINNER. LET'S GO TO A DIFFERENT ROOM.
BIG BROTHER...
IT BEATS ME! I DON'T SEE HOW WE CAN BREAK IT WHEN HE TREATS IT LIKE SOME SORTA TREASURE!
BUT INSIDE THE CRYSTAL IS THE FOURTH STONE THAT HOLDS TAMAHOME'S MEMORIES! NO DA!
WE DON'T HAVE A CHOICE! WE'LL JUST HAVE TO FIND A WAY! NO DA!

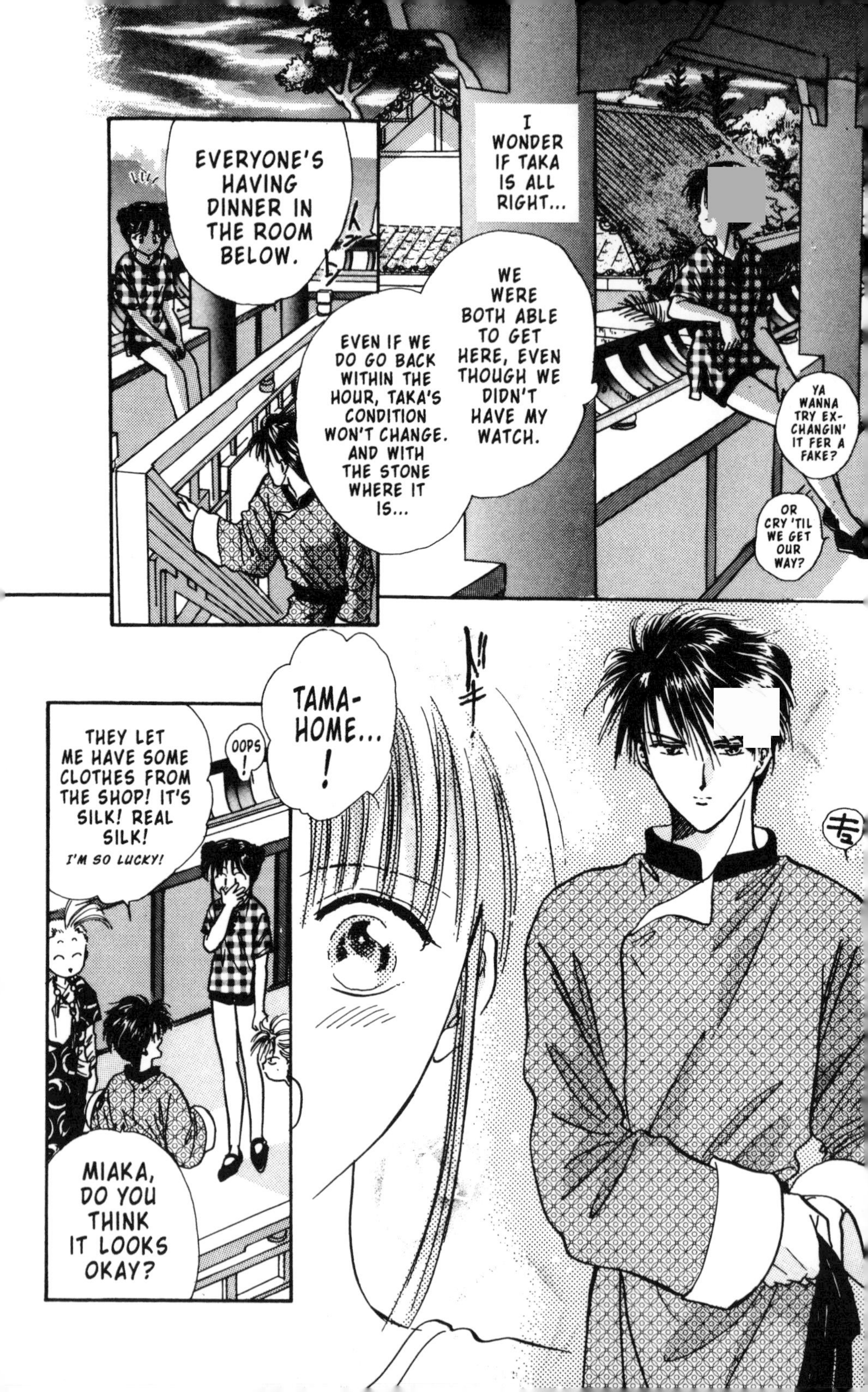
I WONDER IF TAKA IS ALL RIGHT...
WE WERE BOTH ABLE TO GET HERE, EVEN THOUGH WE DIDN'T HAVE MY WATCH.
EVEN IF WE DO GO BACK WITHIN THE HOUR, TAKA'S CONDITION WON'T CHANGE. AND WITH THE STONE WHERE IT IS...
YA WANNA TRY EX-CHANGIN' IT FER A FAKE?
OR CRY 'TIL WE GET OUR WAY?
EVERYONE'S HAVING DINNER IN THE ROOM BELOW.
TAMA-HOME...!
OOPS!
THEY LET ME HAVE SOME CLOTHES FROM THE SHOP! IT'S SILK! REAL SILK!
I'M SO LUCKY!
MIAKA, DO YOU THINK IT LOOKS OKAY?

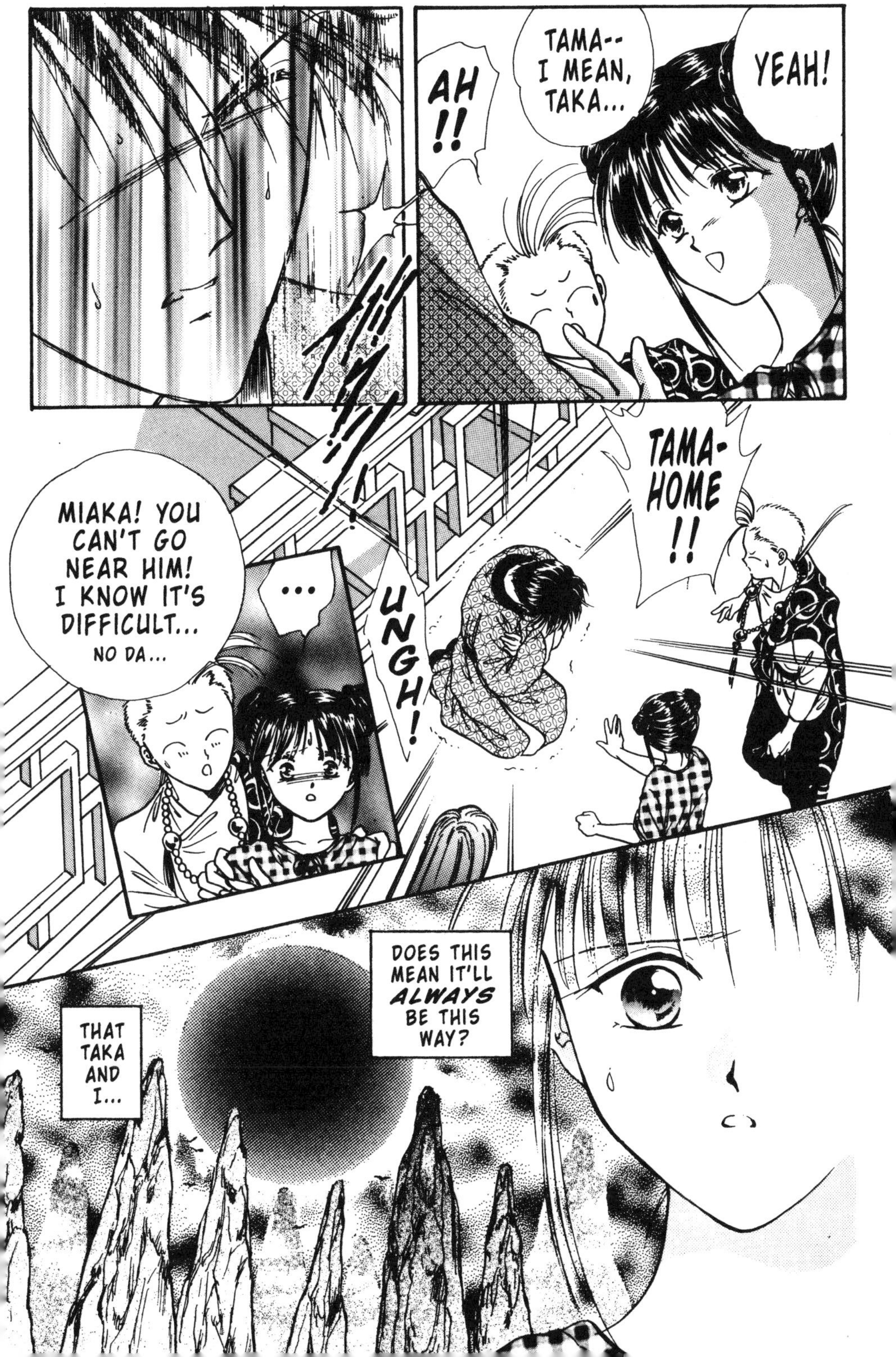
YEAH!
TAMA-- I MEAN, TAKA...
AH!!
TAMA-HOME!!
UNGH!
...
MIAKA! YOU CAN'T GO NEAR HIM! I KNOW IT'S DIFFICULT... NO DA...
DOES THIS MEAN IT'LL ALWAYS BE THIS WAY?
THAT TAKA AND I...

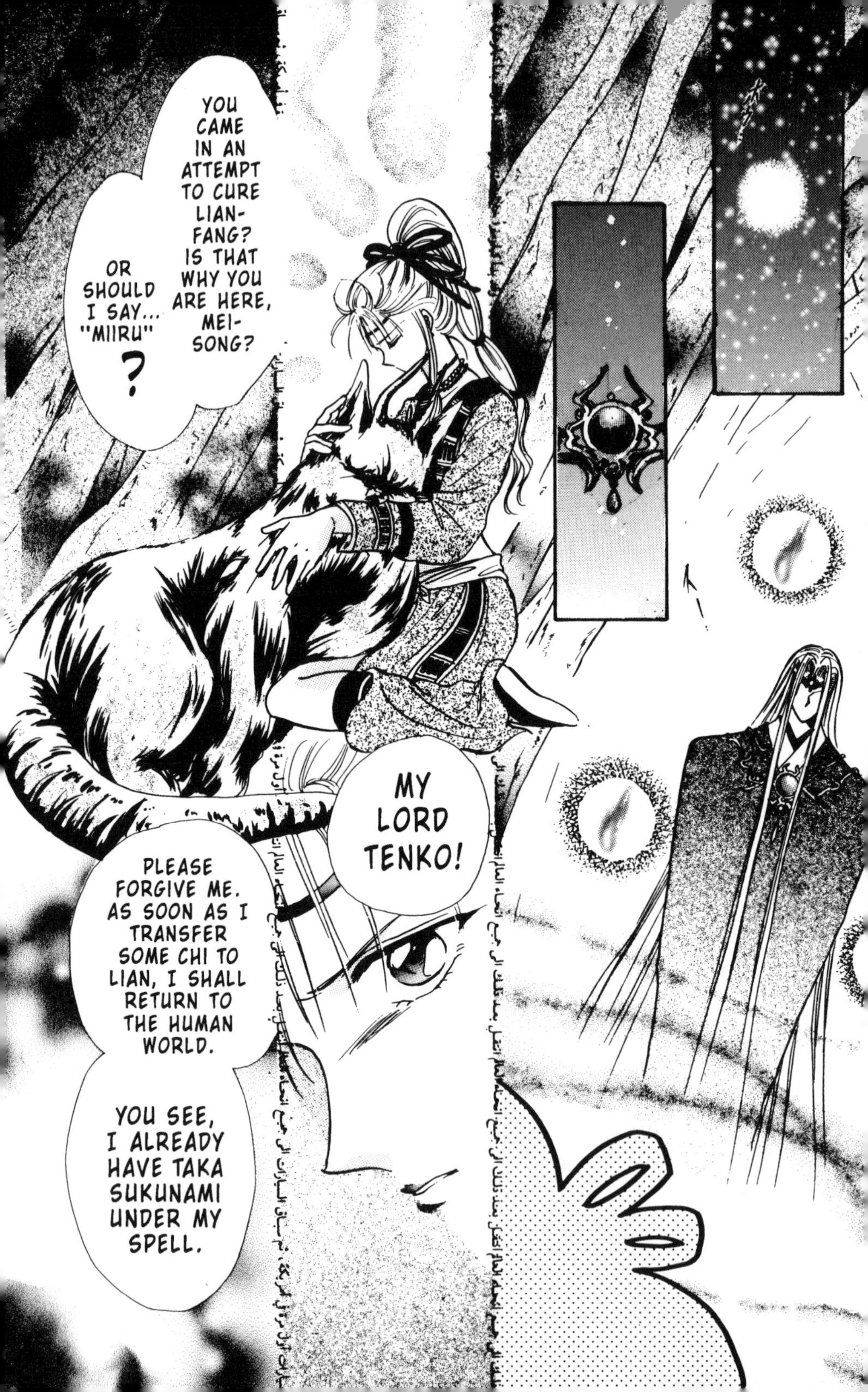
YOU CAME IN AN ATTEMPT TO CURE LIAN-FANG? IS THAT WHY YOU ARE HERE, MEI-SONG?
OR SHOULD I SAY... "MIIRU"?
MY LORD TENKO!
PLEASE FORGIVE ME. AS SOON AS I TRANSFER SOME CHI TO LIAN, I SHALL RETURN TO THE HUMAN WORLD.
YOU SEE, I ALREADY HAVE TAKA SUKUNAMI UNDER MY SPELL.

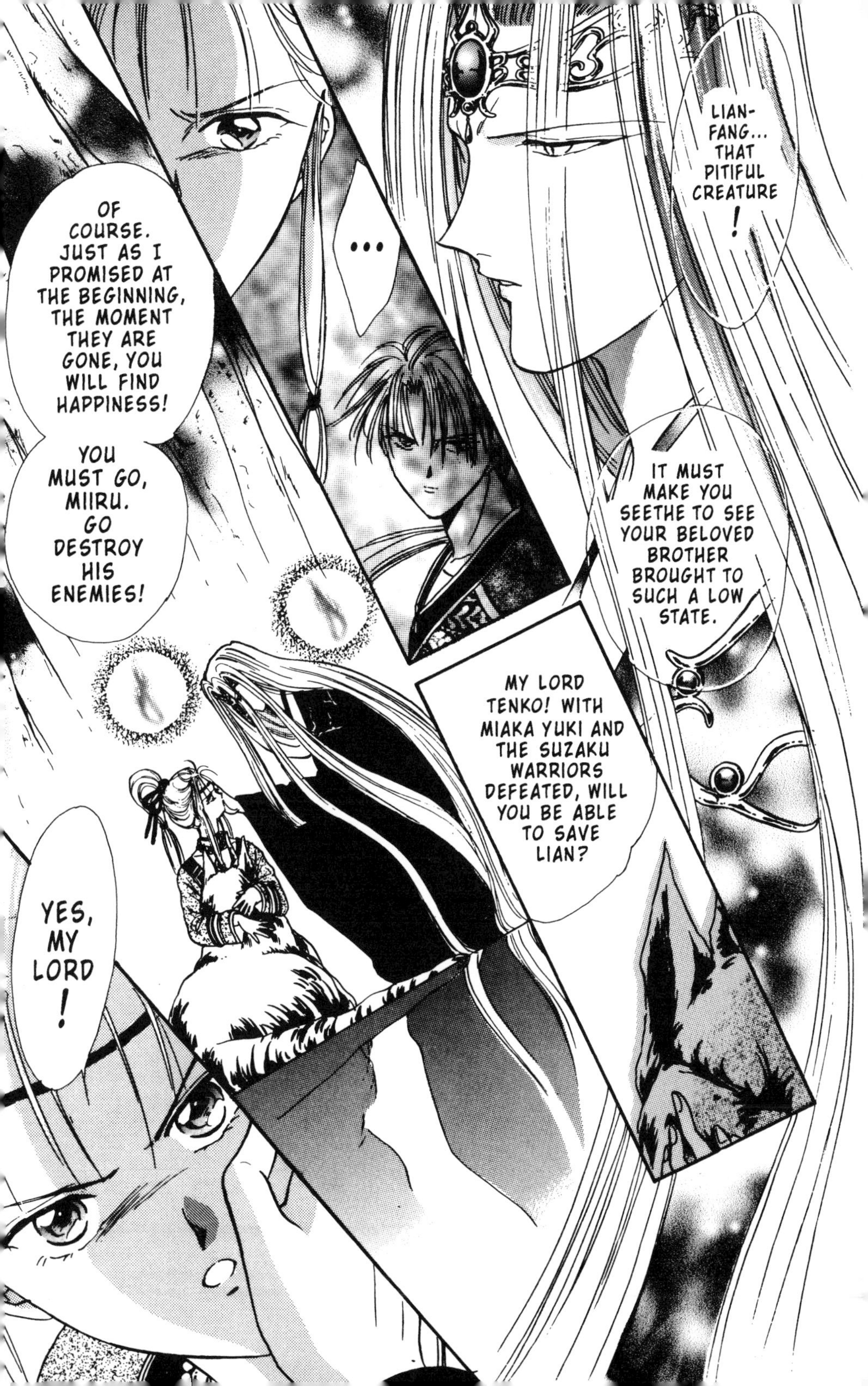
LIAN-FANG... THAT PITIFUL CREATURE!
IT MUST MAKE YOU SEETHE TO SEE YOUR BELOVED BROTHER BROUGHT TO SUCH A LOW STATE.
...
MY LORD TENKO! WITH MIAKA YUKI AND THE SUZAKU WARRIORS DEFEATED, WILL YOU BE ABLE TO SAVE LIAN?
OF COURSE. JUST AS I PROMISED AT THE BEGINNING, THE MOMENT THEY ARE GONE, YOU WILL FIND HAPPINESS!
YOU MUST GO, MIIRU. GO DESTROY HIS ENEMIES!
YES, MY LORD!

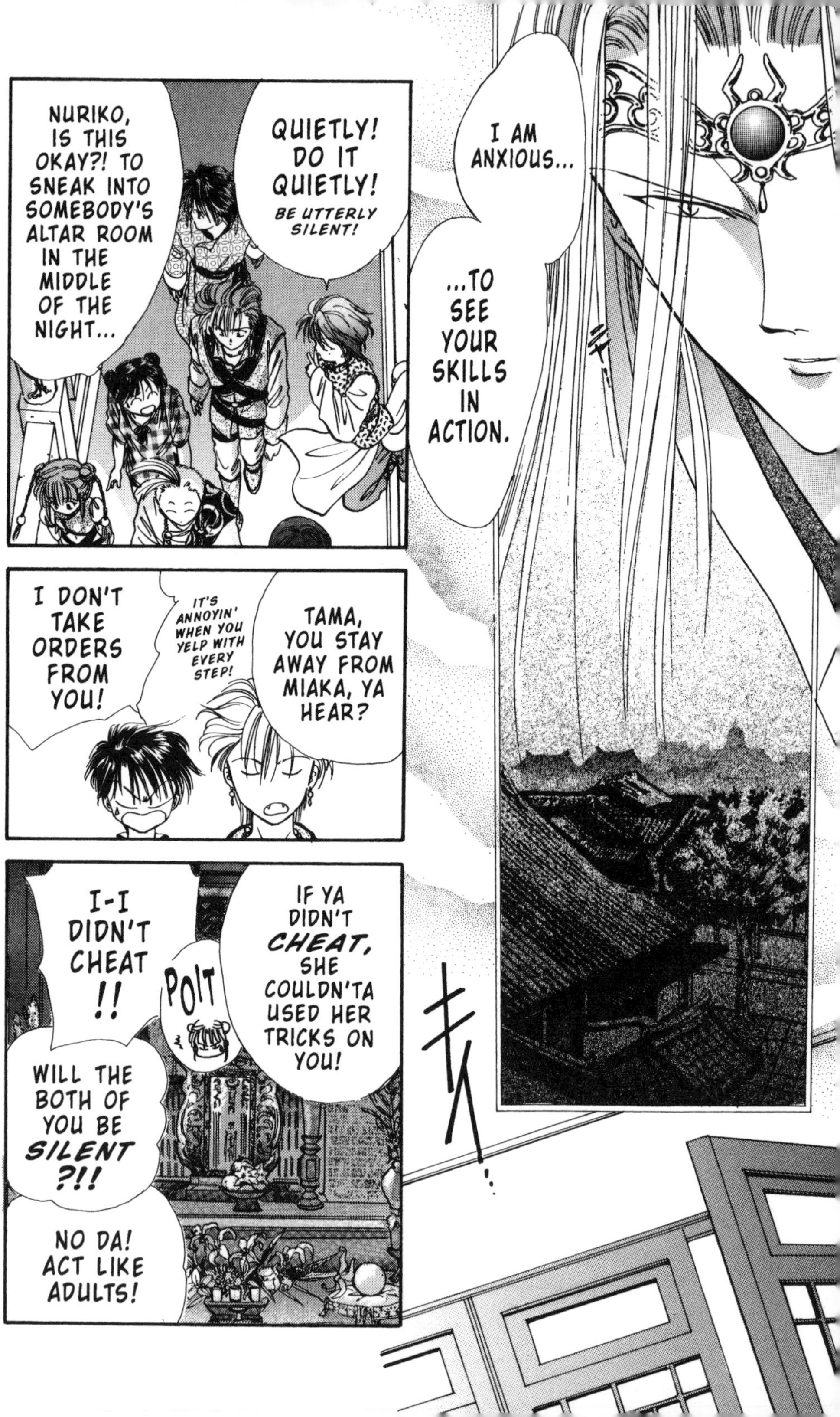
I AM ANXIOUS...
...TO SEE YOUR SKILLS IN ACTION.
キイ...
QUIETLY! DO IT QUIETLY! BE UTTERLY SILENT!
NURIKO, IS THIS OKAY?! TO SNEAK INTO SOMEBODY'S ALTAR ROOM IN THE MIDDLE OF THE NIGHT...
TAMA, YOU STAY AWAY FROM MIAKA, YA HEAR?
IT'S ANNOYIN' WHEN YOU YELP WITH EVERY STEP!
I DON'T TAKE ORDERS FROM YOU!
IF YA DIDN'T CHEAT, SHE COULDN'TA USED HER TRICKS ON YOU!
POIT
I-I DIDN'T CHEAT!!
WILL THE BOTH OF YOU BE SILENT?!!
NO DA! ACT LIKE ADULTS!

In an earlier section, I talked about readers who said that they wouldn't acknowledge fans who became fans just because of the anime. Before long, I got a lot of letters complaining about that opinion saying, "I could cry," or "no fair!" Many said things like this, "Hey, I saw an episode or two of the anime, and I went right out and bought all of the graphic novels! That could be considered becoming a fan through the original work, too!!" Ahh... yeah. ☺ The people writing in have a point. There are people who never had the chance to hear about *Fushigi Yūgi* until the anime came out, but once they did, their love for the series was just as strong as anyone else's. Those people fell in love with the story, and it makes me very happy that the number of fans increased after it became an anime. I can only say I'm moved that a whole lot of new people are emotionally affected by a story that came from the bottom of my heart. People can make a lot of friends through fan groups and have something to talk about. Even if they have different perspectives or have different favorite characters, they can have their worlds expanded by the points of view of others. At least, that's what I'd like to see happen. I'm so mature! If I were childish, I'd want to monopolize the work only for myself! ☺ So, everyone, be sure to go forward with an open heart! Remember there will be new readers too... So to you long-time readers, don't look disparagingly on any new fans!

While I was thinking all of those things, I got this letter that said, "I knew that shojo manga = high school romance, ♥♥♥ so I never read your stuff." *KA-WHUMP.*

A lot of people think shojo manga is boring, huh? No, I understand their point. ☺ When I was in 6th grade, there was someone I knew who said, "Shojo manga are just boring romances," and threw the books out. *But why bring it up now?* Humph! Is all of this just revenge for ancient humiliations? ☺

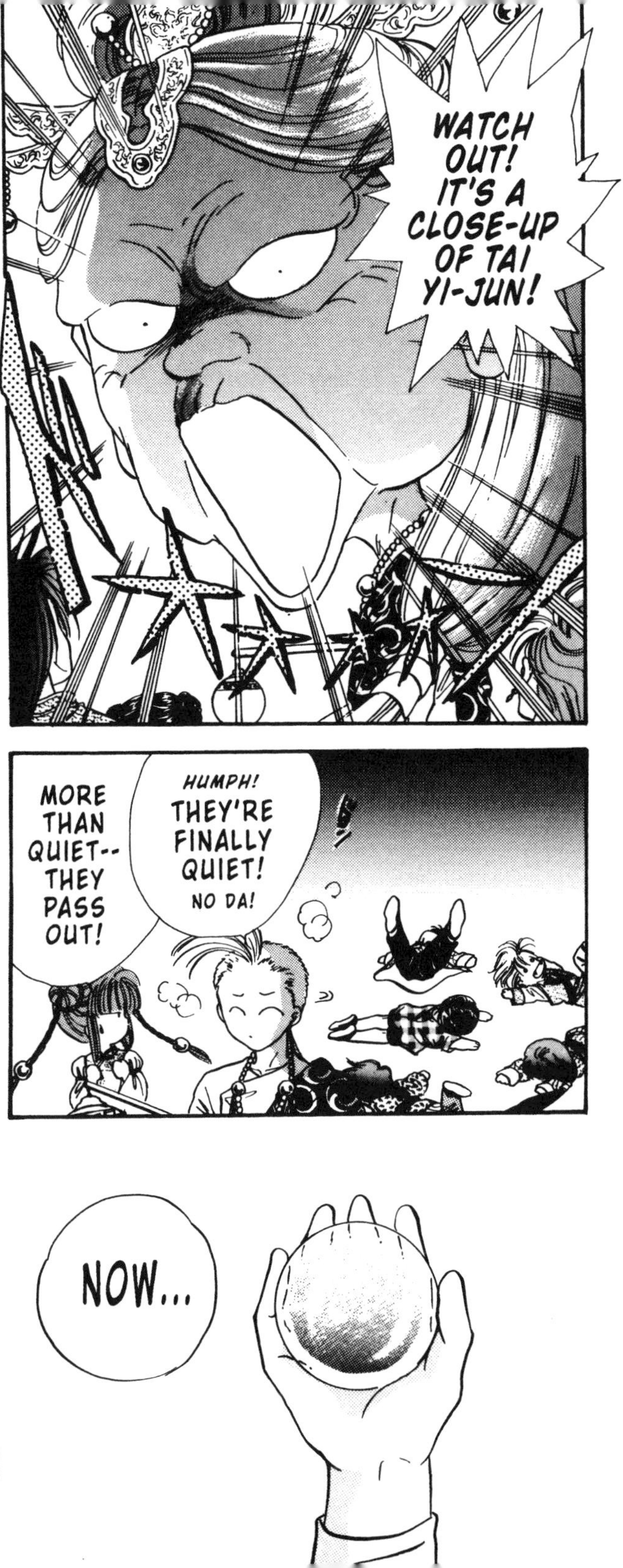
WATCH OUT! IT'S A CLOSE-UP OF TAI YI-JUN!
HUMPH! THEY'RE FINALLY QUIET! NO DA!
MORE THAN QUIET-- THEY PASS OUT!
NOW...

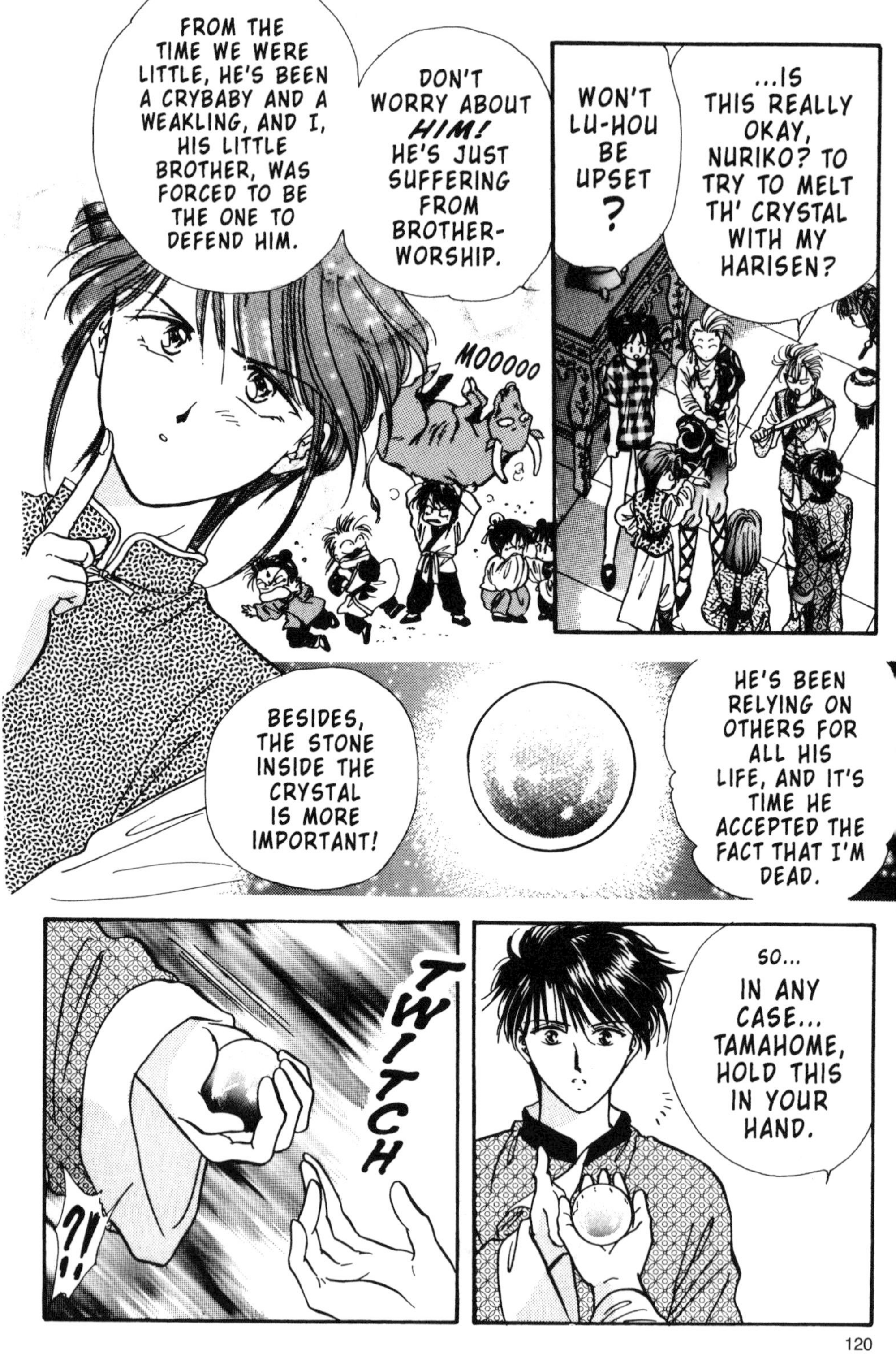
...IS THIS REALLY OKAY, NURIKO? TO TRY TO MELT TH' CRYSTAL WITH MY HARISEN?
WON'T LU-HOU BE UPSET?
DON'T WORRY ABOUT *HIM!* HE'S JUST SUFFERING FROM BROTHER-WORSHIP.
FROM THE TIME WE WERE LITTLE, HE'S BEEN A CRYBABY AND A WEAKLING, AND I, HIS LITTLE BROTHER, WAS FORCED TO BE THE ONE TO DEFEND HIM.
MOOOOO
HE'S BEEN RELYING ON OTHERS FOR ALL HIS LIFE, AND IT'S TIME HE ACCEPTED THE FACT THAT I'M DEAD.
BESIDES, THE STONE INSIDE THE CRYSTAL IS MORE IMPORTANT!
SO... IN ANY CASE... TAMAHOME, HOLD THIS IN YOUR HAND.
TWITCH
?!

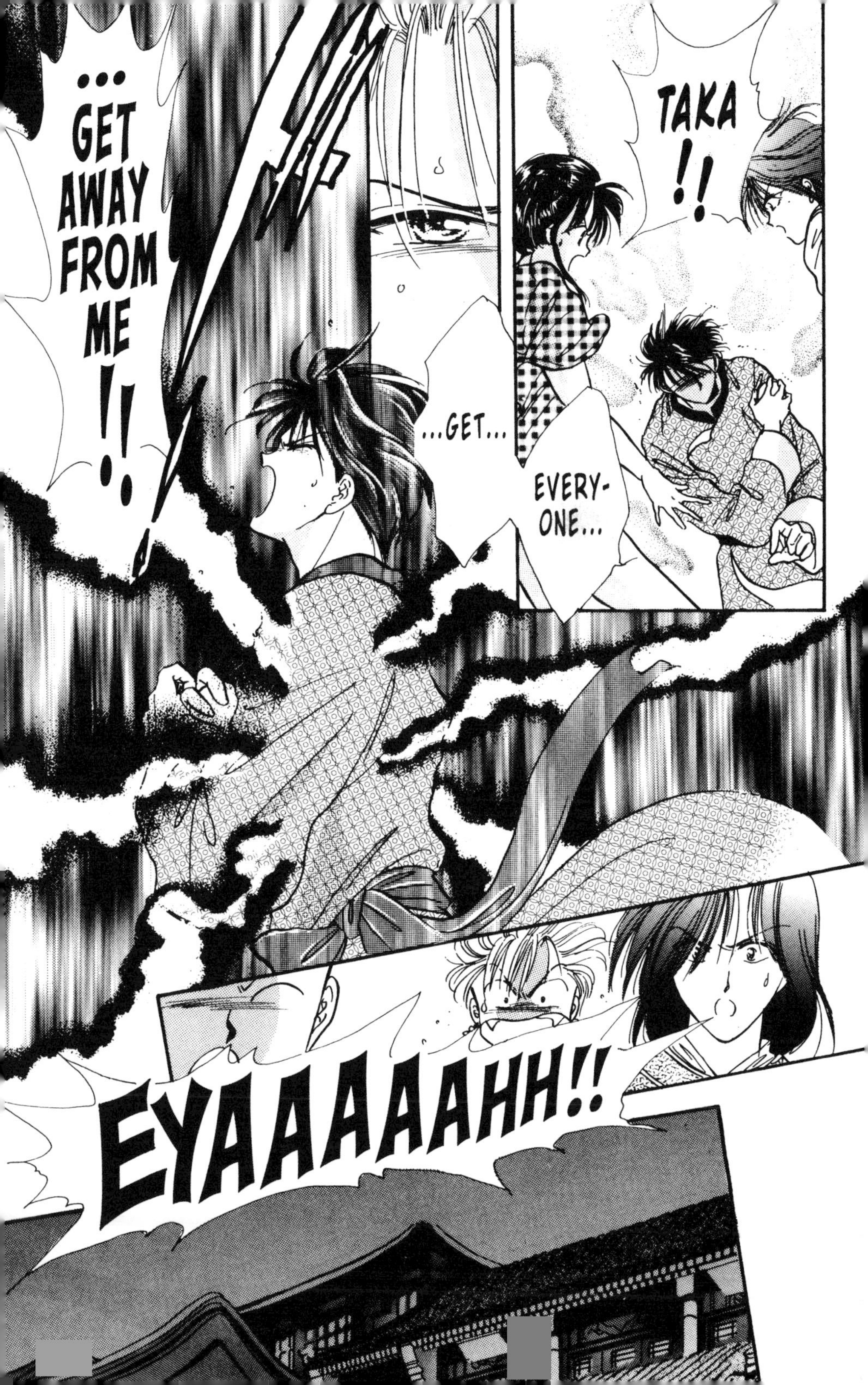
TAKA!!
...GET...
EVERY-ONE...
...GET AWAY FROM ME!!
EYAAAAAAHH!!

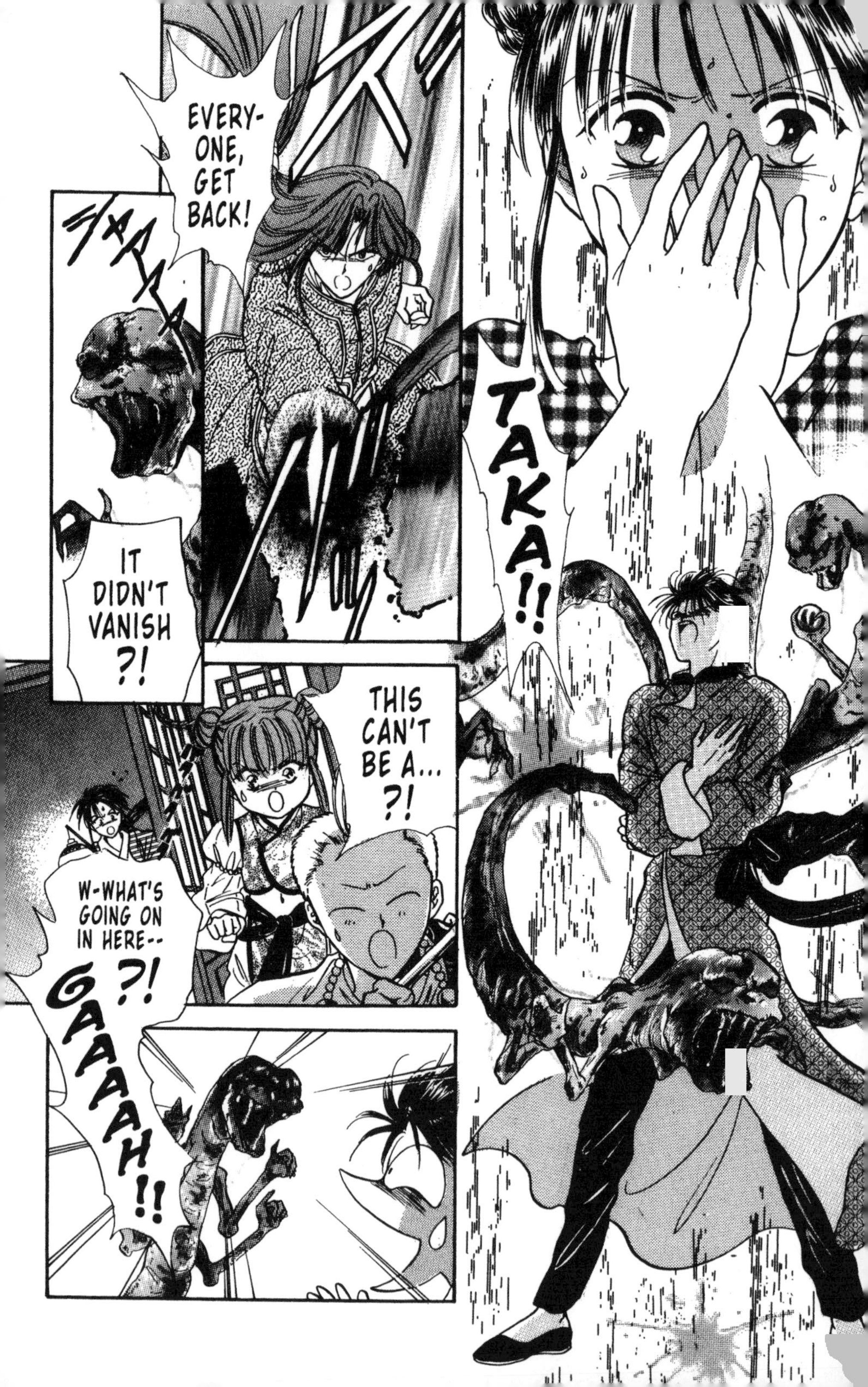
TAKA!!
EVERY-ONE, GET BACK!
IT DIDN'T VANISH?!
THIS CAN'T BE A...?!
W-WHAT'S GOING ON IN HERE--?!
GAAAAAH!!

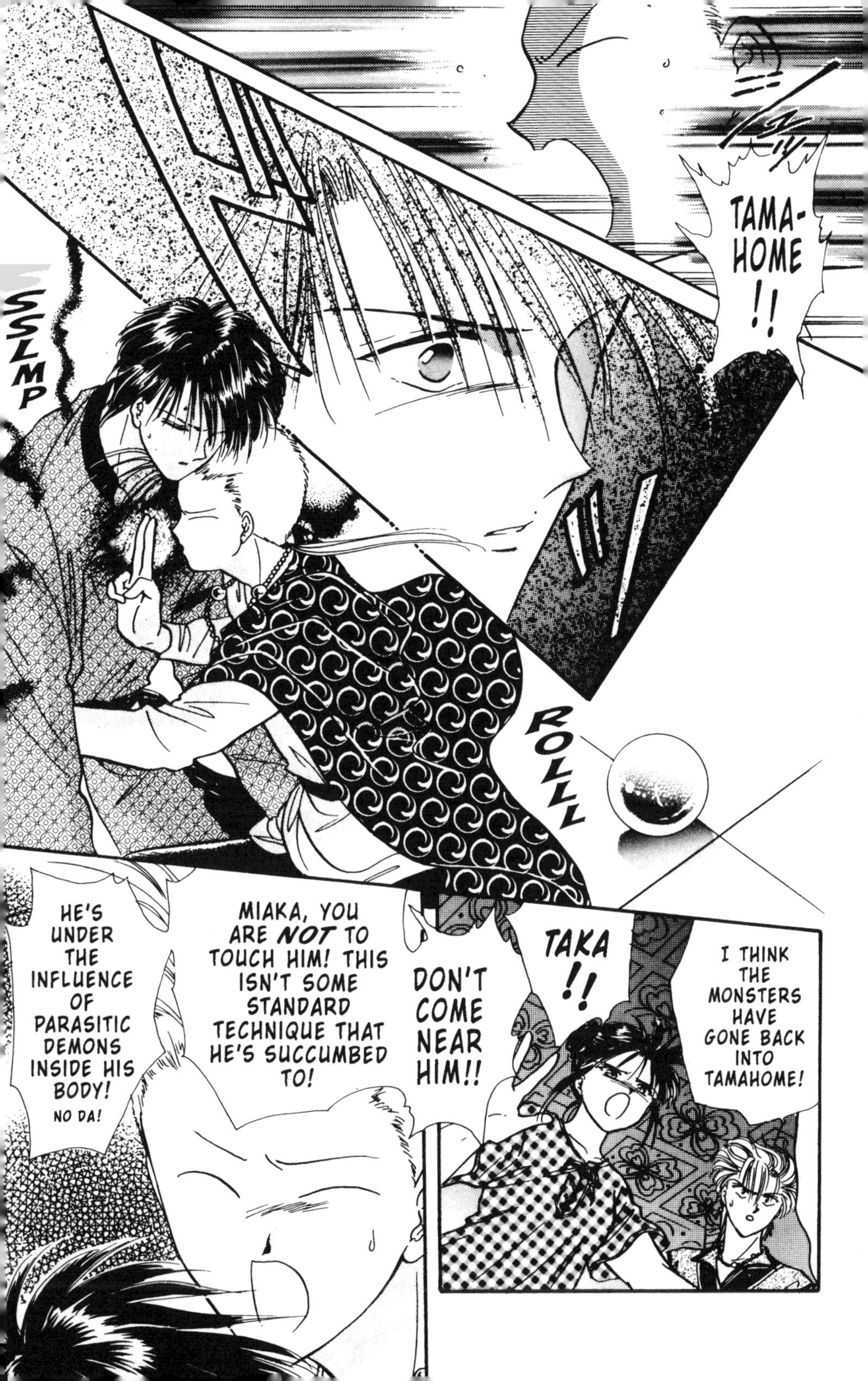
TAMA-HOME!!
SSLMP
ROLLL
I THINK THE MONSTERS HAVE GONE BACK INTO TAMAHOME!
TAKA!!
DON'T COME NEAR HIM!!
MIAKA, YOU ARE *NOT* TO TOUCH HIM! THIS ISN'T SOME STANDARD TECHNIQUE THAT HE'S SUCCUMBED TO!
HE'S UNDER THE INFLUENCE OF PARASITIC DEMONS INSIDE HIS BODY!
NO DA!

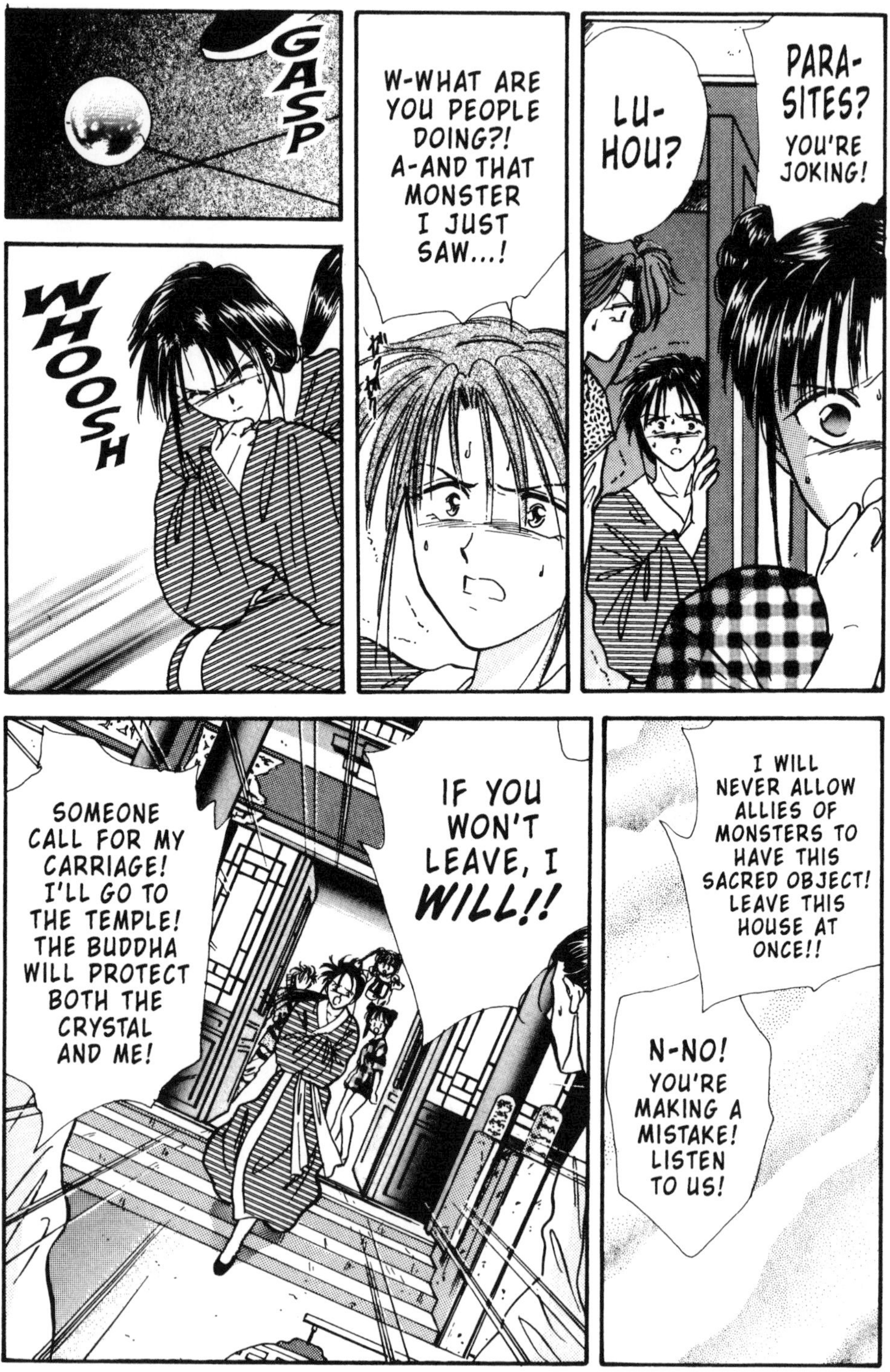
PARA-SITES? YOU'RE JOKING!
LU-HOU?
W-WHAT ARE YOU PEOPLE DOING?! A-AND THAT MONSTER I JUST SAW...!
GASP
WHOOSH
I WILL NEVER ALLOW ALLIES OF MONSTERS TO HAVE THIS SACRED OBJECT! LEAVE THIS HOUSE AT ONCE!!
N-NO! YOU'RE MAKING A MISTAKE! LISTEN TO US!
IF YOU WON'T LEAVE, I *WILL!!*
SOMEONE CALL FOR MY CARRIAGE! I'LL GO TO THE TEMPLE! THE BUDDHA WILL PROTECT BOTH THE CRYSTAL AND ME!

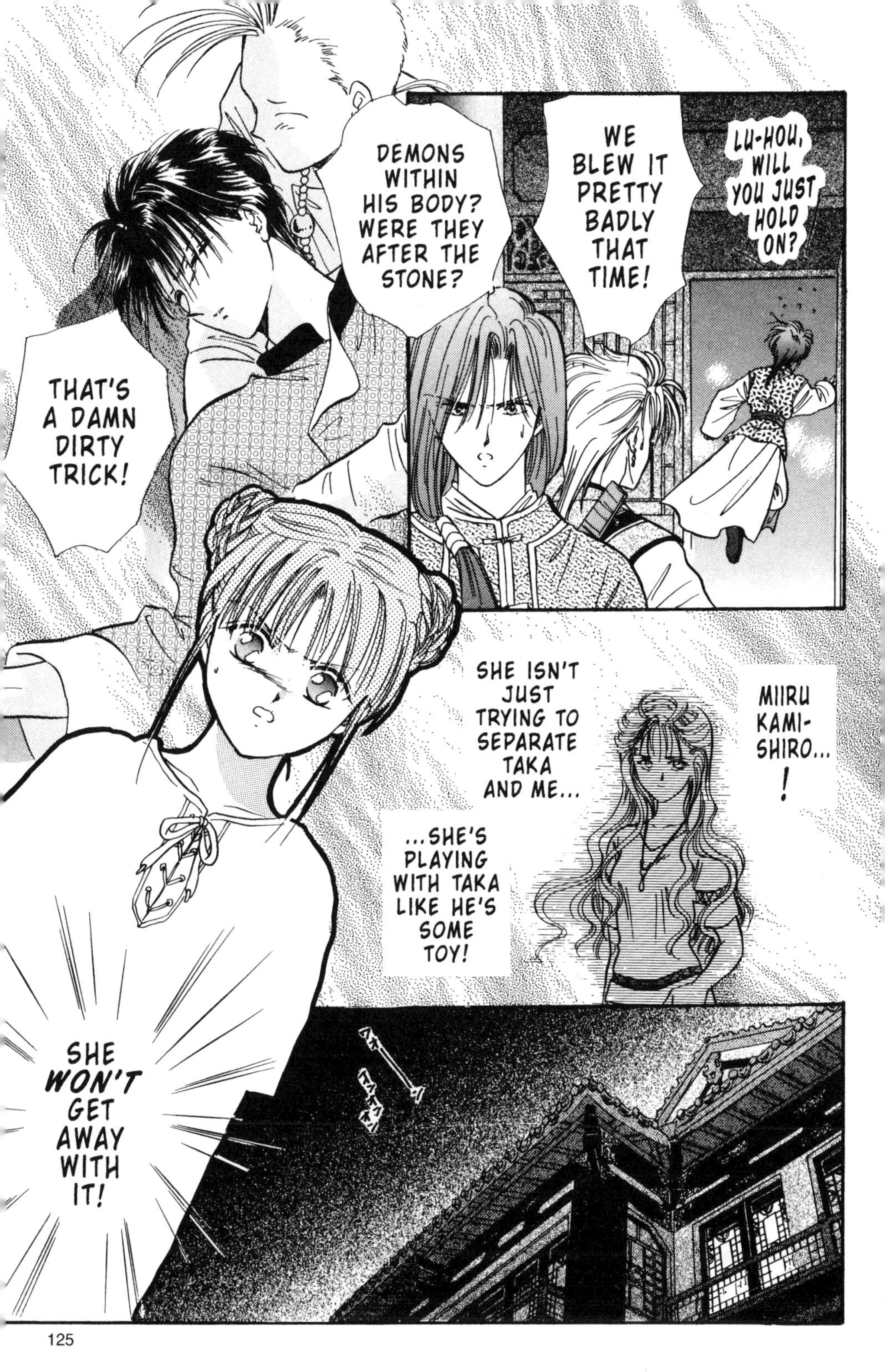
LU-HOU, WILL YOU JUST HOLD ON?
WE BLEW IT PRETTY BADLY THAT TIME!
DEMONS WITHIN HIS BODY? WERE THEY AFTER THE STONE?
THAT'S A DAMN DIRTY TRICK!
MIIRU KAMI-SHIRO... !
SHE ISN'T JUST TRYING TO SEPARATE TAKA AND ME...
...SHE'S PLAYING WITH TAKA LIKE HE'S SOME TOY!
SHE *WON'T* GET AWAY WITH IT!

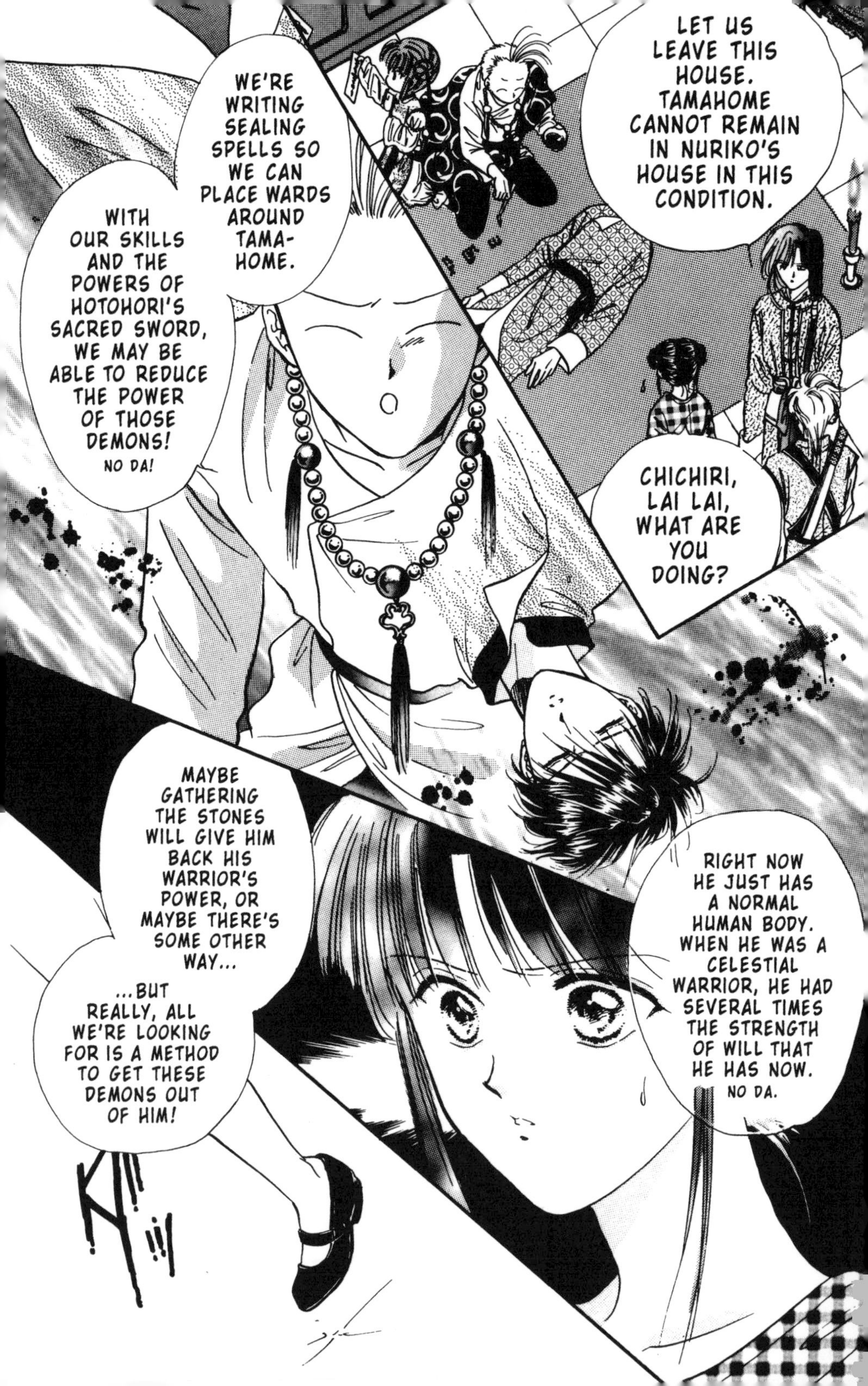

LET US LEAVE THIS HOUSE. TAMAHOME CANNOT REMAIN IN NURIKO'S HOUSE IN THIS CONDITION.
CHICHIRI, LAI LAI, WHAT ARE YOU DOING?
WE'RE WRITING SEALING SPELLS SO WE CAN PLACE WARDS AROUND TAMA-HOME.
WITH OUR SKILLS AND THE POWERS OF HOTOHORI'S SACRED SWORD, WE MAY BE ABLE TO REDUCE THE POWER OF THOSE DEMONS! NO DA!
RIGHT NOW HE JUST HAS A NORMAL HUMAN BODY. WHEN HE WAS A CELESTIAL WARRIOR, HE HAD SEVERAL TIMES THE STRENGTH OF WILL THAT HE HAS NOW. NO DA.
MAYBE GATHERING THE STONES WILL GIVE HIM BACK HIS WARRIOR'S POWER, OR MAYBE THERE'S SOME OTHER WAY...
...BUT REALLY, ALL WE'RE LOOKING FOR IS A METHOD TO GET THESE DEMONS OUT OF HIM!

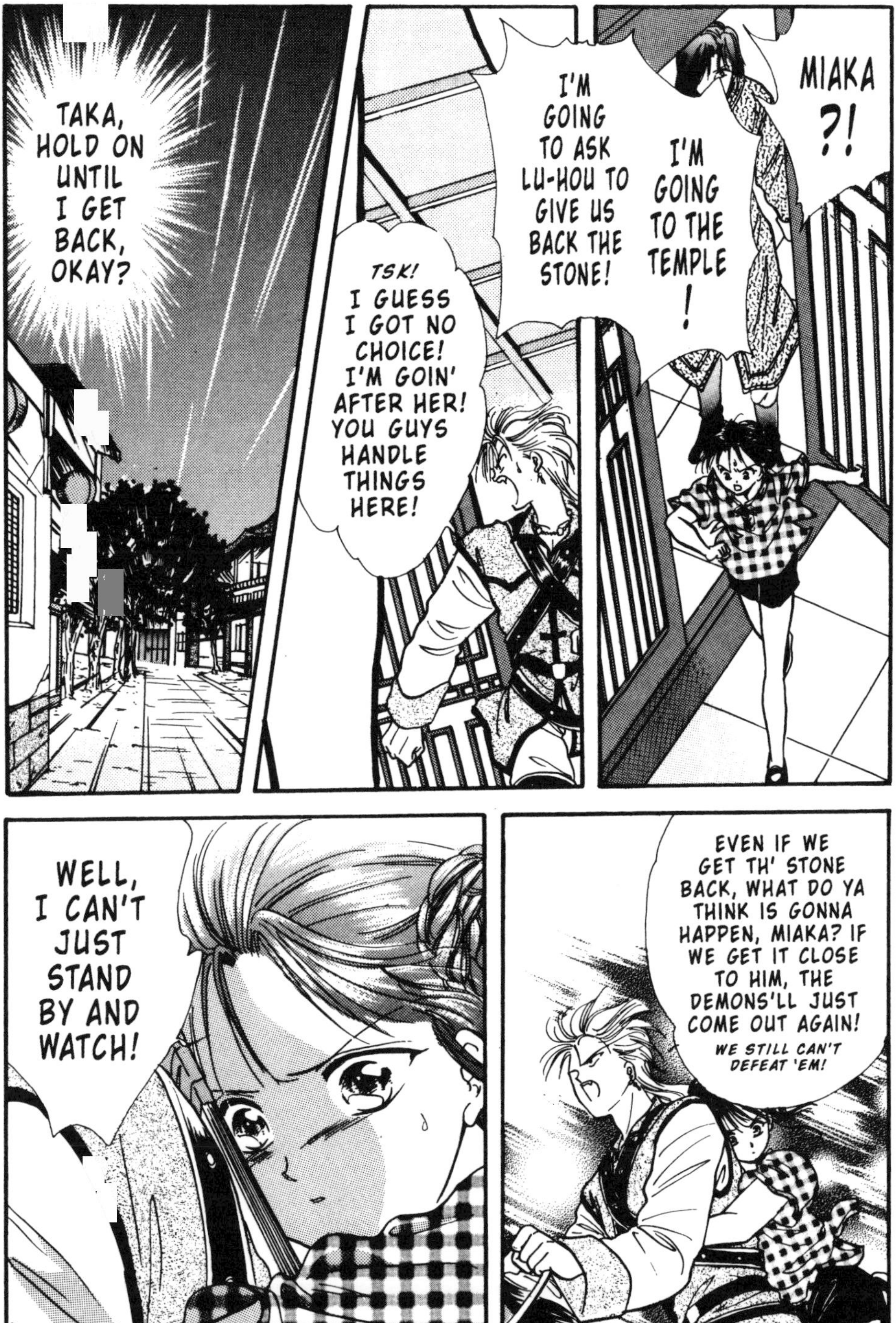
MIAKA ?!
I'M GOING TO THE TEMPLE!
I'M GOING TO ASK LU-HOU TO GIVE US BACK THE STONE!
TSK! I GUESS I GOT NO CHOICE! I'M GOIN' AFTER HER! YOU GUYS HANDLE THINGS HERE!
TAKA, HOLD ON UNTIL I GET BACK, OKAY?
EVEN IF WE GET TH' STONE BACK, WHAT DO YA THINK IS GONNA HAPPEN, MIAKA? IF WE GET IT CLOSE TO HIM, THE DEMONS'LL JUST COME OUT AGAIN! WE STILL CAN'T DEFEAT 'EM!
WELL, I CAN'T JUST STAND BY AND WATCH!

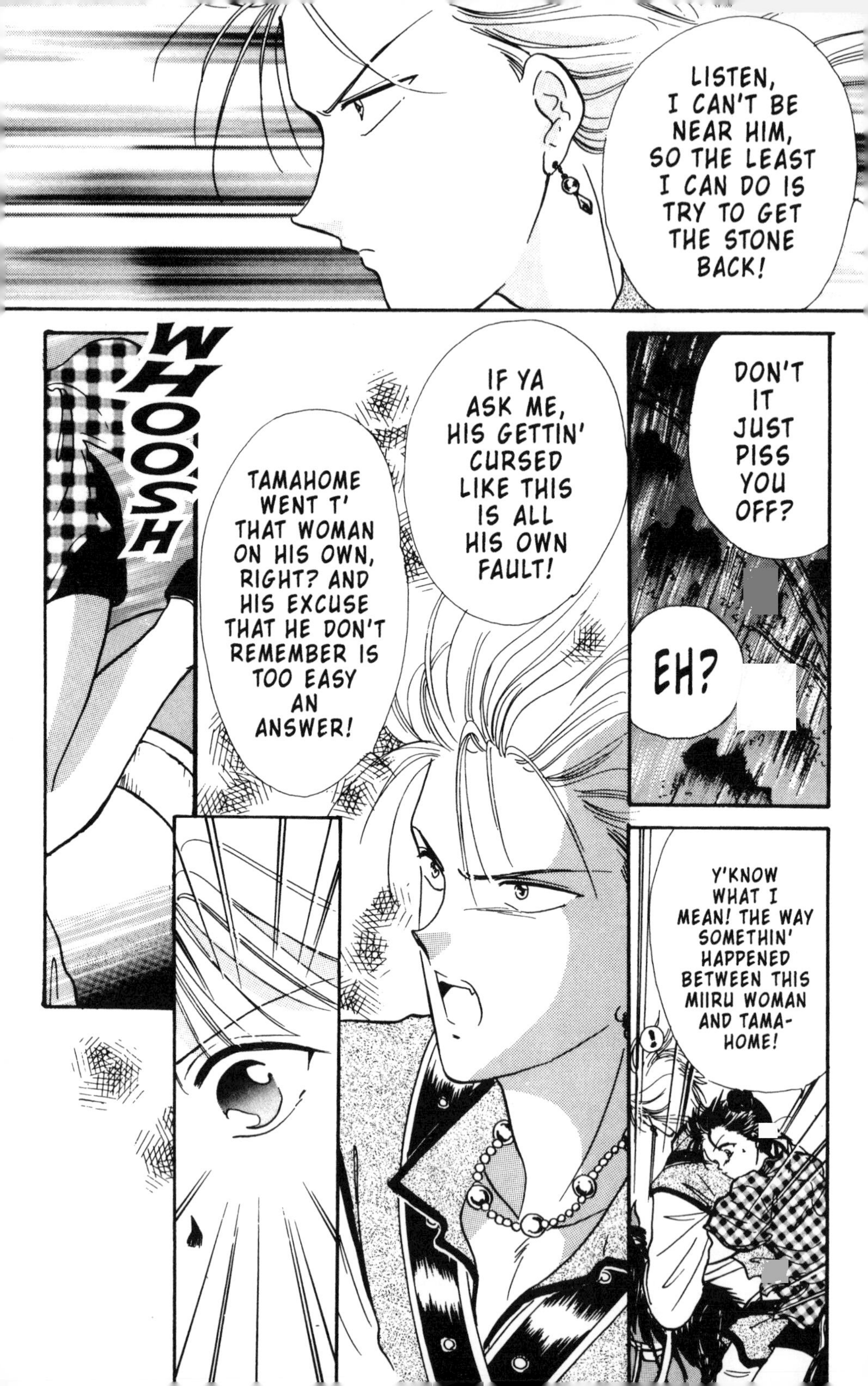
LISTEN, I CAN'T BE NEAR HIM, SO THE LEAST I CAN DO IS TRY TO GET THE STONE BACK!
DON'T IT JUST PISS YOU OFF?
EH?
Y'KNOW WHAT I MEAN! THE WAY SOMETHIN' HAPPENED BETWEEN THIS MIIRU WOMAN AND TAMA-HOME!
!
IF YA ASK ME, HIS GETTIN' CURSED LIKE THIS IS ALL HIS OWN FAULT!
TAMAHOME WENT T' THAT WOMAN ON HIS OWN, RIGHT? AND HIS EXCUSE THAT HE DON'T REMEMBER IS TOO EASY AN ANSWER!
WHOOSH

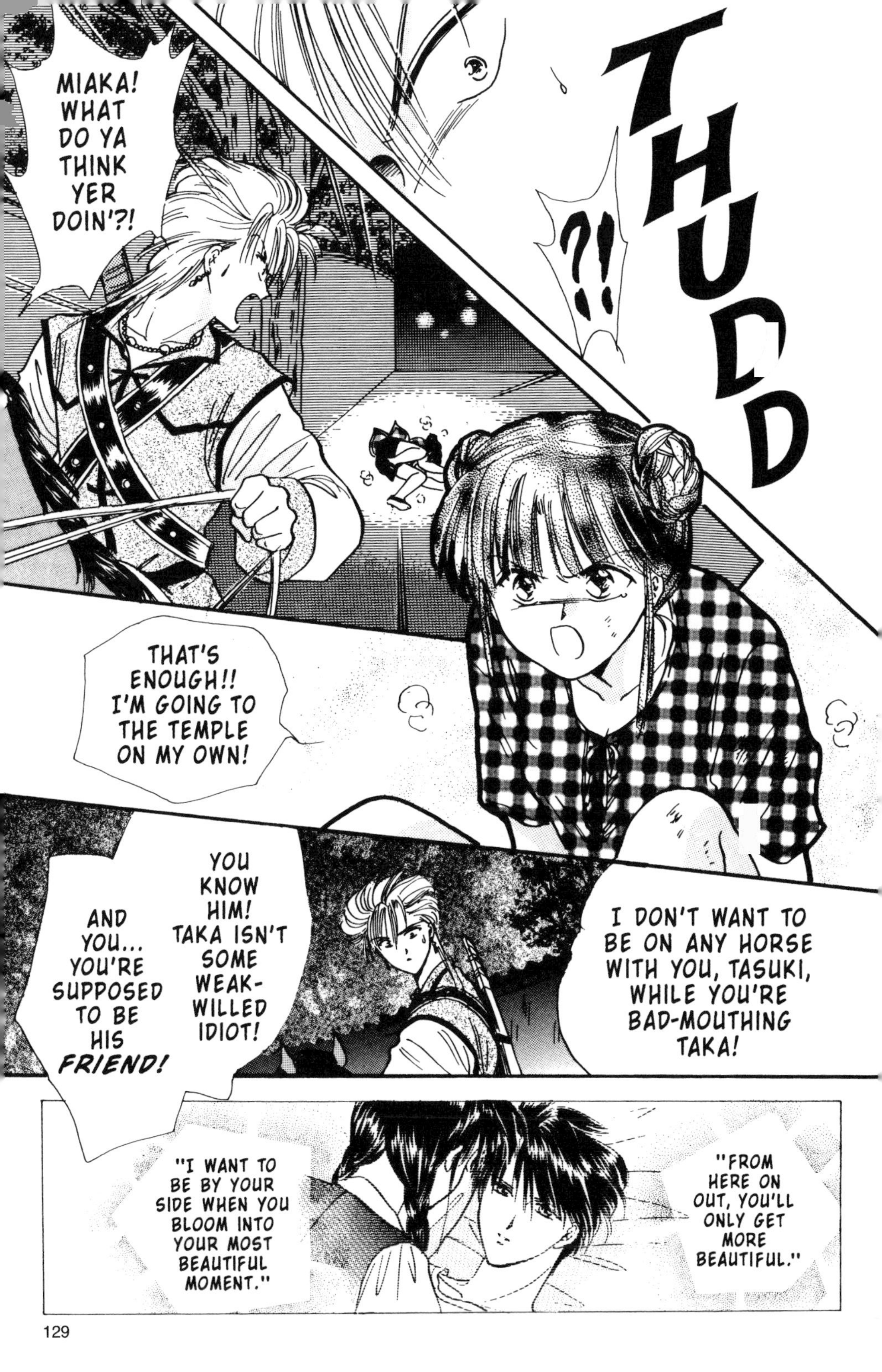
THUDD
?!!
MIAKA! WHAT DO YA THINK YER DOIN'?!
THAT'S ENOUGH!! I'M GOING TO THE TEMPLE ON MY OWN!
I DON'T WANT TO BE ON ANY HORSE WITH YOU, TASUKI, WHILE YOU'RE BAD-MOUTHING TAKA!
YOU KNOW HIM! TAKA ISN'T SOME WEAK-WILLED IDIOT!
AND YOU... YOU'RE SUPPOSED TO BE HIS *FRIEND!*
"FROM HERE ON OUT, YOU'LL ONLY GET MORE BEAUTIFUL."
"I WANT TO BE BY YOUR SIDE WHEN YOU BLOOM INTO YOUR MOST BEAUTIFUL MOMENT."

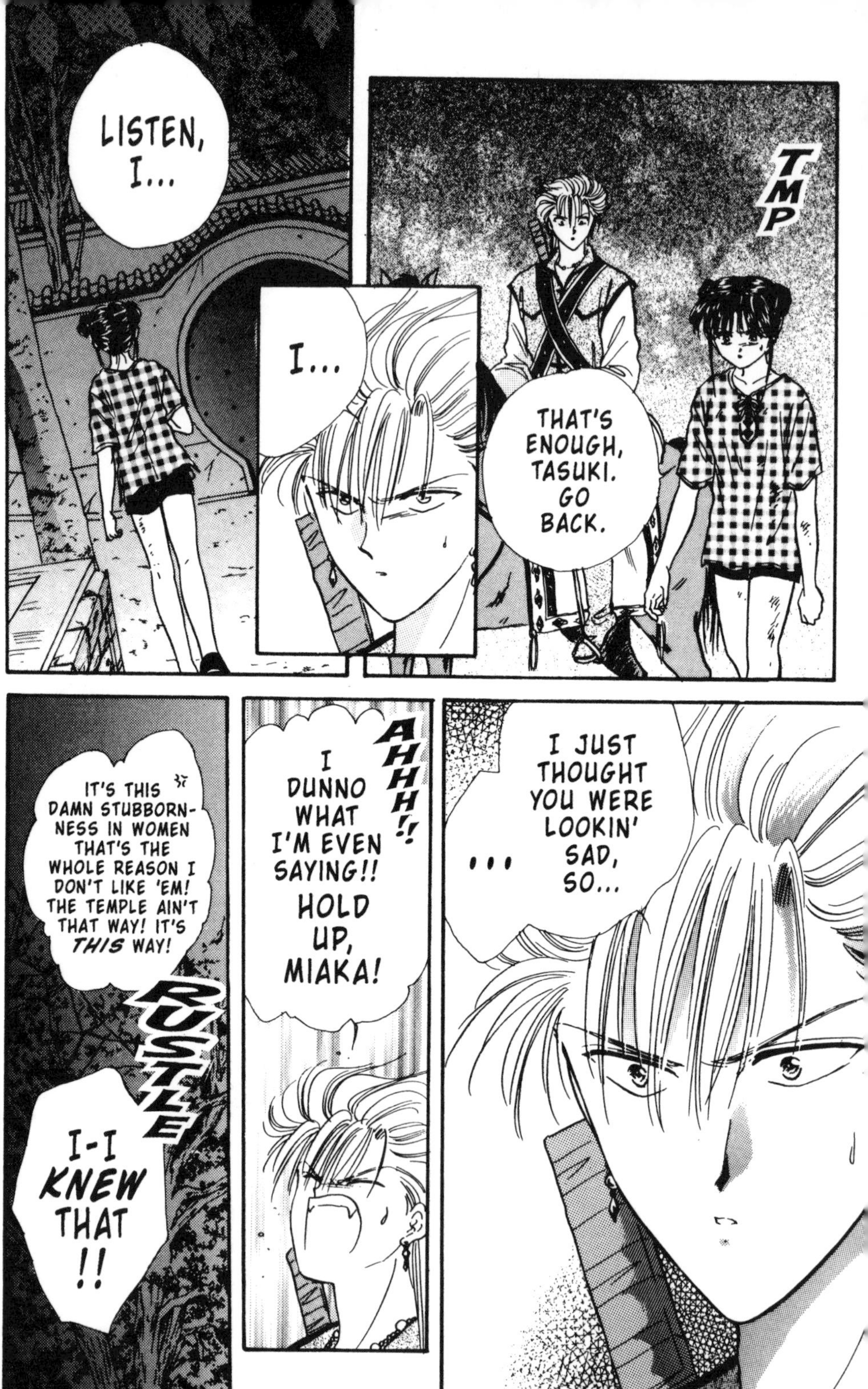
TMP
THAT'S ENOUGH, TASUKI. GO BACK.
I...
LISTEN, I...
I JUST THOUGHT YOU WERE LOOKIN' SAD, SO...
...
AHHHH!!
I DUNNO WHAT I'M EVEN SAYING!! HOLD UP, MIAKA!
IT'S THIS DAMN STUBBORNNESS IN WOMEN THAT'S THE WHOLE REASON I DON'T LIKE 'EM! THE TEMPLE AIN'T THAT WAY! IT'S *THIS* WAY!
RUSTLE
I-I *KNEW* THAT!!

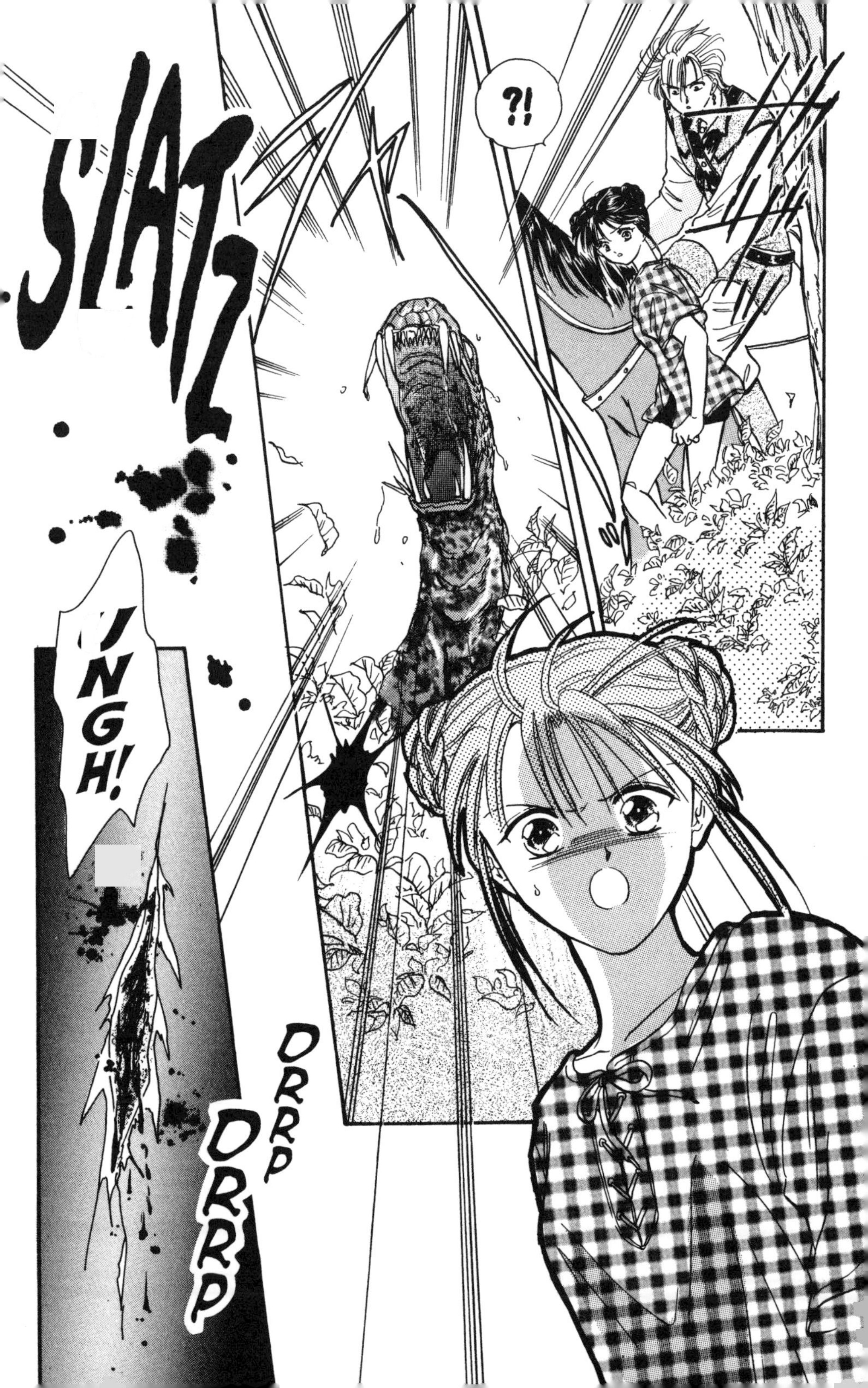
?!
SLAT
NGH!
DRRP
DRRP

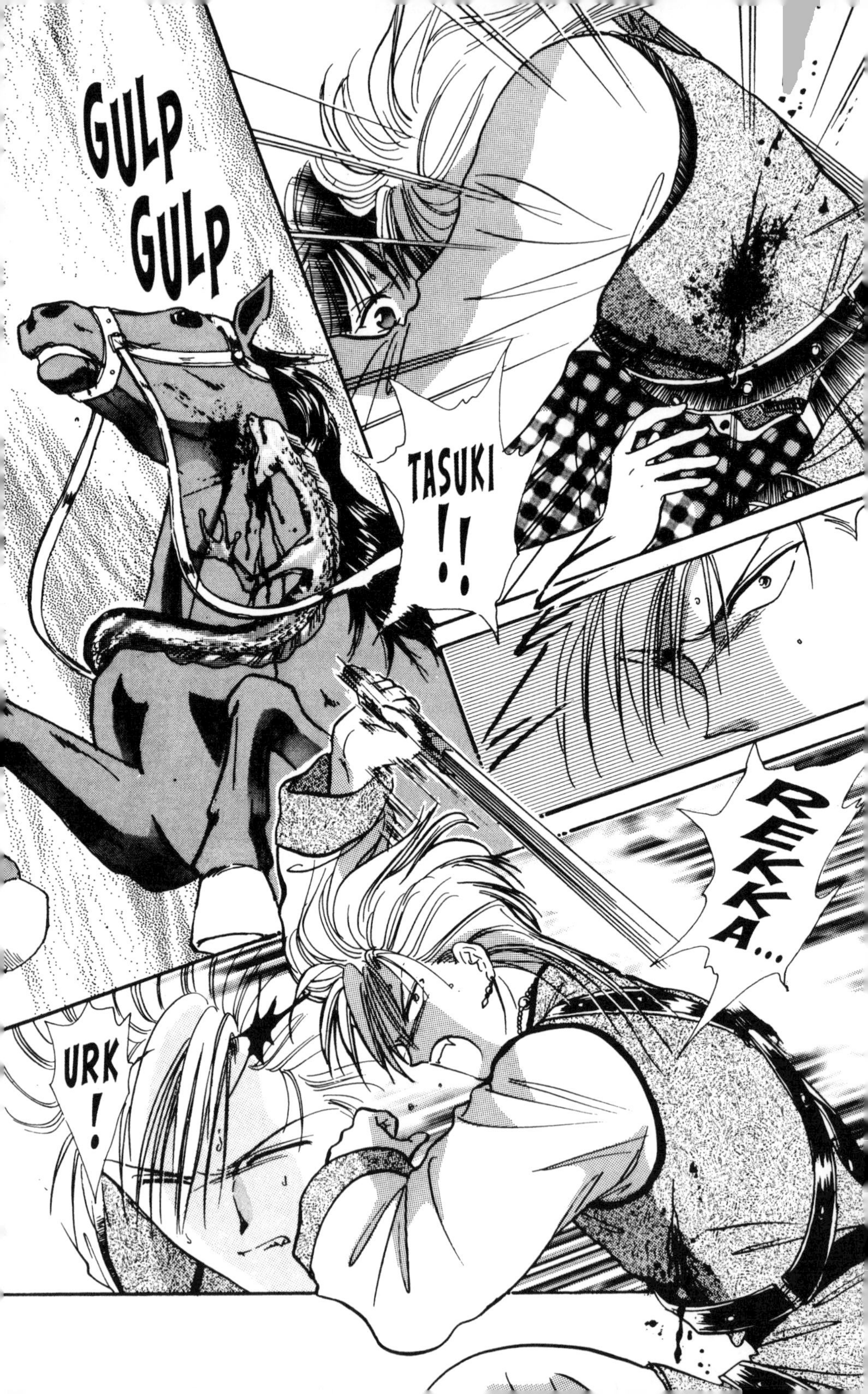
TASUKI!!
REKKA...
GULP GULP
URK!

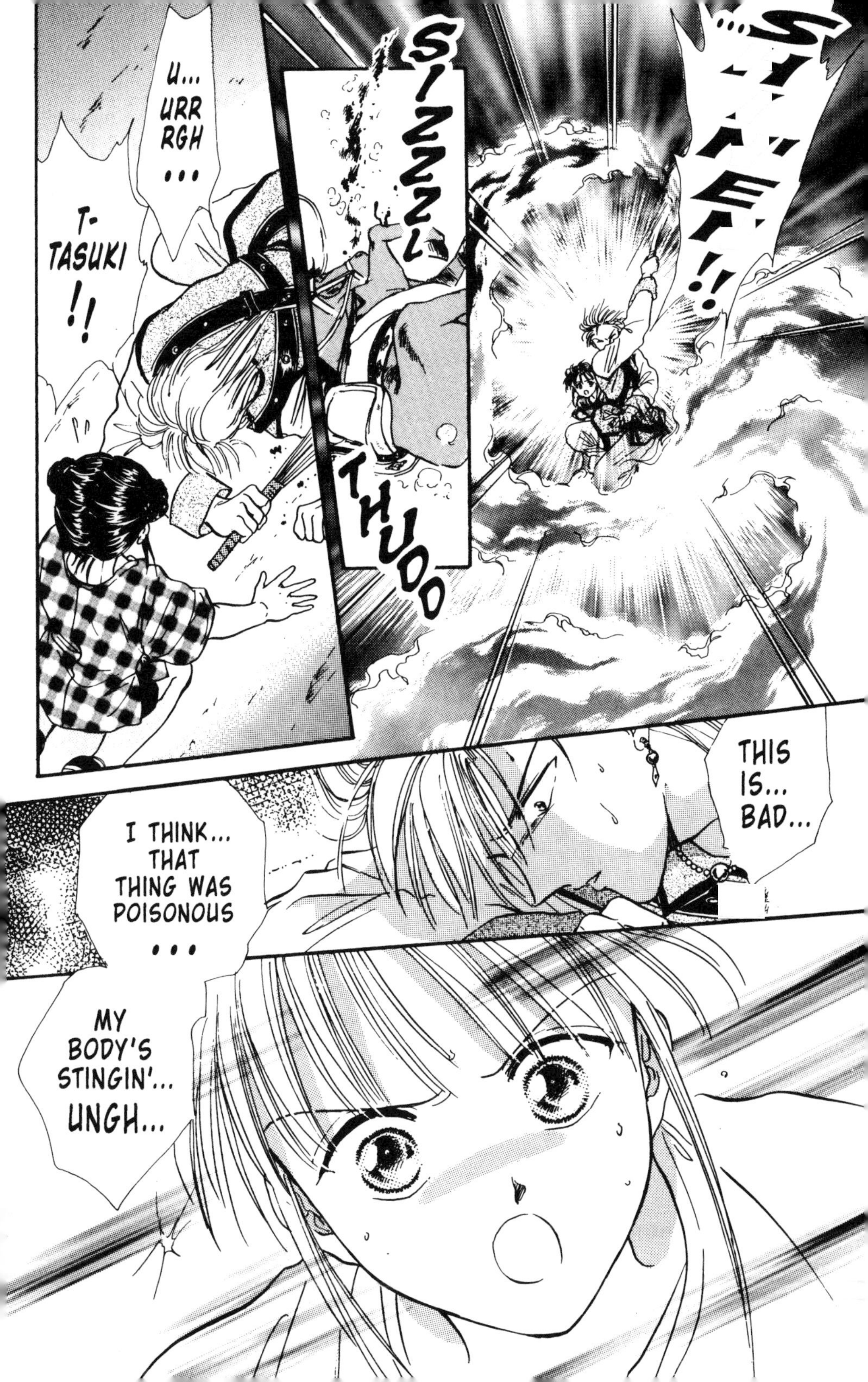
U... URRRGH...
T-TASUKI!!
SIZZZL
THUDD
THIS IS... BAD...
I THINK... THAT THING WAS POISONOUS...
MY BODY'S STINGIN'... UNGH...

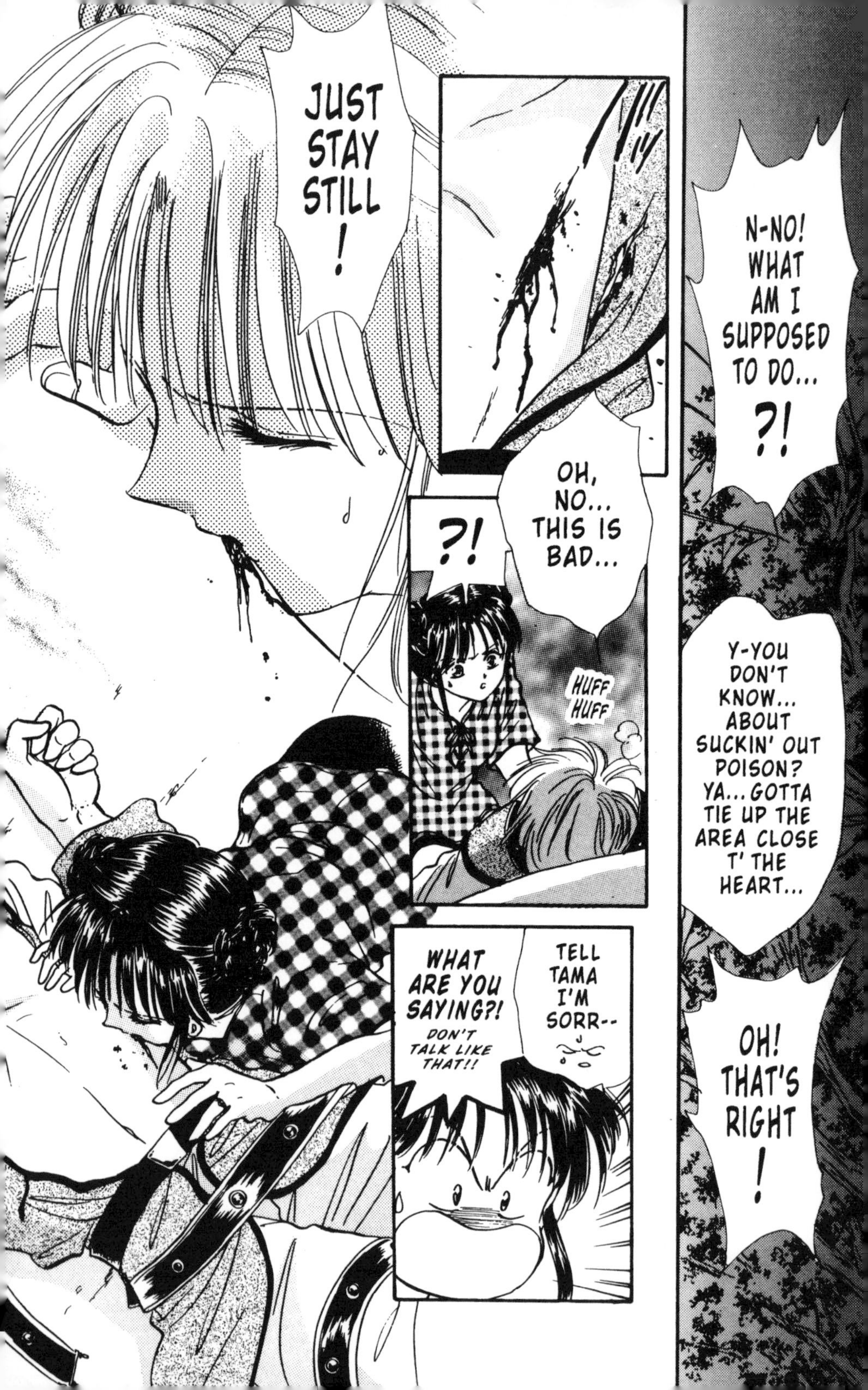
N-NO! WHAT AM I SUPPOSED TO DO... ?!
Y-YOU DON'T KNOW... ABOUT SUCKIN' OUT POISON? YA... GOTTA TIE UP THE AREA CLOSE T' THE HEART...
OH! THAT'S RIGHT!
OH, NO... THIS IS BAD...
?!
HUFF HUFF
TELL TAMA I'M SORR--
WHAT ARE YOU SAYING?!
DON'T TALK LIKE THAT!!
JUST STAY STILL!

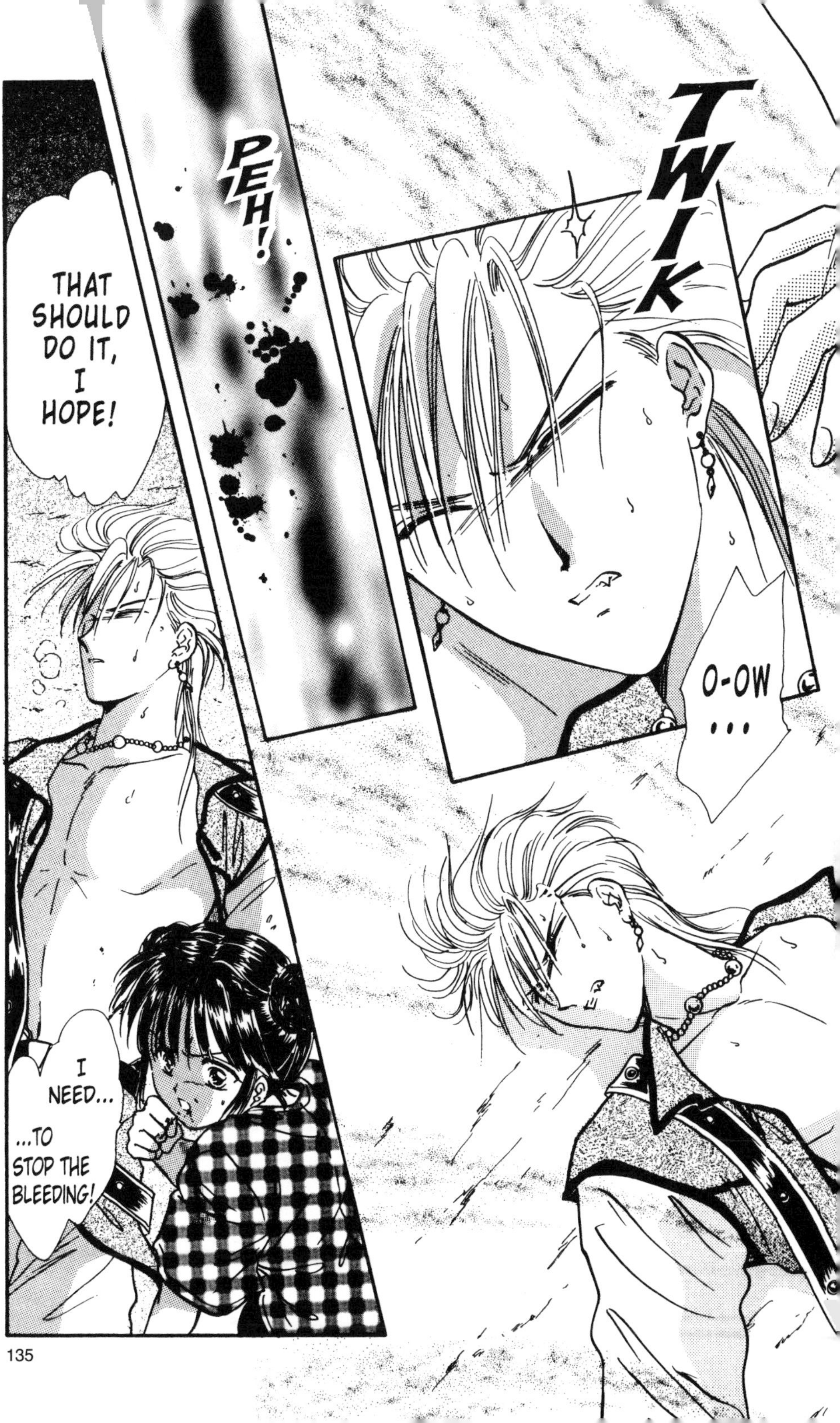
TWIK
O-OW...
PEH!
THAT SHOULD DO IT, I HOPE!
I NEED...
...TO STOP THE BLEEDING!

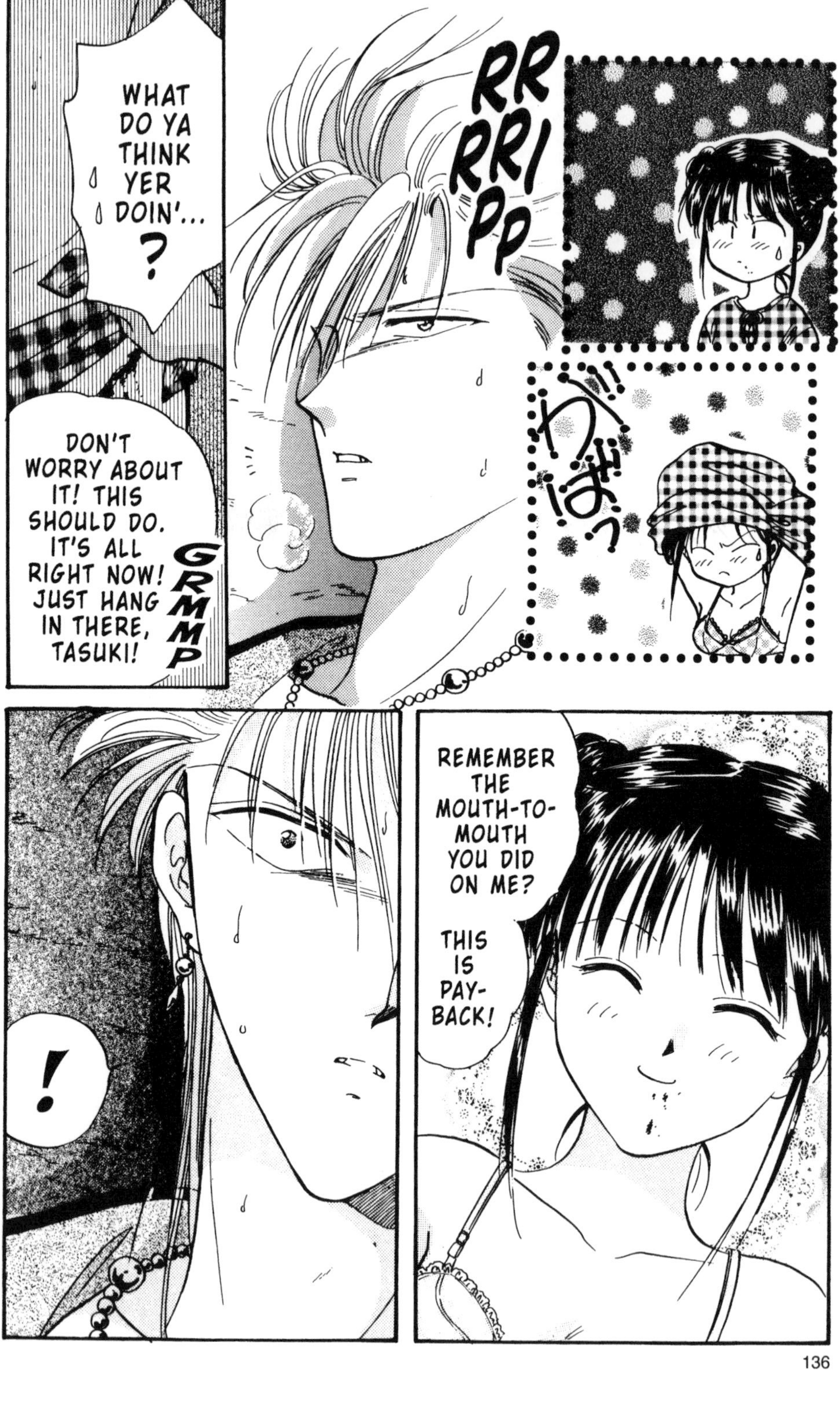
わ゛ばっ!
RRRRIPP
WHAT DO YA THINK YER DOIN'...?
DON'T WORRY ABOUT IT! THIS SHOULD DO. IT'S ALL RIGHT NOW! JUST HANG IN THERE, TASUKI!
GRMMP
REMEMBER THE MOUTH-TO-MOUTH YOU DID ON ME?
THIS IS PAY-BACK!
!

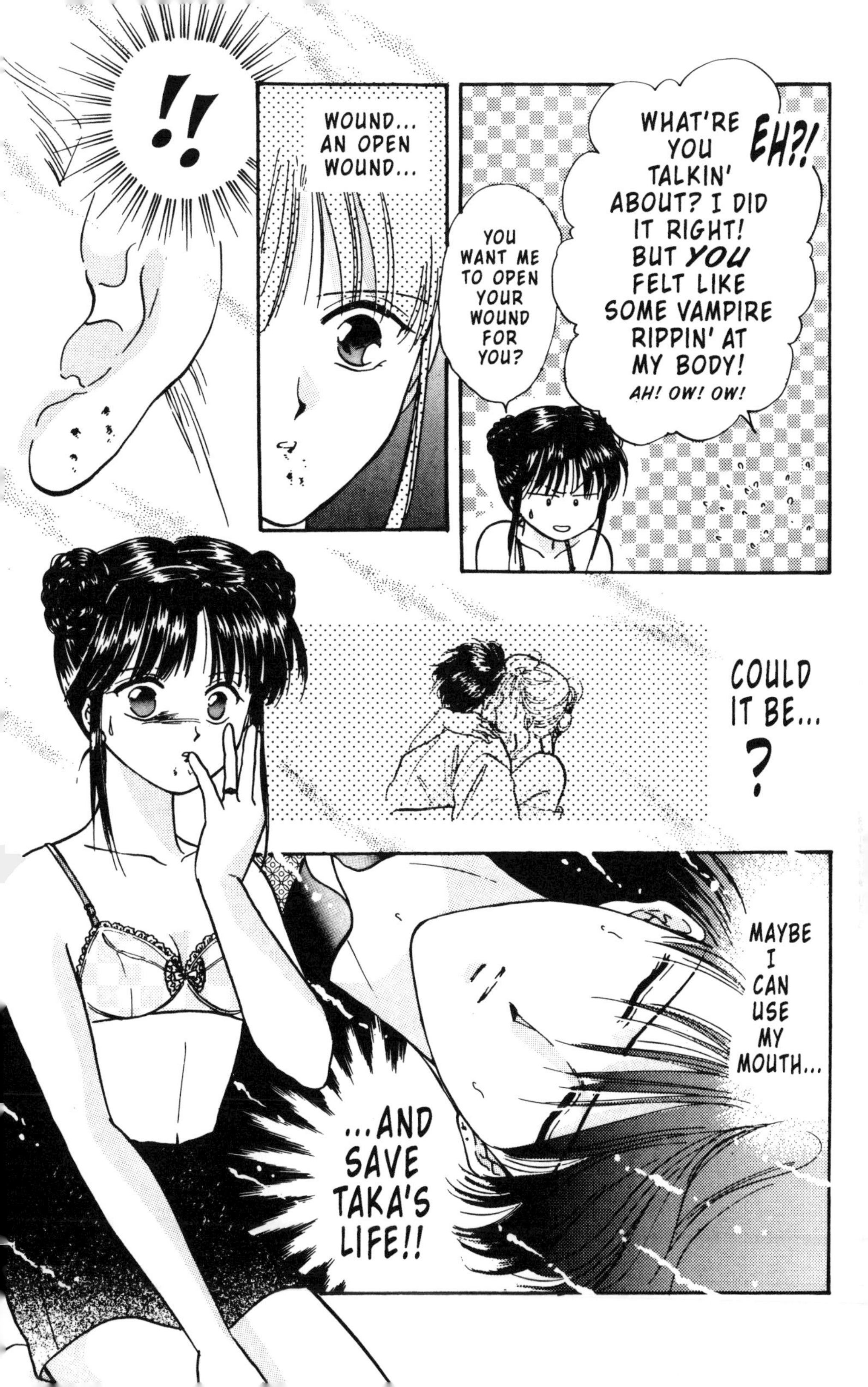
EH?!
WHAT'RE YOU TALKIN' ABOUT? I DID IT RIGHT! BUT YOU FELT LIKE SOME VAMPIRE RIPPIN' AT MY BODY!
AH! OW! OW!
YOU WANT ME TO OPEN YOUR WOUND FOR YOU?
WOUND... AN OPEN WOUND...
!!
COULD IT BE...?
MAYBE I CAN USE MY MOUTH...
...AND SAVE TAKA'S LIFE!!

ふしぎ悪戯

FUSHIGI AKUGI

THE MALICIOUS PLAY (13)

It's now November '95.

Some of the character merchandise things I talked about before were unconfirmed when I talked about them, so don't get upset if you can't find them, okay?

Oh, yeah! There's a jigsaw puzzle from Seika Notebooks! They come in three sizes: small, medium, and large. And the pictures they chose were great! The Suzaku warriors look cool! And the shot with Miaka and Tama is so cute! Another thing! Was everybody able to get their hands on a calendar this year? No, not mine... the two versions of the anime calendar! The pictures in them are beautiful! I love them both, but the one sold by Movic (I mean, the thing's just huge!!)... I'm still wondering about the May/June picture! ☺ Those nudes get me every time! *Fantastic!* ☆ Both the Suzaku and Seiryu are just cool! Nakago and Soi... Now that was just too good!!
Oh, also the phone cards (the ones you can pick up for 20 yen), those are dead-on! Chichiri is especially cool!
He's got a profile on the card!

I wonder if they're still on sale.

Idea by Ms. Rui Suzuki.

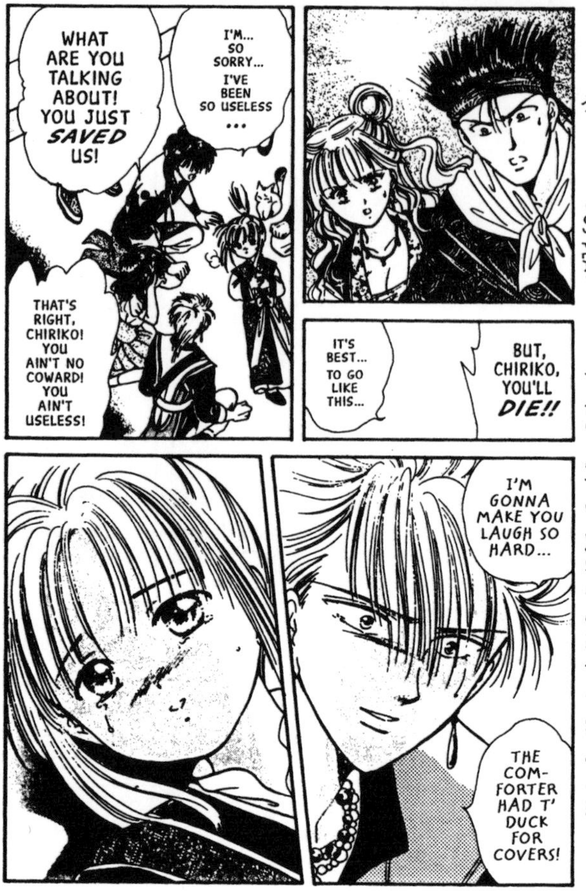
BUT, CHIRIKO, YOU'LL *DIE!!*
IT'S BEST... TO GO LIKE THIS...
I'M... SO SORRY... I'VE BEEN SO USELESS...
WHAT ARE YOU TALKING ABOUT! YOU JUST *SAVED* US!
THAT'S RIGHT, CHIRIKO! YOU AIN'T NO COWARD! YOU AIN'T USELESS!
I'M GONNA MAKE YOU LAUGH SO HARD...
THE COMFORTER HAD T' DUCK FOR COVERS!

The title is "Hey, hey, Tasuki!" Whether you should laugh or cry is up to you.

We all burst out laughing.

• CD Book (5) (All finished!)... Have you all had a chance to listen to it?
Well, Watase just got goosebumps listening to it! The background music by 135 was just terrific! (On book (4), I loved "19"!) The scene where Seiryu consumes Yui! The scene where Miaka begins the chant to call Suzaku!! Nakago being so noble in the tale from long ago! The last scene! I just love the songs! And the brilliant acting by the voice actors! And the wonderful sound effects! I honestly feel that this is the best one yet among the five!
And Nakago's final "Mother!" had his voice overlaid with the voice from his youth! Tra-la! ★★★
Of course, at the scene where Suzaku is summoned, I got all shivery! It's really incredible when they put this to sound! The "Suzaku Theme" they used in the opening was so cool, I fell in love with it!
All the other songs were great too! Nakago's theme was just what the doctor ordered! ☺ And Miaka and Tamahome's theme left me spellbound. I swear, when I heard Subete ni Wo Ai Ni (Everything is Wo Ai Ni) the tears started to flow! And "Sayonara Iranai" (No Need for Goodbyes)!! I was a crying wreck just listening to the songs! ☺ I had this image of the universe and the heavens...
It seems that the songs had an effect on my assistants too. They were a little too on-target. *Waaaah!*
There was some dialog between Nakago and Yui on this CD. It didn't happen in the original, but last time, I talked all about Nakago to the scriptwriters, and maybe that was the reason for it. This stuff was always a part of Nakago's feelings and motivations, but because of page counts and other considerations it was left out. It's like they put it back in just for me... so listen closely!!
Sincerely, to all of the production people, and all of the actors who have stuck with the CD book series for more than three years, and everyone, etc., you guys did such a great job!!

If you readers can get your hands on all five, be sure to give them a listen! Everyone who worked on it is a genius! (No, really. It's true!) But people like Makoto Nagai and the voice actors... I doubt they'll ever gather in the same place again!

Chapter Ninety-Three
The Gulf of Courage

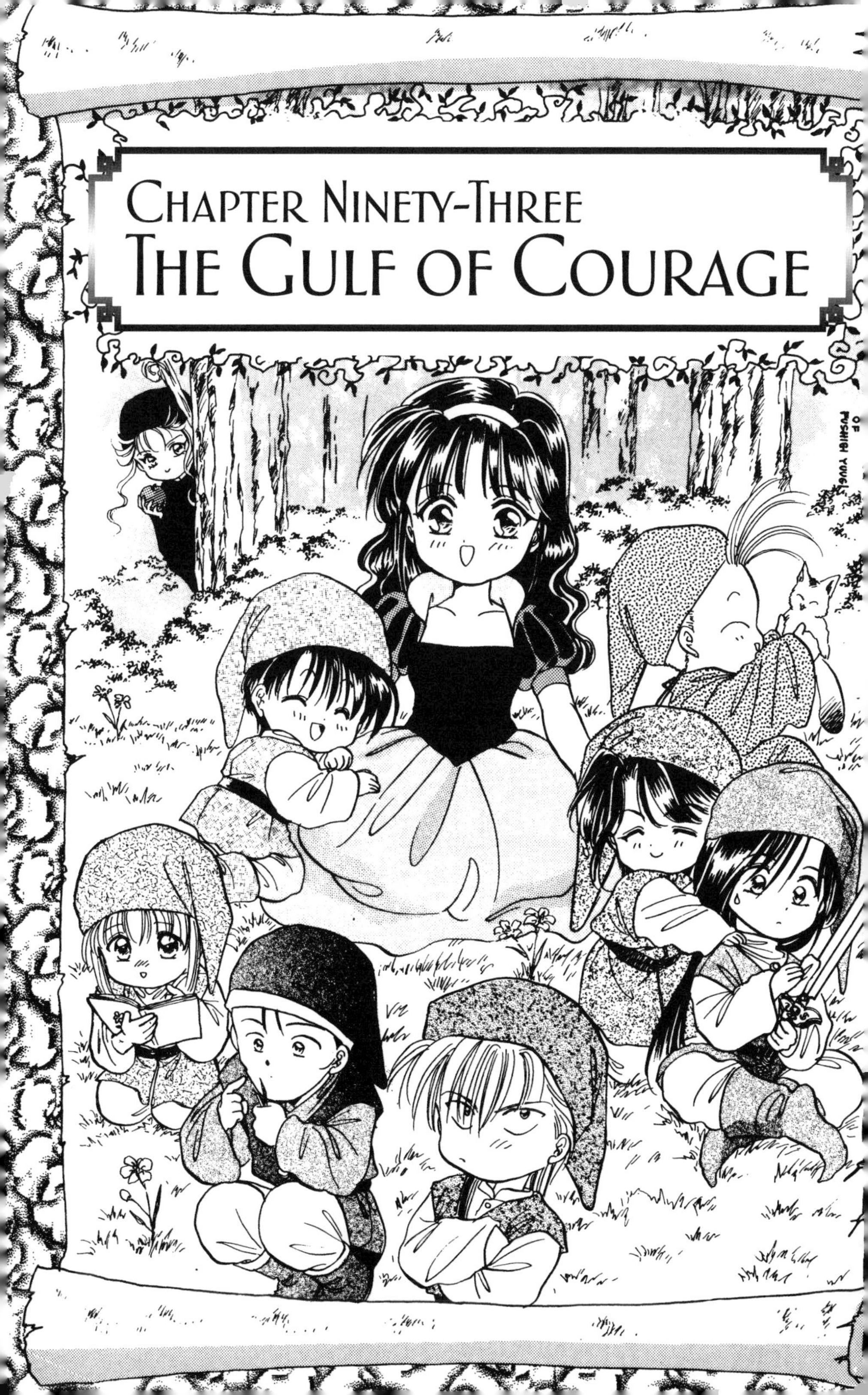
OF FUSHIGI YUUGI

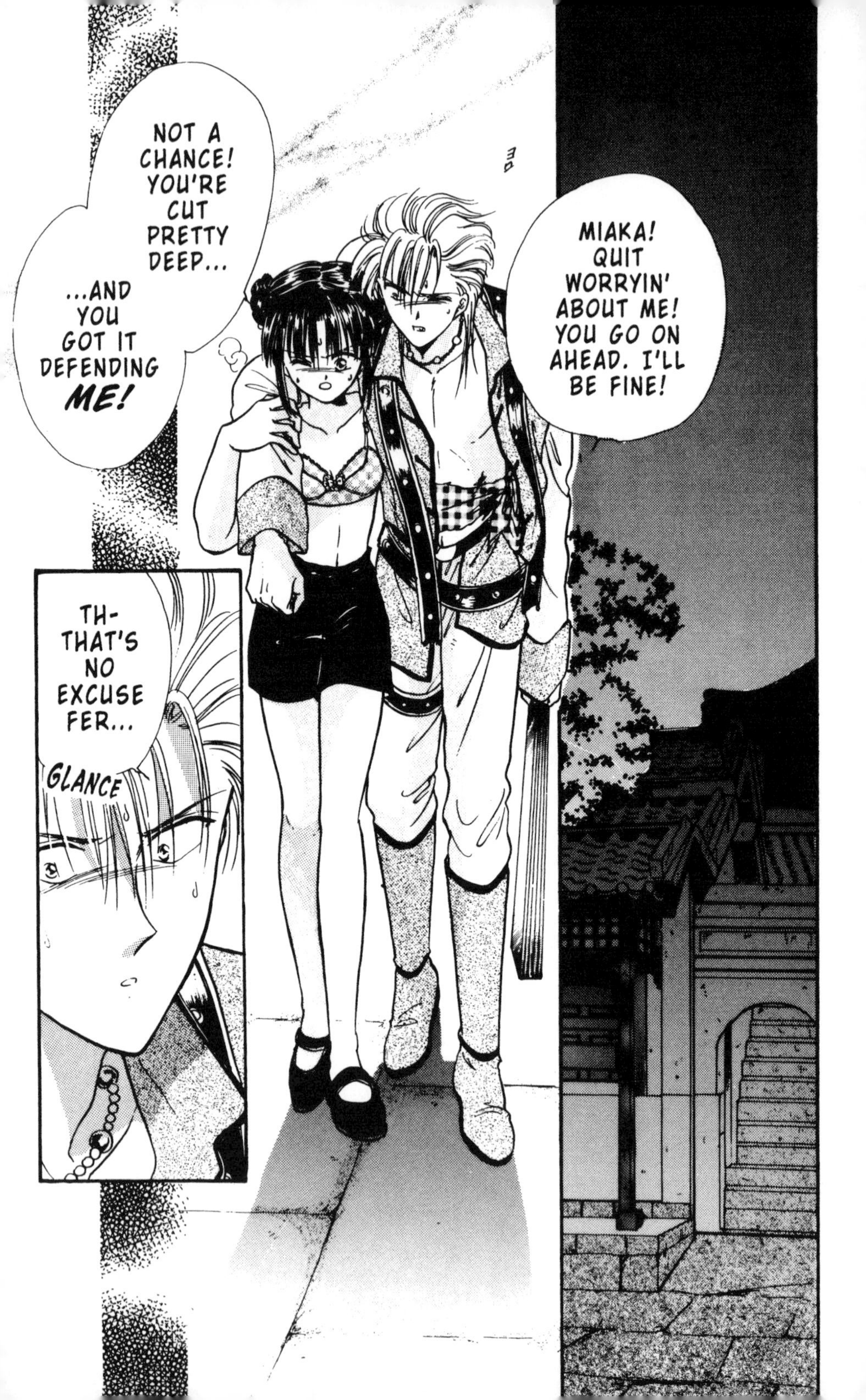
MIAKA! QUIT WORRYIN' ABOUT ME! YOU GO ON AHEAD. I'LL BE FINE!
NOT A CHANCE! YOU'RE CUT PRETTY DEEP...
...AND YOU GOT IT DEFENDING ME!
TH-THAT'S NO EXCUSE FER...
GLANCE

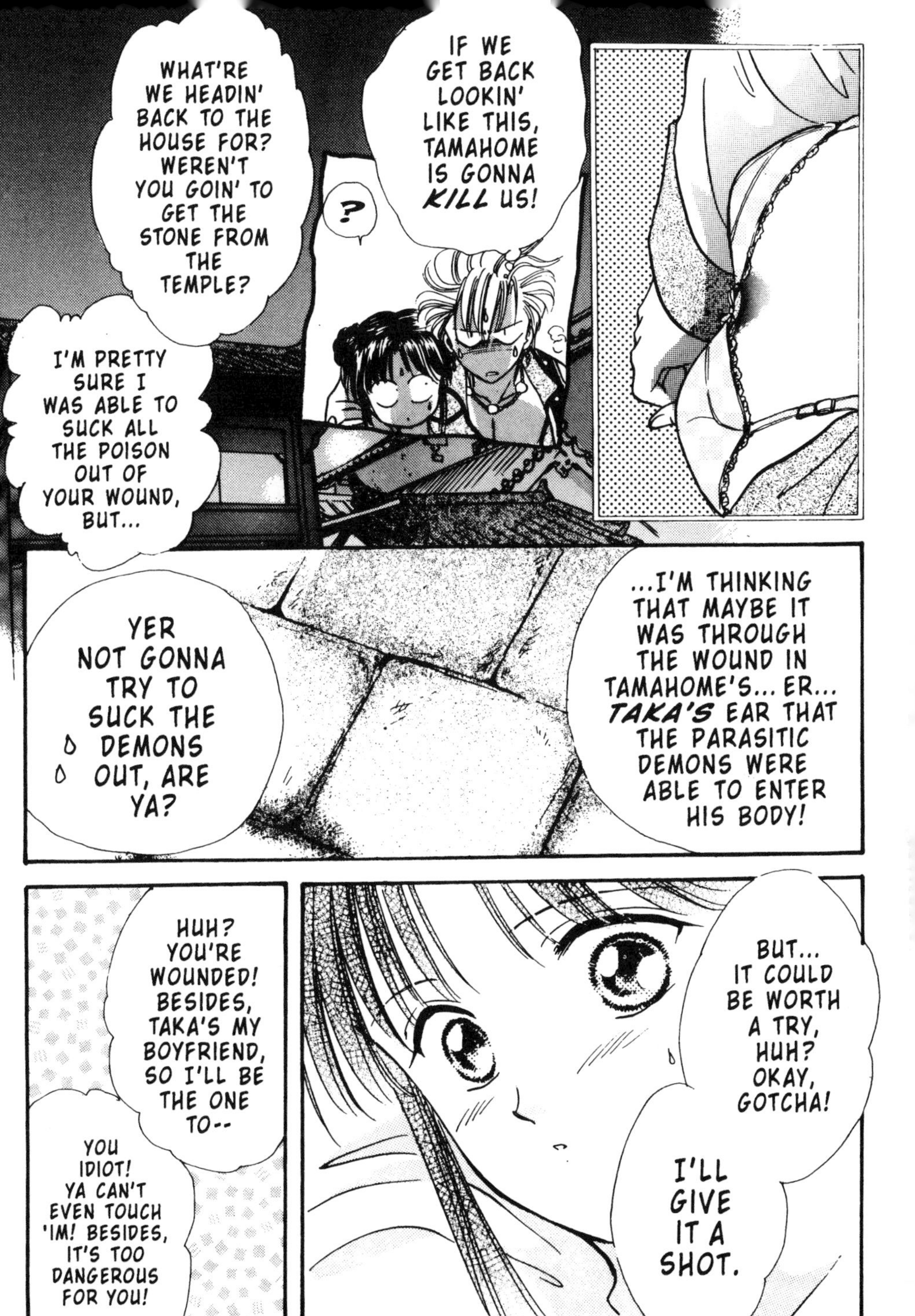
IF WE GET BACK LOOKIN' LIKE THIS, TAMAHOME IS GONNA *KILL* US!
WHAT'RE WE HEADIN' BACK TO THE HOUSE FOR? WEREN'T YOU GOIN' TO GET THE STONE FROM THE TEMPLE?
?
I'M PRETTY SURE I WAS ABLE TO SUCK ALL THE POISON OUT OF YOUR WOUND, BUT...
...I'M THINKING THAT MAYBE IT WAS THROUGH THE WOUND IN TAMAHOME'S... ER... *TAKA'S* EAR THAT THE PARASITIC DEMONS WERE ABLE TO ENTER HIS BODY!
YER NOT GONNA TRY TO SUCK THE DEMONS OUT, ARE YA?
BUT... IT COULD BE WORTH A TRY, HUH? OKAY, GOTCHA!
I'LL GIVE IT A SHOT.
HUH? YOU'RE WOUNDED! BESIDES, TAKA'S MY BOYFRIEND, SO I'LL BE THE ONE TO--
YOU IDIOT! YA CAN'T EVEN TOUCH 'IM! BESIDES, IT'S TOO DANGEROUS FOR YOU!

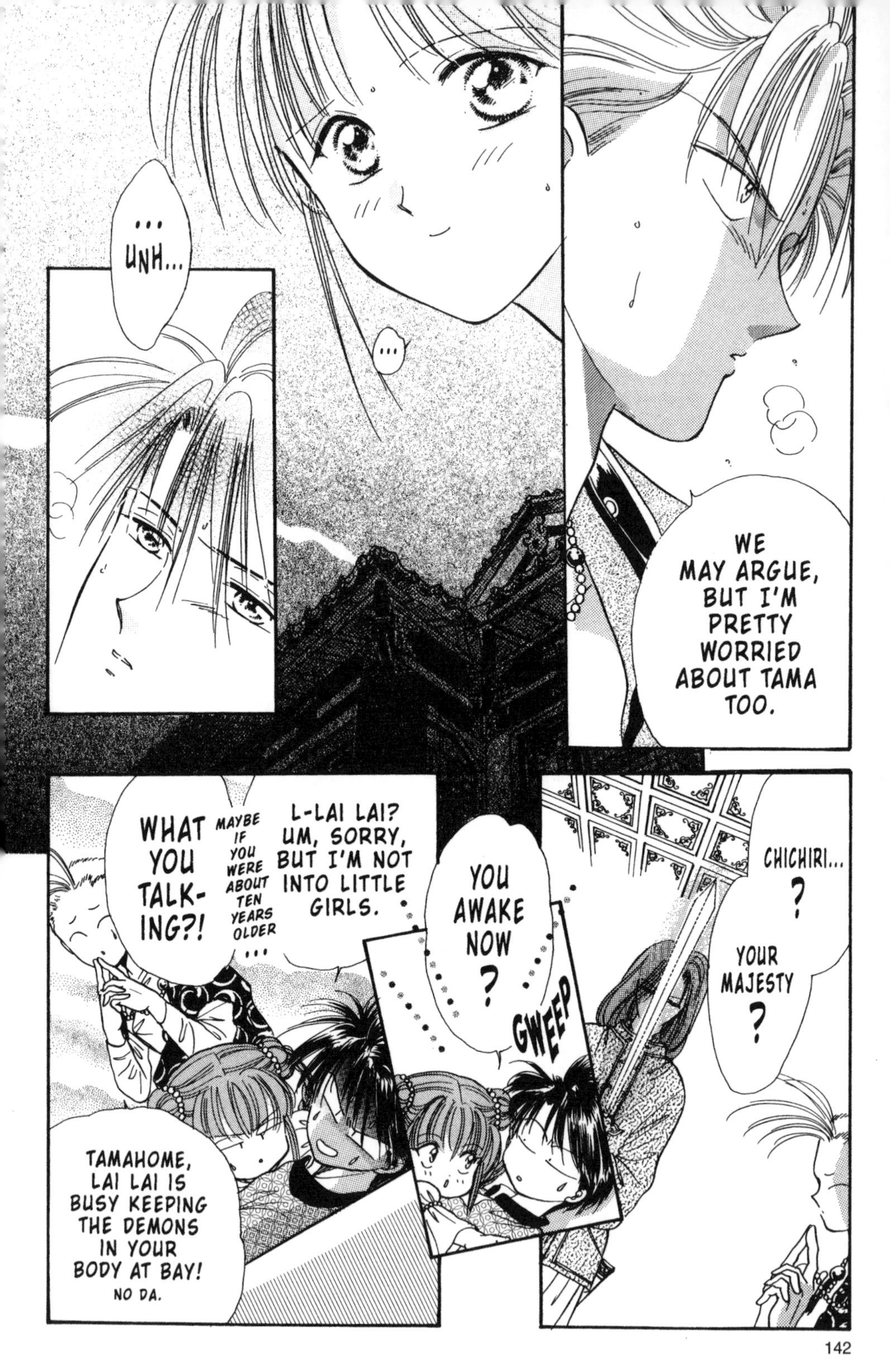
WE MAY ARGUE, BUT I'M PRETTY WORRIED ABOUT TAMA TOO.
...
... UNH...
CHICHIRI... ?
YOUR MAJESTY ?
YOU AWAKE NOW ?
GWEEP
L-LAI LAI? UM, SORRY, BUT I'M NOT INTO LITTLE GIRLS.
MAYBE IF YOU WERE ABOUT TEN YEARS OLDER...
WHAT YOU TALKING?!
TAMAHOME, LAI LAI IS BUSY KEEPING THE DEMONS IN YOUR BODY AT BAY! NO DA.

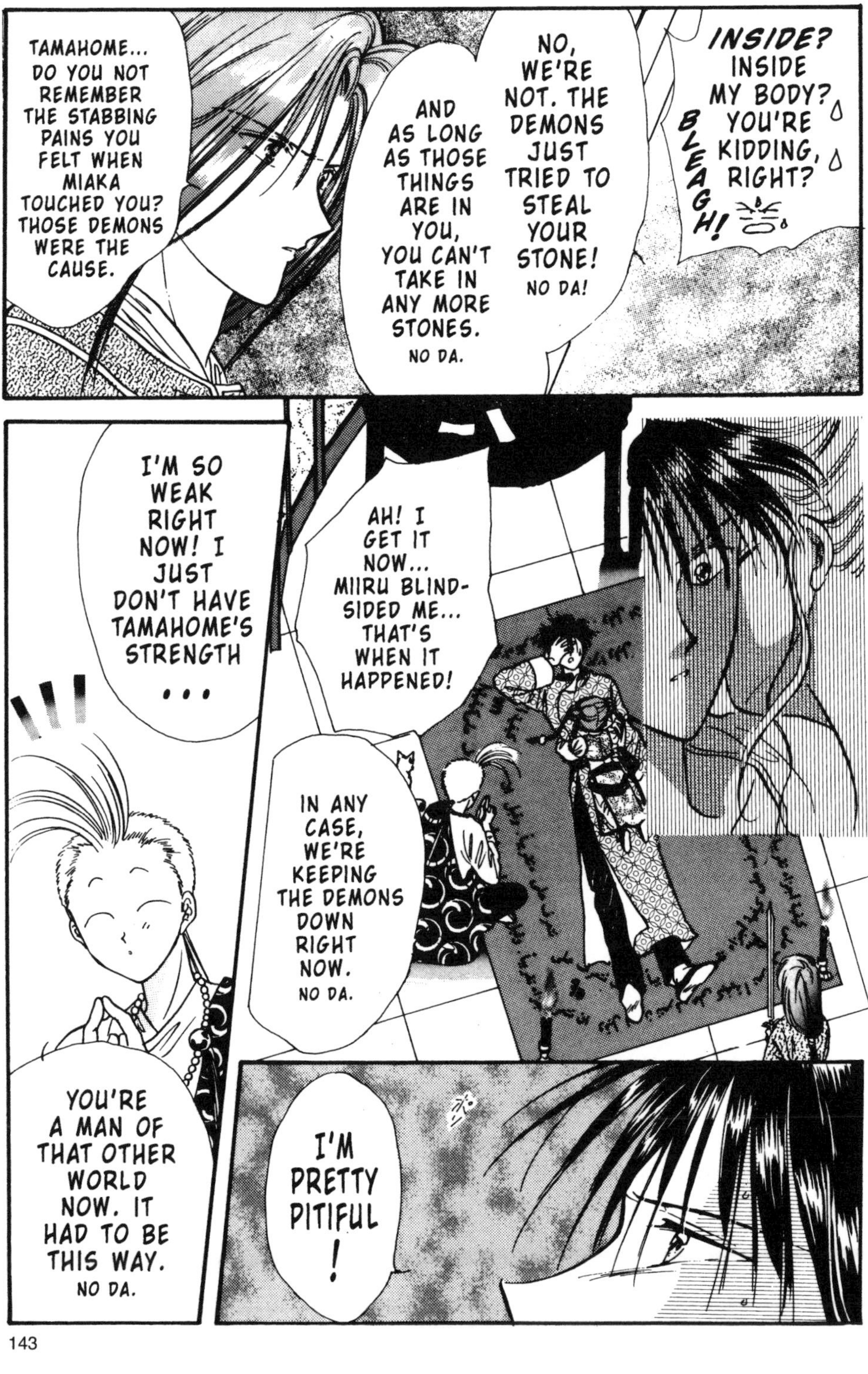
INSIDE? INSIDE MY BODY? YOU'RE KIDDING, RIGHT?
BLEAGH!
NO, WE'RE NOT. THE DEMONS JUST TRIED TO STEAL YOUR STONE! NO DA!
AND AS LONG AS THOSE THINGS ARE IN YOU, YOU CAN'T TAKE IN ANY MORE STONES. NO DA.
TAMAHOME... DO YOU NOT REMEMBER THE STABBING PAINS YOU FELT WHEN MIAKA TOUCHED YOU? THOSE DEMONS WERE THE CAUSE.
AH! I GET IT NOW... MIIRU BLIND-SIDED ME... THAT'S WHEN IT HAPPENED!
IN ANY CASE, WE'RE KEEPING THE DEMONS DOWN RIGHT NOW. NO DA.
I'M PRETTY PITIFUL!
I'M SO WEAK RIGHT NOW! I JUST DON'T HAVE TAMAHOME'S STRENGTH
...
YOU'RE A MAN OF THAT OTHER WORLD NOW. IT HAD TO BE THIS WAY. NO DA.

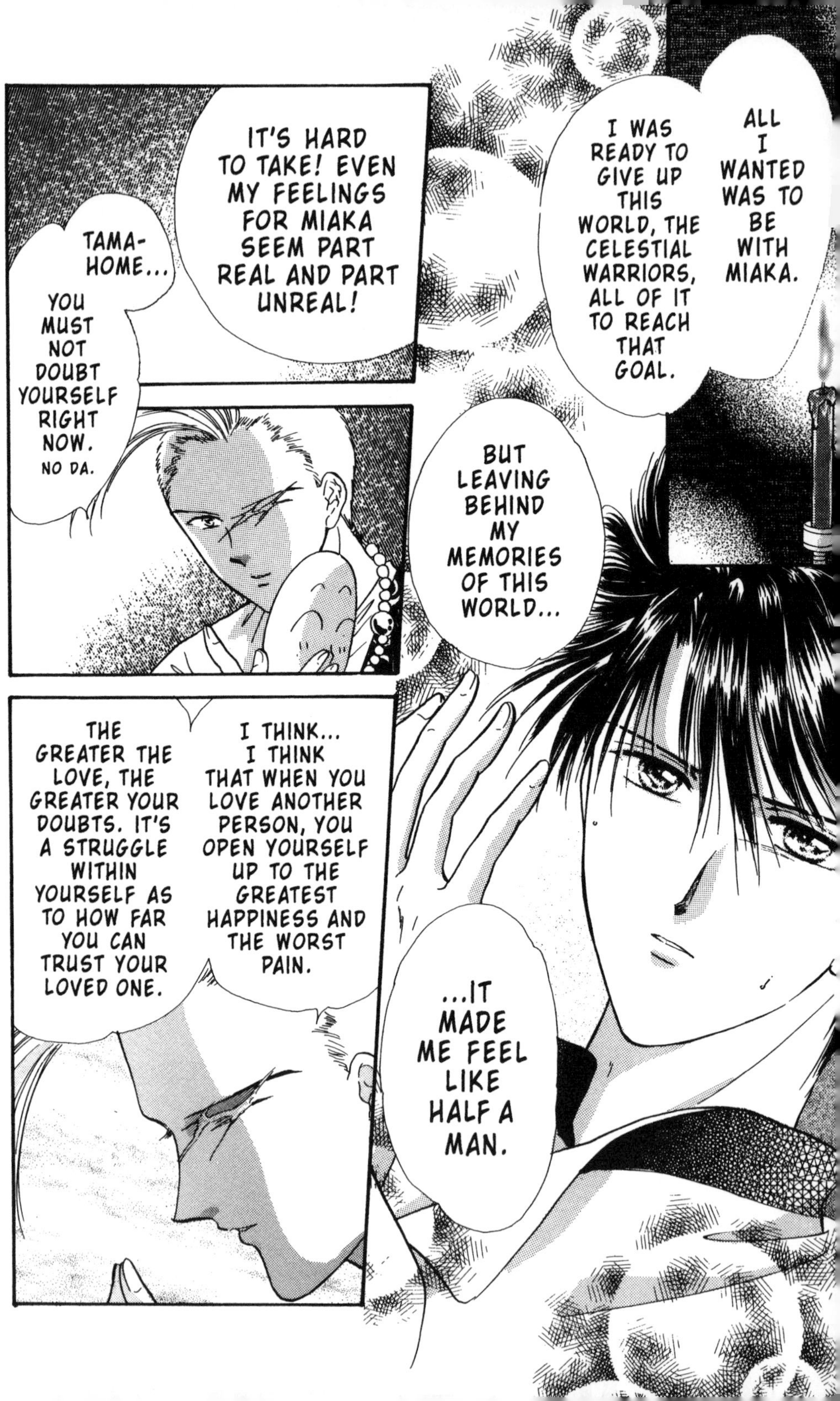
ALL I WANTED WAS TO BE WITH MIAKA.
I WAS READY TO GIVE UP THIS WORLD, THE CELESTIAL WARRIORS, ALL OF IT TO REACH THAT GOAL.
BUT LEAVING BEHIND MY MEMORIES OF THIS WORLD...
...IT MADE ME FEEL LIKE HALF A MAN.
IT'S HARD TO TAKE! EVEN MY FEELINGS FOR MIAKA SEEM PART REAL AND PART UNREAL!
TAMA-HOME...
YOU MUST NOT DOUBT YOURSELF RIGHT NOW. NO DA.
I THINK... I THINK THAT WHEN YOU LOVE ANOTHER PERSON, YOU OPEN YOURSELF UP TO THE GREATEST HAPPINESS AND THE WORST PAIN.
THE GREATER THE LOVE, THE GREATER YOUR DOUBTS. IT'S A STRUGGLE WITHIN YOURSELF AS TO HOW FAR YOU CAN TRUST YOUR LOVED ONE.

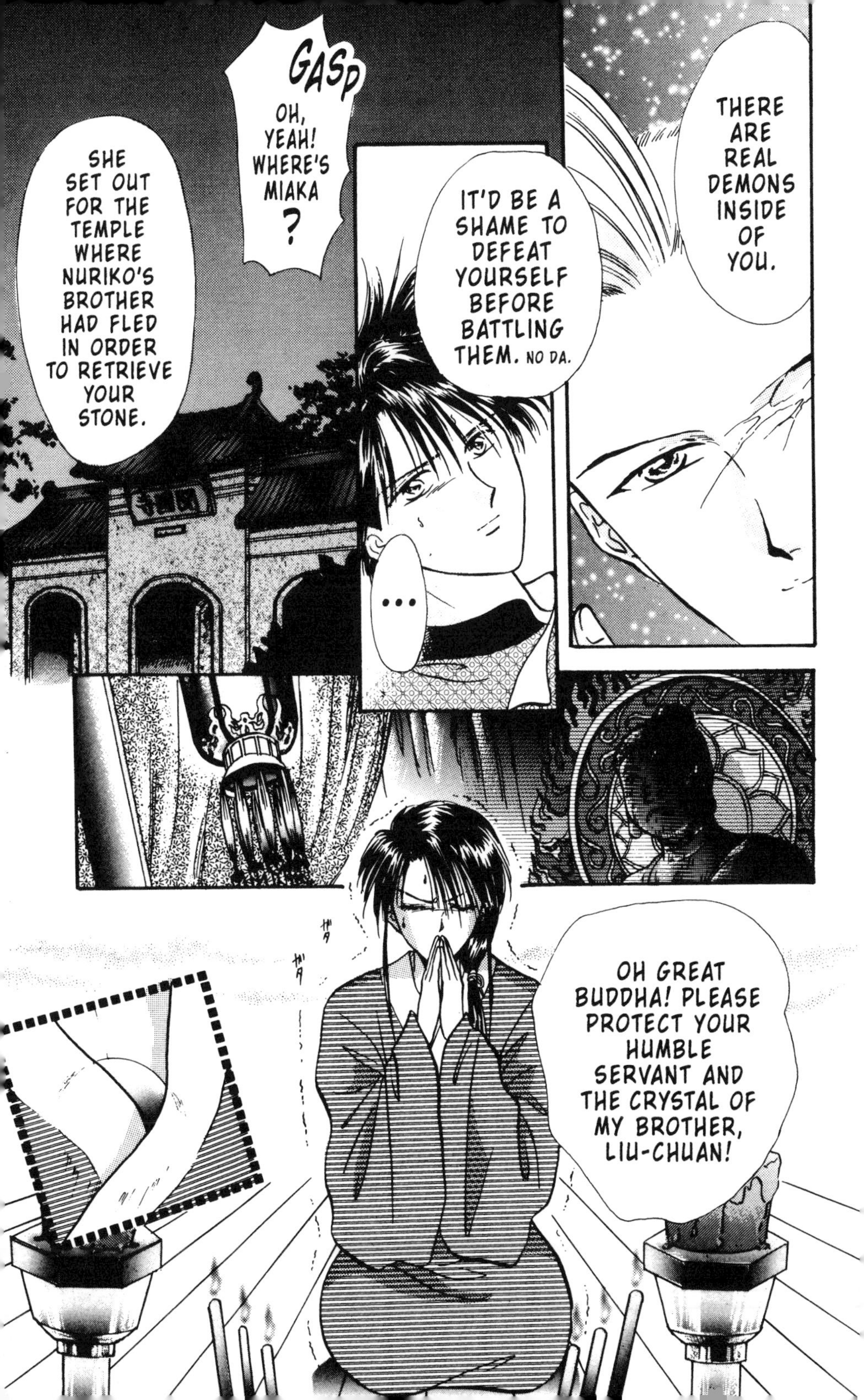
THERE ARE REAL DEMONS INSIDE OF YOU.
IT'D BE A SHAME TO DEFEAT YOURSELF BEFORE BATTLING THEM. NO DA.
...
GASP
OH, YEAH! WHERE'S MIAKA?
SHE SET OUT FOR THE TEMPLE WHERE NURIKO'S BROTHER HAD FLED IN ORDER TO RETRIEVE YOUR STONE.
OH GREAT BUDDHA! PLEASE PROTECT YOUR HUMBLE SERVANT AND THE CRYSTAL OF MY BROTHER, LIU-CHUAN!

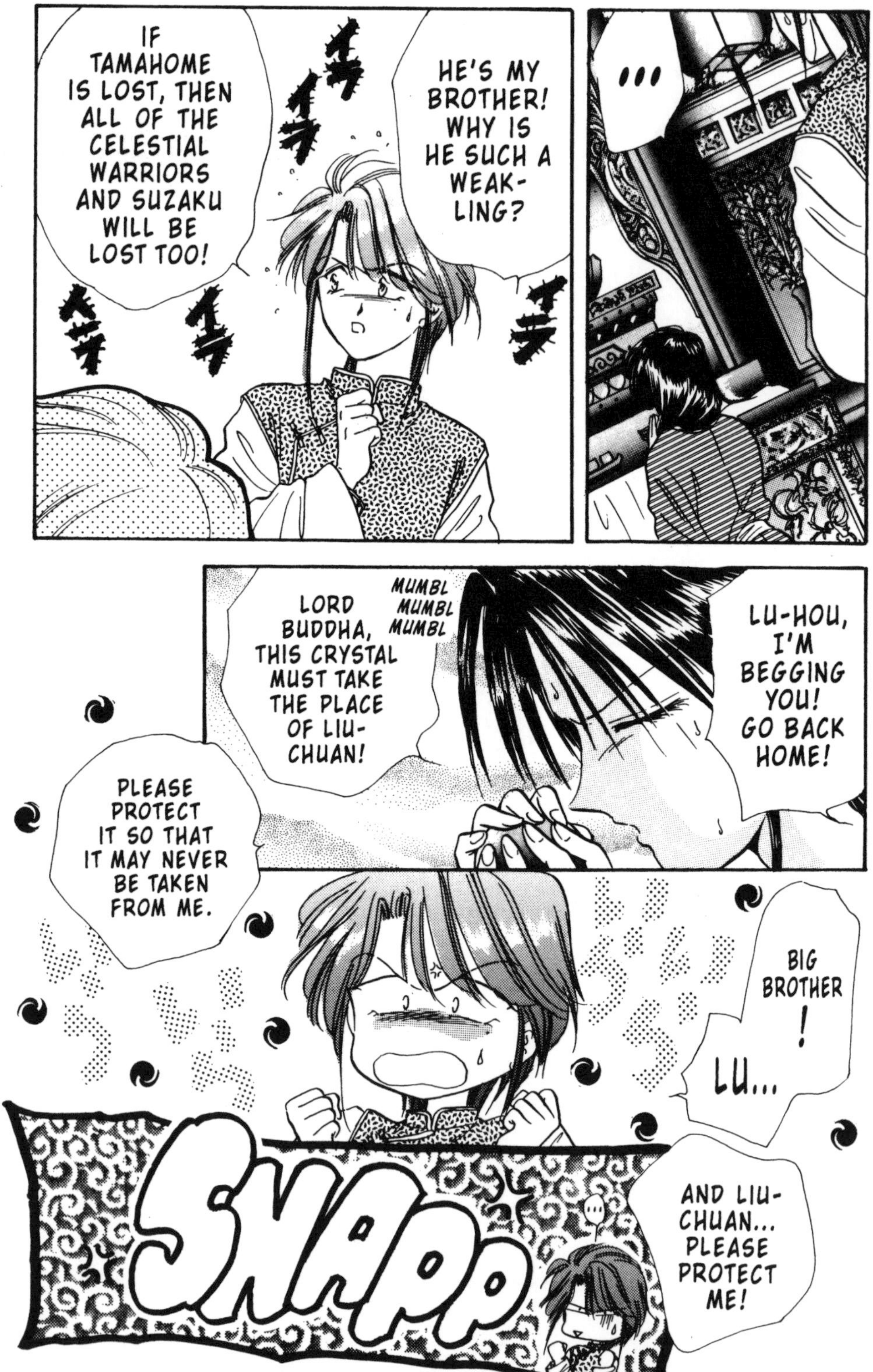
...
HE'S MY BROTHER! WHY IS HE SUCH A WEAK-LING?
IF TAMAHOME IS LOST, THEN ALL OF THE CELESTIAL WARRIORS AND SUZAKU WILL BE LOST TOO!
LU-HOU, I'M BEGGING YOU! GO BACK HOME!
MUMBL MUMBL MUMBL
LORD BUDDHA, THIS CRYSTAL MUST TAKE THE PLACE OF LIU-CHUAN!
PLEASE PROTECT IT SO THAT IT MAY NEVER BE TAKEN FROM ME.
BIG BROTHER!
LU...
AND LIU-CHUAN... PLEASE PROTECT ME!
...
SNAPP

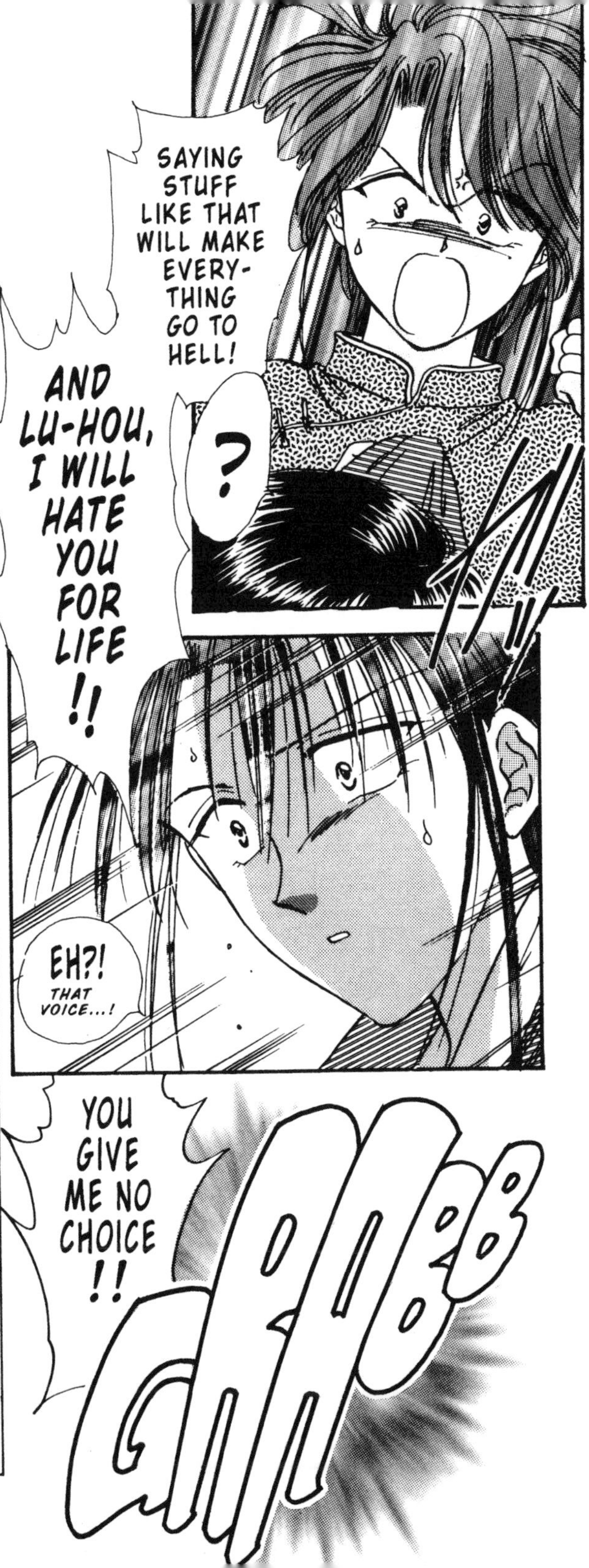
SAYING STUFF LIKE THAT WILL MAKE EVERY-THING GO TO HELL!
AND LU-HOU, I WILL HATE YOU FOR LIFE!!
?
EH?! THAT VOICE...!
YOU GIVE ME NO CHOICE!!

(Continued...)
But since my professional manga debut, it seems like I've come to know the complexities of shojo manga. Never underestimate it! It explores the details of how we express our feelings... It just has some wonderful attributes that shonen manga lacks! It's strongest with stories involving romantic love, but since that wasn't my personal interest early on, I'd say, "Oh God!" and throw it away. But recently, I've come to like the romance more and more. ☺ The ones I like are the "couple fated to be together" stories... the ones where they're hanging all over each other! I can't get enough of them! ☺
When I see a real-life couple walking in the street (not the ones that make you sick! Let's forget those for now), I get this pleasant feeling. I think in the past when I used to say "ugh!" I was just jealous. ☺ One of my assistants is in the habit of saying, "Ahh, that's amore!"
Before my debut, everything I wrote was sort of all over the place. (Really! My settings and situations were really detailed then, but when I go back and read them now, I don't understand what's going on. I had the mistaken impression that throwing people into wild situation after wild situation was interesting, but it isn't.) But no matter what the story, if there is no love in it, it can be pretty dull. When one person is thinking of another, don't you think that's pretty wonderful? ☺
I never intended to be a "shojo manga artist." (I did some shojo manga-style stories, but that's because the magazines were shojo magazines.) But "shojo manga" wasn't what I wanted to draw. I wanted children, adults, everybody to enjoy my manga! (Well... *Fushigi Yûgi* was meant for people in the 3rd year of middle school and up, and that's how I drew it.) I think that this obsession (in the manga world) with aiming stories at a particular segment of the population is extremely strange! Personally I like the general "middle school" feel of my manga, and I want to keep it in my work, ideally. But there are times when I worry about the feel of my manga... ☺

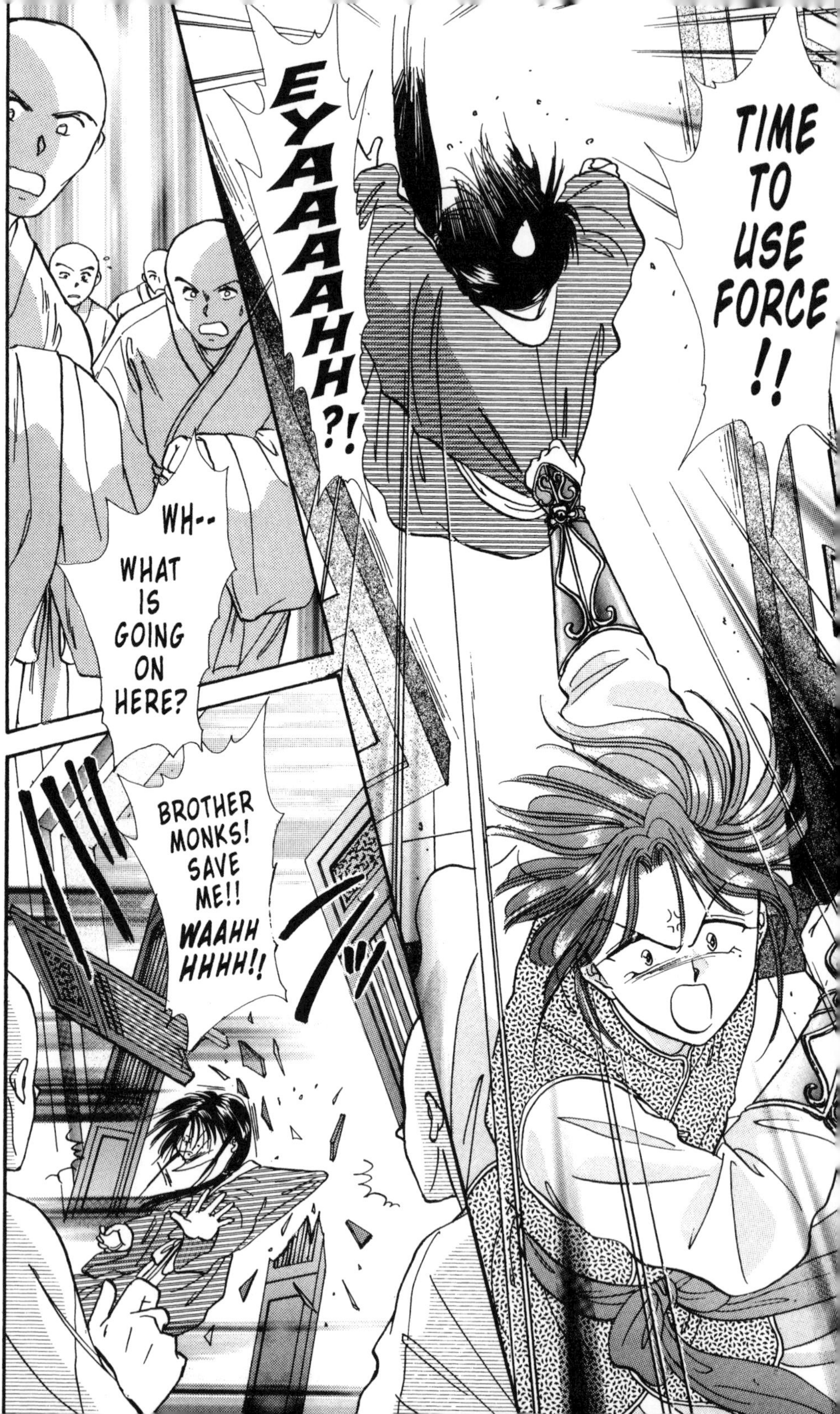
TIME TO USE FORCE!!
EYAAAAHH?!
WH-- WHAT IS GOING ON HERE?
BROTHER MONKS! SAVE ME!! WAAHH HHHH!!

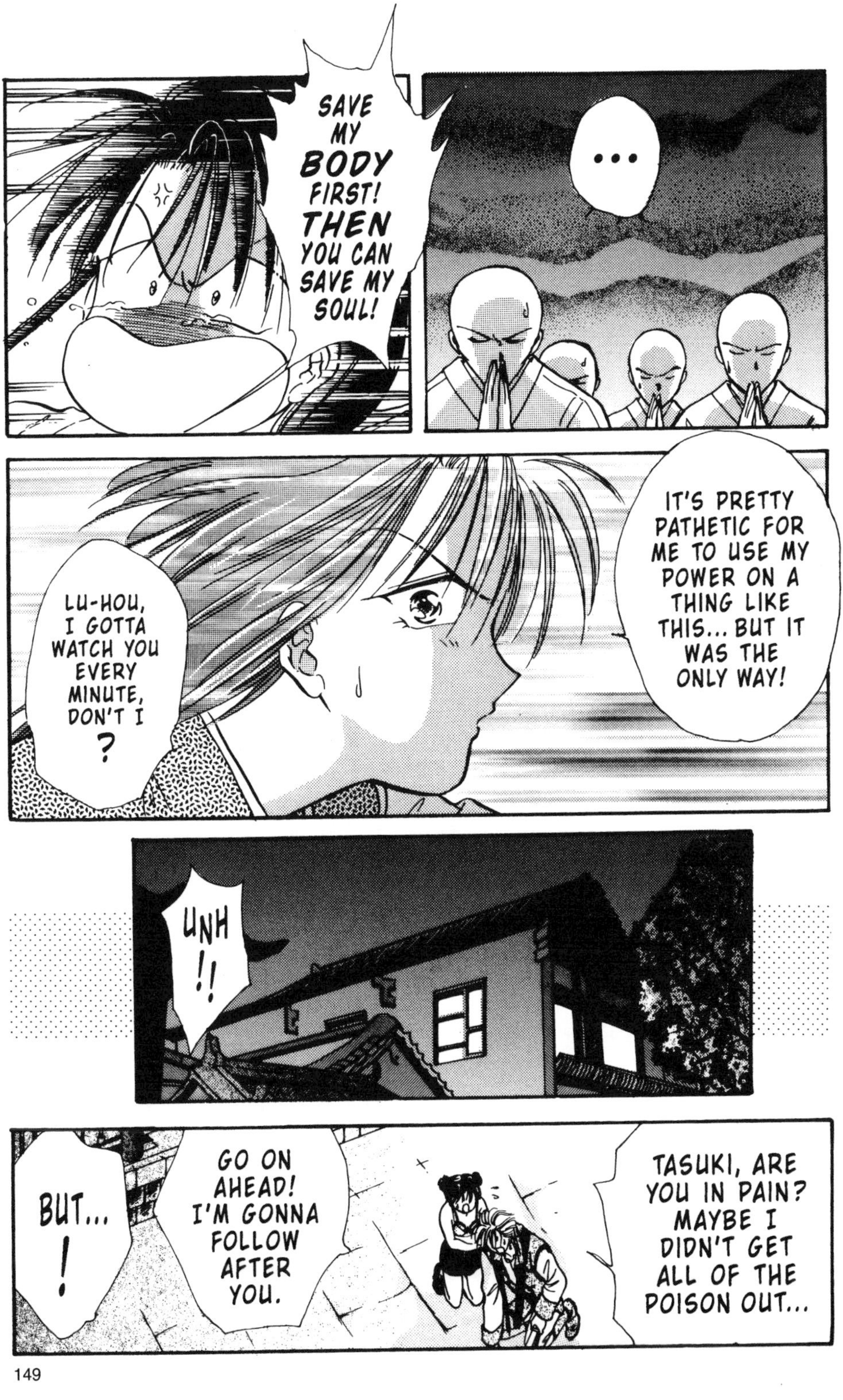
...
SAVE MY BODY FIRST! THEN YOU CAN SAVE MY SOUL!
IT'S PRETTY PATHETIC FOR ME TO USE MY POWER ON A THING LIKE THIS... BUT IT WAS THE ONLY WAY!
LU-HOU, I GOTTA WATCH YOU EVERY MINUTE, DON'T I?
UNH!!
TASUKI, ARE YOU IN PAIN? MAYBE I DIDN'T GET ALL OF THE POISON OUT...
GO ON AHEAD! I'M GONNA FOLLOW AFTER YOU.
BUT...!

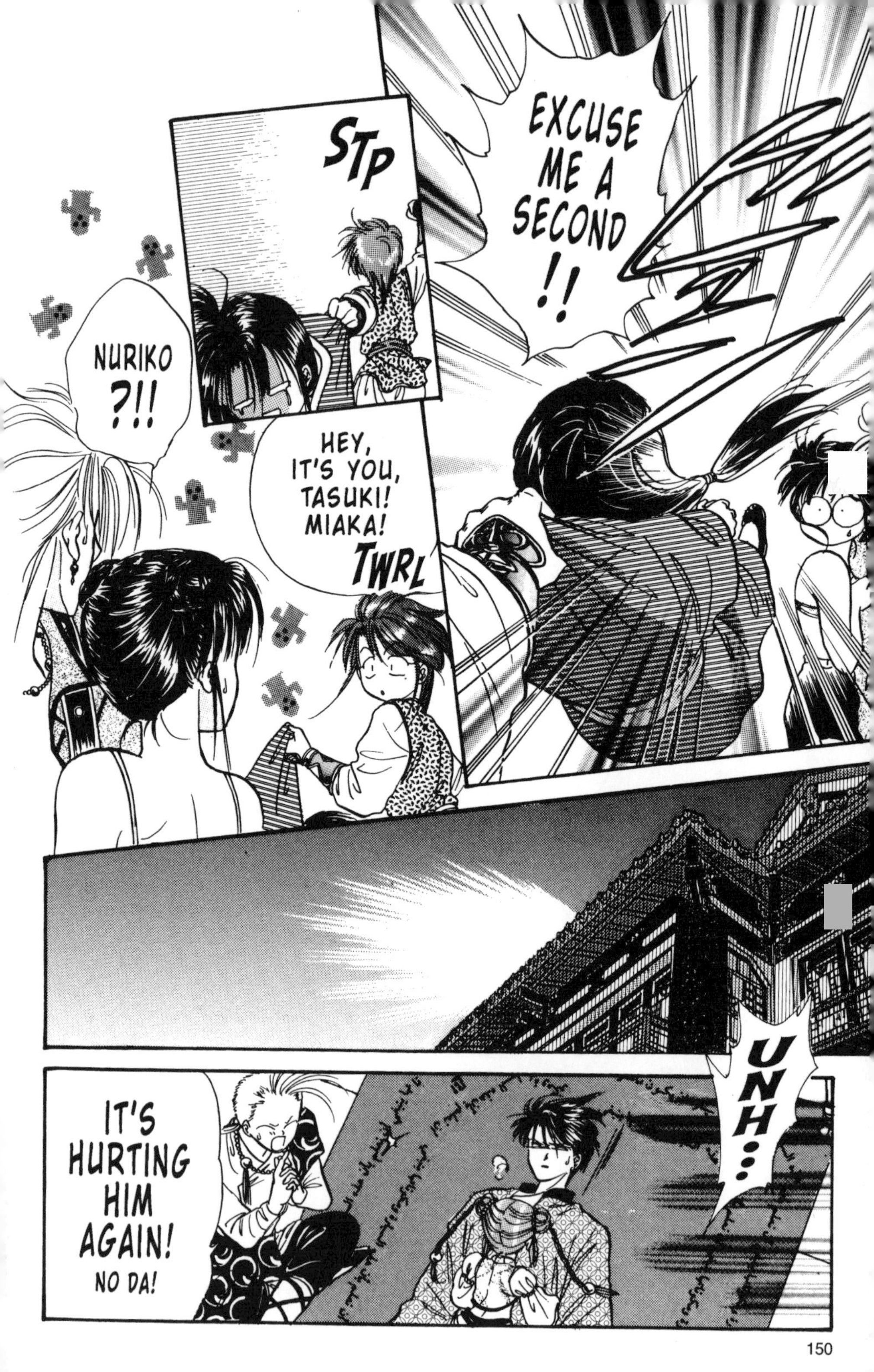
EXCUSE ME A SECOND !!
STP
NURIKO ?!!
HEY, IT'S YOU, TASUKI! MIAKA!
TWRL
UNH...
IT'S HURTING HIM AGAIN! NO DA!

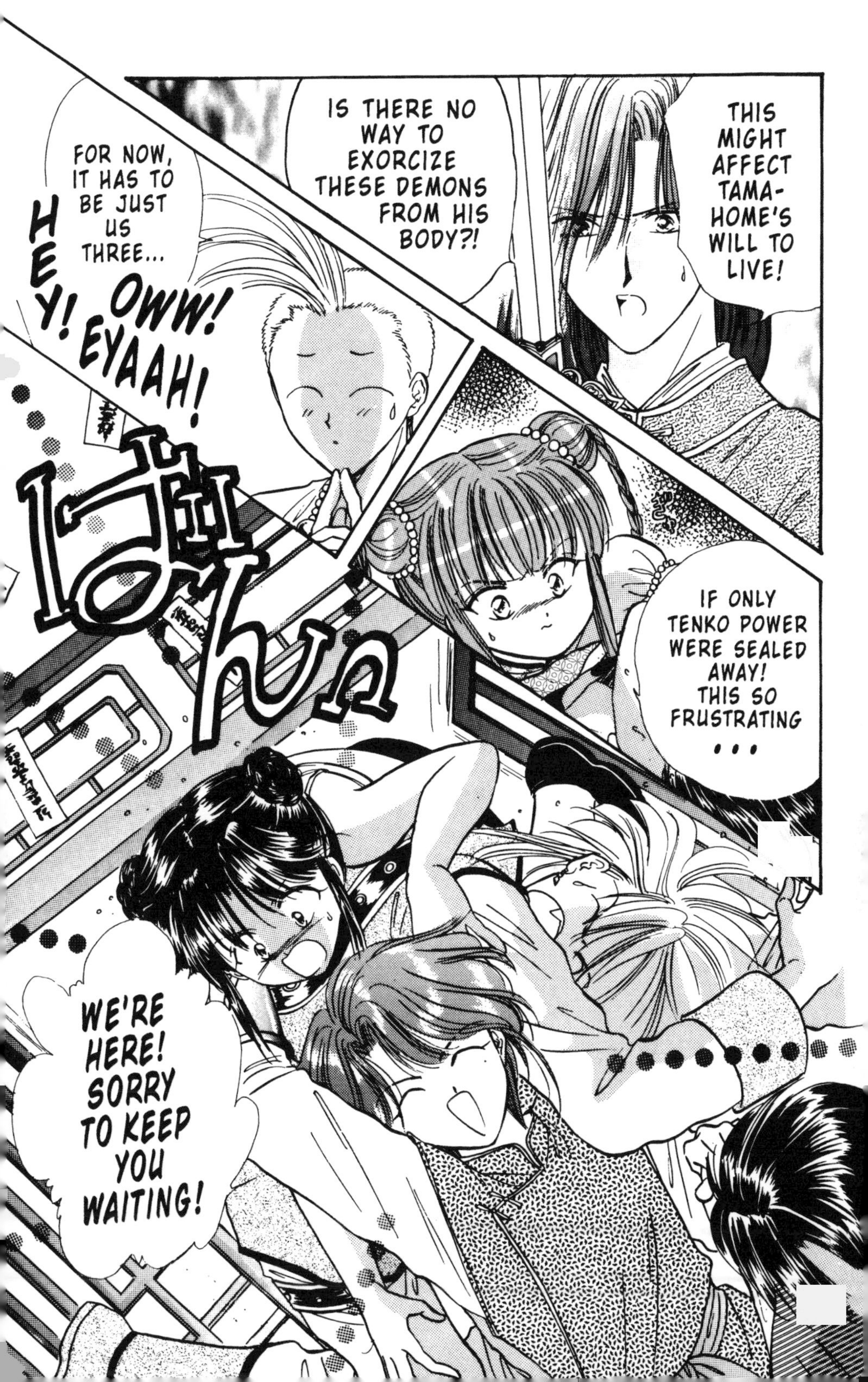
THIS MIGHT AFFECT TAMA-HOME'S WILL TO LIVE!
IS THERE NO WAY TO EXORCIZE THESE DEMONS FROM HIS BODY?!
FOR NOW, IT HAS TO BE JUST US THREE...
OWW! EYAAH!
HEY!
IF ONLY TENKO POWER WERE SEALED AWAY! THIS SO FRUSTRATING...
WE'RE HERE! SORRY TO KEEP YOU WAITING!

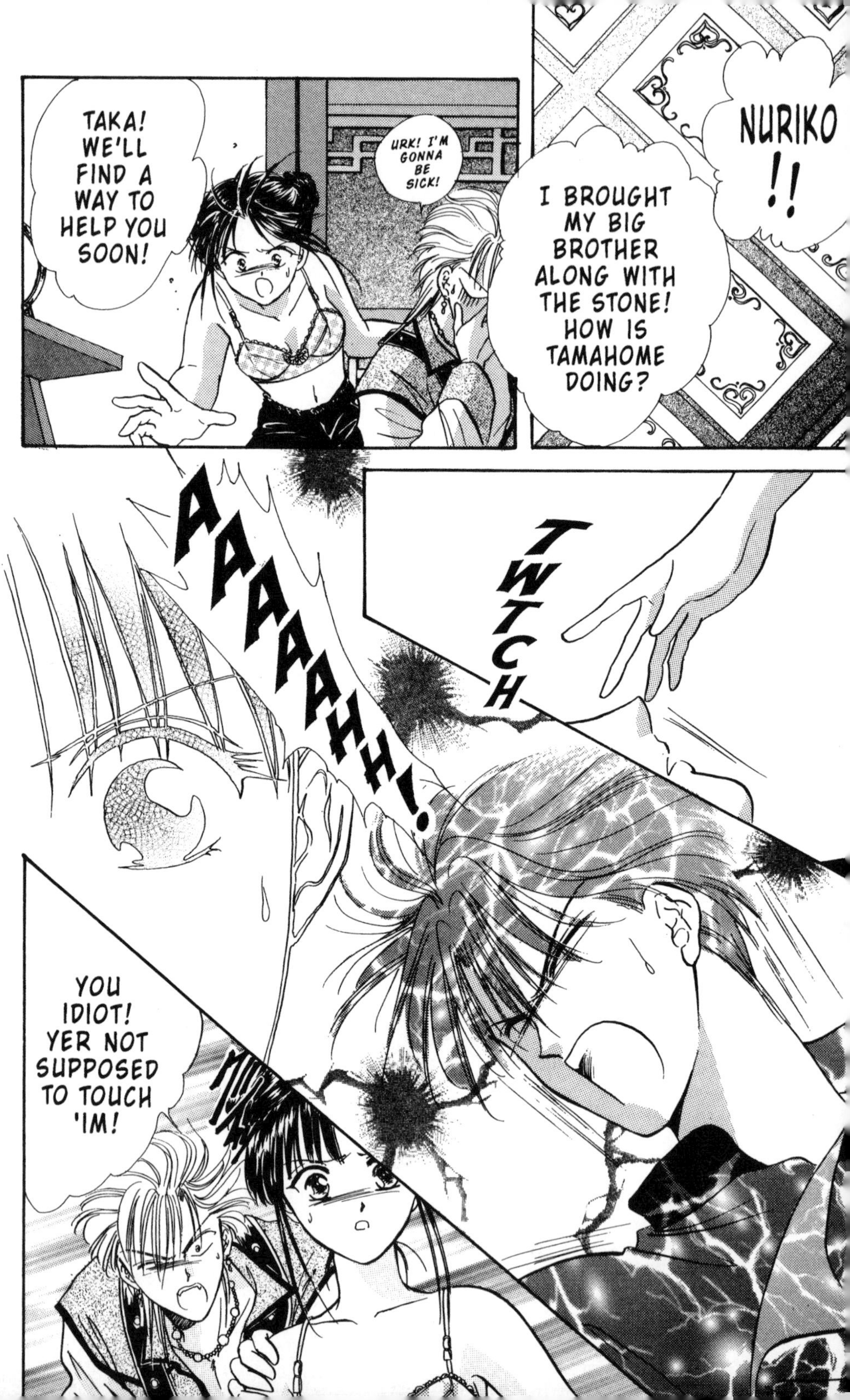
NURIKO !!
I BROUGHT MY BIG BROTHER ALONG WITH THE STONE! HOW IS TAMAHOME DOING?
URK! I'M GONNA BE SICK!
TAKA! WE'LL FIND A WAY TO HELP YOU SOON!
TWTCH
AAAAAHH!
YOU IDIOT! YER NOT SUPPOSED TO TOUCH 'IM!

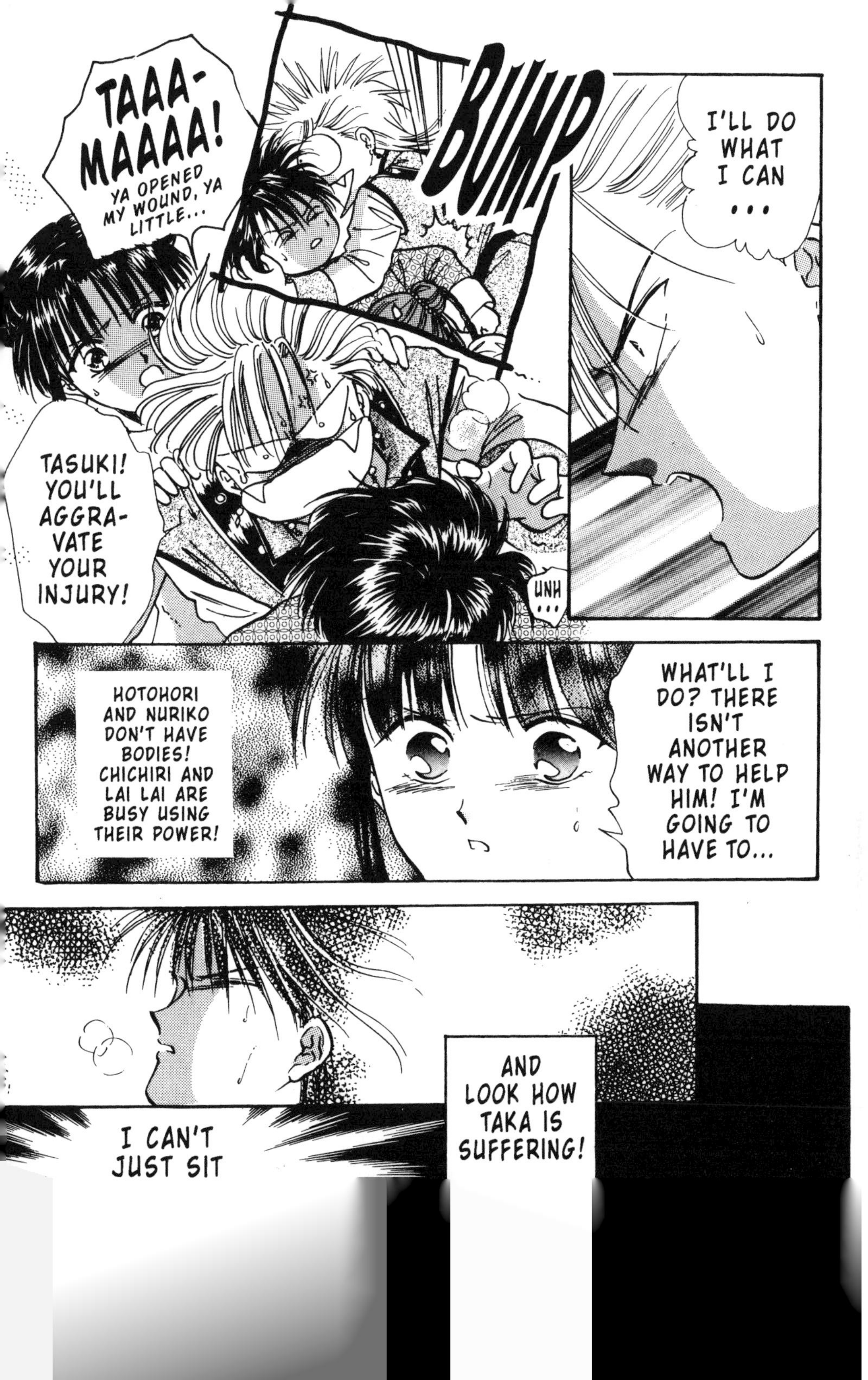
I'LL DO WHAT I CAN ...
BUMP
TAAA-MAAAA!
YA OPENED MY WOUND, YA LITTLE...
UNH ...
TASUKI! YOU'LL AGGRAVATE YOUR INJURY!
WHAT'LL I DO? THERE ISN'T ANOTHER WAY TO HELP HIM! I'M GOING TO HAVE TO...
HOTOHORI AND NURIKO DON'T HAVE BODIES! CHICHIRI AND LAI LAI ARE BUSY USING THEIR POWER!
AND LOOK HOW TAKA IS SUFFERING!
I CAN'T JUST SIT

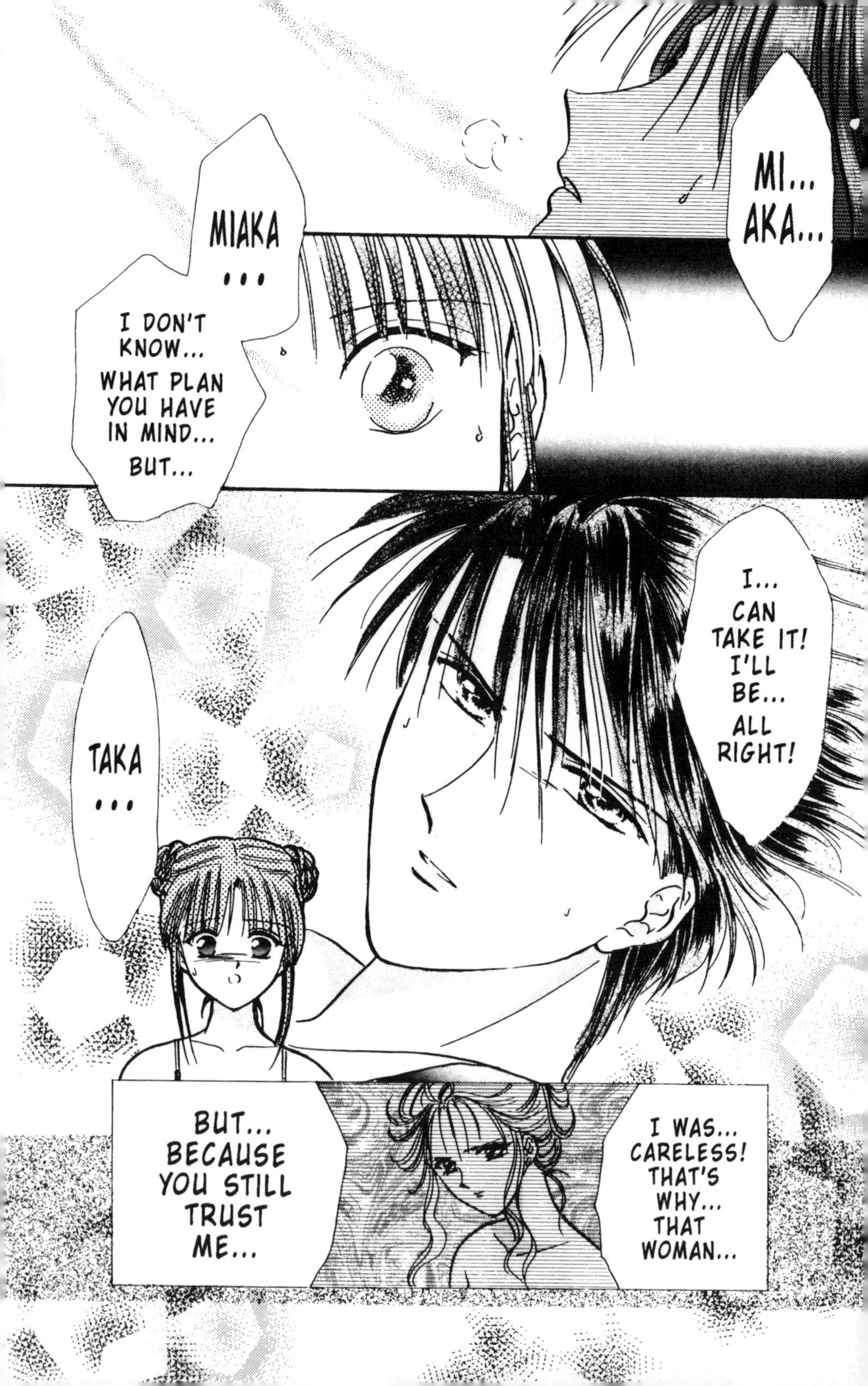
MI... AKA...
MIAKA ...
I DON'T KNOW... WHAT PLAN YOU HAVE IN MIND... BUT...
I... CAN TAKE IT! I'LL BE... ALL RIGHT!
TAKA ...
I WAS... CARELESS! THAT'S WHY... THAT WOMAN...
BUT... BECAUSE YOU STILL TRUST ME...

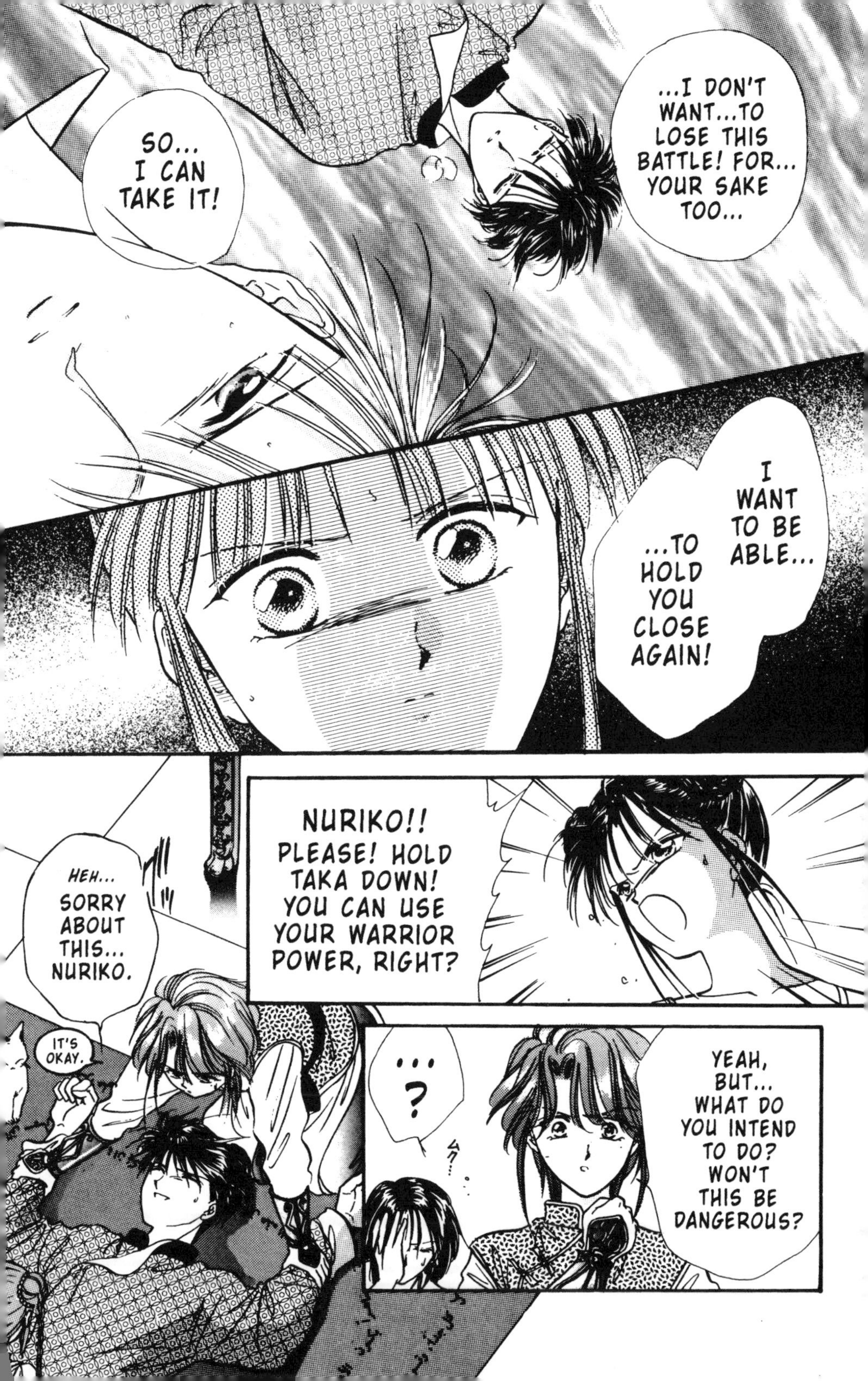
...I DON'T WANT...TO LOSE THIS BATTLE! FOR... YOUR SAKE TOO...
SO... I CAN TAKE IT!
I WANT TO BE ABLE...
...TO HOLD YOU CLOSE AGAIN!
NURIKO!! PLEASE! HOLD TAKA DOWN! YOU CAN USE YOUR WARRIOR POWER, RIGHT?
YEAH, BUT... WHAT DO YOU INTEND TO DO? WON'T THIS BE DANGEROUS?
...?
HEH... SORRY ABOUT THIS... NURIKO.
IT'S OKAY.

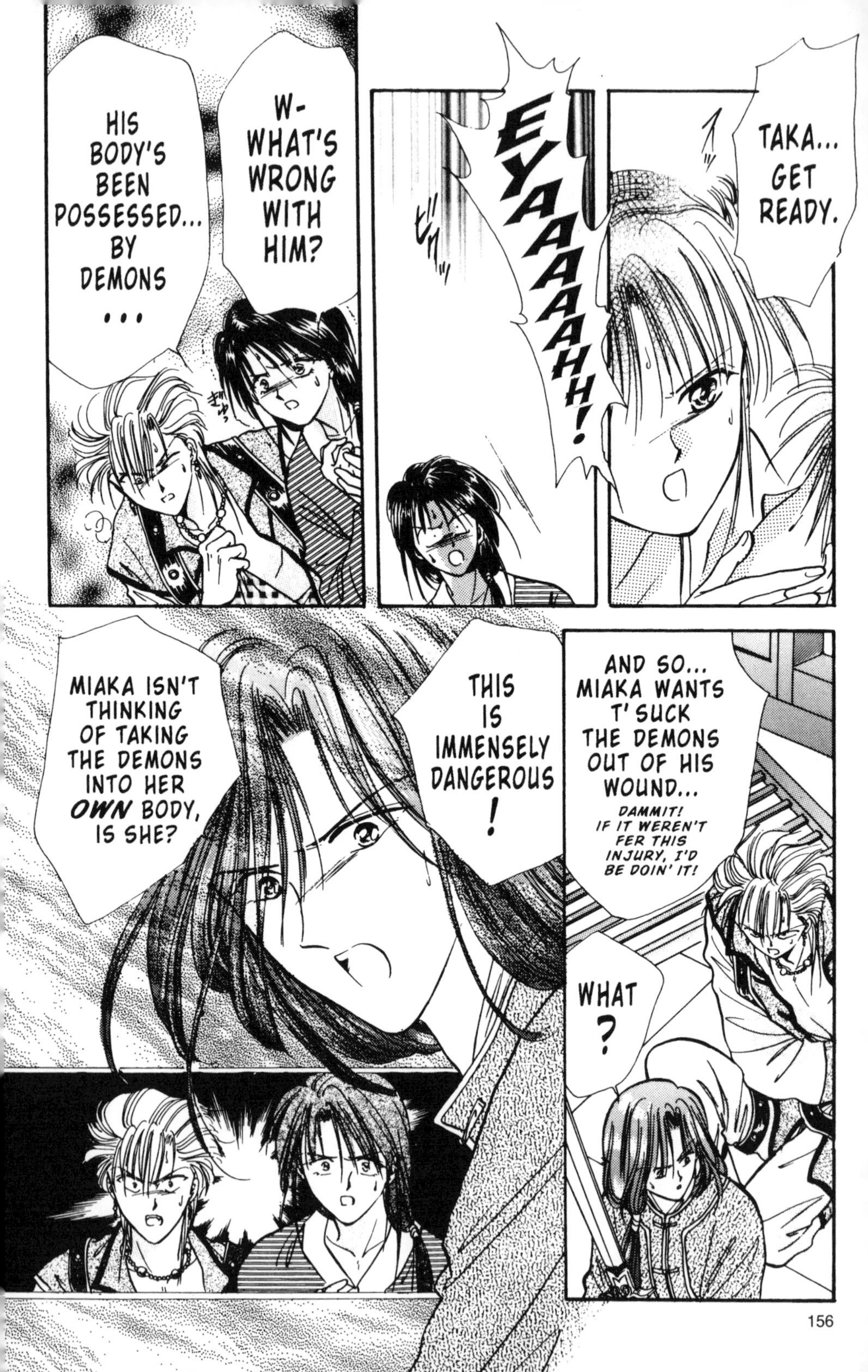
TAKA... GET READY.
EYAAAAAAH!
W- WHAT'S WRONG WITH HIM?
HIS BODY'S BEEN POSSESSED... BY DEMONS ...
AND SO... MIAKA WANTS T' SUCK THE DEMONS OUT OF HIS WOUND...
DAMMIT! IF IT WEREN'T FER THIS INJURY, I'D BE DOIN' IT!
WHAT?
THIS IS IMMENSELY DANGEROUS!
MIAKA ISN'T THINKING OF TAKING THE DEMONS INTO HER *OWN* BODY, IS SHE?

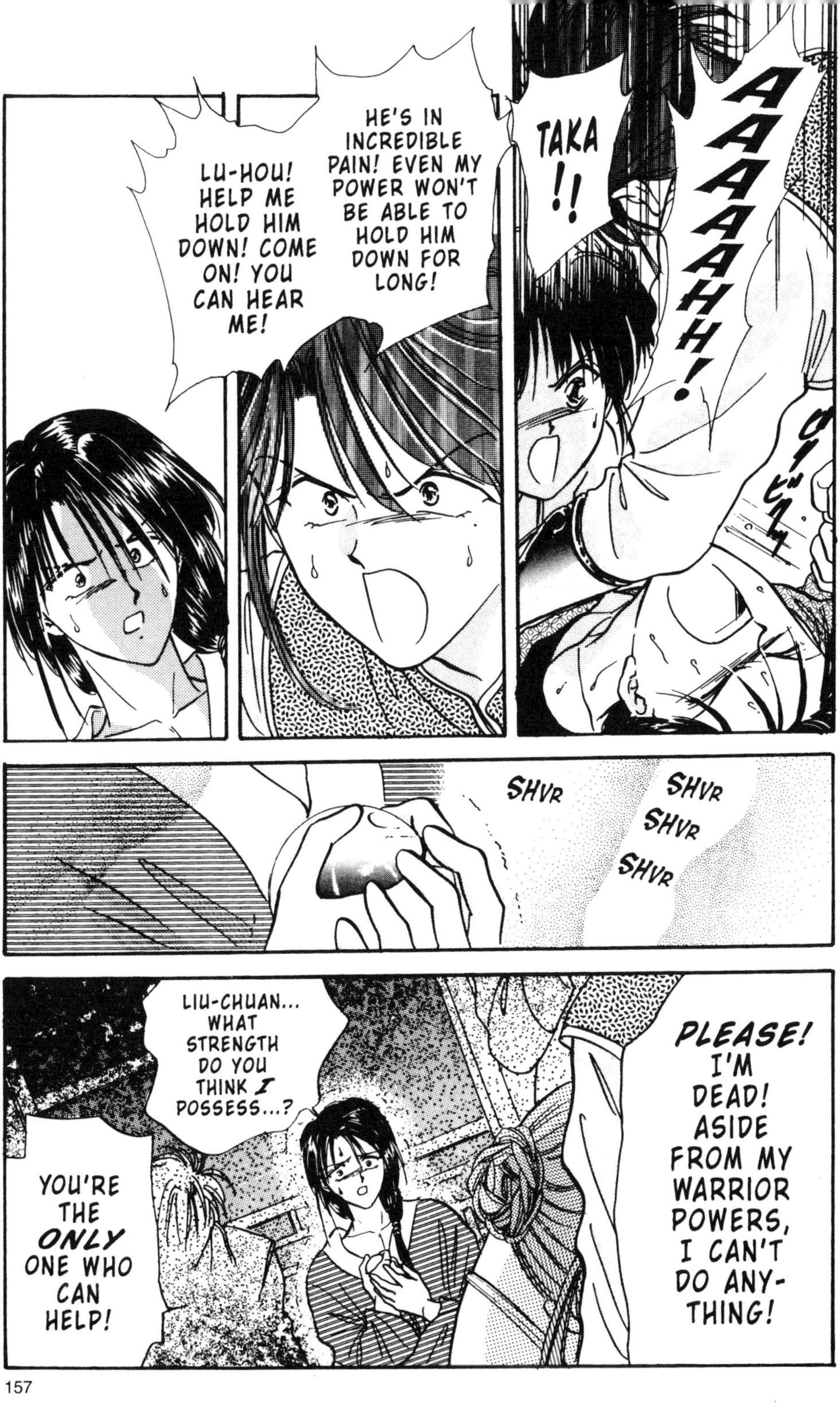
AAAAAAHH!
TAKA!!
HE'S IN INCREDIBLE PAIN! EVEN MY POWER WON'T BE ABLE TO HOLD HIM DOWN FOR LONG!
LU-HOU! HELP ME HOLD HIM DOWN! COME ON! YOU CAN HEAR ME!
SHVR
SHVR
SHVR
SHVR
PLEASE! I'M DEAD! ASIDE FROM MY WARRIOR POWERS, I CAN'T DO ANY-THING!
LIU-CHUAN... WHAT STRENGTH DO YOU THINK I POSSESS...?
YOU'RE THE ONLY ONE WHO CAN HELP!

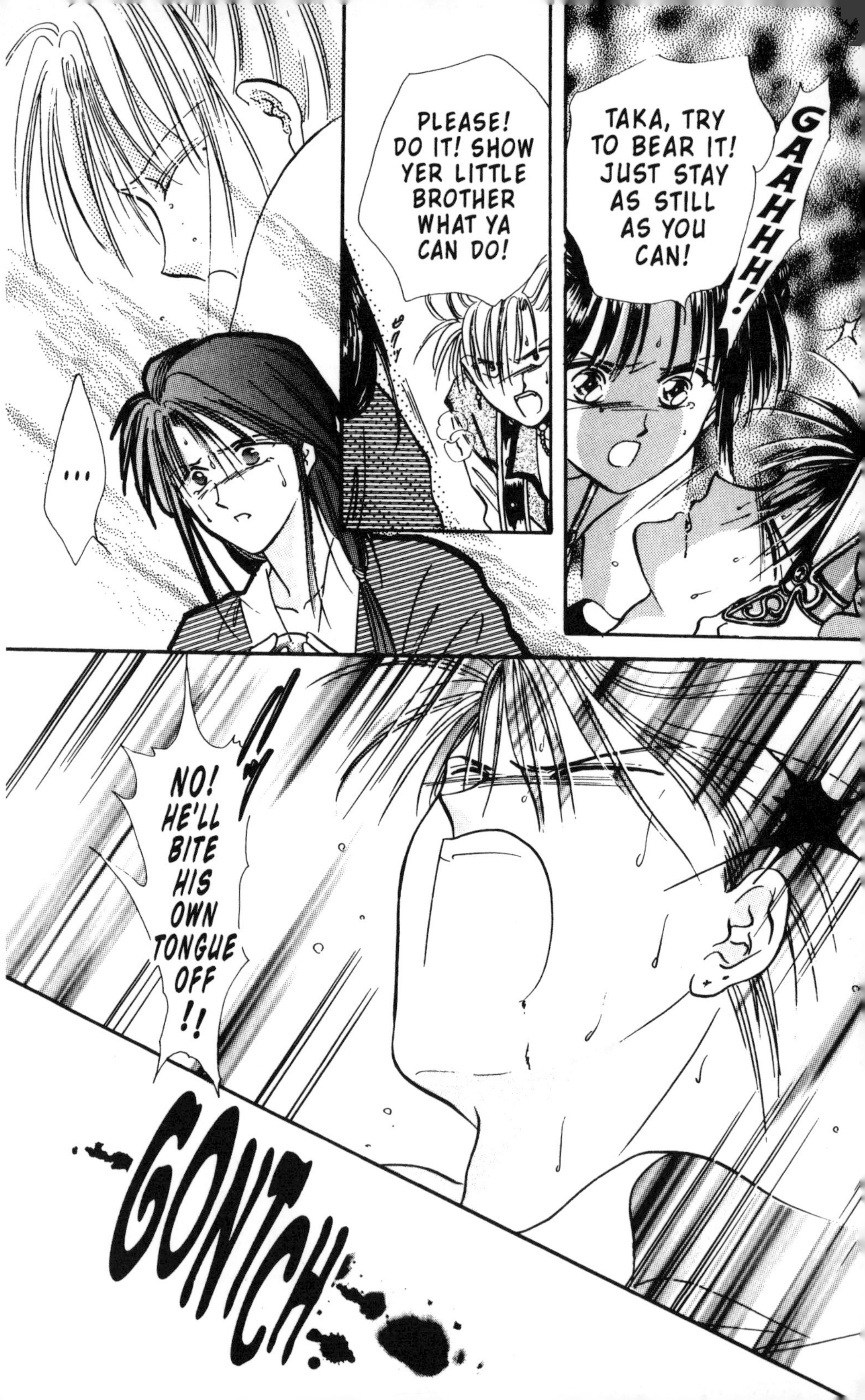
GAAHHHH!
TAKA, TRY TO BEAR IT! JUST STAY AS STILL AS YOU CAN!
PLEASE! DO IT! SHOW YER LITTLE BROTHER WHAT YA CAN DO!
...
NO! HE'LL BITE HIS OWN TONGUE OFF!!
GONTCH

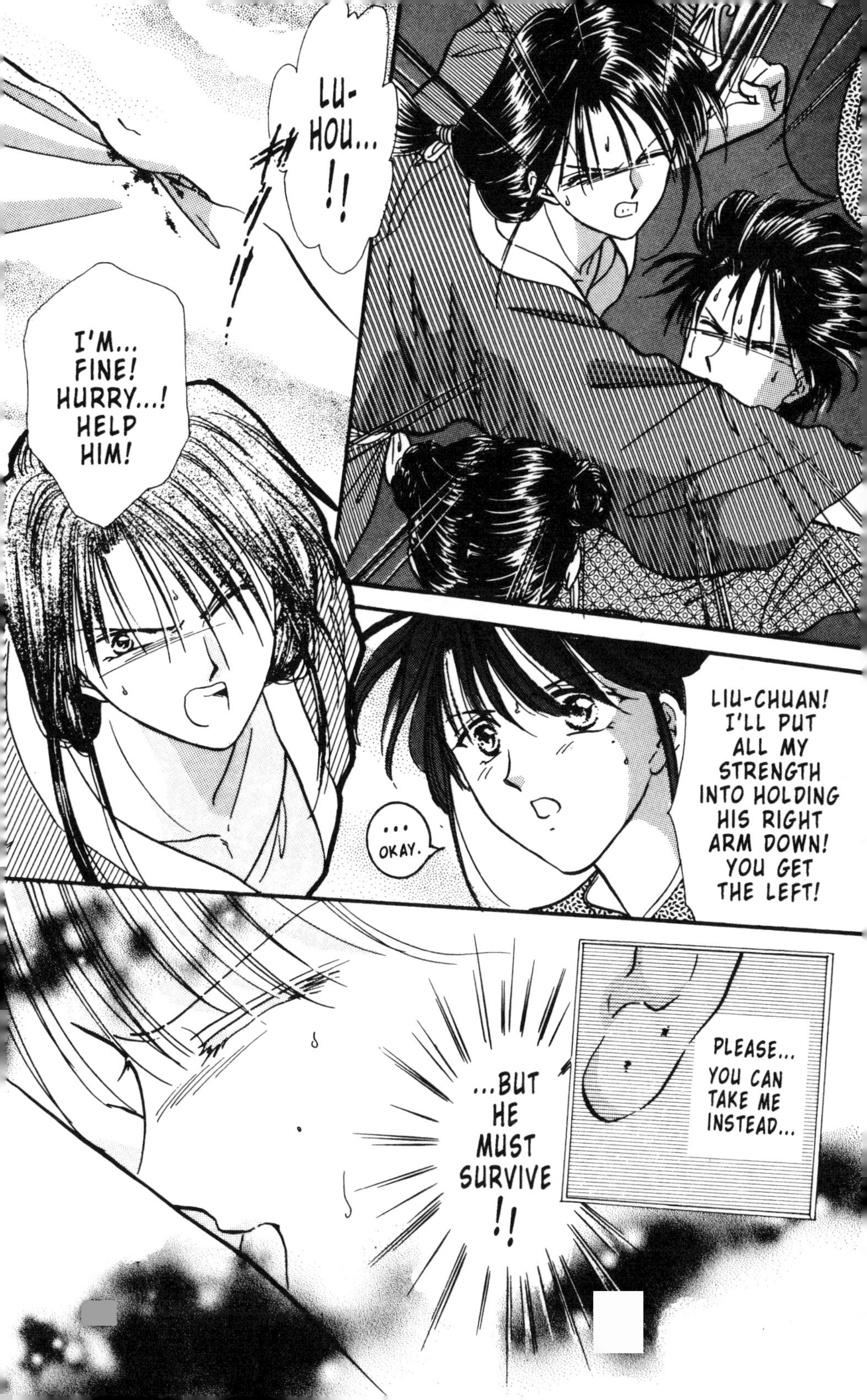
LU-HOU...!!
I'M... FINE! HURRY...! HELP HIM!
LIU-CHUAN! I'LL PUT ALL MY STRENGTH INTO HOLDING HIS RIGHT ARM DOWN! YOU GET THE LEFT!
...OKAY.
PLEASE... YOU CAN TAKE ME INSTEAD...
...BUT HE MUST SURVIVE!!

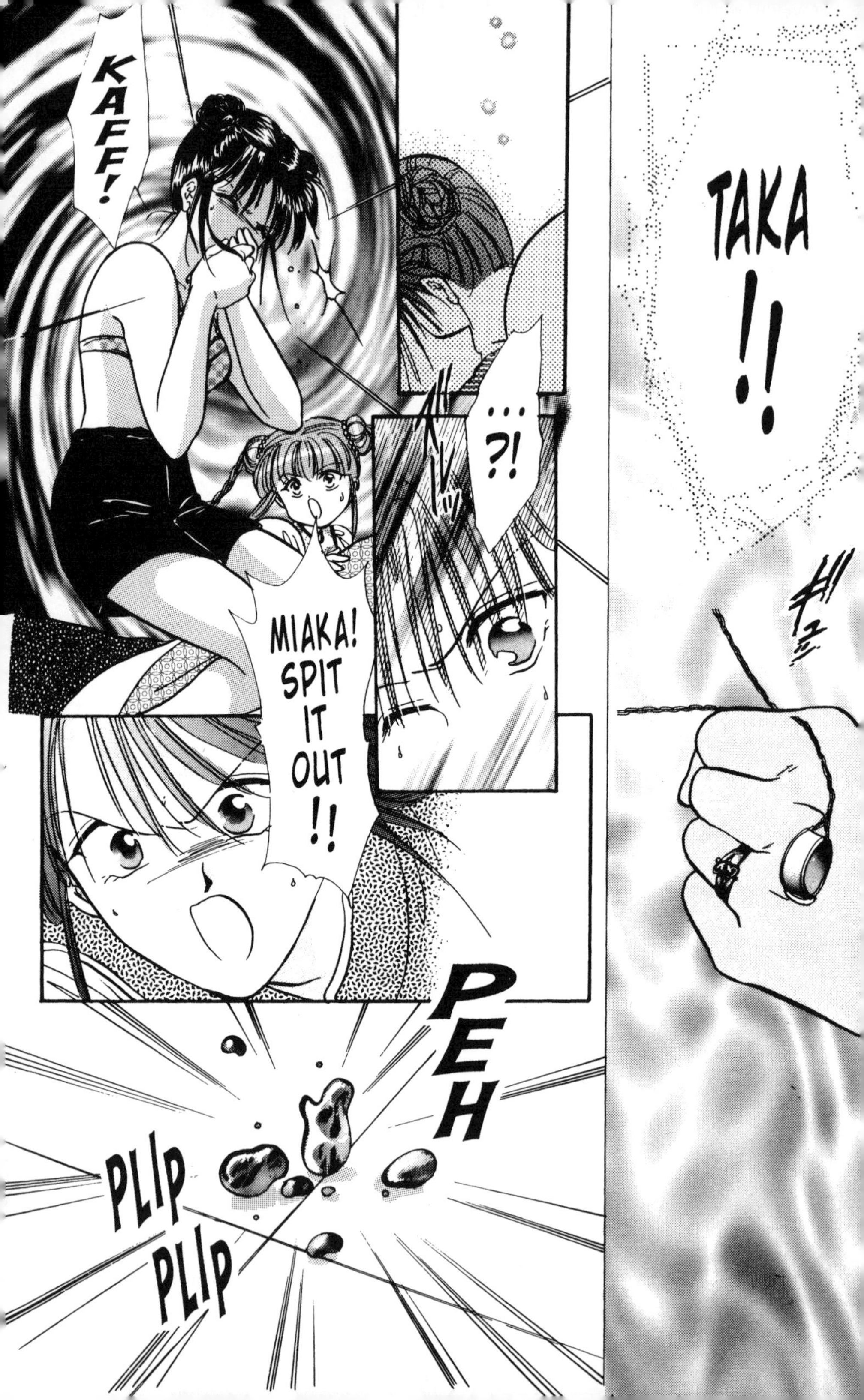
TAKA!!
KAFF!
...?!
MIAKA! SPIT IT OUT!!
PEH
PLIP PLIP

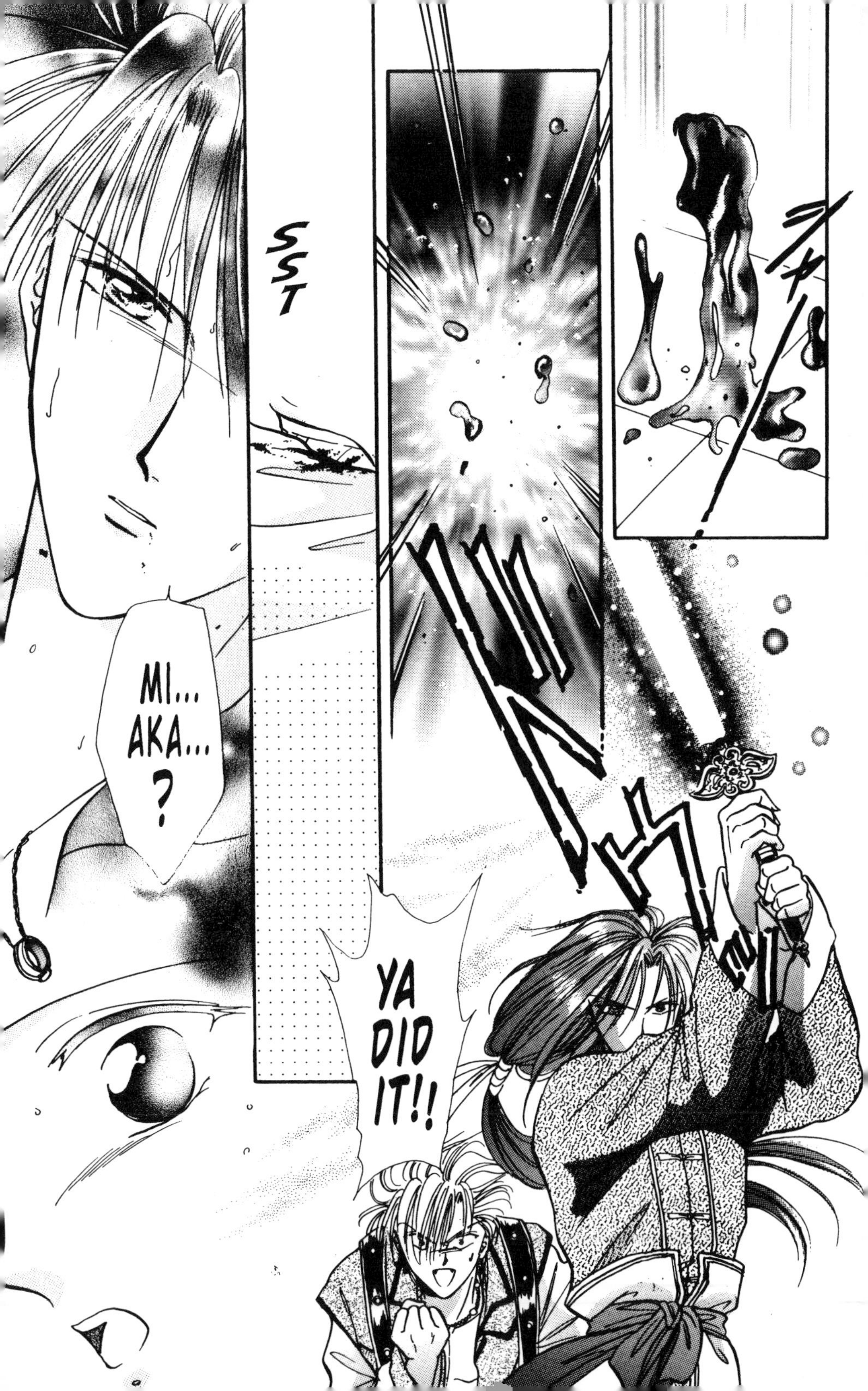
SST
MI... AKA...?
YA DID IT!!

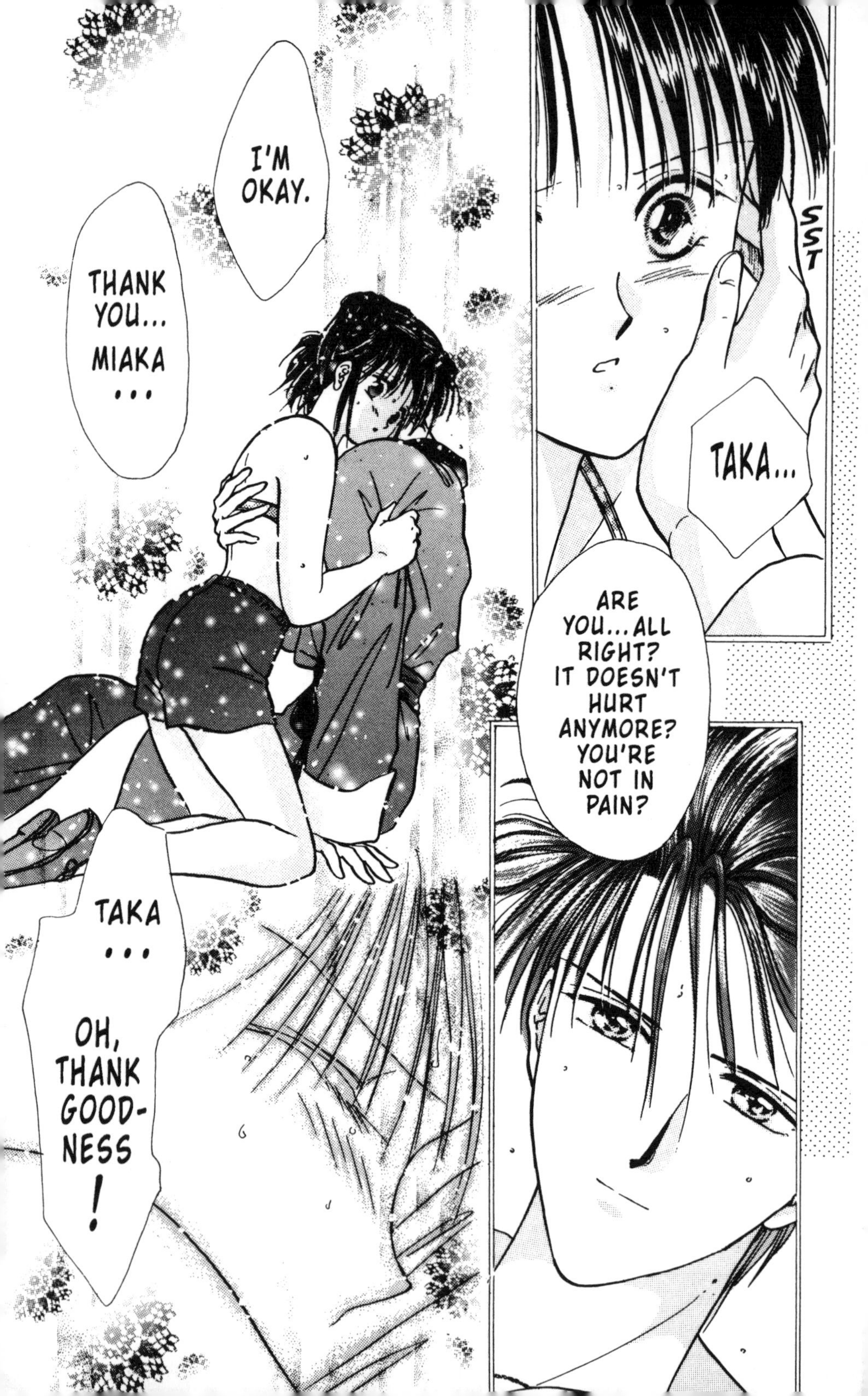
SST
TAKA...
ARE YOU...ALL RIGHT? IT DOESN'T HURT ANYMORE? YOU'RE NOT IN PAIN?
I'M OKAY.
THANK YOU... MIAKA...
TAKA... OH, THANK GOODNESS!

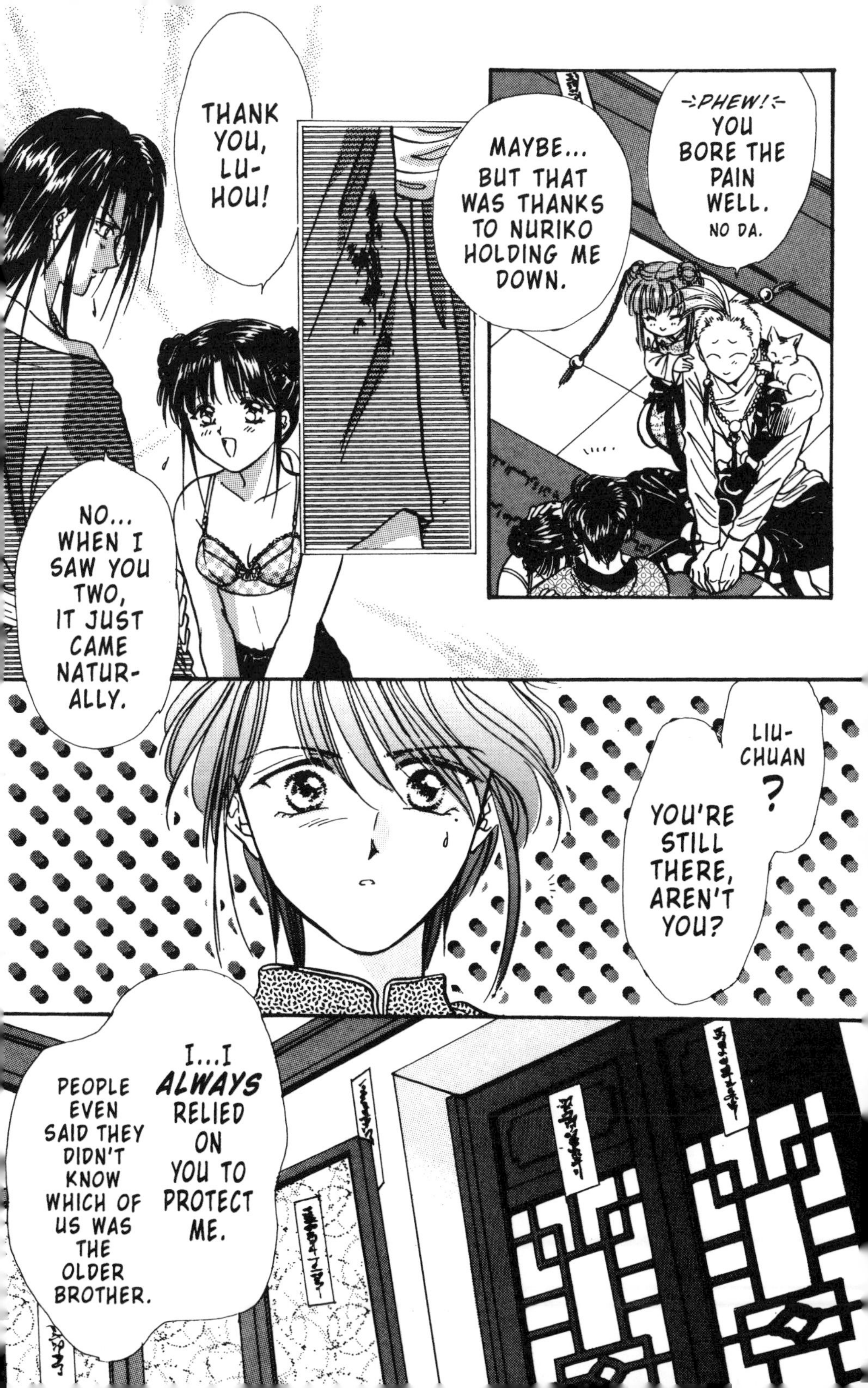

-PHEW!- YOU BORE THE PAIN WELL. NO DA.
MAYBE... BUT THAT WAS THANKS TO NURIKO HOLDING ME DOWN.
THANK YOU, LU-HOU!
NO... WHEN I SAW YOU TWO, IT JUST CAME NATURALLY.
LIU-CHUAN?
YOU'RE STILL THERE, AREN'T YOU?
I...I *ALWAYS* RELIED ON YOU TO PROTECT ME.
PEOPLE EVEN SAID THEY DIDN'T KNOW WHICH OF US WAS THE OLDER BROTHER.

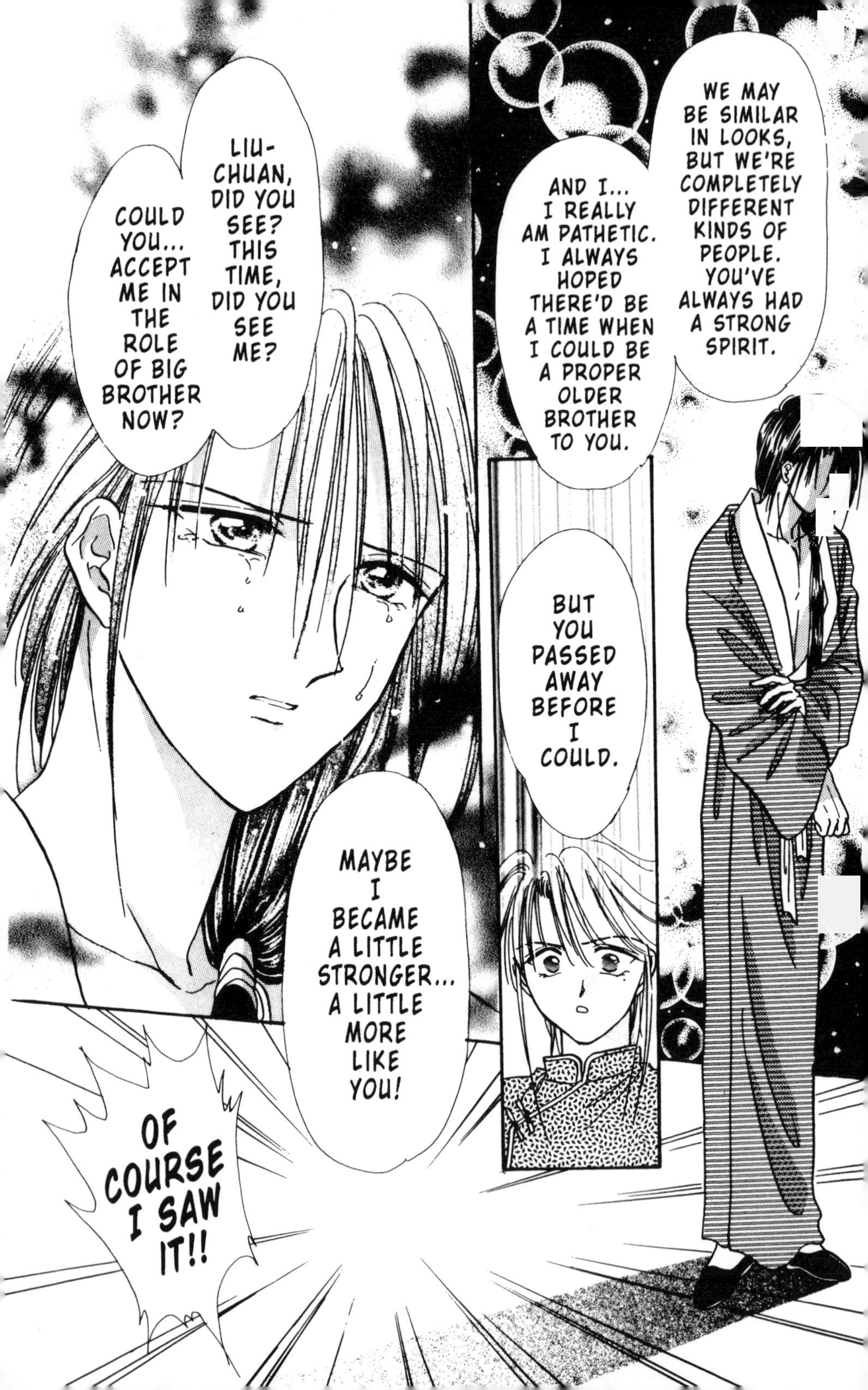
WE MAY BE SIMILAR IN LOOKS, BUT WE'RE COMPLETELY DIFFERENT KINDS OF PEOPLE. YOU'VE ALWAYS HAD A STRONG SPIRIT.
AND I... I REALLY AM PATHETIC. I ALWAYS HOPED THERE'D BE A TIME WHEN I COULD BE A PROPER OLDER BROTHER TO YOU.
BUT YOU PASSED AWAY BEFORE I COULD.
LIU-CHUAN, DID YOU SEE? THIS TIME, DID YOU SEE ME?
COULD YOU... ACCEPT ME IN THE ROLE OF BIG BROTHER NOW?
MAYBE I BECAME A LITTLE STRONGER... A LITTLE MORE LIKE YOU!
OF COURSE I SAW IT!!

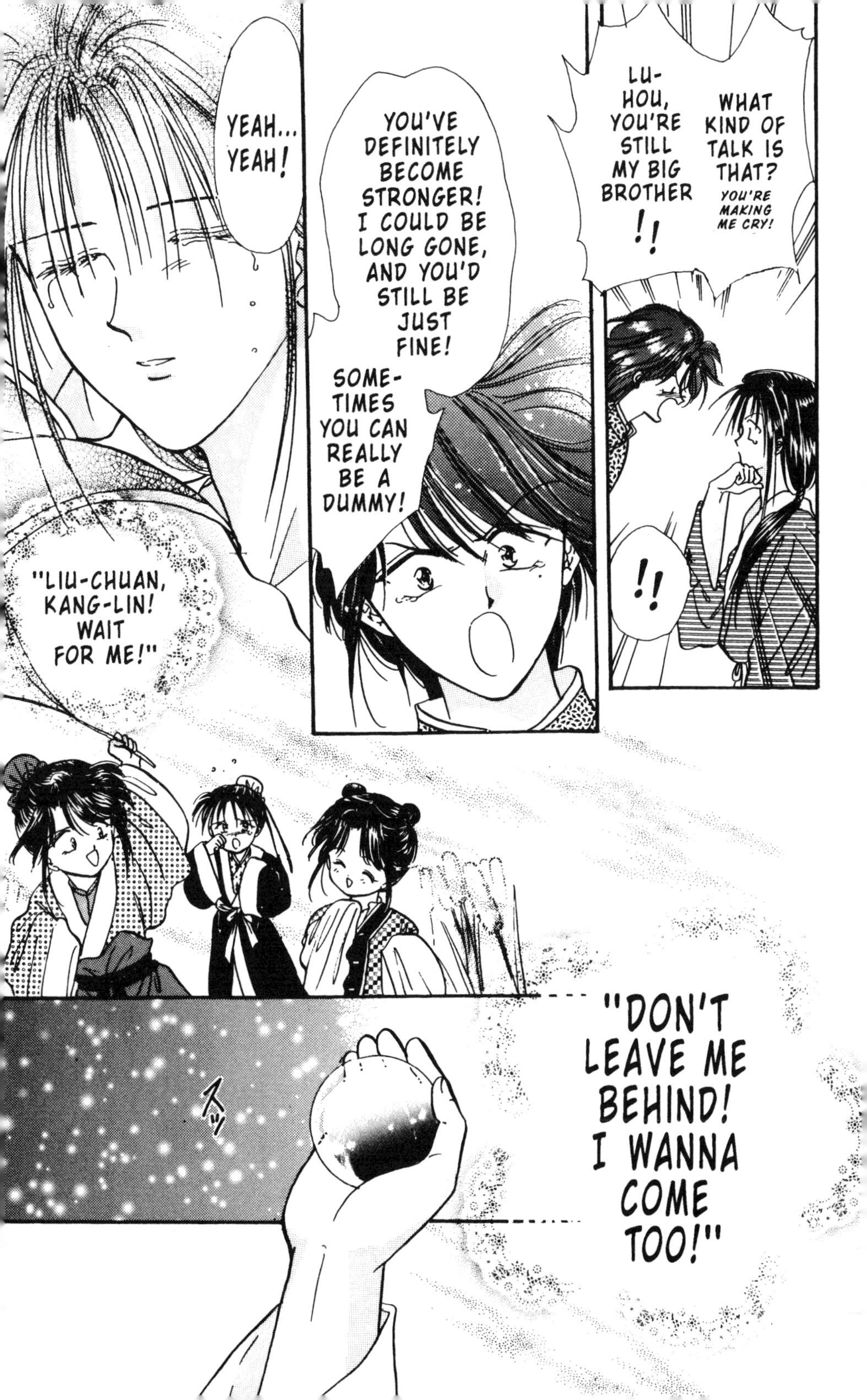
WHAT KIND OF TALK IS THAT? YOU'RE MAKING ME CRY!
LU-HOU, YOU'RE STILL MY BIG BROTHER!!
!!
YOU'VE DEFINITELY BECOME STRONGER! I COULD BE LONG GONE, AND YOU'D STILL BE JUST FINE!
SOMETIMES YOU CAN REALLY BE A DUMMY!
YEAH... YEAH!
"LIU-CHUAN, KANG-LIN! WAIT FOR ME!"
"DON'T LEAVE ME BEHIND! I WANNA COME TOO!"
スッ

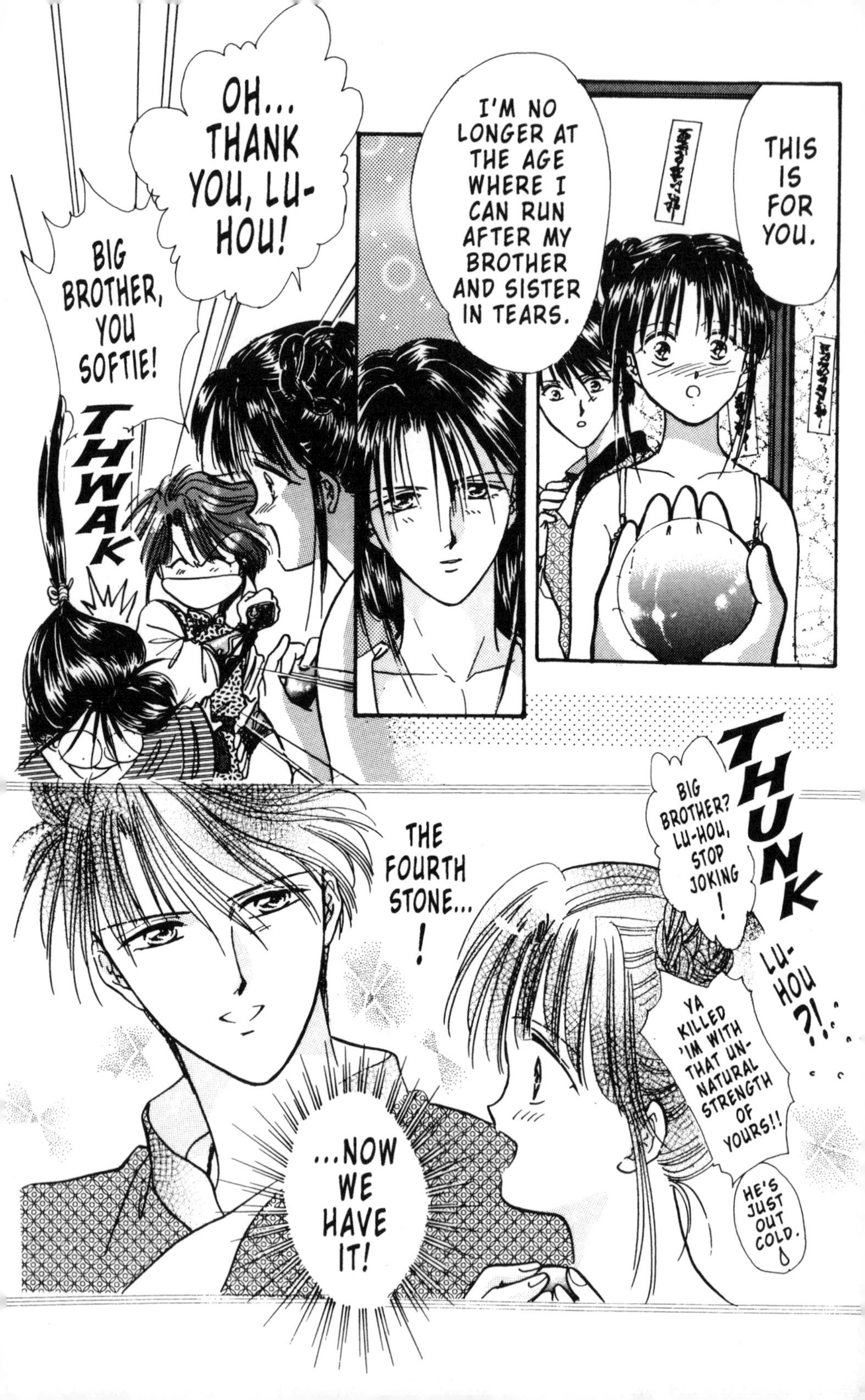
THIS IS FOR YOU.
I'M NO LONGER AT THE AGE WHERE I CAN RUN AFTER MY BROTHER AND SISTER IN TEARS.
OH... THANK YOU, LU-HOU!
BIG BROTHER, YOU SOFTIE!
THWAK
THUNK
BIG BROTHER? LU-HOU, STOP JOKING!
LU-HOU?!
YA KILLED 'IM WITH THAT UN-NATURAL STRENGTH OF YOURS!!
HE'S JUST OUT COLD.
THE FOURTH STONE...!
...NOW WE HAVE IT!

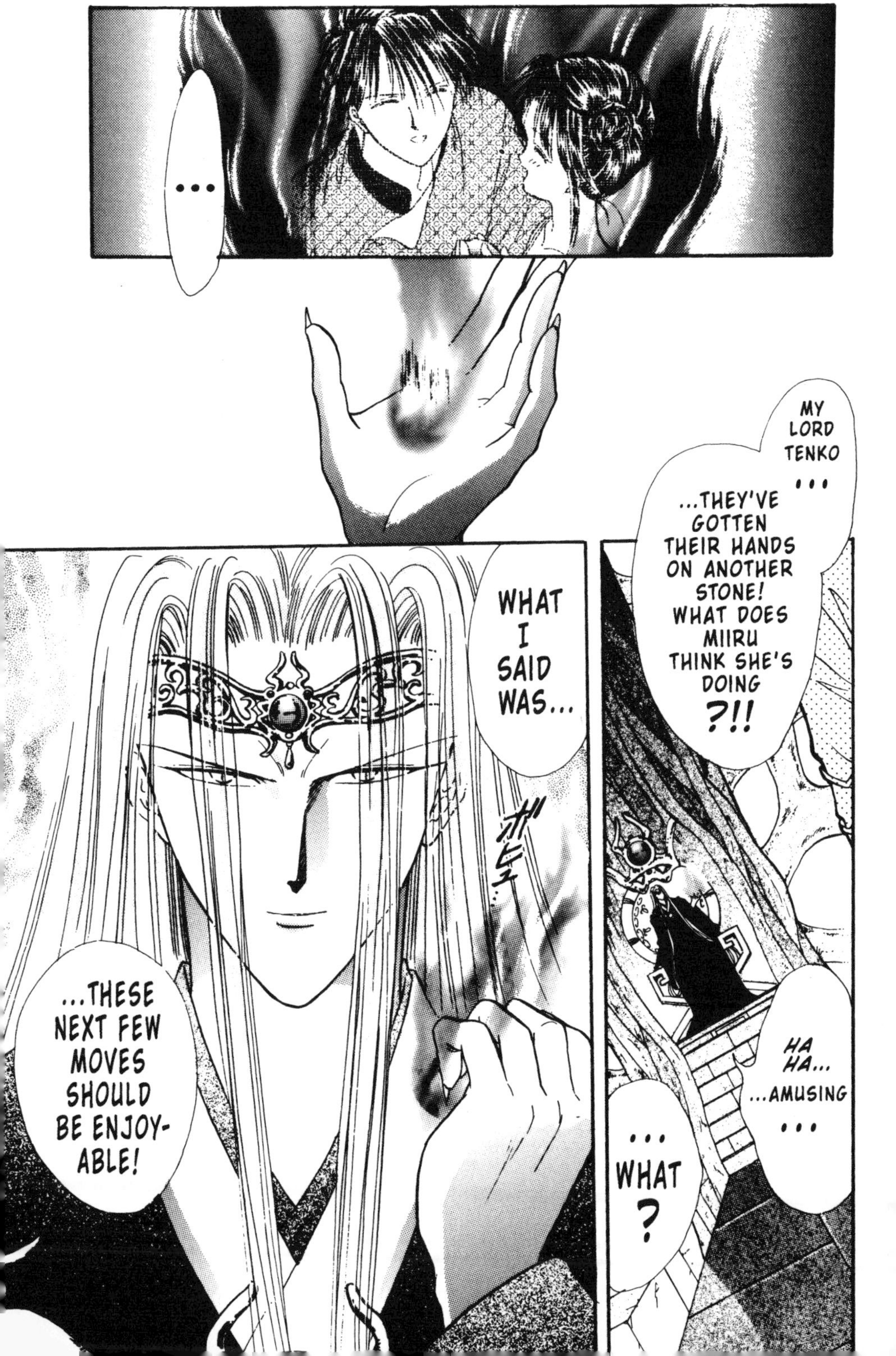
...
MY LORD TENKO ... ...THEY'VE GOTTEN THEIR HANDS ON ANOTHER STONE! WHAT DOES MIIRU THINK SHE'S DOING ?!!
HA HA... ...AMUSING ...
... WHAT ?
WHAT I SAID WAS...
...THESE NEXT FEW MOVES SHOULD BE ENJOY-ABLE!

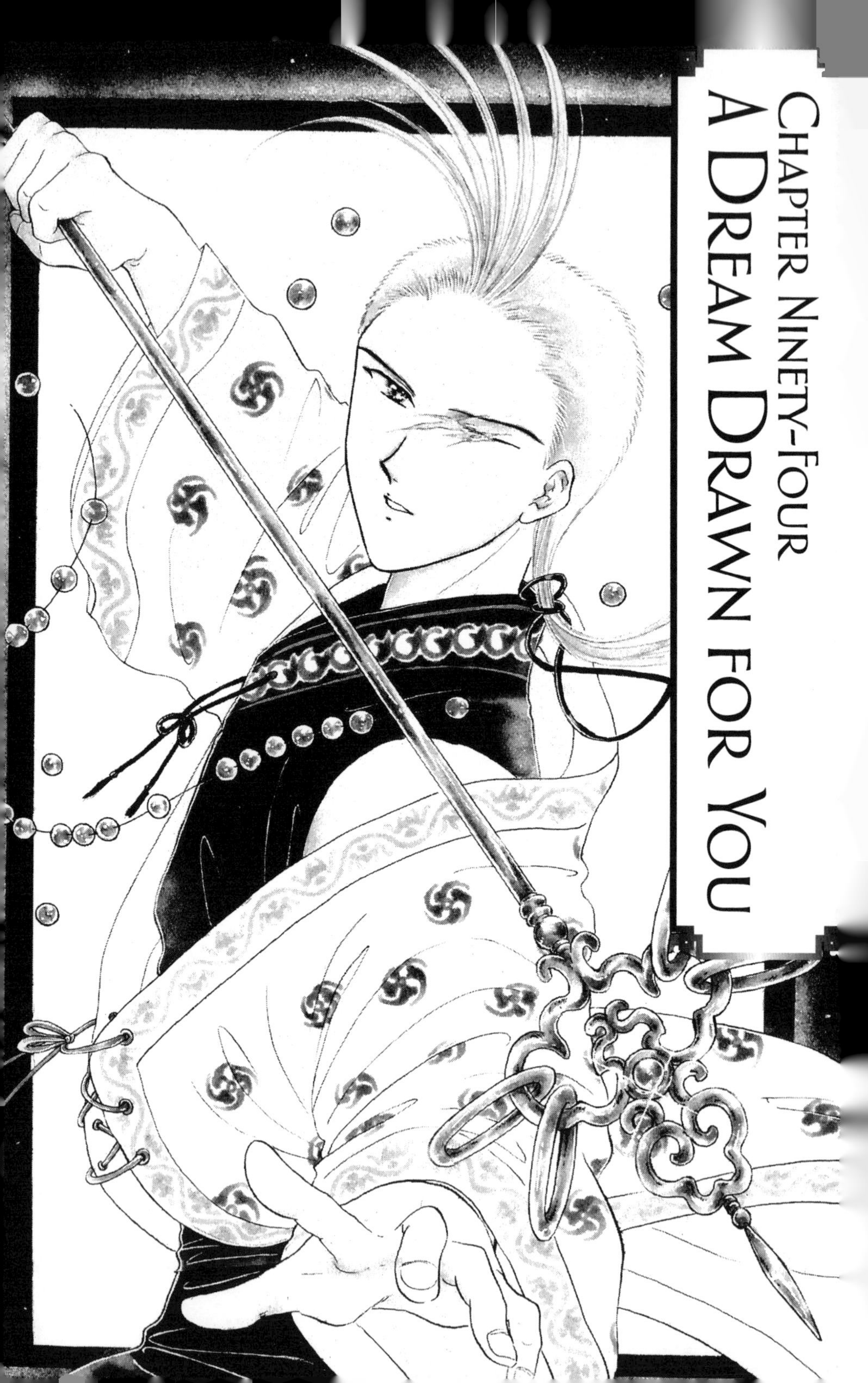
Chapter Ninety-Four
A Dream Drawn for You

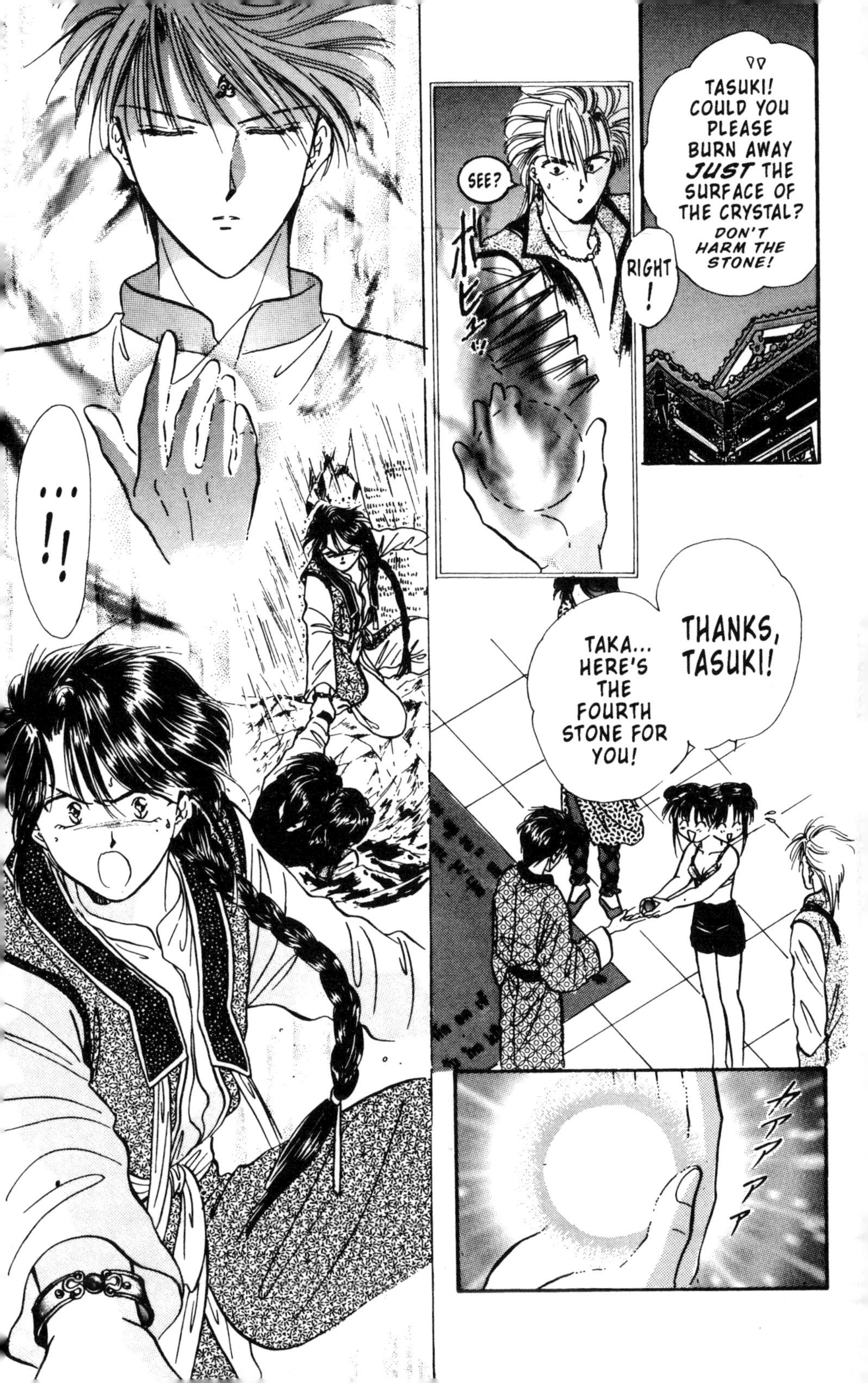
TASUKI! COULD YOU PLEASE BURN AWAY JUST THE SURFACE OF THE CRYSTAL? DON'T HARM THE STONE!
SEE?
RIGHT!
THANKS, TASUKI!
TAKA... HERE'S THE FOURTH STONE FOR YOU!
...!!

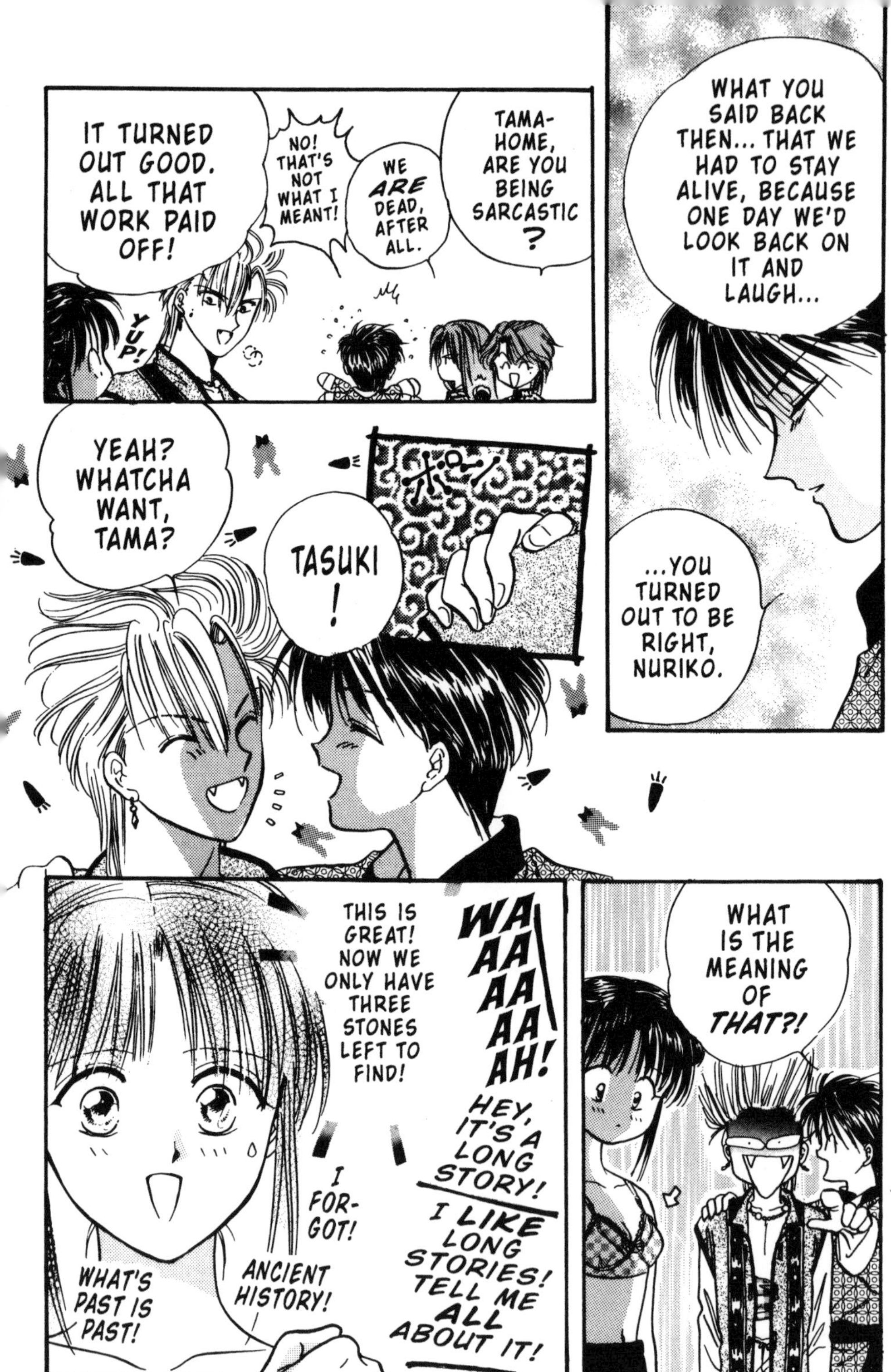
WHAT YOU SAID BACK THEN... THAT WE HAD TO STAY ALIVE, BECAUSE ONE DAY WE'D LOOK BACK ON IT AND LAUGH...
...YOU TURNED OUT TO BE RIGHT, NURIKO.
TAMA-HOME, ARE YOU BEING SARCASTIC?
WE ARE DEAD, AFTER ALL.
NO! THAT'S NOT WHAT I MEANT!
IT TURNED OUT GOOD. ALL THAT WORK PAID OFF!
YUP!
TASUKI!
YEAH? WHATCHA WANT, TAMA?
WHAT IS THE MEANING OF THAT?!
WAAAAAAH!
THIS IS GREAT! NOW WE ONLY HAVE THREE STONES LEFT TO FIND!
HEY, IT'S A LONG STORY!
I LIKE LONG STORIES! TELL ME ALL ABOUT IT!
I FOR-GOT!
ANCIENT HISTORY!
WHAT'S PAST IS PAST!

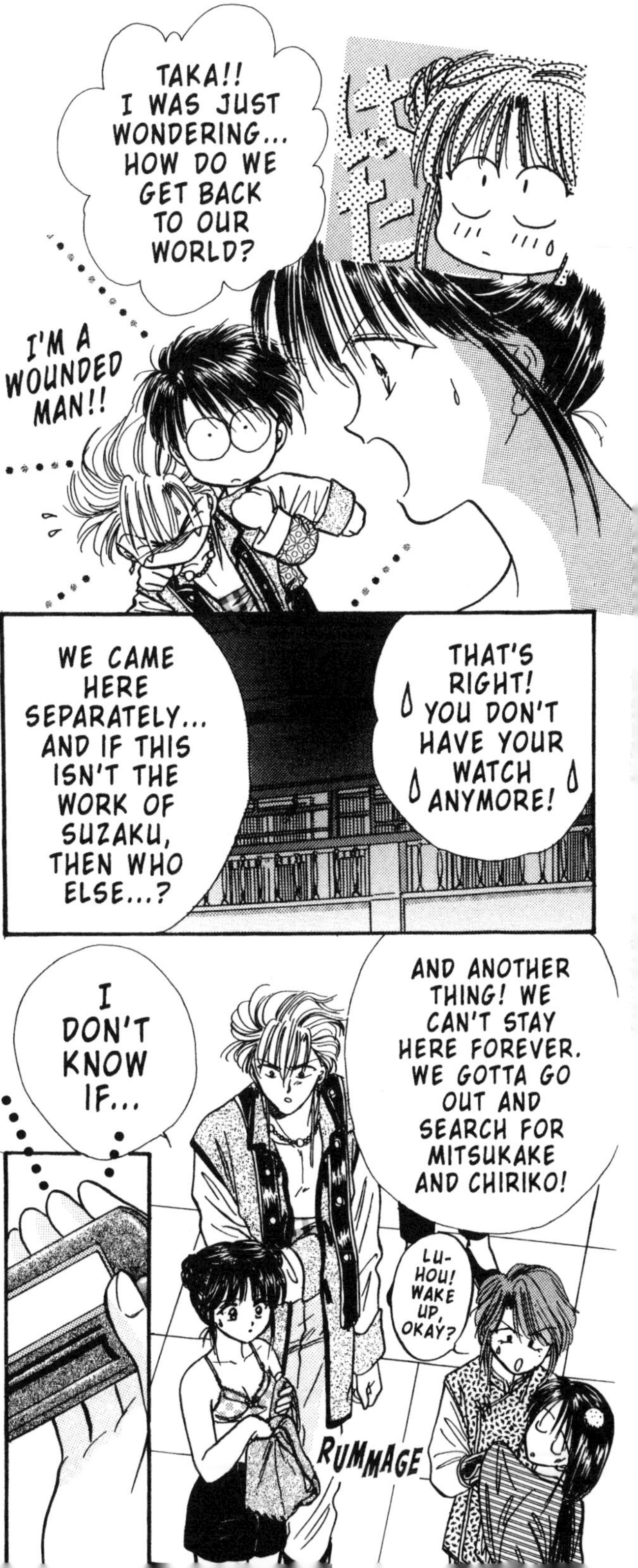
TAKA!! I WAS JUST WONDERING... HOW DO WE GET BACK TO OUR WORLD?
I'M A WOUNDED MAN!!
THAT'S RIGHT! YOU DON'T HAVE YOUR WATCH ANYMORE!
WE CAME HERE SEPARATELY... AND IF THIS ISN'T THE WORK OF SUZAKU, THEN WHO ELSE...?
AND ANOTHER THING! WE CAN'T STAY HERE FOREVER. WE GOTTA GO OUT AND SEARCH FOR MITSUKAKE AND CHIRIKO!
I DON'T KNOW IF...
LU-HOU! WAKE UP, OKAY?
RUMMAGE

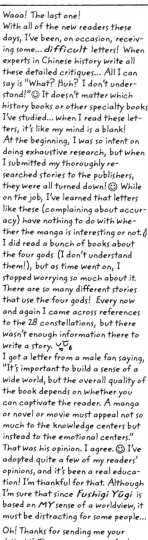

Waaa! The last one!
With all of the new readers these days, I've been, on occasion, receiving some... ***difficult*** letters! When experts in Chinese history write all these detailed critiques... All I can say is "What? Huh? I don't understand!" ☺ It doesn't matter which history books or other specialty books I've studied... when I read these letters, it's like my mind is a blank!
At the beginning, I was so intent on doing exhaustive research, but when I submitted my thoroughly researched stories to the publishers, they were all turned down! ☺ While on the job, I've learned that letters like these (complaining about accuracy) have nothing to do with whether the manga is interesting or not.
I did read a bunch of books about the four gods (I don't understand them!), but as time went on, I stopped worrying so much about it. There are so many different stories that use the four gods! Every now and again I came across references to the 28 constellations, but there wasn't enough information there to write a story.
I got a letter from a male fan saying, "It's important to build a sense of a wide world, but the overall quality of the book depends on whether you can captivate the reader. A manga or novel or movie must appeal not so much to the knowledge centers but instead to the emotional centers." That was his opinion. I agree. ☺ I've adopted quite a few of my readers' opinions, and it's been a real education! I'm thankful for that. Although I'm sure that since *Fushigi Yûgi* is based on *MY* sense of a worldview, it must be distracting for some people...

Oh! Thanks for sending me your dojinshi! They were so much fun! (I wonder if there'll be a lot more coming in...) Hm... Why don't more of you guys send yours in? It's no fair to hog them all to yourselves! ☺ If you think, "The creator will get mad," well... there are a lot of different types of artists out there. And I'm not the type to get angry! I've seen racy books, and I'm fine with them! ☺ So just screw up your courage and send them!! Even just one, send them in! I want to see the-- Ah! I'm going too far! Farewell, everyone! *stomp, stomp, stomp, slam!*

What a weird mangaka! 95. 11. 17.

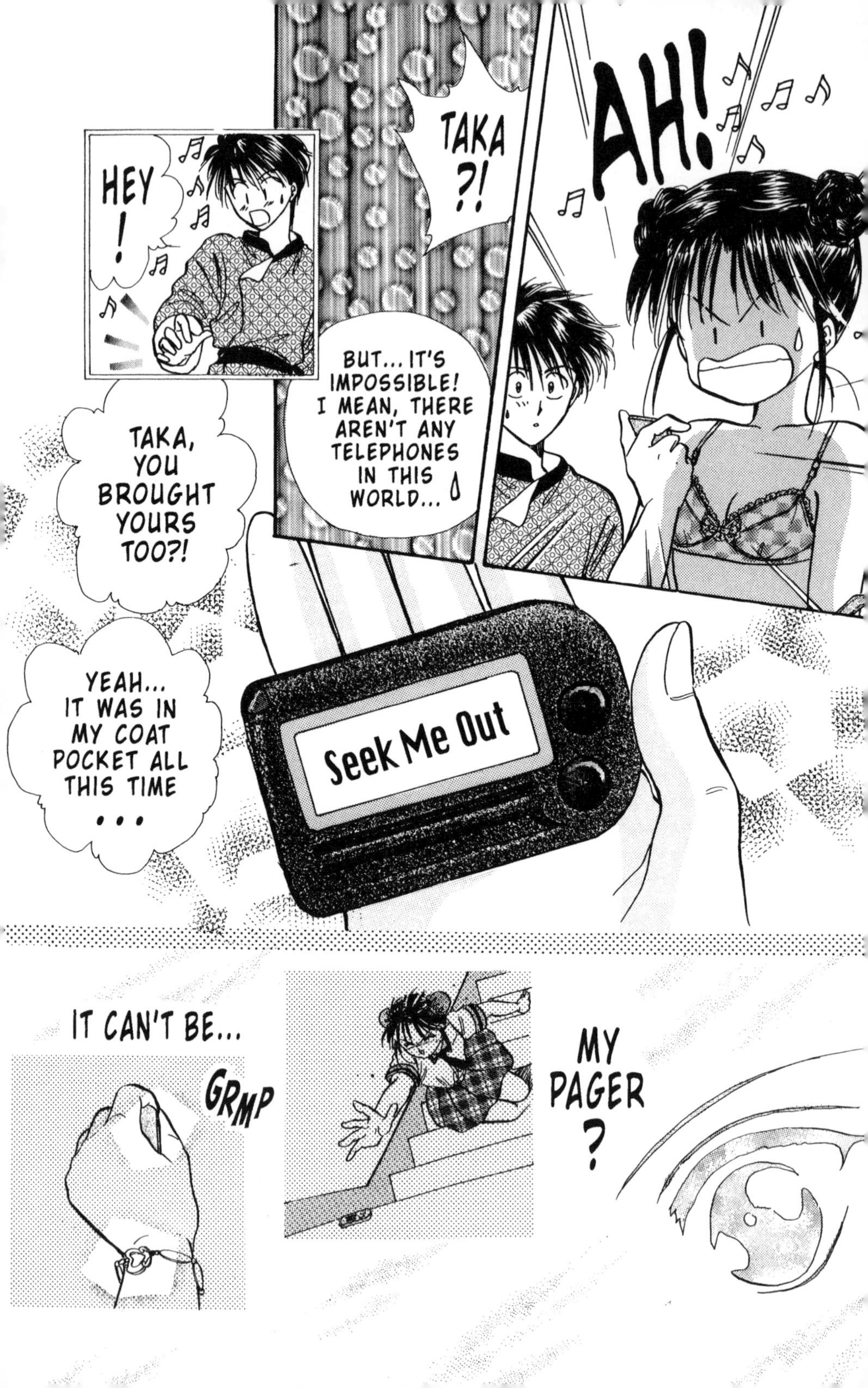
AH!
TAKA ?!
BUT... IT'S IMPOSSIBLE! I MEAN, THERE AREN'T ANY TELEPHONES IN THIS WORLD...
HEY !
Seek Me Out
TAKA, YOU BROUGHT YOURS TOO?!
YEAH... IT WAS IN MY COAT POCKET ALL THIS TIME ...
MY PAGER ?
IT CAN'T BE...
GRMP

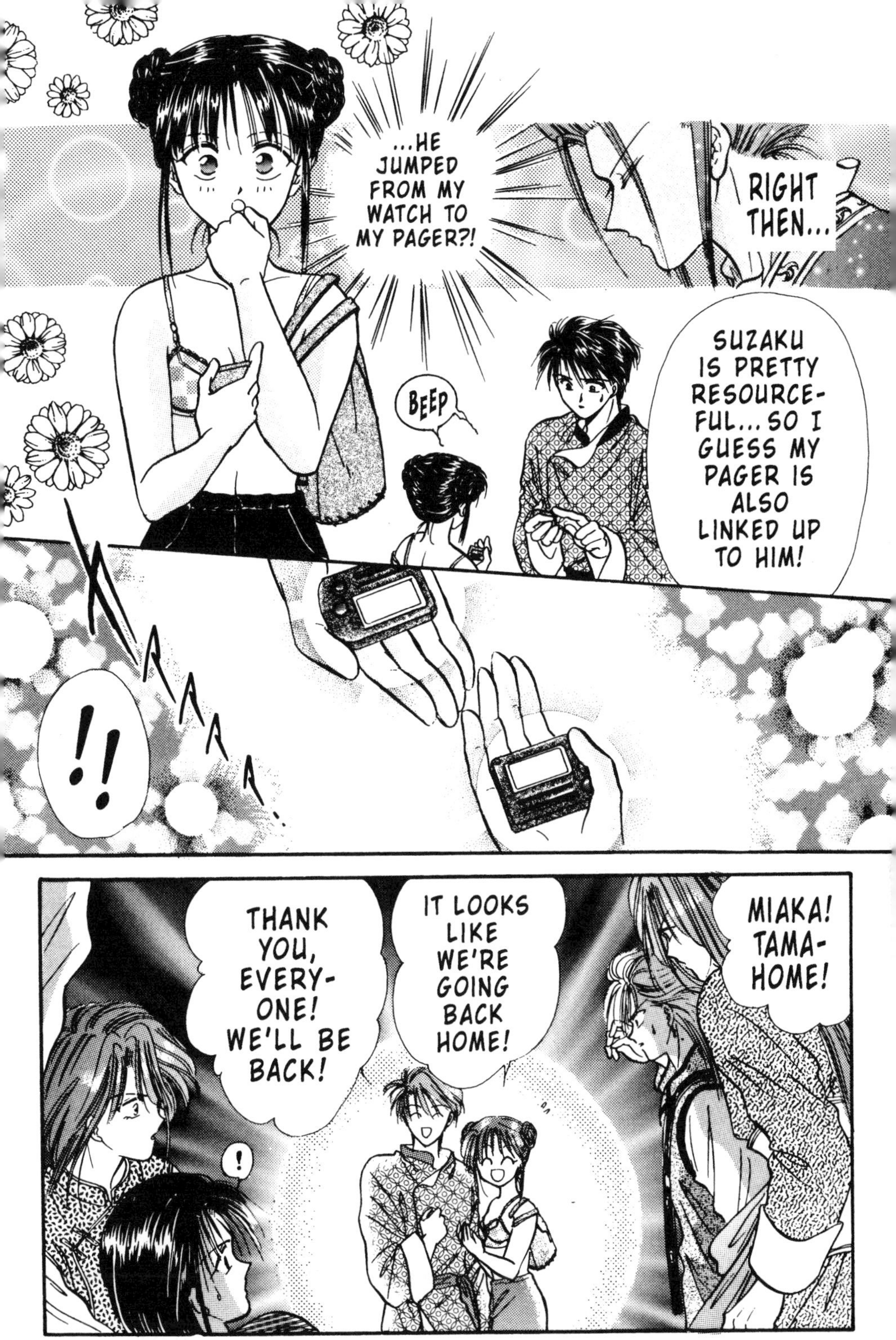
RIGHT THEN...
SUZAKU IS PRETTY RESOURCEFUL... SO I GUESS MY PAGER IS ALSO LINKED UP TO HIM!
BEEP
...HE JUMPED FROM MY WATCH TO MY PAGER?!
!!
MIAKA! TAMAHOME!
IT LOOKS LIKE WE'RE GOING BACK HOME!
THANK YOU, EVERYONE! WE'LL BE BACK!
!

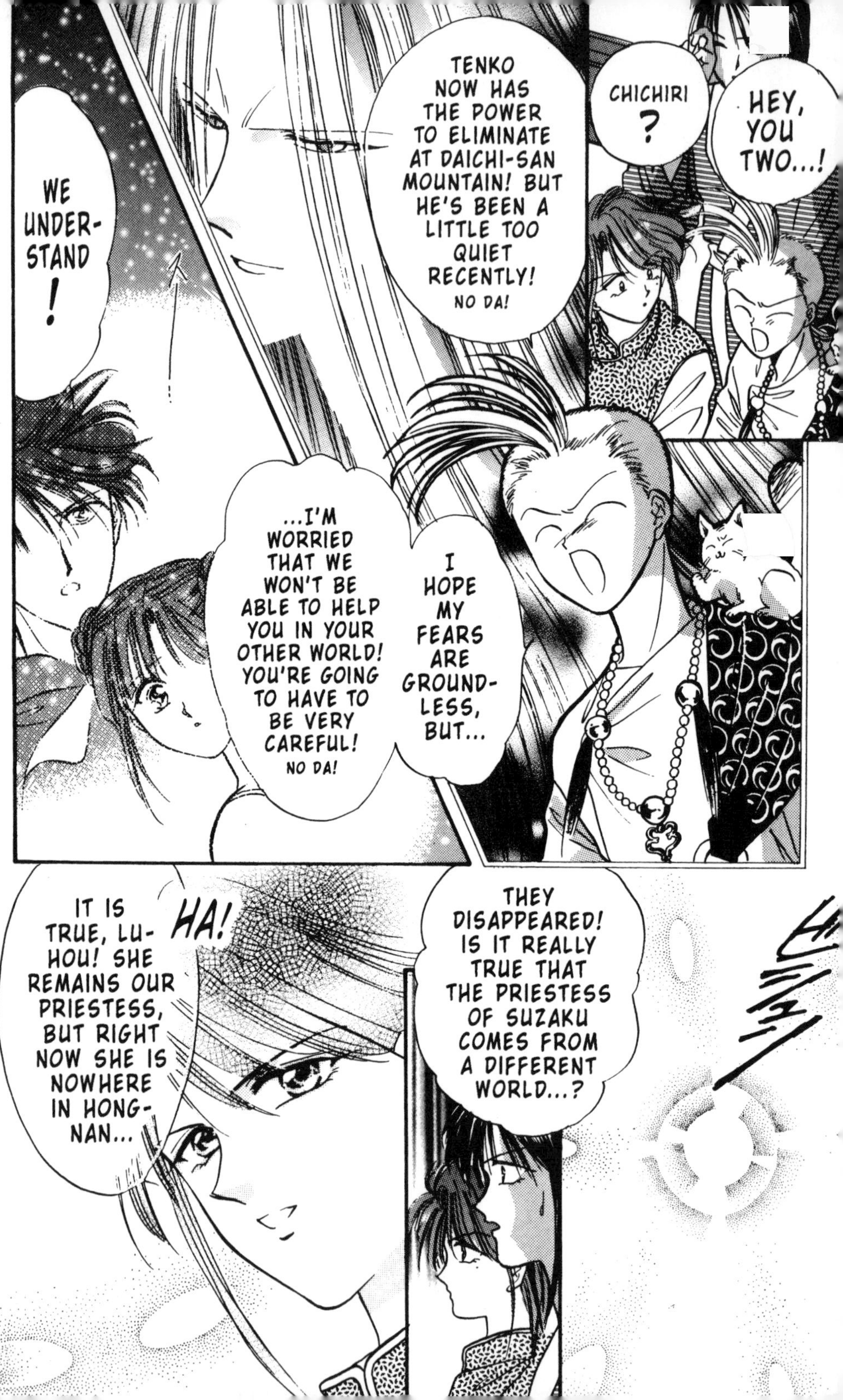
HEY, YOU TWO...!
CHICHIRI ?
TENKO NOW HAS THE POWER TO ELIMINATE AT DAICHI-SAN MOUNTAIN! BUT HE'S BEEN A LITTLE TOO QUIET RECENTLY! NO DA!
I HOPE MY FEARS ARE GROUNDLESS, BUT...
...I'M WORRIED THAT WE WON'T BE ABLE TO HELP YOU IN YOUR OTHER WORLD! YOU'RE GOING TO HAVE TO BE VERY CAREFUL! NO DA!
WE UNDERSTAND !
THEY DISAPPEARED! IS IT REALLY TRUE THAT THE PRIESTESS OF SUZAKU COMES FROM A DIFFERENT WORLD...?
HA!
IT IS TRUE, LU-HOU! SHE REMAINS OUR PRIESTESS, BUT RIGHT NOW SHE IS NOWHERE IN HONG-NAN...

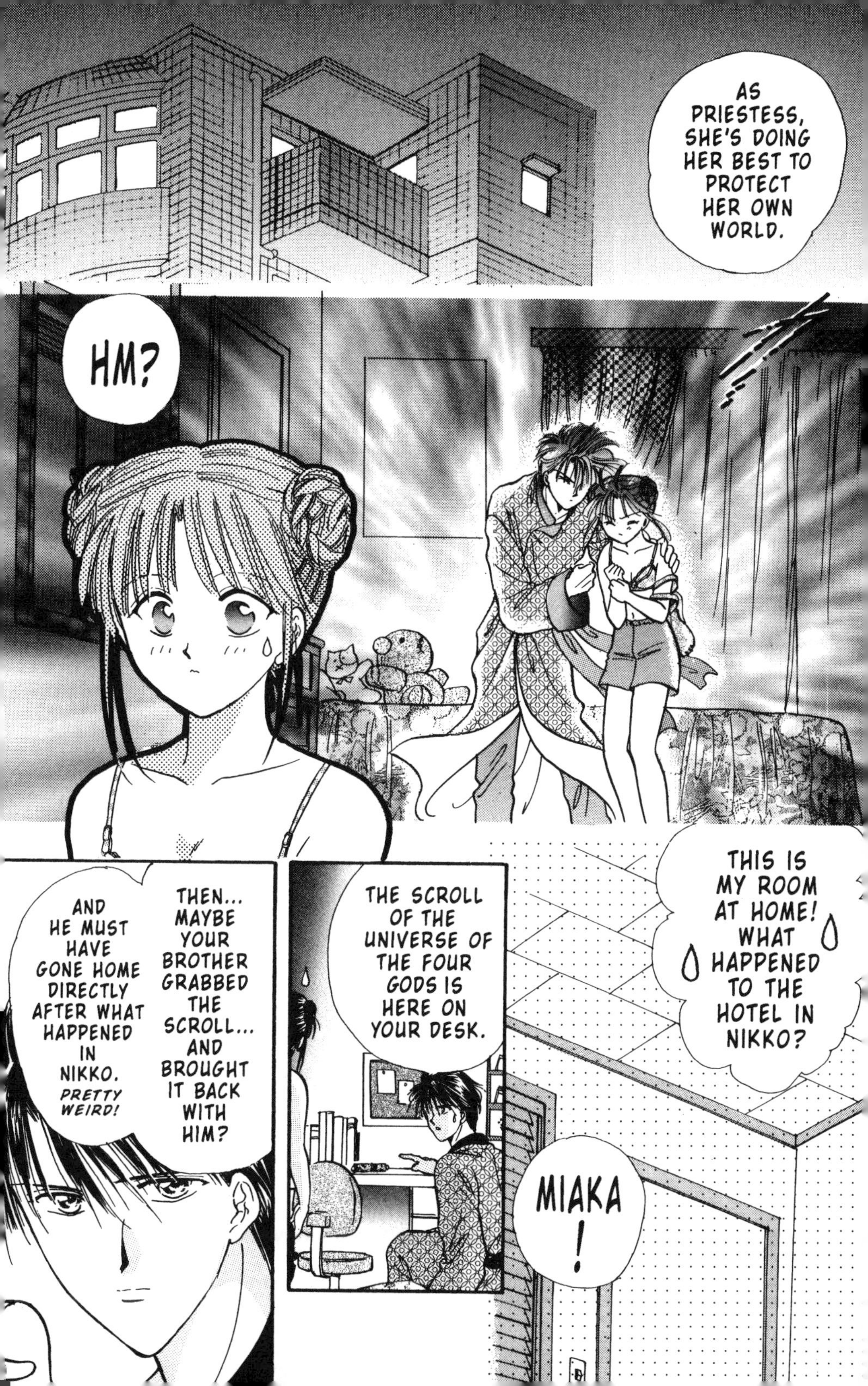
AS PRIESTESS, SHE'S DOING HER BEST TO PROTECT HER OWN WORLD.
HM?
THIS IS MY ROOM AT HOME! WHAT HAPPENED TO THE HOTEL IN NIKKO?
MIAKA!
THE SCROLL OF THE UNIVERSE OF THE FOUR GODS IS HERE ON YOUR DESK.
THEN... MAYBE YOUR BROTHER GRABBED THE SCROLL... AND BROUGHT IT BACK WITH HIM?
AND HE MUST HAVE GONE HOME DIRECTLY AFTER WHAT HAPPENED IN NIKKO. PRETTY WEIRD!

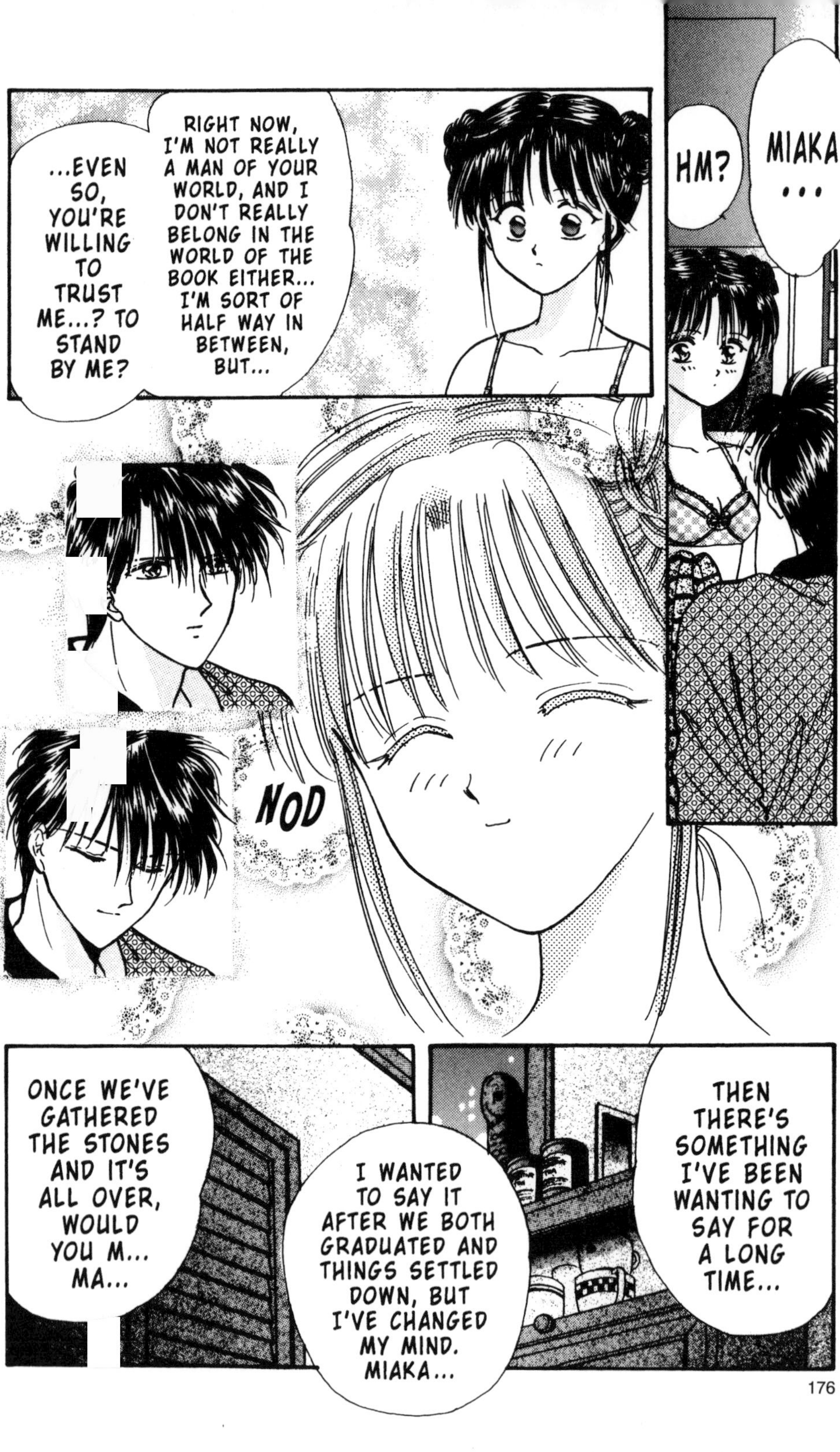
MIAKA ...
HM?
RIGHT NOW, I'M NOT REALLY A MAN OF YOUR WORLD, AND I DON'T REALLY BELONG IN THE WORLD OF THE BOOK EITHER... I'M SORT OF HALF WAY IN BETWEEN, BUT...
...EVEN SO, YOU'RE WILLING TO TRUST ME...? TO STAND BY ME?
NOD
THEN THERE'S SOMETHING I'VE BEEN WANTING TO SAY FOR A LONG TIME...
I WANTED TO SAY IT AFTER WE BOTH GRADUATED AND THINGS SETTLED DOWN, BUT I'VE CHANGED MY MIND. MIAKA...
ONCE WE'VE GATHERED THE STONES AND IT'S ALL OVER, WOULD YOU M... MA...

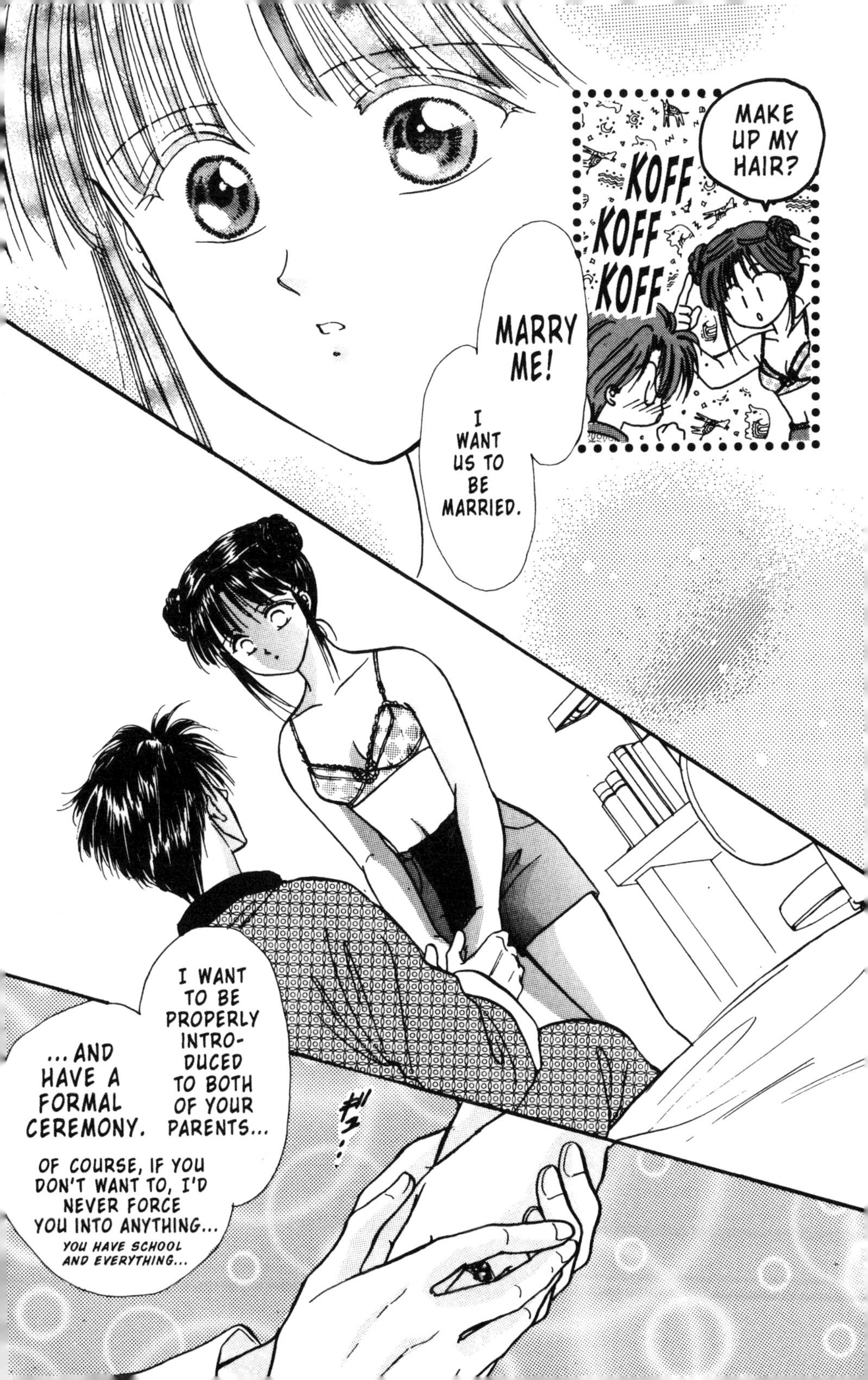
MARRY ME!
I WANT US TO BE MARRIED.
MAKE UP MY HAIR?
KOFF KOFF KOFF
I WANT TO BE PROPERLY INTRO-DUCED TO BOTH OF YOUR PARENTS...
...AND HAVE A FORMAL CEREMONY.
OF COURSE, IF YOU DON'T WANT TO, I'D NEVER FORCE YOU INTO ANYTHING...
YOU HAVE SCHOOL AND EVERYTHING...

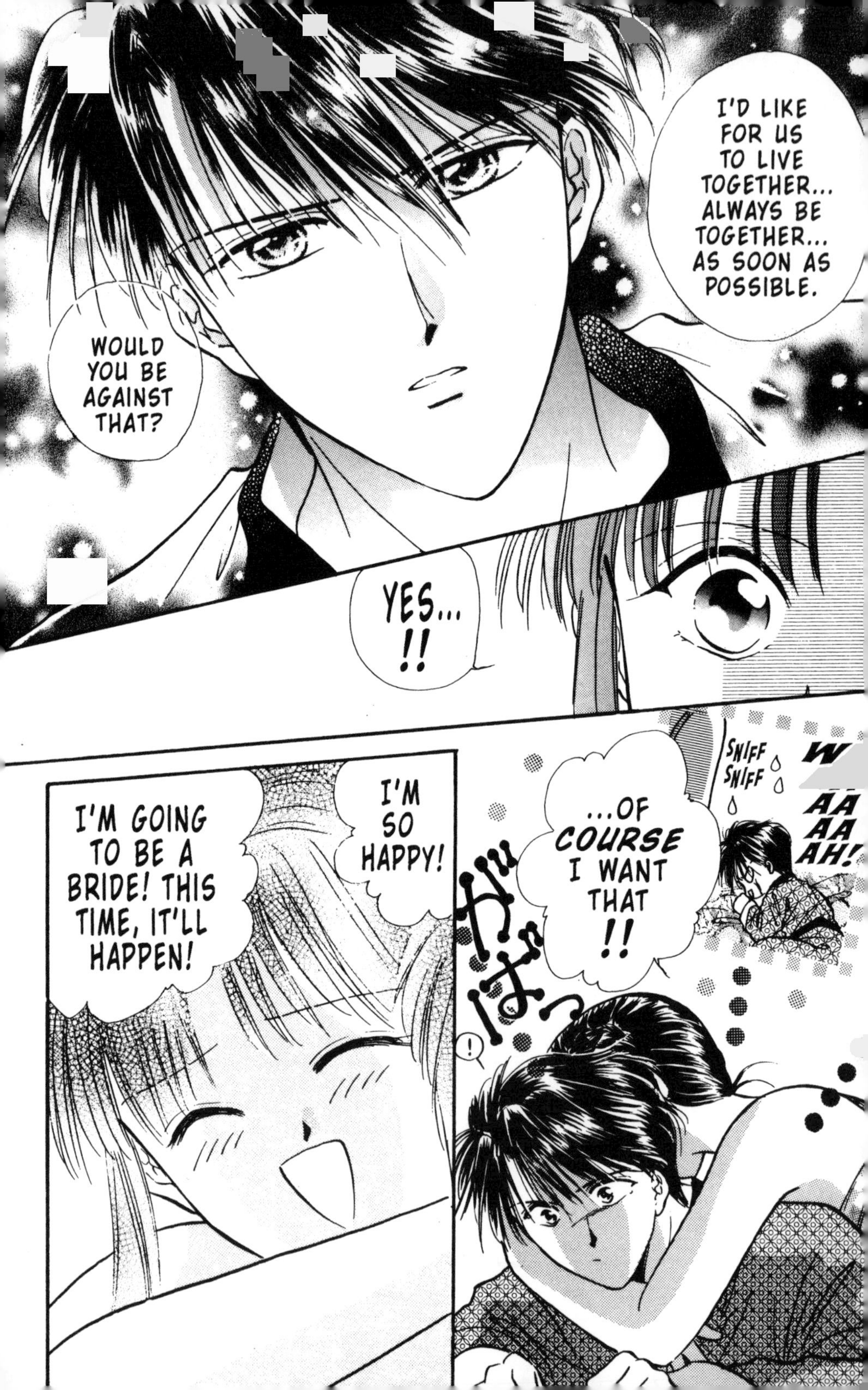
I'D LIKE FOR US TO LIVE TOGETHER... ALWAYS BE TOGETHER... AS SOON AS POSSIBLE.
WOULD YOU BE AGAINST THAT?
YES... !!
WAAAAAH!
SNIFF SNIFF
...OF COURSE I WANT THAT !!
がばっ
!
I'M SO HAPPY!
I'M GOING TO BE A BRIDE! THIS TIME, IT'LL HAPPEN!

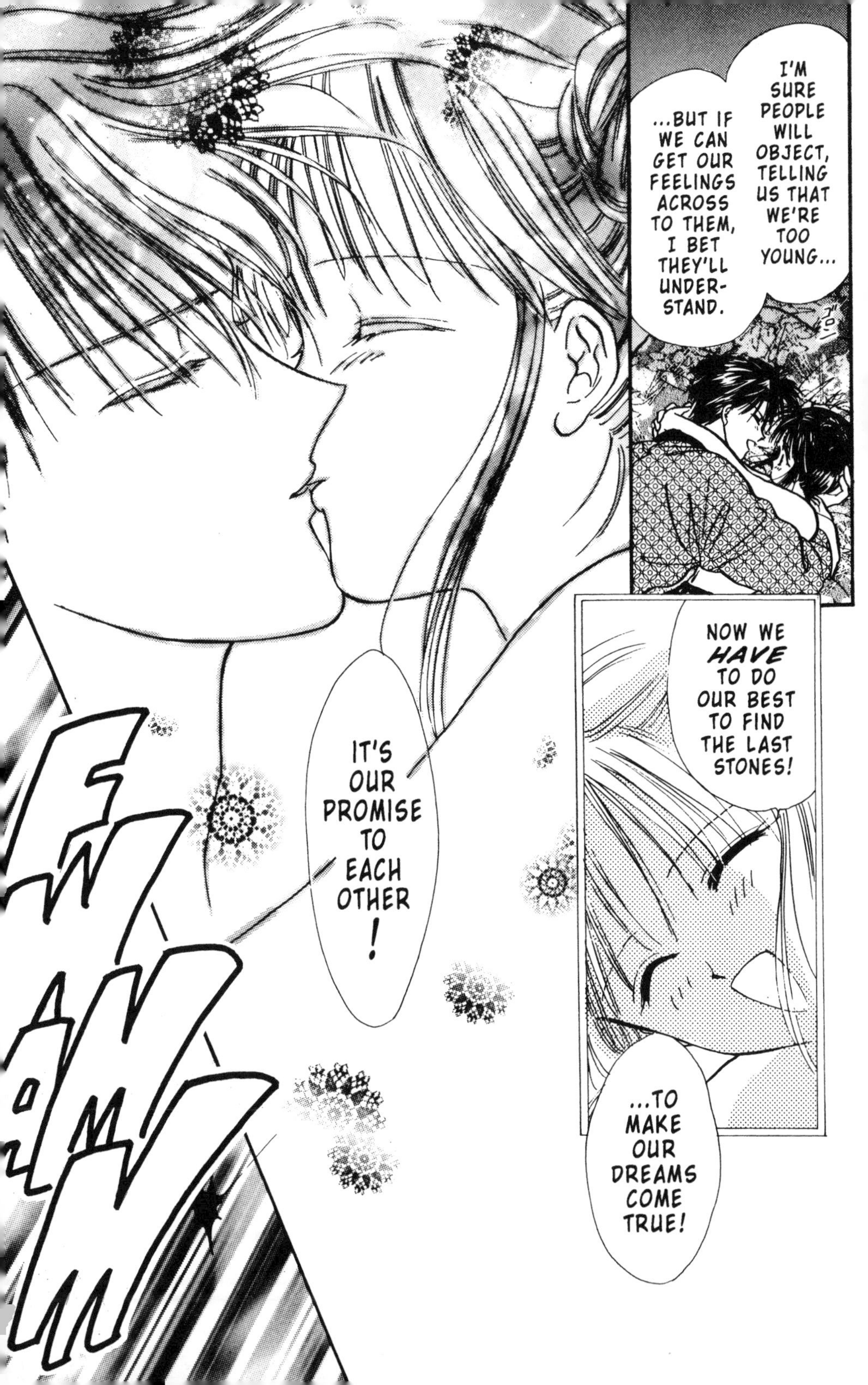
I'M SURE PEOPLE WILL OBJECT, TELLING US THAT WE'RE TOO YOUNG...
...BUT IF WE CAN GET OUR FEELINGS ACROSS TO THEM, I BET THEY'LL UNDER-STAND.
NOW WE *HAVE* TO DO OUR BEST TO FIND THE LAST STONES!
...TO MAKE OUR DREAMS COME TRUE!
IT'S OUR PROMISE TO EACH OTHER!

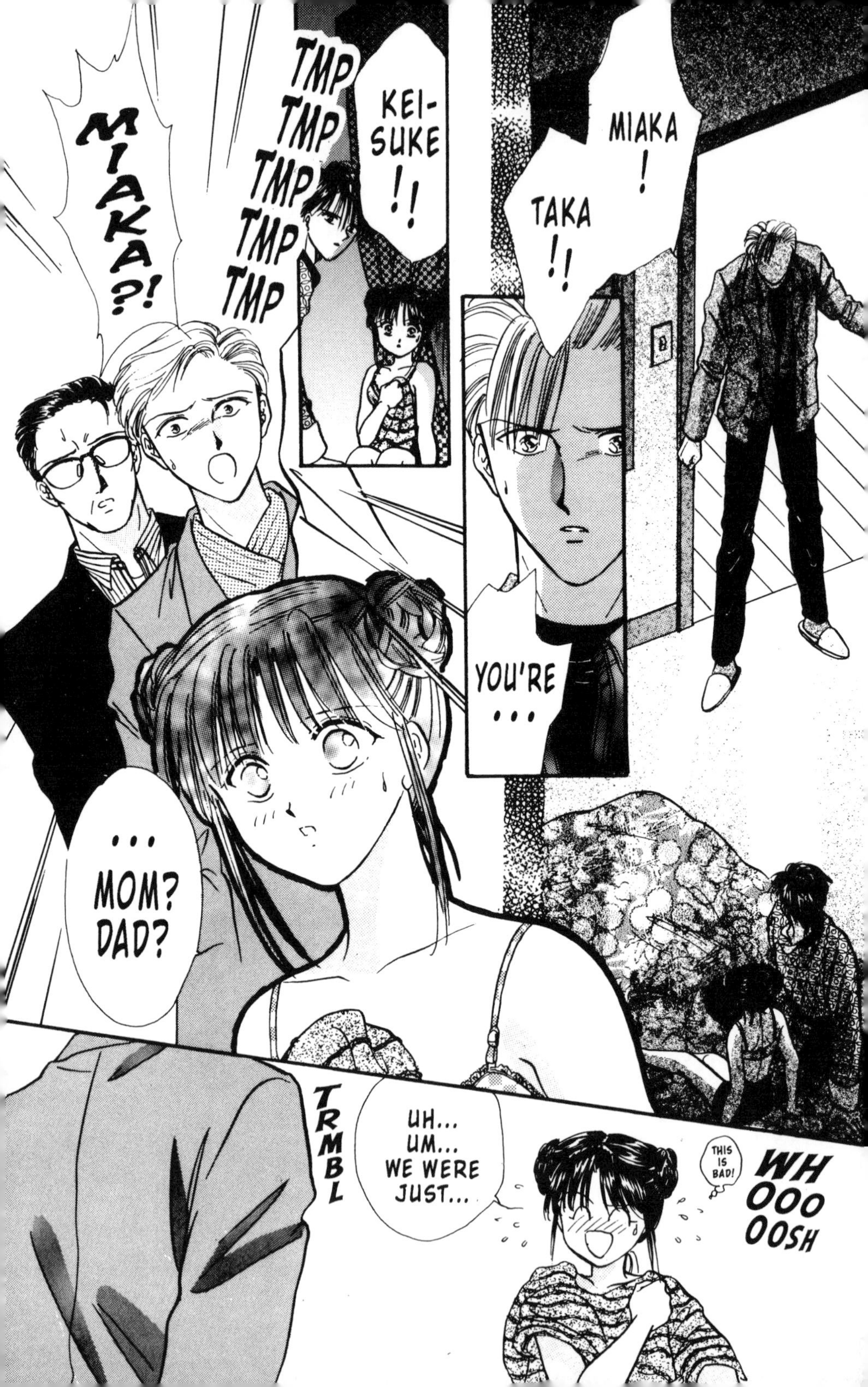
MIAKA!
TAKA!!
KEI-SUKE!!
TMP TMP TMP TMP TMP
MIAKA?!
YOU'RE...
...MOM? DAD?
WHOOOOOSH
THIS IS BAD!
UH... UM... WE WERE JUST...
TRMBL

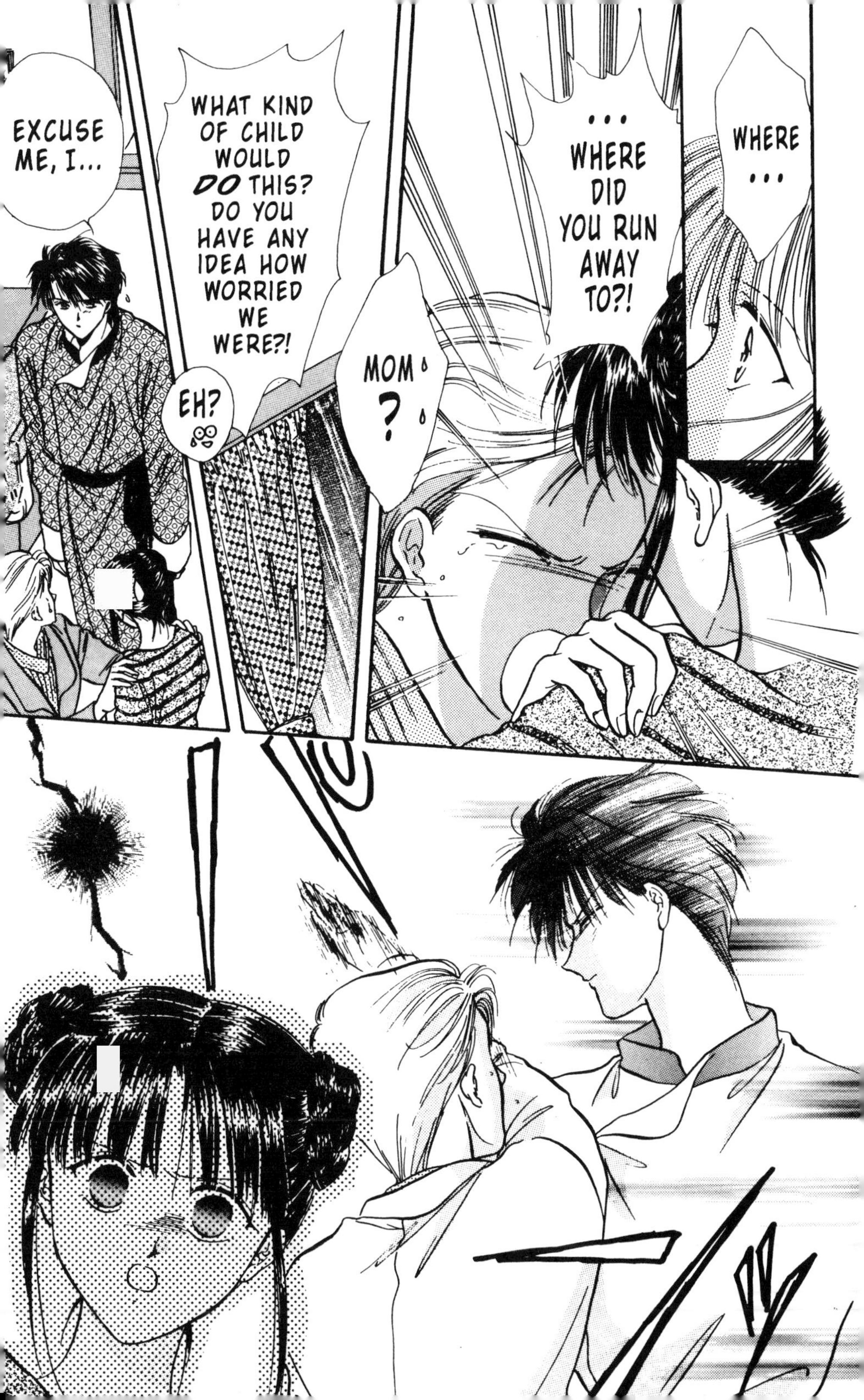
WHERE ...
... WHERE DID YOU RUN AWAY TO?!
MOM ?
WHAT KIND OF CHILD WOULD DO THIS? DO YOU HAVE ANY IDEA HOW WORRIED WE WERE?!
EXCUSE ME, I...
EH?

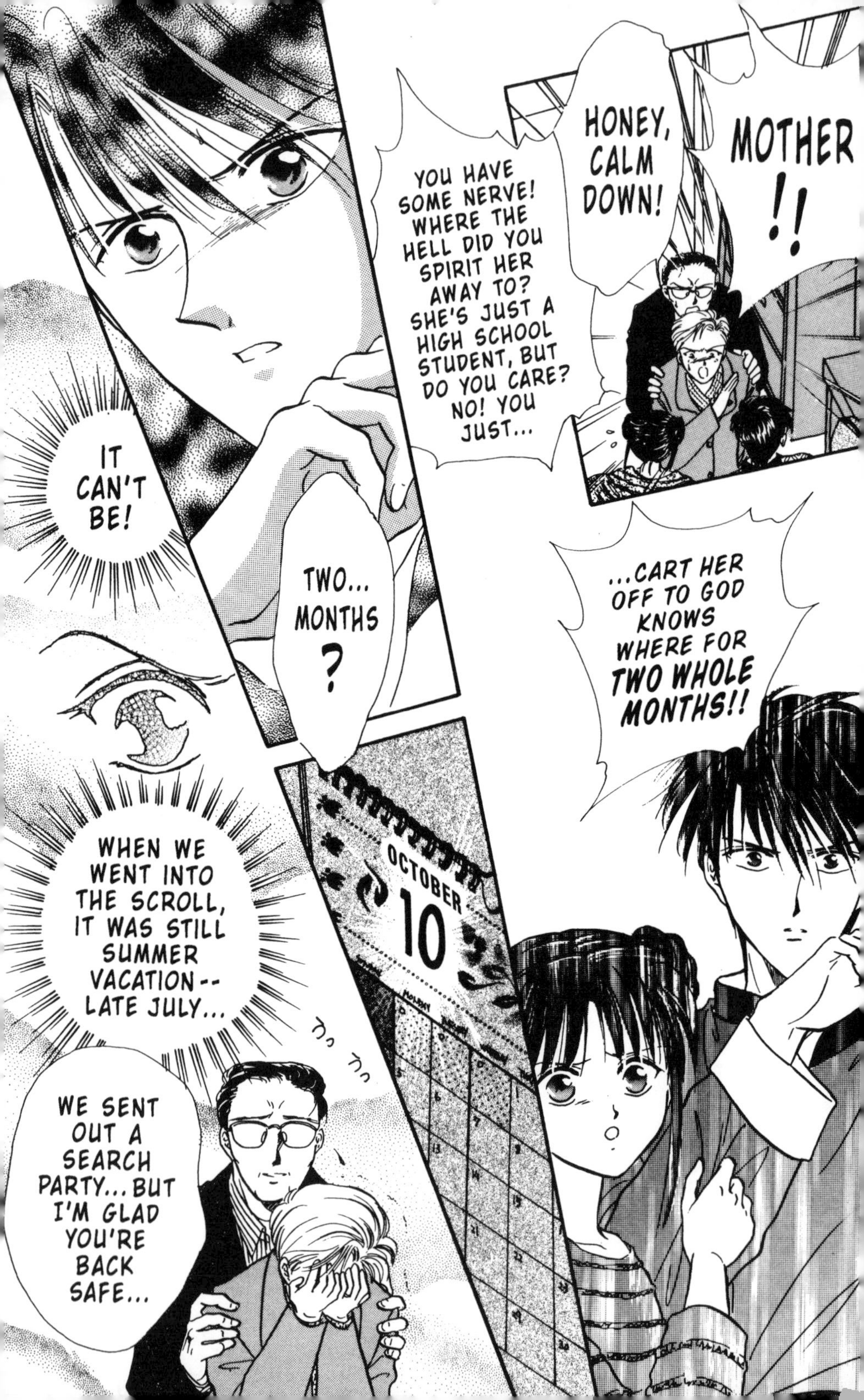
MOTHER!!
HONEY, CALM DOWN!
YOU HAVE SOME NERVE! WHERE THE HELL DID YOU SPIRIT HER AWAY TO? SHE'S JUST A HIGH SCHOOL STUDENT, BUT DO YOU CARE? NO! YOU JUST...
...CART HER OFF TO GOD KNOWS WHERE FOR TWO WHOLE MONTHS!!
TWO... MONTHS?
IT CAN'T BE!
OCTOBER
10
WHEN WE WENT INTO THE SCROLL, IT WAS STILL SUMMER VACATION--LATE JULY...
WE SENT OUT A SEARCH PARTY... BUT I'M GLAD YOU'RE BACK SAFE...

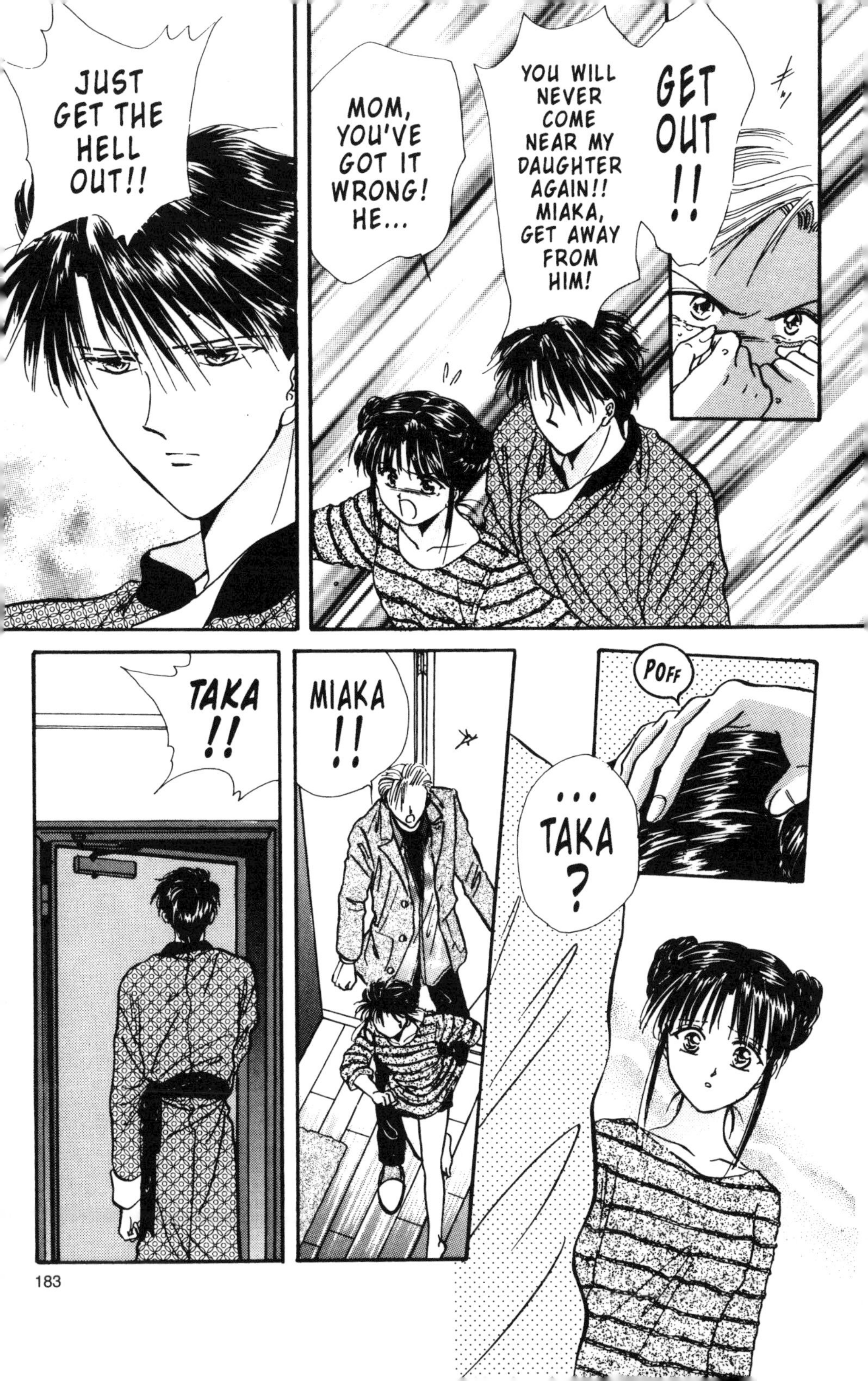
GET OUT!!
YOU WILL NEVER COME NEAR MY DAUGHTER AGAIN!! MIAKA, GET AWAY FROM HIM!
MOM, YOU'VE GOT IT WRONG! HE...
JUST GET THE HELL OUT!!
POFF
...TAKA?
MIAKA!!
TAKA!!

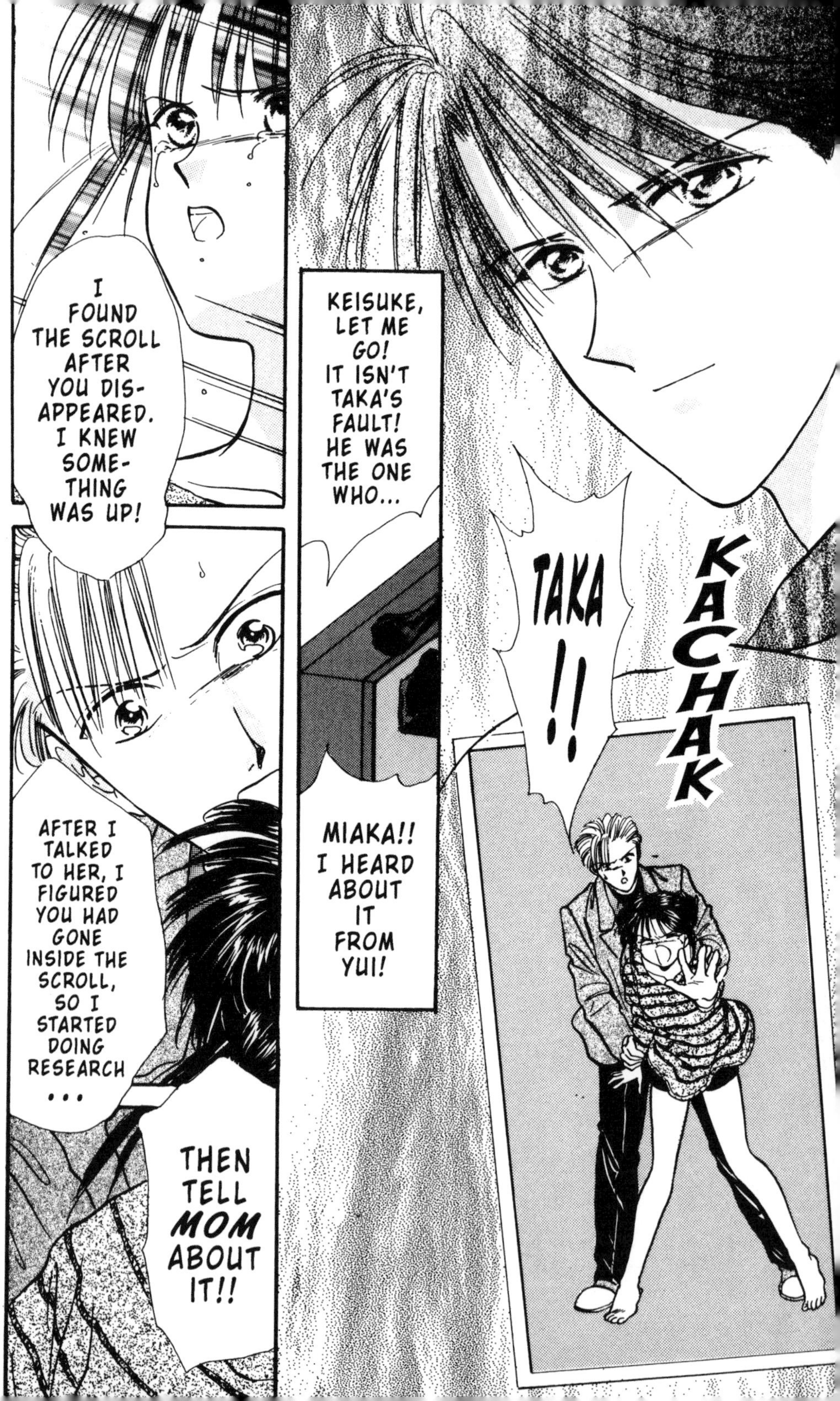

TAKA!!
KACHAK
KEISUKE, LET ME GO! IT ISN'T TAKA'S FAULT! HE WAS THE ONE WHO...
MIAKA!! I HEARD ABOUT IT FROM YUI!
I FOUND THE SCROLL AFTER YOU DIS-APPEARED. I KNEW SOME-THING WAS UP!
AFTER I TALKED TO HER, I FIGURED YOU HAD GONE INSIDE THE SCROLL, SO I STARTED DOING RESEARCH...
THEN TELL MOM ABOUT IT!!

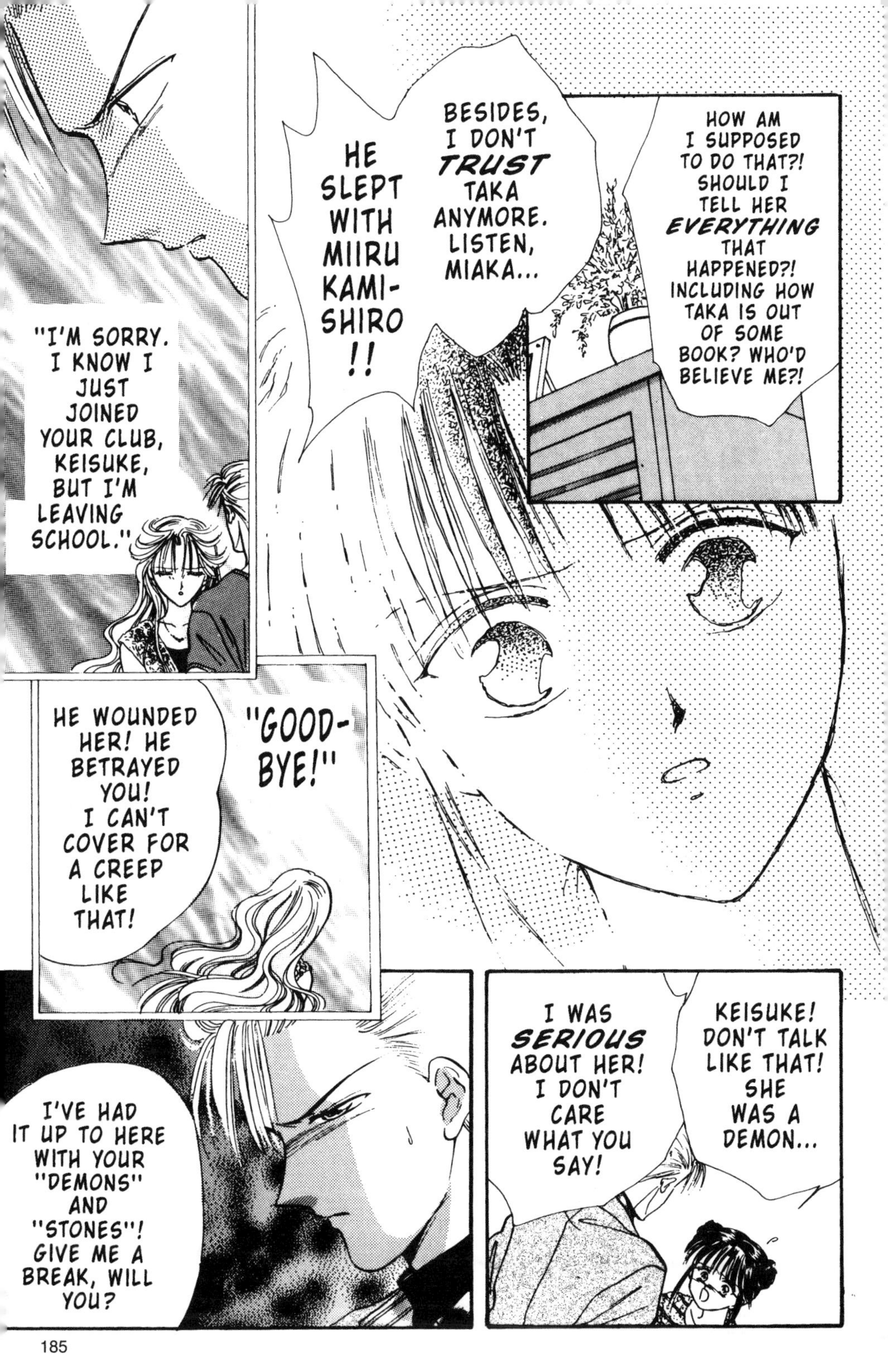

HOW AM I SUPPOSED TO DO THAT?! SHOULD I TELL HER *EVERYTHING* THAT HAPPENED?! INCLUDING HOW TAKA IS OUT OF SOME BOOK? WHO'D BELIEVE ME?!
BESIDES, I DON'T *TRUST* TAKA ANYMORE. LISTEN, MIAKA...
HE SLEPT WITH MIIRU KAMI-SHIRO!!
"I'M SORRY. I KNOW I JUST JOINED YOUR CLUB, KEISUKE, BUT I'M LEAVING SCHOOL."
"GOOD-BYE!"
HE WOUNDED HER! HE BETRAYED YOU! I CAN'T COVER FOR A CREEP LIKE THAT!
KEISUKE! DON'T TALK LIKE THAT! SHE WAS A DEMON...
I WAS *SERIOUS* ABOUT HER! I DON'T CARE WHAT YOU SAY!
I'VE HAD IT UP TO HERE WITH YOUR "DEMONS" AND "STONES"! GIVE ME A BREAK, WILL YOU?

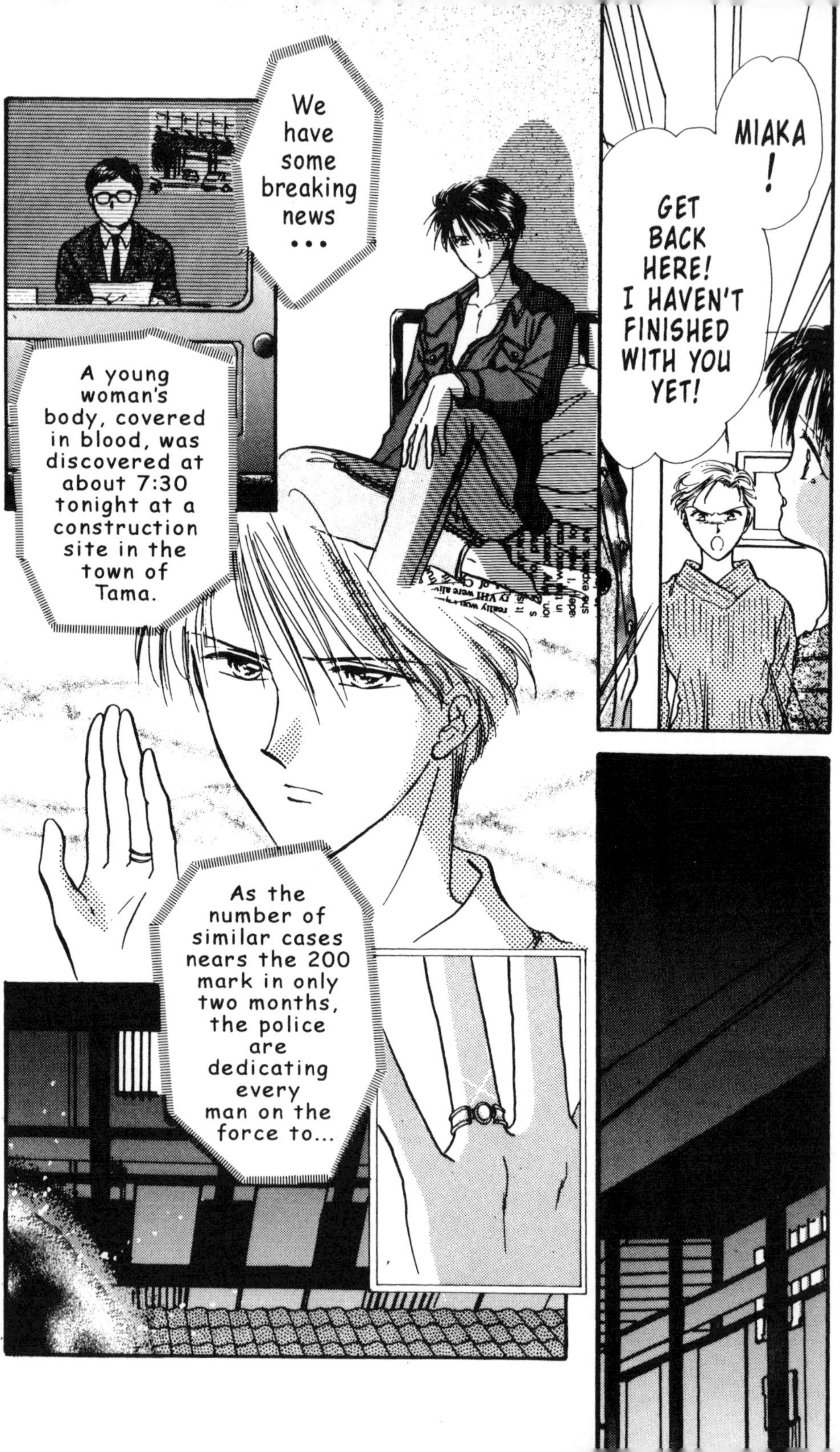
MIAKA!
GET BACK HERE! I HAVEN'T FINISHED WITH YOU YET!
We have some breaking news...
A young woman's body, covered in blood, was discovered at about 7:30 tonight at a construction site in the town of Tama.
As the number of similar cases nears the 200 mark in only two months, the police are dedicating every man on the force to...

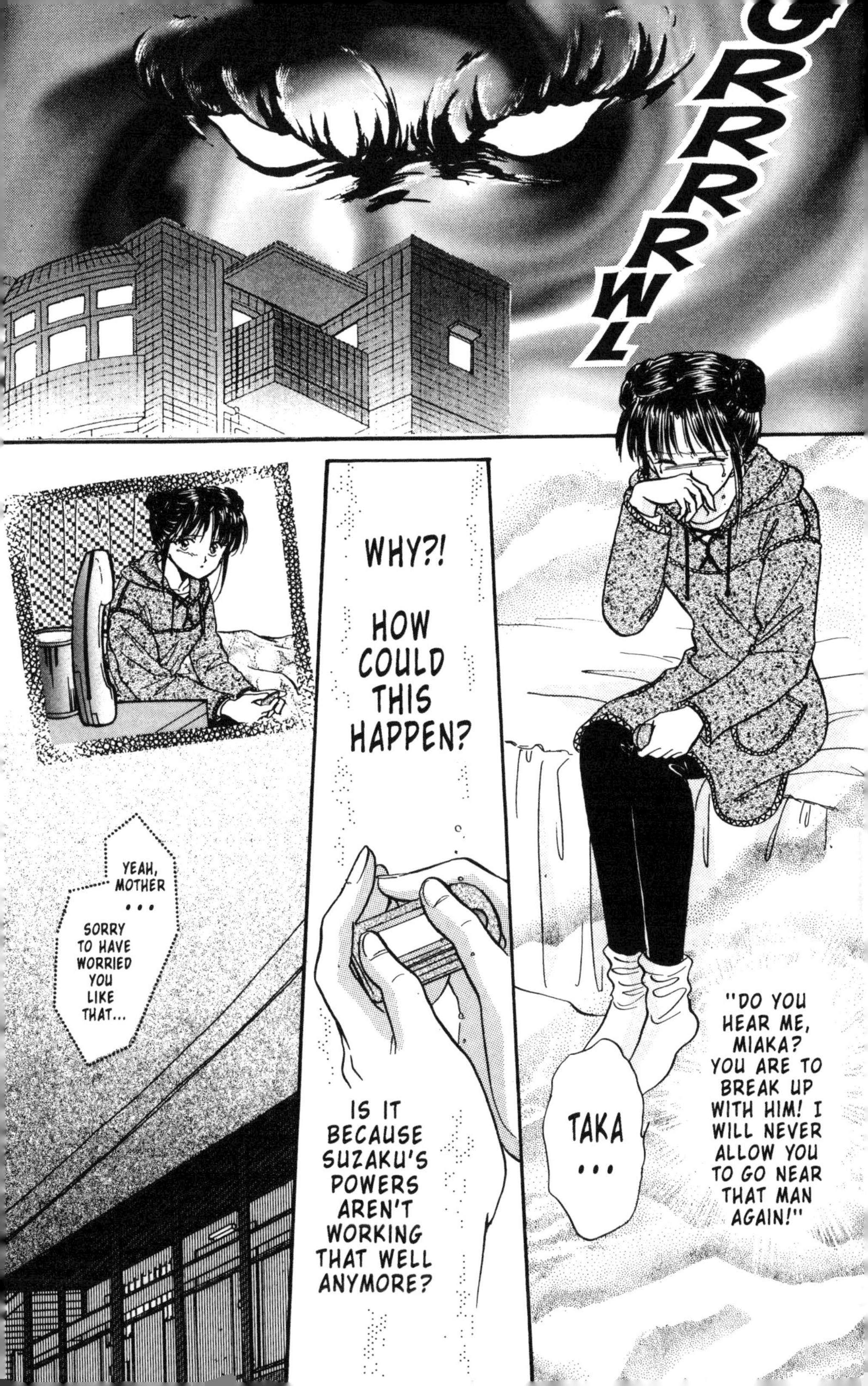
GRRRRWL
"DO YOU HEAR ME, MIAKA? YOU ARE TO BREAK UP WITH HIM! I WILL NEVER ALLOW YOU TO GO NEAR THAT MAN AGAIN!"
TAKA ...
WHY?!
HOW COULD THIS HAPPEN?
IS IT BECAUSE SUZAKU'S POWERS AREN'T WORKING THAT WELL ANYMORE?
YEAH, MOTHER ...
SORRY TO HAVE WORRIED YOU LIKE THAT...

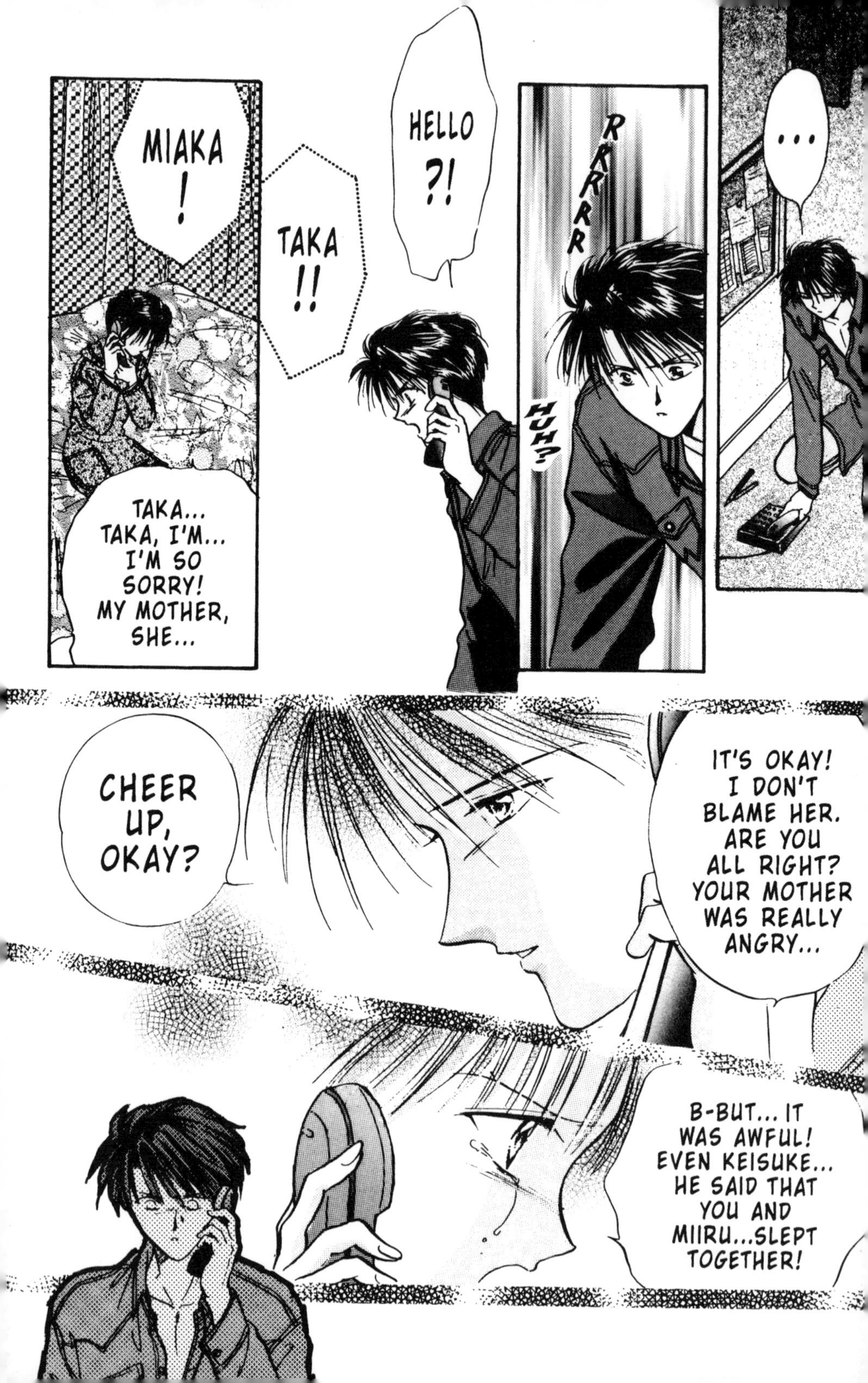
...
RRRRR
HUH?
HELLO ?!
TAKA !!
MIAKA !
TAKA... TAKA, I'M... I'M SO SORRY! MY MOTHER, SHE...
IT'S OKAY! I DON'T BLAME HER. ARE YOU ALL RIGHT? YOUR MOTHER WAS REALLY ANGRY...
CHEER UP, OKAY?
B-BUT... IT WAS AWFUL! EVEN KEISUKE... HE SAID THAT YOU AND MIIRU...SLEPT TOGETHER!

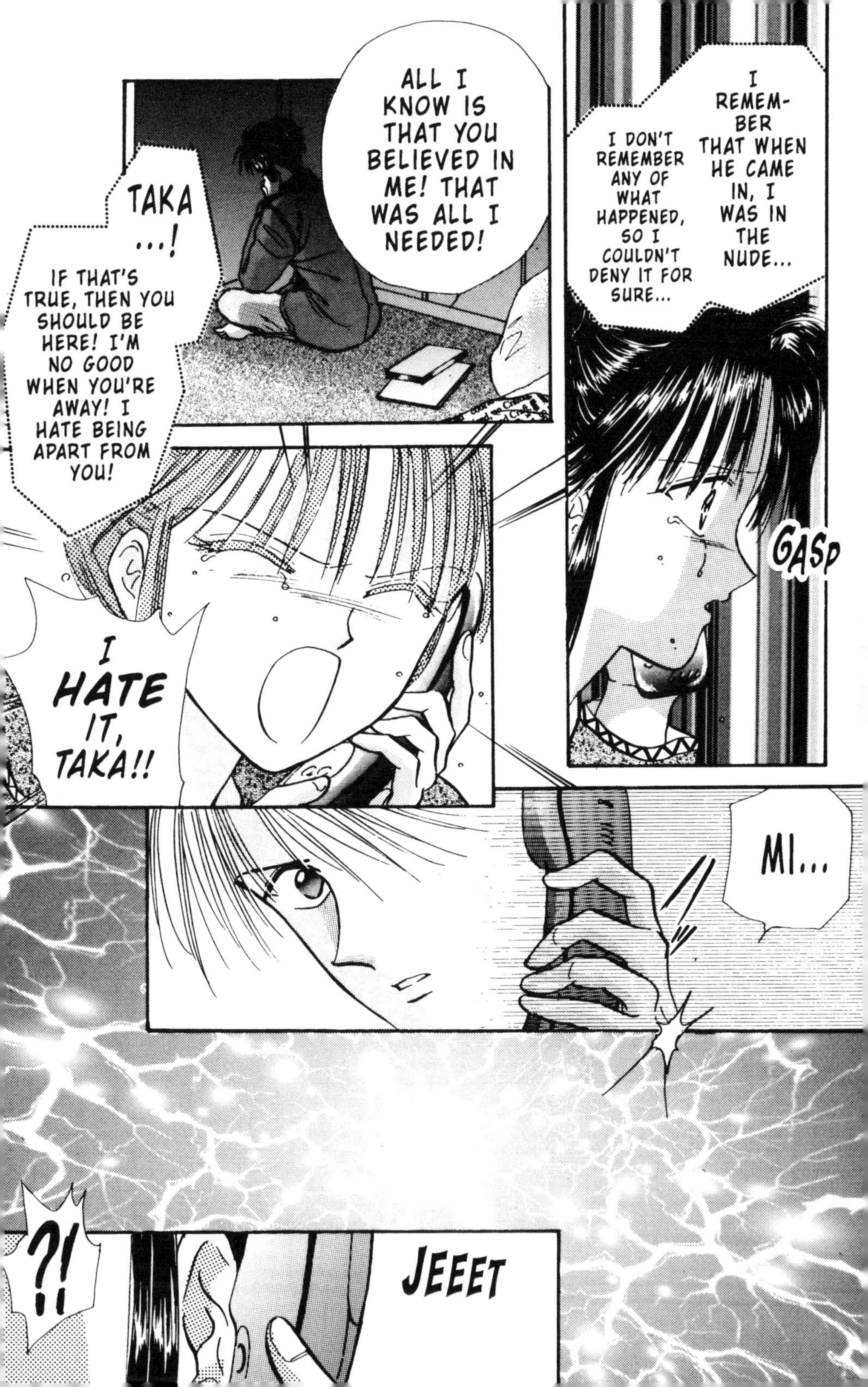
I REMEMBER THAT WHEN HE CAME IN, I WAS IN THE NUDE...
I DON'T REMEMBER ANY OF WHAT HAPPENED, SO I COULDN'T DENY IT FOR SURE...
GASP
ALL I KNOW IS THAT YOU BELIEVED IN ME! THAT WAS ALL I NEEDED!
TAKA ...!
IF THAT'S TRUE, THEN YOU SHOULD BE HERE! I'M NO GOOD WHEN YOU'RE AWAY! I HATE BEING APART FROM YOU!
I HATE IT, TAKA!!
MI...
JEEET
?!

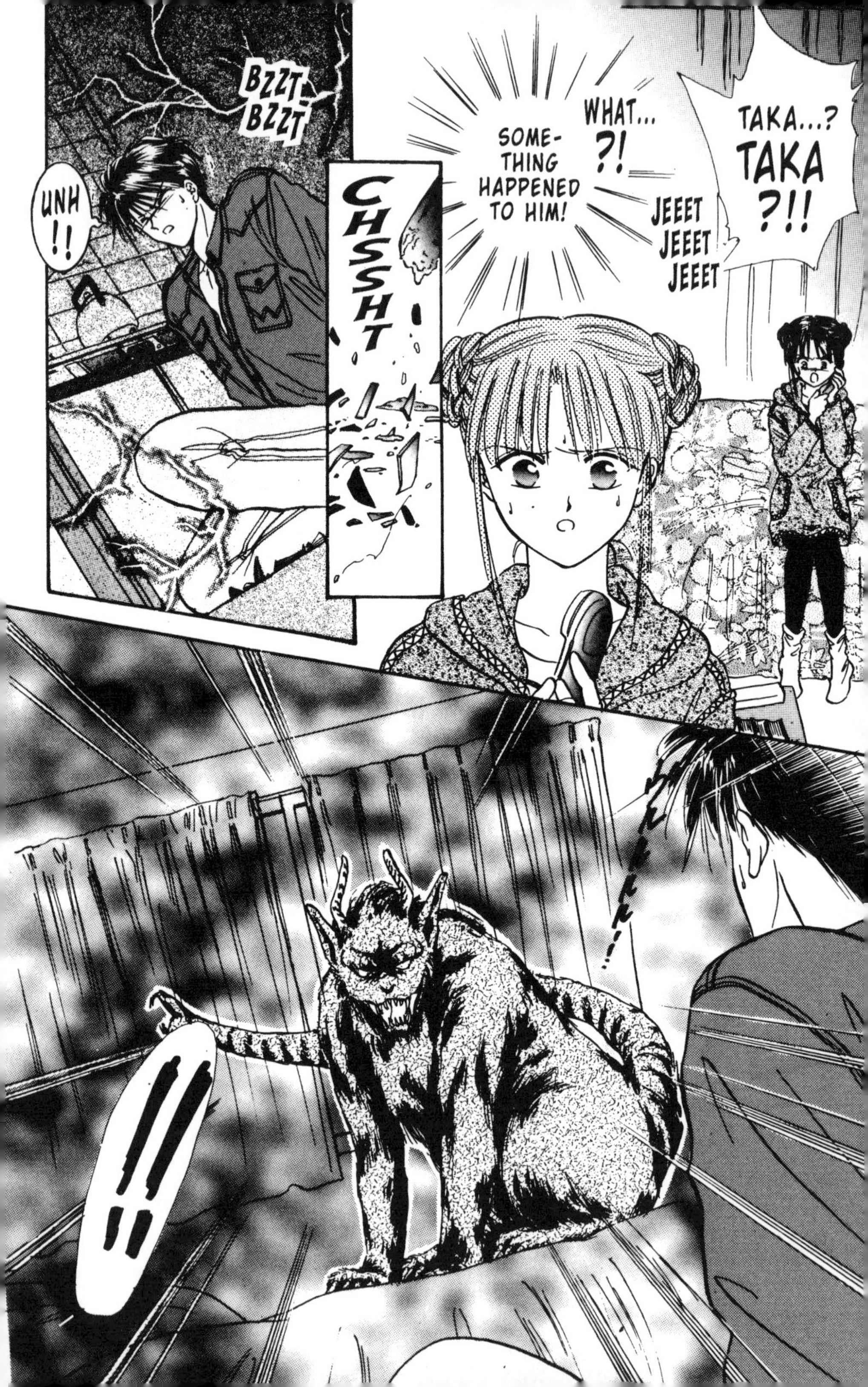
TAKA...? TAKA?!!
WHAT... ?!
JEEET JEEET JEEET
SOME-THING HAPPENED TO HIM!
CHSSHT
BZZT BZZT
UNH!!
!!

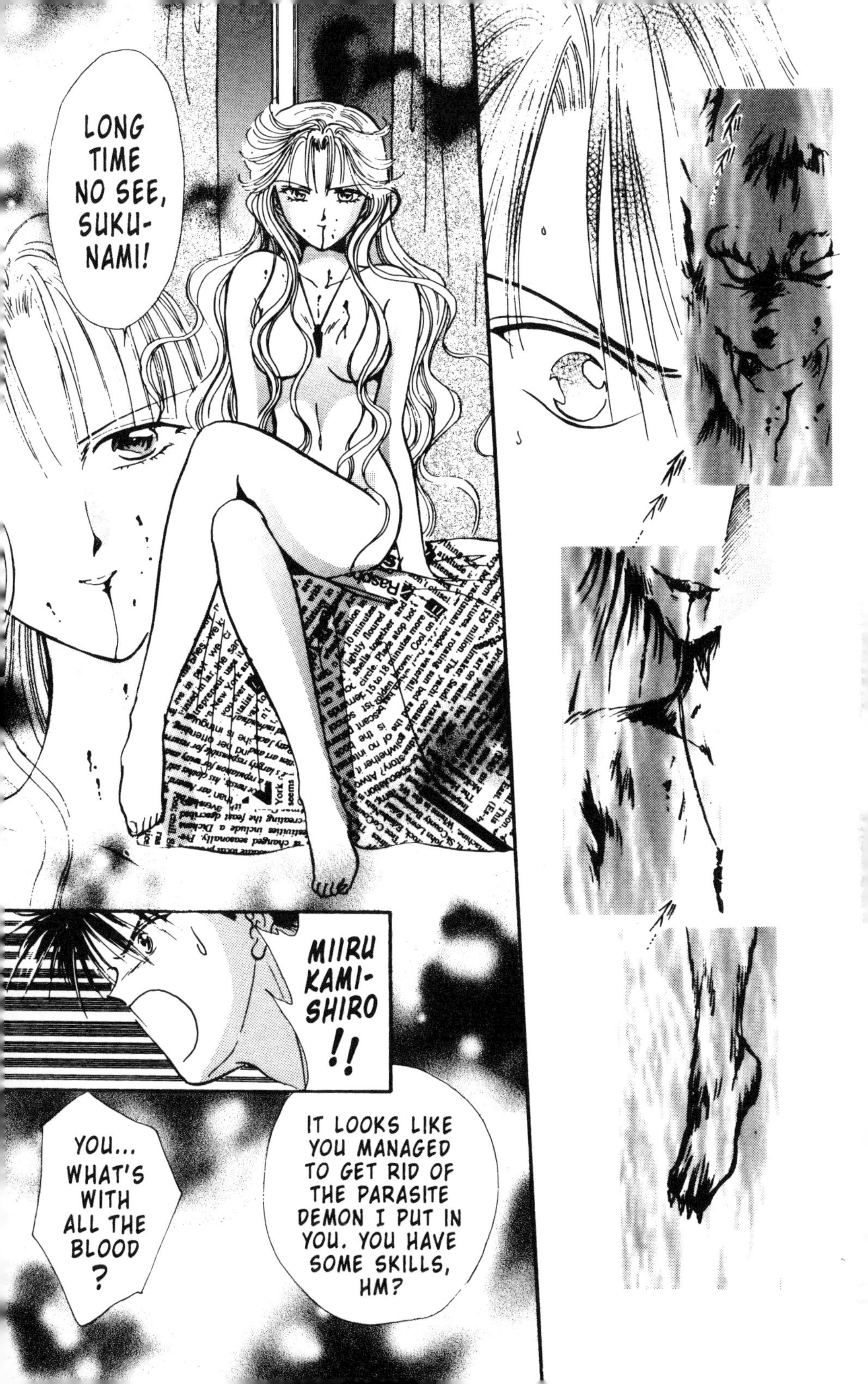
LONG TIME NO SEE, SUKU-NAMI!
MIIRU KAMI-SHIRO!!
IT LOOKS LIKE YOU MANAGED TO GET RID OF THE PARASITE DEMON I PUT IN YOU. YOU HAVE SOME SKILLS, HM?
YOU... WHAT'S WITH ALL THE BLOOD?

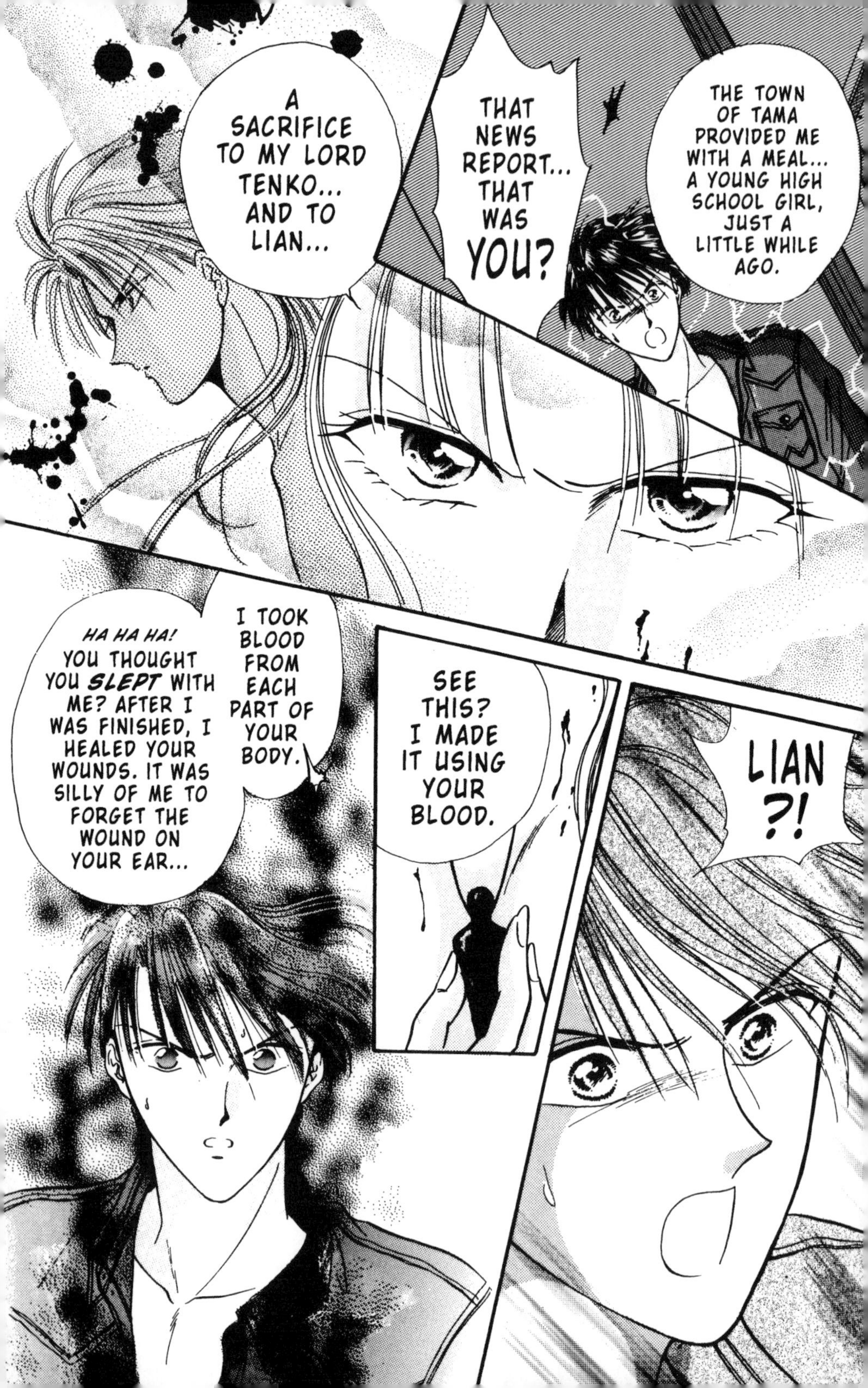
THE TOWN OF TAMA PROVIDED ME WITH A MEAL... A YOUNG HIGH SCHOOL GIRL, JUST A LITTLE WHILE AGO.
THAT NEWS REPORT... THAT WAS YOU?
A SACRIFICE TO MY LORD TENKO... AND TO LIAN...
LIAN ?!
SEE THIS? I MADE IT USING YOUR BLOOD.
I TOOK BLOOD FROM EACH PART OF YOUR BODY.
HA HA HA! YOU THOUGHT YOU SLEPT WITH ME? AFTER I WAS FINISHED, I HEALED YOUR WOUNDS. IT WAS SILLY OF ME TO FORGET THE WOUND ON YOUR EAR...

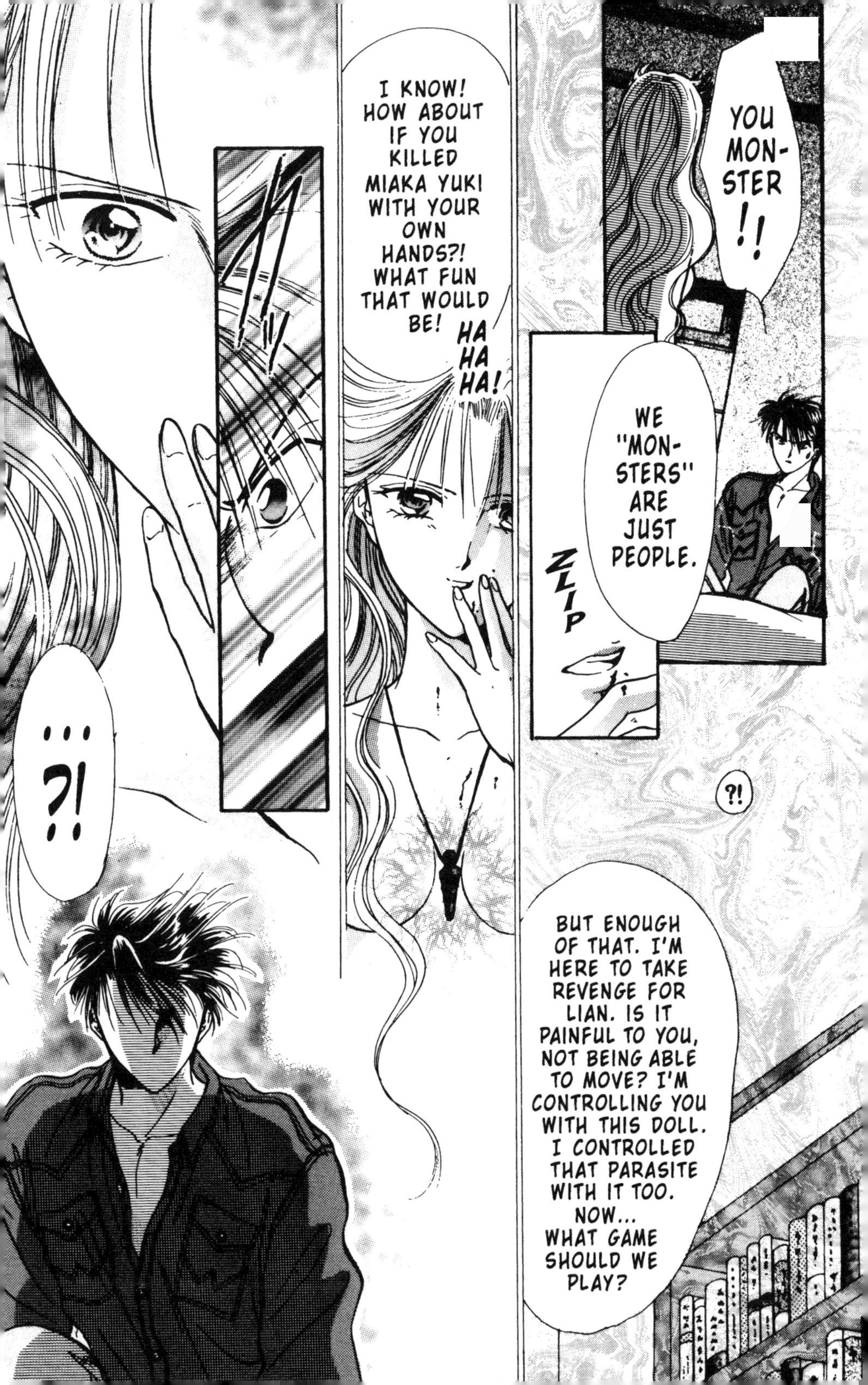
YOU MONSTER!!
WE "MONSTERS" ARE JUST PEOPLE.
ZLIP
?!
BUT ENOUGH OF THAT. I'M HERE TO TAKE REVENGE FOR LIAN. IS IT PAINFUL TO YOU, NOT BEING ABLE TO MOVE? I'M CONTROLLING YOU WITH THIS DOLL. I CONTROLLED THAT PARASITE WITH IT TOO. NOW... WHAT GAME SHOULD WE PLAY?
I KNOW! HOW ABOUT IF YOU KILLED MIAKA YUKI WITH YOUR OWN HANDS?! WHAT FUN THAT WOULD BE!
HA HA HA!
...?!

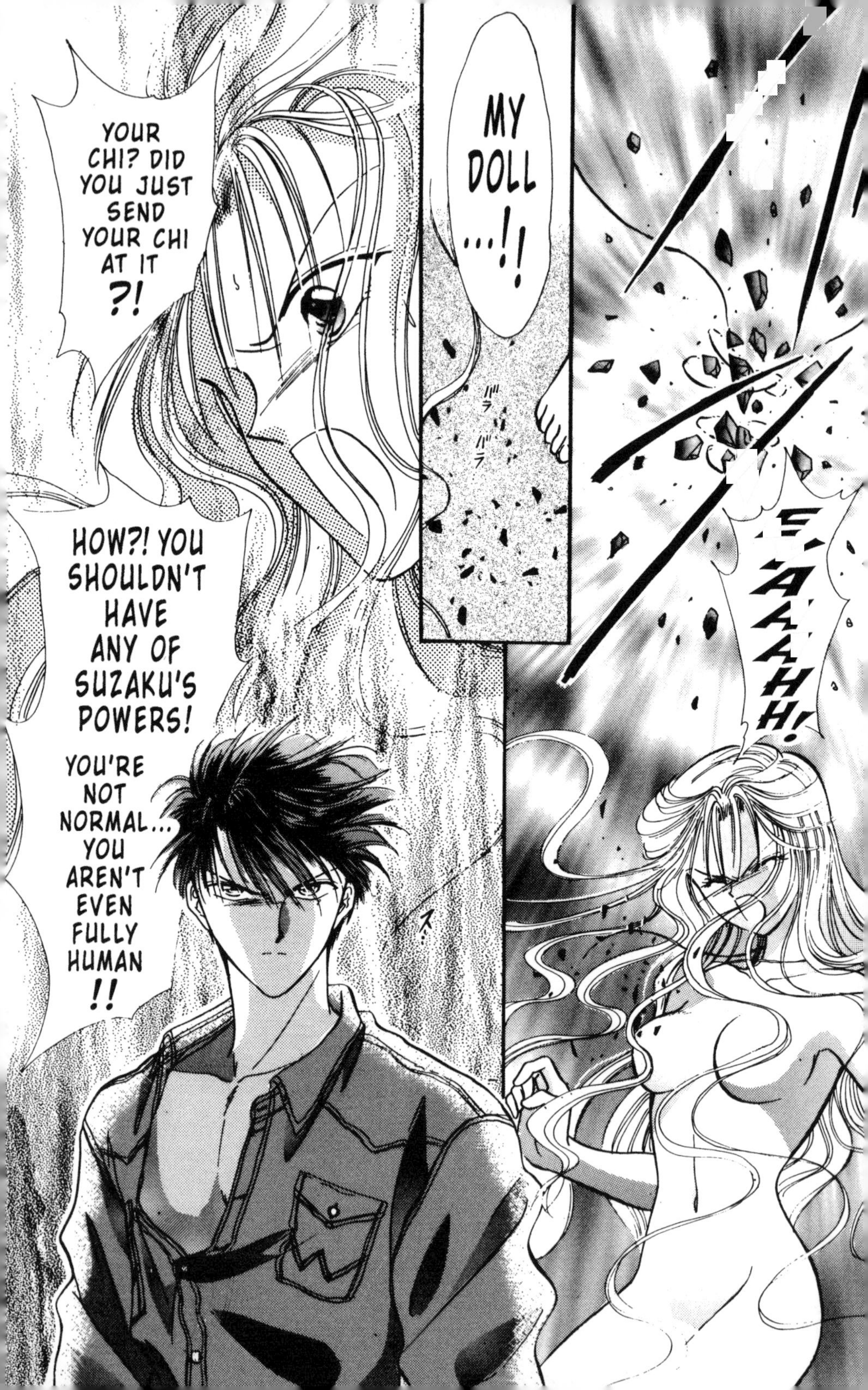
EAAAAHH!
MY DOLL...!!
YOUR CHI? DID YOU JUST SEND YOUR CHI AT IT ?!
HOW?! YOU SHOULDN'T HAVE ANY OF SUZAKU'S POWERS!
YOU'RE NOT NORMAL... YOU AREN'T EVEN FULLY HUMAN !!

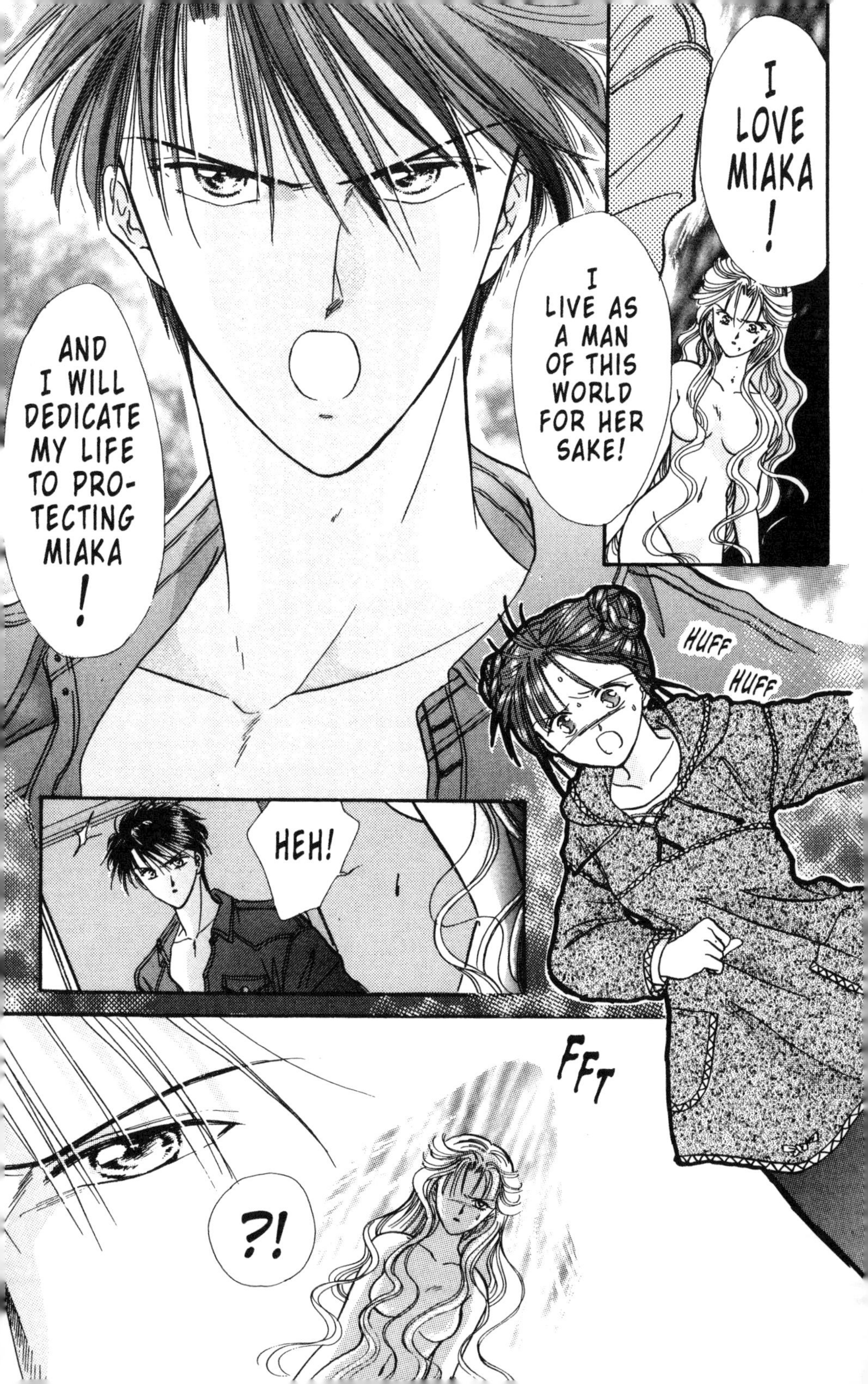
I LOVE MIAKA!
I LIVE AS A MAN OF THIS WORLD FOR HER SAKE!
AND I WILL DEDICATE MY LIFE TO PROTECTING MIAKA!
HUFF
HUFF
HEH!
FFT
?!

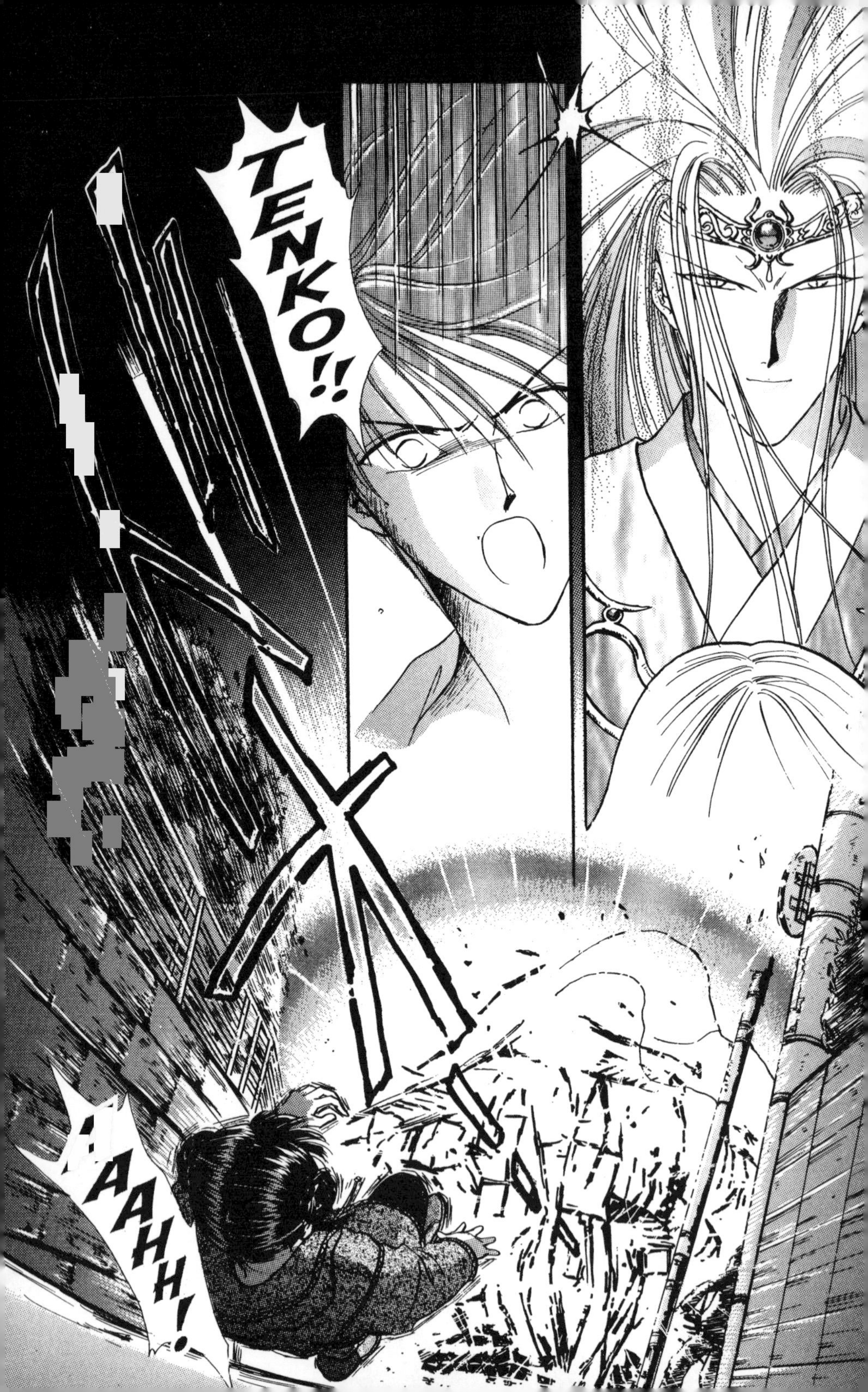
TENKO!!
AAHH!

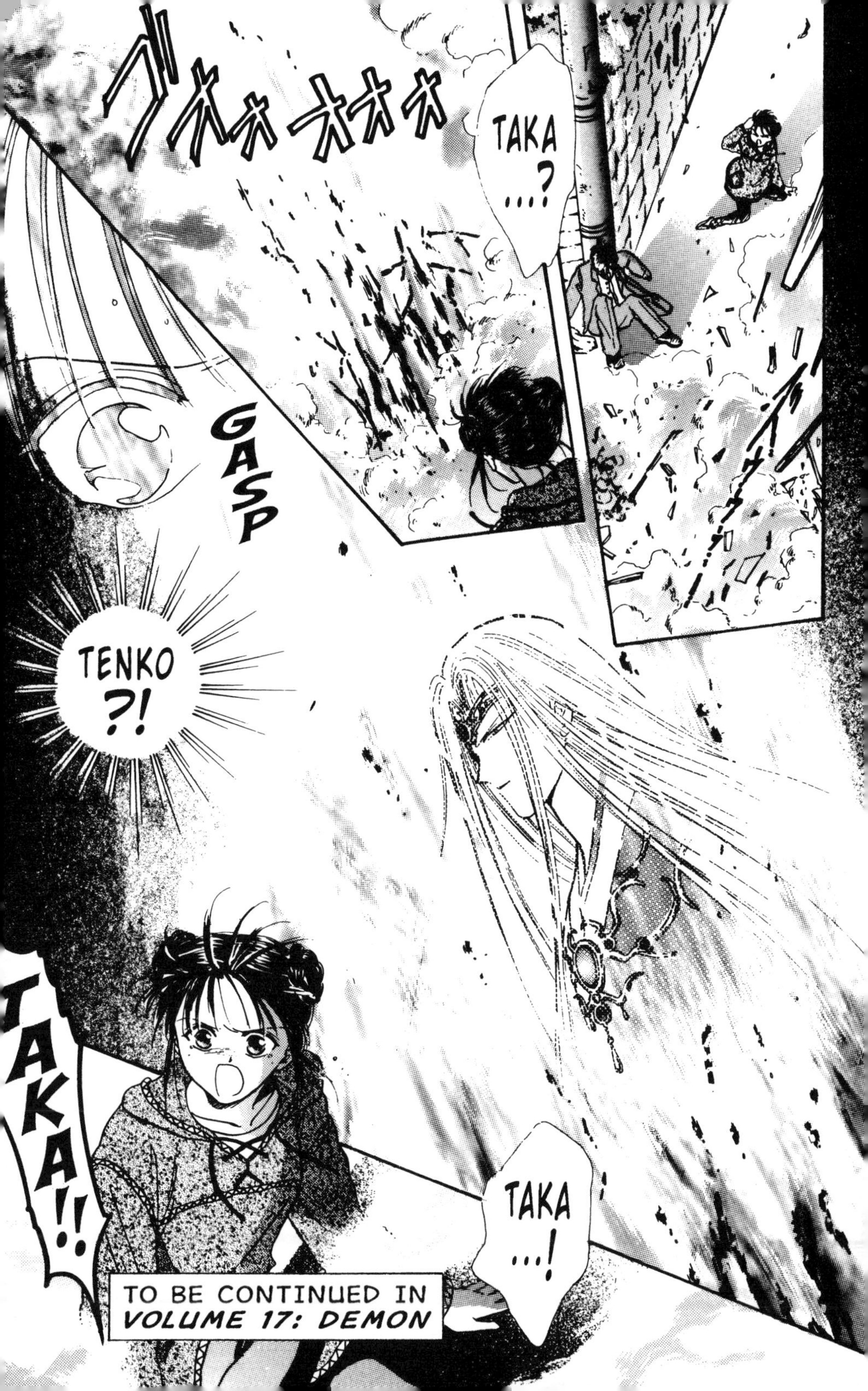

ゴオォオオオ
TAKA ...?
GASP
TENKO ?!
TAKA ...!
TAKA!!
TO BE CONTINUED IN
VOLUME 17: DEMON

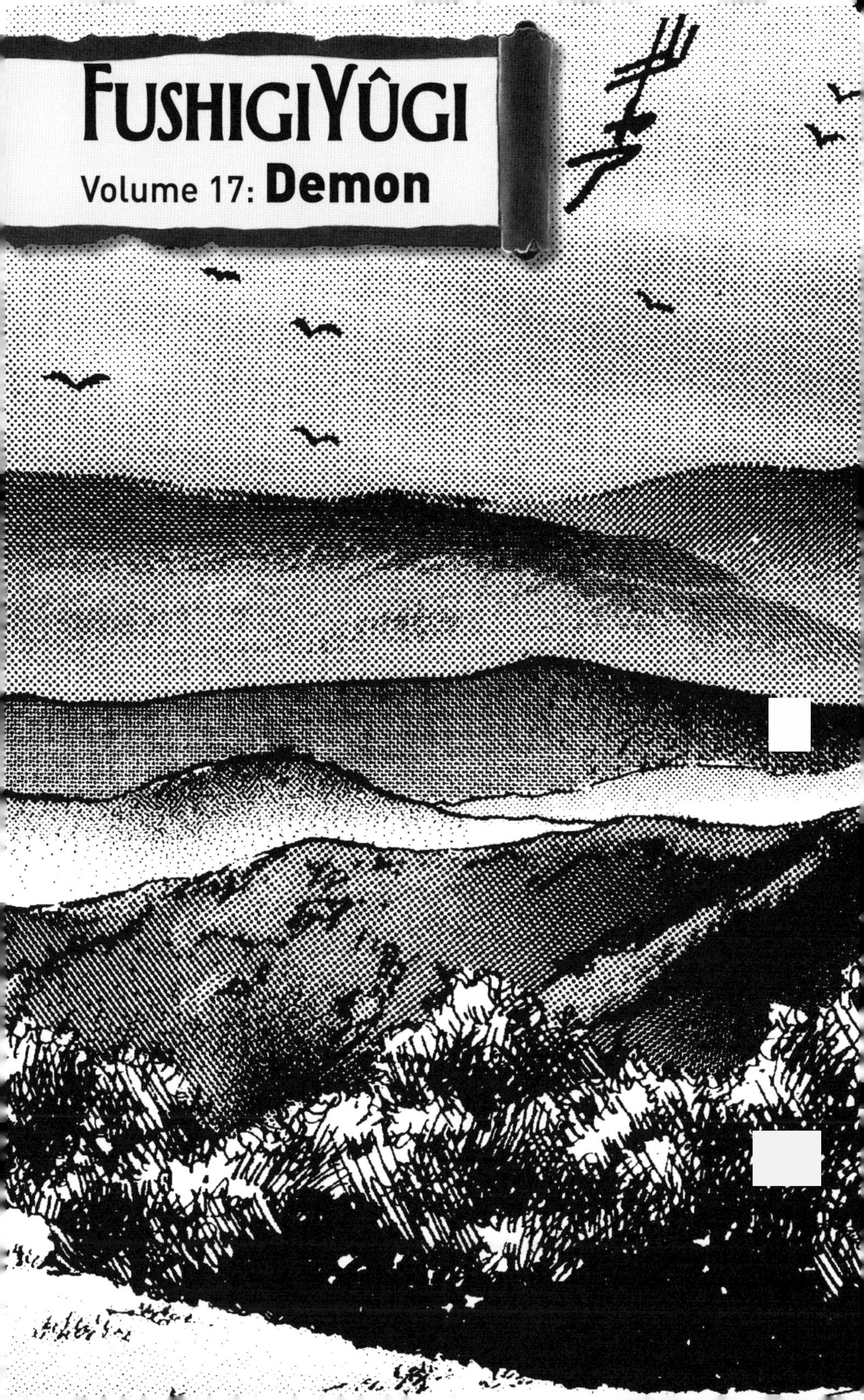
FUSHIGI YÛGI
Volume 17: Demon

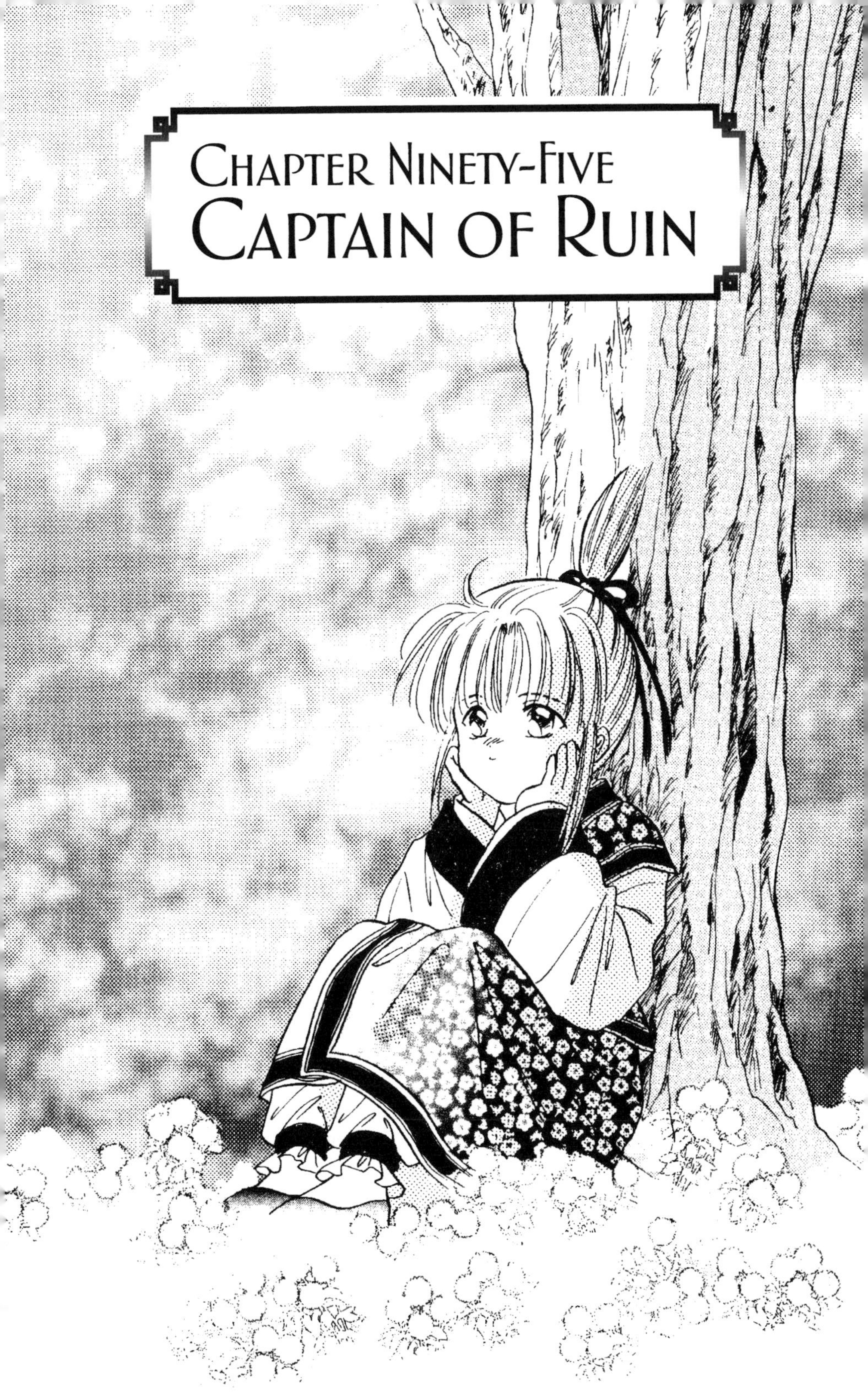
Chapter Ninety-Five
Captain of Ruin

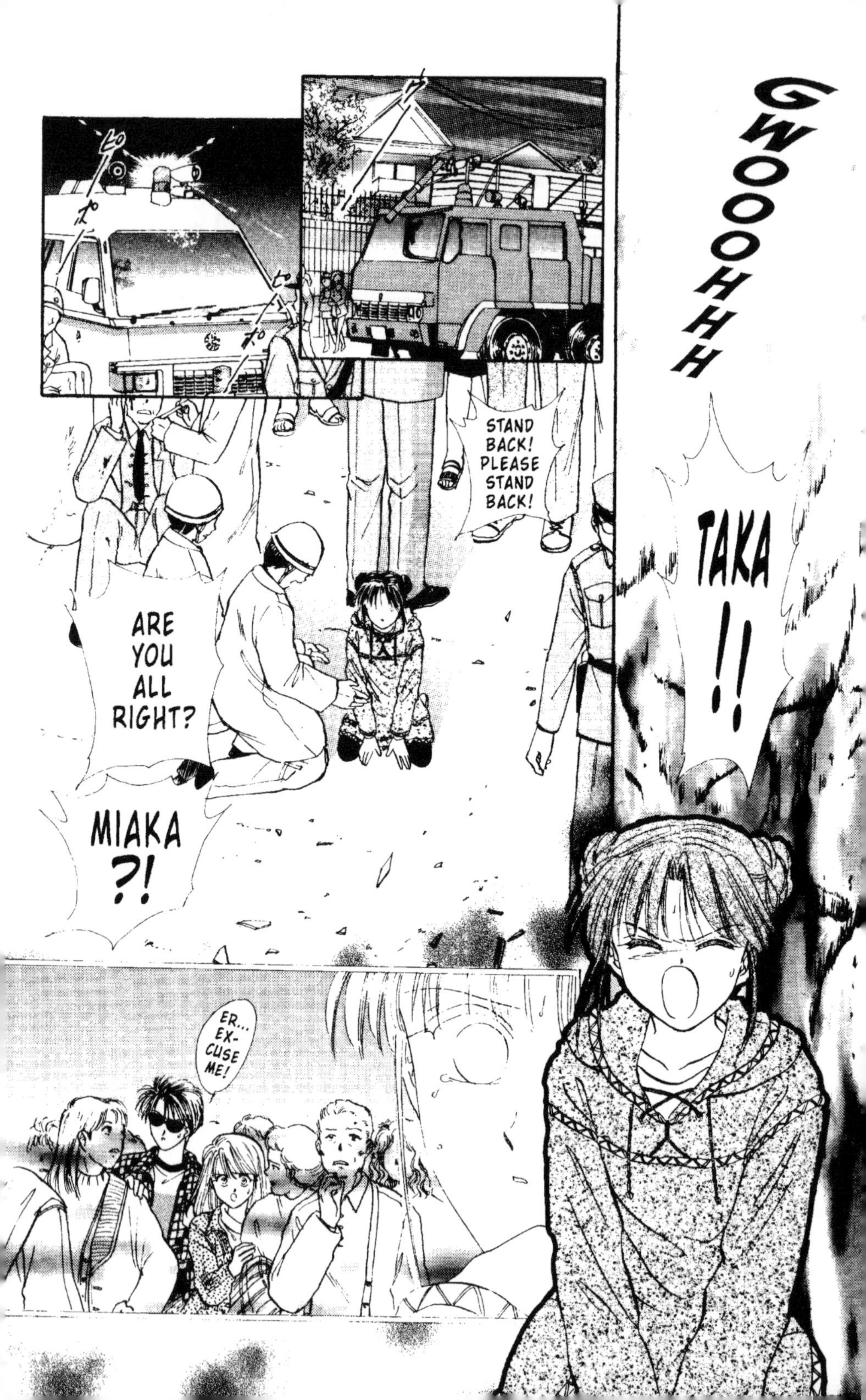
GWOOOOHHHH
TAKA!!
STAND BACK! PLEASE STAND BACK!
ARE YOU ALL RIGHT?
MIAKA?!
ER... EX-CUSE ME!

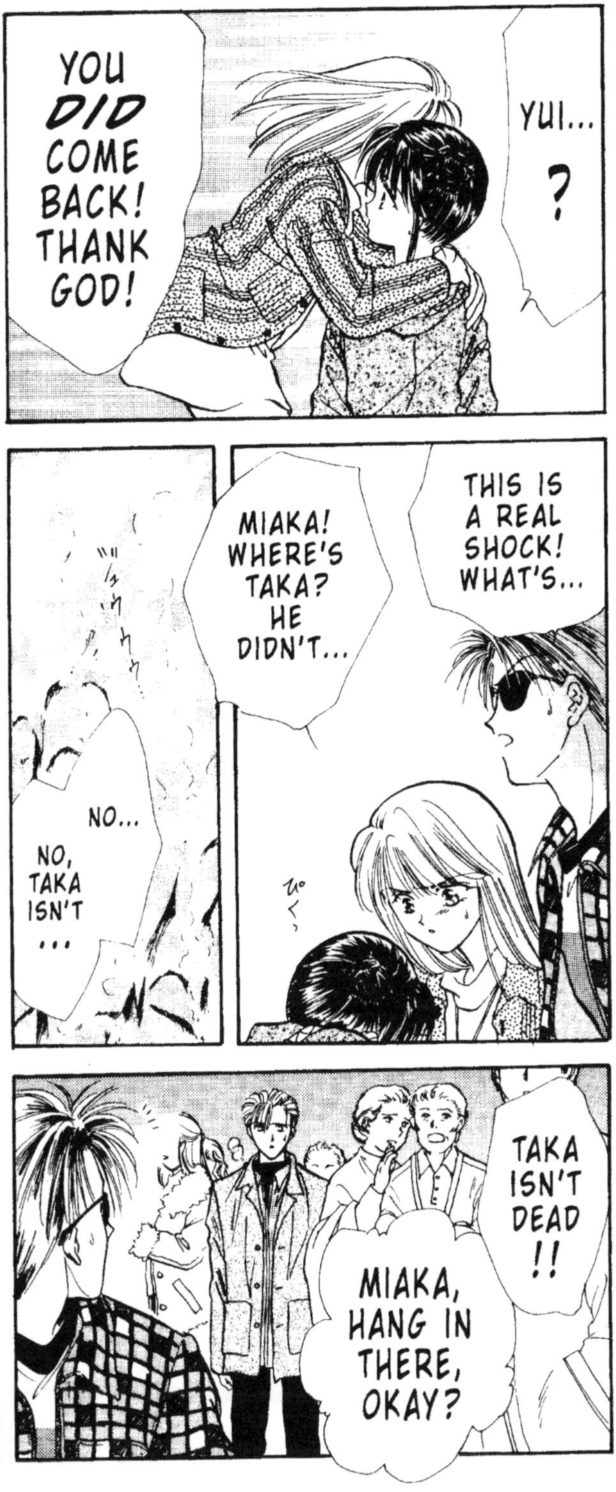
YUI... ?
YOU *DID* COME BACK! THANK GOD!
THIS IS A REAL SHOCK! WHAT'S...
MIAKA! WHERE'S TAKA? HE DIDN'T...
NO...
NO, TAKA ISN'T ...
TAKA ISN'T DEAD !!
MIAKA, HANG IN THERE, OKAY?

Volume 17. Ah, volume 17... Volume 17. *Ah!*
Hello, this is Watase. *Feeling a little sleepy.*
Hmm... By the time this is published, the anime will have finished its run. I'll comment on that in the next volume. *It's only March (1996) while I'm writing this.* Oh, and thanks to all of you, *Fushigi Yûgi* volumes 1-16 have sold a total of over 10 million books! *Thank you all so much!*
Enough of that! Watase is cutting this off! In both the good and the bad meanings of the word! *(What am I talking about?)*
FY, Part 2. I've always called it "Part 2," but in my heart I've called it a "side story" or a "sequel." The main story was from volume 1 to volume 13... At least that's how I feel about it. *Because Part 2 is so short!* Now Part 2...was done by request (with Suzaku as the main god, and with a lot of comings and goings from the real world...). My biggest motivation was that I wanted to draw more of the celestial warriors!! So I agreed and got started. I loved the feel of volume 4, and I wanted to try that again! In Part 1, the situation was so dire and everyone had to be so heroic, there was no time for any real fun among the warriors (although I forced some in there! ☺). I was so happy that I could draw some exciting, crowded scenes after so long. **However...** in the last installment, chapter 94, something missed the mark. And it looks like something big and bad is headed this way. ☺ So just as I was thinking that I would do as I like, the characters started acting the way they wanted to! *Okay guys, have fun and... sorry.*
And the bad way I cut things off is... Around January, I kept on missing deadlines, I never got enough sleep, my stomach hurt, my stress was building, and everything was feeling terrible! When I was mentally and physically at my worst, right in the middle of work, I cut it off. I pulled the trigger............(vacation)..................... ☺ You're just one big dummy, now arntcha? That's what they'd say in my home accent. ϑ϶
That was really an awful thing to do to my assistants. ϑ϶

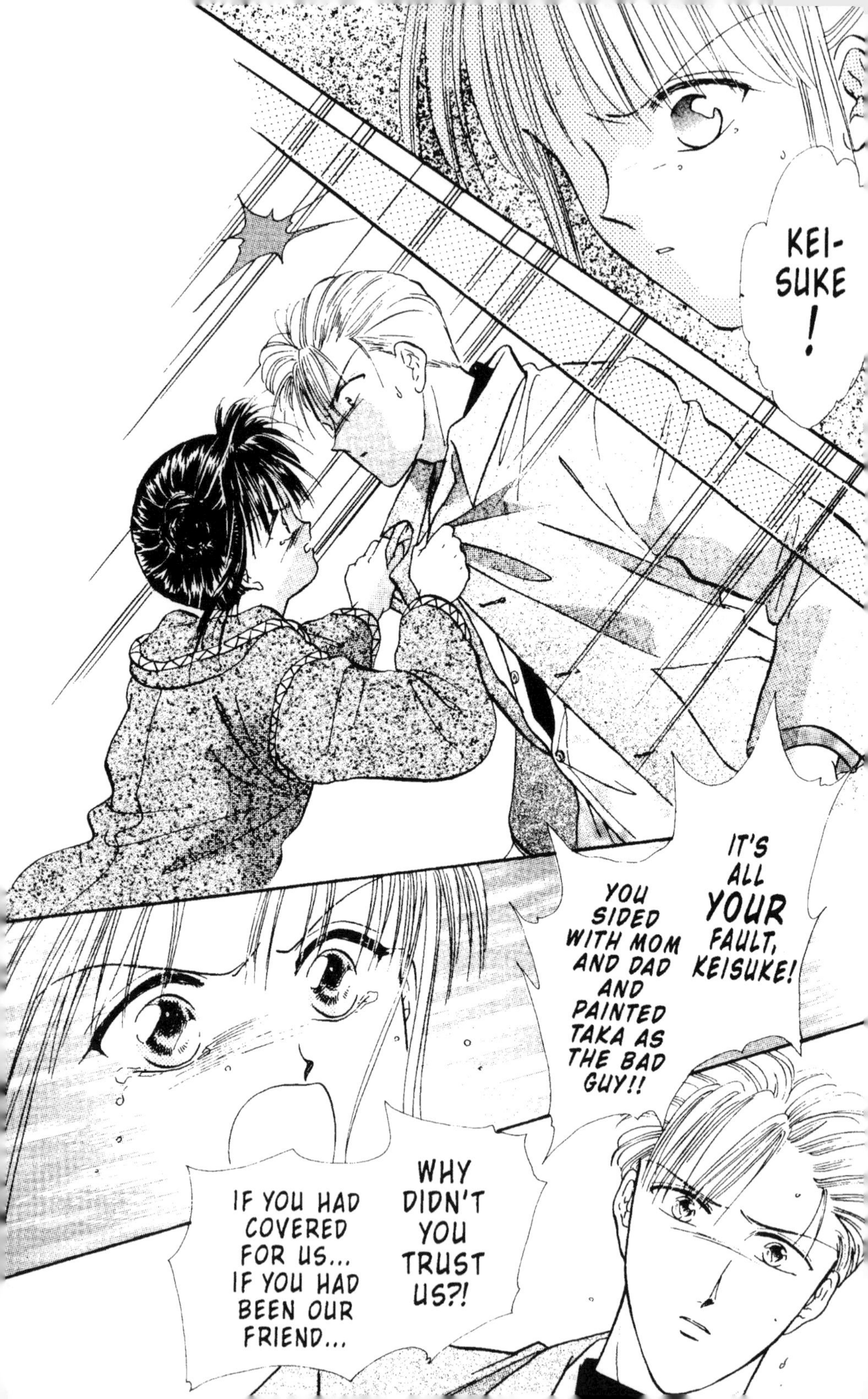
KEI-SUKE!
IT'S ALL YOUR FAULT, KEISUKE!
YOU SIDED WITH MOM AND DAD AND PAINTED TAKA AS THE BAD GUY!!
WHY DIDN'T YOU TRUST US?!
IF YOU HAD COVERED FOR US... IF YOU HAD BEEN OUR FRIEND...

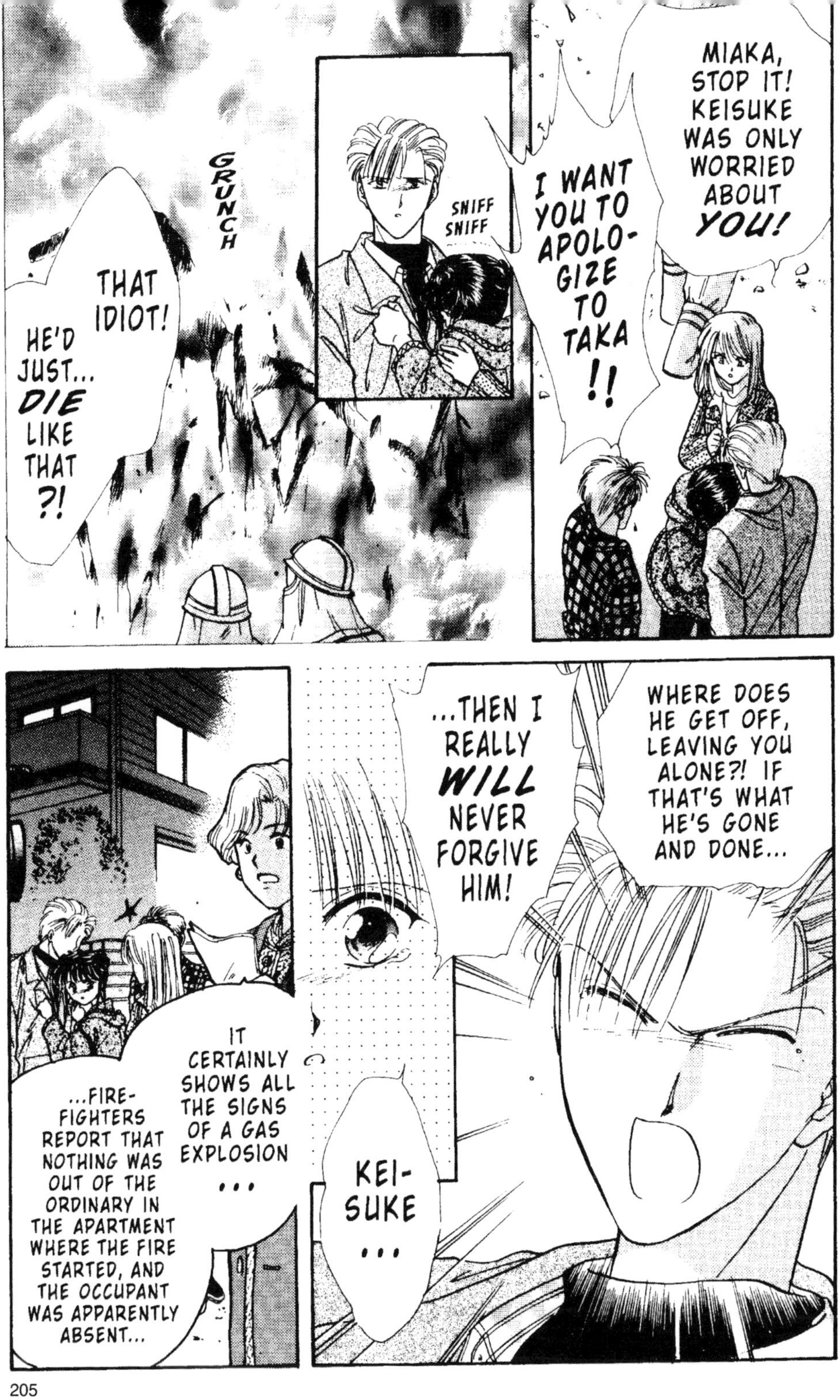
MIAKA, STOP IT! KEISUKE WAS ONLY WORRIED ABOUT YOU!
I WANT YOU TO APOLOGIZE TO TAKA!!
SNIFF SNIFF
GRUNCH
THAT IDIOT!
HE'D JUST... DIE LIKE THAT?!
WHERE DOES HE GET OFF, LEAVING YOU ALONE?! IF THAT'S WHAT HE'S GONE AND DONE...
...THEN I REALLY WILL NEVER FORGIVE HIM!
KEISUKE...
IT CERTAINLY SHOWS ALL THE SIGNS OF A GAS EXPLOSION...
...FIREFIGHTERS REPORT THAT NOTHING WAS OUT OF THE ORDINARY IN THE APARTMENT WHERE THE FIRE STARTED, AND THE OCCUPANT WAS APPARENTLY ABSENT...

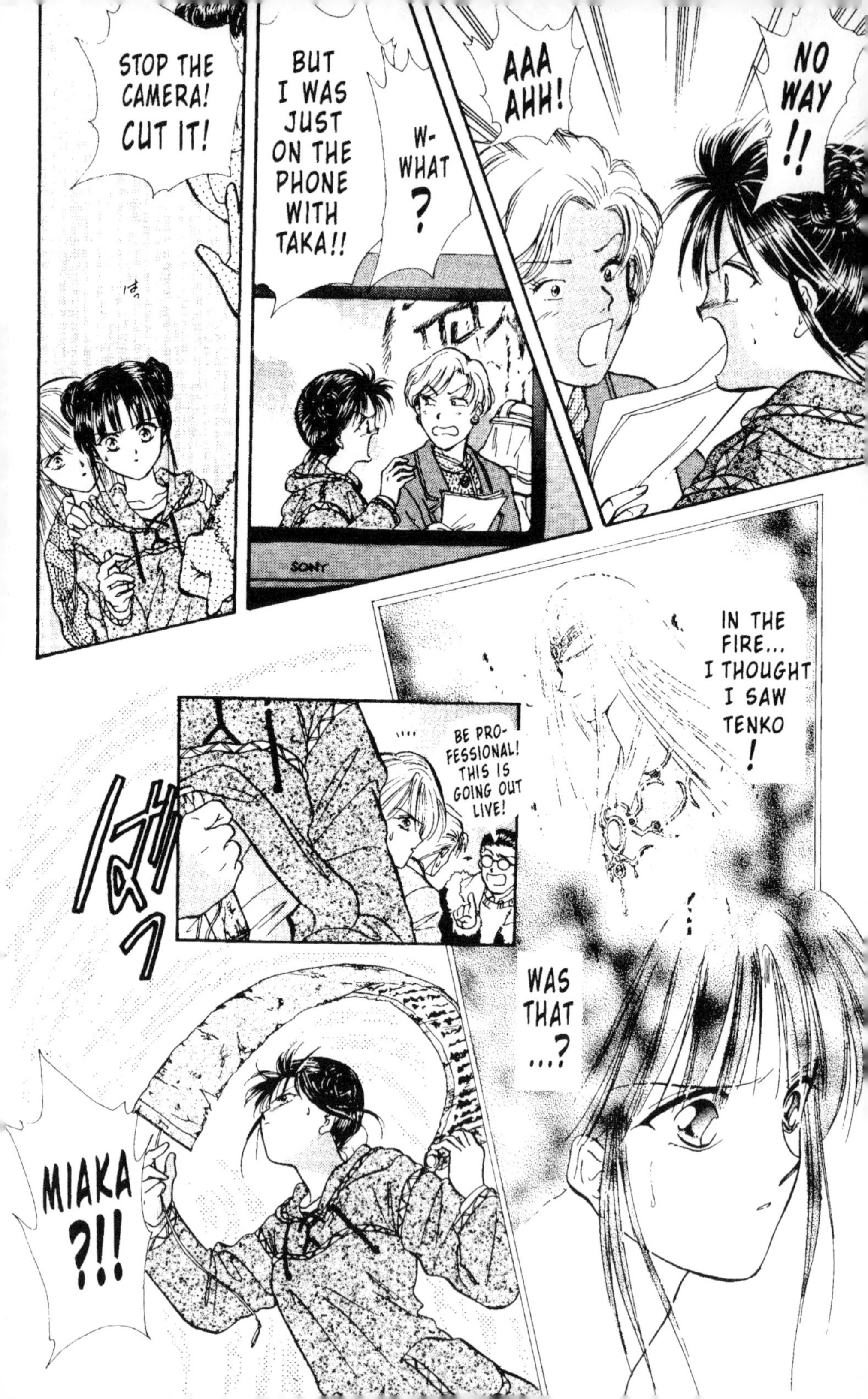
NO WAY!!
AAA AHH!
W-WHAT?
BUT I WAS JUST ON THE PHONE WITH TAKA!!
STOP THE CAMERA! CUT IT!
SONY
IN THE FIRE... I THOUGHT I SAW TENKO!
BE PRO-FESSIONAL! THIS IS GOING OUT LIVE!
WAS THAT ...?
MIAKA?!!

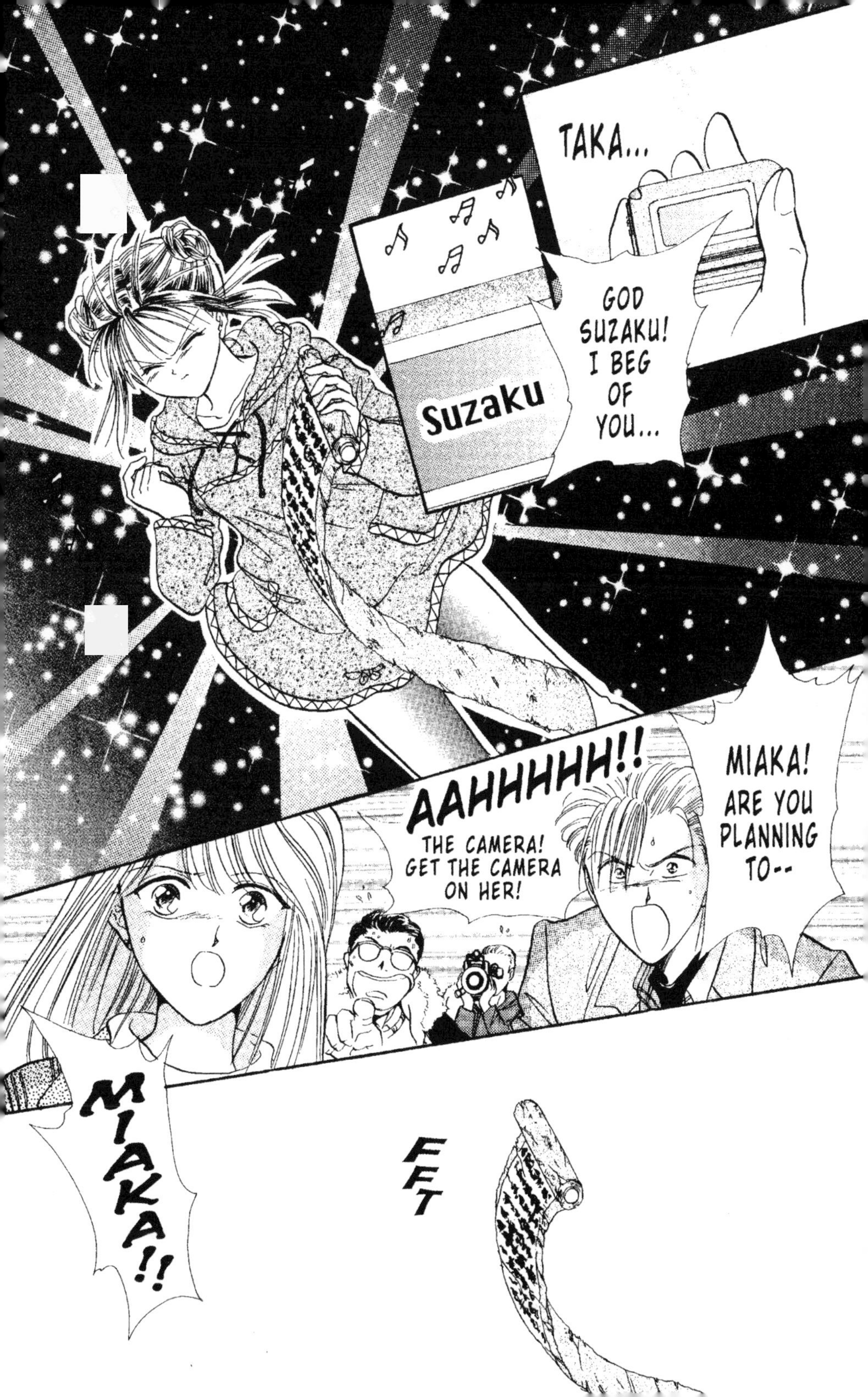
TAKA...
GOD SUZAKU! I BEG OF YOU...
Suzaku
MIAKA! ARE YOU PLANNING TO--
AAHHHHH!!
THE CAMERA! GET THE CAMERA ON HER!
FFT
MIAKA!!

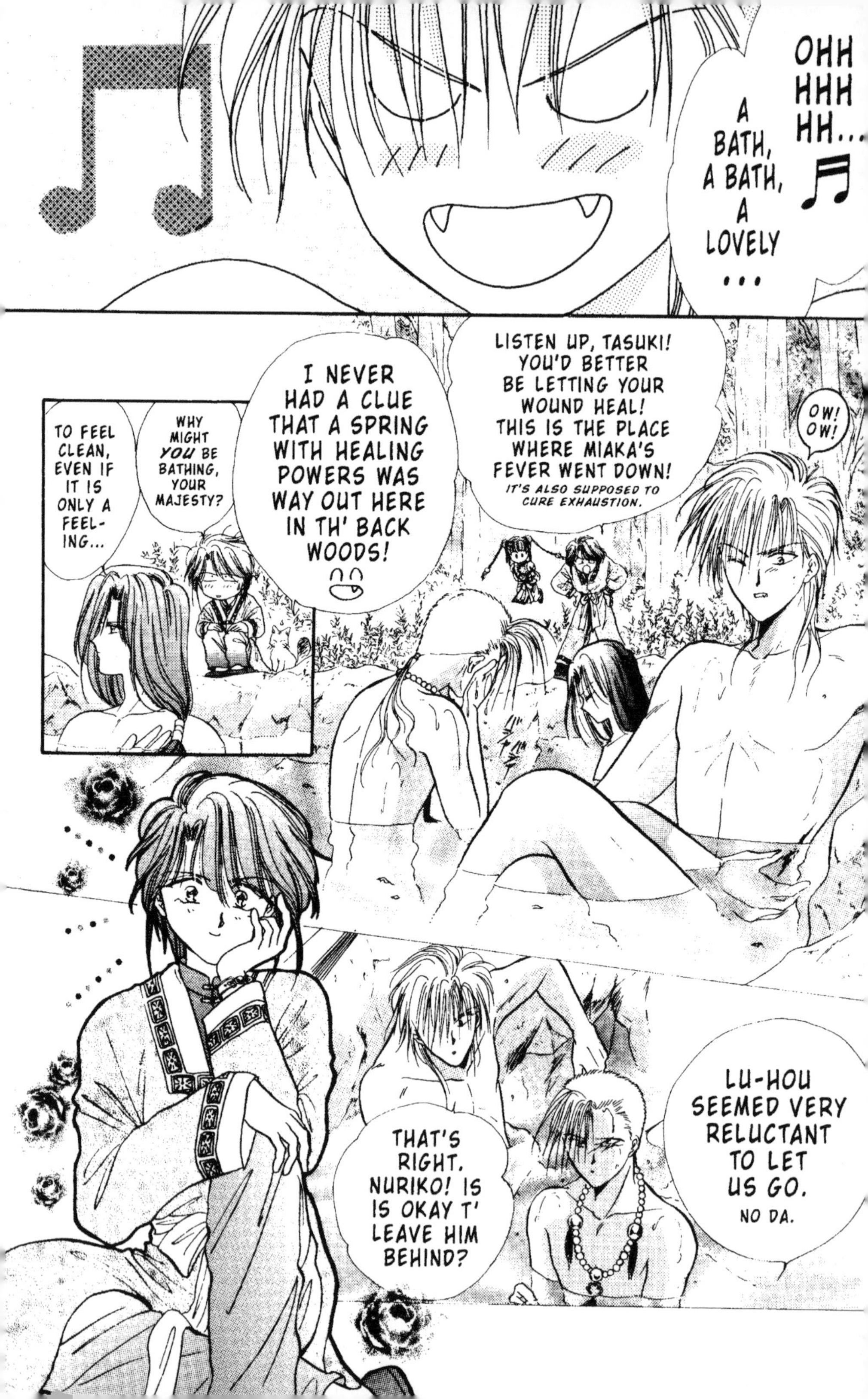
OHHHHHHH... ♬
A BATH, A BATH, A LOVELY ...
OW! OW!
LISTEN UP, TASUKI! YOU'D BETTER BE LETTING YOUR WOUND HEAL! THIS IS THE PLACE WHERE MIAKA'S FEVER WENT DOWN! IT'S ALSO SUPPOSED TO CURE EXHAUSTION.
I NEVER HAD A CLUE THAT A SPRING WITH HEALING POWERS WAS WAY OUT HERE IN TH' BACK WOODS!
WHY MIGHT YOU BE BATHING, YOUR MAJESTY?
TO FEEL CLEAN, EVEN IF IT IS ONLY A FEEL- ING...
LU-HOU SEEMED VERY RELUCTANT TO LET US GO. NO DA.
THAT'S RIGHT. NURIKO! IS IS OKAY T' LEAVE HIM BEHIND?

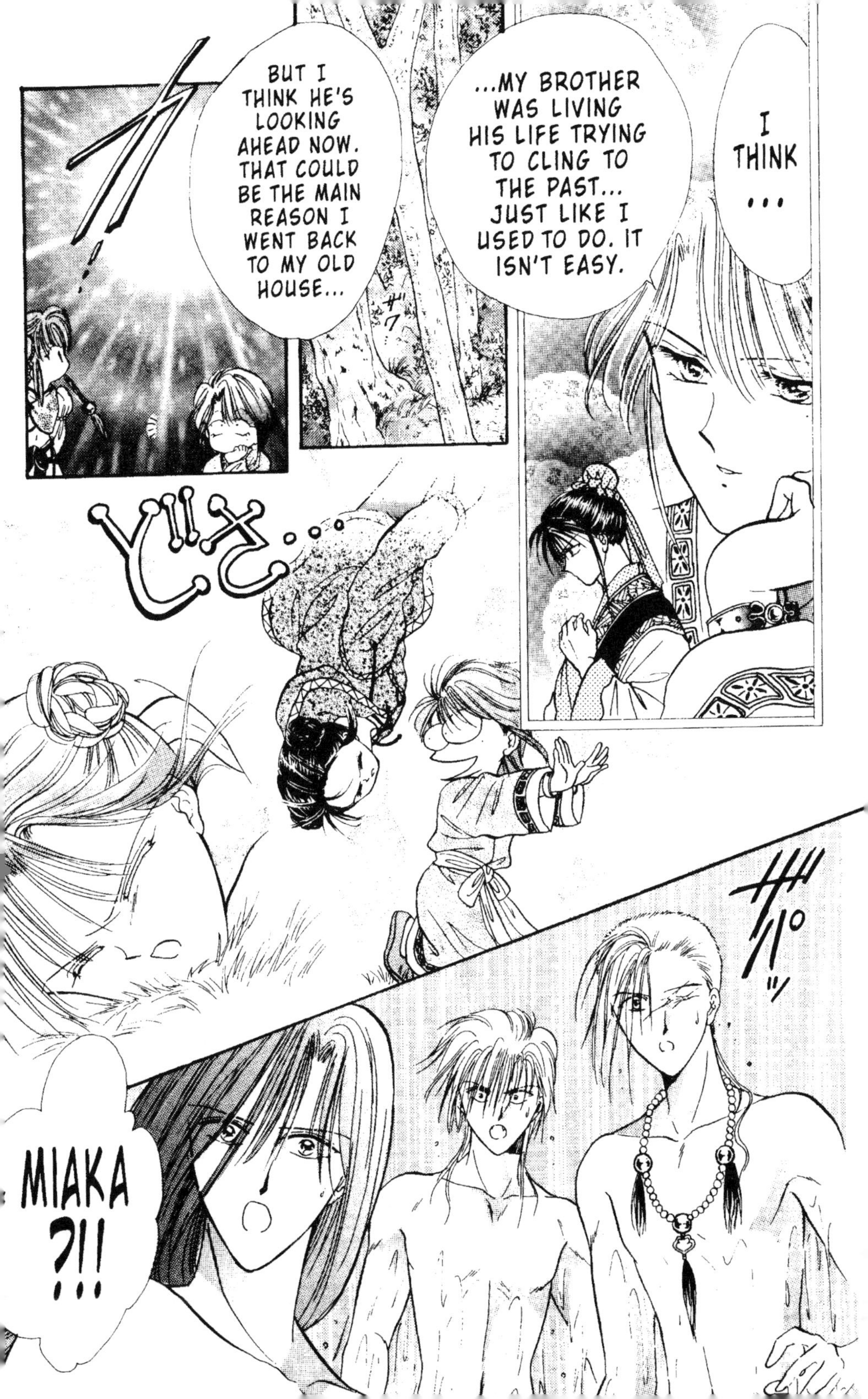
I THINK...
...MY BROTHER WAS LIVING HIS LIFE TRYING TO CLING TO THE PAST... JUST LIKE I USED TO DO. IT ISN'T EASY.
BUT I THINK HE'S LOOKING AHEAD NOW. THAT COULD BE THE MAIN REASON I WENT BACK TO MY OLD HOUSE...
MIAKA?!!...

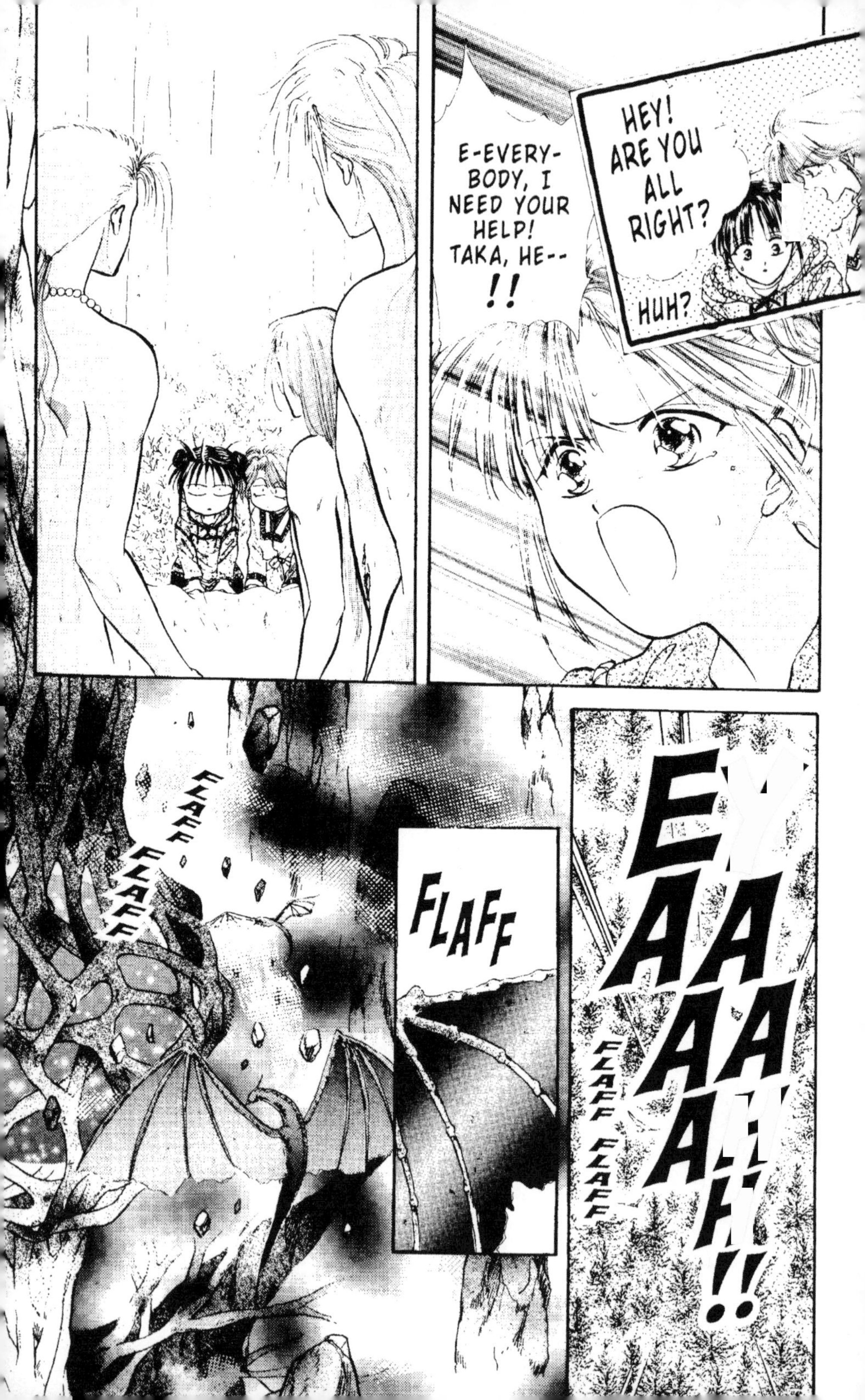
HEY! ARE YOU ALL RIGHT?
HUH?
E-EVERY-BODY, I NEED YOUR HELP! TAKA, HE-- !!
EYAAAAAAH!!
FLAFF FLAFF
FLAFF
FLAFF FLAFF

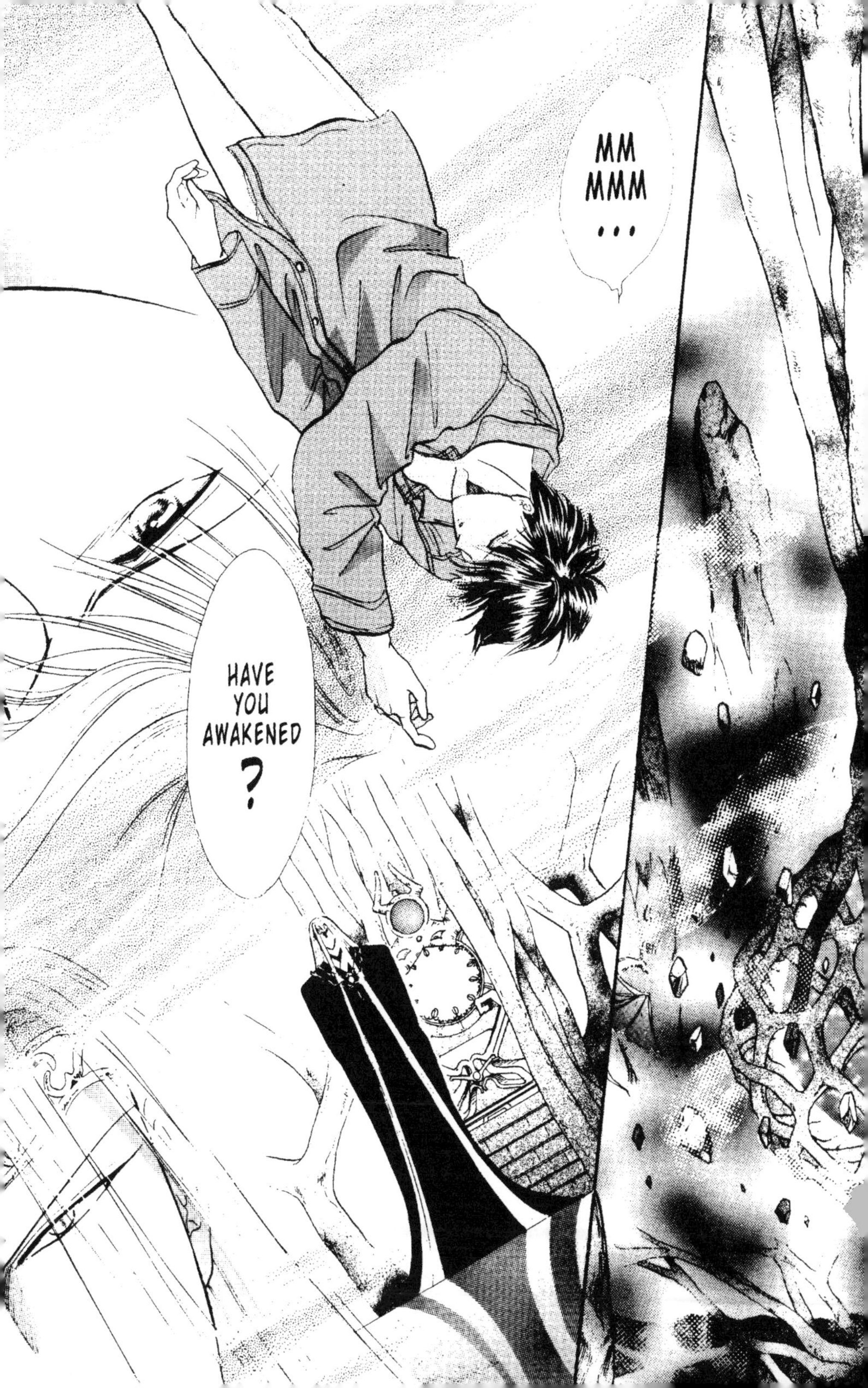
MM MMM...
HAVE YOU AWAKENED?

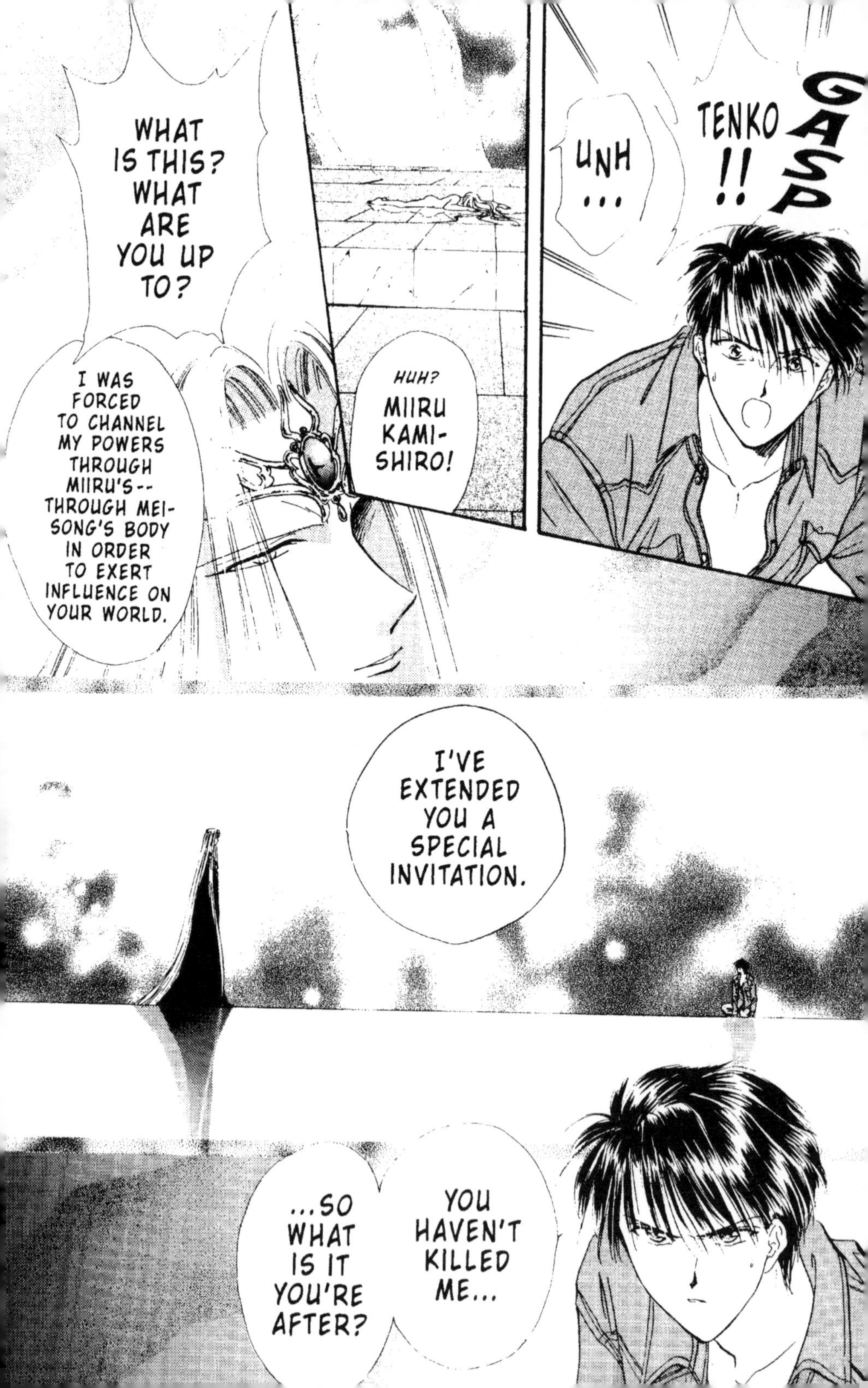
GASP
TENKO!!
UNH...
HUH? MIIRU KAMI-SHIRO!
WHAT IS THIS? WHAT ARE YOU UP TO?
I WAS FORCED TO CHANNEL MY POWERS THROUGH MIIRU'S--THROUGH MEI-SONG'S BODY IN ORDER TO EXERT INFLUENCE ON YOUR WORLD.
I'VE EXTENDED YOU A SPECIAL INVITATION.
YOU HAVEN'T KILLED ME...
...SO WHAT IS IT YOU'RE AFTER?

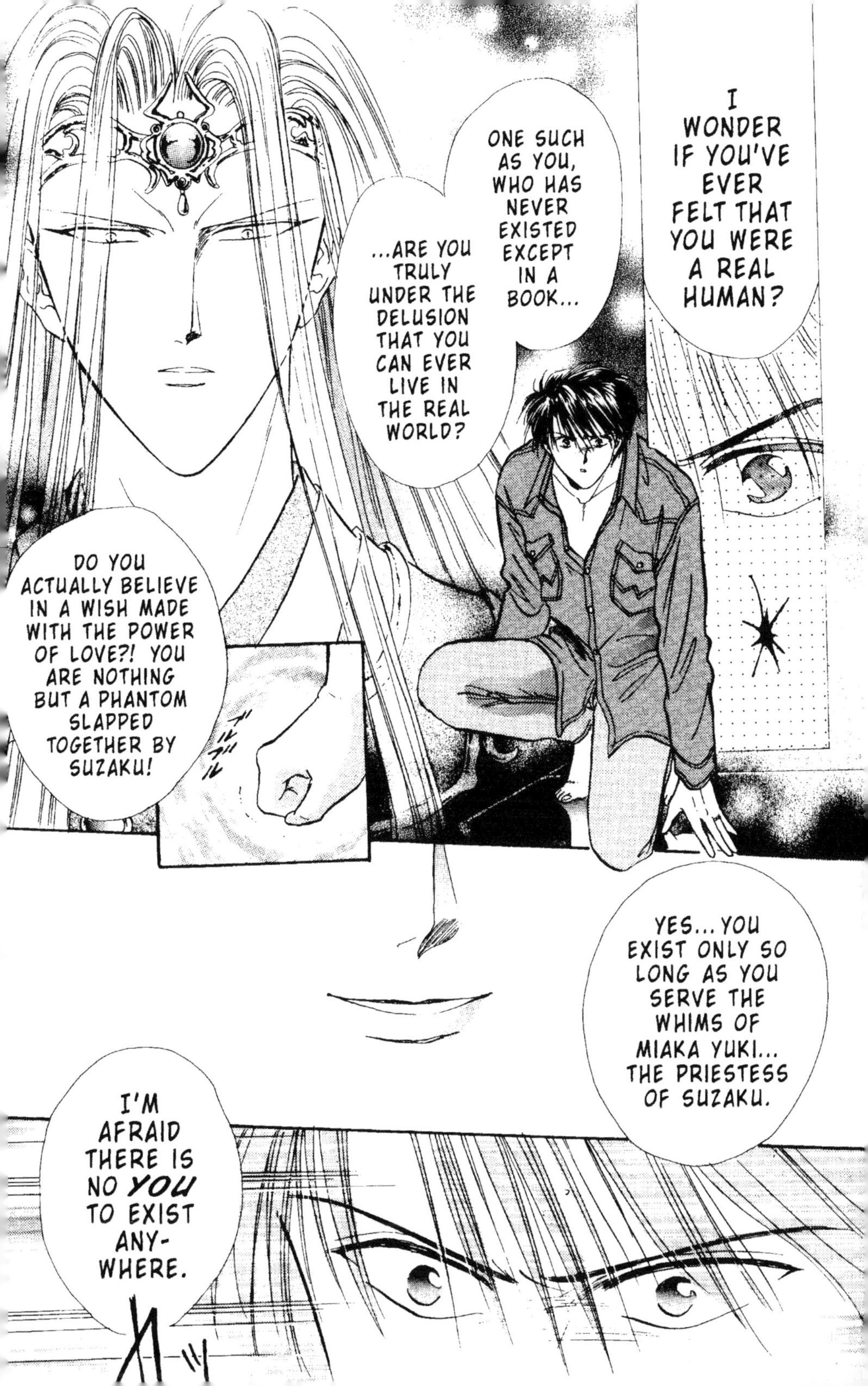
I WONDER IF YOU'VE EVER FELT THAT YOU WERE A REAL HUMAN?
ONE SUCH AS YOU, WHO HAS NEVER EXISTED EXCEPT IN A BOOK...
...ARE YOU TRULY UNDER THE DELUSION THAT YOU CAN EVER LIVE IN THE REAL WORLD?
DO YOU ACTUALLY BELIEVE IN A WISH MADE WITH THE POWER OF LOVE?! YOU ARE NOTHING BUT A PHANTOM SLAPPED TOGETHER BY SUZAKU!
YES... YOU EXIST ONLY SO LONG AS YOU SERVE THE WHIMS OF MIAKA YUKI... THE PRIESTESS OF SUZAKU.
I'M AFRAID THERE IS NO *YOU* TO EXIST ANYWHERE.

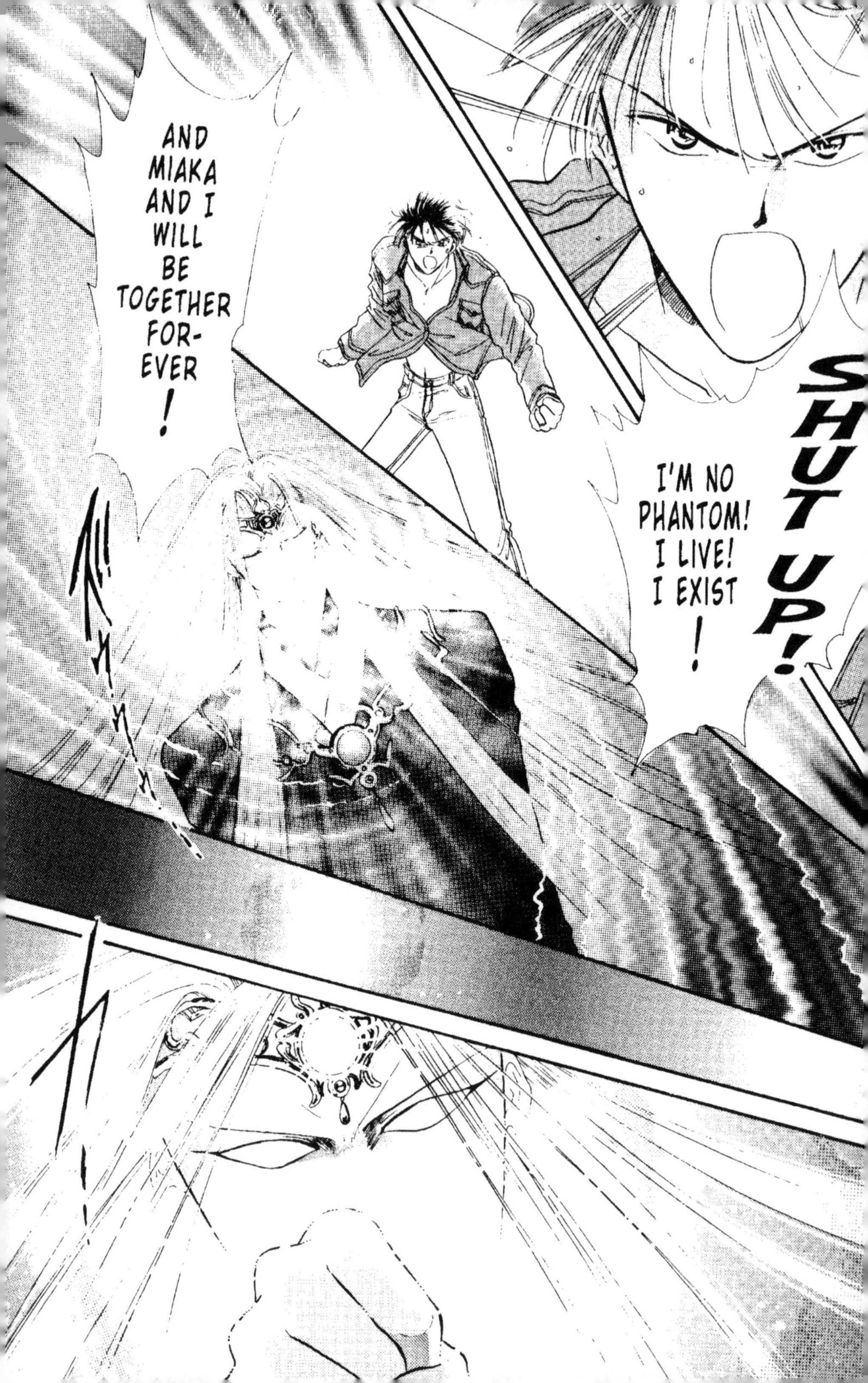
SHUT UP!
I'M NO PHANTOM! I LIVE! I EXIST!
AND MIAKA AND I WILL BE TOGETHER FOR-EVER!

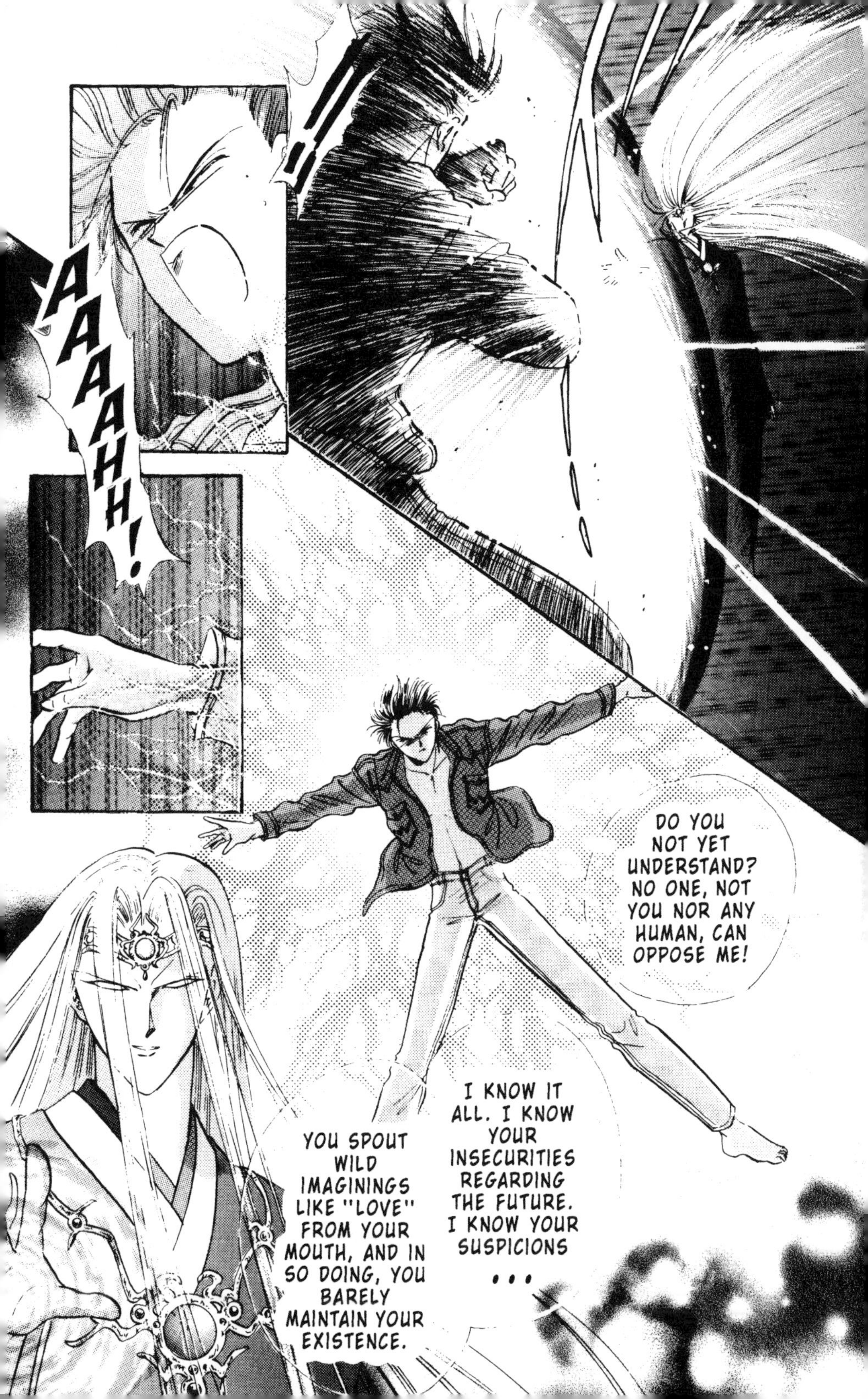
AAAAHH!
DO YOU NOT YET UNDERSTAND? NO ONE, NOT YOU NOR ANY HUMAN, CAN OPPOSE ME!
I KNOW IT ALL. I KNOW YOUR INSECURITIES REGARDING THE FUTURE. I KNOW YOUR SUSPICIONS ...
YOU SPOUT WILD IMAGININGS LIKE "LOVE" FROM YOUR MOUTH, AND IN SO DOING, YOU BARELY MAINTAIN YOUR EXISTENCE.

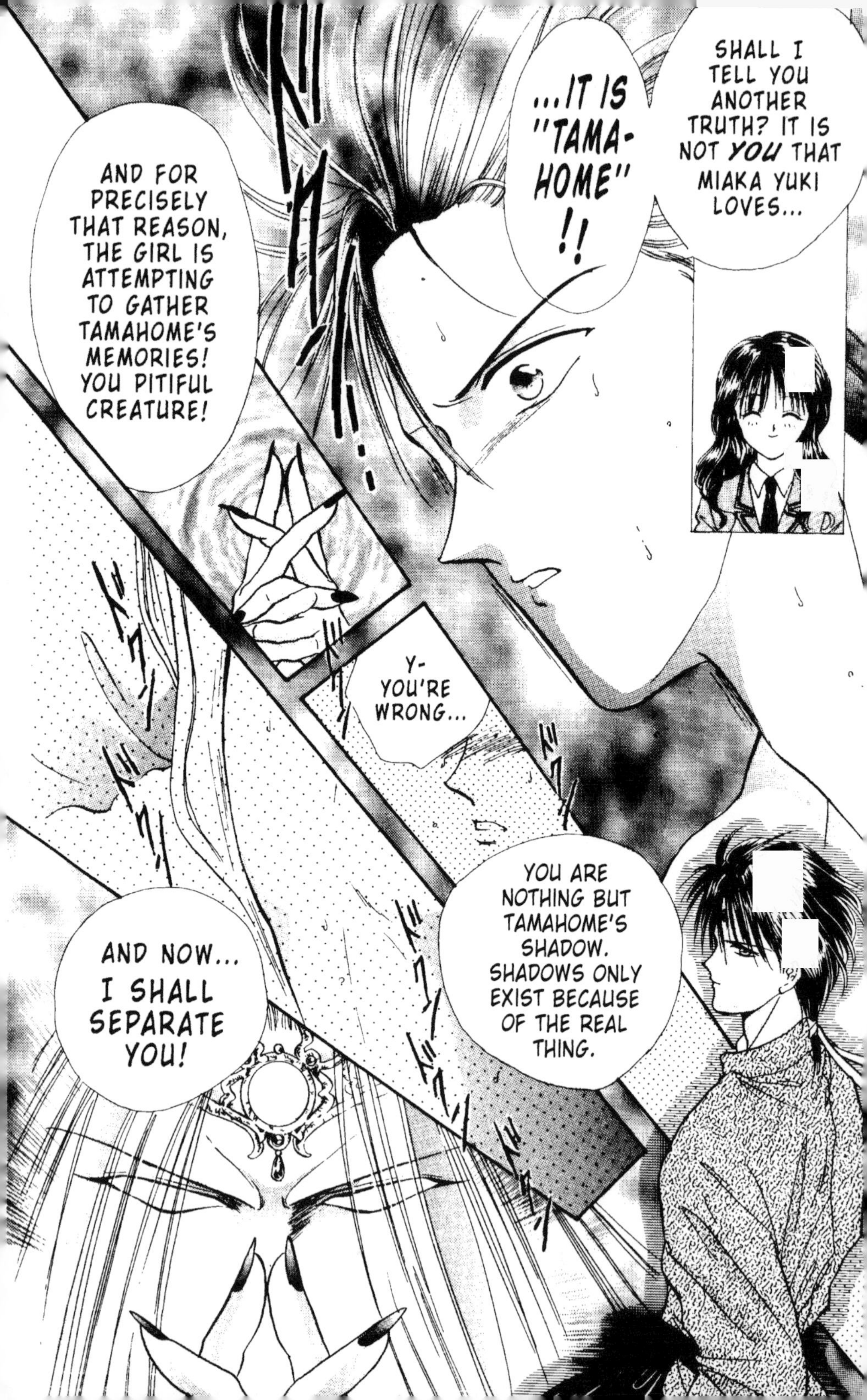
SHALL I TELL YOU ANOTHER TRUTH? IT IS NOT *YOU* THAT MIAKA YUKI LOVES...
...IT IS "TAMAHOME"!!
AND FOR PRECISELY THAT REASON, THE GIRL IS ATTEMPTING TO GATHER TAMAHOME'S MEMORIES! YOU PITIFUL CREATURE!
Y-YOU'RE WRONG...
YOU ARE NOTHING BUT TAMAHOME'S SHADOW. SHADOWS ONLY EXIST BECAUSE OF THE REAL THING.
AND NOW... I SHALL SEPARATE YOU!

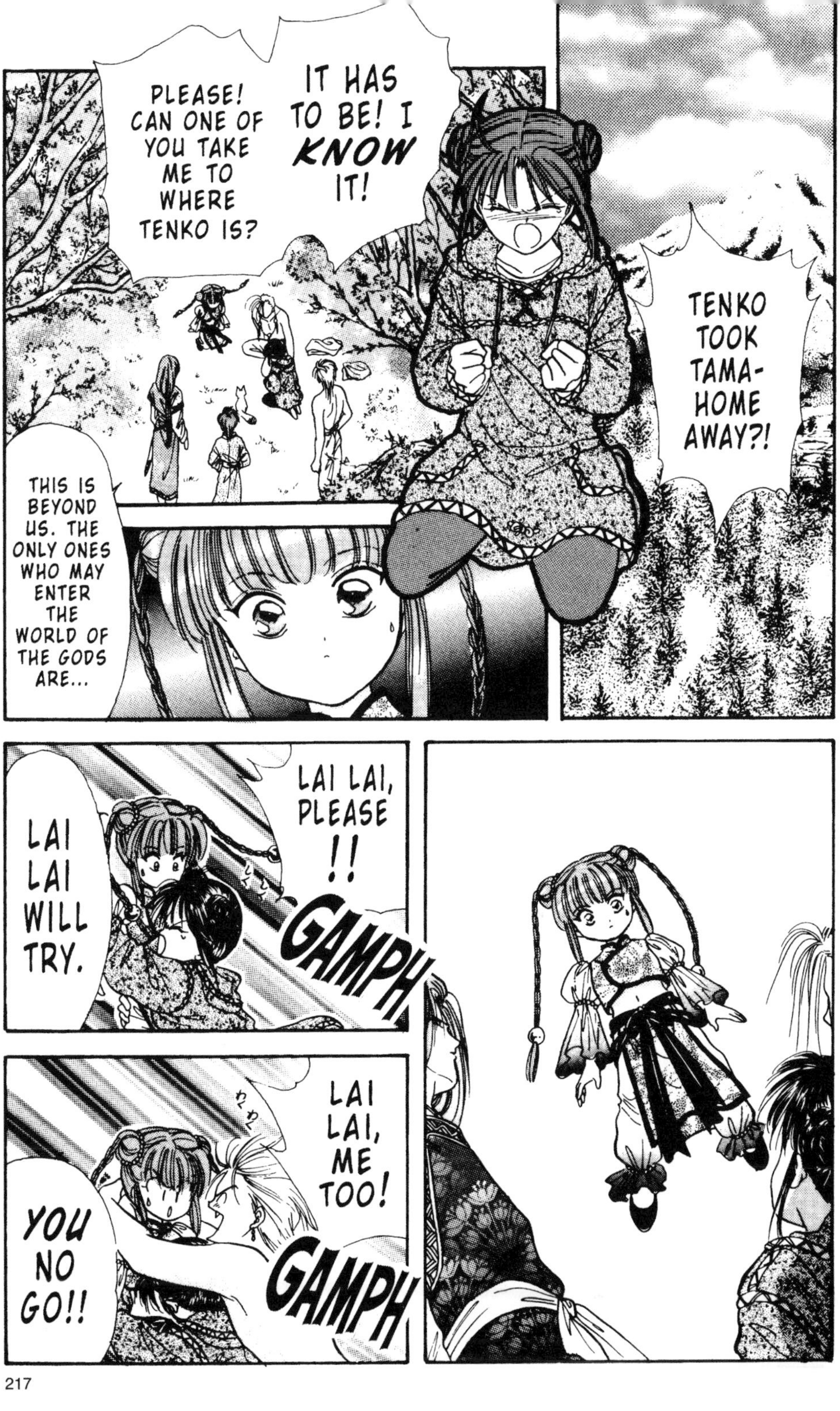
TENKO TOOK TAMA-HOME AWAY?!
IT HAS TO BE! I *KNOW* IT!
PLEASE! CAN ONE OF YOU TAKE ME TO WHERE TENKO IS?
THIS IS BEYOND US. THE ONLY ONES WHO MAY ENTER THE WORLD OF THE GODS ARE...
LAI LAI, PLEASE!!
GAMPH
LAI LAI WILL TRY.
LAI LAI, ME TOO!
GAMPH
YOU NO GO!!

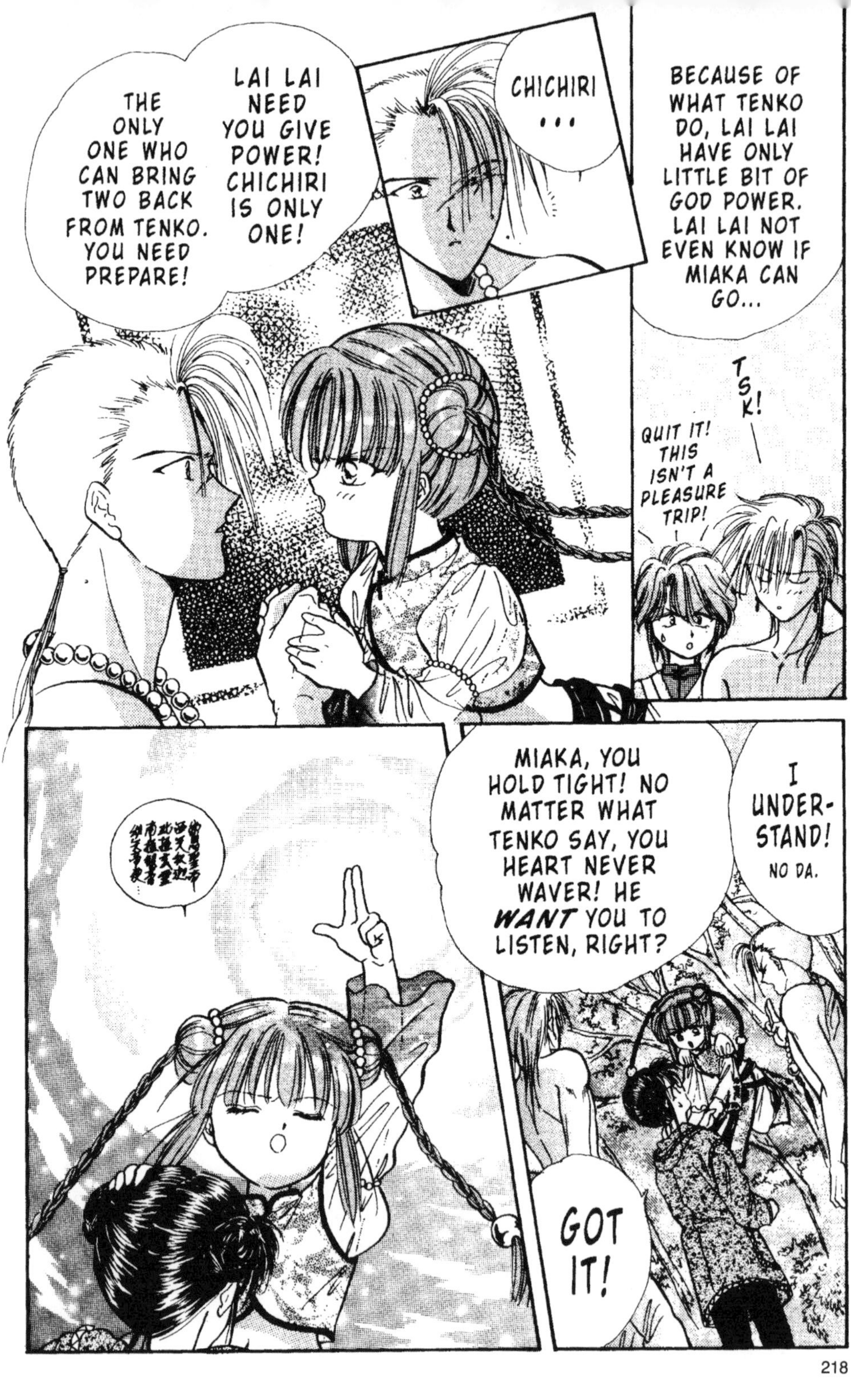
BECAUSE OF WHAT TENKO DO, LAI LAI HAVE ONLY LITTLE BIT OF GOD POWER. LAI LAI NOT EVEN KNOW IF MIAKA CAN GO...
TSK!
QUIT IT! THIS ISN'T A PLEASURE TRIP!
CHICHIRI...
LAI LAI NEED YOU GIVE POWER! CHICHIRI IS ONLY ONE!
THE ONLY ONE WHO CAN BRING TWO BACK FROM TENKO. YOU NEED PREPARE!
I UNDERSTAND! NO DA.
MIAKA, YOU HOLD TIGHT! NO MATTER WHAT TENKO SAY, YOU HEART NEVER WAVER! HE WANT YOU TO LISTEN, RIGHT?
GOT IT!

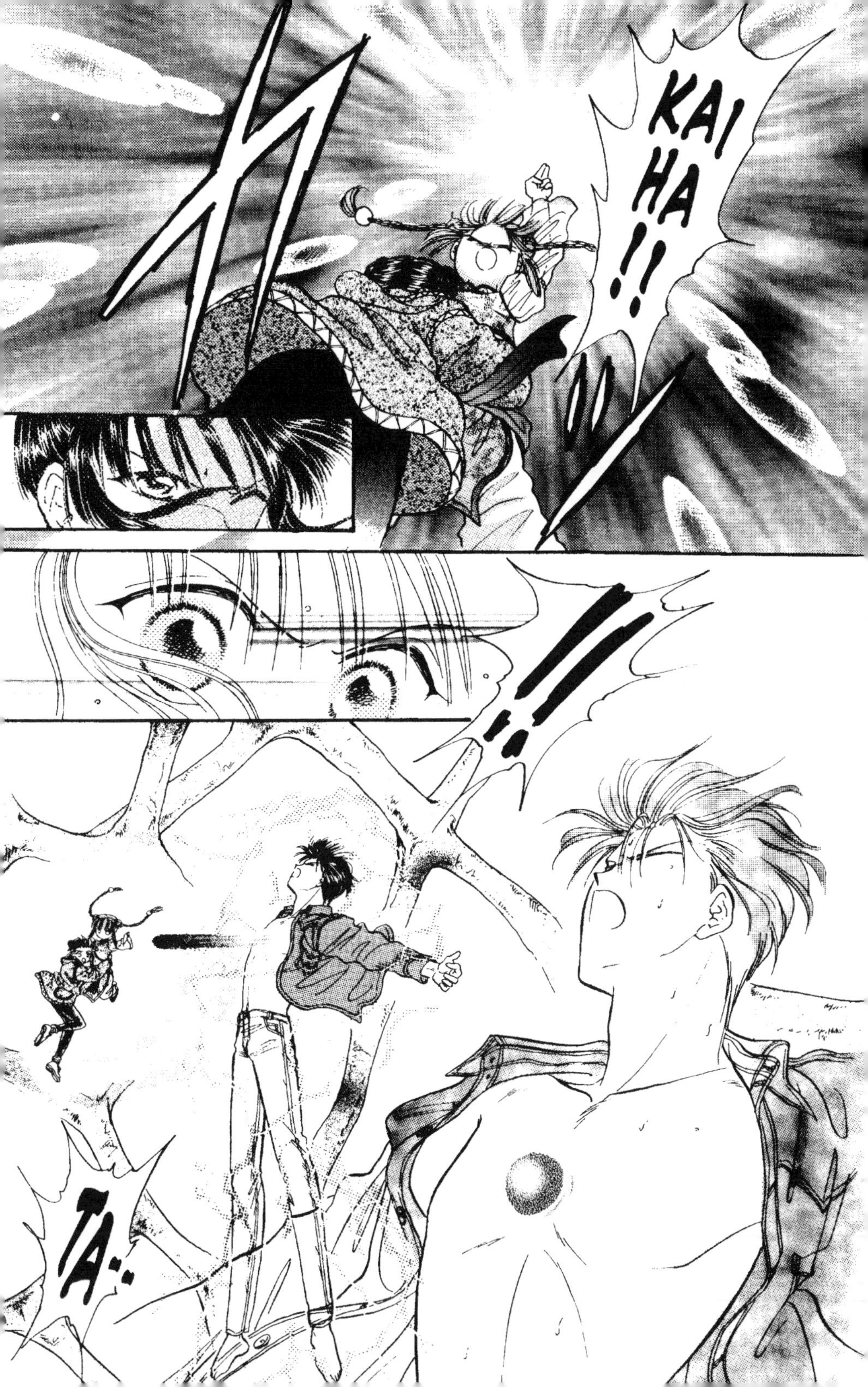
KAI HA!!
!!
TA...

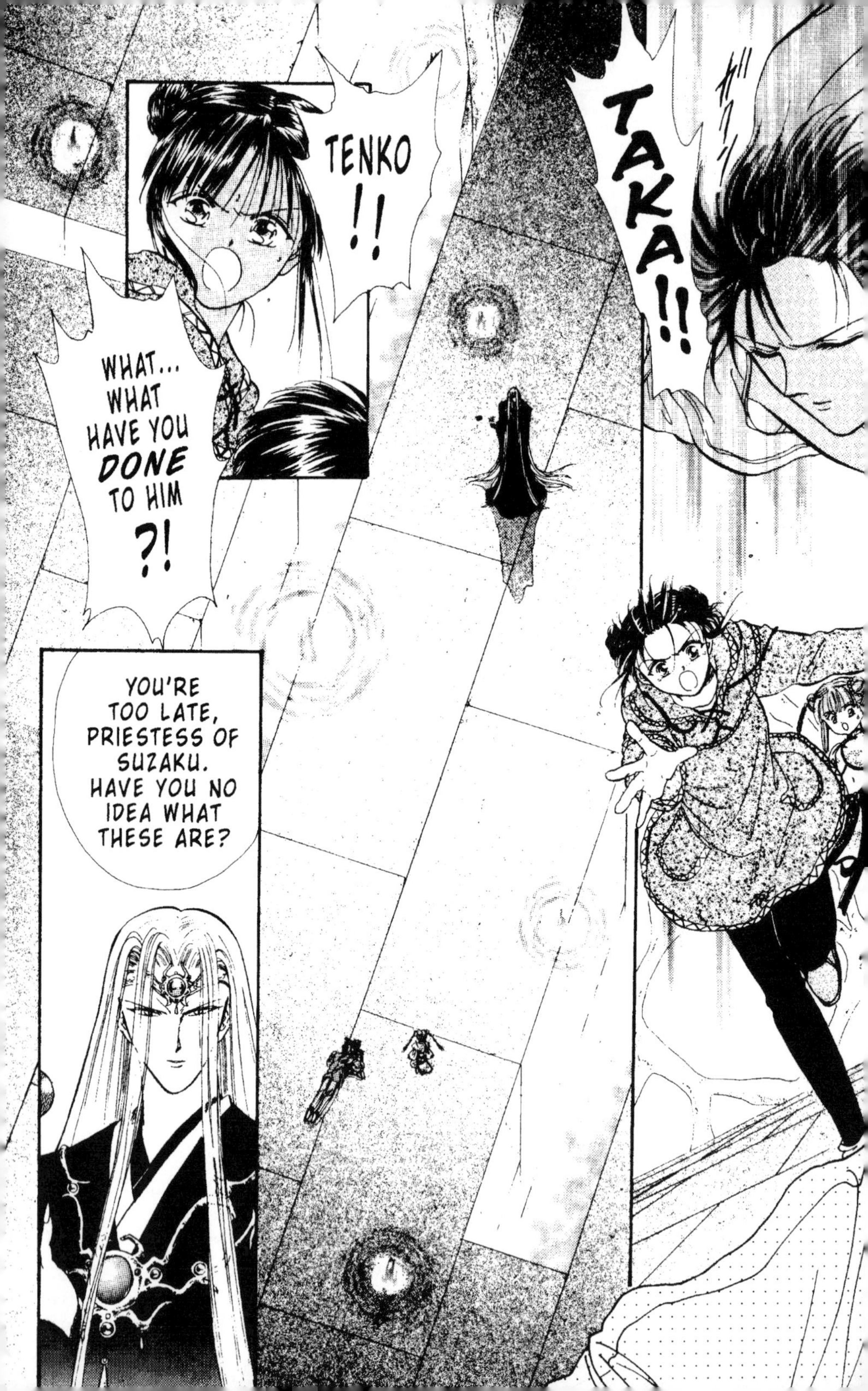
TAKA!!
TENKO!!
WHAT... WHAT HAVE YOU *DONE* TO HIM?!
YOU'RE TOO LATE, PRIESTESS OF SUZAKU. HAVE YOU NO IDEA WHAT THESE ARE?

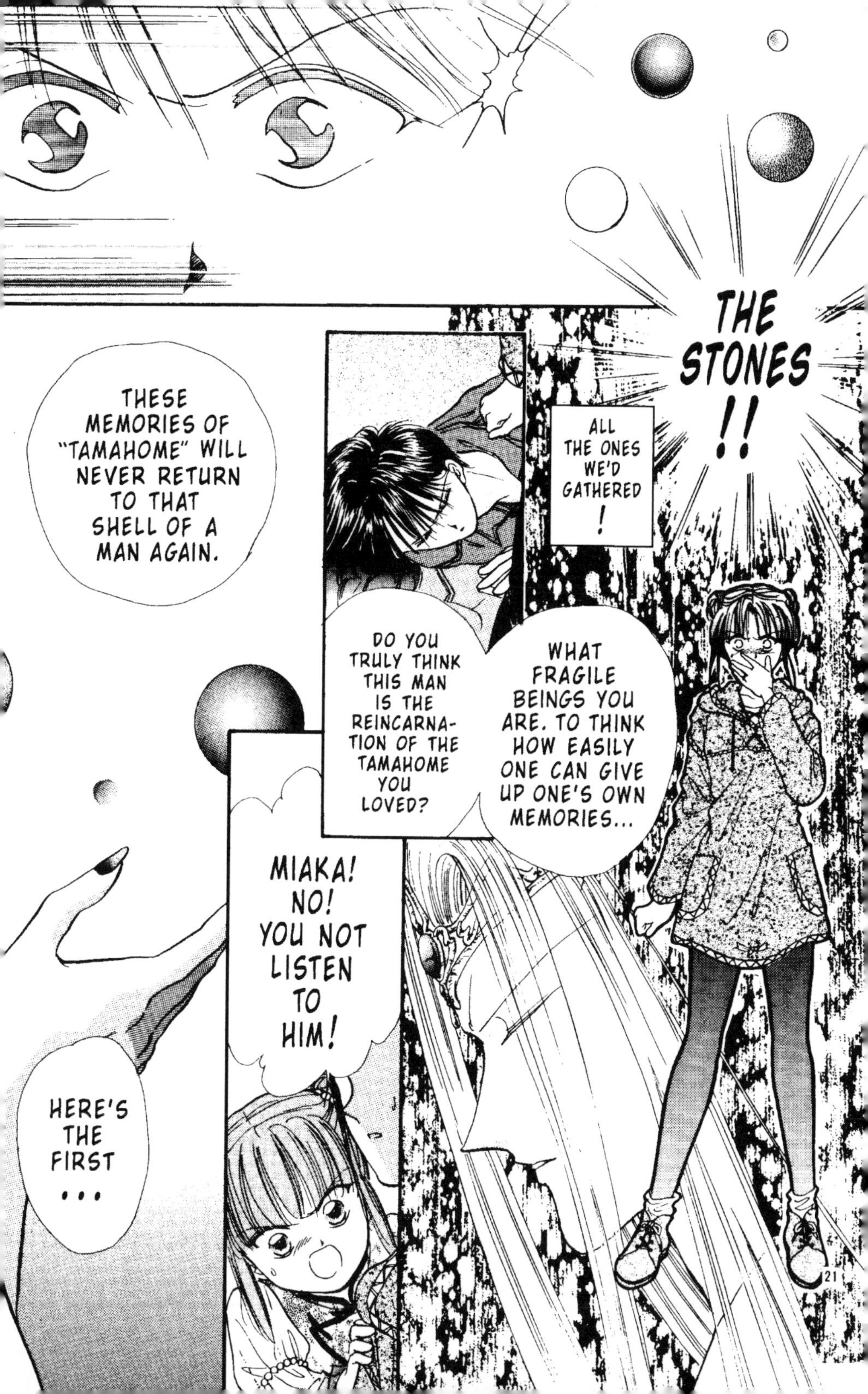
THE STONES!!
ALL THE ONES WE'D GATHERED!
WHAT FRAGILE BEINGS YOU ARE. TO THINK HOW EASILY ONE CAN GIVE UP ONE'S OWN MEMORIES...
DO YOU TRULY THINK THIS MAN IS THE REINCARNATION OF THE TAMAHOME YOU LOVED?
THESE MEMORIES OF "TAMAHOME" WILL NEVER RETURN TO THAT SHELL OF A MAN AGAIN.
MIAKA! NO! YOU NOT LISTEN TO HIM!
HERE'S THE FIRST...

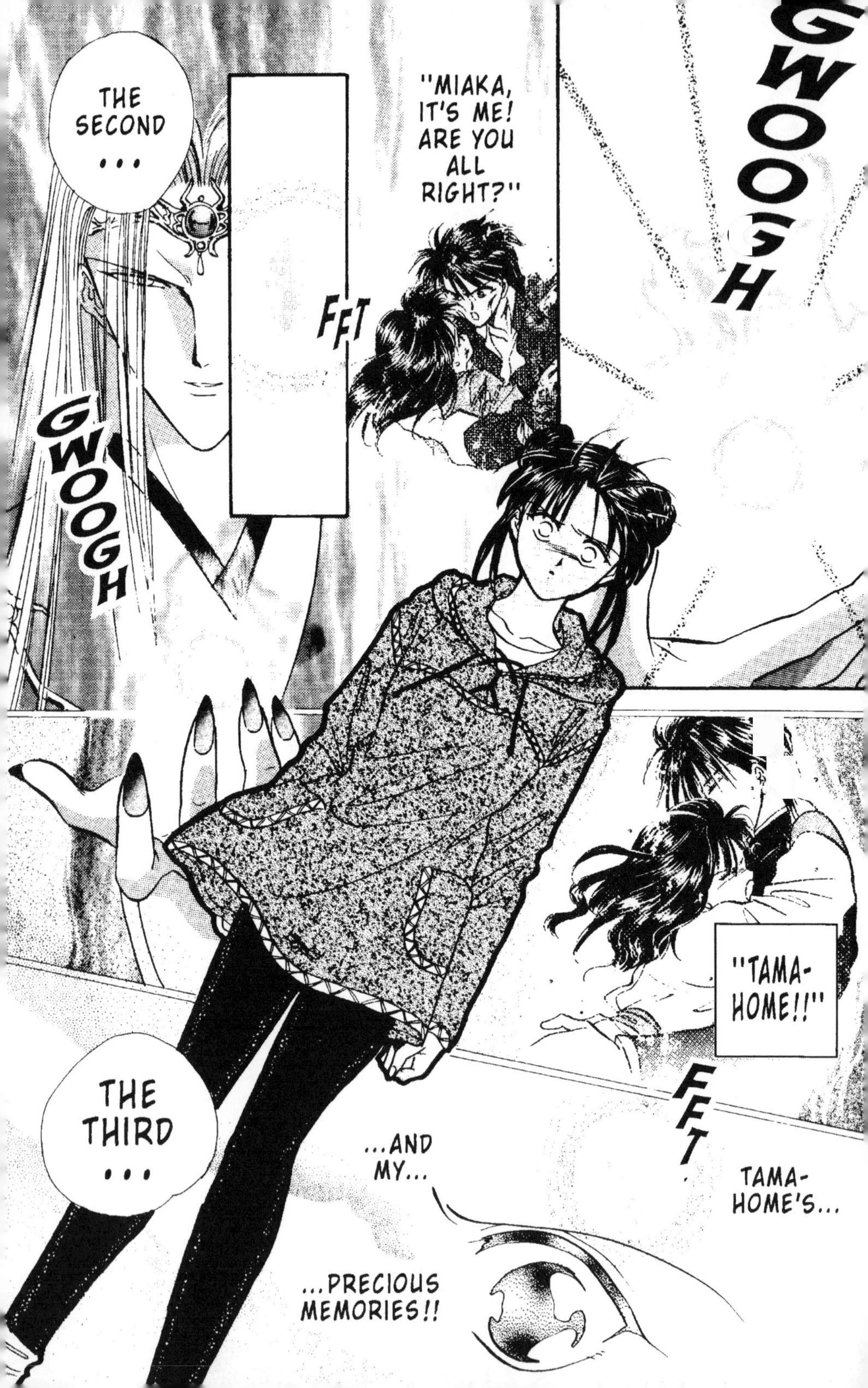
GWOOOGH
"MIAKA, IT'S ME! ARE YOU ALL RIGHT?"
FFT
THE SECOND ...
GWOOGH
"TAMA-HOME!!"
FFT
TAMA-HOME'S...
...AND MY...
...PRECIOUS MEMORIES!!
THE THIRD ...

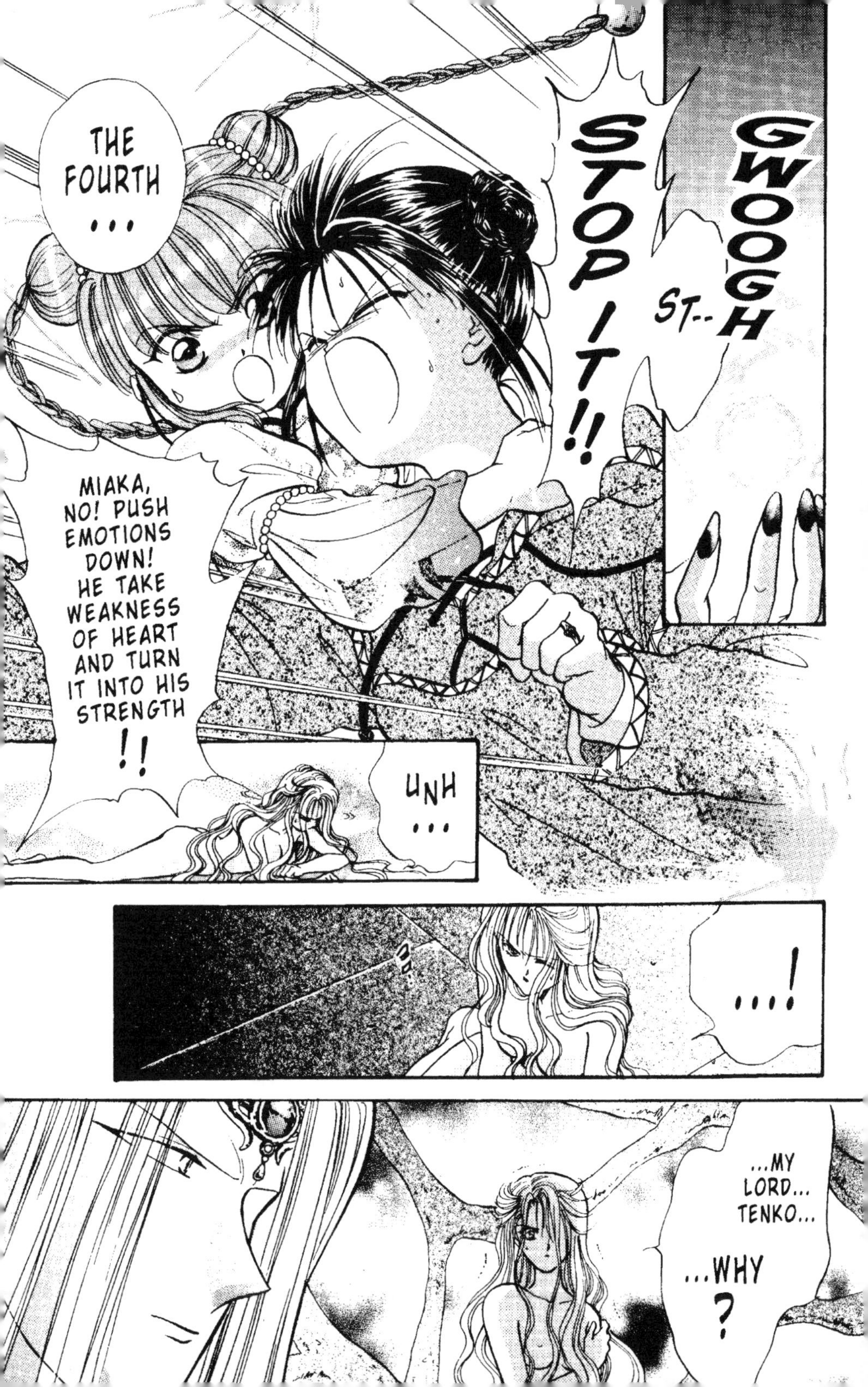
GWOOGH
ST--
STOP IT!!
THE FOURTH ...
MIAKA, NO! PUSH EMOTIONS DOWN! HE TAKE WEAKNESS OF HEART AND TURN IT INTO HIS STRENGTH !!
UNH ...
...!
...MY LORD... TENKO...
...WHY ?

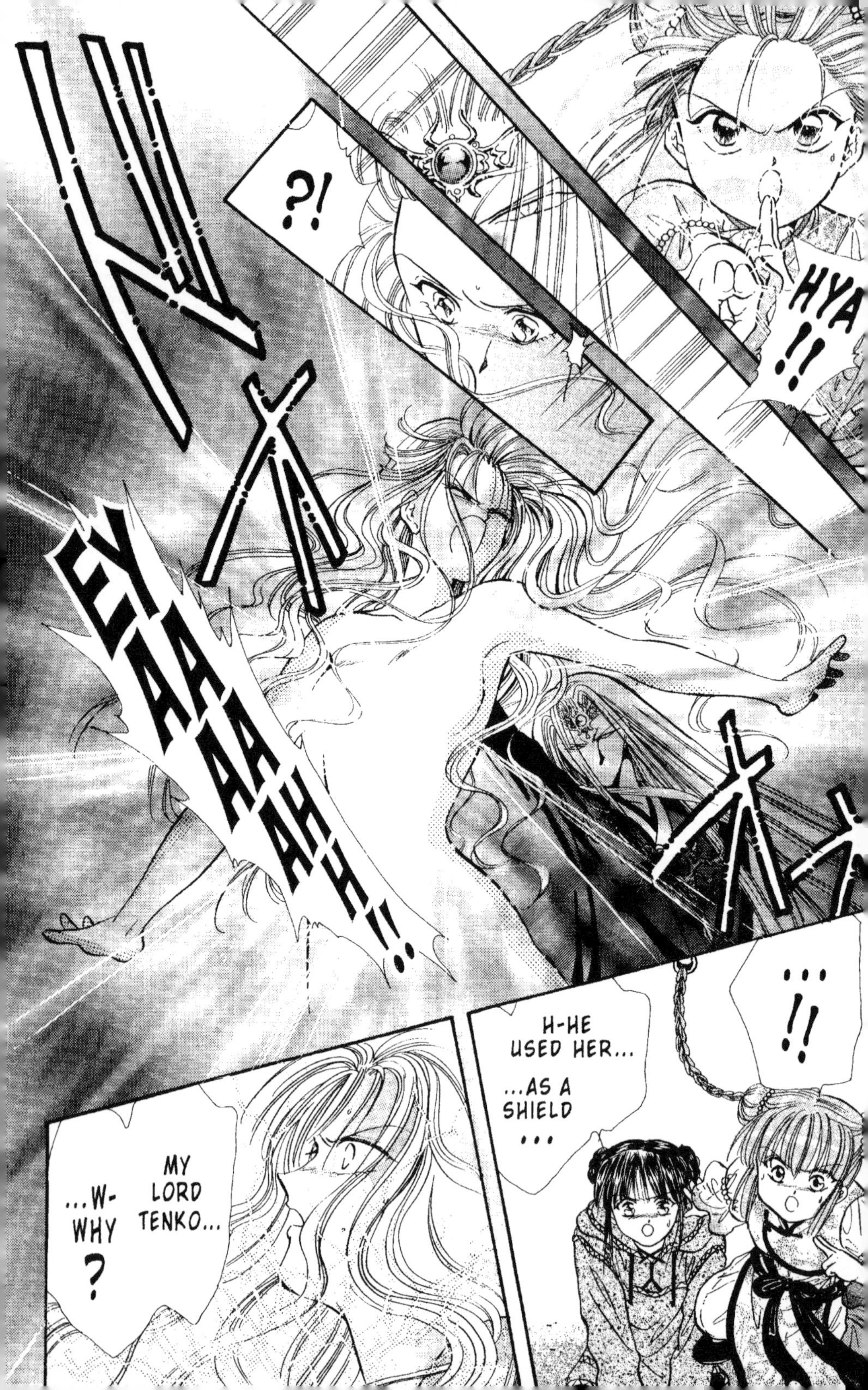
?!
HYA !!
ZU
ZA
EYAAAAAAHH!!
ZA
ZA
...!!
H-HE USED HER...
...AS A SHIELD...
MY LORD TENKO...
...W-WHY?

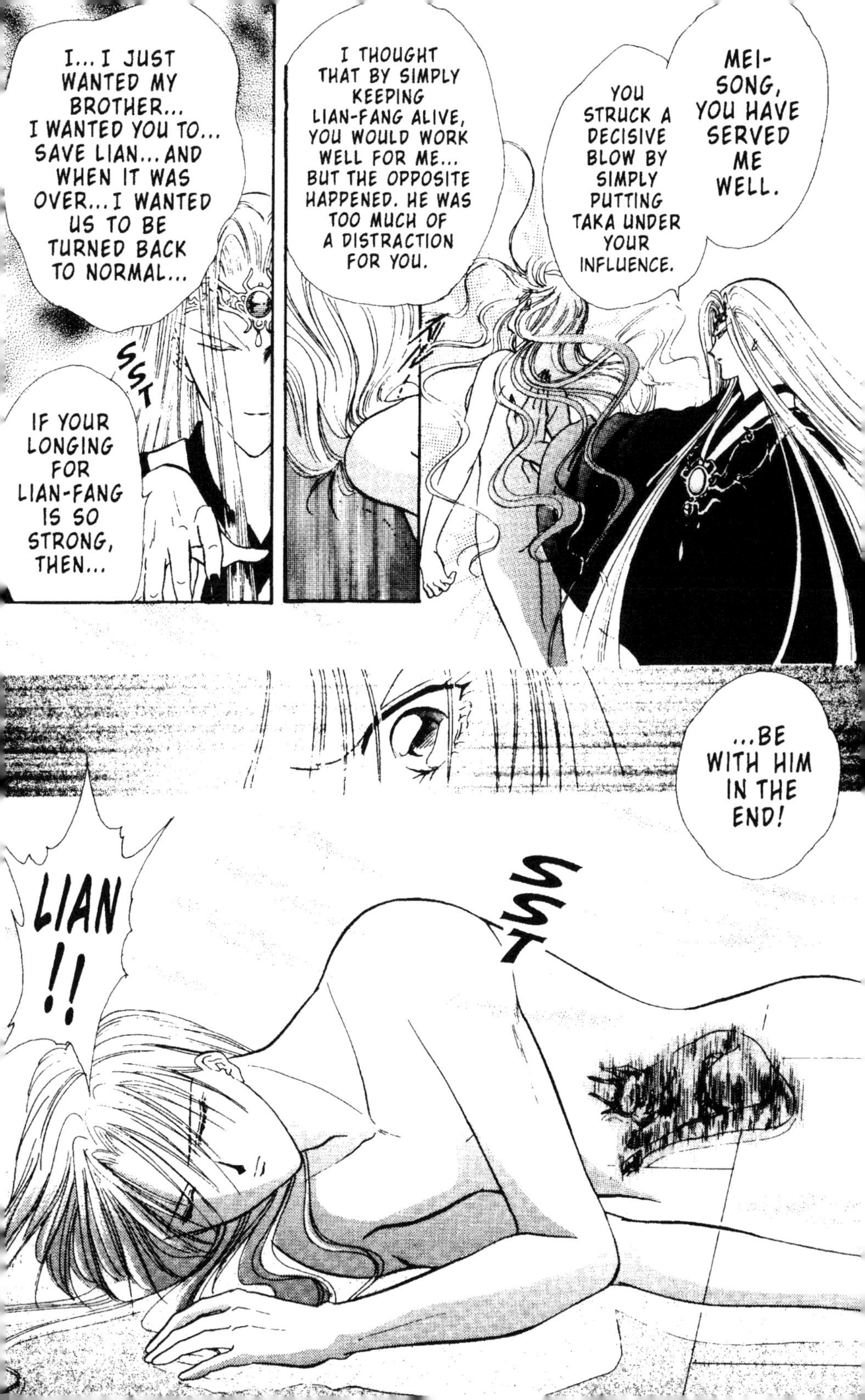

MEI-SONG, YOU HAVE SERVED ME WELL.
YOU STRUCK A DECISIVE BLOW BY SIMPLY PUTTING TAKA UNDER YOUR INFLUENCE.
I THOUGHT THAT BY SIMPLY KEEPING LIAN-FANG ALIVE, YOU WOULD WORK WELL FOR ME... BUT THE OPPOSITE HAPPENED. HE WAS TOO MUCH OF A DISTRACTION FOR YOU.
I... I JUST WANTED MY BROTHER... I WANTED YOU TO... SAVE LIAN... AND WHEN IT WAS OVER... I WANTED US TO BE TURNED BACK TO NORMAL...
SST
IF YOUR LONGING FOR LIAN-FANG IS SO STRONG, THEN...
...BE WITH HIM IN THE END!
SST
LIAN!!

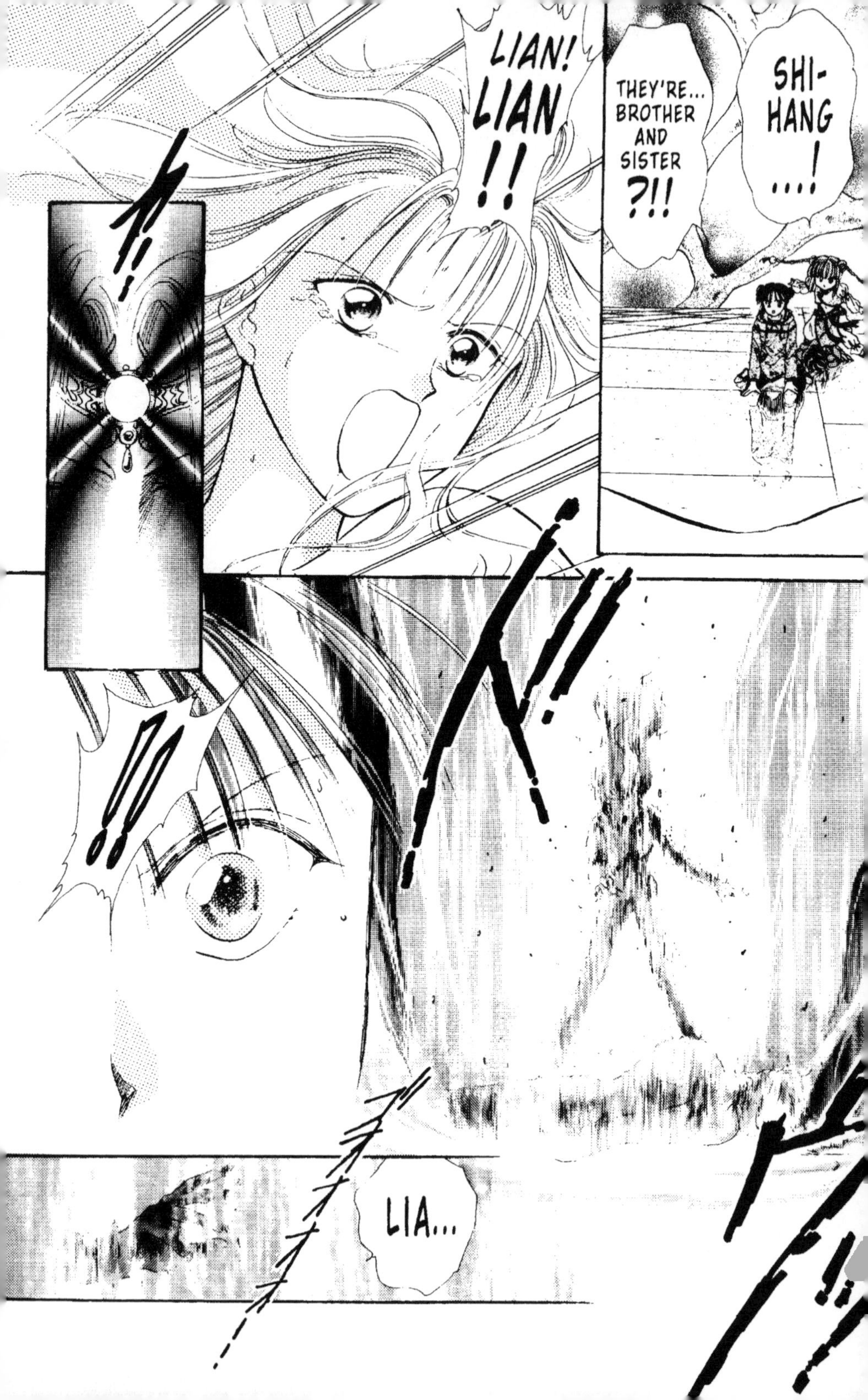
SHI-HANG ...!
THEY'RE... BROTHER AND SISTER ?!!
LIAN! LIAN !!
LIA...

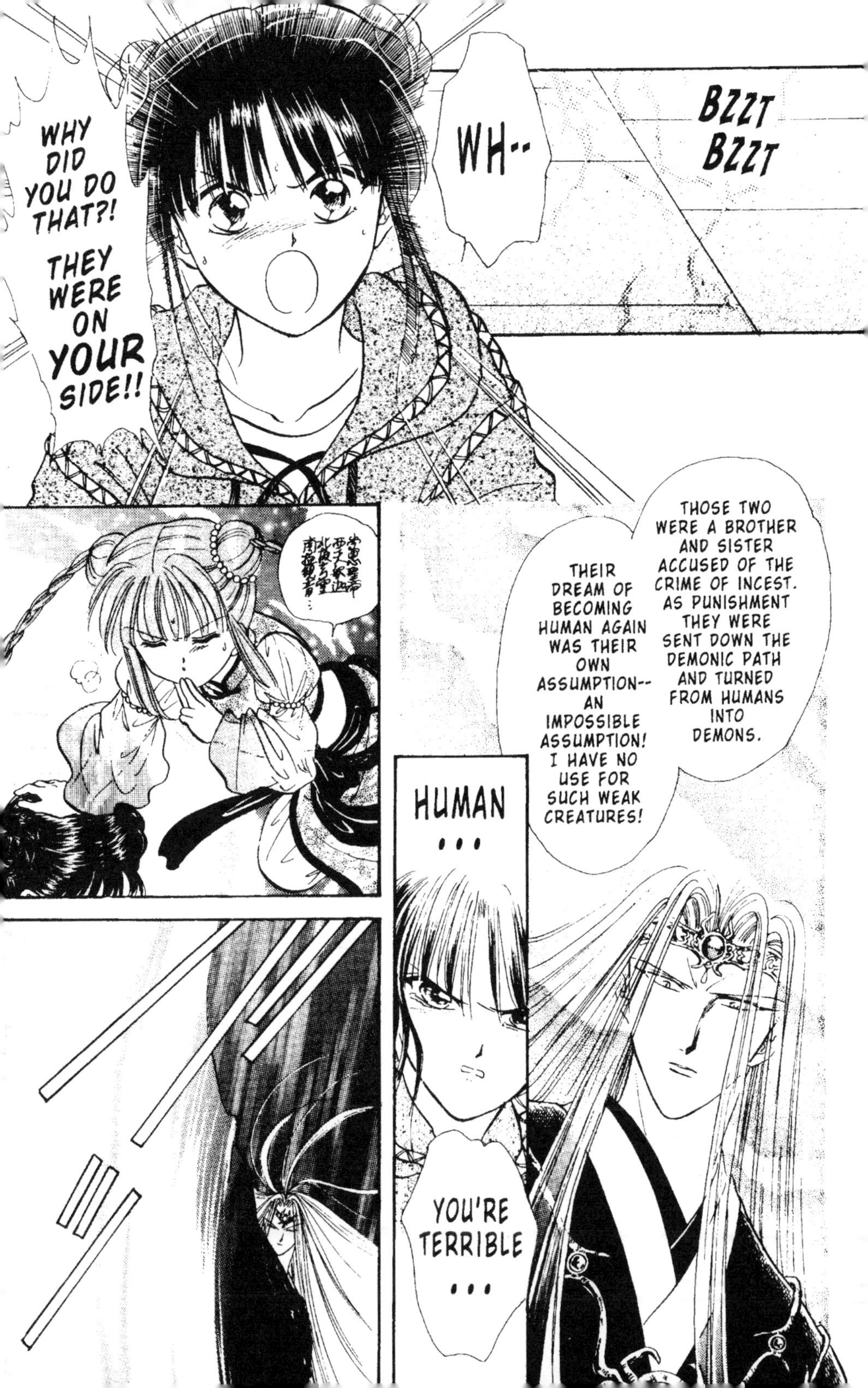
BZZT BZZT
WH--
WHY DID YOU DO THAT?!
THEY WERE ON YOUR SIDE!!
THOSE TWO WERE A BROTHER AND SISTER ACCUSED OF THE CRIME OF INCEST. AS PUNISHMENT THEY WERE SENT DOWN THE DEMONIC PATH AND TURNED FROM HUMANS INTO DEMONS.
THEIR DREAM OF BECOMING HUMAN AGAIN WAS THEIR OWN ASSUMPTION-- AN IMPOSSIBLE ASSUMPTION! I HAVE NO USE FOR SUCH WEAK CREATURES!
HUMAN ...
YOU'RE TERRIBLE ...

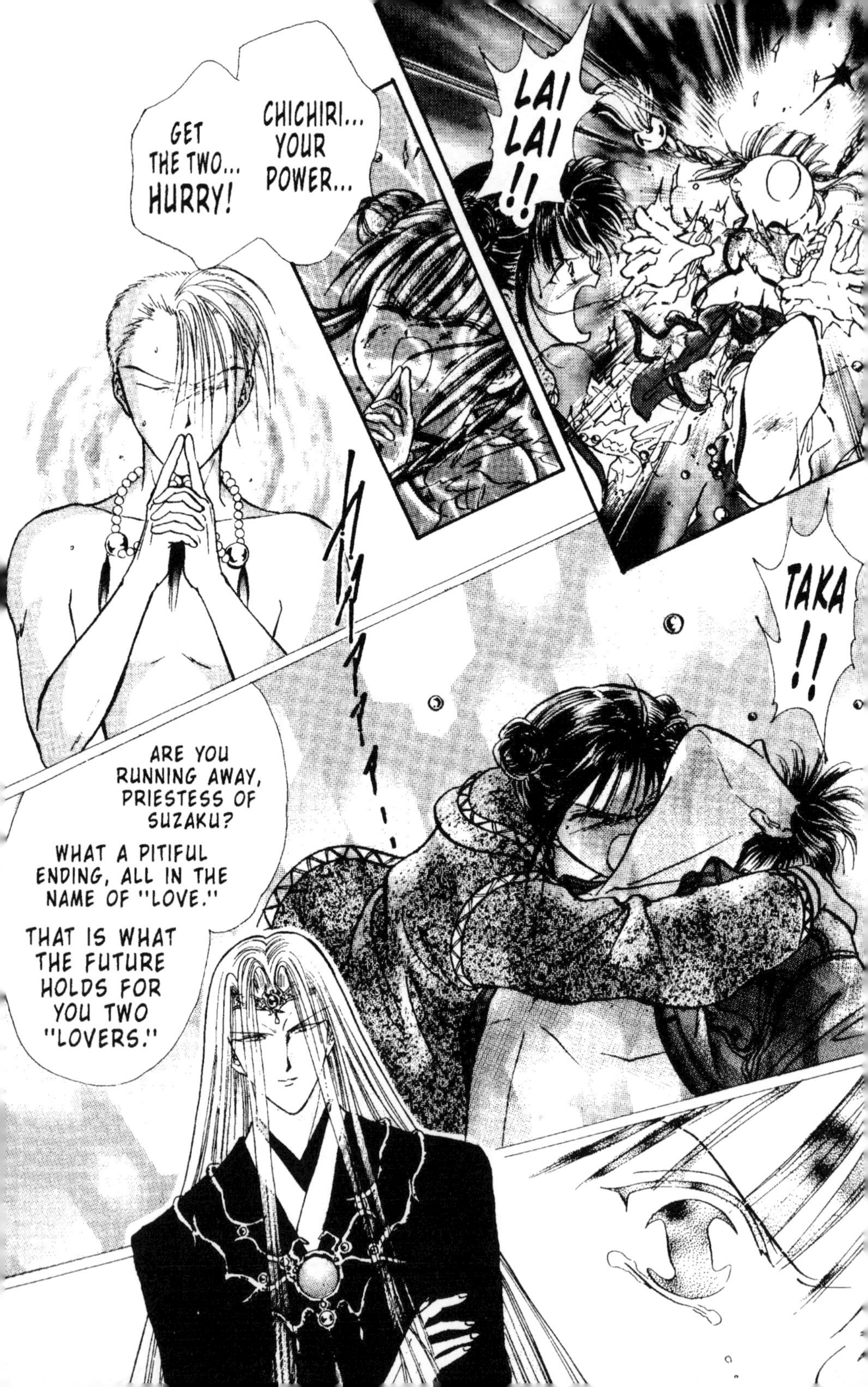
LAI LAI!!
CHICHIRI... YOUR POWER...
GET THE TWO... HURRY!
TAKA!!
ARE YOU RUNNING AWAY, PRIESTESS OF SUZAKU?
WHAT A PITIFUL ENDING, ALL IN THE NAME OF "LOVE."
THAT IS WHAT THE FUTURE HOLDS FOR YOU TWO "LOVERS."

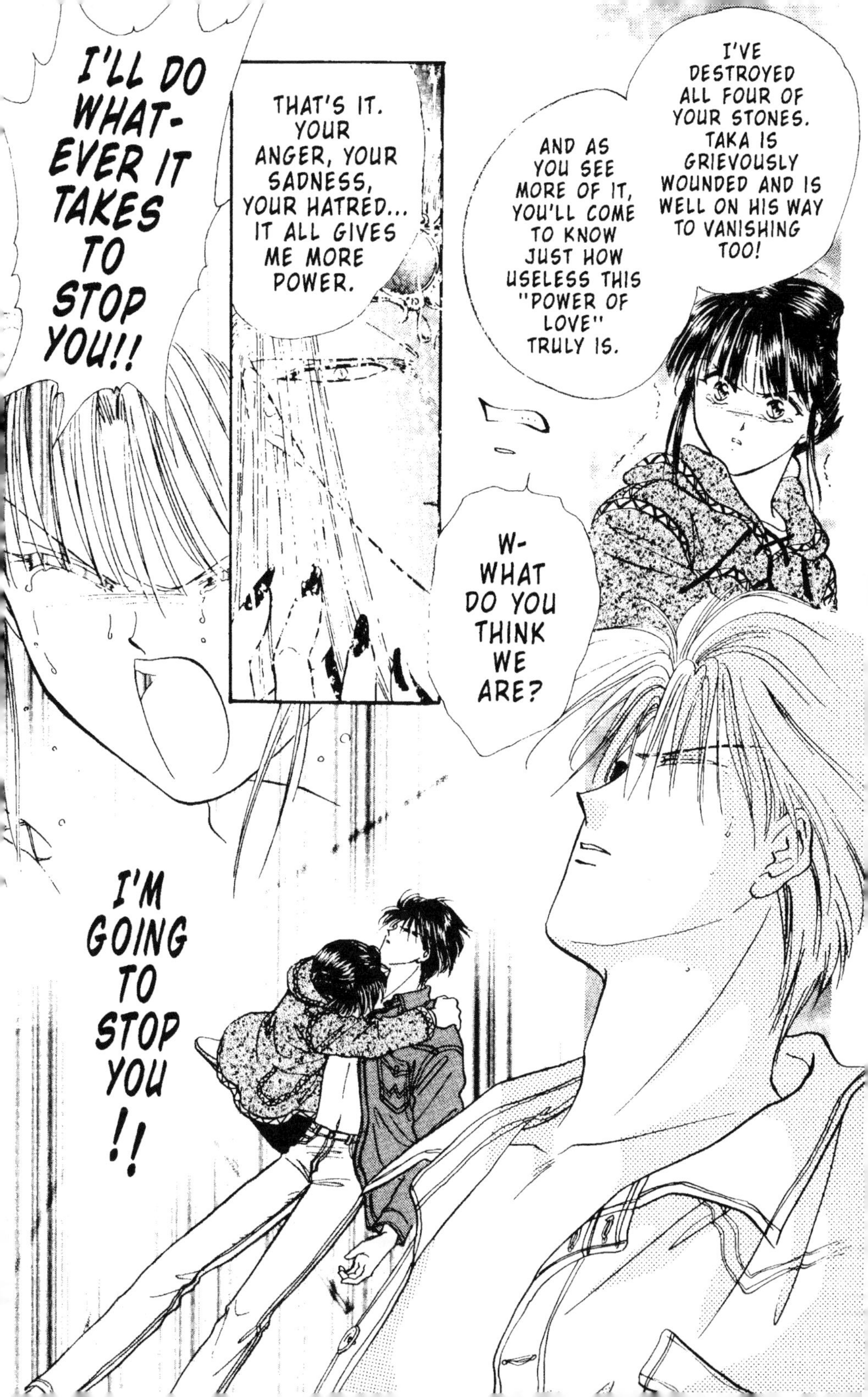
I'VE DESTROYED ALL FOUR OF YOUR STONES. TAKA IS GRIEVOUSLY WOUNDED AND IS WELL ON HIS WAY TO VANISHING TOO!
AND AS YOU SEE MORE OF IT, YOU'LL COME TO KNOW JUST HOW USELESS THIS "POWER OF LOVE" TRULY IS.
THAT'S IT. YOUR ANGER, YOUR SADNESS, YOUR HATRED... IT ALL GIVES ME MORE POWER.
I'LL DO WHAT-EVER IT TAKES TO STOP YOU!!
W-WHAT DO YOU THINK WE ARE?
I'M GOING TO STOP YOU !!

Chapter Ninety-Six
Overflowing Doubt

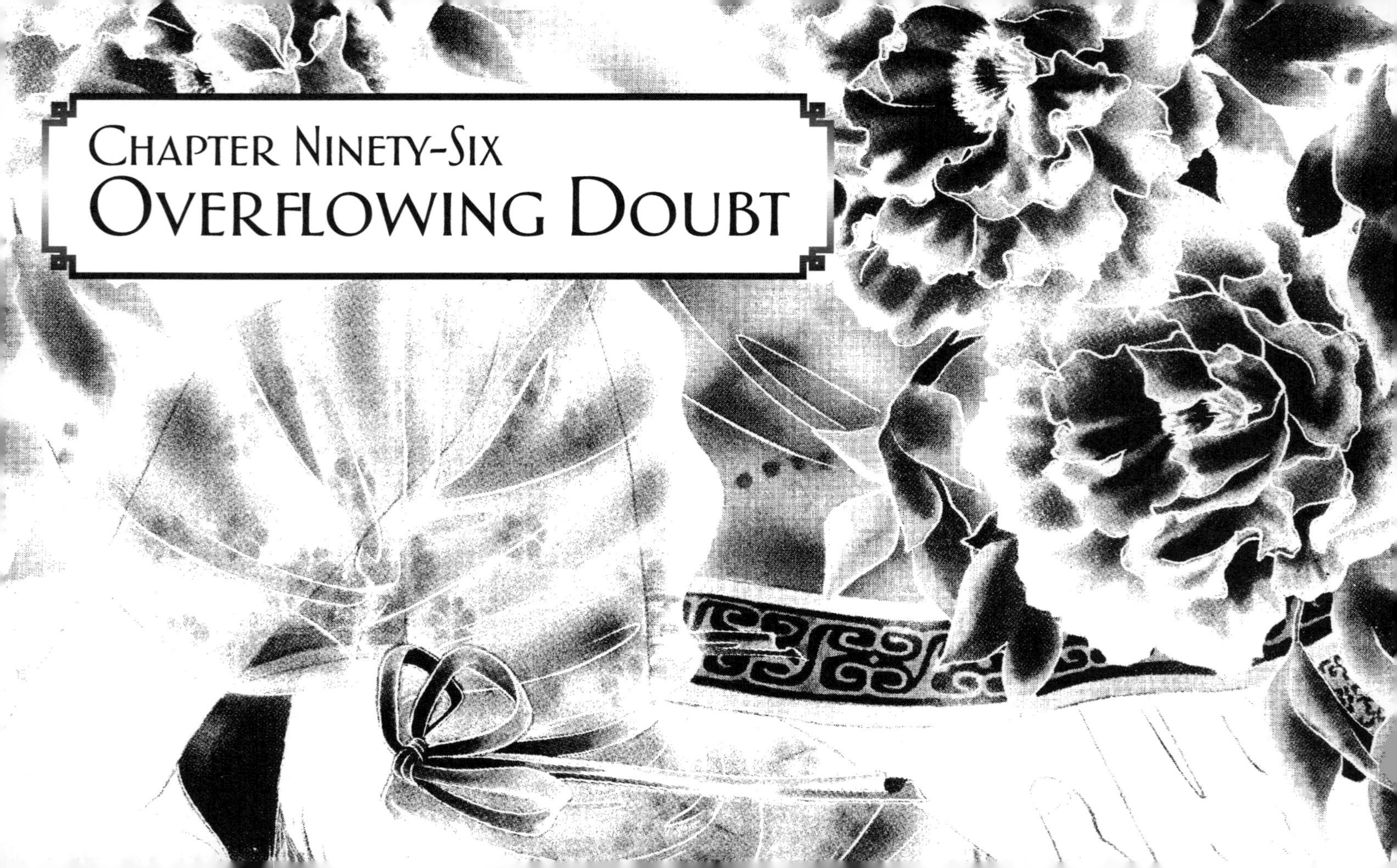

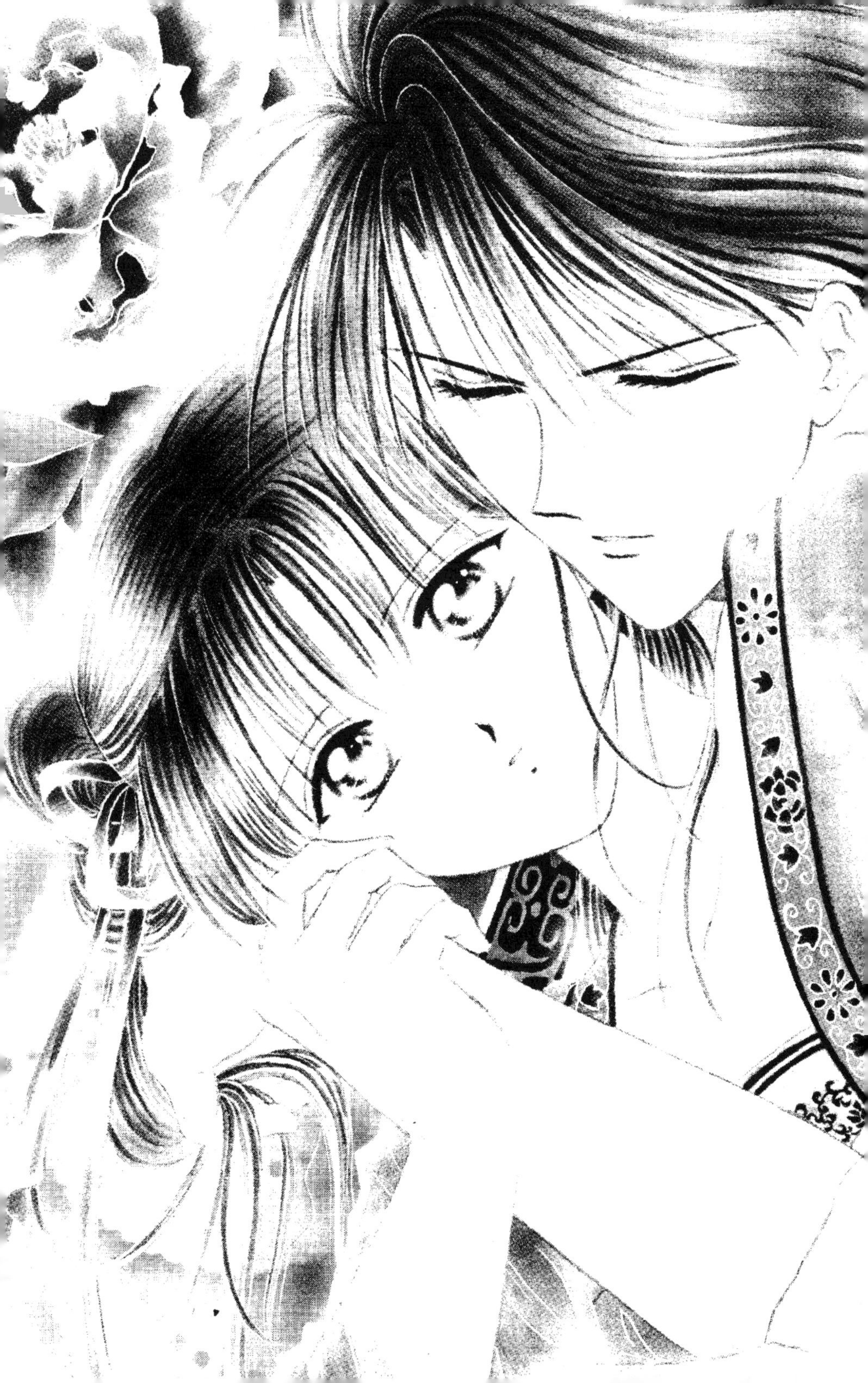

THE TWINS, BY REQUEST →

DEPICTING A SCENE IF THEY BOTH WERE ALIVE TODAY (OF COURSE, ONE IS STILL ALIVE, BUT...). (AT 17-YEARS-OLD VERSION)

What happens when I use an art pen.

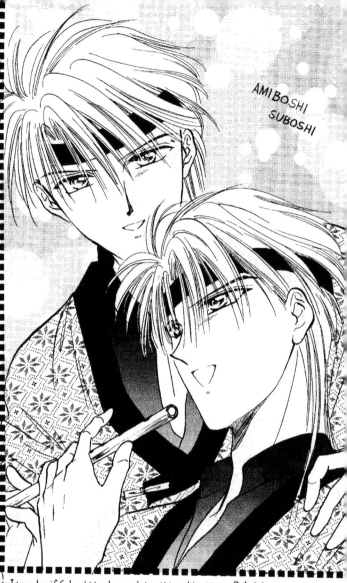

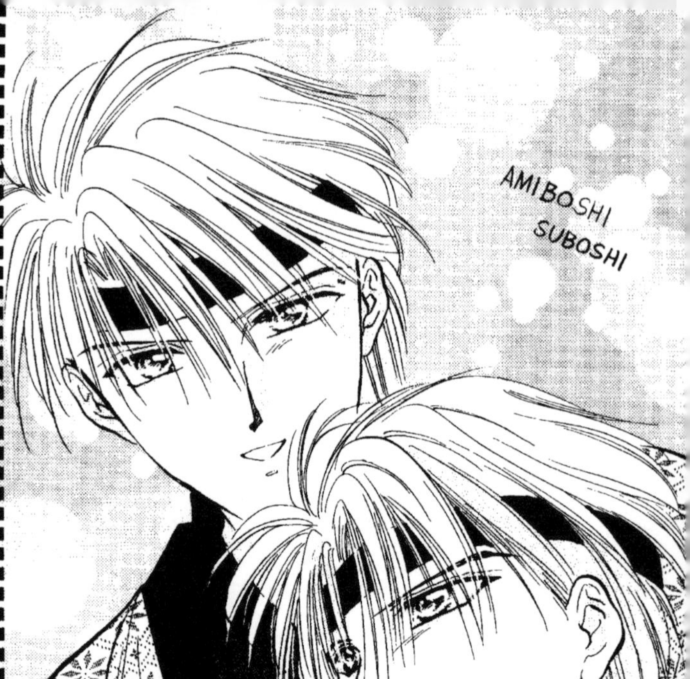
AMIBOSHI
SUBOSHI

I get a lot of calls to trot out Amiboshi again! But as I said previously, this is the story of Suzaku, Part 2, and please accept it as such.
A Suboshi fan said "Poor Suboshi" at the way he died, but it was just karma coming around. In other words, each of them were rewarded or punished as each of their actions warranted.
Suboshi's feelings for Yui never came to anything, but in the end, he even took on his brother's karma.
And Amiboshi... I keep telling you the way he talked to Miaka in volume 10 wasn't born out of romantic feelings! (The images made an impression, but that didn't represent his true feelings. I drew it in an erotic way as a bonus for the fans.) Personally, I think that Amiboshi gives off the feel of a rabbit... Rabbit?!

The anime conveyed that very well!!

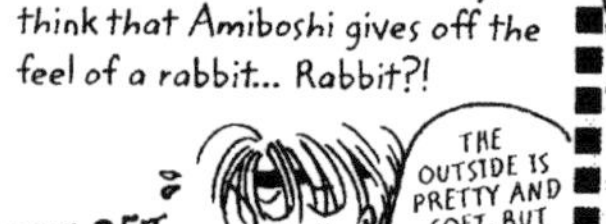
PET PET
PAT PAT
THE OUTSIDE IS PRETTY AND SOFT, BUT THERE'S A CERTAIN SADNESS INSIDE.

I wonder if Suboshi is always doing things like that...? It's no good! No one can ever come between those brothers. They're best together!! ...I think. And now, the two are one. Amiboshi's happiness is a testament to Suboshi's spirit. Amiboshi will always remember Suboshi somewhere in his heart. And when the day comes when he can remember fully... At that time, he'll be a truly mature and strong person. He'll be ready to handle the truth and accept it. Even when Amiboshi was acting as a spy, he always had in mind that Suboshi lived under Nakago, and even if he wanted to betray Nakago, he couldn't. (Nakago is so evil!) The Suzaku warriors really came to like him. If Amiboshi ever heard that Suboshi murdered Tamahome's family, he'd be devestated. One reader said, "I notice that the twins bring out each other's characteristics. Amiboshi brought out the cruelty in Suboshi, and Suboshi brought out the gentleness in Amiboshi." *Heh, heh, heh!*

In the CD album "Seiryu no Gyakushuhen" (Revenge of Seiryu Chapter), Amiboshi's song made me cry. But I wanted Suboshi to sing it! Suboshi's song made me laugh. I mean, it was so cool, but the lyrics are so straightforward. How could he ever bring himself to sing that to Yui? ☺ All the other songs were great! And Hotohori's... Tomo didn't get a song! *Sniff, sniff!*

Buy the CD!

In all honesty, although their ways of showing love may have been wrong, they both loved very deeply.

THANK YOU FOR PUTTING NAKAGO ON THE COVER! THANK YOU!! AND SO, NEXT TIME, I'LL TALK ABOUT NAKAGO...

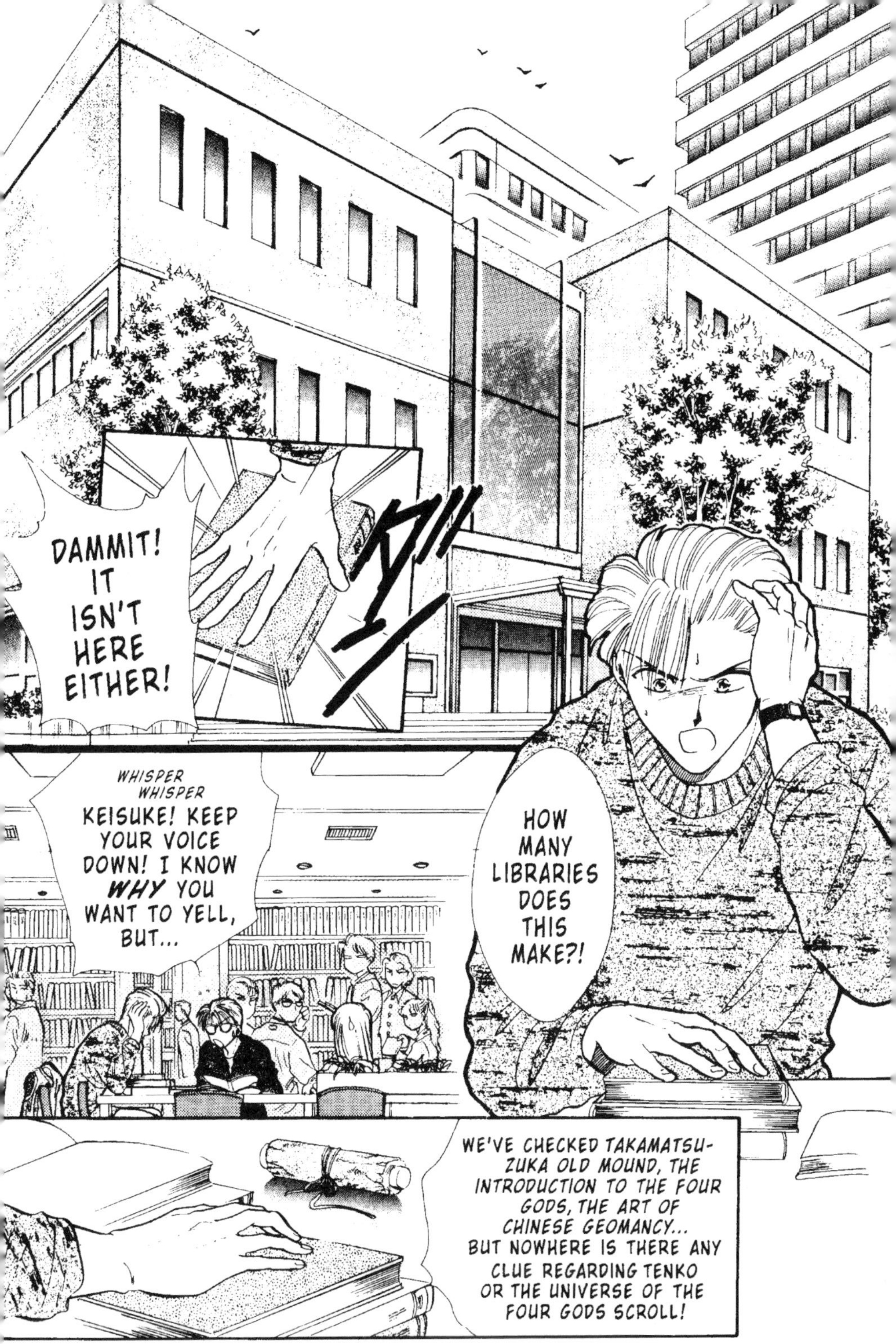
DAMMIT! IT ISN'T HERE EITHER!
HOW MANY LIBRARIES DOES THIS MAKE?!
WHISPER WHISPER
KEISUKE! KEEP YOUR VOICE DOWN! I KNOW *WHY* YOU WANT TO YELL, BUT...
WE'VE CHECKED TAKAMATSU-ZUKA OLD MOUND, THE INTRODUCTION TO THE FOUR GODS, THE ART OF CHINESE GEOMANCY... BUT NOWHERE IS THERE ANY CLUE REGARDING TENKO OR THE UNIVERSE OF THE FOUR GODS SCROLL!

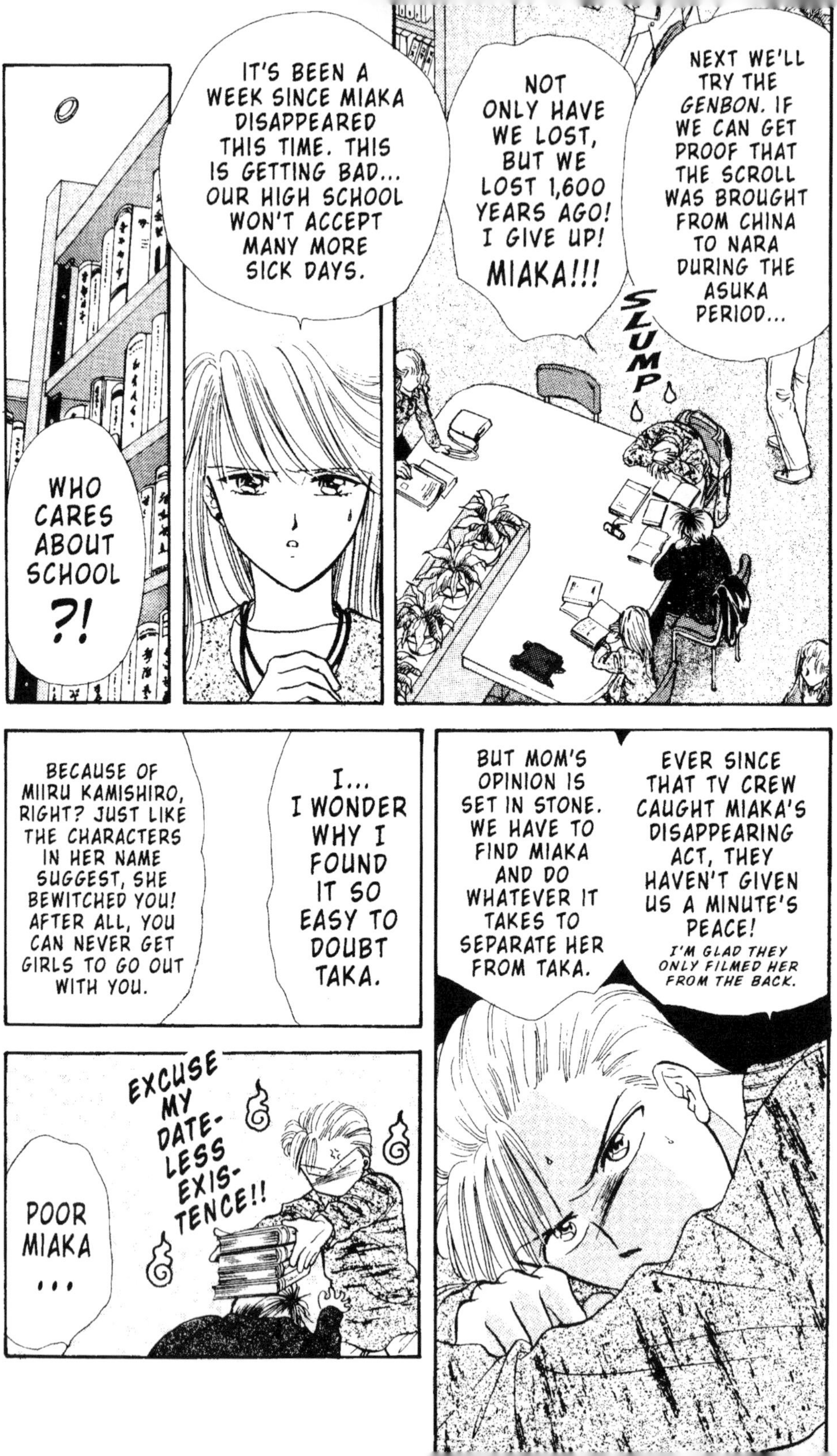
NEXT WE'LL TRY THE GENBON. IF WE CAN GET PROOF THAT THE SCROLL WAS BROUGHT FROM CHINA TO NARA DURING THE ASUKA PERIOD...
NOT ONLY HAVE WE LOST, BUT WE LOST 1,600 YEARS AGO! I GIVE UP! MIAKA!!!
SLUMP
IT'S BEEN A WEEK SINCE MIAKA DISAPPEARED THIS TIME. THIS IS GETTING BAD... OUR HIGH SCHOOL WON'T ACCEPT MANY MORE SICK DAYS.
WHO CARES ABOUT SCHOOL?!
EVER SINCE THAT TV CREW CAUGHT MIAKA'S DISAPPEARING ACT, THEY HAVEN'T GIVEN US A MINUTE'S PEACE!
I'M GLAD THEY ONLY FILMED HER FROM THE BACK.
BUT MOM'S OPINION IS SET IN STONE. WE HAVE TO FIND MIAKA AND DO WHATEVER IT TAKES TO SEPARATE HER FROM TAKA.
I... I WONDER WHY I FOUND IT SO EASY TO DOUBT TAKA.
BECAUSE OF MIIRU KAMISHIRO, RIGHT? JUST LIKE THE CHARACTERS IN HER NAME SUGGEST, SHE BEWITCHED YOU! AFTER ALL, YOU CAN NEVER GET GIRLS TO GO OUT WITH YOU.
EXCUSE MY DATE-LESS EXISTENCE!!
POOR MIAKA...

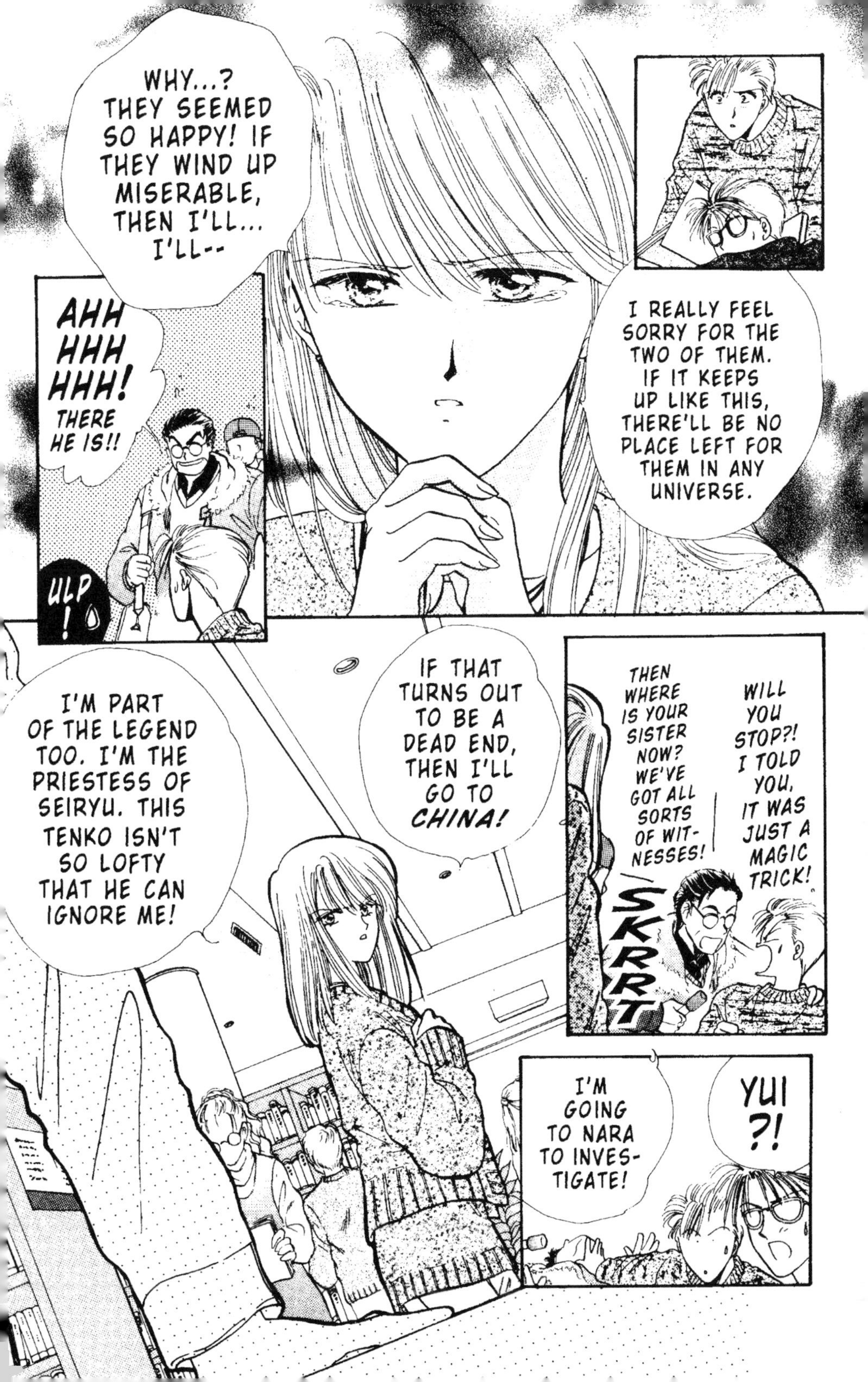
I REALLY FEEL SORRY FOR THE TWO OF THEM. IF IT KEEPS UP LIKE THIS, THERE'LL BE NO PLACE LEFT FOR THEM IN ANY UNIVERSE.
WHY...? THEY SEEMED SO HAPPY! IF THEY WIND UP MISERABLE, THEN I'LL... I'LL--
AHHHHHHHHH! THERE HE IS!!
ULP!
WILL YOU STOP?! I TOLD YOU, IT WAS JUST A MAGIC TRICK!
THEN WHERE IS YOUR SISTER NOW? WE'VE GOT ALL SORTS OF WITNESSES!
SKRRT
YUI?!
I'M GOING TO NARA TO INVESTIGATE!
IF THAT TURNS OUT TO BE A DEAD END, THEN I'LL GO TO CHINA!
I'M PART OF THE LEGEND TOO. I'M THE PRIESTESS OF SEIRYU. THIS TENKO ISN'T SO LOFTY THAT HE CAN IGNORE ME!

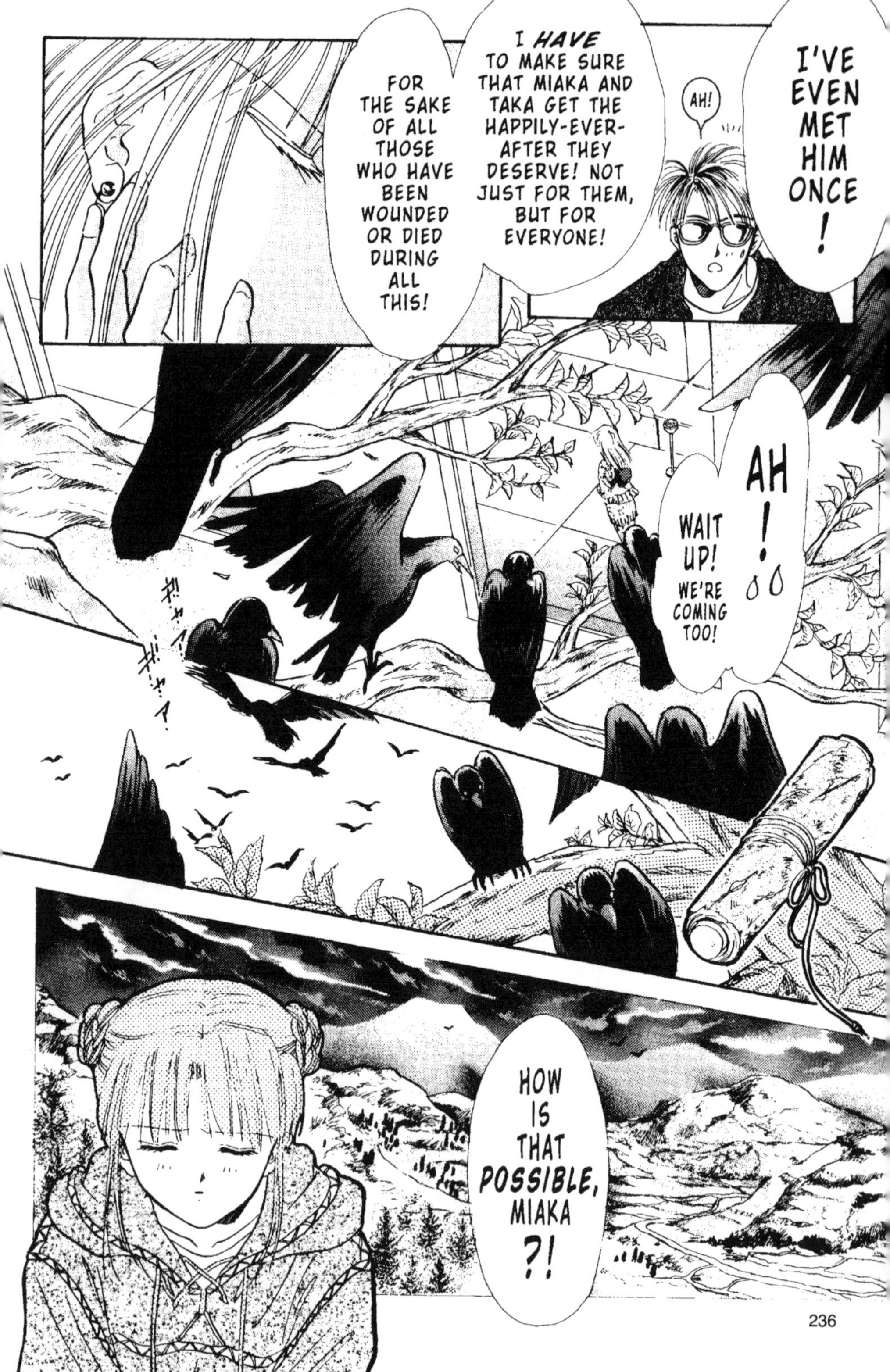
I'VE EVEN MET HIM ONCE!
AH!
I HAVE TO MAKE SURE THAT MIAKA AND TAKA GET THE HAPPILY-EVER-AFTER THEY DESERVE! NOT JUST FOR THEM, BUT FOR EVERYONE!
FOR THE SAKE OF ALL THOSE WHO HAVE BEEN WOUNDED OR DIED DURING ALL THIS!
AH!
WAIT UP! WE'RE COMING TOO!
HOW IS THAT POSSIBLE, MIAKA?!

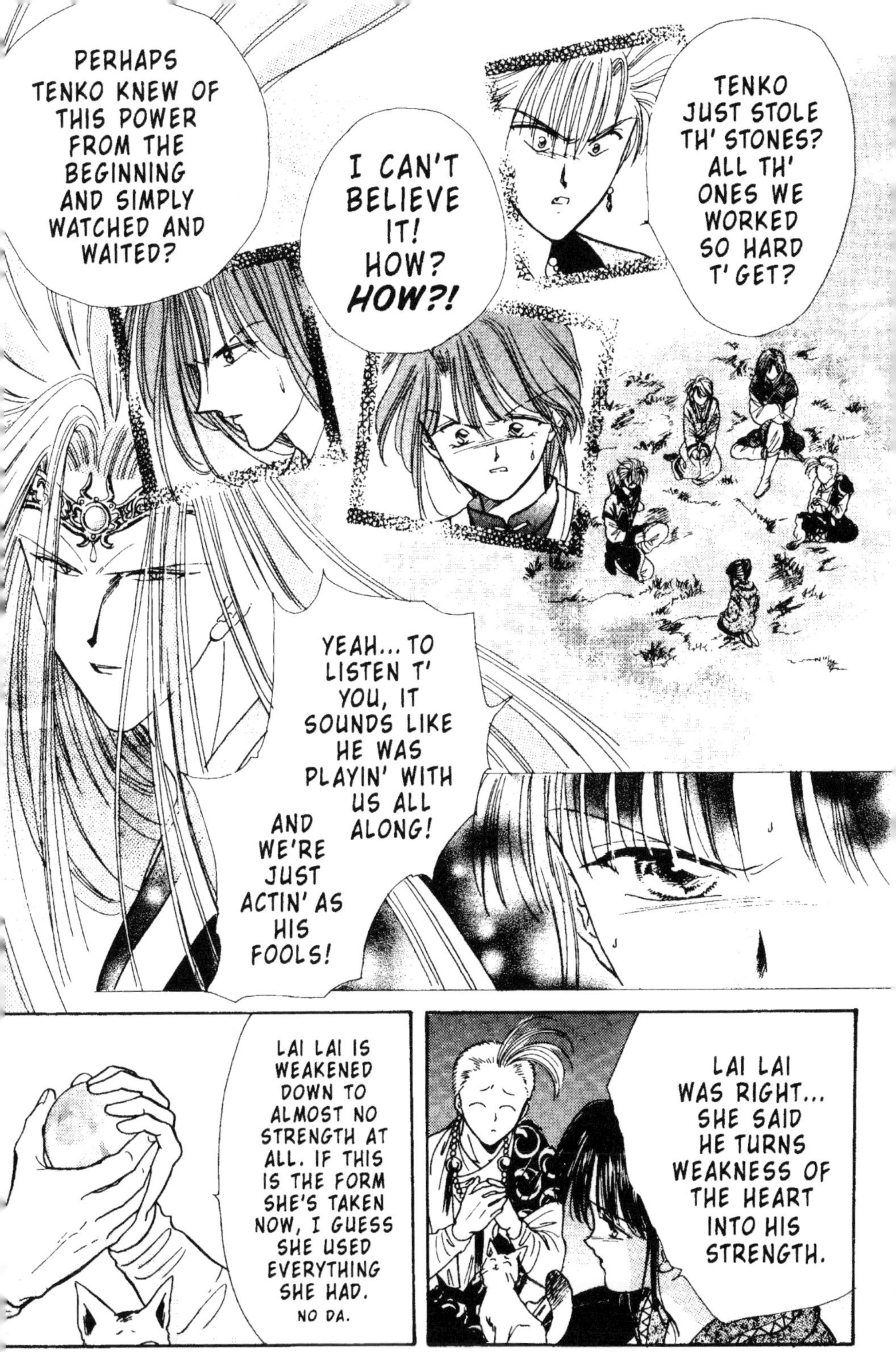
TENKO JUST STOLE TH' STONES? ALL TH' ONES WE WORKED SO HARD T' GET?
I CAN'T BELIEVE IT! HOW? *HOW?!*
PERHAPS TENKO KNEW OF THIS POWER FROM THE BEGINNING AND SIMPLY WATCHED AND WAITED?
YEAH... TO LISTEN T' YOU, IT SOUNDS LIKE HE WAS PLAYIN' WITH US ALL ALONG!
AND WE'RE JUST ACTIN' AS HIS FOOLS!
LAI LAI WAS RIGHT... SHE SAID HE TURNS WEAKNESS OF THE HEART INTO HIS STRENGTH.
LAI LAI IS WEAKENED DOWN TO ALMOST NO STRENGTH AT ALL. IF THIS IS THE FORM SHE'S TAKEN NOW, I GUESS SHE USED EVERYTHING SHE HAD. NO DA.

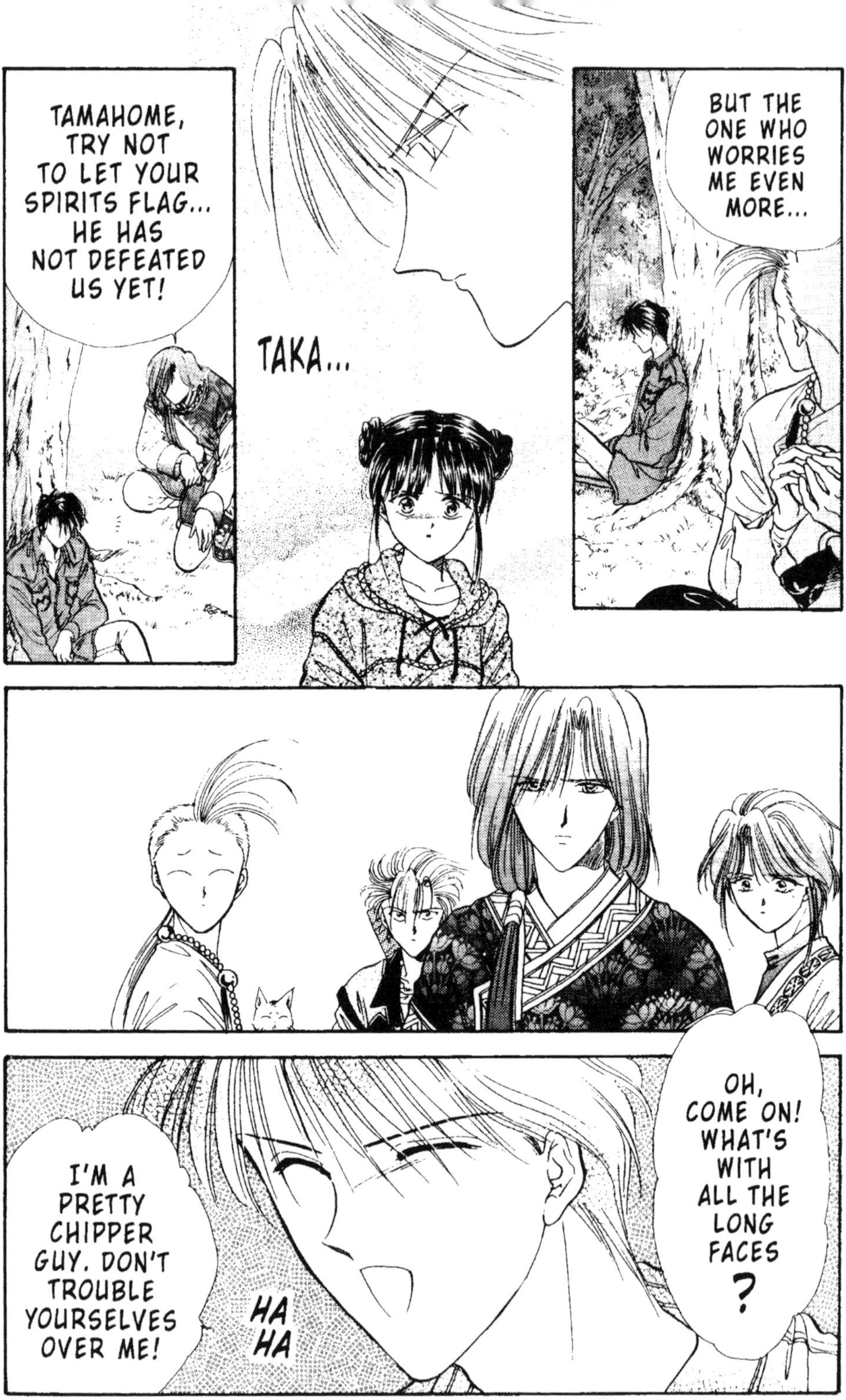
BUT THE ONE WHO WORRIES ME EVEN MORE...
TAKA...
TAMAHOME, TRY NOT TO LET YOUR SPIRITS FLAG... HE HAS NOT DEFEATED US YET!
OH, COME ON! WHAT'S WITH ALL THE LONG FACES?
HA HA
I'M A PRETTY CHIPPER GUY. DON'T TROUBLE YOURSELVES OVER ME!

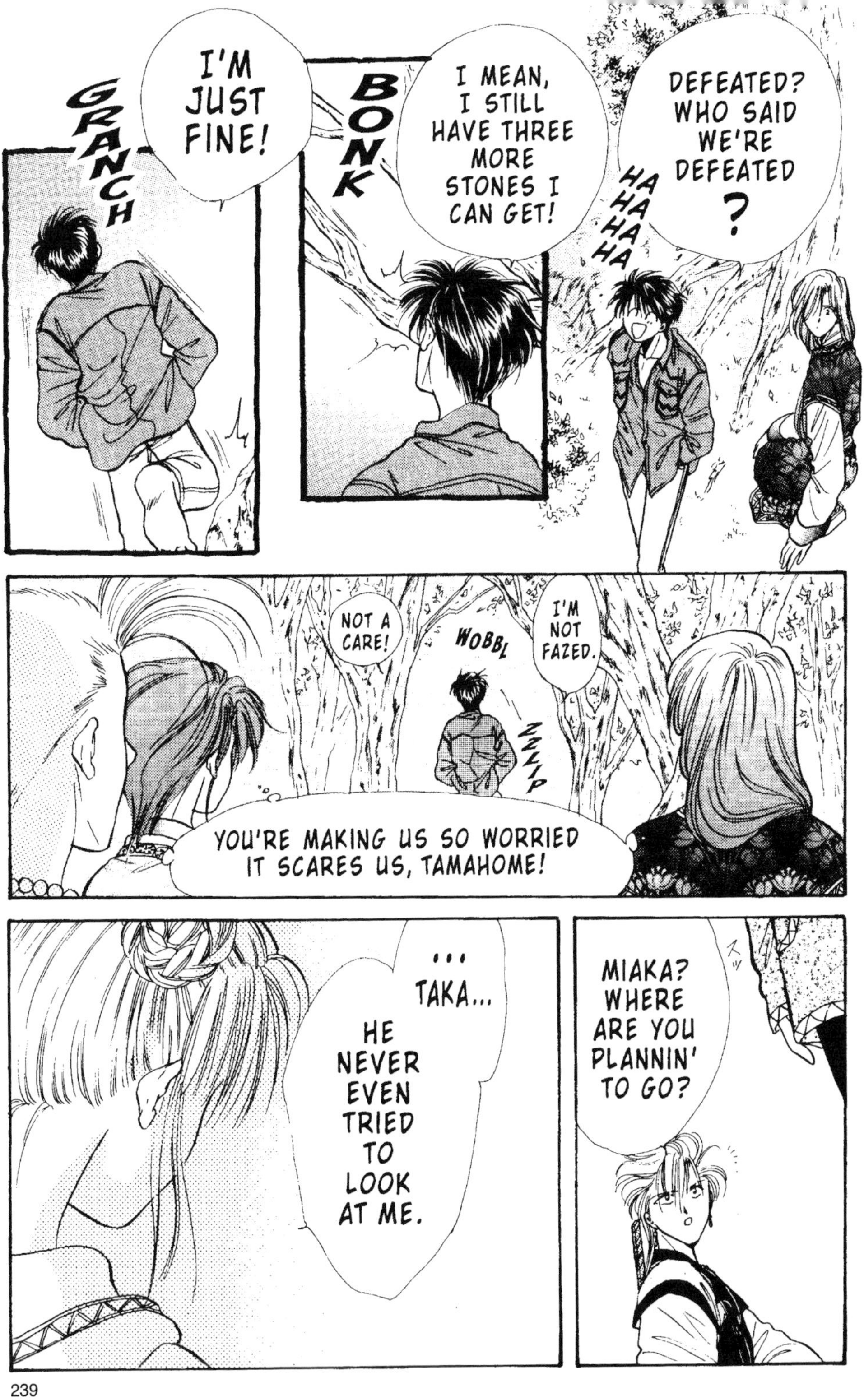
DEFEATED? WHO SAID WE'RE DEFEATED?
HAHAHAHAHA
I MEAN, I STILL HAVE THREE MORE STONES I CAN GET!
BONK
I'M JUST FINE!
GRANCH
I'M NOT FAZED.
ZZZIP
WOBBL
NOT A CARE!
YOU'RE MAKING US SO WORRIED IT SCARES US, TAMAHOME!
スッ
MIAKA? WHERE ARE YOU PLANNIN' TO GO?
... TAKA...
HE NEVER EVEN TRIED TO LOOK AT ME.

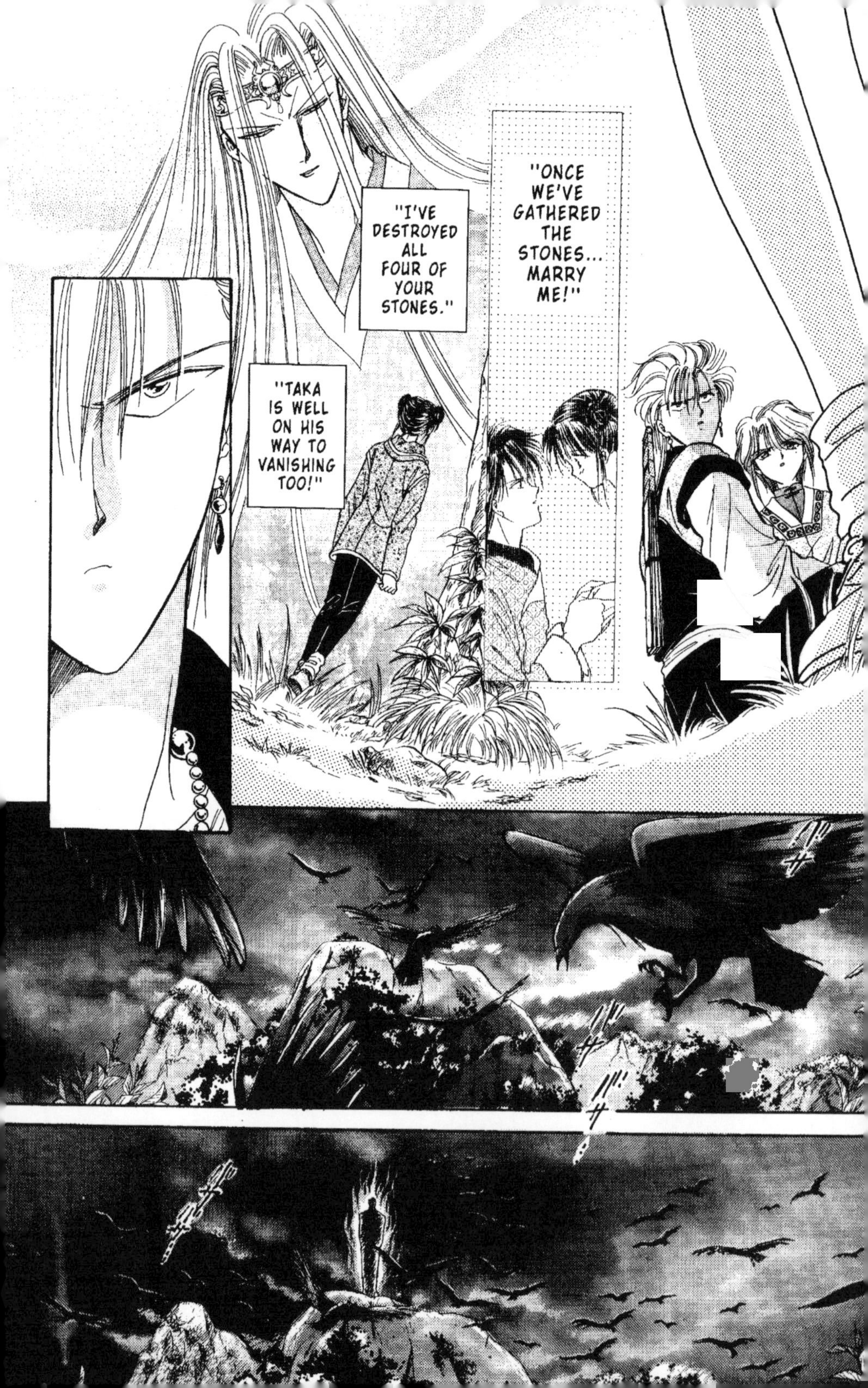
"ONCE WE'VE GATHERED THE STONES... MARRY ME!"
"I'VE DESTROYED ALL FOUR OF YOUR STONES."
"TAKA IS WELL ON HIS WAY TO VANISHING TOO!"

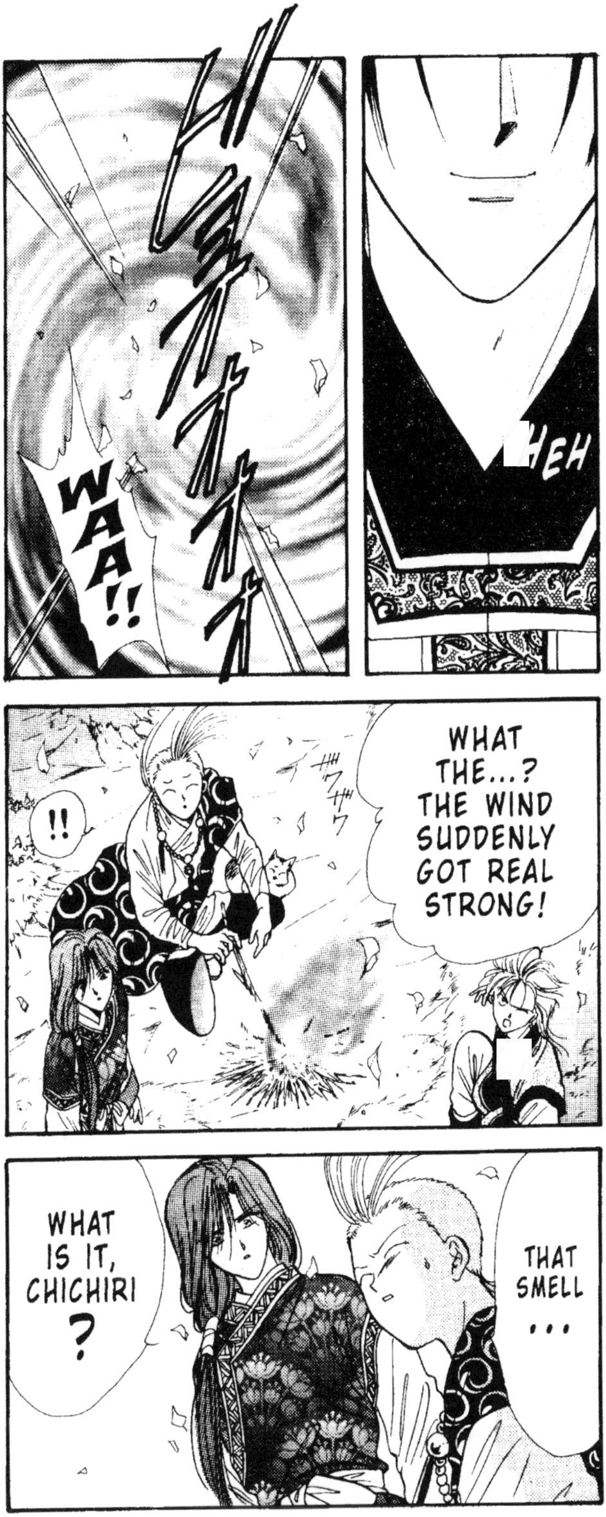
HEH
WAA!!
WHAT THE...? THE WIND SUDDENLY GOT REAL STRONG!
!!
THAT SMELL...
WHAT IS IT, CHICHIRI?

"Aw, I sent off my letter ages ago, and **no reply ever comes!!**" To those fans who feel this, please don't be angry. *I'm positively worn out!* Maybe I'm the only one you write to, but I get cardboard boxes with a thousand letters in each every month! And I feel so relieved when I can finally make the time to read them. I'm sorry, everyone! At least I make every effort to read them! Umm...and even if you put, "Read by X-month, X-day," it still won't help. There have been times when I was only able to open mail long after such deadlines had passed. And please! People who send sign boards or requests for signed pictures... I'm sorry, but I can't do it! I can't even send your pictures back. I'm so sorry! Don't do it even as a joke! Not unless you want me to drop dead from exhaustion! *I keep hearing from the people around me that I look like I'm about to collapse. Isn't that an awful thing to say?*

Now, on to the next subject! (Oh! If you don't already know what goes on in this story, then come back and read this later.) About Tasuki! There was a day when news of Tasuki's rampage spread throughout the entire nation of Japan... *Really?!* Well... among the Tasuki fans (a friend calls them fanatics), the • reaction • was • unbelievable. ☺ And many people across the land heard the scream of indignation. (Okay, that's kind of an exaggeration. It's just written that way to create an image.) There were some good points to the reaction: The guy lost a little of his overwhelming popularity! It's a little scary. The incident certainly split the "angry" fans and the "overjoyed" fans into two distinct groups. As for what Miaka did...(there's a lot of jealousy going around). According to some of the letters I've received, the reaction ranges from "This is what I've been waiting for!" through "With Tasuki's history, what the hell is going on?!" ☺ and finally to people who are angry at Tasuki himself. (He does love her.) One person said, "I'd like you to sympathize with the plight of true love and stop placing obstacles between Miaka and Tama!" *That's so cute!*

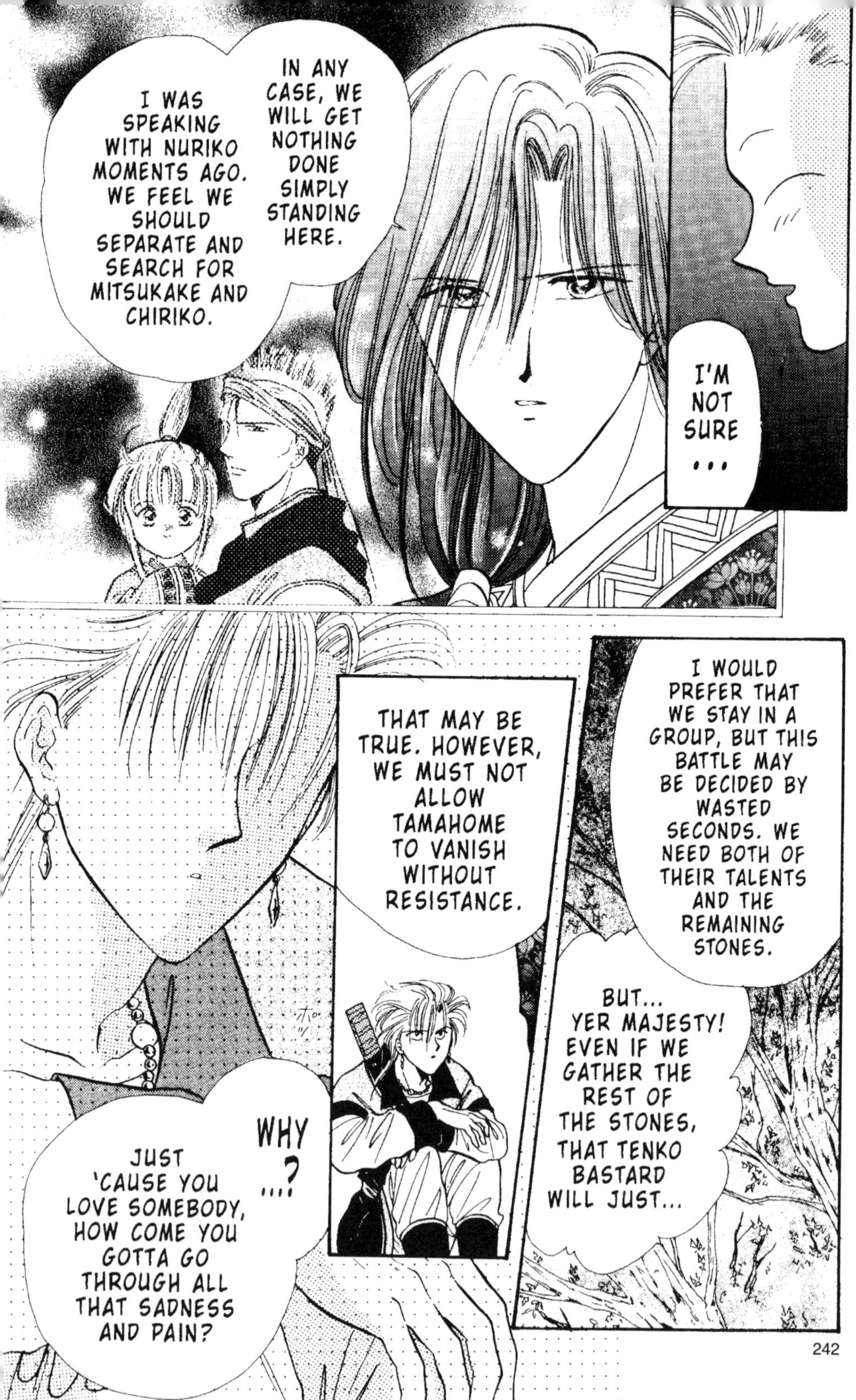
I'M NOT SURE...
IN ANY CASE, WE WILL GET NOTHING DONE SIMPLY STANDING HERE.
I WAS SPEAKING WITH NURIKO MOMENTS AGO. WE FEEL WE SHOULD SEPARATE AND SEARCH FOR MITSUKAKE AND CHIRIKO.
I WOULD PREFER THAT WE STAY IN A GROUP, BUT THIS BATTLE MAY BE DECIDED BY WASTED SECONDS. WE NEED BOTH OF THEIR TALENTS AND THE REMAINING STONES.
BUT... YER MAJESTY! EVEN IF WE GATHER THE REST OF THE STONES, THAT TENKO BASTARD WILL JUST...
THAT MAY BE TRUE. HOWEVER, WE MUST NOT ALLOW TAMAHOME TO VANISH WITHOUT RESISTANCE.
WHY...?
JUST 'CAUSE YOU LOVE SOMEBODY, HOW COME YOU GOTTA GO THROUGH ALL THAT SADNESS AND PAIN?

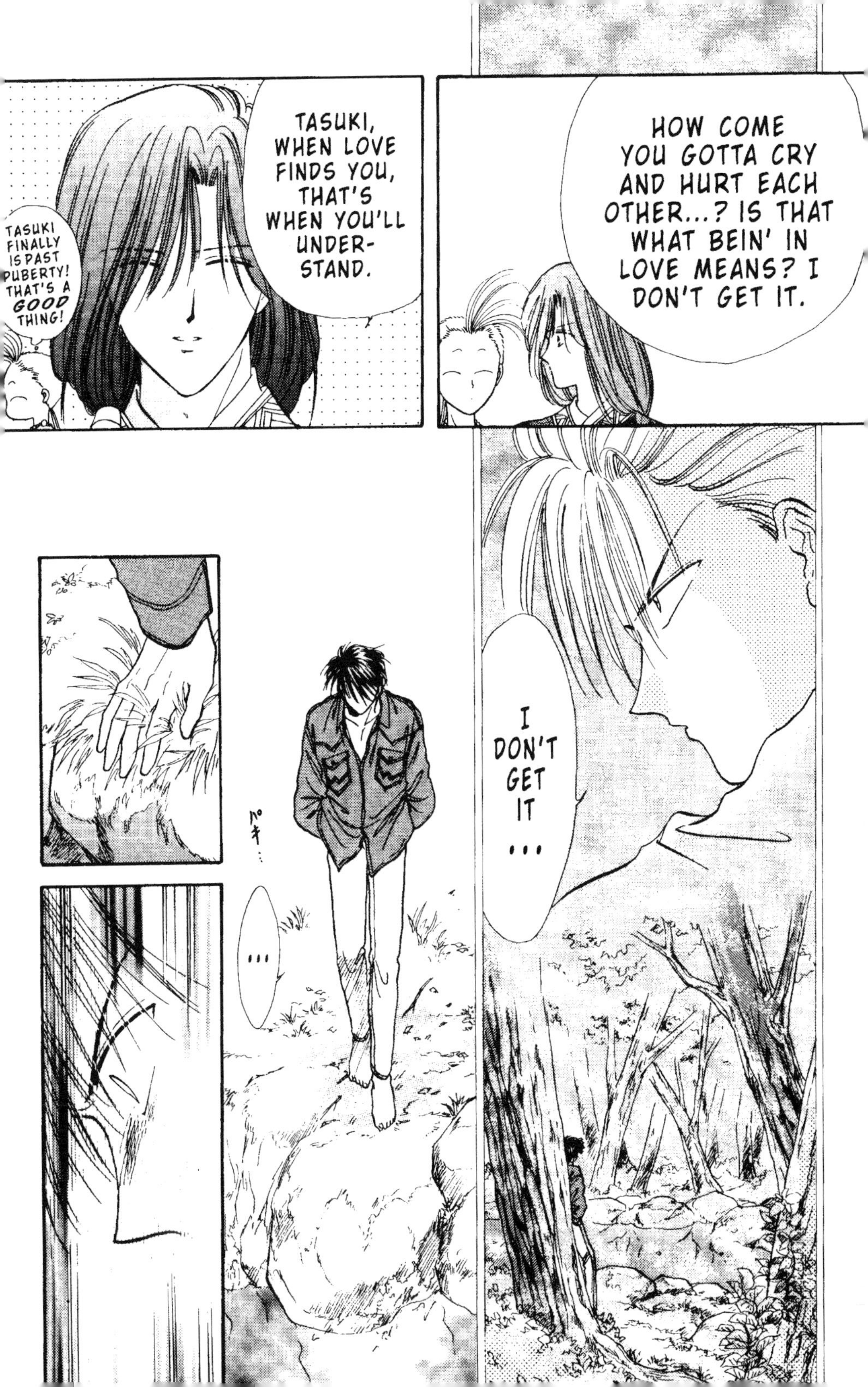
HOW COME YOU GOTTA CRY AND HURT EACH OTHER...? IS THAT WHAT BEIN' IN LOVE MEANS? I DON'T GET IT.
TASUKI, WHEN LOVE FINDS YOU, THAT'S WHEN YOU'LL UNDER-STAND.
TASUKI FINALLY IS PAST PUBERTY! THAT'S A GOOD THING!
I DON'T GET IT ...
パキ...
...

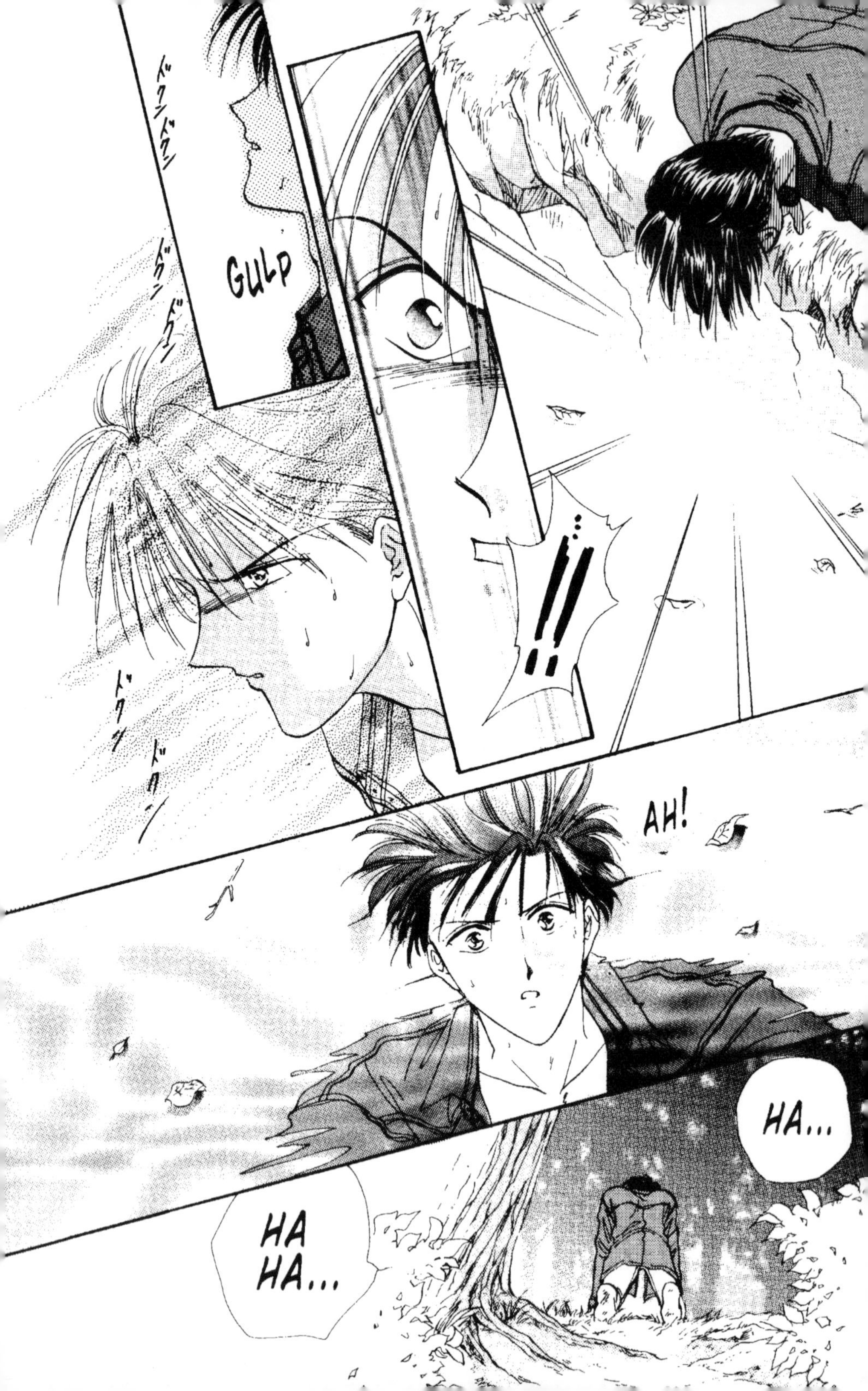
!!
ドクンドクン
GULP
ドクンドクン
ドクン
ドクン
AH!
HA...
HA
HA...

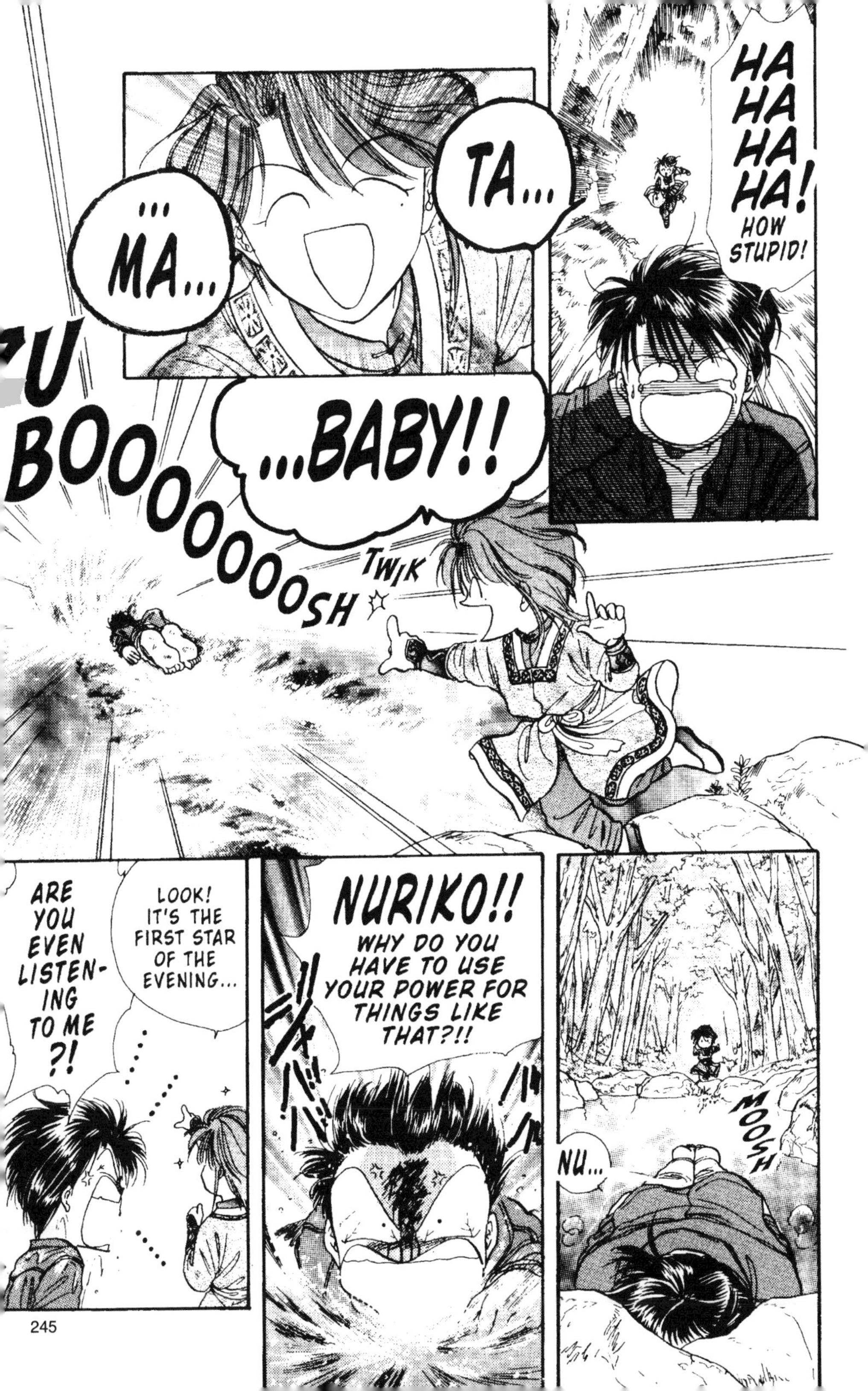
HA HA HA HA! HOW STUPID!
TA...
...MA...
...BABY!!
ZU BOOOOOOOOSH
TWIK
MOOSH
NU...
NURIKO!! WHY DO YOU HAVE TO USE YOUR POWER FOR THINGS LIKE THAT?!!
LOOK! IT'S THE FIRST STAR OF THE EVENING...
ARE YOU EVEN LISTEN-ING TO ME?!
......

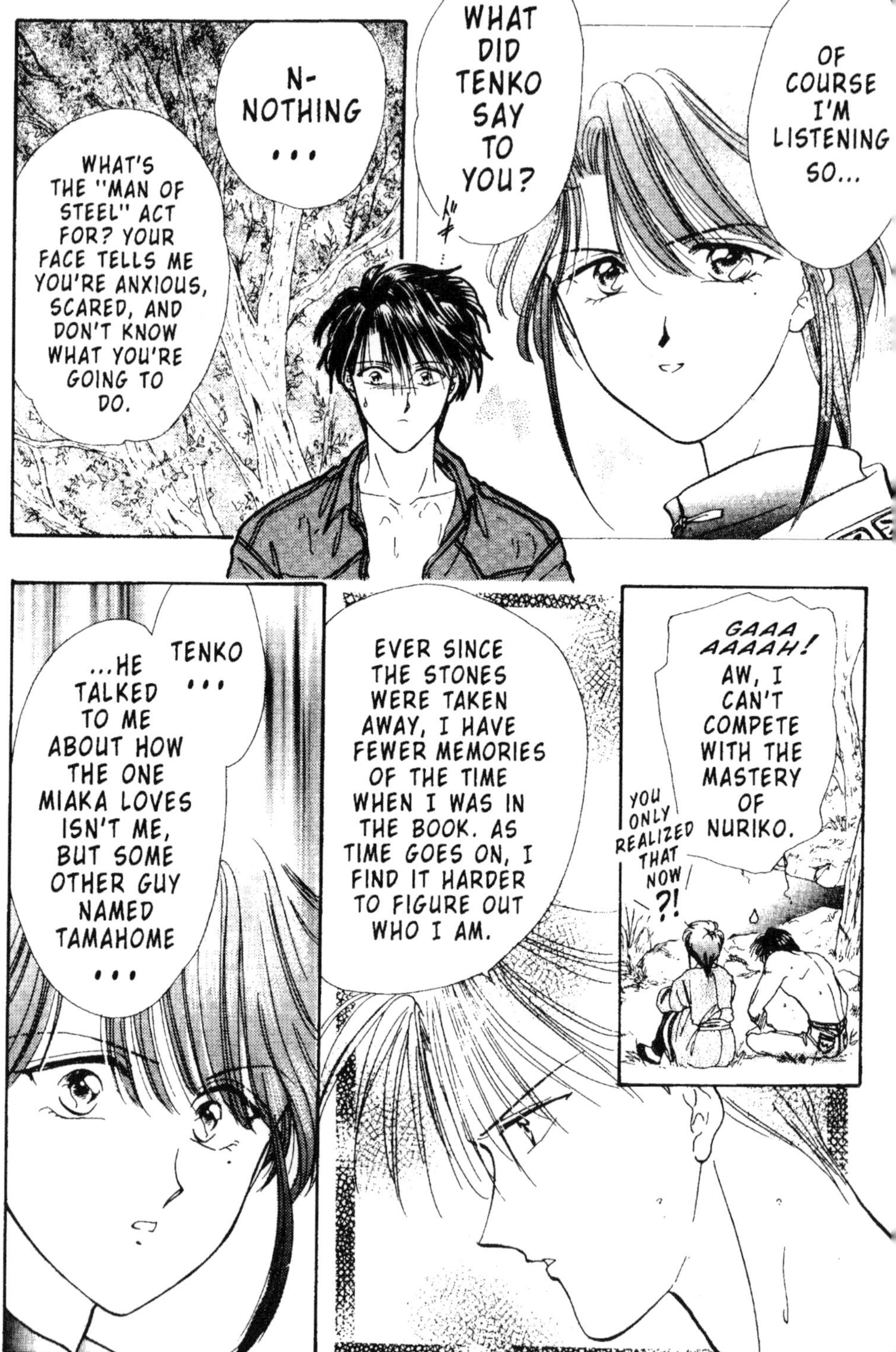
OF COURSE I'M LISTENING SO...
WHAT DID TENKO SAY TO YOU?
N-NOTHING...
WHAT'S THE "MAN OF STEEL" ACT FOR? YOUR FACE TELLS ME YOU'RE ANXIOUS, SCARED, AND DON'T KNOW WHAT YOU'RE GOING TO DO.
GAAA AAAAH! AW, I CAN'T COMPETE WITH THE MASTERY OF NURIKO.
YOU ONLY REALIZED THAT NOW?!
EVER SINCE THE STONES WERE TAKEN AWAY, I HAVE FEWER MEMORIES OF THE TIME WHEN I WAS IN THE BOOK. AS TIME GOES ON, I FIND IT HARDER TO FIGURE OUT WHO I AM.
TENKO...
...HE TALKED TO ME ABOUT HOW THE ONE MIAKA LOVES ISN'T ME, BUT SOME OTHER GUY NAMED TAMAHOME...

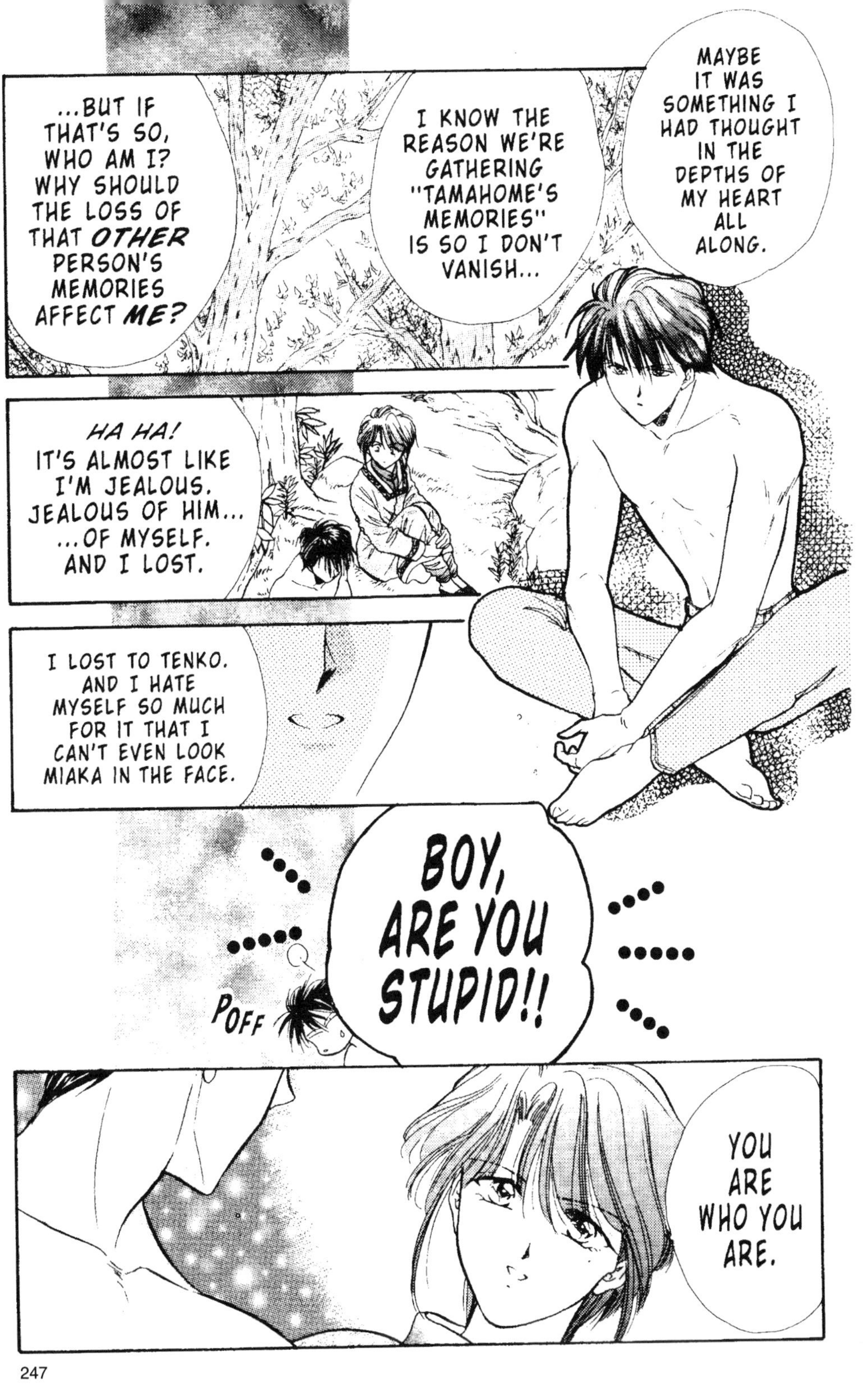
MAYBE IT WAS SOMETHING I HAD THOUGHT IN THE DEPTHS OF MY HEART ALL ALONG.
I KNOW THE REASON WE'RE GATHERING "TAMAHOME'S MEMORIES" IS SO I DON'T VANISH...
...BUT IF THAT'S SO, WHO AM I? WHY SHOULD THE LOSS OF THAT *OTHER* PERSON'S MEMORIES AFFECT *ME?*
HA HA! IT'S ALMOST LIKE I'M JEALOUS. JEALOUS OF HIM... ...OF MYSELF. AND I LOST.
I LOST TO TENKO. AND I HATE MYSELF SO MUCH FOR IT THAT I CAN'T EVEN LOOK MIAKA IN THE FACE.
BOY, ARE YOU STUPID!!
POFF
YOU ARE WHO YOU ARE.

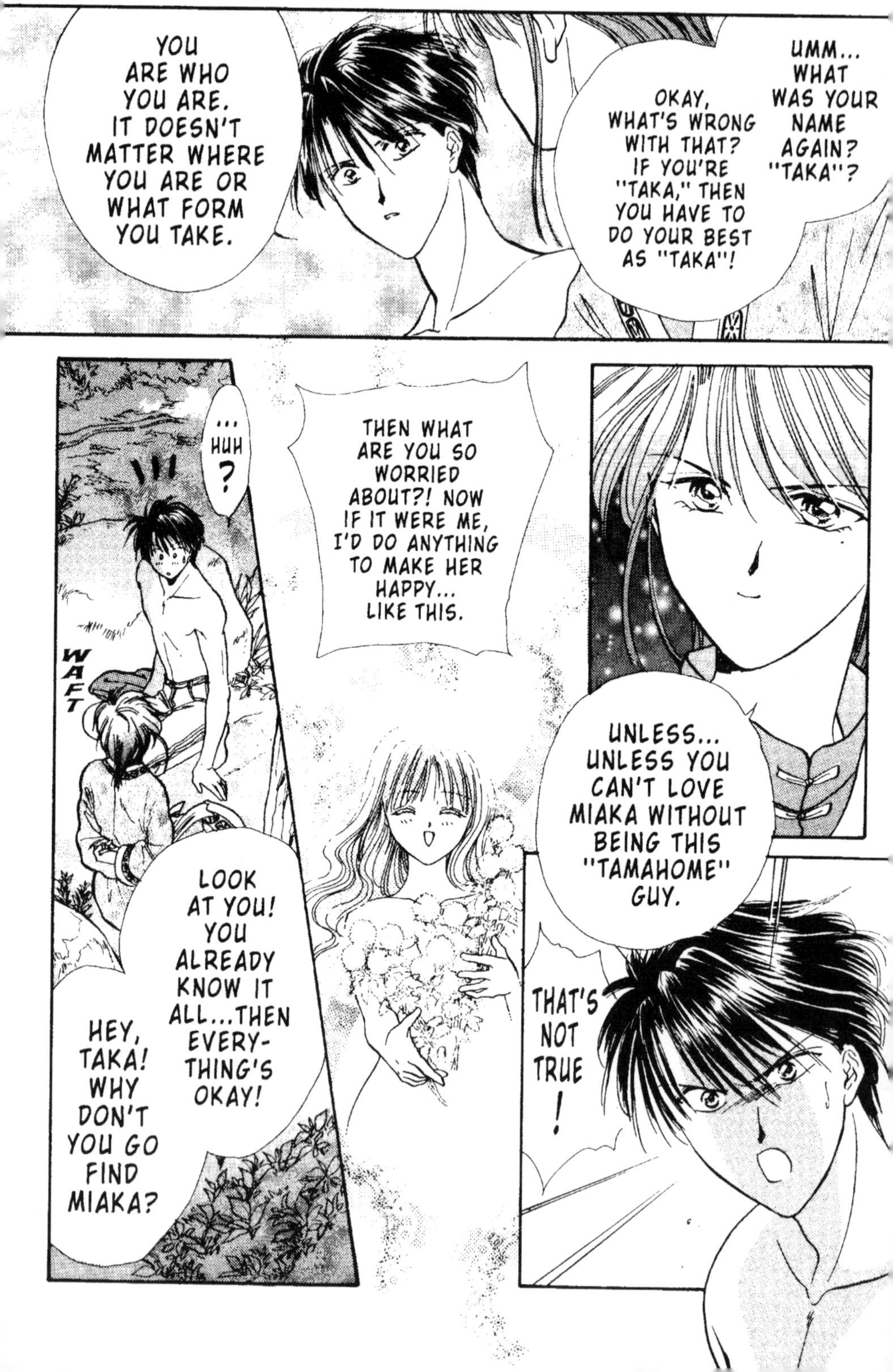
UMM... WHAT WAS YOUR NAME AGAIN? "TAKA"?
OKAY, WHAT'S WRONG WITH THAT? IF YOU'RE "TAKA," THEN YOU HAVE TO DO YOUR BEST AS "TAKA"!
YOU ARE WHO YOU ARE. IT DOESN'T MATTER WHERE YOU ARE OR WHAT FORM YOU TAKE.
UNLESS... UNLESS YOU CAN'T LOVE MIAKA WITHOUT BEING THIS "TAMAHOME" GUY.
THAT'S NOT TRUE!
THEN WHAT ARE YOU SO WORRIED ABOUT?! NOW IF IT WERE ME, I'D DO ANYTHING TO MAKE HER HAPPY... LIKE THIS.
...HUH?
WAFT
LOOK AT YOU! YOU ALREADY KNOW IT ALL...THEN EVERYTHING'S OKAY!
HEY, TAKA! WHY DON'T YOU GO FIND MIAKA?

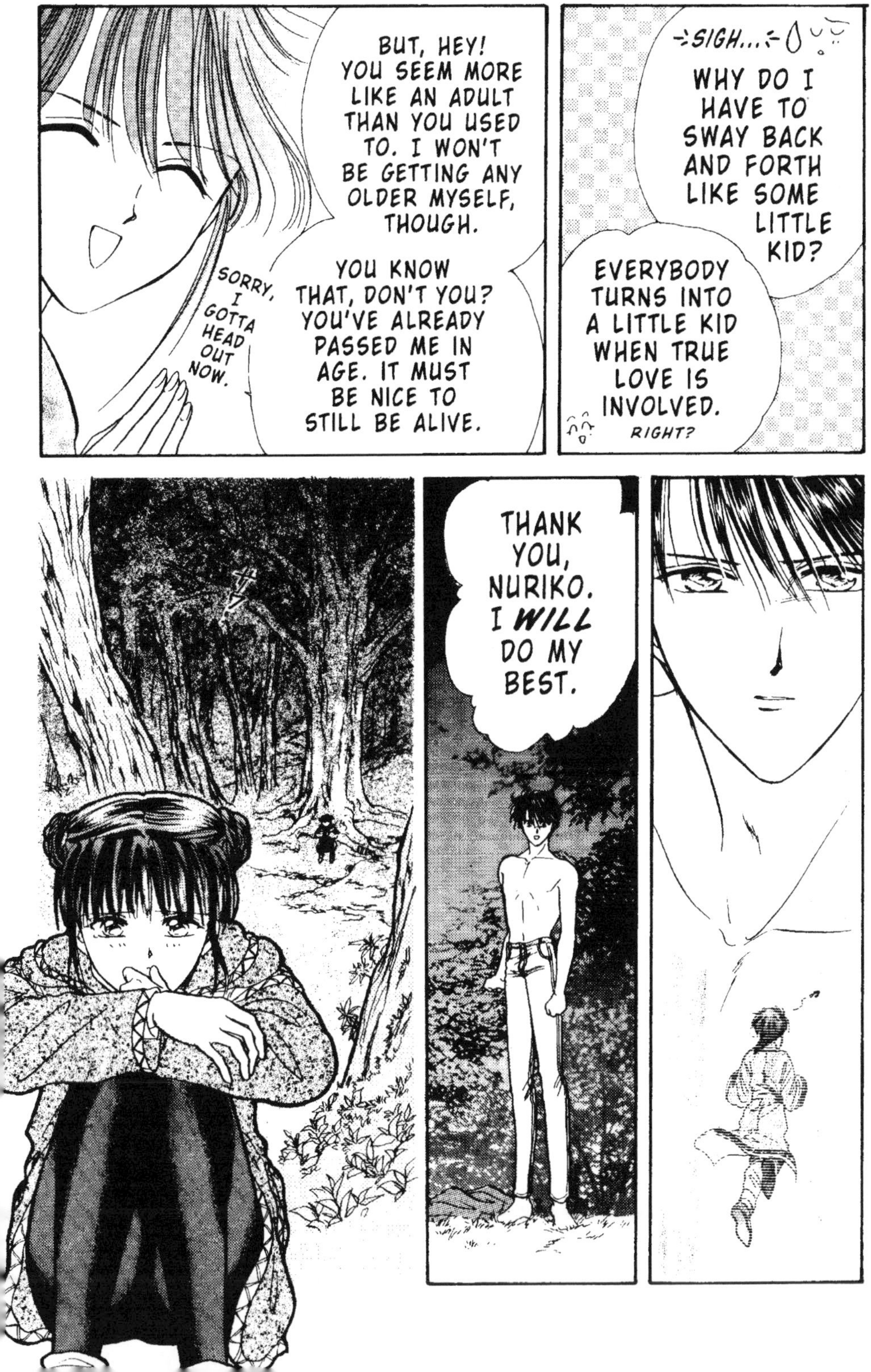
-:-SIGH...-:-
WHY DO I HAVE TO SWAY BACK AND FORTH LIKE SOME LITTLE KID?
EVERYBODY TURNS INTO A LITTLE KID WHEN TRUE LOVE IS INVOLVED.
RIGHT?
BUT, HEY! YOU SEEM MORE LIKE AN ADULT THAN YOU USED TO. I WON'T BE GETTING ANY OLDER MYSELF, THOUGH.
YOU KNOW THAT, DON'T YOU? YOU'VE ALREADY PASSED ME IN AGE. IT MUST BE NICE TO STILL BE ALIVE.
SORRY, I GOTTA HEAD OUT NOW.
THANK YOU, NURIKO. I *WILL* DO MY BEST.

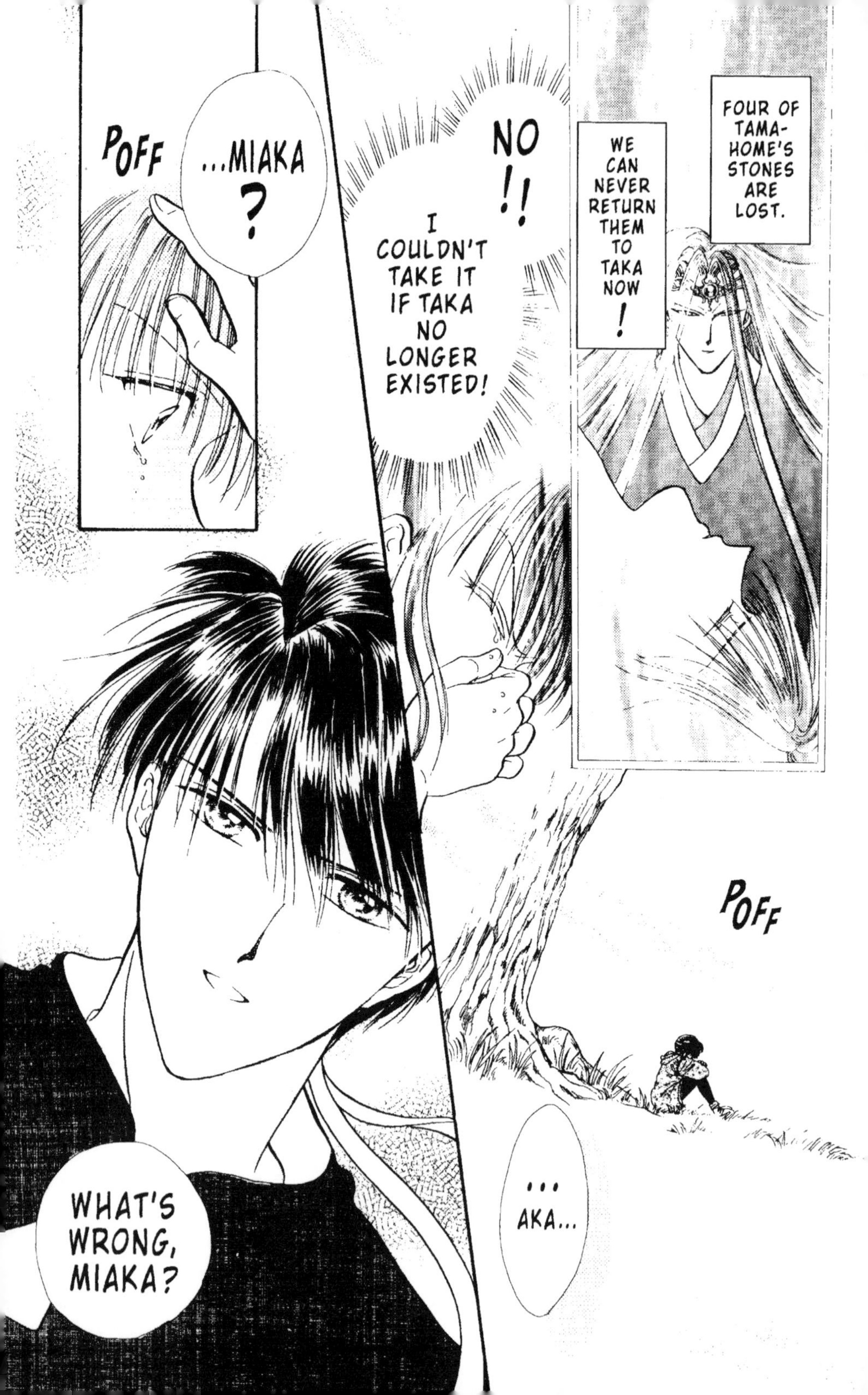
FOUR OF TAMA-HOME'S STONES ARE LOST.
WE CAN NEVER RETURN THEM TO TAKA NOW!
NO!!
I COULDN'T TAKE IT IF TAKA NO LONGER EXISTED!
POFF
...MIAKA?
POFF
...AKA...
WHAT'S WRONG, MIAKA?

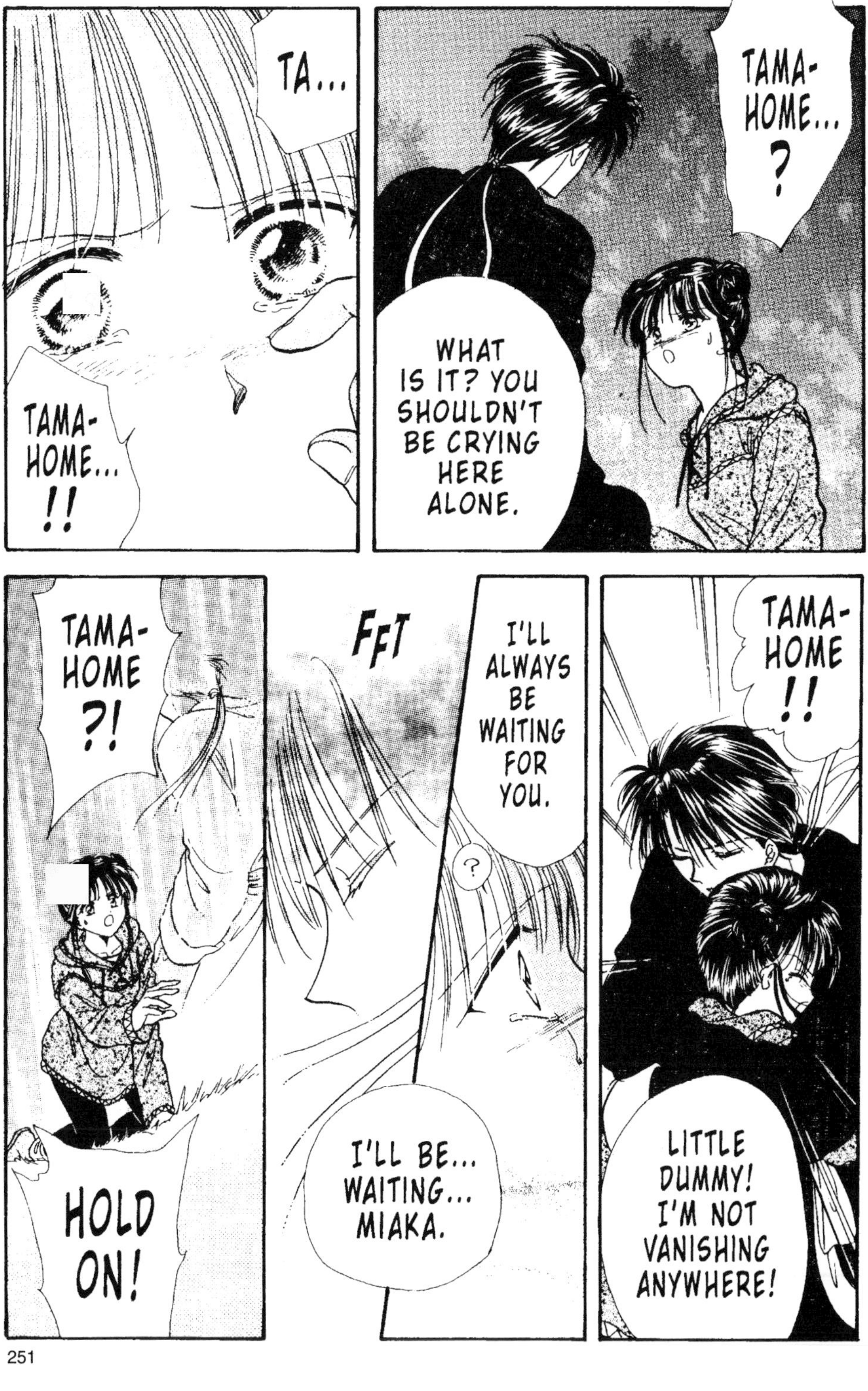
TAMA-HOME...?
WHAT IS IT? YOU SHOULDN'T BE CRYING HERE ALONE.
TA...
TAMA-HOME...!!
TAMA-HOME!!
LITTLE DUMMY! I'M NOT VANISHING ANYWHERE!
I'LL ALWAYS BE WAITING FOR YOU.
FFT
?
I'LL BE... WAITING... MIAKA.
TAMA-HOME?!
HOLD ON!

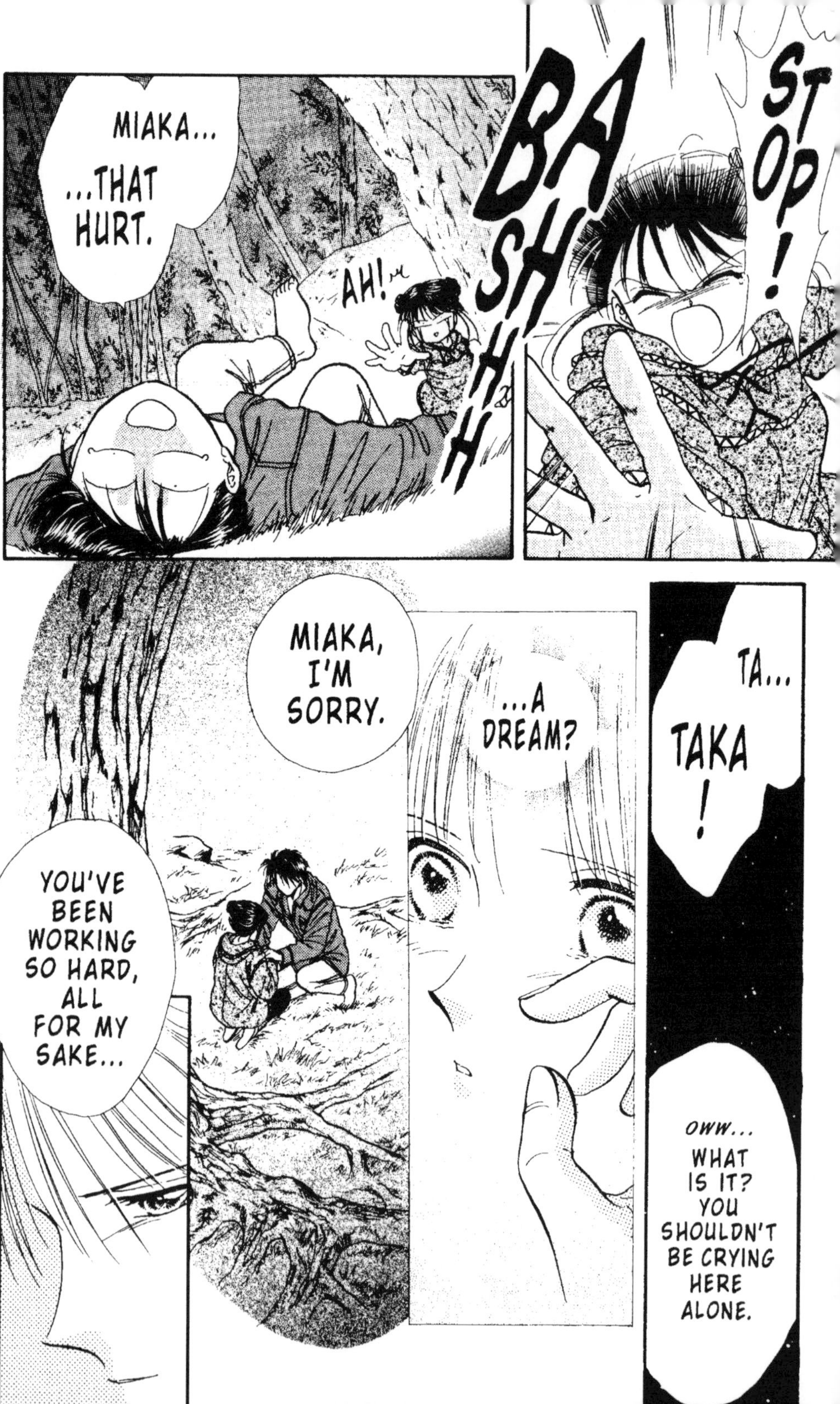
STOP!
BASHHHHH
AH!
MIAKA...
...THAT HURT.
TA...
TAKA!
OWW... WHAT IS IT? YOU SHOULDN'T BE CRYING HERE ALONE.
...A DREAM?
MIAKA, I'M SORRY.
YOU'VE BEEN WORKING SO HARD, ALL FOR MY SAKE...

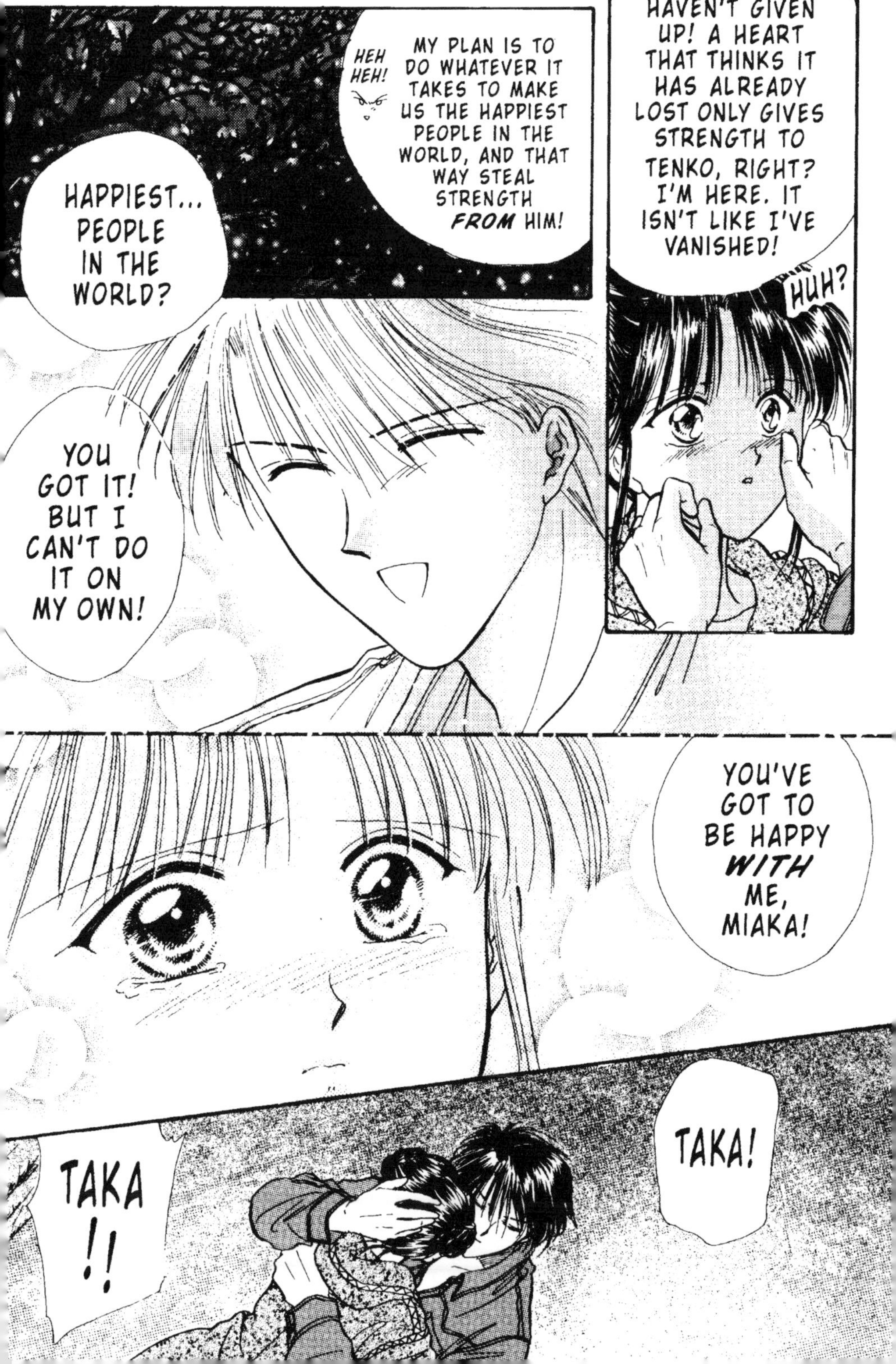
BUT I HAVEN'T GIVEN UP! A HEART THAT THINKS IT HAS ALREADY LOST ONLY GIVES STRENGTH TO TENKO, RIGHT? I'M HERE. IT ISN'T LIKE I'VE VANISHED!
HUH?
MY PLAN IS TO DO WHATEVER IT TAKES TO MAKE US THE HAPPIEST PEOPLE IN THE WORLD, AND THAT WAY STEAL STRENGTH *FROM* HIM!
HEH HEH!
HAPPIEST... PEOPLE IN THE WORLD?
YOU GOT IT! BUT I CAN'T DO IT ON MY OWN!
YOU'VE GOT TO BE HAPPY *WITH* ME, MIAKA!
TAKA!
TAKA!!

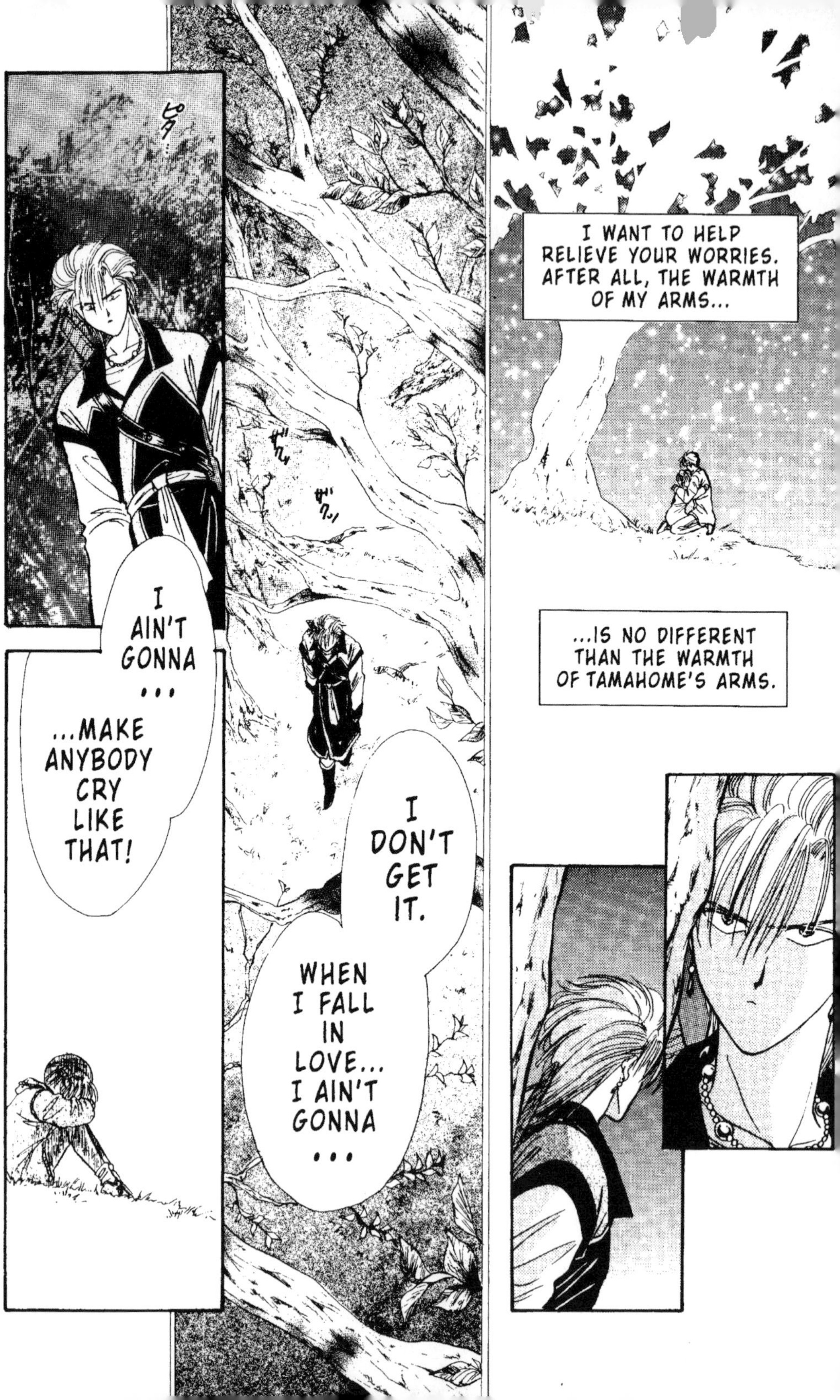
I WANT TO HELP RELIEVE YOUR WORRIES. AFTER ALL, THE WARMTH OF MY ARMS...
...IS NO DIFFERENT THAN THE WARMTH OF TAMAHOME'S ARMS.
I DON'T GET IT.
WHEN I FALL IN LOVE... I AIN'T GONNA...
ピタ…
I AIN'T GONNA...
...MAKE ANYBODY CRY LIKE THAT!

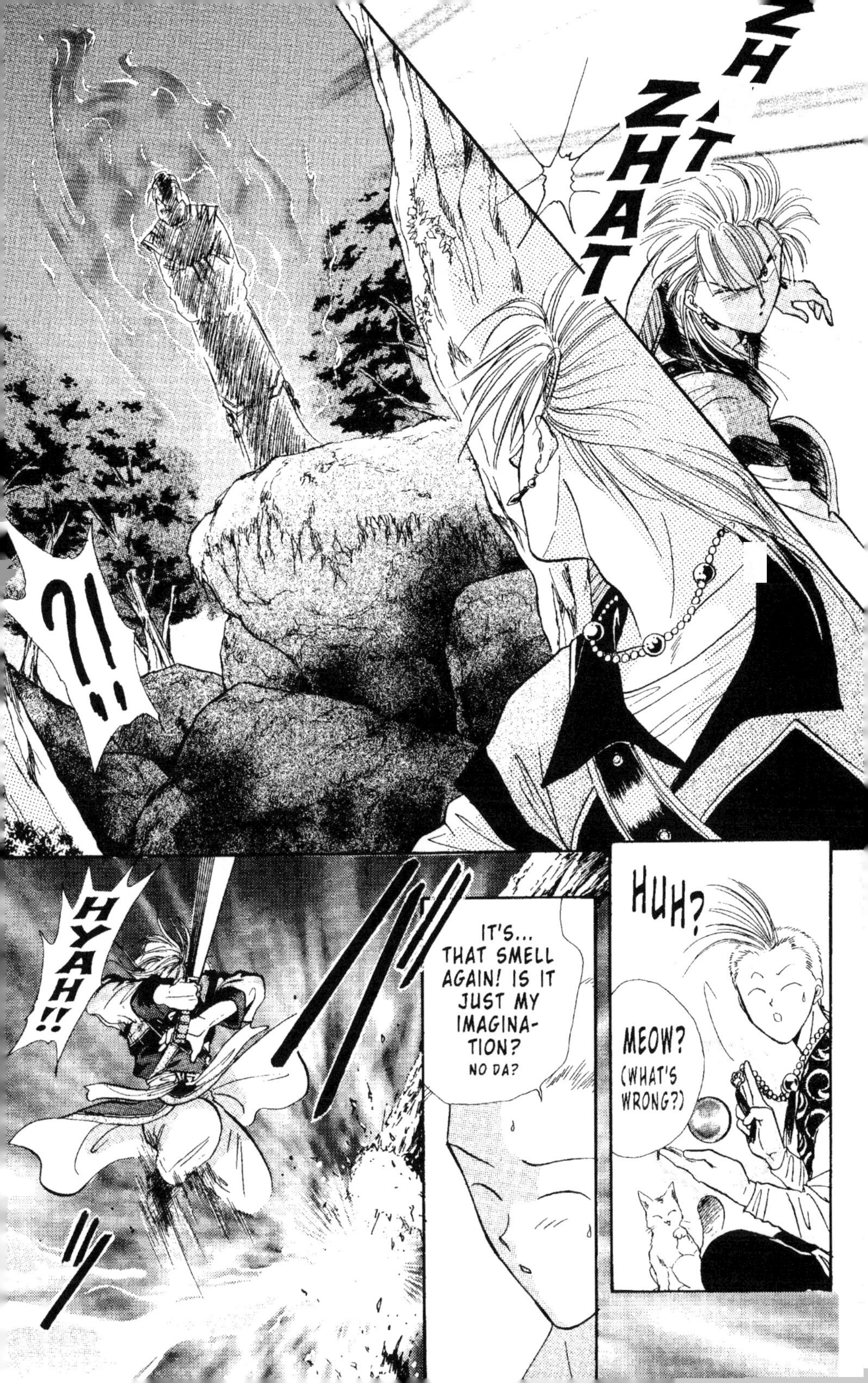
ZHAT
ZHAT
?!!
HUH?
MEOW? (WHAT'S WRONG?)
IT'S... THAT SMELL AGAIN! IS IT JUST MY IMAGINATION? NO DA?
HYAAH!!

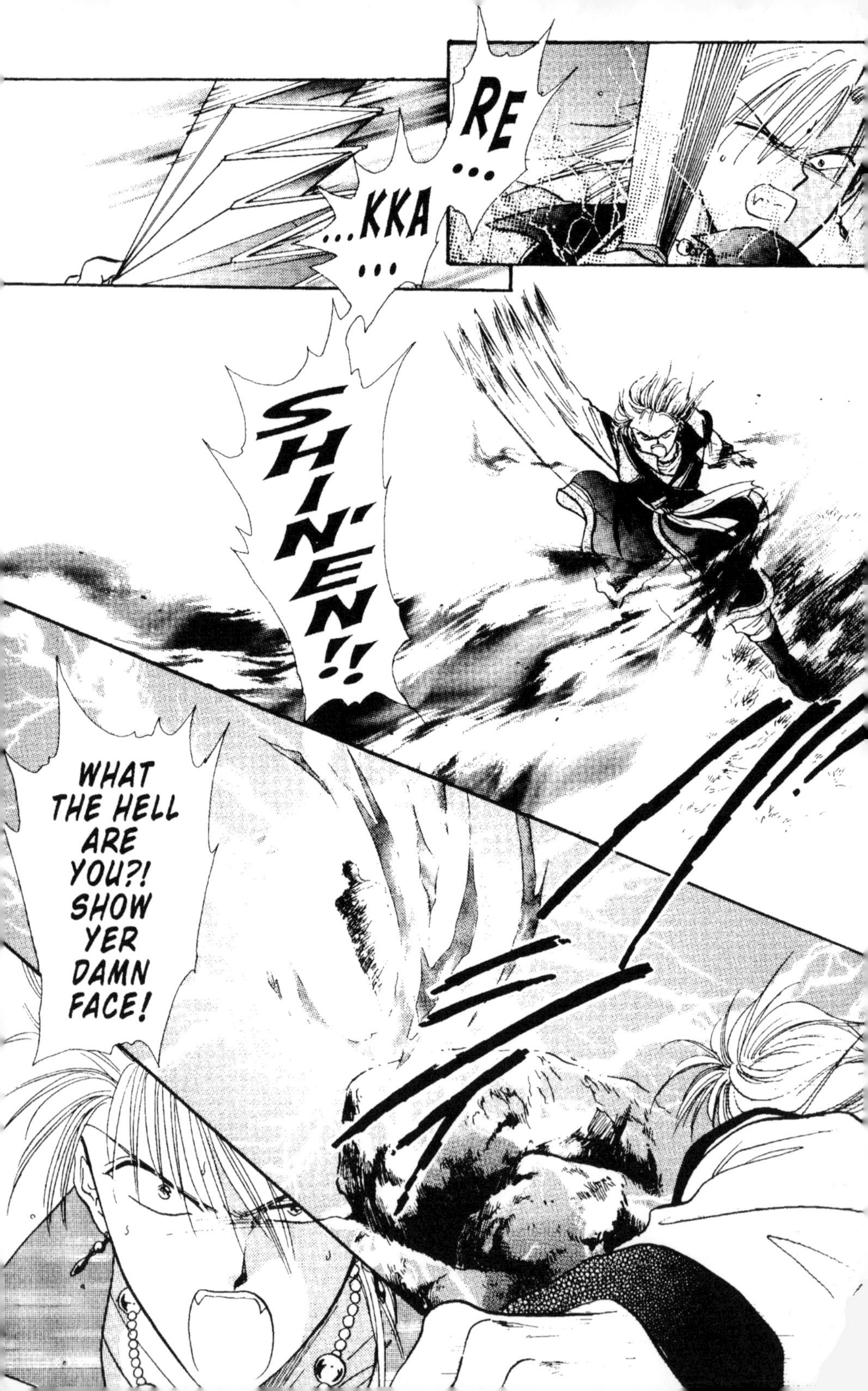
RE...
...KKA...
SHIN'EN!!
WHAT THE HELL ARE YOU?! SHOW YER DAMN FACE!

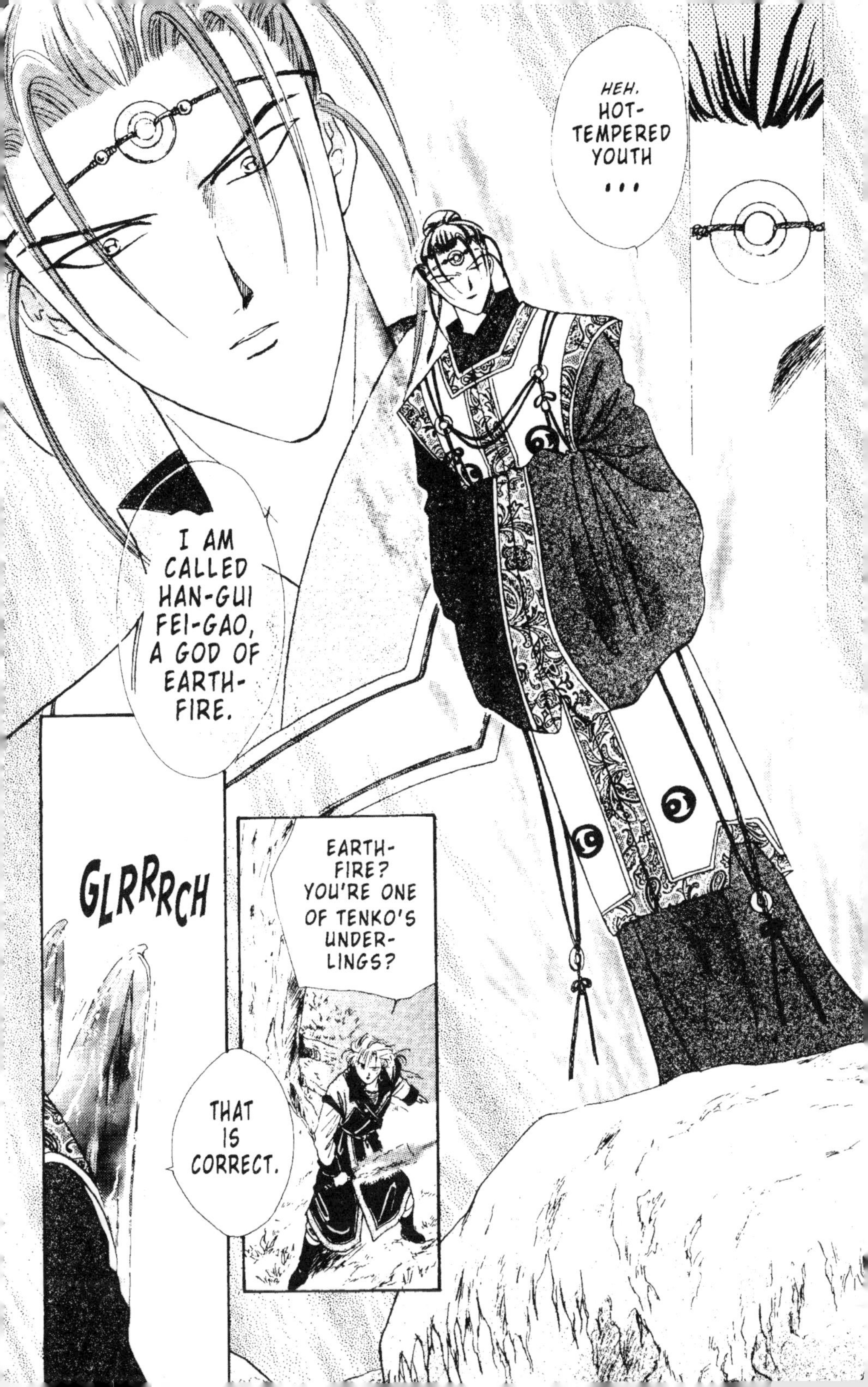
HEH. HOT-TEMPERED YOUTH...
I AM CALLED HAN-GUI FEI-GAO, A GOD OF EARTH-FIRE.
EARTH-FIRE? YOU'RE ONE OF TENKO'S UNDER-LINGS?
THAT IS CORRECT.
GLRRRCH

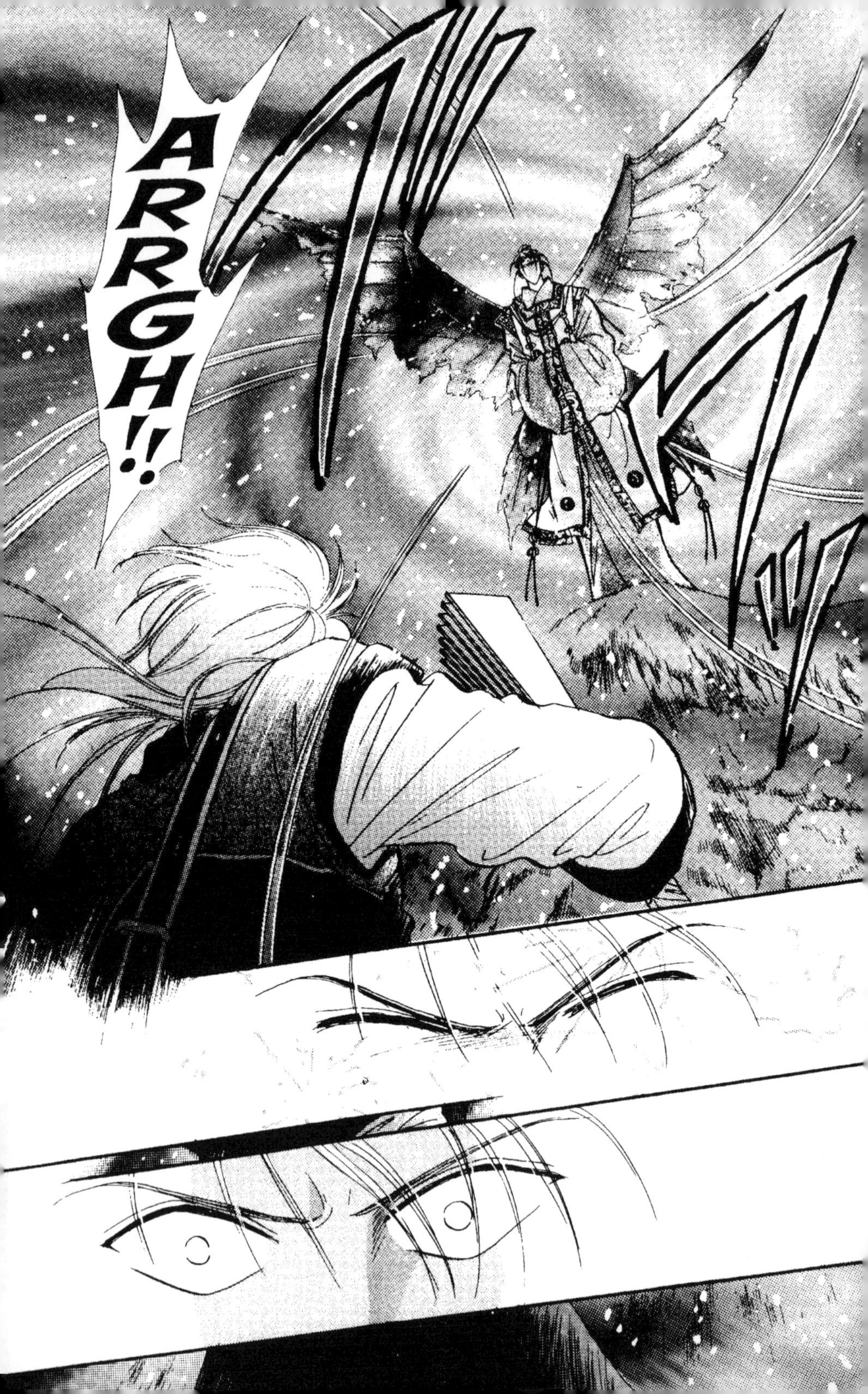
ARRGH!!

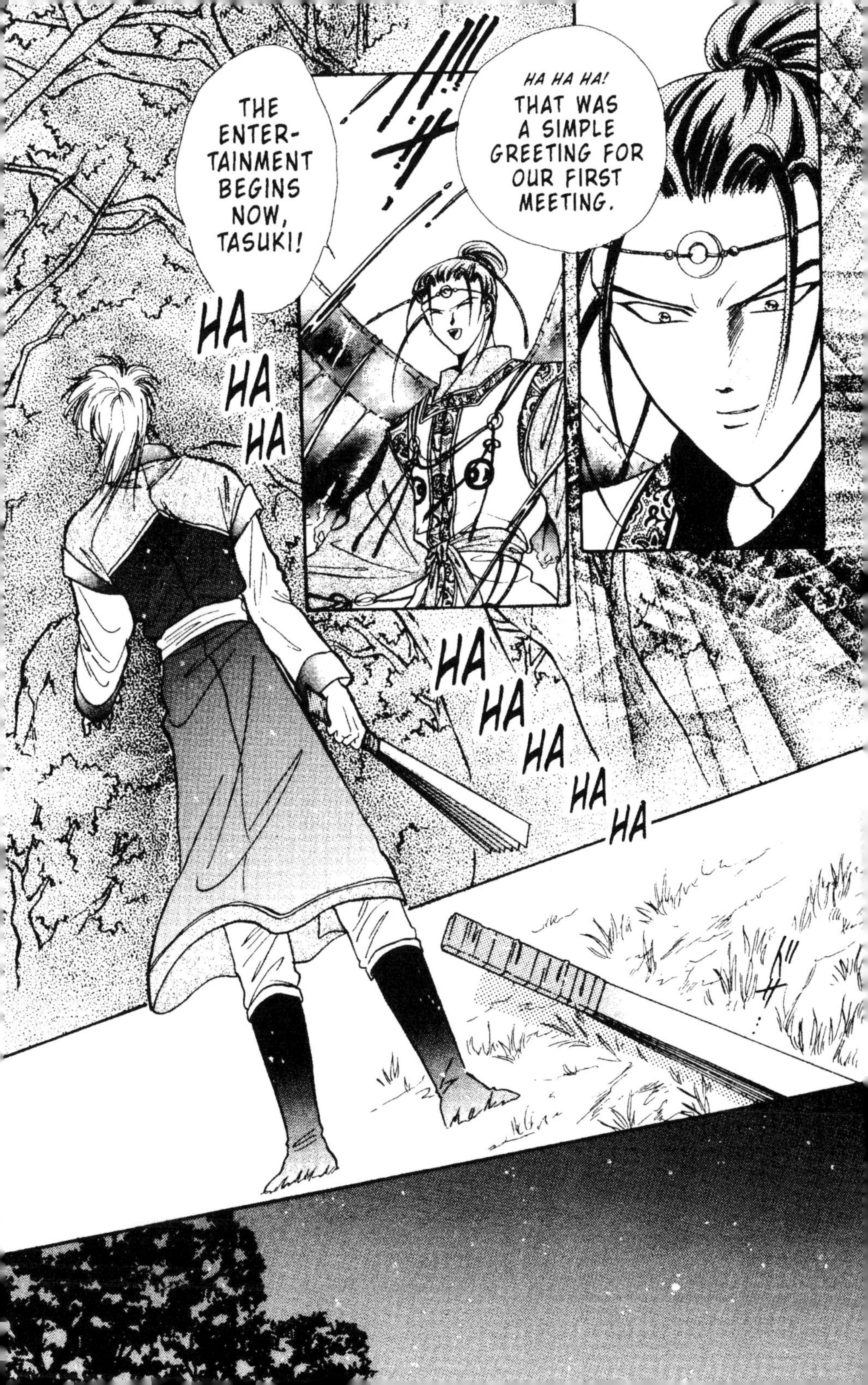
HA HA HA!
THAT WAS A SIMPLE GREETING FOR OUR FIRST MEETING.
THE ENTER-TAINMENT BEGINS NOW, TASUKI!
HA HA HA
HA HA HA HA HA

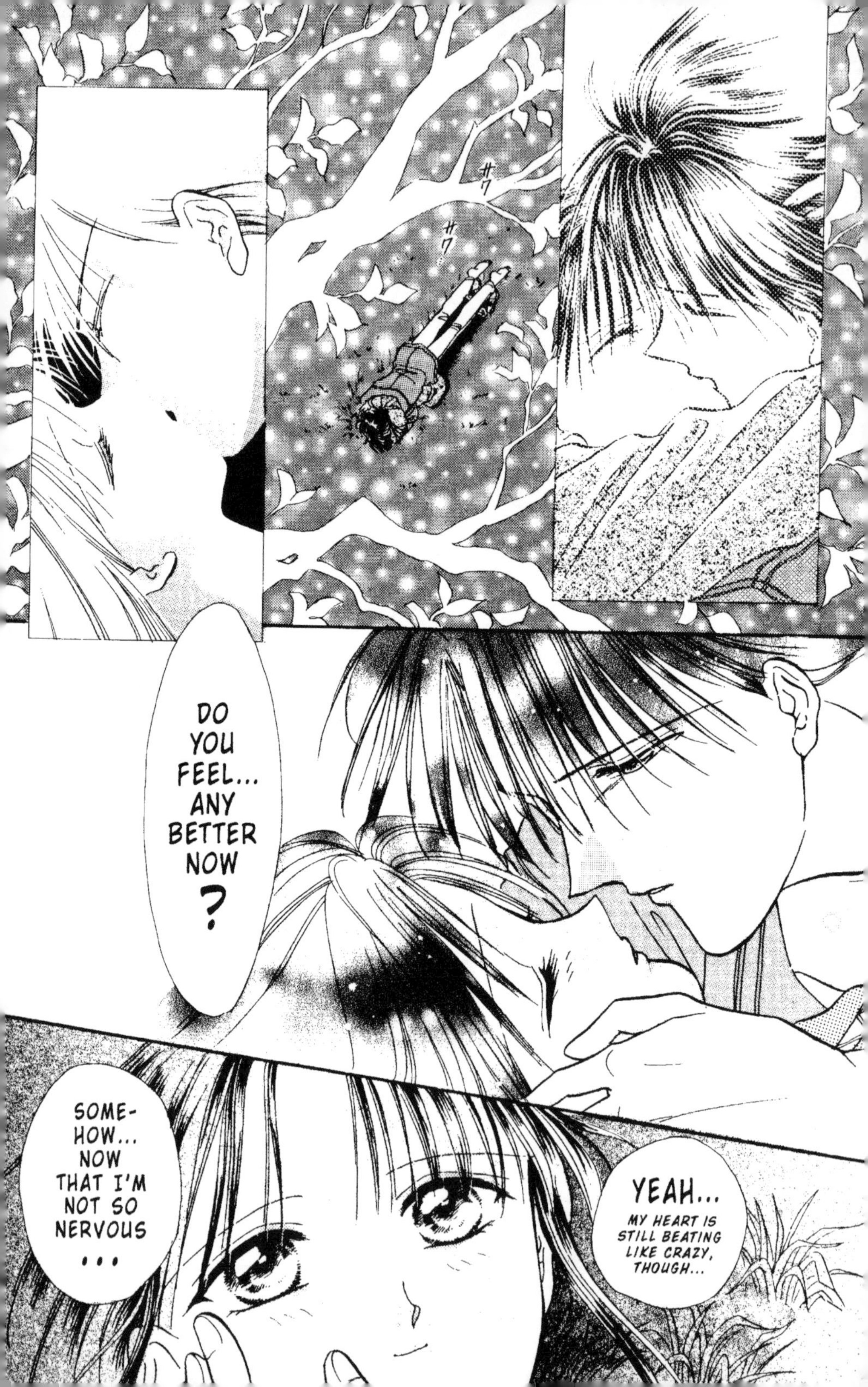
ザワ
ザワ
DO YOU FEEL... ANY BETTER NOW?
YEAH... MY HEART IS STILL BEATING LIKE CRAZY, THOUGH...
SOME-HOW... NOW THAT I'M NOT SO NERVOUS...

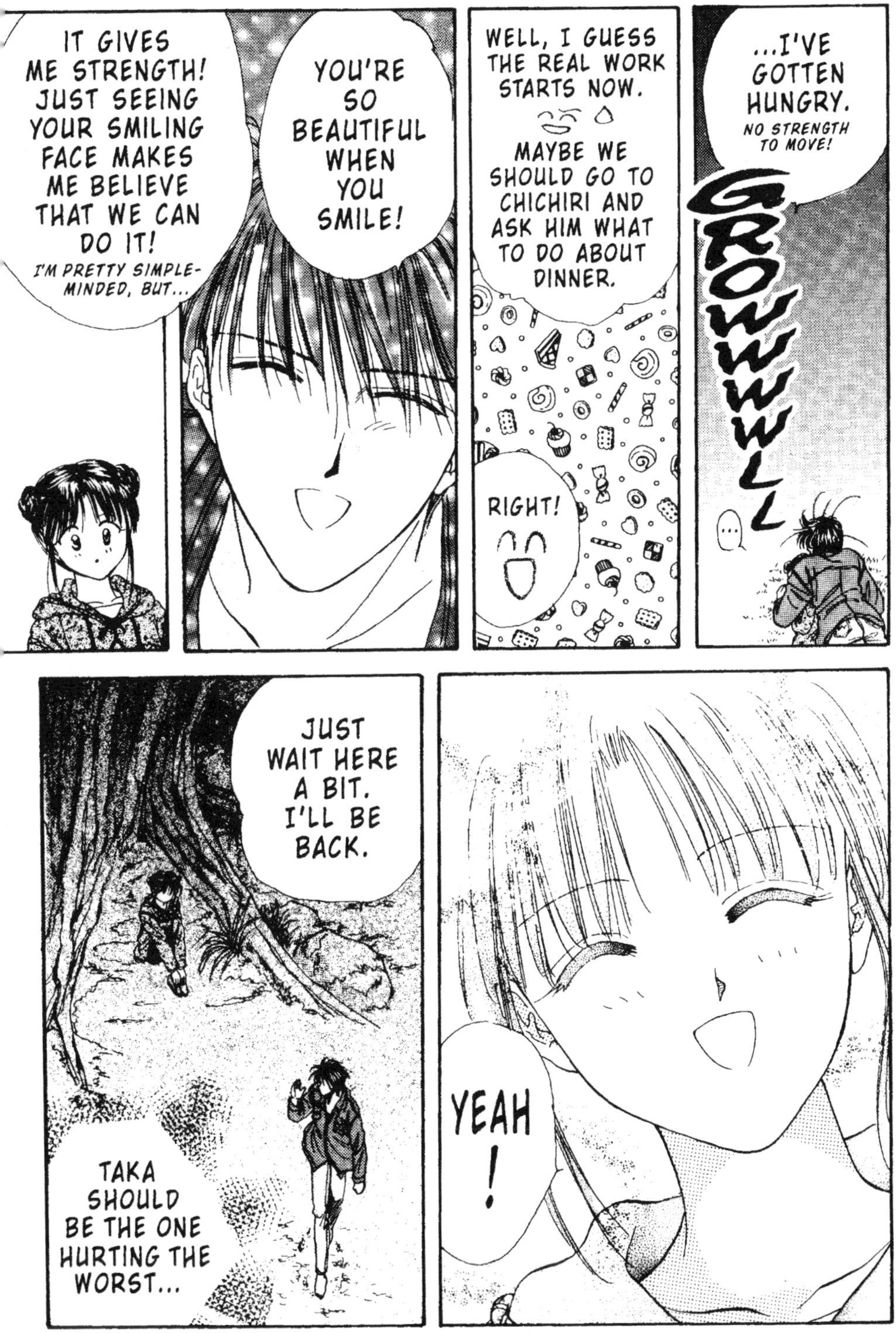
...I'VE GOTTEN HUNGRY.
NO STRENGTH TO MOVE!
GROWWWWLL
...
WELL, I GUESS THE REAL WORK STARTS NOW.
MAYBE WE SHOULD GO TO CHICHIRI AND ASK HIM WHAT TO DO ABOUT DINNER.
RIGHT!
YOU'RE SO BEAUTIFUL WHEN YOU SMILE!
IT GIVES ME STRENGTH! JUST SEEING YOUR SMILING FACE MAKES ME BELIEVE THAT WE CAN DO IT!
I'M PRETTY SIMPLE-MINDED, BUT...
YEAH!
JUST WAIT HERE A BIT. I'LL BE BACK.
TAKA SHOULD BE THE ONE HURTING THE WORST...

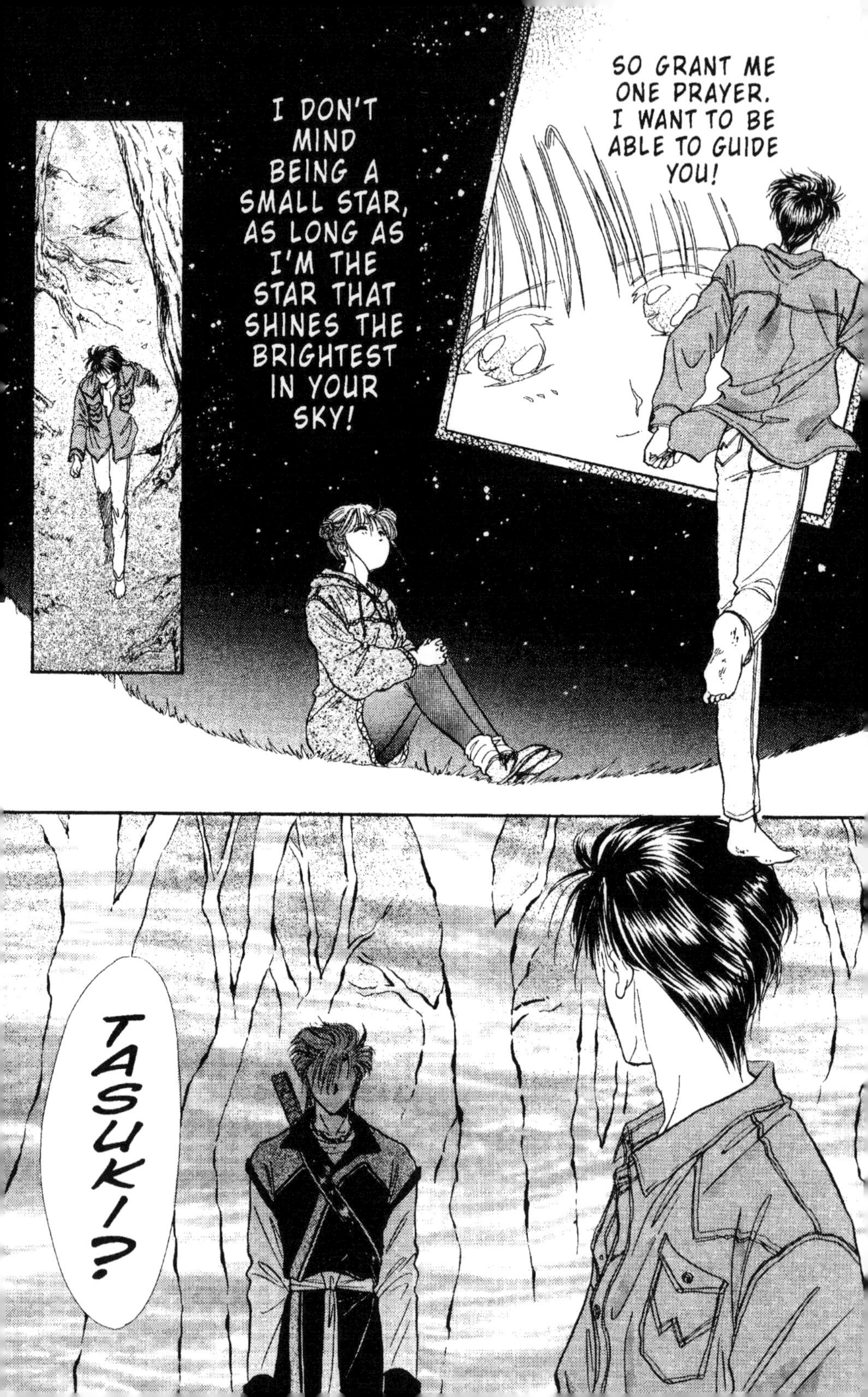
SO GRANT ME ONE PRAYER. I WANT TO BE ABLE TO GUIDE YOU!
I DON'T MIND BEING A SMALL STAR, AS LONG AS I'M THE STAR THAT SHINES THE BRIGHTEST IN YOUR SKY!
TASUKI?

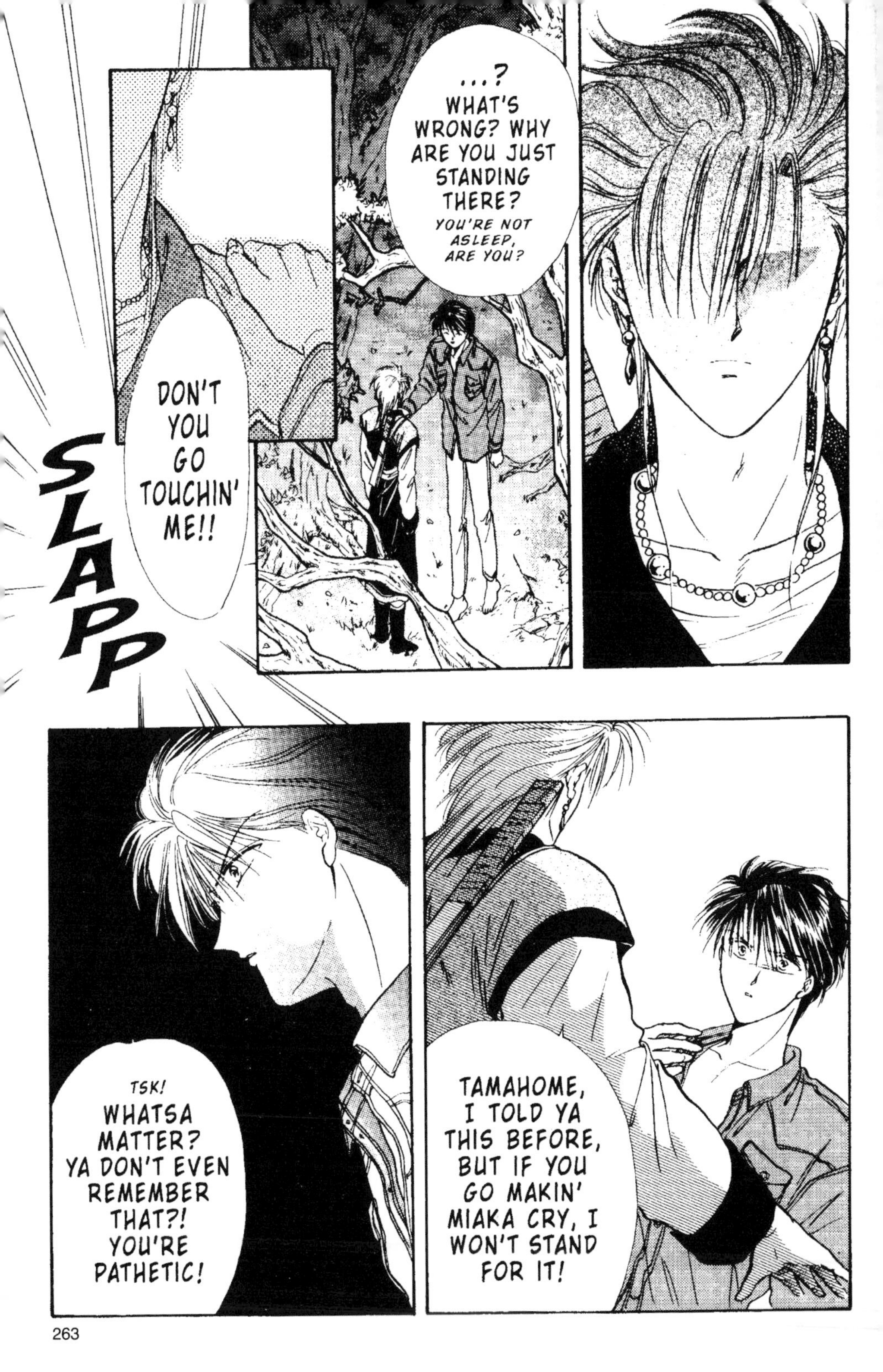
...? WHAT'S WRONG? WHY ARE YOU JUST STANDING THERE?
YOU'RE NOT ASLEEP, ARE YOU?
DON'T YOU GO TOUCHIN' ME!!
SLAPP
TAMAHOME, I TOLD YA THIS BEFORE, BUT IF YOU GO MAKIN' MIAKA CRY, I WON'T STAND FOR IT!
TSK!
WHATSA MATTER? YA DON'T EVEN REMEMBER THAT?! YOU'RE PATHETIC!

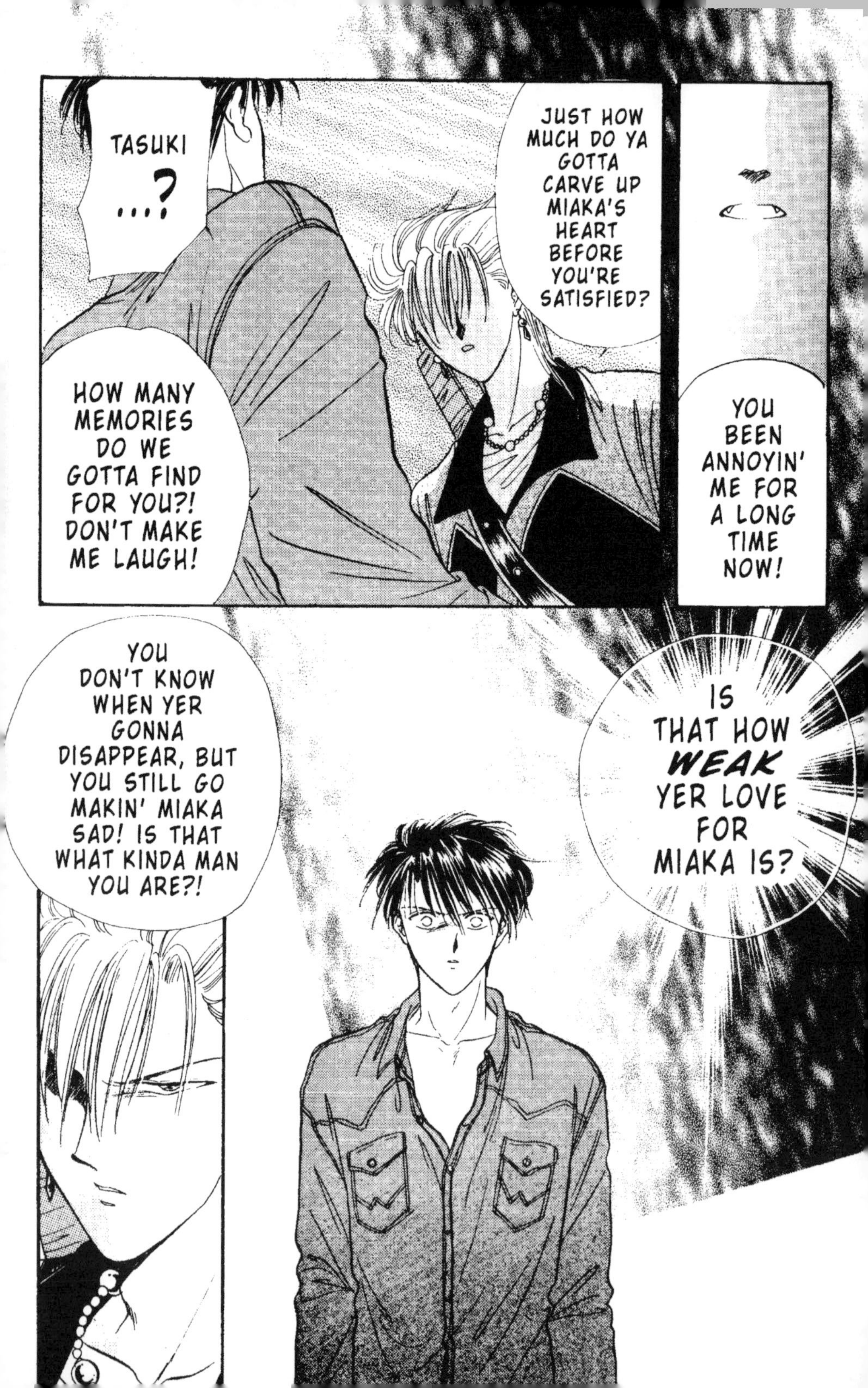
YOU BEEN ANNOYIN' ME FOR A LONG TIME NOW!
JUST HOW MUCH DO YA GOTTA CARVE UP MIAKA'S HEART BEFORE YOU'RE SATISFIED?
TASUKI ...?
HOW MANY MEMORIES DO WE GOTTA FIND FOR YOU?! DON'T MAKE ME LAUGH!
IS THAT HOW ***WEAK*** YER LOVE FOR MIAKA IS?
YOU DON'T KNOW WHEN YER GONNA DISAPPEAR, BUT YOU STILL GO MAKIN' MIAKA SAD! IS THAT WHAT KINDA MAN YOU ARE?!

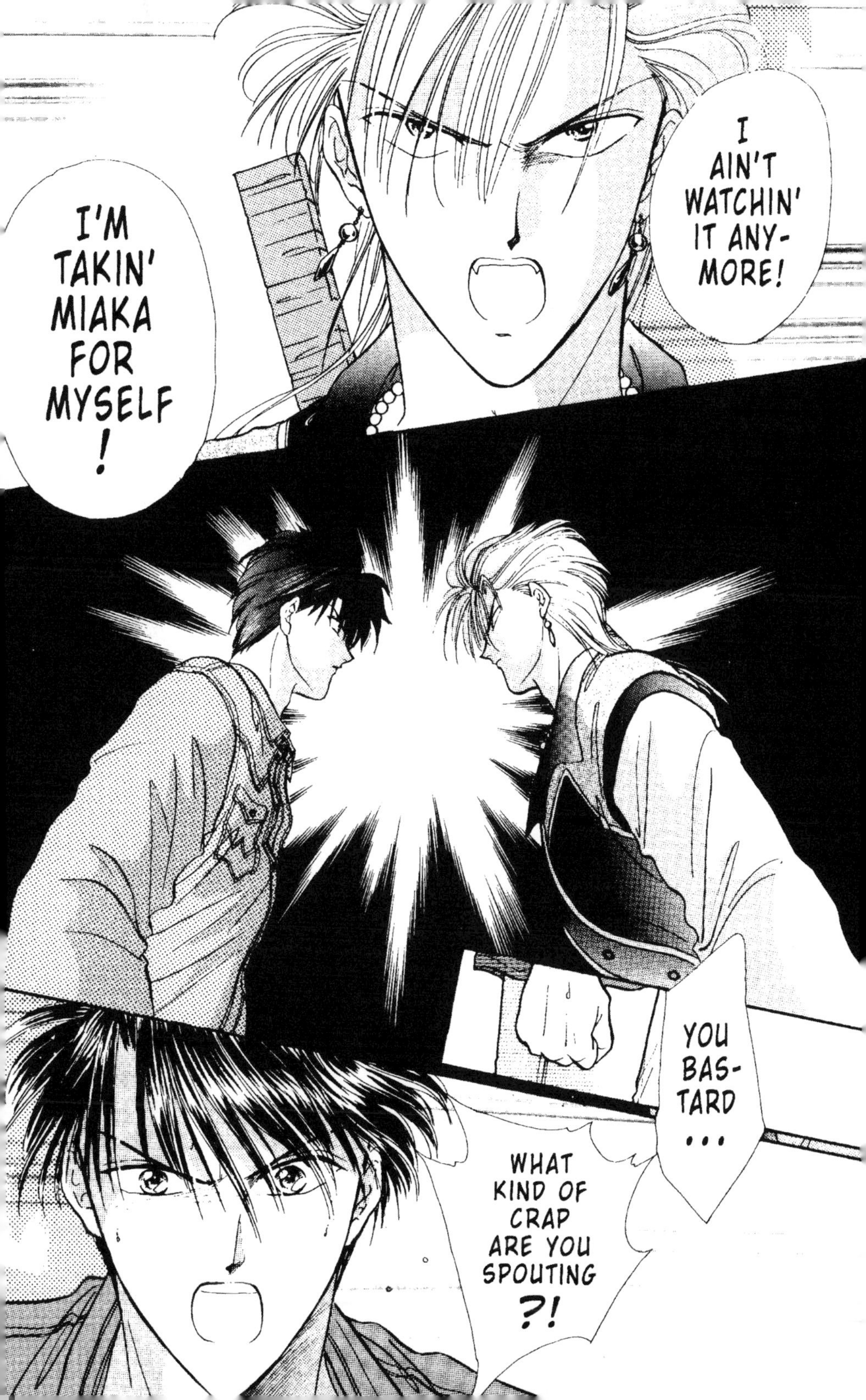
I AIN'T WATCHIN' IT ANY-MORE!
I'M TAKIN' MIAKA FOR MYSELF!
YOU BAS-TARD...
WHAT KIND OF CRAP ARE YOU SPOUTING?!

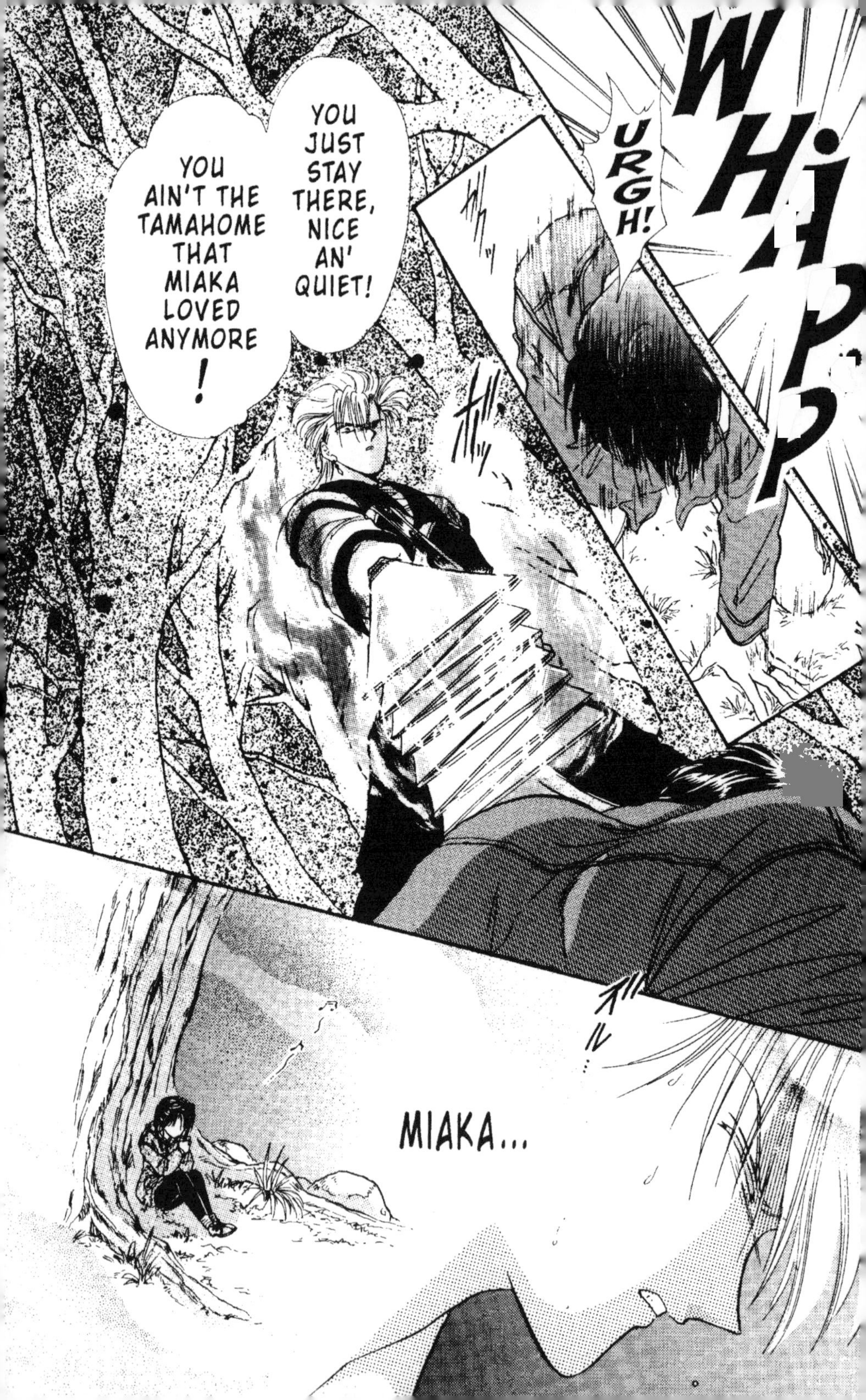
WHiPP
URGH!
YOU JUST STAY THERE, NICE AN' QUIET!
YOU AIN'T THE TAMAHOME THAT MIAKA LOVED ANYMORE!
MIAKA...

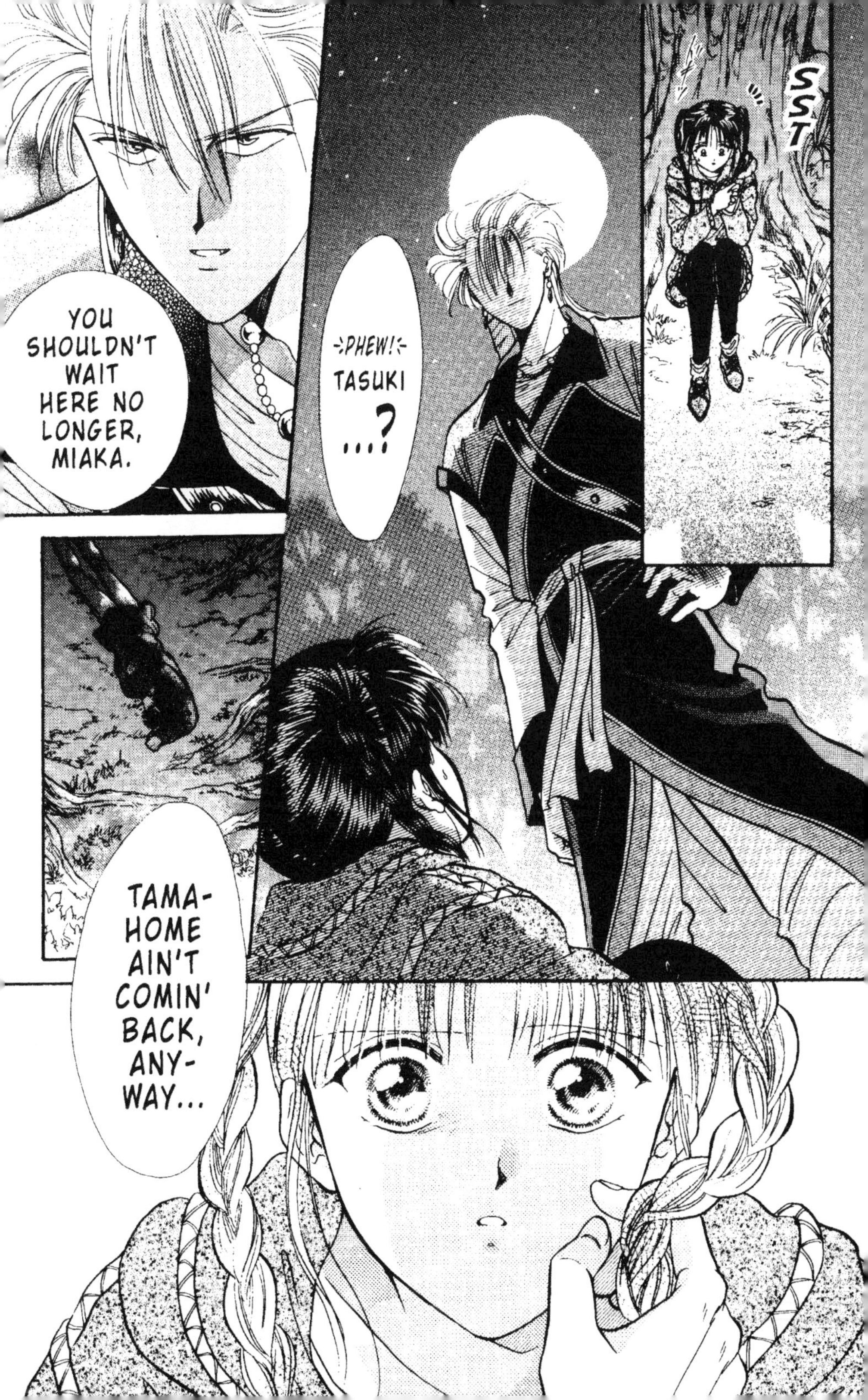
SST
-PHEW!-
TASUKI
...?
YOU SHOULDN'T WAIT HERE NO LONGER, MIAKA.
TAMA-HOME AIN'T COMIN' BACK, ANY-WAY...

ふしぎ悪戯
FUSHIGI AKUGI
THE MALICIOUS PLAY

IDEA BY:
MY
ASSISTANT H.
☺

(14)

PAPER,
SCISSORS
...!!

I'M
TAKING
YOU
ON!

SHUT
UP
!

ROCK!

HERE'S SOME INFORMATION!
The CD Books are coming out again! For Part 2!! "I can't believe it!" is what I thought, but they're actually coming out... sometime around June (1996)! And... they're pulling the songs by the voice actors on the previous five volumes and gathering them into their own CD Book, "Best of Fushigi Yûgi"! (I think that's what it's called.) Yes, they're really all together in one place, and for only 1,800 yen! What a bargain!! So for all those people who think that five volumes is a little much, this is for you!! 💕 Anyway, I'll be creating original art for the cover and the liner notes. There'll be 17 songs in all (including one from the phantom Zen-Play CD.) ☺

Thanks to everyone for the Valentine's Day gifts this year (1996)!!

I wasn't able to make the White Day (3/14) deadline, but I did get replies out to everybody! I thought I was gonna die! 💦 I mean... I GOT THEM FROM 184 PEOPLE!!! I'm sorry! As I expected, I couldn't eat them all myself. My editor said to me, "Don't eat all those! If you try, you'll wind up in the hospital!" and he stopped me. 💦 But if I had even one bite of each, it means I accept!! I thank you all for your gifts of love! Most of them (2/3rds?) were made by hand! Inside there were cookies, those senbei crackers I really like, Nakago dolls, scarves...they all made me very happy! (But about the handmade foods... I'm happy for the thought, but there were some I wasn't able to taste before they spoiled! 💦)

A TRUE STORY!

THERE WERE 410 ITEMS DELIVERED TO THE CHARACTERS!!

ON FEBRUARY 14, 15, 16... I STANK OF MY TREASURE TROVE OF CHOCOLATES! Burp...

AND THE REST...

NUMBER 1!!

BEST 10!!

NUMBER 3

JUST BARELY MADE A NEW RECORD FOR HIM! CONGRATULATIONS!

IT'S ONLY NATURAL!

TASUKI!! (76 ITEMS)

NUMBER 2

THANK YOU!

NURIKO! (62 ITEMS)

NO DA?

CHICHIRI! (56 ITEMS)

NO.4! TAKA (41 ITEMS) DAMMIT!!	NO.5! CHIRIKO (32 ITEMS)	NO.6! HOTOHORI (30 ITEMS)	NO.7! MITSUKAKE (25 ITEMS)
NO.8 WATASE (18 ITEMS)	NO.9 AMIBOSHI (14 ITEMS)	NO.10 SUBOSHI (7 ITEMS)	NO.11 NAKAGO (6 ITEMS)	NO.12 MIAKA (5 ITEMS)	NO.13 (3 ITEMS)	TOKAKI KNEI-GONG (KÔJI) TOMO

Chapter Ninety-Seven
The Night Wandering

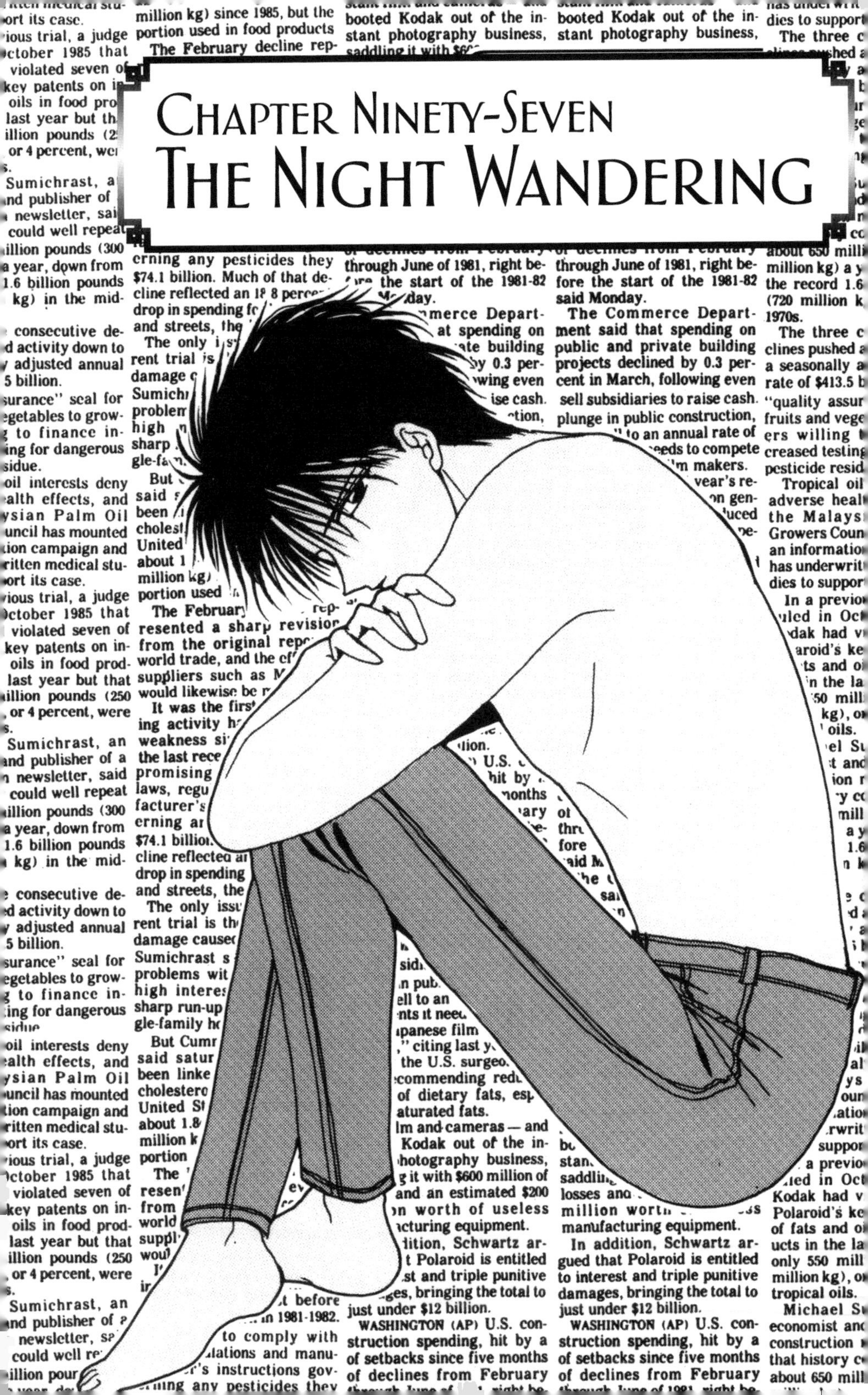

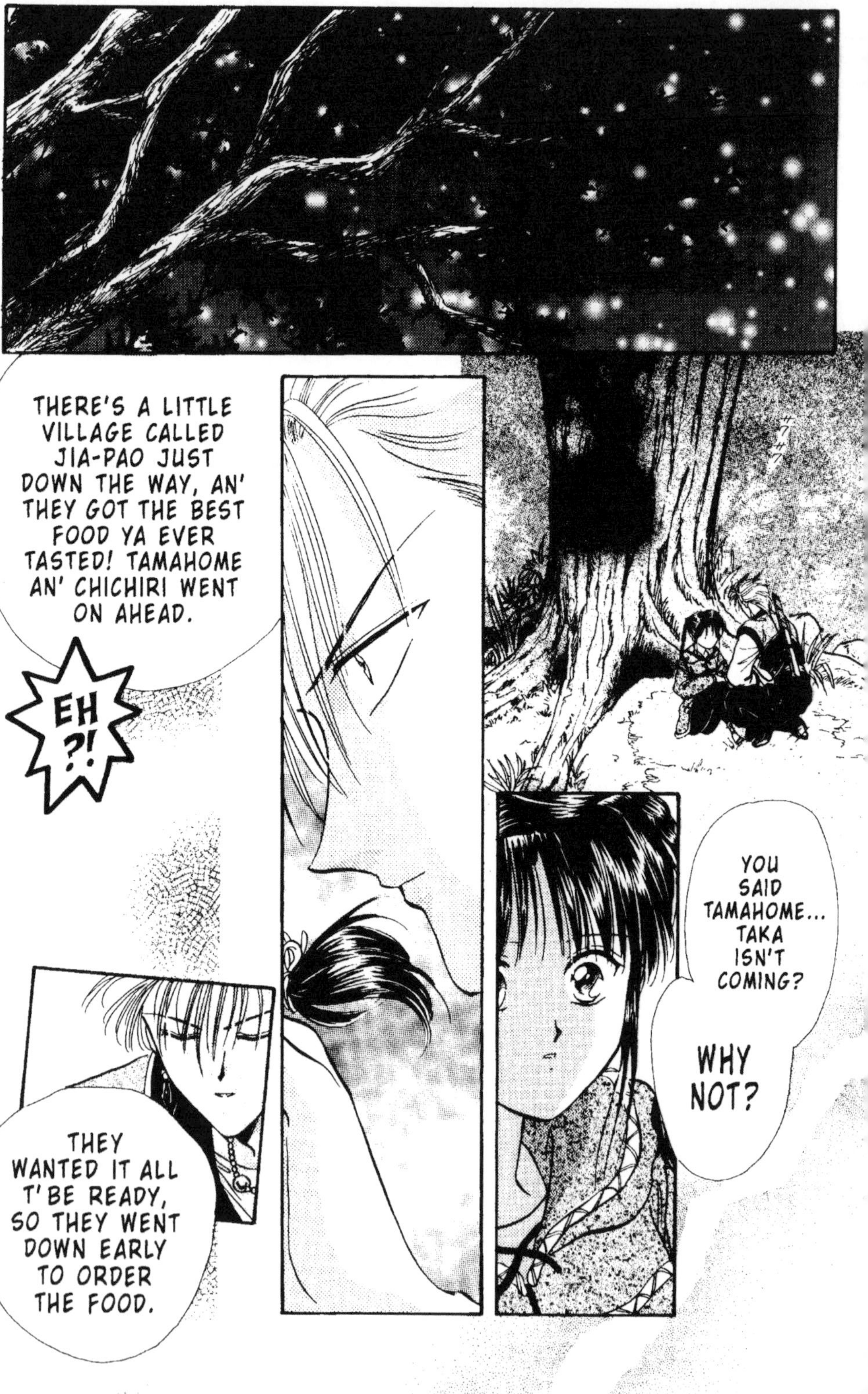

THERE'S A LITTLE VILLAGE CALLED JIA-PAO JUST DOWN THE WAY, AN' THEY GOT THE BEST FOOD YA EVER TASTED! TAMAHOME AN' CHICHIRI WENT ON AHEAD.
EH ?!
YOU SAID TAMAHOME... TAKA ISN'T COMING?
WHY NOT?
THEY WANTED IT ALL T'BE READY, SO THEY WENT DOWN EARLY TO ORDER THE FOOD.

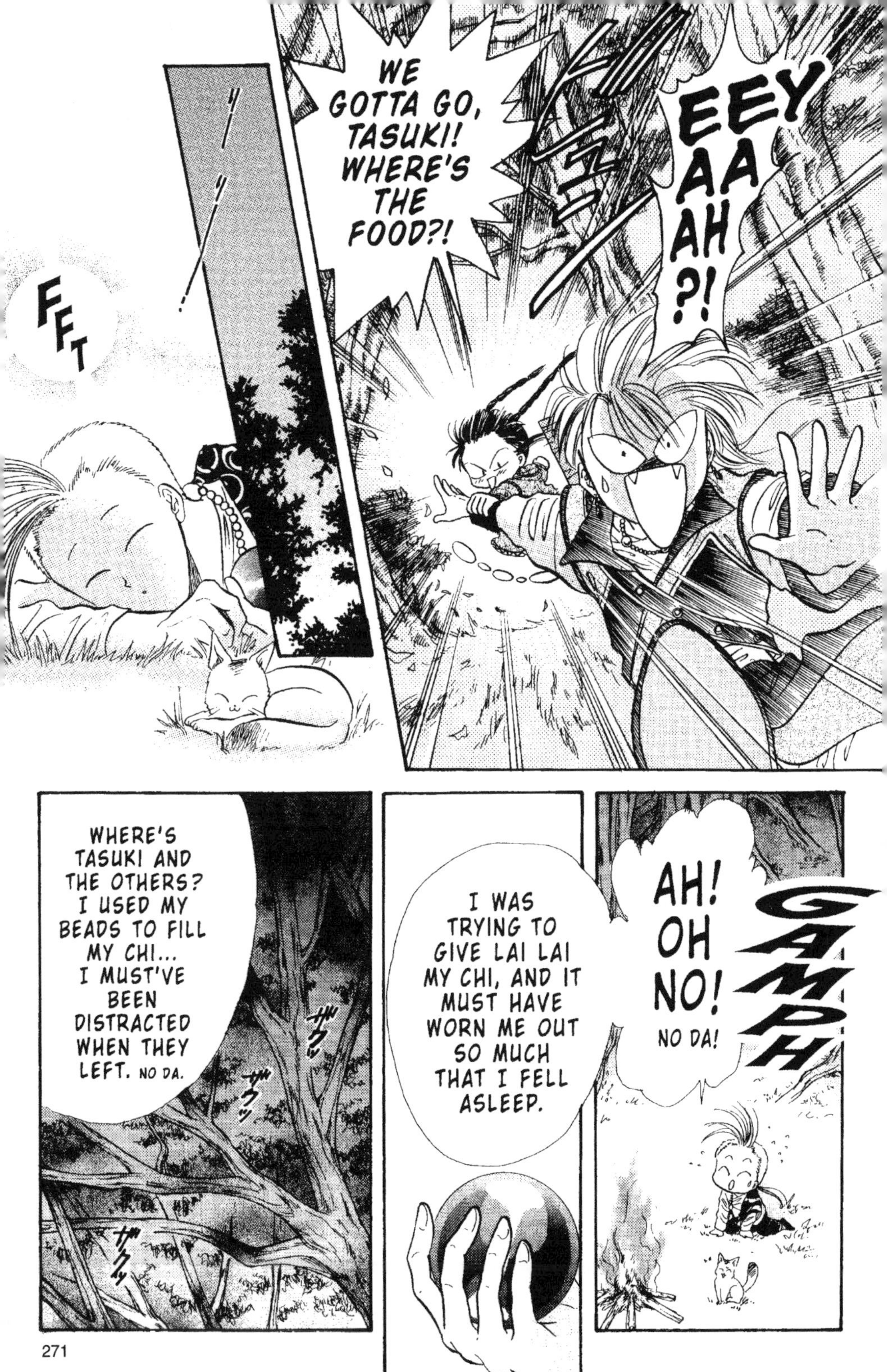

WE GOTTA GO, TASUKI! WHERE'S THE FOOD?!
EEYAAAH?!
FFT
AH! OH NO! NO DA!
GAMPH
I WAS TRYING TO GIVE LAI LAI MY CHI, AND IT MUST HAVE WORN ME OUT SO MUCH THAT I FELL ASLEEP.
WHERE'S TASUKI AND THE OTHERS? I USED MY BEADS TO FILL MY CHI... I MUST'VE BEEN DISTRACTED WHEN THEY LEFT. NO DA.

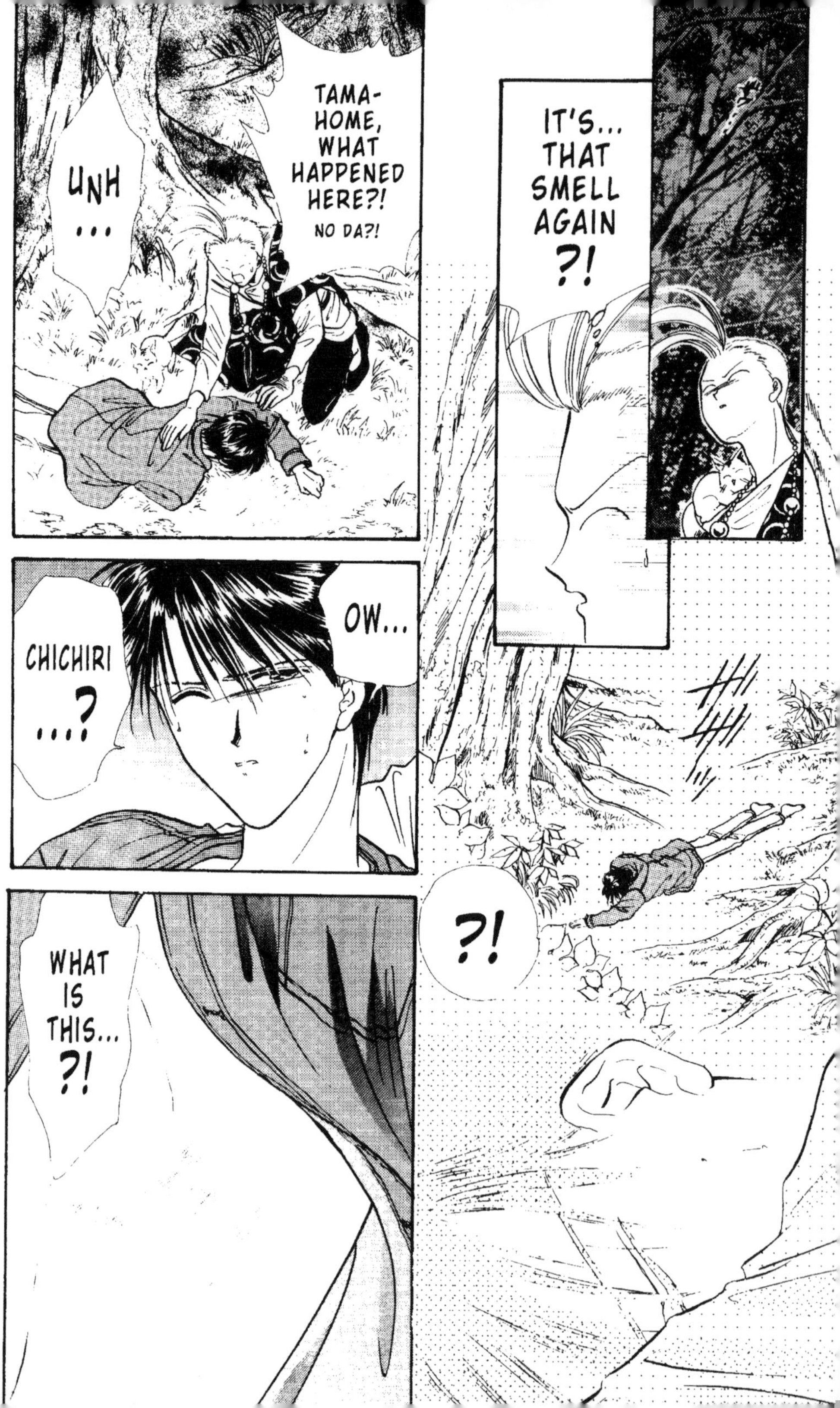
IT'S... THAT SMELL AGAIN ?!
?!
TAMA-HOME, WHAT HAPPENED HERE?!
NO DA?!
UNH ...
OW...
CHICHIRI ...?
WHAT IS THIS... ?!

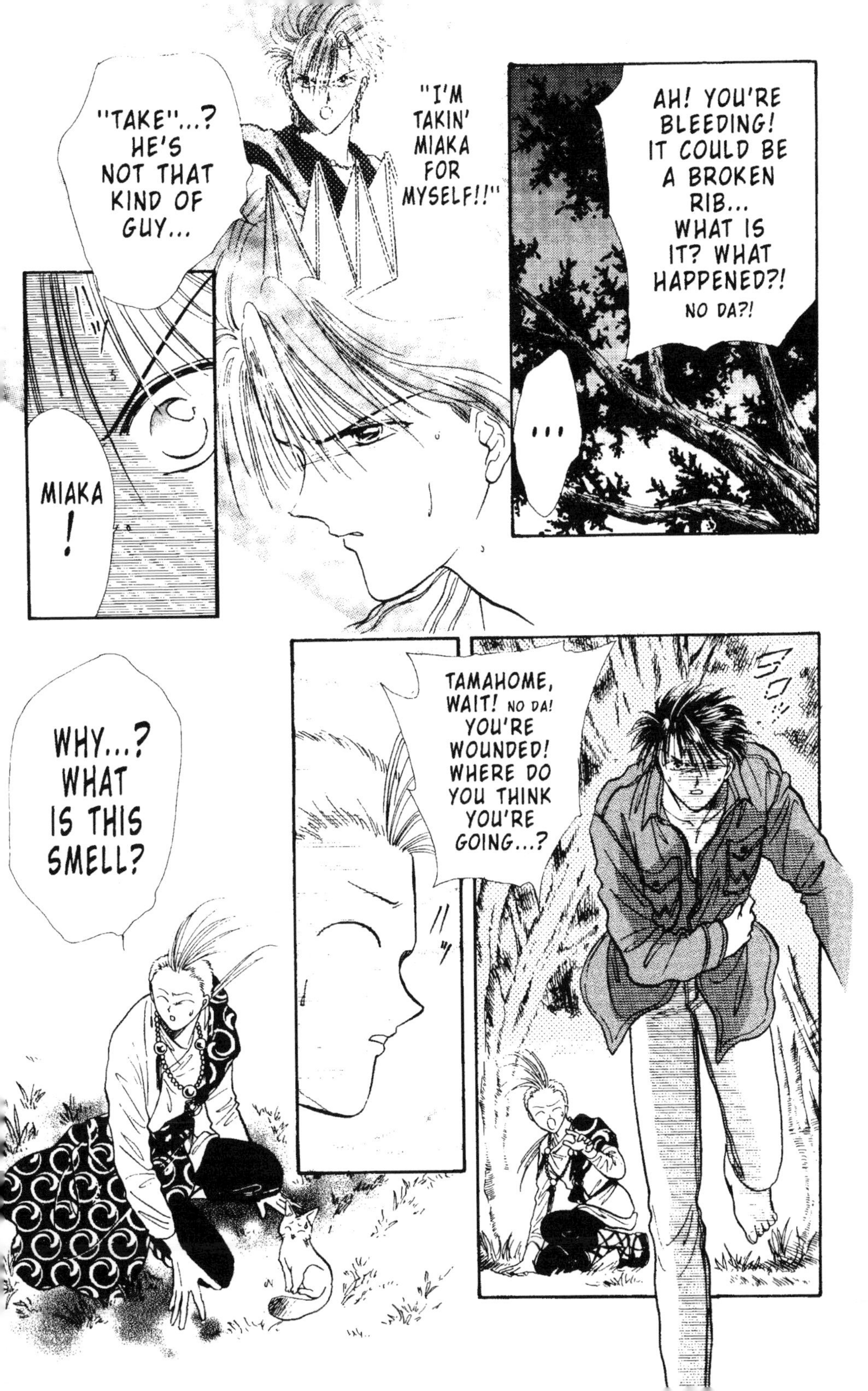
AH! YOU'RE BLEEDING! IT COULD BE A BROKEN RIB... WHAT IS IT? WHAT HAPPENED?! NO DA?!
...
"I'M TAKIN' MIAKA FOR MYSELF!!"
"TAKE"...? HE'S NOT THAT KIND OF GUY...
MIAKA!
TAMAHOME, WAIT! NO DA! YOU'RE WOUNDED! WHERE DO YOU THINK YOU'RE GOING...?
WHY...? WHAT IS THIS SMELL?

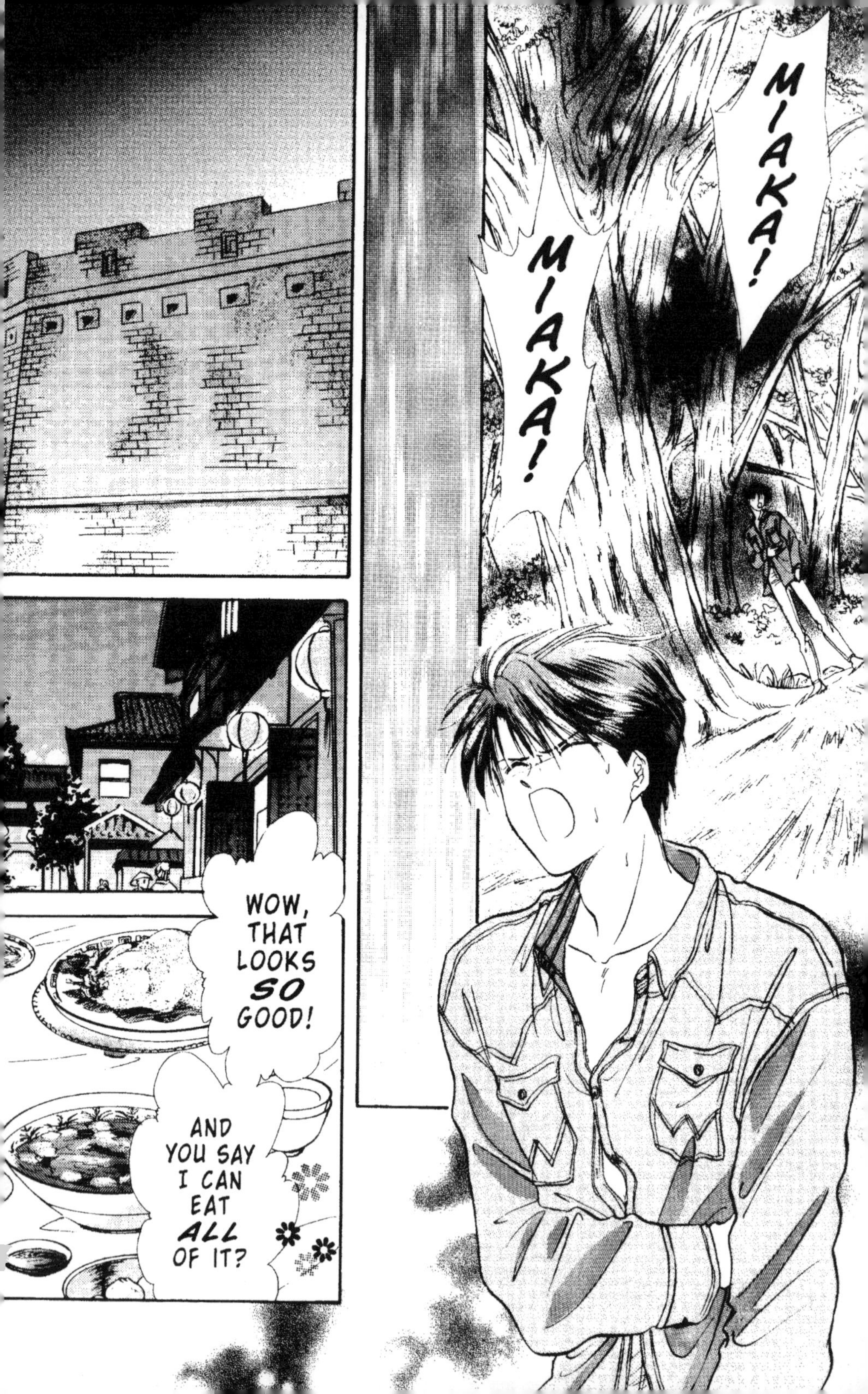
MIAKA!
MIAKA!
WOW, THAT LOOKS SO GOOD!
AND YOU SAY I CAN EAT ALL OF IT?

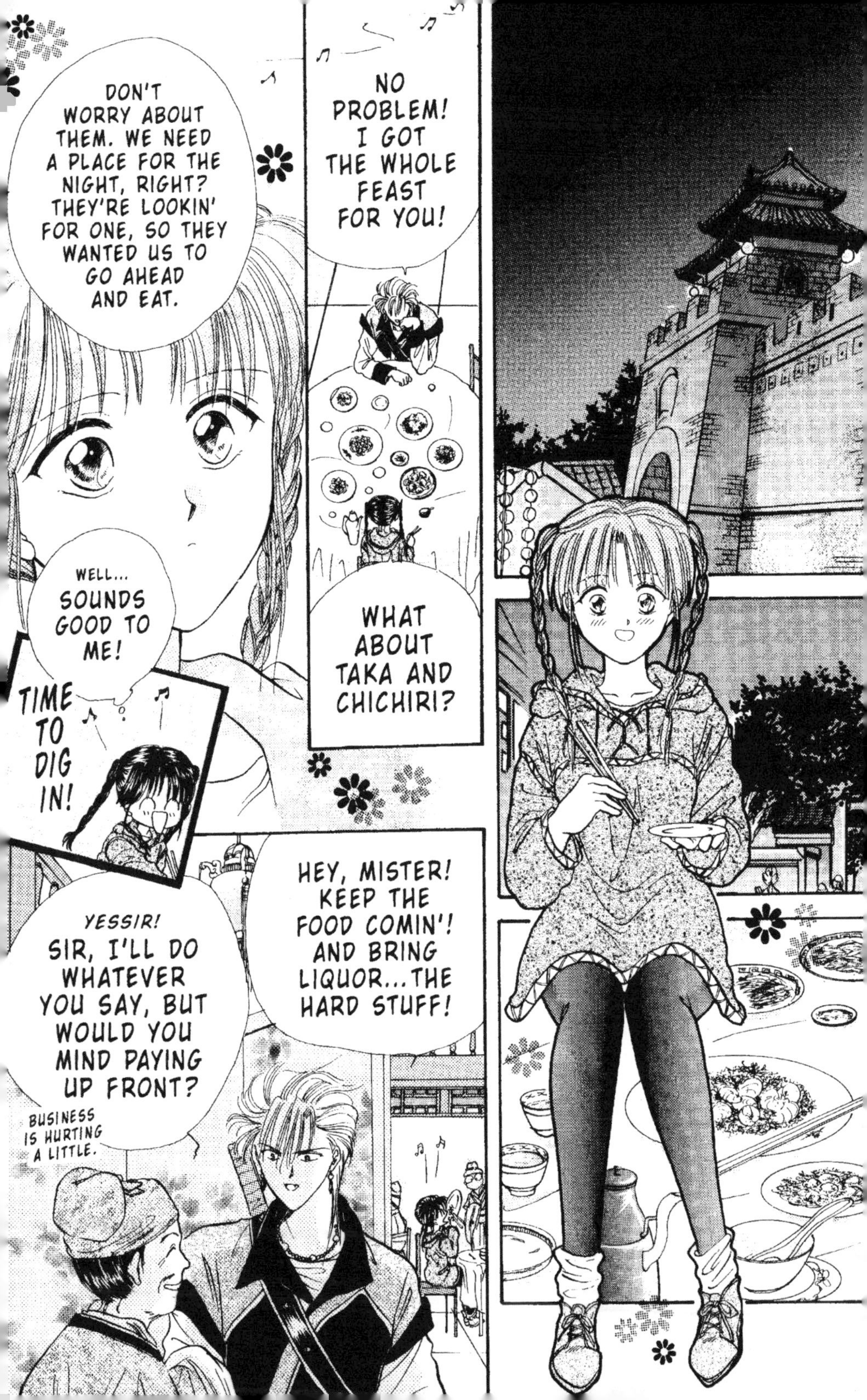
NO PROBLEM! I GOT THE WHOLE FEAST FOR YOU!
WHAT ABOUT TAKA AND CHICHIRI?
DON'T WORRY ABOUT THEM. WE NEED A PLACE FOR THE NIGHT, RIGHT? THEY'RE LOOKIN' FOR ONE, SO THEY WANTED US TO GO AHEAD AND EAT.
WELL... SOUNDS GOOD TO ME!
TIME TO DIG IN!
HEY, MISTER! KEEP THE FOOD COMIN'! AND BRING LIQUOR... THE HARD STUFF!
YESSIR! SIR, I'LL DO WHATEVER YOU SAY, BUT WOULD YOU MIND PAYING UP FRONT?
BUSINESS IS HURTING A LITTLE.

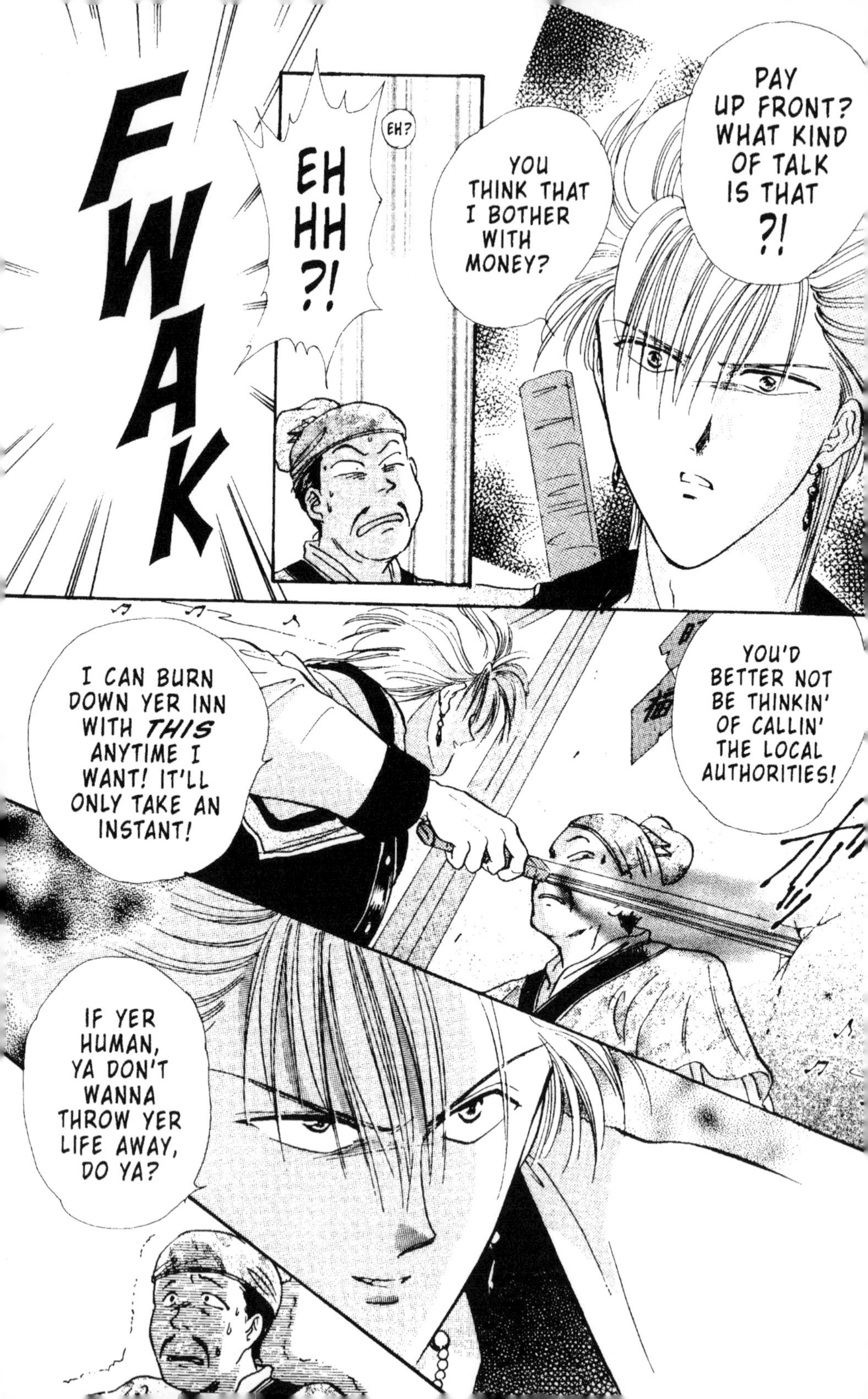
PAY UP FRONT? WHAT KIND OF TALK IS THAT ?!
YOU THINK THAT I BOTHER WITH MONEY?
EH?
EHHH?!
FWAK
YOU'D BETTER NOT BE THINKIN' OF CALLIN' THE LOCAL AUTHORITIES!
I CAN BURN DOWN YER INN WITH *THIS* ANYTIME I WANT! IT'LL ONLY TAKE AN INSTANT!
IF YER HUMAN, YA DON'T WANNA THROW YER LIFE AWAY, DO YA?

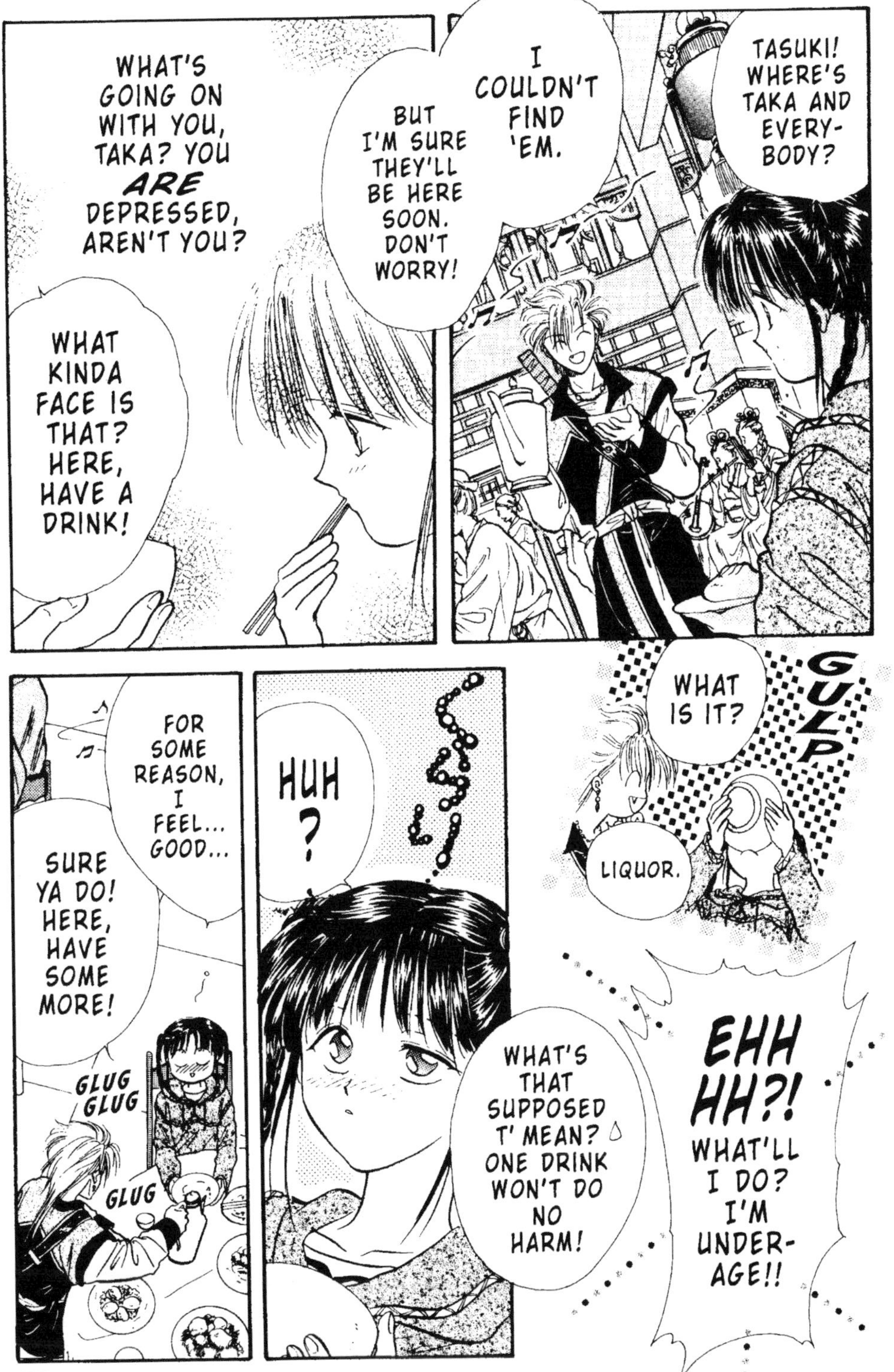
TASUKI! WHERE'S TAKA AND EVERY-BODY?
I COULDN'T FIND 'EM.
BUT I'M SURE THEY'LL BE HERE SOON. DON'T WORRY!
WHAT'S GOING ON WITH YOU, TAKA? YOU *ARE* DEPRESSED, AREN'T YOU?
WHAT KINDA FACE IS THAT? HERE, HAVE A DRINK!
WHAT IS IT?
GULP
LIQUOR.
EHHHH?! WHAT'LL I DO? I'M UNDER-AGE!!
HUH?
WHAT'S THAT SUPPOSED T' MEAN? ONE DRINK WON'T DO NO HARM!
FOR SOME REASON, I FEEL... GOOD...
SURE YA DO! HERE, HAVE SOME MORE!
GLUG GLUG
GLUG

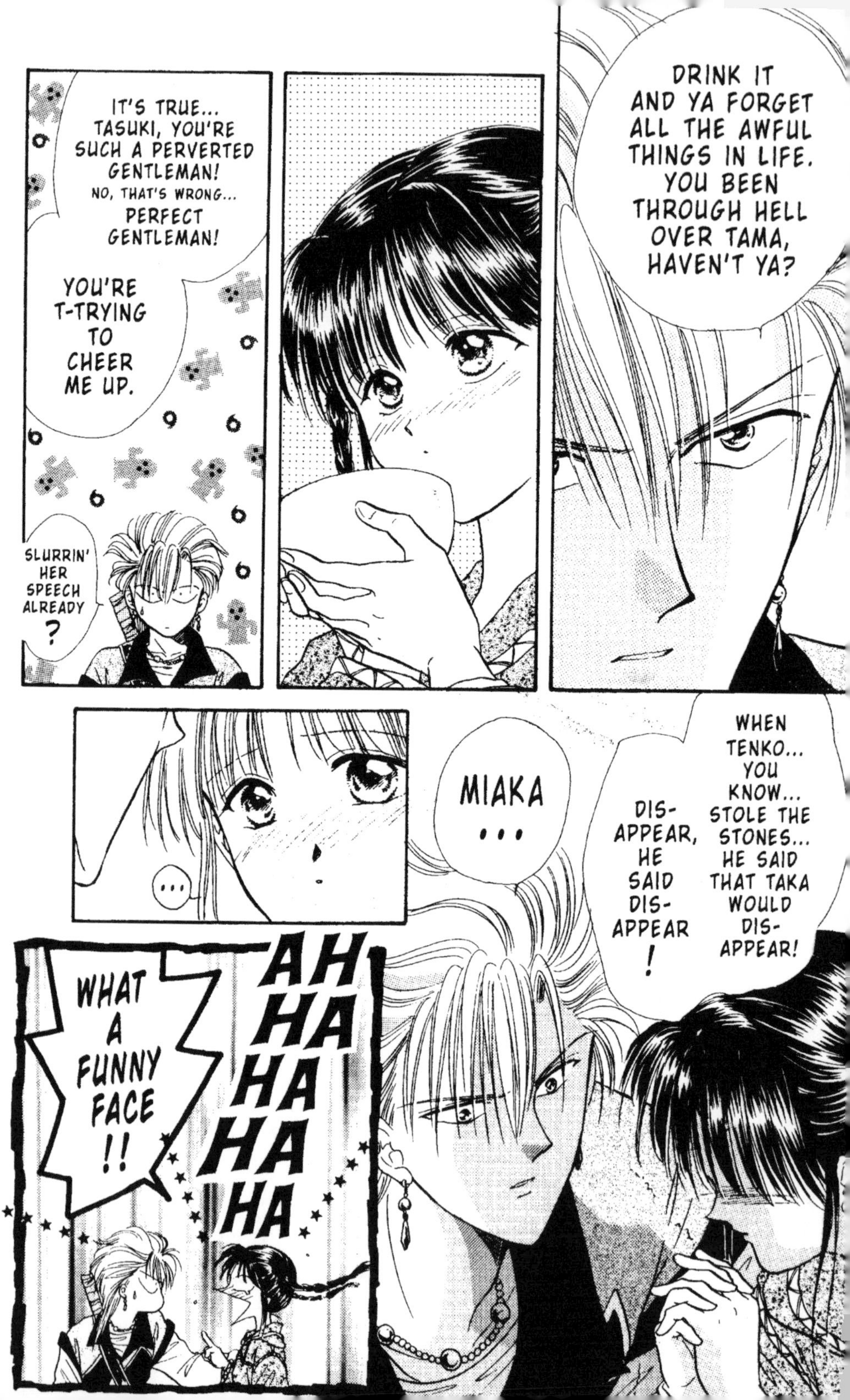
DRINK IT AND YA FORGET ALL THE AWFUL THINGS IN LIFE. YOU BEEN THROUGH HELL OVER TAMA, HAVEN'T YA?
IT'S TRUE... TASUKI, YOU'RE SUCH A PERVERTED GENTLEMAN! NO, THAT'S WRONG... PERFECT GENTLEMAN!
YOU'RE T-TRYING TO CHEER ME UP.
SLURRIN' HER SPEECH ALREADY?
WHEN TENKO... YOU KNOW... STOLE THE STONES... HE SAID THAT TAKA WOULD DIS-APPEAR!
DIS-APPEAR, HE SAID DIS-APPEAR!
MIAKA...
...
AH HA HA HA HA HA
WHAT A FUNNY FACE!!

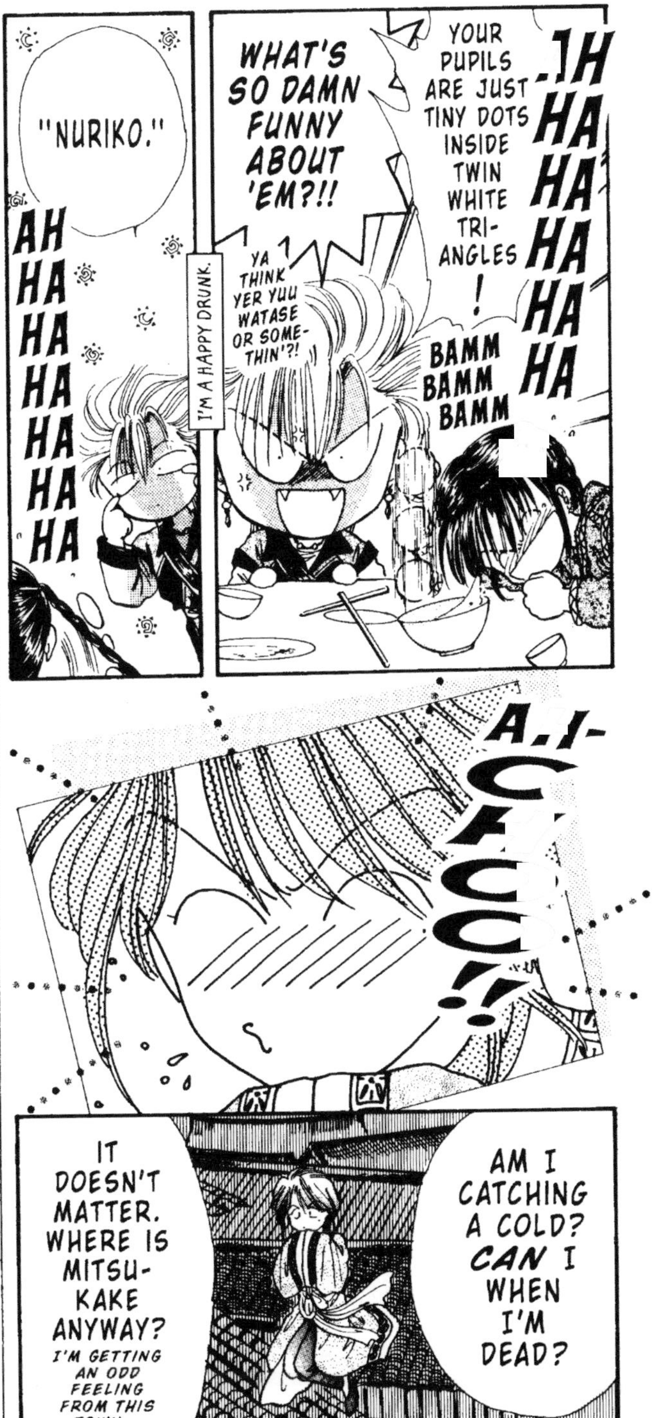

YOUR PUPILS ARE JUST TINY DOTS INSIDE TWIN WHITE TRI-ANGLES!
HA HA HA HA HA HA
WHAT'S SO DAMN FUNNY ABOUT 'EM?!!
YA THINK YER YUU WATASE OR SOME-THIN'?!
BAMM BAMM BAMM
I'M A HAPPY DRUNK.
"NURIKO."
AH HA HA HA HA HA HA HA
A, I-
AM I CATCHING A COLD? CAN I WHEN I'M DEAD?
IT DOESN'T MATTER. WHERE IS MITSU-KAKE ANYWAY?
I'M GETTING AN ODD FEELING FROM THIS TOWN...

Once Part 2 started, Tasuki's popularity went up and up! And it looks like it happened when he gained some sex appeal. It's true that he matured after the end of Part 1, but I didn't try to draw him sexier on purpose. It's just that after we settled on it being two years later, I drew him a little more grown up... just naturally. I did the same for the others, as if they were really alive. *And they are alive! Kind of.* In this story arc too, another one of those "Don" sound effect scenes popped up. If your question is, "Huh? Why would Tasuki do that sort of thing?!" then all I can say is that it just worked out that way. But we're getting into some impressive territory! Things that Miaka has never done up to this point! Is this really revealing true feelings? And if it is, then it's a different problem from the "evil Tama" we had before. *By the way, water is a symbol for the subconscious.*

At one point when we finished work early, all the assistants started talking about whether Tasuki was really in love with Miaka. One assistant, H, had the same reaction as me. "Hmm..." But M (a Tasuki fan--oh, and by the way, H is a very vocal fan of Amiboshi and Suboshi) said, "This is the day I've been waiting for! He really DOES love her!"

H said, "...But it always seemed like love for a little sister."

M replied, "No! In Part 1, it was just friendship, but this is Part 2! He didn't realize it before, but after they separated, he finally understood his feelings!"

"Ahh... Now that he sees her so in love with Tama..."

"Right! Now she's shown up again, and more than that, Miaka's constantly unhappy!"

"To do that to a girl who was your friend? That's pathetic!"

"But..." I said. And in my heart, I got the image of a brother who dotes too much on his little sister...then goes too far and attempts rape. *(A scandalous thought!)*

But M answered, "Tasuki isn't so much of a beast to do that with a girl he doesn't even like!" *That's true.* ☺ And after that, they began to digress.

"Did he ever get her underwear off?"

"Oh, normally they just come off along with the pants." Or maybe she's been wandering around all this time with no panties at all! " Would any-body do that?! *Miaka would be crying...!*

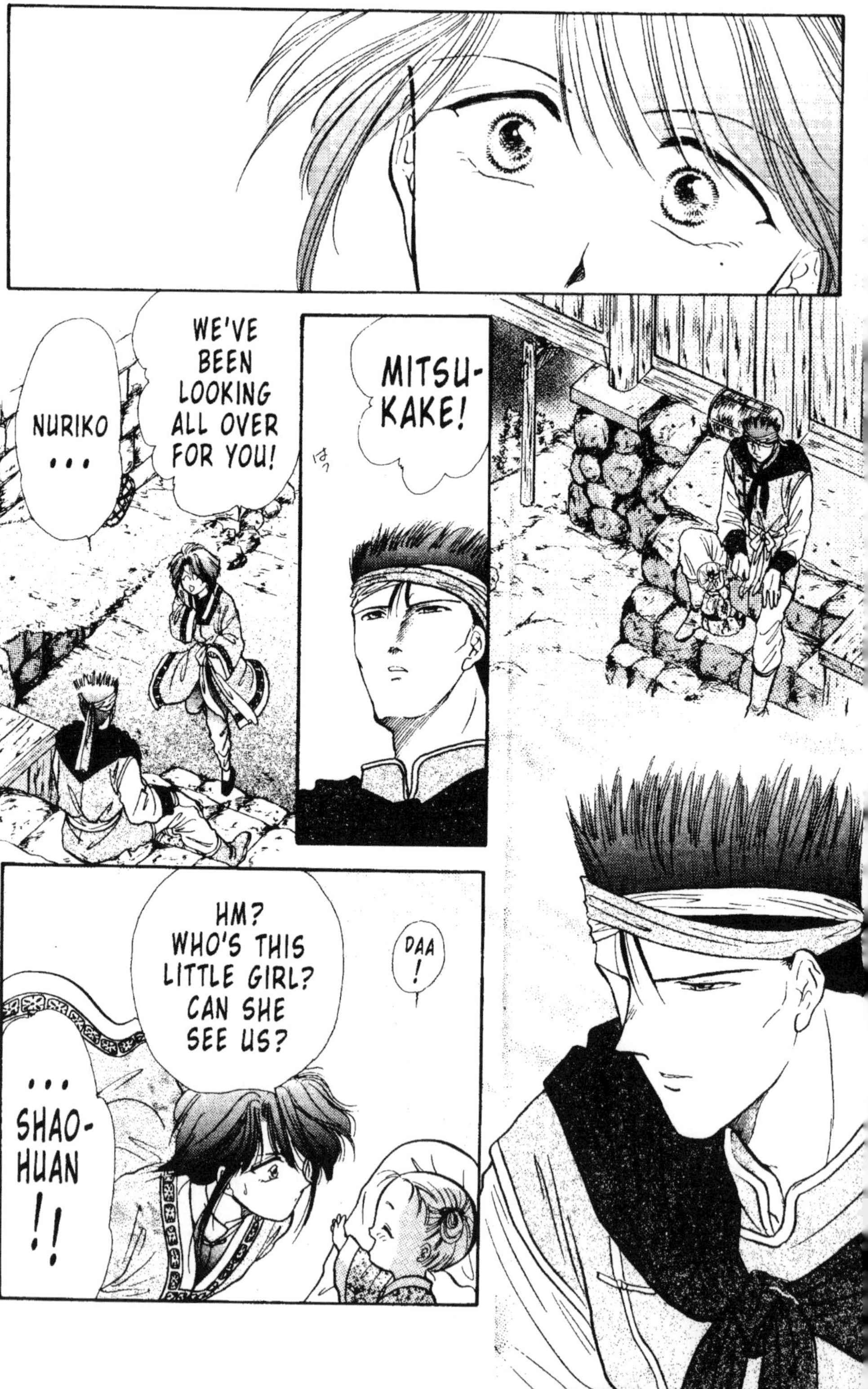
MITSU-KAKE!
は
WE'VE BEEN LOOKING ALL OVER FOR YOU!
NURIKO...
HM? WHO'S THIS LITTLE GIRL? CAN SHE SEE US?
DAA!
...SHAO-HUAN!!

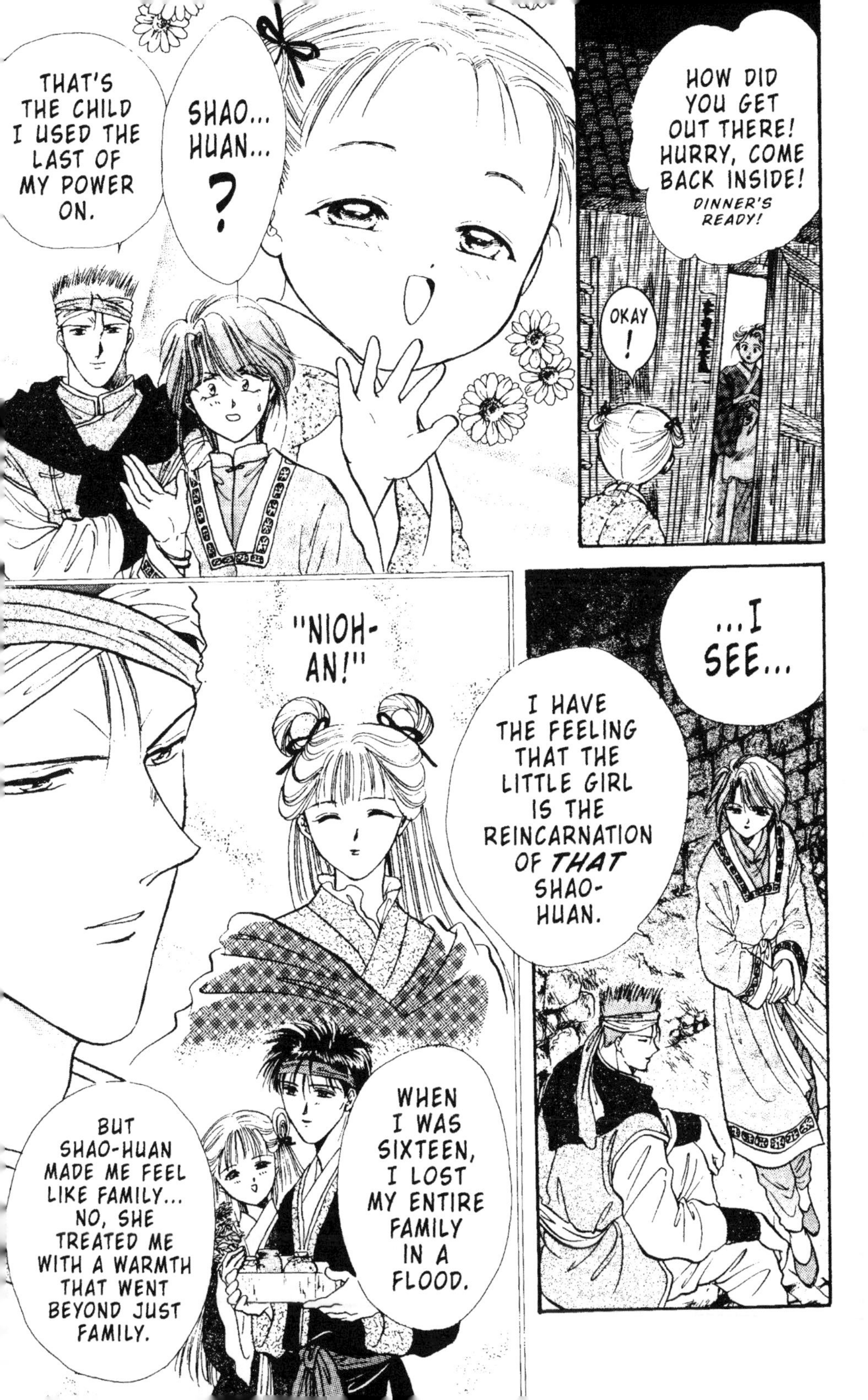
HOW DID YOU GET OUT THERE! HURRY, COME BACK INSIDE!
DINNER'S READY!
OKAY!
SHAO... HUAN... ?
THAT'S THE CHILD I USED THE LAST OF MY POWER ON.
...I SEE...
I HAVE THE FEELING THAT THE LITTLE GIRL IS THE REINCARNATION OF *THAT* SHAO-HUAN.
"NIOH-AN!"
WHEN I WAS SIXTEEN, I LOST MY ENTIRE FAMILY IN A FLOOD.
BUT SHAO-HUAN MADE ME FEEL LIKE FAMILY... NO, SHE TREATED ME WITH A WARMTH THAT WENT BEYOND JUST FAMILY.

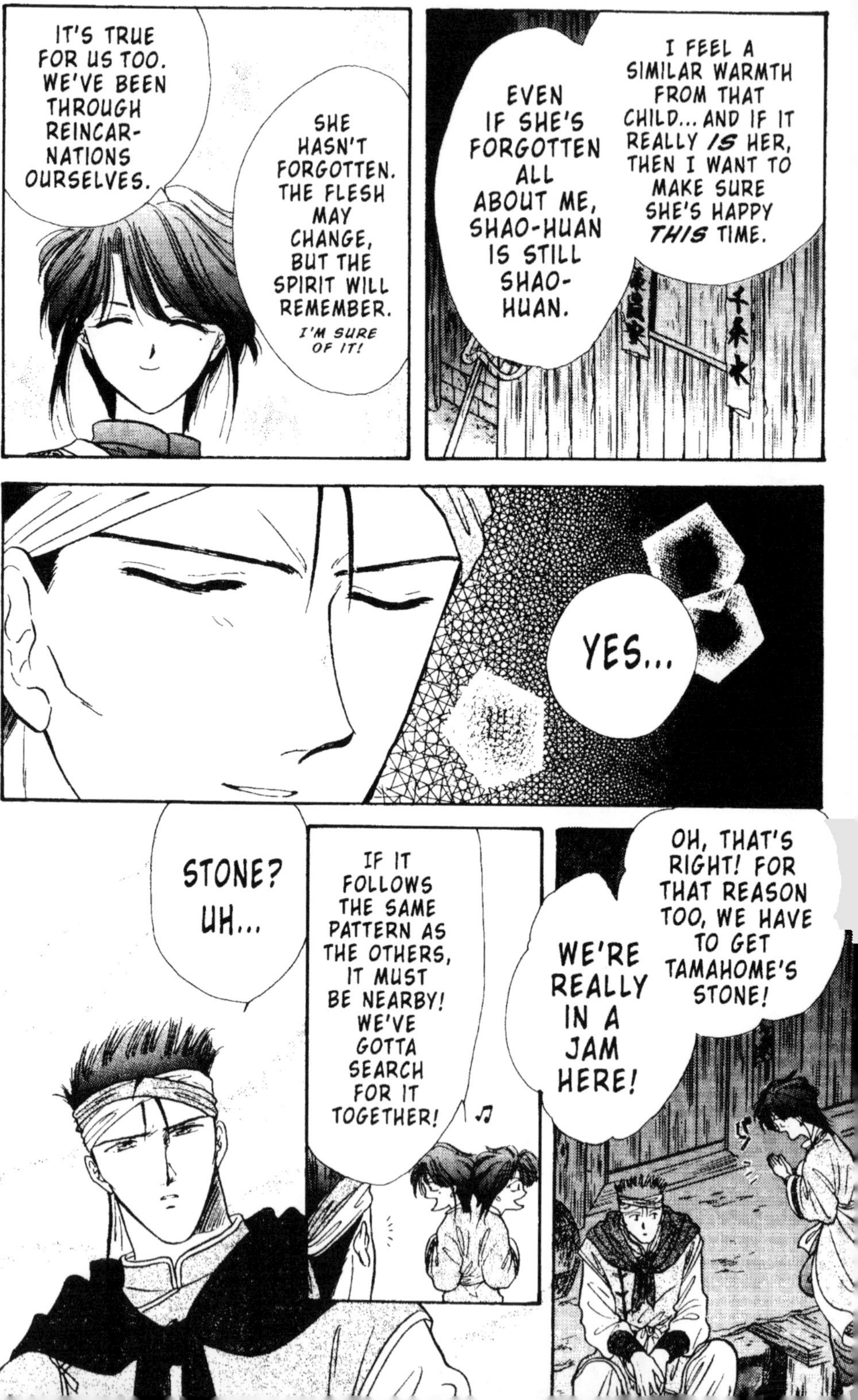
I FEEL A SIMILAR WARMTH FROM THAT CHILD... AND IF IT REALLY *IS* HER, THEN I WANT TO MAKE SURE SHE'S HAPPY *THIS* TIME.
EVEN IF SHE'S FORGOTTEN ALL ABOUT ME, SHAO-HUAN IS STILL SHAO-HUAN.
SHE HASN'T FORGOTTEN. THE FLESH MAY CHANGE, BUT THE SPIRIT WILL REMEMBER.
I'M SURE OF IT!
IT'S TRUE FOR US TOO. WE'VE BEEN THROUGH REINCARNATIONS OURSELVES.
YES...
OH, THAT'S RIGHT! FOR THAT REASON TOO, WE HAVE TO GET TAMAHOME'S STONE!
WE'RE REALLY IN A JAM HERE!
IF IT FOLLOWS THE SAME PATTERN AS THE OTHERS, IT MUST BE NEARBY! WE'VE GOTTA SEARCH FOR IT TOGETHER!
STONE? UH...

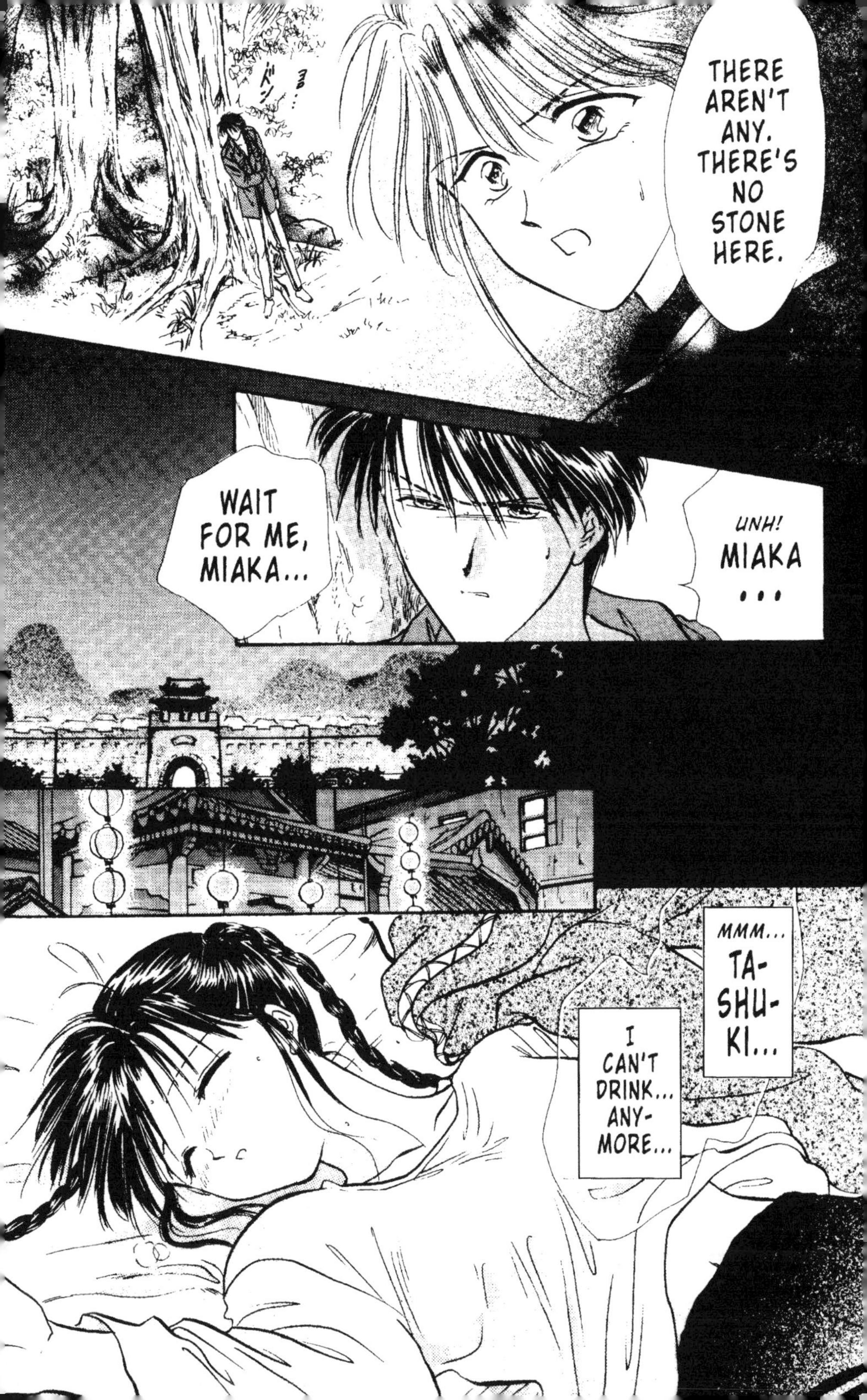
THERE AREN'T ANY. THERE'S NO STONE HERE.
UNH! MIAKA ...
WAIT FOR ME, MIAKA...
MMM... TA-SHU-KI...
I CAN'T DRINK... ANY-MORE...

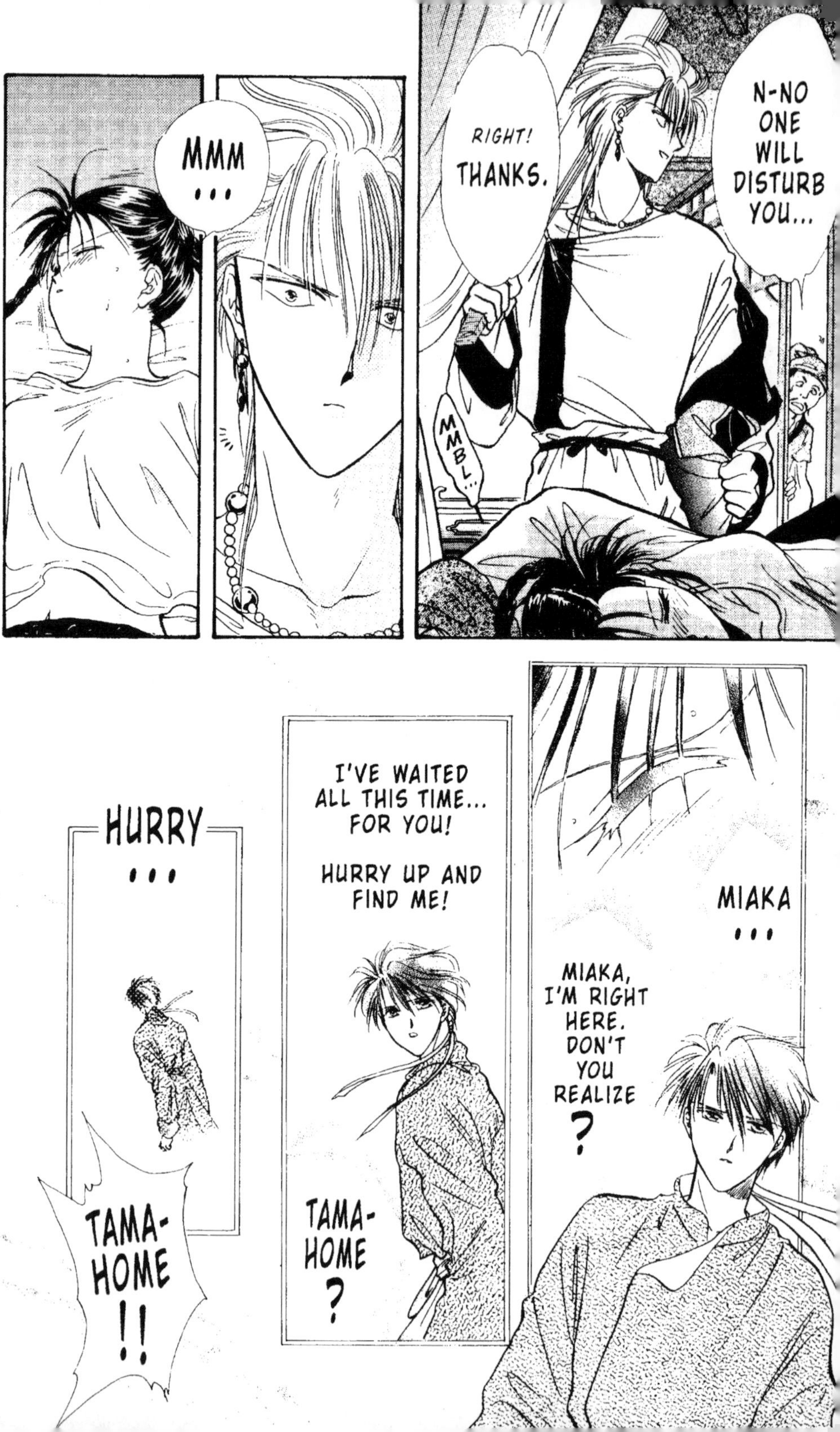
N-NO ONE WILL DISTURB YOU...
RIGHT! THANKS.
MMBL...
MMM ...
MIAKA ...
MIAKA, I'M RIGHT HERE. DON'T YOU REALIZE ?
I'VE WAITED ALL THIS TIME... FOR YOU!
HURRY UP AND FIND ME!
TAMA-HOME ?
HURRY ...
TAMA-HOME !!

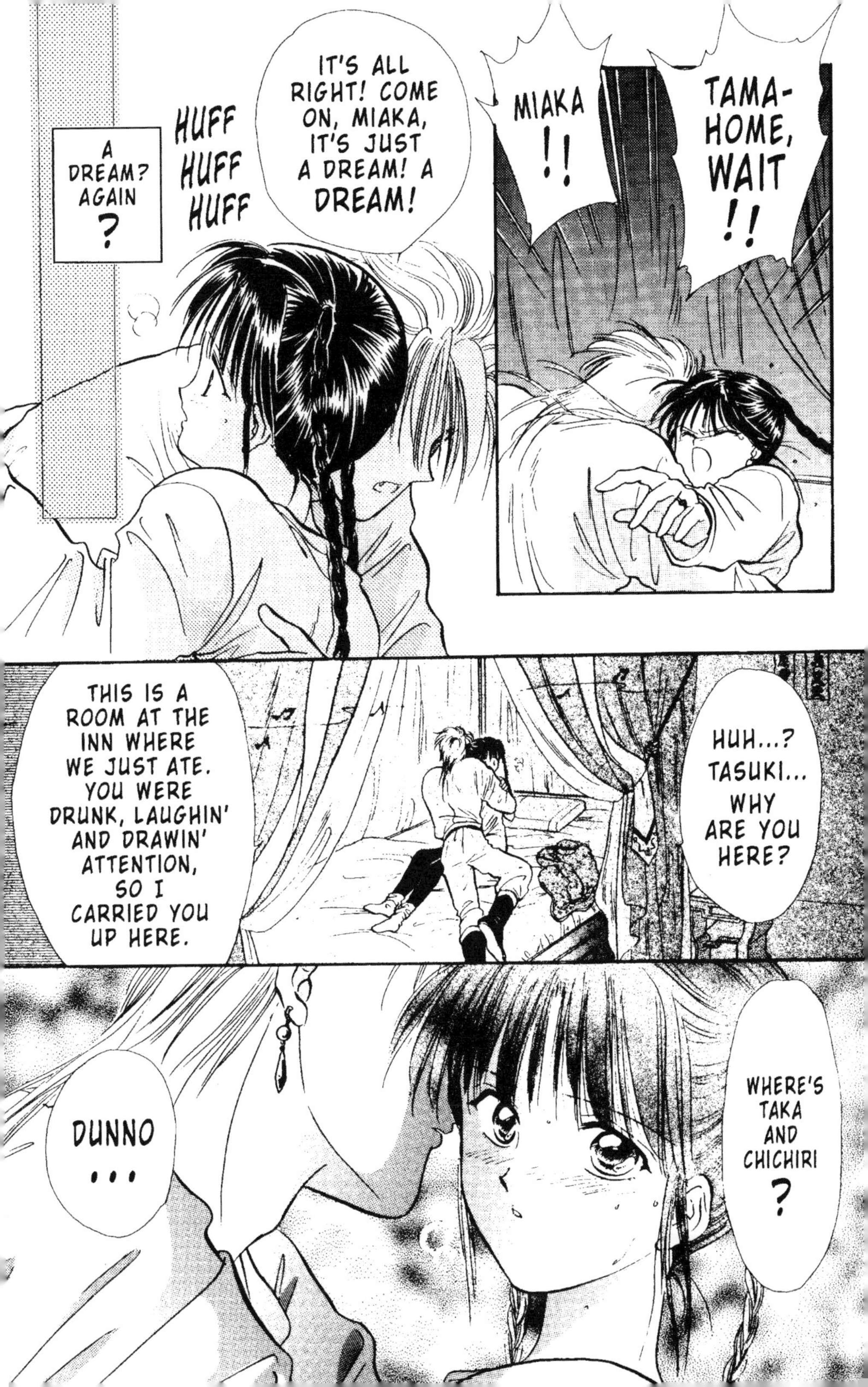

TAMA-HOME, WAIT!!
MIAKA!!
IT'S ALL RIGHT! COME ON, MIAKA, IT'S JUST A DREAM! A DREAM!
HUFF HUFF HUFF
A DREAM? AGAIN?
HUH...? TASUKI... WHY ARE YOU HERE?
THIS IS A ROOM AT THE INN WHERE WE JUST ATE. YOU WERE DRUNK, LAUGHIN' AND DRAWIN' ATTENTION, SO I CARRIED YOU UP HERE.
WHERE'S TAKA AND CHICHIRI?
DUNNO...

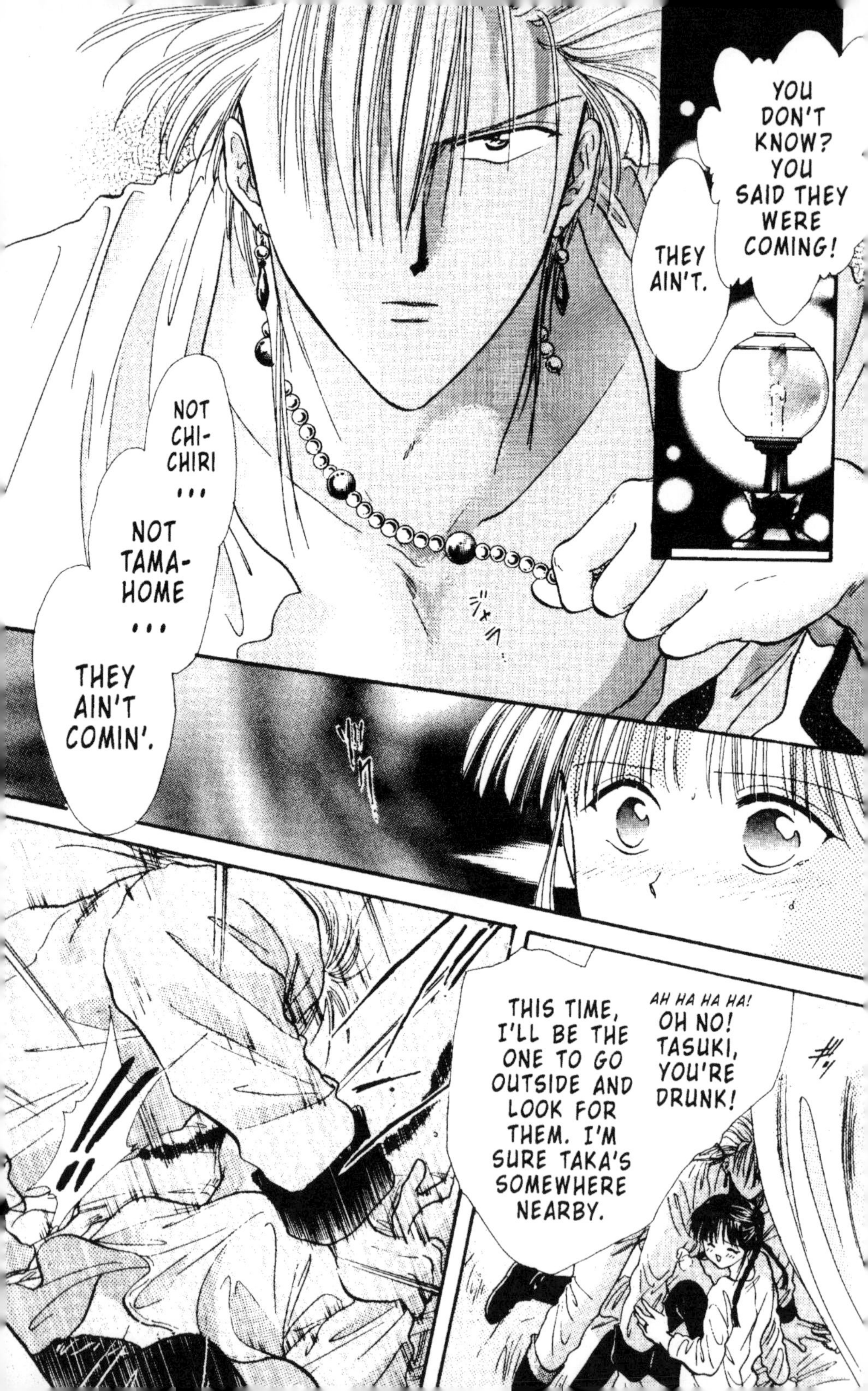
YOU DON'T KNOW? YOU SAID THEY WERE COMING!
THEY AIN'T.
NOT CHICHIRI...
NOT TAMAHOME...
THEY AIN'T COMIN'.
AH HA HA HA! OH NO! TASUKI, YOU'RE DRUNK!
THIS TIME, I'LL BE THE ONE TO GO OUTSIDE AND LOOK FOR THEM. I'M SURE TAKA'S SOMEWHERE NEARBY.

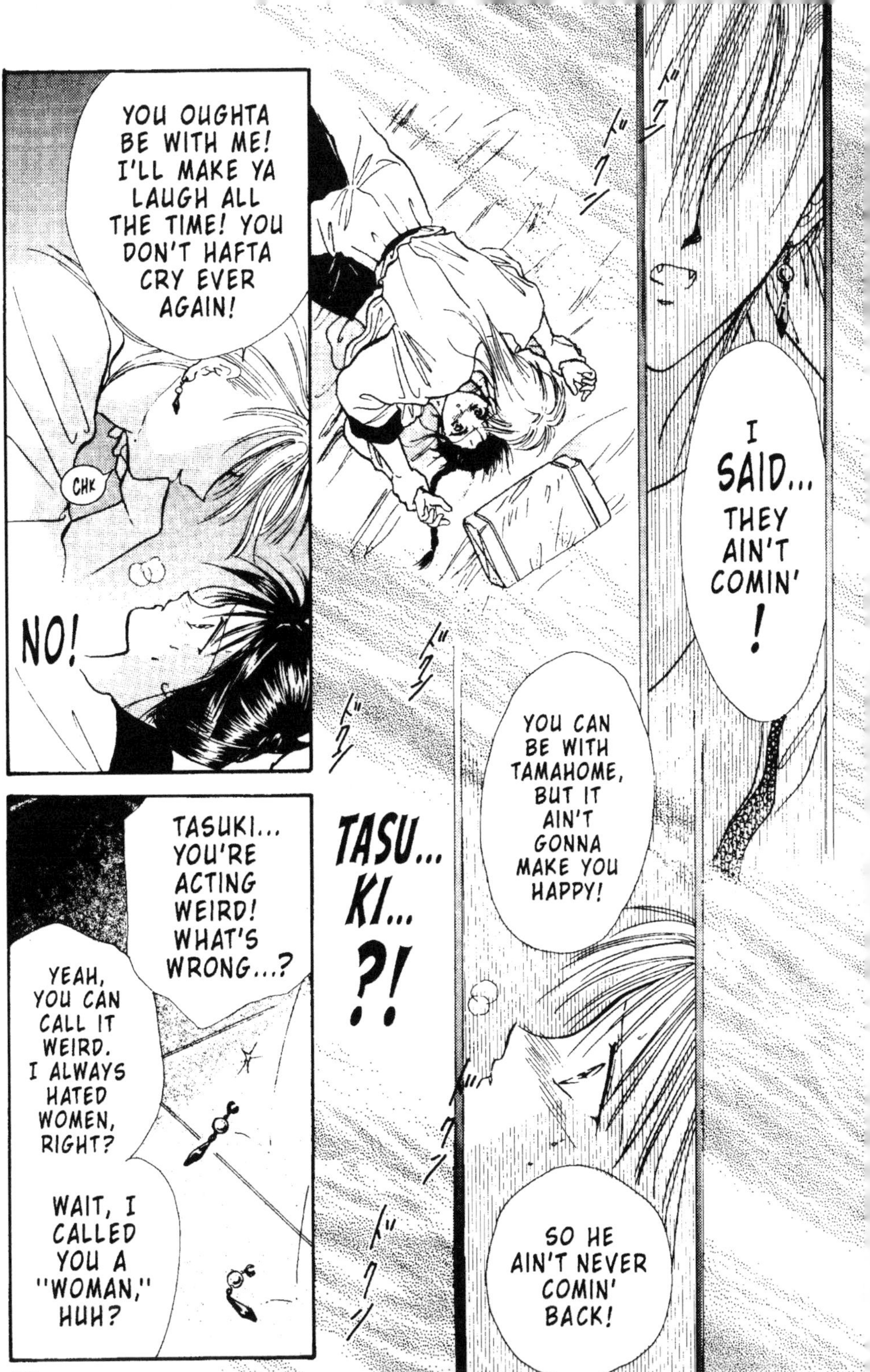
I SAID... THEY AIN'T COMIN'!
YOU CAN BE WITH TAMAHOME, BUT IT AIN'T GONNA MAKE YOU HAPPY!
SO HE AIN'T NEVER COMIN' BACK!
TASU... KI... ?!
YOU OUGHTA BE WITH ME! I'LL MAKE YA LAUGH ALL THE TIME! YOU DON'T HAFTA CRY EVER AGAIN!
CHK
NO!
TASUKI... YOU'RE ACTING WEIRD! WHAT'S WRONG...?
YEAH, YOU CAN CALL IT WEIRD. I ALWAYS HATED WOMEN, RIGHT?
WAIT, I CALLED YOU A "WOMAN," HUH?

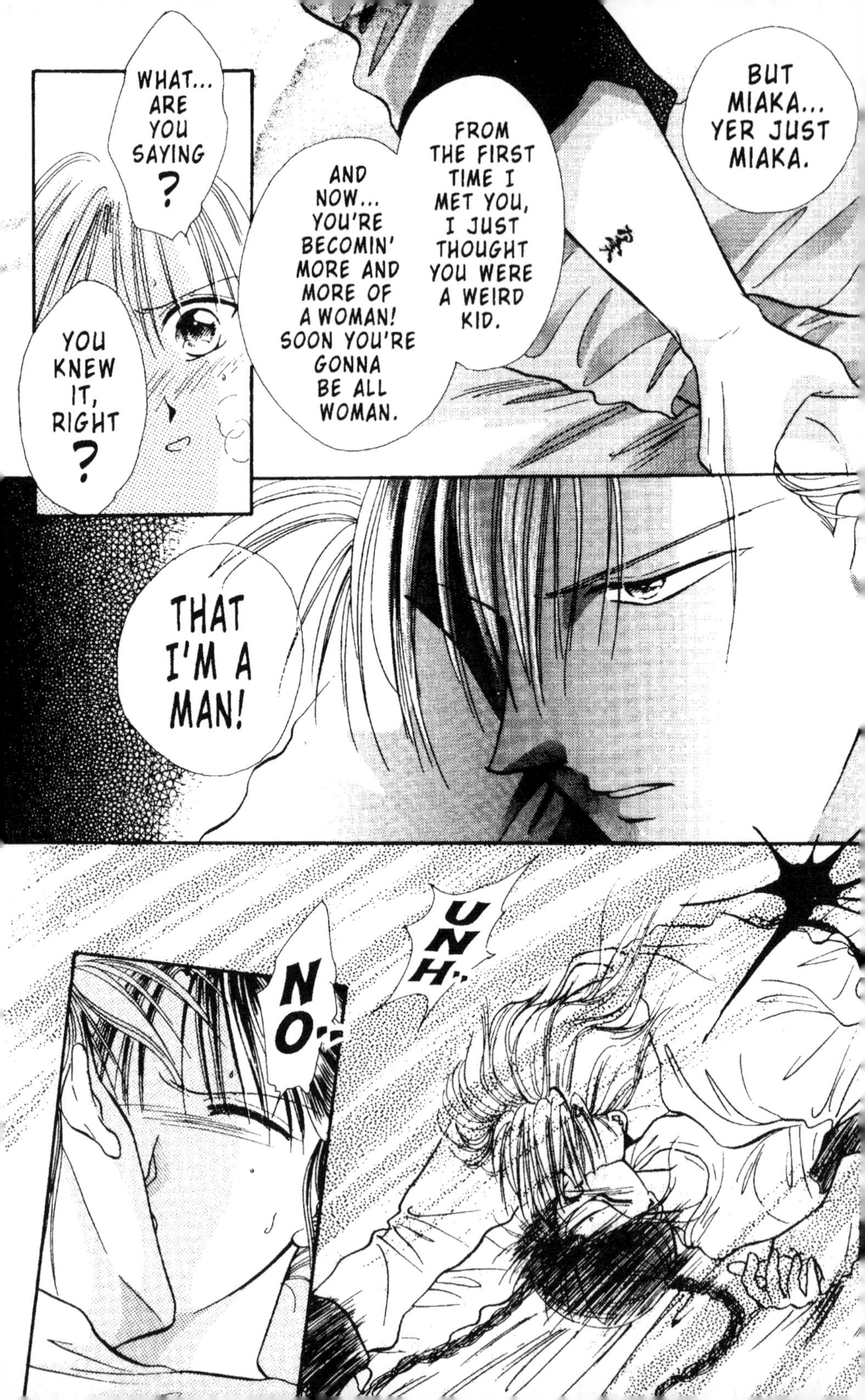
BUT MIAKA... YER JUST MIAKA.
FROM THE FIRST TIME I MET YOU, I JUST THOUGHT YOU WERE A WEIRD KID.
AND NOW... YOU'RE BECOMIN' MORE AND MORE OF A WOMAN! SOON YOU'RE GONNA BE ALL WOMAN.
WHAT... ARE YOU SAYING?
YOU KNEW IT, RIGHT?
THAT I'M A MAN!
UNH..
NO..

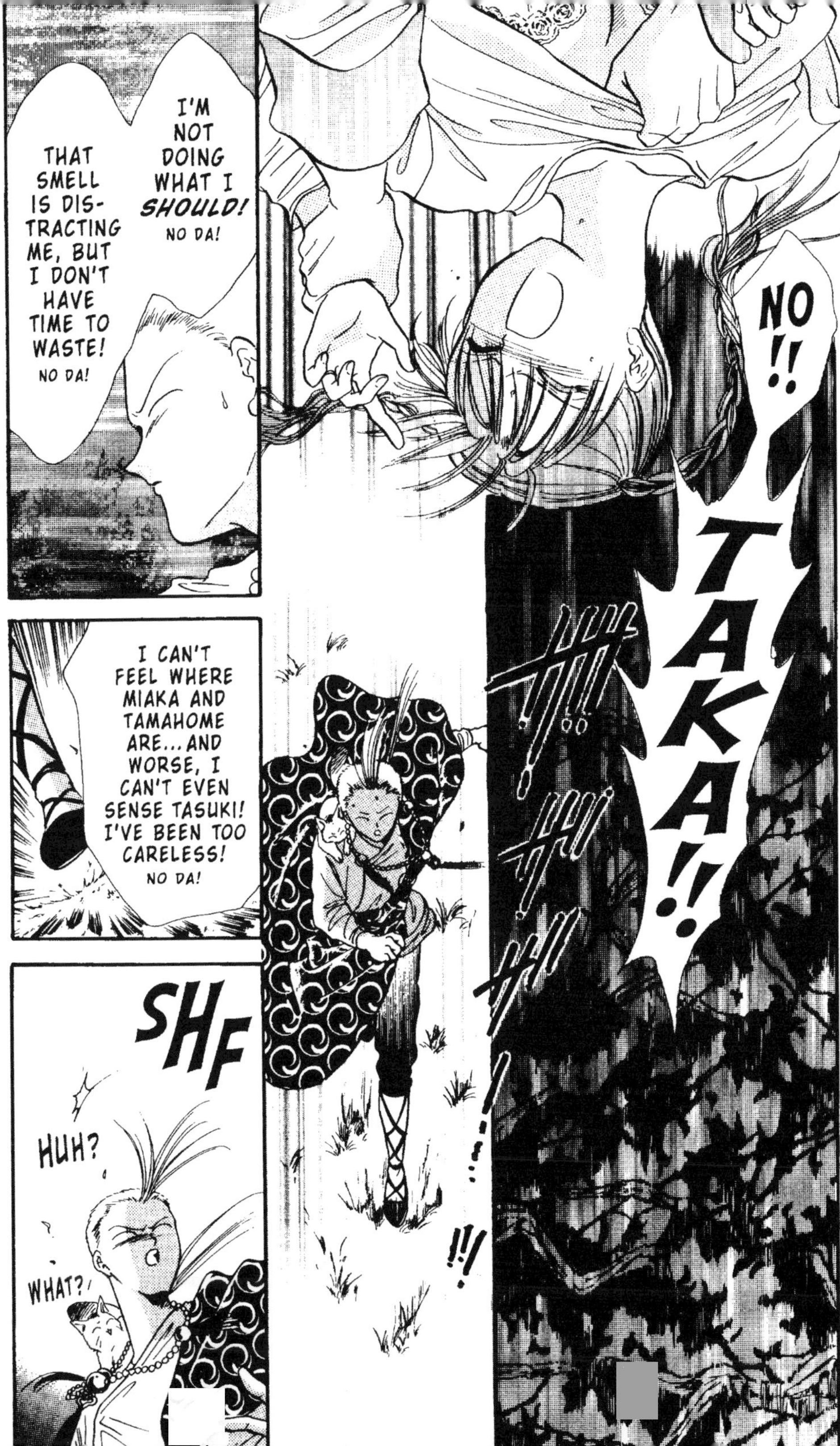
NO!!
TAKA!!
!!!
I'M NOT DOING WHAT I *SHOULD!* NO DA!
THAT SMELL IS DISTRACTING ME, BUT I DON'T HAVE TIME TO WASTE! NO DA!
I CAN'T FEEL WHERE MIAKA AND TAMAHOME ARE...AND WORSE, I CAN'T EVEN SENSE TASUKI! I'VE BEEN TOO CARELESS! NO DA!
SHF
HUH?
WHAT?

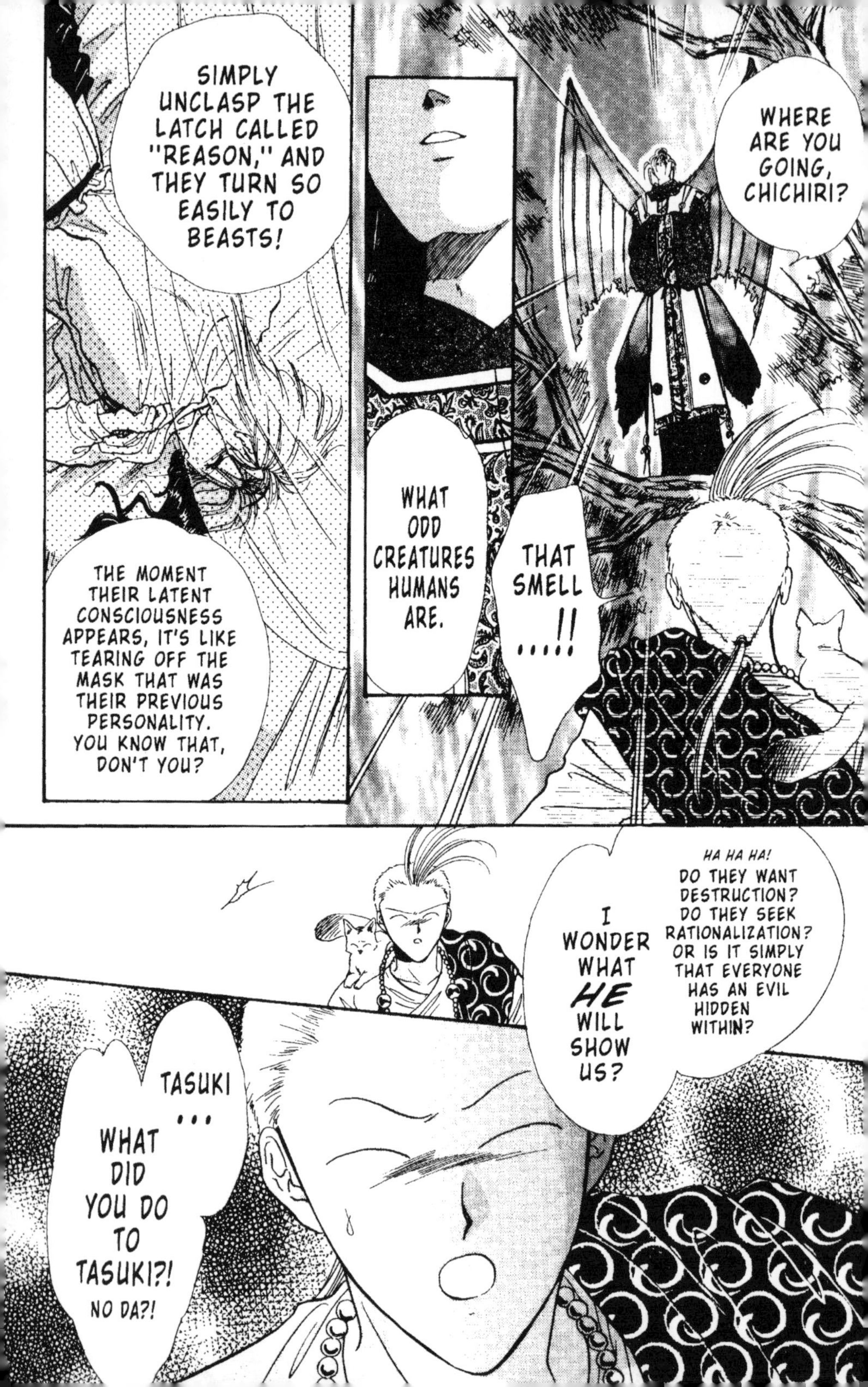
WHERE ARE YOU GOING, CHICHIRI?
THAT SMELL ....!!
WHAT ODD CREATURES HUMANS ARE.
SIMPLY UNCLASP THE LATCH CALLED "REASON," AND THEY TURN SO EASILY TO BEASTS!
THE MOMENT THEIR LATENT CONSCIOUSNESS APPEARS, IT'S LIKE TEARING OFF THE MASK THAT WAS THEIR PREVIOUS PERSONALITY. YOU KNOW THAT, DON'T YOU?
HA HA HA! DO THEY WANT DESTRUCTION? DO THEY SEEK RATIONALIZATION? OR IS IT SIMPLY THAT EVERYONE HAS AN EVIL HIDDEN WITHIN?
I WONDER WHAT HE WILL SHOW US?
TASUKI ... WHAT DID YOU DO TO TASUKI?! NO DA?!

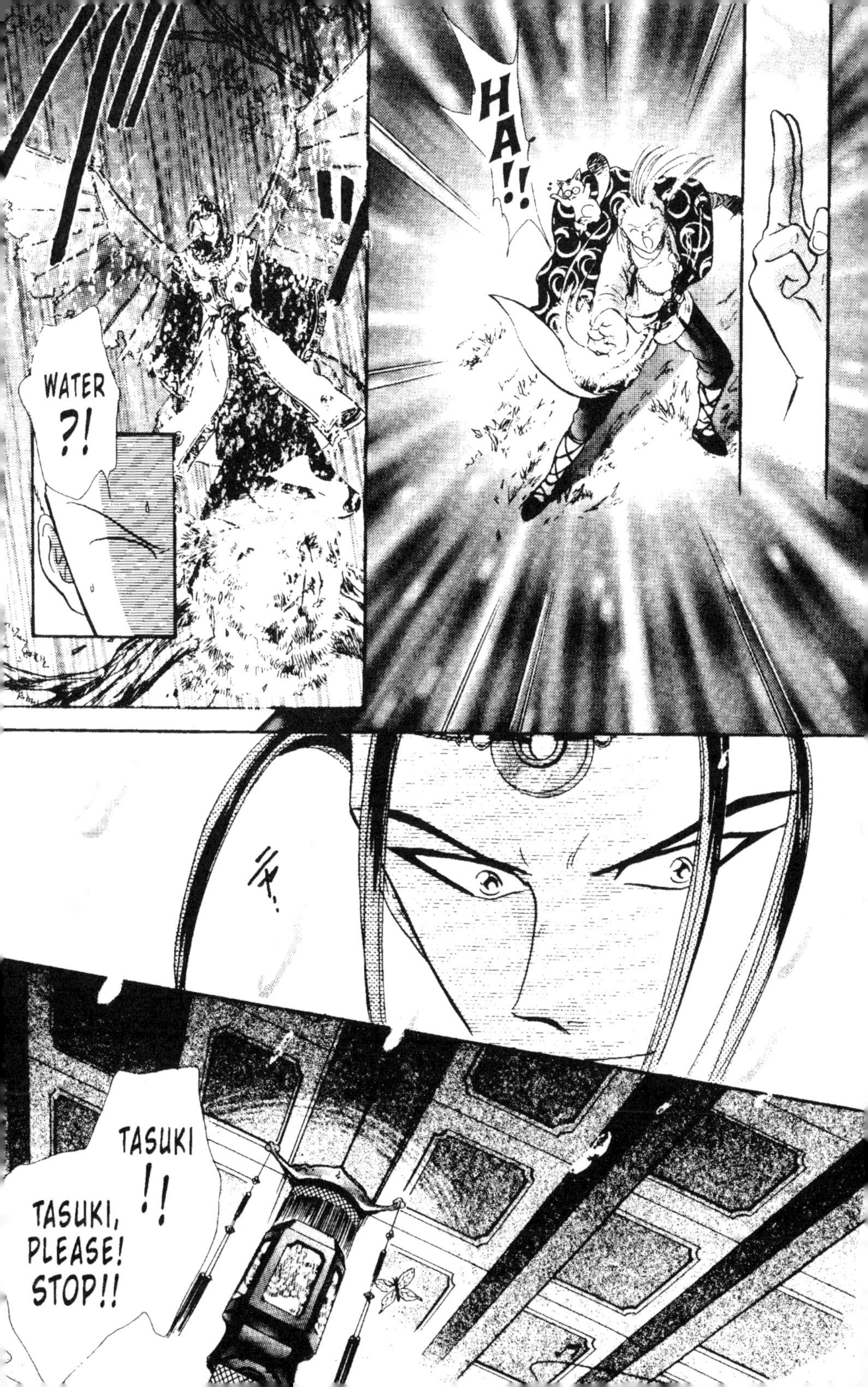
HA!!
WATER ?!
TASUKI !!
TASUKI, PLEASE! STOP!!

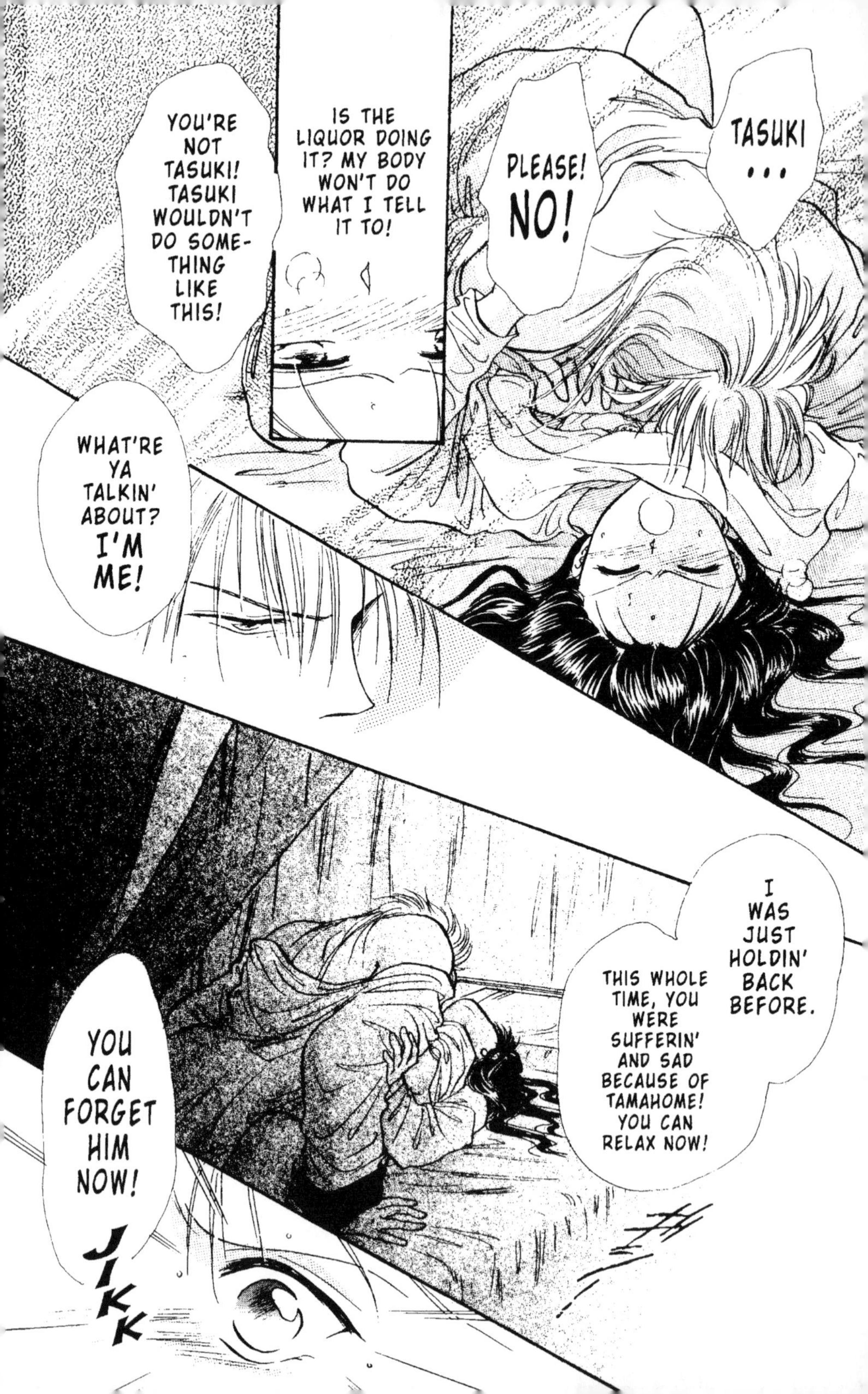
TASUKI ...
PLEASE! NO!
IS THE LIQUOR DOING IT? MY BODY WON'T DO WHAT I TELL IT TO!
YOU'RE NOT TASUKI! TASUKI WOULDN'T DO SOME-THING LIKE THIS!
WHAT'RE YA TALKIN' ABOUT? I'M ME!
I WAS JUST HOLDIN' BACK BEFORE.
THIS WHOLE TIME, YOU WERE SUFFERIN' AND SAD BECAUSE OF TAMAHOME! YOU CAN RELAX NOW!
YOU CAN FORGET HIM NOW!
JIKK

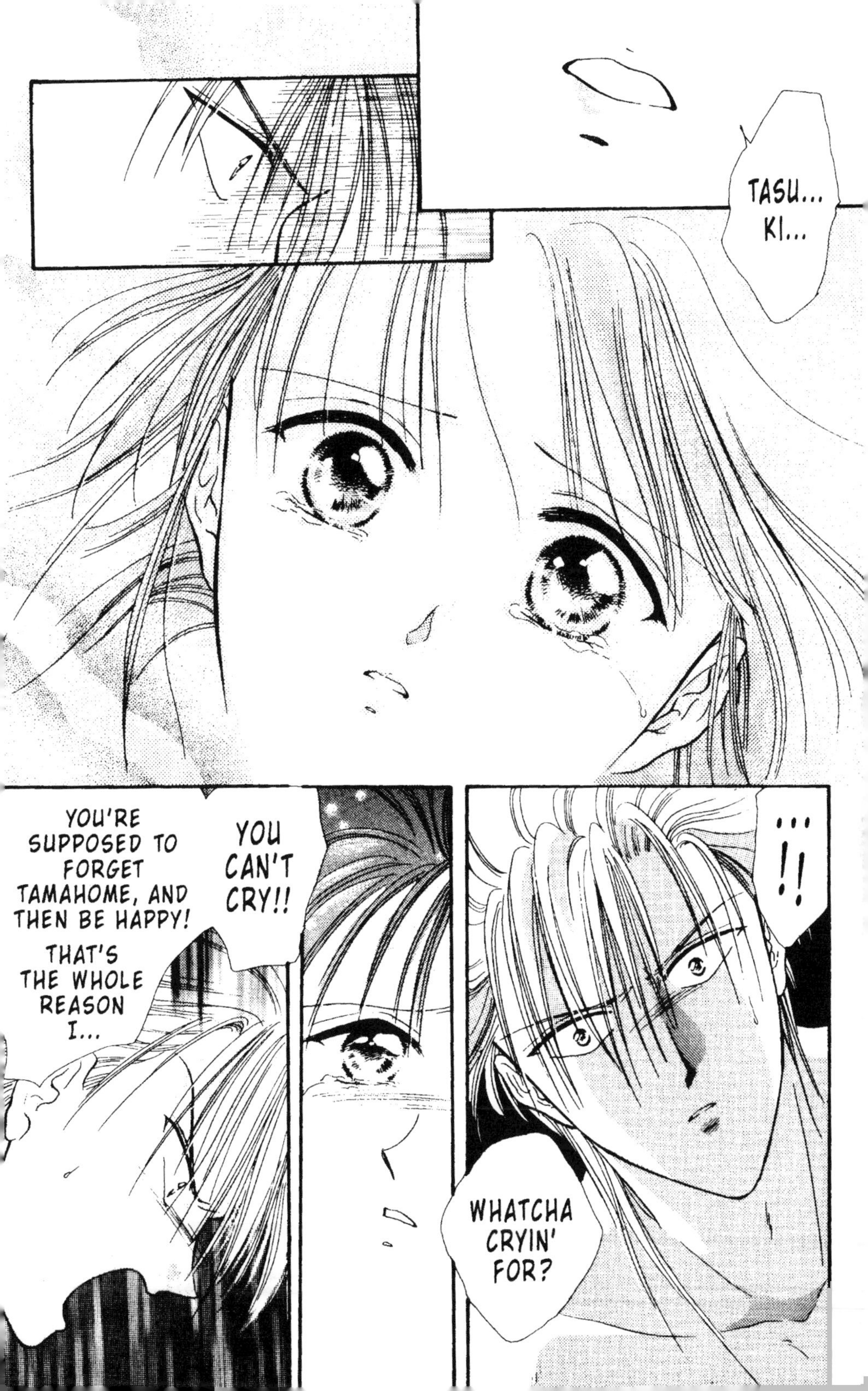
TASU... KI...
...!!
YOU CAN'T CRY!!
YOU'RE SUPPOSED TO FORGET TAMAHOME, AND THEN BE HAPPY!
THAT'S THE WHOLE REASON I...
WHATCHA CRYIN' FOR?

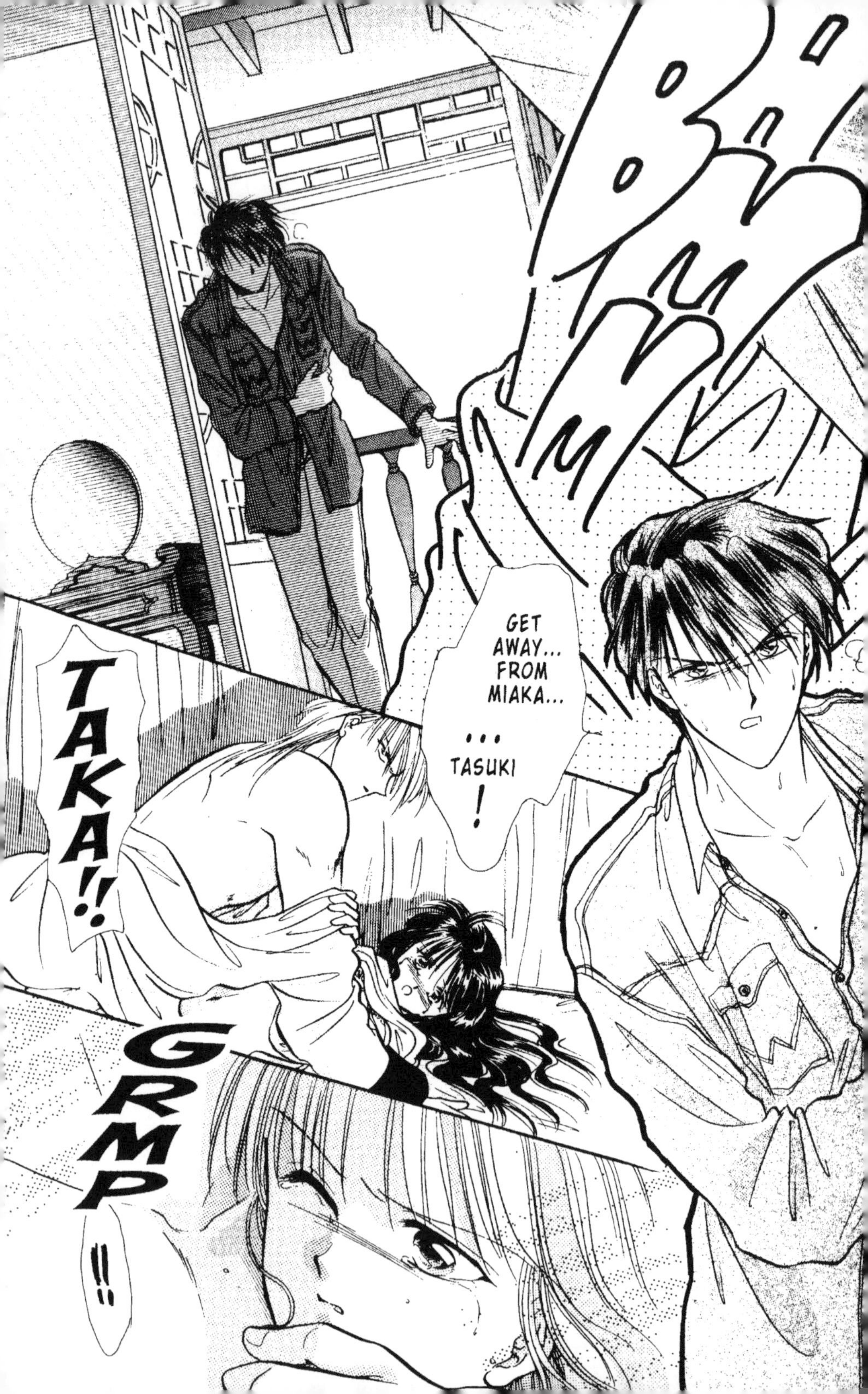
DOMM
GET AWAY... FROM MIAKA...
... TASUKI !
TAKA!!
GRMP !!!

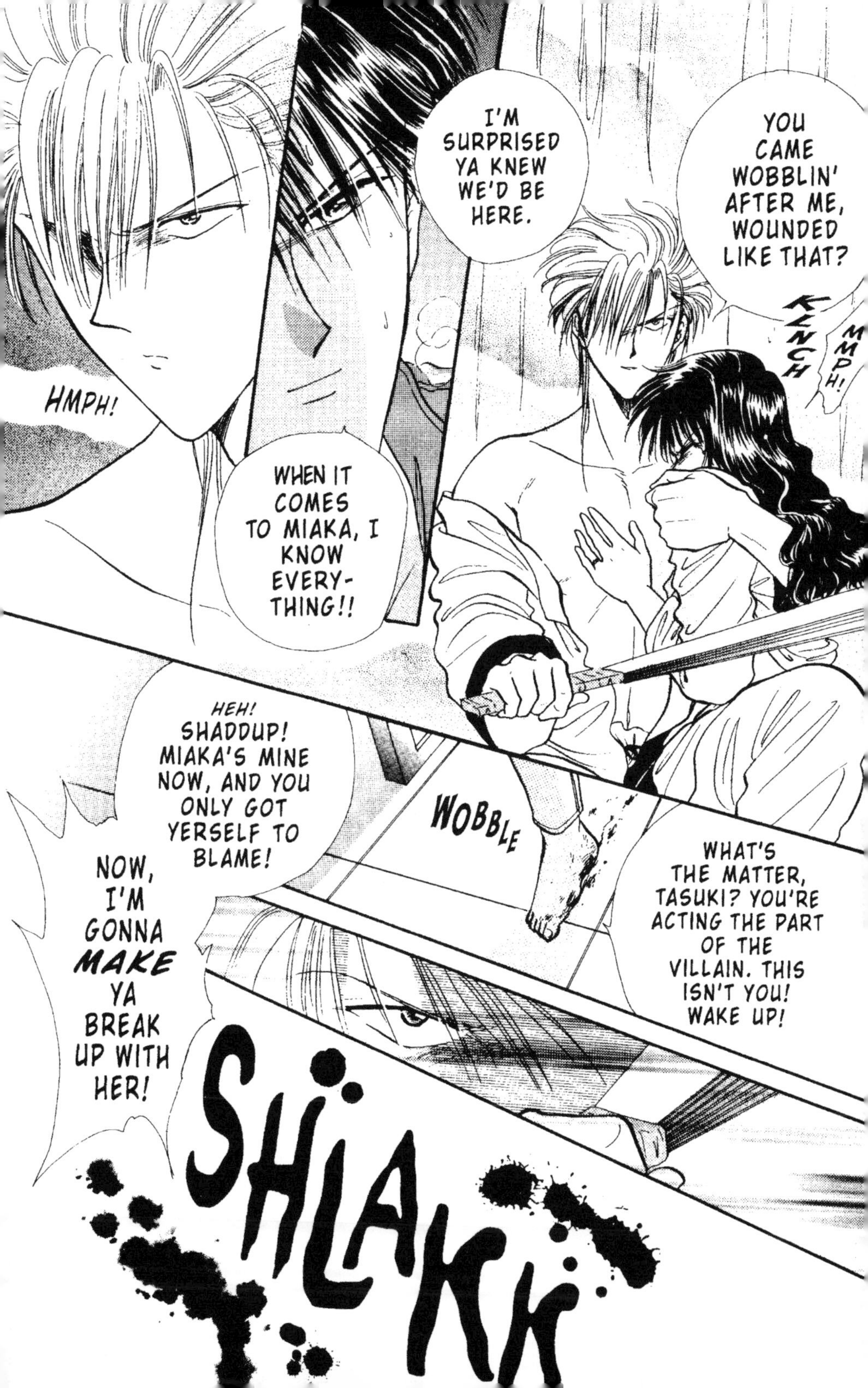

YOU CAME WOBBLIN' AFTER ME, WOUNDED LIKE THAT?
KLENCH
MMPH!
I'M SURPRISED YA KNEW WE'D BE HERE.
WHEN IT COMES TO MIAKA, I KNOW EVERY-THING!!
HMPH!
WHAT'S THE MATTER, TASUKI? YOU'RE ACTING THE PART OF THE VILLAIN. THIS ISN'T YOU! WAKE UP!
WOBBLE
HEH! SHADDUP! MIAKA'S MINE NOW, AND YOU ONLY GOT YERSELF TO BLAME!
NOW, I'M GONNA MAKE YA BREAK UP WITH HER!
SHLAKK

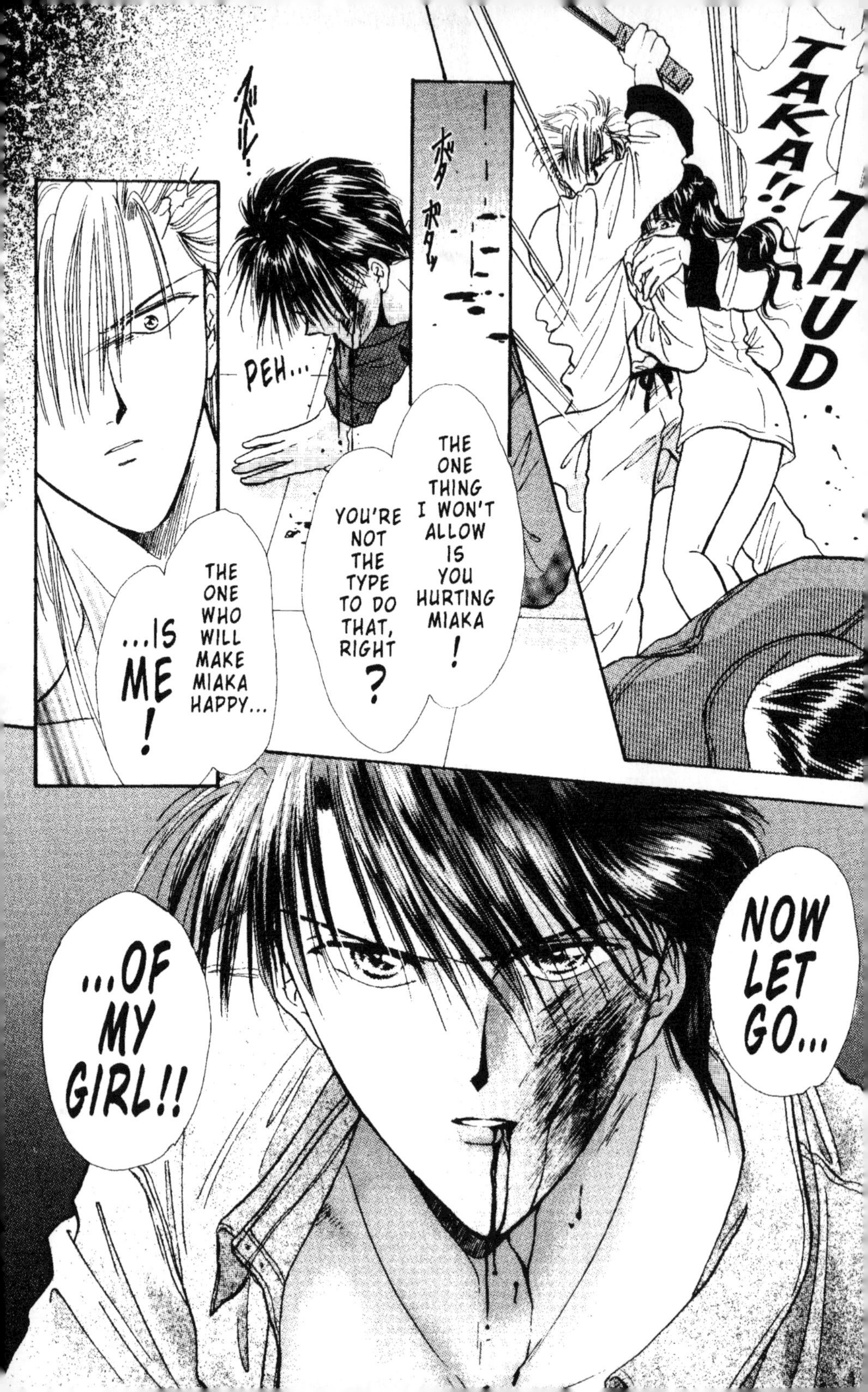
TAKA!!
THUD
THE ONE THING I WON'T ALLOW IS YOU HURTING MIAKA!
YOU'RE NOT THE TYPE TO DO THAT, RIGHT?
PEH...
THE ONE WHO WILL MAKE MIAKA HAPPY...
...IS ME!
NOW LET GO...
...OF MY GIRL!!

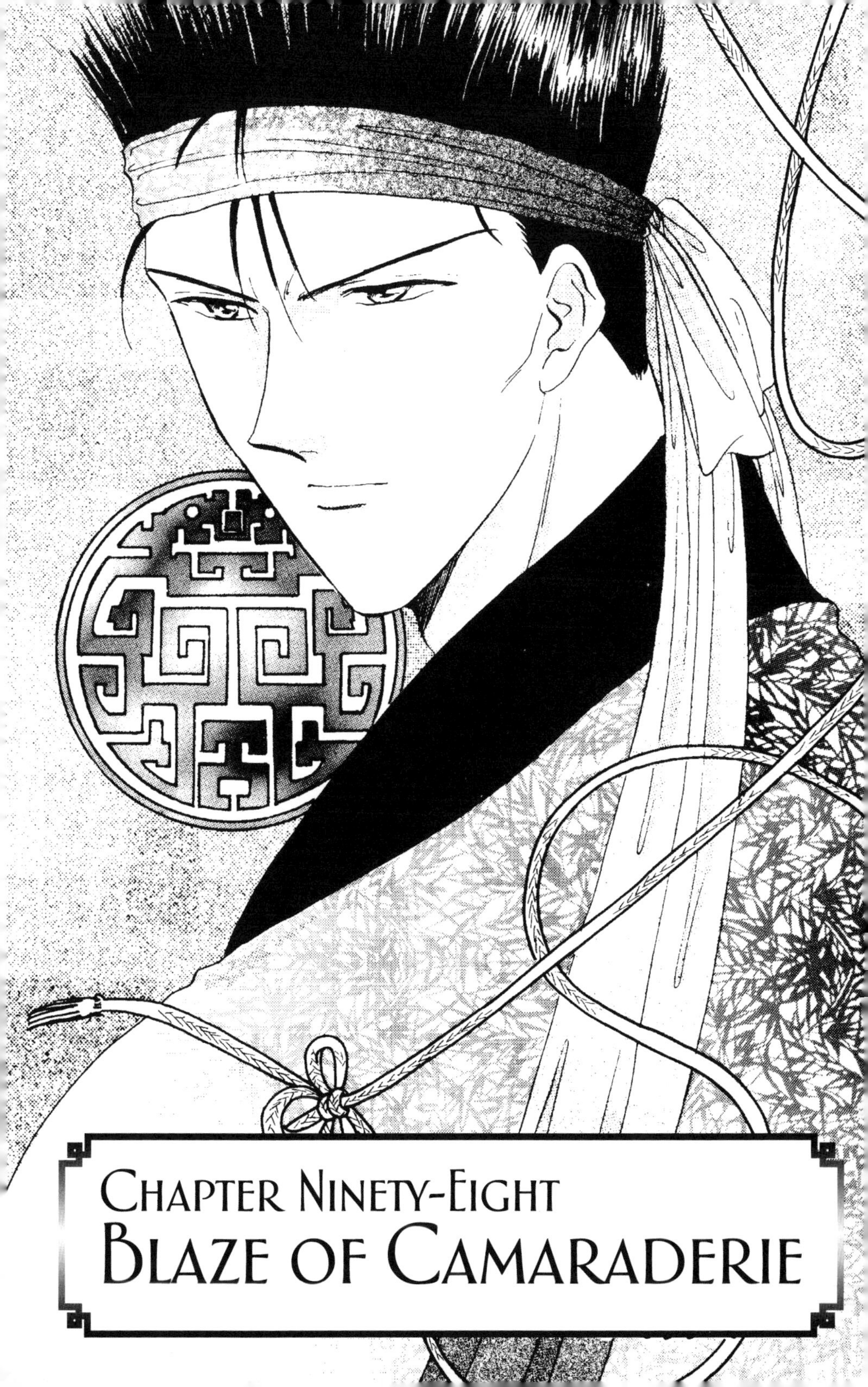

Chapter Ninety-Eight
Blaze of Camaraderie

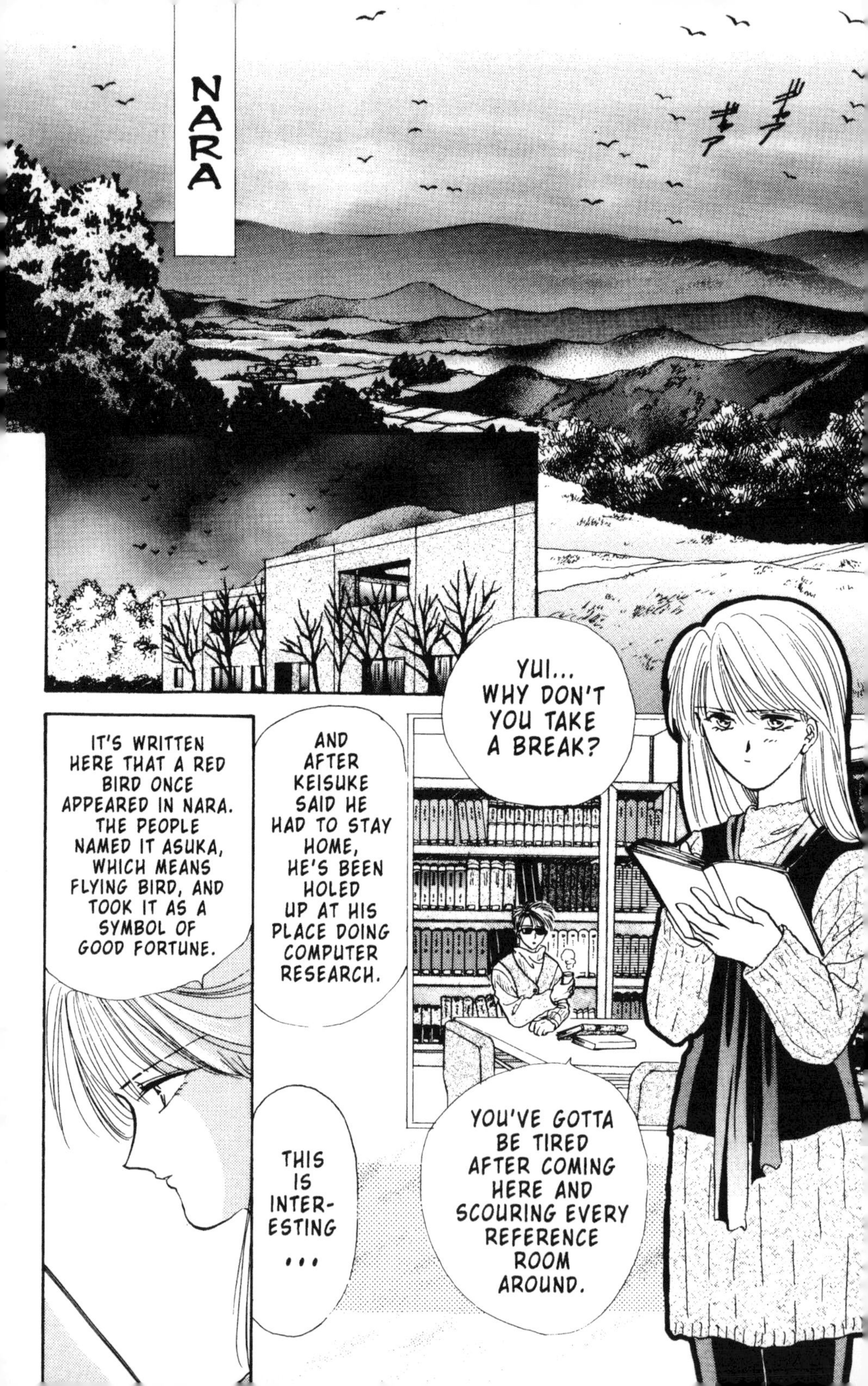
NARA
YUI... WHY DON'T YOU TAKE A BREAK?
AND AFTER KEISUKE SAID HE HAD TO STAY HOME, HE'S BEEN HOLED UP AT HIS PLACE DOING COMPUTER RESEARCH.
YOU'VE GOTTA BE TIRED AFTER COMING HERE AND SCOURING EVERY REFERENCE ROOM AROUND.
THIS IS INTER-ESTING...
IT'S WRITTEN HERE THAT A RED BIRD ONCE APPEARED IN NARA. THE PEOPLE NAMED IT ASUKA, WHICH MEANS FLYING BIRD, AND TOOK IT AS A SYMBOL OF GOOD FORTUNE.

CON-TINUED... "I agree that he loves her -- a friendship turned into something more."
"Upon receiving artificial respiration, he suddenly becomes aware of women."
"It isn't as if Tasuki's aversion to girls makes him completely uninterested in women from a physical standpoint. ☺"
Yeah, his basic male urges coming to the fore has a pretty deep meaning, and that is: Just because he's a friend, it doesn't mean that you should let your guard down! *Scary!*
"This is terrible for Miaka! The worst! Quite a shock! He's her friend. She probably thought of him as an older brother, and he tries to rape her!"
That's pretty frightening, right? But the thing that made me laugh was what one assistant had seen on TV, *Kare no Iru Onna wo Kukoku Hō*, (*How He Seduces His Girl*), and she said that Tasuki tried every method mentioned in the show! ☺ The last method on the program was holding her down and having his way. For a drinker like Tasuki to spend the night not drinking means that it was all planned. In the future, he might become good at picking up the girls.
...But actually, all I wanted to do was wound Tasuki a little. He makes me mad sometimes! ☺ It means that he gets very hurt and loses his friends... but he's the only character who hadn't hurt himself yet.
But in growing up, you have to risk getting wounded. He's displaying his ignorance of love! He has a lot of bad points too, you know! You've all seen how he blurts things out without thinking! ☺ But a side of him that he would never want people to see came out here. A part that he himself didn't know about. I know it's a hard thing, but I think it would have been even worse if Taka hadn't dealt with it like an adult. ☺
And it all ended with that sound effect, "Don." (My assistants were so shocked they cried.) And in the end, "What's this? So Taka and Tasuki like each other after all!" ☺
Looking at the situation, the way Tasuki shows love is more represented by his repartee with Taka than by what he does to Miaka. He just built up resentment toward Taka without understanding what true "strength" is.
This time, the background music is "Love Phantom" by B'z!!

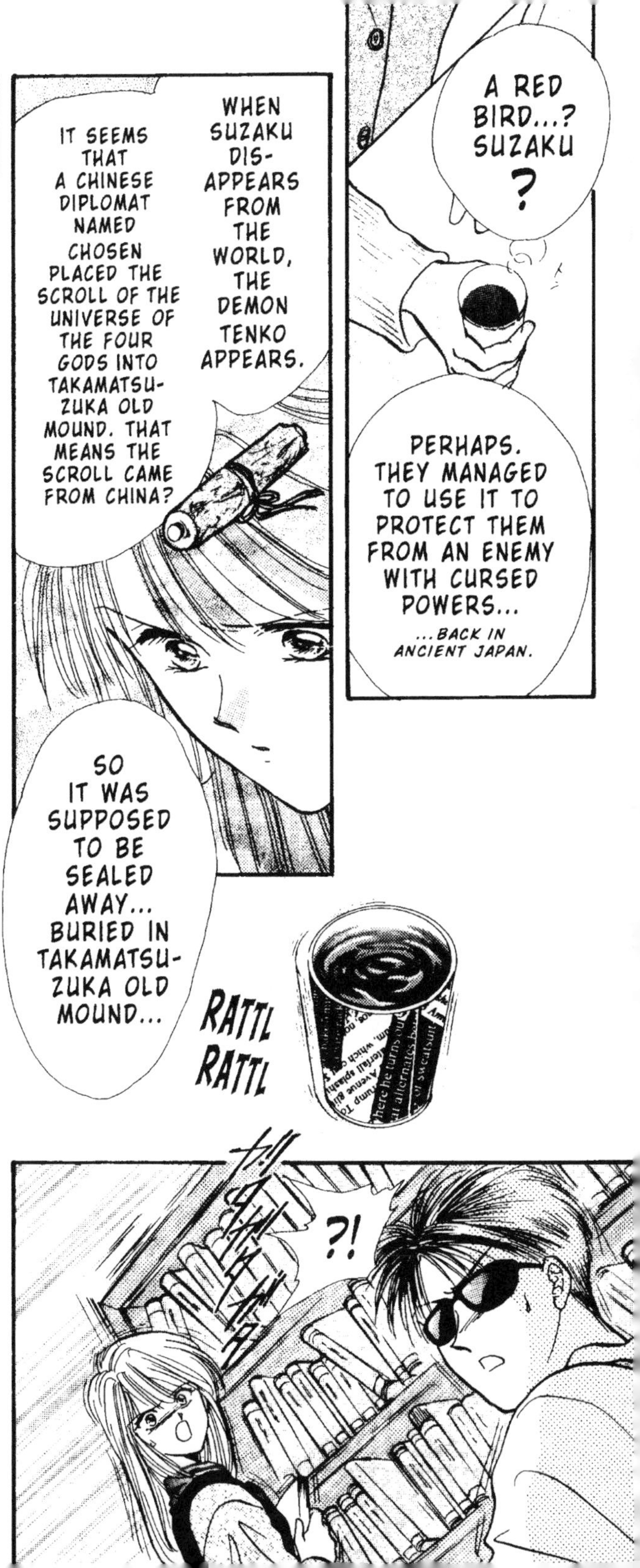
A RED BIRD...? SUZAKU ?
PERHAPS. THEY MANAGED TO USE IT TO PROTECT THEM FROM AN ENEMY WITH CURSED POWERS...
...BACK IN ANCIENT JAPAN.
WHEN SUZAKU DISAPPEARS FROM THE WORLD, THE DEMON TENKO APPEARS.
IT SEEMS THAT A CHINESE DIPLOMAT NAMED CHOSEN PLACED THE SCROLL OF THE UNIVERSE OF THE FOUR GODS INTO TAKAMATSUZUKA OLD MOUND. THAT MEANS THE SCROLL CAME FROM CHINA?
SO IT WAS SUPPOSED TO BE SEALED AWAY... BURIED IN TAKAMATSUZUKA OLD MOUND...
RATTL RATTL
?!

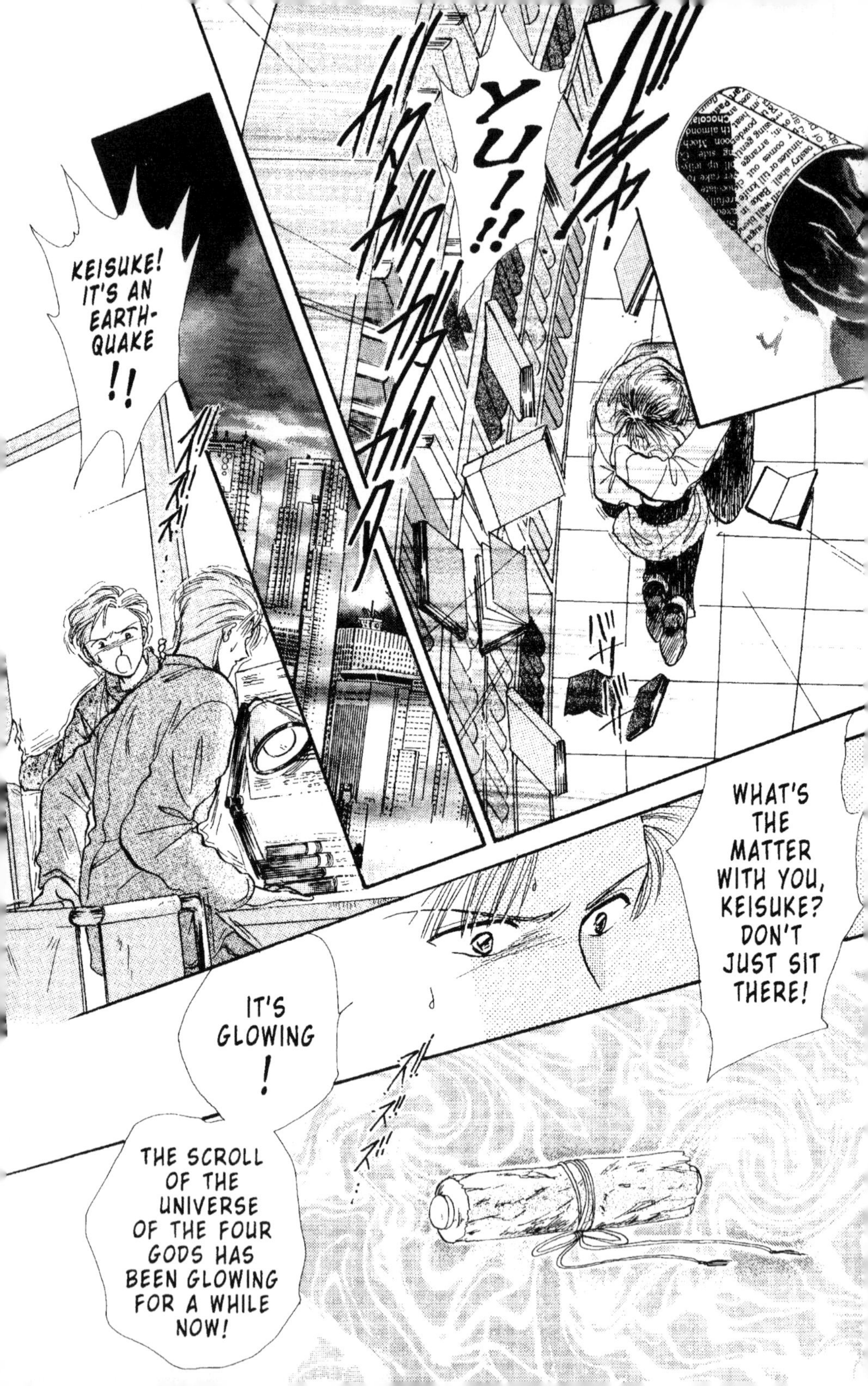
KEISUKE! IT'S AN EARTHQUAKE!!
WHAT'S THE MATTER WITH YOU, KEISUKE? DON'T JUST SIT THERE!
IT'S GLOWING!
THE SCROLL OF THE UNIVERSE OF THE FOUR GODS HAS BEEN GLOWING FOR A WHILE NOW!

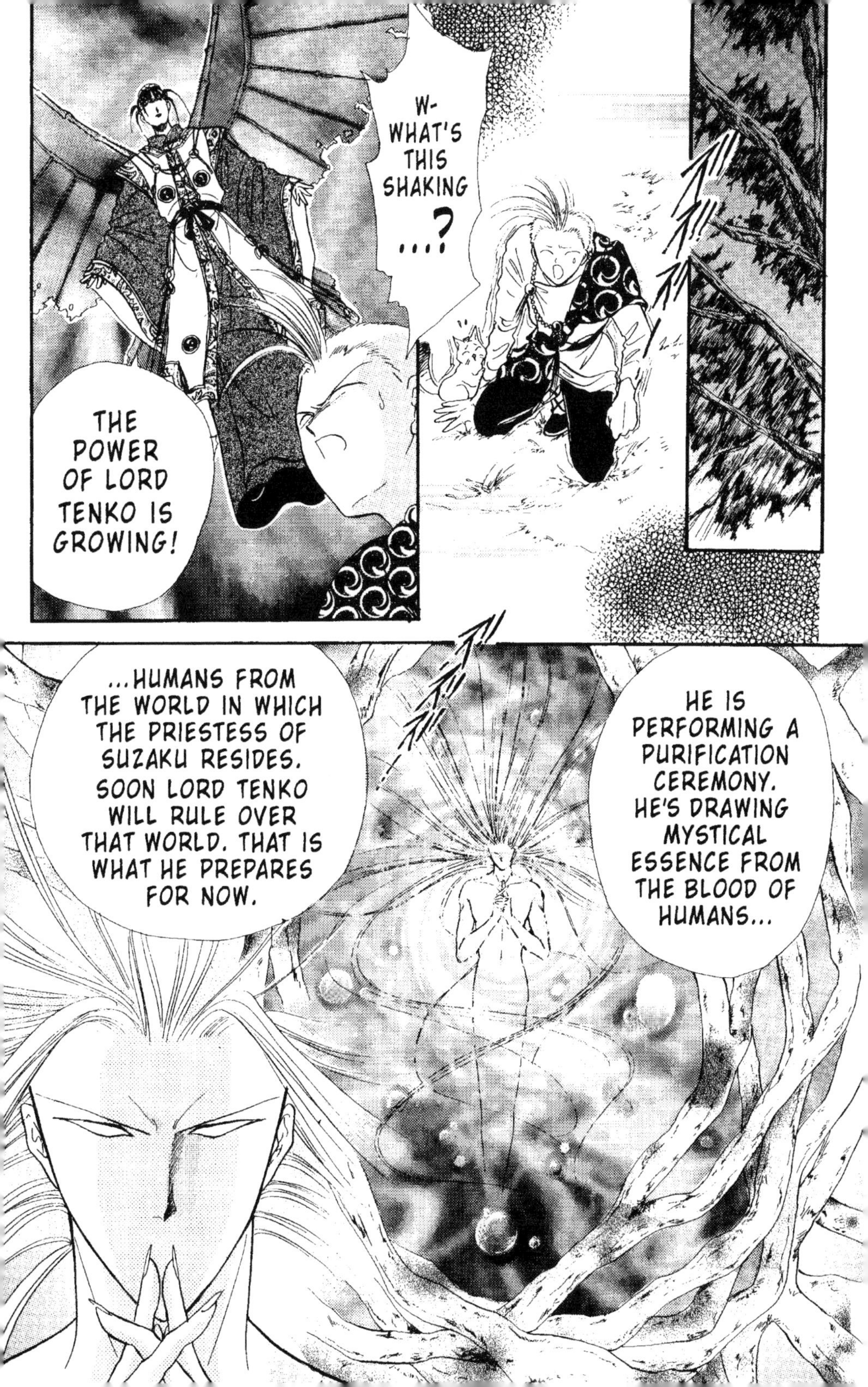
W-WHAT'S THIS SHAKING ...?
THE POWER OF LORD TENKO IS GROWING!
HE IS PERFORMING A PURIFICATION CEREMONY. HE'S DRAWING MYSTICAL ESSENCE FROM THE BLOOD OF HUMANS...
...HUMANS FROM THE WORLD IN WHICH THE PRIESTESS OF SUZAKU RESIDES. SOON LORD TENKO WILL RULE OVER THAT WORLD. THAT IS WHAT HE PREPARES FOR NOW.

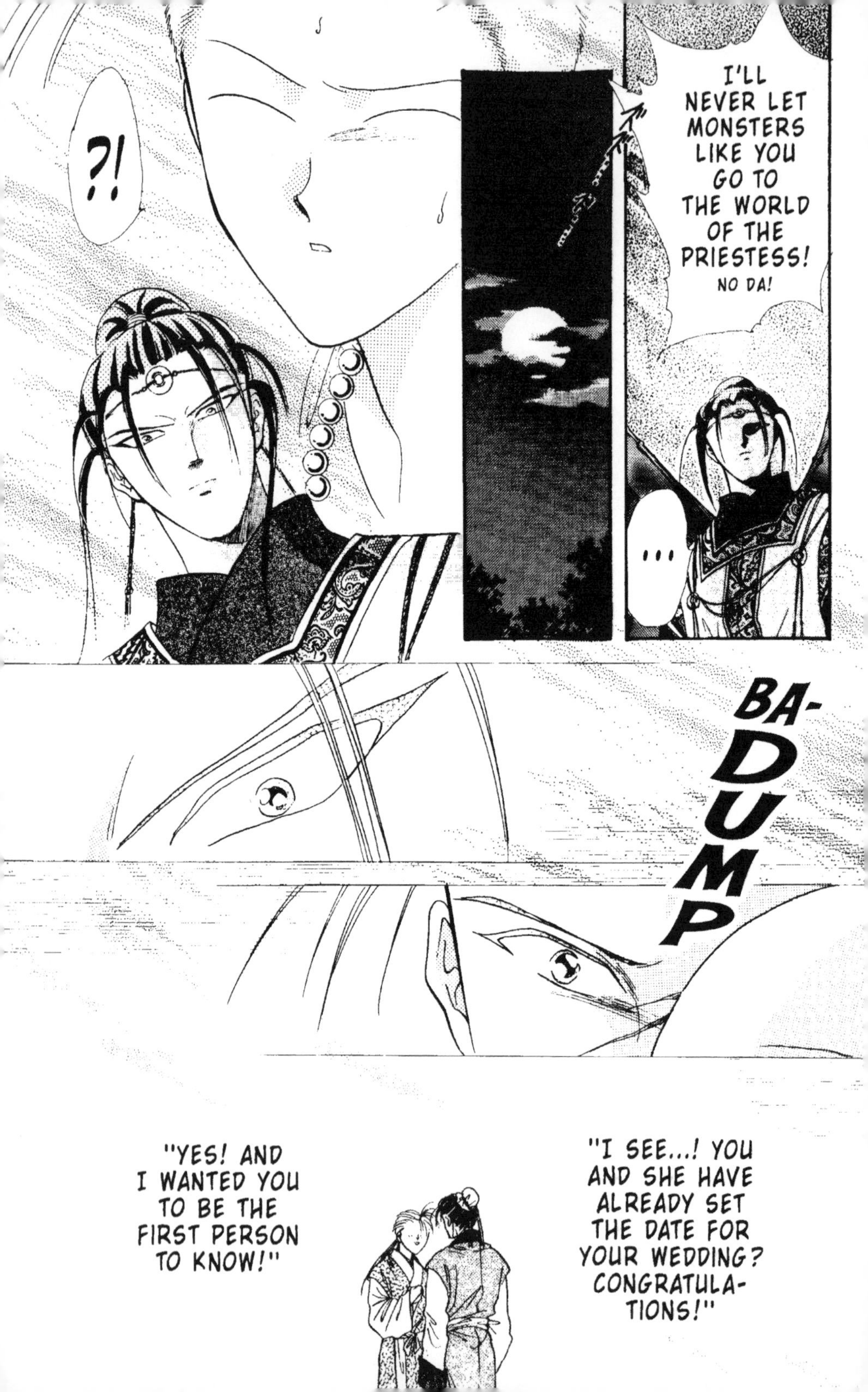
I'LL NEVER LET MONSTERS LIKE YOU GO TO THE WORLD OF THE PRIESTESS!
NO DA!
...
?!
BA-DUMP
"I SEE...! YOU AND SHE HAVE ALREADY SET THE DATE FOR YOUR WEDDING? CONGRATULA-TIONS!"
"YES! AND I WANTED YOU TO BE THE FIRST PERSON TO KNOW!"

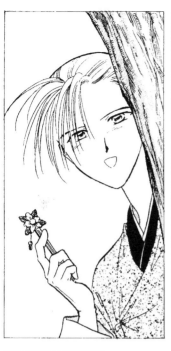

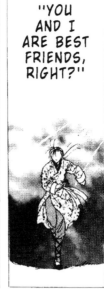

"YOU WILL CELEBRATE WITH US, RIGHT?"
"OF COURSE I WILL! AFTER ALL, WE THREE GREW UP TOGETHER!"
"YOU AND I ARE BEST FRIENDS, RIGHT?"
WHY ?
WHY ...?

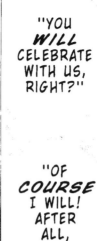

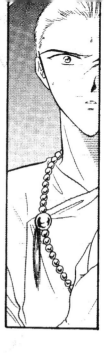

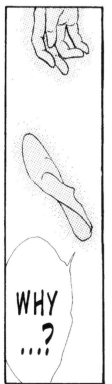

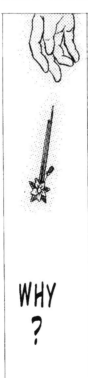

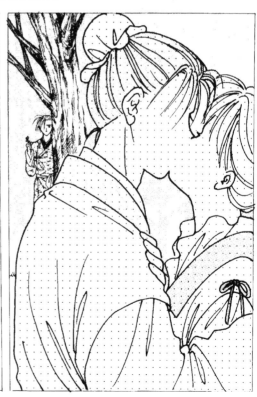

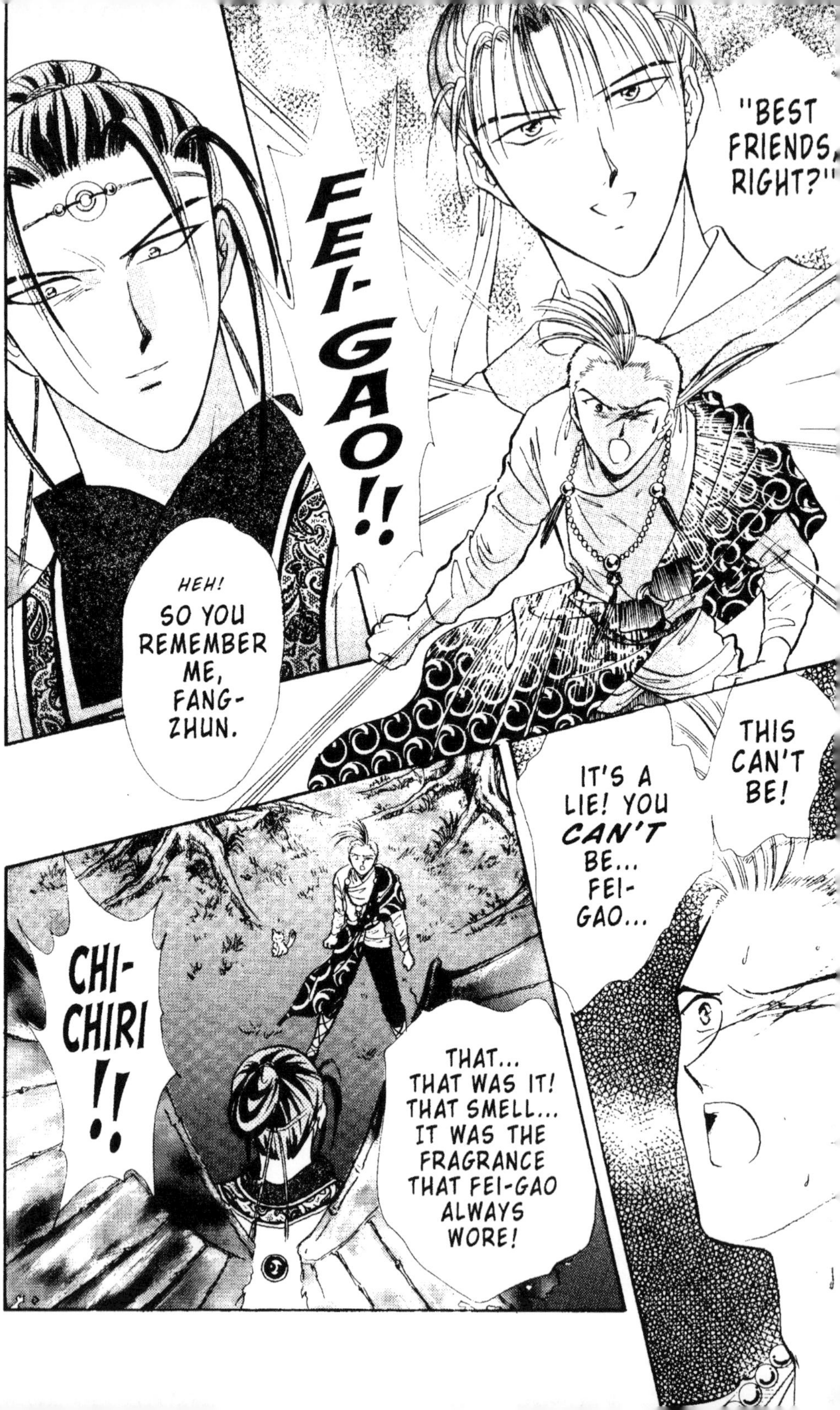
"BEST FRIENDS, RIGHT?"
FEI-GAO!!
HEH! SO YOU REMEMBER ME, FANG-ZHUN.
THIS CAN'T BE!
IT'S A LIE! YOU *CAN'T* BE... FEI-GAO...
CHI-CHIRI!!
THAT... THAT WAS IT! THAT SMELL... IT WAS THE FRAGRANCE THAT FEI-GAO ALWAYS WORE!

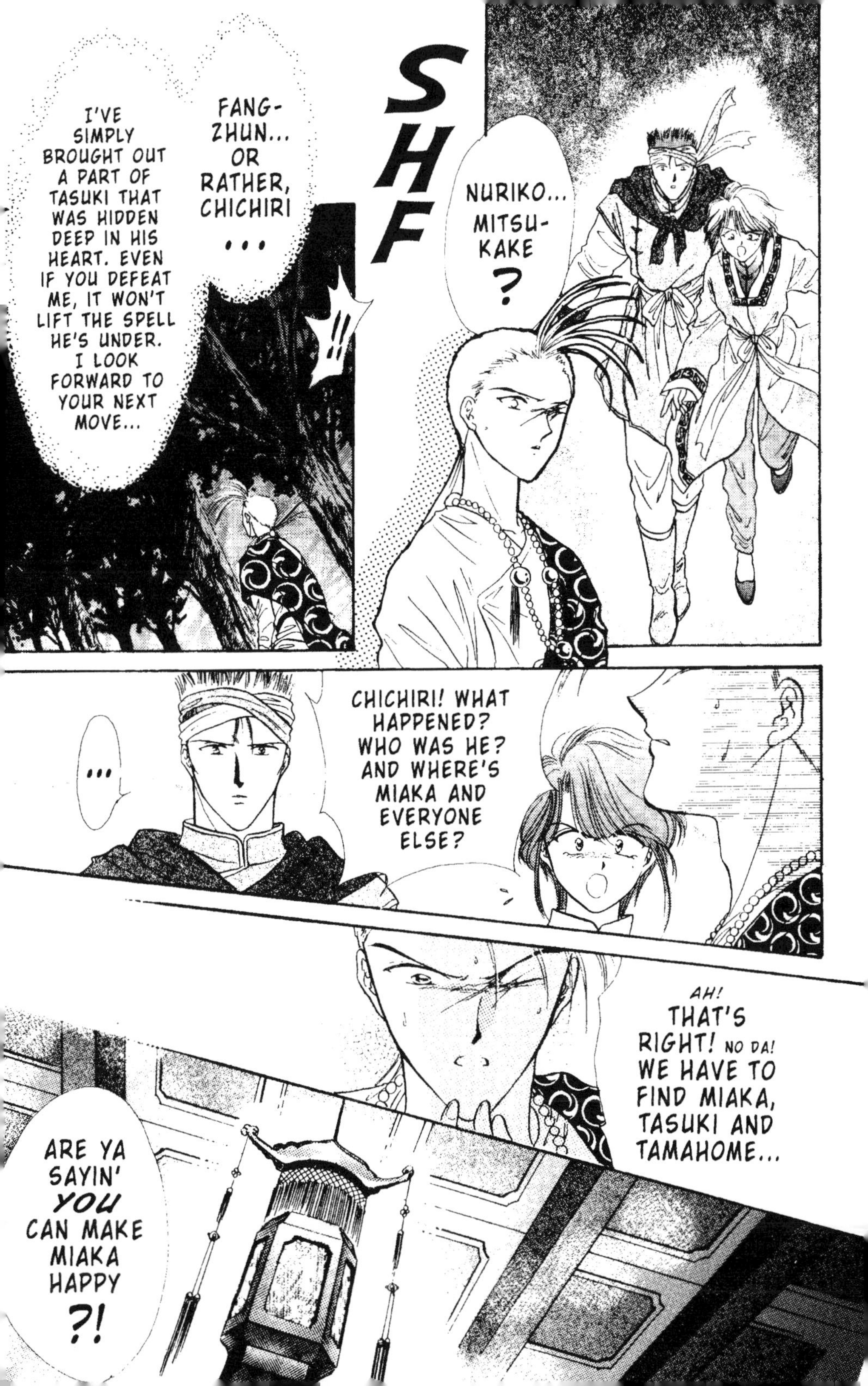
SHF
NURIKO... MITSUKAKE?
!!
FANG-ZHUN... OR RATHER, CHICHIRI...
I'VE SIMPLY BROUGHT OUT A PART OF TASUKI THAT WAS HIDDEN DEEP IN HIS HEART. EVEN IF YOU DEFEAT ME, IT WON'T LIFT THE SPELL HE'S UNDER. I LOOK FORWARD TO YOUR NEXT MOVE...
CHICHIRI! WHAT HAPPENED? WHO WAS HE? AND WHERE'S MIAKA AND EVERYONE ELSE?
...
AH! THAT'S RIGHT! NO DA! WE HAVE TO FIND MIAKA, TASUKI AND TAMAHOME...
ARE YA SAYIN' YOU CAN MAKE MIAKA HAPPY?!

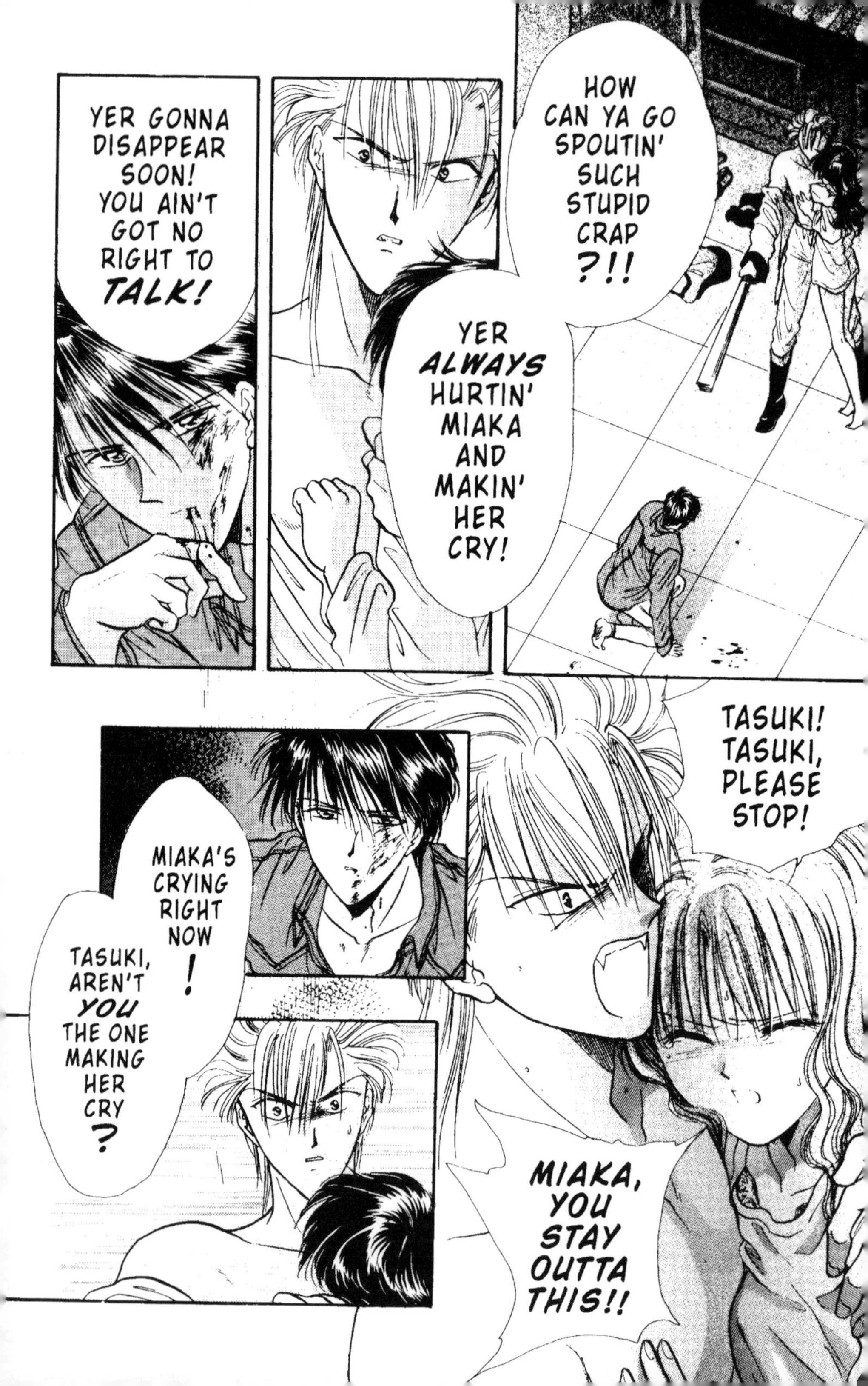
HOW CAN YA GO SPOUTIN' SUCH STUPID CRAP?!!
YER ALWAYS HURTIN' MIAKA AND MAKIN' HER CRY!
YER GONNA DISAPPEAR SOON! YOU AIN'T GOT NO RIGHT TO TALK!
TASUKI! TASUKI, PLEASE STOP!
MIAKA, YOU STAY OUTTA THIS!!
MIAKA'S CRYING RIGHT NOW!
TASUKI, AREN'T YOU THE ONE MAKING HER CRY?

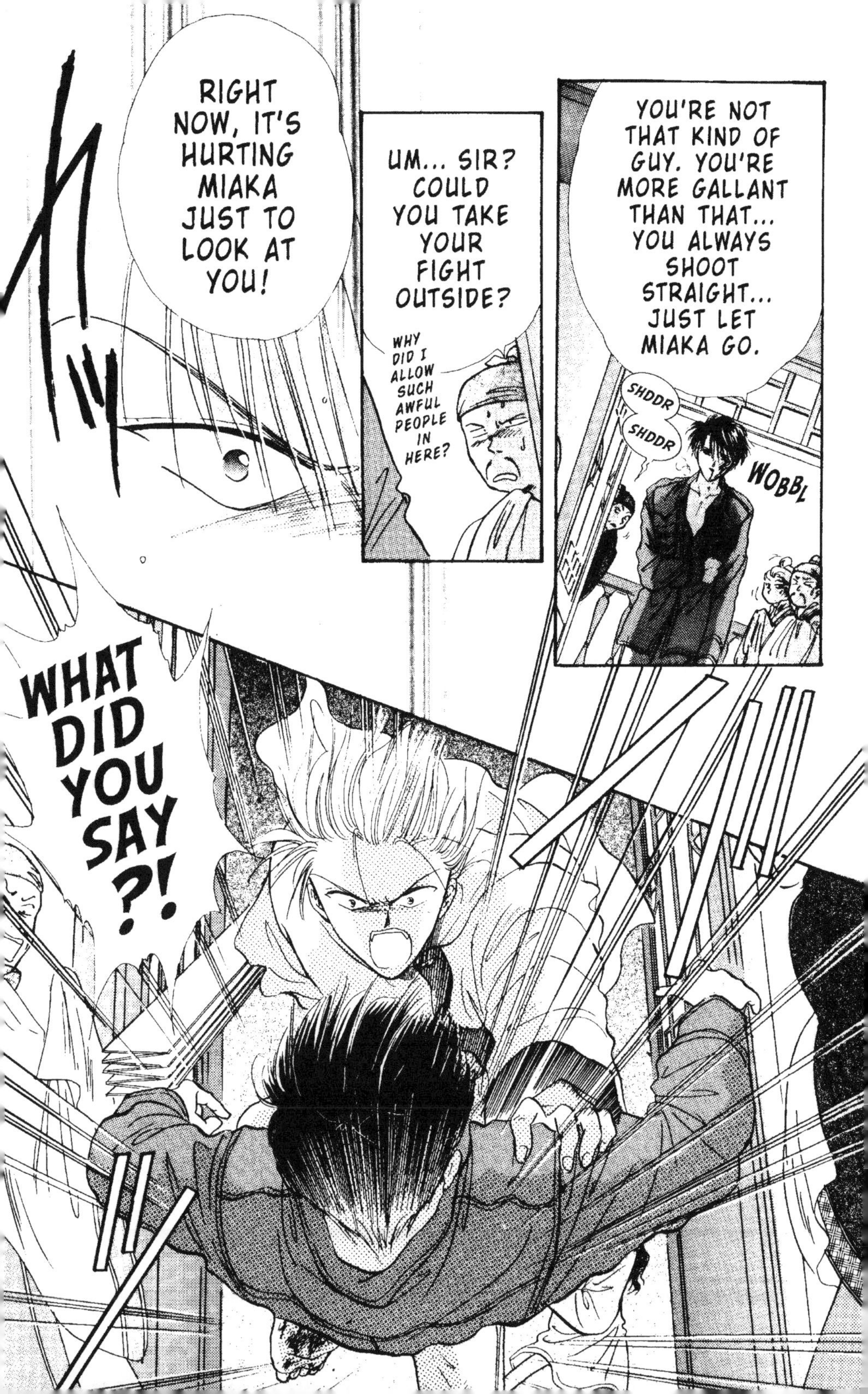
YOU'RE NOT THAT KIND OF GUY. YOU'RE MORE GALLANT THAN THAT... YOU ALWAYS SHOOT STRAIGHT... JUST LET MIAKA GO.
SHDDR
SHDDR
WOBBL
UM... SIR? COULD YOU TAKE YOUR FIGHT OUTSIDE?
WHY DID I ALLOW SUCH AWFUL PEOPLE IN HERE?
RIGHT NOW, IT'S HURTING MIAKA JUST TO LOOK AT YOU!
WHAT DID YOU SAY?!

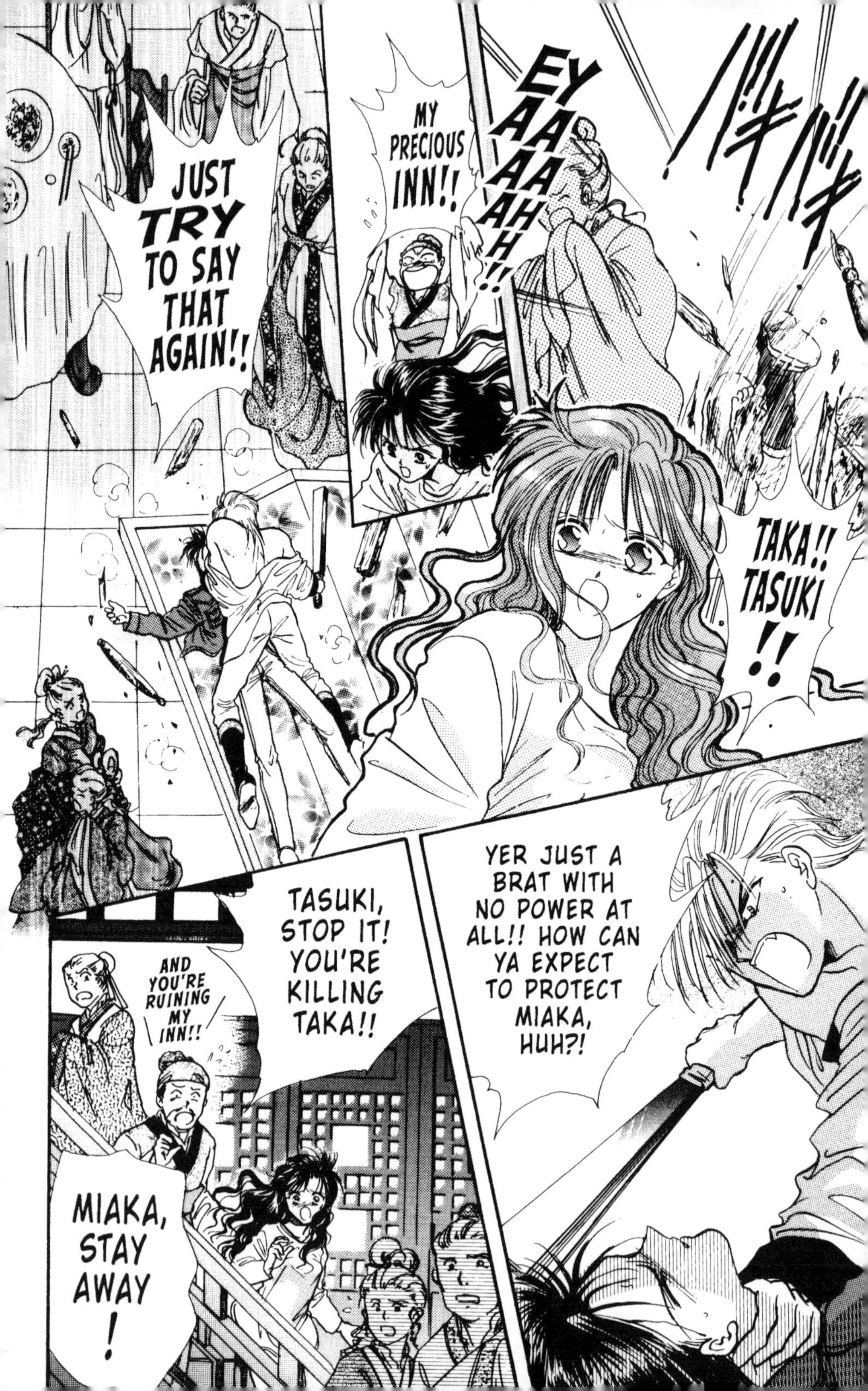

バキバキ
EYAAAAAAAH!!
MY PRECIOUS INN!!
TAKA!! TASUKI!!
JUST TRY TO SAY THAT AGAIN!!
YER JUST A BRAT WITH NO POWER AT ALL!! HOW CAN YA EXPECT TO PROTECT MIAKA, HUH?!
TASUKI, STOP IT! YOU'RE KILLING TAKA!!
AND YOU'RE RUINING MY INN!!
MIAKA, STAY AWAY!

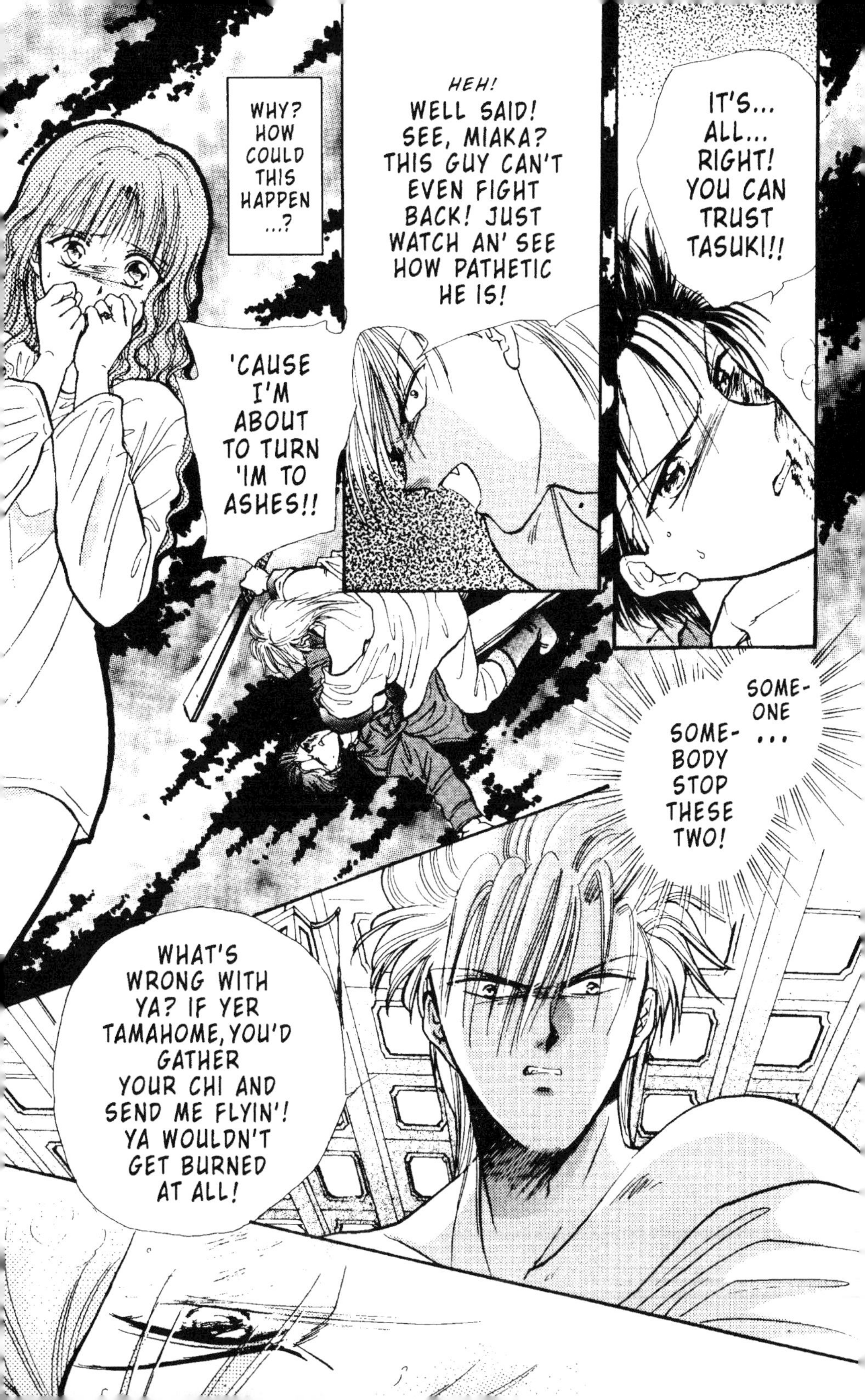
IT'S... ALL... RIGHT! YOU CAN TRUST TASUKI!!
HEH!
WELL SAID! SEE, MIAKA? THIS GUY CAN'T EVEN FIGHT BACK! JUST WATCH AN' SEE HOW PATHETIC HE IS!
'CAUSE I'M ABOUT TO TURN 'IM TO ASHES!!
WHY? HOW COULD THIS HAPPEN ...?
SOME-ONE ...
SOME-BODY STOP THESE TWO!
WHAT'S WRONG WITH YA? IF YER TAMAHOME, YOU'D GATHER YOUR CHI AND SEND ME FLYIN'! YA WOULDN'T GET BURNED AT ALL!

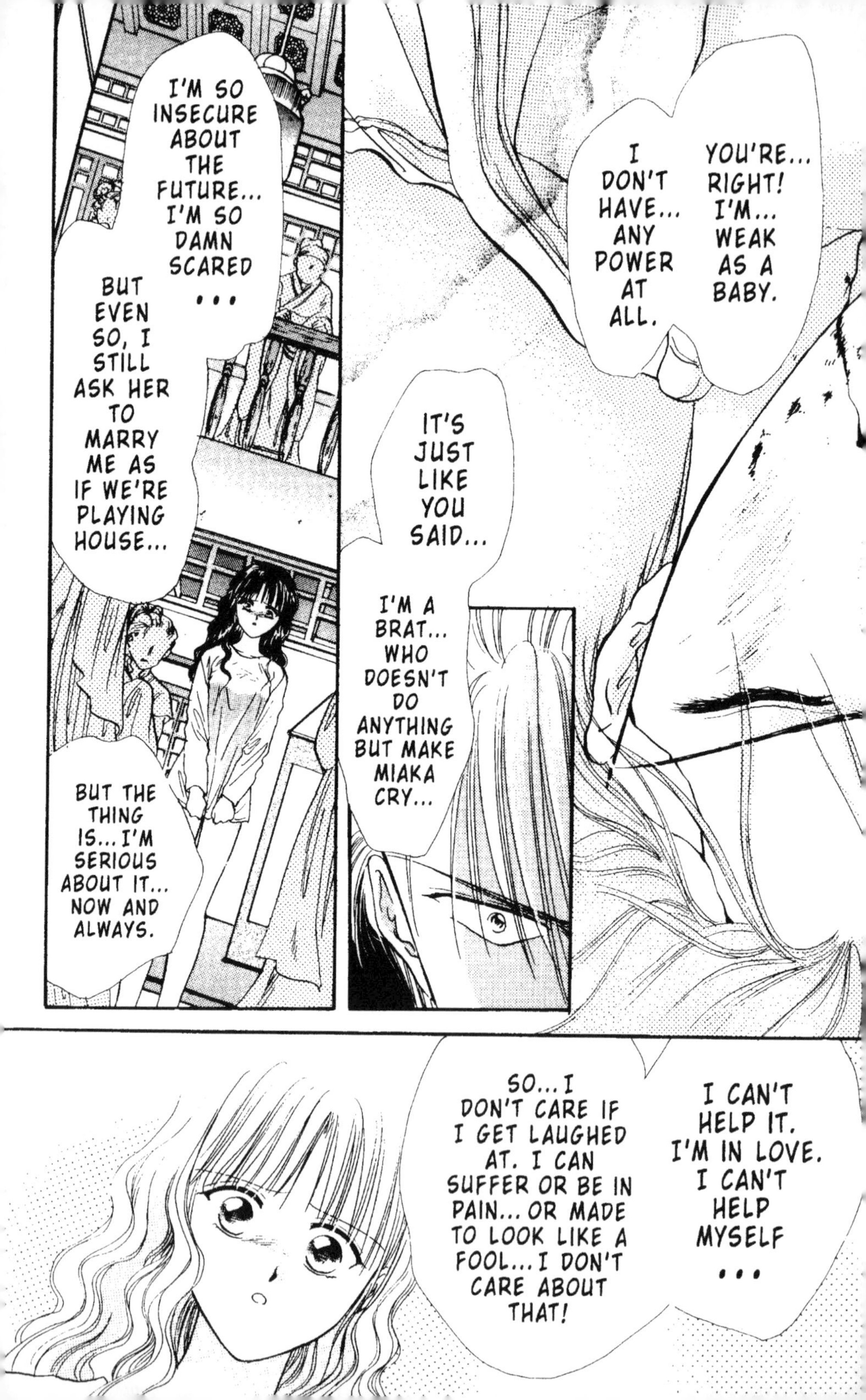
YOU'RE... RIGHT! I'M... WEAK AS A BABY.
I DON'T HAVE... ANY POWER AT ALL.
IT'S JUST LIKE YOU SAID...
I'M A BRAT... WHO DOESN'T DO ANYTHING BUT MAKE MIAKA CRY...
I'M SO INSECURE ABOUT THE FUTURE... I'M SO DAMN SCARED...
BUT EVEN SO, I STILL ASK HER TO MARRY ME AS IF WE'RE PLAYING HOUSE...
BUT THE THING IS... I'M SERIOUS ABOUT IT... NOW AND ALWAYS.
I CAN'T HELP IT. I'M IN LOVE. I CAN'T HELP MYSELF...
SO... I DON'T CARE IF I GET LAUGHED AT. I CAN SUFFER OR BE IN PAIN... OR MADE TO LOOK LIKE A FOOL... I DON'T CARE ABOUT THAT!

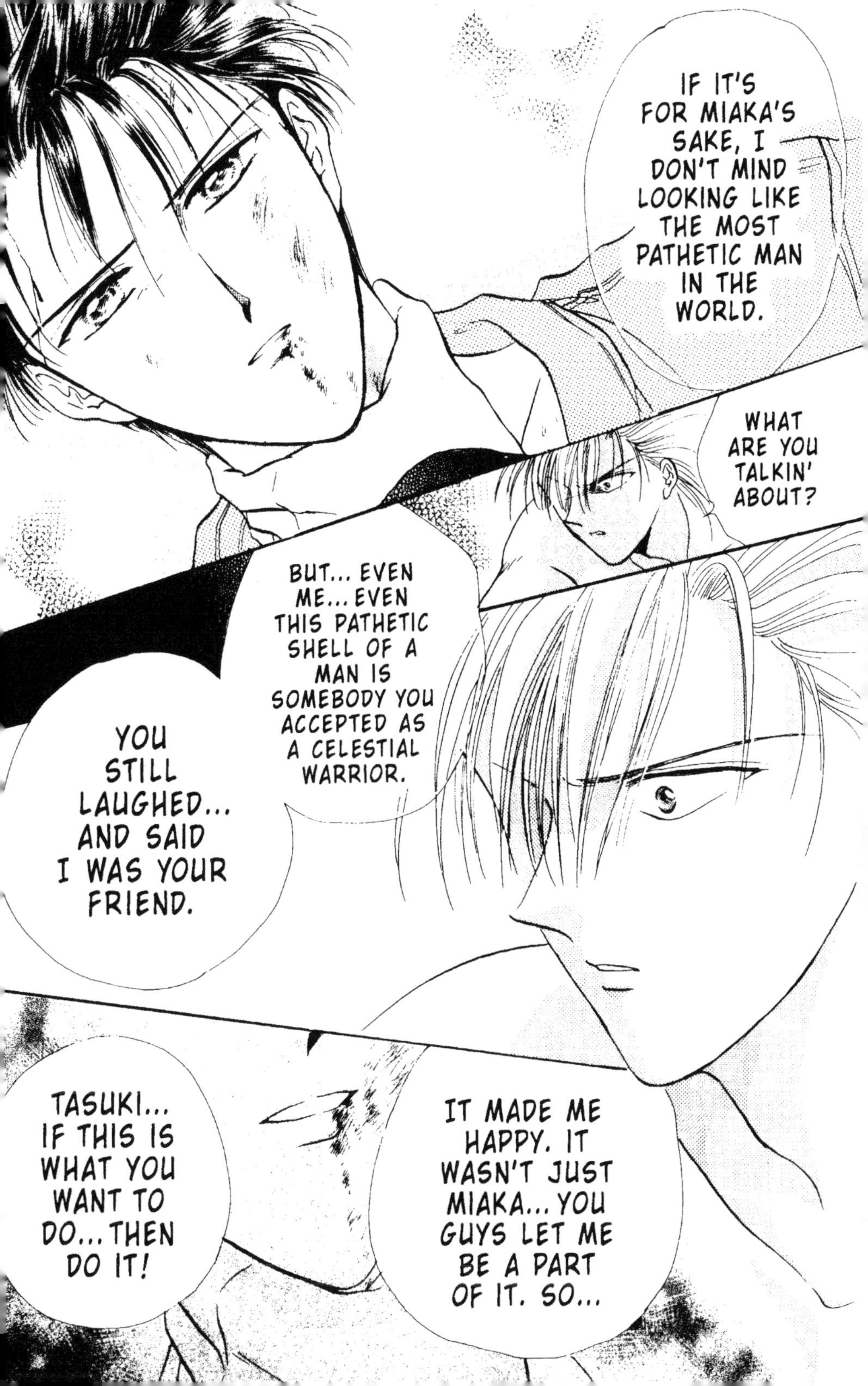
IF IT'S FOR MIAKA'S SAKE, I DON'T MIND LOOKING LIKE THE MOST PATHETIC MAN IN THE WORLD.
WHAT ARE YOU TALKIN' ABOUT?
BUT... EVEN ME... EVEN THIS PATHETIC SHELL OF A MAN IS SOMEBODY YOU ACCEPTED AS A CELESTIAL WARRIOR.
YOU STILL LAUGHED... AND SAID I WAS YOUR FRIEND.
IT MADE ME HAPPY. IT WASN'T JUST MIAKA... YOU GUYS LET ME BE A PART OF IT. SO...
TASUKI... IF THIS IS WHAT YOU WANT TO DO... THEN DO IT!

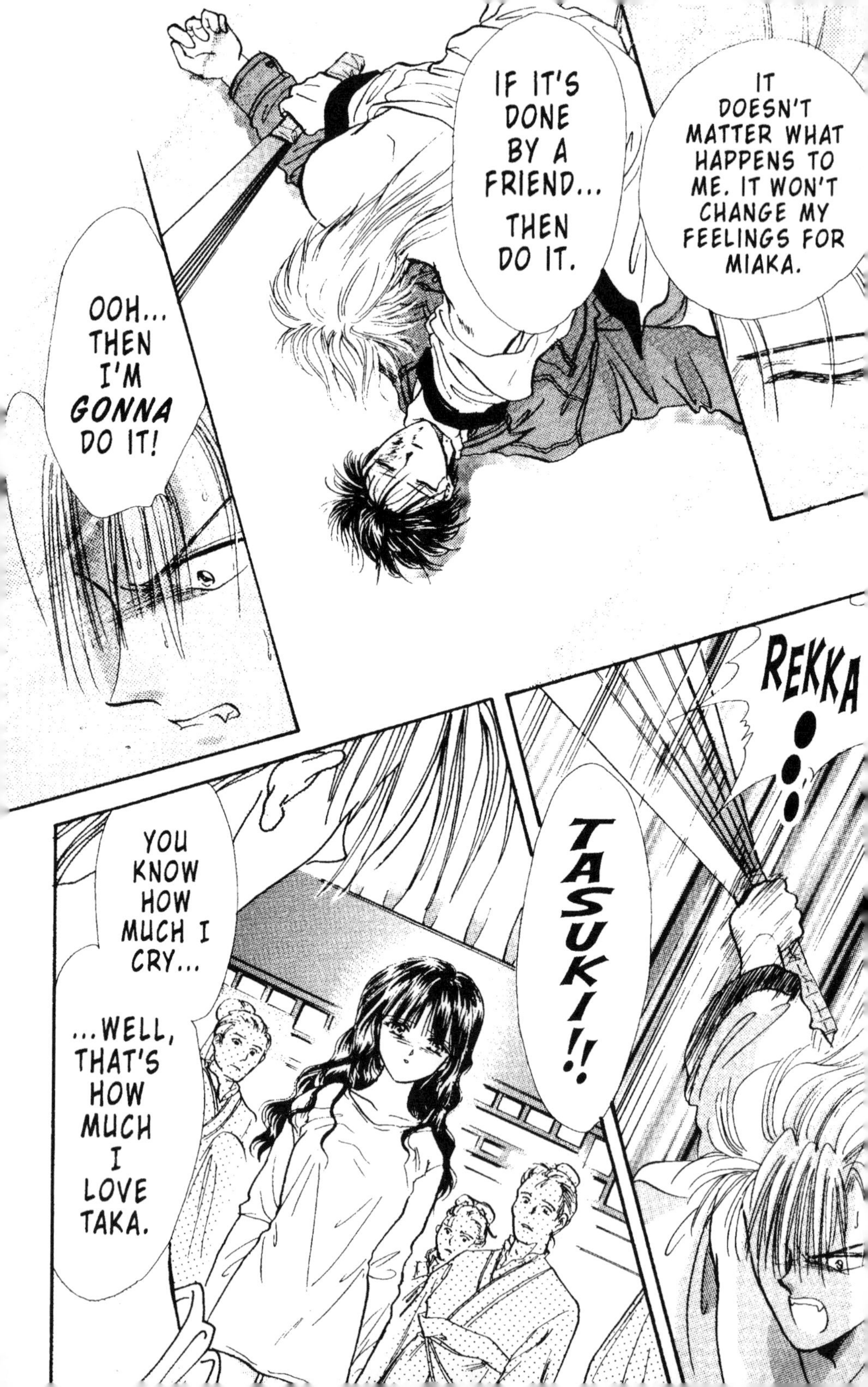

IT DOESN'T MATTER WHAT HAPPENS TO ME. IT WON'T CHANGE MY FEELINGS FOR MIAKA.
IF IT'S DONE BY A FRIEND...
THEN DO IT.
OOH... THEN I'M *GONNA* DO IT!
REKKA...
TASUKI!!
YOU KNOW HOW MUCH I CRY...
...WELL, THAT'S HOW MUCH I LOVE TAKA.

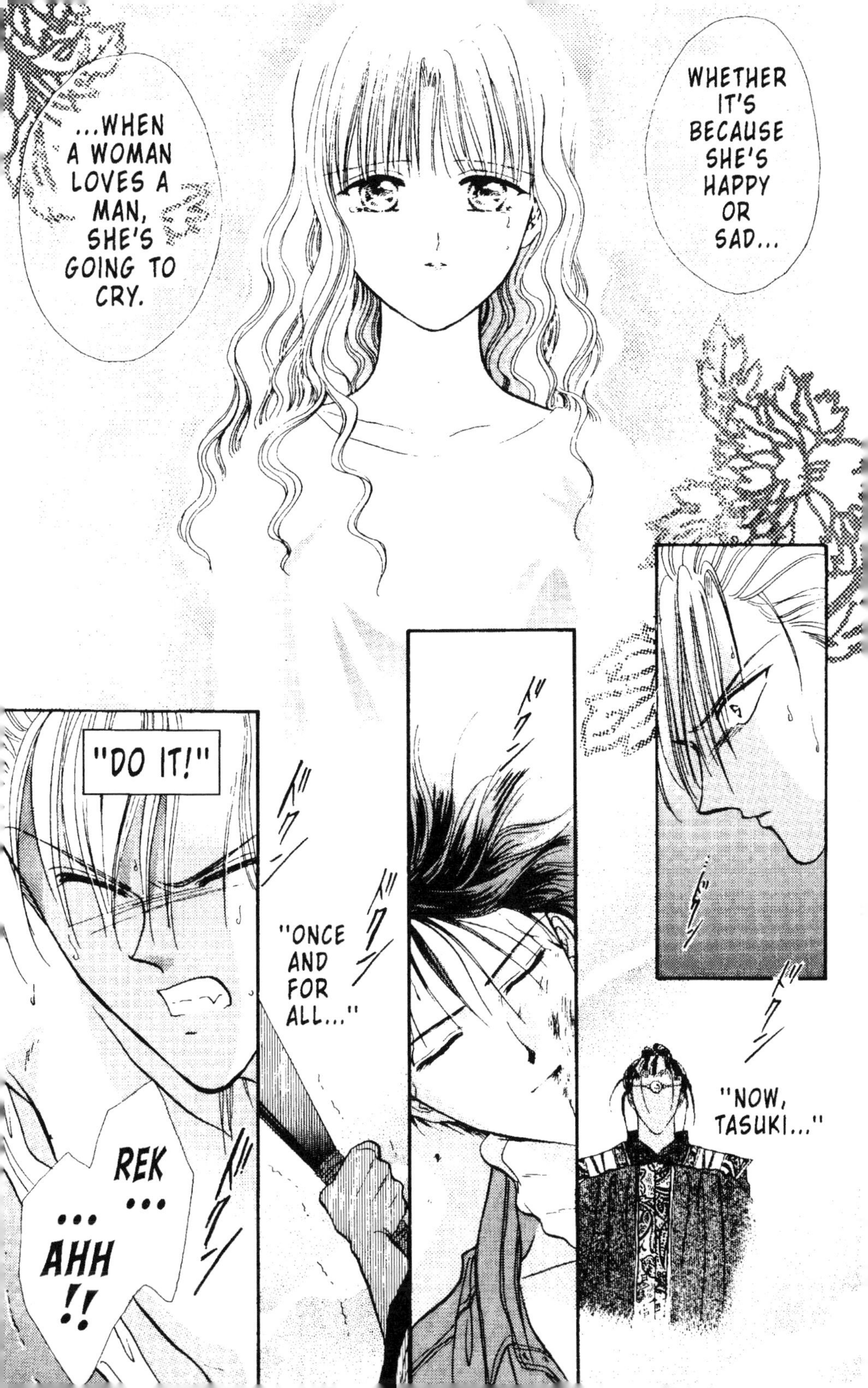
WHETHER IT'S BECAUSE SHE'S HAPPY OR SAD...
...WHEN A WOMAN LOVES A MAN, SHE'S GOING TO CRY.
"NOW, TASUKI..."
"ONCE AND FOR ALL..."
"DO IT!"
REK... ...AHH!!

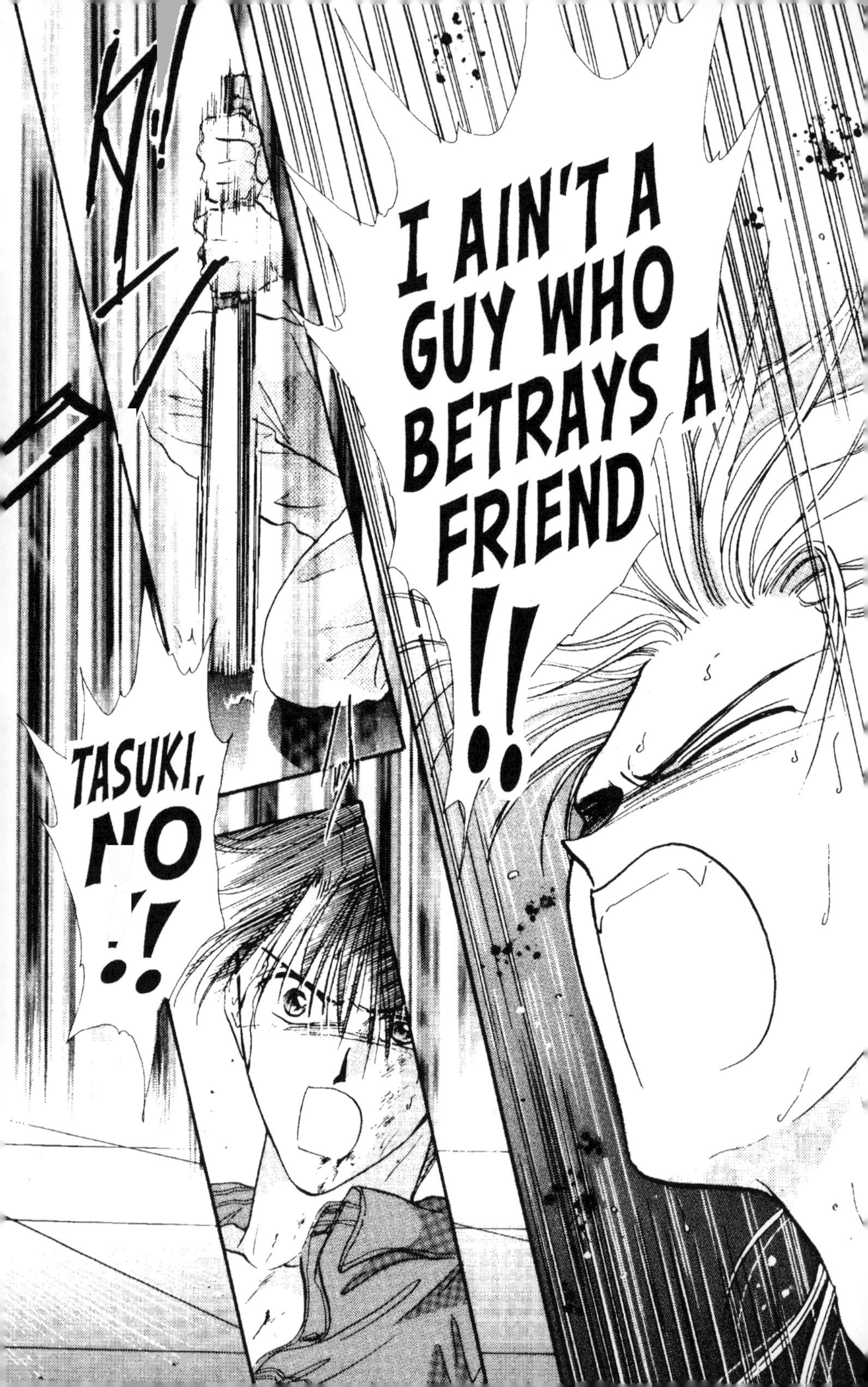
I AIN'T A GUY WHO BETRAYS A FRIEND!!
TASUKI, NO!!

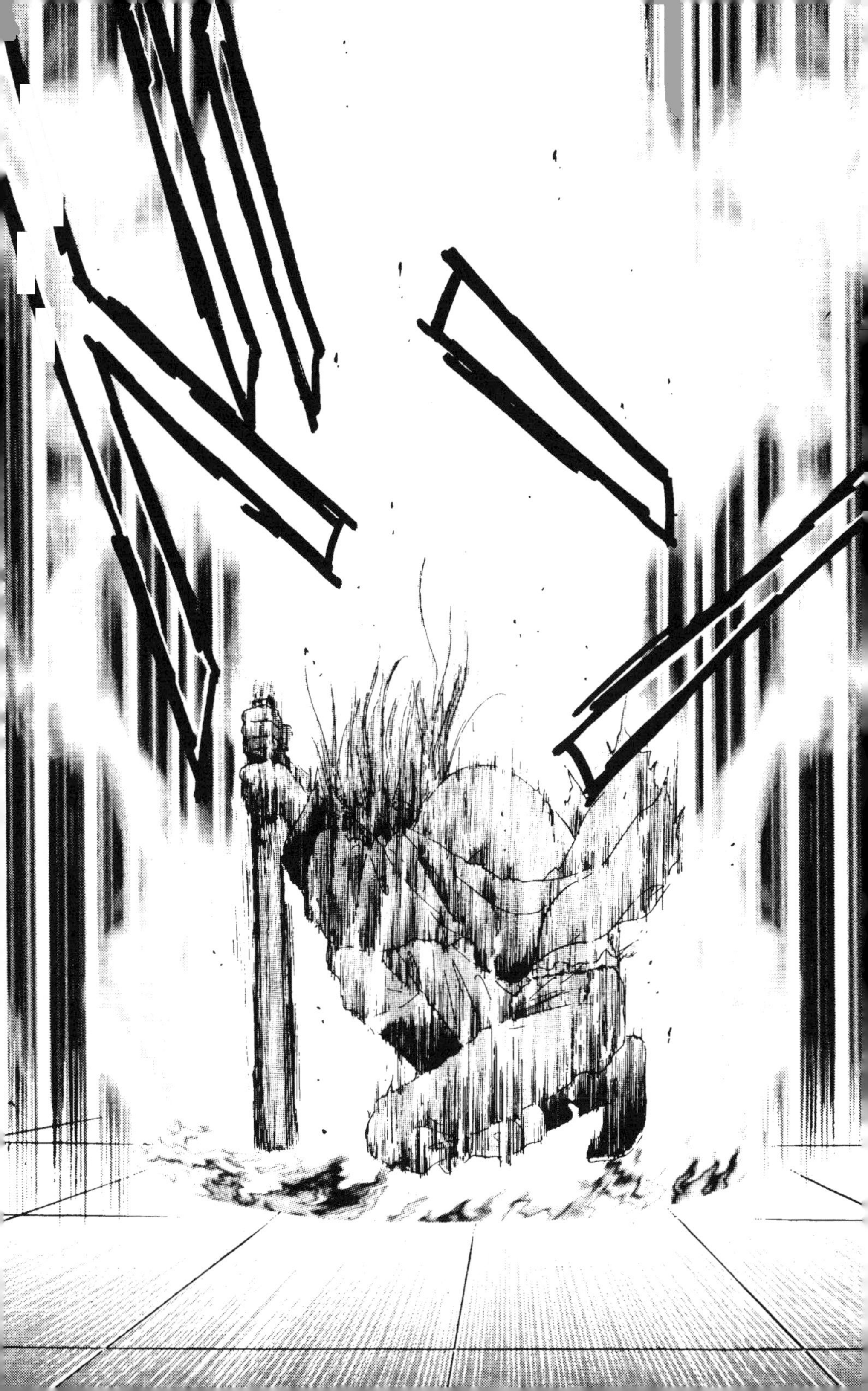

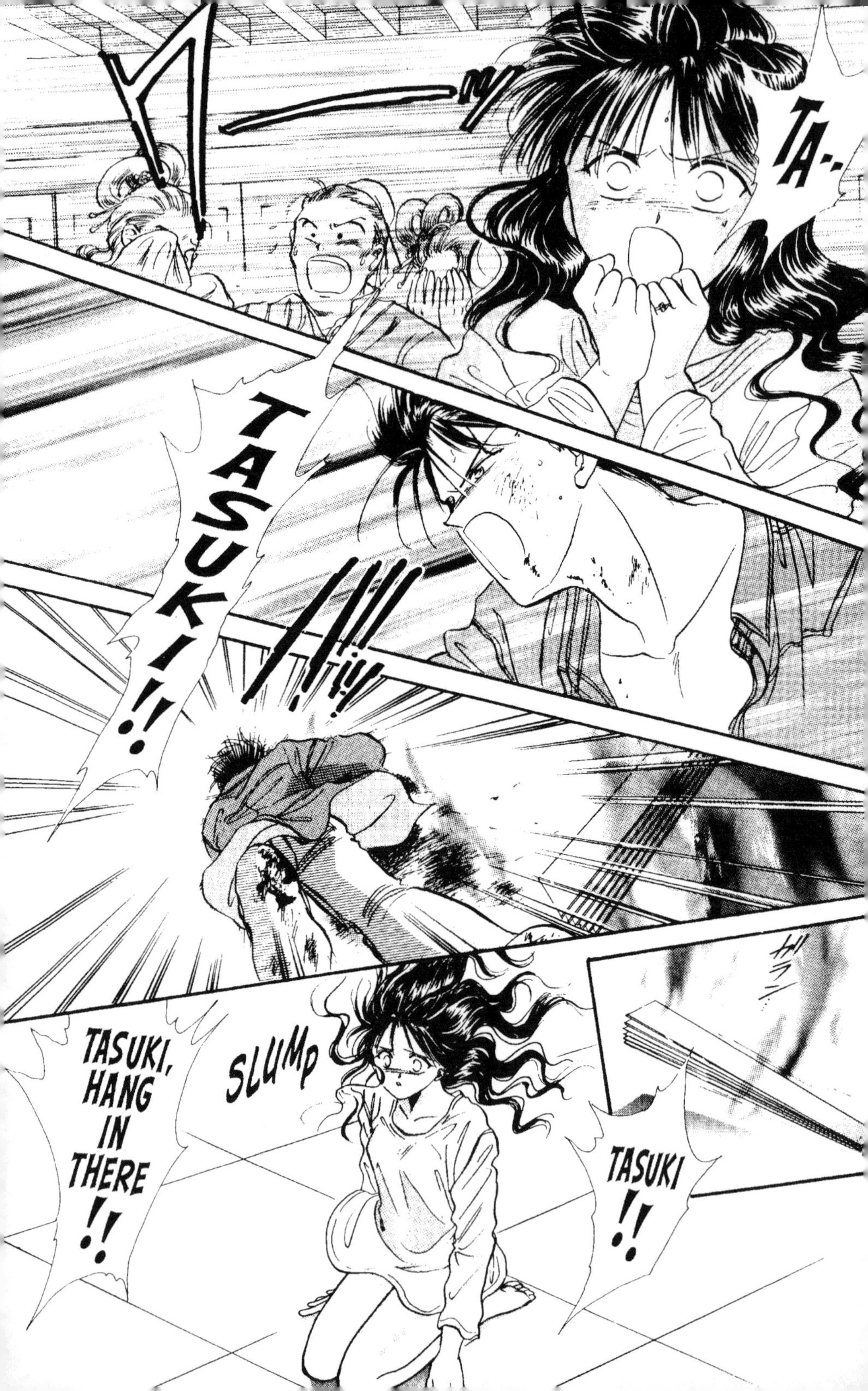
TA--
N------NN
TASUKI!!
SLUMP
TASUKI!!
TASUKI, HANG IN THERE!!

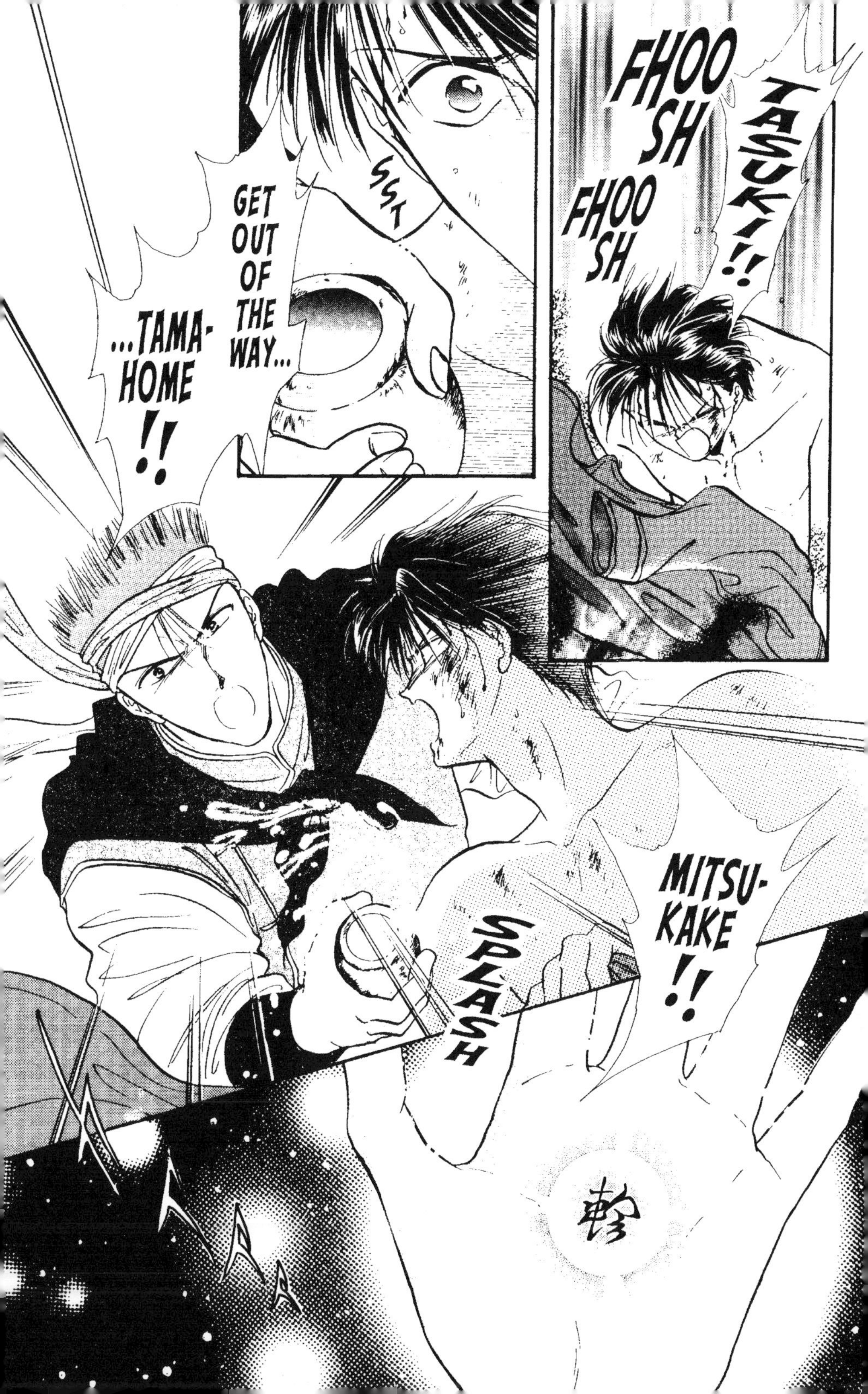
TASUKI!!
FHOOSH
FHOOSH
GET OUT OF THE WAY...
...TAMA-HOME!!
MITSU-KAKE!!
SPLASH

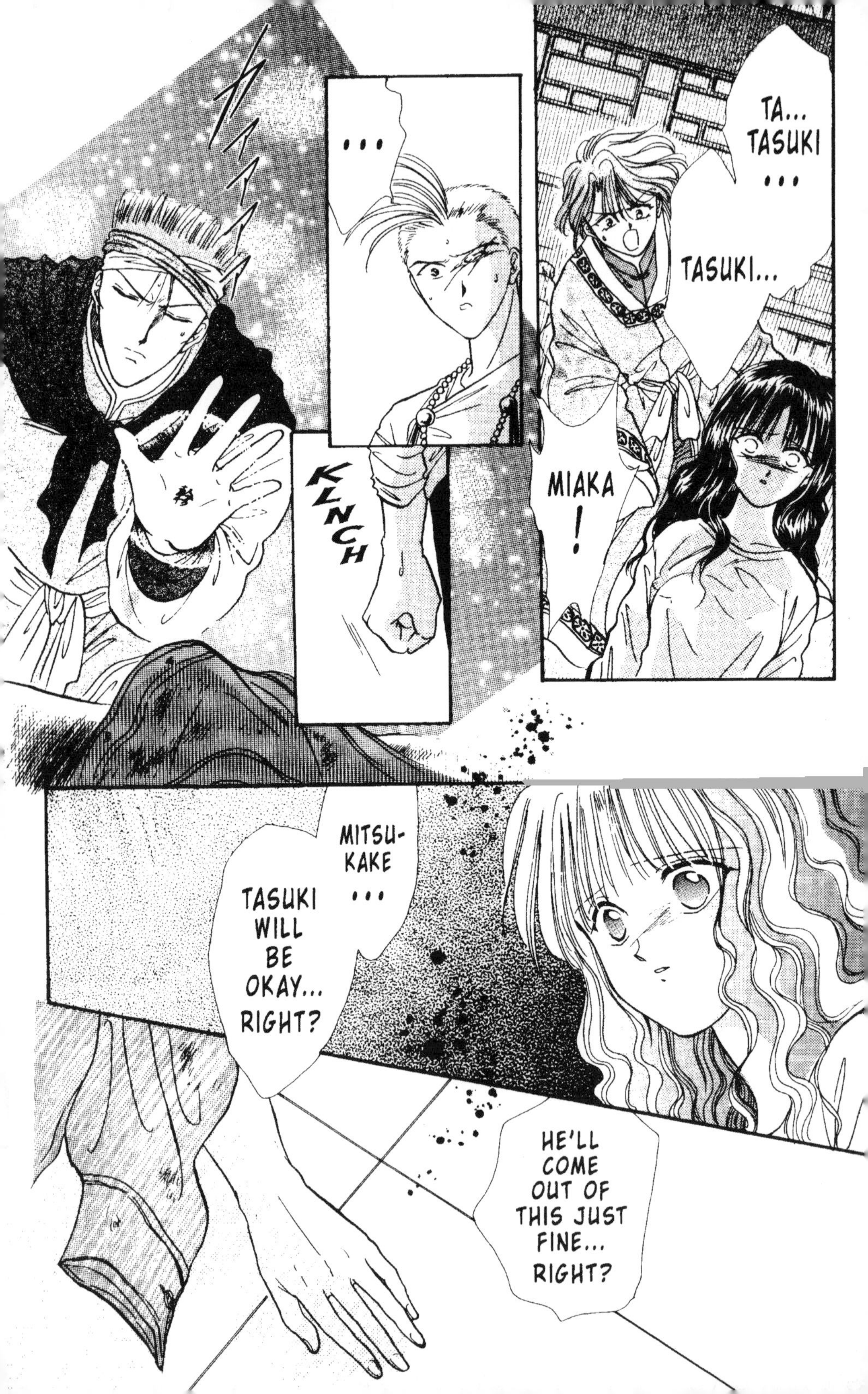
TA... TASUKI...
TASUKI...
MIAKA!
...
KLINCH
MITSU-KAKE...
TASUKI WILL BE OKAY... RIGHT?
HE'LL COME OUT OF THIS JUST FINE... RIGHT?

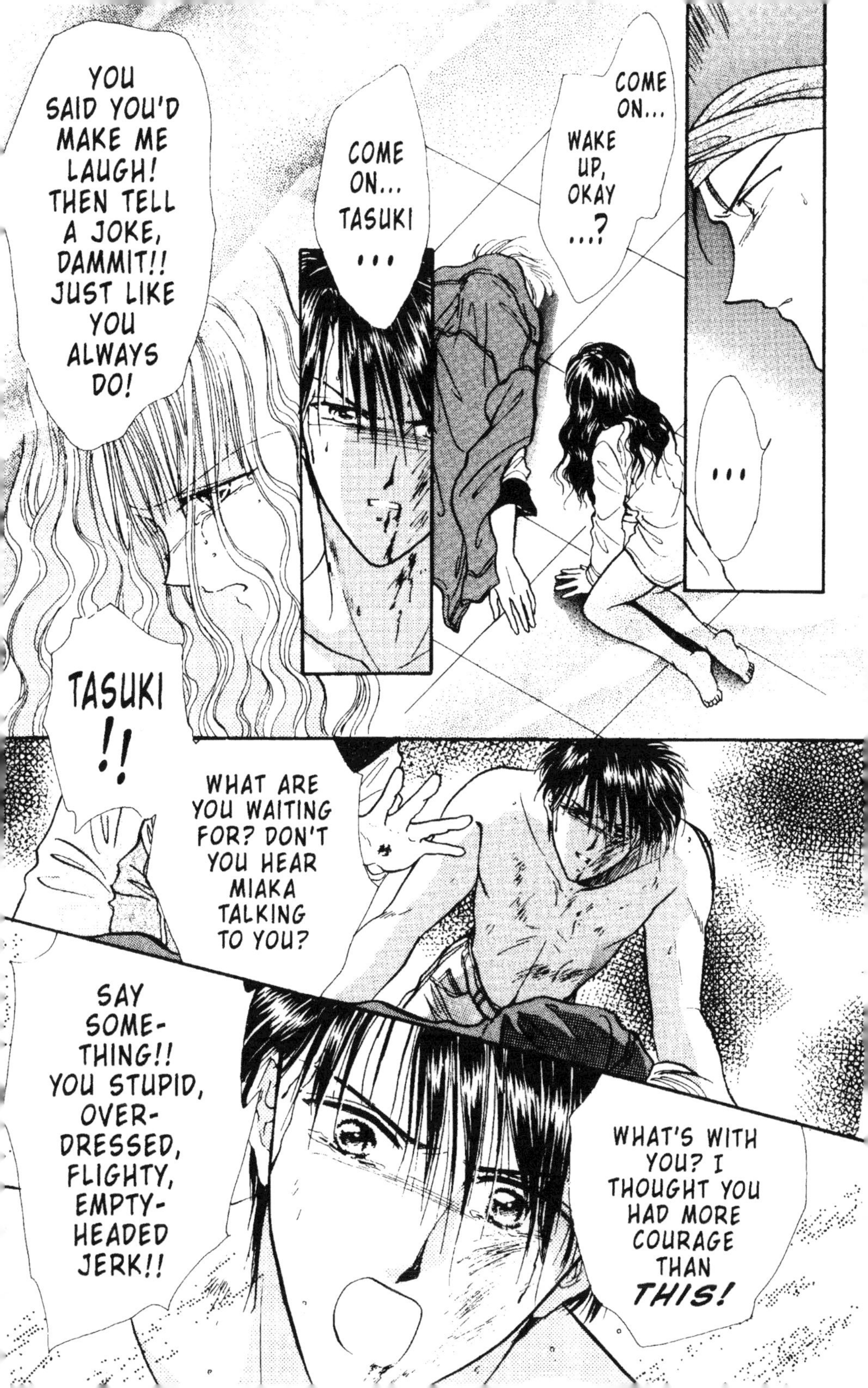
...
COME ON... WAKE UP, OKAY ...?
COME ON... TASUKI ...
YOU SAID YOU'D MAKE ME LAUGH! THEN TELL A JOKE, DAMMIT!! JUST LIKE YOU ALWAYS DO!
TASUKI !!
WHAT ARE YOU WAITING FOR? DON'T YOU HEAR MIAKA TALKING TO YOU?
WHAT'S WITH YOU? I THOUGHT YOU HAD MORE COURAGE THAN *THIS!*
SAY SOME-THING!! YOU STUPID, OVER-DRESSED, FLIGHTY, EMPTY-HEADED JERK!!

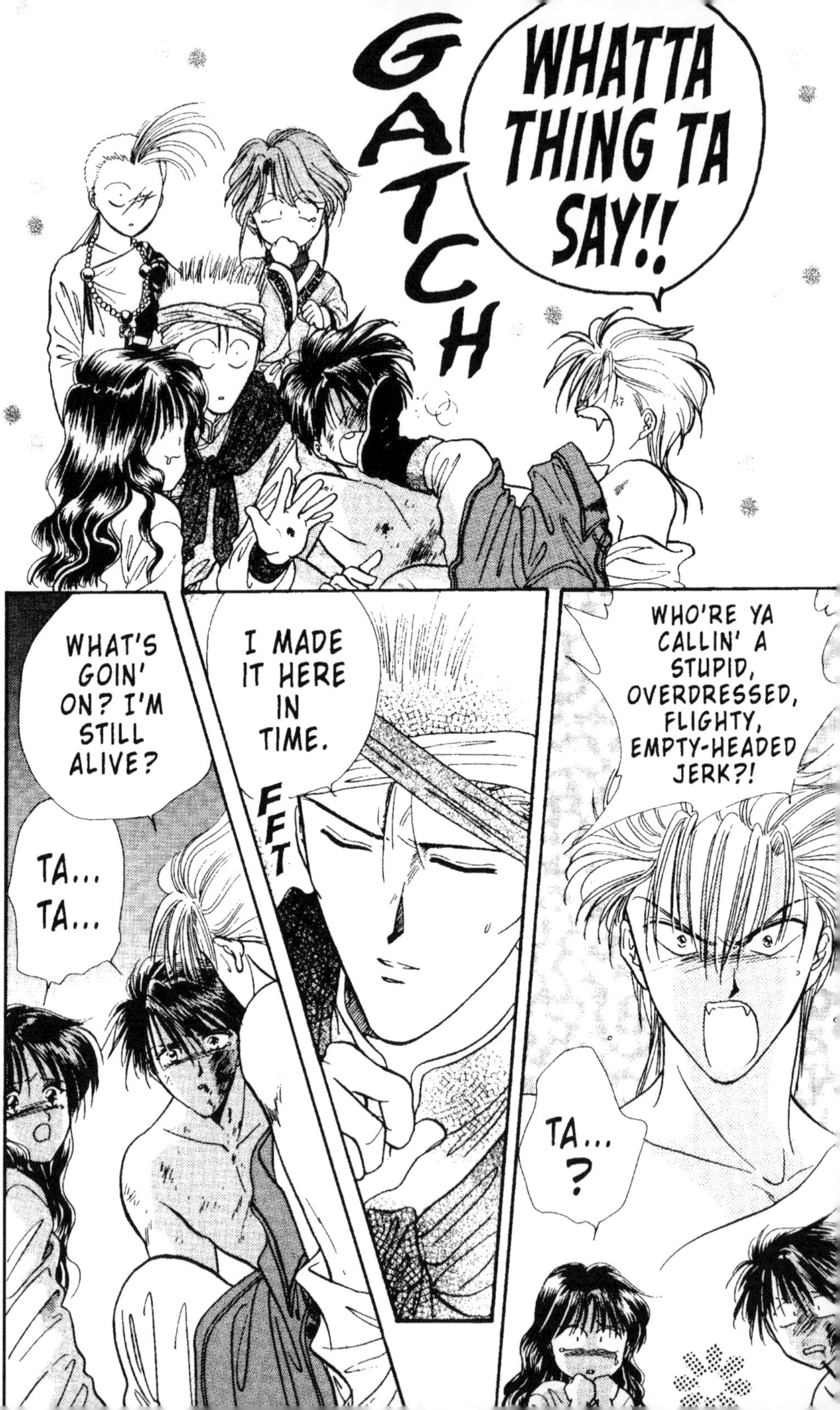
WHATTA THING TA SAY!!
GATCH
WHO'RE YA CALLIN' A STUPID, OVERDRESSED, FLIGHTY, EMPTY-HEADED JERK?!
TA... ?
I MADE IT HERE IN TIME.
FFT
WHAT'S GOIN' ON? I'M STILL ALIVE?
TA... TA...

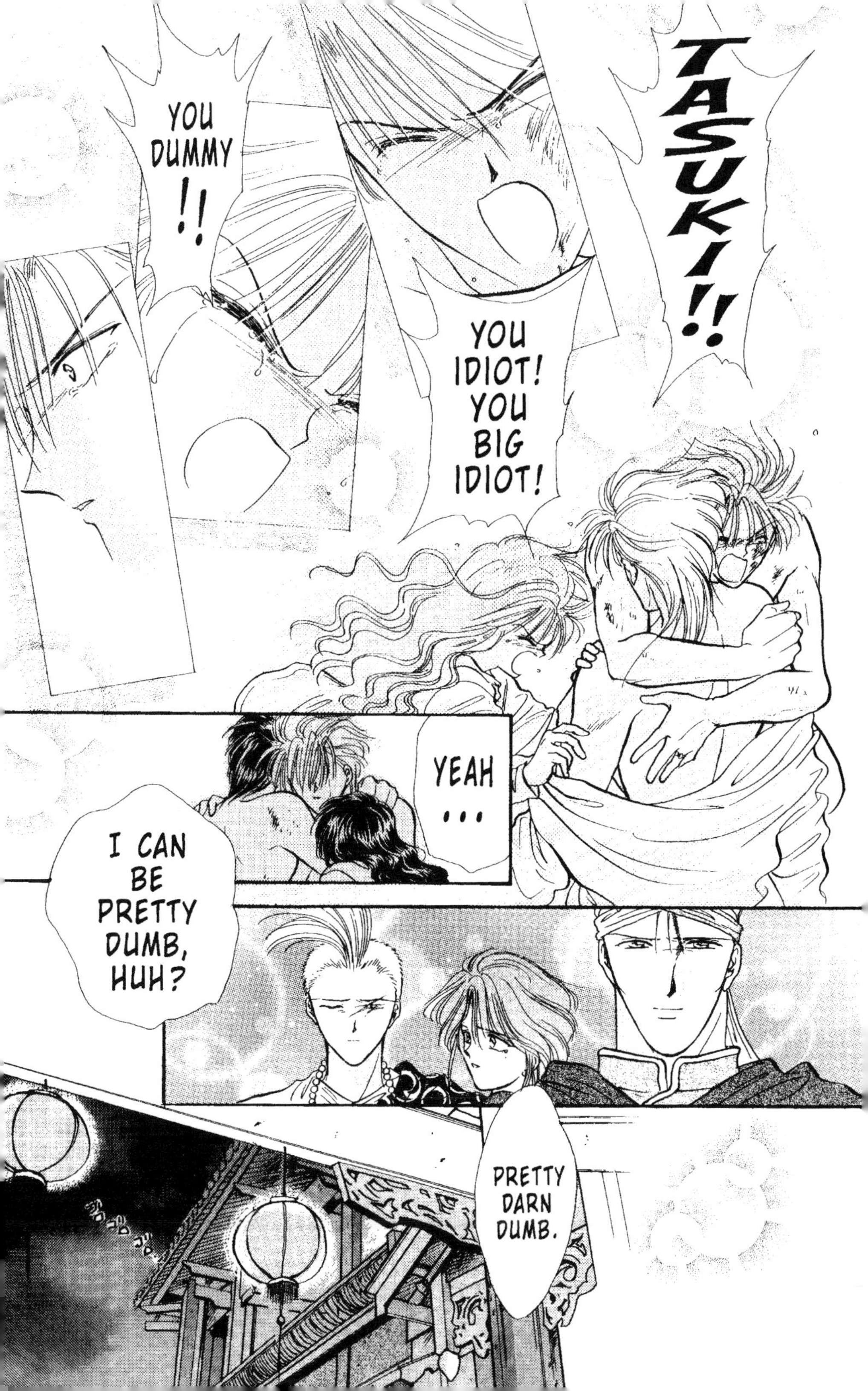
TASUKI!!
YOU IDIOT! YOU BIG IDIOT!
YOU DUMMY!!
YEAH...
I CAN BE PRETTY DUMB, HUH?
PRETTY DARN DUMB.

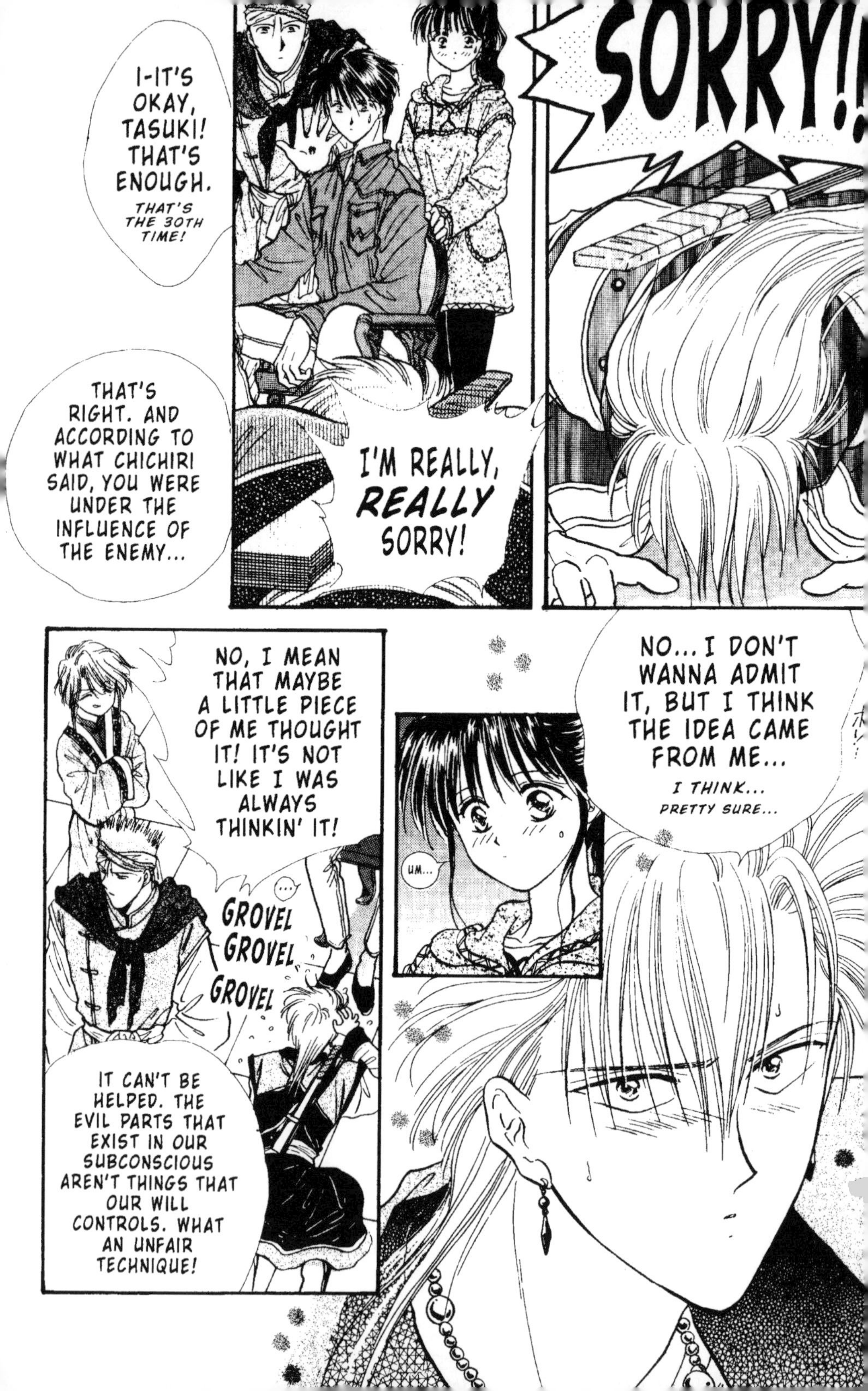
SORRY!!
I'M REALLY, REALLY SORRY!
I-IT'S OKAY, TASUKI! THAT'S ENOUGH.
THAT'S THE 30TH TIME!
THAT'S RIGHT. AND ACCORDING TO WHAT CHICHIRI SAID, YOU WERE UNDER THE INFLUENCE OF THE ENEMY...
NO... I DON'T WANNA ADMIT IT, BUT I THINK THE IDEA CAME FROM ME...
I THINK... PRETTY SURE...
UM...
NO, I MEAN THAT MAYBE A LITTLE PIECE OF ME THOUGHT IT! IT'S NOT LIKE I WAS ALWAYS THINKIN' IT!
...
GROVEL GROVEL GROVEL
IT CAN'T BE HELPED. THE EVIL PARTS THAT EXIST IN OUR SUBCONSCIOUS AREN'T THINGS THAT OUR WILL CONTROLS. WHAT AN UNFAIR TECHNIQUE!

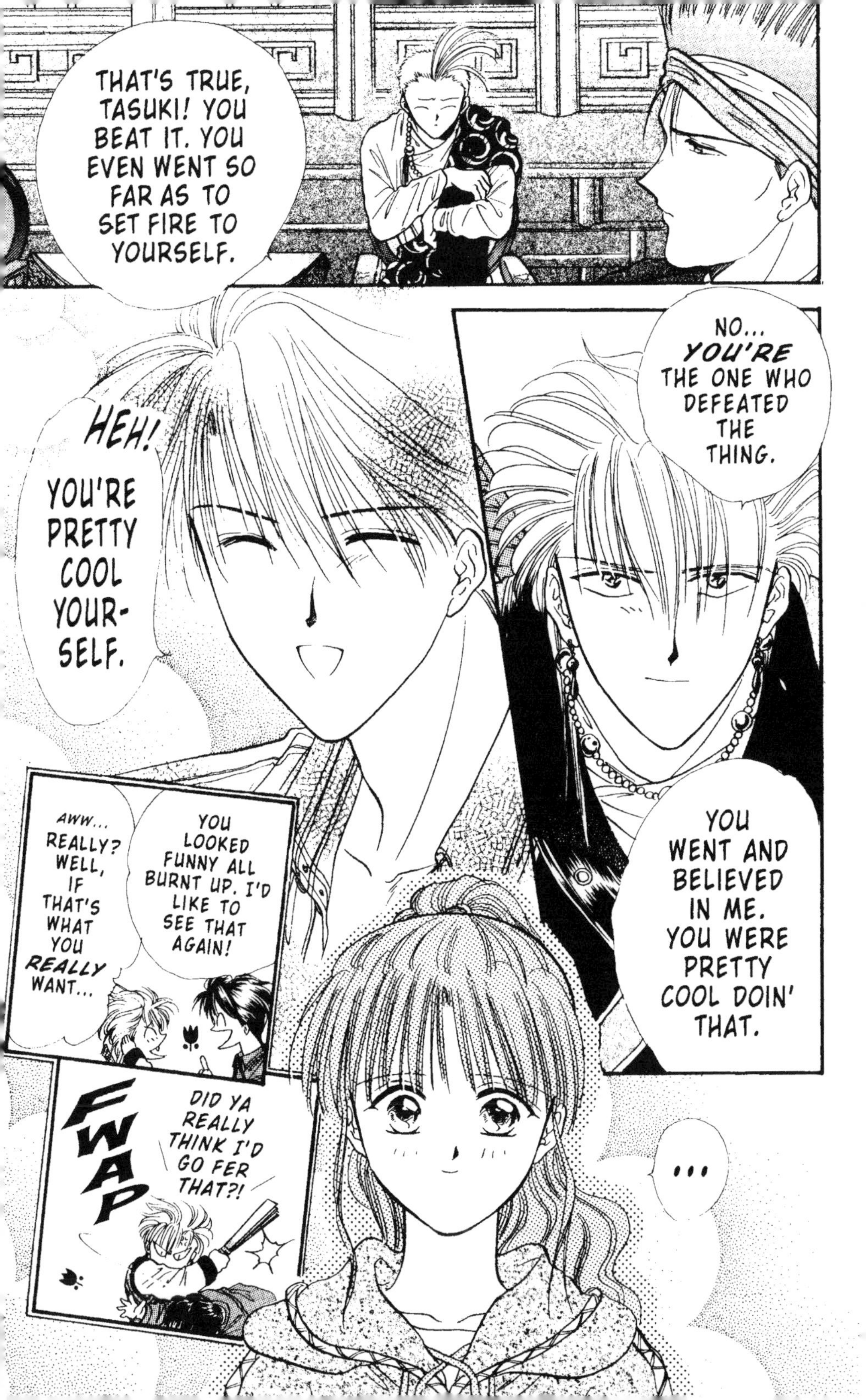
THAT'S TRUE, TASUKI! YOU BEAT IT. YOU EVEN WENT SO FAR AS TO SET FIRE TO YOURSELF.
NO... YOU'RE THE ONE WHO DEFEATED THE THING.
YOU WENT AND BELIEVED IN ME. YOU WERE PRETTY COOL DOIN' THAT.
HEH!
YOU'RE PRETTY COOL YOUR-SELF.
...
YOU LOOKED FUNNY ALL BURNT UP. I'D LIKE TO SEE THAT AGAIN!
AWW... REALLY? WELL, IF THAT'S WHAT YOU REALLY WANT...
DID YA REALLY THINK I'D GO FER THAT?!
FWAP

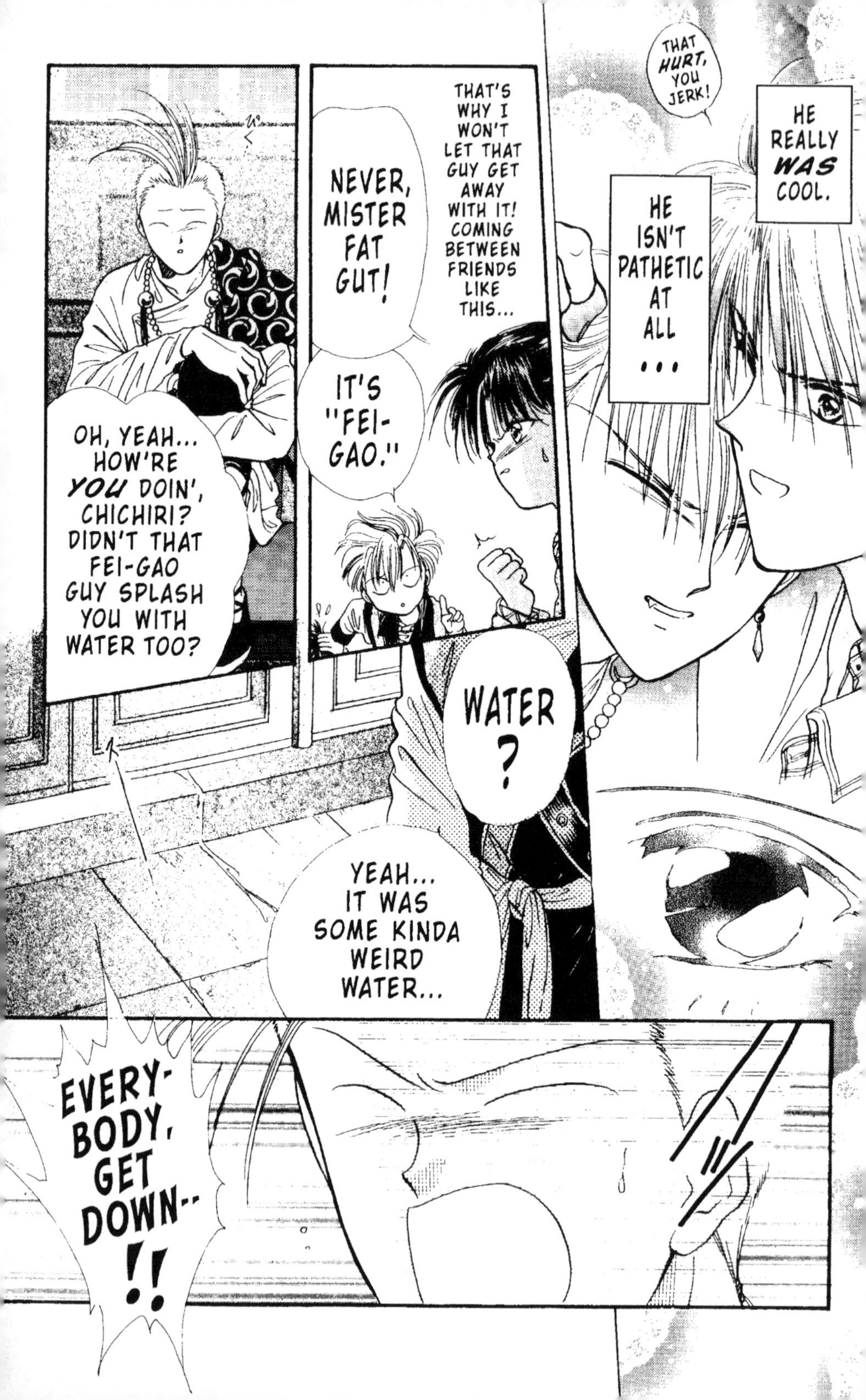
THAT HURT, YOU JERK!
HE REALLY WAS COOL.
HE ISN'T PATHETIC AT ALL...
THAT'S WHY I WON'T LET THAT GUY GET AWAY WITH IT! COMING BETWEEN FRIENDS LIKE THIS...
NEVER, MISTER FAT GUT!
IT'S "FEI-GAO."
OH, YEAH... HOW'RE YOU DOIN', CHICHIRI? DIDN'T THAT FEI-GAO GUY SPLASH YOU WITH WATER TOO?
WATER?
YEAH... IT WAS SOME KINDA WEIRD WATER...
EVERY-BODY, GET DOWN--!!

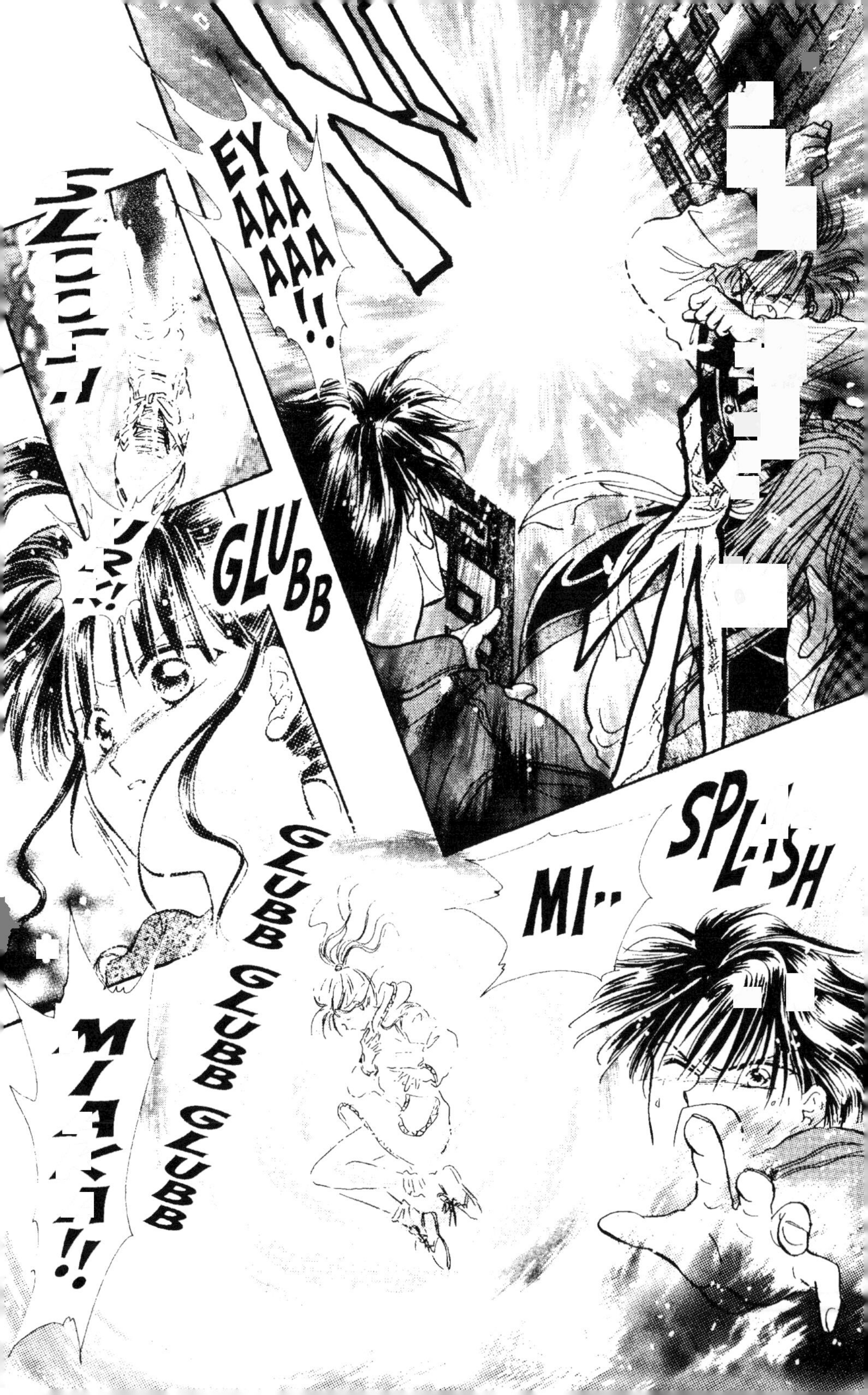
EY AAAAAA!!
SPLASH
MI..
GLUBB
GLUBB GLUBB GLUBB GLUBB

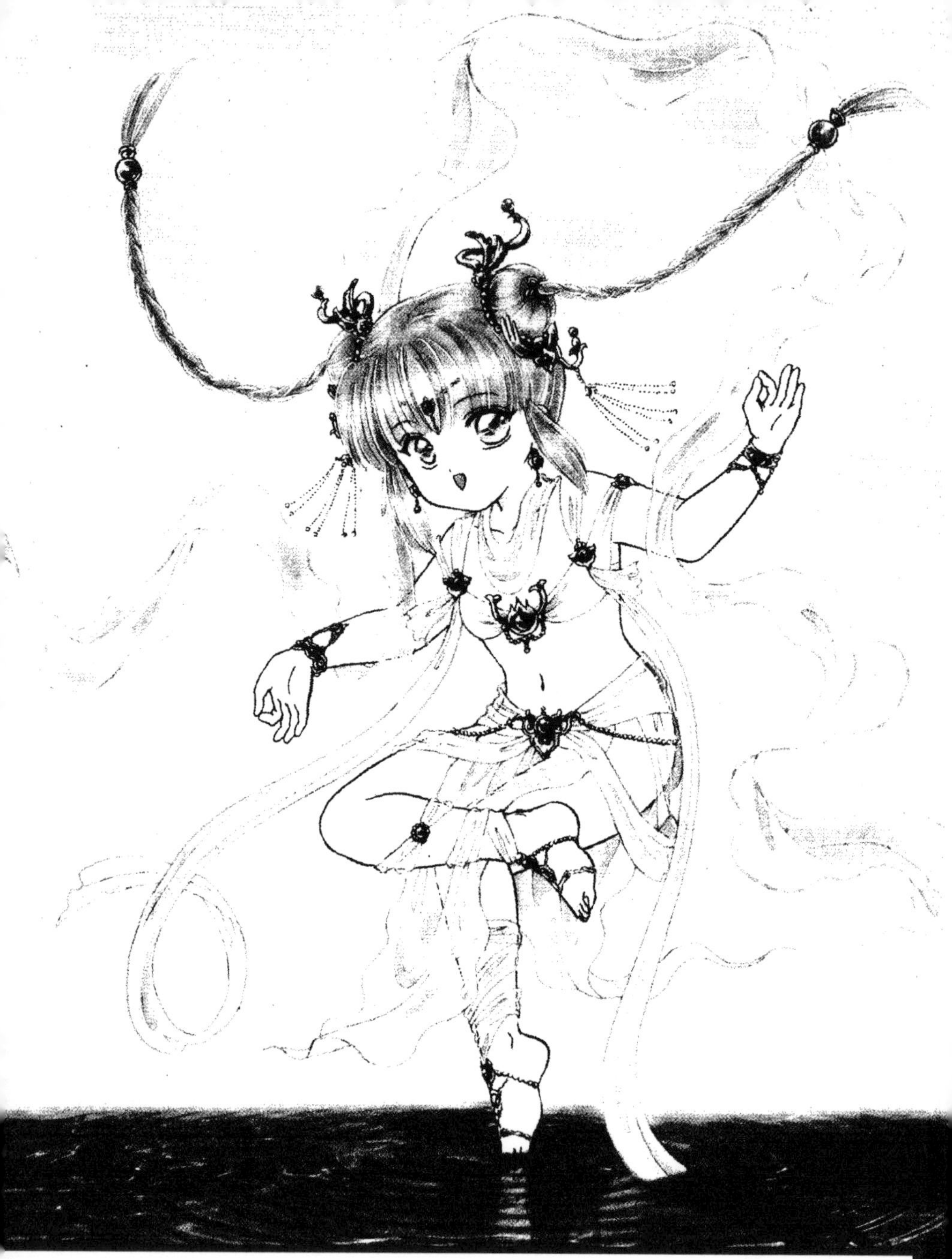

Chapter Ninety-Nine
The Tragic Transmigration

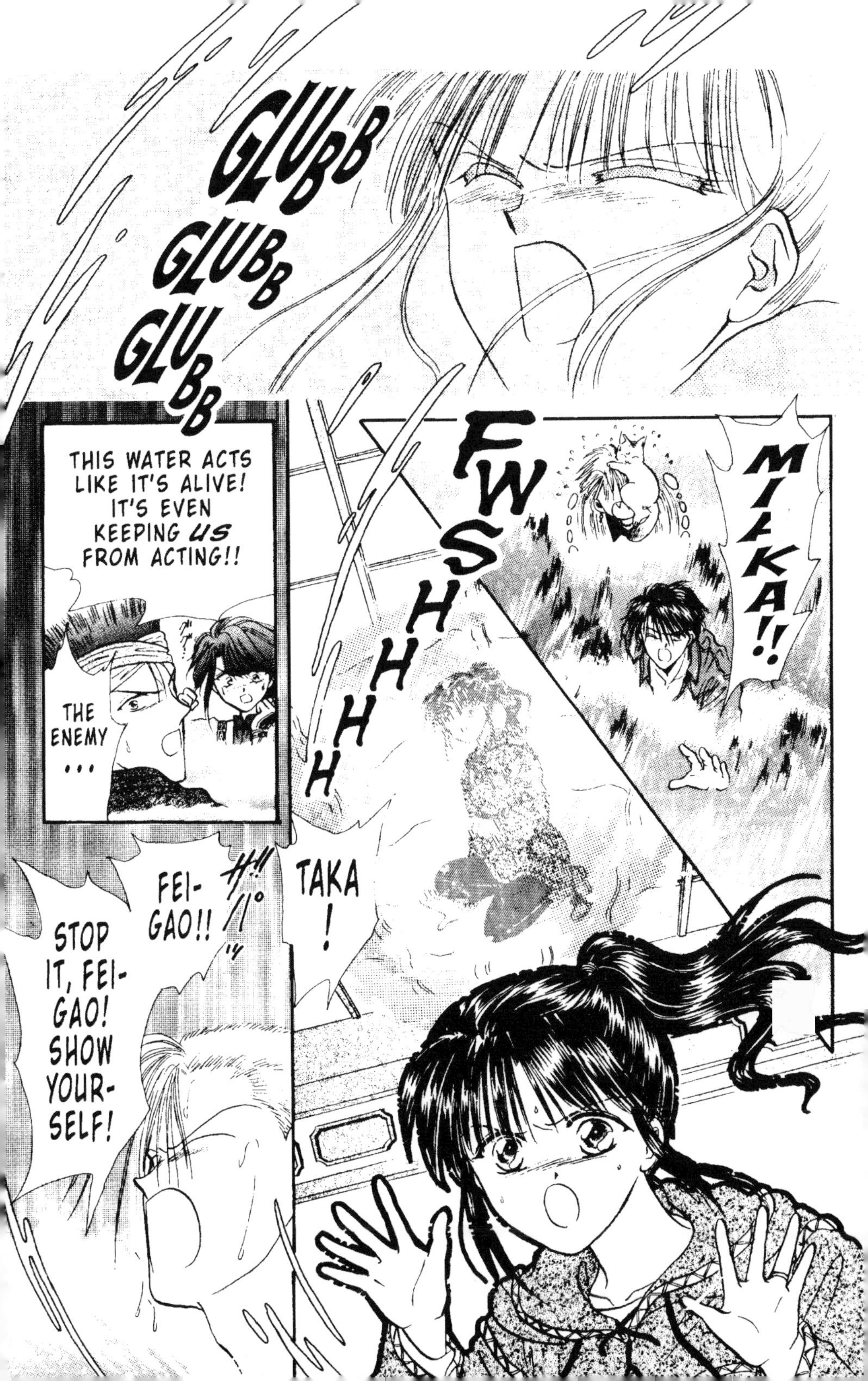
GLUBB
GLUBB
GLUBB
FWSHHHHH
MIKKA!!
THIS WATER ACTS LIKE IT'S ALIVE! IT'S EVEN KEEPING US FROM ACTING!!
THE ENEMY...
TAKA!
FEI-GAO!!
STOP IT, FEI-GAO! SHOW YOURSELF!

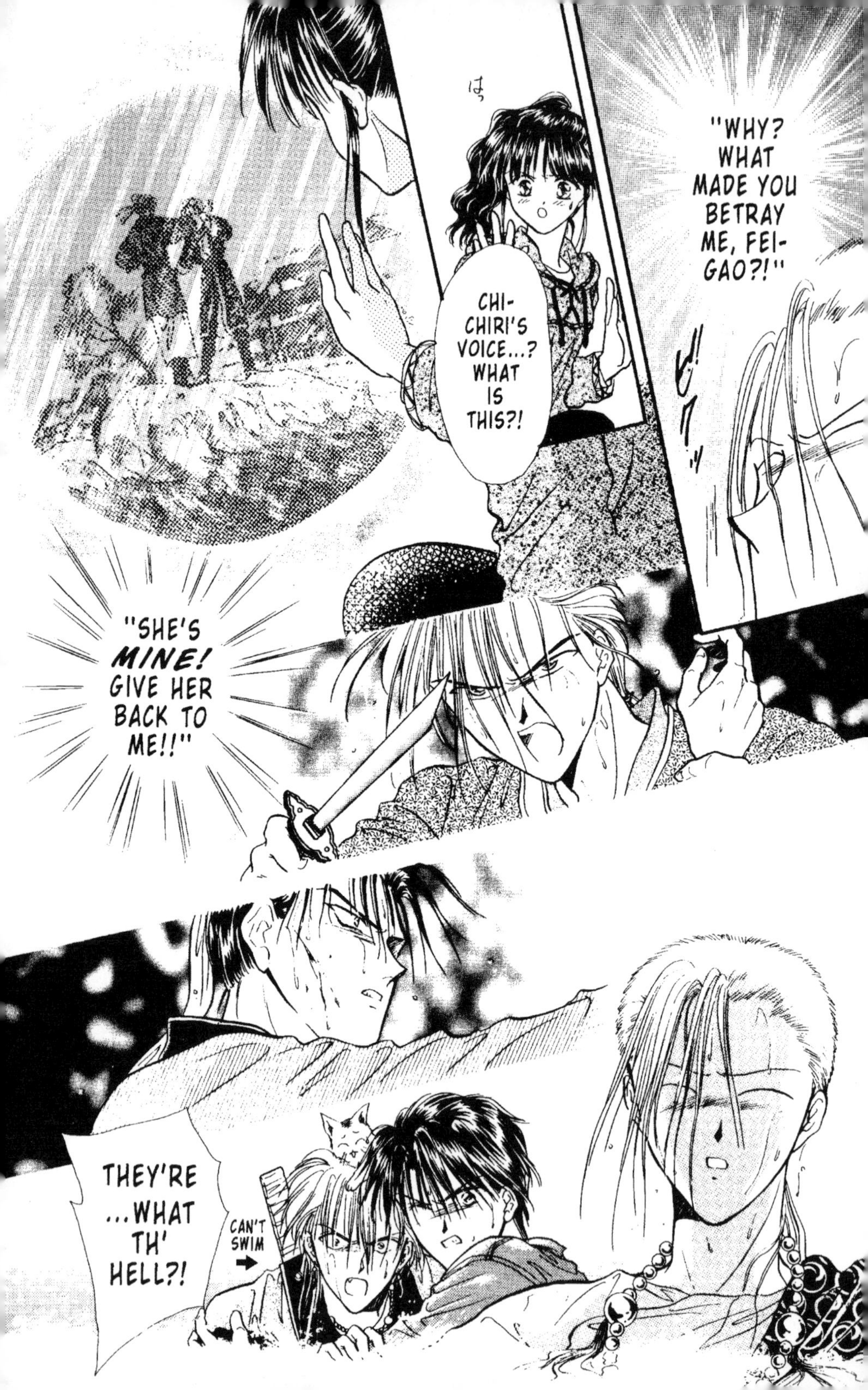
"WHY? WHAT MADE YOU BETRAY ME, FEI-GAO?!"
はっ
CHI-CHIRI'S VOICE...? WHAT IS THIS?!
"SHE'S MINE! GIVE HER BACK TO ME!!"
THEY'RE ...WHAT TH' HELL?!
CAN'T SWIM

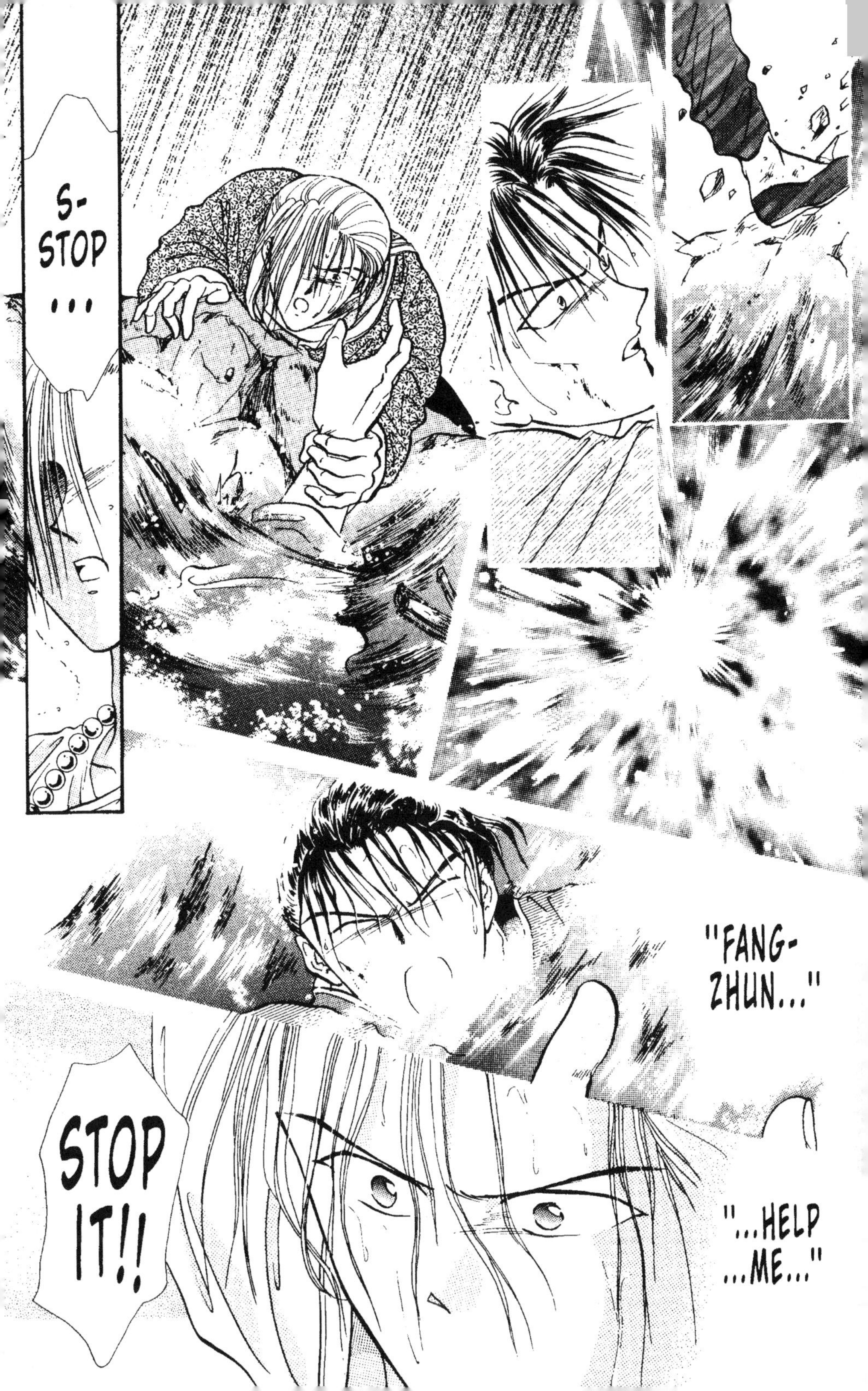
S-STOP...
"FANG-ZHUN..."
"...HELP ...ME..."
STOP IT!!

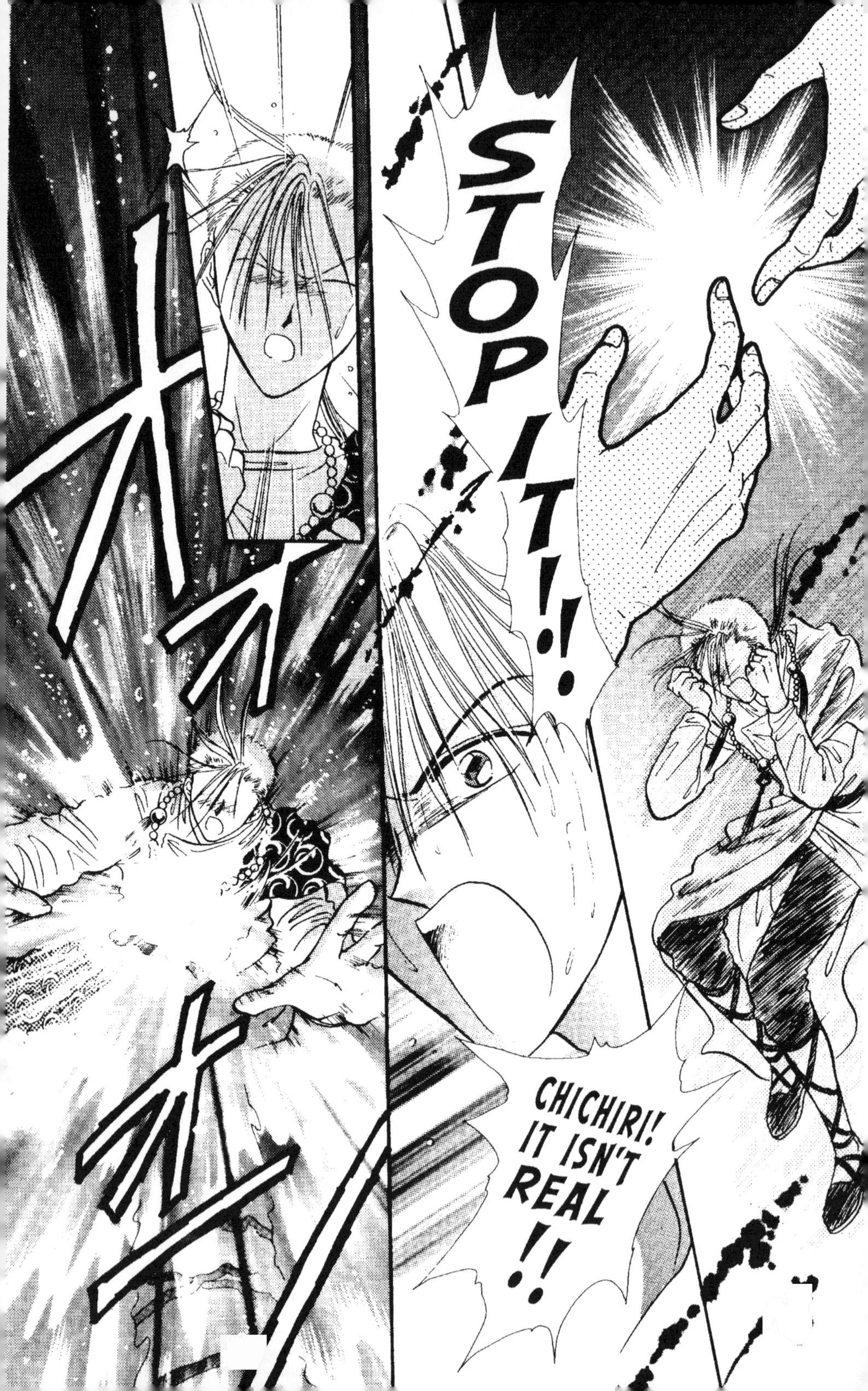
STOP IT!!!
CHICHIRI! IT ISN'T REAL!!

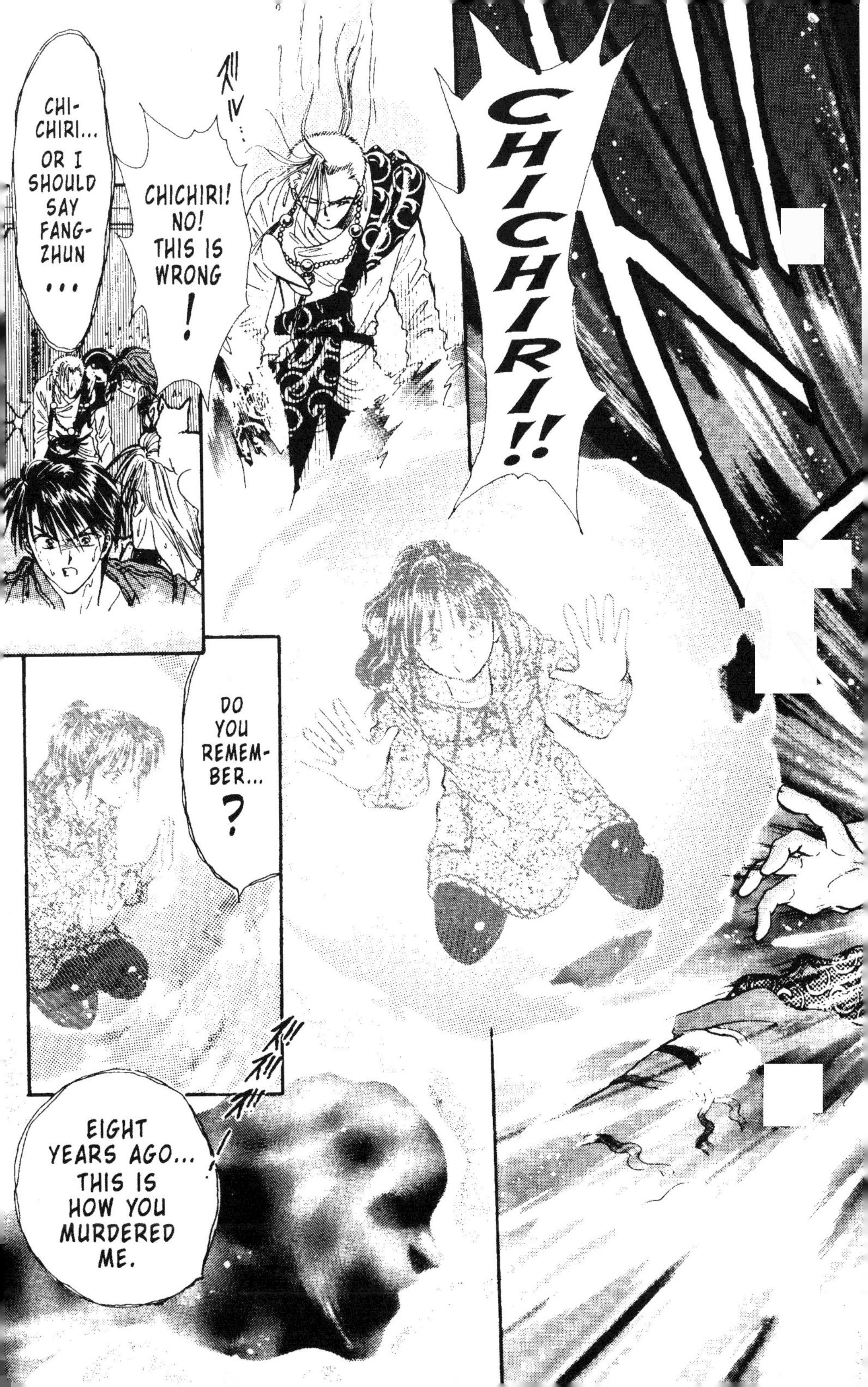
CHICHIRI!!
CHICHIRI! NO! THIS IS WRONG!
CHI-CHIRI... OR I SHOULD SAY FANG-ZHUN...
DO YOU REMEMBER...?
EIGHT YEARS AGO... THIS IS HOW YOU MURDERED ME.

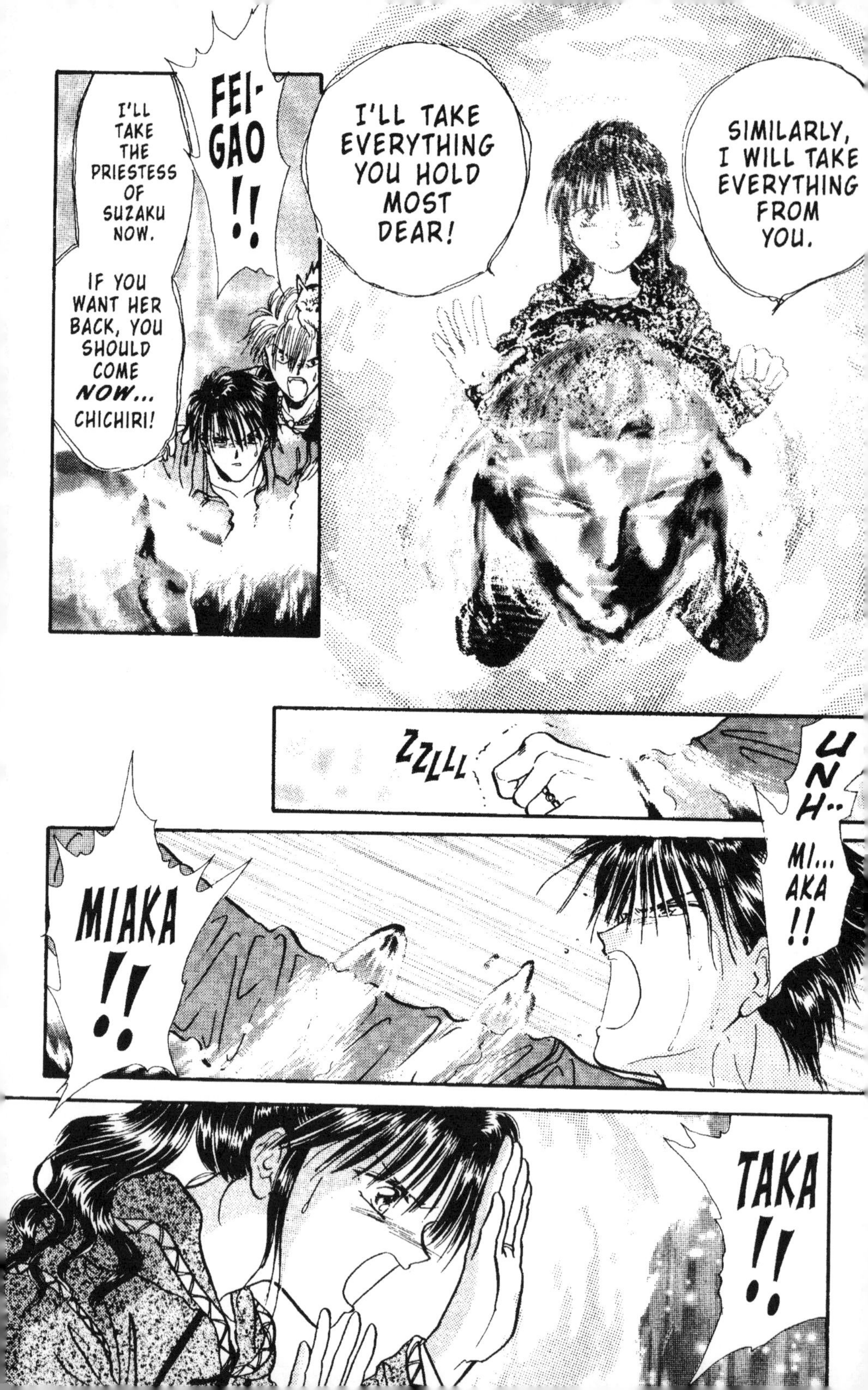
SIMILARLY, I WILL TAKE EVERYTHING FROM YOU.
I'LL TAKE EVERYTHING YOU HOLD MOST DEAR!
FEI-GAO!!
I'LL TAKE THE PRIESTESS OF SUZAKU NOW.
IF YOU WANT HER BACK, YOU SHOULD COME NOW... CHICHIRI!
UNH..
ZZLLL
MI... AKA!!
MIAKA!!
TAKA!!

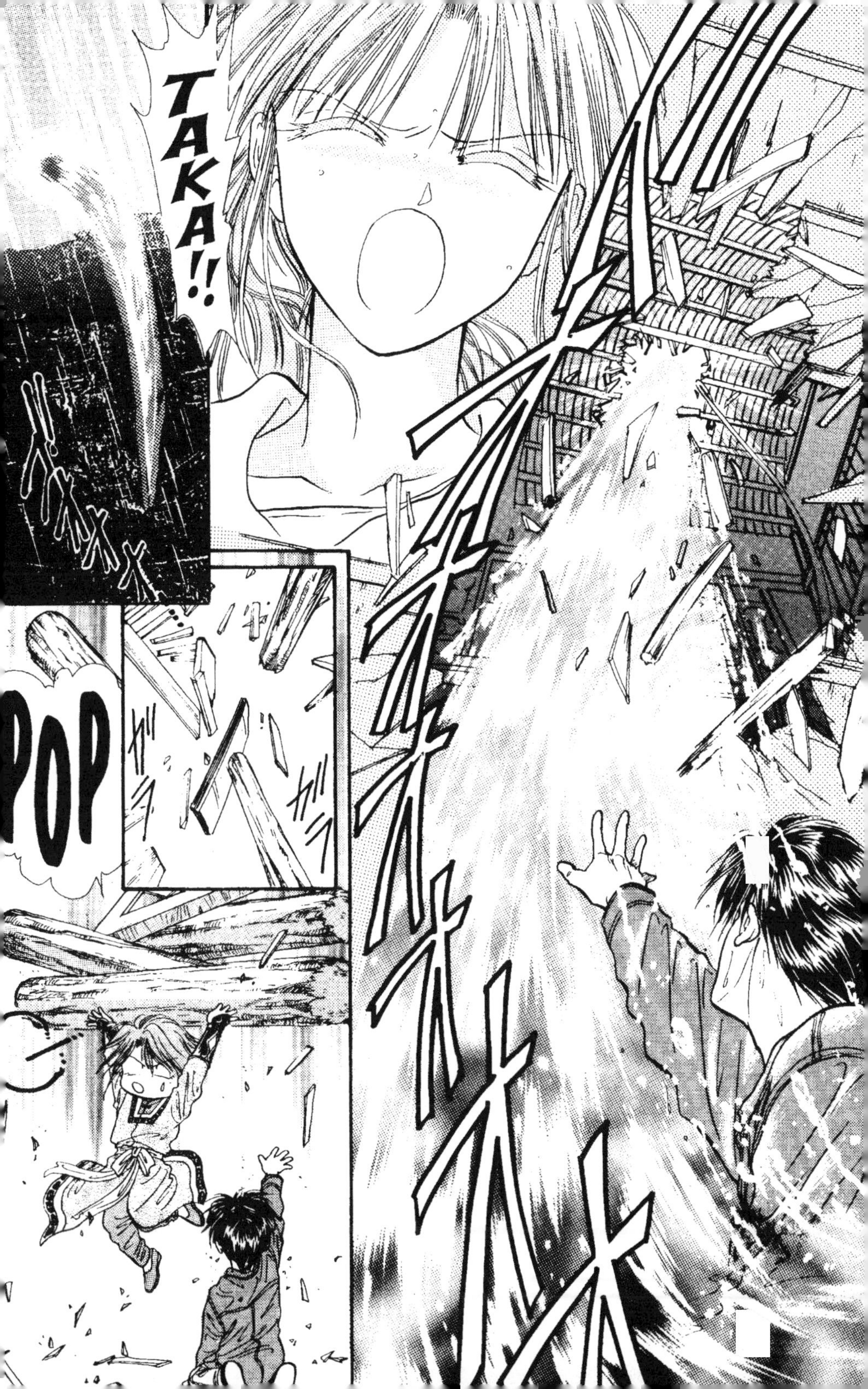
TAKA!!
POP

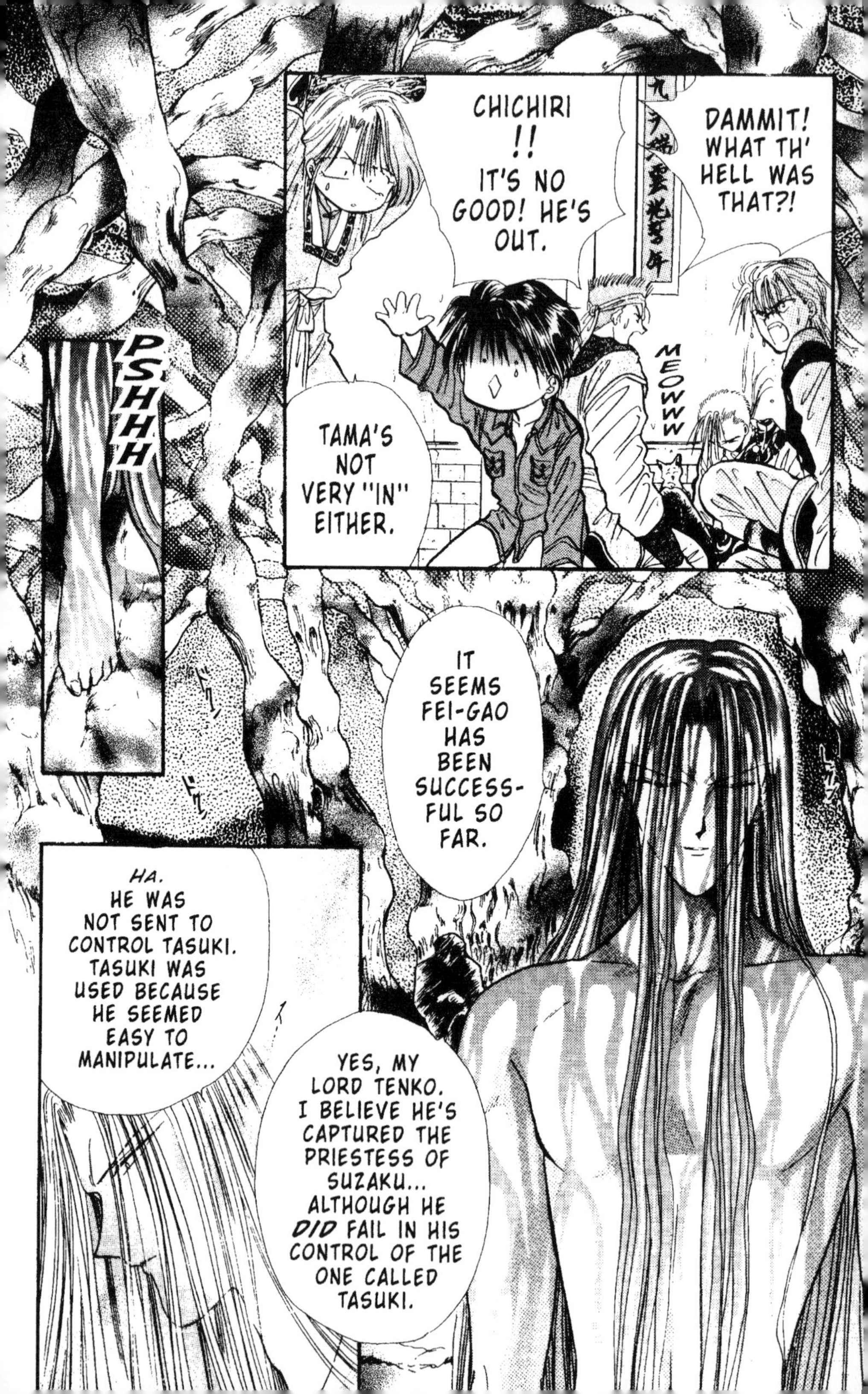

DAMMIT! WHAT TH' HELL WAS THAT?!
CHICHIRI !! IT'S NO GOOD! HE'S OUT.
MEOWWW
TAMA'S NOT VERY "IN" EITHER.
PSHHHH
IT SEEMS FEI-GAO HAS BEEN SUCCESS-FUL SO FAR.
YES, MY LORD TENKO. I BELIEVE HE'S CAPTURED THE PRIESTESS OF SUZAKU... ALTHOUGH HE *DID* FAIL IN HIS CONTROL OF THE ONE CALLED TASUKI.
HA. HE WAS NOT SENT TO CONTROL TASUKI. TASUKI WAS USED BECAUSE HE SEEMED EASY TO MANIPULATE...

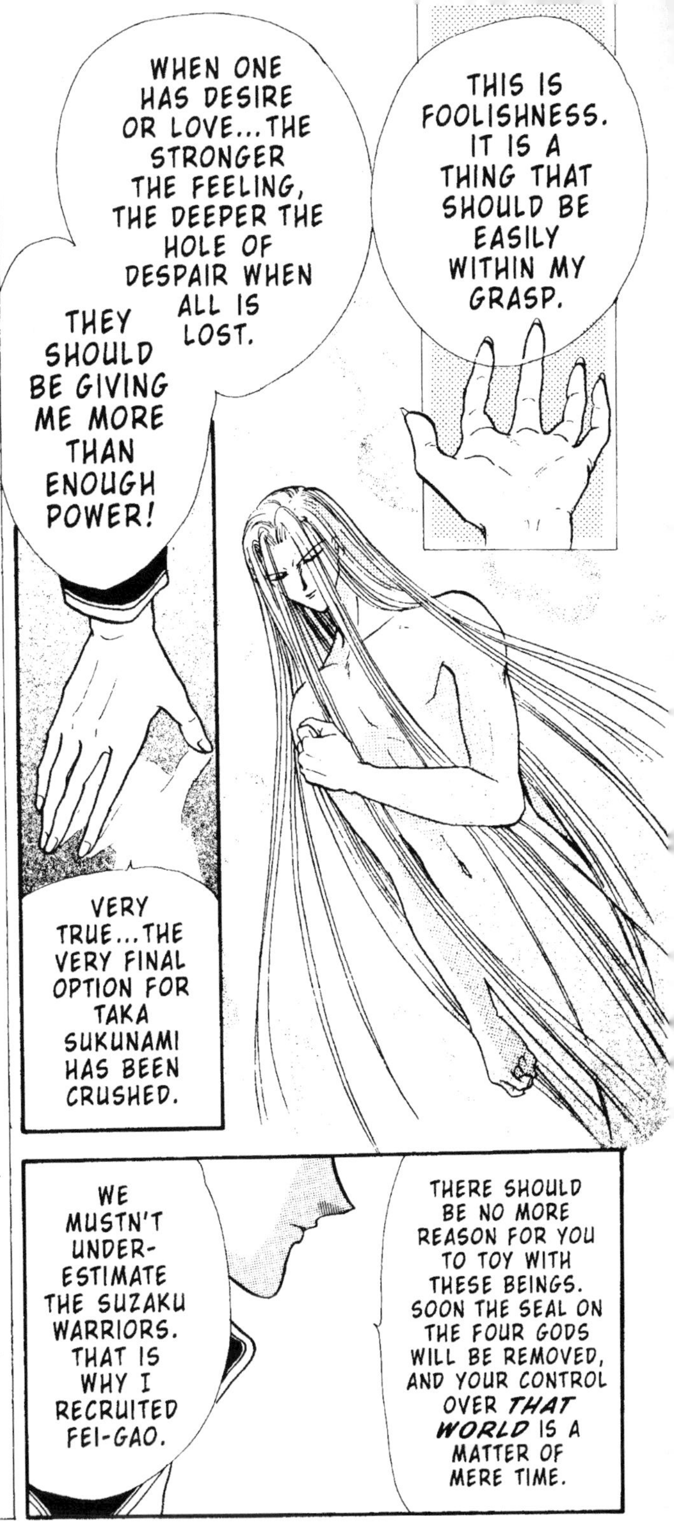
THIS IS FOOLISHNESS. IT IS A THING THAT SHOULD BE EASILY WITHIN MY GRASP.
WHEN ONE HAS DESIRE OR LOVE... THE STRONGER THE FEELING, THE DEEPER THE HOLE OF DESPAIR WHEN ALL IS LOST.
THEY SHOULD BE GIVING ME MORE THAN ENOUGH POWER!
VERY TRUE... THE VERY FINAL OPTION FOR TAKA SUKUNAMI HAS BEEN CRUSHED.
THERE SHOULD BE NO MORE REASON FOR YOU TO TOY WITH THESE BEINGS. SOON THE SEAL ON THE FOUR GODS WILL BE REMOVED, AND YOUR CONTROL OVER *THAT WORLD* IS A MATTER OF MERE TIME.
WE MUSTN'T UNDER-ESTIMATE THE SUZAKU WARRIORS. THAT IS WHY I RECRUITED FEI-GAO.

CON-TINUED... But according to my assistants, "Tasuki isn't so much after sex as wanting to give himself to someone else." Hm. That's deep. Good luck growing up, Tasuki! If I were Miaka, you'd be my number one guy! (But actually, I love Taka.)

The big break was Chichiri! The shadowy man who was putting pressure on the celestial warriors had pressure put on him by Chichiri fans throughout the entire country. (How many artists have the ego to say a thing like that?!) Sorry for keeping you waiting! Chichiri is a very strong and able warrior, but he's been living his life punishing himself for the wounds he's inflicted on others. The charms of a man who can pierce through his own defenses has really caught the eye of women everywhere (including housewives!). But, to be fair, Tasuki also has a large group of manic housewives as fans. Tama does too. Countless numbers! That's such an exaggeration!☺ And...there is a faction that's been clamoring to hear about Chichiri's past, so they should be happy...but I'll bet that soon I'll hear from a group that DIDN'T want to know! I didn't do it to please the fans, but to show his past to the other celestial warriors. Chichiri is the type to pierce through the shadows, but with the pain of this one part of his past, he probably felt that he wasn't good enough to become a Celestial Warrior. It could be that if he allowed himself to be swayed just a little more by self-doubt, he might never have joined the others. So from Chichiri's point of view, he might have done something terrible (Tasuki too), but even so, the others just take the information in without a trace of blame. Isn't that what being a friend means? (He did tell Miaka once, but it must have been a painful revelation for him. Still, he was doing it to cheer her up.)

All people, no matter who they are, have their bad sides and weaknesses. In the end, Nuriko and Chiriko beat theirs. Tamahome is fighting his inner demons even now. And since Chichiri is human too, he had to face his pain...not by fighting it, but by realizing nothing can be done about it and accepting it. That point might have been the awakening of his powers... in the midst of his sadness. But it's probably his understanding of how evil people can be that made him want to become the kind of person whom other people could depend on for protection. He's a nice guy after all.

BACKGROUND MUSIC: "SHA•RION" BY ERI. THE FIGHT SCENES ARE THE THIRD SONG FROM PANZER DRAGOON.

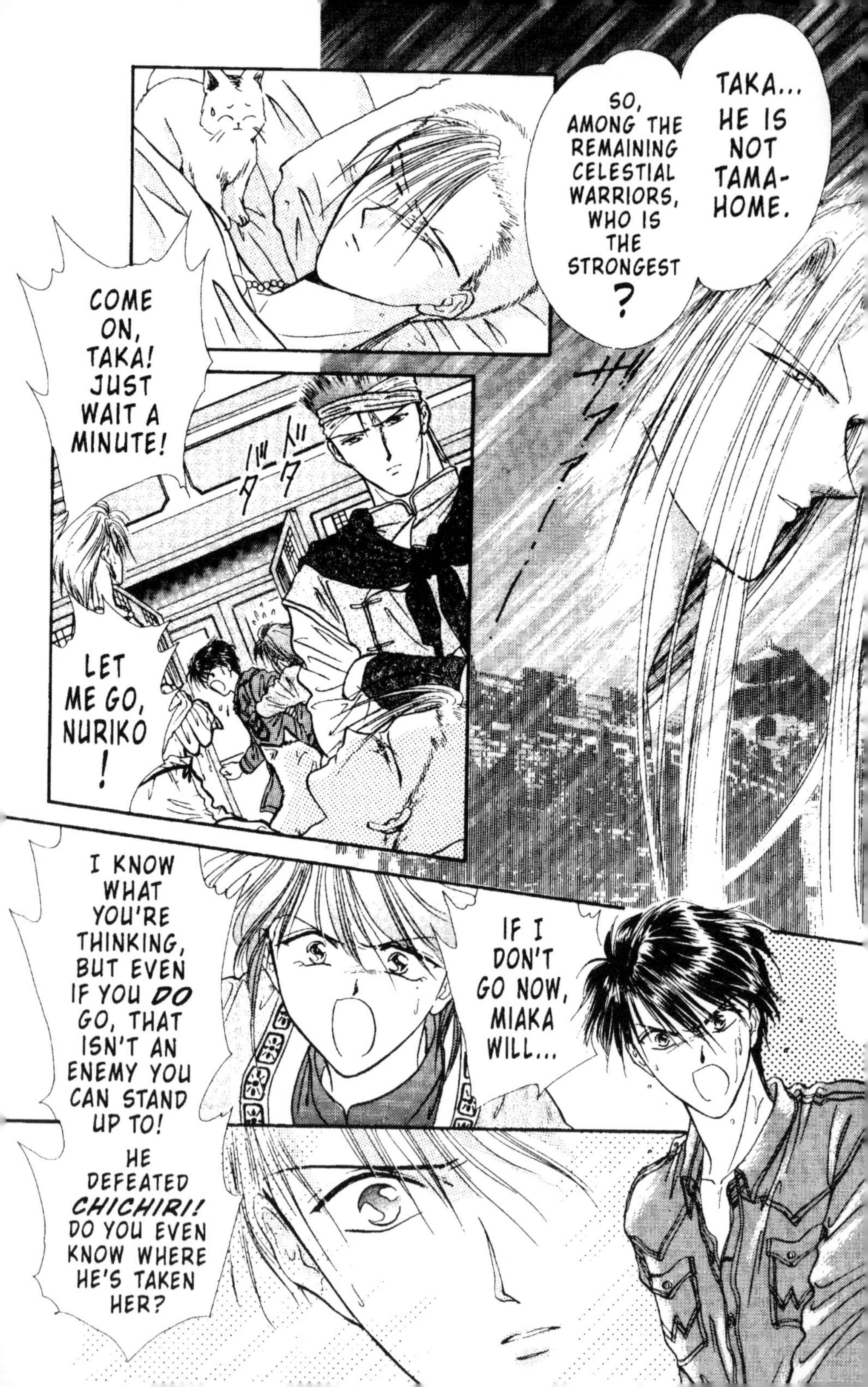
TAKA... HE IS NOT TAMA-HOME.
SO, AMONG THE REMAINING CELESTIAL WARRIORS, WHO IS THE STRONGEST?
COME ON, TAKA! JUST WAIT A MINUTE!
LET ME GO, NURIKO!
IF I DON'T GO NOW, MIAKA WILL...
I KNOW WHAT YOU'RE THINKING, BUT EVEN IF YOU *DO* GO, THAT ISN'T AN ENEMY YOU CAN STAND UP TO!
HE DEFEATED *CHICHIRI!* DO YOU EVEN KNOW WHERE HE'S TAKEN HER?

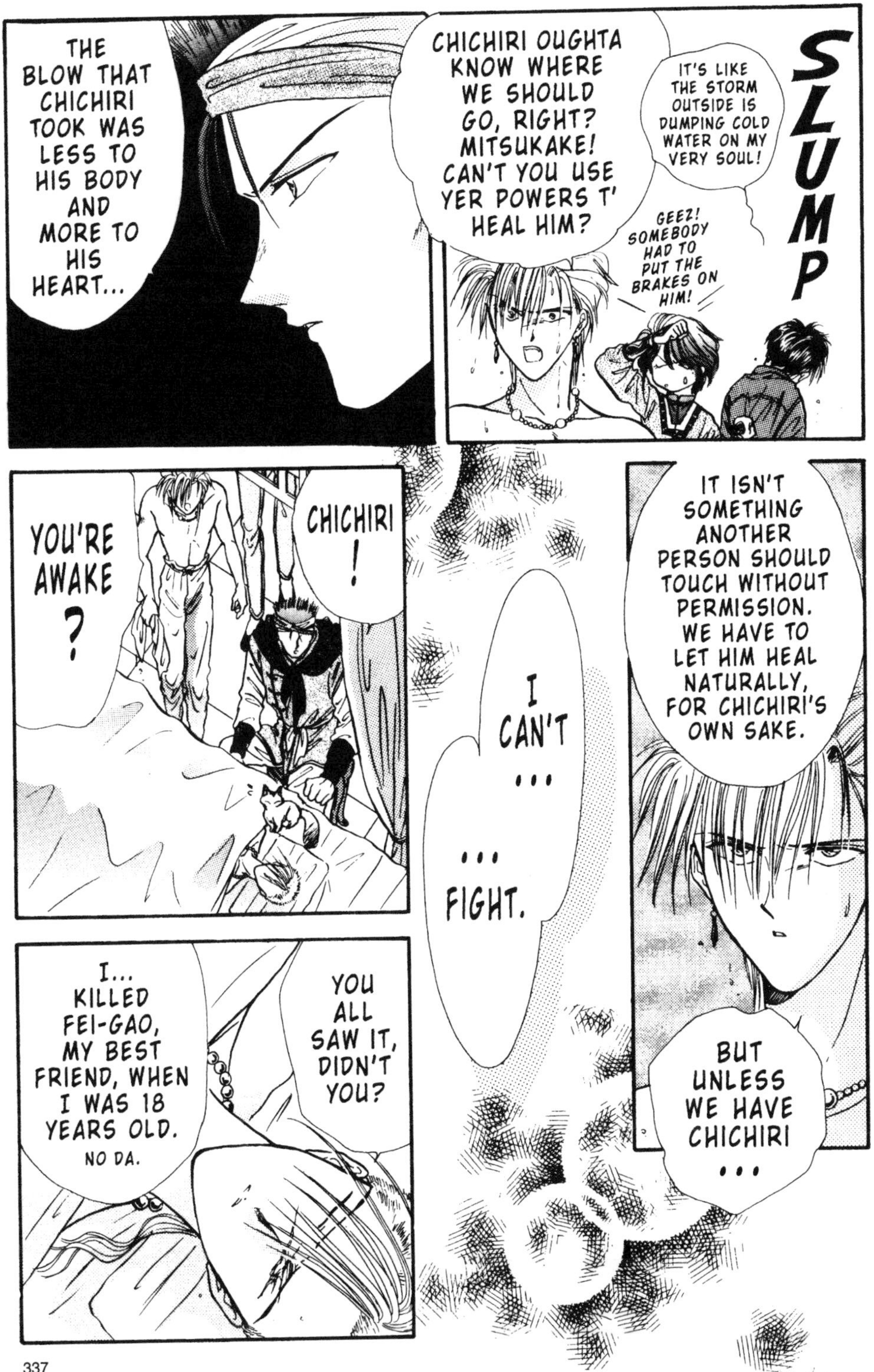
SLUMP
IT'S LIKE THE STORM OUTSIDE IS DUMPING COLD WATER ON MY VERY SOUL!
CHICHIRI OUGHTA KNOW WHERE WE SHOULD GO, RIGHT? MITSUKAKE! CAN'T YOU USE YER POWERS T' HEAL HIM?
GEEZ! SOMEBODY HAD TO PUT THE BRAKES ON HIM!
THE BLOW THAT CHICHIRI TOOK WAS LESS TO HIS BODY AND MORE TO HIS HEART...
IT ISN'T SOMETHING ANOTHER PERSON SHOULD TOUCH WITHOUT PERMISSION. WE HAVE TO LET HIM HEAL NATURALLY, FOR CHICHIRI'S OWN SAKE.
BUT UNLESS WE HAVE CHICHIRI...
I CAN'T...
...FIGHT.
CHICHIRI!
YOU'RE AWAKE?
YOU ALL SAW IT, DIDN'T YOU?
I... KILLED FEI-GAO, MY BEST FRIEND, WHEN I WAS 18 YEARS OLD. NO DA.

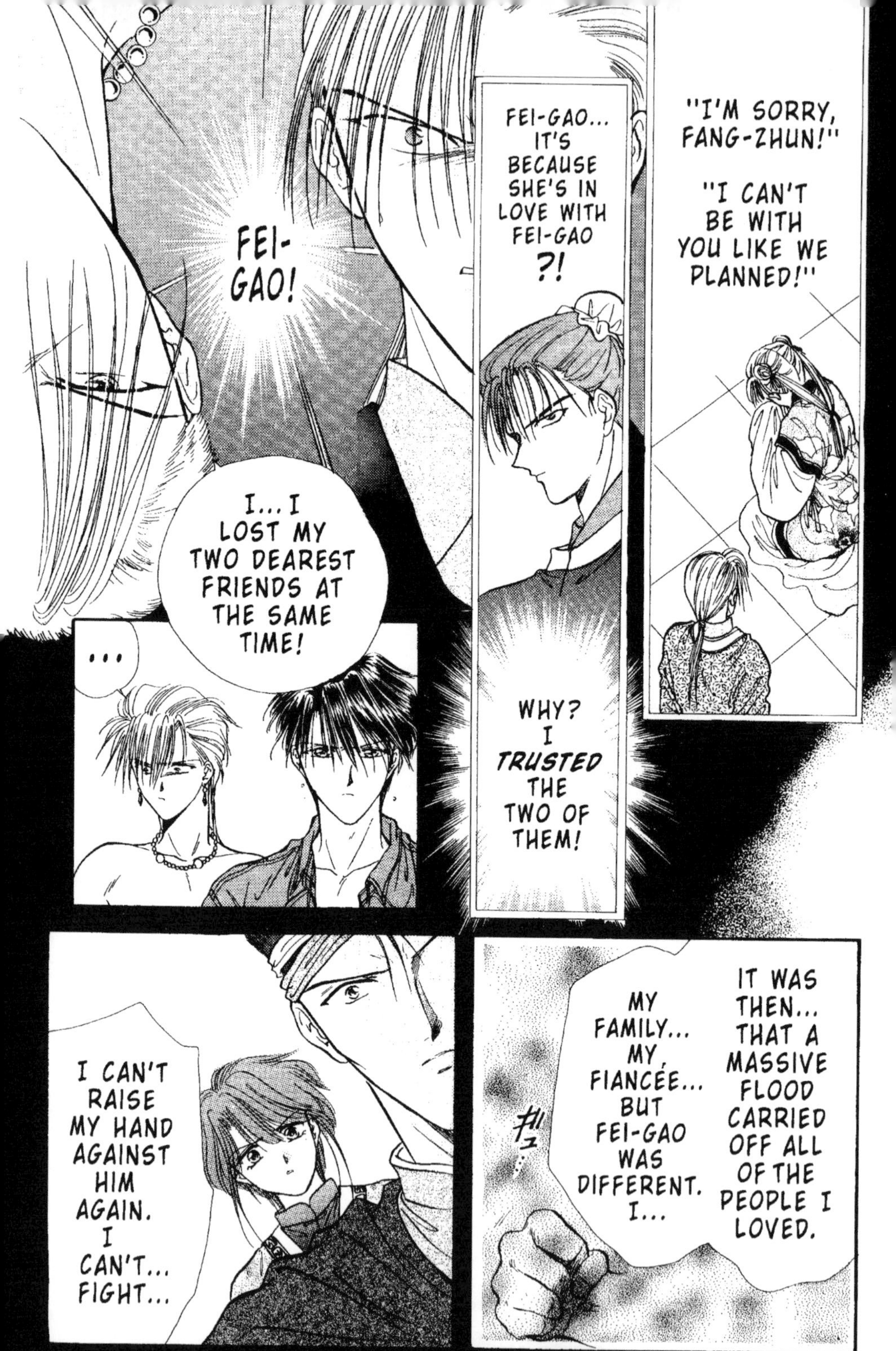
"I'M SORRY, FANG-ZHUN!"
"I CAN'T BE WITH YOU LIKE WE PLANNED!"
FEI-GAO... IT'S BECAUSE SHE'S IN LOVE WITH FEI-GAO ?!
WHY? I ***TRUSTED*** THE TWO OF THEM!
FEI-GAO!
I... I LOST MY TWO DEAREST FRIENDS AT THE SAME TIME!
...
IT WAS THEN... THAT A MASSIVE FLOOD CARRIED OFF ALL OF THE PEOPLE I LOVED.
MY FAMILY... MY FIANCÉE... BUT FEI-GAO WAS DIFFERENT. I...
ギュ...
I CAN'T RAISE MY HAND AGAINST HIM AGAIN. I CAN'T... FIGHT...

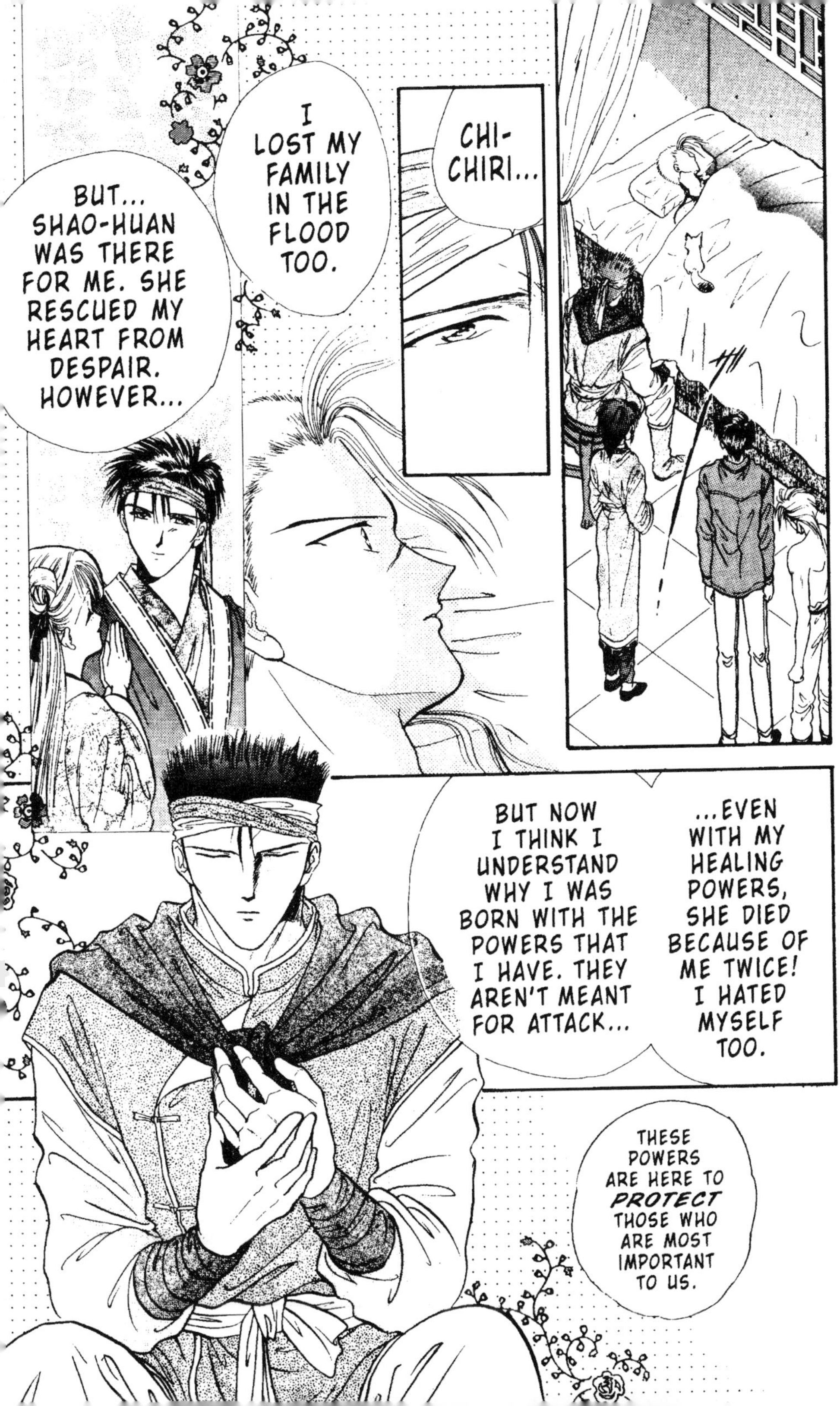
CHI-CHIRI...
I LOST MY FAMILY IN THE FLOOD TOO.
BUT... SHAO-HUAN WAS THERE FOR ME. SHE RESCUED MY HEART FROM DESPAIR. HOWEVER...
...EVEN WITH MY HEALING POWERS, SHE DIED BECAUSE OF ME TWICE! I HATED MYSELF TOO.
BUT NOW I THINK I UNDERSTAND WHY I WAS BORN WITH THE POWERS THAT I HAVE. THEY AREN'T MEANT FOR ATTACK...
THESE POWERS ARE HERE TO *PROTECT* THOSE WHO ARE MOST IMPORTANT TO US.

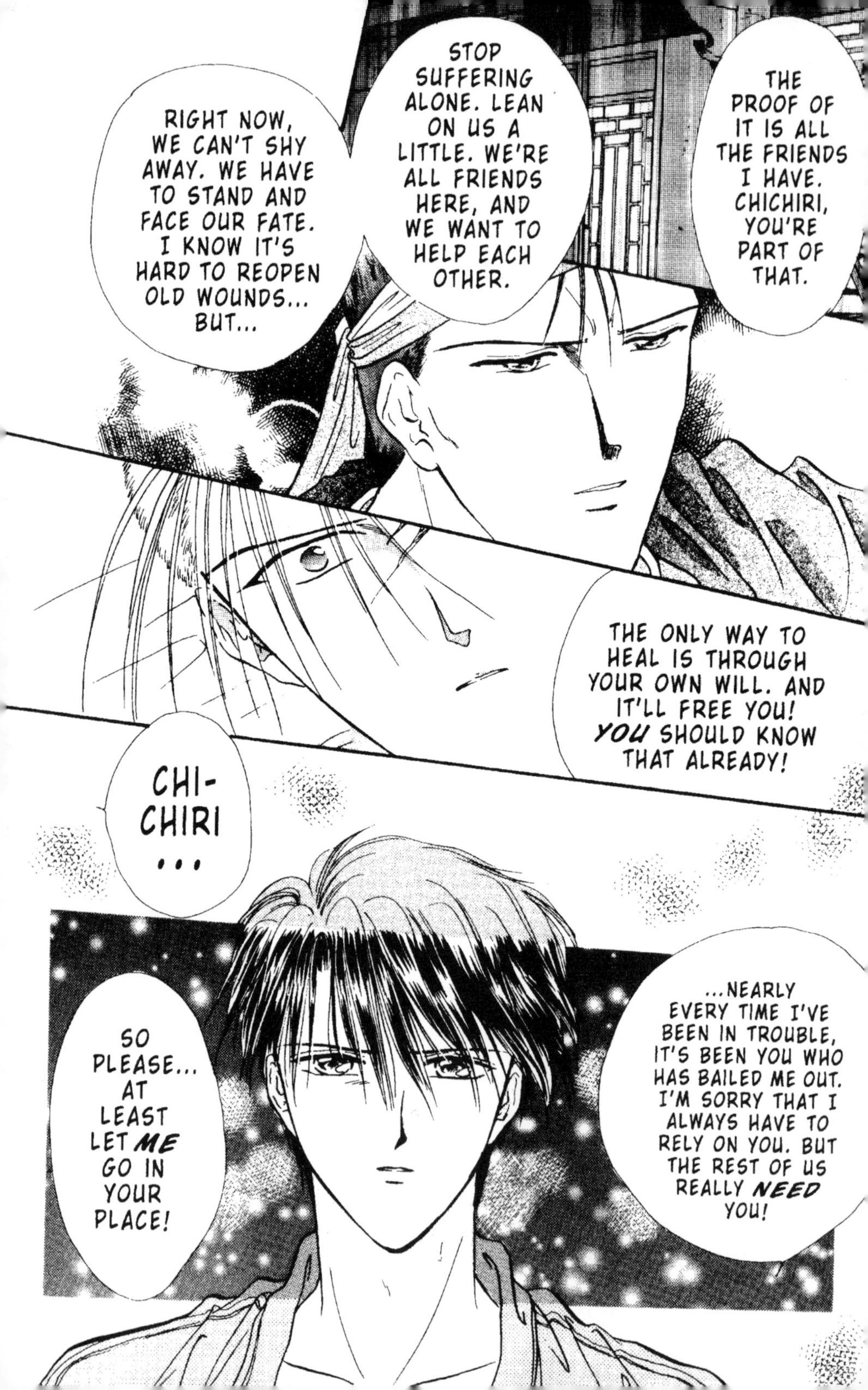
THE PROOF OF IT IS ALL THE FRIENDS I HAVE. CHICHIRI, YOU'RE PART OF THAT.
STOP SUFFERING ALONE. LEAN ON US A LITTLE. WE'RE ALL FRIENDS HERE, AND WE WANT TO HELP EACH OTHER.
RIGHT NOW, WE CAN'T SHY AWAY. WE HAVE TO STAND AND FACE OUR FATE. I KNOW IT'S HARD TO REOPEN OLD WOUNDS... BUT...
THE ONLY WAY TO HEAL IS THROUGH YOUR OWN WILL. AND IT'LL FREE YOU! *YOU* SHOULD KNOW THAT ALREADY!
CHI-CHIRI ...
...NEARLY EVERY TIME I'VE BEEN IN TROUBLE, IT'S BEEN YOU WHO HAS BAILED ME OUT. I'M SORRY THAT I ALWAYS HAVE TO RELY ON YOU. BUT THE REST OF US REALLY *NEED* YOU!
SO PLEASE... AT LEAST LET *ME* GO IN YOUR PLACE!

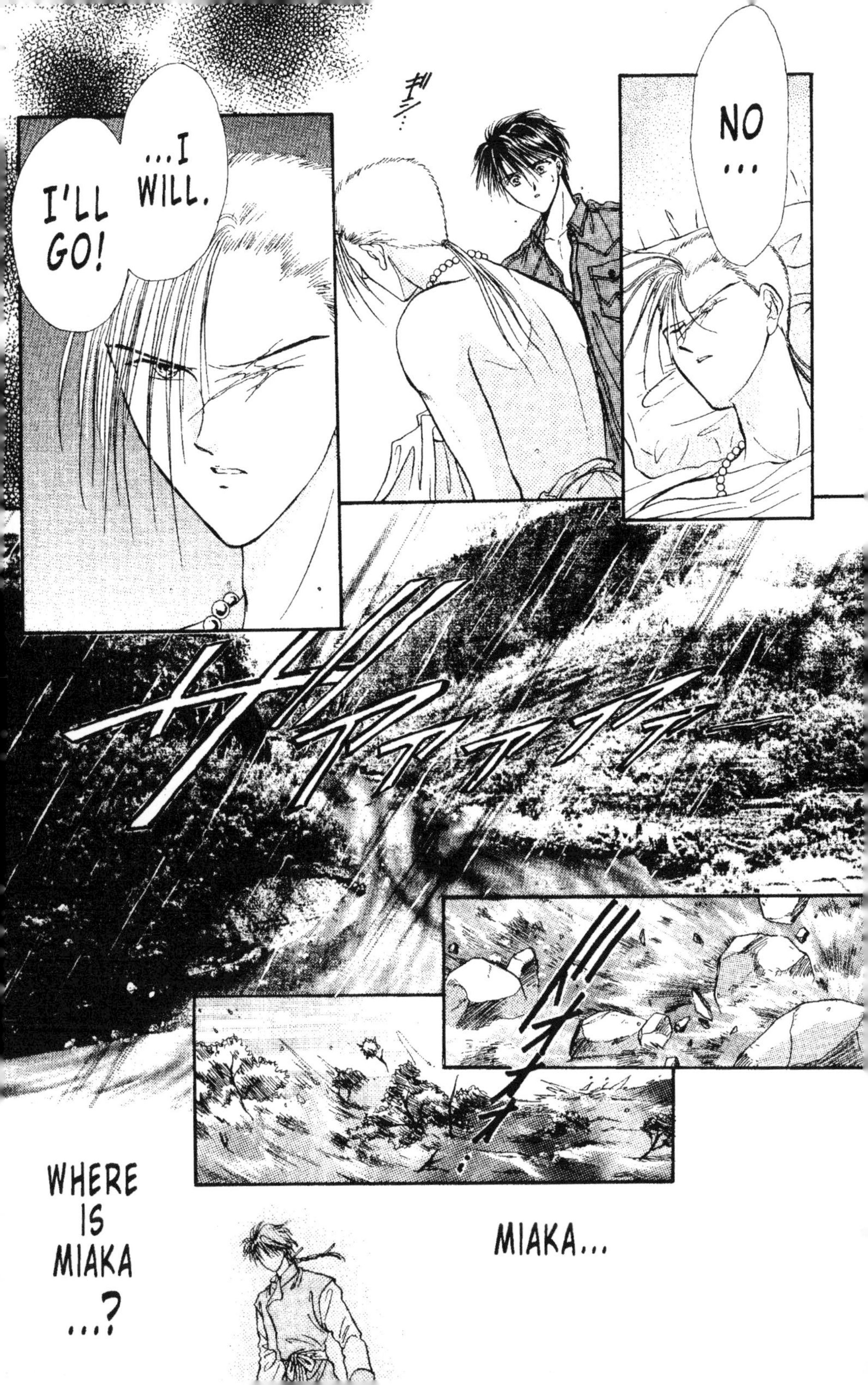
NO...
...I WILL.
I'LL GO!
MIAKA...
WHERE IS MIAKA ...?

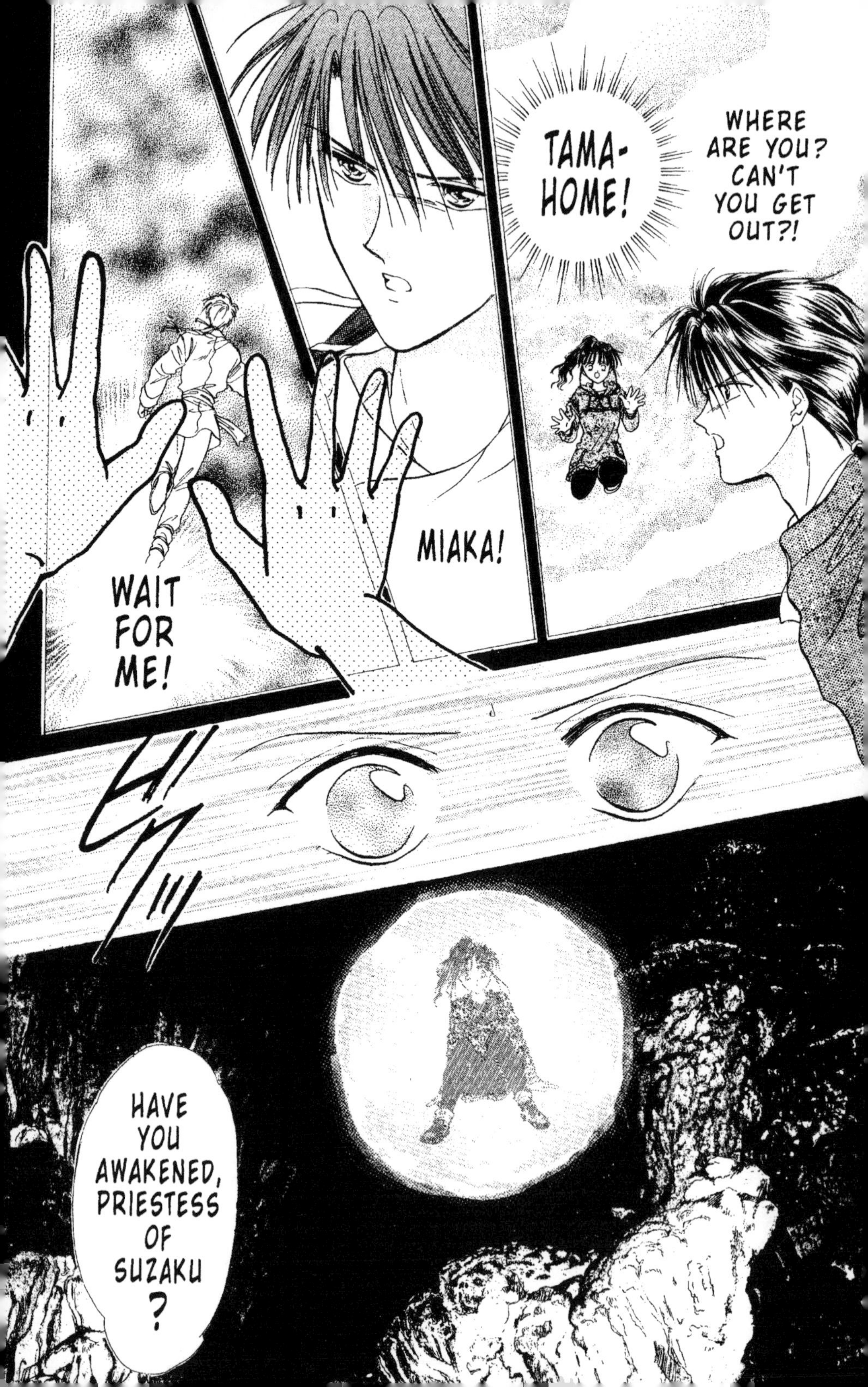
WHERE ARE YOU? CAN'T YOU GET OUT?!
TAMA-HOME!
MIAKA!
WAIT FOR ME!
HAVE YOU AWAKENED, PRIESTESS OF SUZAKU?

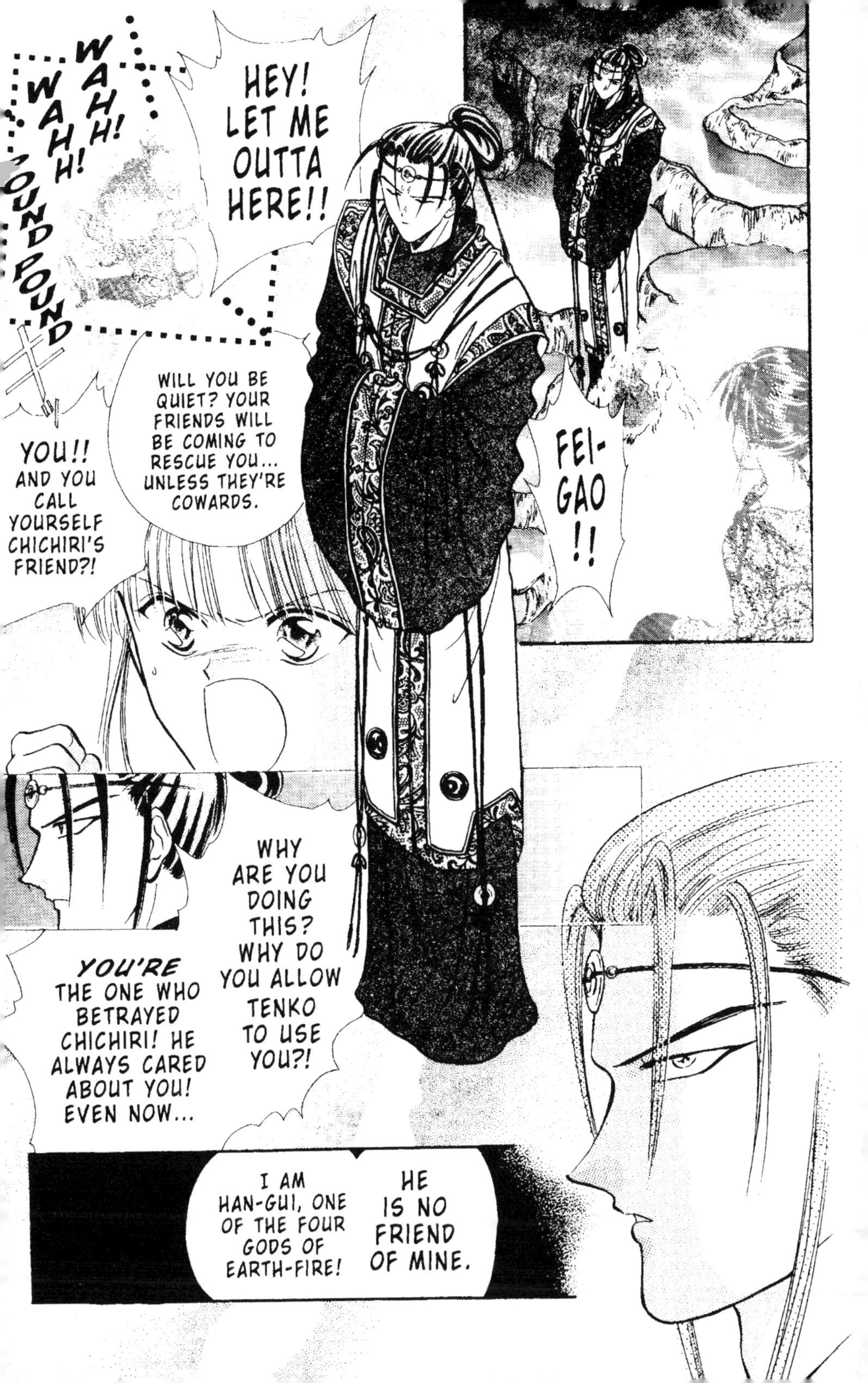
FEI-GAO!!
HEY! LET ME OUTTA HERE!!
WAHH! WAHH!
POUND POUND
WILL YOU BE QUIET? YOUR FRIENDS WILL BE COMING TO RESCUE YOU... UNLESS THEY'RE COWARDS.
YOU!! AND YOU CALL YOURSELF CHICHIRI'S FRIEND?!
WHY ARE YOU DOING THIS? WHY DO YOU ALLOW TENKO TO USE YOU?!
YOU'RE THE ONE WHO BETRAYED CHICHIRI! HE ALWAYS CARED ABOUT YOU! EVEN NOW...
HE IS NO FRIEND OF MINE.
I AM HAN-GUI, ONE OF THE FOUR GODS OF EARTH-FIRE!

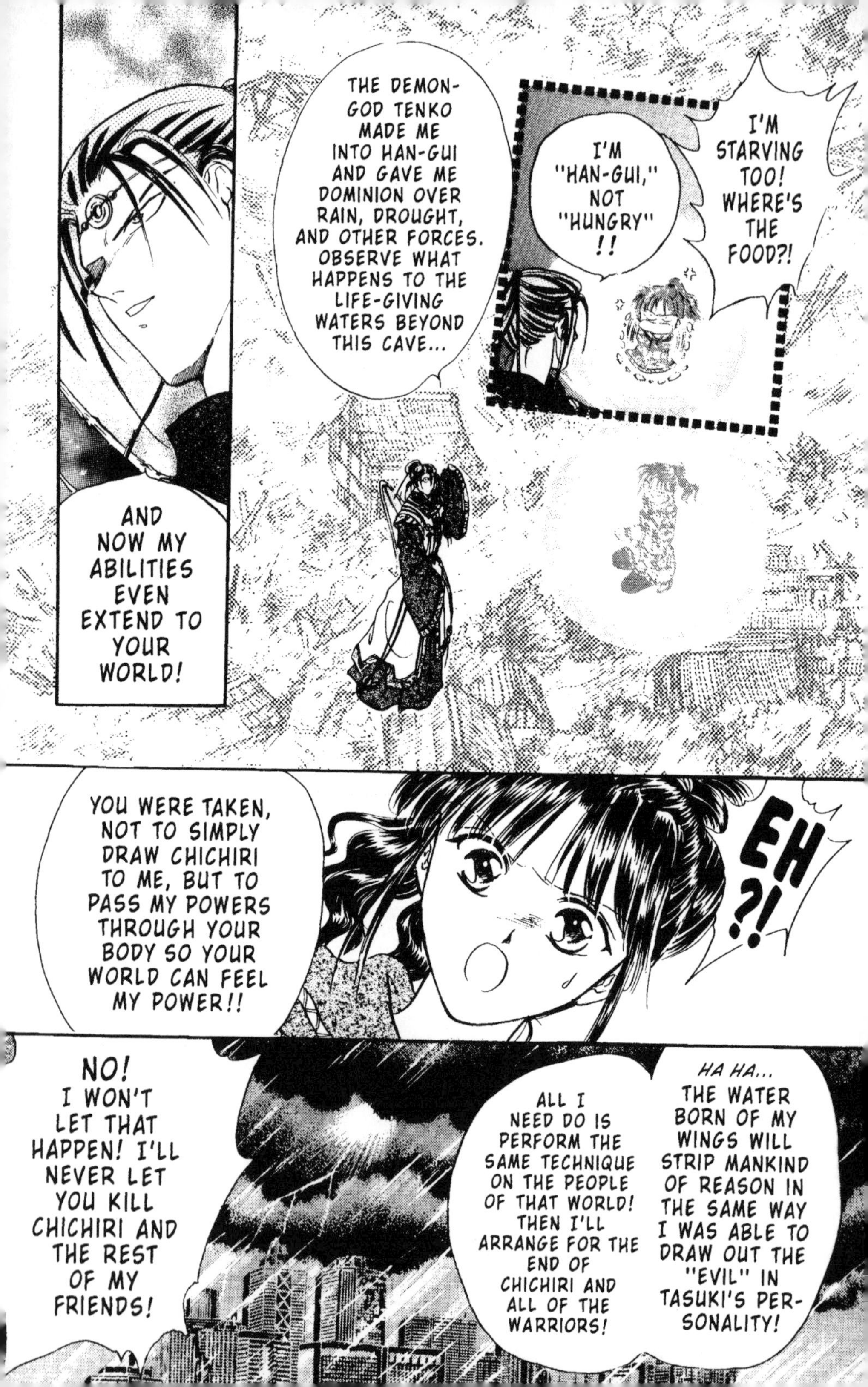
I'M STARVING TOO! WHERE'S THE FOOD?!
I'M "HAN-GUI," NOT "HUNGRY"!!
THE DEMON-GOD TENKO MADE ME INTO HAN-GUI AND GAVE ME DOMINION OVER RAIN, DROUGHT, AND OTHER FORCES. OBSERVE WHAT HAPPENS TO THE LIFE-GIVING WATERS BEYOND THIS CAVE...
AND NOW MY ABILITIES EVEN EXTEND TO YOUR WORLD!
EH?!
YOU WERE TAKEN, NOT TO SIMPLY DRAW CHICHIRI TO ME, BUT TO PASS MY POWERS THROUGH YOUR BODY SO YOUR WORLD CAN FEEL MY POWER!!
HA HA... THE WATER BORN OF MY WINGS WILL STRIP MANKIND OF REASON IN THE SAME WAY I WAS ABLE TO DRAW OUT THE "EVIL" IN TASUKI'S PERSONALITY!
ALL I NEED DO IS PERFORM THE SAME TECHNIQUE ON THE PEOPLE OF THAT WORLD! THEN I'LL ARRANGE FOR THE END OF CHICHIRI AND ALL OF THE WARRIORS!
NO! I WON'T LET THAT HAPPEN! I'LL NEVER LET YOU KILL CHICHIRI AND THE REST OF MY FRIENDS!

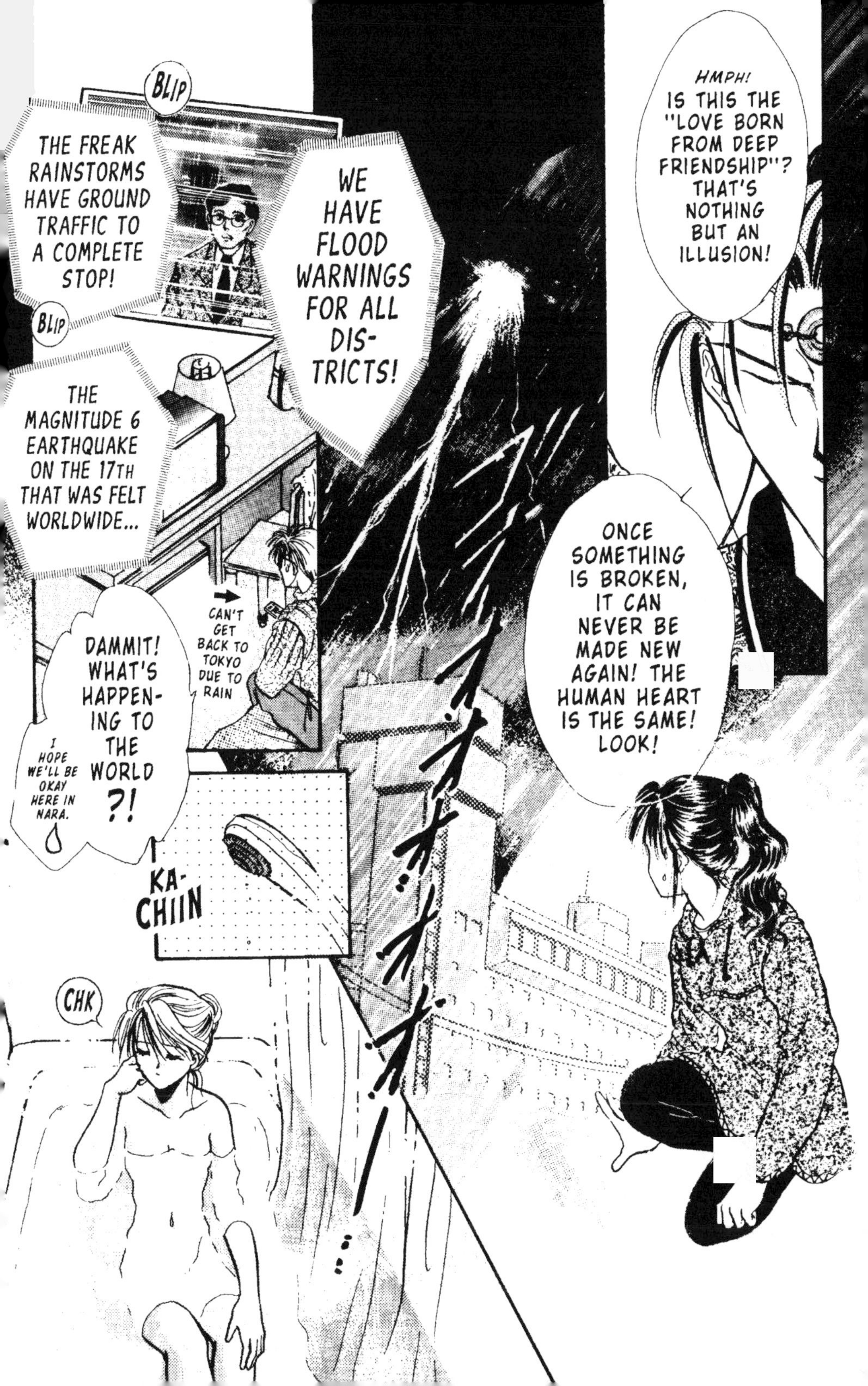
HMPH! IS THIS THE "LOVE BORN FROM DEEP FRIENDSHIP"? THAT'S NOTHING BUT AN ILLUSION!
ONCE SOMETHING IS BROKEN, IT CAN NEVER BE MADE NEW AGAIN! THE HUMAN HEART IS THE SAME! LOOK!
BLIP
THE FREAK RAINSTORMS HAVE GROUND TRAFFIC TO A COMPLETE STOP!
WE HAVE FLOOD WARNINGS FOR ALL DIS-TRICTS!
BLIP
THE MAGNITUDE 6 EARTHQUAKE ON THE 17TH THAT WAS FELT WORLDWIDE...
CAN'T GET BACK TO TOKYO DUE TO RAIN
DAMMIT! WHAT'S HAPPEN-ING TO THE WORLD ?!
I HOPE WE'LL BE OKAY HERE IN NARA.
KA-CHIIN
...
CHK

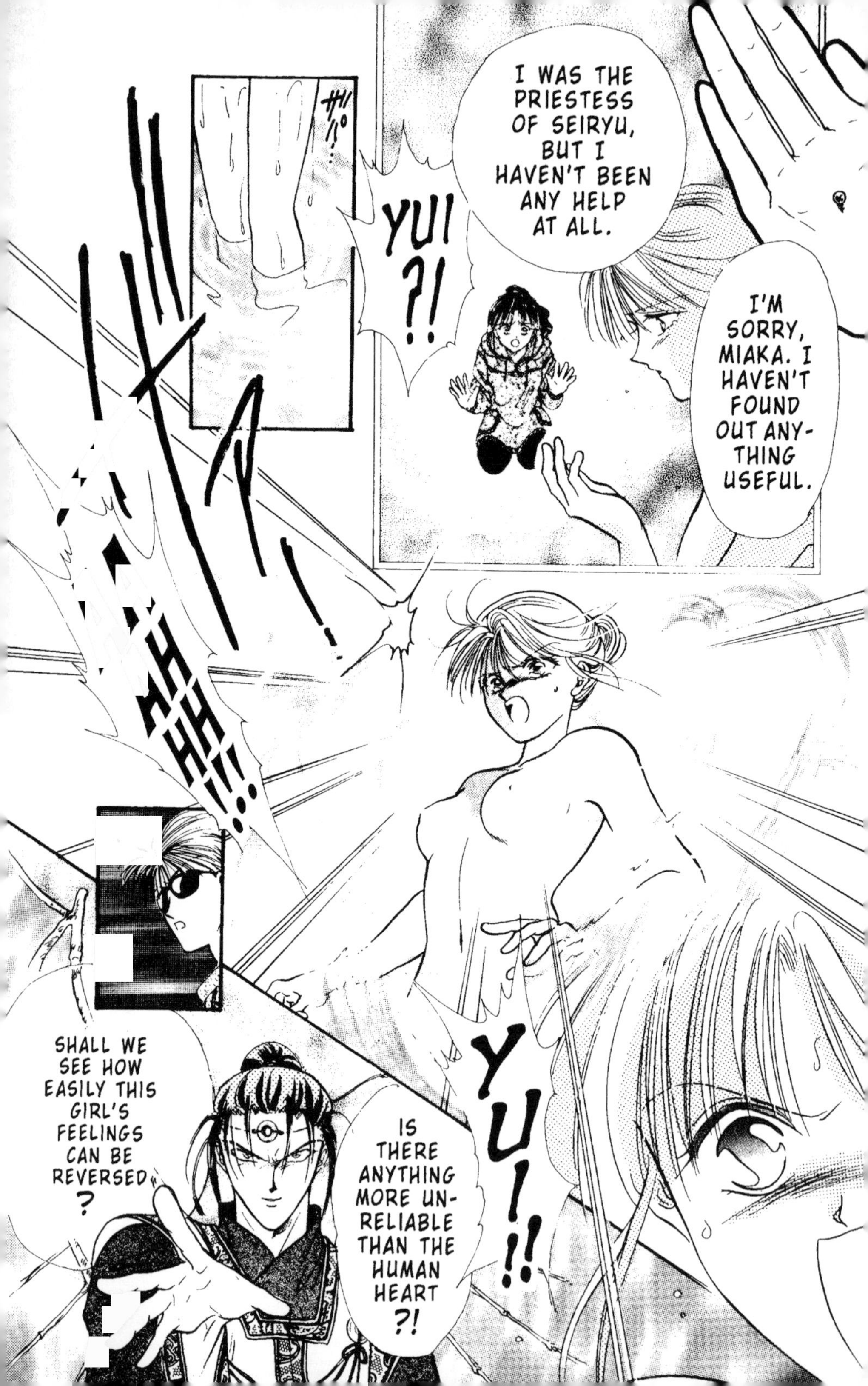
I WAS THE PRIESTESS OF SEIRYU, BUT I HAVEN'T BEEN ANY HELP AT ALL.
I'M SORRY, MIAKA. I HAVEN'T FOUND OUT ANY-THING USEFUL.
YUI?!
YUI!!
IS THERE ANYTHING MORE UN-RELIABLE THAN THE HUMAN HEART?!
SHALL WE SEE HOW EASILY THIS GIRL'S FEELINGS CAN BE REVERSED?

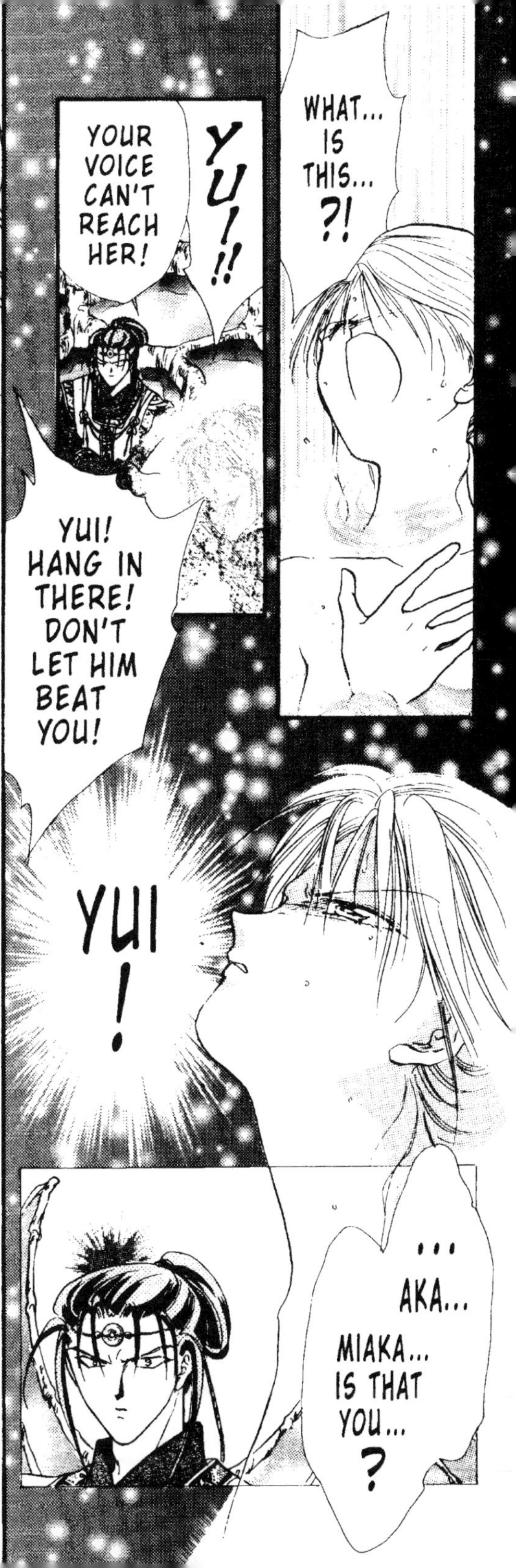
WHAT... IS THIS... ?!
YUI!!
YOUR VOICE CAN'T REACH HER!
YUI! HANG IN THERE! DON'T LET HIM BEAT YOU!
YUI!
...AKA... MIAKA... IS THAT YOU...?
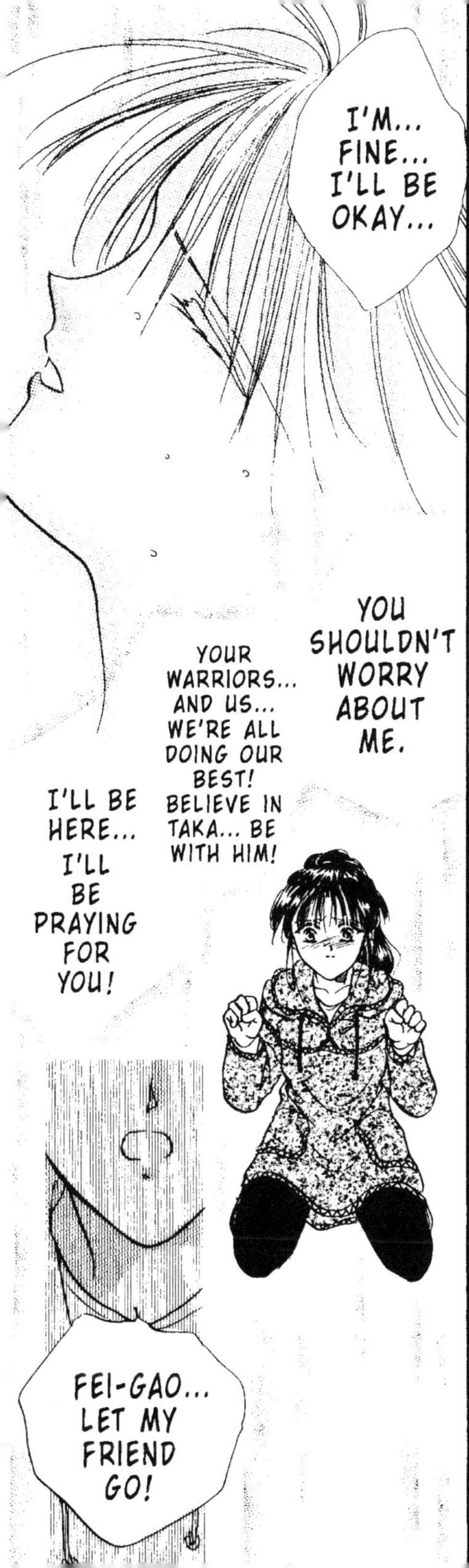
I'M... FINE... I'LL BE OKAY...
YOU SHOULDN'T WORRY ABOUT ME.
YOUR WARRIORS... AND US... WE'RE ALL DOING OUR BEST! BELIEVE IN TAKA... BE WITH HIM!
I'LL BE HERE... I'LL BE PRAYING FOR YOU!
FEI-GAO... LET MY FRIEND GO!

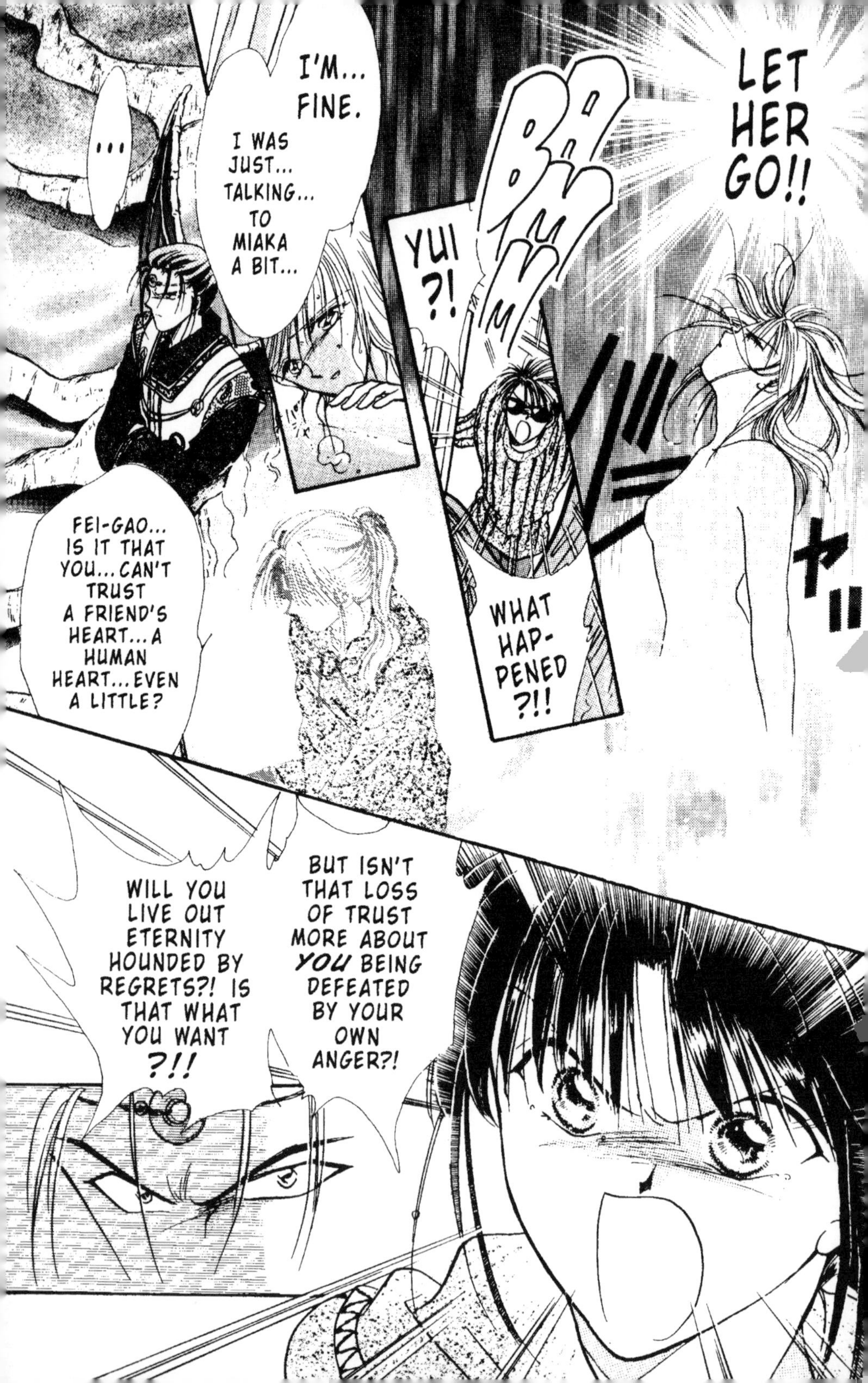
LET HER GO!!
BAMMM
YUI?!
WHAT HAPPENED?!!
I'M... FINE.
I WAS JUST... TALKING... TO MIAKA A BIT...
...
FEI-GAO... IS IT THAT YOU... CAN'T TRUST A FRIEND'S HEART... A HUMAN HEART... EVEN A LITTLE?
BUT ISN'T THAT LOSS OF TRUST MORE ABOUT *YOU* BEING DEFEATED BY YOUR OWN ANGER?!
WILL YOU LIVE OUT ETERNITY HOUNDED BY REGRETS?! IS THAT WHAT YOU WANT ?!!

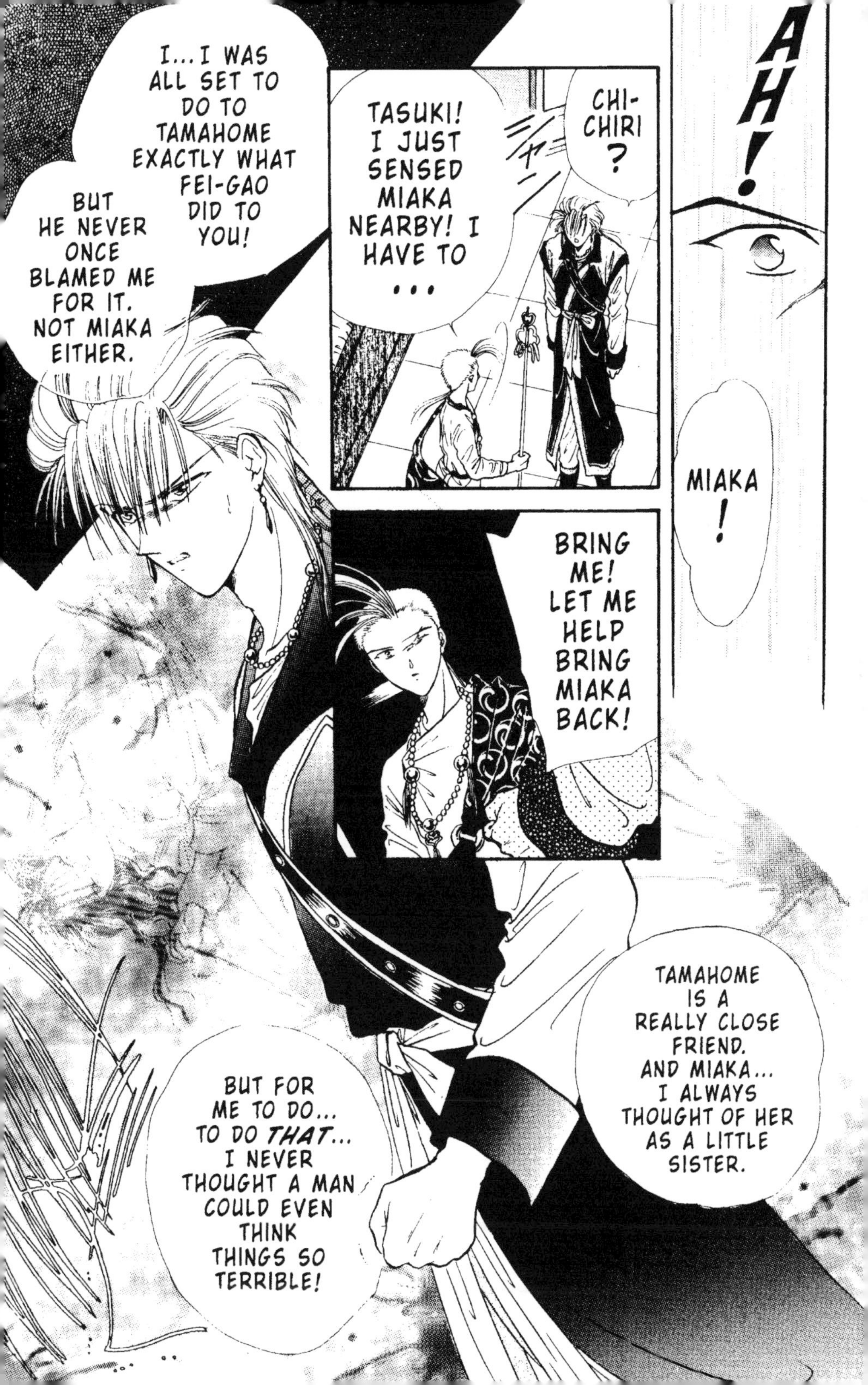
AH!
MIAKA!
CHI-CHIRI?
TASUKI! I JUST SENSED MIAKA NEARBY! I HAVE TO ...
I... I WAS ALL SET TO DO TO TAMAHOME EXACTLY WHAT FEI-GAO DID TO YOU!
BUT HE NEVER ONCE BLAMED ME FOR IT. NOT MIAKA EITHER.
BRING ME! LET ME HELP BRING MIAKA BACK!
TAMAHOME IS A REALLY CLOSE FRIEND. AND MIAKA... I ALWAYS THOUGHT OF HER AS A LITTLE SISTER.
BUT FOR ME TO DO... TO DO *THAT*... I NEVER THOUGHT A MAN COULD EVEN THINK THINGS SO TERRIBLE!

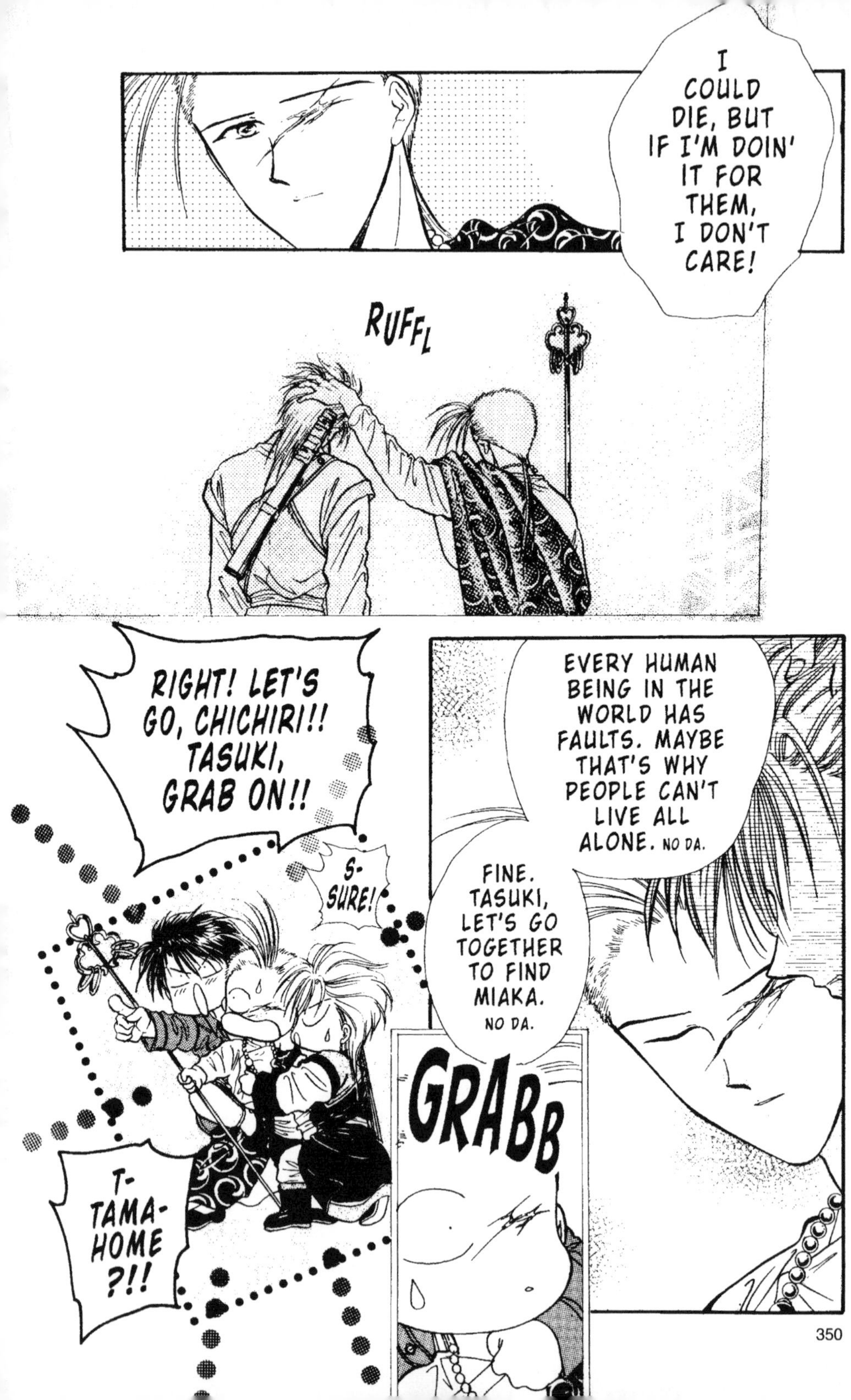
I COULD DIE, BUT IF I'M DOIN' IT FOR THEM, I DON'T CARE!
RUFFL
EVERY HUMAN BEING IN THE WORLD HAS FAULTS. MAYBE THAT'S WHY PEOPLE CAN'T LIVE ALL ALONE. NO DA.
FINE. TASUKI, LET'S GO TOGETHER TO FIND MIAKA. NO DA.
GRABB
RIGHT! LET'S GO, CHICHIRI!! TASUKI, GRAB ON!!
S-SURE!
T-TAMA-HOME?!!

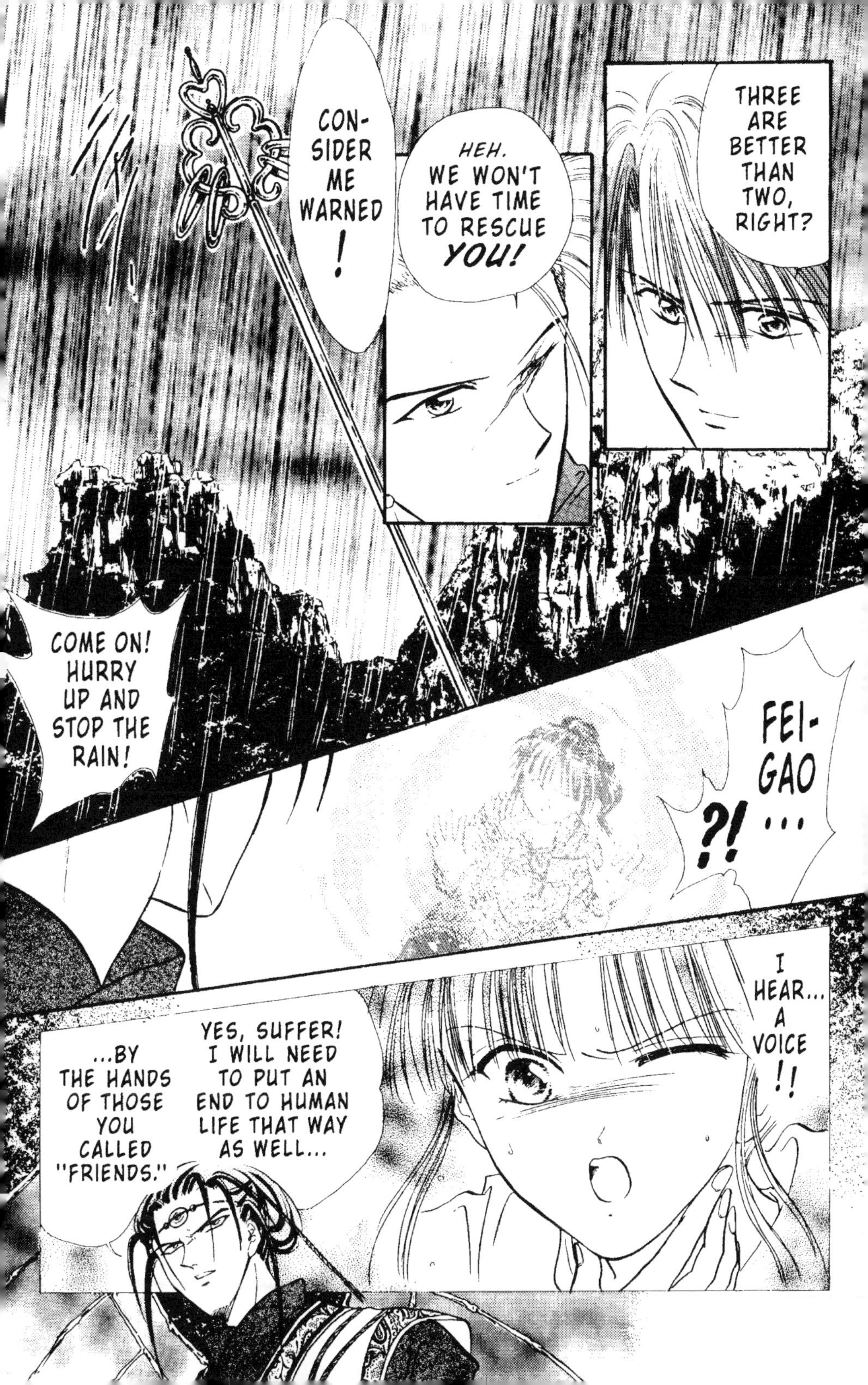
THREE ARE BETTER THAN TWO, RIGHT?
HEH. WE WON'T HAVE TIME TO RESCUE YOU!
CON-SIDER ME WARNED!
COME ON! HURRY UP AND STOP THE RAIN!
FEI-GAO...
?!
I HEAR... A VOICE!!
YES, SUFFER! I WILL NEED TO PUT AN END TO HUMAN LIFE THAT WAY AS WELL...
...BY THE HANDS OF THOSE YOU CALLED "FRIENDS."

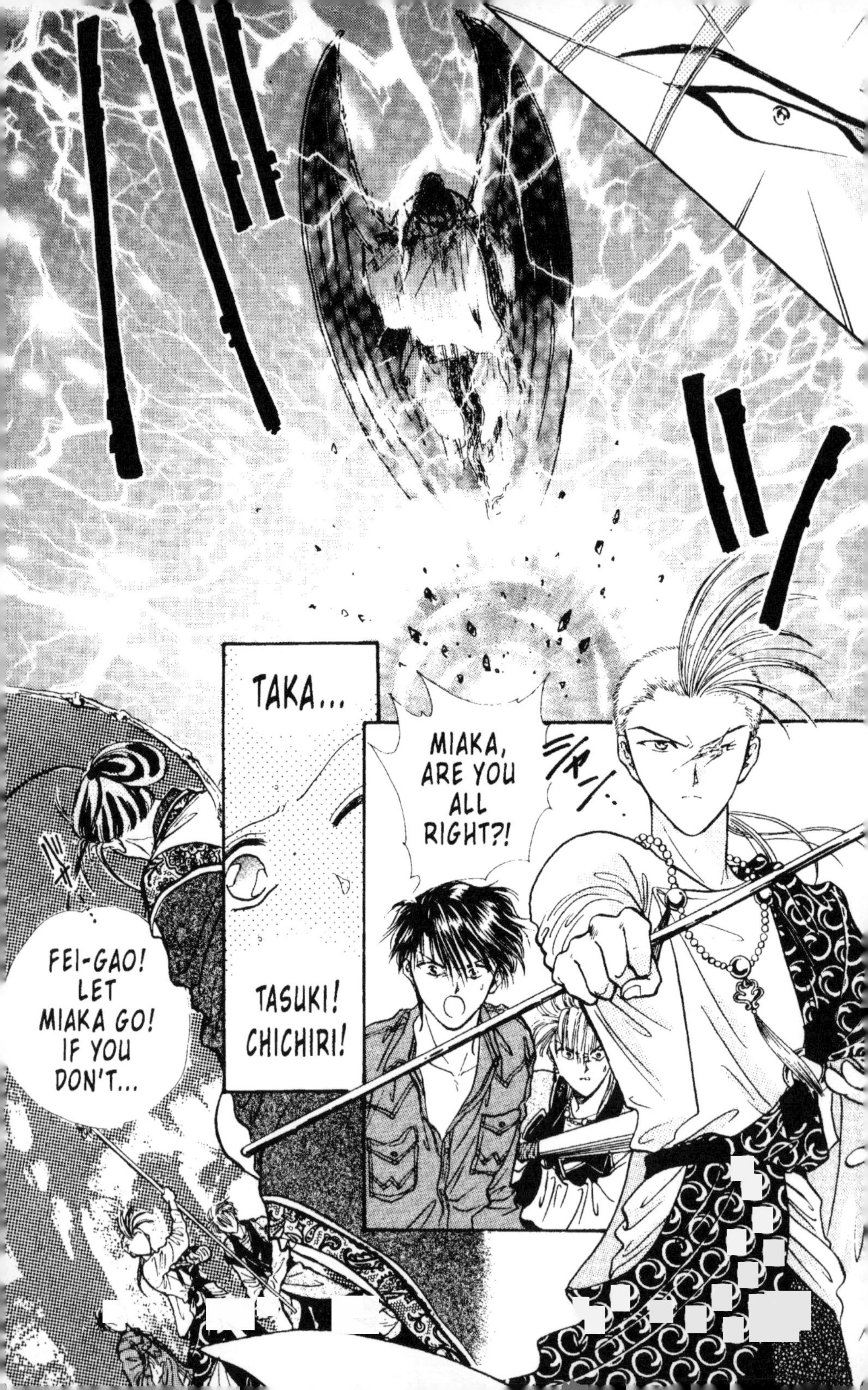
MIAKA, ARE YOU ALL RIGHT?!
TAKA...
TASUKI! CHICHIRI!
FEI-GAO! LET MIAKA GO! IF YOU DON'T...

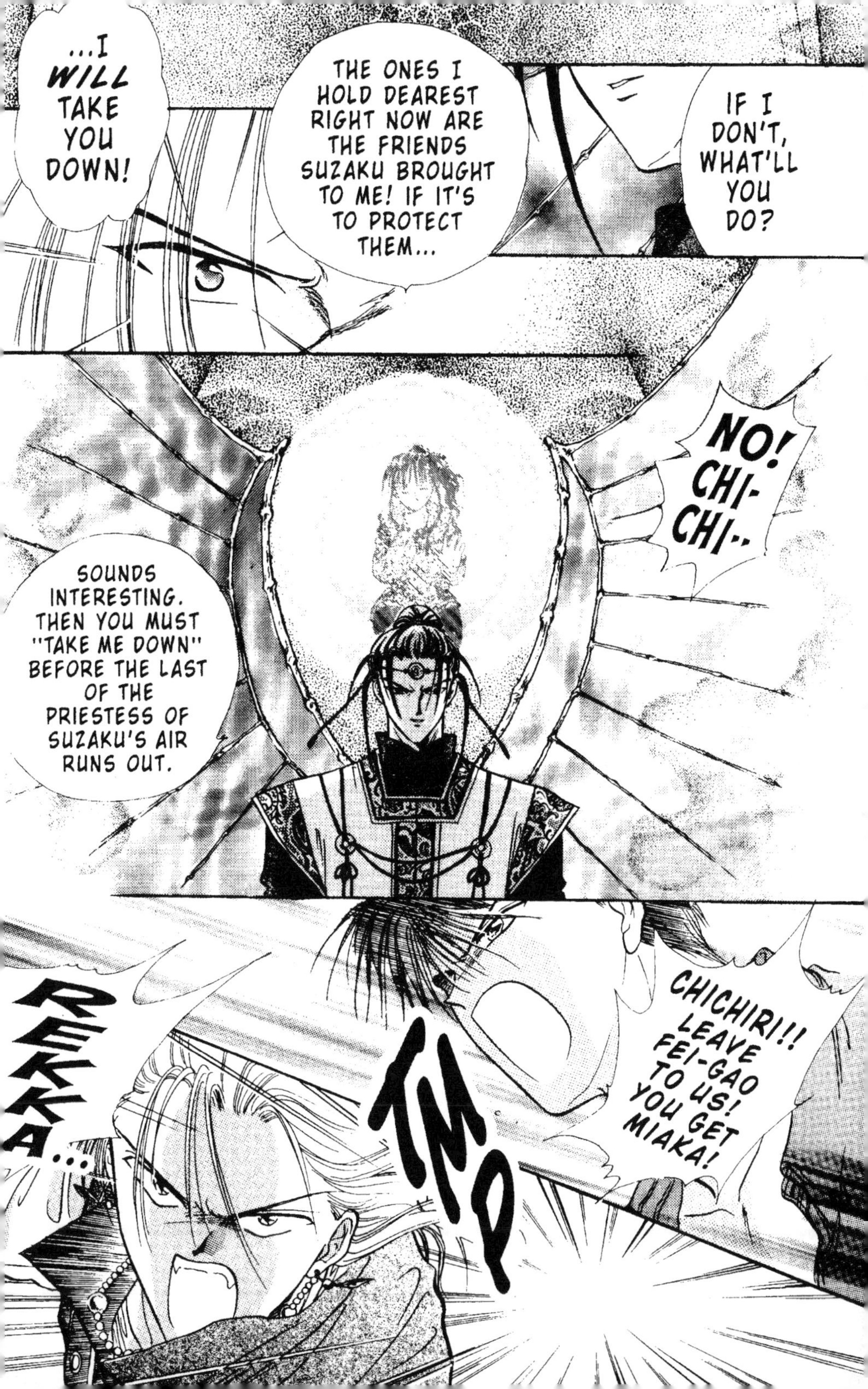
IF I DON'T, WHAT'LL YOU DO?
THE ONES I HOLD DEAREST RIGHT NOW ARE THE FRIENDS SUZAKU BROUGHT TO ME! IF IT'S TO PROTECT THEM...
...I WILL TAKE YOU DOWN!
NO! CHI-CHI..
SOUNDS INTERESTING. THEN YOU MUST "TAKE ME DOWN" BEFORE THE LAST OF THE PRIESTESS OF SUZAKU'S AIR RUNS OUT.
CHICHIRI!! LEAVE FEI-GAO TO US! YOU GET MIAKA!
TMP
REKKA...

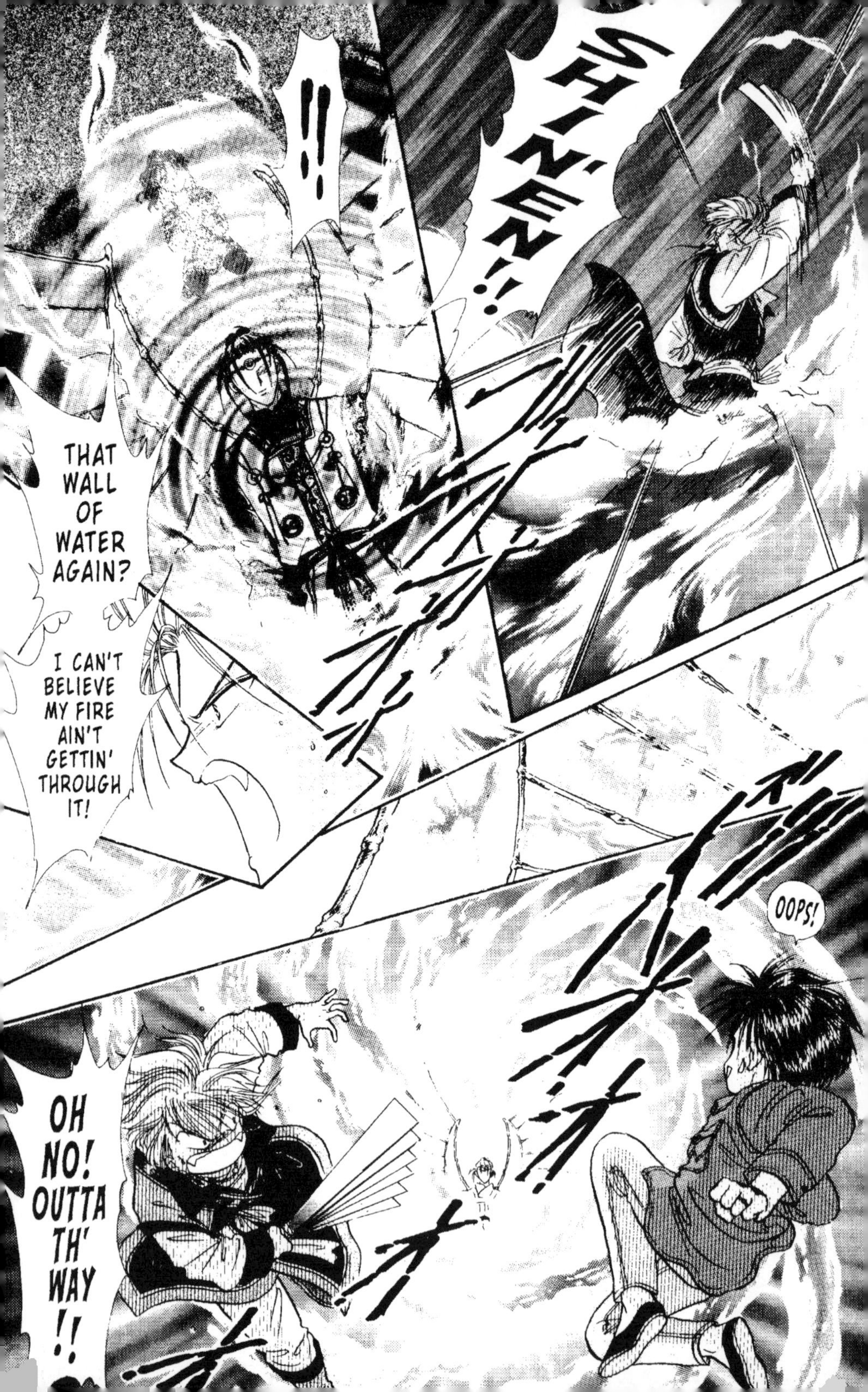
SHIN'EN!!
!!!
THAT WALL OF WATER AGAIN?
I CAN'T BELIEVE MY FIRE AIN'T GETTIN' THROUGH IT!
OOPS!
OH NO! OUTTA TH' WAY!!

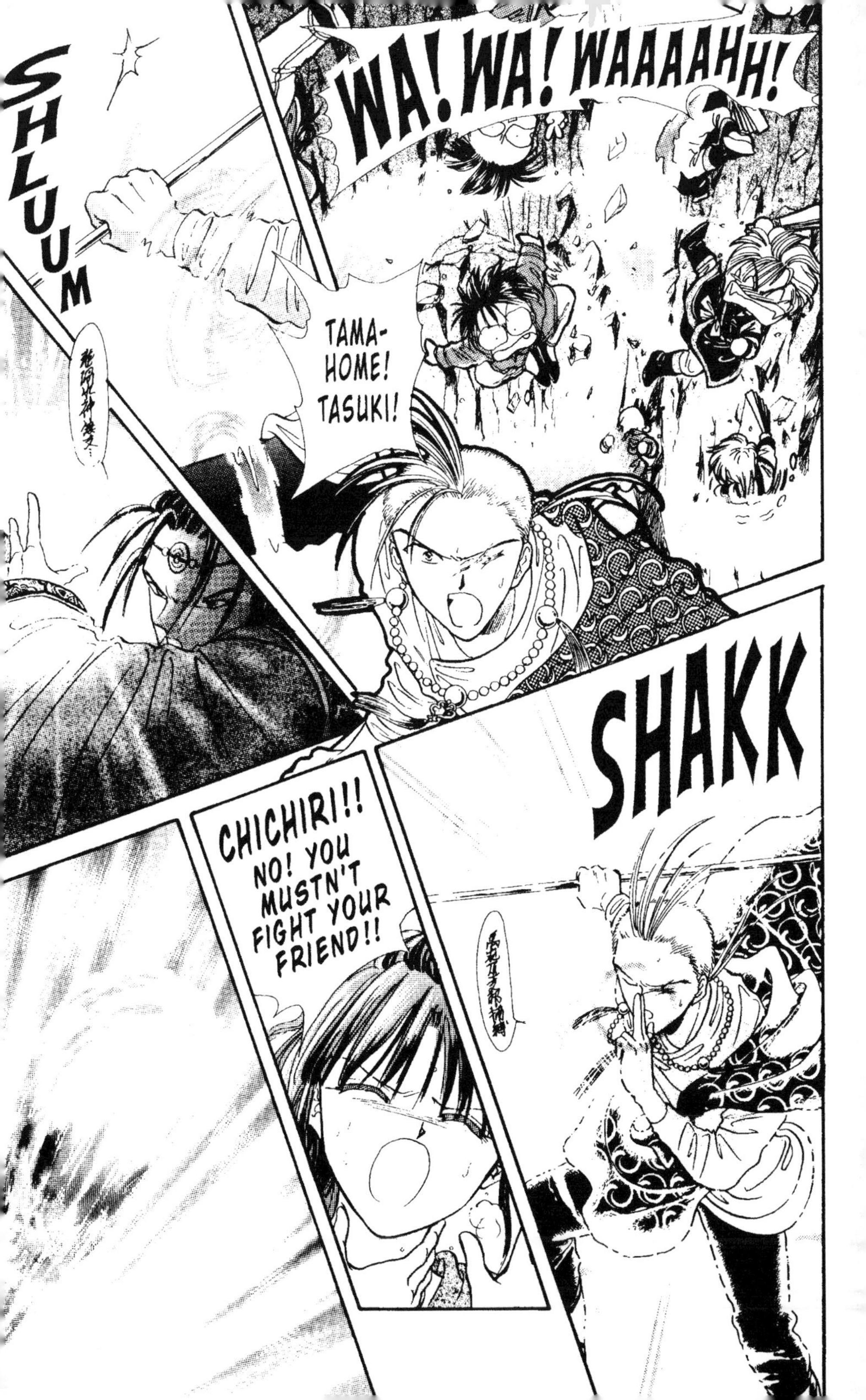
WA! WA! WAAAAHH!
TAMA-HOME! TASUKI!
SHLUUM
SHAKK
CHICHIRI!! NO! YOU MUSTN'T FIGHT YOUR FRIEND!!

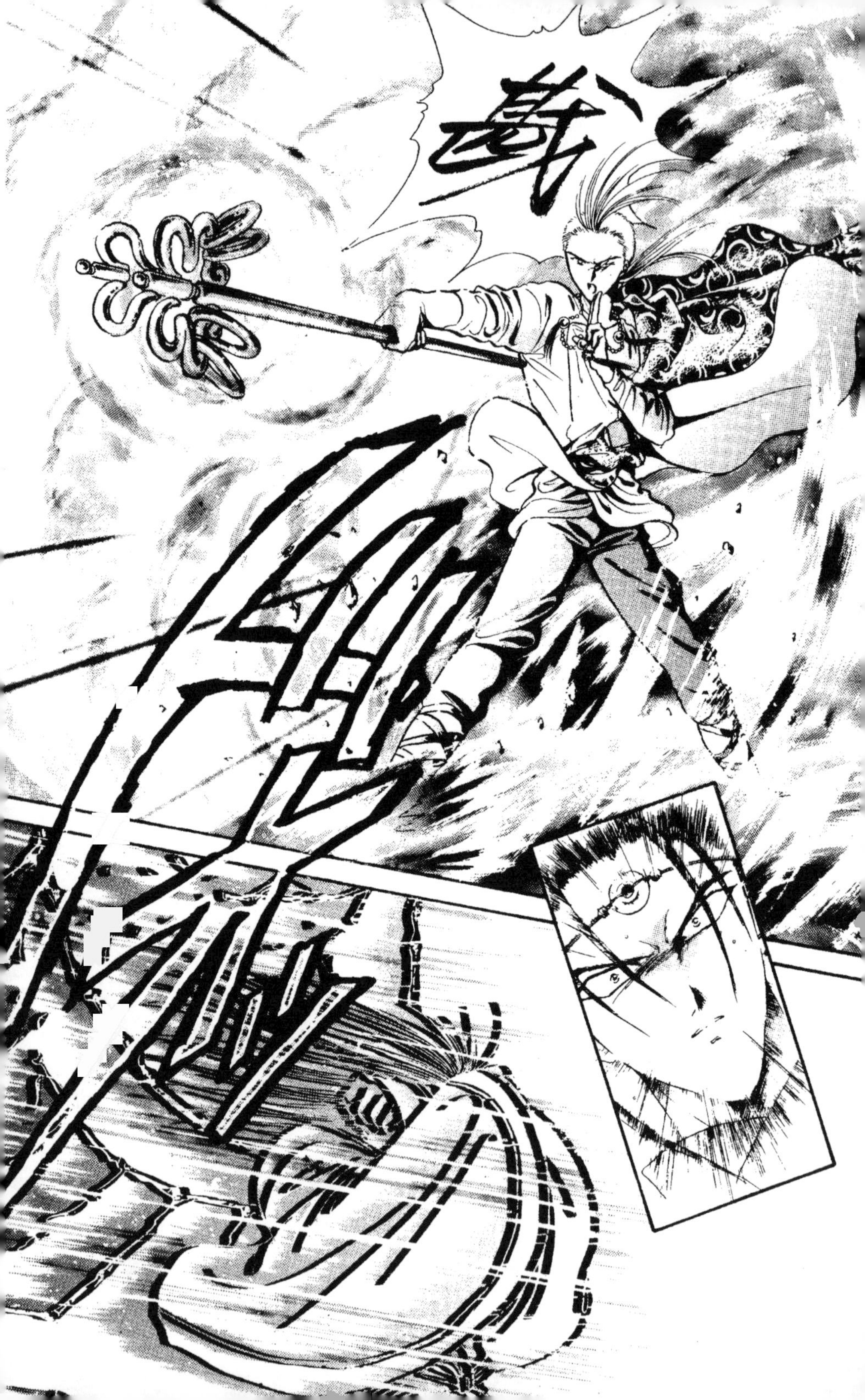

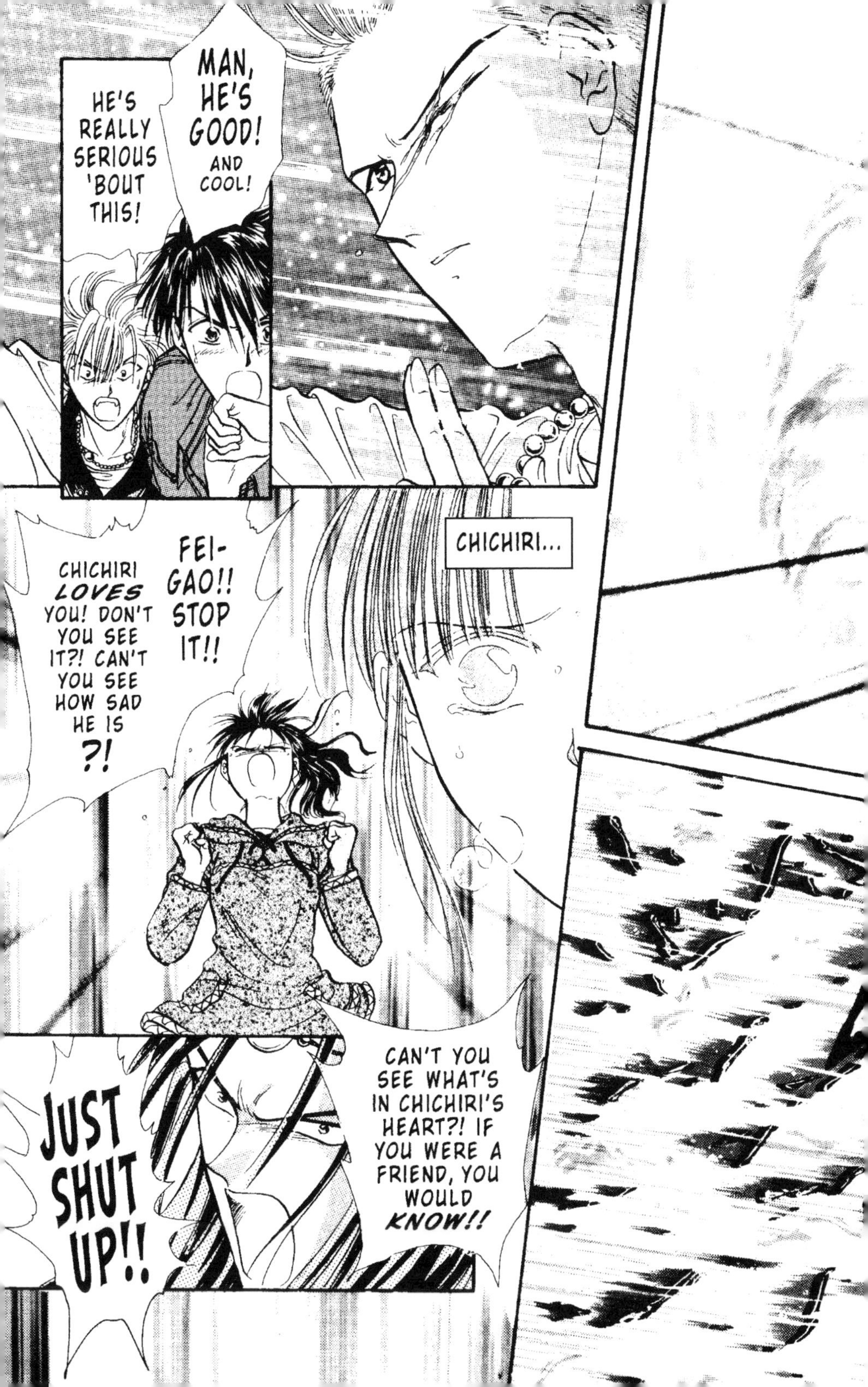

MAN, HE'S GOOD! AND COOL!
HE'S REALLY SERIOUS 'BOUT THIS!
CHICHIRI...
FEI-GAO!! STOP IT!!
CHICHIRI *LOVES* YOU! DON'T YOU SEE IT?! CAN'T YOU SEE HOW SAD HE IS ?!
CAN'T YOU SEE WHAT'S IN CHICHIRI'S HEART?! IF YOU WERE A FRIEND, YOU WOULD *KNOW!!*
JUST SHUT UP!!

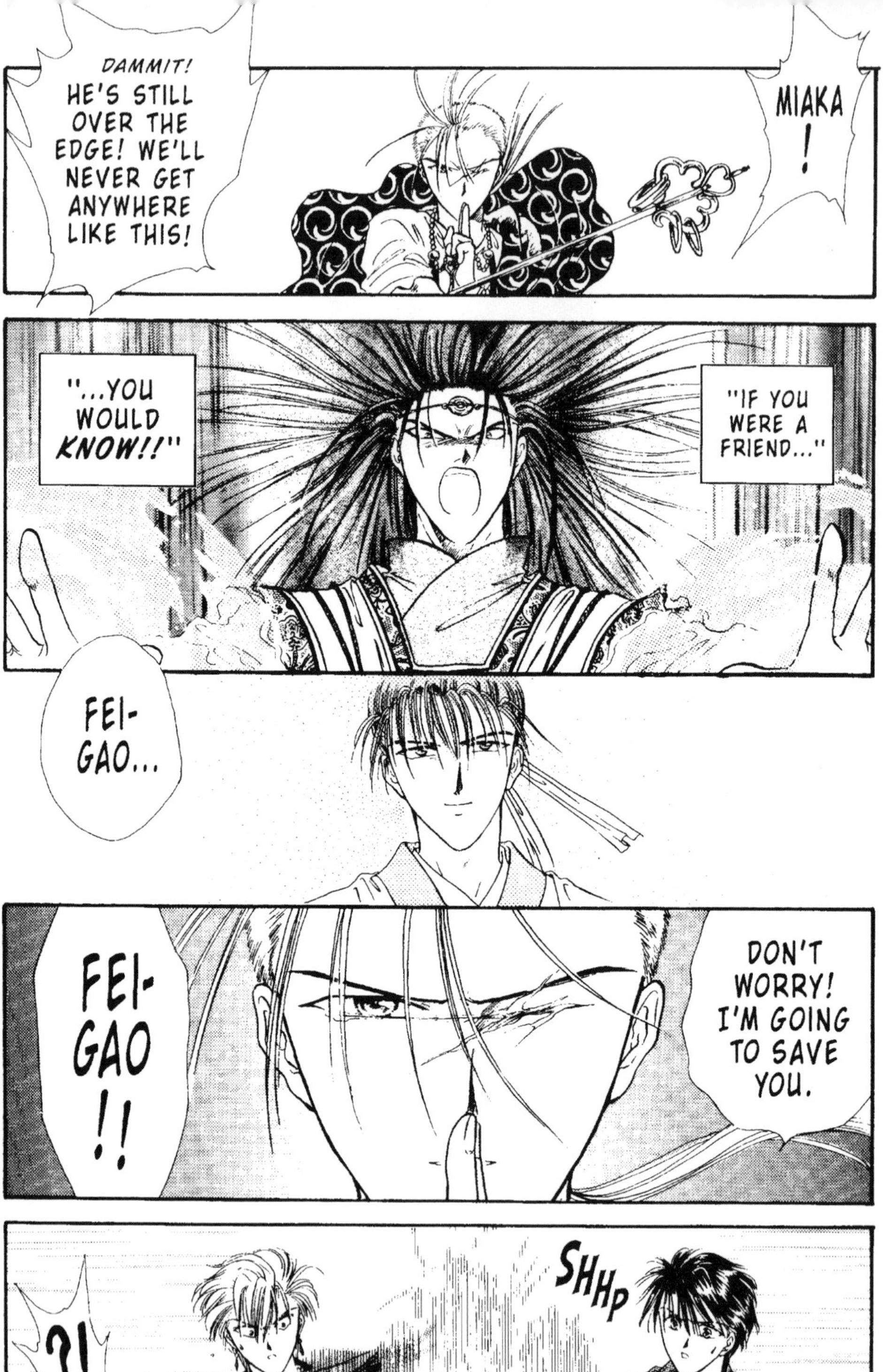
MIAKA!
DAMMIT! HE'S STILL OVER THE EDGE! WE'LL NEVER GET ANYWHERE LIKE THIS!
"IF YOU WERE A FRIEND..."
"...YOU WOULD KNOW!!"
FEI-GAO...
DON'T WORRY! I'M GOING TO SAVE YOU.
FEI-GAO!!
SHHP
?!

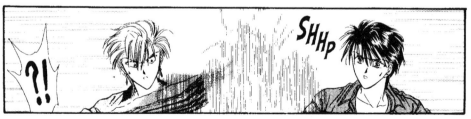

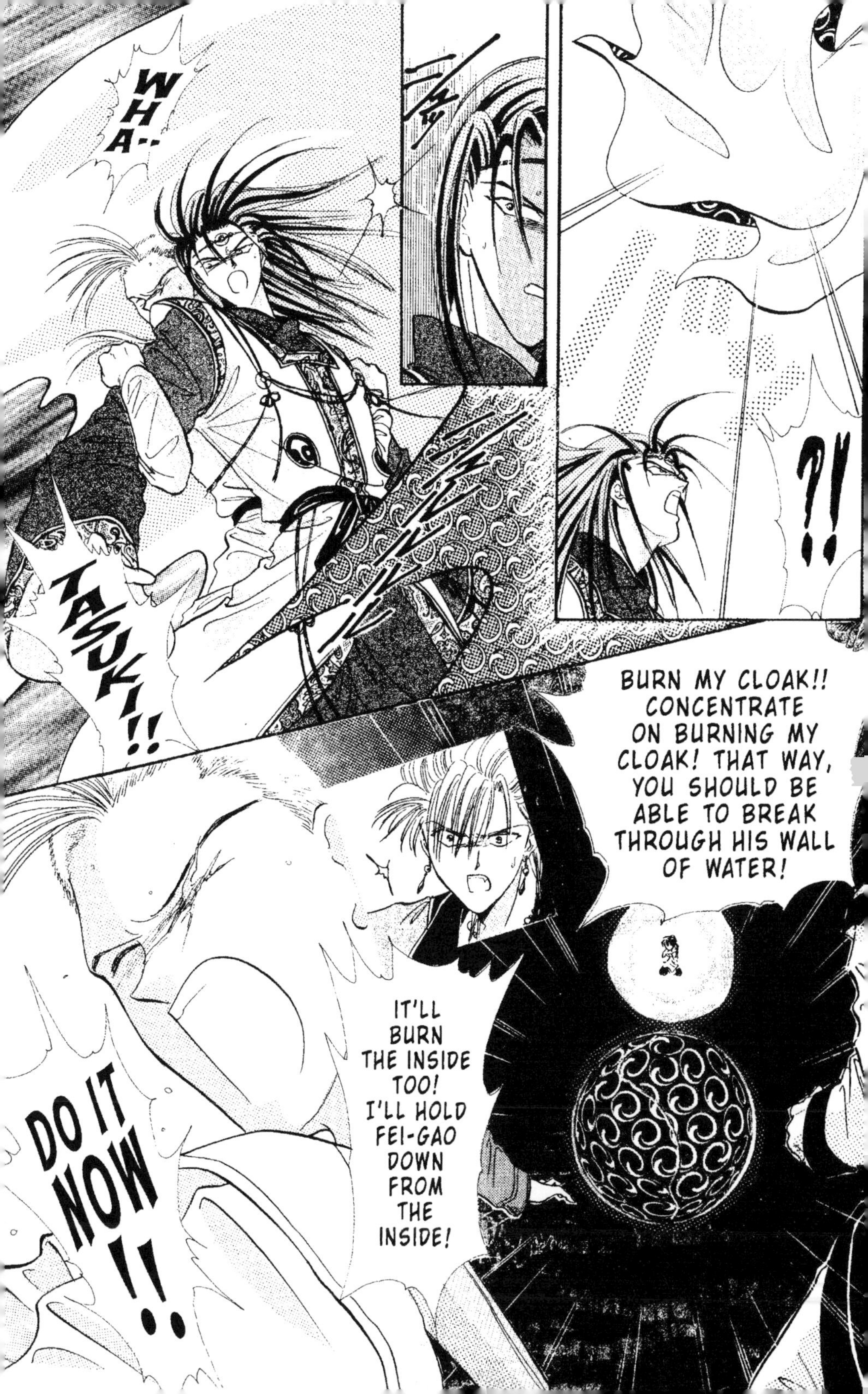
?!!
WHA--
TASUKI!!
BURN MY CLOAK!! CONCENTRATE ON BURNING MY CLOAK! THAT WAY, YOU SHOULD BE ABLE TO BREAK THROUGH HIS WALL OF WATER!
IT'LL BURN THE INSIDE TOO! I'LL HOLD FEI-GAO DOWN FROM THE INSIDE!
DO IT NOW!!

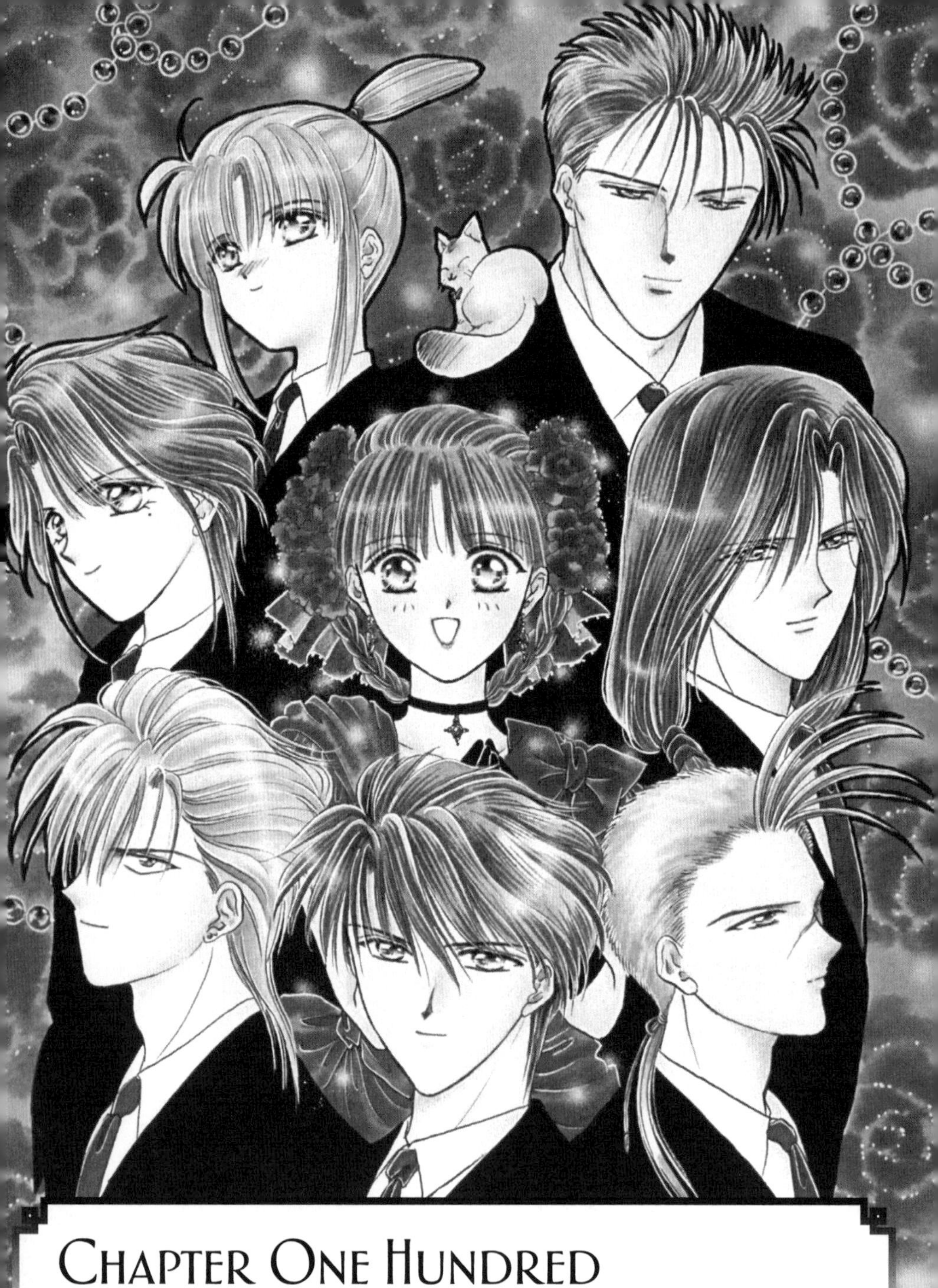

Chapter One Hundred
The Ephemeral Reflection in the Water

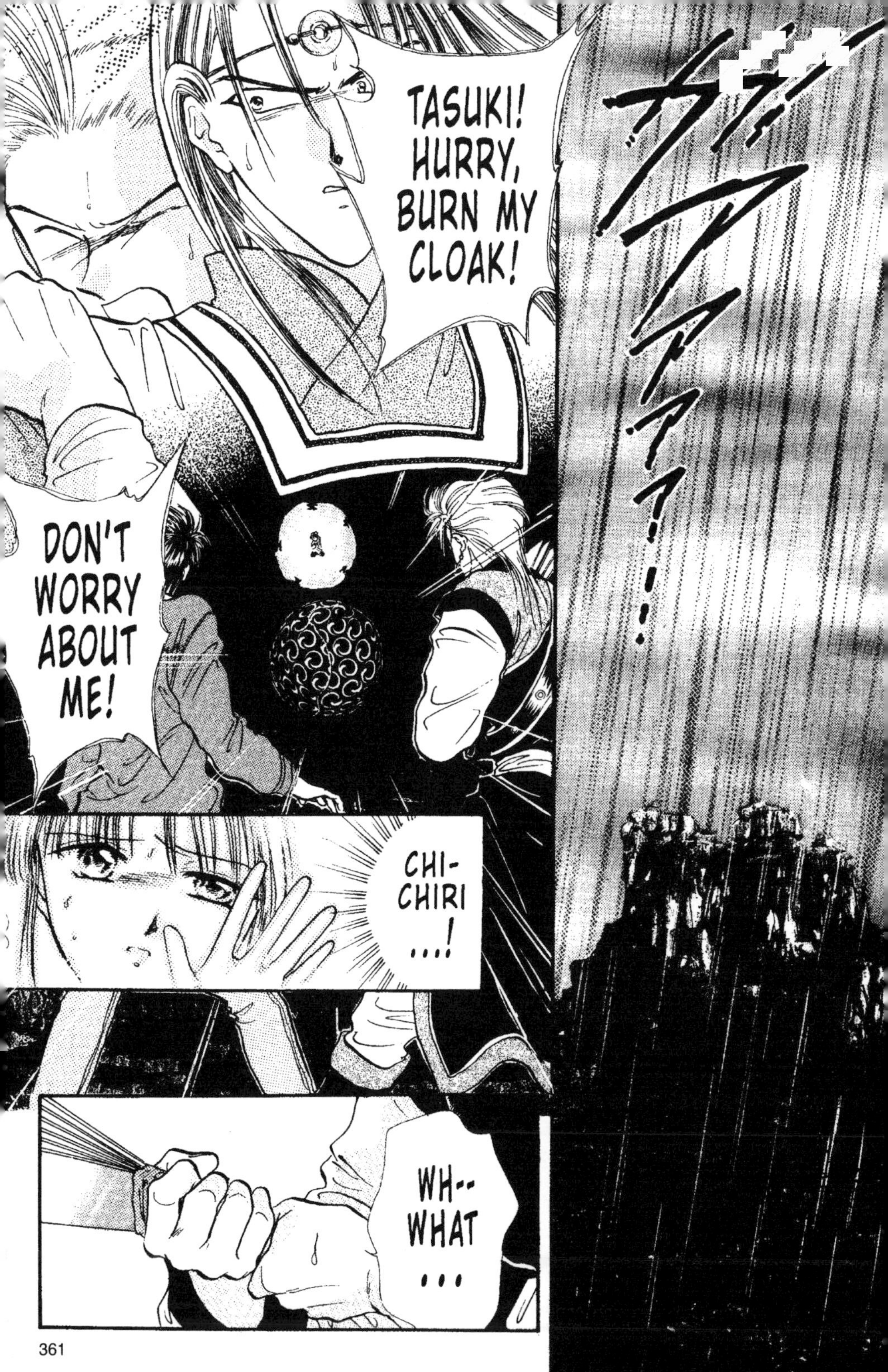
TASUKI! HURRY, BURN MY CLOAK!
DON'T WORRY ABOUT ME!
CHI-CHIRI ...!
WH-- WHAT ...

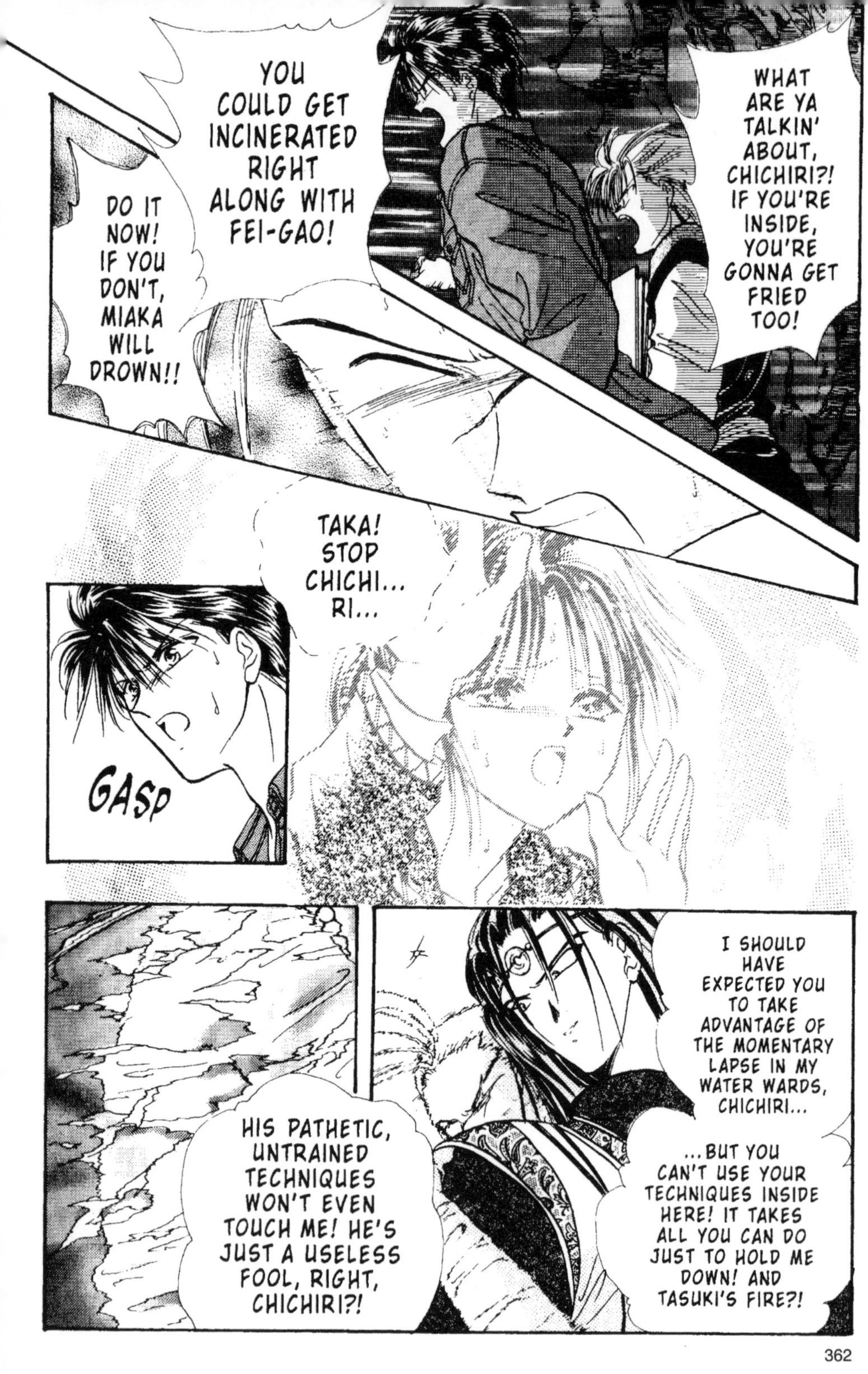
WHAT ARE YA TALKIN' ABOUT, CHICHIRI?! IF YOU'RE INSIDE, YOU'RE GONNA GET FRIED TOO!
YOU COULD GET INCINERATED RIGHT ALONG WITH FEI-GAO!
DO IT NOW! IF YOU DON'T, MIAKA WILL DROWN!!
TAKA! STOP CHICHI... RI...
GASP
I SHOULD HAVE EXPECTED YOU TO TAKE ADVANTAGE OF THE MOMENTARY LAPSE IN MY WATER WARDS, CHICHIRI...
...BUT YOU CAN'T USE YOUR TECHNIQUES INSIDE HERE! IT TAKES ALL YOU CAN DO JUST TO HOLD ME DOWN! AND TASUKI'S FIRE?!
HIS PATHETIC, UNTRAINED TECHNIQUES WON'T EVEN TOUCH ME! HE'S JUST A USELESS FOOL, RIGHT, CHICHIRI?!

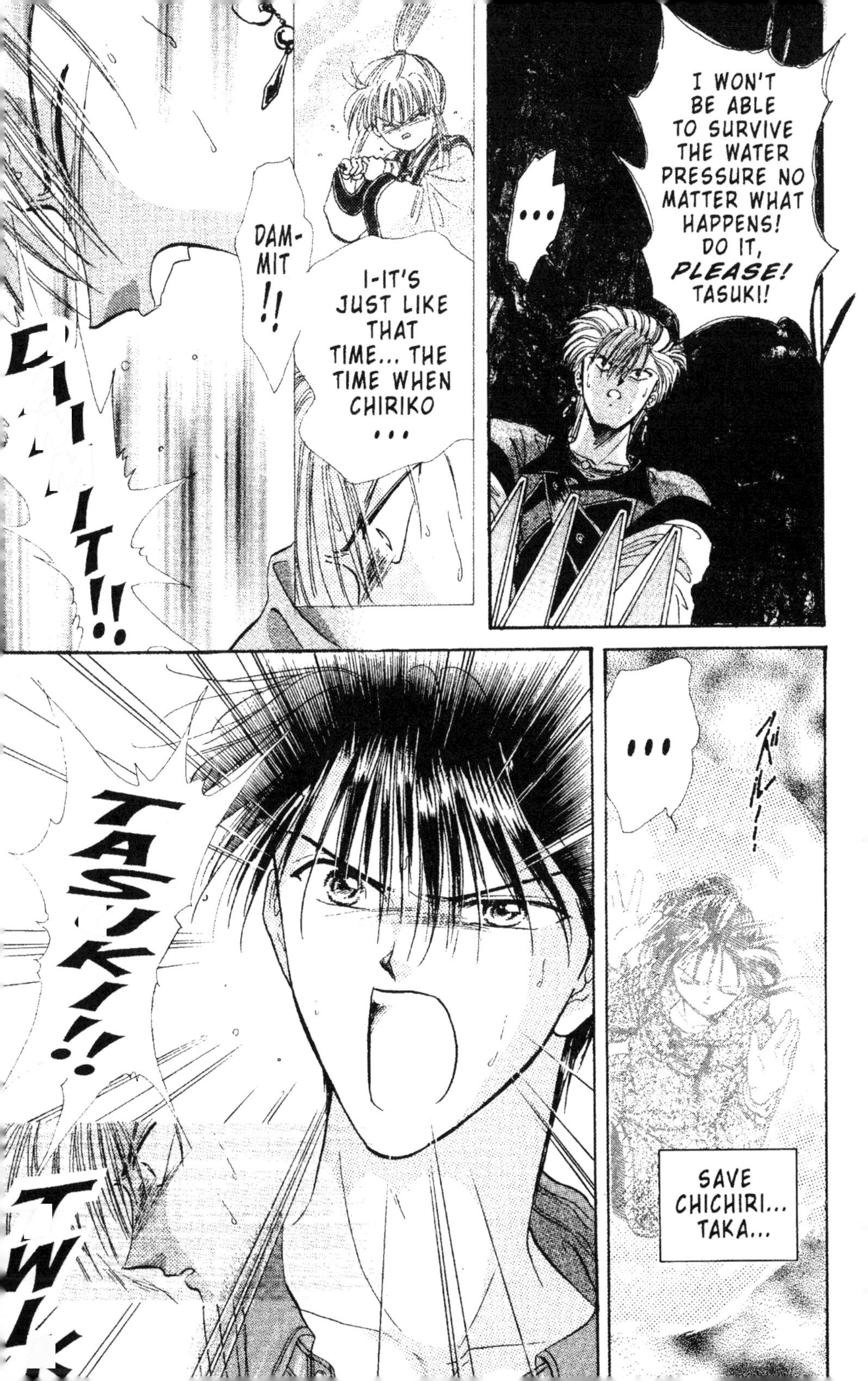
I WON'T BE ABLE TO SURVIVE THE WATER PRESSURE NO MATTER WHAT HAPPENS! DO IT, *PLEASE!* TASUKI!
...
I-IT'S JUST LIKE THAT TIME... THE TIME WHEN CHIRIKO ...
DAM-MIT !!
DAMMIT!!
...
SAVE CHICHIRI... TAKA...
TASUKI!!
TWI

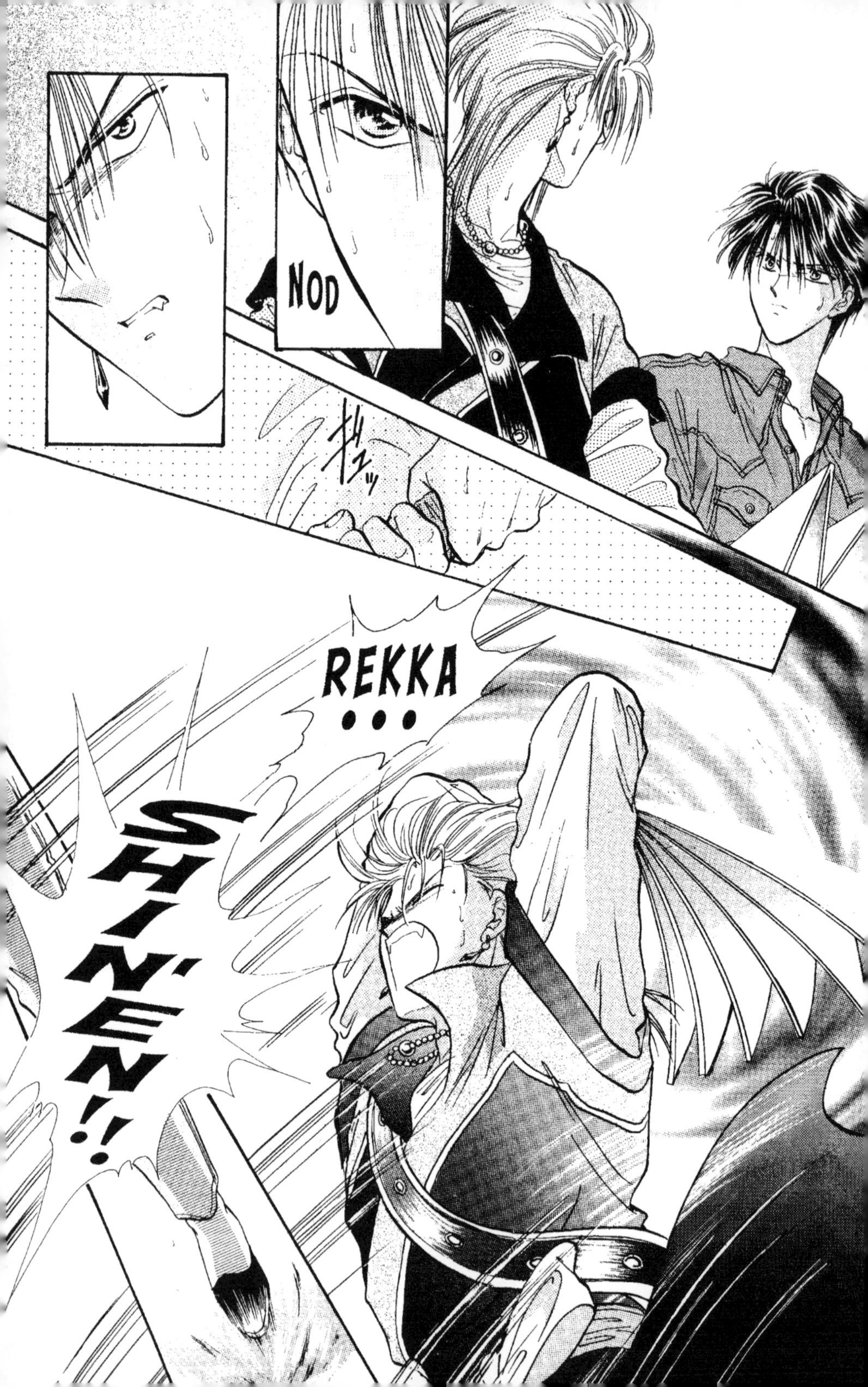
NOD
ギュッ
REKKA
...
SHIN'EN!!

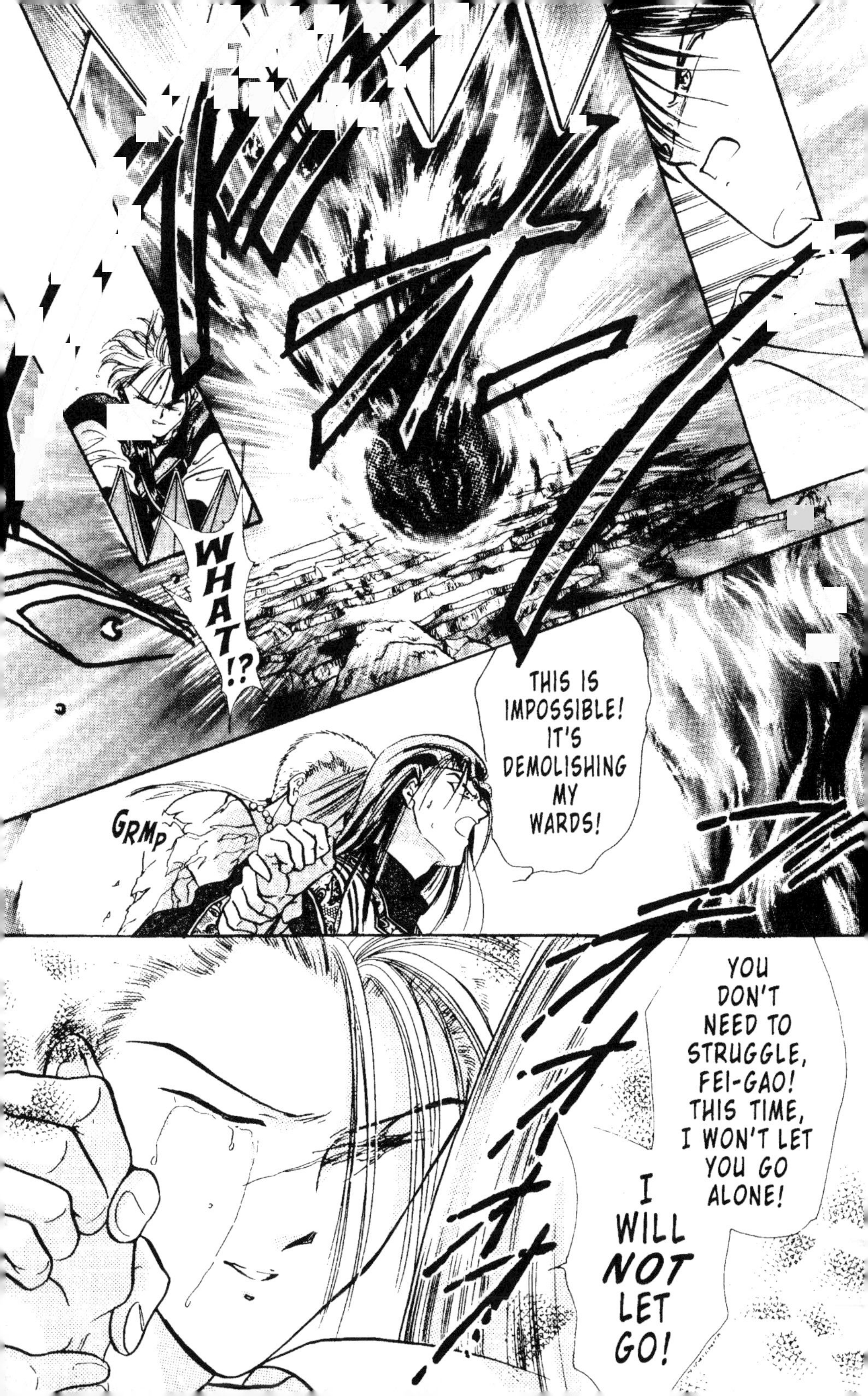
WHAT!?
THIS IS IMPOSSIBLE! IT'S DEMOLISHING MY WARDS!
GRMP
YOU DON'T NEED TO STRUGGLE, FEI-GAO! THIS TIME, I WON'T LET YOU GO ALONE!
I WILL NOT LET GO!

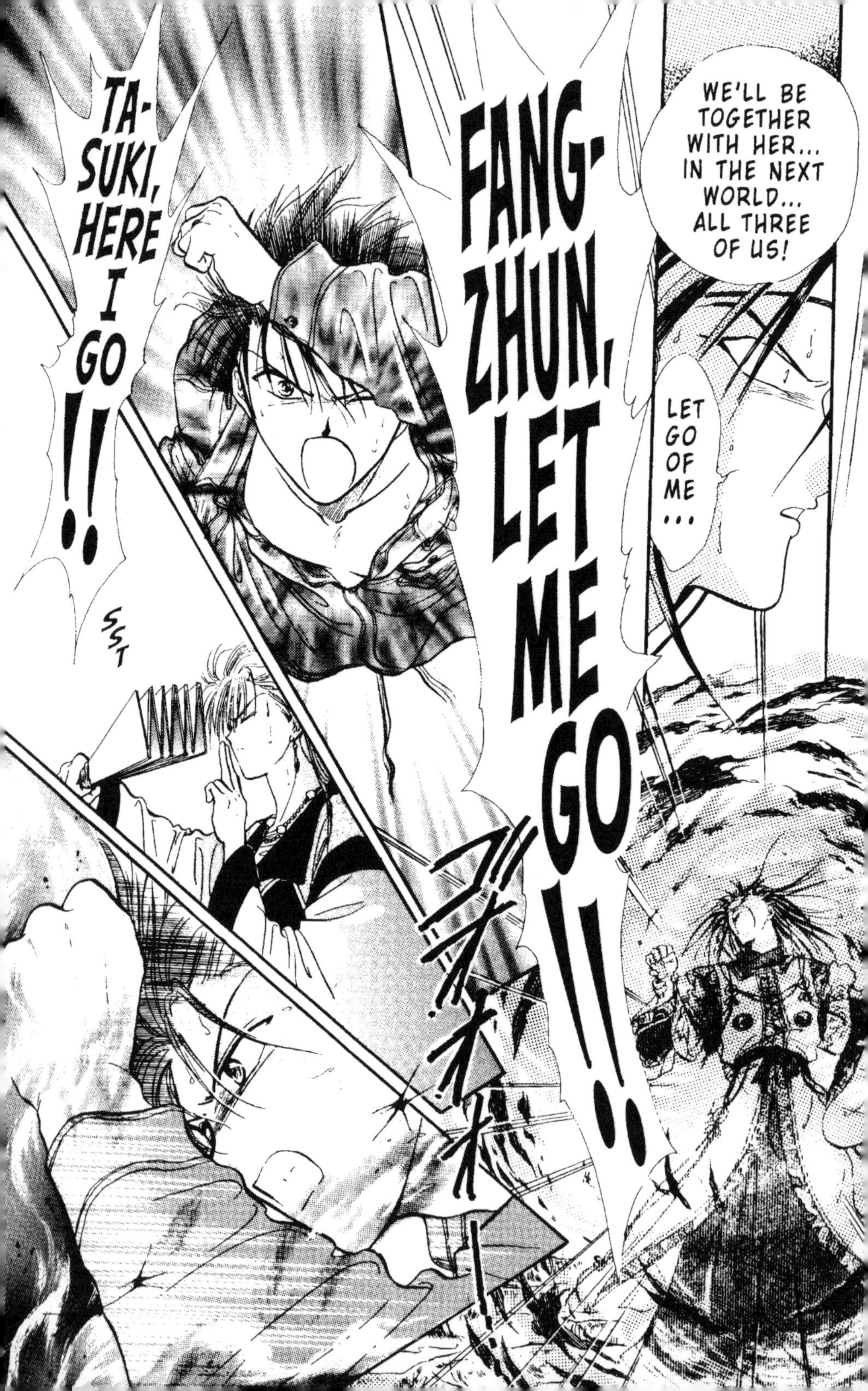
WE'LL BE TOGETHER WITH HER... IN THE NEXT WORLD... ALL THREE OF US!
LET GO OF ME...
FANG-ZHUN, LET ME GO!!
TA-SUKI, HERE I GO!!
SST

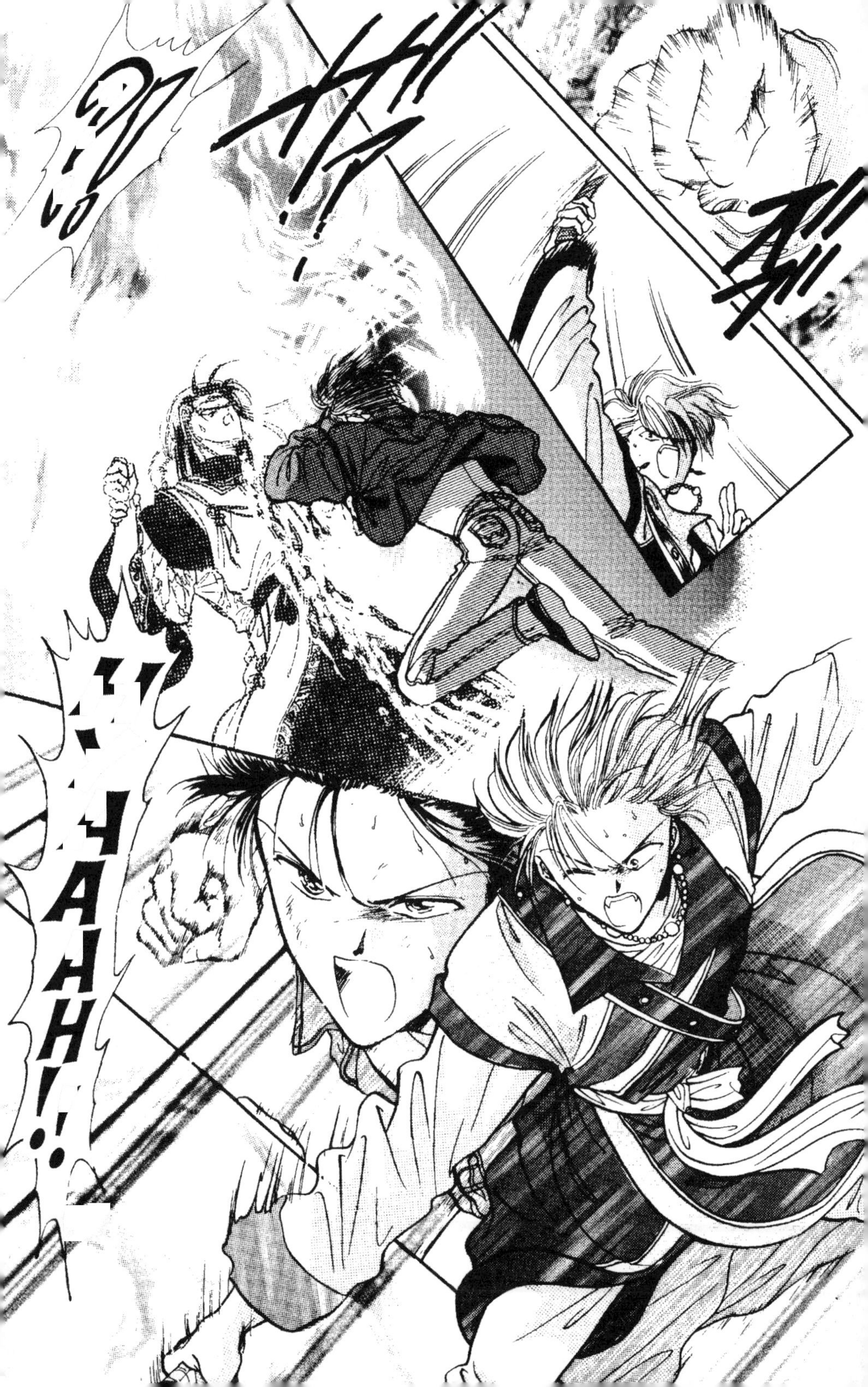
YAAAH!!

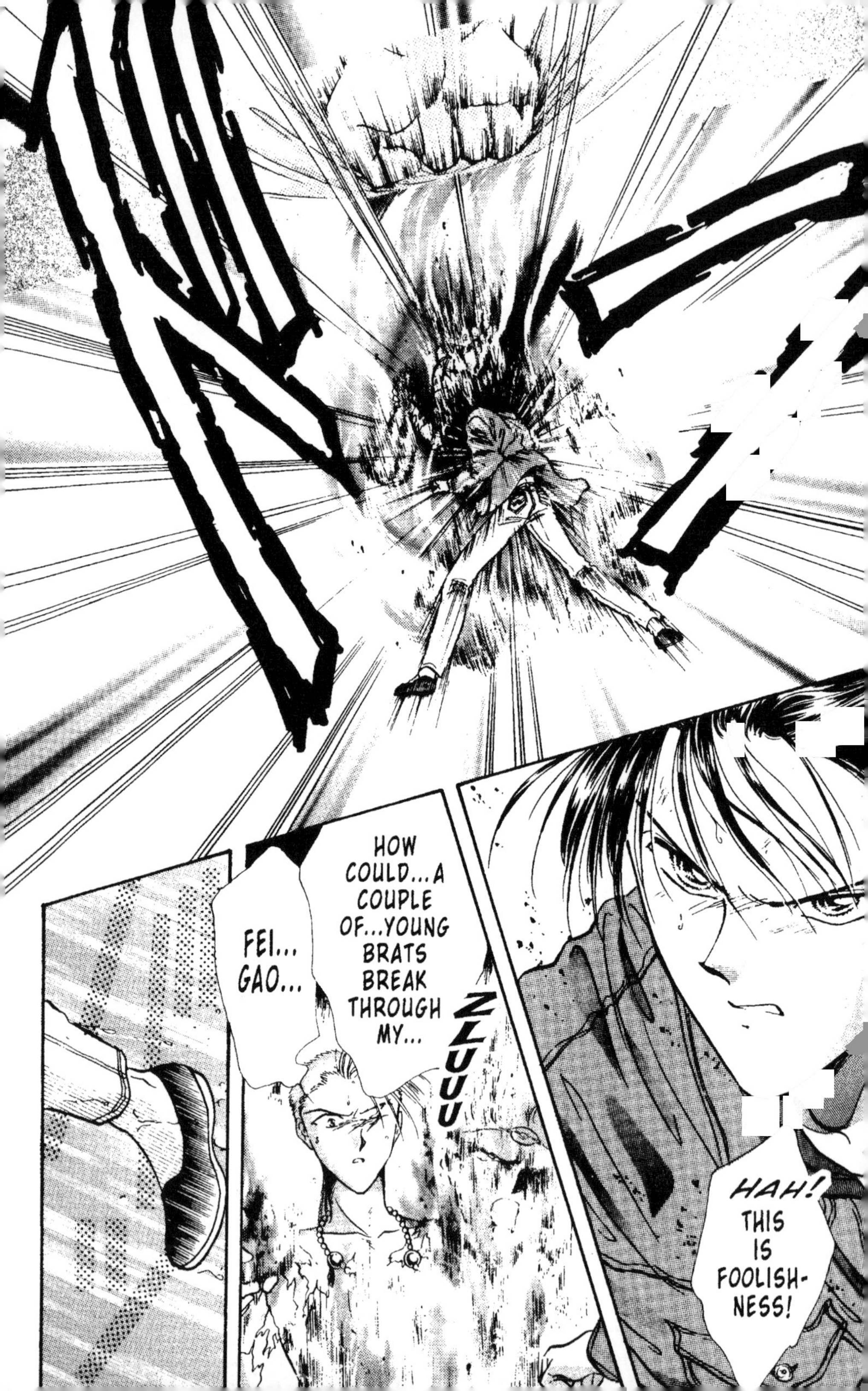
HAH! THIS IS FOOLISHNESS!
HOW COULD... A COUPLE OF... YOUNG BRATS BREAK THROUGH MY...
FEI... GAO...
ZLUUUU

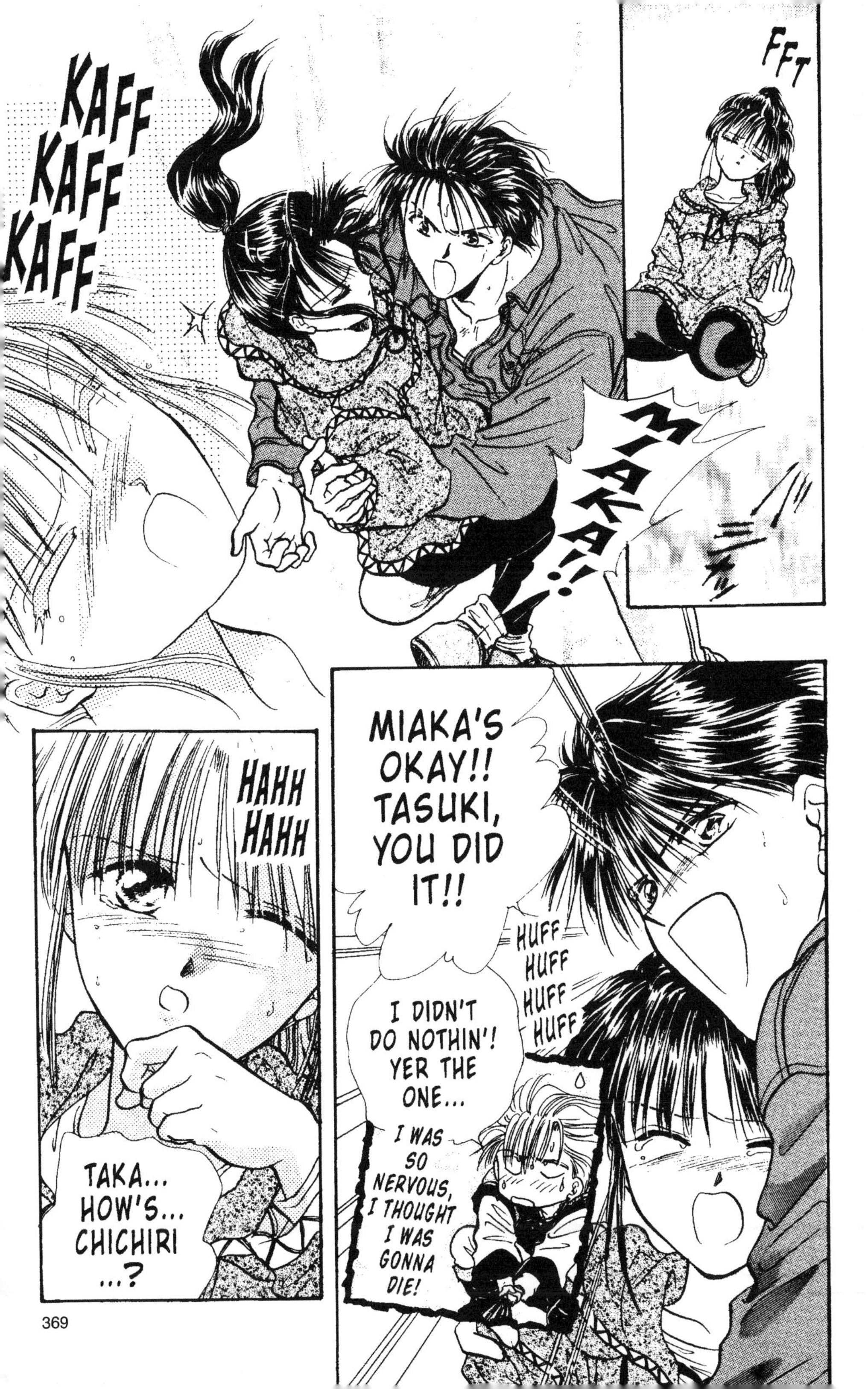
FFT
MIAKA!!
KAFF KAFF KAFF
MIAKA'S OKAY!! TASUKI, YOU DID IT!!
HUFF HUFF HUFF HUFF
I DIDN'T DO NOTHIN'! YER THE ONE...
I WAS SO NERVOUS, I THOUGHT I WAS GONNA DIE!
HAHH HAHH
TAKA... HOW'S... CHICHIRI ...?

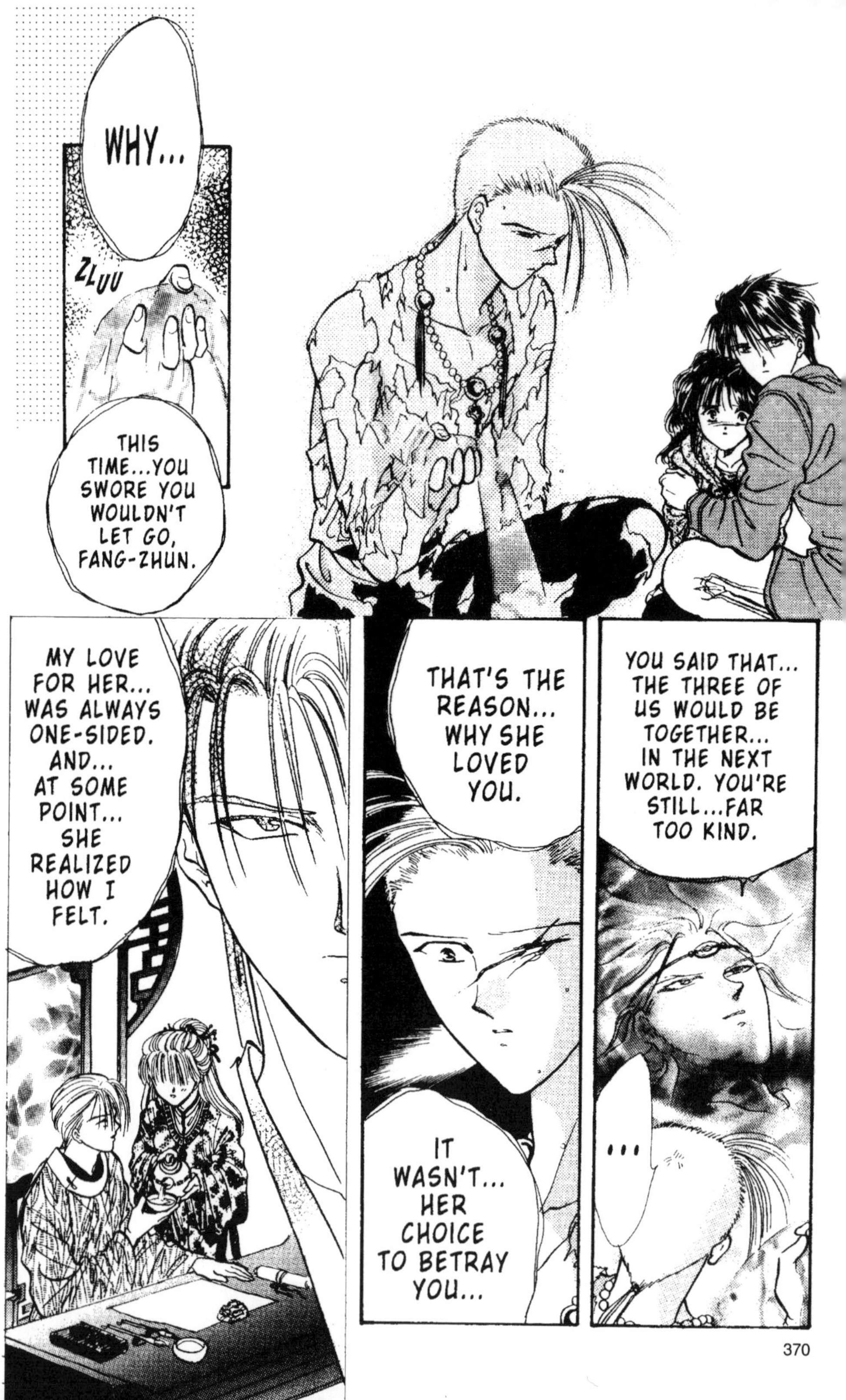
WHY...
ZLUU
THIS TIME...YOU SWORE YOU WOULDN'T LET GO, FANG-ZHUN.
YOU SAID THAT... THE THREE OF US WOULD BE TOGETHER... IN THE NEXT WORLD. YOU'RE STILL...FAR TOO KIND.
...
THAT'S THE REASON... WHY SHE LOVED YOU.
IT WASN'T... HER CHOICE TO BETRAY YOU...
MY LOVE FOR HER... WAS ALWAYS ONE-SIDED. AND... AT SOME POINT... SHE REALIZED HOW I FELT.

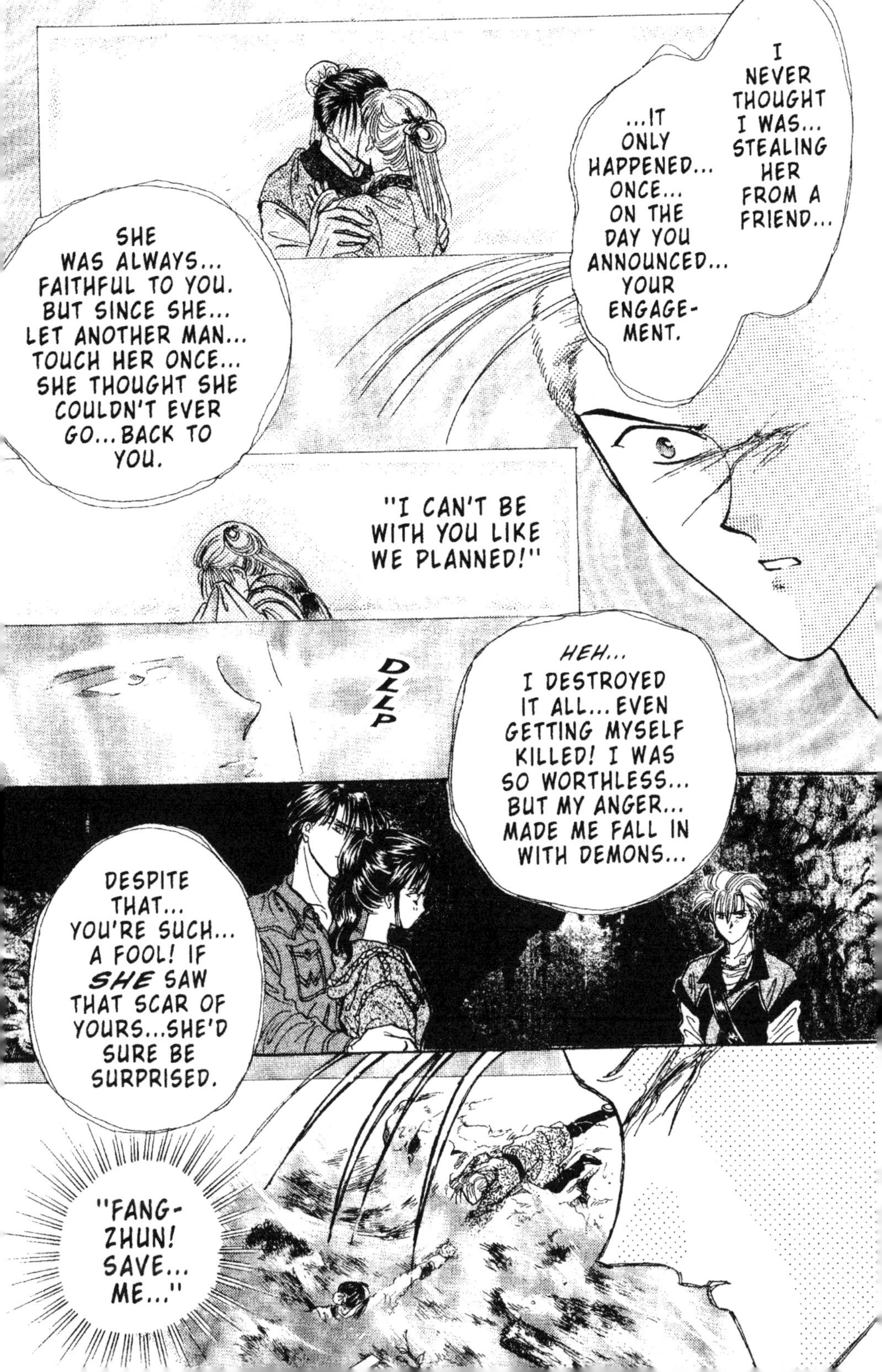
I NEVER THOUGHT I WAS... STEALING HER FROM A FRIEND...
...IT ONLY HAPPENED... ONCE... ON THE DAY YOU ANNOUNCED... YOUR ENGAGE-MENT.
SHE WAS ALWAYS... FAITHFUL TO YOU. BUT SINCE SHE... LET ANOTHER MAN... TOUCH HER ONCE... SHE THOUGHT SHE COULDN'T EVER GO... BACK TO YOU.
"I CAN'T BE WITH YOU LIKE WE PLANNED!"
DLLP
HEH... I DESTROYED IT ALL... EVEN GETTING MYSELF KILLED! I WAS SO WORTHLESS... BUT MY ANGER... MADE ME FALL IN WITH DEMONS...
DESPITE THAT... YOU'RE SUCH... A FOOL! IF SHE SAW THAT SCAR OF YOURS...SHE'D SURE BE SURPRISED.
"FANG-ZHUN! SAVE... ME..."

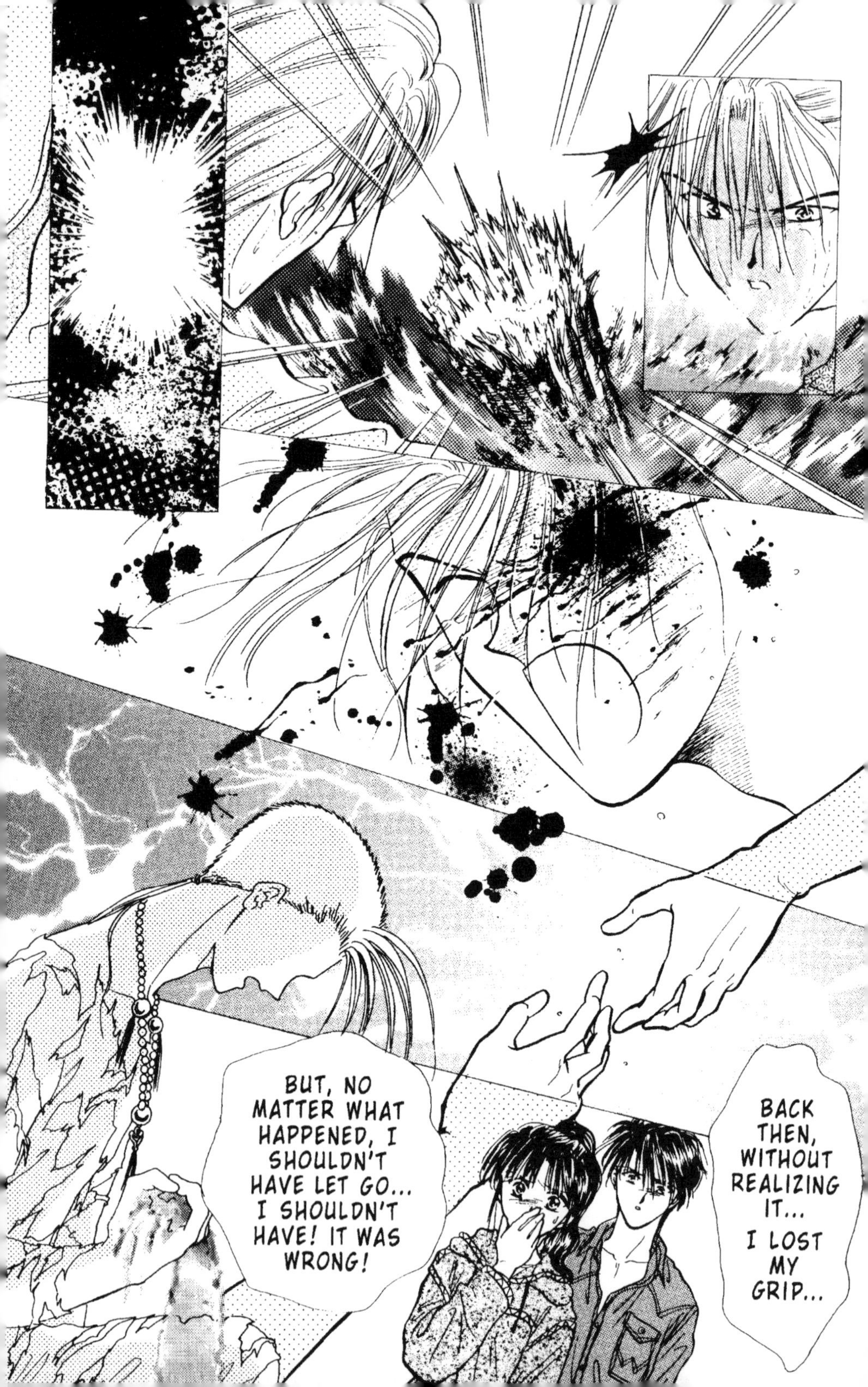
BACK THEN, WITHOUT REALIZING IT... I LOST MY GRIP...
BUT, NO MATTER WHAT HAPPENED, I SHOULDN'T HAVE LET GO... I SHOULDN'T HAVE! IT WAS WRONG!

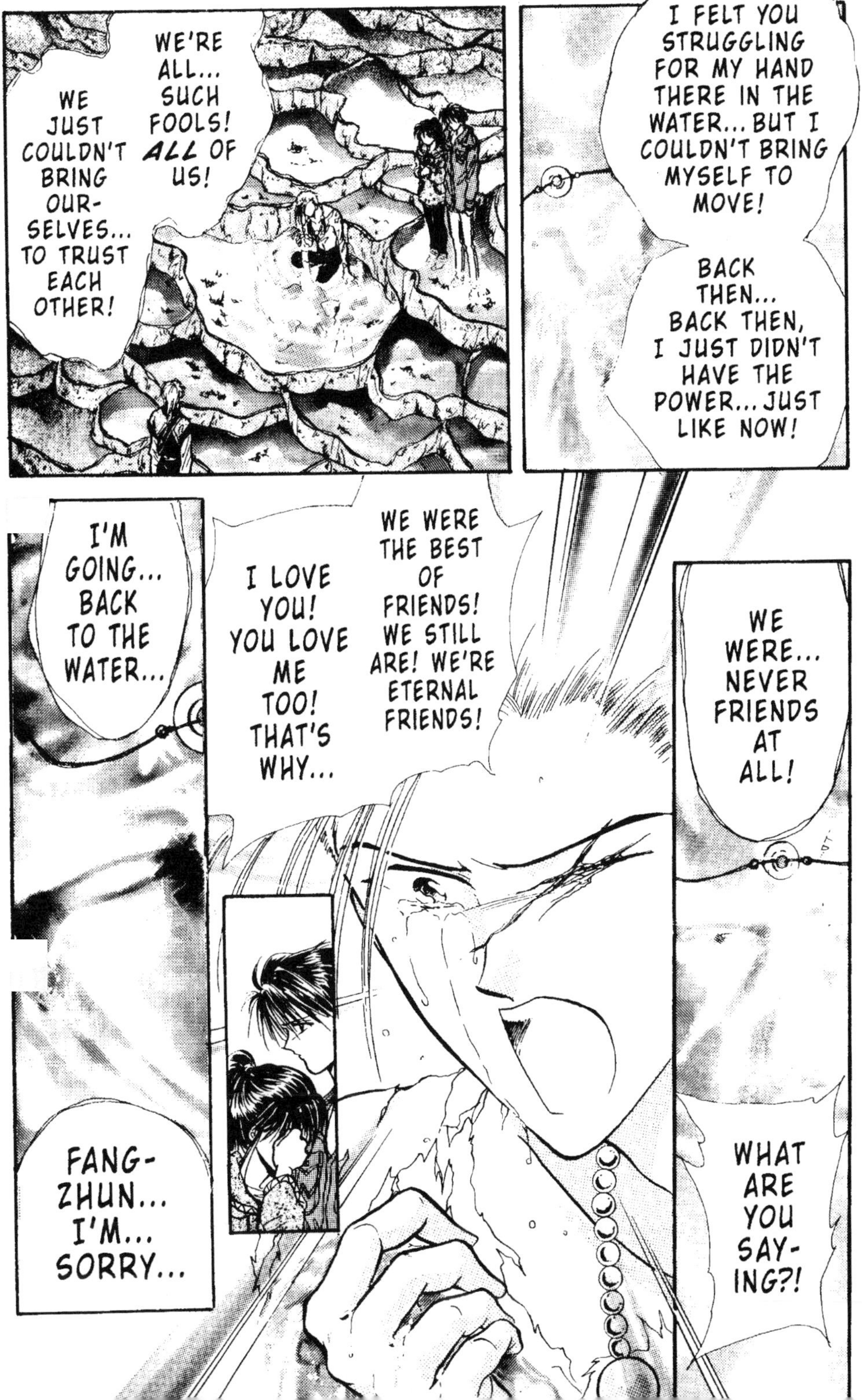
I FELT YOU STRUGGLING FOR MY HAND THERE IN THE WATER... BUT I COULDN'T BRING MYSELF TO MOVE!
BACK THEN... BACK THEN, I JUST DIDN'T HAVE THE POWER... JUST LIKE NOW!
WE'RE ALL... SUCH FOOLS! *ALL* OF US!
WE JUST COULDN'T BRING OURSELVES... TO TRUST EACH OTHER!
WE WERE... NEVER FRIENDS AT ALL!
WHAT ARE YOU SAYING?!
WE WERE THE BEST OF FRIENDS! WE STILL ARE! WE'RE ETERNAL FRIENDS!
I LOVE YOU! YOU LOVE ME TOO! THAT'S WHY...
I'M GOING... BACK TO THE WATER...
FANG-ZHUN... I'M... SORRY...

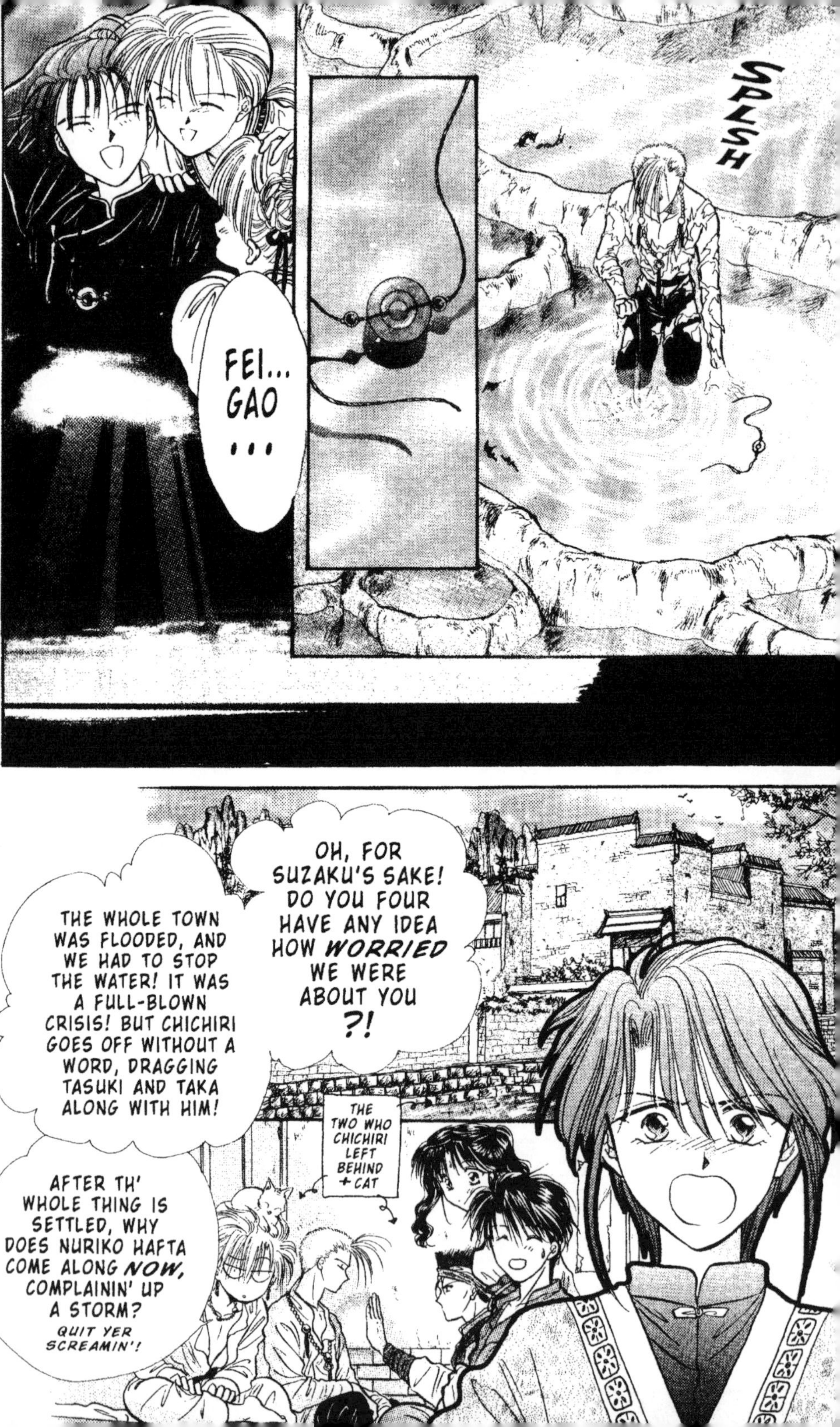
SPLSH
FEI... GAO ...
OH, FOR SUZAKU'S SAKE! DO YOU FOUR HAVE ANY IDEA HOW WORRIED WE WERE ABOUT YOU ?!
THE WHOLE TOWN WAS FLOODED, AND WE HAD TO STOP THE WATER! IT WAS A FULL-BLOWN CRISIS! BUT CHICHIRI GOES OFF WITHOUT A WORD, DRAGGING TASUKI AND TAKA ALONG WITH HIM!
THE TWO WHO CHICHIRI LEFT BEHIND + CAT
AFTER TH' WHOLE THING IS SETTLED, WHY DOES NURIKO HAFTA COME ALONG NOW, COMPLAININ' UP A STORM?
QUIT YER SCREAMIN'!

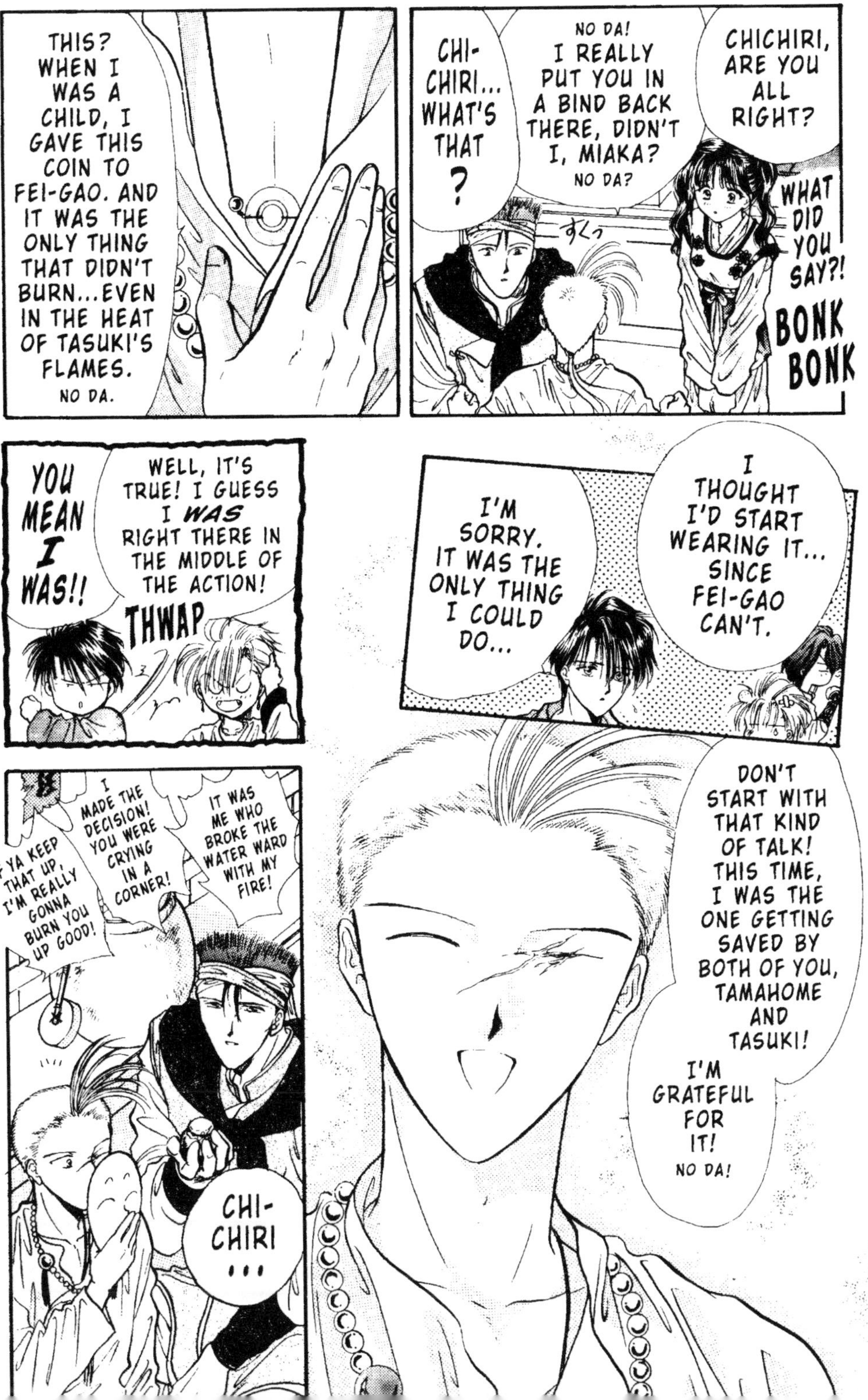
CHICHIRI, ARE YOU ALL RIGHT?
WHAT DID YOU SAY?!
BONK BONK
NO DA! I REALLY PUT YOU IN A BIND BACK THERE, DIDN'T I, MIAKA? NO DA?
すくっ
CHI-CHIRI... WHAT'S THAT ?
THIS? WHEN I WAS A CHILD, I GAVE THIS COIN TO FEI-GAO. AND IT WAS THE ONLY THING THAT DIDN'T BURN...EVEN IN THE HEAT OF TASUKI'S FLAMES. NO DA.
I THOUGHT I'D START WEARING IT... SINCE FEI-GAO CAN'T.
I'M SORRY. IT WAS THE ONLY THING I COULD DO...
WELL, IT'S TRUE! I GUESS I *WAS* RIGHT THERE IN THE MIDDLE OF THE ACTION!
YOU MEAN I WAS!!
THWAP
DON'T START WITH THAT KIND OF TALK! THIS TIME, I WAS THE ONE GETTING SAVED BY BOTH OF YOU, TAMAHOME AND TASUKI!
I'M GRATEFUL FOR IT! NO DA!
IT WAS ME WHO BROKE THE WATER WARD WITH MY FIRE!
I MADE THE DECISION! YOU WERE CRYING IN A CORNER!
IF YA KEEP THAT UP, I'M REALLY GONNA BURN YOU UP GOOD!
CHI-CHIRI...

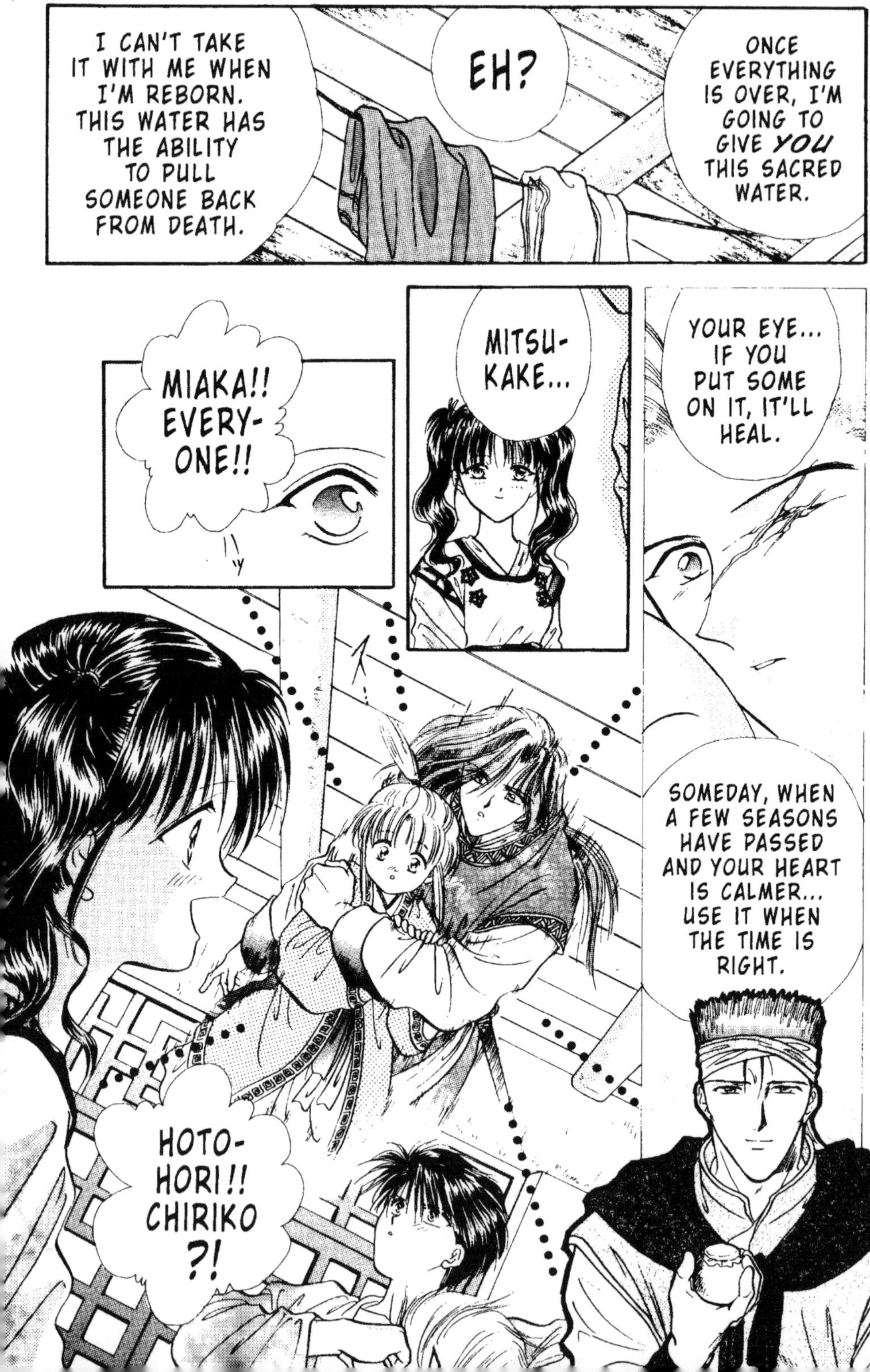
ONCE EVERYTHING IS OVER, I'M GOING TO GIVE *YOU* THIS SACRED WATER.
EH?
I CAN'T TAKE IT WITH ME WHEN I'M REBORN. THIS WATER HAS THE ABILITY TO PULL SOMEONE BACK FROM DEATH.
YOUR EYE... IF YOU PUT SOME ON IT, IT'LL HEAL.
SOMEDAY, WHEN A FEW SEASONS HAVE PASSED AND YOUR HEART IS CALMER... USE IT WHEN THE TIME IS RIGHT.
MITSU-KAKE...
MIAKA!! EVERY-ONE!!
HOTO-HORI!! CHIRIKO ?!

One of my assistants saw Chichiri unconscious and said, "Big brother's passed out!!" ☺ It's what made the rest of the "family" (Miaka and the warriors) realize just how valuable he is. Well, everybody comments on how they all resemble a family. (But at first glance, Mitsukake seems like the eldest brother -- or maybe the father!) ☺

Mitsukake had a small but good part to play this time.

Assistant H said, "Mitchi was so cool!" when he rescued Tasuki, but actually I think she was paying closer attention to Chichiri.

There are so many scenes in this volume that I just love! But the scene where Chichiri ruffled up Tasuki's hair (p. 350) is among my absolute favorites! I think that is where Chichiri is the coolest character! "Big brother!!" *I'm going to start calling him that, too!* ☺ Tasuki is so tall, but he still acts like a child. From volume 14 on, I'm sure there are people following each character, but in Part 2, you can see how I've reached the pinnacle of my love for these characters. ☺ Even if they don't have much of a part in the story, that doesn't mean that my love for them is any less! *Ah, how I love Chiriko!* Nuriko too! It's true that Nuriko showed just how cool a character can be up until volume 8, so this time I wanted to draw "Childlike Nuriko" a little! The relationship of Lu-Hou to Nuriko was the same as Nuriko's to Kang-Lin, right? I tried to make that clear in the drawings. Hotohori affirmed his love for his child, wife, and himself. Mitsukake finally was able to save the life of each warrior. Tasuki and Taka fired up their friendship. (Actually Taka is a fan of Tasuki. Once again it was an assistant who said, "In that scene where he nodded to Tasuki, Taka was seeing his father there." Oh, come on! At least say, "big brother"!) And Chichiri, who was saved by the two of them, is also happy from the bottom of his "big brother" heart. And finally there's Chiriko. Go to it, Chi-ri-ko!! You too, Miaka and Taka! Your final trials are almost here! *Since we're nearing the end.*

I always wanted to have a fight scene where the two of them act as a combo!

Now... Will "love"... I mean... "the Human Race" win the day? Everything depends on what's inside your heart!!

So, I'll see you all in volume 18!

96.3/3

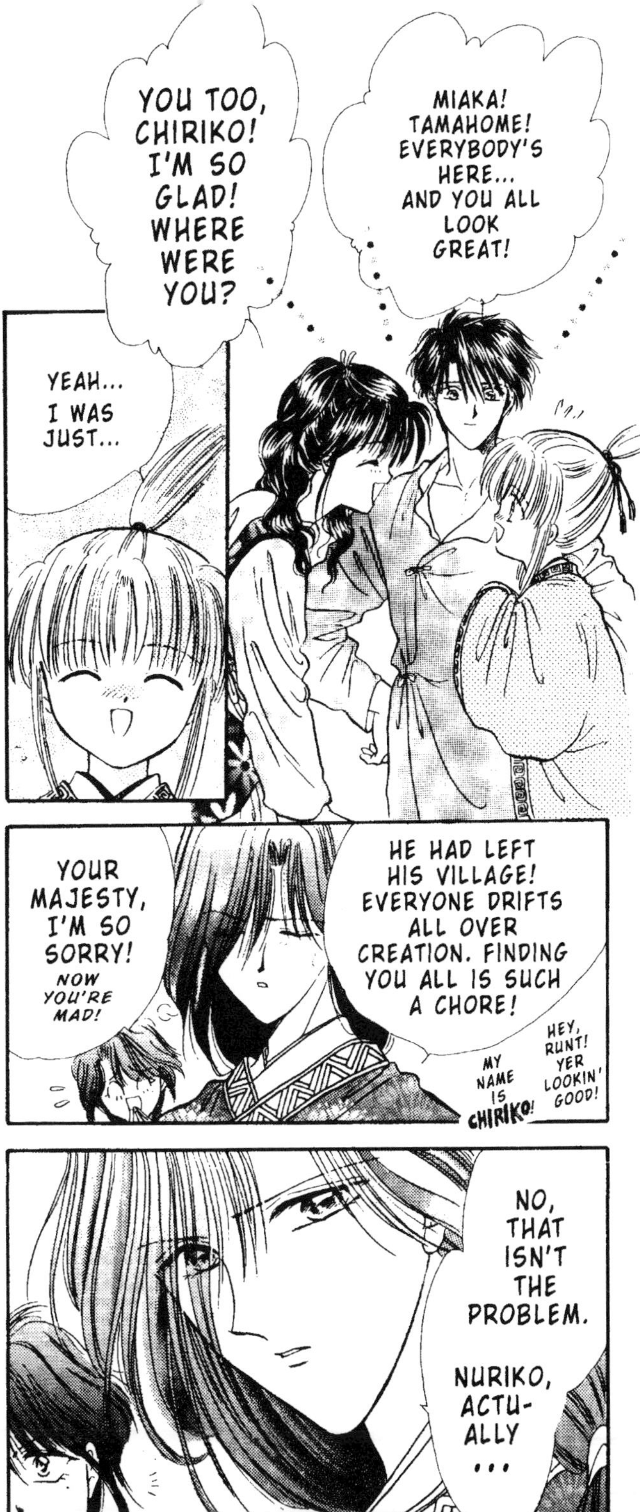

MIAKA! TAMAHOME! EVERYBODY'S HERE... AND YOU ALL LOOK GREAT!
YOU TOO, CHIRIKO! I'M SO GLAD! WHERE WERE YOU?
YEAH... I WAS JUST...
HE HAD LEFT HIS VILLAGE! EVERYONE DRIFTS ALL OVER CREATION. FINDING YOU ALL IS SUCH A CHORE!
HEY, RUNT! YER LOOKIN' GOOD!
MY NAME IS CHIRIKO!
YOUR MAJESTY, I'M SO SORRY!
NOW YOU'RE MAD!
NO, THAT ISN'T THE PROBLEM.
NURIKO, ACTUALLY...

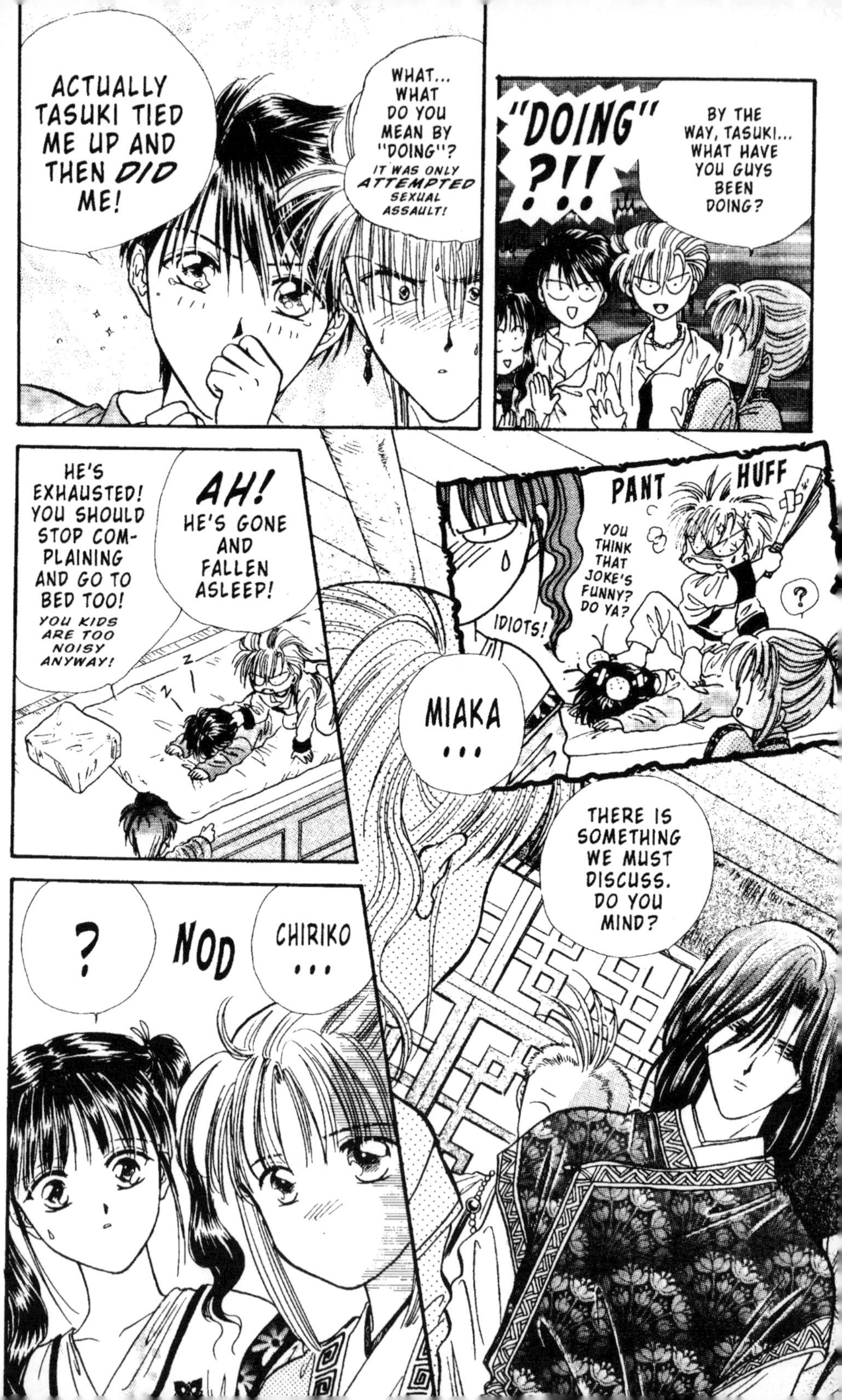
BY THE WAY, TASUKI... WHAT HAVE YOU GUYS BEEN DOING?
"DOING" ?!!
WHAT... WHAT DO YOU MEAN BY "DOING"? IT WAS ONLY ATTEMPTED SEXUAL ASSAULT!
ACTUALLY TASUKI TIED ME UP AND THEN DID ME!
PANT
HUFF
YOU THINK THAT JOKE'S FUNNY? DO YA?
?
IDIOTS!
AH! HE'S GONE AND FALLEN ASLEEP!
HE'S EXHAUSTED! YOU SHOULD STOP COM-PLAINING AND GO TO BED TOO! YOU KIDS ARE TOO NOISY ANYWAY!
MIAKA...
THERE IS SOMETHING WE MUST DISCUSS. DO YOU MIND?
CHIRIKO...
NOD
?

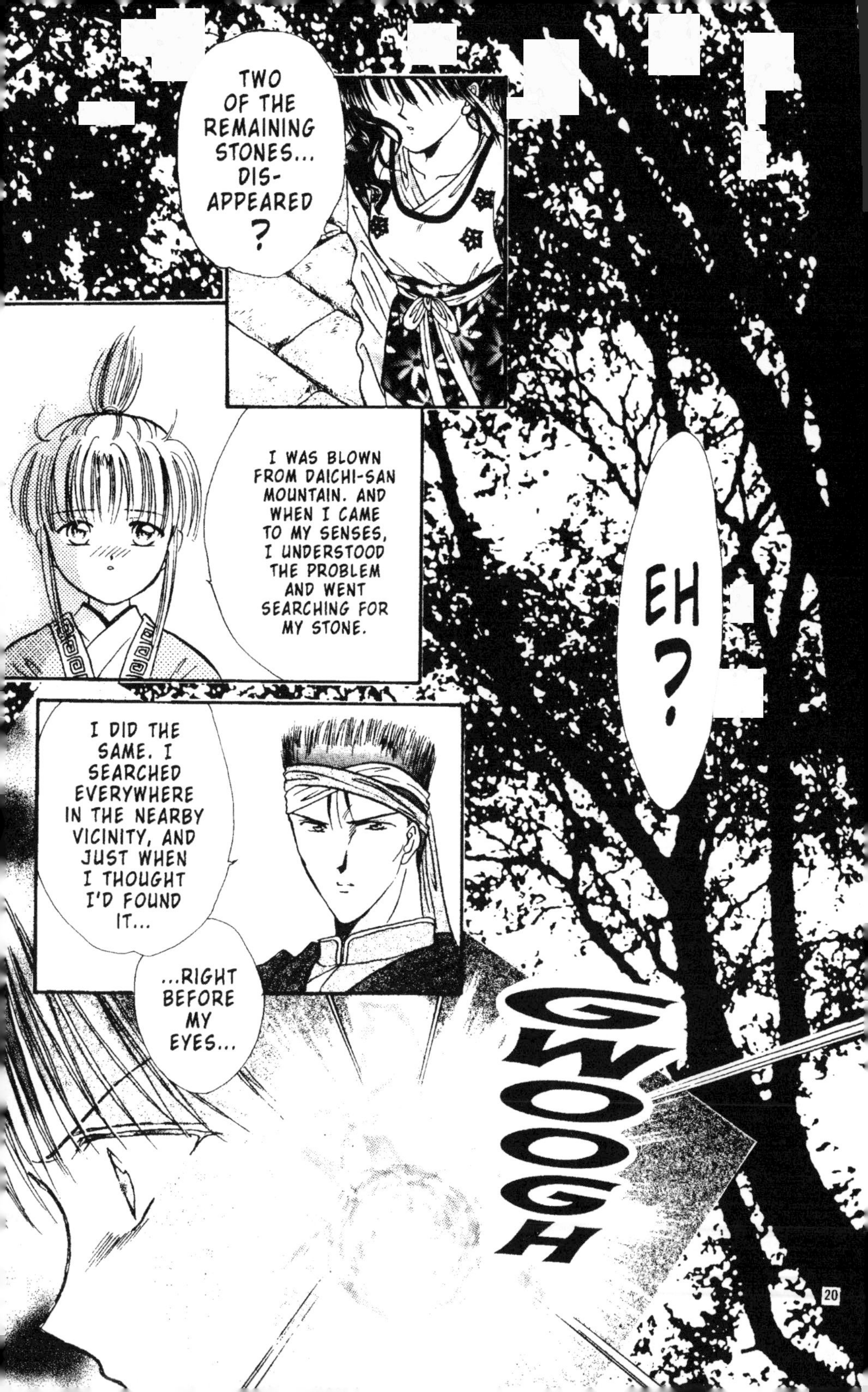

TWO OF THE REMAINING STONES... DIS-APPEARED?
EH?
I WAS BLOWN FROM DAICHI-SAN MOUNTAIN. AND WHEN I CAME TO MY SENSES, I UNDERSTOOD THE PROBLEM AND WENT SEARCHING FOR MY STONE.
I DID THE SAME. I SEARCHED EVERYWHERE IN THE NEARBY VICINITY, AND JUST WHEN I THOUGHT I'D FOUND IT...
...RIGHT BEFORE MY EYES...
GWOOGH

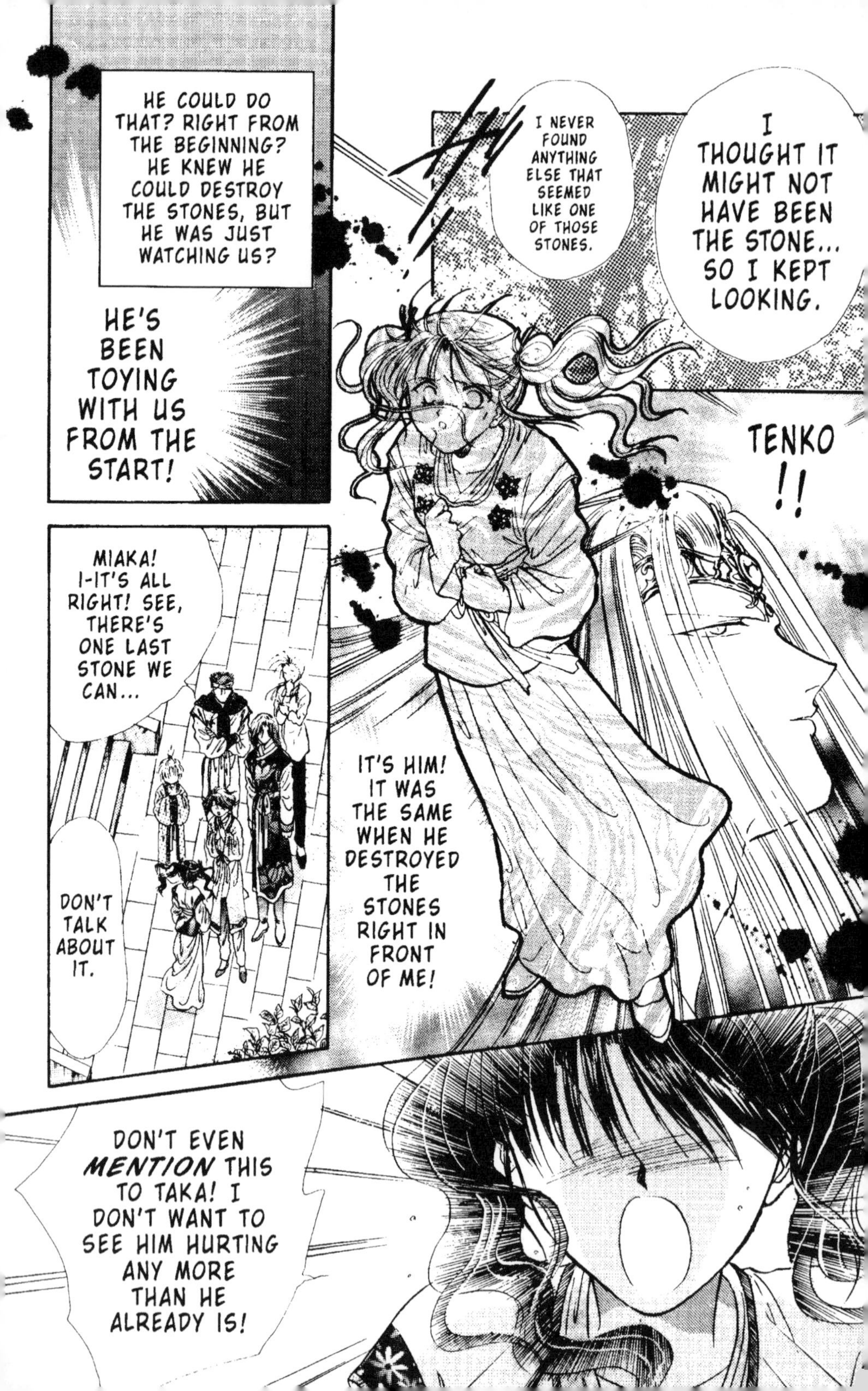
I THOUGHT IT MIGHT NOT HAVE BEEN THE STONE... SO I KEPT LOOKING.
I NEVER FOUND ANYTHING ELSE THAT SEEMED LIKE ONE OF THOSE STONES.
TENKO!!
IT'S HIM! IT WAS THE SAME WHEN HE DESTROYED THE STONES RIGHT IN FRONT OF ME!
HE COULD DO THAT? RIGHT FROM THE BEGINNING? HE KNEW HE COULD DESTROY THE STONES, BUT HE WAS JUST WATCHING US?
HE'S BEEN TOYING WITH US FROM THE START!
MIAKA! I-IT'S ALL RIGHT! SEE, THERE'S ONE LAST STONE WE CAN...
DON'T TALK ABOUT IT.
DON'T EVEN *MENTION* THIS TO TAKA! I DON'T WANT TO SEE HIM HURTING ANY MORE THAN HE ALREADY IS!

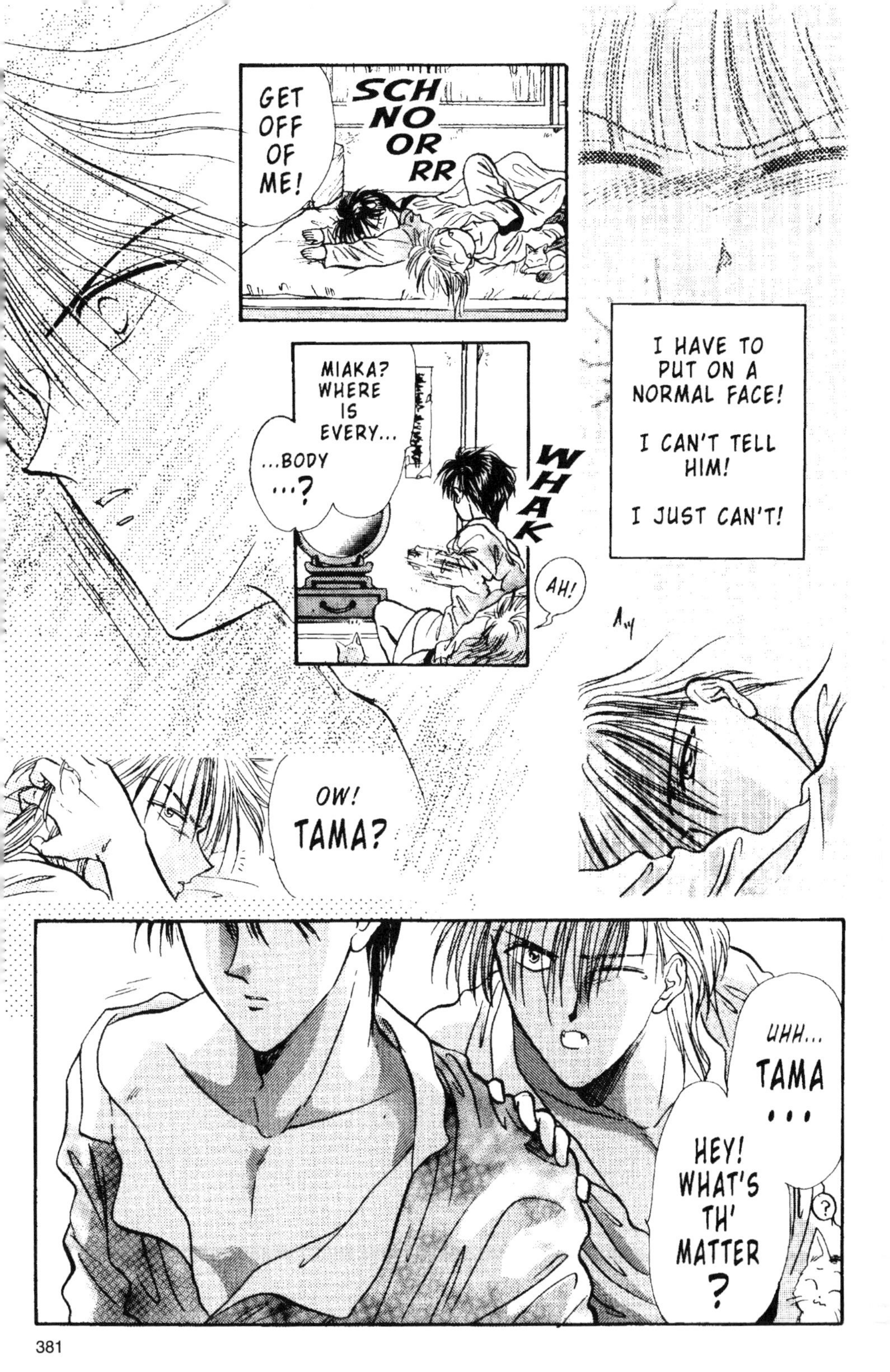
SCH NO OR RR
GET OFF OF ME!
I HAVE TO PUT ON A NORMAL FACE!
I CAN'T TELL HIM!
I JUST CAN'T!
MIAKA? WHERE IS EVERY...
...BODY ...?
WHAK
AH!
Ay
OW! TAMA?
UHH... TAMA ...
HEY! WHAT'S TH' MATTER ?
?

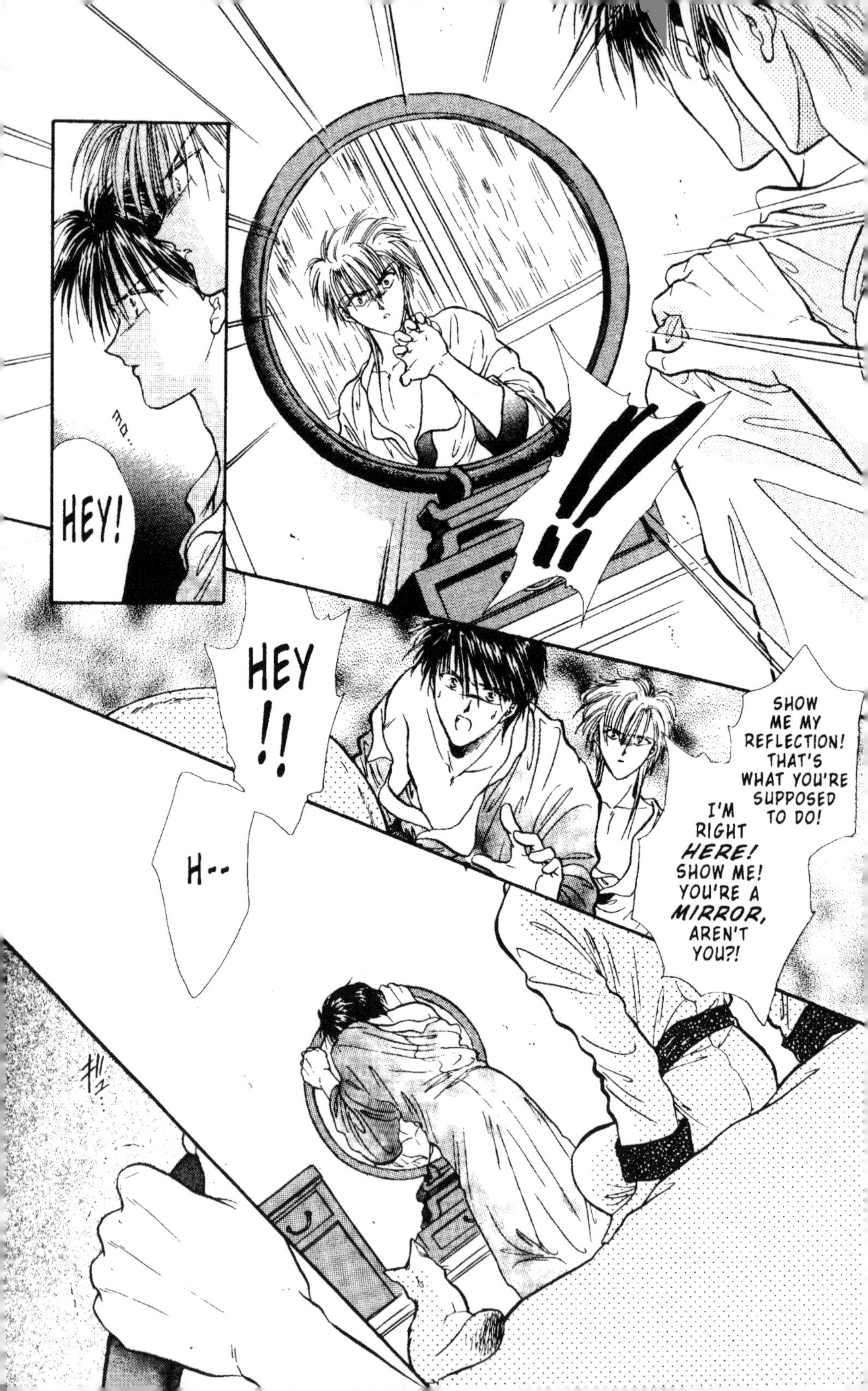

!!
ma...
HEY!
SHOW ME MY REFLECTION! THAT'S WHAT YOU'RE SUPPOSED TO DO!
I'M RIGHT *HERE!* SHOW ME! YOU'RE A *MIRROR,* AREN'T YOU?!
HEY !!
H--

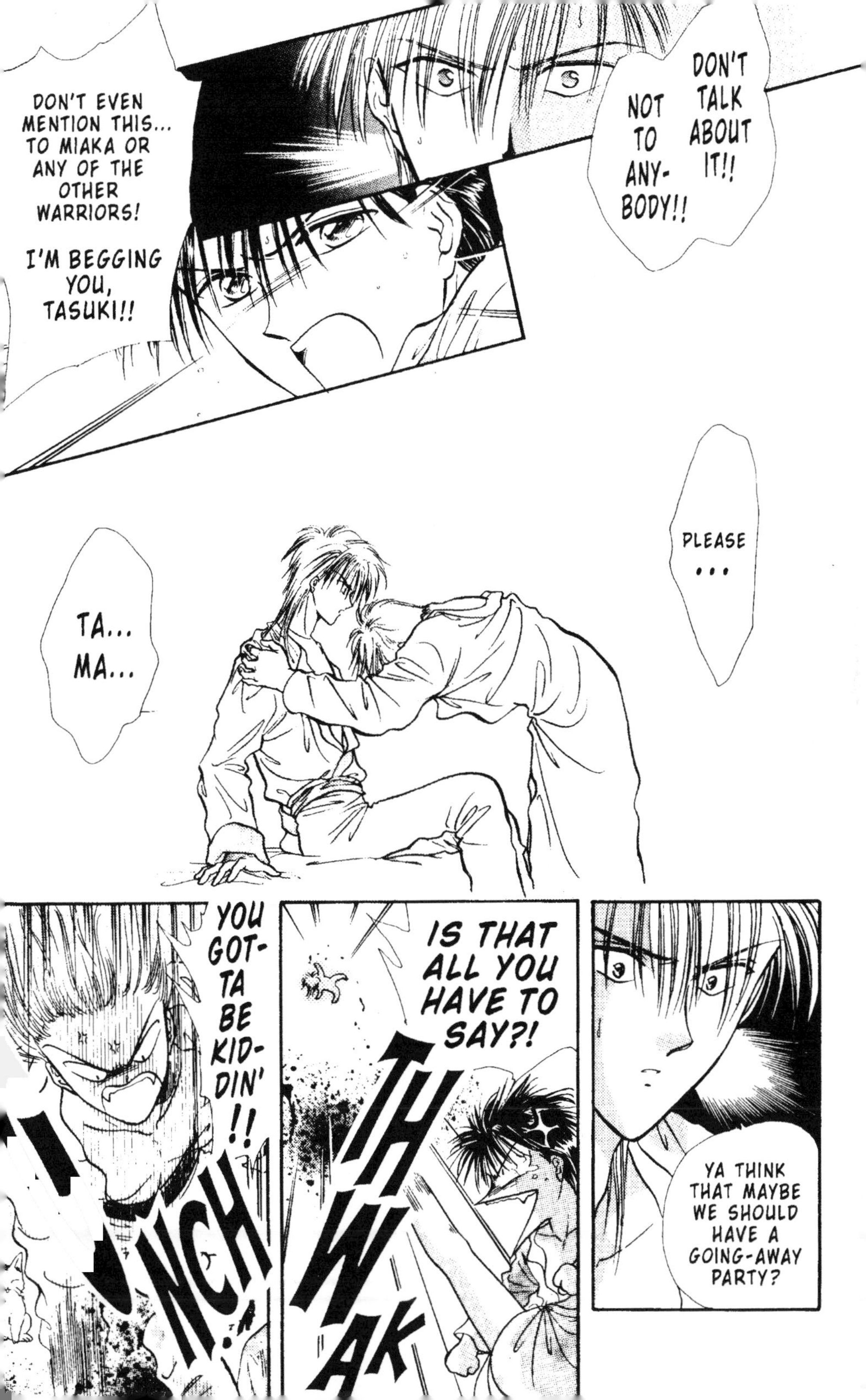
DON'T TALK ABOUT IT!!
NOT TO ANY-BODY!!
DON'T EVEN MENTION THIS... TO MIAKA OR ANY OF THE OTHER WARRIORS!
I'M BEGGING YOU, TASUKI!!
PLEASE...
TA... MA...
YA THINK THAT MAYBE WE SHOULD HAVE A GOING-AWAY PARTY?
IS THAT ALL YOU HAVE TO SAY?!
THWAK
YOU GOT-TA BE KID-DIN'!!
NCH!

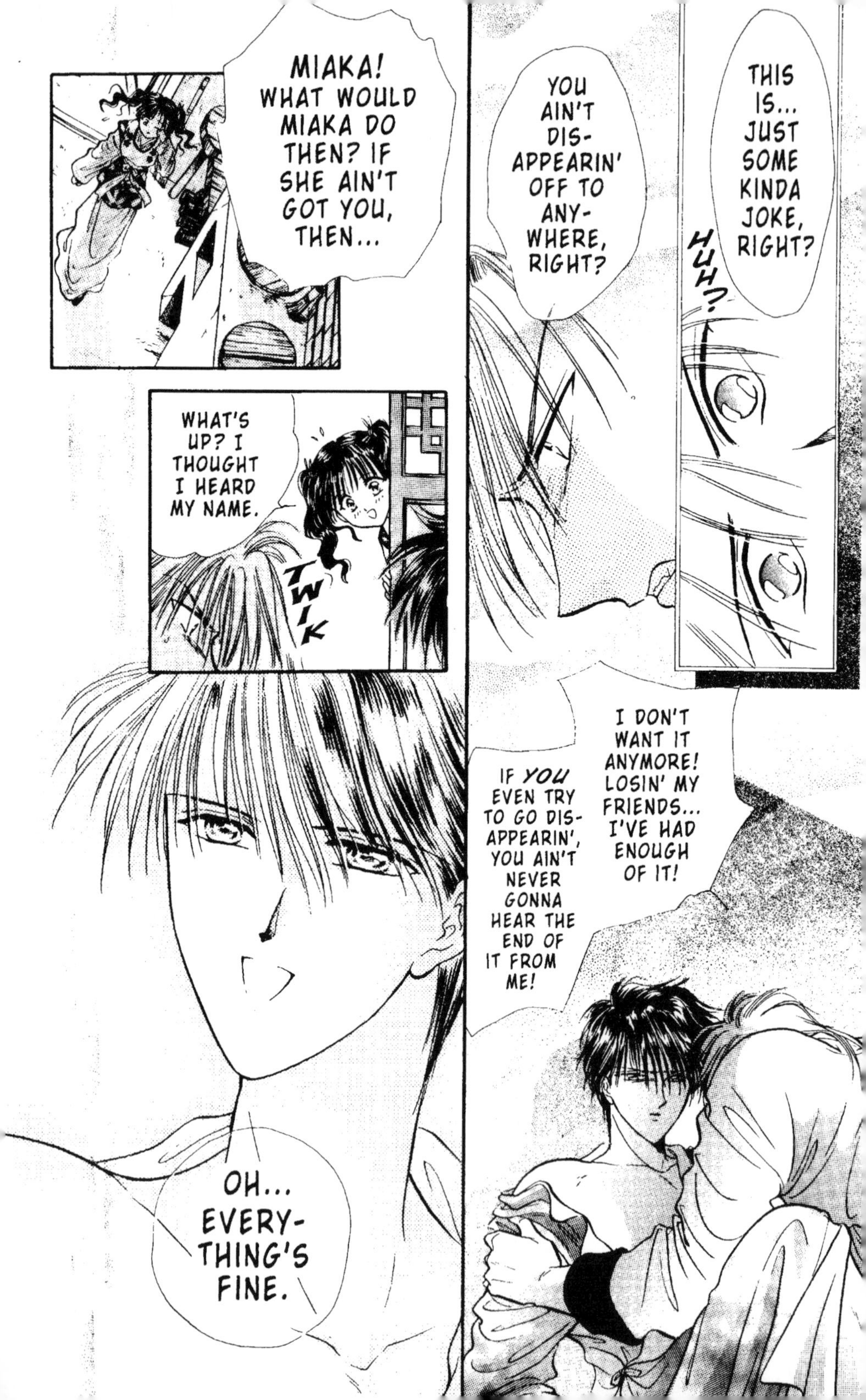
THIS IS... JUST SOME KINDA JOKE, RIGHT?
HUH?
YOU AIN'T DIS-APPEARIN' OFF TO ANY-WHERE, RIGHT?
I DON'T WANT IT ANYMORE! LOSIN' MY FRIENDS... I'VE HAD ENOUGH OF IT!
IF *YOU* EVEN TRY TO GO DIS-APPEARIN', YOU AIN'T NEVER GONNA HEAR THE END OF IT FROM ME!
MIAKA! WHAT WOULD MIAKA DO THEN? IF SHE AIN'T GOT YOU, THEN...
WHAT'S UP? I THOUGHT I HEARD MY NAME.
TWIK
OH... EVERY-THING'S FINE.

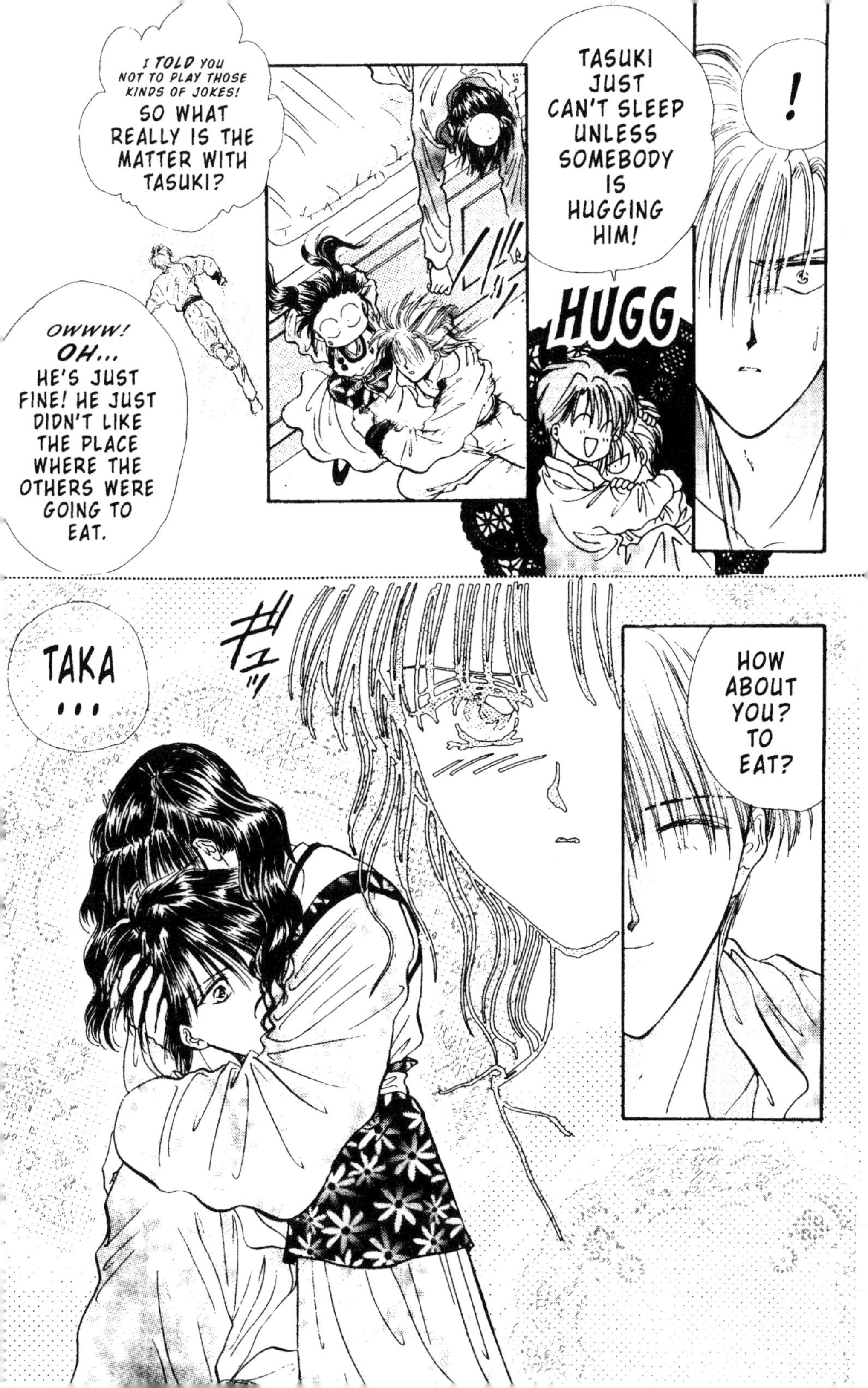
!
TASUKI JUST CAN'T SLEEP UNLESS SOMEBODY IS HUGGING HIM!
HUGG
I TOLD YOU NOT TO PLAY THOSE KINDS OF JOKES! SO WHAT REALLY IS THE MATTER WITH TASUKI?
OWWW! OH... HE'S JUST FINE! HE JUST DIDN'T LIKE THE PLACE WHERE THE OTHERS WERE GOING TO EAT.
HOW ABOUT YOU? TO EAT?
TAKA ...

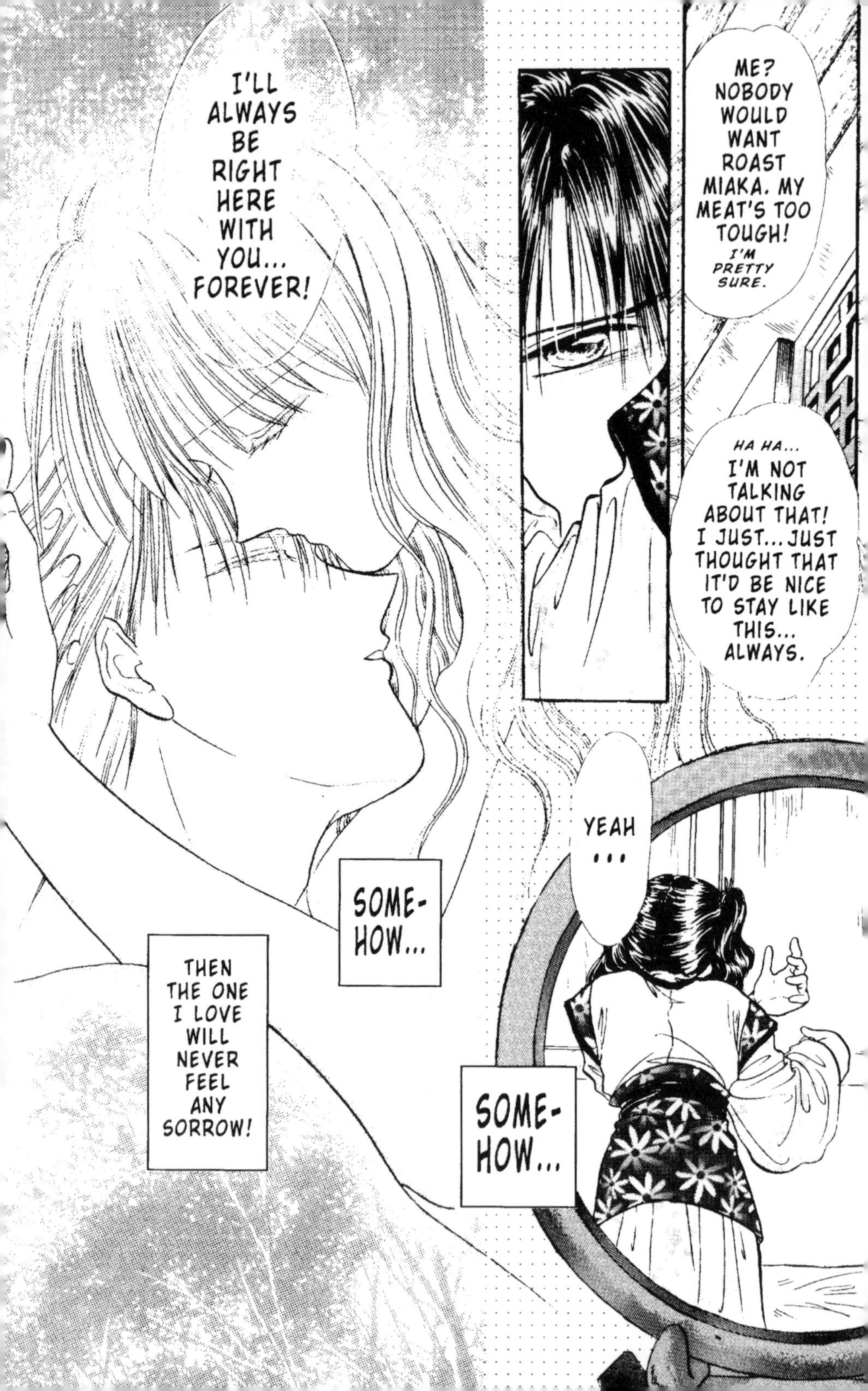
ME? NOBODY WOULD WANT ROAST MIAKA. MY MEAT'S TOO TOUGH!
I'M PRETTY SURE.
HA HA... I'M NOT TALKING ABOUT THAT! I JUST... JUST THOUGHT THAT IT'D BE NICE TO STAY LIKE THIS... ALWAYS.
YEAH...
SOME-HOW...
I'LL ALWAYS BE RIGHT HERE WITH YOU... FOREVER!
SOME-HOW...
THEN THE ONE I LOVE WILL NEVER FEEL ANY SORROW!

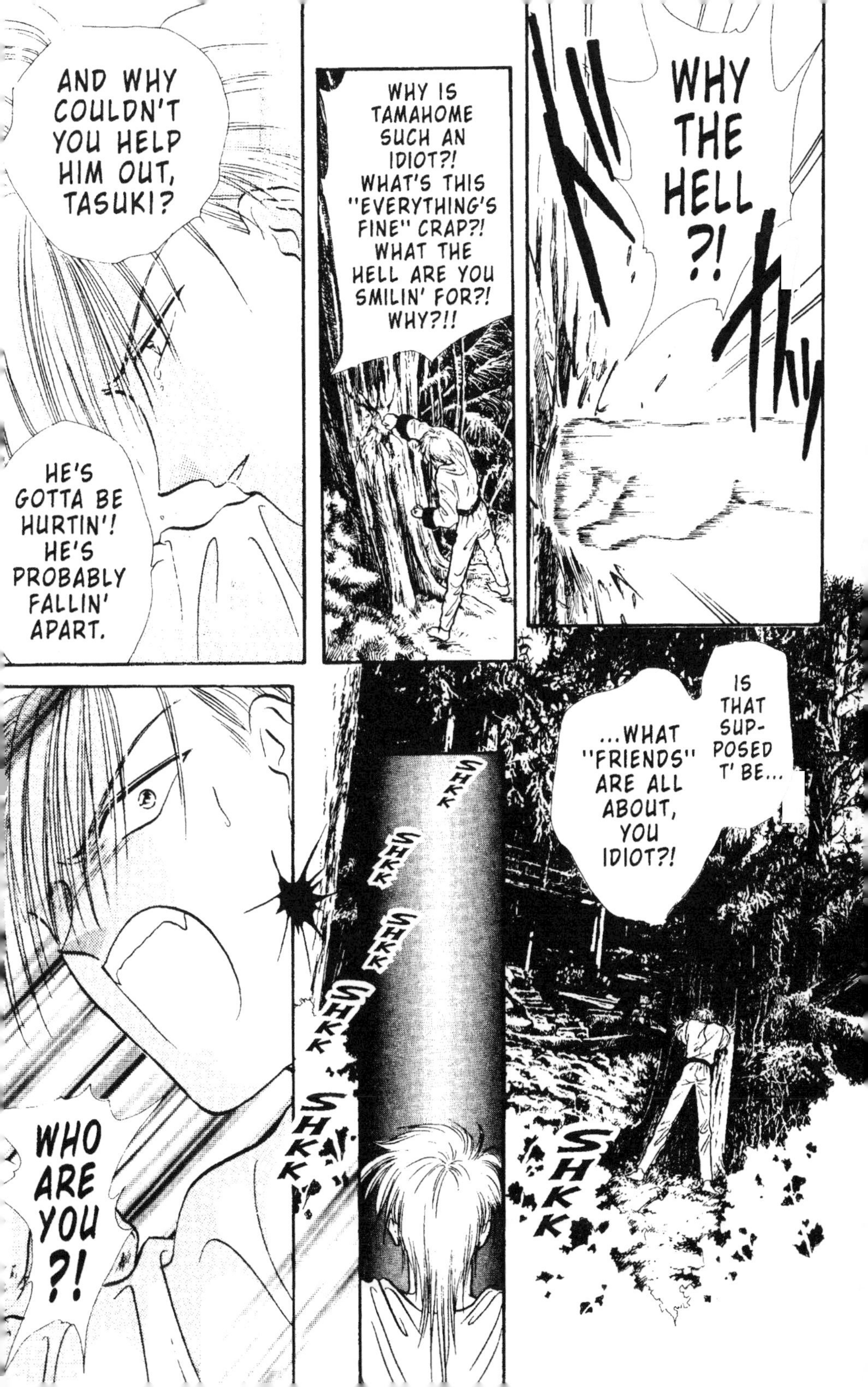
WHY THE HELL ?!
WHY IS TAMAHOME SUCH AN IDIOT?! WHAT'S THIS "EVERYTHING'S FINE" CRAP?! WHAT THE HELL ARE YOU SMILIN' FOR?! WHY?!!
AND WHY COULDN'T YOU HELP HIM OUT, TASUKI?
HE'S GOTTA BE HURTIN'! HE'S PROBABLY FALLIN' APART.
IS THAT SUP-POSED T' BE...
...WHAT "FRIENDS" ARE ALL ABOUT, YOU IDIOT?!
SHKK
SHKK
SHKK
SHKK
SHKK
SHKK
SHKK
WHO ARE YOU ?!

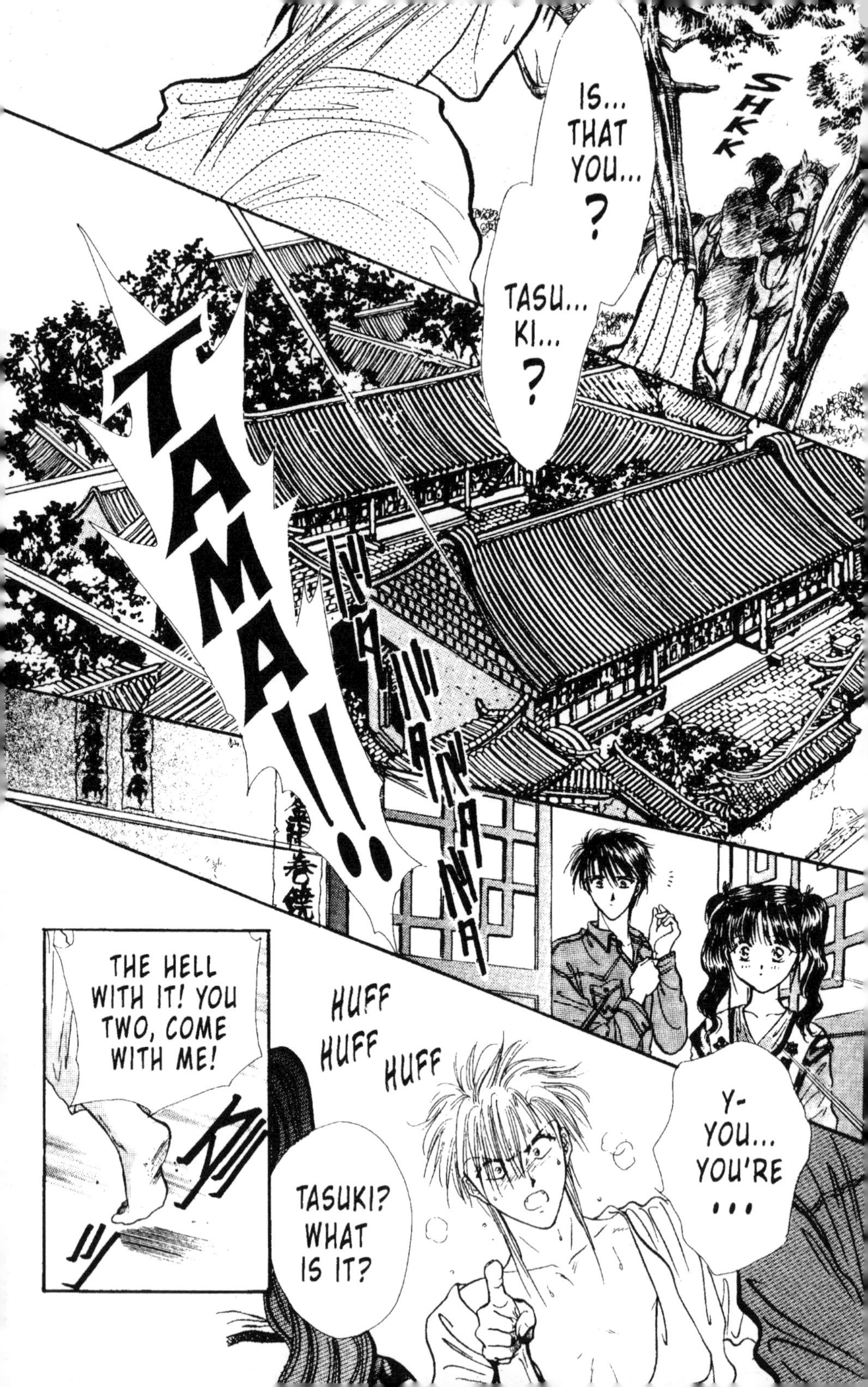
IS... THAT YOU... ?
TASU... KI... ?
SHKK
TAMA!!!..
Y-YOU... YOU'RE ...
TASUKI? WHAT IS IT?
HUFF HUFF HUFF
THE HELL WITH IT! YOU TWO, COME WITH ME!

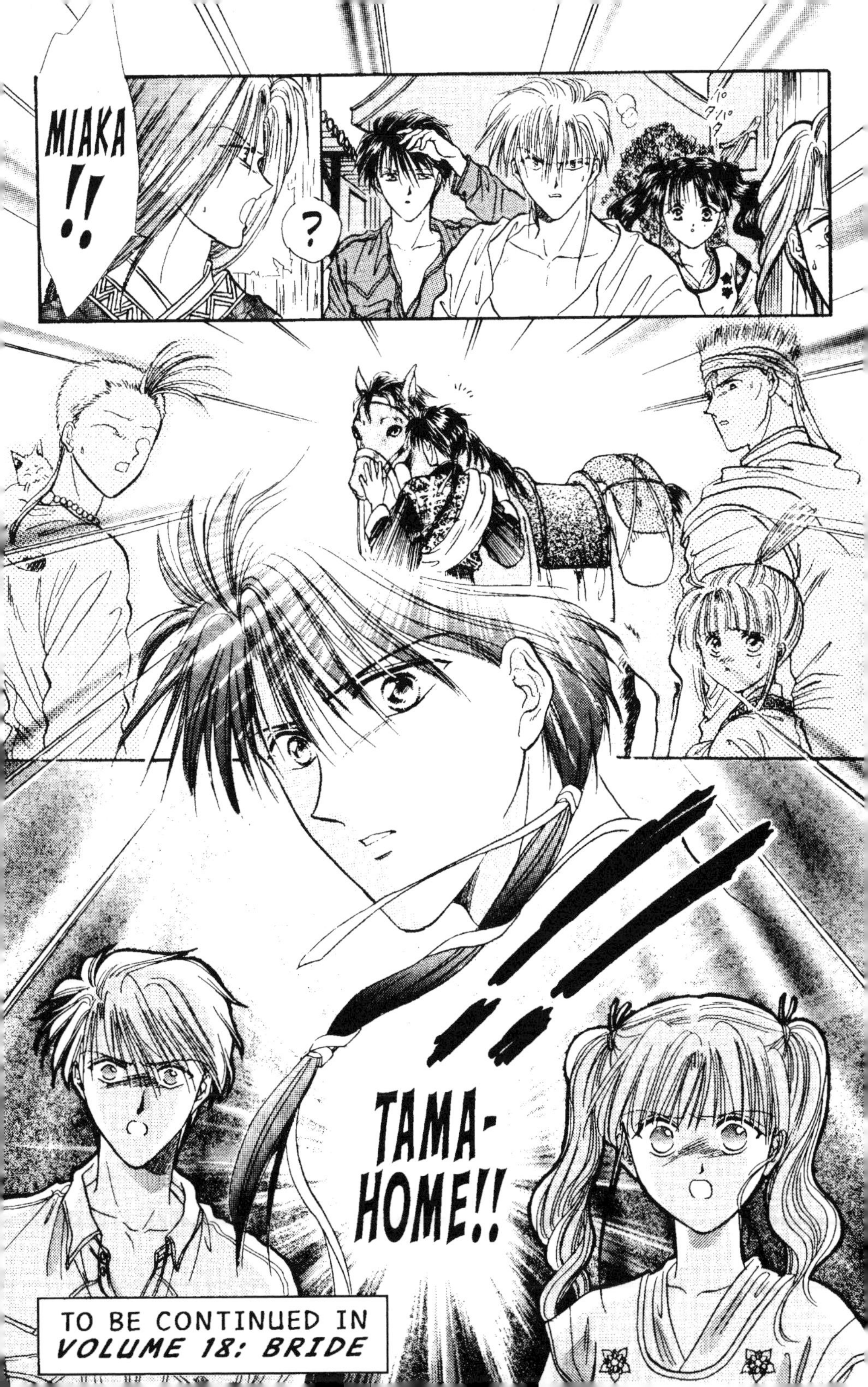
?
MIAKA!!
TAMA-HOME!!
TO BE CONTINUED IN VOLUME 18: BRIDE

FUSHIGI YÛGI

Volume 18: **Bride**

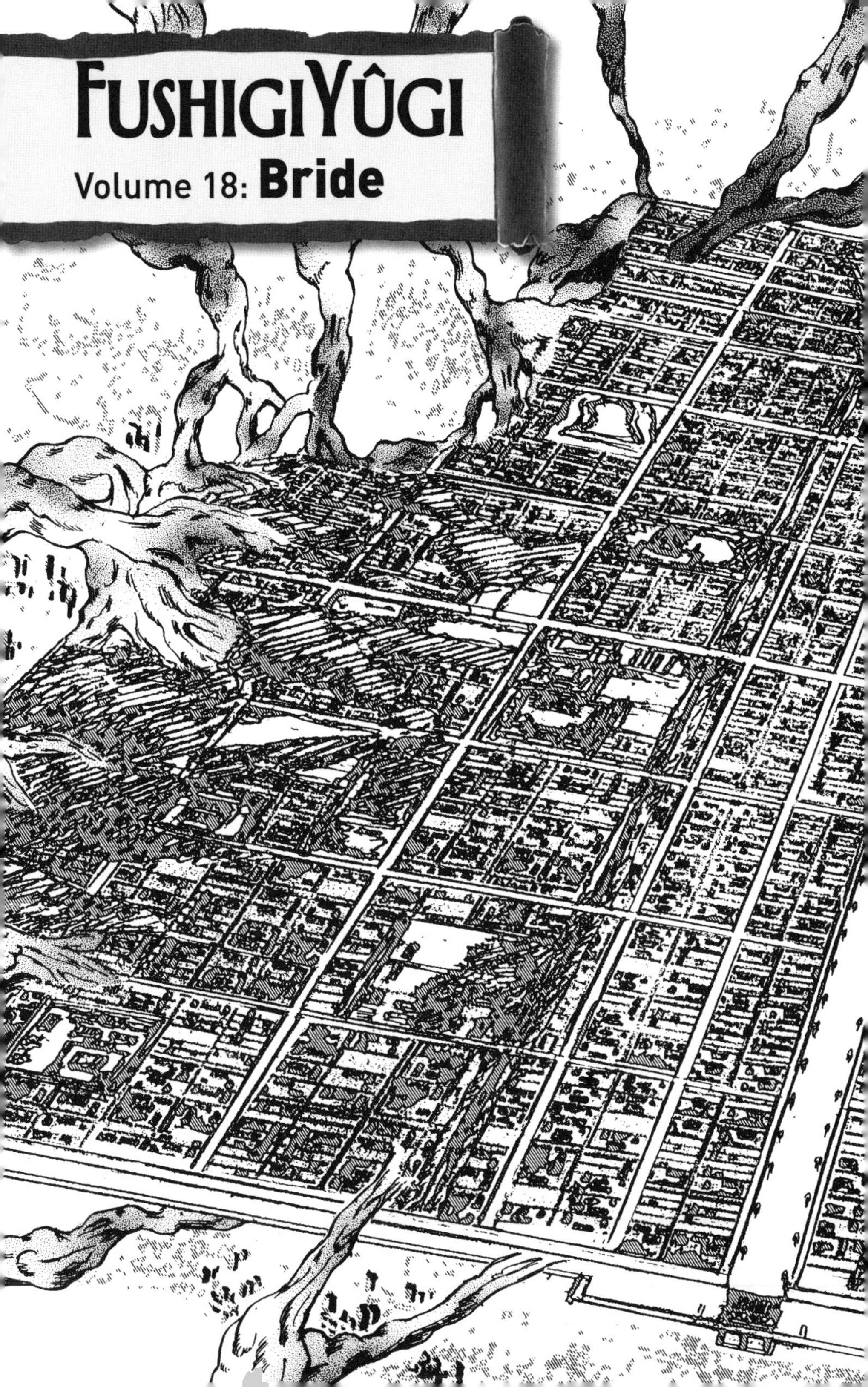

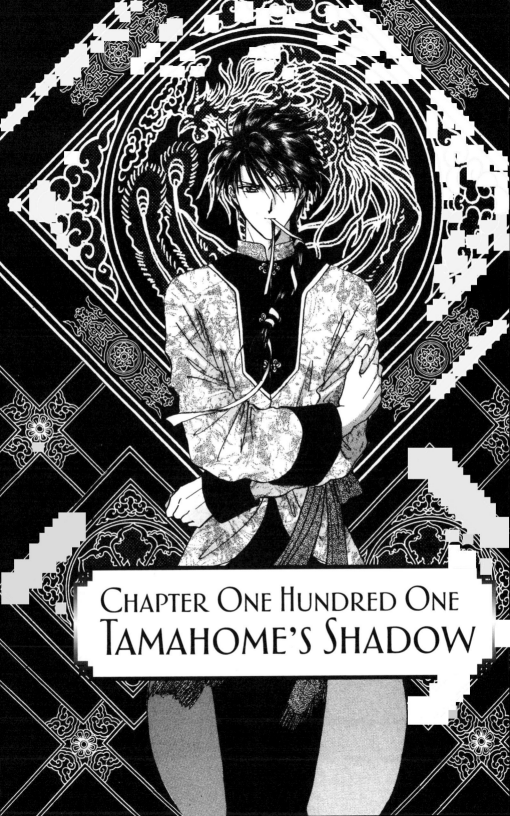

CHAPTER ONE HUNDRED ONE
TAMAHOME'S SHADOW

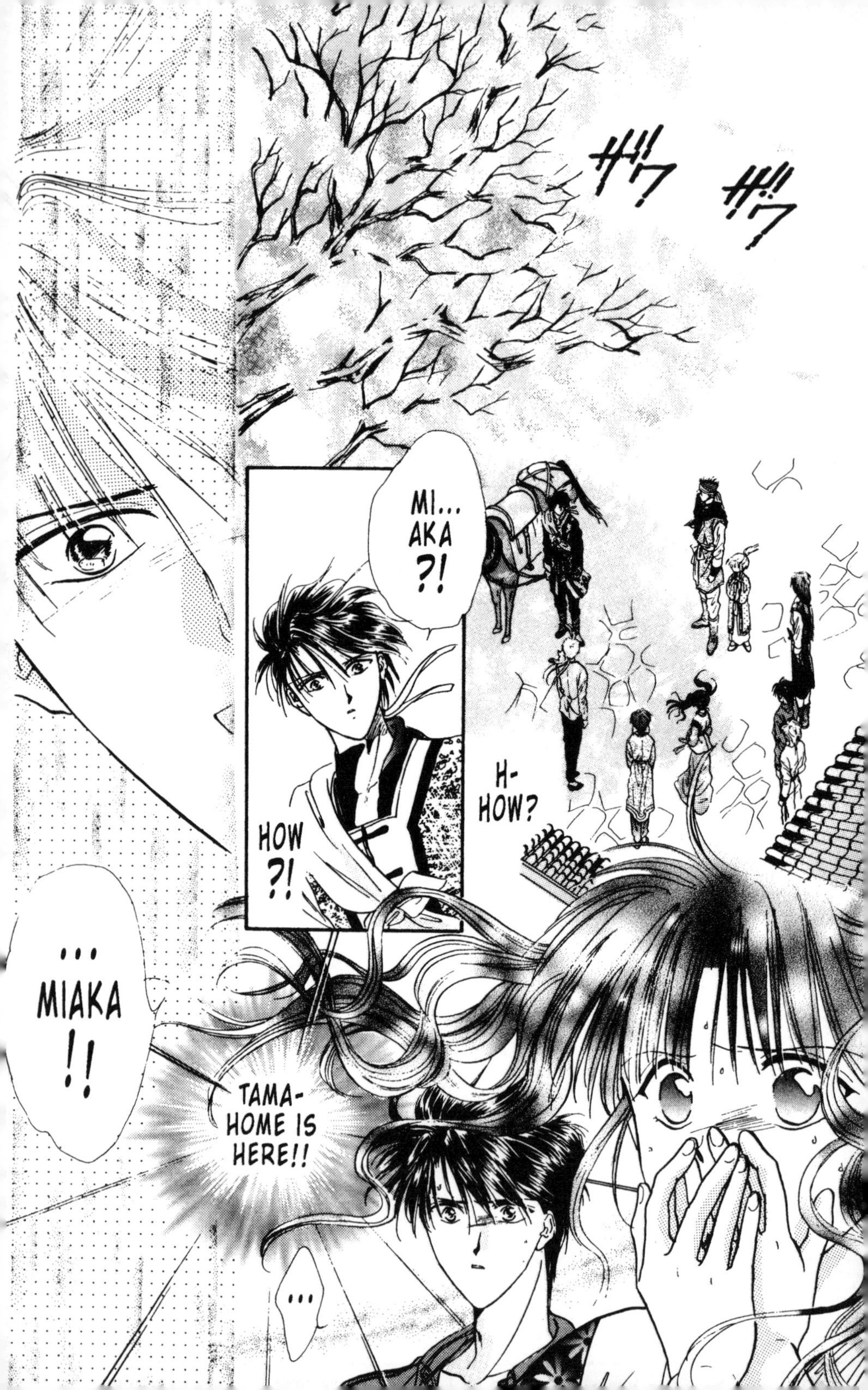
ザワ ザワ
H- HOW?
MI... AKA ?!
HOW ?!
TAMA-HOME IS HERE!!
...
... MIAKA !!

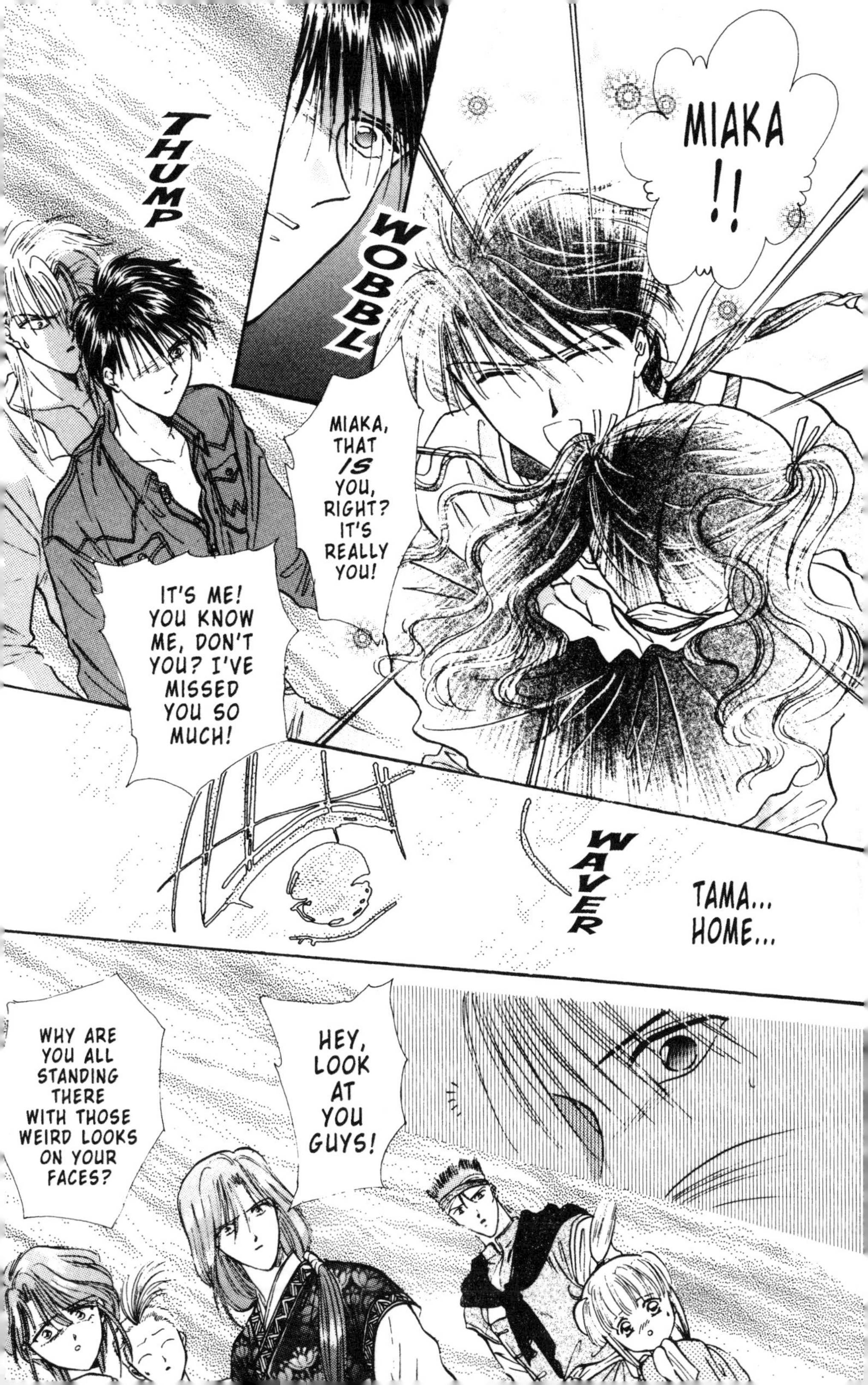
MIAKA !!
WOBBL
MIAKA, THAT IS YOU, RIGHT? IT'S REALLY YOU!
IT'S ME! YOU KNOW ME, DON'T YOU? I'VE MISSED YOU SO MUCH!
THUMP
TAMA... HOME...
WAVER
HEY, LOOK AT YOU GUYS!
WHY ARE YOU ALL STANDING THERE WITH THOSE WEIRD LOOKS ON YOUR FACES?

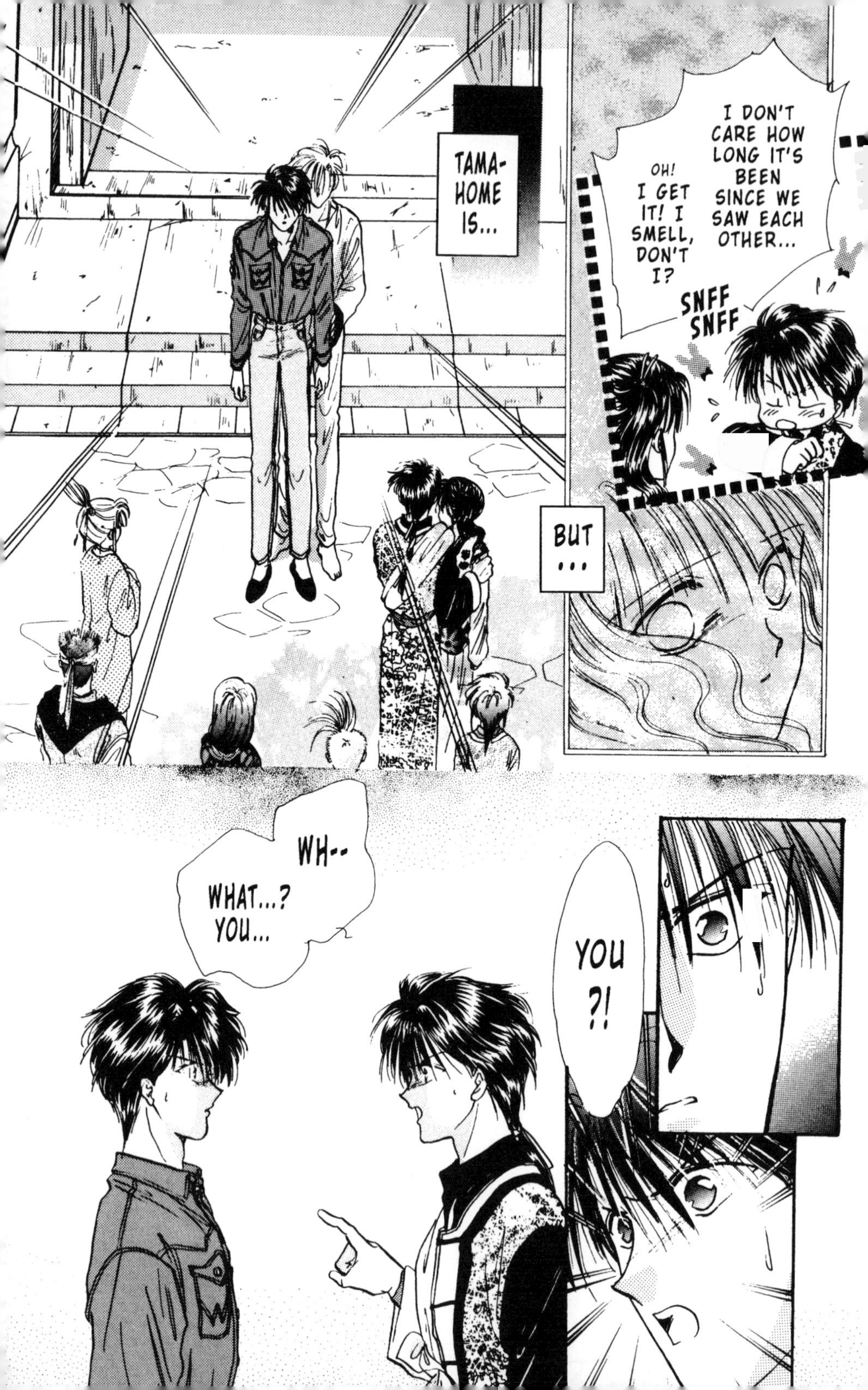
I DON'T CARE HOW LONG IT'S BEEN SINCE WE SAW EACH OTHER...
OH! I GET IT! I SMELL, DON'T I?
SNFF SNFF
BUT...
TAMA-HOME IS...
YOU ?!
WH-- WHAT...? YOU...

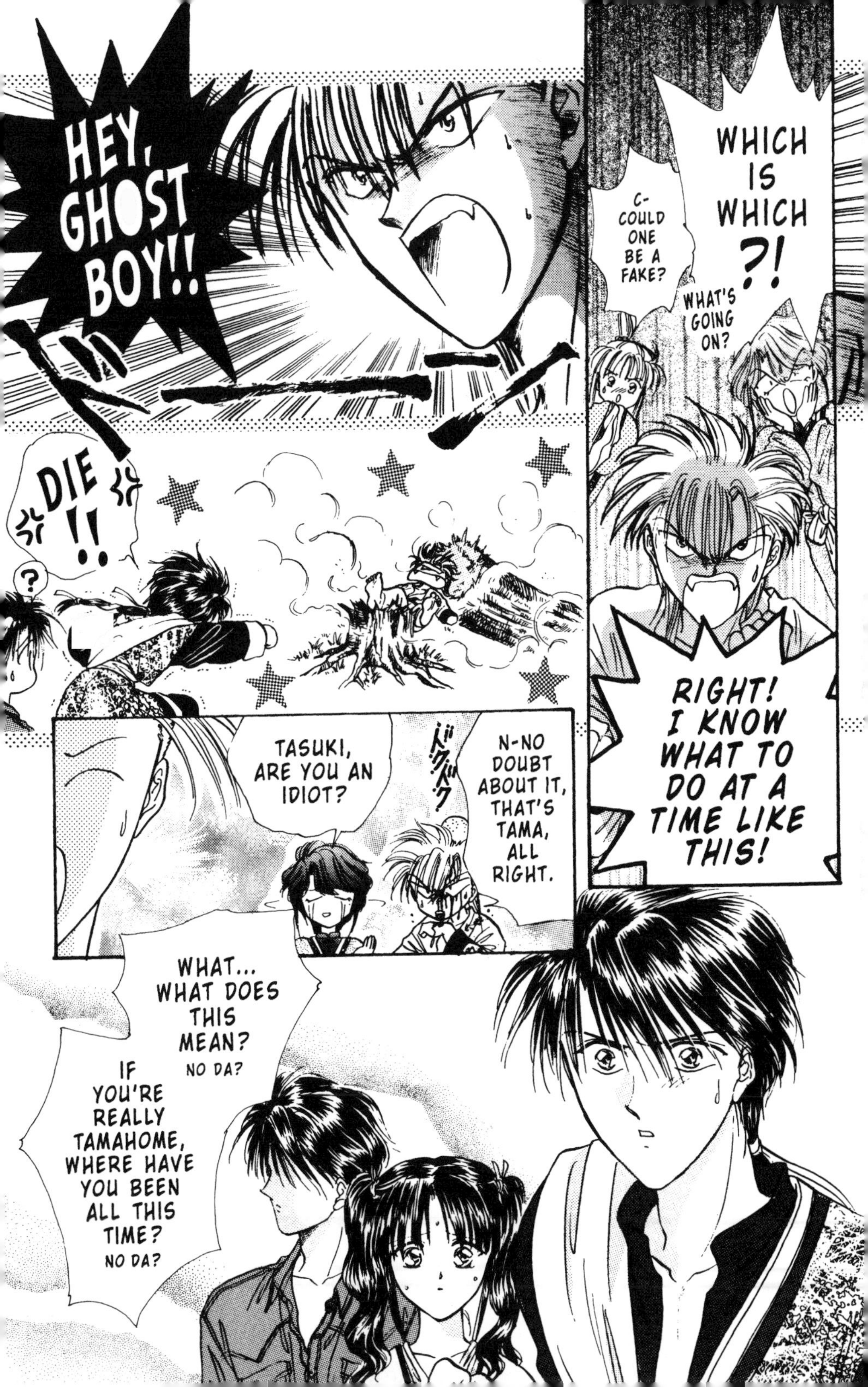
WHICH IS WHICH ?!
C-COULD ONE BE A FAKE?
WHAT'S GOING ON?
RIGHT! I KNOW WHAT TO DO AT A TIME LIKE THIS!
HEY, GHOST BOY!!
DIE!!
?
N-NO DOUBT ABOUT IT, THAT'S TAMA, ALL RIGHT.
TASUKI, ARE YOU AN IDIOT?
WHAT... WHAT DOES THIS MEAN? NO DA?
IF YOU'RE REALLY TAMAHOME, WHERE HAVE YOU BEEN ALL THIS TIME? NO DA?

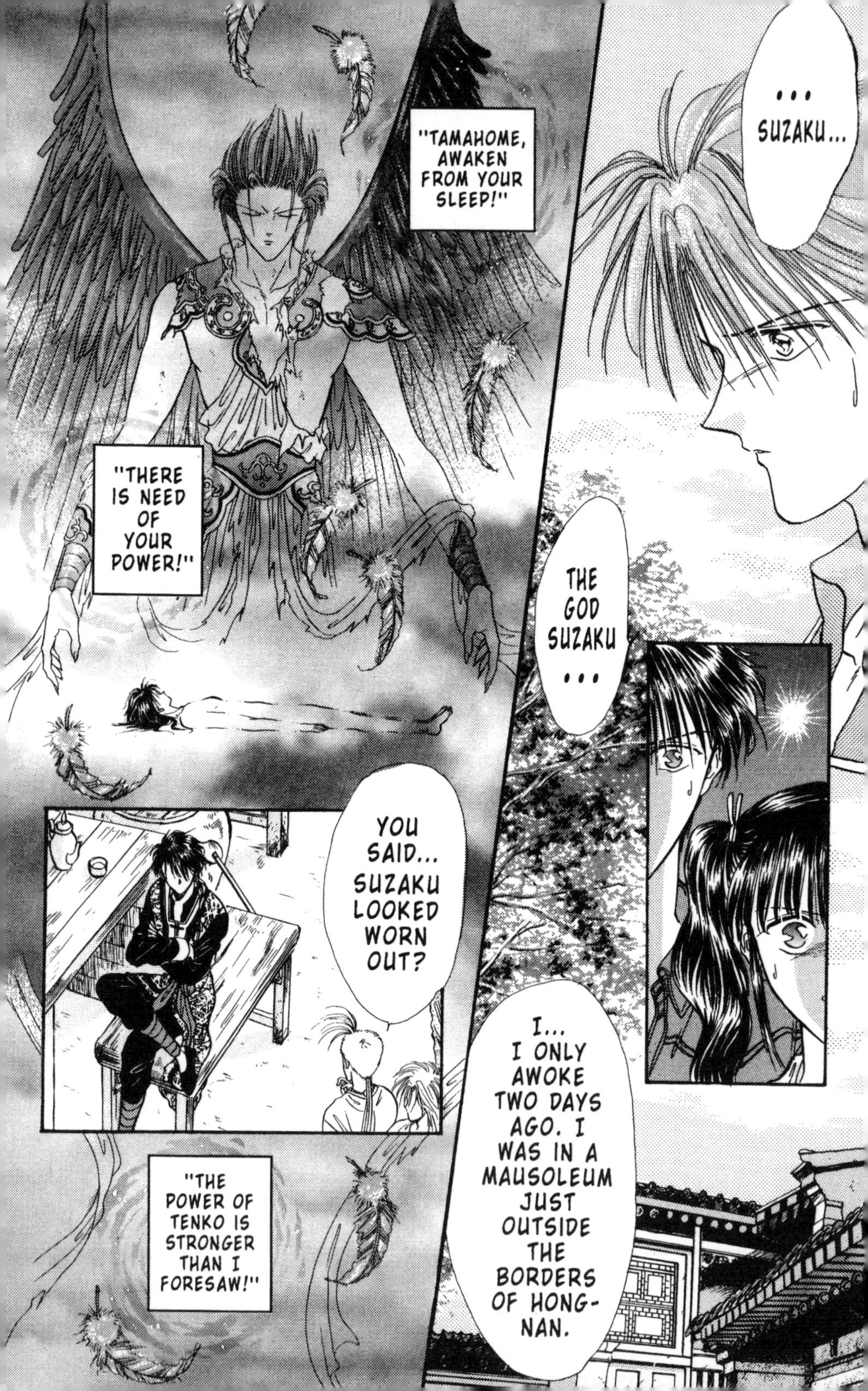
... SUZAKU...
THE GOD SUZAKU...
I... I ONLY AWOKE TWO DAYS AGO. I WAS IN A MAUSOLEUM JUST OUTSIDE THE BORDERS OF HONG-NAN.
"TAMAHOME, AWAKEN FROM YOUR SLEEP!"
"THERE IS NEED OF YOUR POWER!"
YOU SAID... SUZAKU LOOKED WORN OUT?
"THE POWER OF TENKO IS STRONGER THAN I FORESAW!"

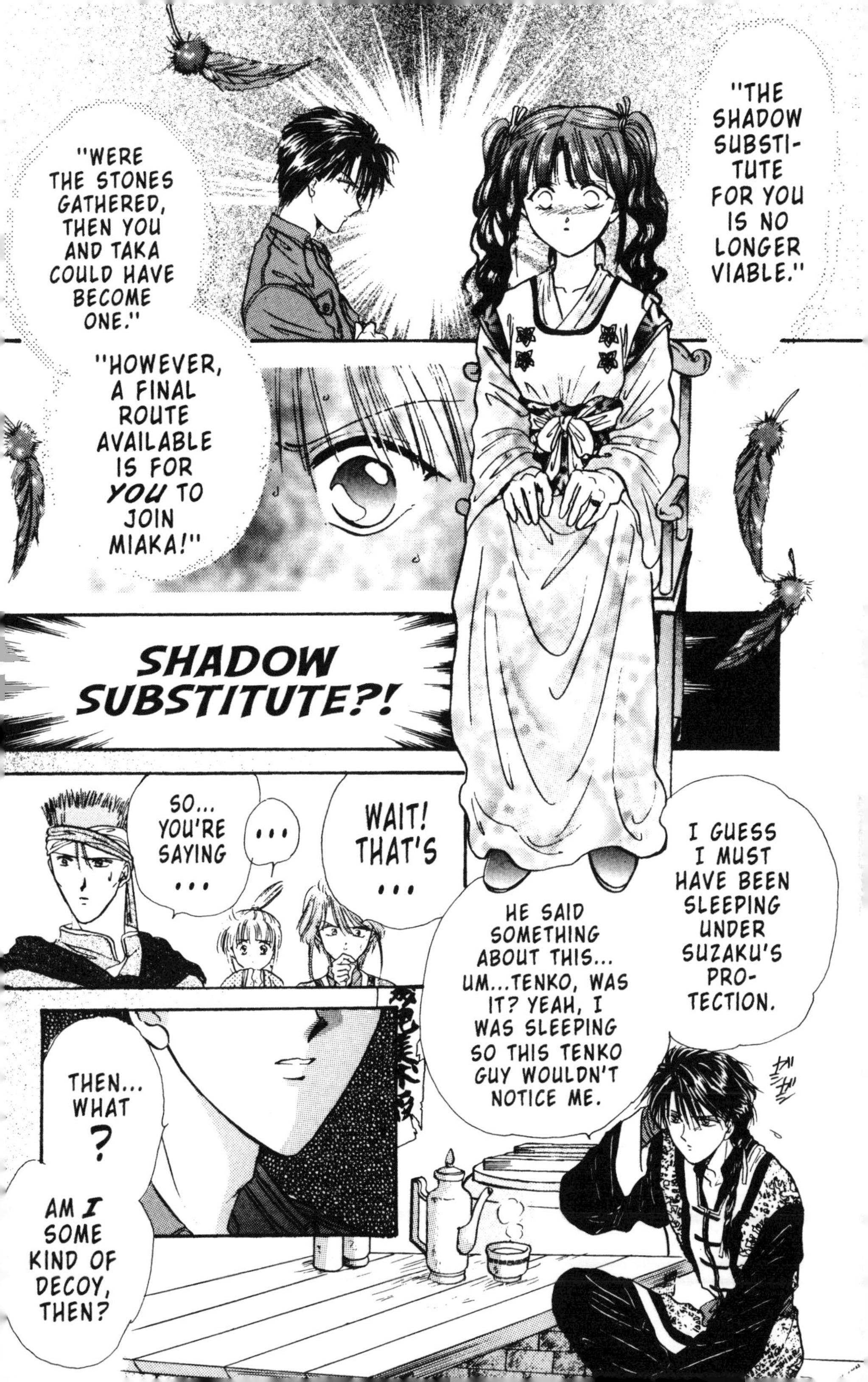
"THE SHADOW SUBSTITUTE FOR YOU IS NO LONGER VIABLE."
"WERE THE STONES GATHERED, THEN YOU AND TAKA COULD HAVE BECOME ONE."
"HOWEVER, A FINAL ROUTE AVAILABLE IS FOR *YOU* TO JOIN MIAKA!"
SHADOW SUBSTITUTE?!
WAIT! THAT'S ...
...
SO... YOU'RE SAYING ...
I GUESS I MUST HAVE BEEN SLEEPING UNDER SUZAKU'S PROTECTION.
HE SAID SOMETHING ABOUT THIS... UM...TENKO, WAS IT? YEAH, I WAS SLEEPING SO THIS TENKO GUY WOULDN'T NOTICE ME.
THEN... WHAT ?
AM *I* SOME KIND OF DECOY, THEN?

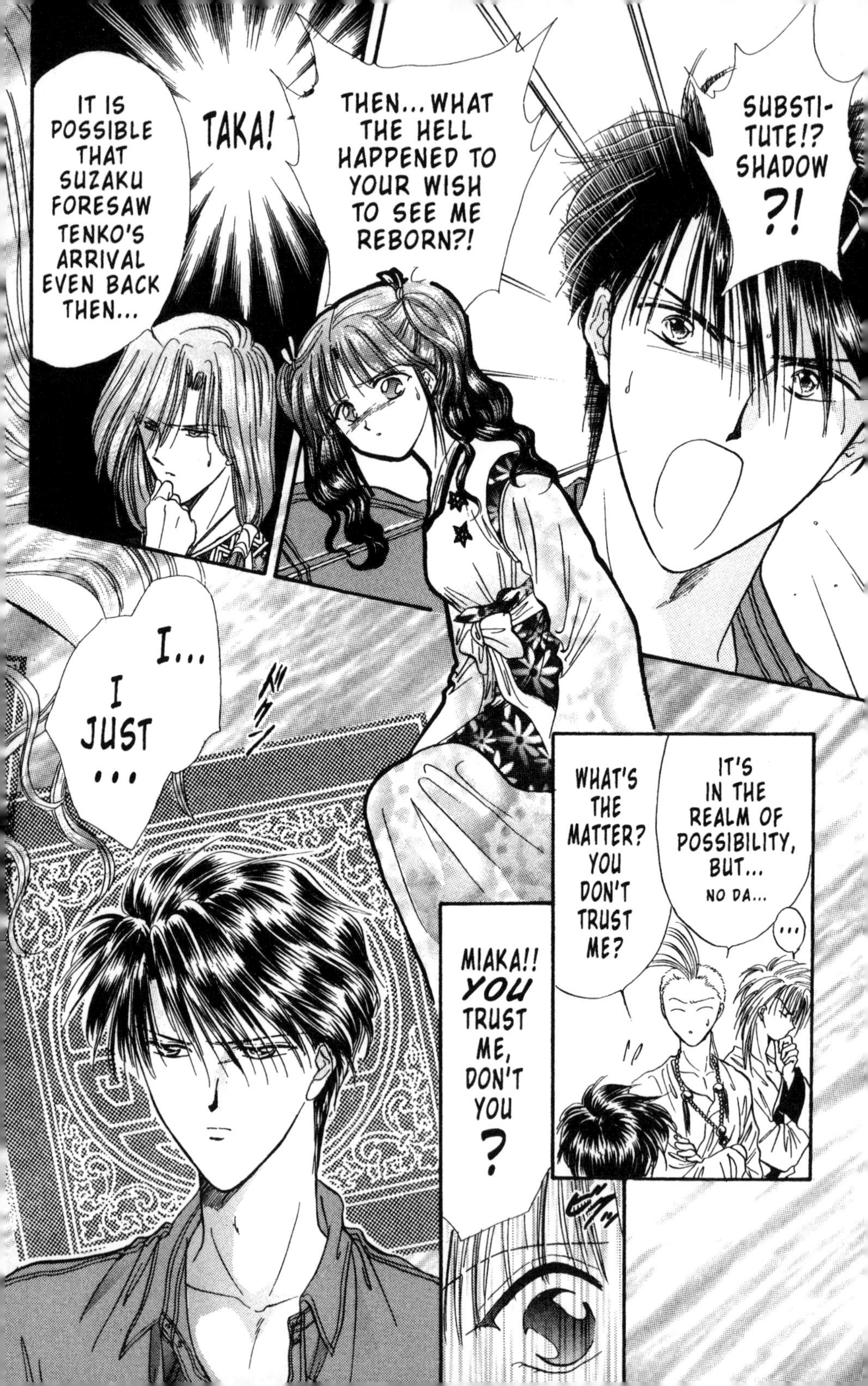
SUBSTITUTE!? SHADOW ?!
THEN...WHAT THE HELL HAPPENED TO YOUR WISH TO SEE ME REBORN?!
TAKA!
IT IS POSSIBLE THAT SUZAKU FORESAW TENKO'S ARRIVAL EVEN BACK THEN...
IT'S IN THE REALM OF POSSIBILITY, BUT... NO DA...
...
WHAT'S THE MATTER? YOU DON'T TRUST ME?
MIAKA!! YOU TRUST ME, DON'T YOU ?
I... I JUST ...

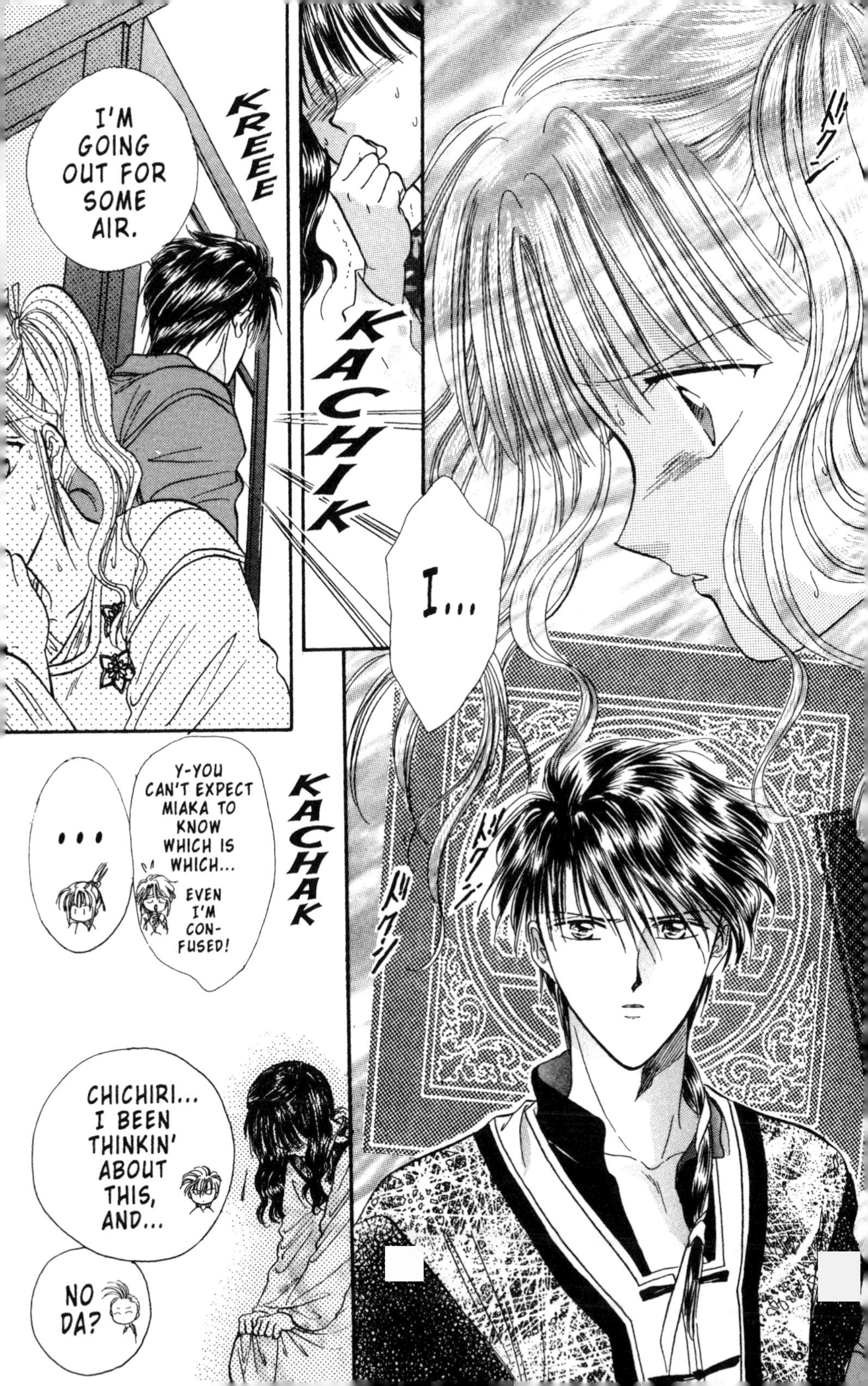
I...
KACHIK
KREEE
I'M GOING OUT FOR SOME AIR.
Y-YOU CAN'T EXPECT MIAKA TO KNOW WHICH IS WHICH...
EVEN I'M CON-FUSED!
...
KACHAK
CHICHIRI... I BEEN THINKIN' ABOUT THIS, AND...
NO DA?

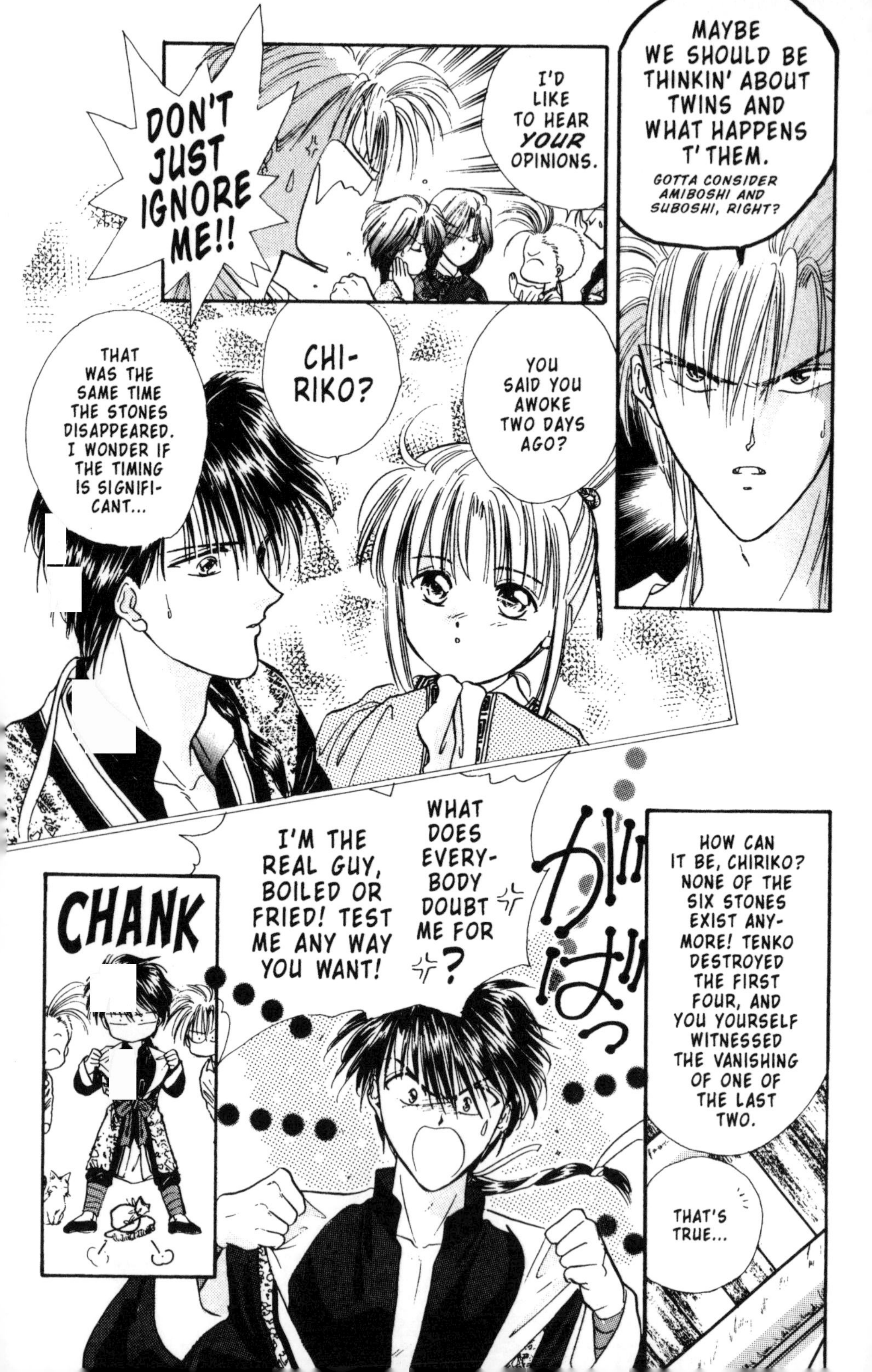
MAYBE WE SHOULD BE THINKIN' ABOUT TWINS AND WHAT HAPPENS T' THEM.
GOTTA CONSIDER AMIBOSHI AND SUBOSHI, RIGHT?
I'D LIKE TO HEAR *YOUR* OPINIONS.
DON'T JUST IGNORE ME!!
YOU SAID YOU AWOKE TWO DAYS AGO?
CHI-RIKO?
THAT WAS THE SAME TIME THE STONES DISAPPEARED. I WONDER IF THE TIMING IS SIGNIFI-CANT...
HOW CAN IT BE, CHIRIKO? NONE OF THE SIX STONES EXIST ANY-MORE! TENKO DESTROYED THE FIRST FOUR, AND YOU YOURSELF WITNESSED THE VANISHING OF ONE OF THE LAST TWO.
THAT'S TRUE...
WHAT DOES EVERY-BODY DOUBT ME FOR?
I'M THE REAL GUY, BOILED OR FRIED! TEST ME ANY WAY YOU WANT!
CHANK

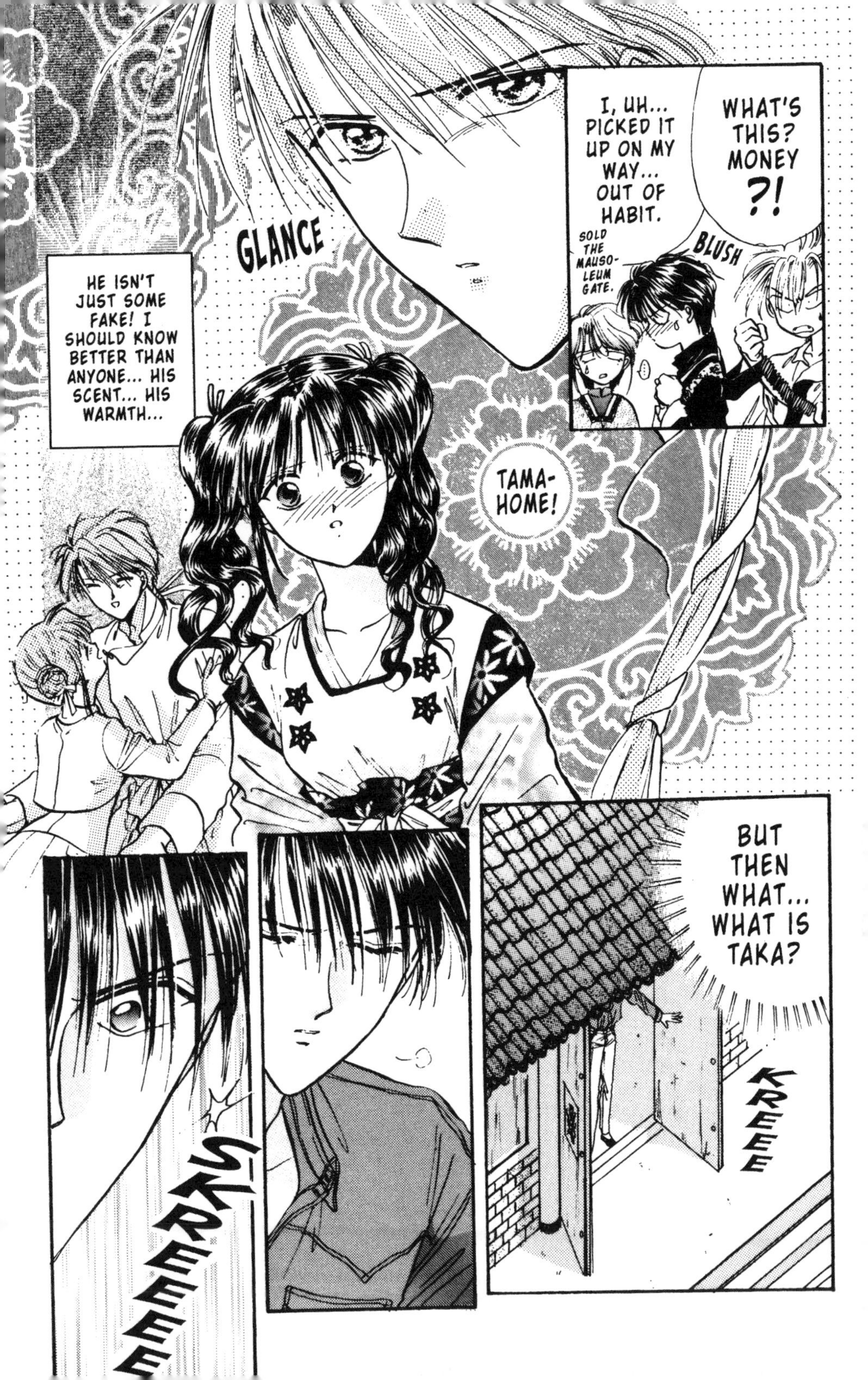
WHAT'S THIS? MONEY ?!
I, UH... PICKED IT UP ON MY WAY... OUT OF HABIT.
BLUSH
SOLD THE MAUSO-LEUM GATE.
GLANCE
HE ISN'T JUST SOME FAKE! I SHOULD KNOW BETTER THAN ANYONE... HIS SCENT... HIS WARMTH...
TAMA-HOME!
BUT THEN WHAT... WHAT IS TAKA?
KREEE
SKREEEEE

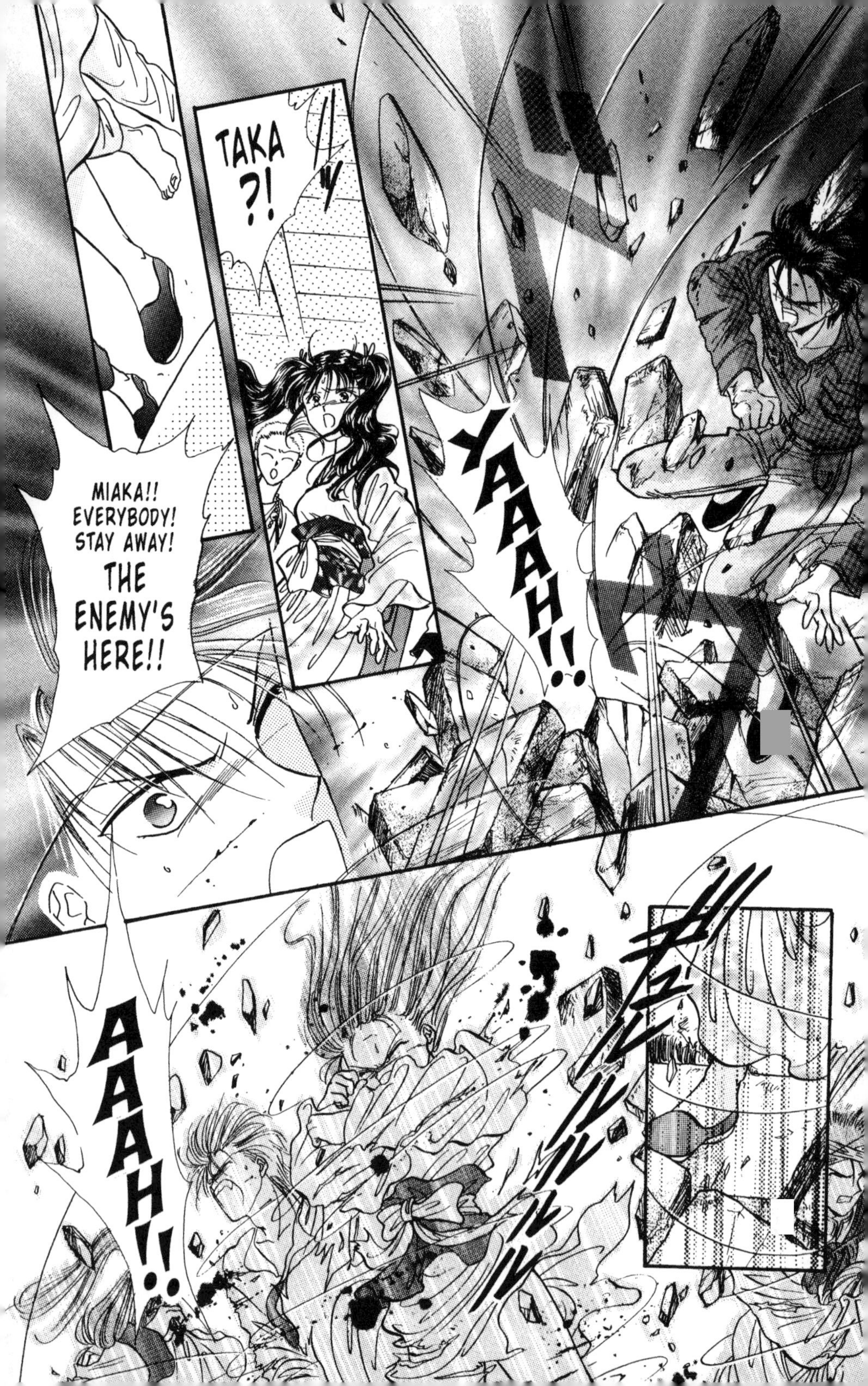
YAAAH!!
TAKA ?!
MIAKA!! EVERYBODY! STAY AWAY! THE ENEMY'S HERE!!
AAAH!!

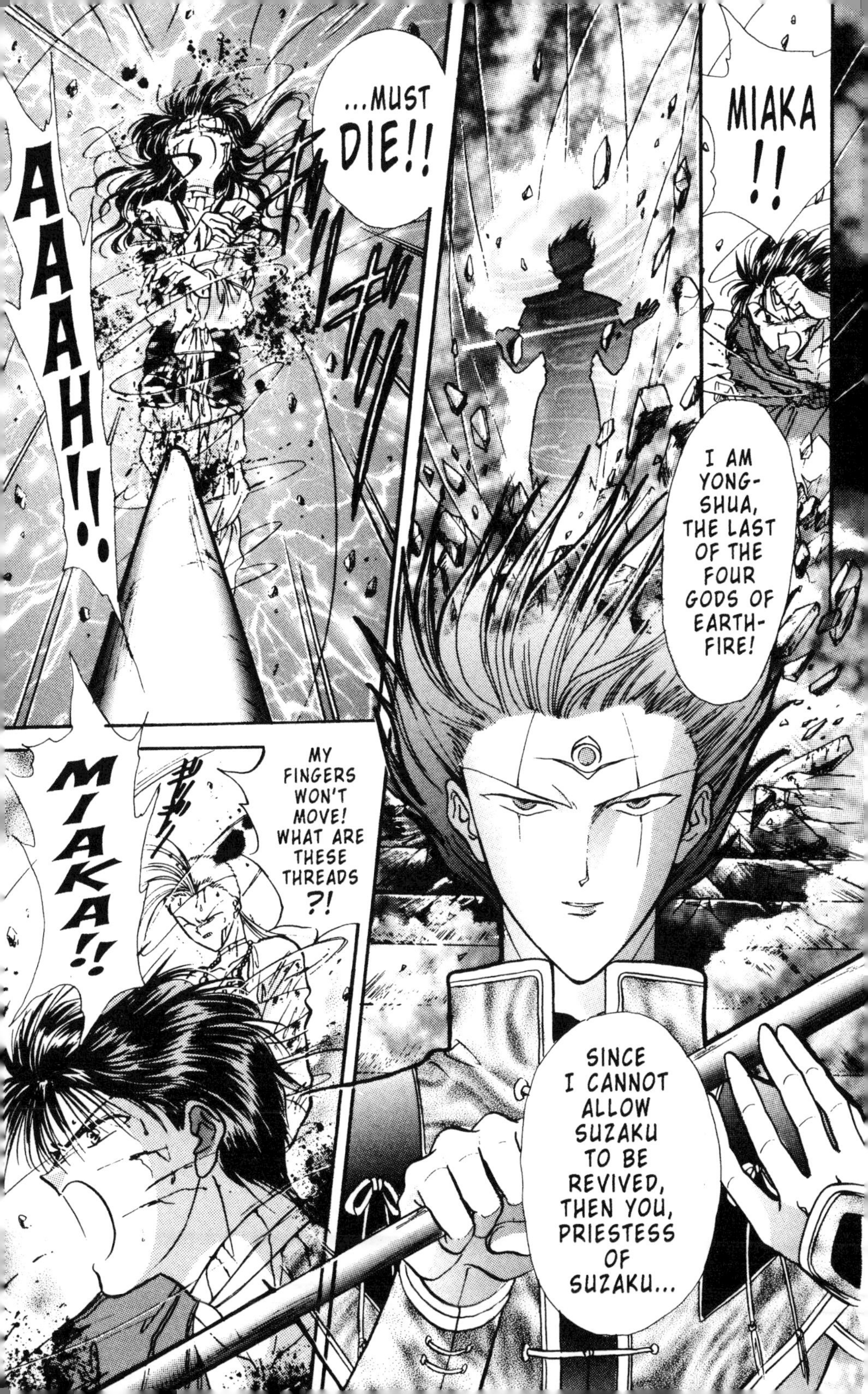
MIAKA!!
I AM YONG-SHUA, THE LAST OF THE FOUR GODS OF EARTH-FIRE!
SINCE I CANNOT ALLOW SUZAKU TO BE REVIVED, THEN YOU, PRIESTESS OF SUZAKU...
...MUST DIE!!
AAAAH!!
MY FINGERS WON'T MOVE! WHAT ARE THESE THREADS?!
MIAKA!!

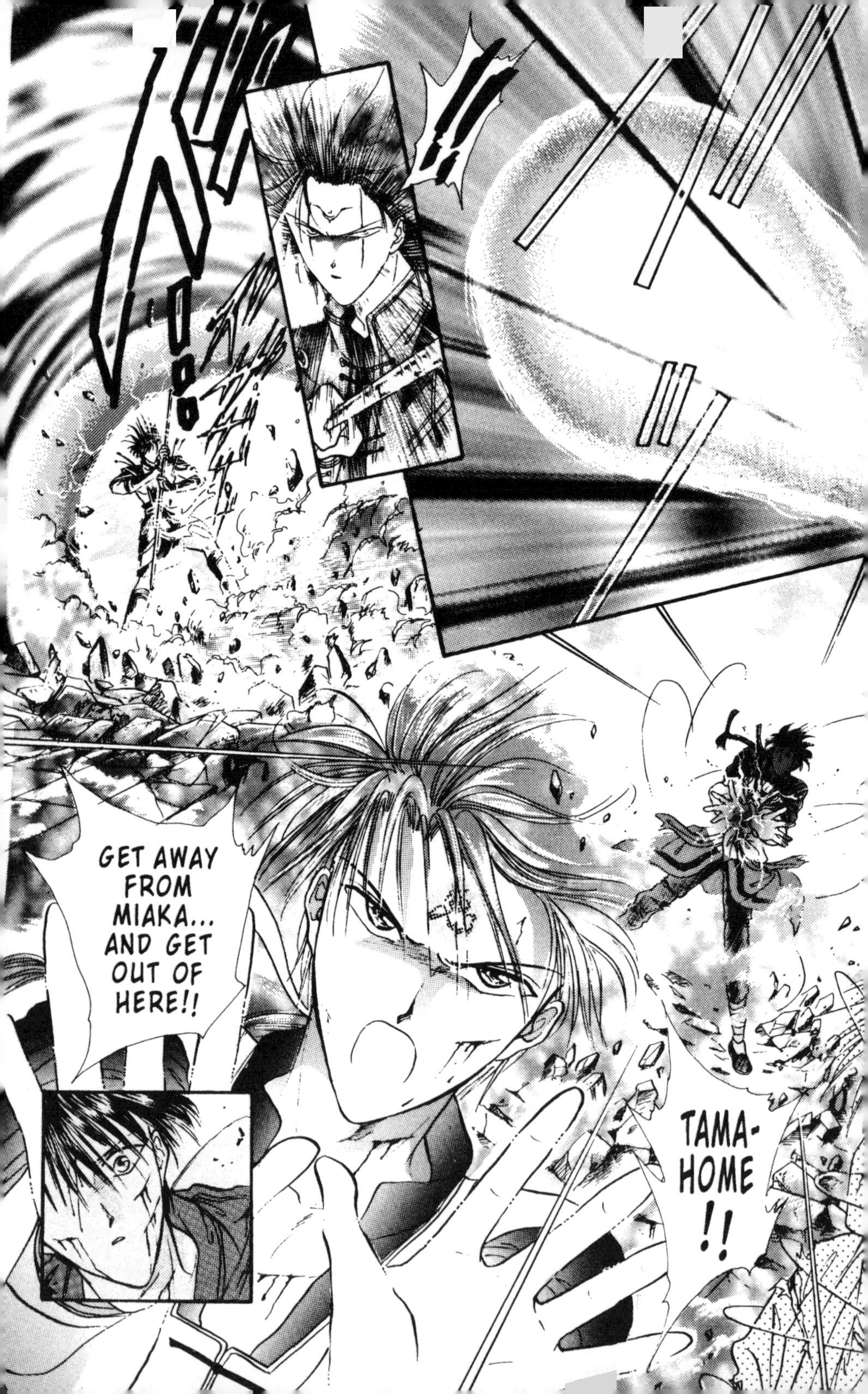
GET AWAY FROM MIAKA... AND GET OUT OF HERE!!
TAMA-HOME!!

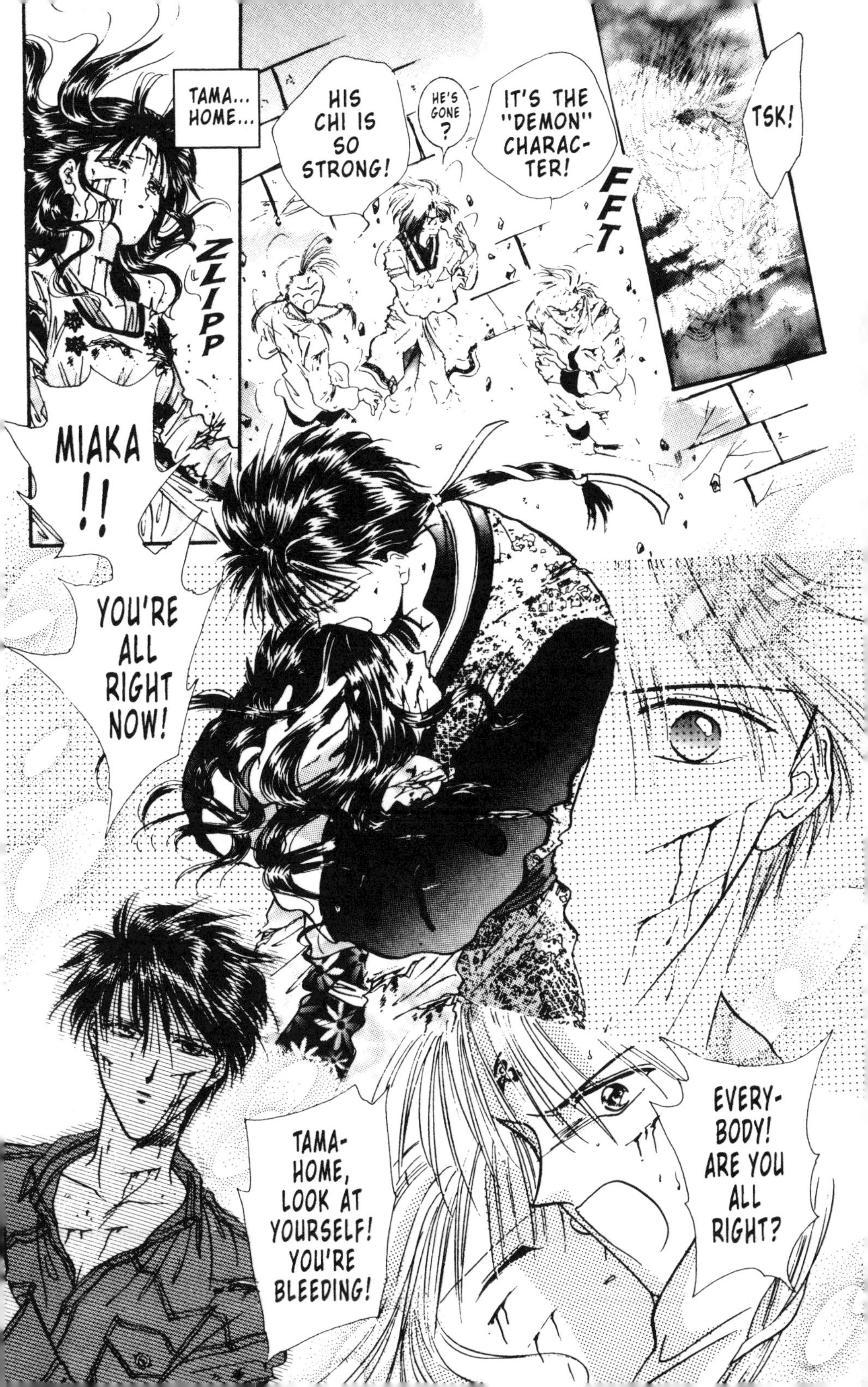
TSK!
IT'S THE "DEMON" CHARACTER!
HE'S GONE?
HIS CHI IS SO STRONG!
FFT
TAMA... HOME...
ZZLIPP
MIAKA!!
YOU'RE ALL RIGHT NOW!
EVERYBODY! ARE YOU ALL RIGHT?
TAMAHOME, LOOK AT YOURSELF! YOU'RE BLEEDING!

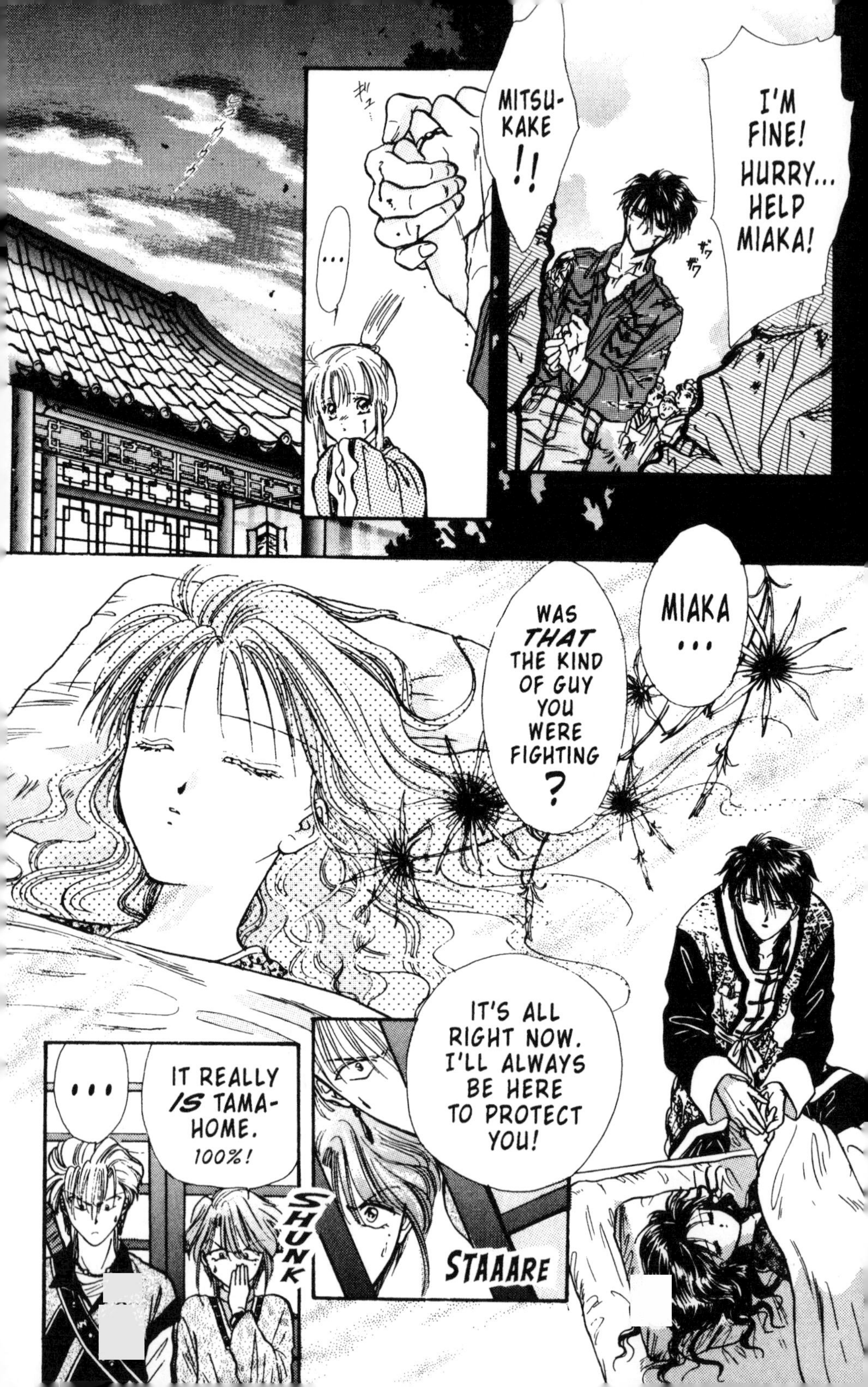
MITSU-KAKE !!
I'M FINE! HURRY... HELP MIAKA!
...
MIAKA ...
WAS THAT THE KIND OF GUY YOU WERE FIGHTING ?
IT'S ALL RIGHT NOW. I'LL ALWAYS BE HERE TO PROTECT YOU!
STAAARE
SHUNK
IT REALLY IS TAMA-HOME. 100%!
...

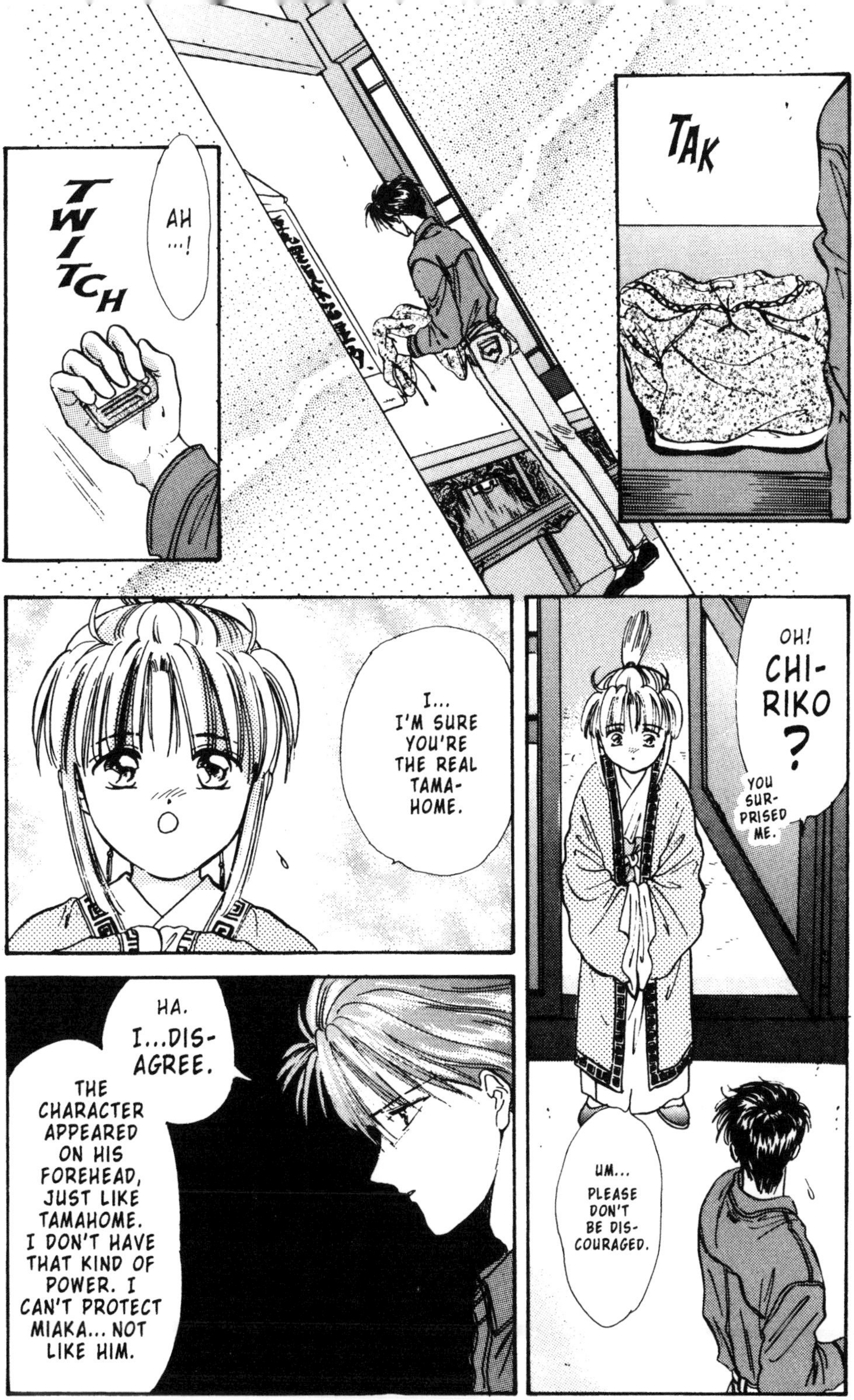
TAK
TWITCH
AH ...!
OH! CHI-RIKO?
YOU SURPRISED ME.
UM... PLEASE DON'T BE DISCOURAGED.
I... I'M SURE YOU'RE THE REAL TAMA-HOME.
HA. I...DIS-AGREE.
THE CHARACTER APPEARED ON HIS FOREHEAD, JUST LIKE TAMAHOME. I DON'T HAVE THAT KIND OF POWER. I CAN'T PROTECT MIAKA... NOT LIKE HIM.

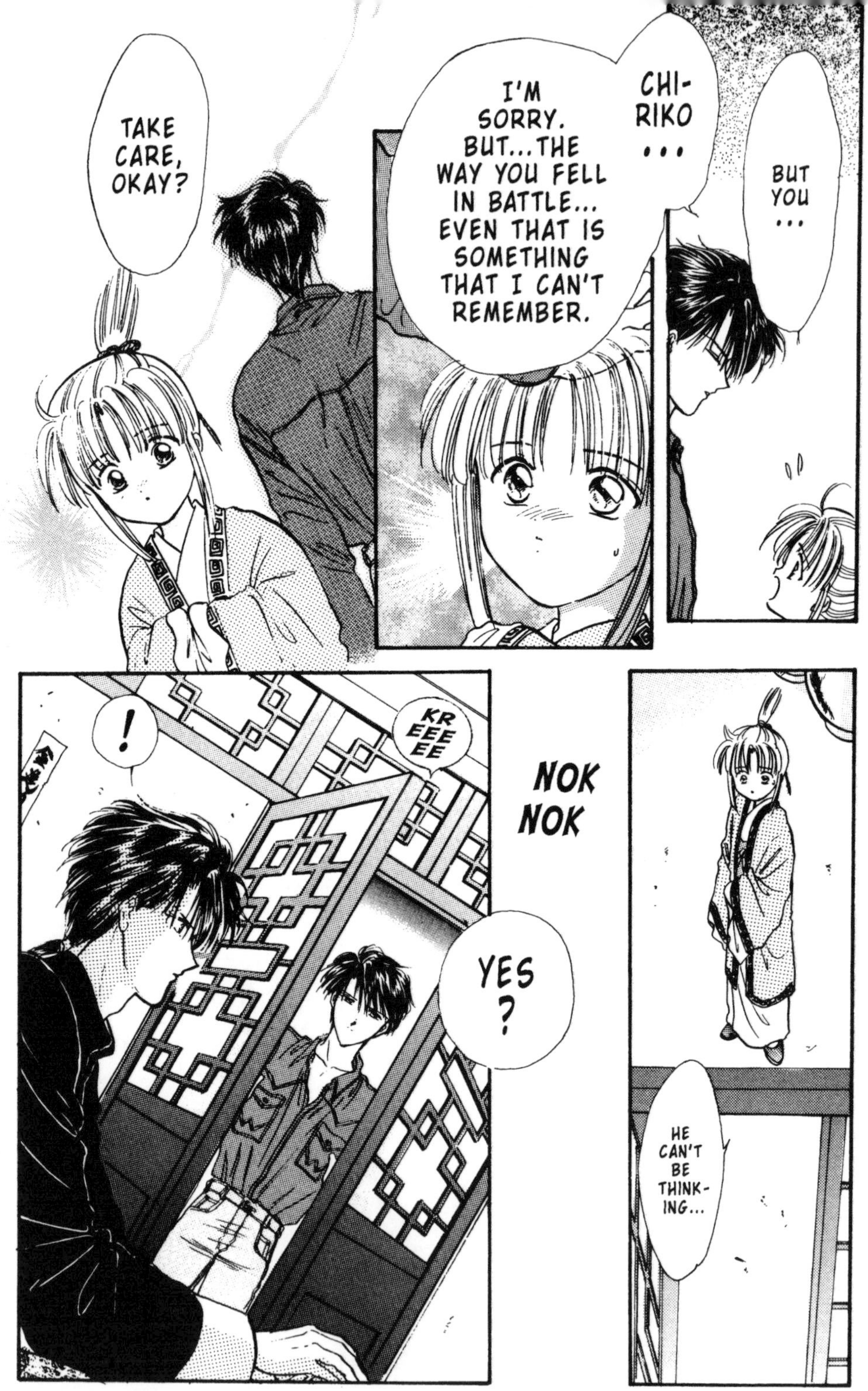
BUT YOU...
CHI-RIKO...
I'M SORRY. BUT...THE WAY YOU FELL IN BATTLE... EVEN THAT IS SOMETHING THAT I CAN'T REMEMBER.
TAKE CARE, OKAY?
HE CAN'T BE THINKING...
NOK NOK
KREEEEEE
!
YES?

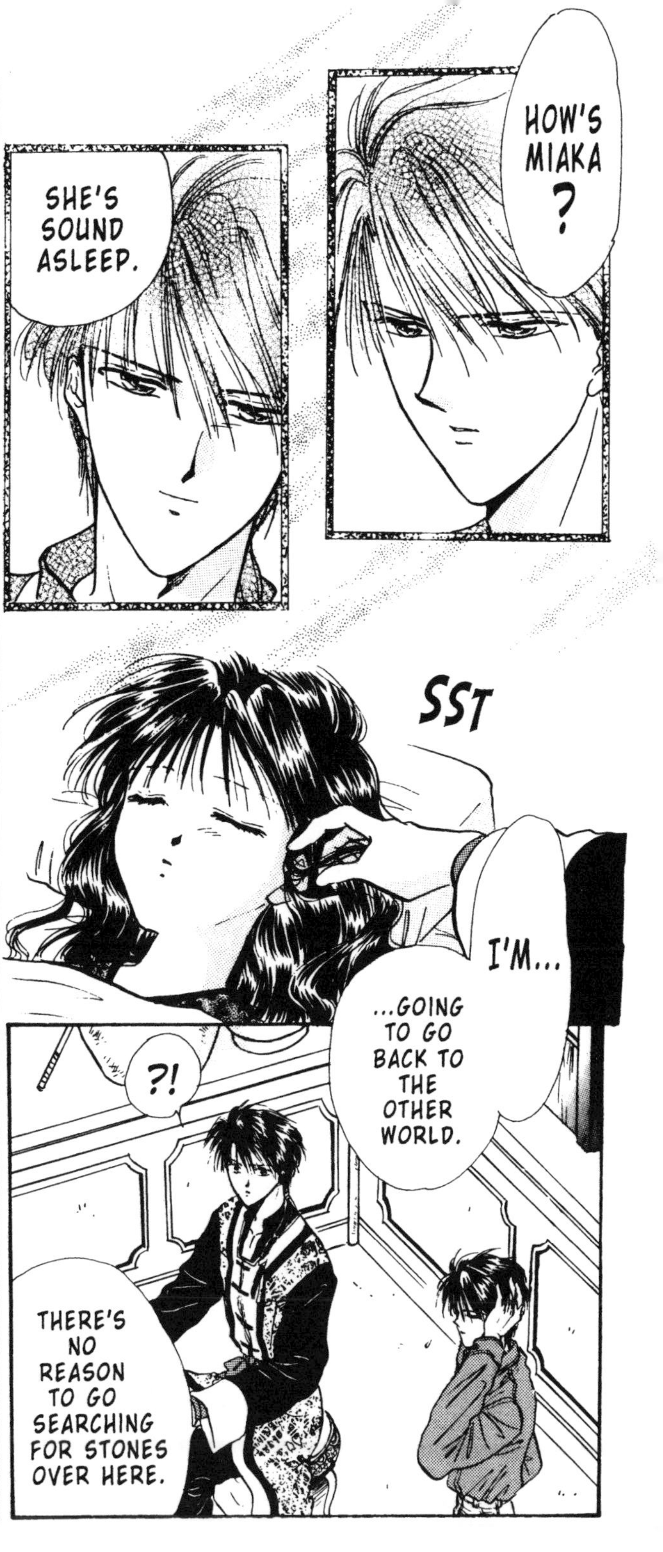
HOW'S MIAKA ?
SHE'S SOUND ASLEEP.
SST
I'M...
...GOING TO GO BACK TO THE OTHER WORLD.
?!
THERE'S NO REASON TO GO SEARCHING FOR STONES OVER HERE.

WHAT THE HECK?!

FUSHIGI YŪGI has reached its final volume!!
...And because of this, when it ended its run in the magazine, I received a whole lot of tear-stained letters. I can only pass along my thanks and my love to the fans. Speaking of endings... the anime! "Why is it only Part 1?!" Well, it was only one year from beginning to end. I'm just thankful that it had a chance to end well. It impressed me in many ways, but as the creator, I have to say that I sure learned from it!
I met so many wonderful professional people, and it was a year that really bore fruit for me!
They had episodes in the anime that I never got the chance to draw (stuff with Keisuke and Tetsuya, and with Tatara and Suzuno...), and they were able to do scenes that surpassed my imagination! They even said, "Can we do it this way?" and asked my opinion on scenes! I was so happy! Before production started, everyone around me was warning me, "Don't get your hopes up too high!" When I think of that now, I can only wonder, "What was I so worked up about?" ☺ But everybody on the staff should get all the credit! The producers (all of them), the directors, the voice actors... everybody talked it over and tried really hard to wrestle with the concepts and come up with the best way to bring them to the screen. I was inspired to do that more myself! ☺ The colors were so beautiful! They struggled over Chichiri's hair and the backgrounds... I, as creator, heard many different opinions from the fans, but on the whole, I'd say that the production was really great! From the bottom of my heart, I think everyone on the staff was just wonderful! Although I'm not quite sure exactly what some of them do... but I really would like to thank the entire staff, one by one, for their contribution. Thank you so much, everyone! It's kind of strange, but when I watched the very final episode, I felt such peace of mind. (I felt like begging to be the anime director's disciple.) It made me question whether I was actually the creator behind this anime!! I was so amazed at the results! I'm so happy with it! Really! Rent it if you have to, but see it! *There are OAVs too! The people of Studio Pierrot took the scenes I had in my heart and animated them! I have absolutely no regrets!*

And that's good, right?

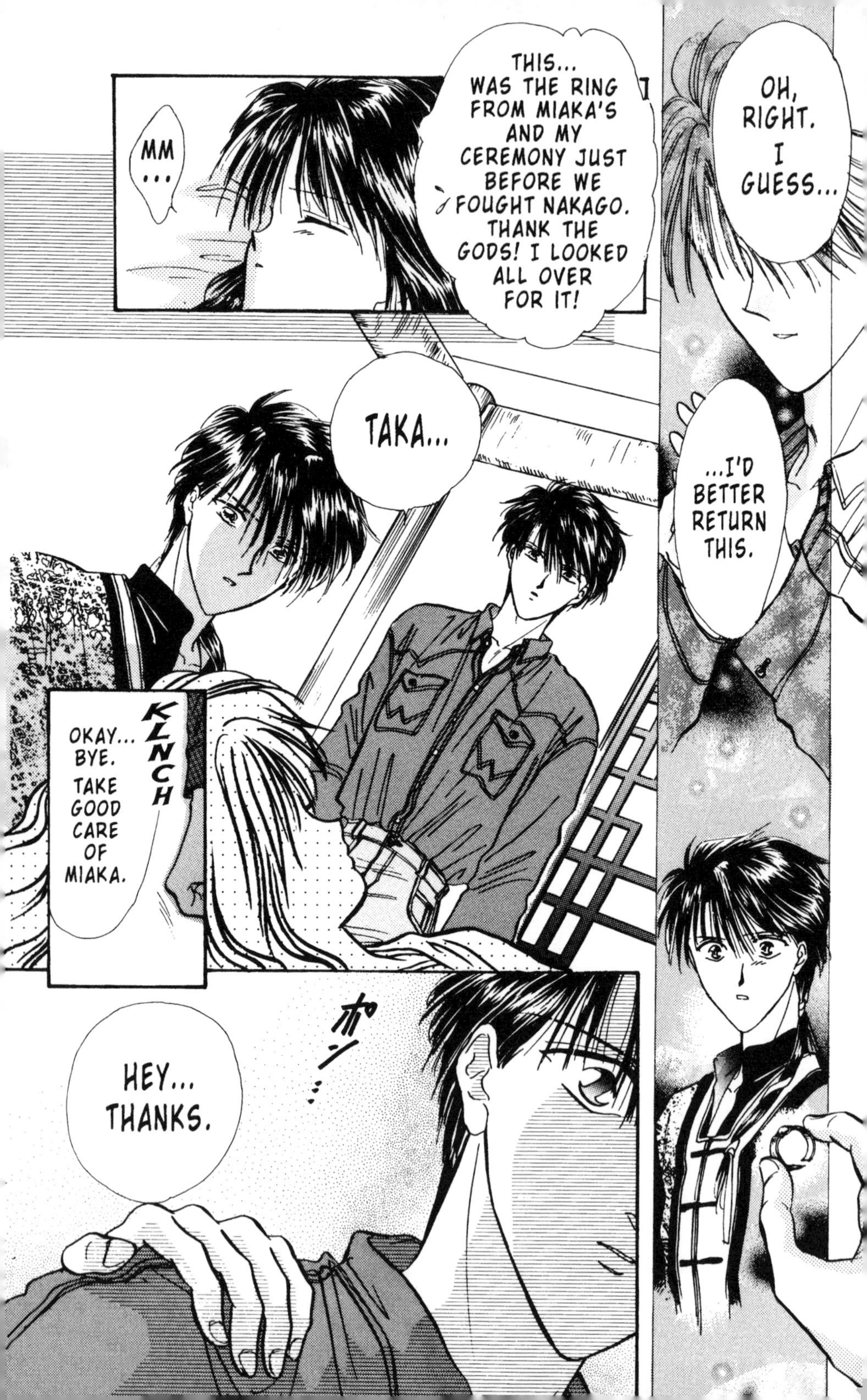
OH, RIGHT. I GUESS...
...I'D BETTER RETURN THIS.
THIS... WAS THE RING FROM MIAKA'S AND MY CEREMONY JUST BEFORE WE FOUGHT NAKAGO. THANK THE GODS! I LOOKED ALL OVER FOR IT!
MM...
TAKA...
KLNCH
OKAY... BYE. TAKE GOOD CARE OF MIAKA.
ポン...
HEY... THANKS.

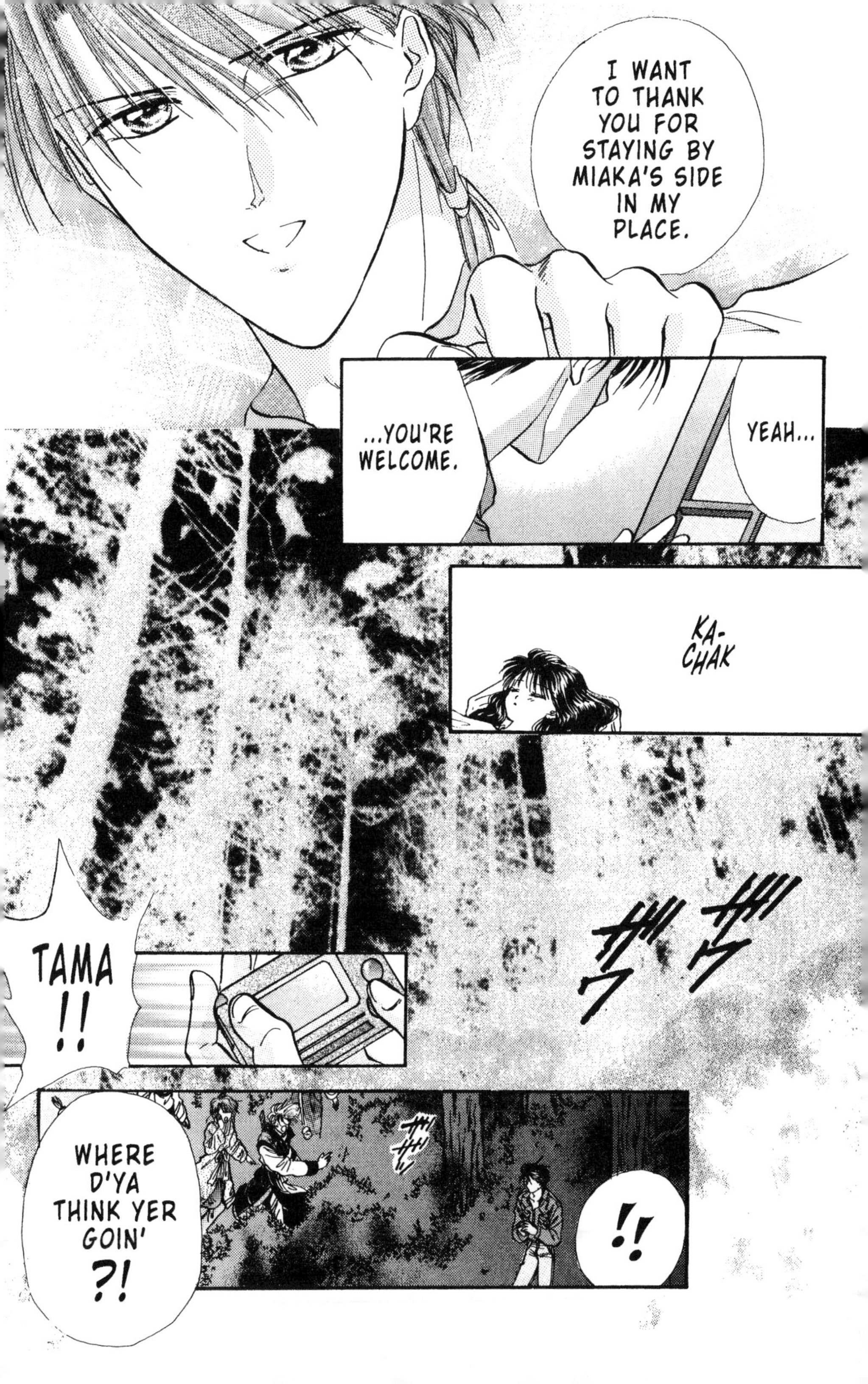
I WANT TO THANK YOU FOR STAYING BY MIAKA'S SIDE IN MY PLACE.
YEAH...
...YOU'RE WELCOME.
KA-CHAK
TAMA!!
!!
WHERE D'YA THINK YER GOIN'?!

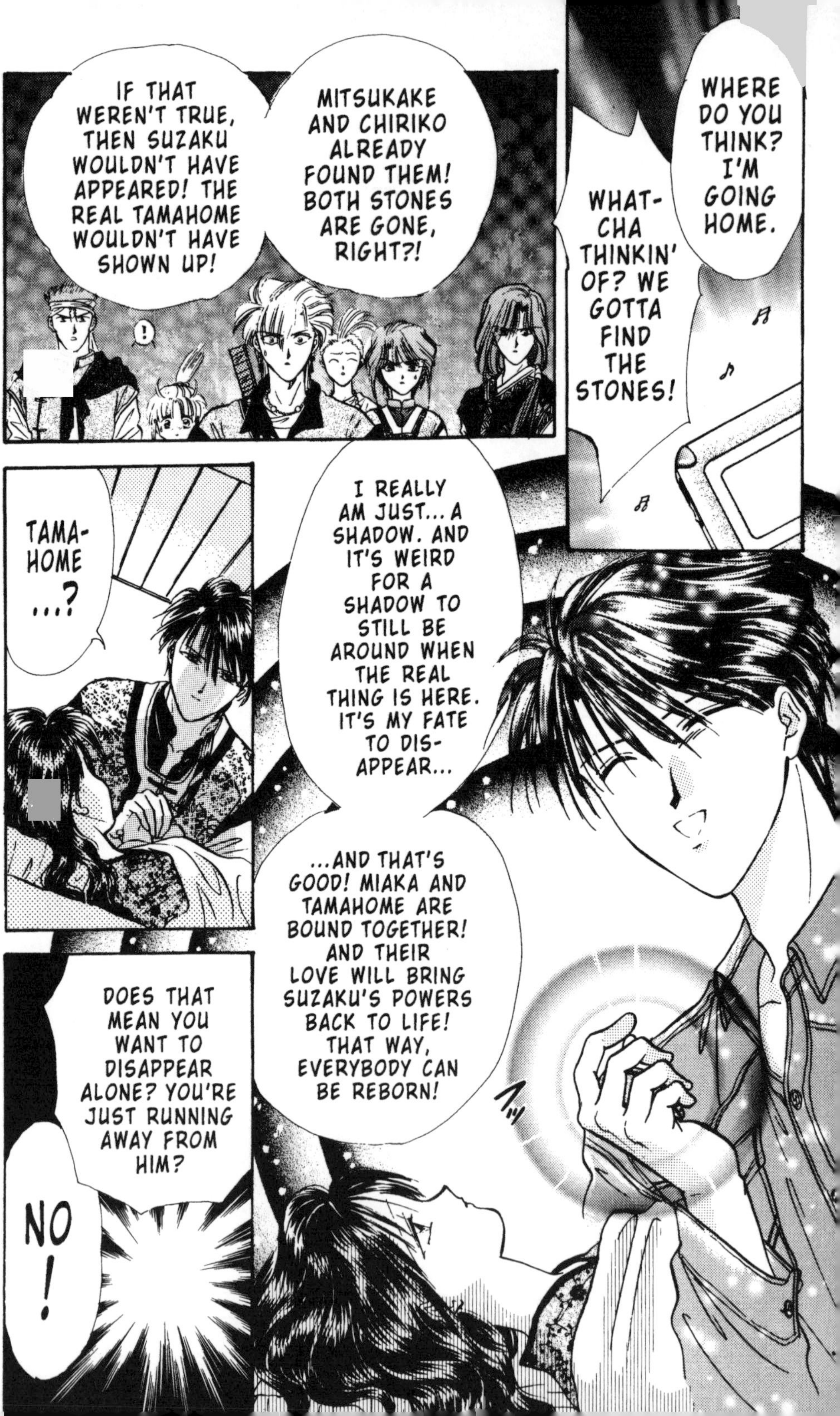
WHERE DO YOU THINK? I'M GOING HOME.
WHAT-CHA THINKIN' OF? WE GOTTA FIND THE STONES!
MITSUKAKE AND CHIRIKO ALREADY FOUND THEM! BOTH STONES ARE GONE, RIGHT?!
IF THAT WEREN'T TRUE, THEN SUZAKU WOULDN'T HAVE APPEARED! THE REAL TAMAHOME WOULDN'T HAVE SHOWN UP!
!
I REALLY AM JUST... A SHADOW. AND IT'S WEIRD FOR A SHADOW TO STILL BE AROUND WHEN THE REAL THING IS HERE. IT'S MY FATE TO DIS-APPEAR...
...AND THAT'S GOOD! MIAKA AND TAMAHOME ARE BOUND TOGETHER! AND THEIR LOVE WILL BRING SUZAKU'S POWERS BACK TO LIFE! THAT WAY, EVERYBODY CAN BE REBORN!
TAMA-HOME ...?
DOES THAT MEAN YOU WANT TO DISAPPEAR ALONE? YOU'RE JUST RUNNING AWAY FROM HIM?
NO!

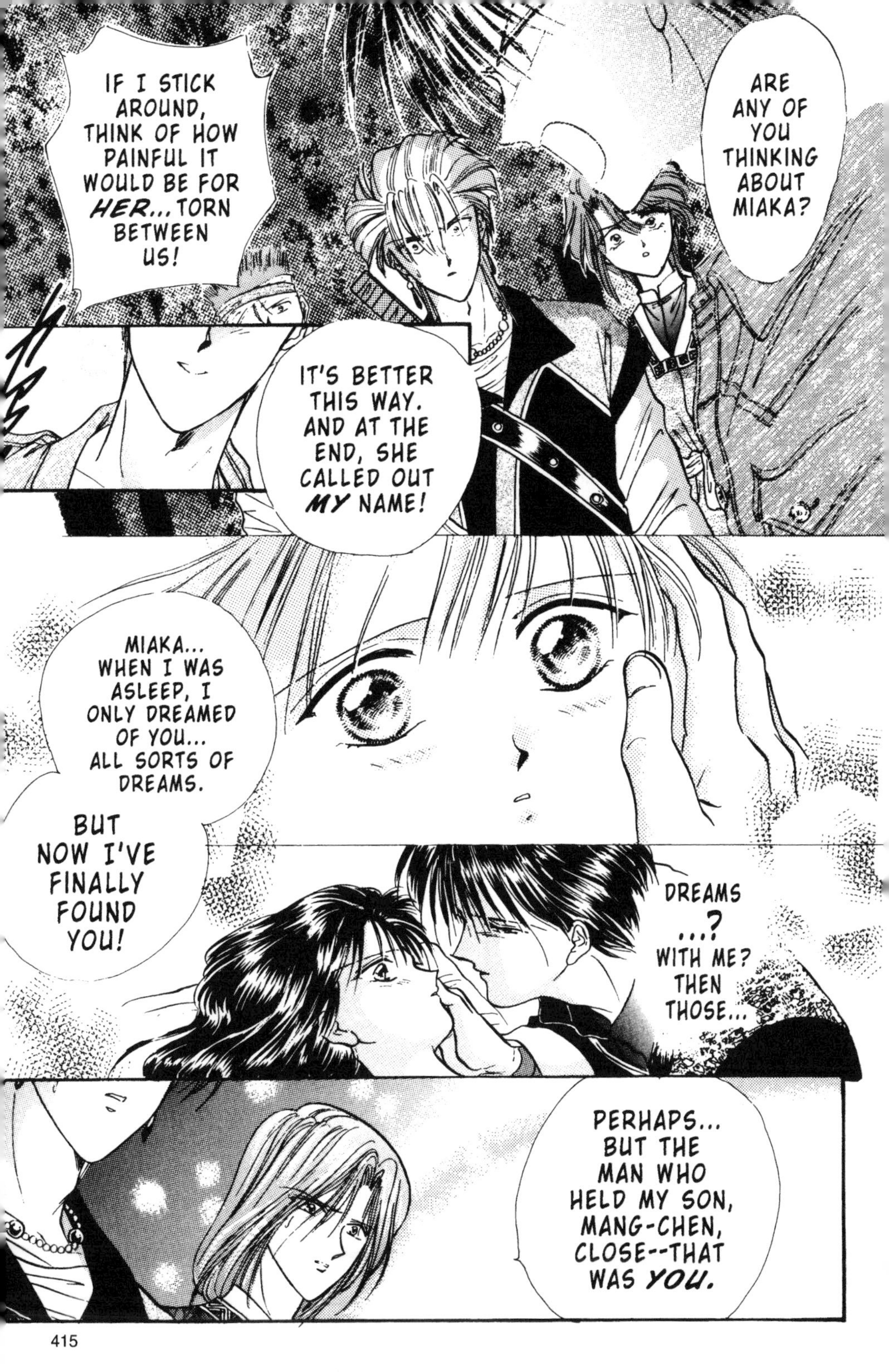
ARE ANY OF YOU THINKING ABOUT MIAKA?
IF I STICK AROUND, THINK OF HOW PAINFUL IT WOULD BE FOR *HER*... TORN BETWEEN US!
IT'S BETTER THIS WAY. AND AT THE END, SHE CALLED OUT *MY* NAME!
MIAKA... WHEN I WAS ASLEEP, I ONLY DREAMED OF YOU... ALL SORTS OF DREAMS.
BUT NOW I'VE FINALLY FOUND YOU!
DREAMS ...? WITH ME? THEN THOSE...
PERHAPS... BUT THE MAN WHO HELD MY SON, MANG-CHEN, CLOSE--THAT WAS *YOU*.

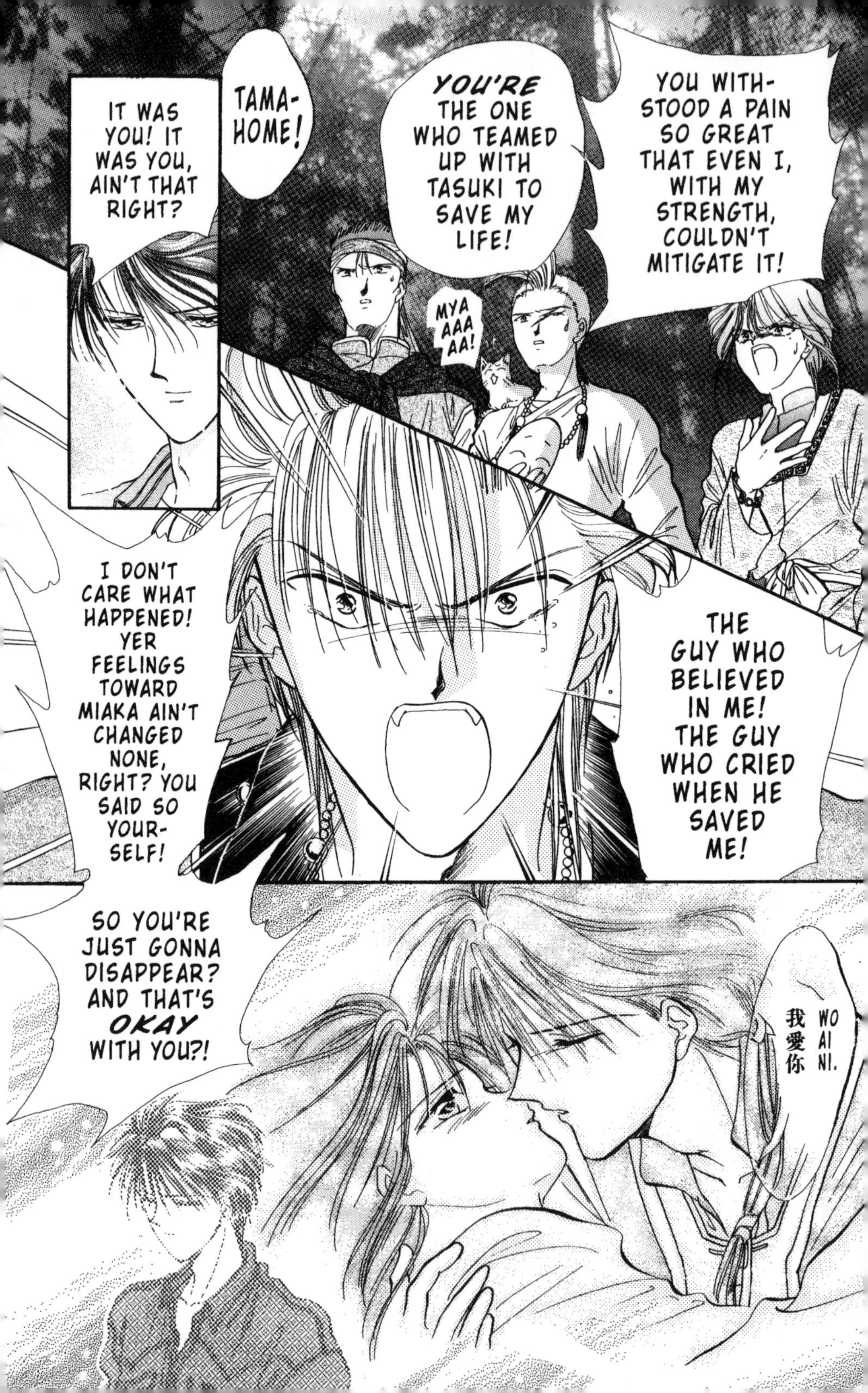
YOU WITH-STOOD A PAIN SO GREAT THAT EVEN I, WITH MY STRENGTH, COULDN'T MITIGATE IT!
YOU'RE THE ONE WHO TEAMED UP WITH TASUKI TO SAVE MY LIFE!
TAMA-HOME!
MYA AAA AA!
IT WAS YOU! IT WAS YOU, AIN'T THAT RIGHT?
THE GUY WHO BELIEVED IN ME! THE GUY WHO CRIED WHEN HE SAVED ME!
I DON'T CARE WHAT HAPPENED! YER FEELINGS TOWARD MIAKA AIN'T CHANGED NONE, RIGHT? YOU SAID SO YOUR-SELF!
WO AI NI. 我愛你
SO YOU'RE JUST GONNA DISAPPEAR? AND THAT'S *OKAY* WITH YOU?!

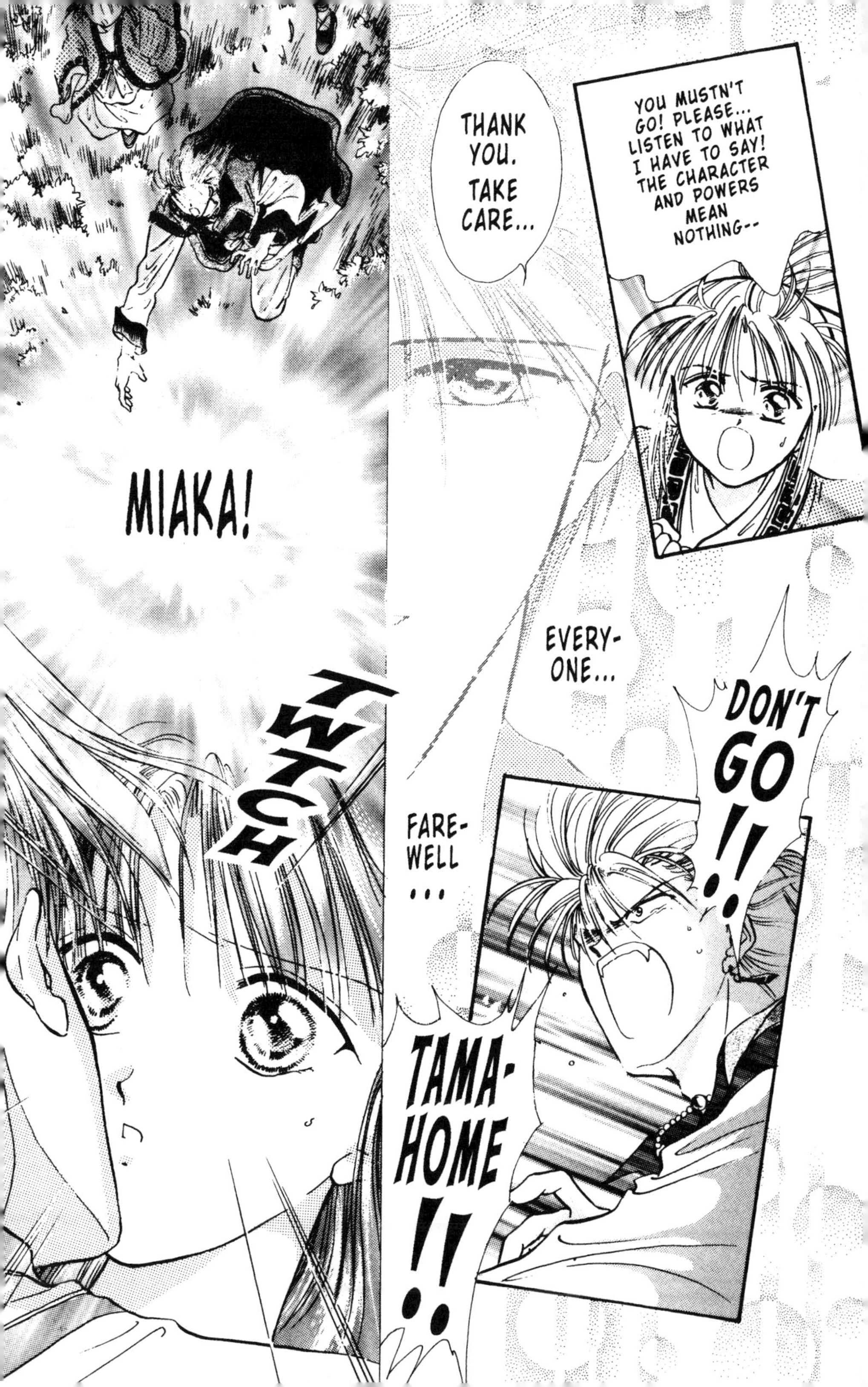
YOU MUSTN'T GO! PLEASE... LISTEN TO WHAT I HAVE TO SAY! THE CHARACTER AND POWERS MEAN NOTHING--
THANK YOU. TAKE CARE...
EVERY-ONE...
DON'T GO!!
FARE-WELL...
TAMA-HOME!!
MIAKA!
TWITCH

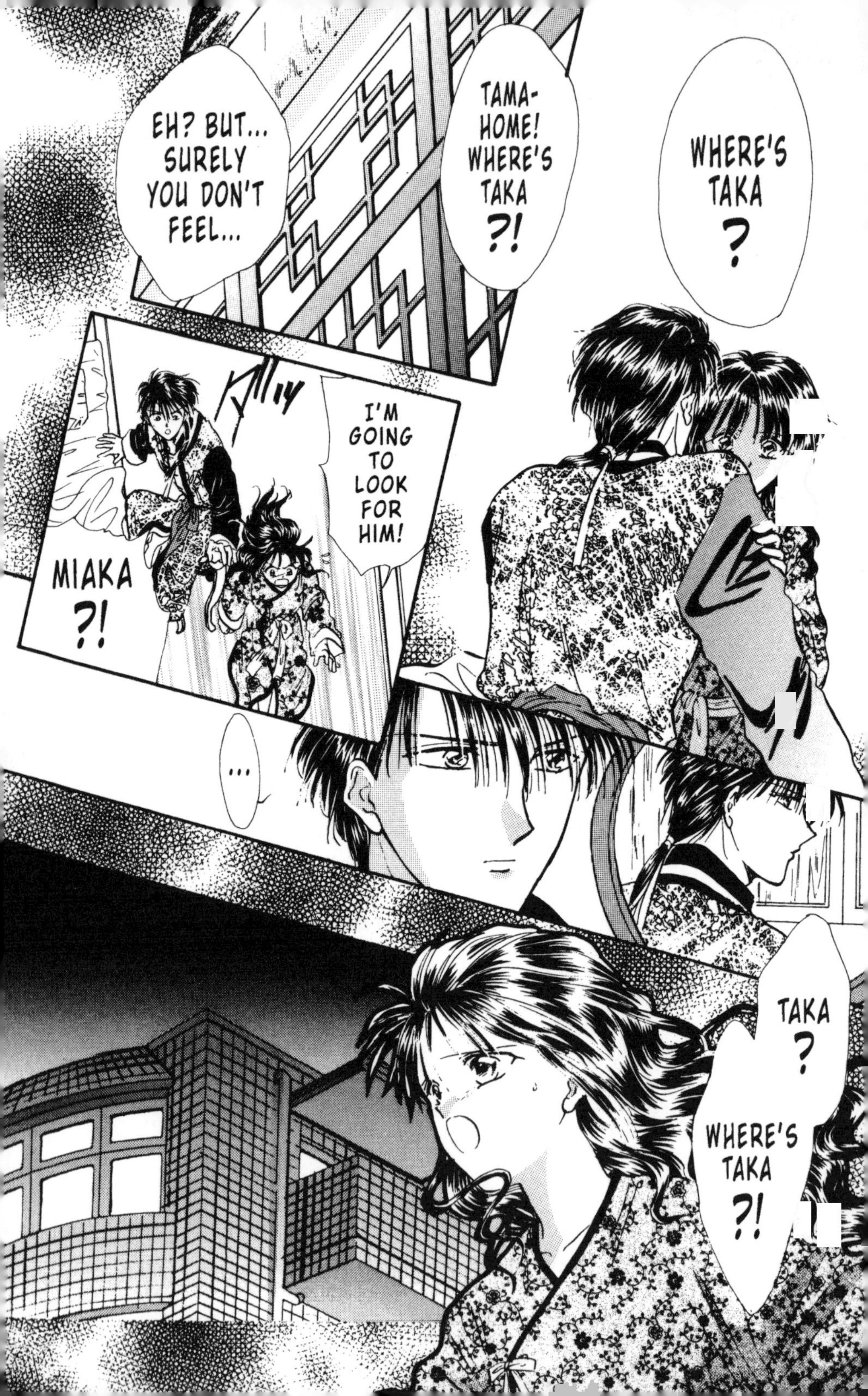
WHERE'S TAKA?
TAMA-HOME! WHERE'S TAKA?!
EH? BUT... SURELY YOU DON'T FEEL...
I'M GOING TO LOOK FOR HIM!
MIAKA?!
...
TAKA?
WHERE'S TAKA?!

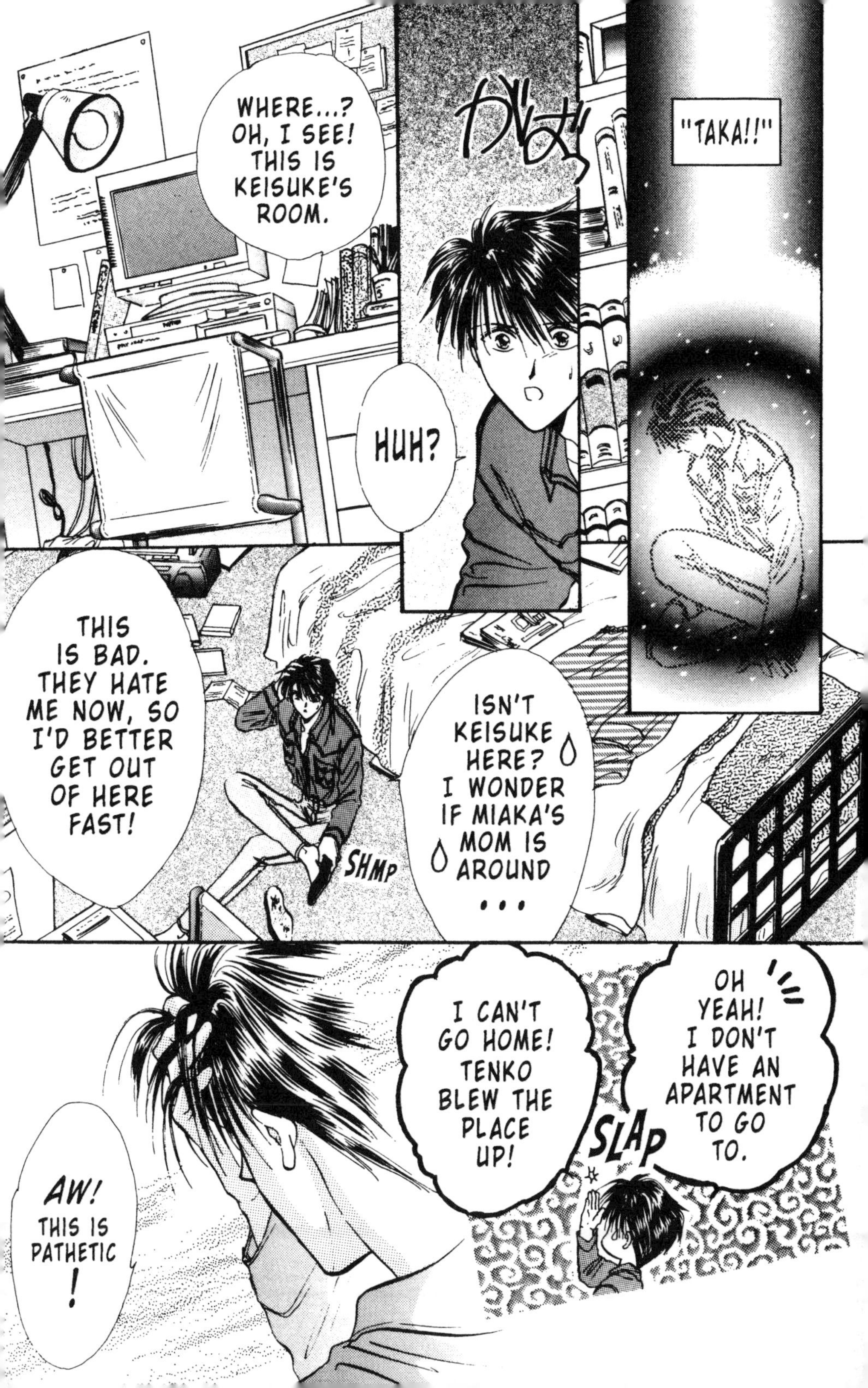
"TAKA!!"
がばっ
HUH?
WHERE...? OH, I SEE! THIS IS KEISUKE'S ROOM.
ISN'T KEISUKE HERE? I WONDER IF MIAKA'S MOM IS AROUND...
SHMP
THIS IS BAD. THEY HATE ME NOW, SO I'D BETTER GET OUT OF HERE FAST!
OH YEAH! I DON'T HAVE AN APARTMENT TO GO TO.
SLAP
I CAN'T GO HOME! TENKO BLEW THE PLACE UP!
AW! THIS IS PATHETIC!

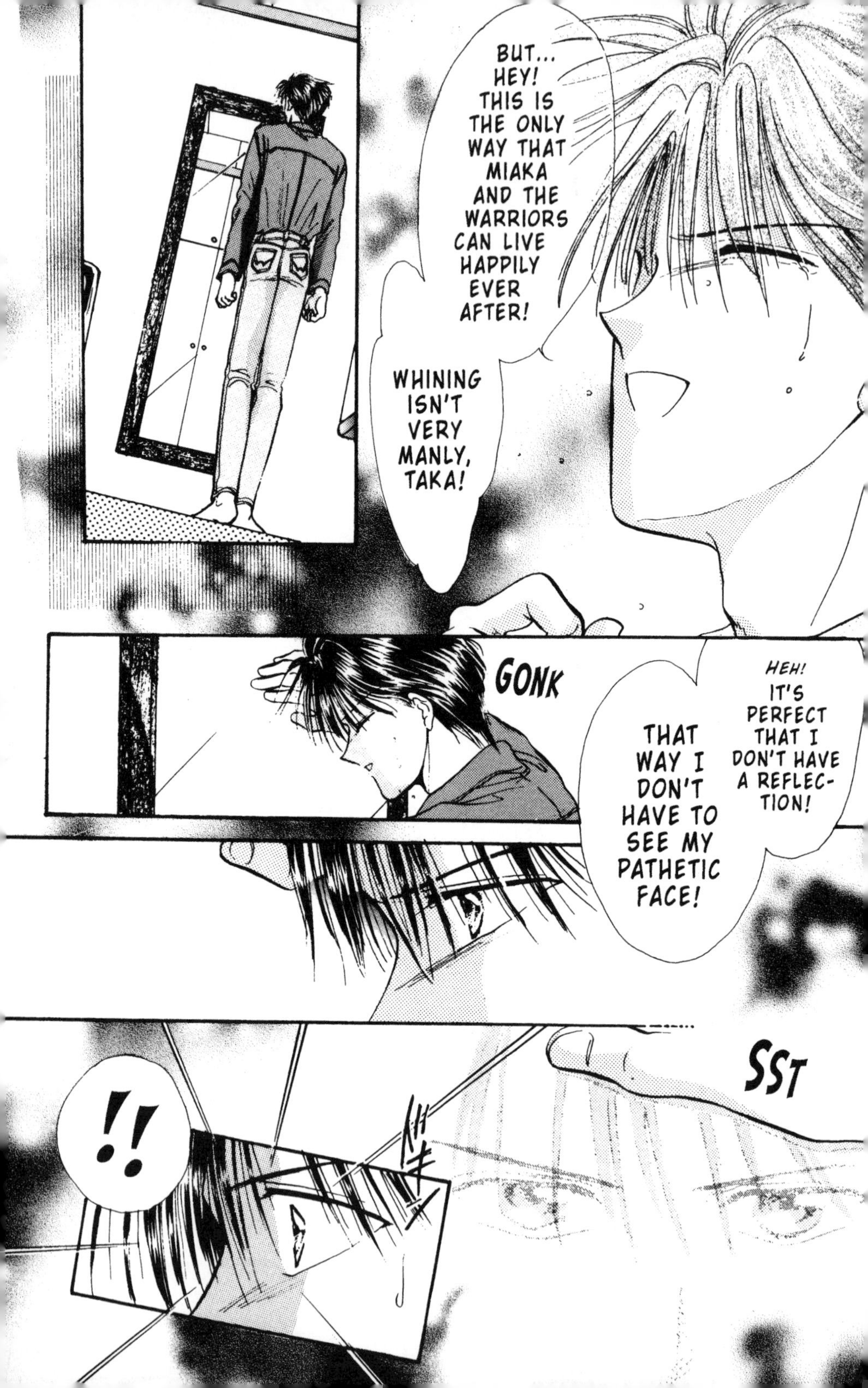
BUT... HEY! THIS IS THE ONLY WAY THAT MIAKA AND THE WARRIORS CAN LIVE HAPPILY EVER AFTER!
WHINING ISN'T VERY MANLY, TAKA!
HEH! IT'S PERFECT THAT I DON'T HAVE A REFLECTION!
THAT WAY I DON'T HAVE TO SEE MY PATHETIC FACE!
GONK
SST
!!

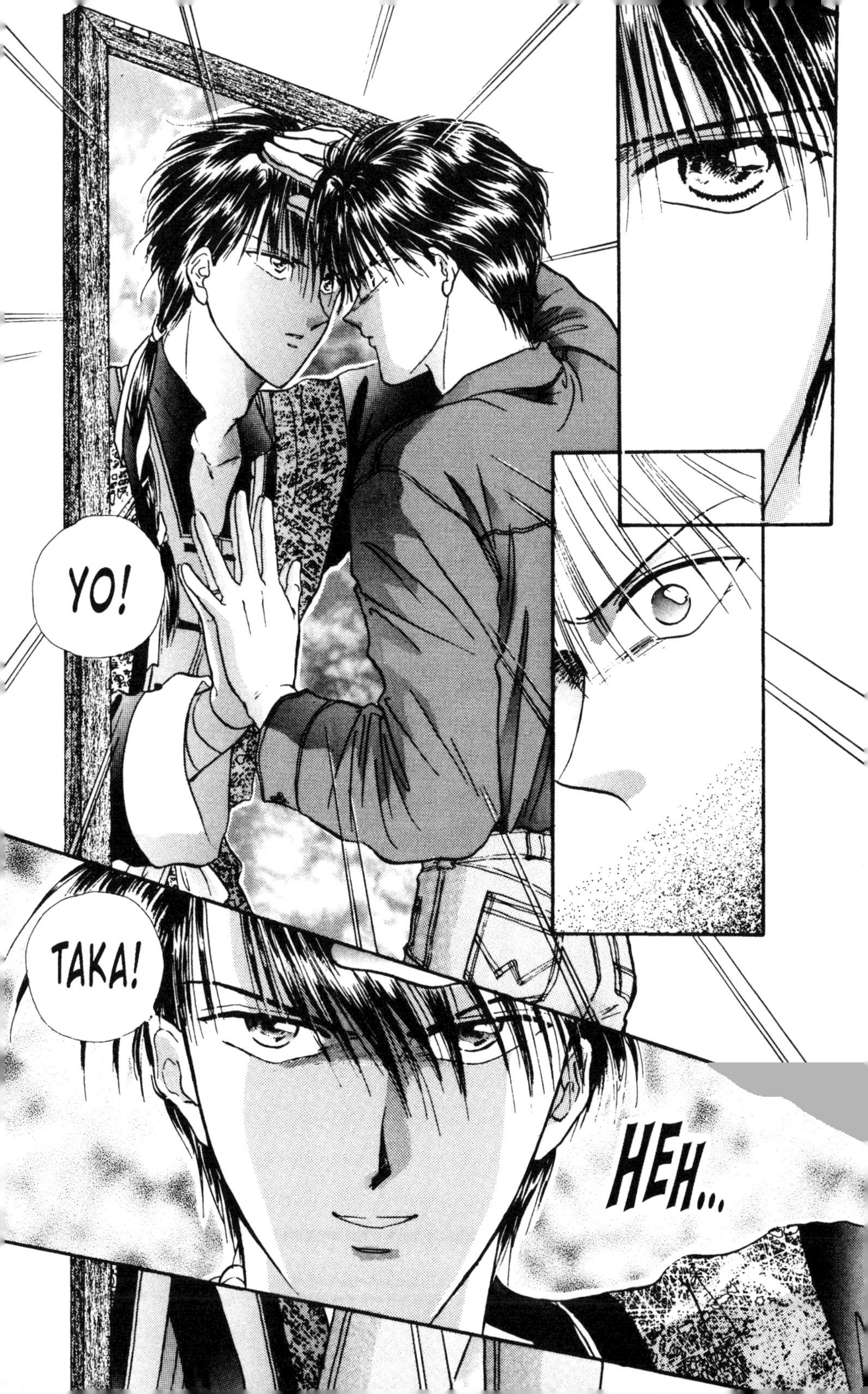
YO!
TAKA!
HEH...

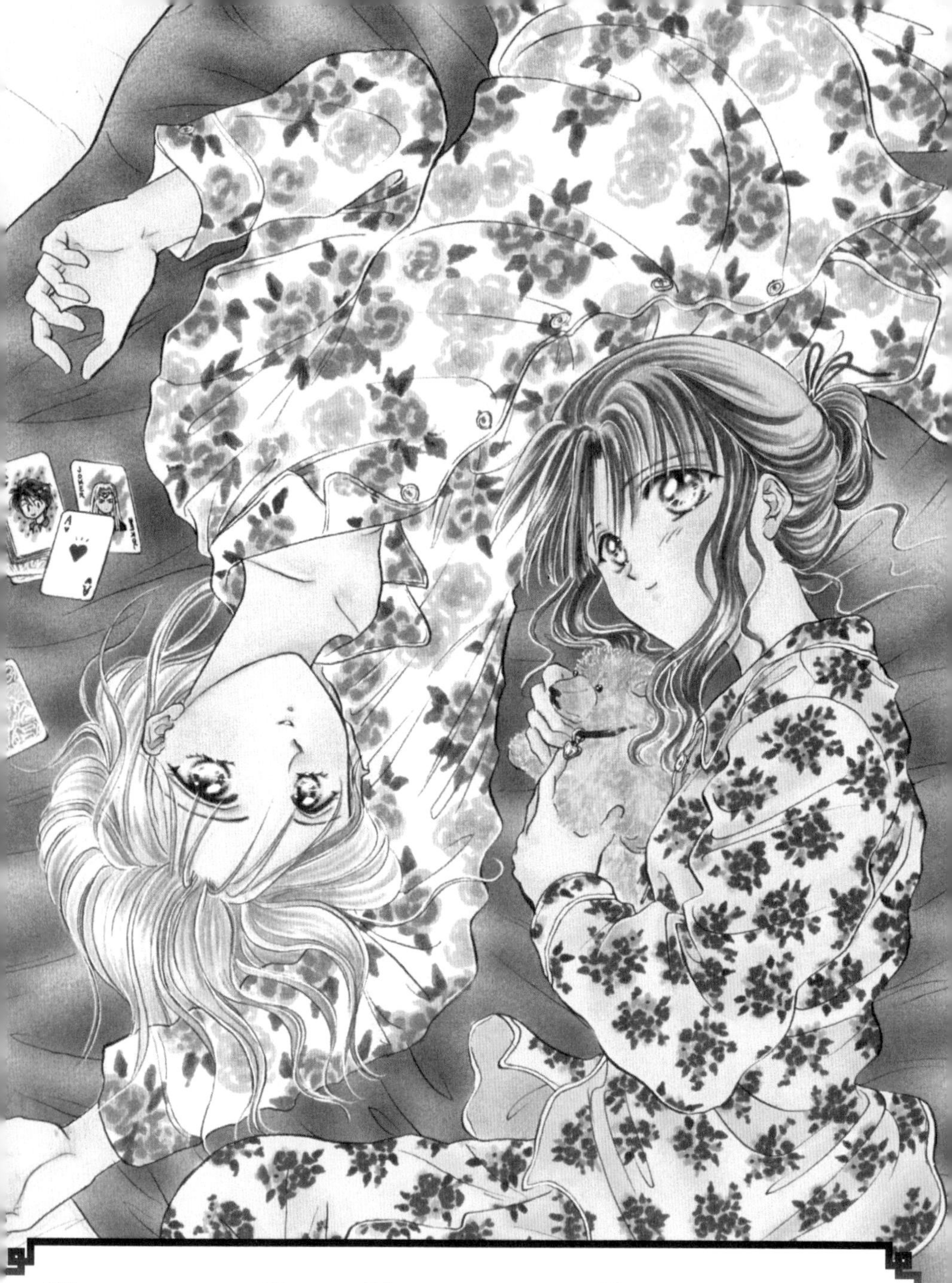

Chapter One Hundred Two
Souls Seeking Their Mates

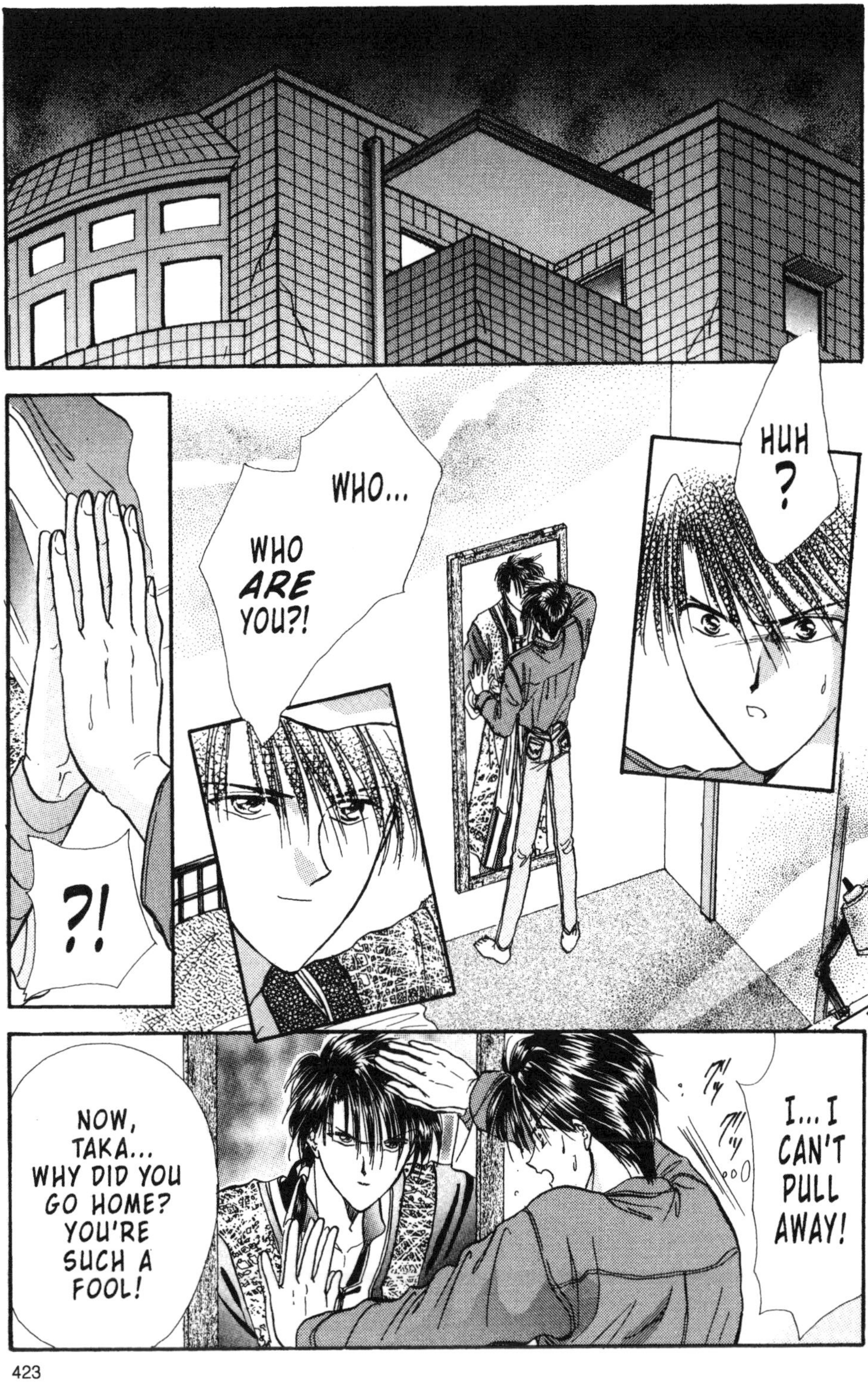
HUH ?
WHO...
WHO ARE YOU?!
?!
I... I CAN'T PULL AWAY!
NOW, TAKA... WHY DID YOU GO HOME? YOU'RE SUCH A FOOL!

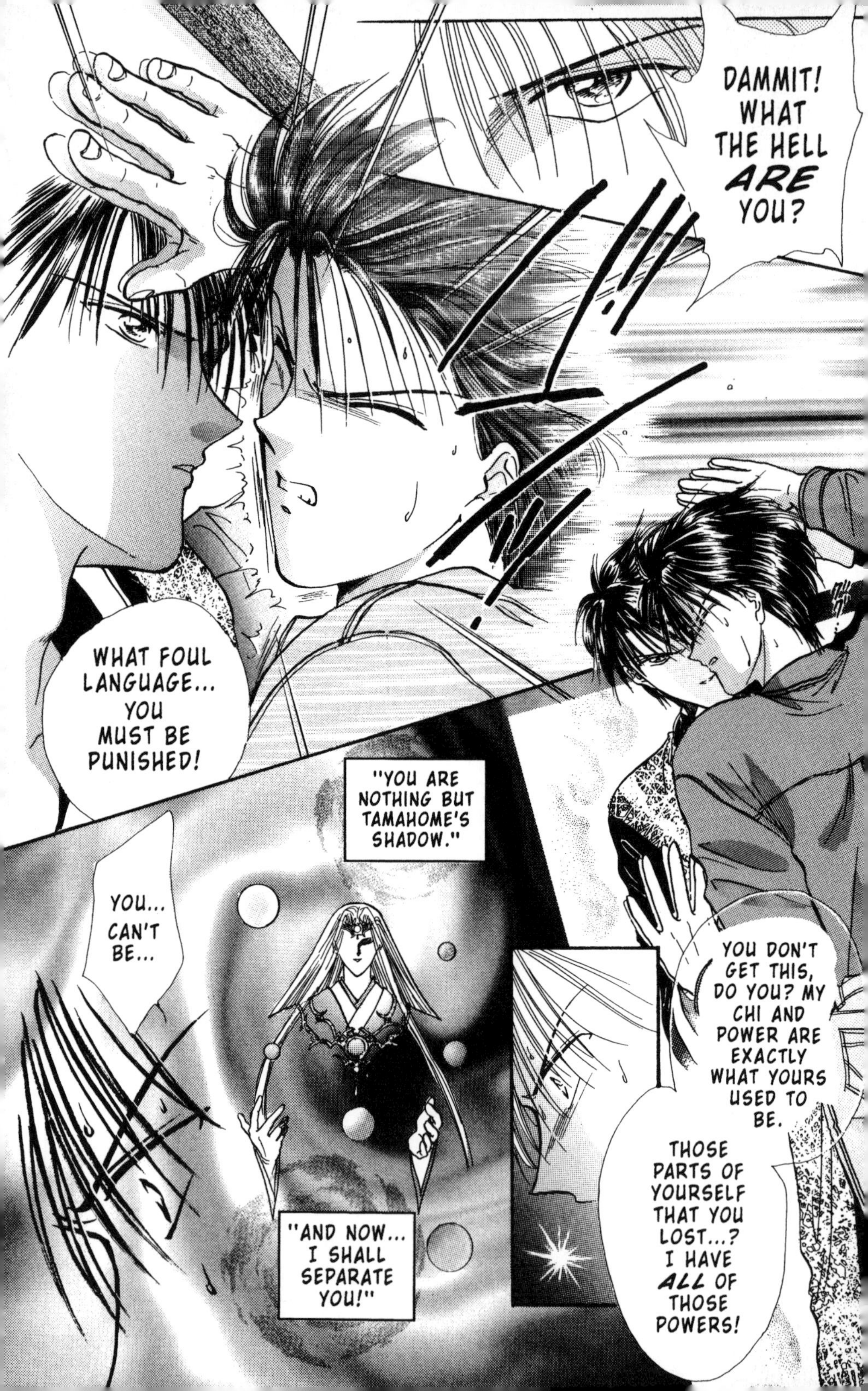
DAMMIT! WHAT THE HELL *ARE* YOU?
WHAT FOUL LANGUAGE... YOU MUST BE PUNISHED!
YOU DON'T GET THIS, DO YOU? MY CHI AND POWER ARE EXACTLY WHAT YOURS USED TO BE.
THOSE PARTS OF YOURSELF THAT YOU LOST...? I HAVE *ALL* OF THOSE POWERS!
"YOU ARE NOTHING BUT TAMAHOME'S SHADOW."
"AND NOW... I SHALL SEPARATE YOU!"
YOU... CAN'T BE...

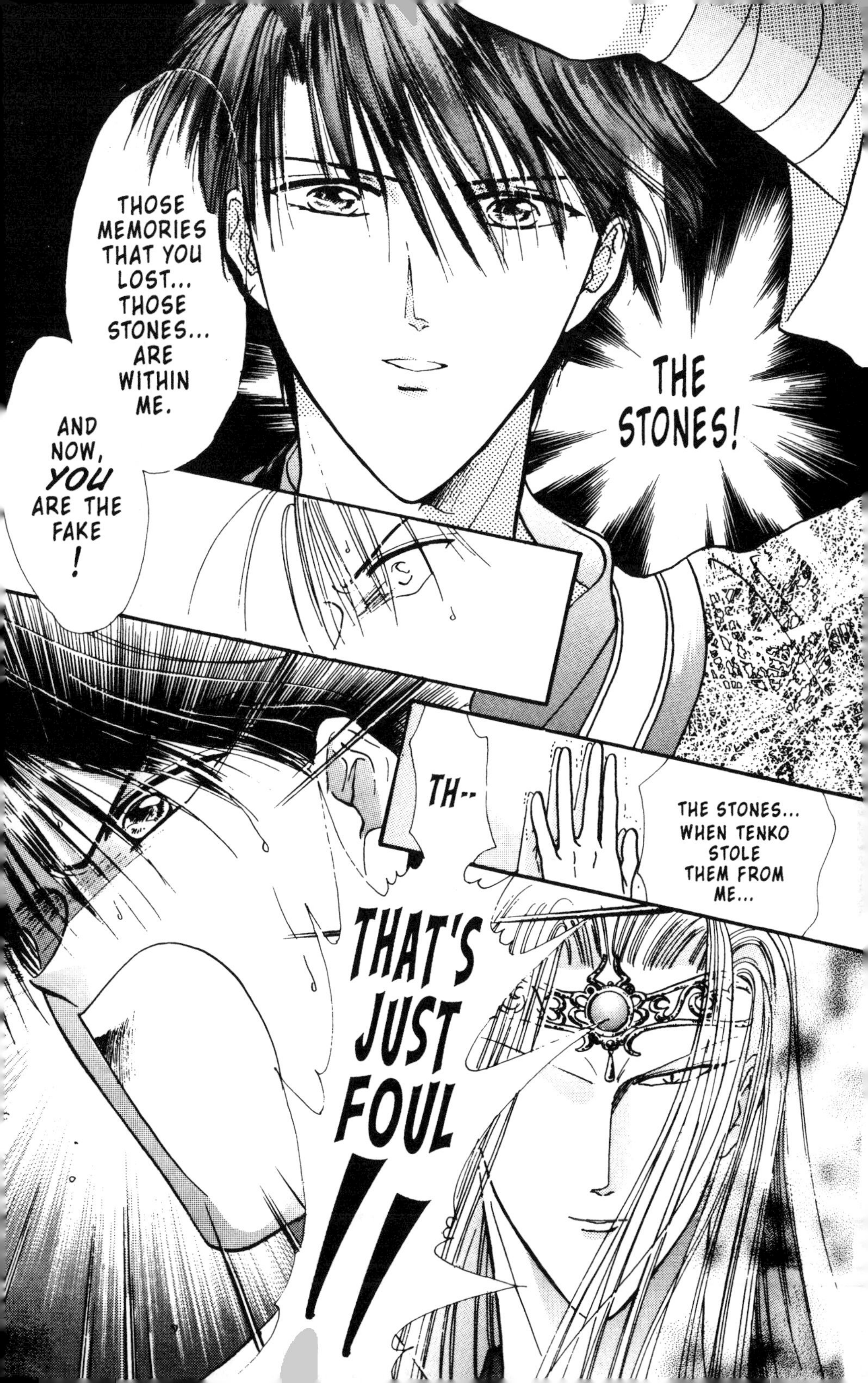
THOSE MEMORIES THAT YOU LOST... THOSE STONES... ARE WITHIN ME.
AND NOW, ***YOU*** ARE THE FAKE!
THE STONES!
THE STONES... WHEN TENKO STOLE THEM FROM ME...
TH--
THAT'S JUST FOUL!!

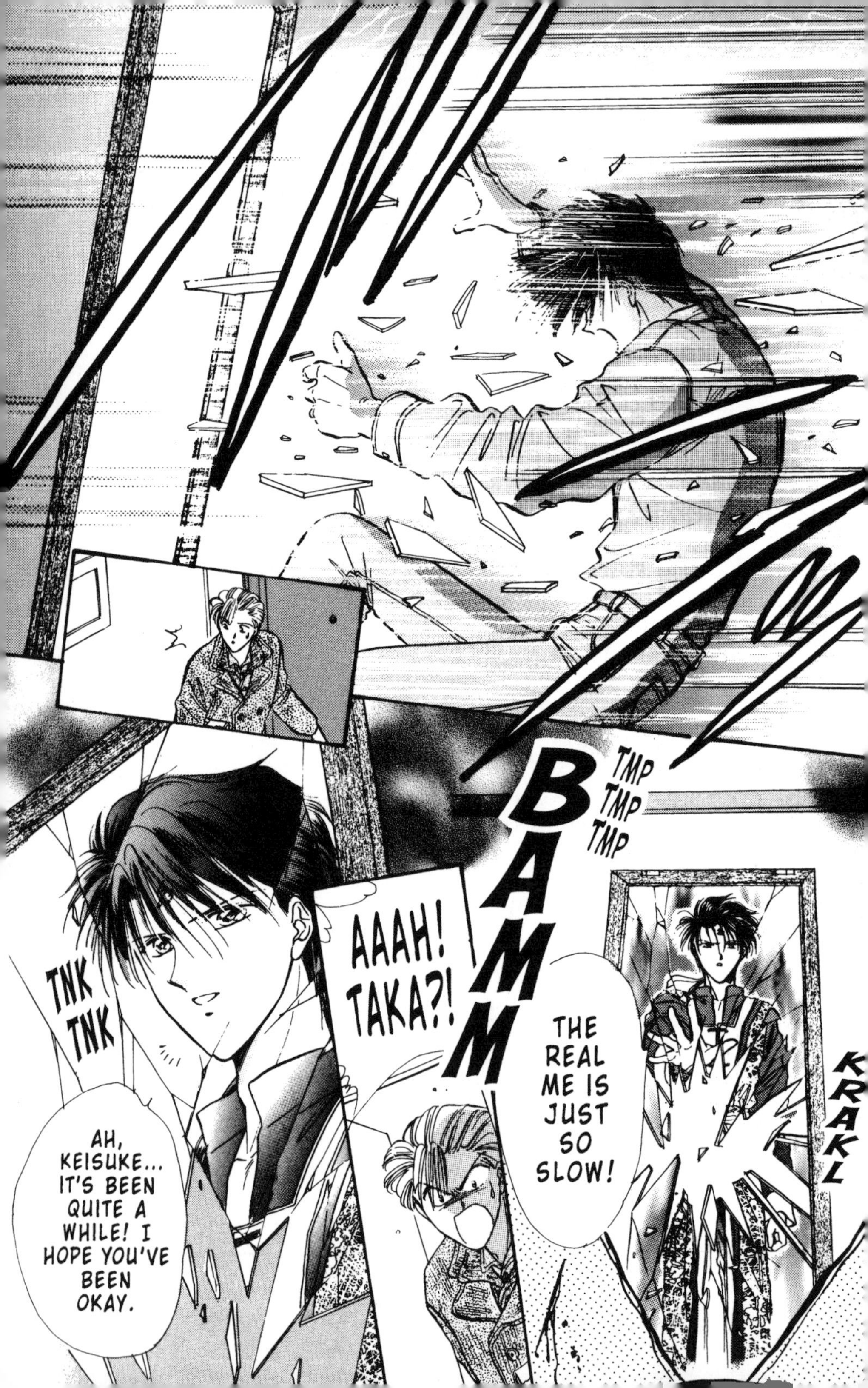
TMP TMP TMP
BAMM
KRAKL
THE REAL ME IS JUST SO SLOW!
AAAH! TAKA?!
TNK TNK
AH, KEISUKE... IT'S BEEN QUITE A WHILE! I HOPE YOU'VE BEEN OKAY.

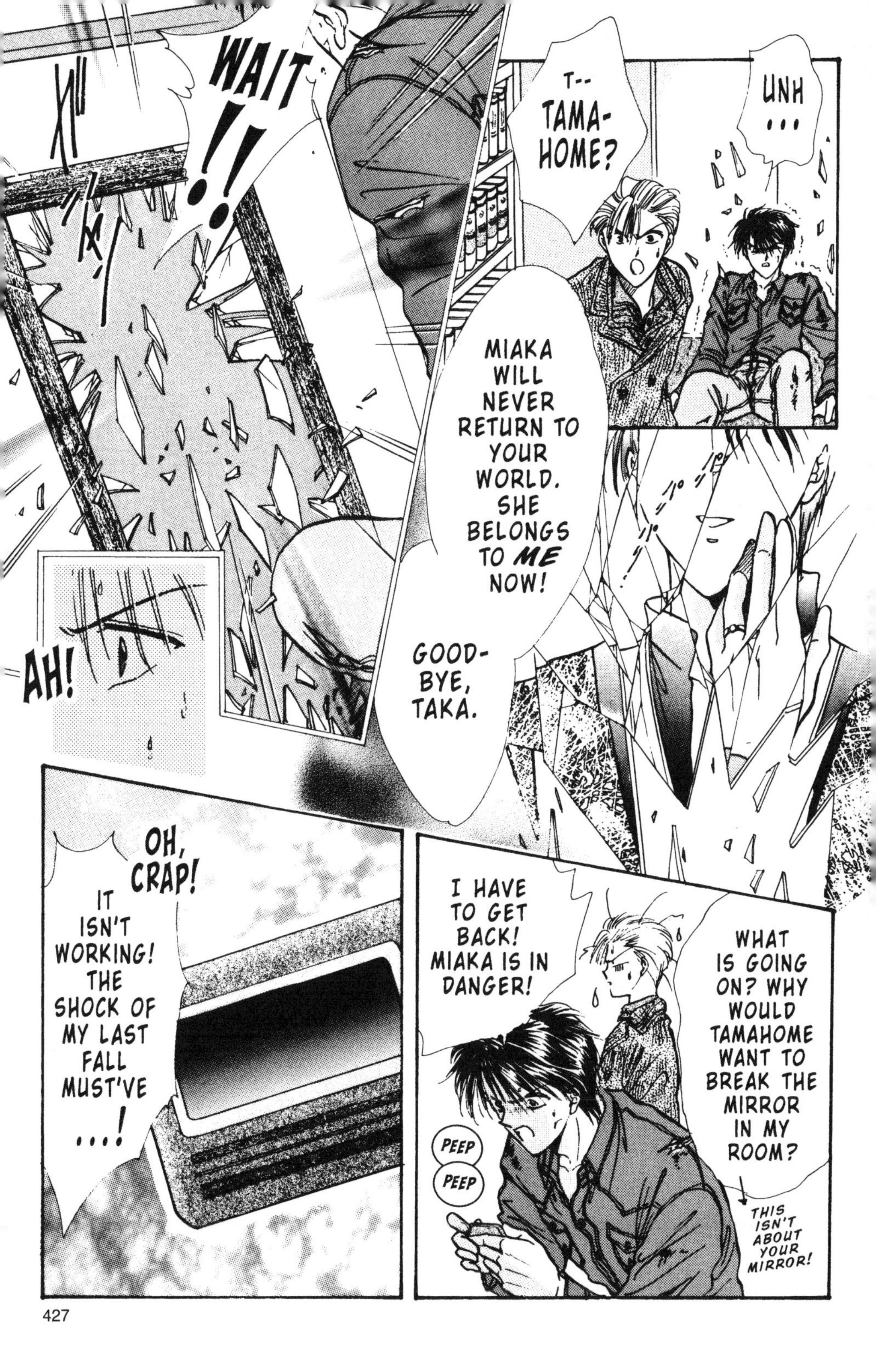
UNH ...
T-- TAMA-HOME?
MIAKA WILL NEVER RETURN TO YOUR WORLD. SHE BELONGS TO *ME* NOW!
GOOD-BYE, TAKA.
WAIT!!
AH!
WHAT IS GOING ON? WHY WOULD TAMAHOME WANT TO BREAK THE MIRROR IN MY ROOM?
I HAVE TO GET BACK! MIAKA IS IN DANGER!
PEEP
PEEP
THIS ISN'T ABOUT YOUR MIRROR!
OH, CRAP!
IT ISN'T WORKING! THE SHOCK OF MY LAST FALL MUST'VE ...!

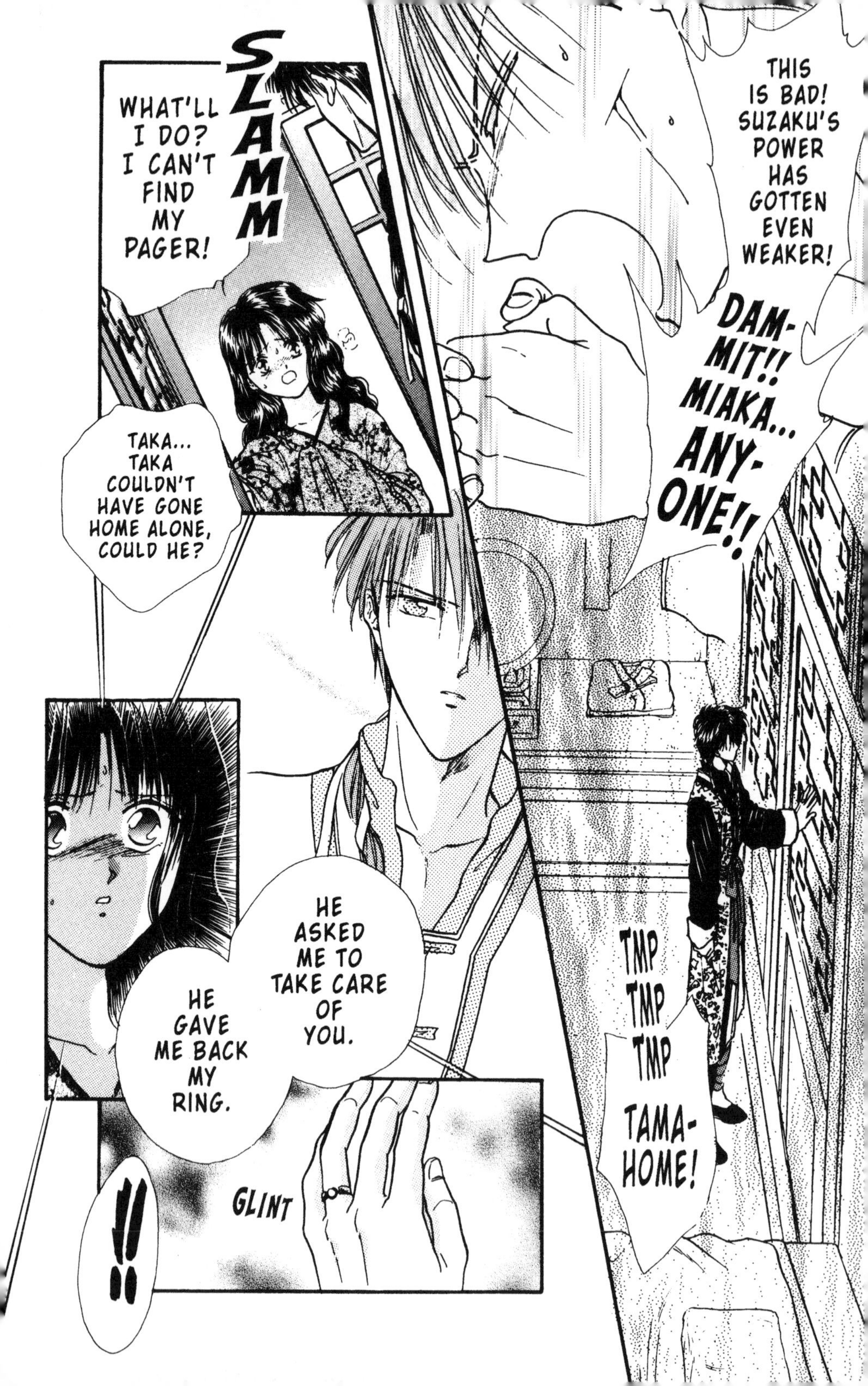
THIS IS BAD! SUZAKU'S POWER HAS GOTTEN EVEN WEAKER!
DAM-MIT!! MIAKA... ANY-ONE!!
SLAMM
WHAT'LL I DO? I CAN'T FIND MY PAGER!
TAKA... TAKA COULDN'T HAVE GONE HOME ALONE, COULD HE?
TMP TMP TMP
TAMA-HOME!
HE ASKED ME TO TAKE CARE OF YOU.
HE GAVE ME BACK MY RING.
GLINT
!!

THE *FUSHIGI YŪGI* TRENDS AND COUNTERMEASURES CORNER (?)

※ ONLY FOR THOSE WHO HAVE READ ALL THE WAY TO THE END!!

I really like Taka. (To be blunt.)

At first, the Tamahome fans would say things like, "There's something not the same about him," or, "It's like he's a completely different person," etc., but I like him! I know I've talked a lot about Nakago and Tasuki, and said a lot of other things, but now that the end is here, I consider Taka to be one of the most important characters I've ever created. Love♡!!

(There are spoilers ahead, folks!)

Tamahome and Taka are the same, but different. Why? It's because Taka changed between his existence as Tamahome and becoming Taka. Sure, the change of names and situations took care of some of it, but there was also the change of Tamahome (the boy) to Taka (the man). By the way, when Taka first appeared minus his stones (memories), the first reaction to him was that he seemed less "human" and more like a "doll" or "puppet." Some people said that he didn't have his "spirit" anymore. That's only natural -- he was made by Suzaku. He had no memories. Taka was pretty much a blank slate inside. And in some ways, for a young girl (Miaka), that was an ideal situation. He's an older guy, cute and gentle. What is a "human" anyway?

(Speaking of dolls, the most recent fans may not know about this but there was a Chichiri doll created for some UFO-Catcher-style crane machine games, and I was credited as designer! *It was made for a Shojo Comics event.*)

Anyway, I'd like all of you to read the books and see Taka's growth. Do you see the change? No, I don't mean that his hair got longer! *No? You don't see it?* Waaaaaah! ���

× × ×

And so, I played Part 2 as if the main character was Miaka, but actually it was Taka! The adult will never again be the child. The most important thing wasn't gathering those stones! It was going through the experiences that will finally allow Taka to accept himself as Taka. Also, the people around him have to accept him as well. That's the kind of story this is!! On the other hand, *Fushigi Yūgi* has always been a work that built on the feelings of its readers. Or something like that...right?

429

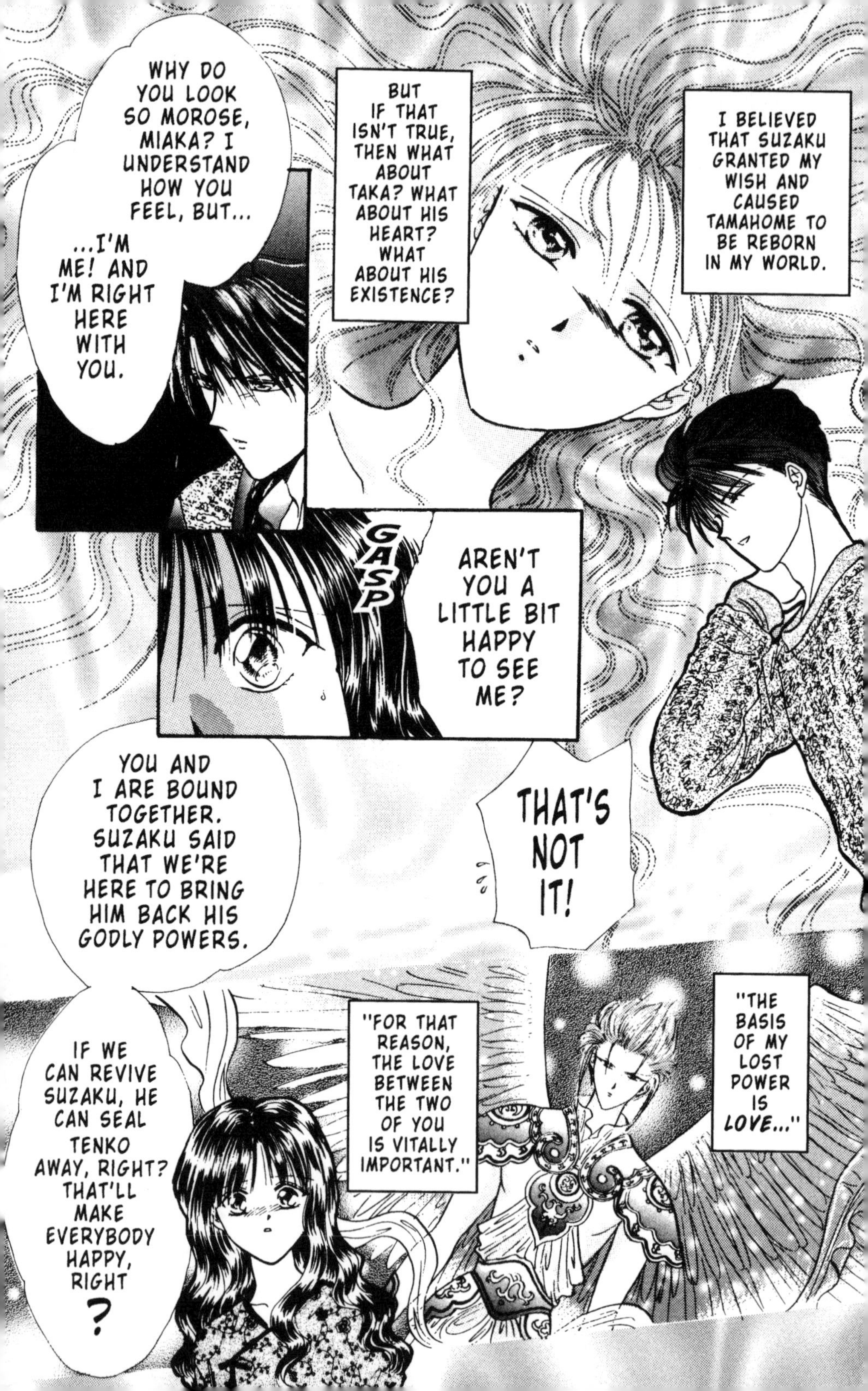
I BELIEVED THAT SUZAKU GRANTED MY WISH AND CAUSED TAMAHOME TO BE REBORN IN MY WORLD.
BUT IF THAT ISN'T TRUE, THEN WHAT ABOUT TAKA? WHAT ABOUT HIS HEART? WHAT ABOUT HIS EXISTENCE?
WHY DO YOU LOOK SO MOROSE, MIAKA? I UNDERSTAND HOW YOU FEEL, BUT...
...I'M ME! AND I'M RIGHT HERE WITH YOU.
GASP
AREN'T YOU A LITTLE BIT HAPPY TO SEE ME?
THAT'S NOT IT!
YOU AND I ARE BOUND TOGETHER. SUZAKU SAID THAT WE'RE HERE TO BRING HIM BACK HIS GODLY POWERS.
"THE BASIS OF MY LOST POWER IS *LOVE*..."
"FOR THAT REASON, THE LOVE BETWEEN THE TWO OF YOU IS VITALLY IMPORTANT."
IF WE CAN REVIVE SUZAKU, HE CAN SEAL TENKO AWAY, RIGHT? THAT'LL MAKE EVERYBODY HAPPY, RIGHT?

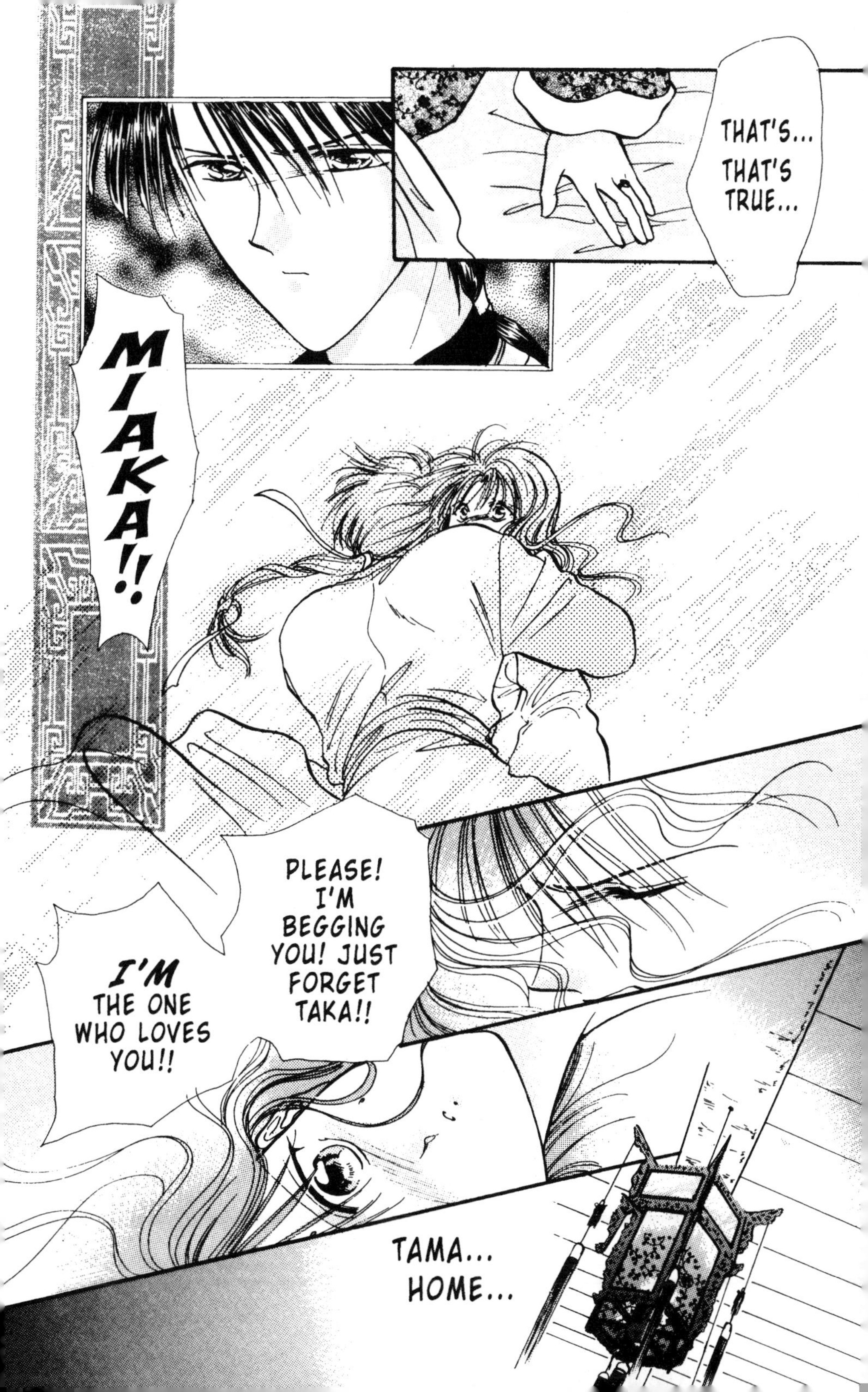
THAT'S... THAT'S TRUE...
MIAKA!!
PLEASE! I'M BEGGING YOU! JUST FORGET TAKA!!
I'M THE ONE WHO LOVES YOU!!
TAMA... HOME...

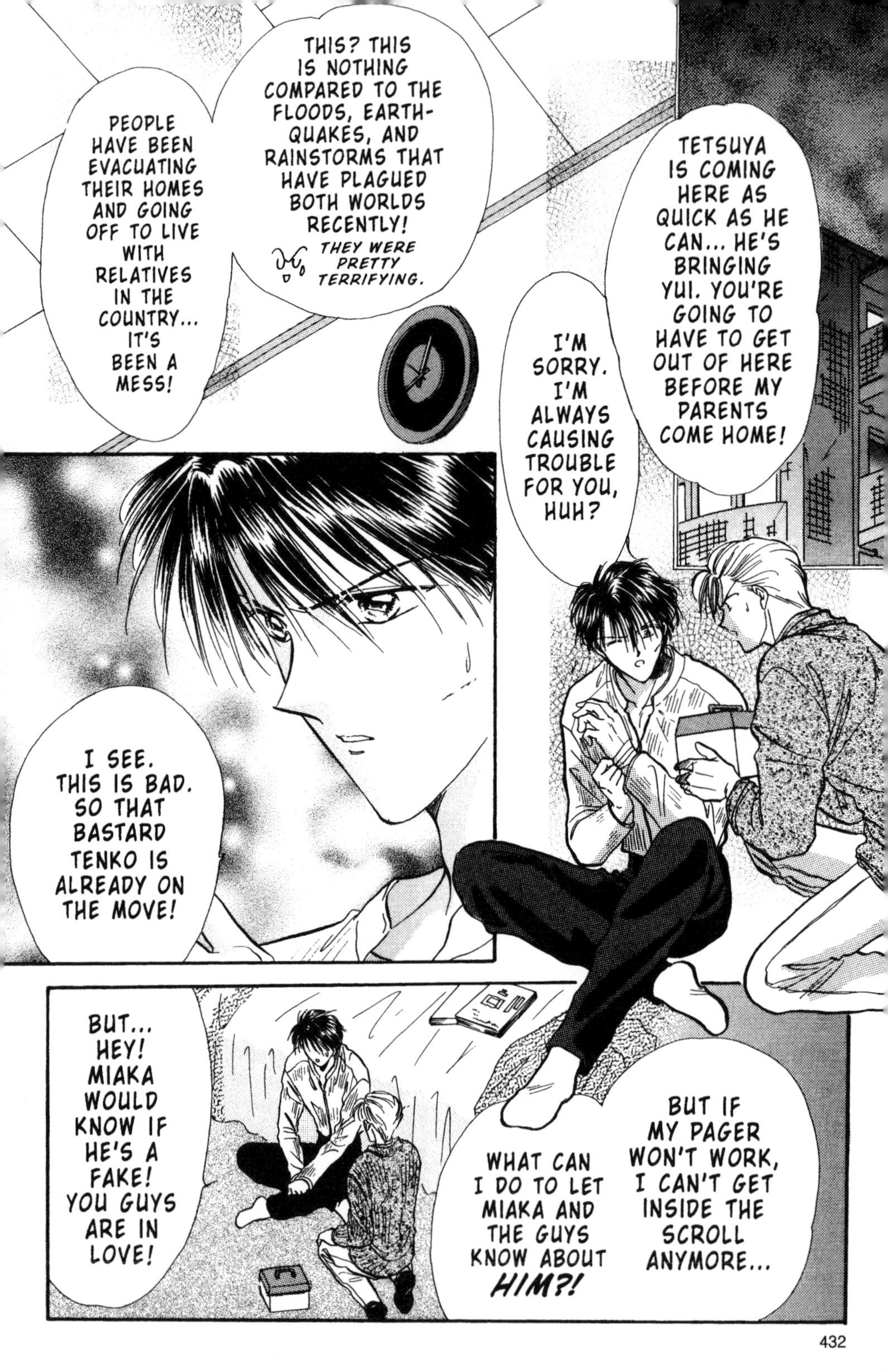
TETSUYA IS COMING HERE AS QUICK AS HE CAN... HE'S BRINGING YUI. YOU'RE GOING TO HAVE TO GET OUT OF HERE BEFORE MY PARENTS COME HOME!
I'M SORRY. I'M ALWAYS CAUSING TROUBLE FOR YOU, HUH?
THIS? THIS IS NOTHING COMPARED TO THE FLOODS, EARTH-QUAKES, AND RAINSTORMS THAT HAVE PLAGUED BOTH WORLDS RECENTLY!
THEY WERE PRETTY TERRIFYING.
PEOPLE HAVE BEEN EVACUATING THEIR HOMES AND GOING OFF TO LIVE WITH RELATIVES IN THE COUNTRY... IT'S BEEN A MESS!
I SEE. THIS IS BAD. SO THAT BASTARD TENKO IS ALREADY ON THE MOVE!
BUT IF MY PAGER WON'T WORK, I CAN'T GET INSIDE THE SCROLL ANYMORE...
WHAT CAN I DO TO LET MIAKA AND THE GUYS KNOW ABOUT HIM?!
BUT... HEY! MIAKA WOULD KNOW IF HE'S A FAKE! YOU GUYS ARE IN LOVE!

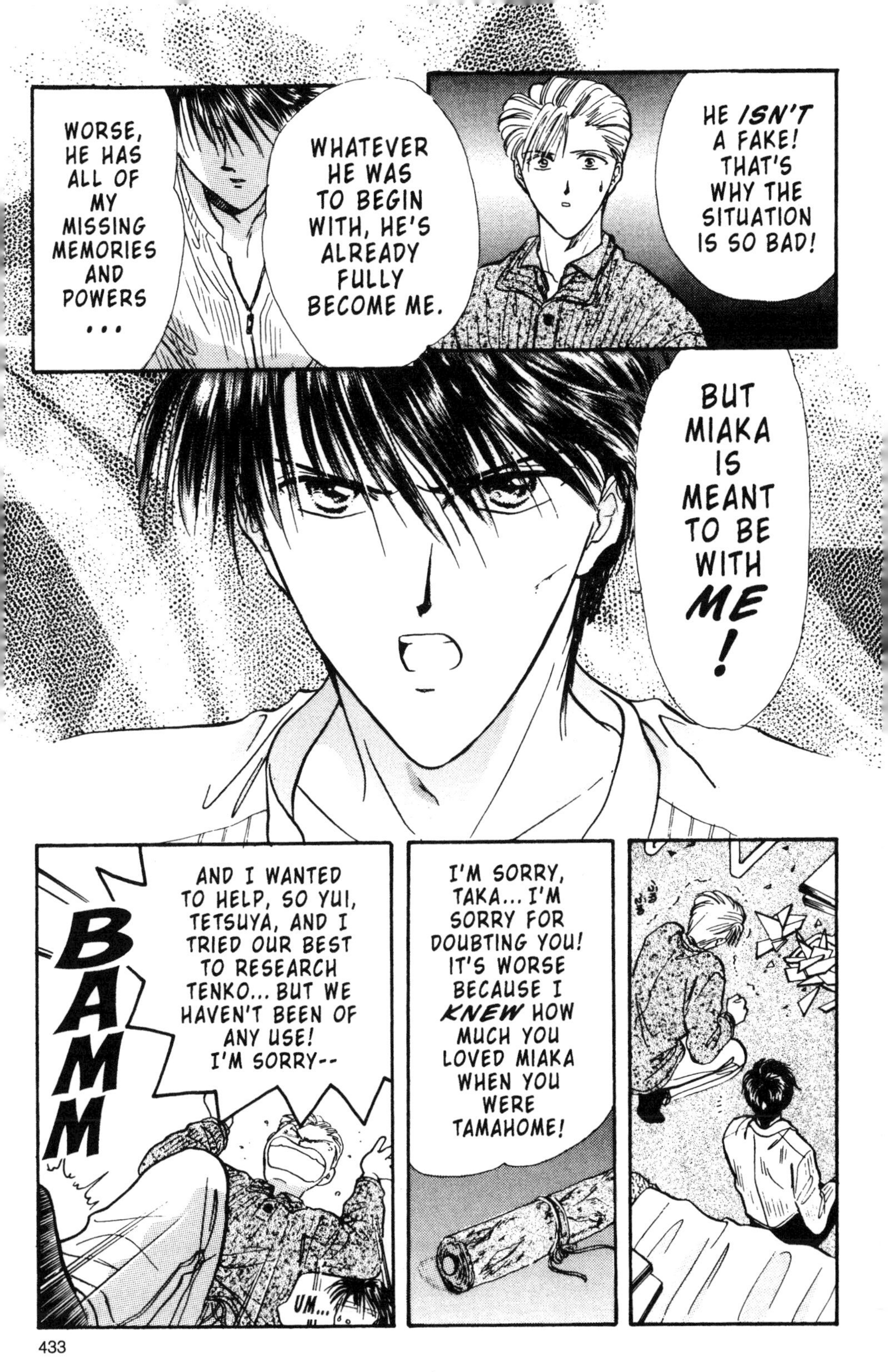

HE *ISN'T* A FAKE! THAT'S WHY THE SITUATION IS SO BAD!
WHATEVER HE WAS TO BEGIN WITH, HE'S ALREADY FULLY BECOME ME.
WORSE, HE HAS ALL OF MY MISSING MEMORIES AND POWERS...
BUT MIAKA IS MEANT TO BE WITH *ME*!
I'M SORRY, TAKA... I'M SORRY FOR DOUBTING YOU! IT'S WORSE BECAUSE I *KNEW* HOW MUCH YOU LOVED MIAKA WHEN YOU WERE TAMAHOME!
AND I WANTED TO HELP, SO YUI, TETSUYA, AND I TRIED OUR BEST TO RESEARCH TENKO... BUT WE HAVEN'T BEEN OF ANY USE! I'M SORRY--
BAMM
UM...

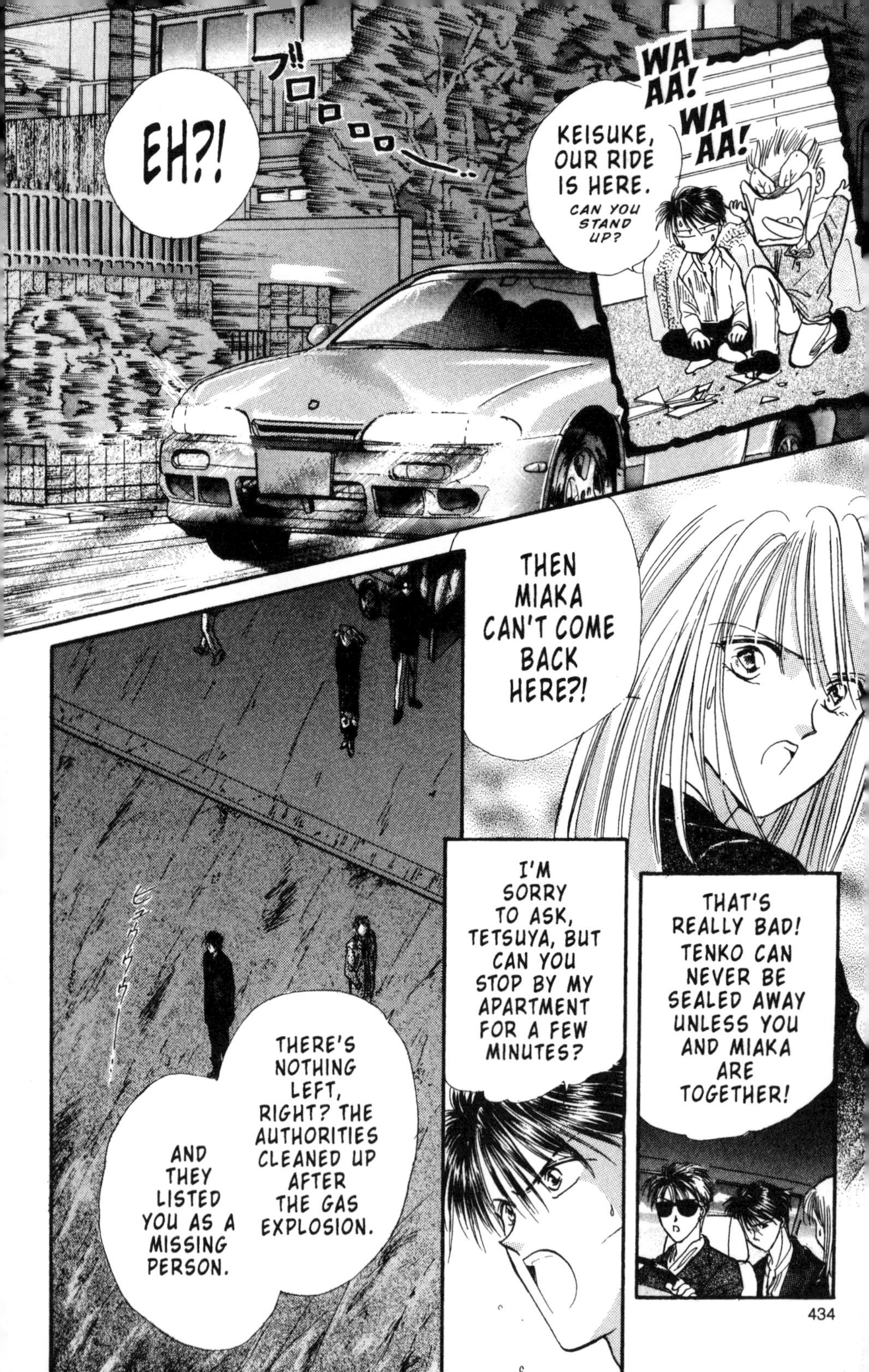
WA AA! WA AA!
KEISUKE, OUR RIDE IS HERE. CAN YOU STAND UP?
ブ!! ロロロロ
EH?!
THEN MIAKA CAN'T COME BACK HERE?!
THAT'S REALLY BAD! TENKO CAN NEVER BE SEALED AWAY UNLESS YOU AND MIAKA ARE TOGETHER!
I'M SORRY TO ASK, TETSUYA, BUT CAN YOU STOP BY MY APARTMENT FOR A FEW MINUTES?
THERE'S NOTHING LEFT, RIGHT? THE AUTHORITIES CLEANED UP AFTER THE GAS EXPLOSION.
AND THEY LISTED YOU AS A MISSING PERSON.

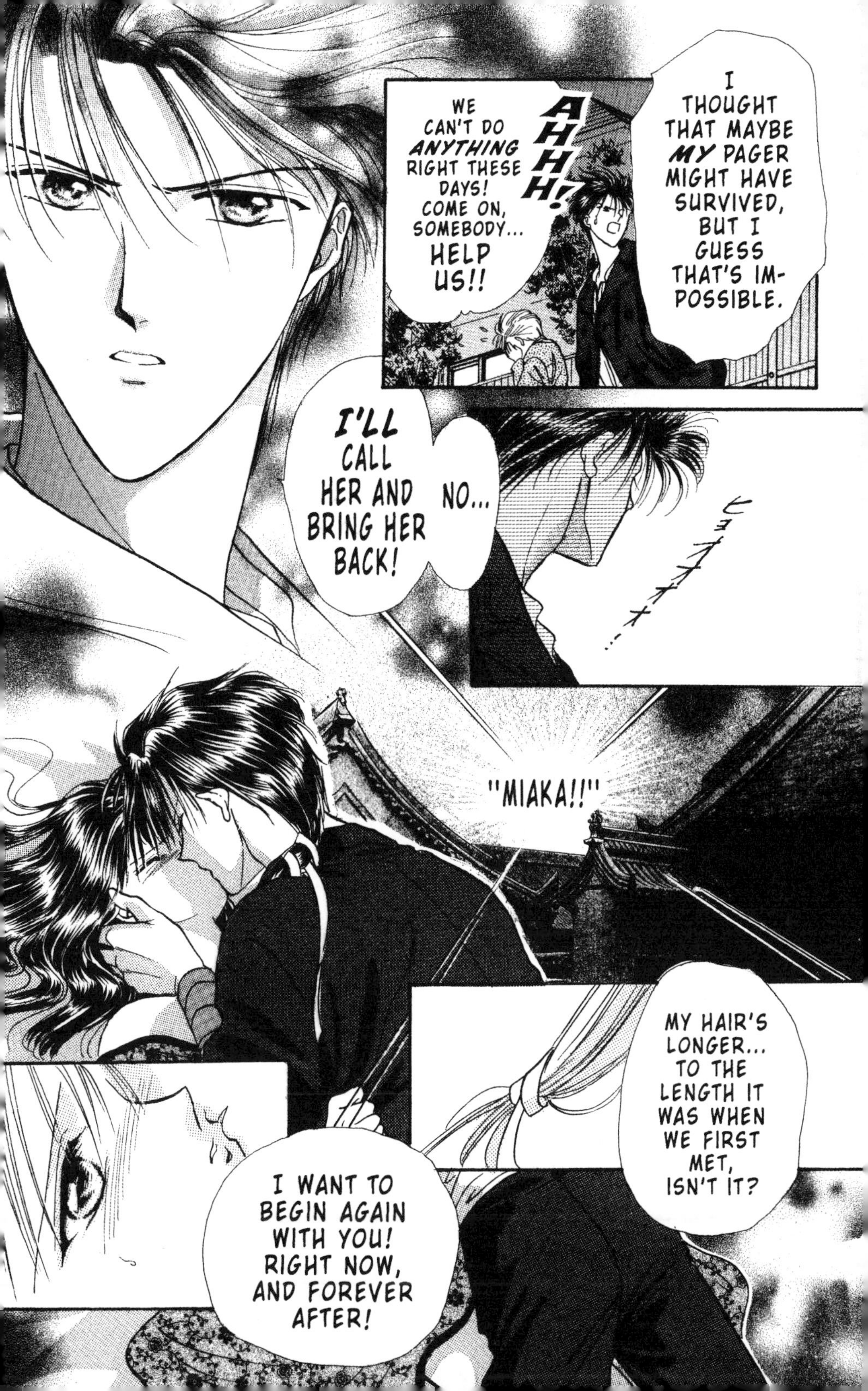
I THOUGHT THAT MAYBE *MY* PAGER MIGHT HAVE SURVIVED, BUT I GUESS THAT'S IM-POSSIBLE.
AHHHH!
WE CAN'T DO *ANYTHING* RIGHT THESE DAYS! COME ON, SOMEBODY... HELP US!!
NO...
I'LL CALL HER AND BRING HER BACK!
"MIAKA!!"
MY HAIR'S LONGER... TO THE LENGTH IT WAS WHEN WE FIRST MET, ISN'T IT?
I WANT TO BEGIN AGAIN WITH YOU! RIGHT NOW, AND FOREVER AFTER!

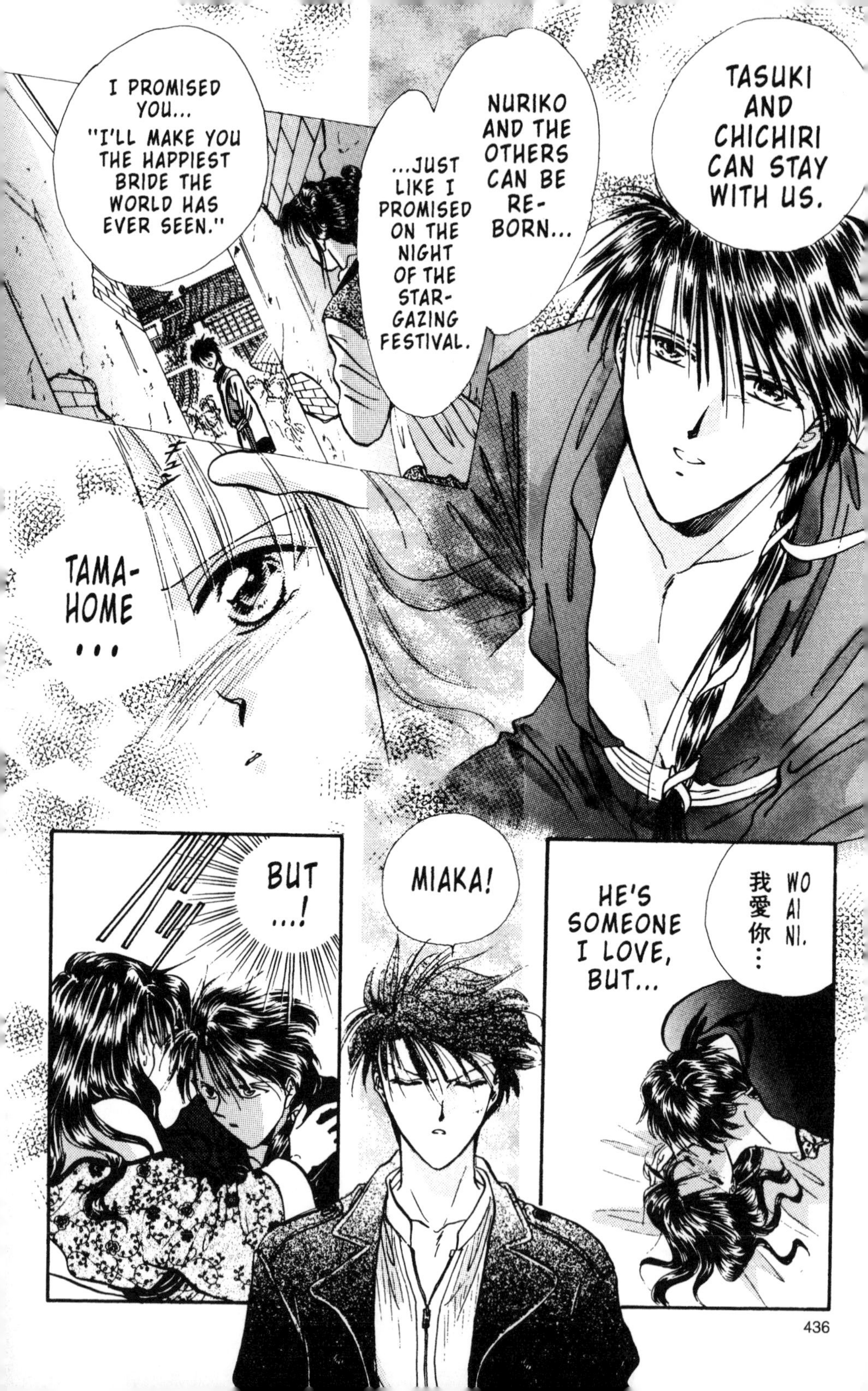
TASUKI AND CHICHIRI CAN STAY WITH US.
NURIKO AND THE OTHERS CAN BE RE-BORN...
...JUST LIKE I PROMISED ON THE NIGHT OF THE STAR-GAZING FESTIVAL.
I PROMISED YOU... "I'LL MAKE YOU THE HAPPIEST BRIDE THE WORLD HAS EVER SEEN."
TAMA-HOME...
WO AI NI. 我愛你…
HE'S SOMEONE I LOVE, BUT...
MIAKA!
BUT ...!

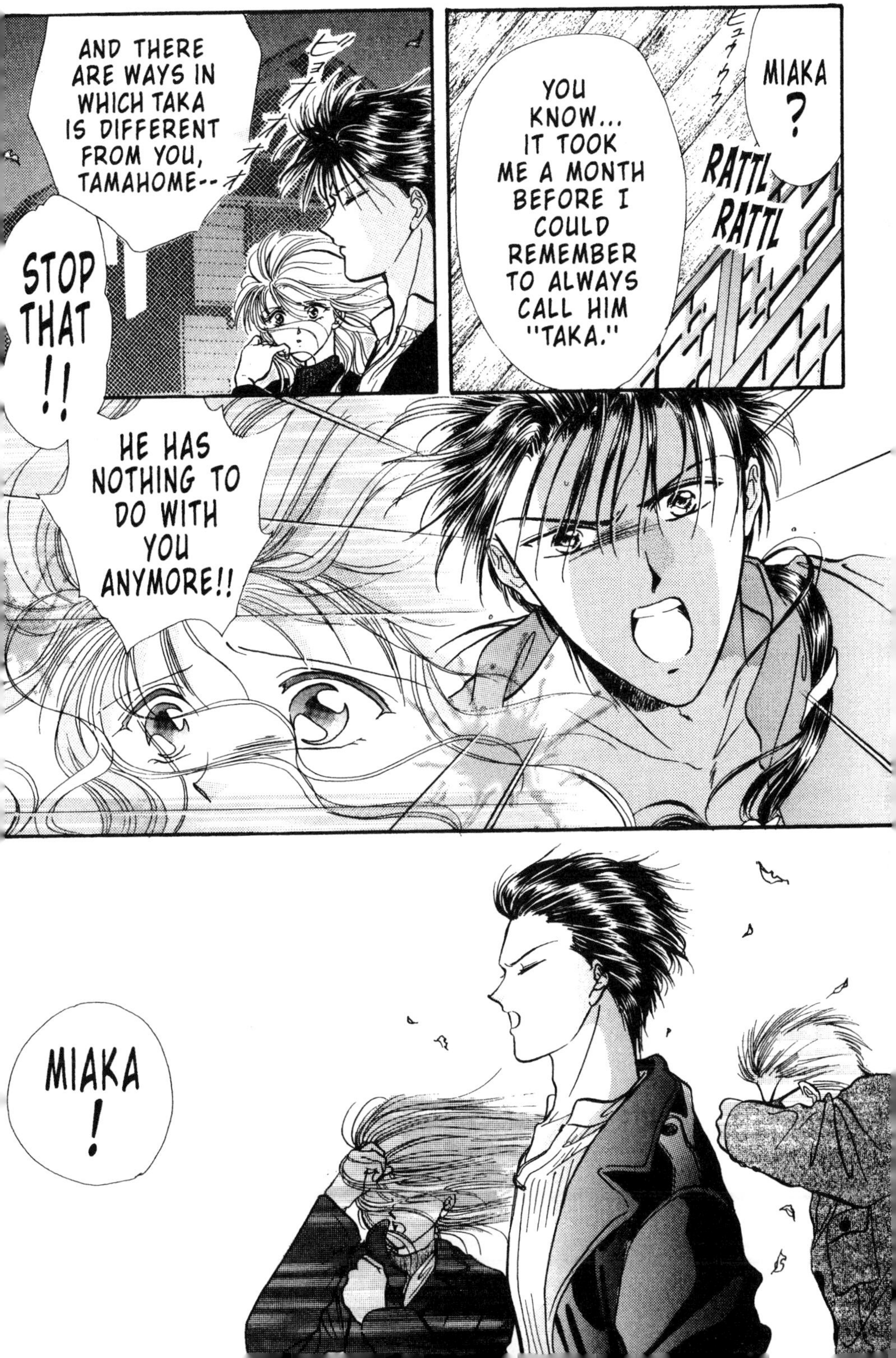
MIAKA ?
RATTL RATTL
YOU KNOW... IT TOOK ME A MONTH BEFORE I COULD REMEMBER TO ALWAYS CALL HIM "TAKA."
AND THERE ARE WAYS IN WHICH TAKA IS DIFFERENT FROM YOU, TAMAHOME--
STOP THAT !!
HE HAS NOTHING TO DO WITH YOU ANYMORE!!
MIAKA !

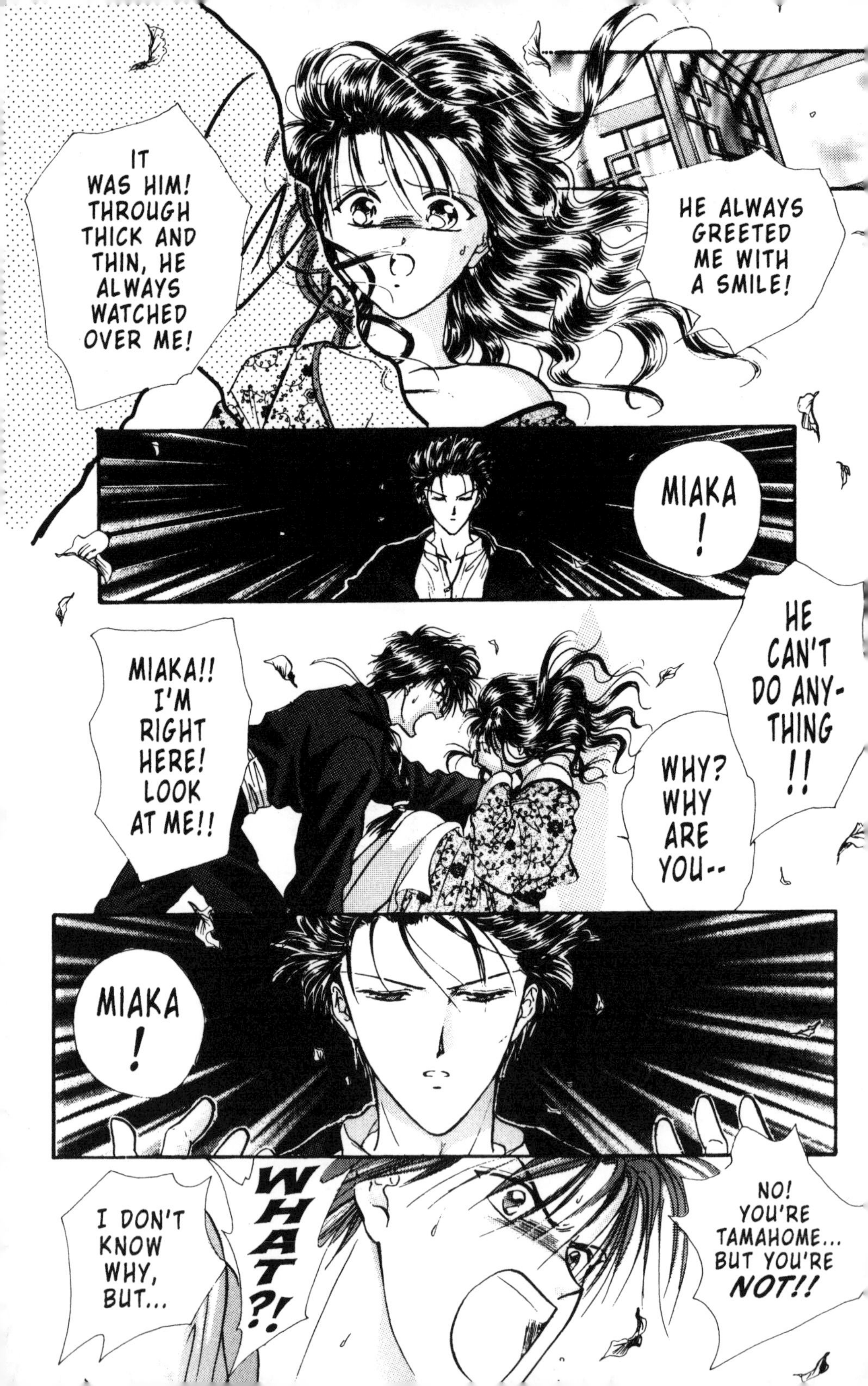
HE ALWAYS GREETED ME WITH A SMILE!
IT WAS HIM! THROUGH THICK AND THIN, HE ALWAYS WATCHED OVER ME!
MIAKA!
HE CAN'T DO ANYTHING!!
WHY? WHY ARE YOU--
MIAKA!! I'M RIGHT HERE! LOOK AT ME!!
MIAKA!
NO! YOU'RE TAMAHOME... BUT YOU'RE NOT!!
WHAT?!
I DON'T KNOW WHY, BUT...

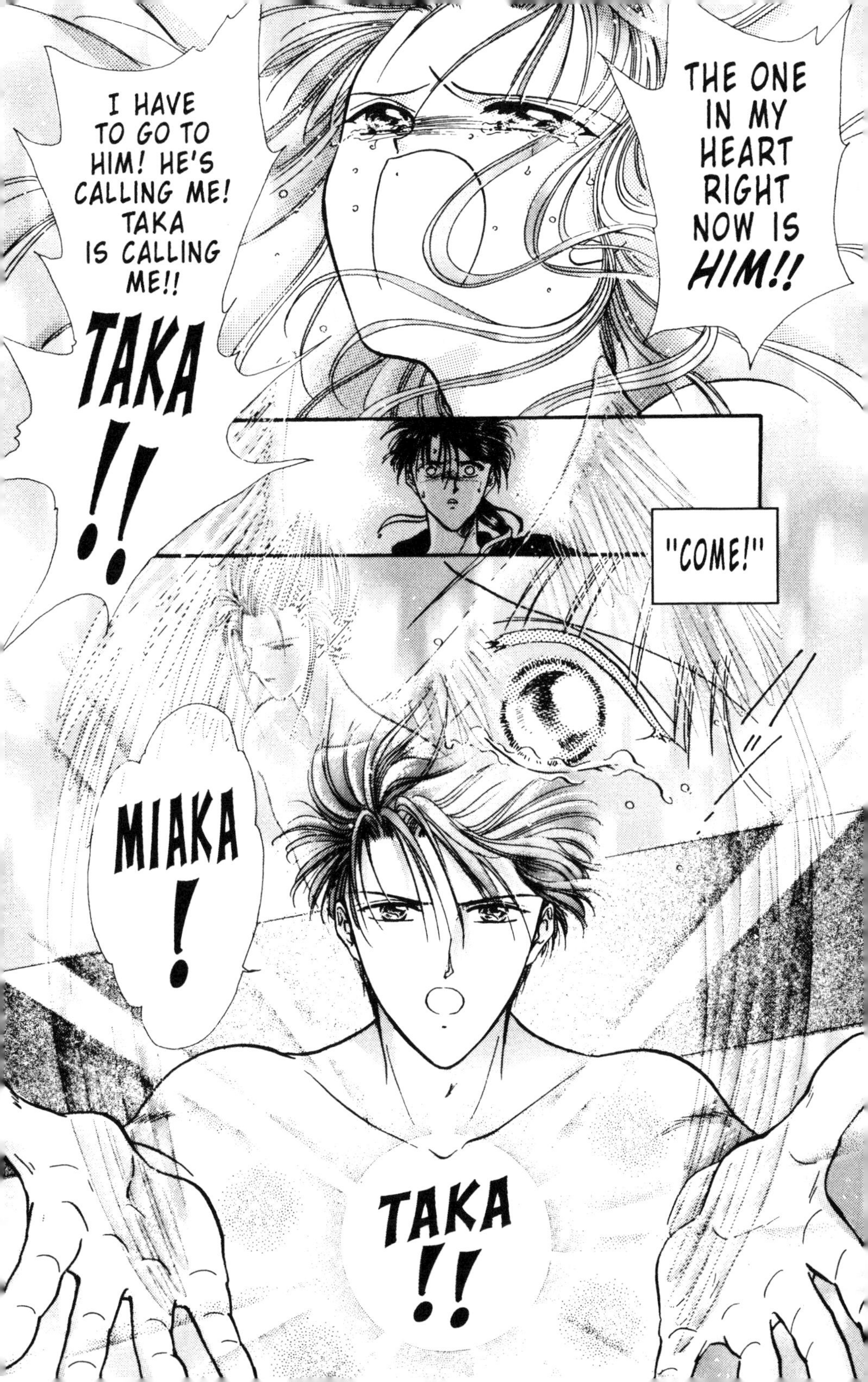
THE ONE IN MY HEART RIGHT NOW IS HIM!!
I HAVE TO GO TO HIM! HE'S CALLING ME! TAKA IS CALLING ME!!
TAKA!!
"COME!"
MIAKA!
TAKA!!

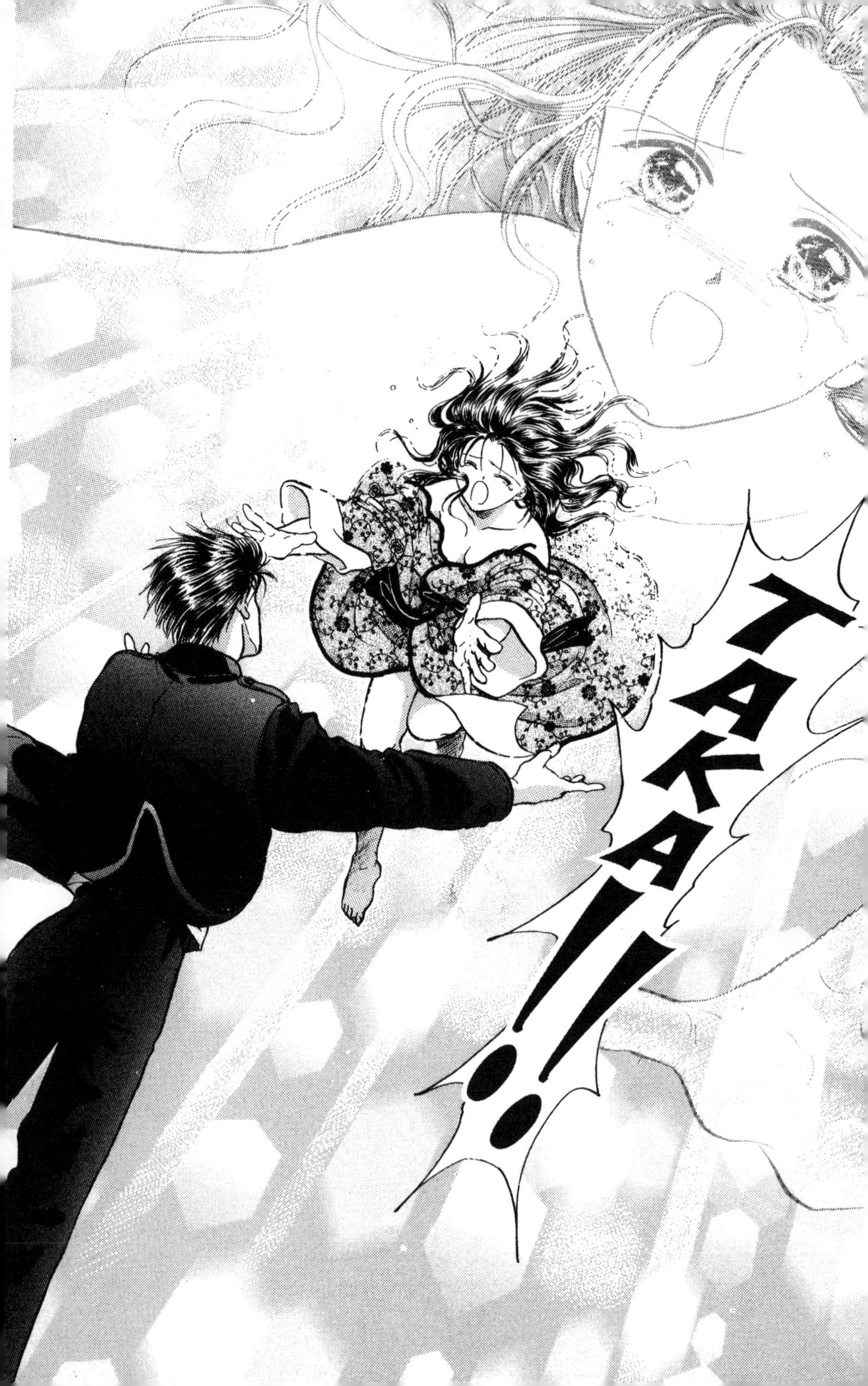
TAKAI!!

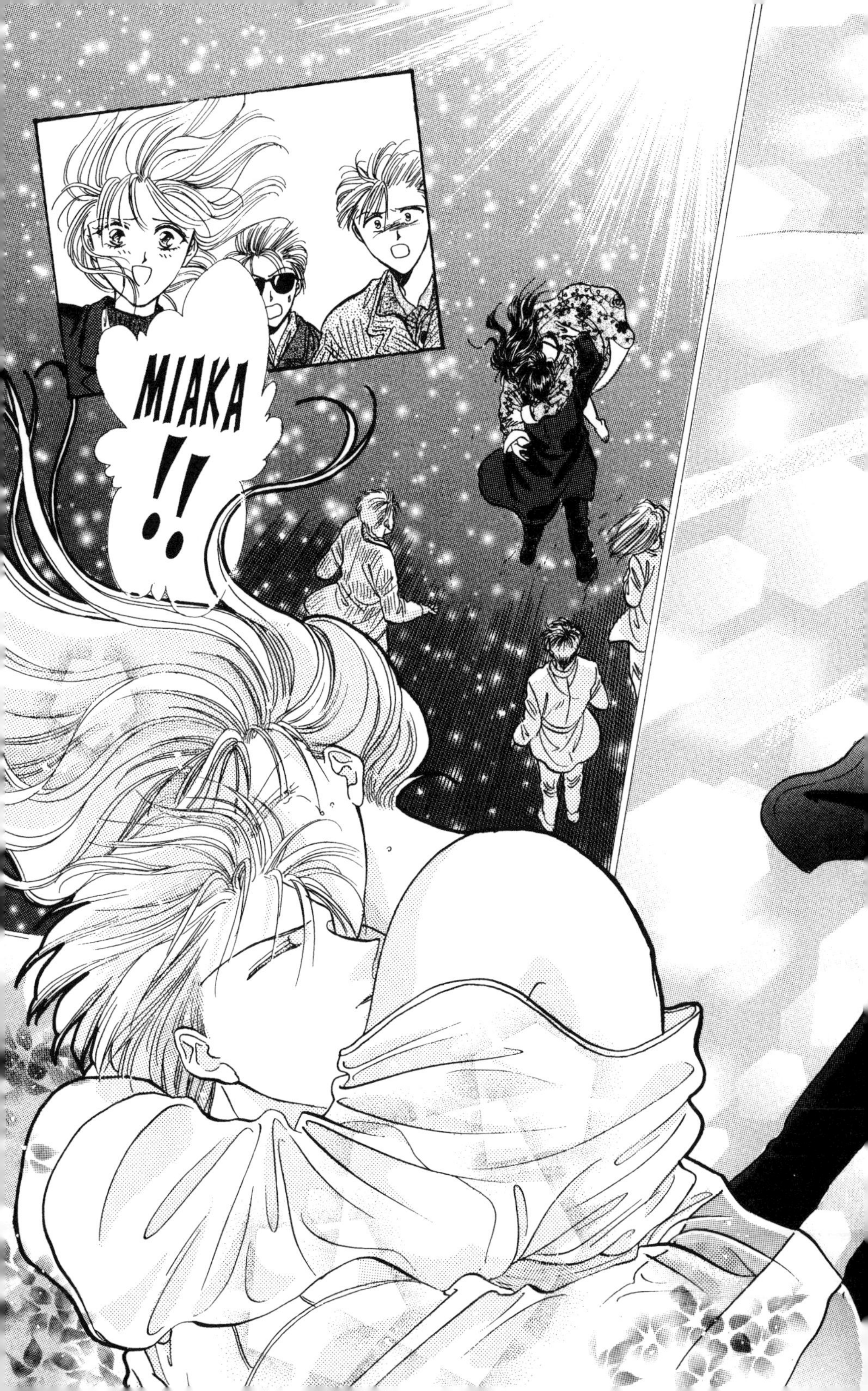
MIAKA!!

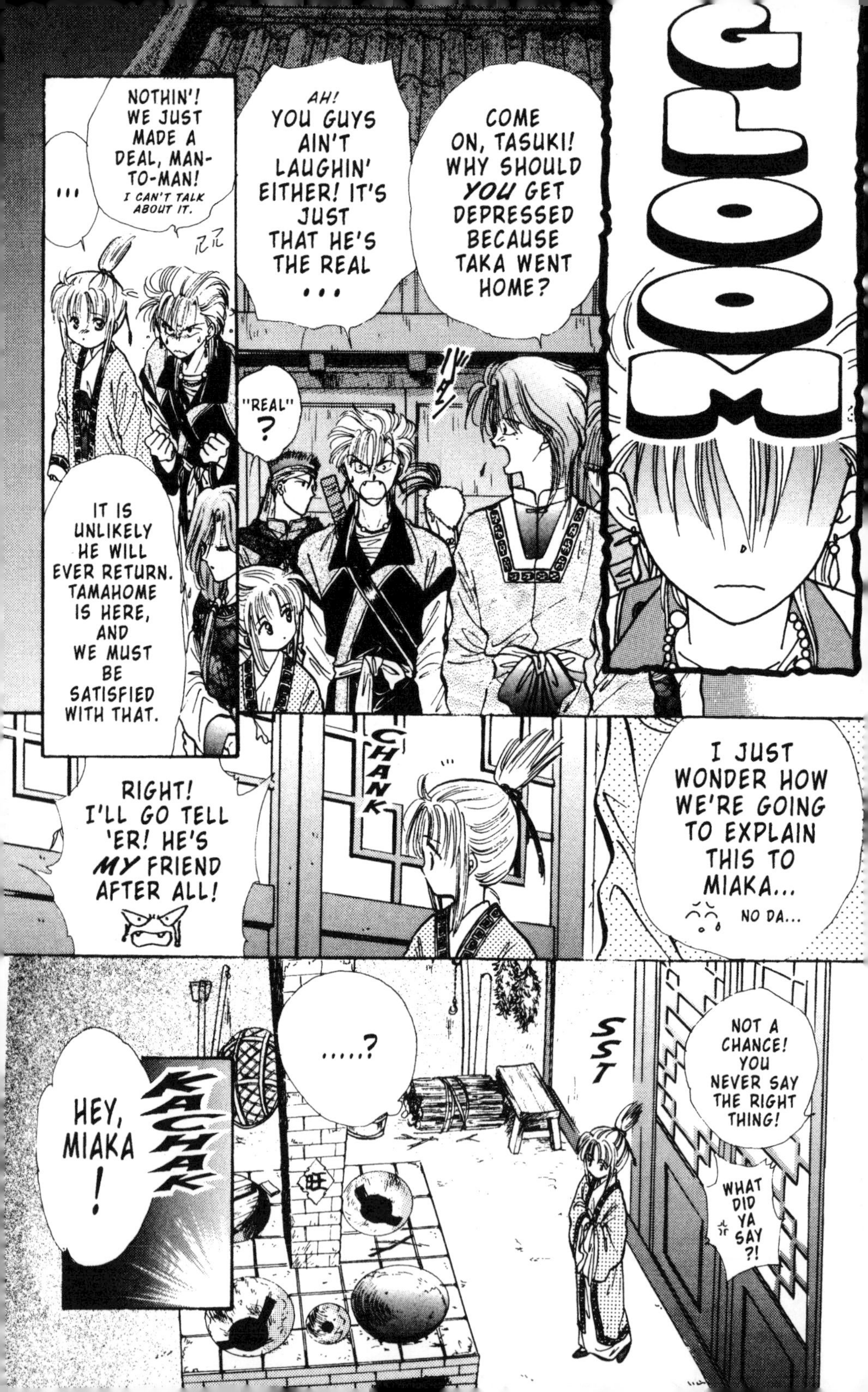
GLOOM
COME ON, TASUKI! WHY SHOULD YOU GET DEPRESSED BECAUSE TAKA WENT HOME?
AH! YOU GUYS AIN'T LAUGHIN' EITHER! IT'S JUST THAT HE'S THE REAL . . .
"REAL" ?
NOTHIN'! WE JUST MADE A DEAL, MAN-TO-MAN! I CAN'T TALK ABOUT IT.
...
IT IS UNLIKELY HE WILL EVER RETURN. TAMAHOME IS HERE, AND WE MUST BE SATISFIED WITH THAT.
I JUST WONDER HOW WE'RE GOING TO EXPLAIN THIS TO MIAKA... NO DA...
CHANK
RIGHT! I'LL GO TELL 'ER! HE'S MY FRIEND AFTER ALL!
SST
NOT A CHANCE! YOU NEVER SAY THE RIGHT THING!
WHAT DID YA SAY?!
.....?
KACHAK
HEY, MIAKA!

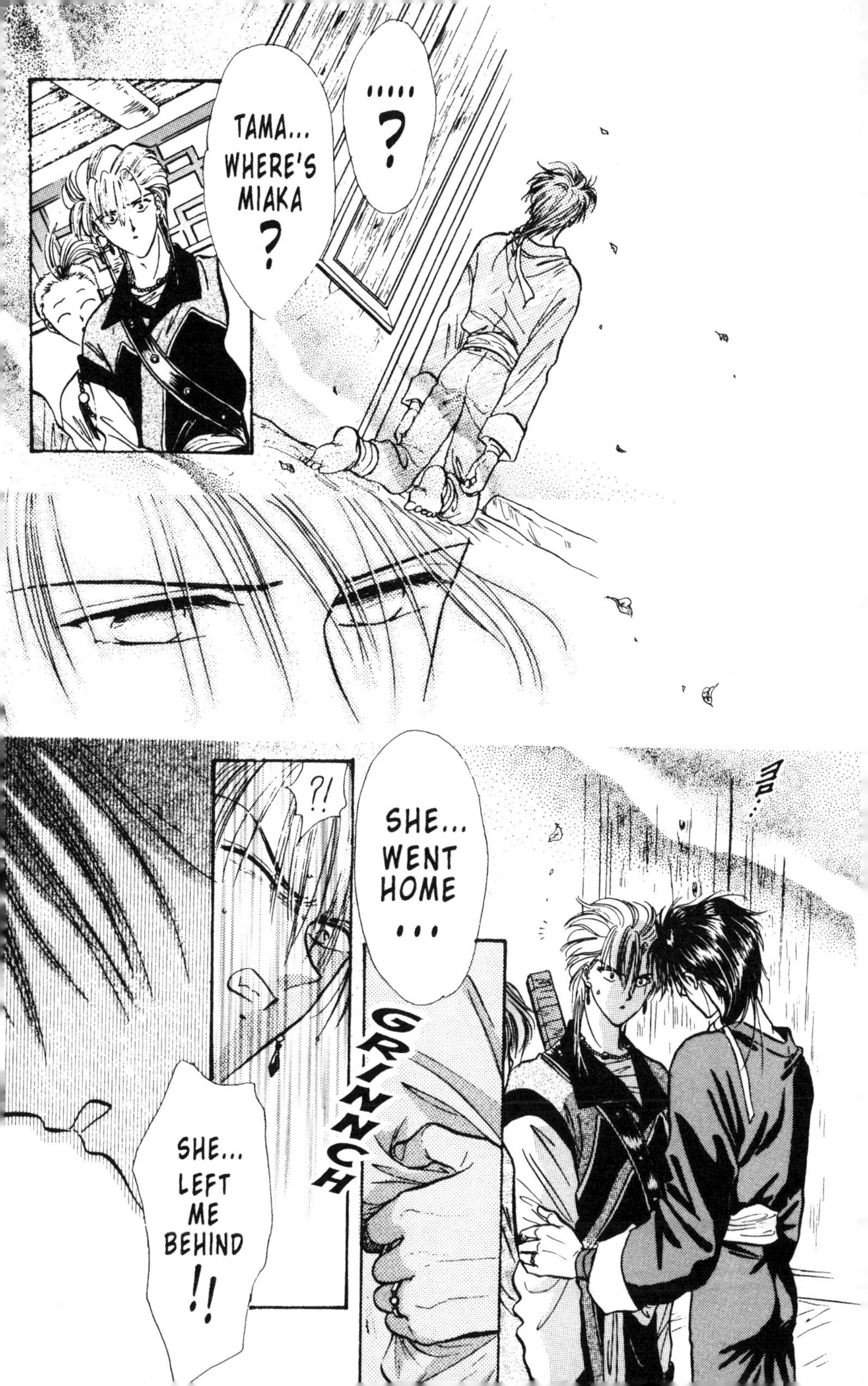
.....?
TAMA... WHERE'S MIAKA?
SHE... WENT HOME...
?!
GRINNCH
SHE... LEFT ME BEHIND!!

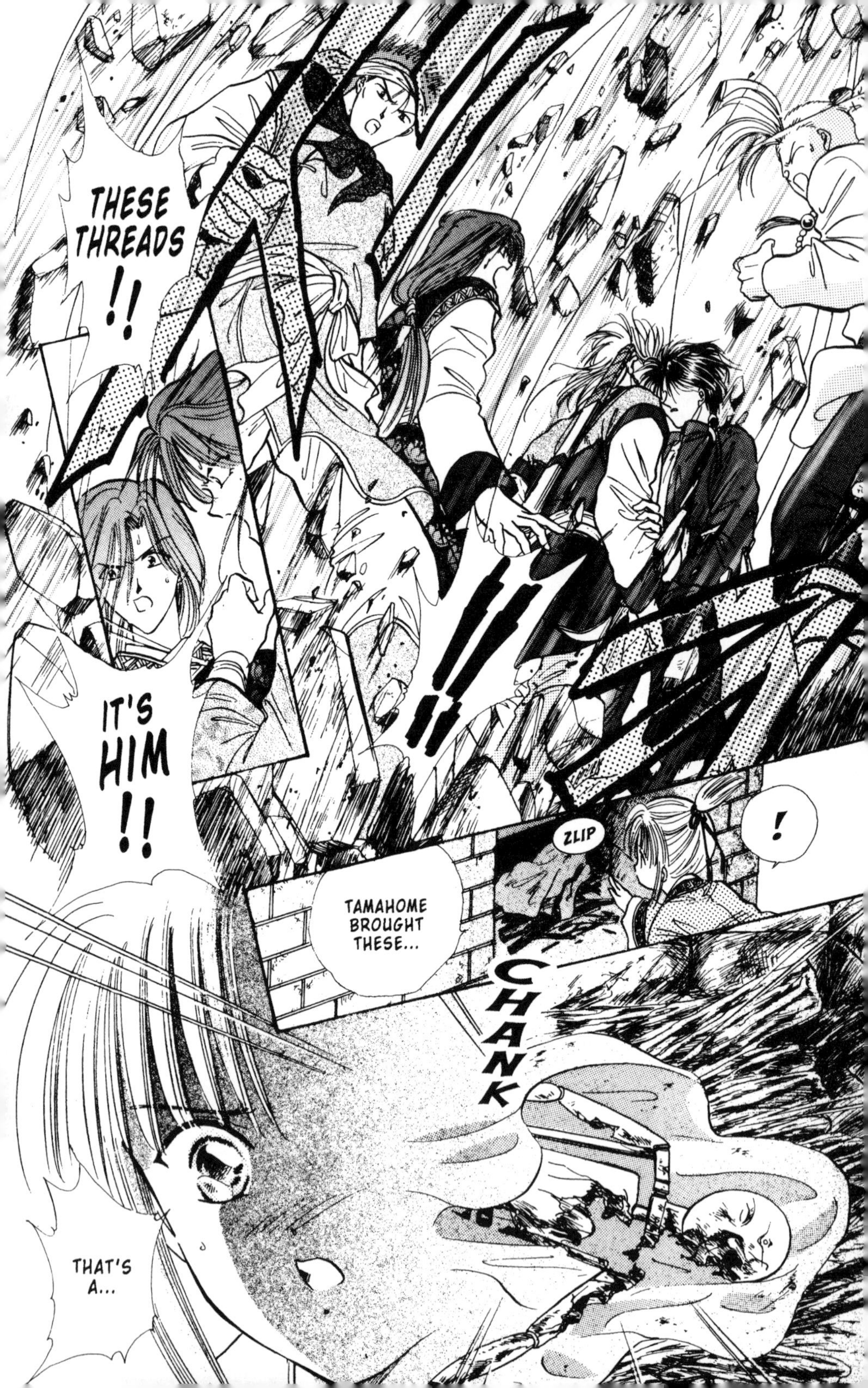
THESE THREADS!!
IT'S HIM!!
!
ZLIP
TAMAHOME BROUGHT THESE...
CHANK
THAT'S A...

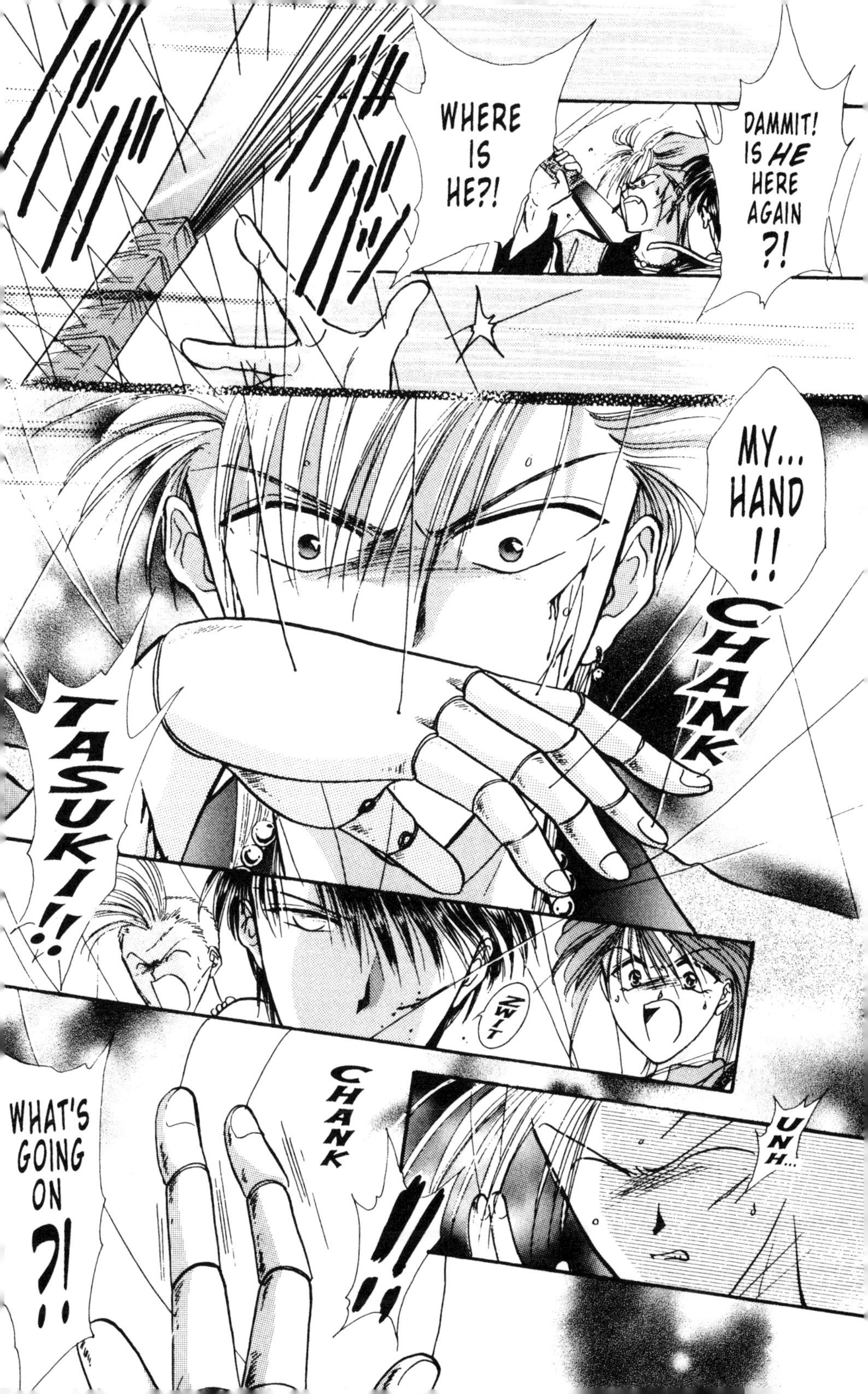
DAMMIT! IS HE HERE AGAIN?!
WHERE IS HE?!
MY... HAND!!
CHANK
TASUKI!!!
ZWIT
UNH...
CHANK
WHAT'S GOING ON?!

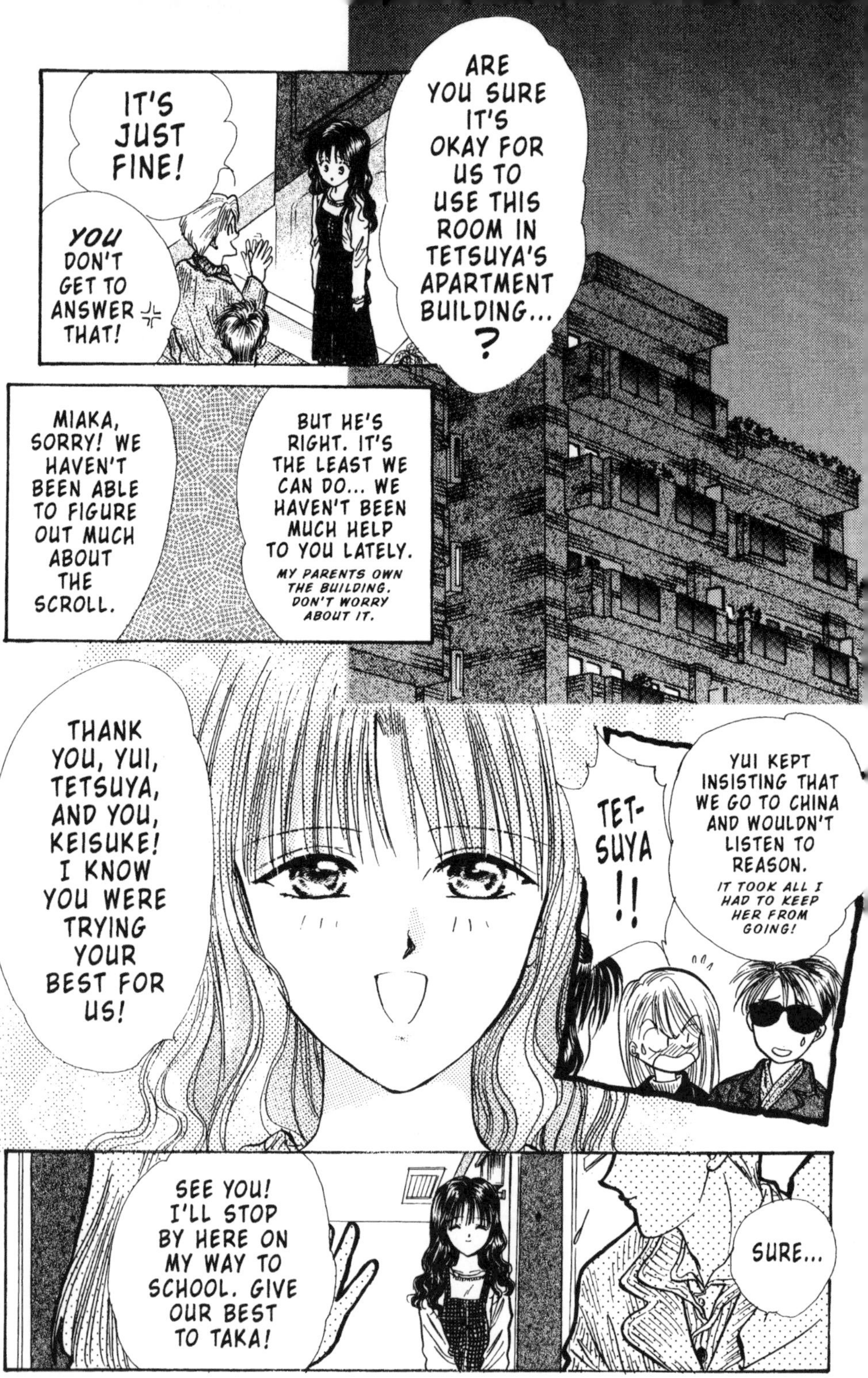
ARE YOU SURE IT'S OKAY FOR US TO USE THIS ROOM IN TETSUYA'S APARTMENT BUILDING...?
IT'S JUST FINE!
YOU DON'T GET TO ANSWER THAT!
BUT HE'S RIGHT. IT'S THE LEAST WE CAN DO... WE HAVEN'T BEEN MUCH HELP TO YOU LATELY.
MY PARENTS OWN THE BUILDING. DON'T WORRY ABOUT IT.
MIAKA, SORRY! WE HAVEN'T BEEN ABLE TO FIGURE OUT MUCH ABOUT THE SCROLL.
YUI KEPT INSISTING THAT WE GO TO CHINA AND WOULDN'T LISTEN TO REASON.
IT TOOK ALL I HAD TO KEEP HER FROM GOING!
TET-SUYA!!
THANK YOU, YUI, TETSUYA, AND YOU, KEISUKE! I KNOW YOU WERE TRYING YOUR BEST FOR US!
SURE...
SEE YOU! I'LL STOP BY HERE ON MY WAY TO SCHOOL. GIVE OUR BEST TO TAKA!

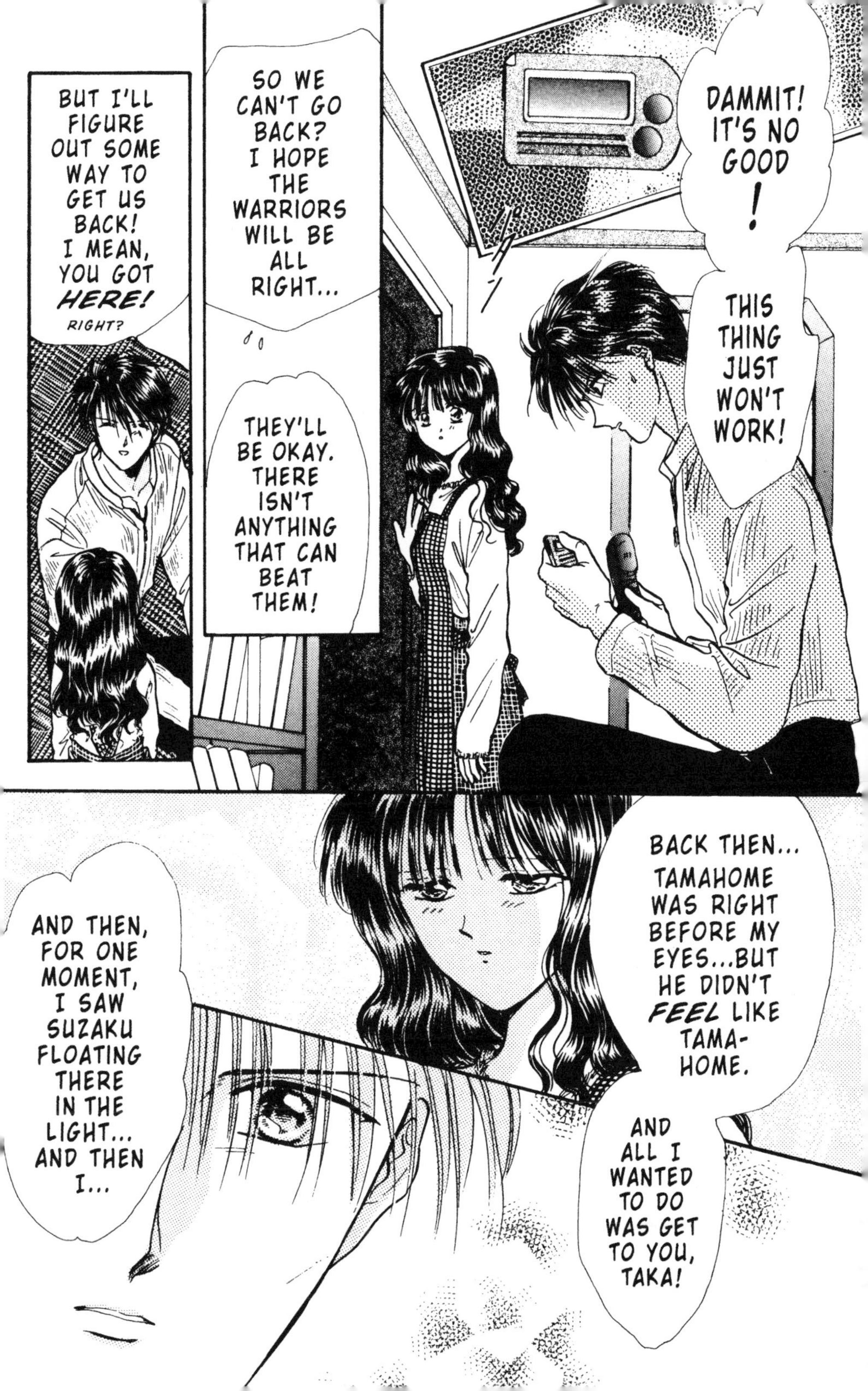
DAMMIT! IT'S NO GOOD!
THIS THING JUST WON'T WORK!
SO WE CAN'T GO BACK? I HOPE THE WARRIORS WILL BE ALL RIGHT...
THEY'LL BE OKAY. THERE ISN'T ANYTHING THAT CAN BEAT THEM!
BUT I'LL FIGURE OUT SOME WAY TO GET US BACK! I MEAN, YOU GOT *HERE!* RIGHT?
BACK THEN... TAMAHOME WAS RIGHT BEFORE MY EYES...BUT HE DIDN'T *FEEL* LIKE TAMA-HOME.
AND THEN, FOR ONE MOMENT, I SAW SUZAKU FLOATING THERE IN THE LIGHT... AND THEN I...
AND ALL I WANTED TO DO WAS GET TO YOU, TAKA!

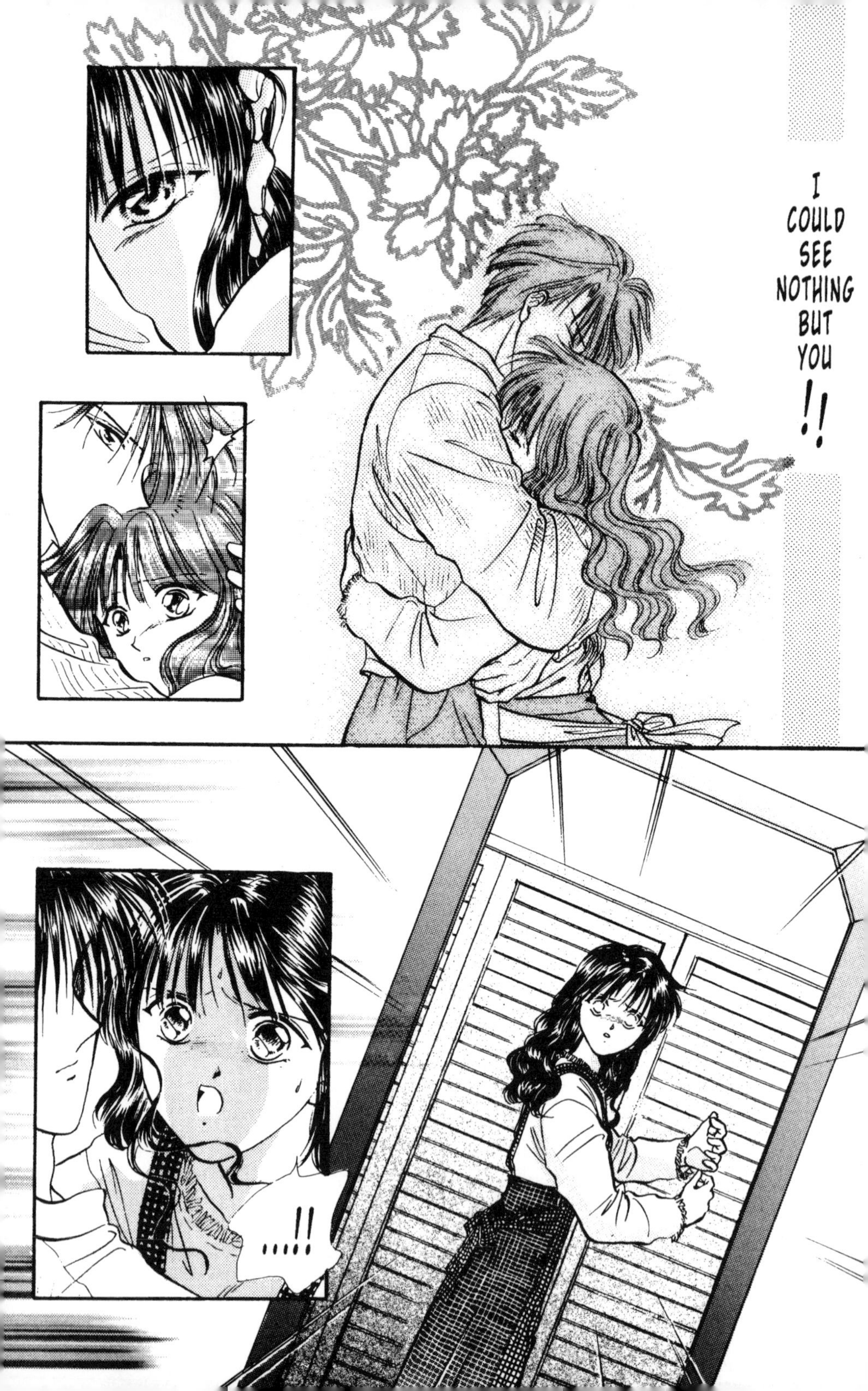
I COULD SEE NOTHING BUT YOU !!
...!!

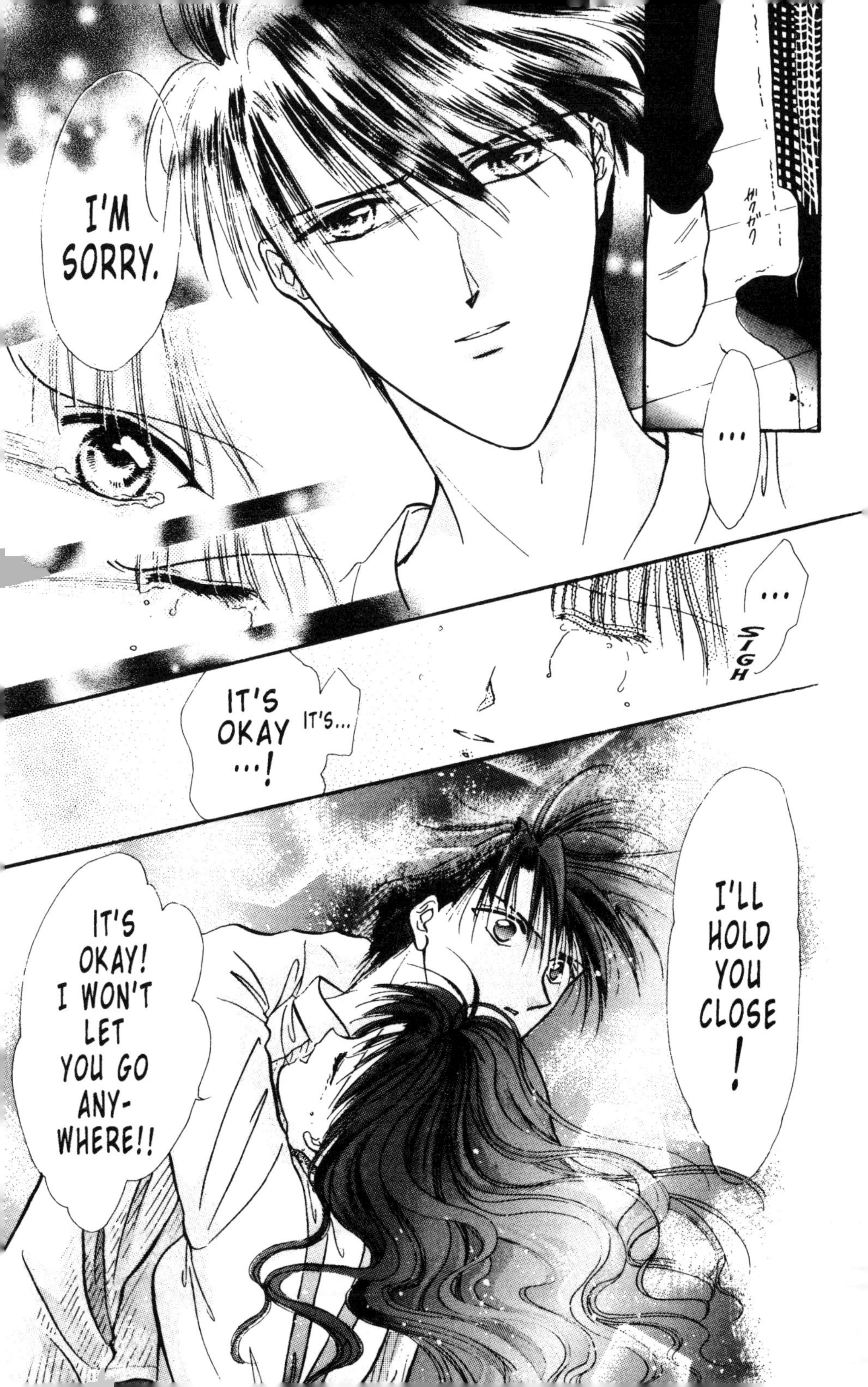
ガクガク
I'M SORRY.
...
...
SIGH
IT'S OKAY IT'S... ...!
I'LL HOLD YOU CLOSE!
IT'S OKAY! I WON'T LET YOU GO ANY-WHERE!!

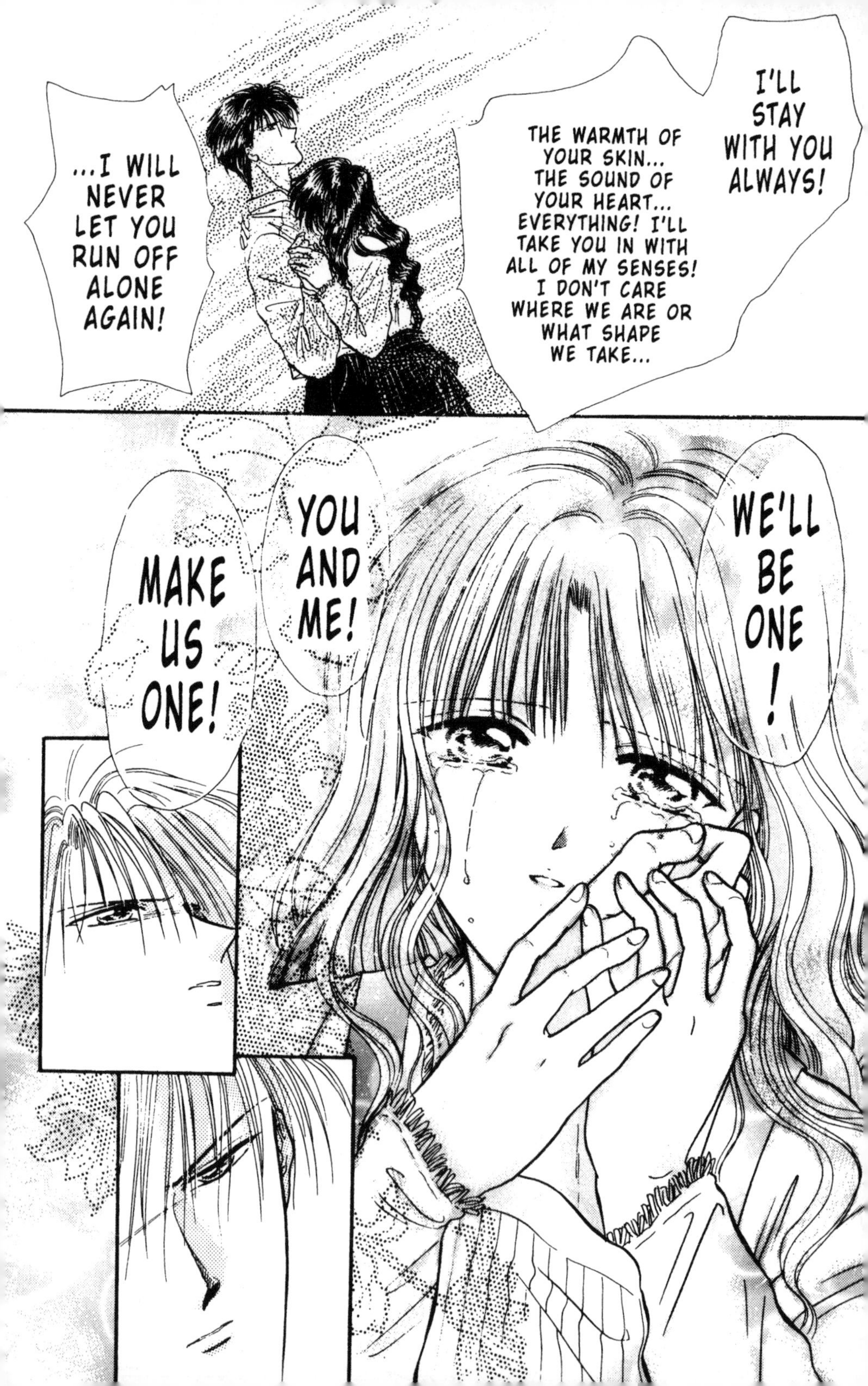
I'LL STAY WITH YOU ALWAYS!
THE WARMTH OF YOUR SKIN... THE SOUND OF YOUR HEART... EVERYTHING! I'LL TAKE YOU IN WITH ALL OF MY SENSES! I DON'T CARE WHERE WE ARE OR WHAT SHAPE WE TAKE...
...I WILL NEVER LET YOU RUN OFF ALONE AGAIN!
WE'LL BE ONE!
YOU AND ME!
MAKE US ONE!

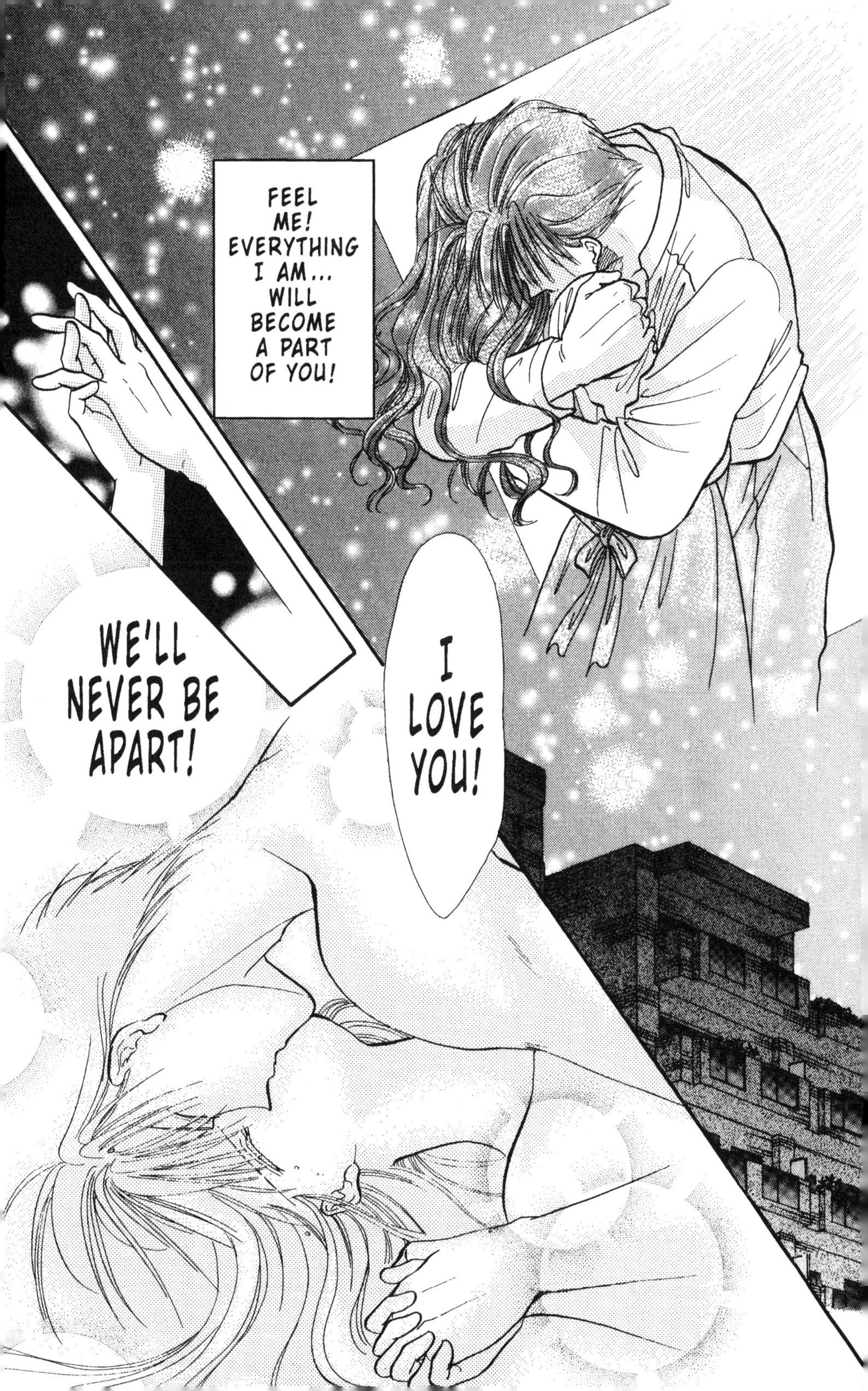
FEEL ME! EVERYTHING I AM... WILL BECOME A PART OF YOU!
I LOVE YOU!
WE'LL NEVER BE APART!

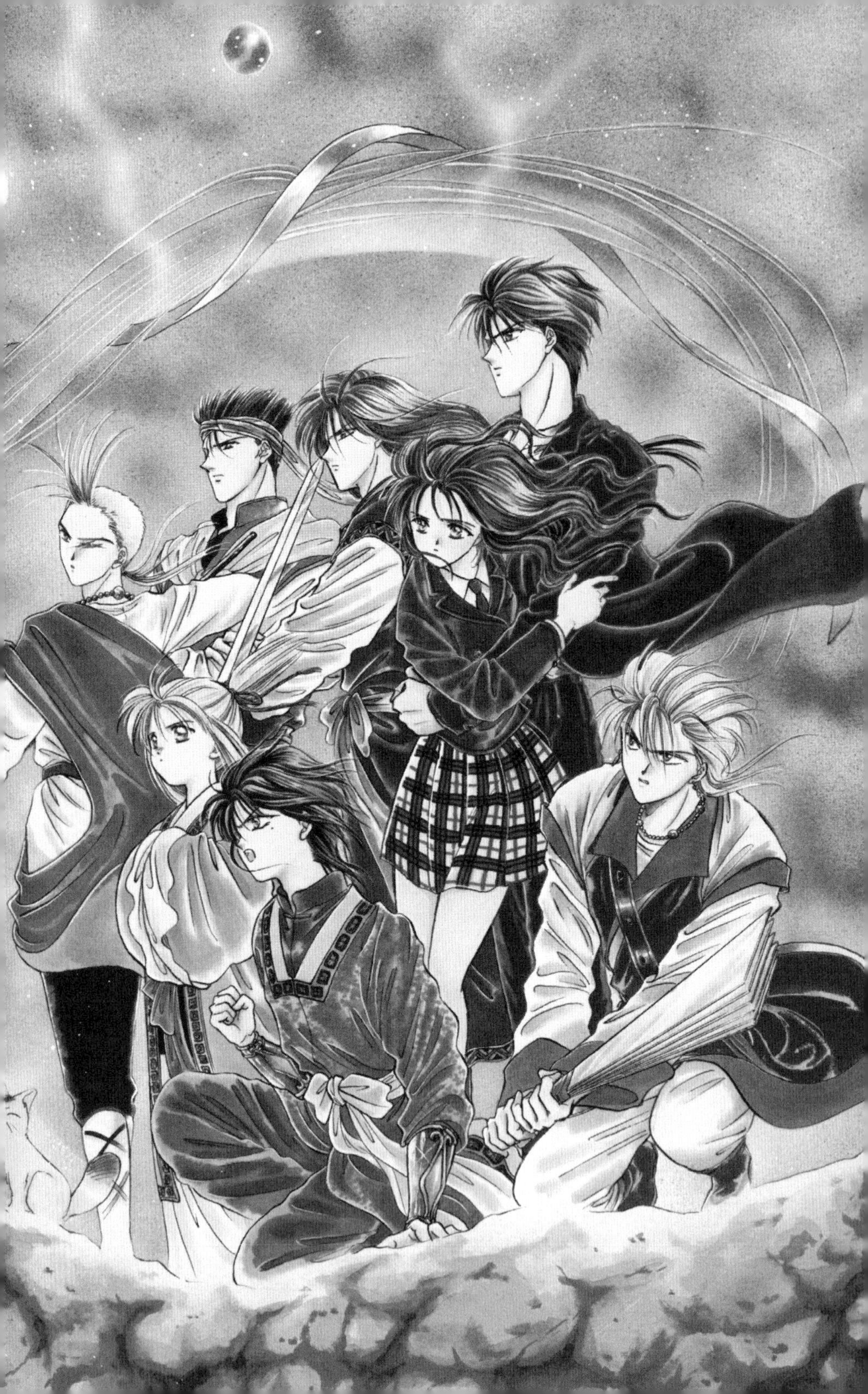

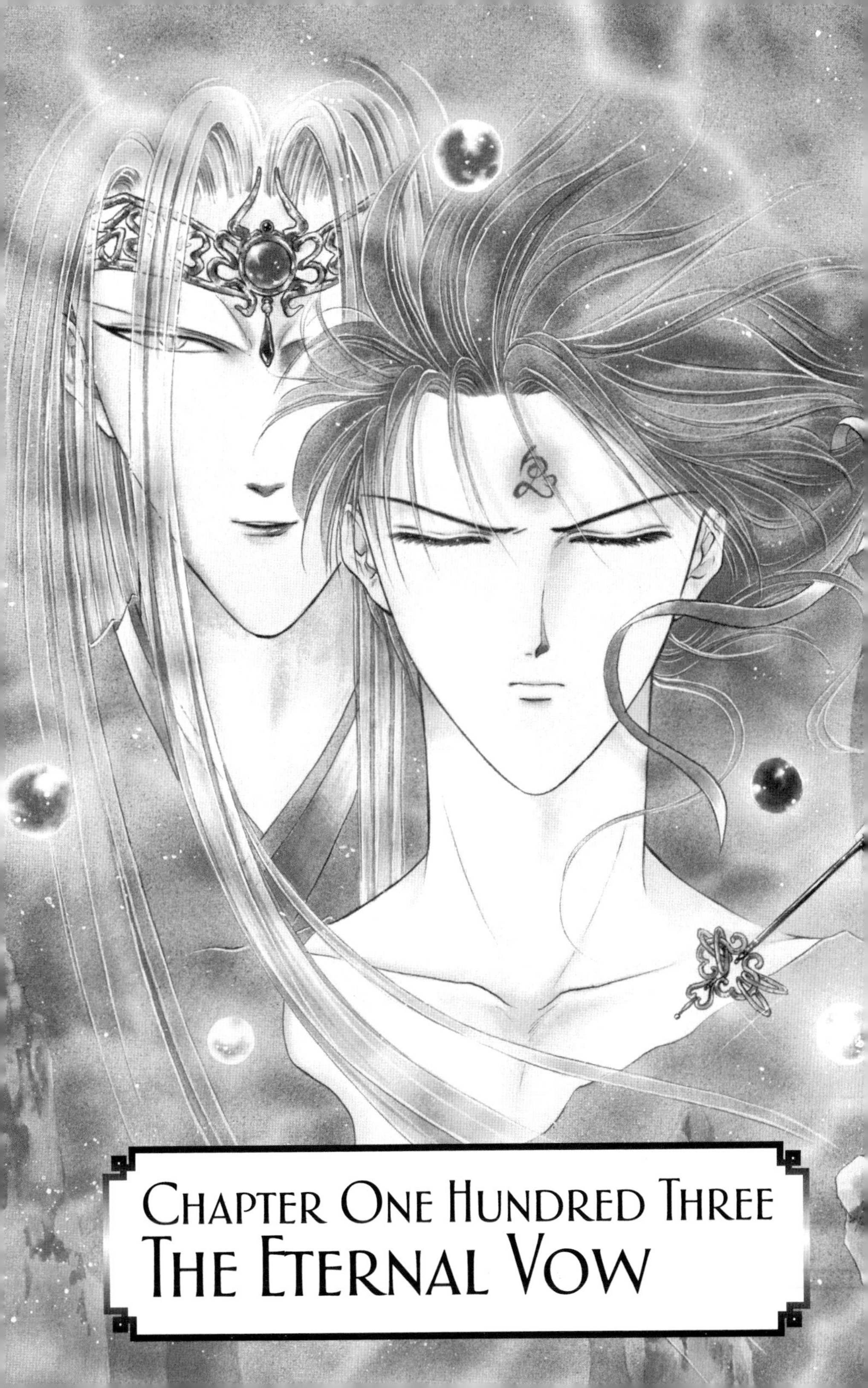

Chapter One Hundred Three
The Eternal Vow

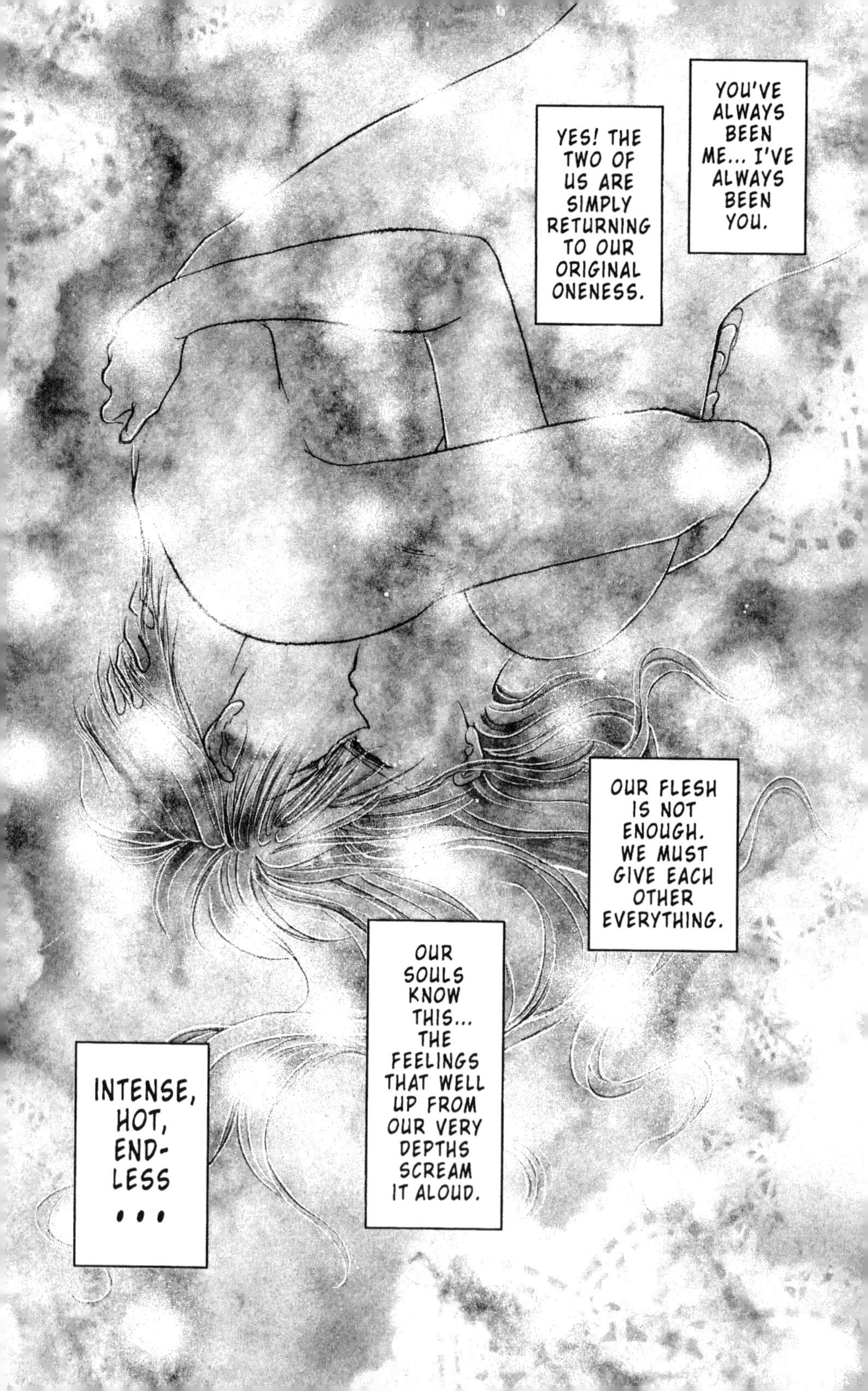
YOU'VE ALWAYS BEEN ME... I'VE ALWAYS BEEN YOU.
YES! THE TWO OF US ARE SIMPLY RETURNING TO OUR ORIGINAL ONENESS.
OUR FLESH IS NOT ENOUGH. WE MUST GIVE EACH OTHER EVERYTHING.
OUR SOULS KNOW THIS... THE FEELINGS THAT WELL UP FROM OUR VERY DEPTHS SCREAM IT ALOUD.
INTENSE, HOT, END-LESS ...

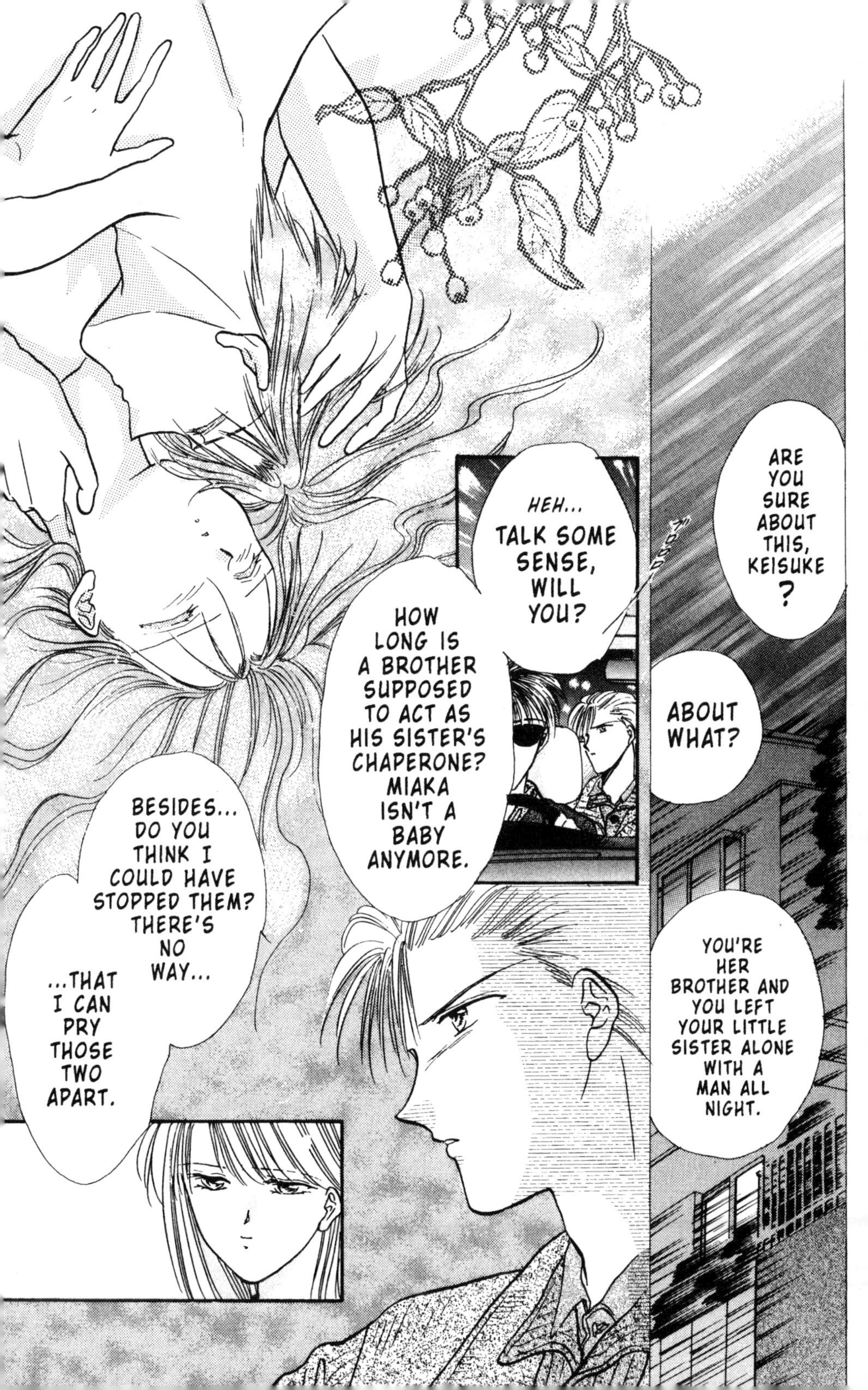

ARE YOU SURE ABOUT THIS, KEISUKE?
ABOUT WHAT?
YOU'RE HER BROTHER AND YOU LEFT YOUR LITTLE SISTER ALONE WITH A MAN ALL NIGHT.
HEH... TALK SOME SENSE, WILL YOU?
HOW LONG IS A BROTHER SUPPOSED TO ACT AS HIS SISTER'S CHAPERONE? MIAKA ISN'T A BABY ANYMORE.
BESIDES... DO YOU THINK I COULD HAVE STOPPED THEM? THERE'S NO WAY...
...THAT I CAN PRY THOSE TWO APART.

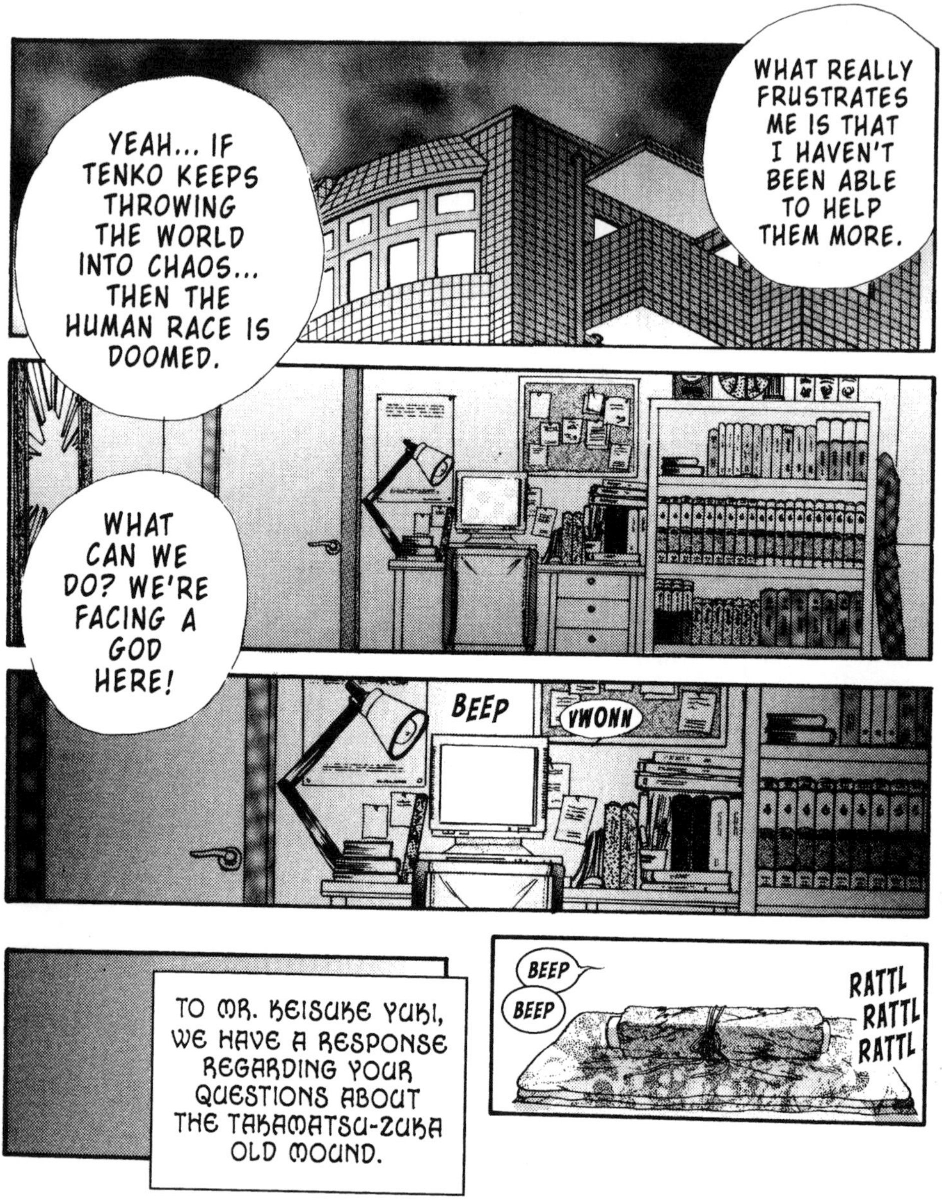
WHAT REALLY FRUSTRATES ME IS THAT I HAVEN'T BEEN ABLE TO HELP THEM MORE.
YEAH... IF TENKO KEEPS THROWING THE WORLD INTO CHAOS... THEN THE HUMAN RACE IS DOOMED.
WHAT CAN WE DO? WE'RE FACING A GOD HERE!
BEEP
VWONN
RATTL RATTL RATTL
BEEP
BEEP
TO MR. KEISUKE YUKI, WE HAVE A RESPONSE REGARDING YOUR QUESTIONS ABOUT THE TAKAMATSU-ZUKA OLD MOUND.

TENKO IS NO GOD.

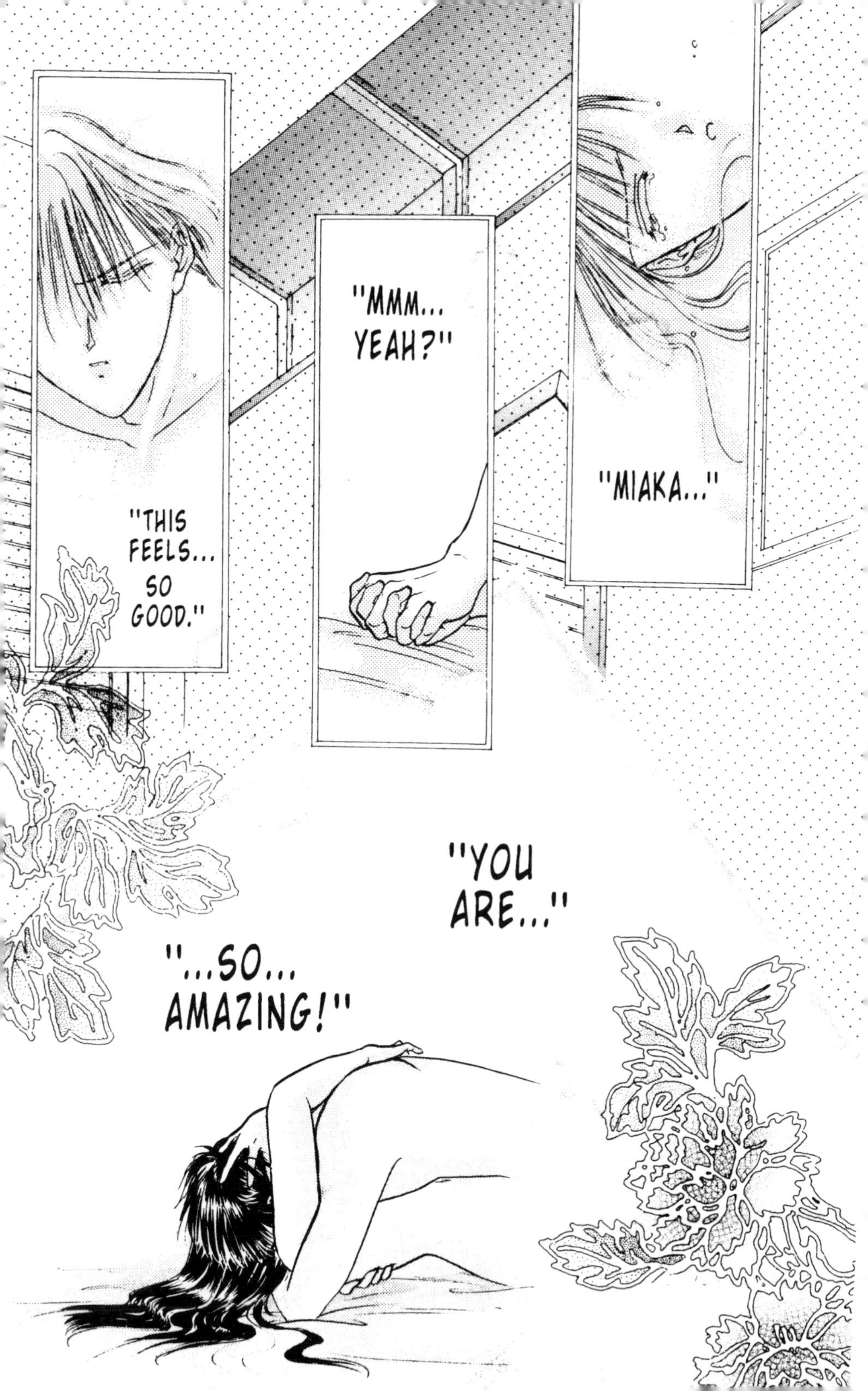
"MIAKA..."
"MMM... YEAH?"
"THIS FEELS... SO GOOD."
"YOU ARE..."
"...SO... AMAZING!"

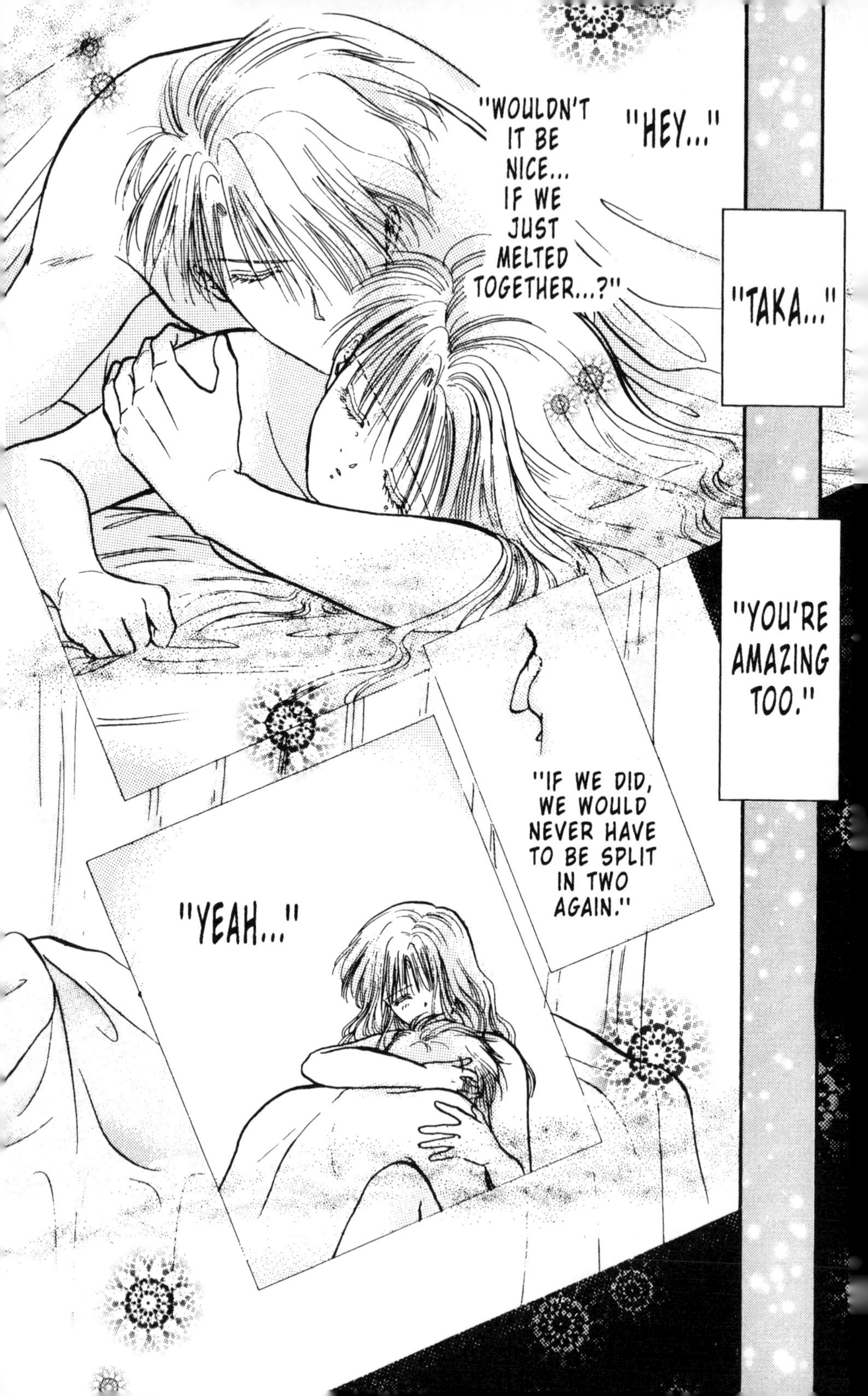
"TAKA..."
"YOU'RE AMAZING TOO."
"HEY..."
"WOULDN'T IT BE NICE... IF WE JUST MELTED TOGETHER...?"
"IF WE DID, WE WOULD NEVER HAVE TO BE SPLIT IN TWO AGAIN."
"YEAH..."

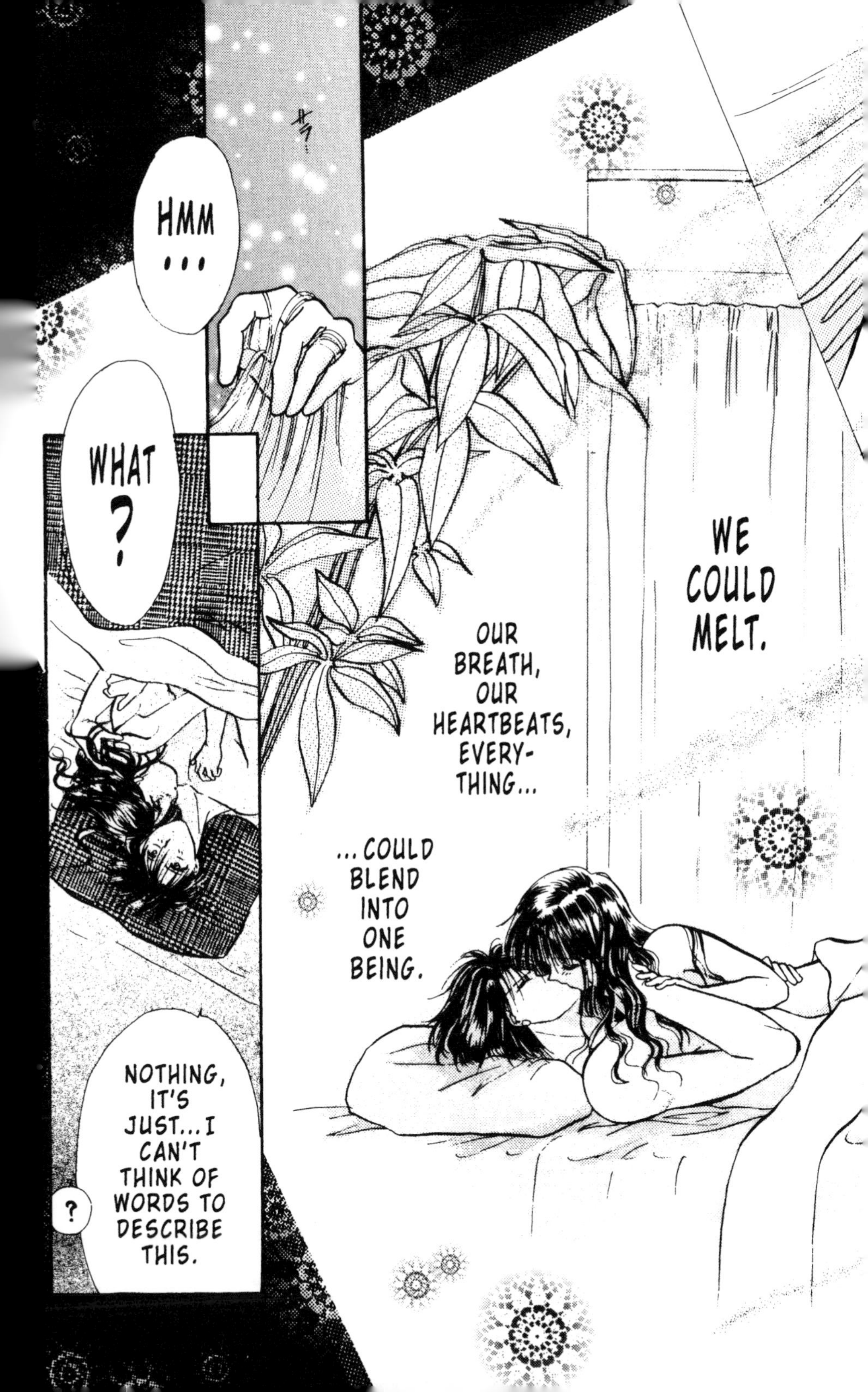
WE COULD MELT.
OUR BREATH, OUR HEARTBEATS, EVERY-THING...
...COULD BLEND INTO ONE BEING.
HMM...
WHAT?
NOTHING, IT'S JUST...I CAN'T THINK OF WORDS TO DESCRIBE THIS.
?

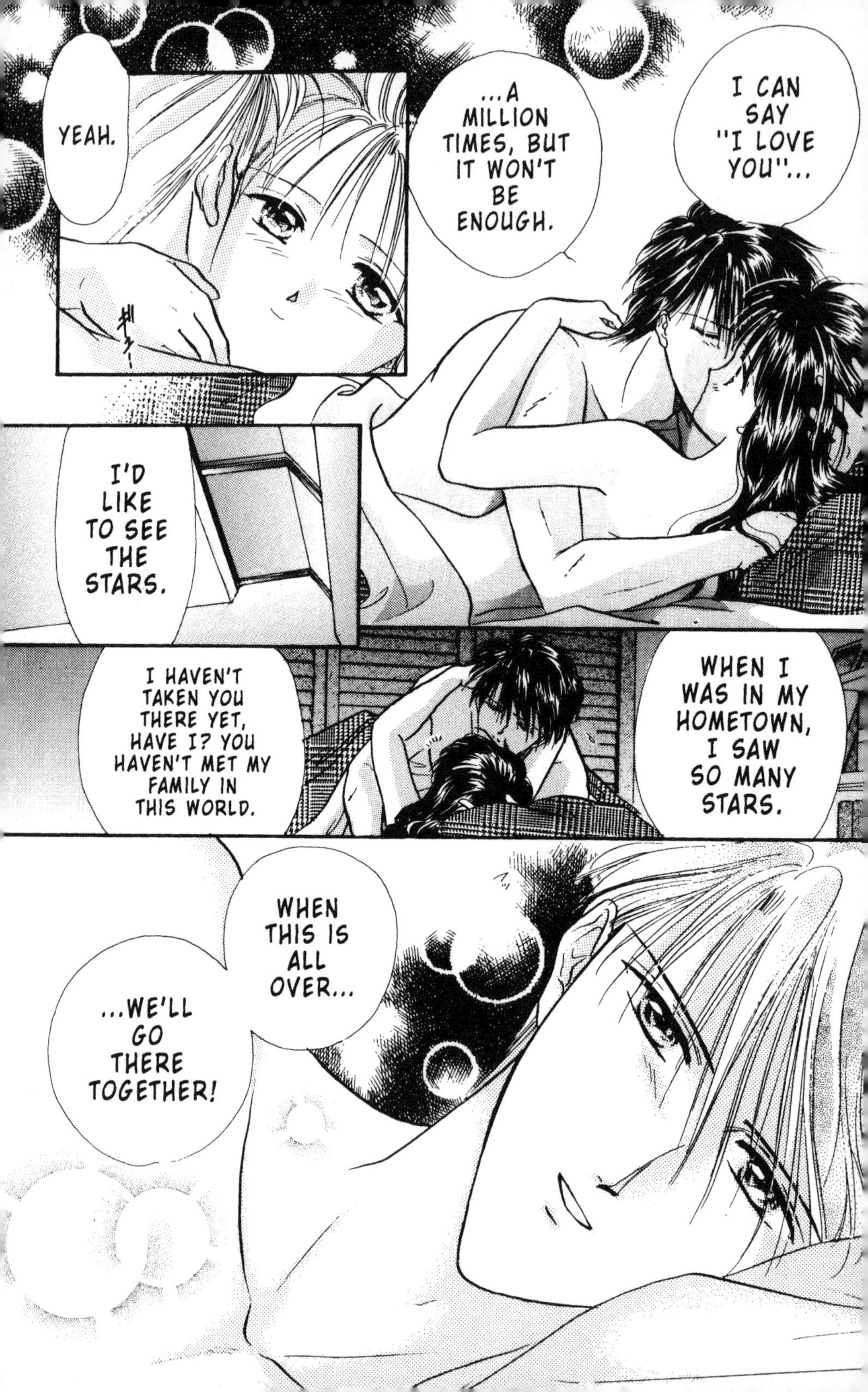
I CAN SAY "I LOVE YOU"...
...A MILLION TIMES, BUT IT WON'T BE ENOUGH.
YEAH.
I'D LIKE TO SEE THE STARS.
WHEN I WAS IN MY HOMETOWN, I SAW SO MANY STARS.
I HAVEN'T TAKEN YOU THERE YET, HAVE I? YOU HAVEN'T MET MY FAMILY IN THIS WORLD.
WHEN THIS IS ALL OVER...
...WE'LL GO THERE TOGETHER!

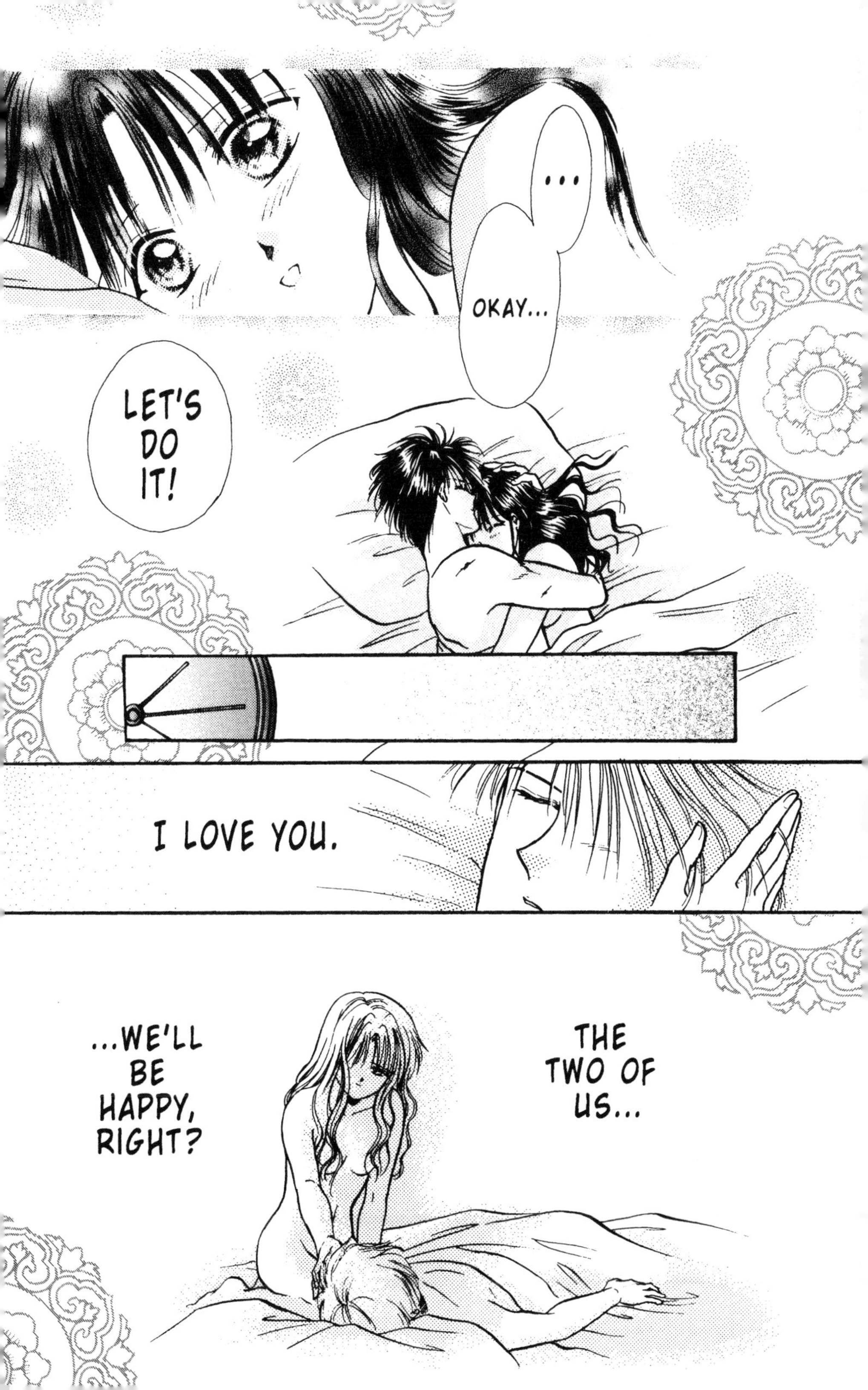
...
OKAY...
LET'S DO IT!
I LOVE YOU.
THE TWO OF US...
...WE'LL BE HAPPY, RIGHT?

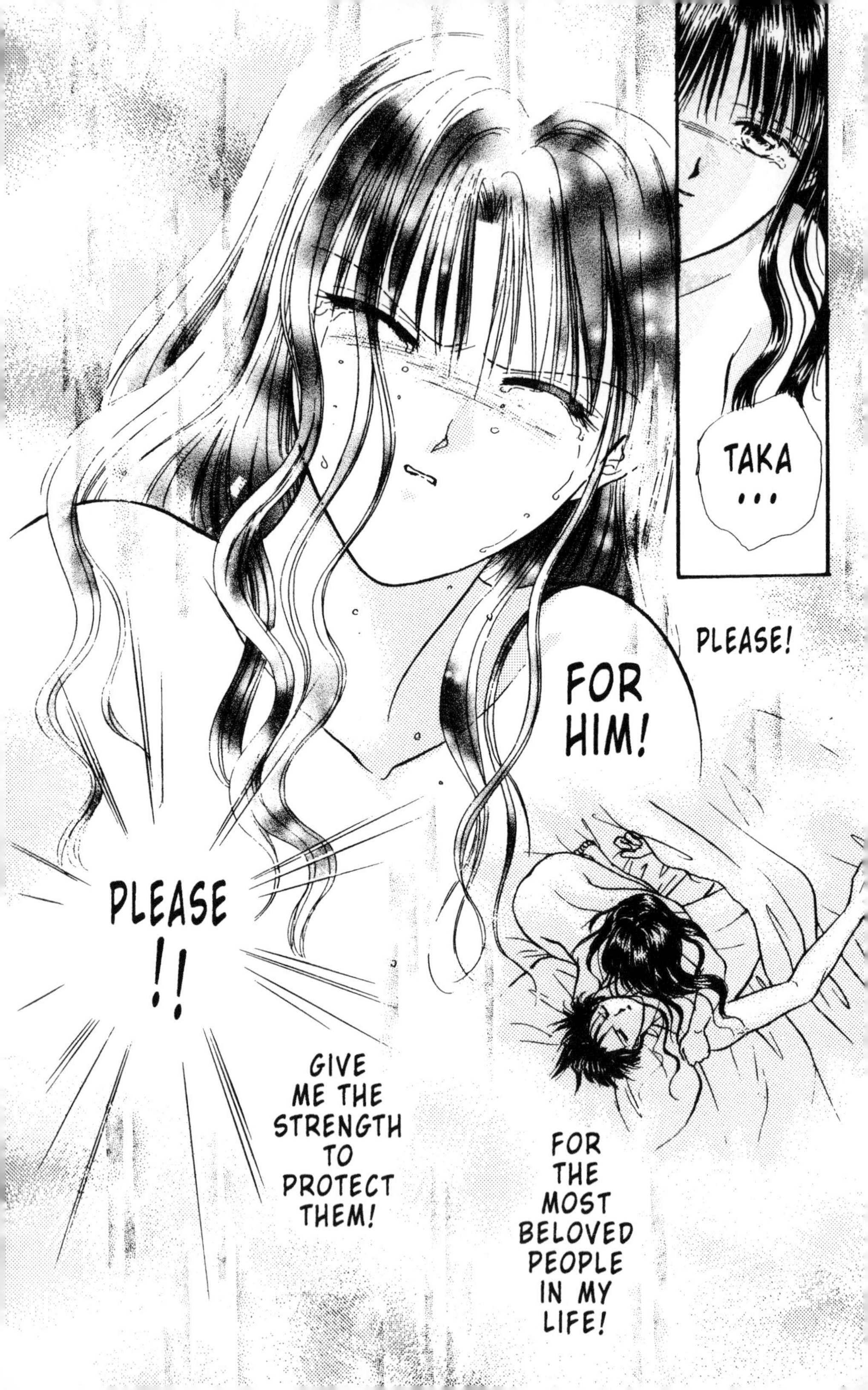

TAKA...
PLEASE!
FOR HIM!
PLEASE!!
GIVE ME THE STRENGTH TO PROTECT THEM!
FOR THE MOST BELOVED PEOPLE IN MY LIFE!

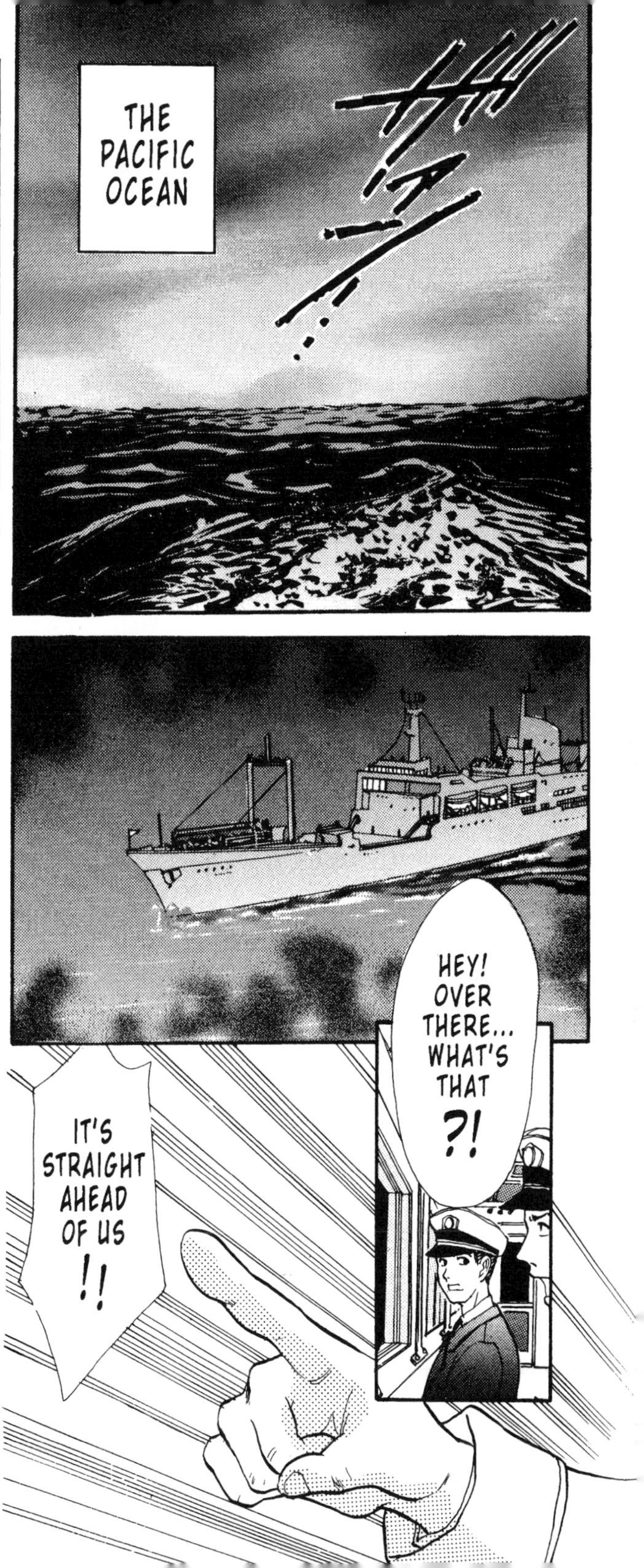
THE PACIFIC OCEAN
HEY! OVER THERE... WHAT'S THAT ?!
IT'S STRAIGHT AHEAD OF US !!

I heard this from a whole bunch of people: "I thought the artist who drew this story was older!" Do I seem like such an old lady to you?! Or at least that was my first reaction...but I guess that wasn't what they meant. ☺ If you wonder why I'm commenting on this, I've heard from a bunch of people who say that Part 2 was a very adult story, or that children shouldn't be allowed to read it. *Oh no! People may take that comment as being all about sex! (But the people who go on about sex...they DO know it's a 22.3-year-old woman writing this, right? It's what was in my heart at the time, and...um, I'll just end it there!)* There's the possibility of a book coming out that delves into the meanings of *Fushigi Yûgi* Parts 1 and 2, the dialog, and installments (really?). If they really did a thorough study, I could imagine it filling two or three books! ☺ The number of people who write letters analyzing my intentions for the story are very few, but... I think that after all the volumes are out, if my readers set the story aside and, after gaining more life experience or maturing into adulthood, they go back and read it one more time, they may get something different out of the story. Although I think it would be interesting to see a book written that explains the story from volume 1 to the end (a players' guide?), I think it's an impossible task. ☺ It just wouldn't fit in one book. I'm sure of that. And would it really serve the readers? You don't have to understand ***everything!*** Some of the stuff is just me being fanatical about the work. I planned out the story from the beginning of the series to the last scene of volume 13 in one go. And I followed that plan, so I never got off track, but there were times when my calculations were off or when a character started developing on his/her own. ☺ *Sometimes I just can't control them!* Wasn't Chiriko supposed to live until the big war? And wasn't Mitsukake supposed to die in a much flashier fashion, in his previous town? And wasn't Hotohori supposed to capture Tamahome's loving gaze...and leave Miaka stranded in the world of the book? ☺ *Now that **would** have been a problem!* About the villains... Certainly the installments with Lian made me say, "That's it!" According to my assistants, they were "hard" and "shadowy." ☺ The Seiryu Warriors were pretty straightforward and a little cute. The villains for Part 2 really attack your insides! From Lian to Miiru to Fei-Gao to Yong-Shua... You can see the emphasis move from the exterior to the interior as you read from start to finish. *But I'm still not very good at this. ბბბ I guess it's not a big deal...*

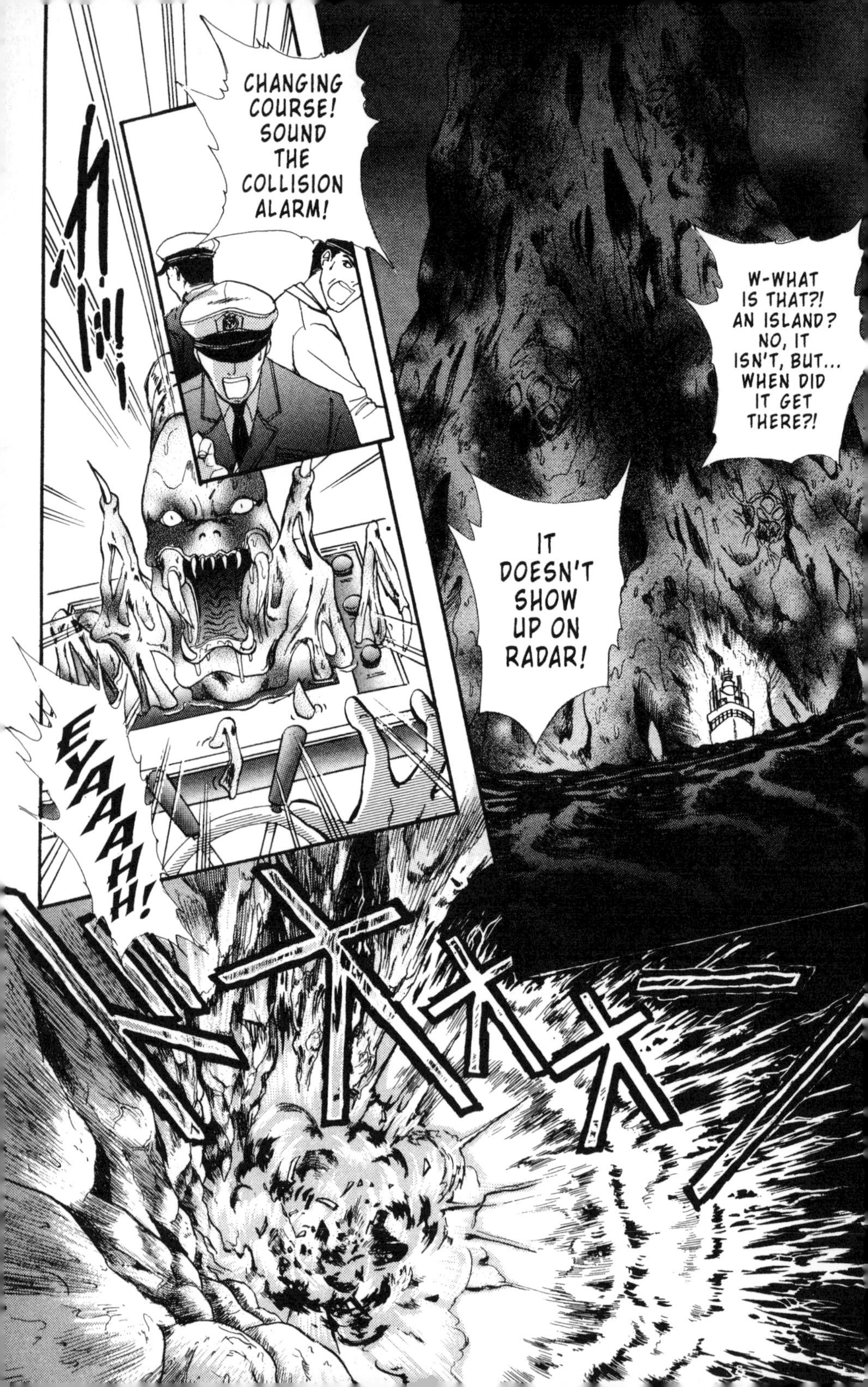
W-WHAT IS THAT?! AN ISLAND? NO, IT ISN'T, BUT... WHEN DID IT GET THERE?!
IT DOESN'T SHOW UP ON RADAR!
CHANGING COURSE! SOUND THE COLLISION ALARM!
EYAAAAH!

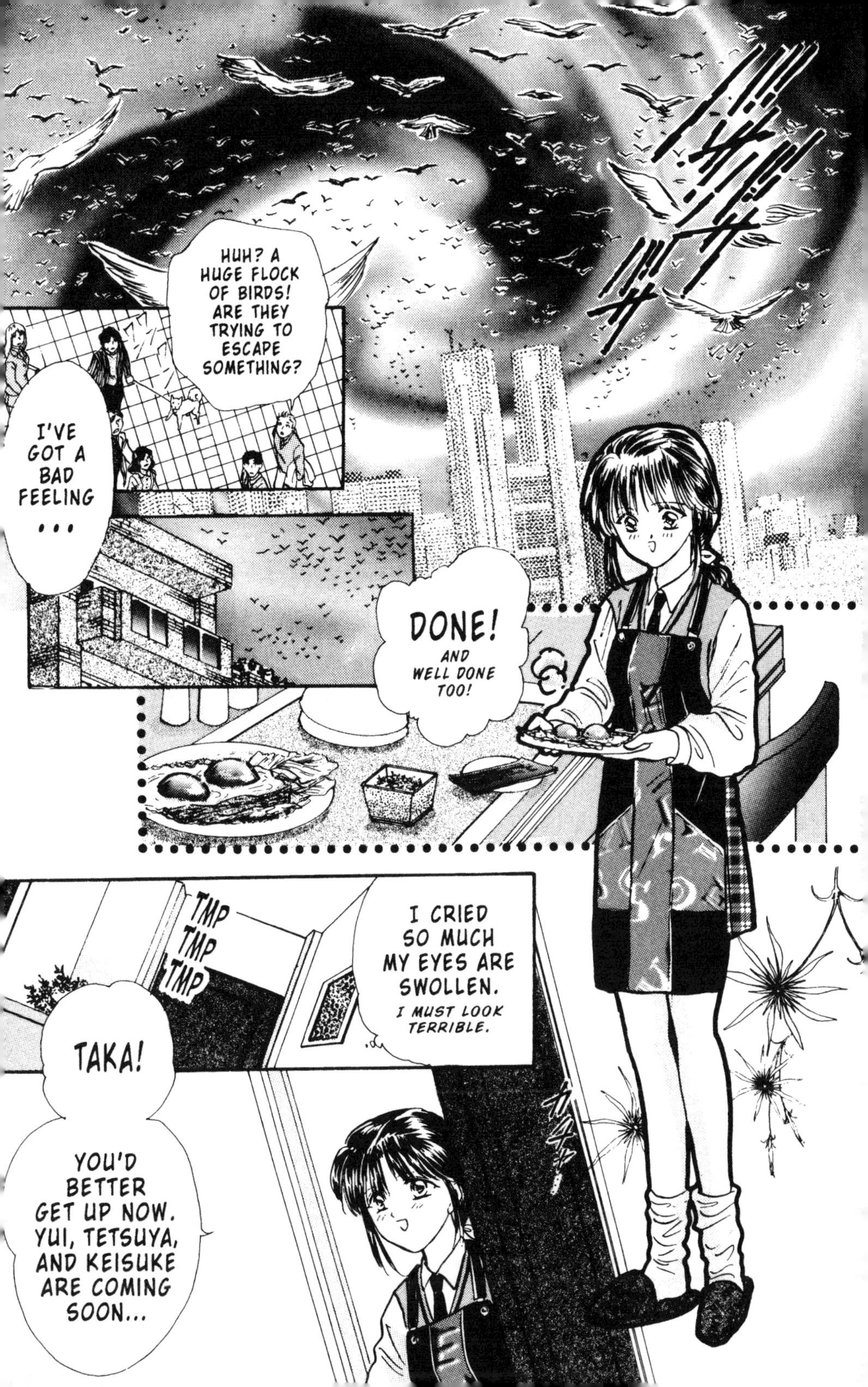
HUH? A HUGE FLOCK OF BIRDS! ARE THEY TRYING TO ESCAPE SOMETHING?
I'VE GOT A BAD FEELING...
DONE! AND WELL DONE TOO!
TMP TMP TMP
I CRIED SO MUCH MY EYES ARE SWOLLEN. I MUST LOOK TERRIBLE.
TAKA!
YOU'D BETTER GET UP NOW. YUI, TETSUYA, AND KEISUKE ARE COMING SOON...

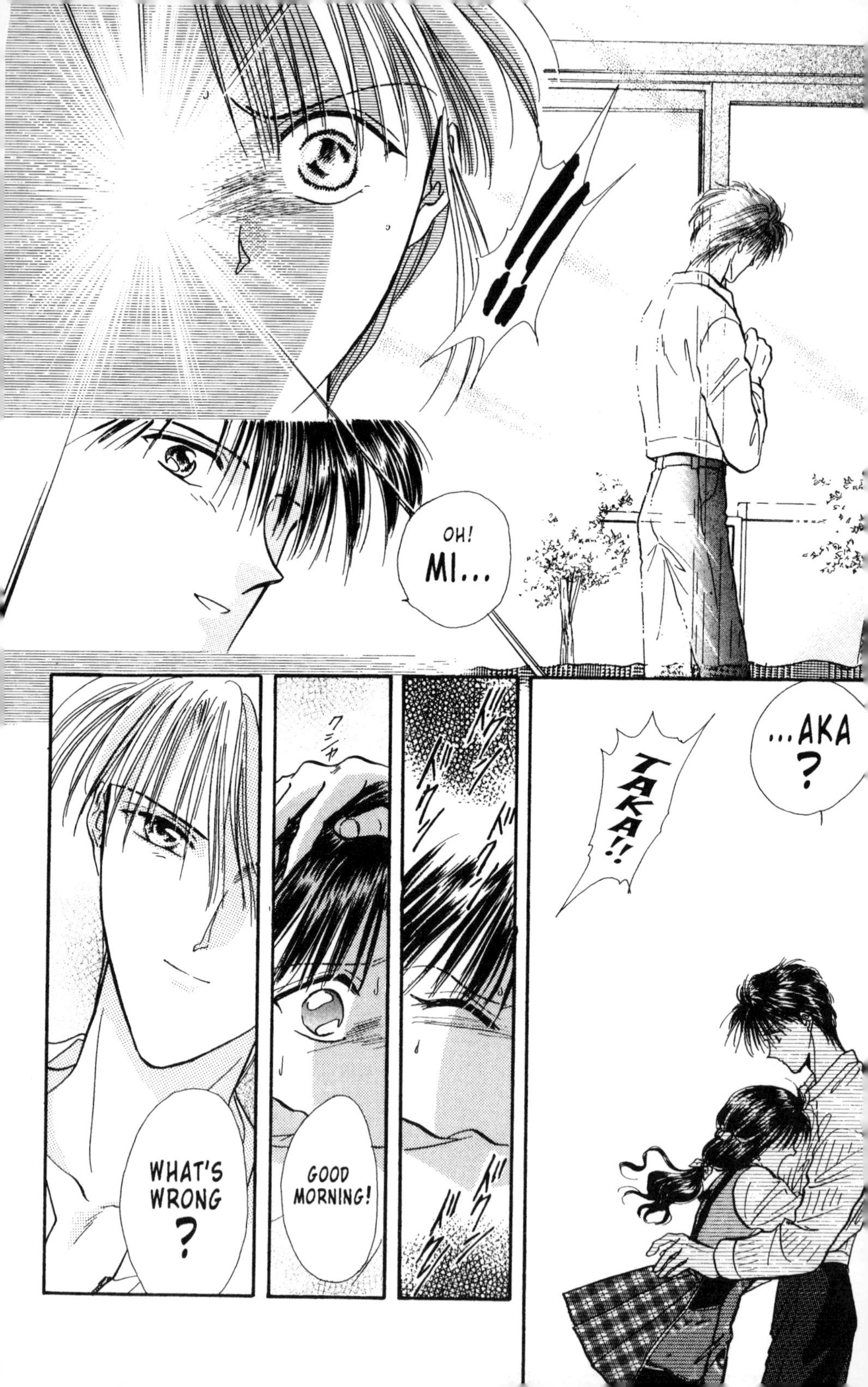

OH! MI...
...AKA?
TAKA!!
クシャ
GOOD MORNING!
WHAT'S WRONG?

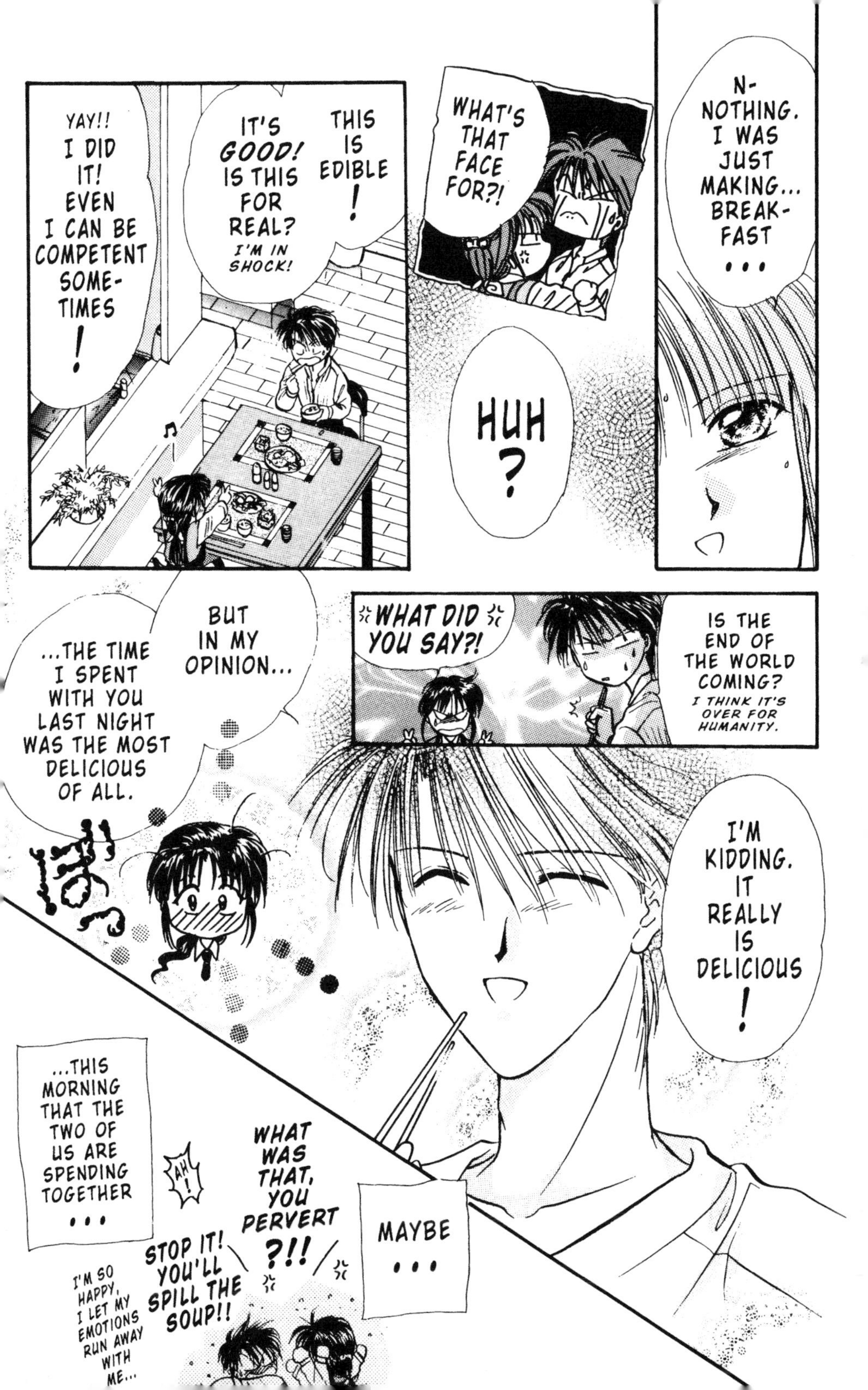
N- NOTHING. I WAS JUST MAKING... BREAK-FAST ...
WHAT'S THAT FACE FOR?!
HUH ?
THIS IS EDIBLE !
IT'S GOOD! IS THIS FOR REAL?
I'M IN SHOCK!
YAY!! I DID IT! EVEN I CAN BE COMPETENT SOME-TIMES !
IS THE END OF THE WORLD COMING?
I THINK IT'S OVER FOR HUMANITY.
WHAT DID YOU SAY?!
I'M KIDDING. IT REALLY IS DELICIOUS !
BUT IN MY OPINION...
...THE TIME I SPENT WITH YOU LAST NIGHT WAS THE MOST DELICIOUS OF ALL.
...THIS MORNING THAT THE TWO OF US ARE SPENDING TOGETHER ...
MAYBE ...
WHAT WAS THAT, YOU PERVERT ?!!
AH!
STOP IT! YOU'LL SPILL THE SOUP!!
I'M SO HAPPY, I LET MY EMOTIONS RUN AWAY WITH ME...

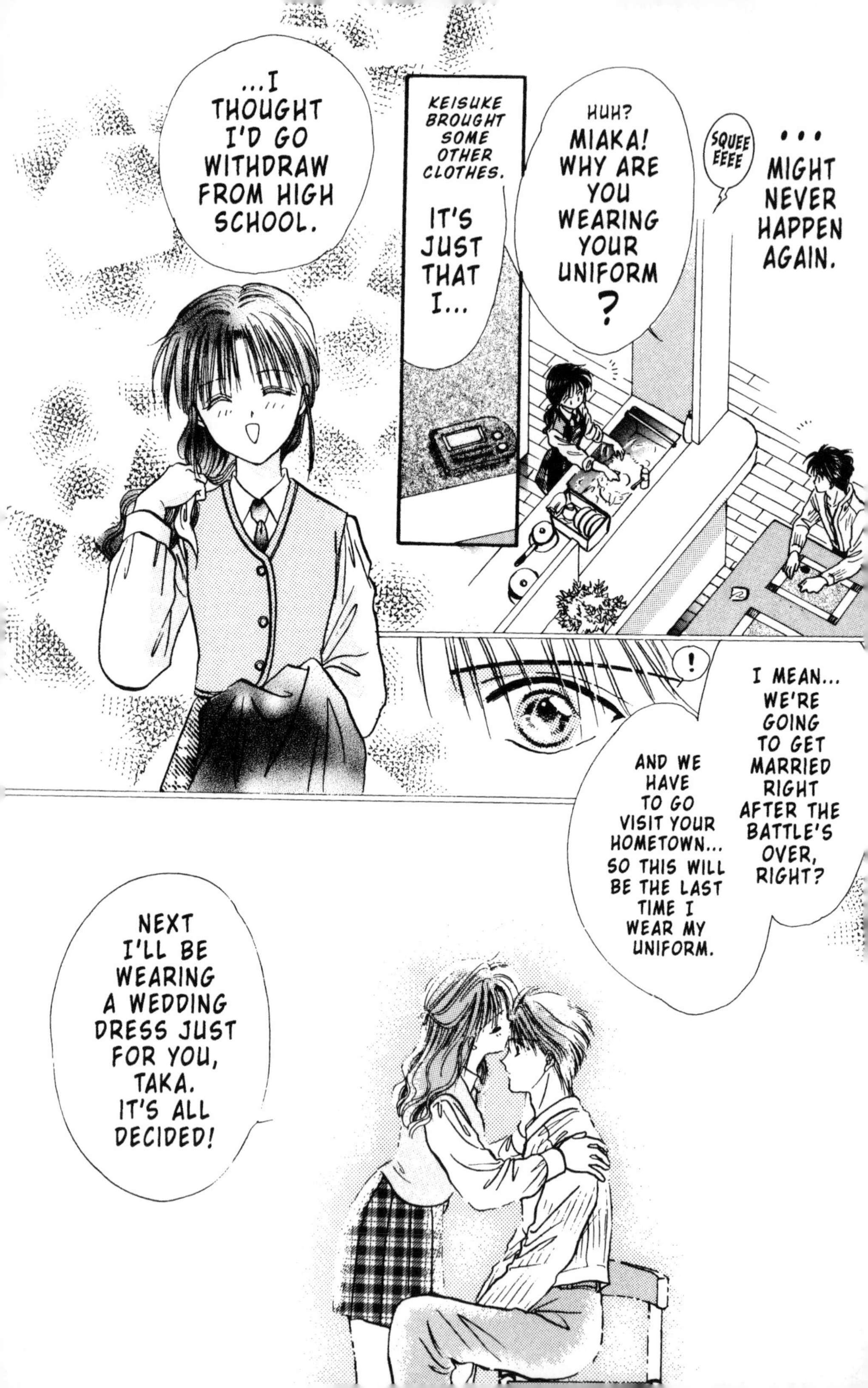

... MIGHT NEVER HAPPEN AGAIN.
SQUEEEEEE
HUH? MIAKA! WHY ARE YOU WEARING YOUR UNIFORM?
KEISUKE BROUGHT SOME OTHER CLOTHES.
IT'S JUST THAT I...
...I THOUGHT I'D GO WITHDRAW FROM HIGH SCHOOL.
!
I MEAN... WE'RE GOING TO GET MARRIED RIGHT AFTER THE BATTLE'S OVER, RIGHT?
AND WE HAVE TO GO VISIT YOUR HOMETOWN... SO THIS WILL BE THE LAST TIME I WEAR MY UNIFORM.
NEXT I'LL BE WEARING A WEDDING DRESS JUST FOR YOU, TAKA. IT'S ALL DECIDED!

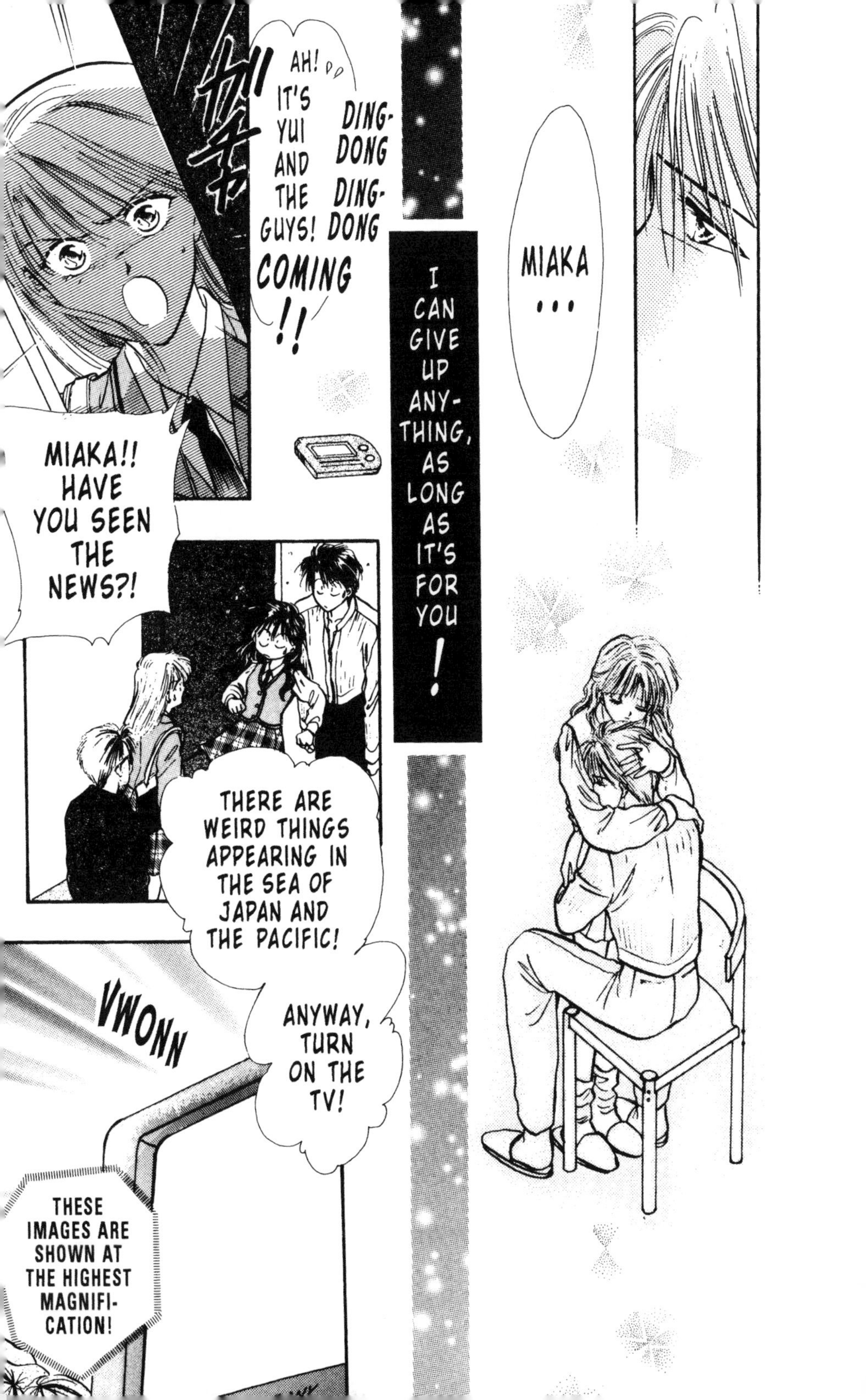

MIAKA...
I CAN GIVE UP ANYTHING, AS LONG AS IT'S FOR YOU!
DING-DONG DING-DONG
AH! IT'S YUI AND THE GUYS!
COMING!!
MIAKA!! HAVE YOU SEEN THE NEWS?!
THERE ARE WEIRD THINGS APPEARING IN THE SEA OF JAPAN AND THE PACIFIC!
ANYWAY, TURN ON THE TV!
VWONN
THESE IMAGES ARE SHOWN AT THE HIGHEST MAGNIFICATION!

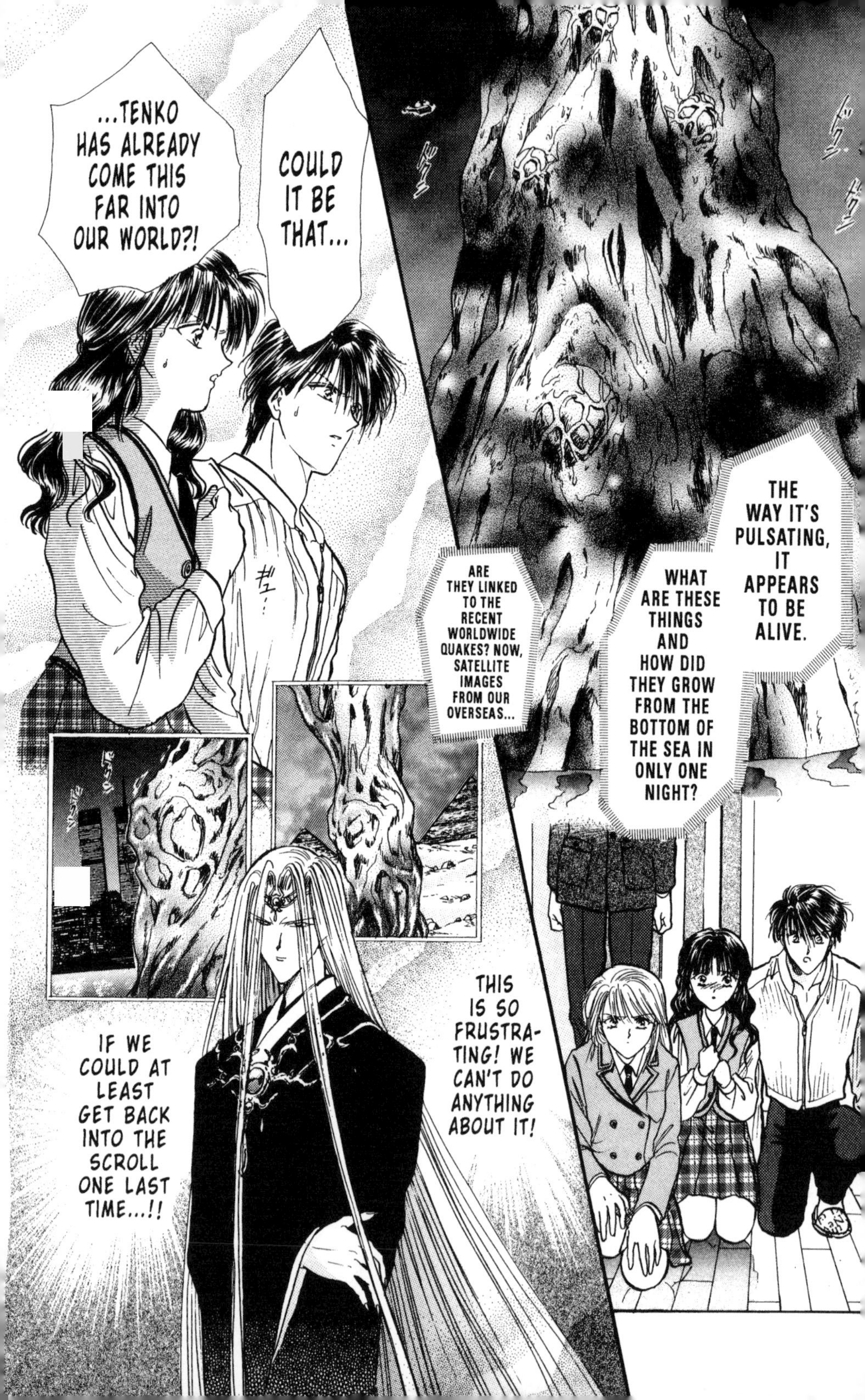
THE WAY IT'S PULSATING, IT APPEARS TO BE ALIVE.
WHAT ARE THESE THINGS AND HOW DID THEY GROW FROM THE BOTTOM OF THE SEA IN ONLY ONE NIGHT?
ARE THEY LINKED TO THE RECENT WORLDWIDE QUAKES? NOW, SATELLITE IMAGES FROM OUR OVERSEAS...
COULD IT BE THAT...
...TENKO HAS ALREADY COME THIS FAR INTO OUR WORLD?!
THIS IS SO FRUSTRA-TING! WE CAN'T DO ANYTHING ABOUT IT!
IF WE COULD AT LEAST GET BACK INTO THE SCROLL ONE LAST TIME...!!

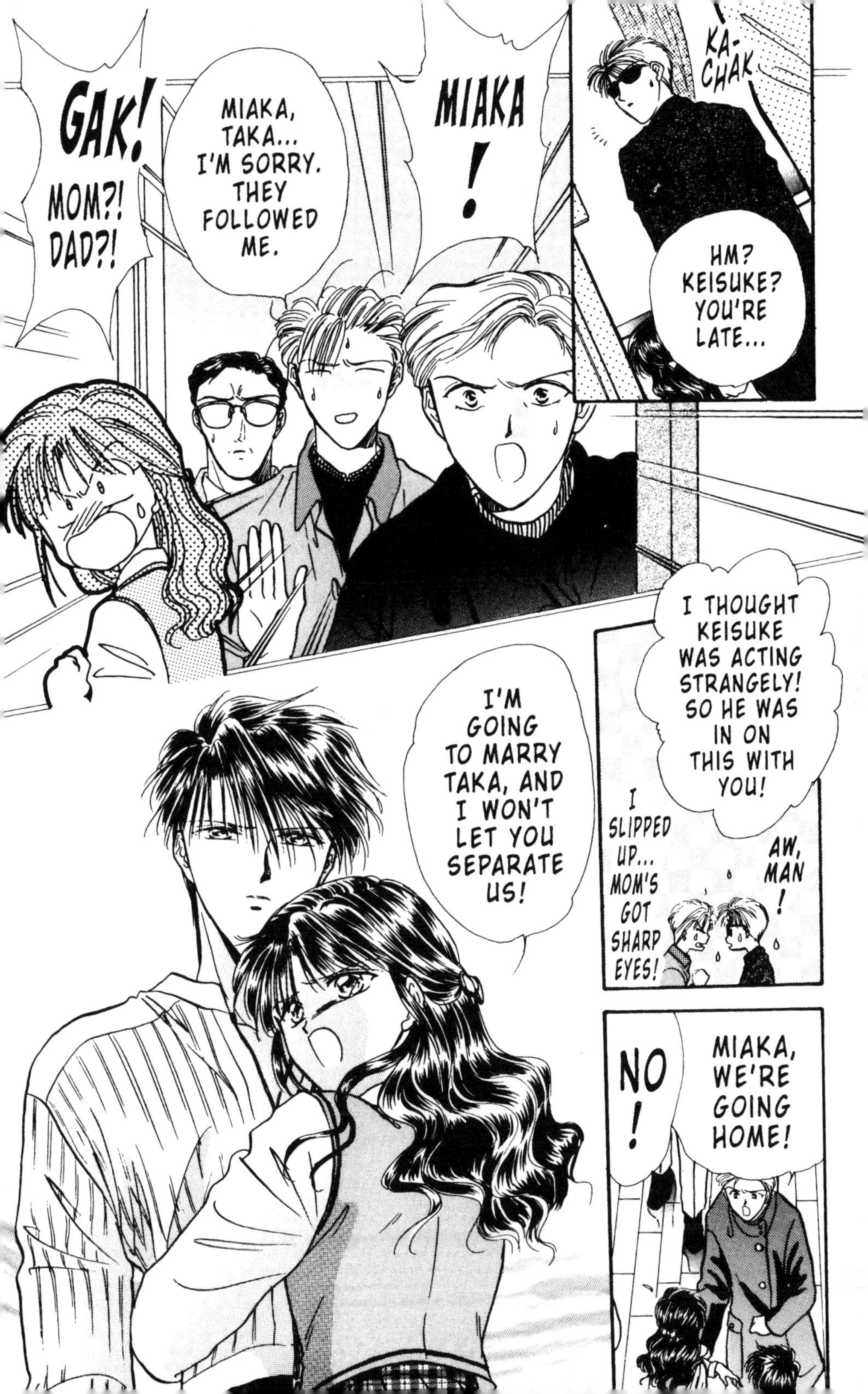
KA-CHAK
HM? KEISUKE? YOU'RE LATE...
MIAKA!
MIAKA, TAKA... I'M SORRY. THEY FOLLOWED ME.
GAK!
MOM?! DAD?!
I THOUGHT KEISUKE WAS ACTING STRANGELY! SO HE WAS IN ON THIS WITH YOU!
AW, MAN!
I SLIPPED UP... MOM'S GOT SHARP EYES!
MIAKA, WE'RE GOING HOME!
NO!
I'M GOING TO MARRY TAKA, AND I WON'T LET YOU SEPARATE US!

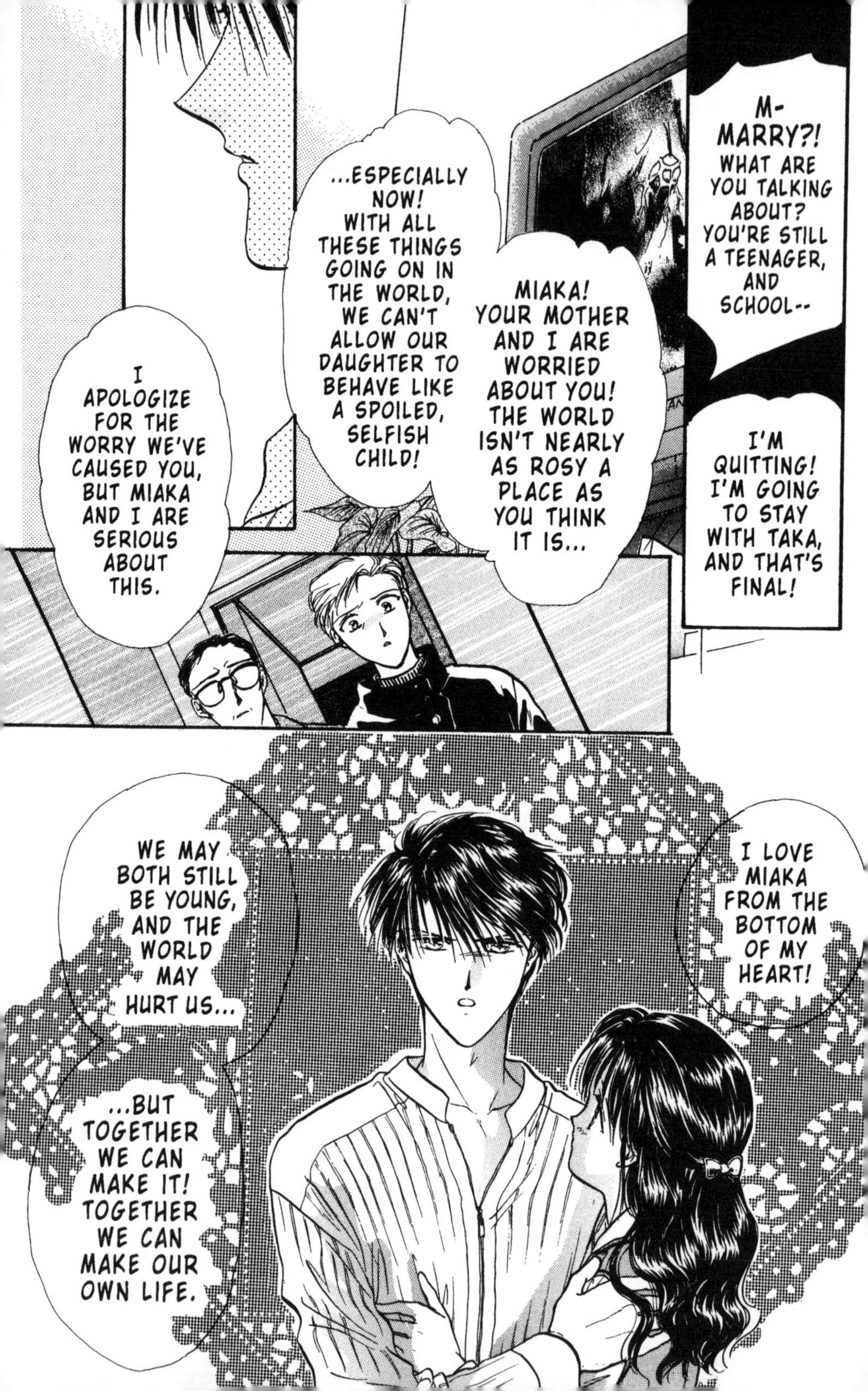
M-MARRY?! WHAT ARE YOU TALKING ABOUT? YOU'RE STILL A TEENAGER, AND SCHOOL--
I'M QUITTING! I'M GOING TO STAY WITH TAKA, AND THAT'S FINAL!
MIAKA! YOUR MOTHER AND I ARE WORRIED ABOUT YOU! THE WORLD ISN'T NEARLY AS ROSY A PLACE AS YOU THINK IT IS...
...ESPECIALLY NOW! WITH ALL THESE THINGS GOING ON IN THE WORLD, WE CAN'T ALLOW OUR DAUGHTER TO BEHAVE LIKE A SPOILED, SELFISH CHILD!
I APOLOGIZE FOR THE WORRY WE'VE CAUSED YOU, BUT MIAKA AND I ARE SERIOUS ABOUT THIS.
I LOVE MIAKA FROM THE BOTTOM OF MY HEART!
WE MAY BOTH STILL BE YOUNG, AND THE WORLD MAY HURT US...
...BUT TOGETHER WE CAN MAKE IT! TOGETHER WE CAN MAKE OUR OWN LIFE.

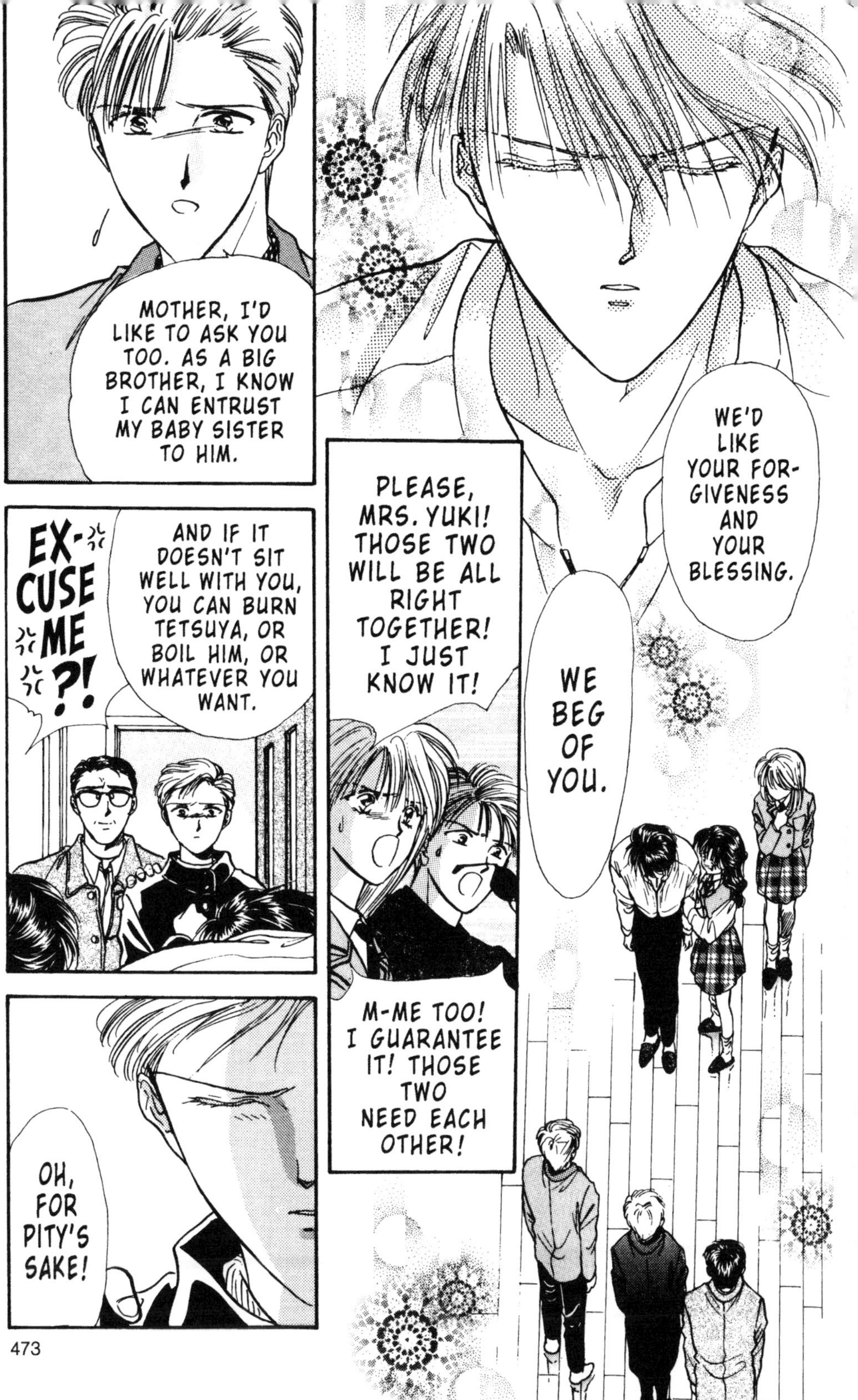
WE'D LIKE YOUR FOR-GIVENESS AND YOUR BLESSING.
WE BEG OF YOU.
PLEASE, MRS. YUKI! THOSE TWO WILL BE ALL RIGHT TOGETHER! I JUST KNOW IT!
M-ME TOO! I GUARANTEE IT! THOSE TWO NEED EACH OTHER!
MOTHER, I'D LIKE TO ASK YOU TOO. AS A BIG BROTHER, I KNOW I CAN ENTRUST MY BABY SISTER TO HIM.
AND IF IT DOESN'T SIT WELL WITH YOU, YOU CAN BURN TETSUYA, OR BOIL HIM, OR WHATEVER YOU WANT.
EX-CUSE ME?!
OH, FOR PITY'S SAKE!

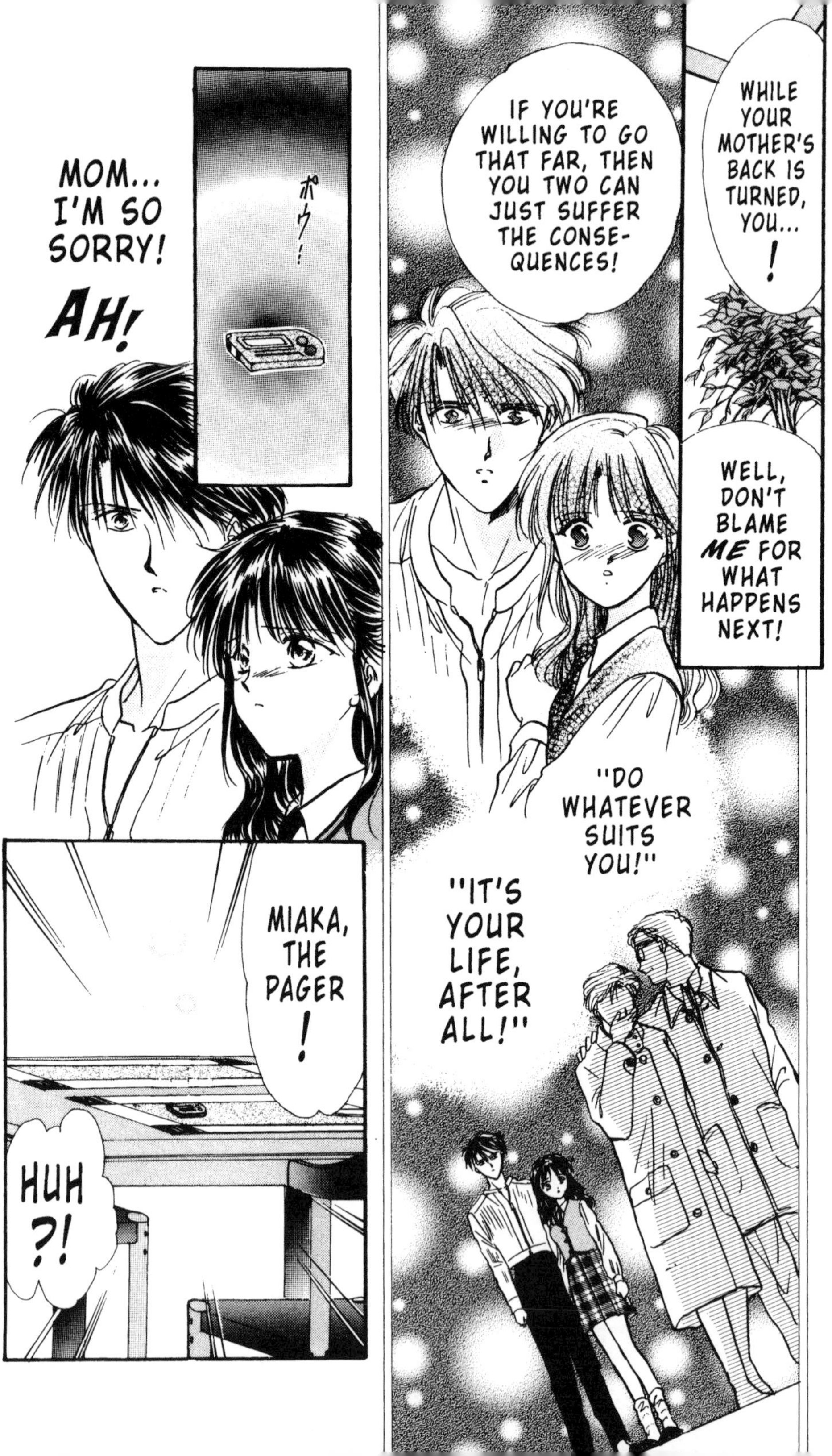
WHILE YOUR MOTHER'S BACK IS TURNED, YOU...!
IF YOU'RE WILLING TO GO THAT FAR, THEN YOU TWO CAN JUST SUFFER THE CONSE-QUENCES!
WELL, DON'T BLAME ME FOR WHAT HAPPENS NEXT!
"DO WHATEVER SUITS YOU!"
"IT'S YOUR LIFE, AFTER ALL!"
ポゥ・・
MOM... I'M SO SORRY!
AH!
MIAKA, THE PAGER!
HUH?!

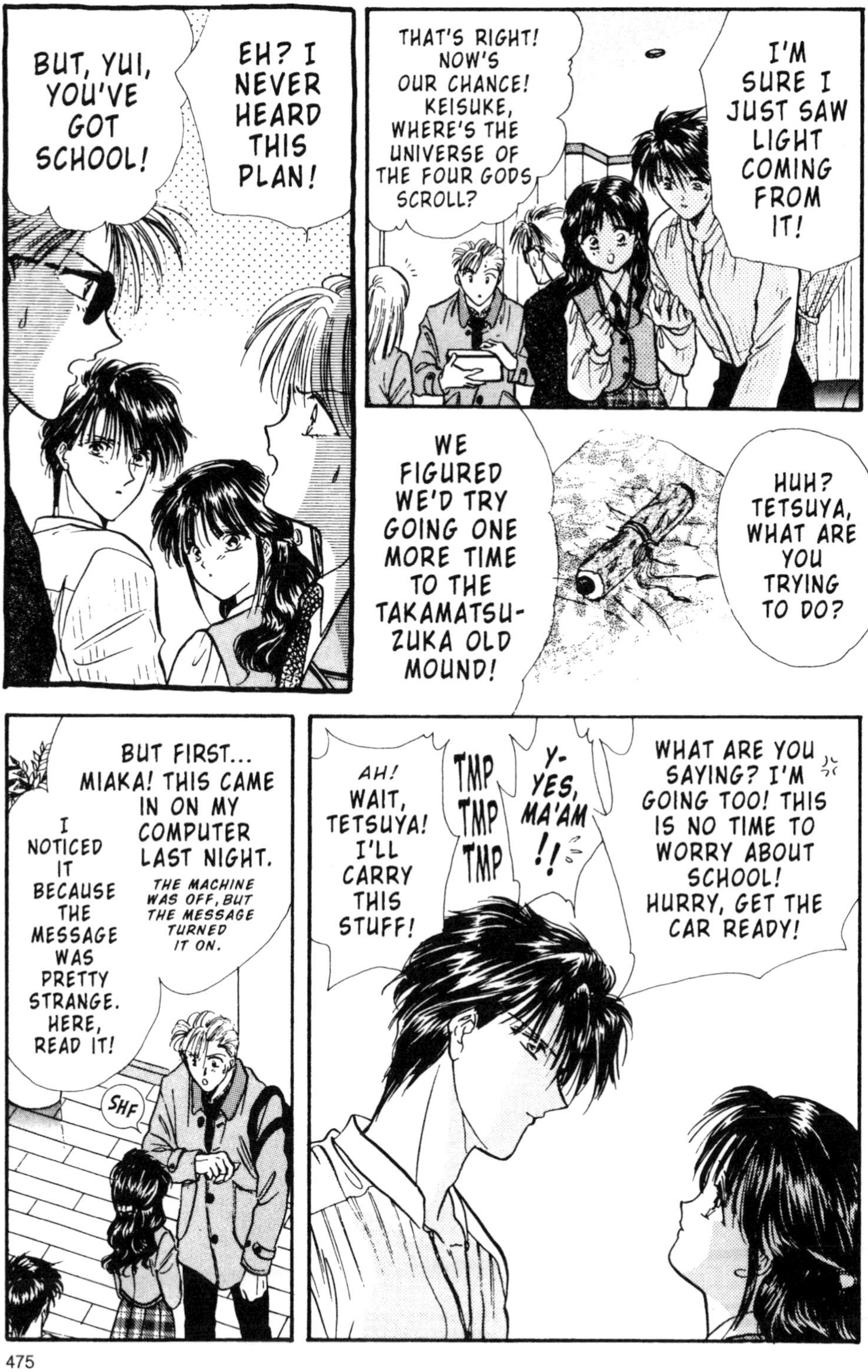
I'M SURE I JUST SAW LIGHT COMING FROM IT!
THAT'S RIGHT! NOW'S OUR CHANCE! KEISUKE, WHERE'S THE UNIVERSE OF THE FOUR GODS SCROLL?
HUH? TETSUYA, WHAT ARE YOU TRYING TO DO?
WE FIGURED WE'D TRY GOING ONE MORE TIME TO THE TAKAMATSU-ZUKA OLD MOUND!
EH? I NEVER HEARD THIS PLAN!
BUT, YUI, YOU'VE GOT SCHOOL!
WHAT ARE YOU SAYING? I'M GOING TOO! THIS IS NO TIME TO WORRY ABOUT SCHOOL! HURRY, GET THE CAR READY!
Y-YES, MA'AM!!
TMP TMP TMP
AH! WAIT, TETSUYA! I'LL CARRY THIS STUFF!
BUT FIRST... MIAKA! THIS CAME IN ON MY COMPUTER LAST NIGHT.
THE MACHINE WAS OFF, BUT THE MESSAGE TURNED IT ON.
I NOTICED IT BECAUSE THE MESSAGE WAS PRETTY STRANGE. HERE, READ IT!
SHF

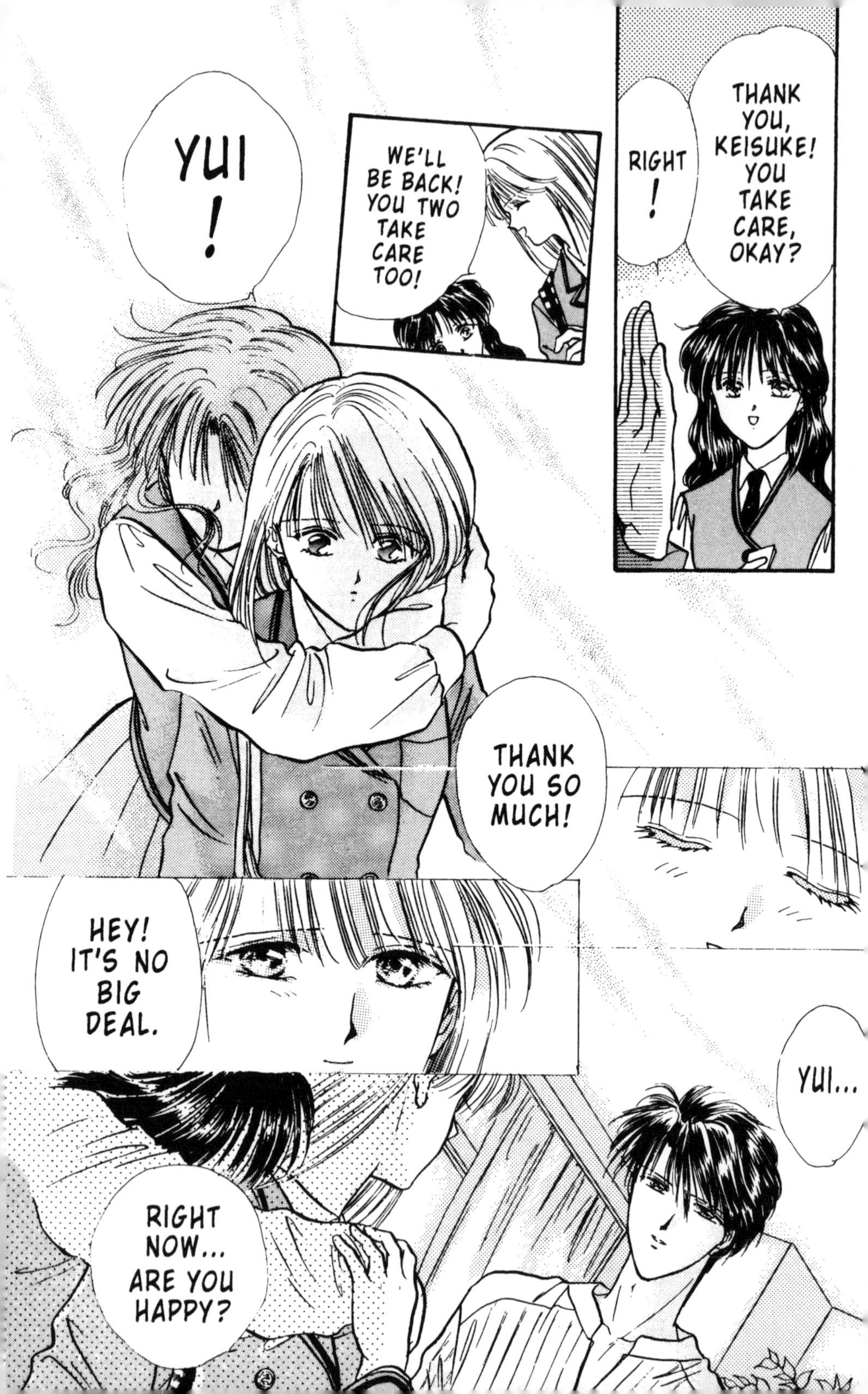
THANK YOU, KEISUKE! YOU TAKE CARE, OKAY?
RIGHT!
WE'LL BE BACK! YOU TWO TAKE CARE TOO!
YUI!
THANK YOU SO MUCH!
HEY! IT'S NO BIG DEAL.
YUI...
RIGHT NOW... ARE YOU HAPPY?

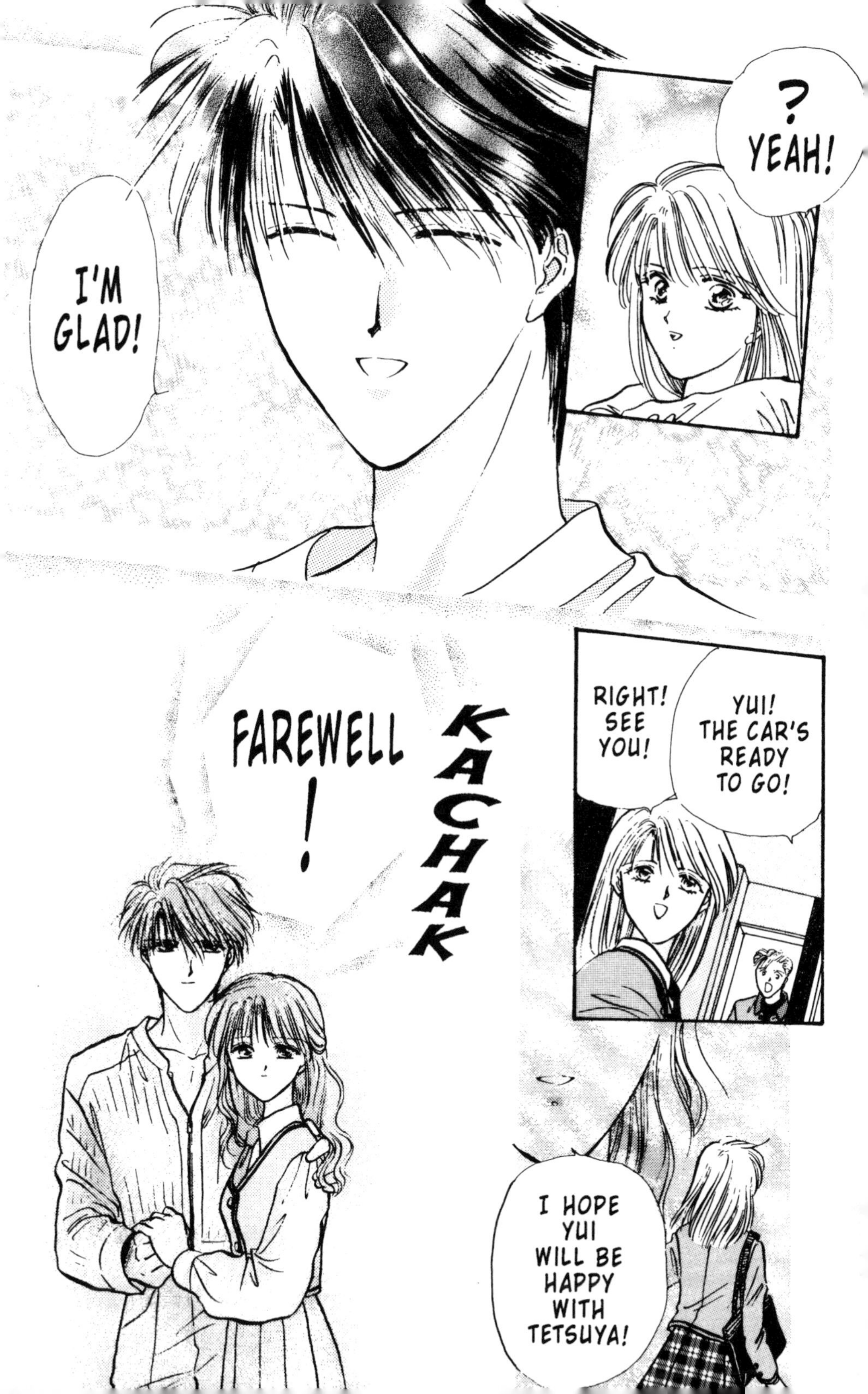
? YEAH!
I'M GLAD!
YUI! THE CAR'S READY TO GO!
RIGHT! SEE YOU!
I HOPE YUI WILL BE HAPPY WITH TETSUYA!
FAREWELL!
KACHAK

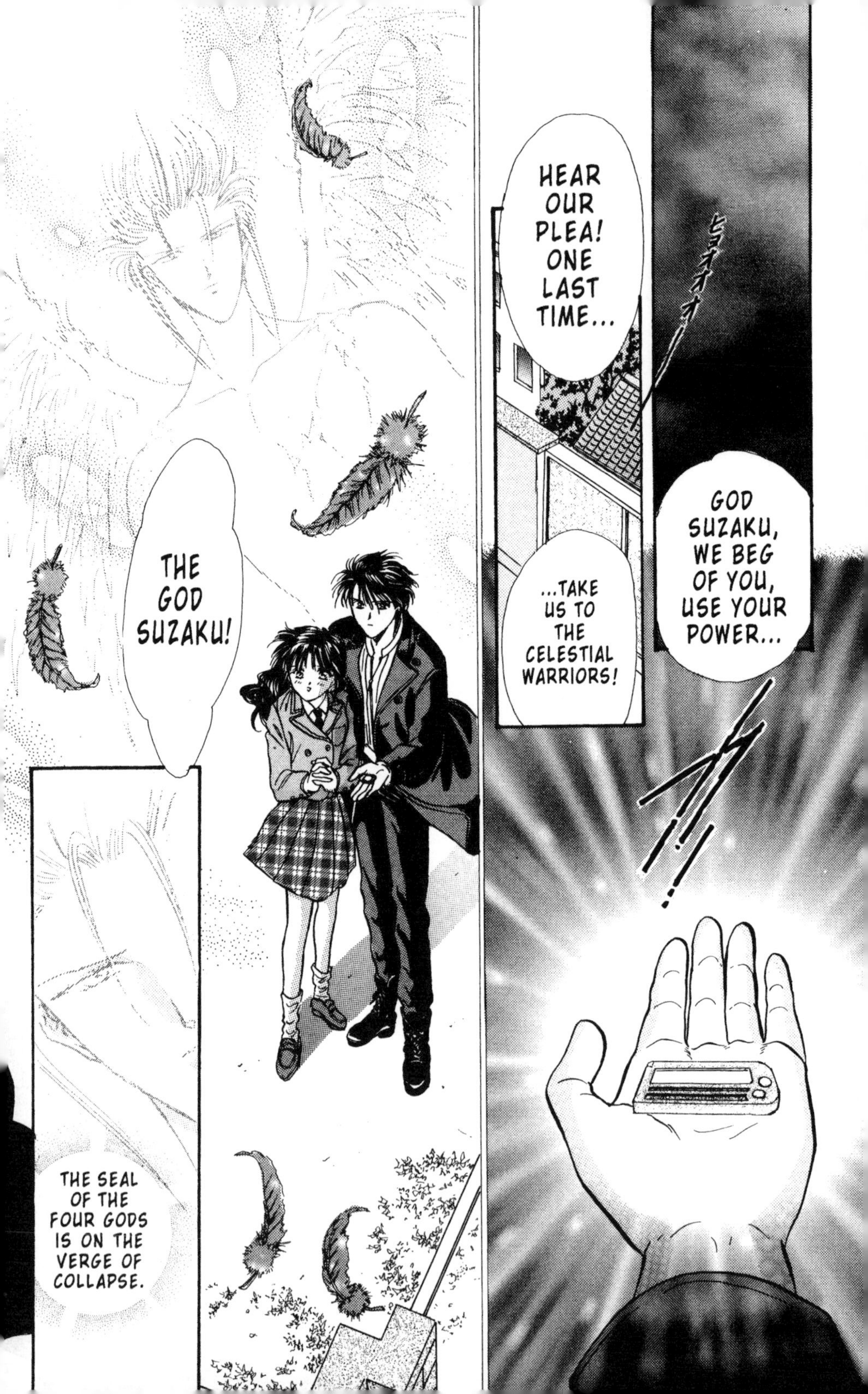
HEAR OUR PLEA! ONE LAST TIME...
ヒュオオオー
...TAKE US TO THE CELESTIAL WARRIORS!
GOD SUZAKU, WE BEG OF YOU, USE YOUR POWER...
THE GOD SUZAKU!
THE SEAL OF THE FOUR GODS IS ON THE VERGE OF COLLAPSE.

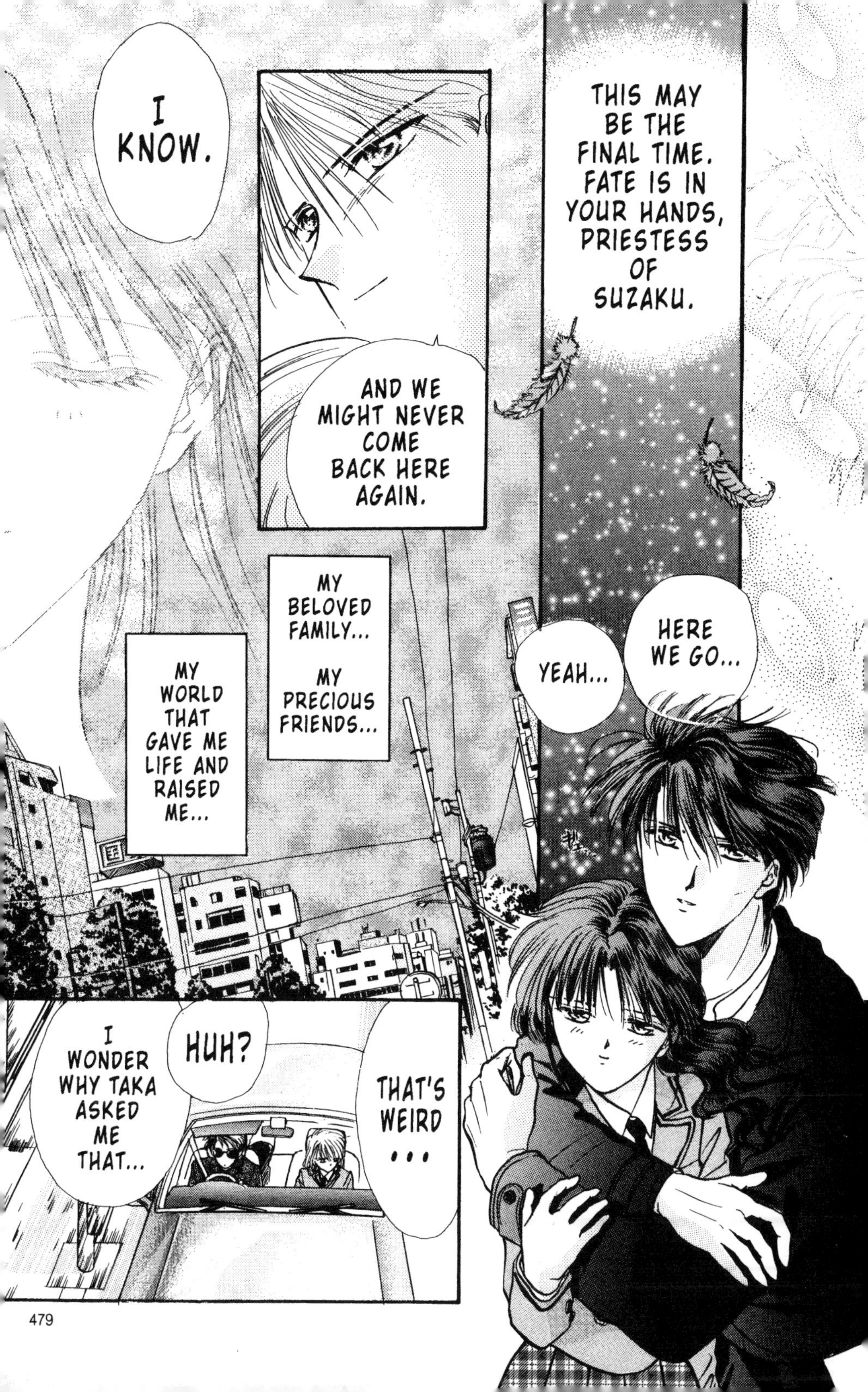
THIS MAY BE THE FINAL TIME. FATE IS IN YOUR HANDS, PRIESTESS OF SUZAKU.
AND WE MIGHT NEVER COME BACK HERE AGAIN.
I KNOW.
HERE WE GO...
YEAH...
MY BELOVED FAMILY...
MY PRECIOUS FRIENDS...
MY WORLD THAT GAVE ME LIFE AND RAISED ME...
THAT'S WEIRD...
HUH?
I WONDER WHY TAKA ASKED ME THAT...

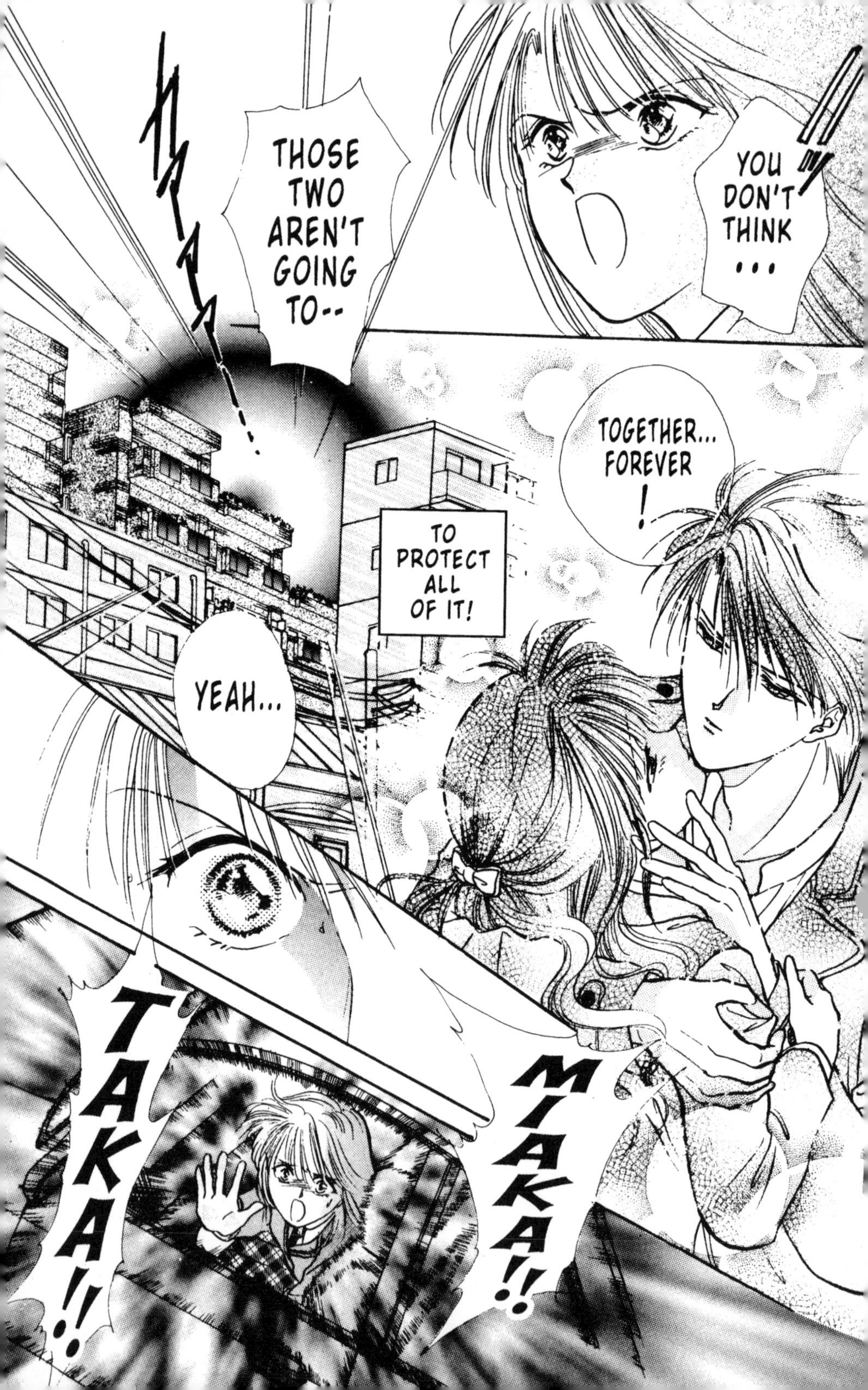
YOU DON'T THINK...
THOSE TWO AREN'T GOING TO--
TOGETHER... FOREVER!
TO PROTECT ALL OF IT!
YEAH...
MIAKA!!
TAKA!!

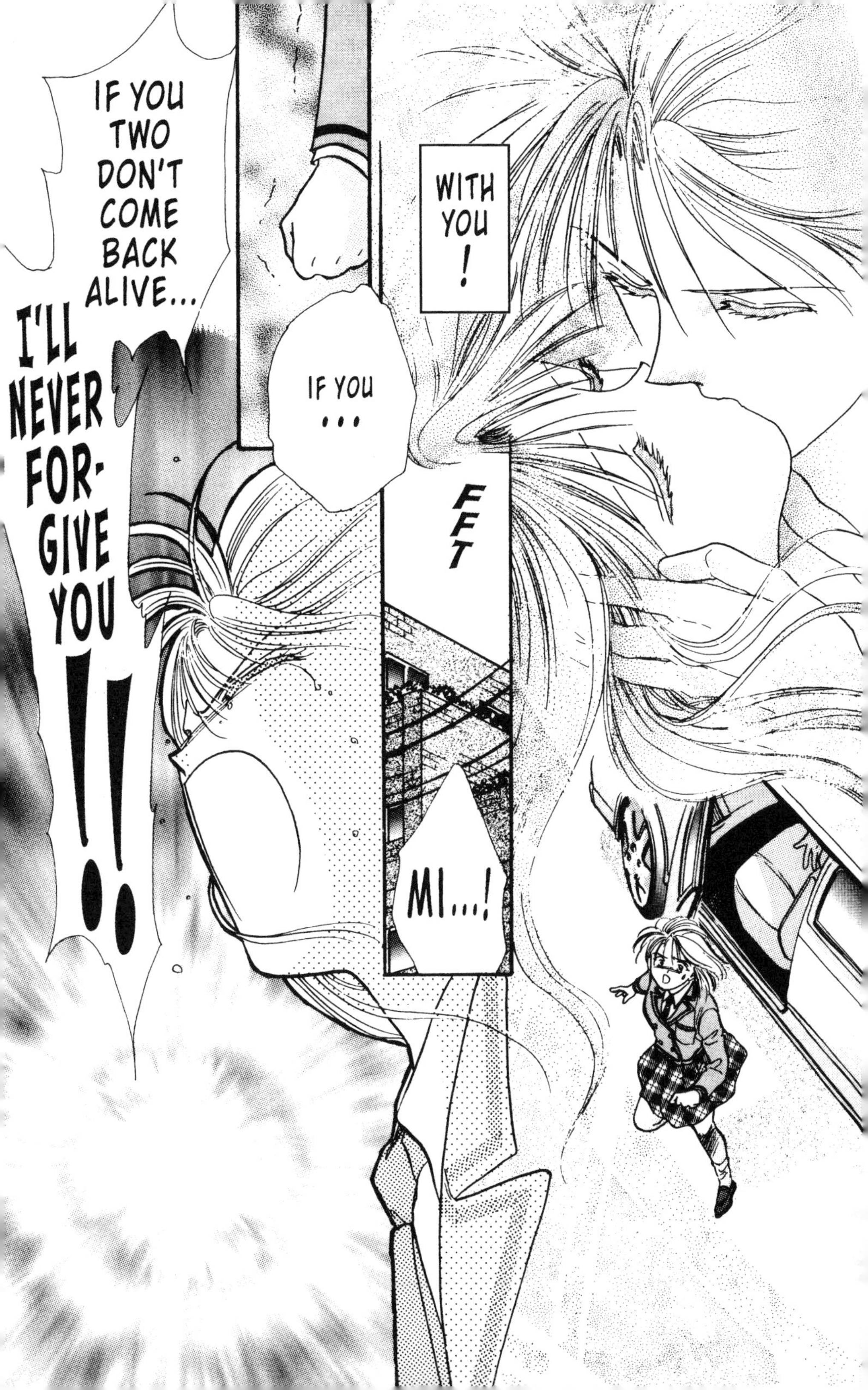
WITH YOU!
IF YOU...
FFT
MI...!
IF YOU TWO DON'T COME BACK ALIVE...
I'LL NEVER FOR-GIVE YOU!!

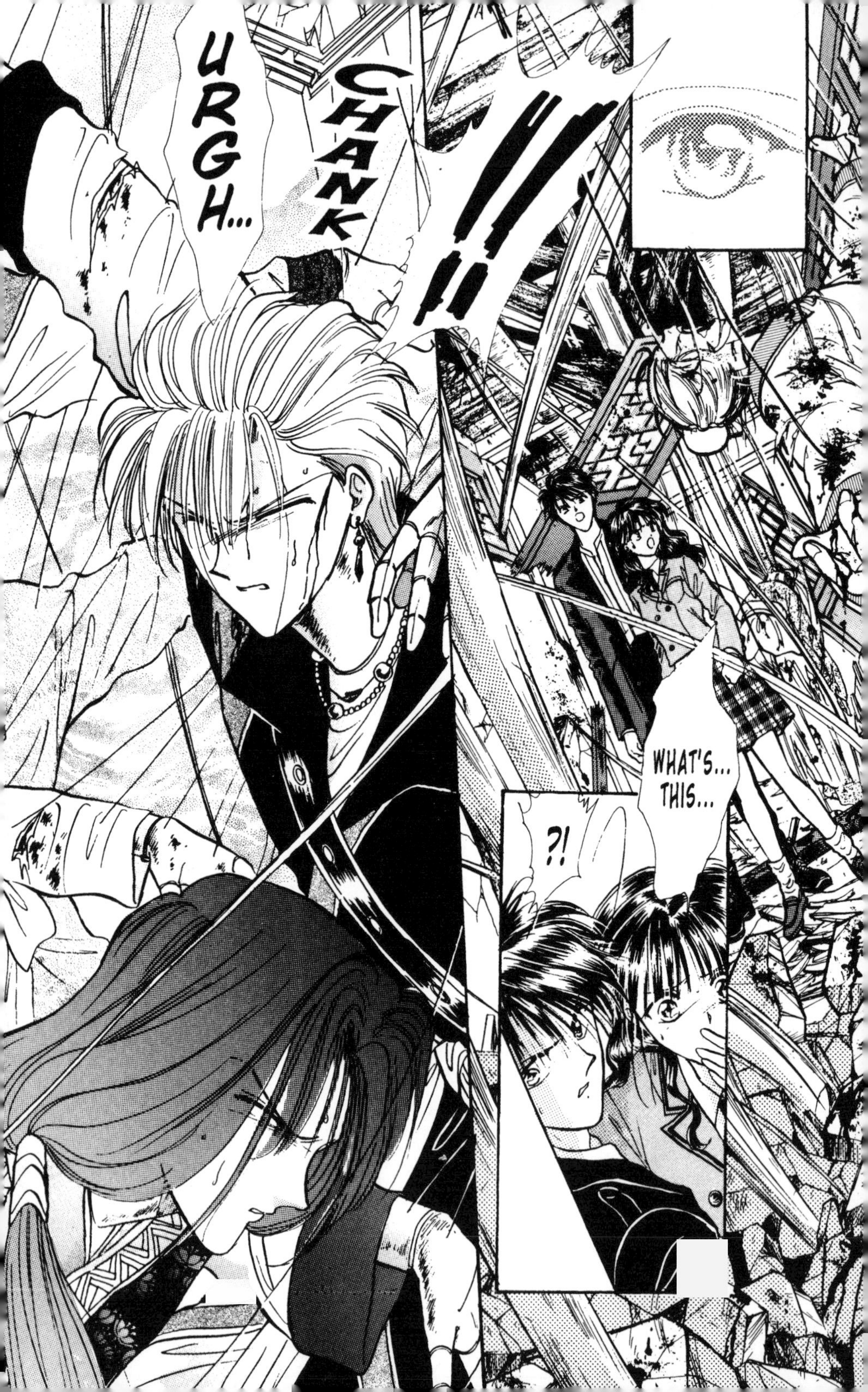
WHAT'S... THIS...
?!
CHANK
URGH...

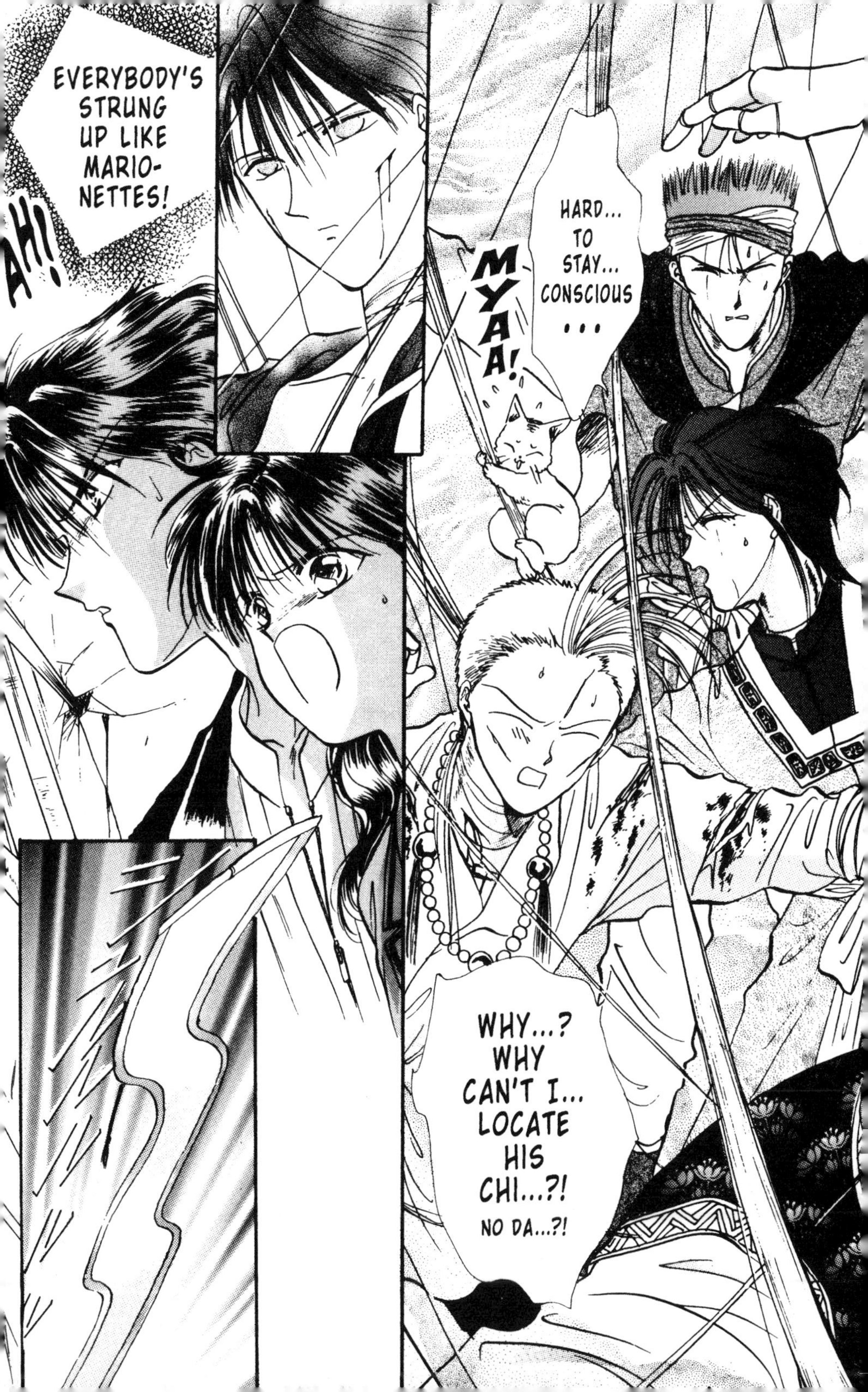
HARD... TO STAY... CONSCIOUS ...
MYAA!
WHY...? WHY CAN'T I... LOCATE HIS CHI...?! NO DA...?!
EVERYBODY'S STRUNG UP LIKE MARIO-NETTES!
AH!!

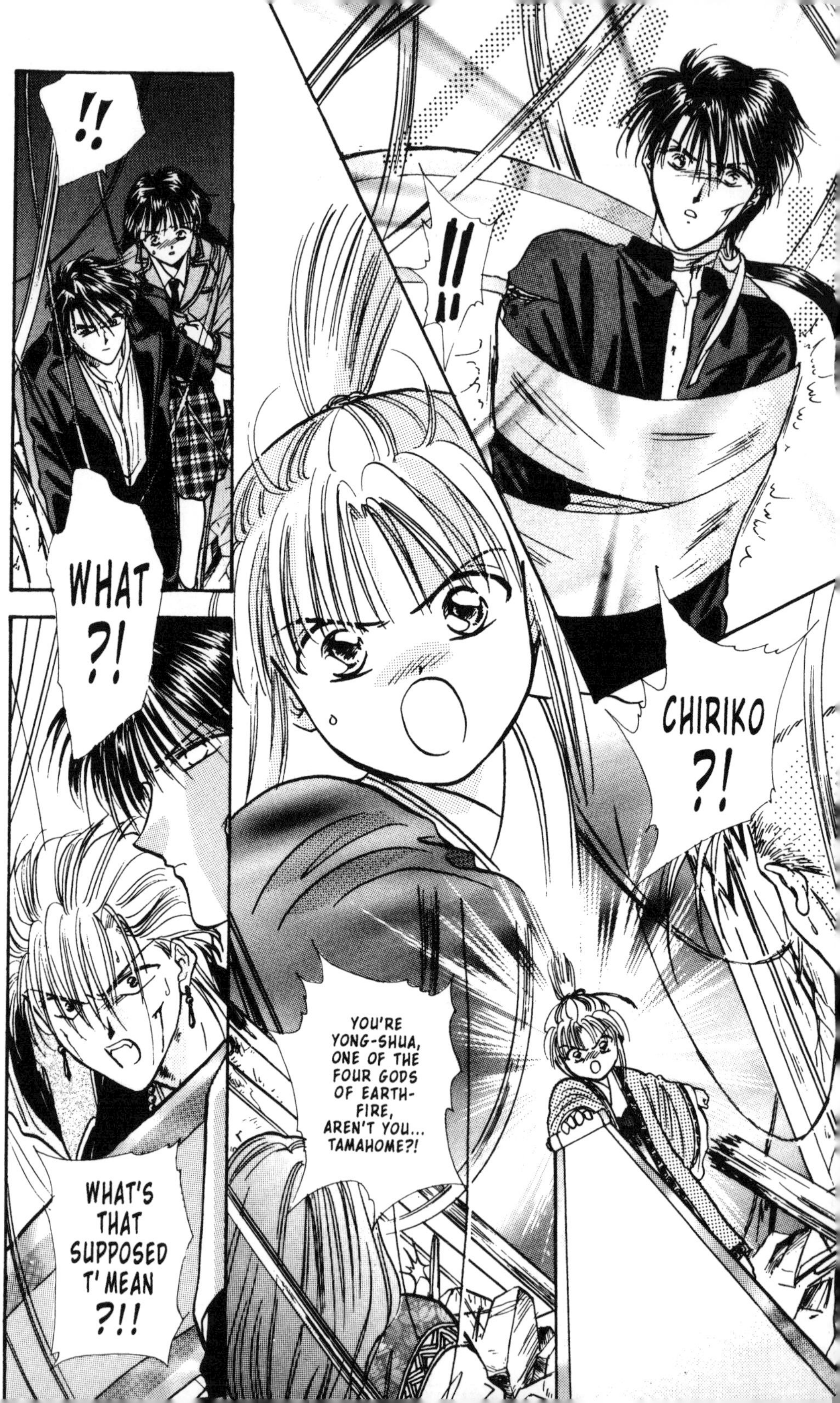
!!
CHIRIKO ?!
YOU'RE YONG-SHUA, ONE OF THE FOUR GODS OF EARTH-FIRE, AREN'T YOU... TAMAHOME?!
!!
WHAT ?!
WHAT'S THAT SUPPOSED T' MEAN ?!!

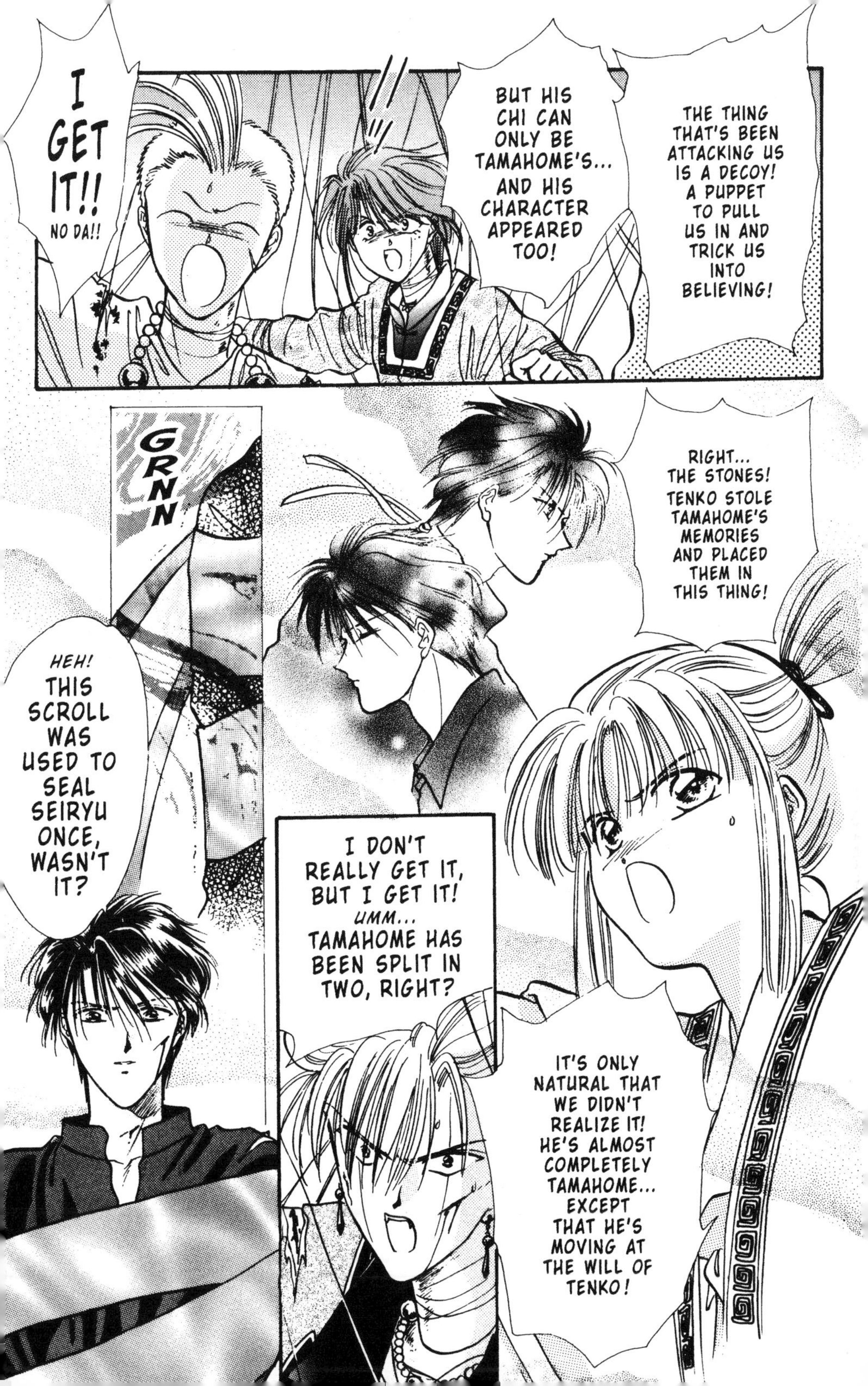
THE THING THAT'S BEEN ATTACKING US IS A DECOY! A PUPPET TO PULL US IN AND TRICK US INTO BELIEVING!
BUT HIS CHI CAN ONLY BE TAMAHOME'S... AND HIS CHARACTER APPEARED TOO!
I GET IT!! NO DA!!
RIGHT... THE STONES! TENKO STOLE TAMAHOME'S MEMORIES AND PLACED THEM IN THIS THING!
I DON'T REALLY GET IT, BUT I GET IT! UMM... TAMAHOME HAS BEEN SPLIT IN TWO, RIGHT?
IT'S ONLY NATURAL THAT WE DIDN'T REALIZE IT! HE'S ALMOST COMPLETELY TAMAHOME... EXCEPT THAT HE'S MOVING AT THE WILL OF TENKO!
GRNN
HEH! THIS SCROLL WAS USED TO SEAL SEIRYU ONCE, WASN'T IT?

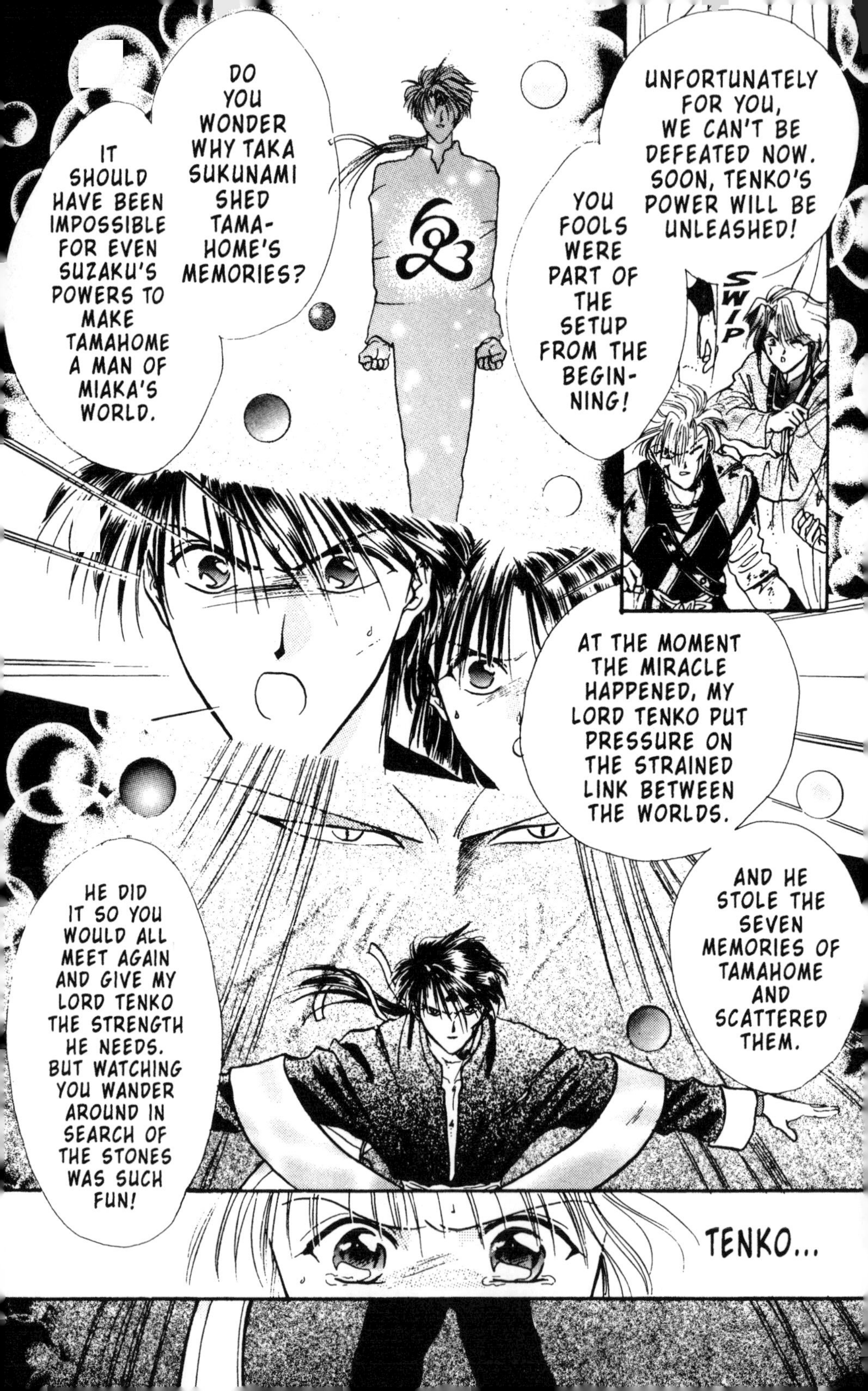
UNFORTUNATELY FOR YOU, WE CAN'T BE DEFEATED NOW. SOON, TENKO'S POWER WILL BE UNLEASHED!
YOU FOOLS WERE PART OF THE SETUP FROM THE BEGIN- NING!
SWIP
DO YOU WONDER WHY TAKA SUKUNAMI SHED TAMA- HOME'S MEMORIES?
IT SHOULD HAVE BEEN IMPOSSIBLE FOR EVEN SUZAKU'S POWERS TO MAKE TAMAHOME A MAN OF MIAKA'S WORLD.
AT THE MOMENT THE MIRACLE HAPPENED, MY LORD TENKO PUT PRESSURE ON THE STRAINED LINK BETWEEN THE WORLDS.
AND HE STOLE THE SEVEN MEMORIES OF TAMAHOME AND SCATTERED THEM.
HE DID IT SO YOU WOULD ALL MEET AGAIN AND GIVE MY LORD TENKO THE STRENGTH HE NEEDS. BUT WATCHING YOU WANDER AROUND IN SEARCH OF THE STONES WAS SUCH FUN!
TENKO...

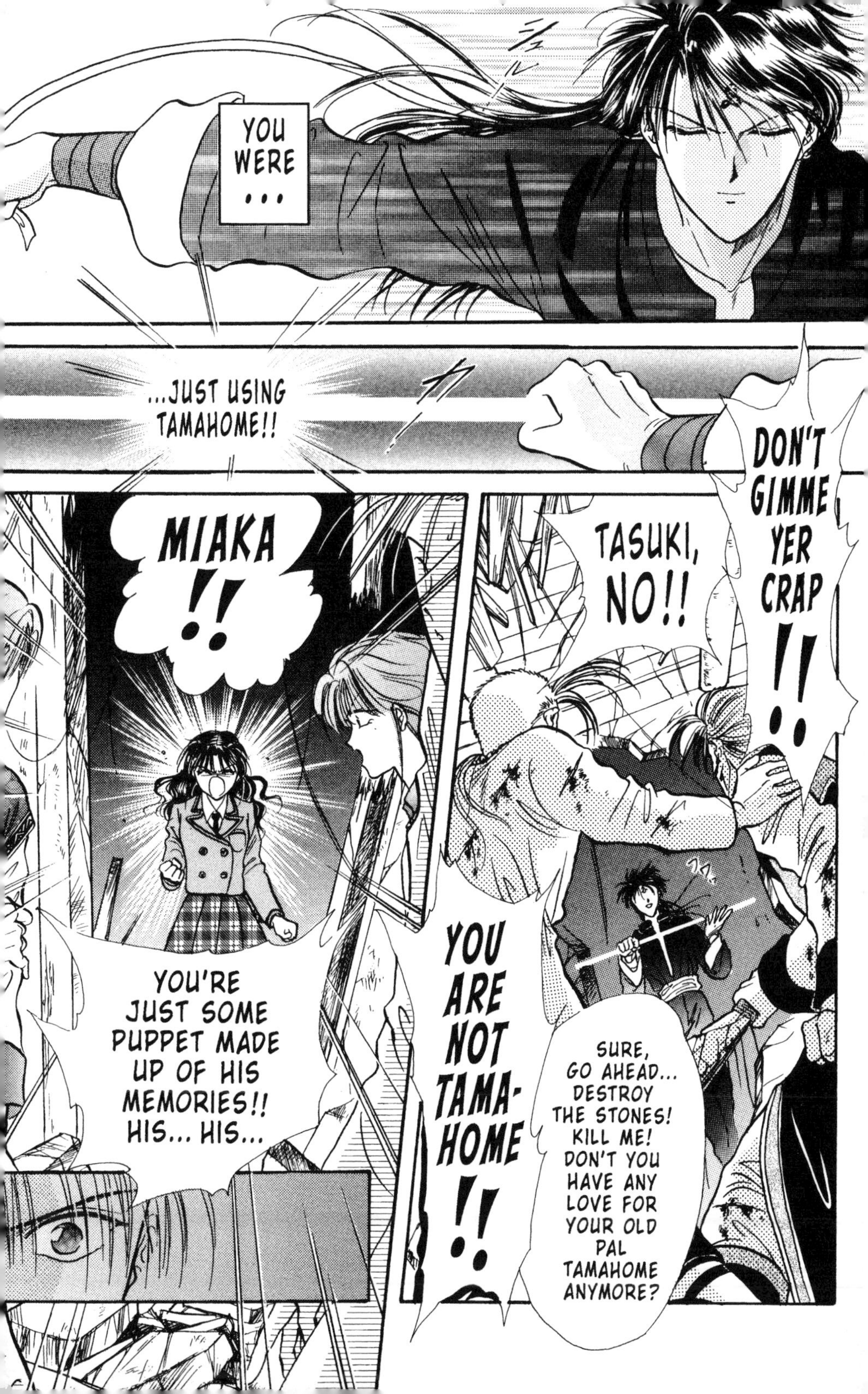
YOU WERE...
...JUST USING TAMAHOME!!
DON'T GIMME YER CRAP!!
TASUKI, NO!!
SURE, GO AHEAD... DESTROY THE STONES! KILL ME! DON'T YOU HAVE ANY LOVE FOR YOUR OLD PAL TAMAHOME ANYMORE?
MIAKA!!
YOU'RE JUST SOME PUPPET MADE UP OF HIS MEMORIES!! HIS... HIS...
YOU ARE NOT TAMAHOME!!

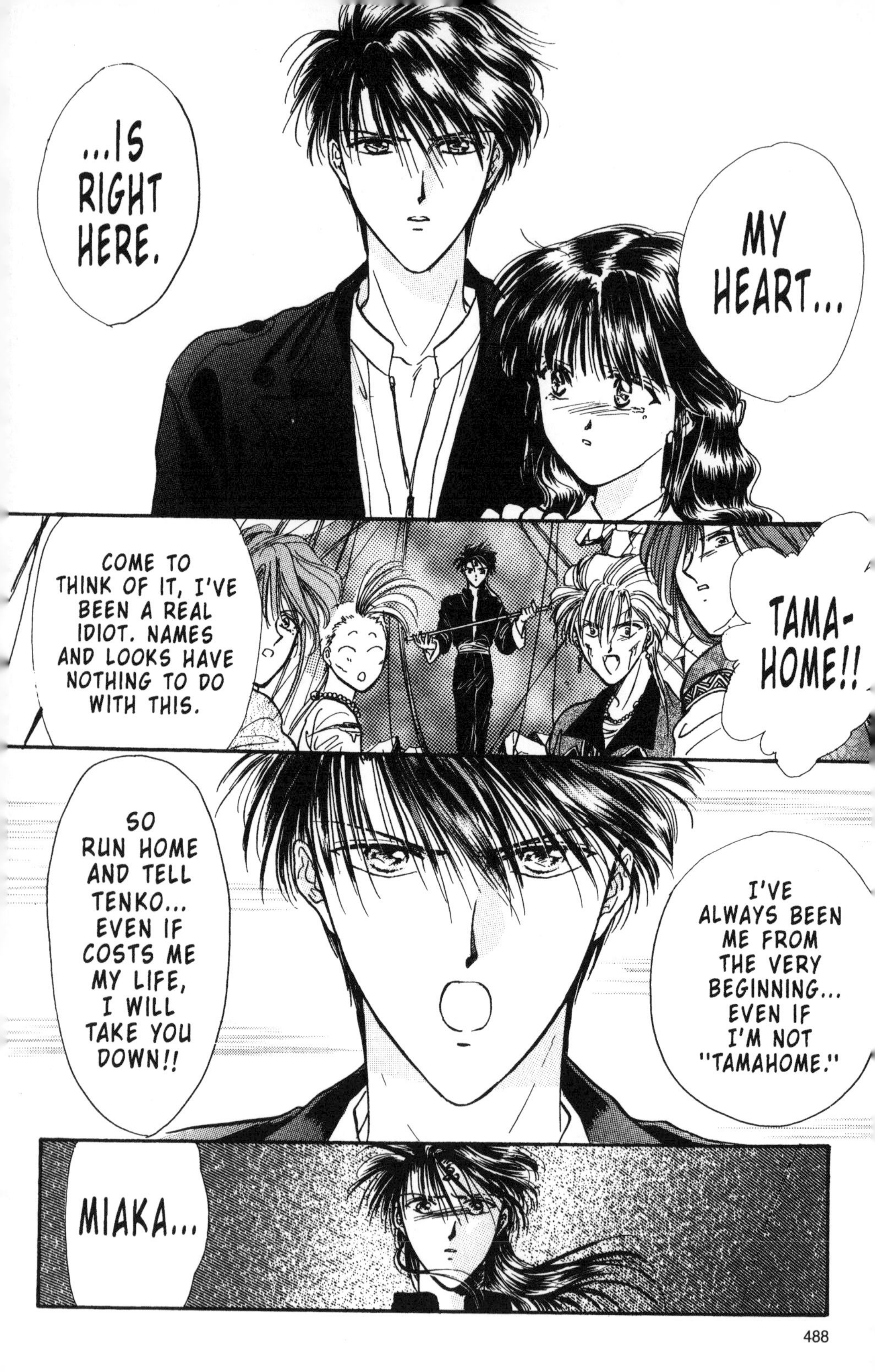
MY HEART...
...IS RIGHT HERE.
TAMA-HOME!!
COME TO THINK OF IT, I'VE BEEN A REAL IDIOT. NAMES AND LOOKS HAVE NOTHING TO DO WITH THIS.
I'VE ALWAYS BEEN ME FROM THE VERY BEGINNING... EVEN IF I'M NOT "TAMAHOME."
SO RUN HOME AND TELL TENKO... EVEN IF COSTS ME MY LIFE, I WILL TAKE YOU DOWN!!
MIAKA...

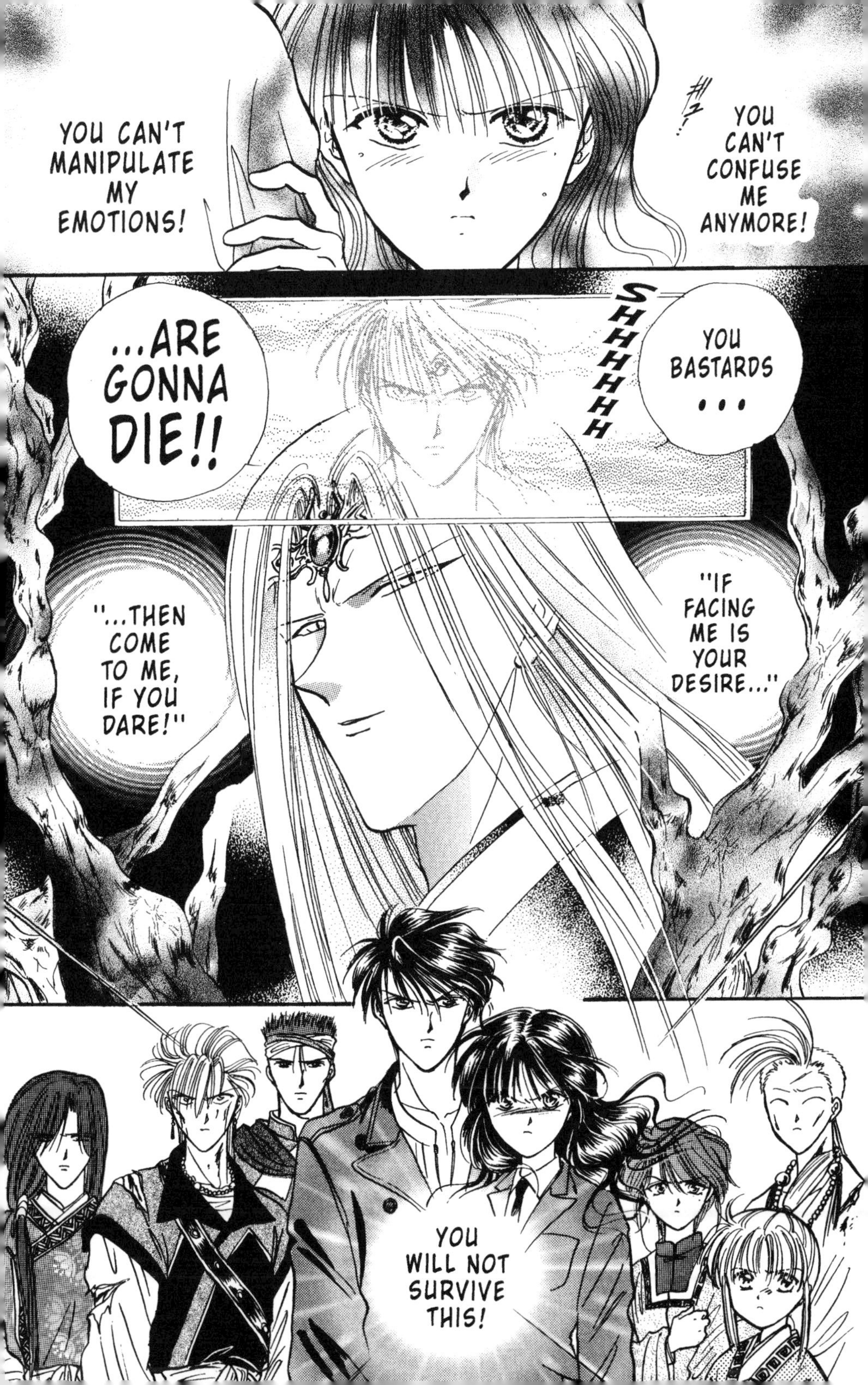
YOU CAN'T CONFUSE ME ANYMORE!
YOU CAN'T MANIPULATE MY EMOTIONS!
YOU BASTARDS...
SHHHHHHH
...ARE GONNA DIE!!
"IF FACING ME IS YOUR DESIRE..."
"...THEN COME TO ME, IF YOU DARE!"
YOU WILL NOT SURVIVE THIS!

GEE, IT'S BEEN SO LONG! THE SECRETS OF "FUSHIGI YŪGI"

Number...Um... What number is this again?

Q1. How come Chichiri's mask can do all those things?
A. Actually, it's one of Chichiri's techniques -- a special power. He can make it rigid or flexible. But to put an expression on it or make it move like a real face, he has to actually wear the mask. But at other times, when he's using other powers or techniques, he takes it off. If another person were to try to use it, that person would need Chichiri's cooperation to make the mask work.

Q2. Can anybody use Tasuki's harisen (metal fan)?
A. From the time when Tai Yi-Jun gave everyone their powered-up equipment, the only person able to use the harisen was Tasuki. (He's able to use the harisen for some other powers too.) When he uses it, he has to concentrate really hard if he wants to limit the flames to only the thing he wants to burn, so it's very difficult. Especially when he shouts, "Dammit, Tama!!" and pulls it out to toast somebody. *But those are just jokes.*

Q3. Why can the dead Celestial Warriors still use their powers?
A. Because their powers are not tied to their bodies, but to their life forces.

Q4. I understood that in Part 1, Miaka could understand everybody because she was sucked into a Japanese translation of the original book, but Part 2 uses the Chinese version. How does she communicate?
A. In Part 2, Miaka is sent to the world of the book directly by the god Suzaku, and since Suzaku can speak both Chinese and Japanese, it only stands to reason that he can give Miaka and Taka his power to communicate as well. (But it's the thought that counts.)
Also, about Tasuki's Kansai accent (let it go, folks. If you're too picky about detail, manga will never be fun!) ...Anyway, think of Hong-Nan as Japan. The capital is Tokyo, and Ko Prefecture (where Tasuki was born) would be near the Kansai area where Osaka and Kobe are.

Q5. What about Taka's real-world family?
A. He has both his parents, a younger brother and a younger sister, and he is the eldest son of a farm family who live in a natural setting in the country. They're never short of food. Isn't that great, Miaka? I'm sure Taka's family is very much like Tamahome's family.

Q6. When you use names like Taiitsukun (Tai Yi-Jun) and Suzaku-seikun (The God Suzaku), why do you put "-kun" at the end?
A. This is completely different than when you call a boy "Yamada-kun" in Japan today. Ages ago when you really wanted to show respect for someone who was much higher in status than yourself, you added "no kimi" to their names, and the "kimi" uses the same kanji as "kun."

Q7. So why did you decide to use the name "Taka"?
A. I wanted to use the "demon" character, and a long time ago in China there was a country name that used Taka's character (pronounced "Gi"). In ancient times in what was called The Third Year of Seiryu, the Japanese Queen Himiko was given the "Four Gods Mirror" by the country of Gi.

Q8. The biggest question!! How does Miaka eat so much and never get fat?!
A. She moves around a lot. She also has a lot of worries and nervous energy.

• LONELY GUY •

KNOCK, KNOCK! WHO'S THERE?
IT'S ME, KNEI-GONG, WHOSE HEART WENT OUT T' THOSE SAD FANS BECAUSE I NEVER HAD A CHANCE T' SHOW UP IN PART 2!
WELL, COME IN! DON'T MIND IF I DO!
NOW... HUAN-LANG GOT SO CONCERNED 'BOUT HIS FAMILY THAT HE LEFT THE MOUNTAIN, AND TH' LAST FEW MONTHS HAVE BEEN SO BORING!
WHO'S HE TALKIN' TO?
BEATS ME!
BUT EVERYTHING'S OKAY!
I GOT MY ROOM! SEE?
A COLLECTION OF HUAN-LANG IMAGES DRAWN BY THE BANDITS!
1ST PRIZE
NOW I'M NEVER LONELY, EVEN AT NIGHT!
KNEI-GONG, IF YOU DON'T SHAPE UP, I AIN'T NEVER COMIN' BACK!!
TRMBL TRMBL

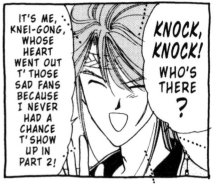

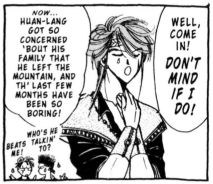

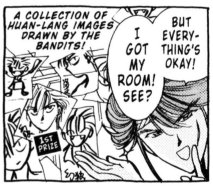

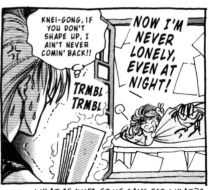

WHAT IF KNEI-GONG SAYS, "SO WHAT?" WHAT'LL YOU DO THEN?!

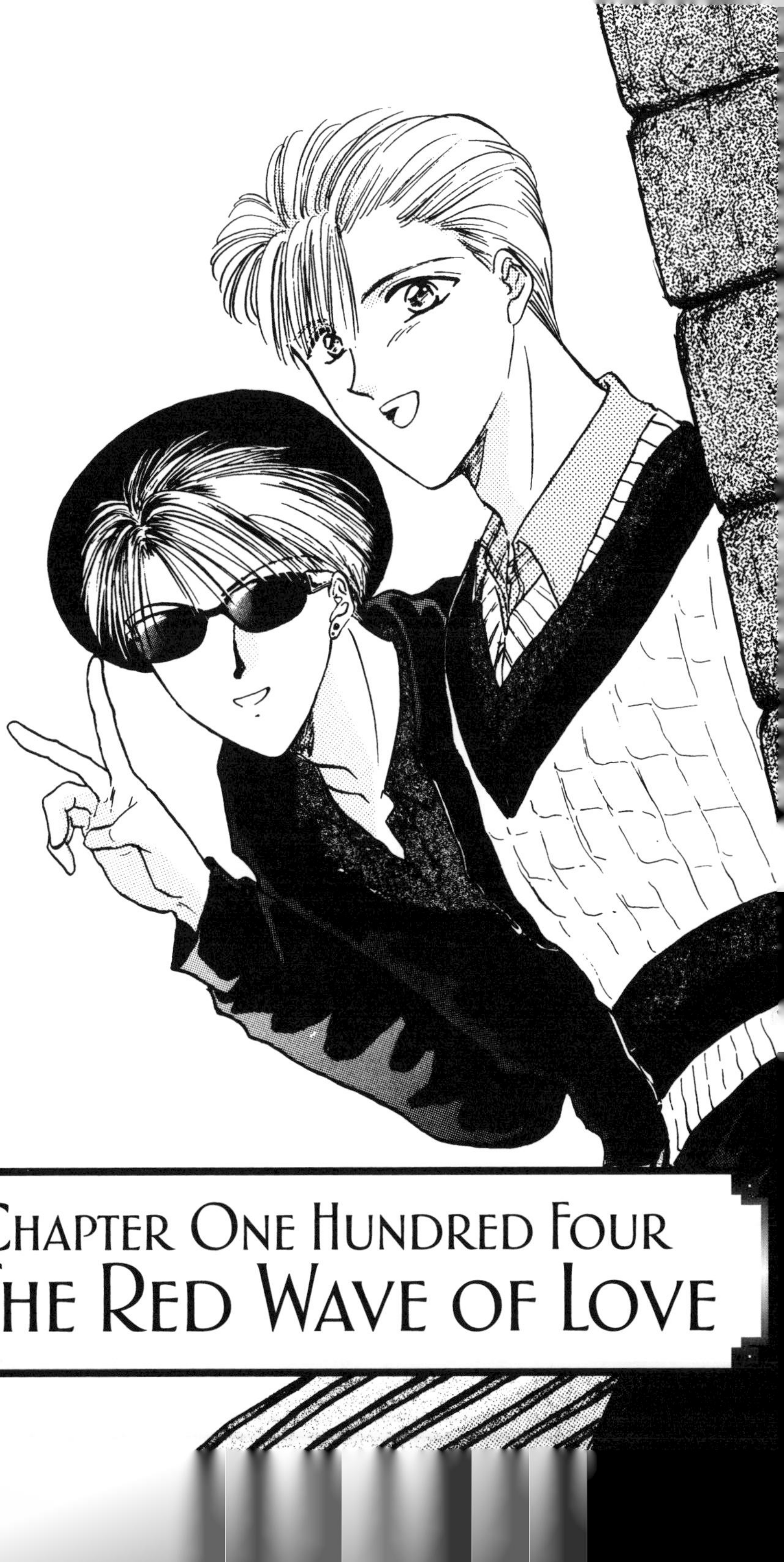

Chapter One Hundred Four
The Red Wave of Love

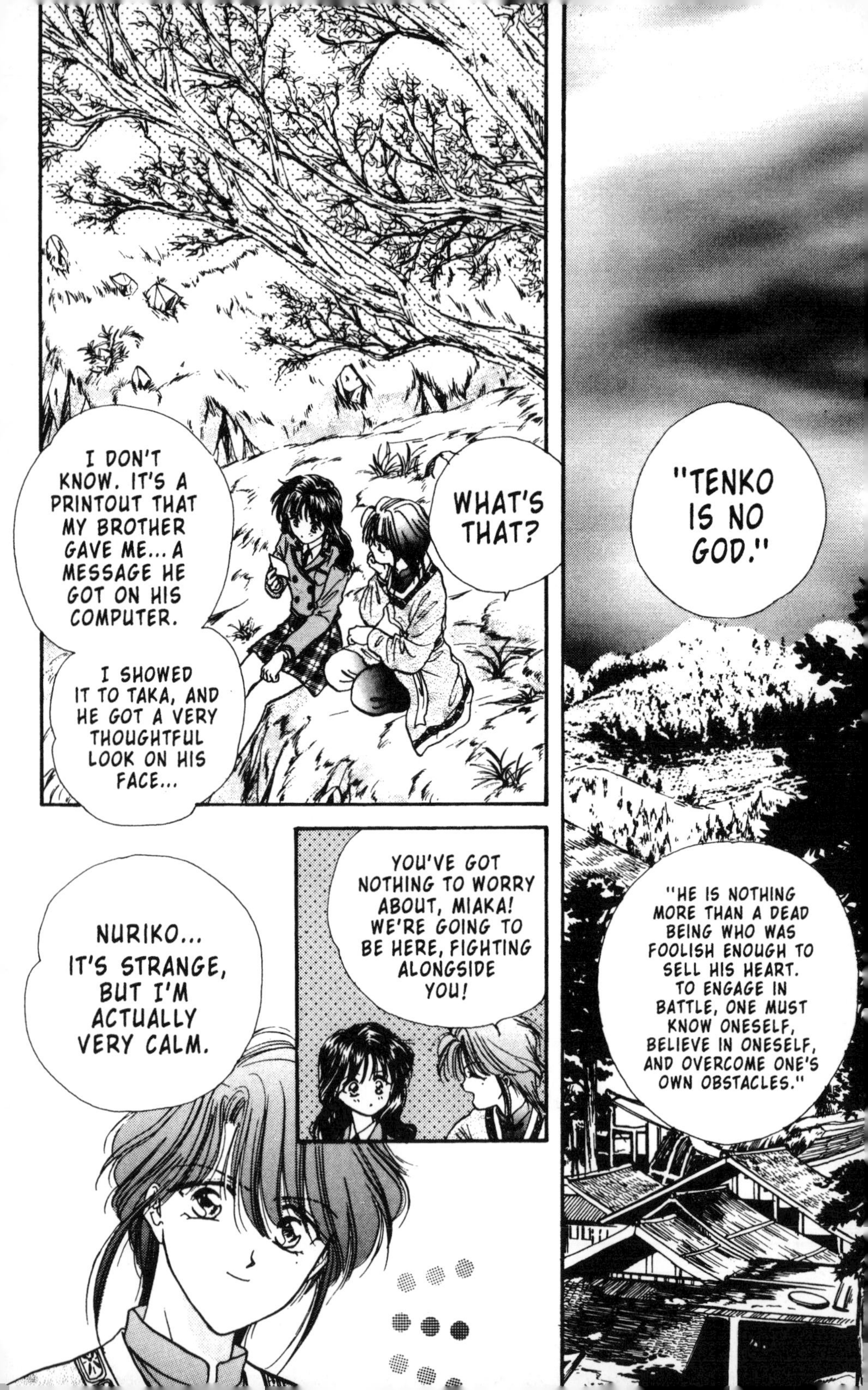
"TENKO IS NO GOD."
"HE IS NOTHING MORE THAN A DEAD BEING WHO WAS FOOLISH ENOUGH TO SELL HIS HEART. TO ENGAGE IN BATTLE, ONE MUST KNOW ONESELF, BELIEVE IN ONESELF, AND OVERCOME ONE'S OWN OBSTACLES."
WHAT'S THAT?
I DON'T KNOW. IT'S A PRINTOUT THAT MY BROTHER GAVE ME... A MESSAGE HE GOT ON HIS COMPUTER.
I SHOWED IT TO TAKA, AND HE GOT A VERY THOUGHTFUL LOOK ON HIS FACE...
YOU'VE GOT NOTHING TO WORRY ABOUT, MIAKA! WE'RE GOING TO BE HERE, FIGHTING ALONGSIDE YOU!
NURIKO... IT'S STRANGE, BUT I'M ACTUALLY VERY CALM.

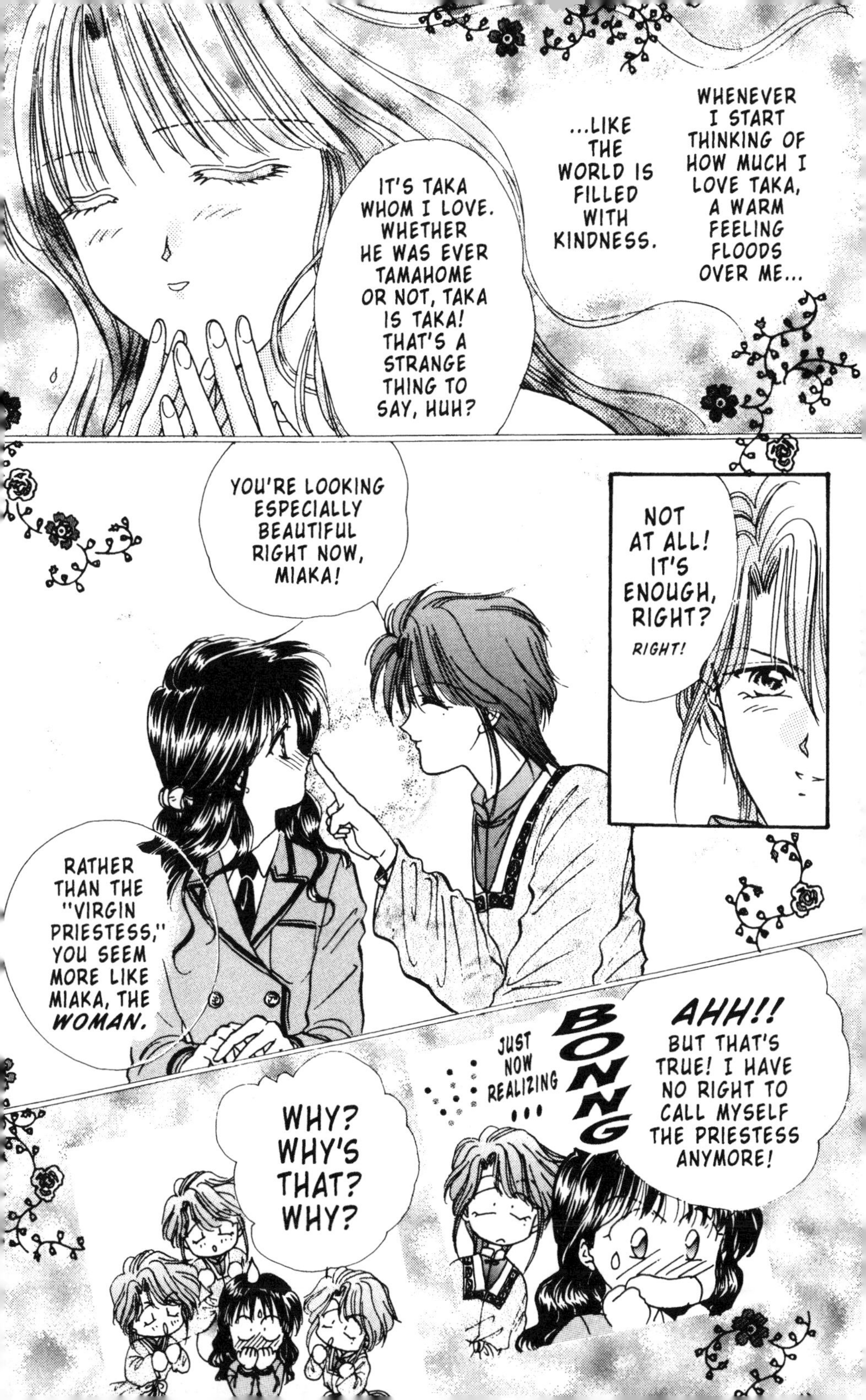
WHENEVER I START THINKING OF HOW MUCH I LOVE TAKA, A WARM FEELING FLOODS OVER ME...
...LIKE THE WORLD IS FILLED WITH KINDNESS.
IT'S TAKA WHOM I LOVE. WHETHER HE WAS EVER TAMAHOME OR NOT, TAKA IS TAKA! THAT'S A STRANGE THING TO SAY, HUH?
NOT AT ALL! IT'S ENOUGH, RIGHT?
RIGHT!
YOU'RE LOOKING ESPECIALLY BEAUTIFUL RIGHT NOW, MIAKA!
RATHER THAN THE "VIRGIN PRIESTESS," YOU SEEM MORE LIKE MIAKA, THE *WOMAN.*
AHH!! BUT THAT'S TRUE! I HAVE NO RIGHT TO CALL MYSELF THE PRIESTESS ANYMORE!
BONNG
JUST NOW REALIZING...
WHY? WHY'S THAT? WHY?

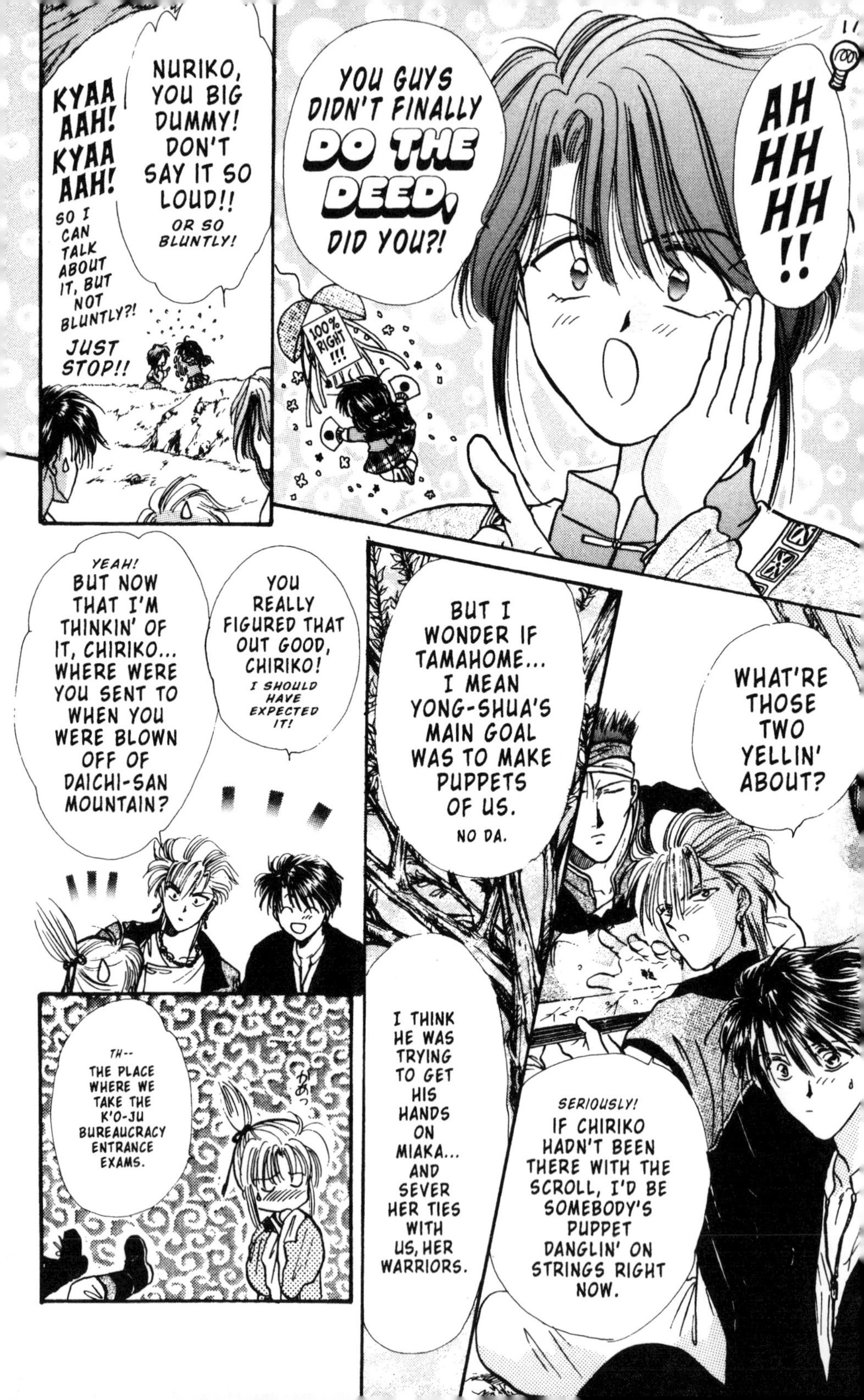
AHHHHHH!!
YOU GUYS DIDN'T FINALLY DO THE DEED, DID YOU?!
100% RIGHT!!!
NURIKO, YOU BIG DUMMY! DON'T SAY IT SO LOUD!! OR SO BLUNTLY!
KYAA AAH! KYAA AAH! SO I CAN TALK ABOUT IT, BUT NOT BLUNTLY?!
JUST STOP!!
WHAT'RE THOSE TWO YELLIN' ABOUT?
BUT I WONDER IF TAMAHOME... I MEAN YONG-SHUA'S MAIN GOAL WAS TO MAKE PUPPETS OF US. NO DA.
I THINK HE WAS TRYING TO GET HIS HANDS ON MIAKA... AND SEVER HER TIES WITH US, HER WARRIORS.
SERIOUSLY! IF CHIRIKO HADN'T BEEN THERE WITH THE SCROLL, I'D BE SOMEBODY'S PUPPET DANGLIN' ON STRINGS RIGHT NOW.
YOU REALLY FIGURED THAT OUT GOOD, CHIRIKO! I SHOULD HAVE EXPECTED IT!
YEAH! BUT NOW THAT I'M THINKIN' OF IT, CHIRIKO... WHERE WERE YOU SENT TO WHEN YOU WERE BLOWN OFF OF DAICHI-SAN MOUNTAIN?
TH-- THE PLACE WHERE WE TAKE THE K'O-JU BUREAUCRACY ENTRANCE EXAMS.

I don't have the right to ask, but...
Don't read this until you finish the story!

There are people out there who are just like Lian. Um... I mean, people with charisma...the type who naturally become leaders. Charismatic people falling from rooftops is getting a little into the dark areas, but...oh well. And Miiru... There are girls like her out there, too -- women who think of men as prey they can eat up. They're both self-destructive. For the men, unless they realize what they're doing, they can bring everyone else down with them (like their friends and family). Then there's Fei-Gao and the love triangle. If you don't treat friendship well, you can destroy it. Then there's Yong-Shua... I mean Tamahome... I talked about dolls tied up with strings a little earlier, but if you think of the very earliest Taka in the story, he was a doll without strings-- just the opposite of what was happening with Yong-Shua/Tamahome. Then, when Miaka gets hit with the strings, that's a way of symbolizing a man's jealousy. Still, that only happened because love was there... But if you handle jealousy wrong, you could lose the one you love forever. It's a tough thing to balance. Tenko, this time, may seem like an extension of Nakago, done to a greater degree... but that isn't the case. He's a symbol. (By the way, in the original setup, he possessed stones of much the same variety that Miaka and Taka had to deal with.) For Taka, the real enemy was actually HIMSELF in the form of Tamahome.
I'm sure that if Tenko never existed, Taka would have been able to collect all of the parts of his heart and turn into the complete Taka, but... That wouldn't have allowed Taka to mature as Taka, and in the last scene where he is able to take Tamahome into himself, he wouldn't have come out as strong, right? What that scene shows is a man who is able to accept a part of himself, even though that part murdered his lover. I don't think strength is something a person can see. That's why I kept the scenes of Taka fighting to a bare minimum. There's nothing "pathetic" about a man worrying or crying. If tomorrow you're stronger (even just a little), then I think that's good enough. An assistant said that she felt the most kindness emanating from Taka, and although he didn't talk of love nearly as much as Tamahome (did he lose interest during the story?). One could really feel the depth of his emotions at times.

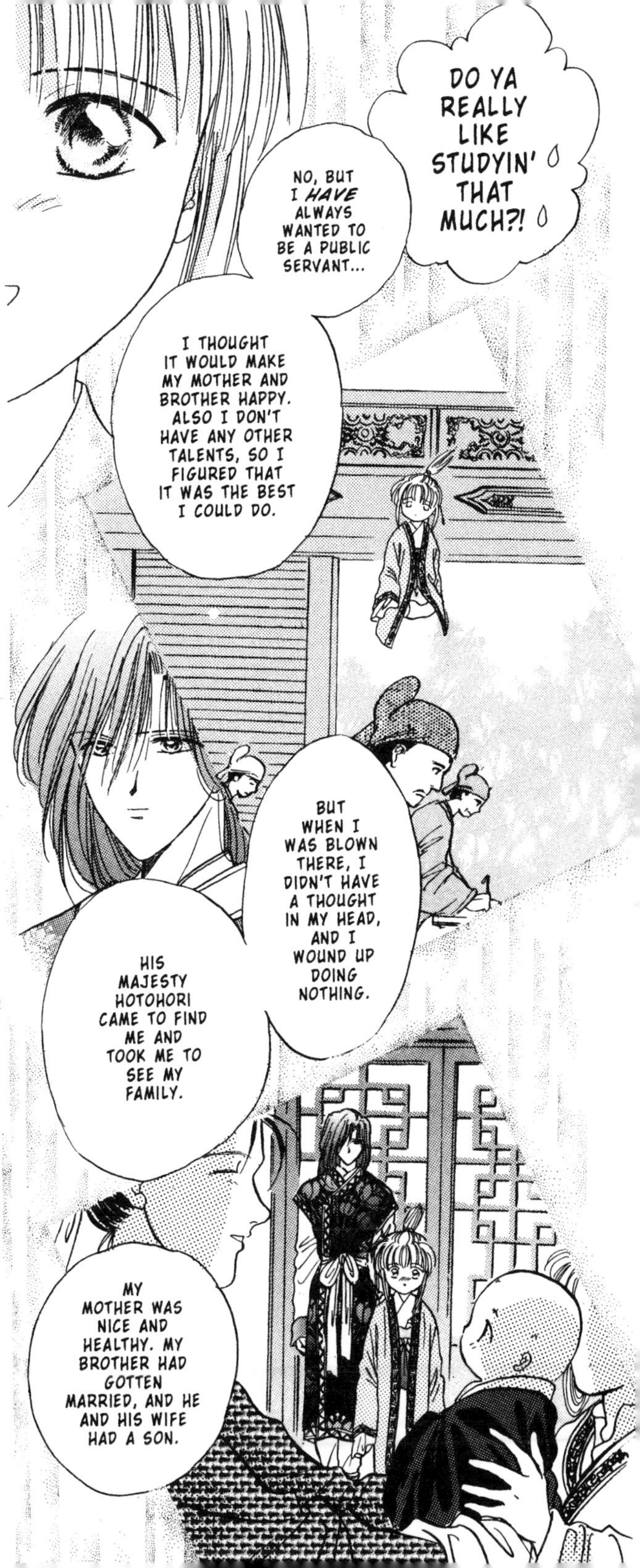

DO YA REALLY LIKE STUDYIN' THAT MUCH?!
NO, BUT I *HAVE* ALWAYS WANTED TO BE A PUBLIC SERVANT...
I THOUGHT IT WOULD MAKE MY MOTHER AND BROTHER HAPPY. ALSO I DON'T HAVE ANY OTHER TALENTS, SO I FIGURED THAT IT WAS THE BEST I COULD DO.
BUT WHEN I WAS BLOWN THERE, I DIDN'T HAVE A THOUGHT IN MY HEAD, AND I WOUND UP DOING NOTHING.
HIS MAJESTY HOTOHORI CAME TO FIND ME AND TOOK ME TO SEE MY FAMILY.
MY MOTHER WAS NICE AND HEALTHY. MY BROTHER HAD GOTTEN MARRIED, AND HE AND HIS WIFE HAD A SON.

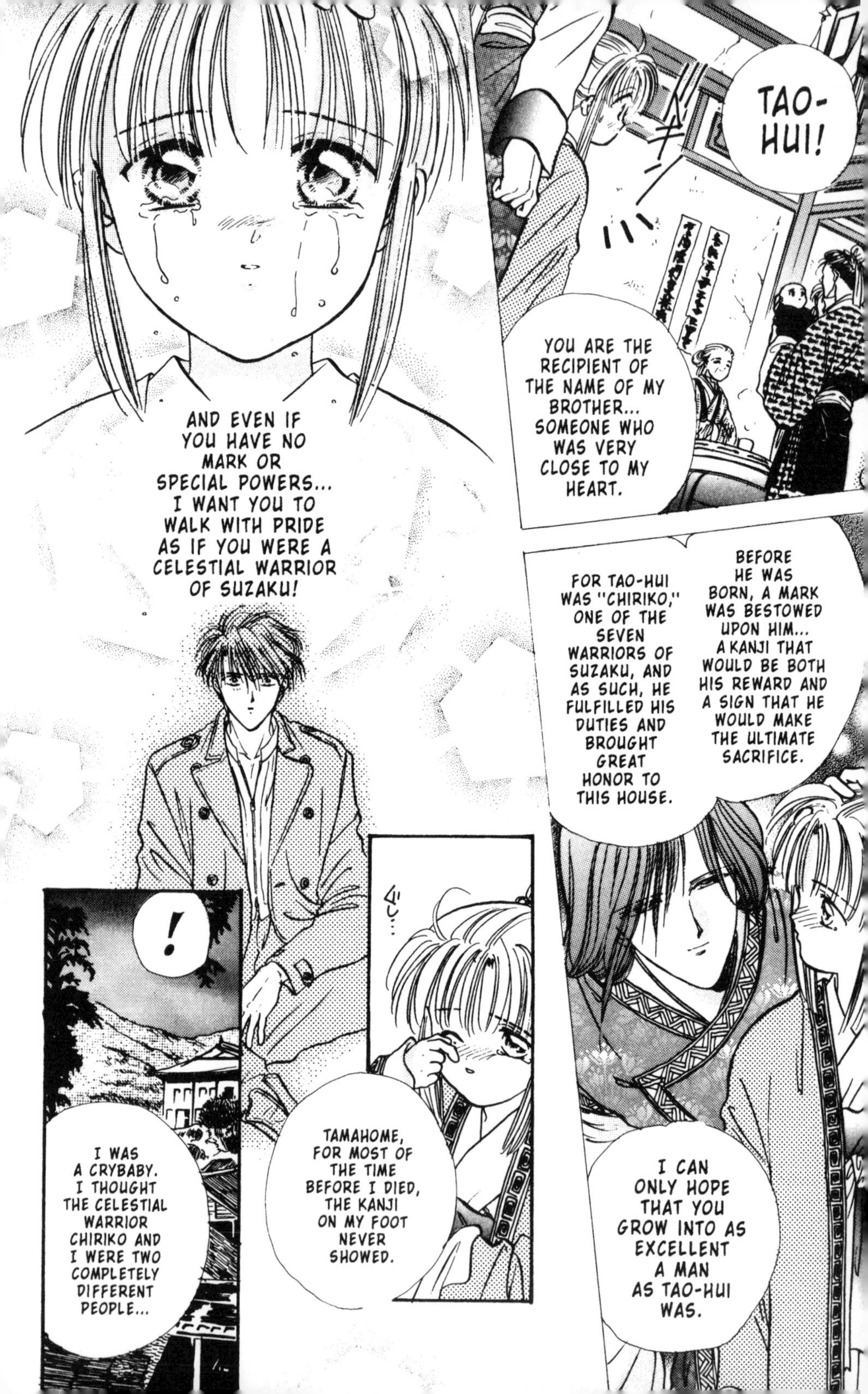
TAO-HUI!
YOU ARE THE RECIPIENT OF THE NAME OF MY BROTHER... SOMEONE WHO WAS VERY CLOSE TO MY HEART.
BEFORE HE WAS BORN, A MARK WAS BESTOWED UPON HIM... A KANJI THAT WOULD BE BOTH HIS REWARD AND A SIGN THAT HE WOULD MAKE THE ULTIMATE SACRIFICE.
FOR TAO-HUI WAS "CHIRIKO," ONE OF THE SEVEN WARRIORS OF SUZAKU, AND AS SUCH, HE FULFILLED HIS DUTIES AND BROUGHT GREAT HONOR TO THIS HOUSE.
I CAN ONLY HOPE THAT YOU GROW INTO AS EXCELLENT A MAN AS TAO-HUI WAS.
AND EVEN IF YOU HAVE NO MARK OR SPECIAL POWERS... I WANT YOU TO WALK WITH PRIDE AS IF YOU WERE A CELESTIAL WARRIOR OF SUZAKU!
ぐし…
TAMAHOME, FOR MOST OF THE TIME BEFORE I DIED, THE KANJI ON MY FOOT NEVER SHOWED.
!
I WAS A CRYBABY. I THOUGHT THE CELESTIAL WARRIOR CHIRIKO AND I WERE TWO COMPLETELY DIFFERENT PEOPLE...

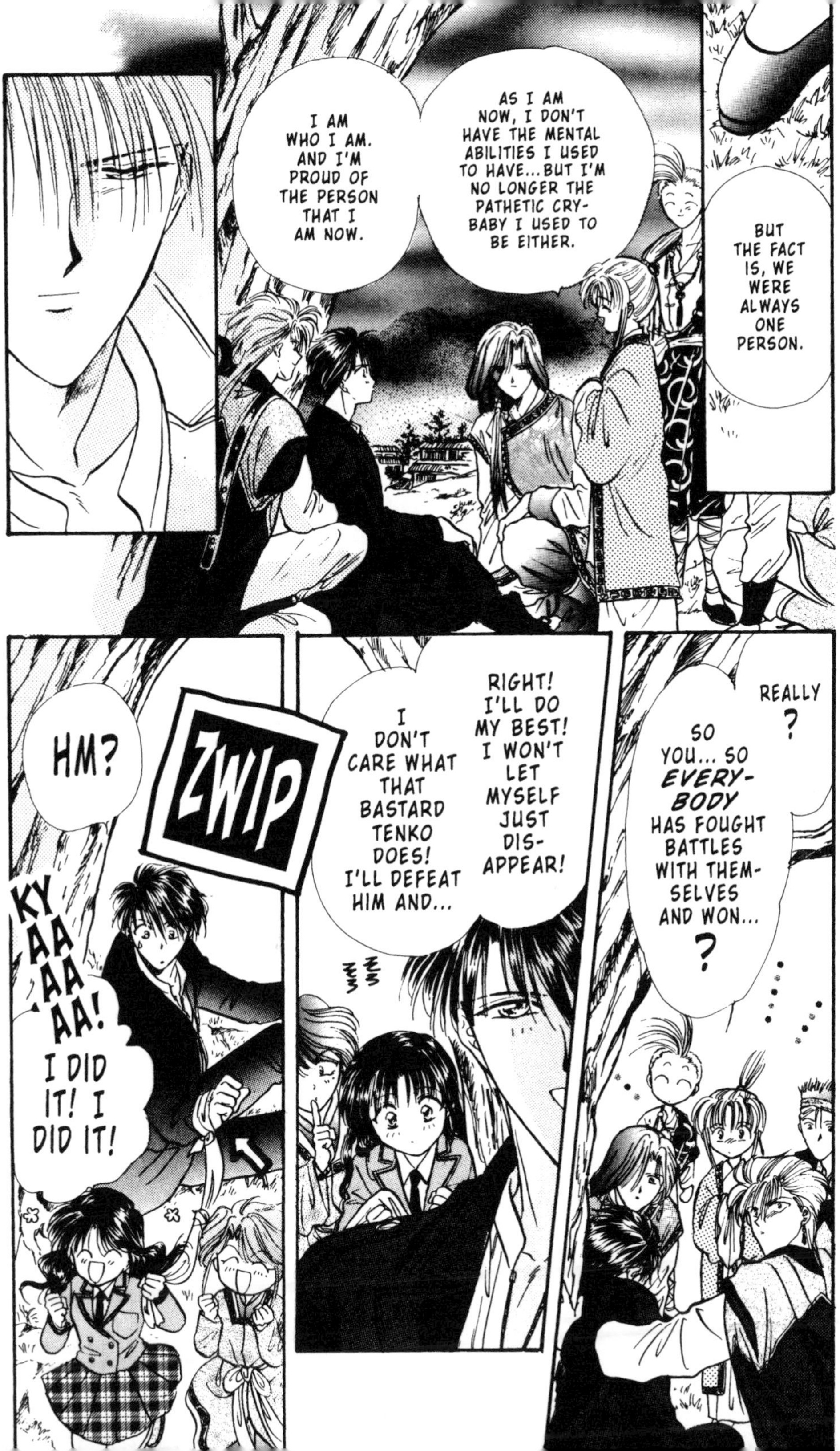
BUT THE FACT IS, WE WERE ALWAYS ONE PERSON.
AS I AM NOW, I DON'T HAVE THE MENTAL ABILITIES I USED TO HAVE... BUT I'M NO LONGER THE PATHETIC CRY-BABY I USED TO BE EITHER.
I AM WHO I AM. AND I'M PROUD OF THE PERSON THAT I AM NOW.
REALLY?
SO YOU... SO EVERY-BODY HAS FOUGHT BATTLES WITH THEM-SELVES AND WON...?
RIGHT! I'LL DO MY BEST! I WON'T LET MYSELF JUST DIS-APPEAR!
I DON'T CARE WHAT THAT BASTARD TENKO DOES! I'LL DEFEAT HIM AND...
ZWIP
HM?
KYAAAAAA!
I DID IT! I DID IT!

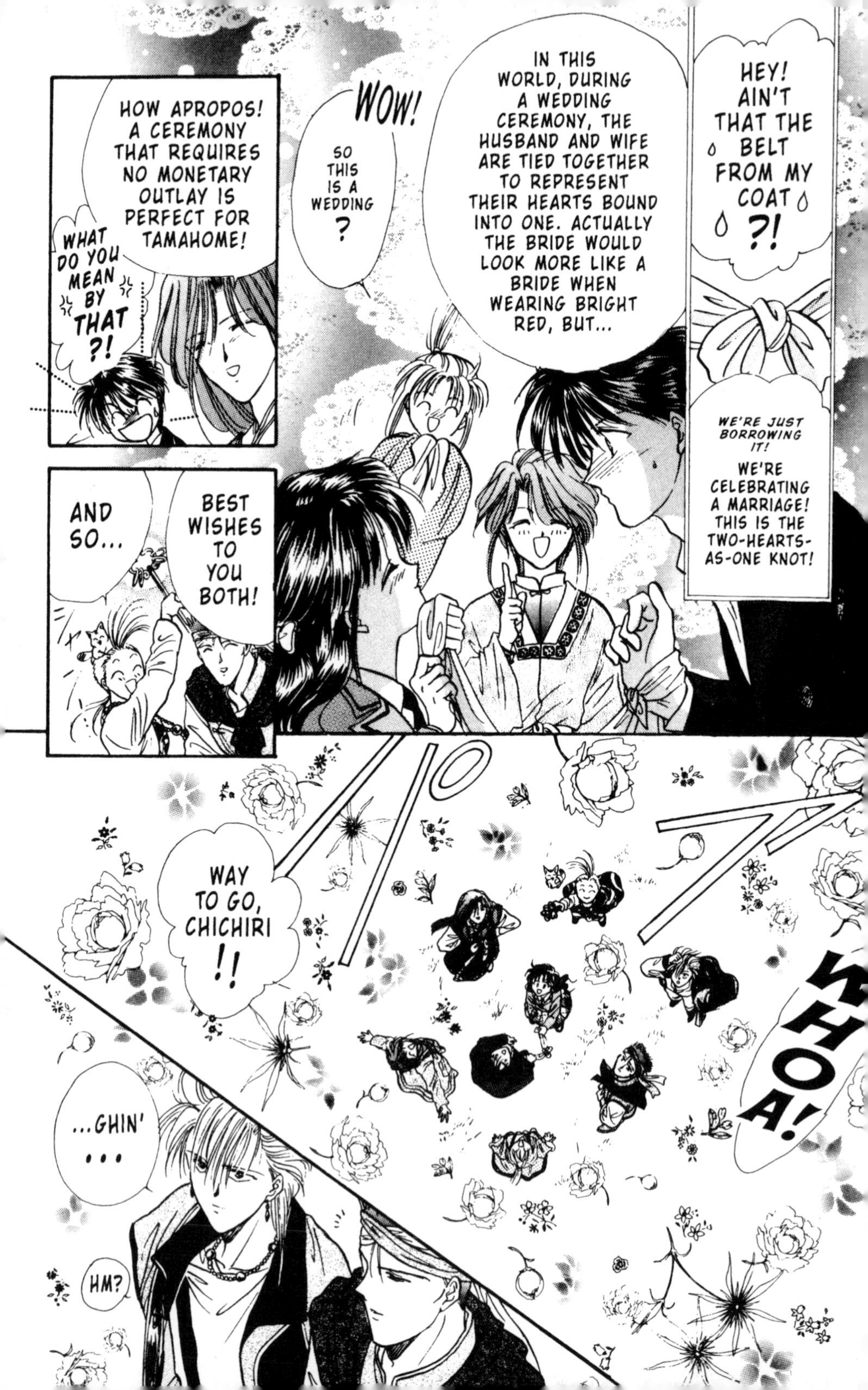
HEY! AIN'T THAT THE BELT FROM MY COAT ?!
WE'RE JUST BORROWING IT!
WE'RE CELEBRATING A MARRIAGE! THIS IS THE TWO-HEARTS-AS-ONE KNOT!
IN THIS WORLD, DURING A WEDDING CEREMONY, THE HUSBAND AND WIFE ARE TIED TOGETHER TO REPRESENT THEIR HEARTS BOUND INTO ONE. ACTUALLY THE BRIDE WOULD LOOK MORE LIKE A BRIDE WHEN WEARING BRIGHT RED, BUT...
WOW!
SO THIS IS A WEDDING ?
HOW APROPOS! A CEREMONY THAT REQUIRES NO MONETARY OUTLAY IS PERFECT FOR TAMAHOME!
WHAT DO YOU MEAN BY THAT ?!
BEST WISHES TO YOU BOTH!
AND SO...
WHOA!
WAY TO GO, CHICHIRI !!
...GHIN' ...
HM?

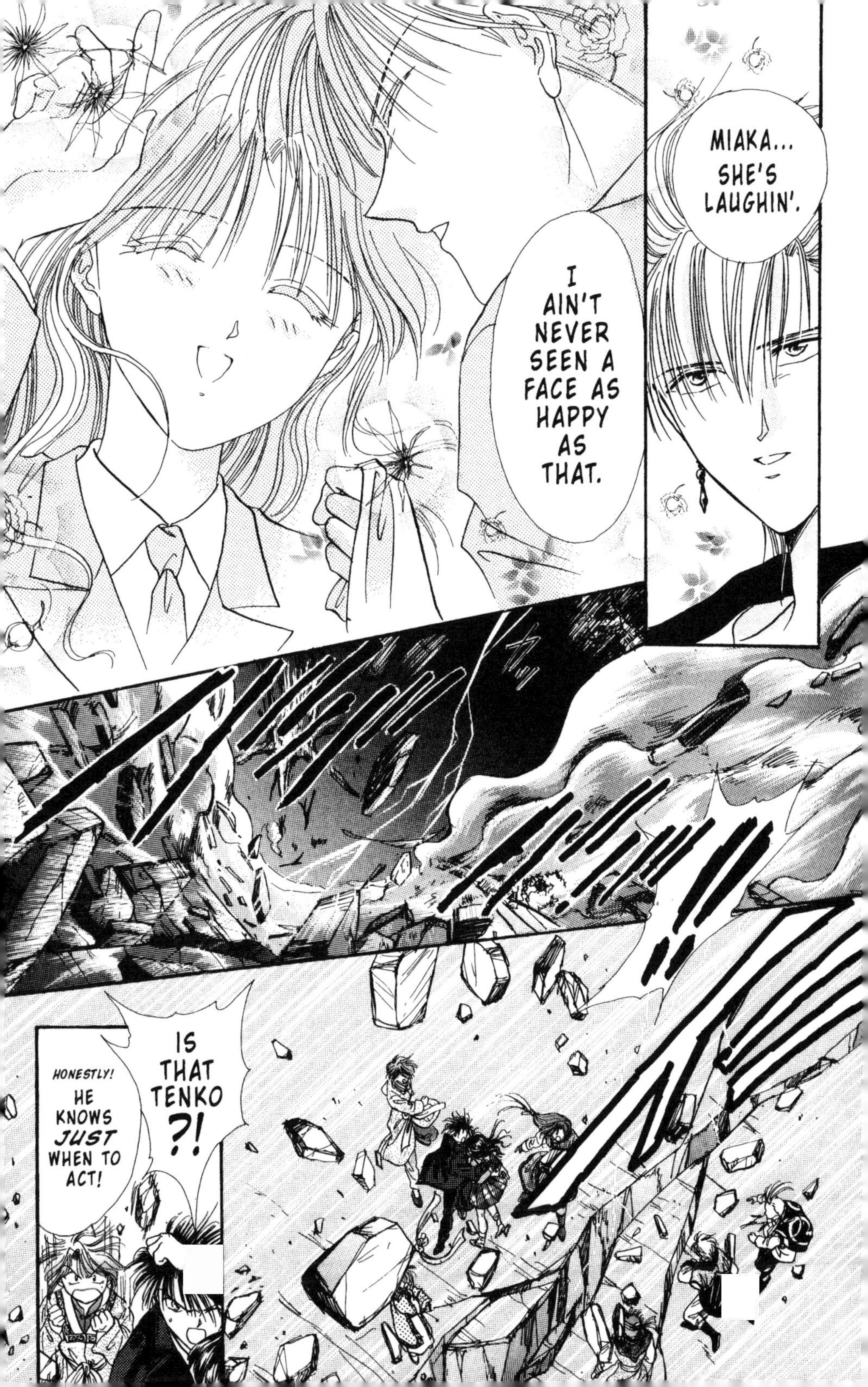
MIAKA... SHE'S LAUGHIN'.
I AIN'T NEVER SEEN A FACE AS HAPPY AS THAT.
IS THAT TENKO ?!
HONESTLY! HE KNOWS JUST WHEN TO ACT!

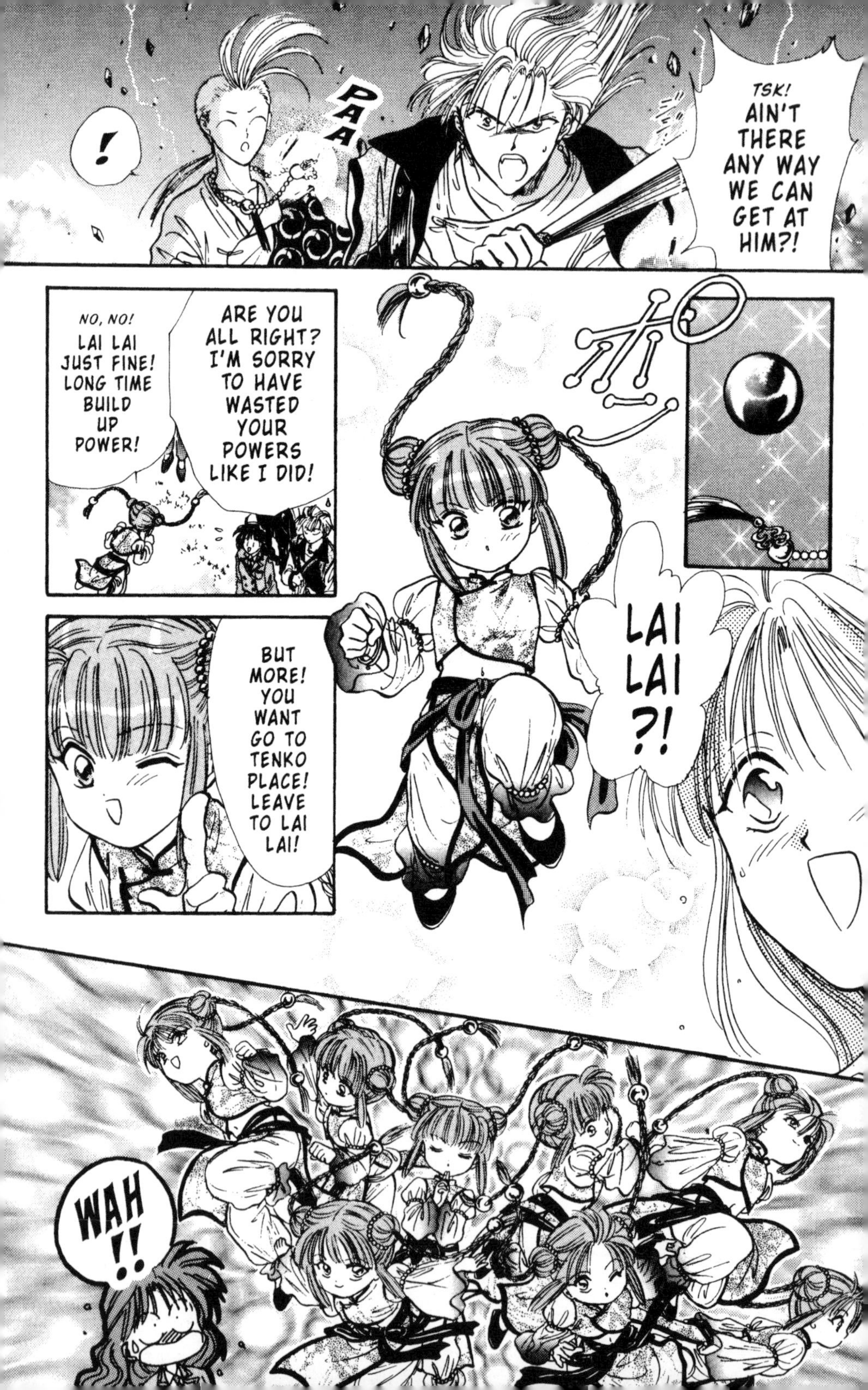
TSK! AIN'T THERE ANY WAY WE CAN GET AT HIM?!
PAA
!
LAI LAI ?!
ARE YOU ALL RIGHT? I'M SORRY TO HAVE WASTED YOUR POWERS LIKE I DID!
NO, NO! LAI LAI JUST FINE! LONG TIME BUILD UP POWER!
BUT MORE! YOU WANT GO TO TENKO PLACE! LEAVE TO LAI LAI!
WAH !!

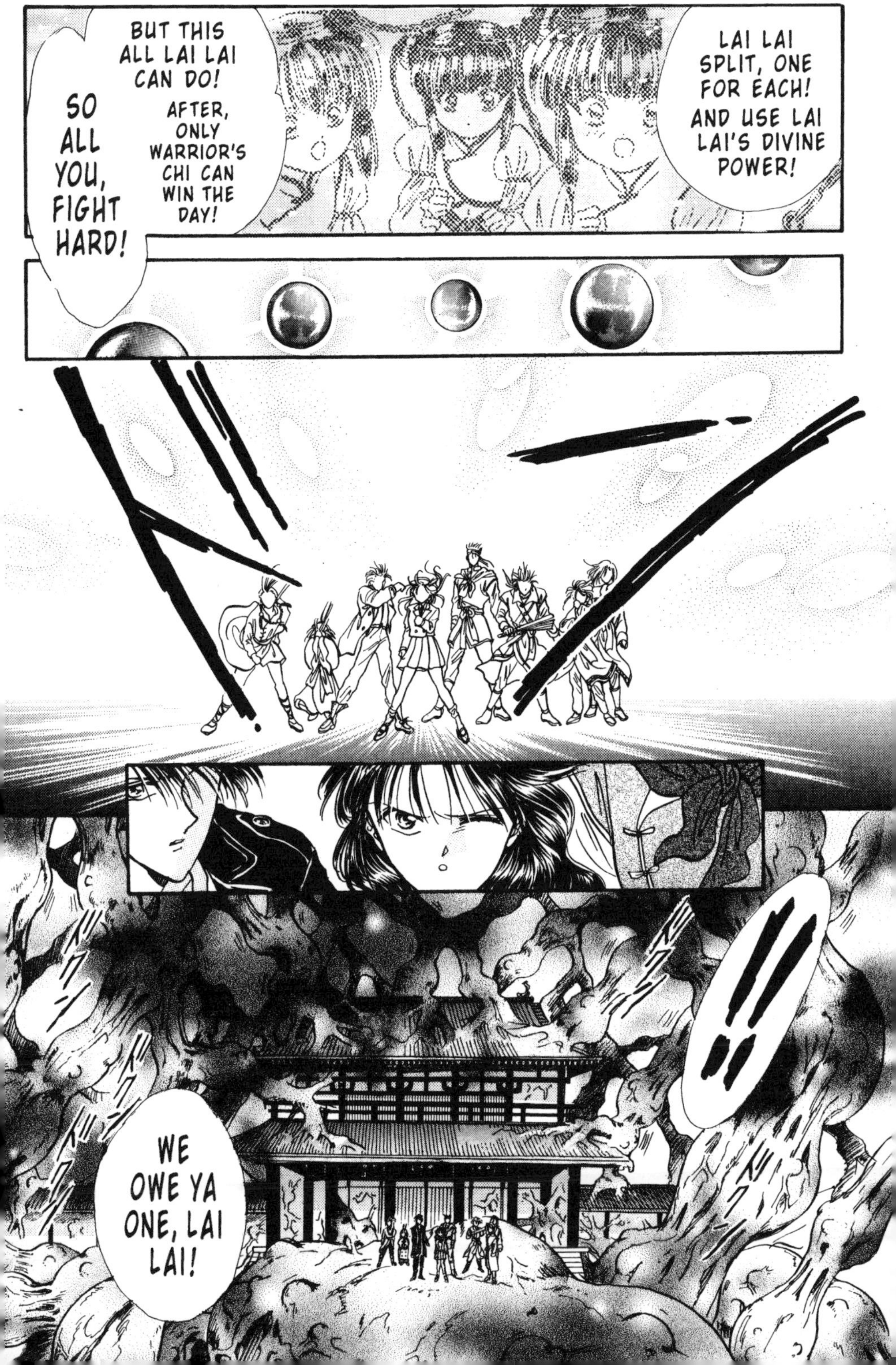
LAI LAI SPLIT, ONE FOR EACH! AND USE LAI LAI'S DIVINE POWER!
BUT THIS ALL LAI LAI CAN DO!
AFTER, ONLY WARRIOR'S CHI CAN WIN THE DAY!
SO ALL YOU, FIGHT HARD!
!!
WE OWE YA ONE, LAI LAI!

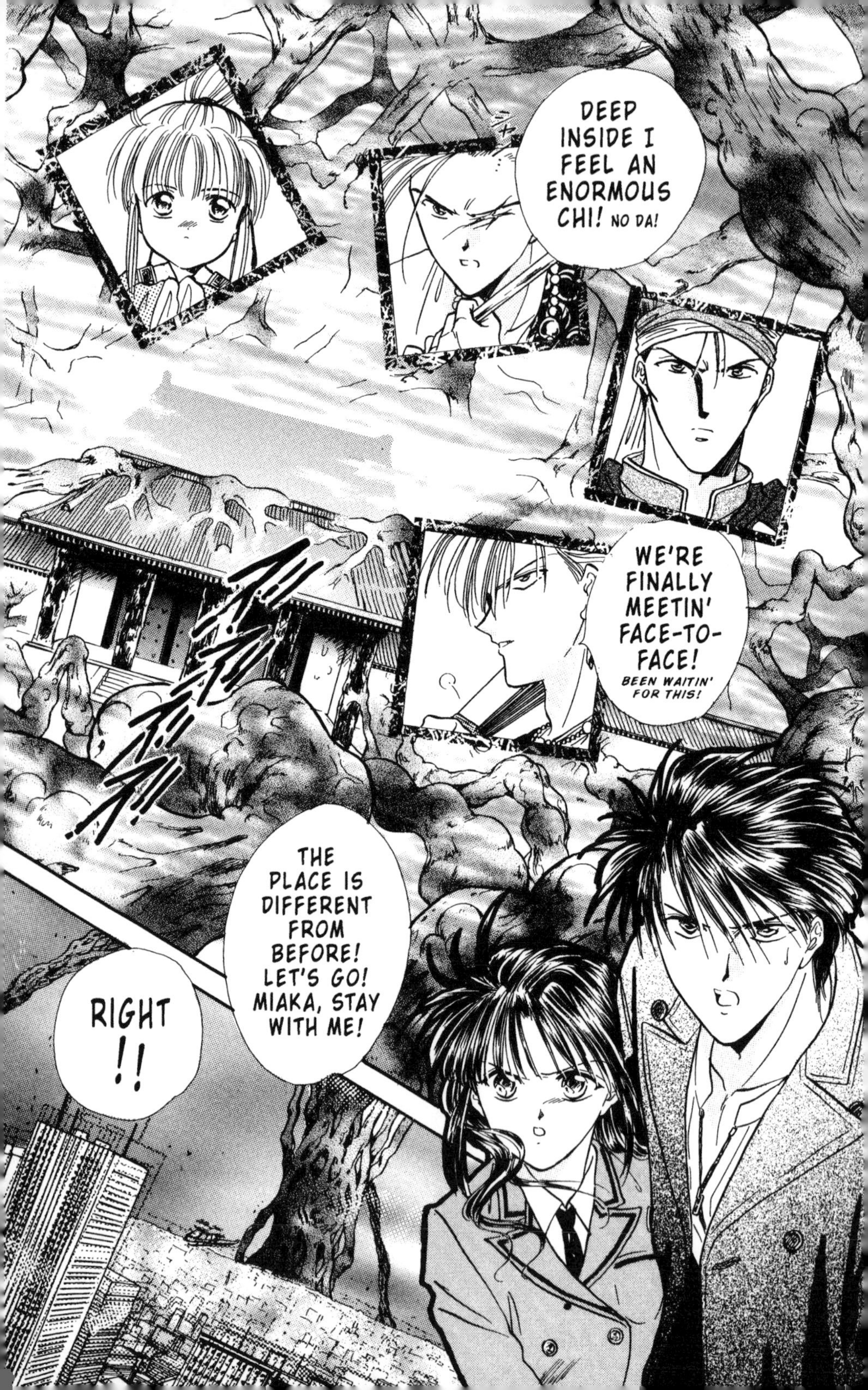
DEEP INSIDE I FEEL AN ENORMOUS CHI! NO DA!
WE'RE FINALLY MEETIN' FACE-TO-FACE! BEEN WAITIN' FOR THIS!
THE PLACE IS DIFFERENT FROM BEFORE! LET'S GO! MIAKA, STAY WITH ME!
RIGHT!!

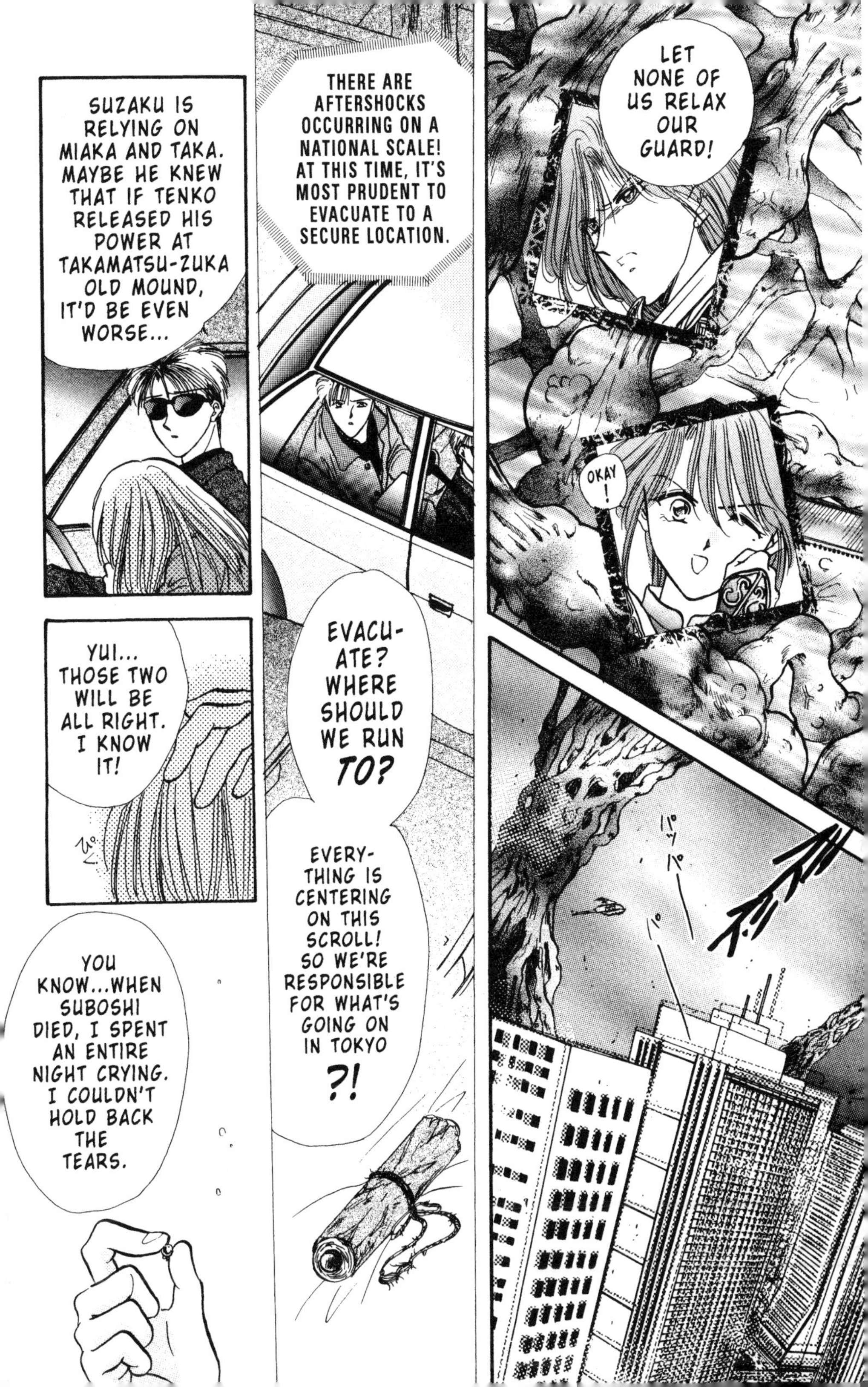
LET NONE OF US RELAX OUR GUARD!
OKAY!
THERE ARE AFTERSHOCKS OCCURRING ON A NATIONAL SCALE! AT THIS TIME, IT'S MOST PRUDENT TO EVACUATE TO A SECURE LOCATION.
EVACU-ATE? WHERE SHOULD WE RUN TO?
EVERY-THING IS CENTERING ON THIS SCROLL! SO WE'RE RESPONSIBLE FOR WHAT'S GOING ON IN TOKYO ?!
SUZAKU IS RELYING ON MIAKA AND TAKA. MAYBE HE KNEW THAT IF TENKO RELEASED HIS POWER AT TAKAMATSU-ZUKA OLD MOUND, IT'D BE EVEN WORSE...
YUI... THOSE TWO WILL BE ALL RIGHT. I KNOW IT!
YOU KNOW...WHEN SUBOSHI DIED, I SPENT AN ENTIRE NIGHT CRYING. I COULDN'T HOLD BACK THE TEARS.

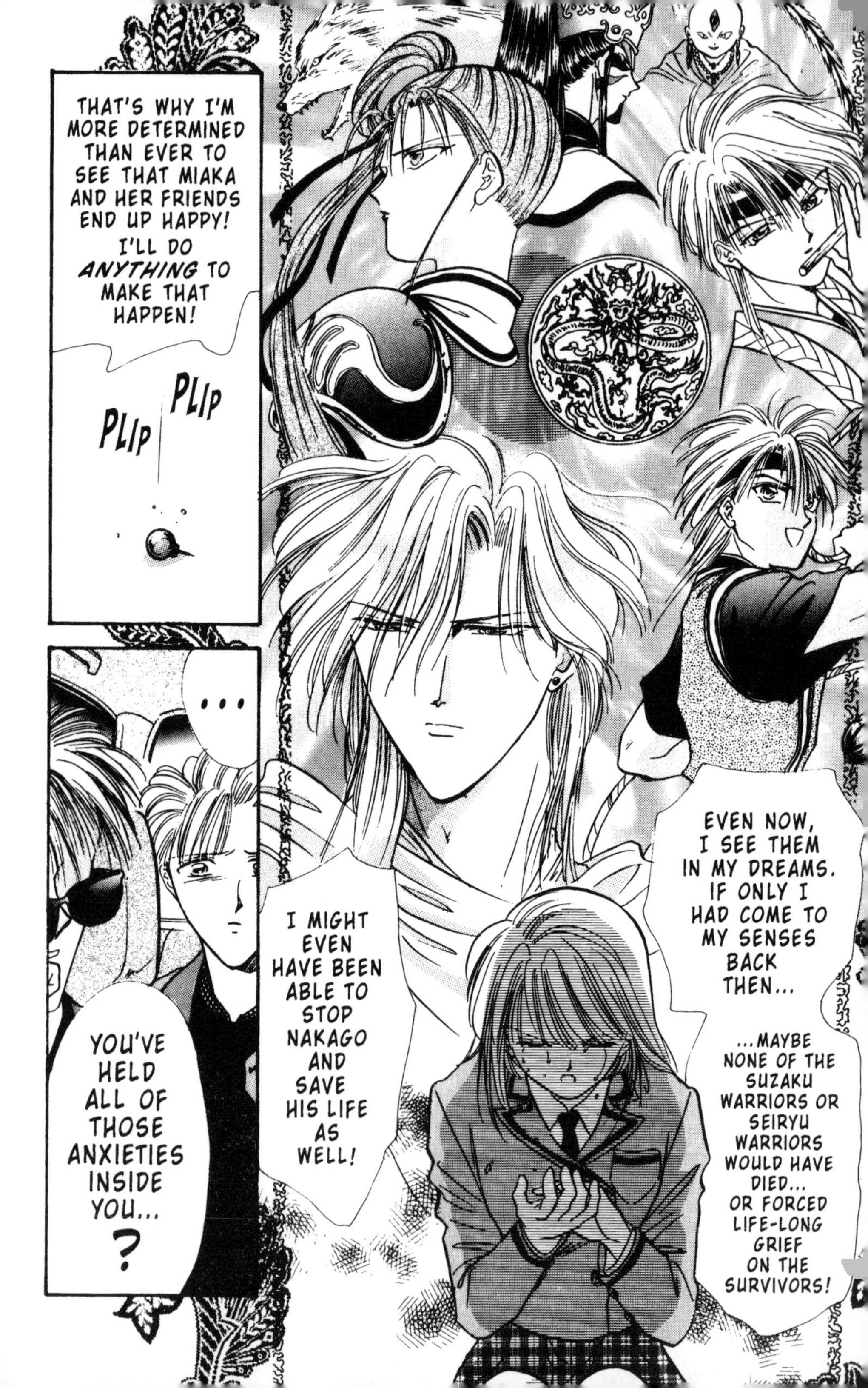
EVEN NOW, I SEE THEM IN MY DREAMS. IF ONLY I HAD COME TO MY SENSES BACK THEN...
...MAYBE NONE OF THE SUZAKU WARRIORS OR SEIRYU WARRIORS WOULD HAVE DIED... OR FORCED LIFE-LONG GRIEF ON THE SURVIVORS!
I MIGHT EVEN HAVE BEEN ABLE TO STOP NAKAGO AND SAVE HIS LIFE AS WELL!
THAT'S WHY I'M MORE DETERMINED THAN EVER TO SEE THAT MIAKA AND HER FRIENDS END UP HAPPY! I'LL DO *ANYTHING* TO MAKE THAT HAPPEN!
PLIP
PLIP
...
YOU'VE HELD ALL OF THOSE ANXIETIES INSIDE YOU...?

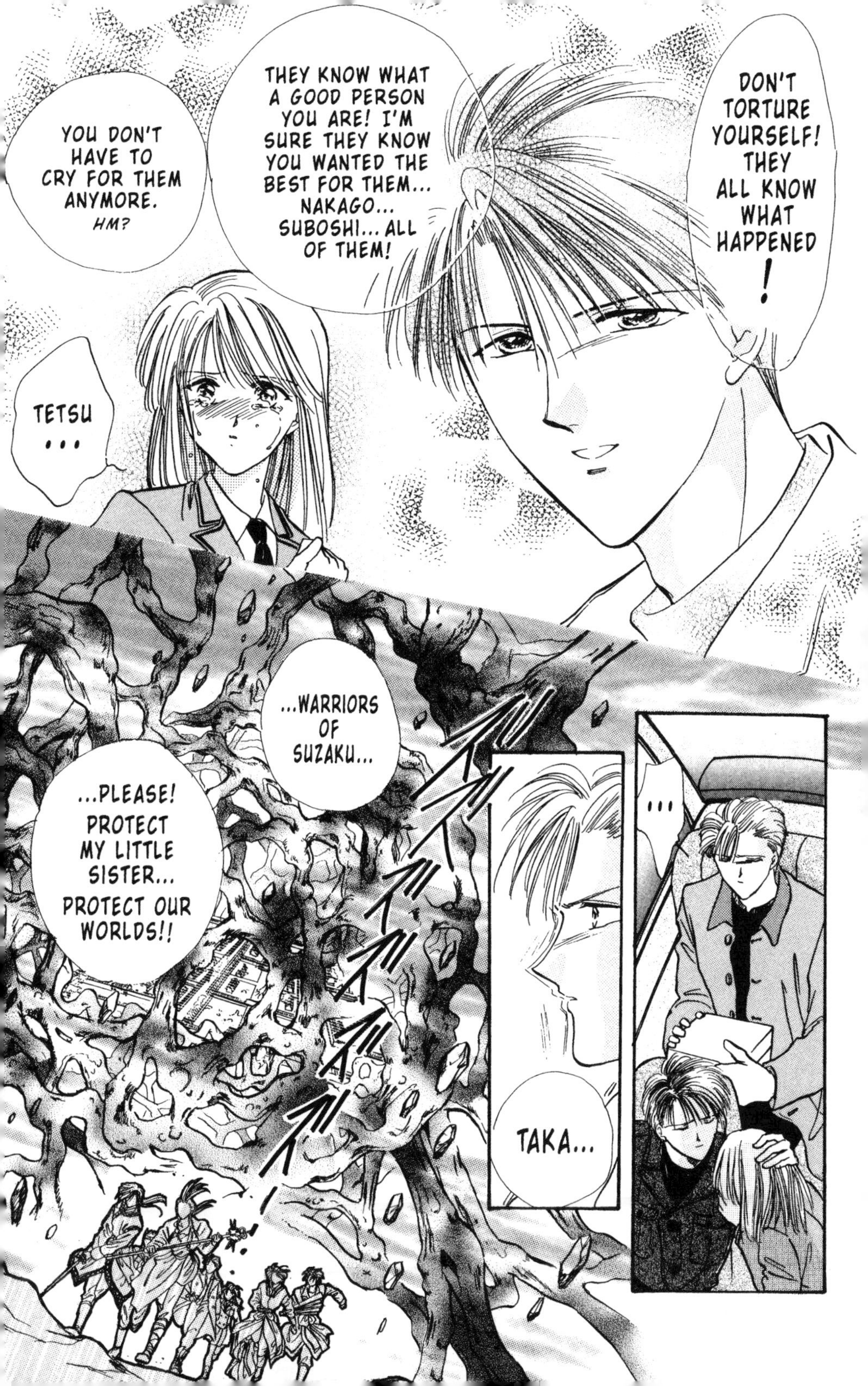
DON'T TORTURE YOURSELF! THEY ALL KNOW WHAT HAPPENED!
THEY KNOW WHAT A GOOD PERSON YOU ARE! I'M SURE THEY KNOW YOU WANTED THE BEST FOR THEM... NAKAGO... SUBOSHI... ALL OF THEM!
YOU DON'T HAVE TO CRY FOR THEM ANYMORE. HM?
TETSU...
...
TAKA...
...WARRIORS OF SUZAKU...
...PLEASE! PROTECT MY LITTLE SISTER... PROTECT OUR WORLDS!!

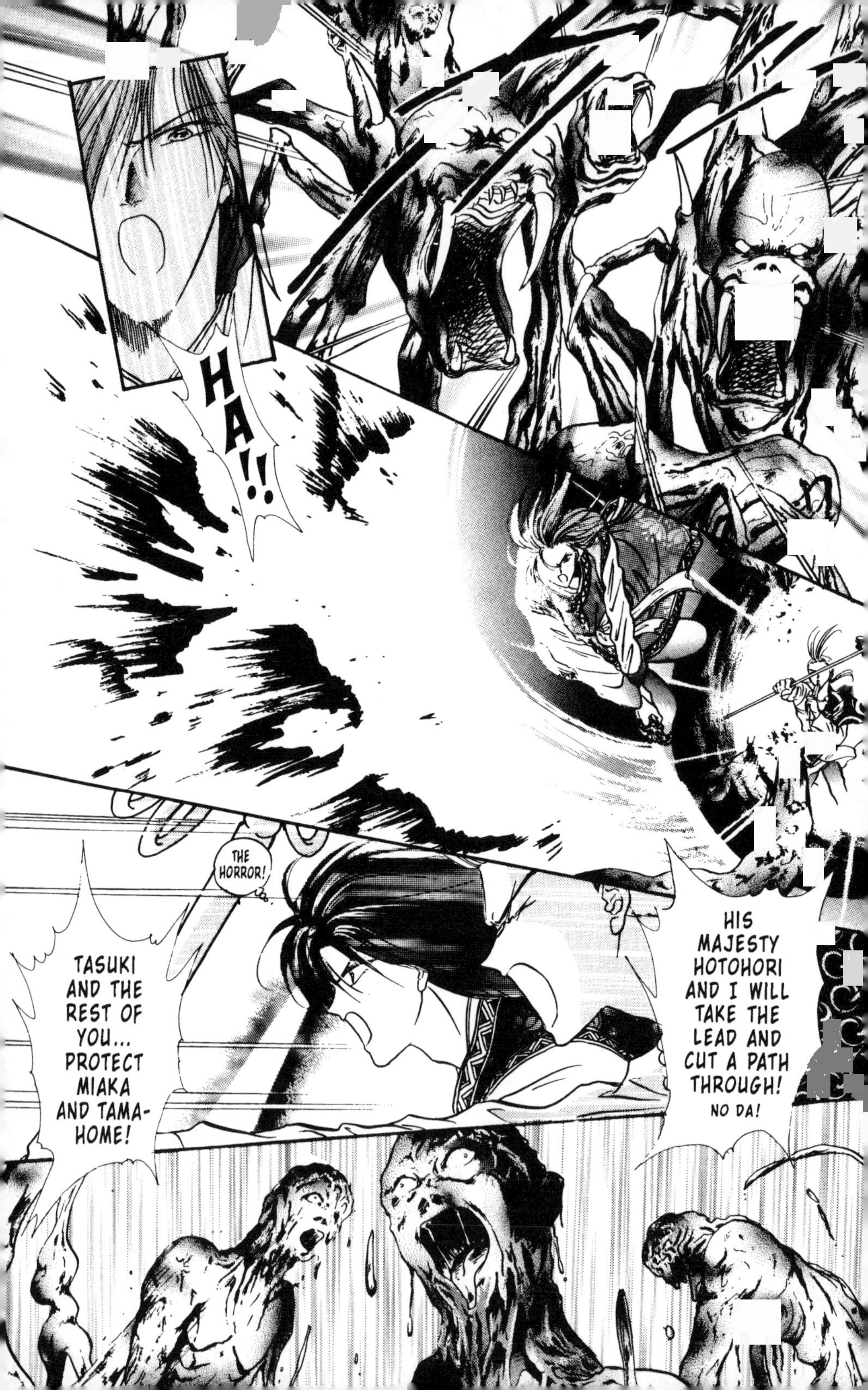
HA!!
HIS MAJESTY HOTOHORI AND I WILL TAKE THE LEAD AND CUT A PATH THROUGH! NO DA!
THE HORROR!
TASUKI AND THE REST OF YOU... PROTECT MIAKA AND TAMA-HOME!

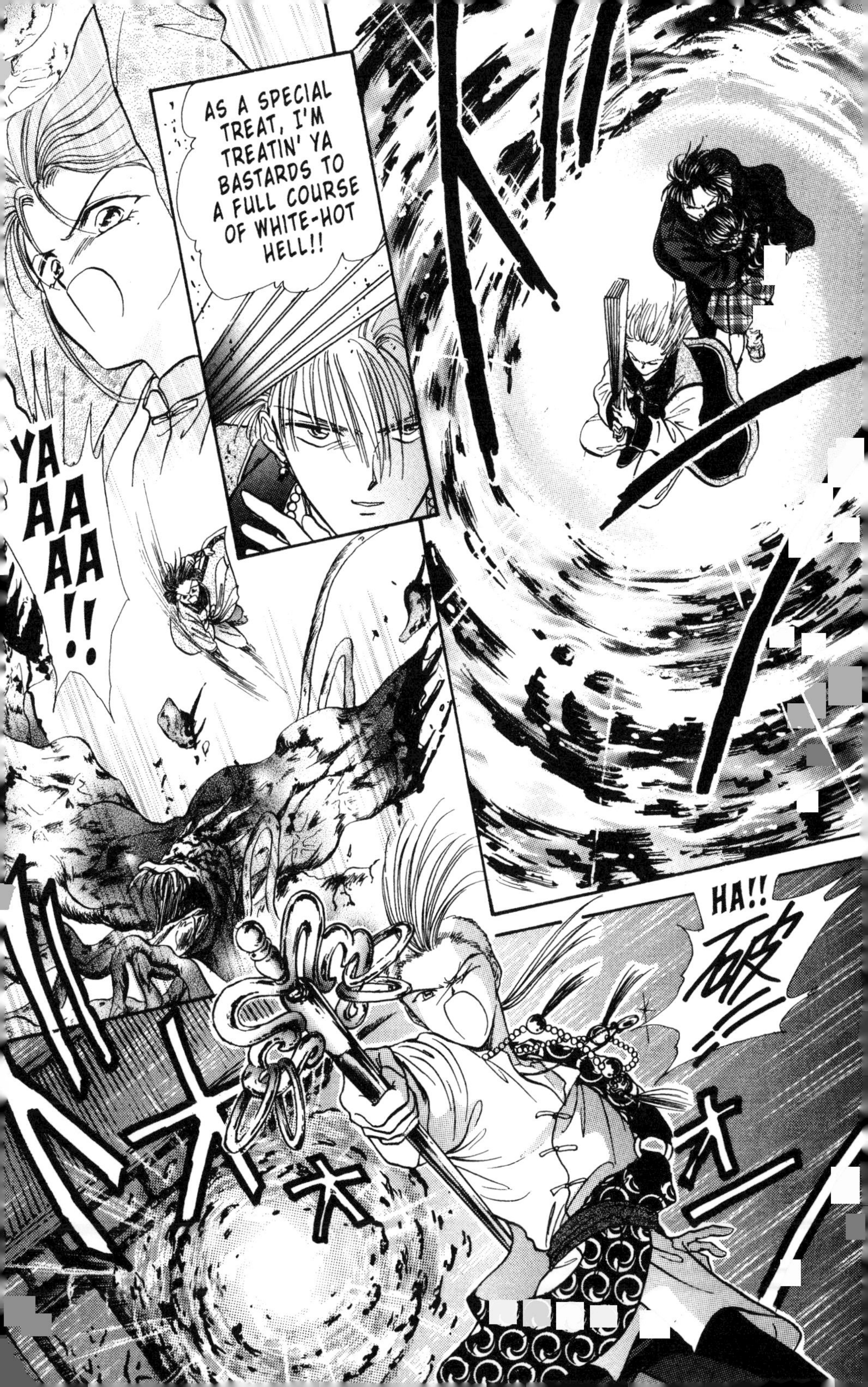
AS A SPECIAL TREAT, I'M TREATIN' YA BASTARDS TO A FULL COURSE OF WHITE-HOT HELL!!
YAAAAA!!
HA!!
破!!

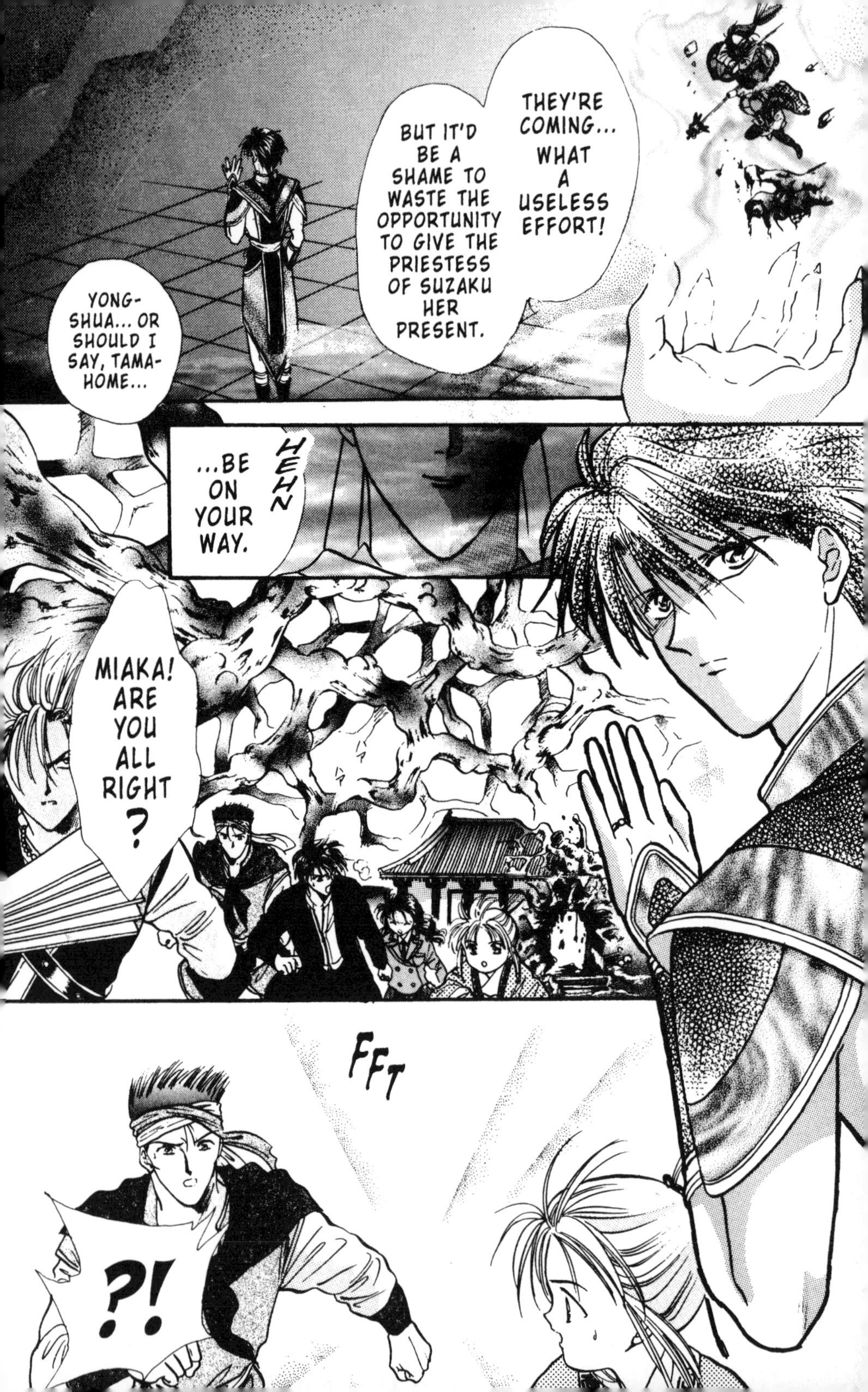
THEY'RE COMING... WHAT A USELESS EFFORT!
BUT IT'D BE A SHAME TO WASTE THE OPPORTUNITY TO GIVE THE PRIESTESS OF SUZAKU HER PRESENT.
YONG-SHUA... OR SHOULD I SAY, TAMA-HOME...
HEHN
...BE ON YOUR WAY.
MIAKA! ARE YOU ALL RIGHT?
FFT
?!

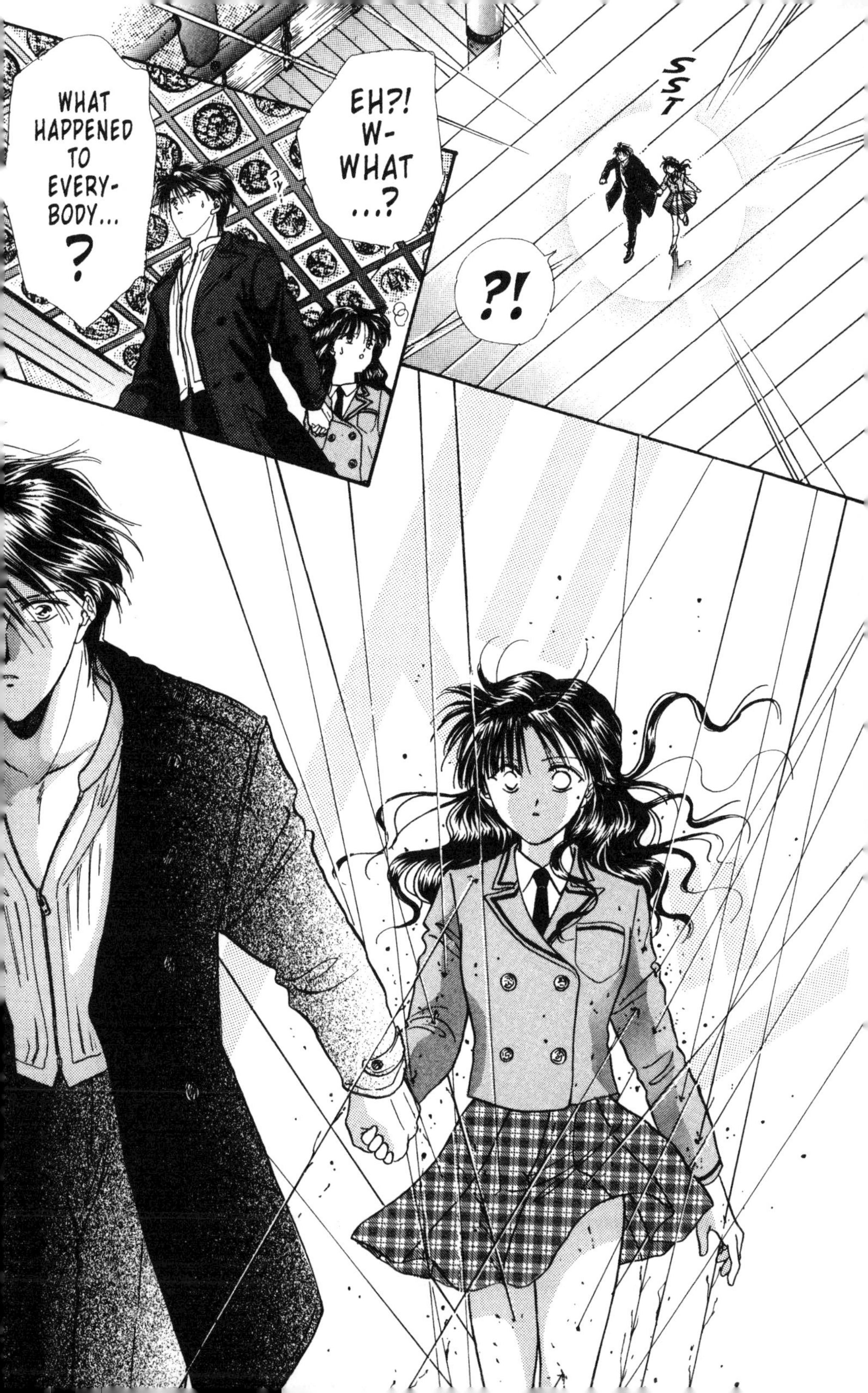
SST
?!
EH?! W-WHAT...?
WHAT HAPPENED TO EVERY-BODY...?

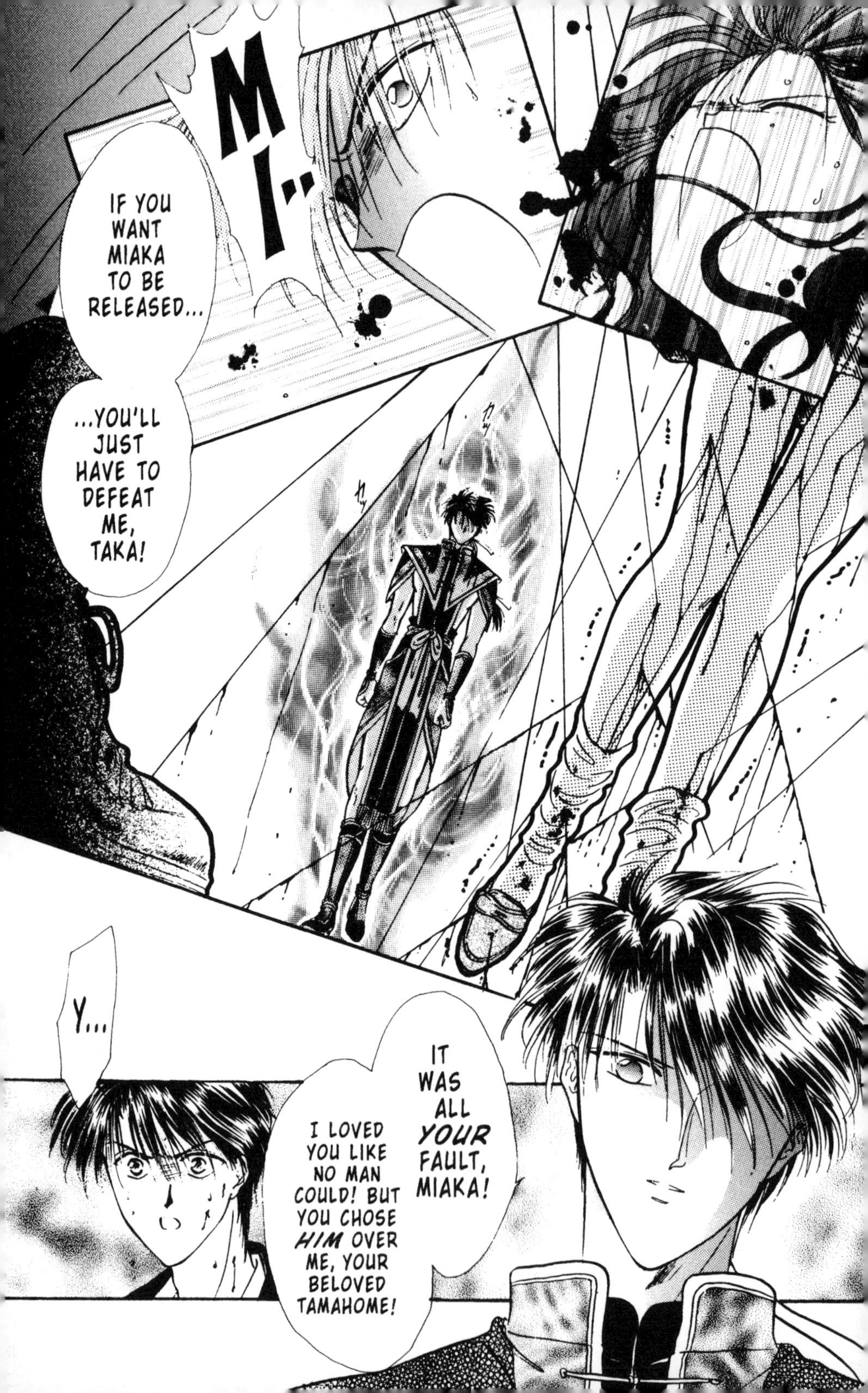
MI..
IF YOU WANT MIAKA TO BE RELEASED...
...YOU'LL JUST HAVE TO DEFEAT ME, TAKA!
IT WAS ALL *YOUR* FAULT, MIAKA!
I LOVED YOU LIKE NO MAN COULD! BUT YOU CHOSE *HIM* OVER ME, YOUR BELOVED TAMAHOME!
Y...

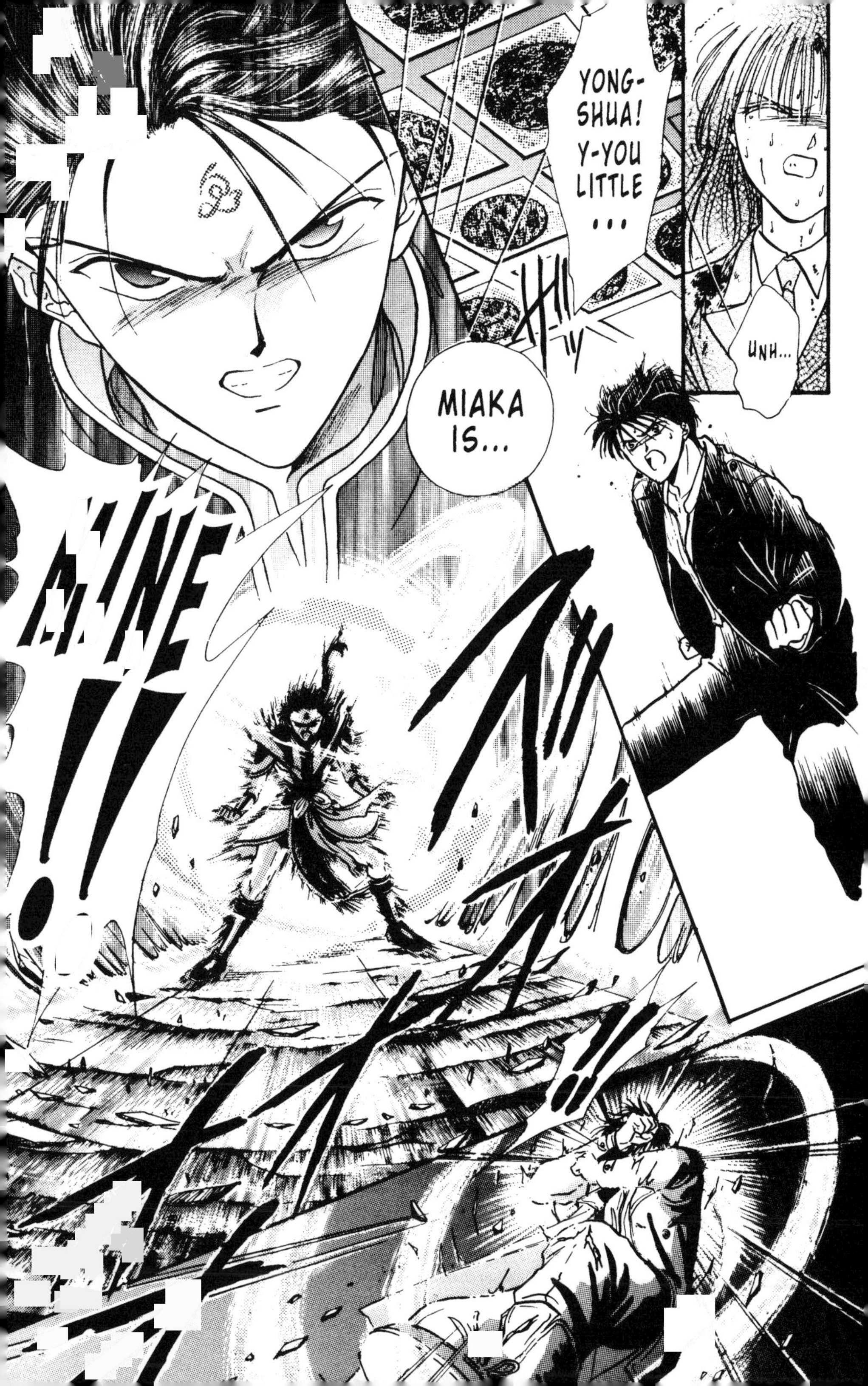
YONG-SHUA! Y-YOU LITTLE...
UNH...
MIAKA IS...
MINE!!

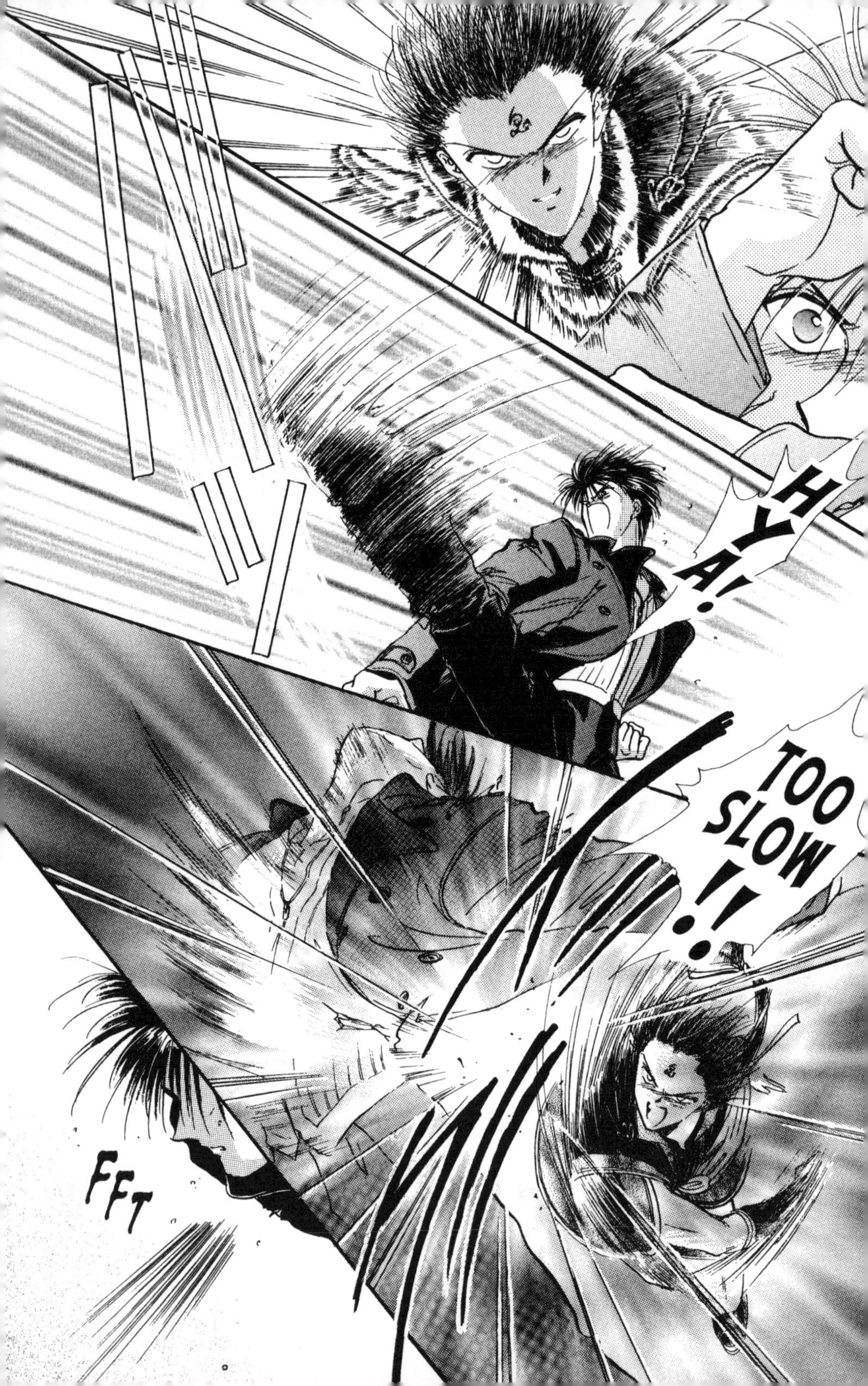
HYA!
TOO SLOW!!
FFT

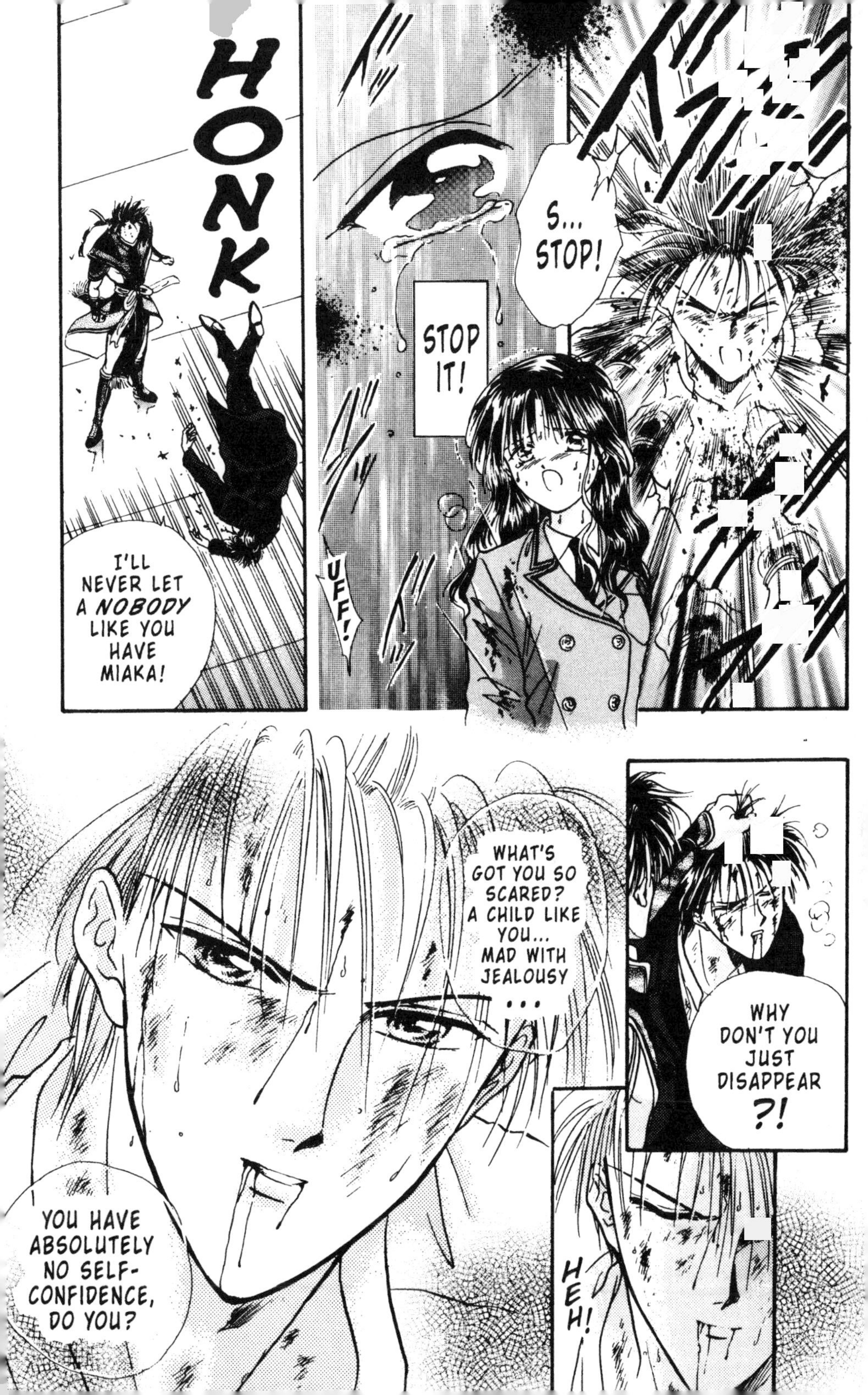
S... STOP!
STOP IT!
UFF!
HONK
I'LL NEVER LET A *NOBODY* LIKE YOU HAVE MIAKA!
WHY DON'T YOU JUST DISAPPEAR ?!
HEH!
WHAT'S GOT YOU SO SCARED? A CHILD LIKE YOU... MAD WITH JEALOUSY ...
YOU HAVE ABSOLUTELY NO SELF-CONFIDENCE, DO YOU?

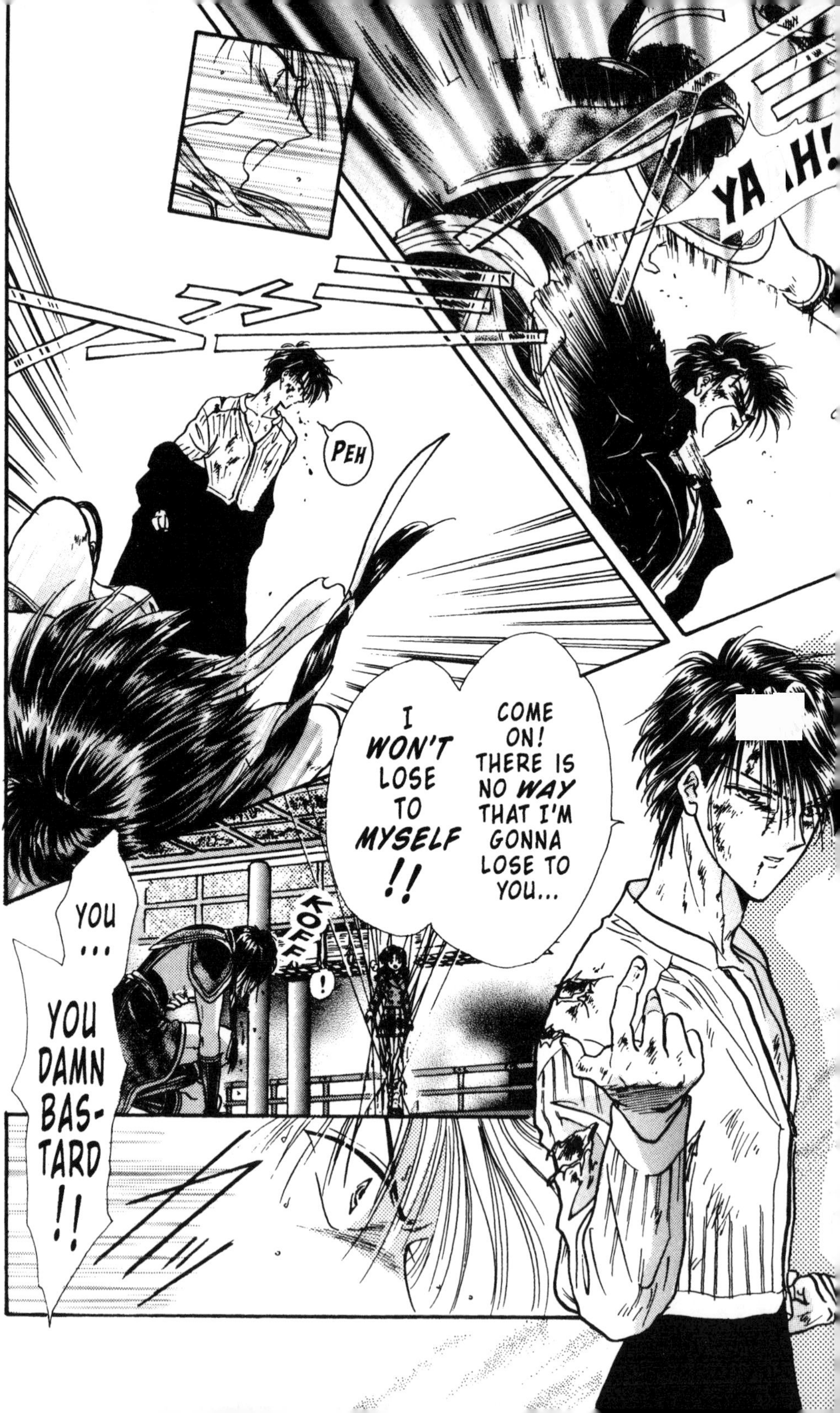
YA H!
PEH
COME ON! THERE IS NO WAY THAT I'M GONNA LOSE TO YOU...
I WON'T LOSE TO MYSELF!!
KOFF
!
YOU... YOU DAMN BASTARD!!

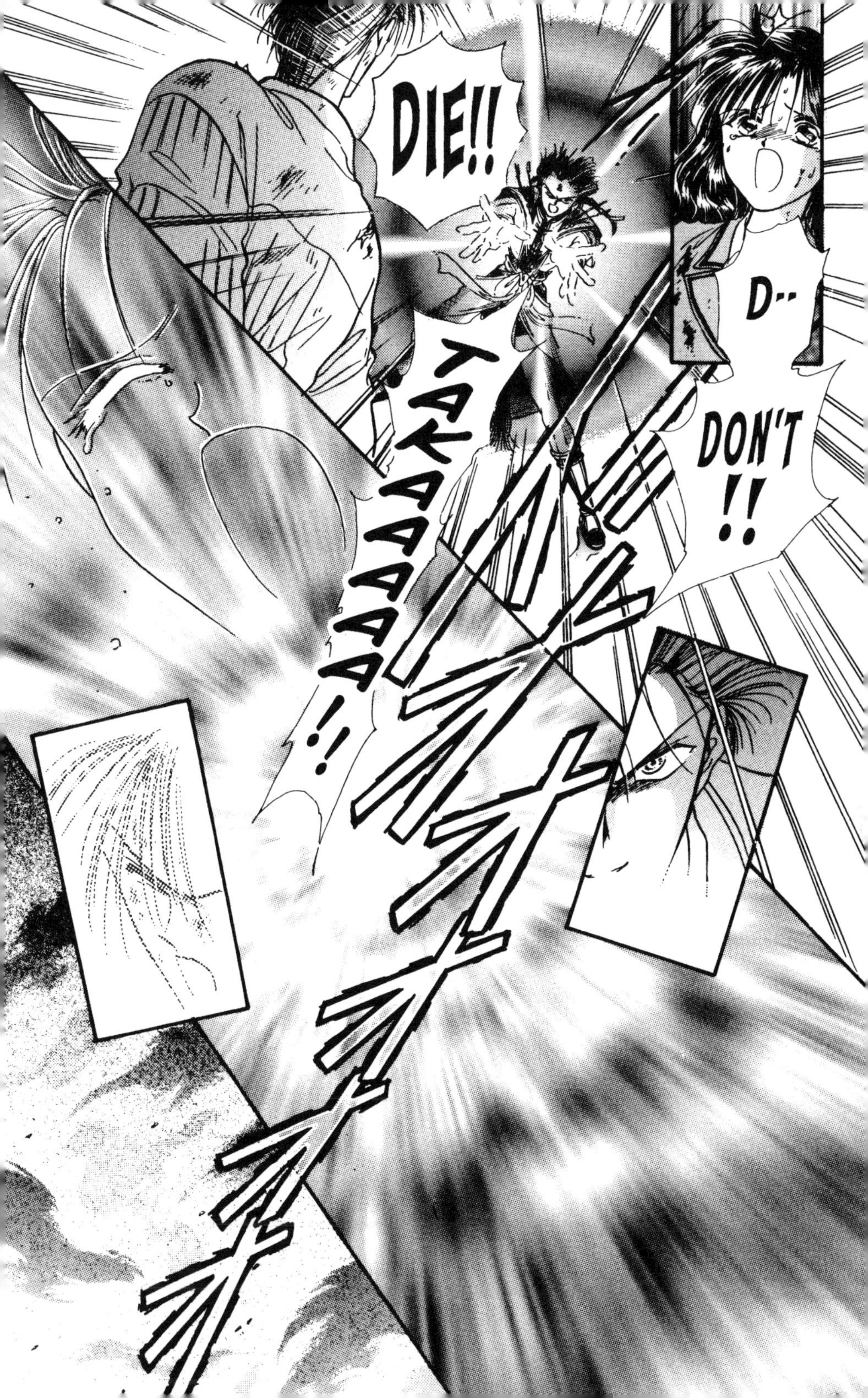
D--
DON'T!!
DIE!!
TAKAAAAAAA!!

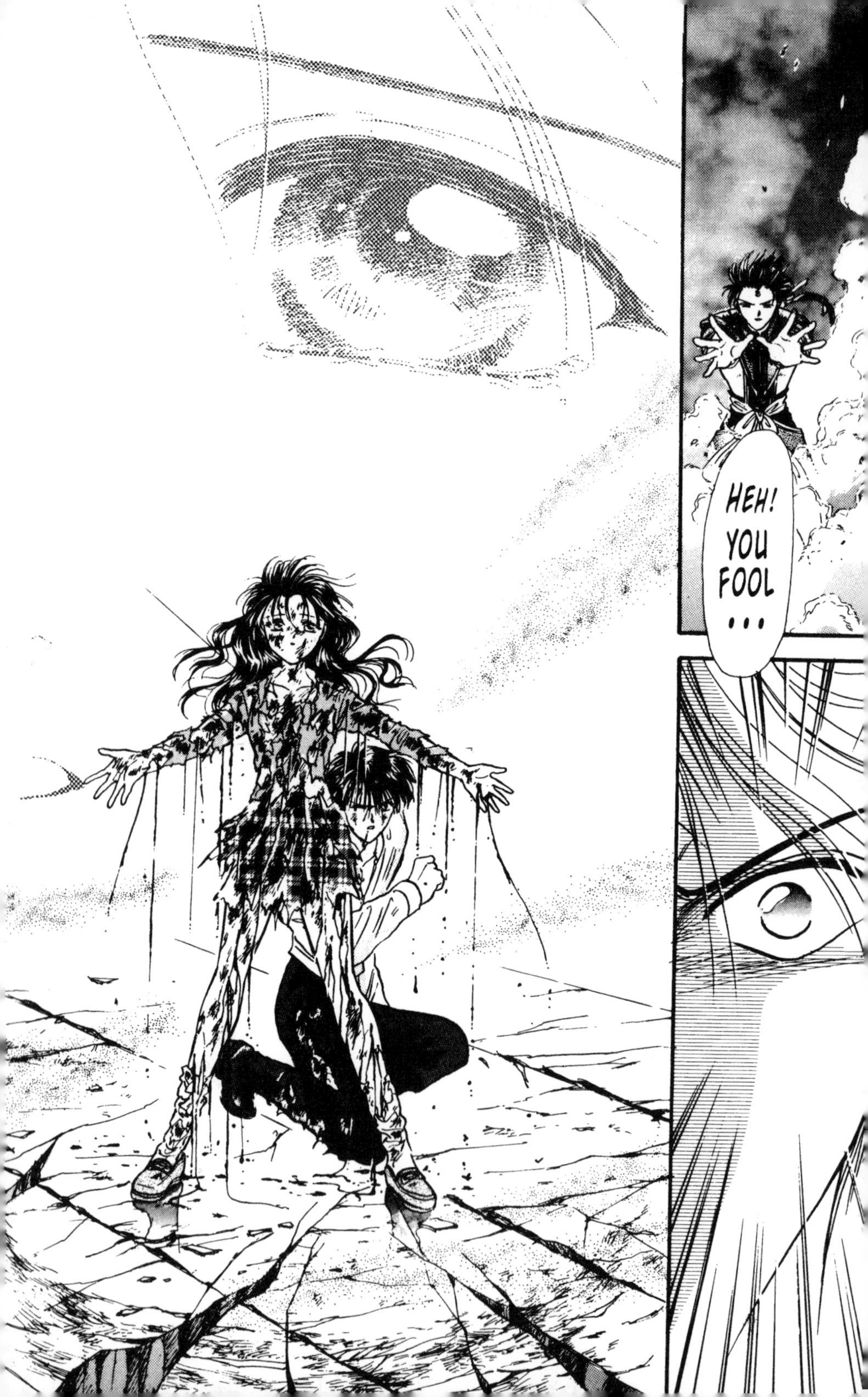
HEH! YOU FOOL ...

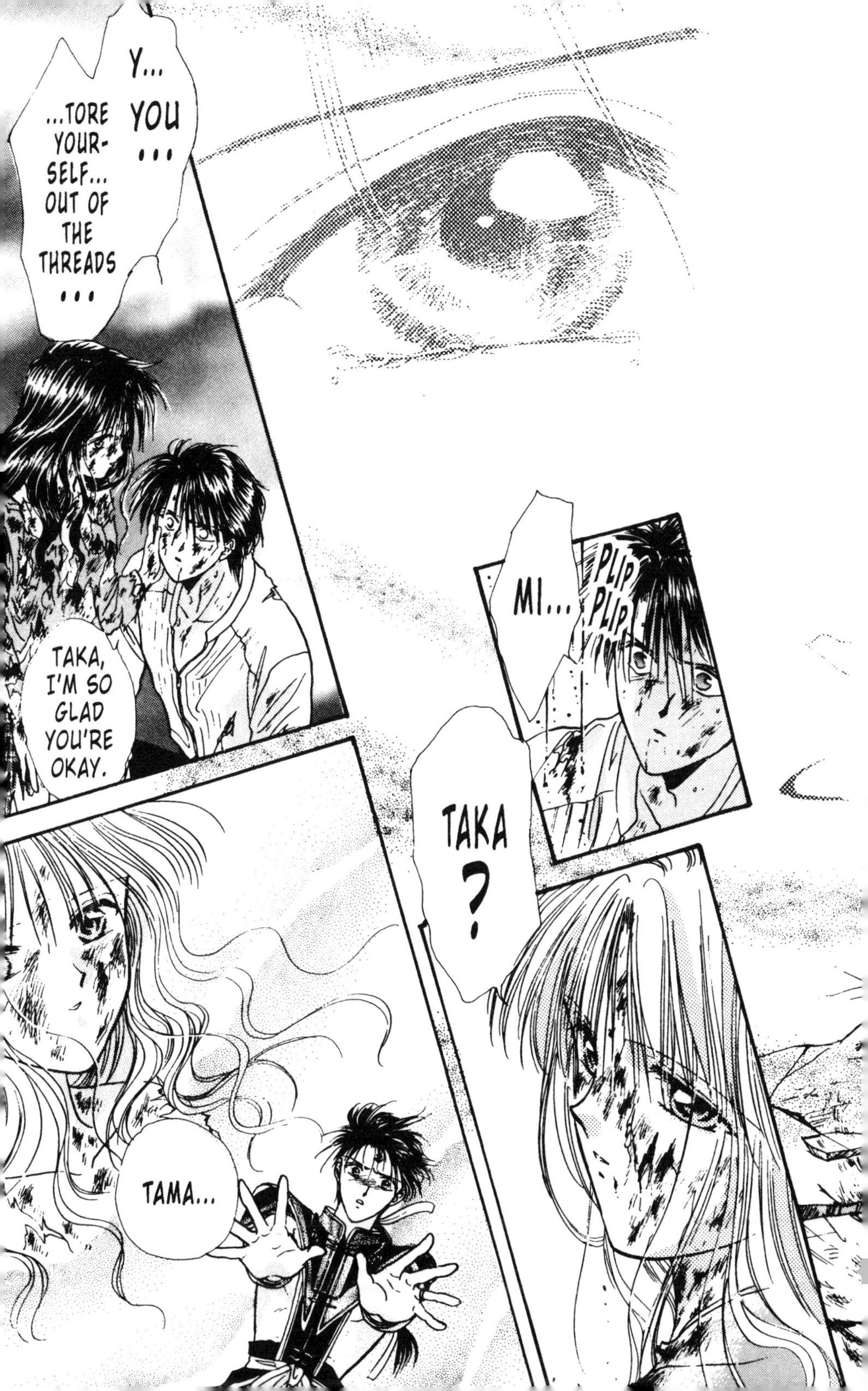

Y... YOU...
...TORE YOURSELF... OUT OF THE THREADS...
TAKA, I'M SO GLAD YOU'RE OKAY.
PLIP PLIP
MI...
TAKA?
TAMA...

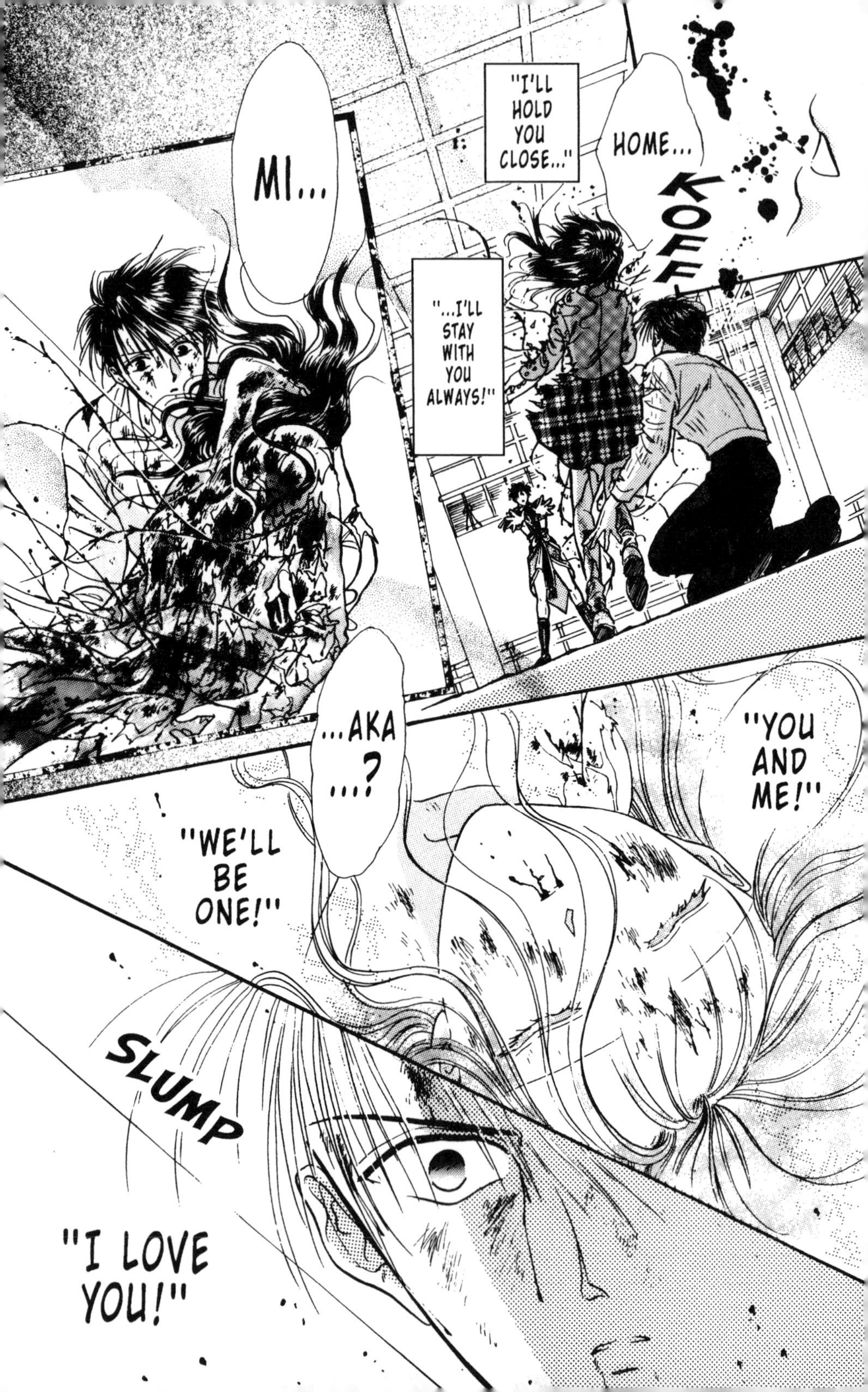
HOME...
KOFF
"I'LL HOLD YOU CLOSE..."
"...I'LL STAY WITH YOU ALWAYS!"
MI...
"YOU AND ME!"
...AKA ...?
"WE'LL BE ONE!"
SLUMP
"I LOVE YOU!"

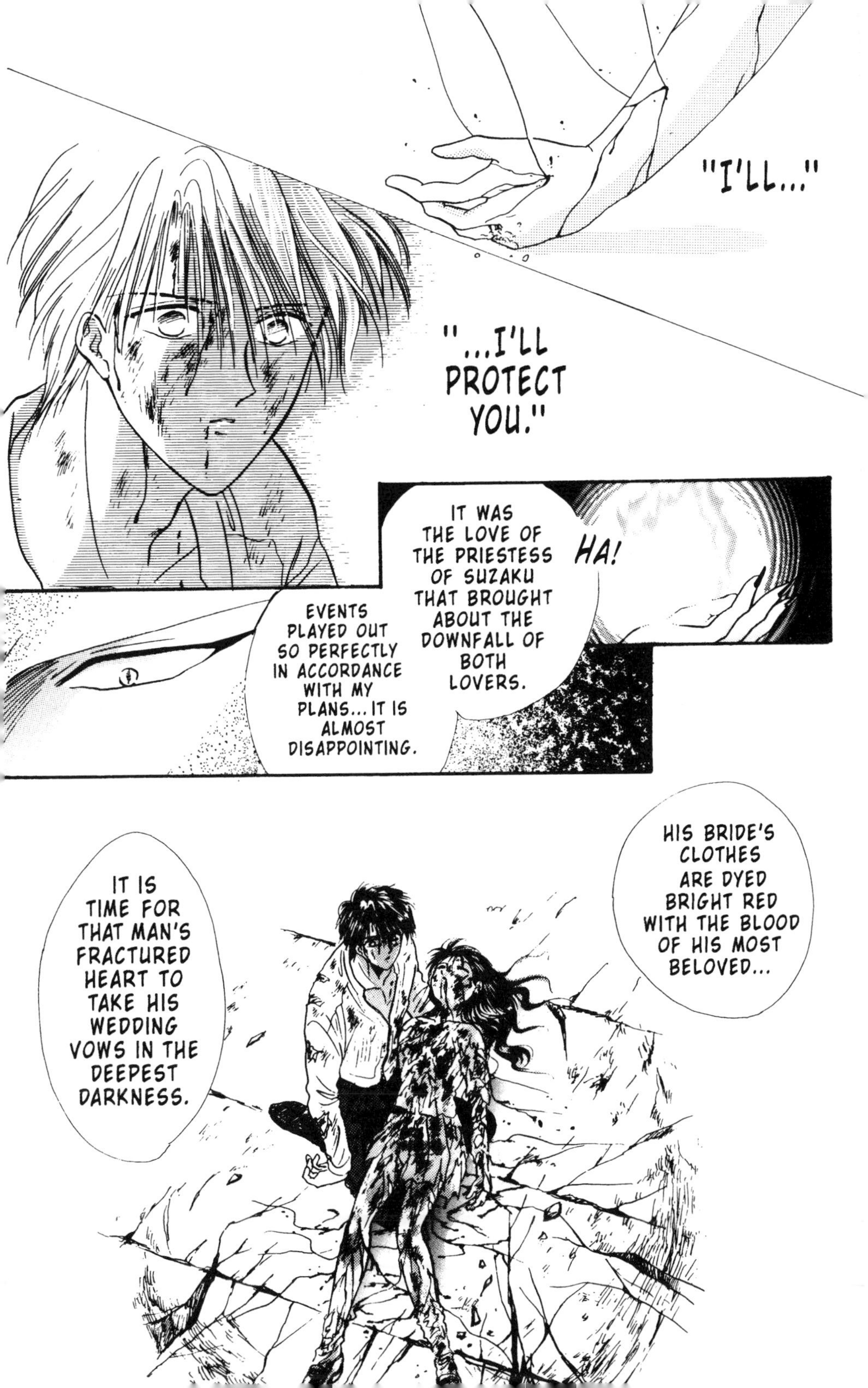
"I'LL..."
"...I'LL PROTECT YOU."
HA!
IT WAS THE LOVE OF THE PRIESTESS OF SUZAKU THAT BROUGHT ABOUT THE DOWNFALL OF BOTH LOVERS.
EVENTS PLAYED OUT SO PERFECTLY IN ACCORDANCE WITH MY PLANS... IT IS ALMOST DISAPPOINTING.
HIS BRIDE'S CLOTHES ARE DYED BRIGHT RED WITH THE BLOOD OF HIS MOST BELOVED...
IT IS TIME FOR THAT MAN'S FRACTURED HEART TO TAKE HIS WEDDING VOWS IN THE DEEPEST DARKNESS.

NAKAGO...

At a meeting, I had decided that I would have him live until nearly the very end. I was determined for him to be the villain (it didn't quite work). Maybe that's the reason why he's the most controversial character among readers, with fans having so many different mental images of him. (I thought so!) Anyway, to me, Nakago is both sad and lonely. He's the fragile little boy who cries in the darkness. Others call him "a big bad guy," or "cool and strong"... Actually, lots of different things. But Nakago is, even now, extremely popular (in Part 1 he was unstoppable!☺) It seems that there are a lot of people who, when reading what happened at the end, went, "Wow!"

Nakago said that he wants to "become a god," and that he wants to "control the world," but really, that was just him trying his hardest to figure out a purpose that would allow him to go on living. In reality, his heart was a complete void. Even if he wanted to die, he couldn't figure out a death where his mother would be on the other side waiting for him... so he couldn't die yet. It's very possible that he hated himself when he lost control of his power, and he even probably was glad his defeat came at the hands of Tamahome (a man who, unlike himself, had a heart that was straight and true). When Yui was questioning Nakago, he probably could easily have lied, but at the time, he just didn't care anymore. I think the scene of Ashitare's death was still playing out in his head. What Ashitare did broke a few centimeters through the armor that surrounds Nakago's heart.

A 12.3-year-old reader wrote a letter saying something to the effect of, "I once said that there was no other place for Nakago to go but Hell, but now I don't think so. Hell is a place where not even one person loves you." As a woman, I can't help but believe that a woman's emotions and actions that are powerful enough to move the heart of a man are incredibly important to their relationship. Nakago has been said to have an enormous sadness... Still, the image of Nakago that persists within me isn't of a strong person at all. That's why, even though he played the role of the bad guy, he wasn't a bad person. While I was drawing Part 2, I came to this realization about Part 1: The strong ones were the girls. They gave a love as strong as that fabled mother's love to their men. Now that's strong!

● INFORMATION! (CIRCA 1996)

● Speaking of Nakago... On July 25, the "Fushigi Yūgi Special" Parts 1 & 2 will come out on video!! (2900 yen.) This one will sell out quick! It covers a lot of ground, and it has a short animated segment for "Nakago Shikkari-shinasai!" ("Hang In There, Nakago!") Let's all watch how pathetic he can be! ☺

● For October, they're planning a series of videos (bonus animation and funny stuff) with Suboshi and Amiboshi...? Tomo and Nakago and Tenko and a super-sexy Tamahome... Everything you've been waiting for! The story is supposed to take place between Parts 1 & 2, and you might be surprised and shout out, "Huh? THAT happened?!"

● Be sure to pick up the very last CD Book, "Eien Wo Ai Ni" (Eternal I Love You)! It's a CD, but it also comes with an old jewel case that came out during an "All That Sho-Comi" event at Animate.

● Also, there are anime CDs, soundtracks, "Itoshii Hito no Tame ni" (for the One I Love) off of a mini album by Akemi Sato, "Seiryu no Gyakushu-hen" (Revenge of the Seiryu Warriors), and songs, and drama disks... a huge number of really great CDs out there! Get them at your neighborhood CD shop. They say they're going to release soundtrack CDs for the OAVs! I'm really looking forward to them! ♫

One other thing. According to my assistants, the Fushigi Yūgi theme song for Part 1 is trf's "Boy Meets Girl" (Remix ●3). Take a listen!

I'm also hooked on "Access"!

Mr. Furusawa (the man who played Nakago in the anime) once told me, "I think that Nakago actually loved Soi. And that's how I played the part." Maybe now they're happy together.

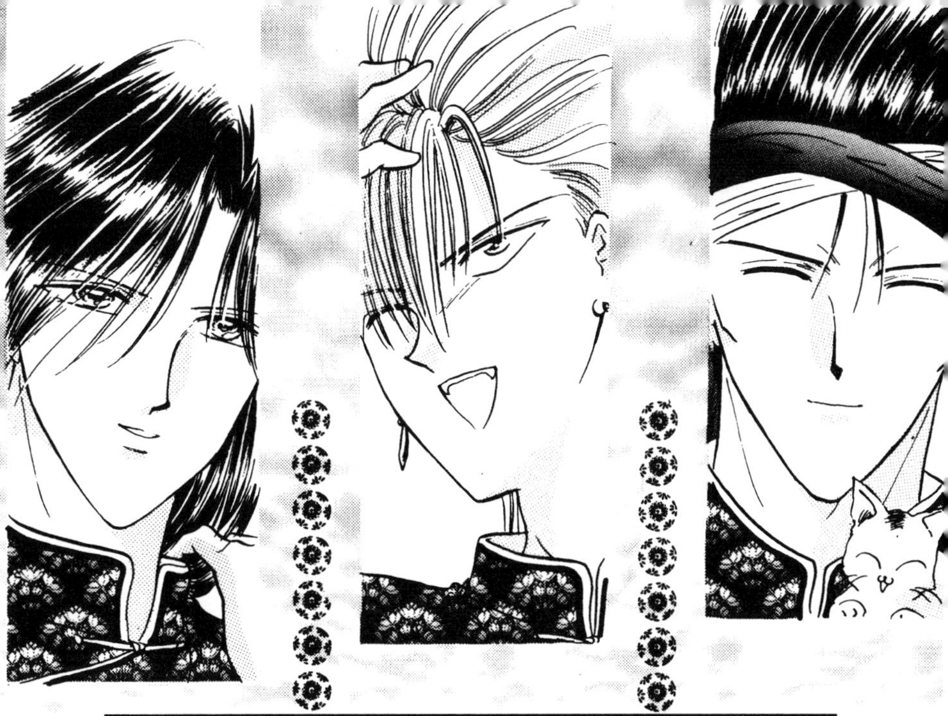

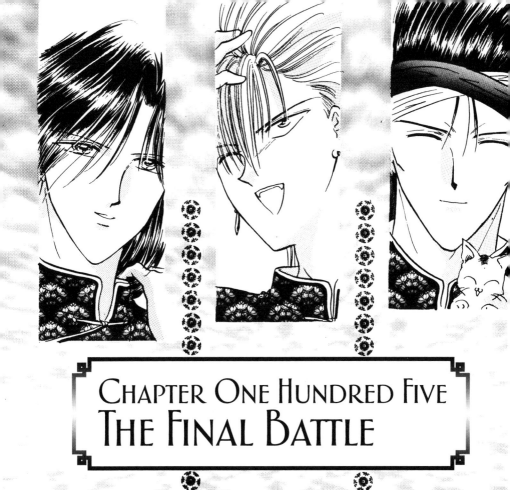

Chapter One Hundred Five
The Final Battle

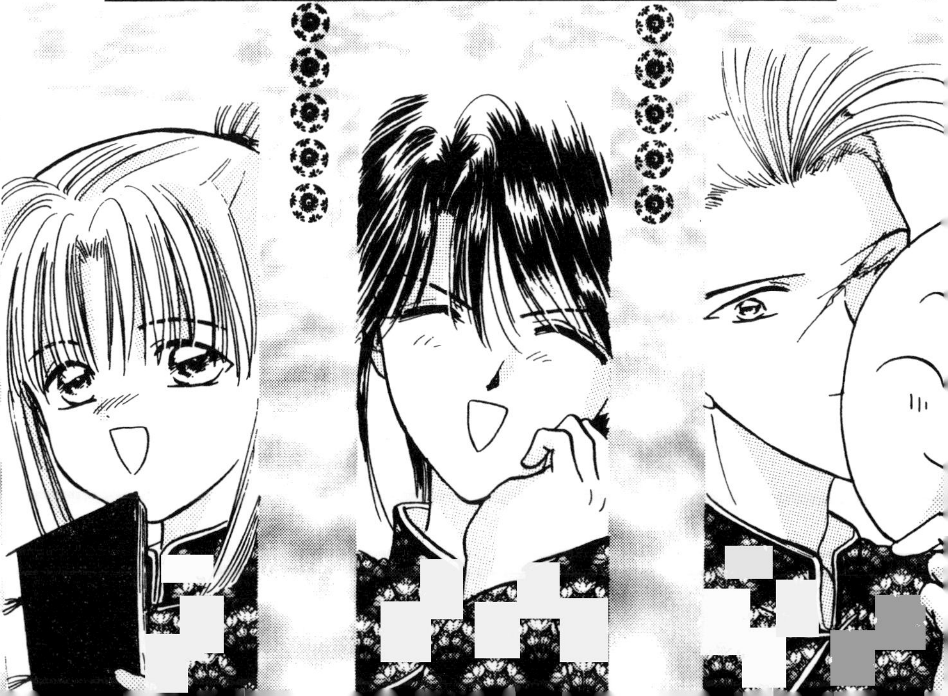

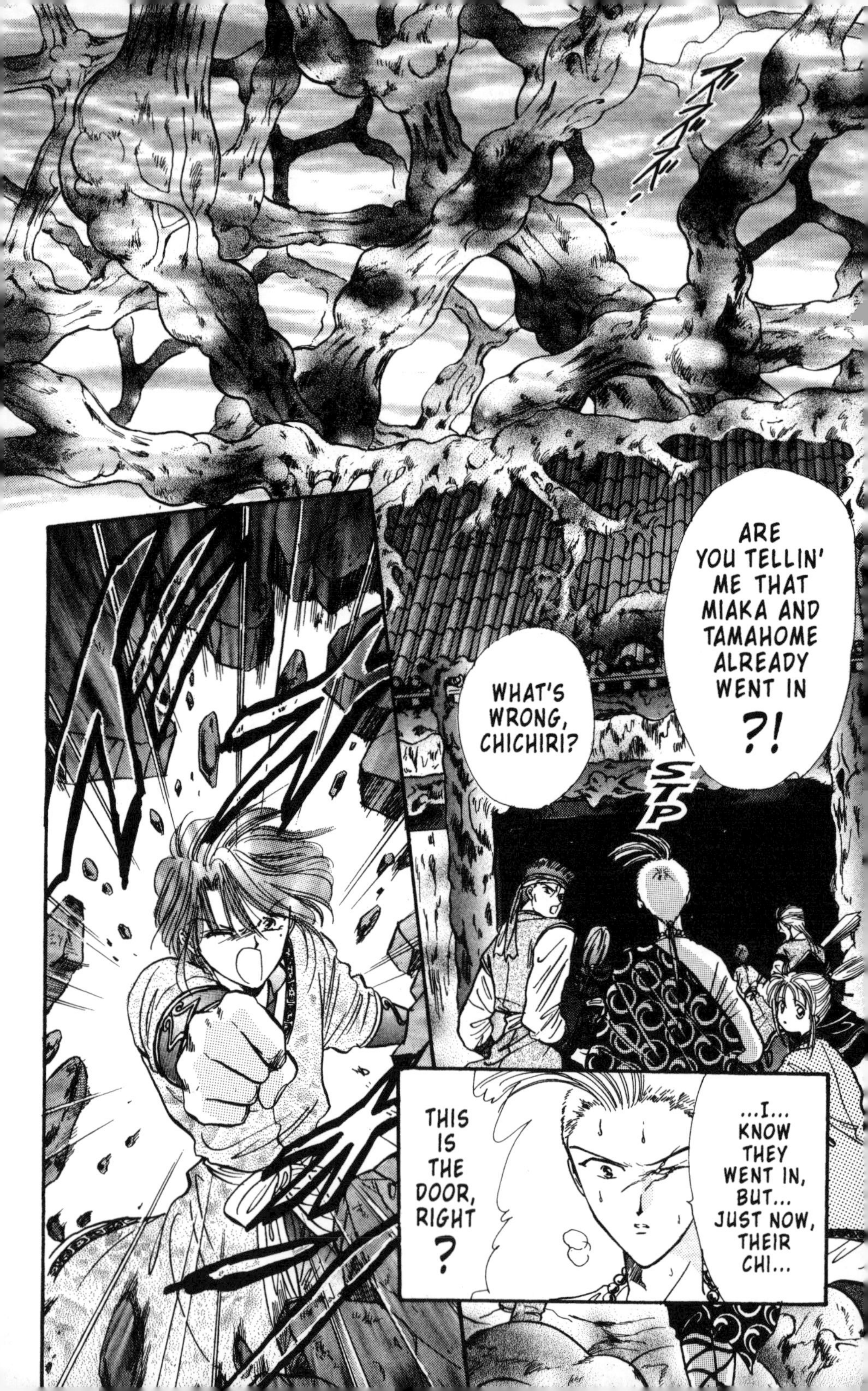
ARE YOU TELLIN' ME THAT MIAKA AND TAMAHOME ALREADY WENT IN ?!
WHAT'S WRONG, CHICHIRI?
STP
...I... KNOW THEY WENT IN, BUT... JUST NOW, THEIR CHI...
THIS IS THE DOOR, RIGHT?

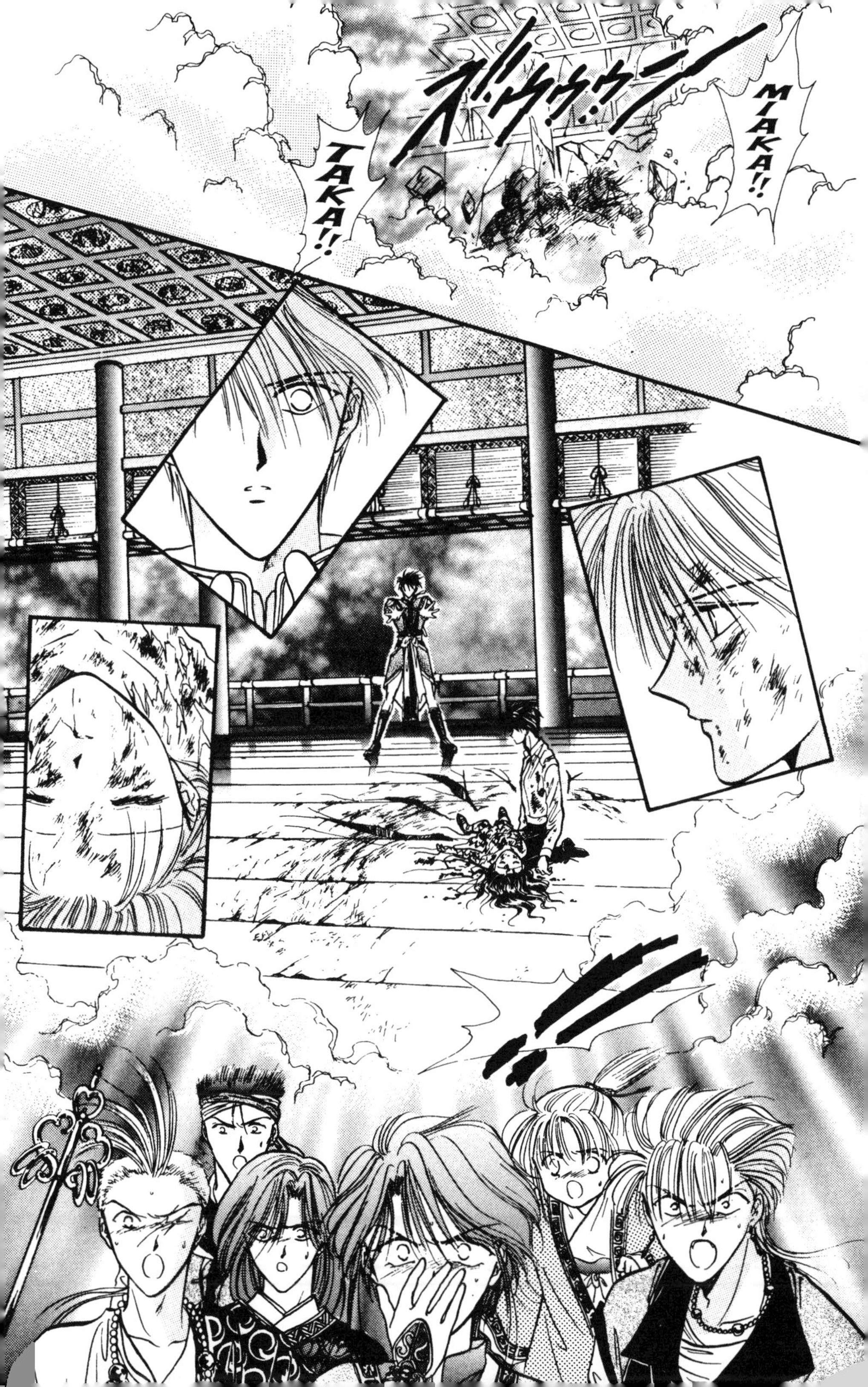

MIAKA!!
ズバウウウン
TAKA!!

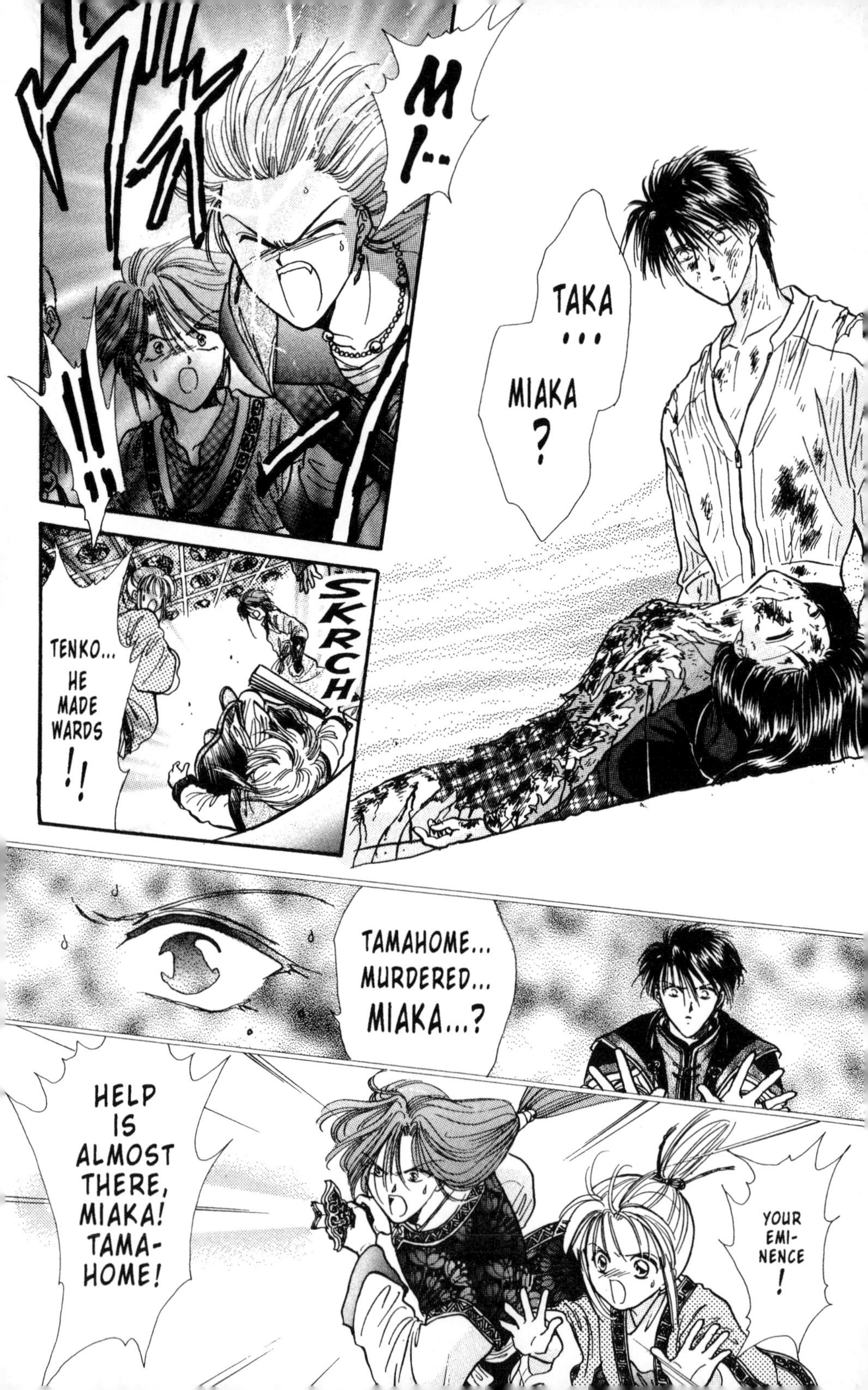
TAKA... MIAKA?
M!...
!!
TENKO... HE MADE WARDS!!
SKRCH
TAMAHOME... MURDERED... MIAKA...?
YOUR EMI-NENCE!
HELP IS ALMOST THERE, MIAKA! TAMA-HOME!

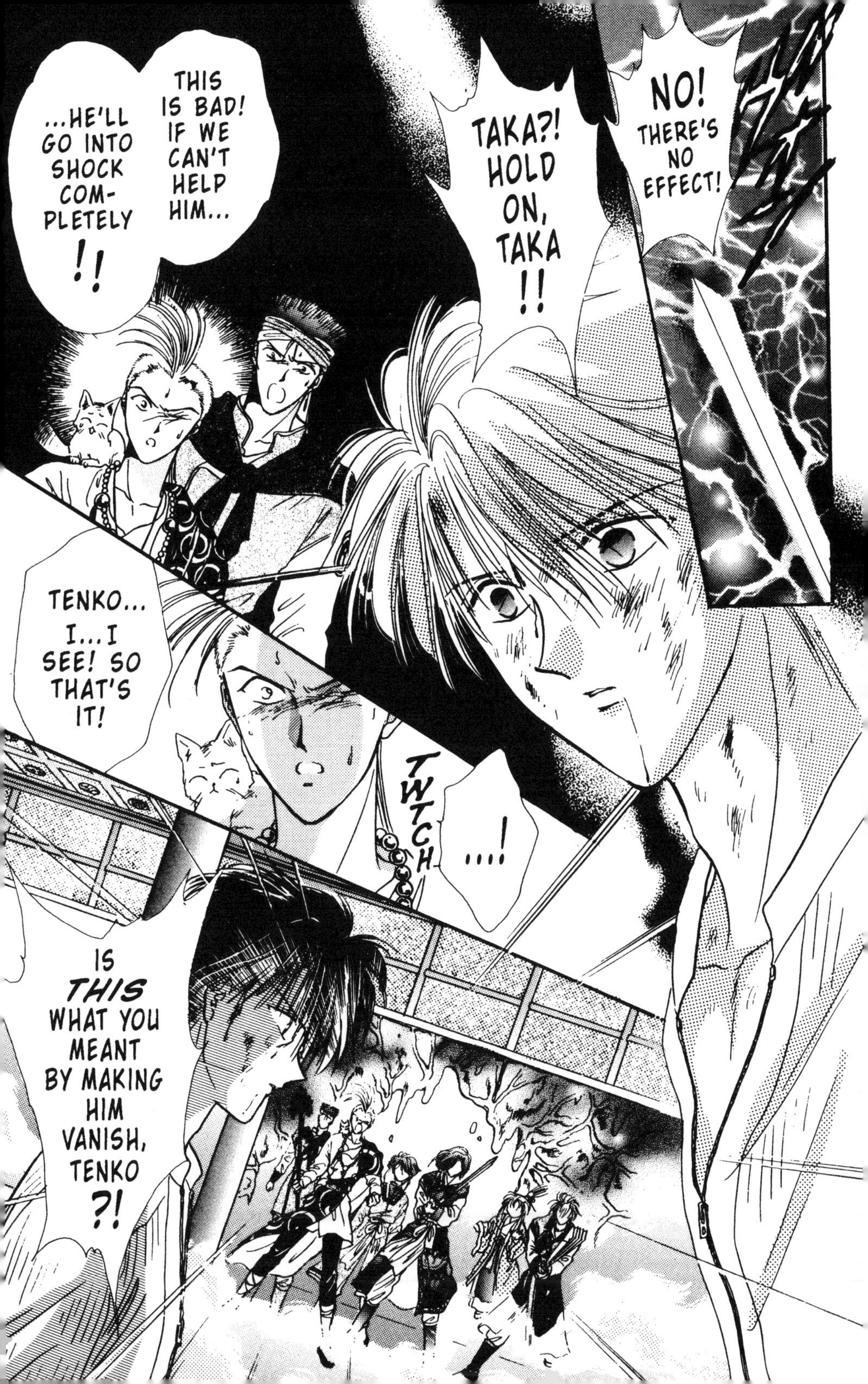
NO! THERE'S NO EFFECT!
TAKA?! HOLD ON, TAKA!!
THIS IS BAD! IF WE CAN'T HELP HIM...
...HE'LL GO INTO SHOCK COMPLETELY!!
TENKO... I...I SEE! SO THAT'S IT!
TWTCH
...!
IS *THIS* WHAT YOU MEANT BY MAKING HIM VANISH, TENKO?!

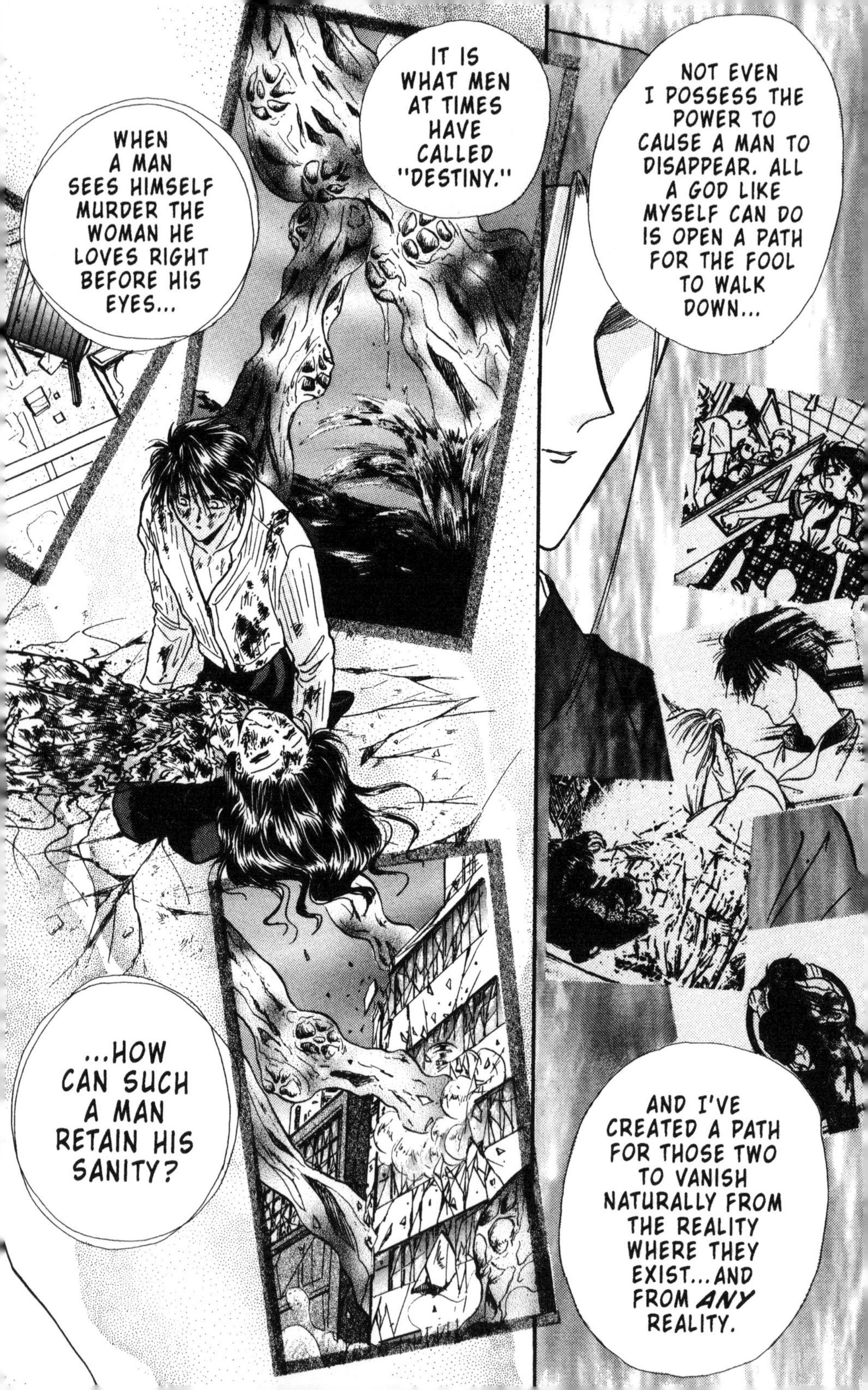
NOT EVEN I POSSESS THE POWER TO CAUSE A MAN TO DISAPPEAR. ALL A GOD LIKE MYSELF CAN DO IS OPEN A PATH FOR THE FOOL TO WALK DOWN...
AND I'VE CREATED A PATH FOR THOSE TWO TO VANISH NATURALLY FROM THE REALITY WHERE THEY EXIST...AND FROM *ANY* REALITY.
IT IS WHAT MEN AT TIMES HAVE CALLED "DESTINY."
WHEN A MAN SEES HIMSELF MURDER THE WOMAN HE LOVES RIGHT BEFORE HIS EYES...
...HOW CAN SUCH A MAN RETAIN HIS SANITY?

Tamahome is the kind of guy who runs flat-out, full speed ahead, and that's one way in which he and Taka are different. But Tamahome only exists because Taka exists...so the two really are one person. *By the way...* The coat that Taka always wears is the same as the coat Tamahome wore in volumes 12 and 13. *Did you notice?*
Since I thought of Tamahome as a "shojo manga hero," I had him spout out some pretty clichéd lines. But he really meant them when he said them. There were some people who didn't like him because of his corny dialog, but he was sincere. It's just proof of how dumb some characters can be--just like Miaka! They're just so emotional. But with all his insecurities, he threw away the part of himself named Tamahome. "He" had vanished for Taka... by an act of Taka's will. Do you remember that drawing at the end with Tamahome in the clouds? The tears were streaming down while I was drawing that. I was thinking, "Wow, he was one incredible man!" Even my assistants said, "Before anybody says anything bad about him, just look at how far the guy goes to show his love! He made himself vanish for the woman he loves!" They were all worked up! ☺ And so, Taka was born. Those last words by the god Suzaku...! These are just the thoughts in my head, but Taka was reborn eighteen years ago... even before Miaka was born. That first time when Miaka went to the library and opened the book, Taka already existed. He had the ring, and he was waiting for the day when he would meet that girl. But it could be the opposite... that because Tamahome existed, Taka existed too. I leave that one to my readers' imaginations. But that may mean that the Seven Suzaku Celestial Warriors exist somewhere as well. ☺ Even though the world changes over the ages. ...Maybe some of you out there may meet them. *Ah... the romance of it! They may be close to you even now!*

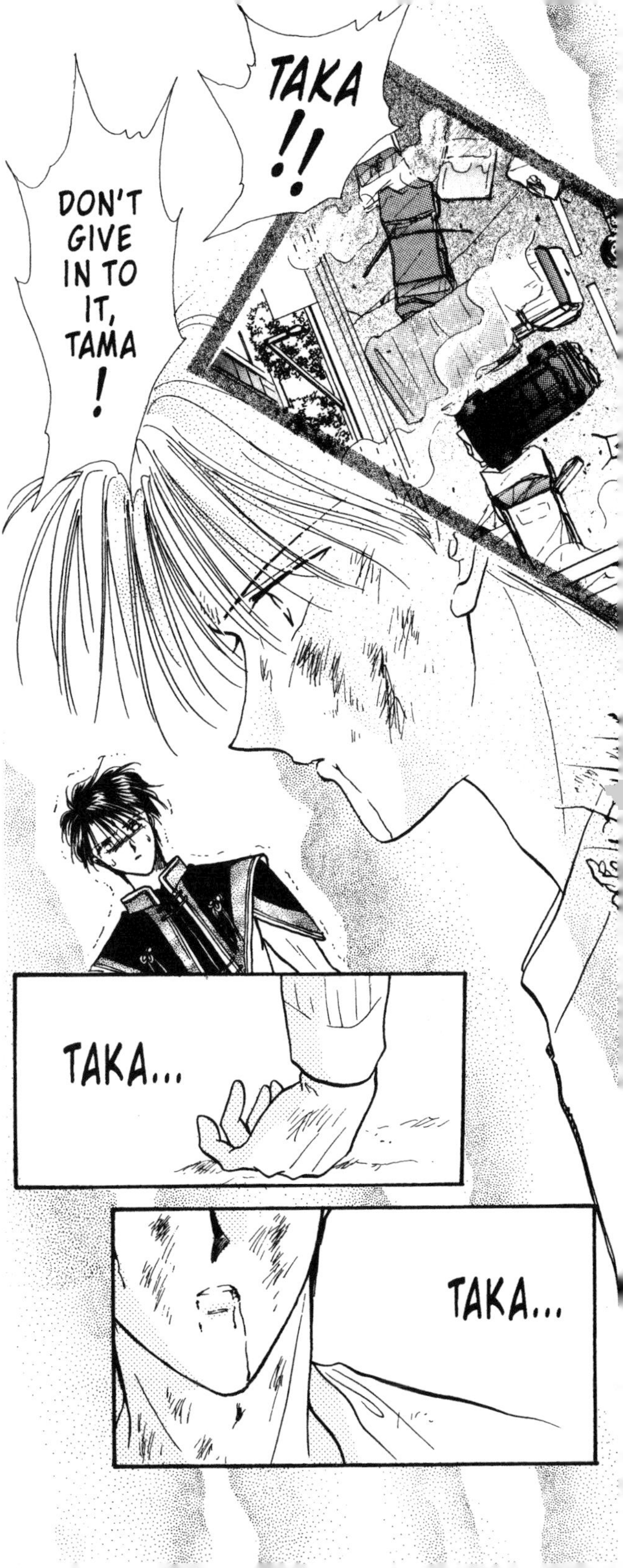

TAKA !!
DON'T GIVE IN TO IT, TAMA!
TAKA...
TAKA...

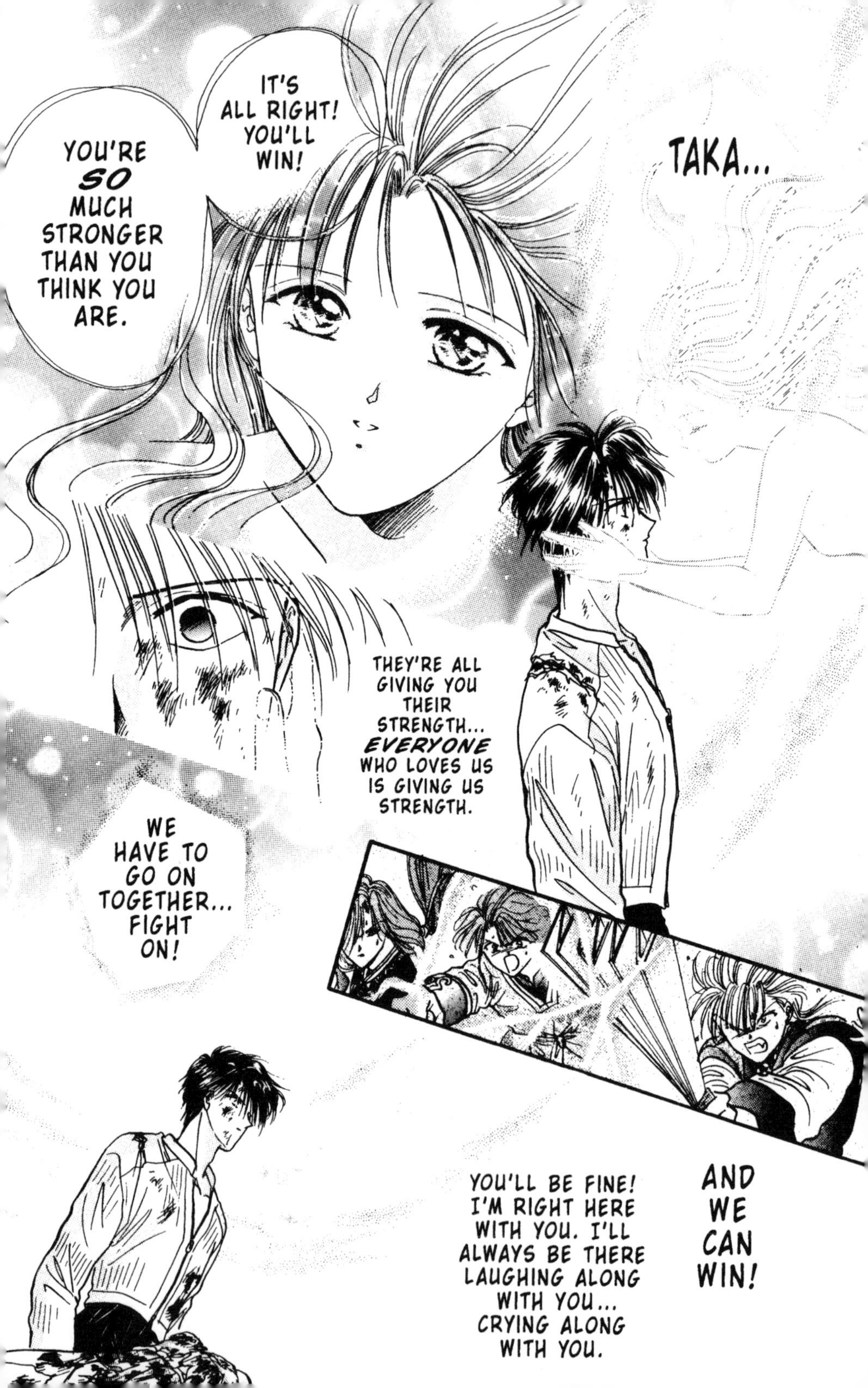
TAKA...
IT'S ALL RIGHT! YOU'LL WIN!
YOU'RE *SO* MUCH STRONGER THAN YOU THINK YOU ARE.
THEY'RE ALL GIVING YOU THEIR STRENGTH... *EVERYONE* WHO LOVES US IS GIVING US STRENGTH.
WE HAVE TO GO ON TOGETHER... FIGHT ON!
YOU'LL BE FINE! I'M RIGHT HERE WITH YOU. I'LL ALWAYS BE THERE LAUGHING ALONG WITH YOU... CRYING ALONG WITH YOU.
AND WE CAN WIN!

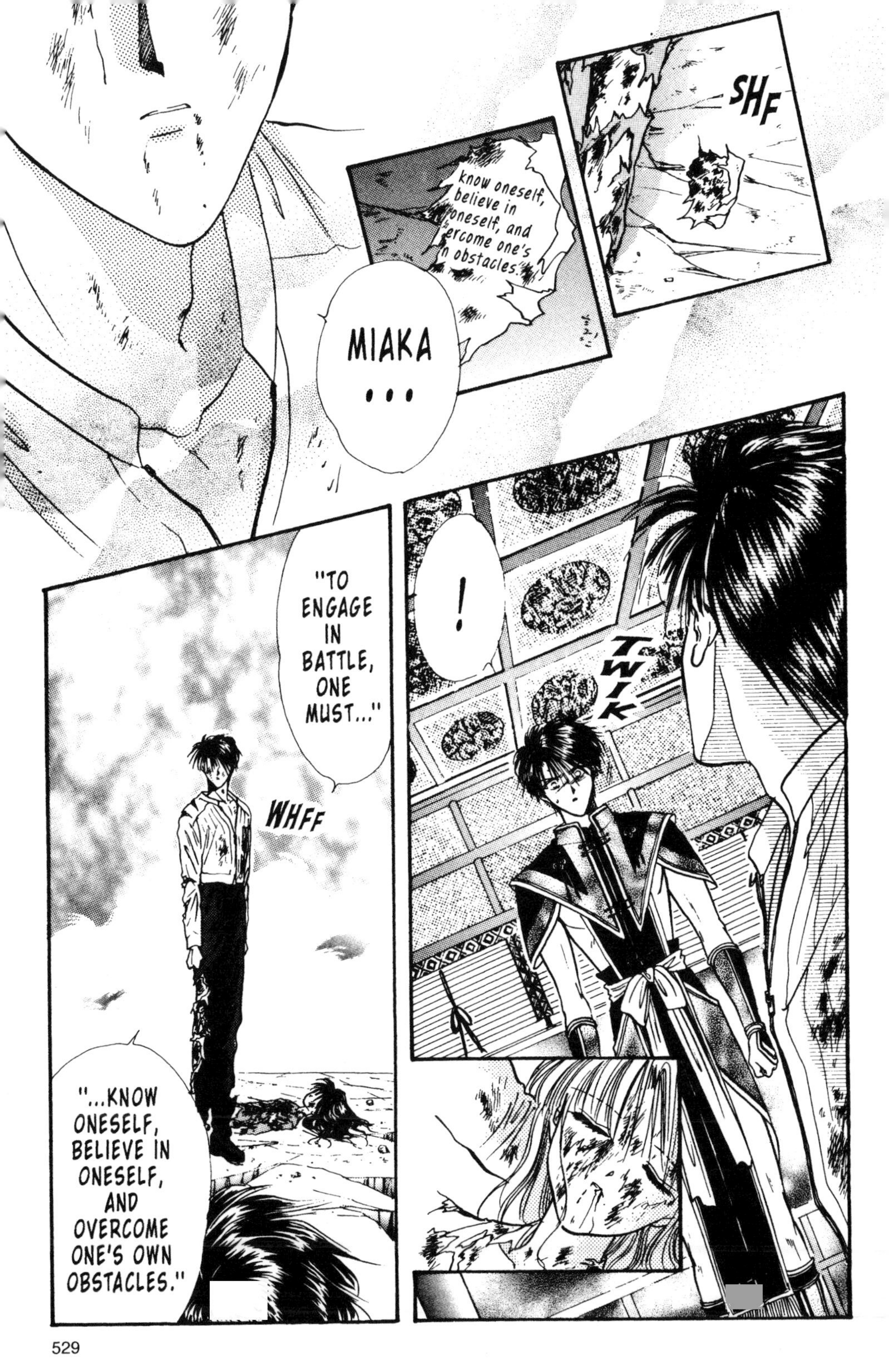
SHF
know oneself, believe in oneself, and ercome one's n obstacles.
MIAKA ...
!
TWIK
"TO ENGAGE IN BATTLE, ONE MUST..."
WHFF
"...KNOW ONESELF, BELIEVE IN ONESELF, AND OVERCOME ONE'S OWN OBSTACLES."

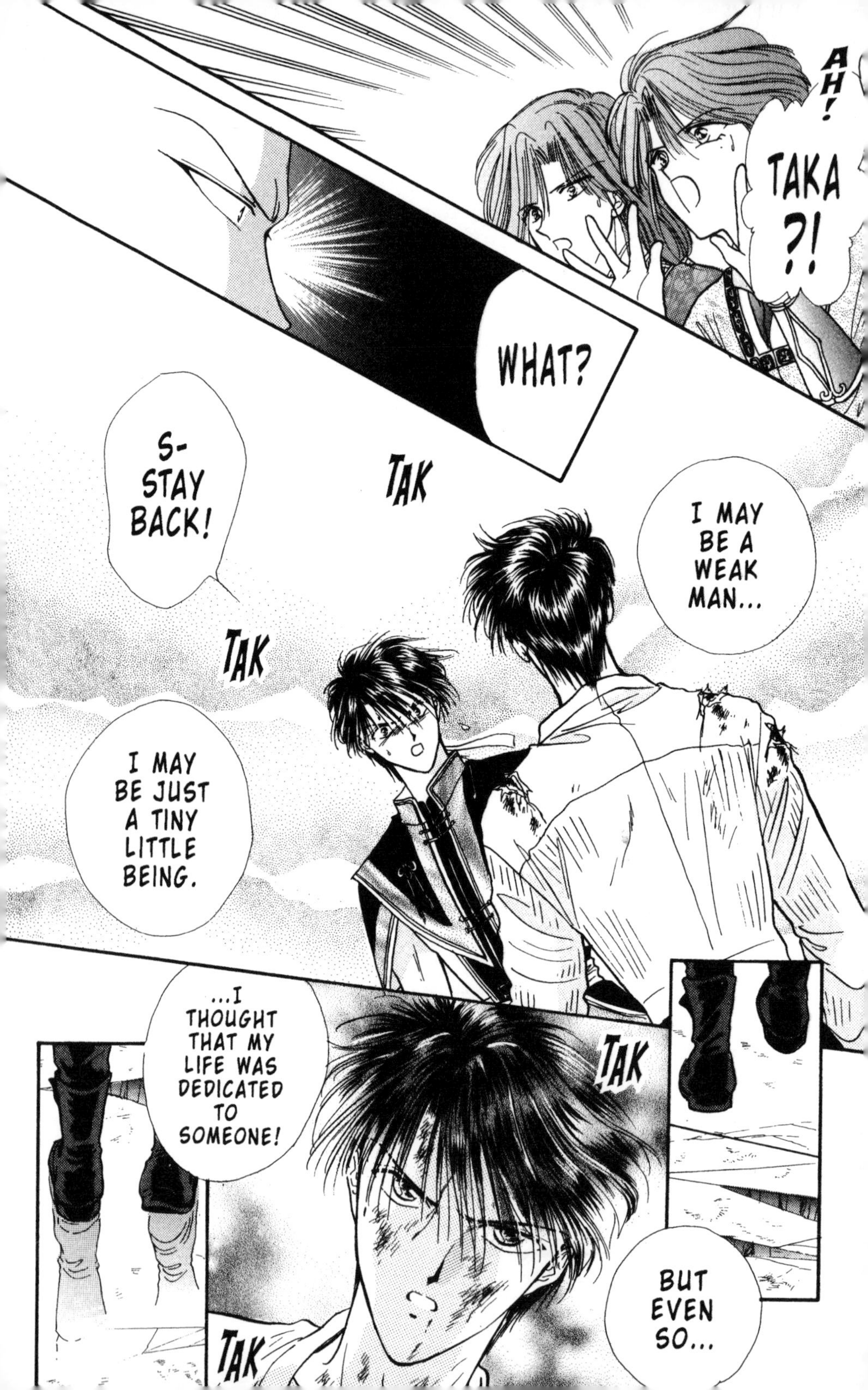
AH!
TAKA?!
WHAT?
I MAY BE A WEAK MAN...
TAK
S-STAY BACK!
TAK
I MAY BE JUST A TINY LITTLE BEING.
TAK
...I THOUGHT THAT MY LIFE WAS DEDICATED TO SOMEONE!
BUT EVEN SO...
TAK

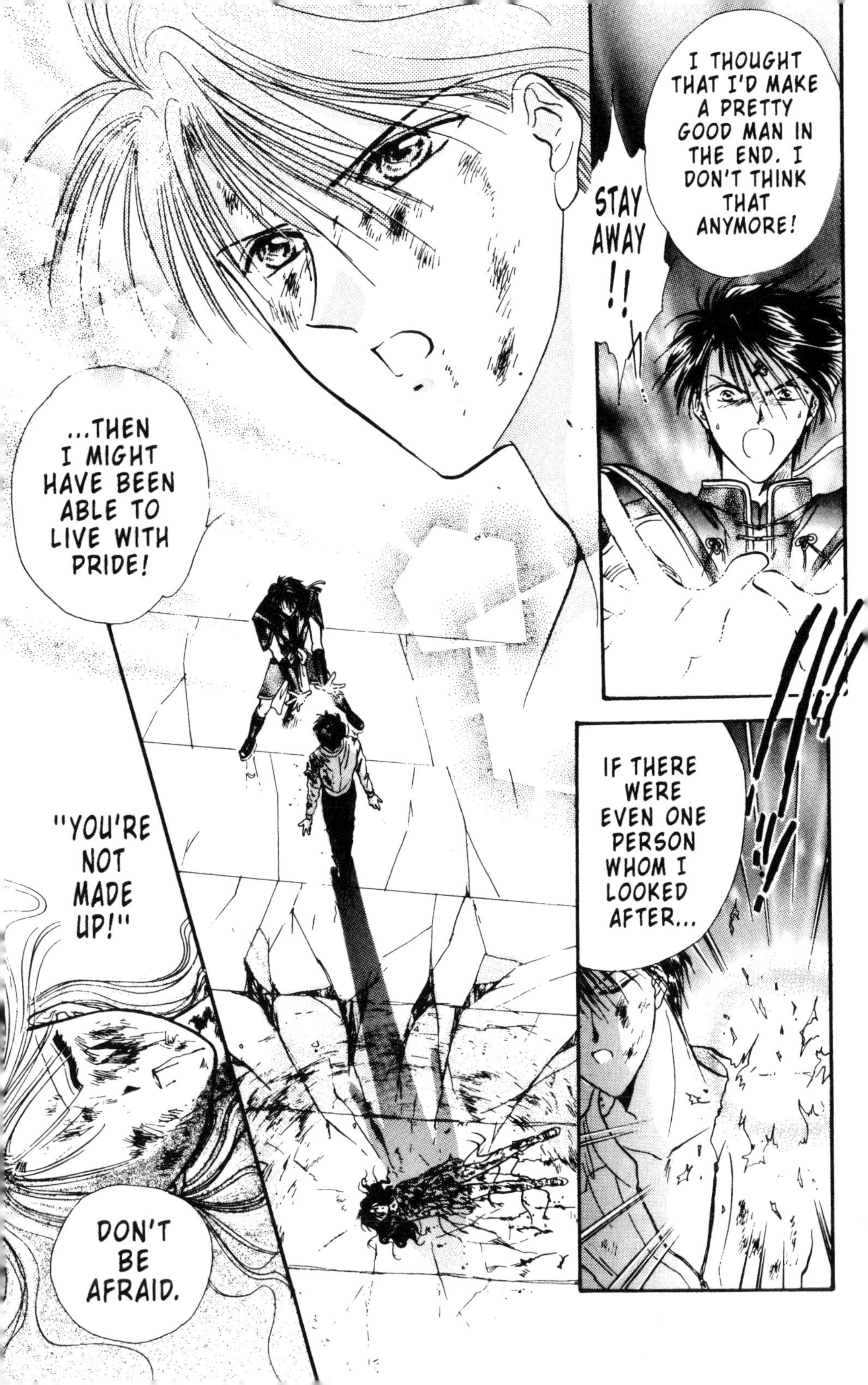
I THOUGHT THAT I'D MAKE A PRETTY GOOD MAN IN THE END. I DON'T THINK THAT ANYMORE!
STAY AWAY!!
IF THERE WERE EVEN ONE PERSON WHOM I LOOKED AFTER...
...THEN I MIGHT HAVE BEEN ABLE TO LIVE WITH PRIDE!
"YOU'RE NOT MADE UP!"
DON'T BE AFRAID.

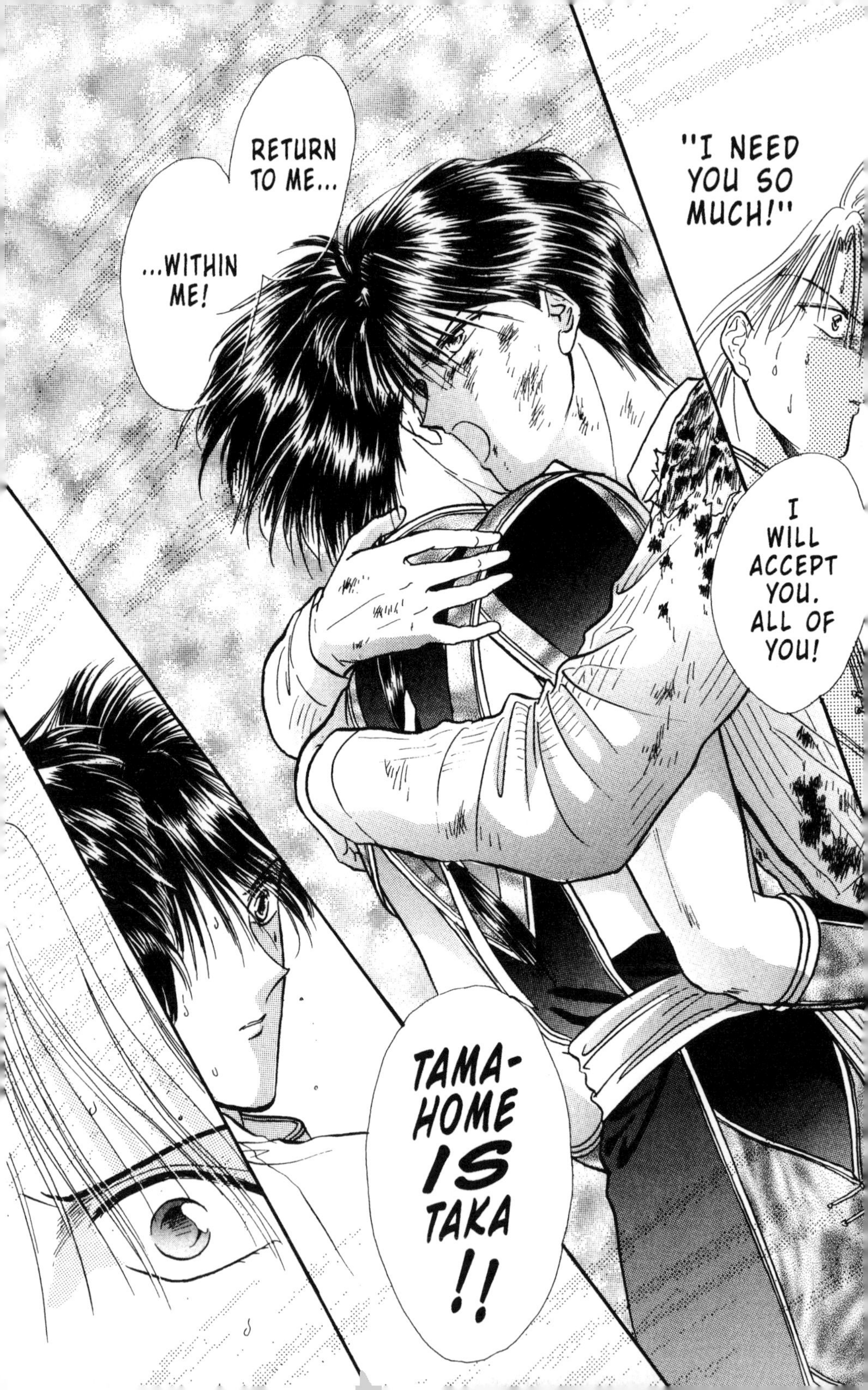
"I NEED YOU SO MUCH!"
RETURN TO ME...
...WITHIN ME!
I WILL ACCEPT YOU. ALL OF YOU!
TAMA-HOME IS TAKA!!

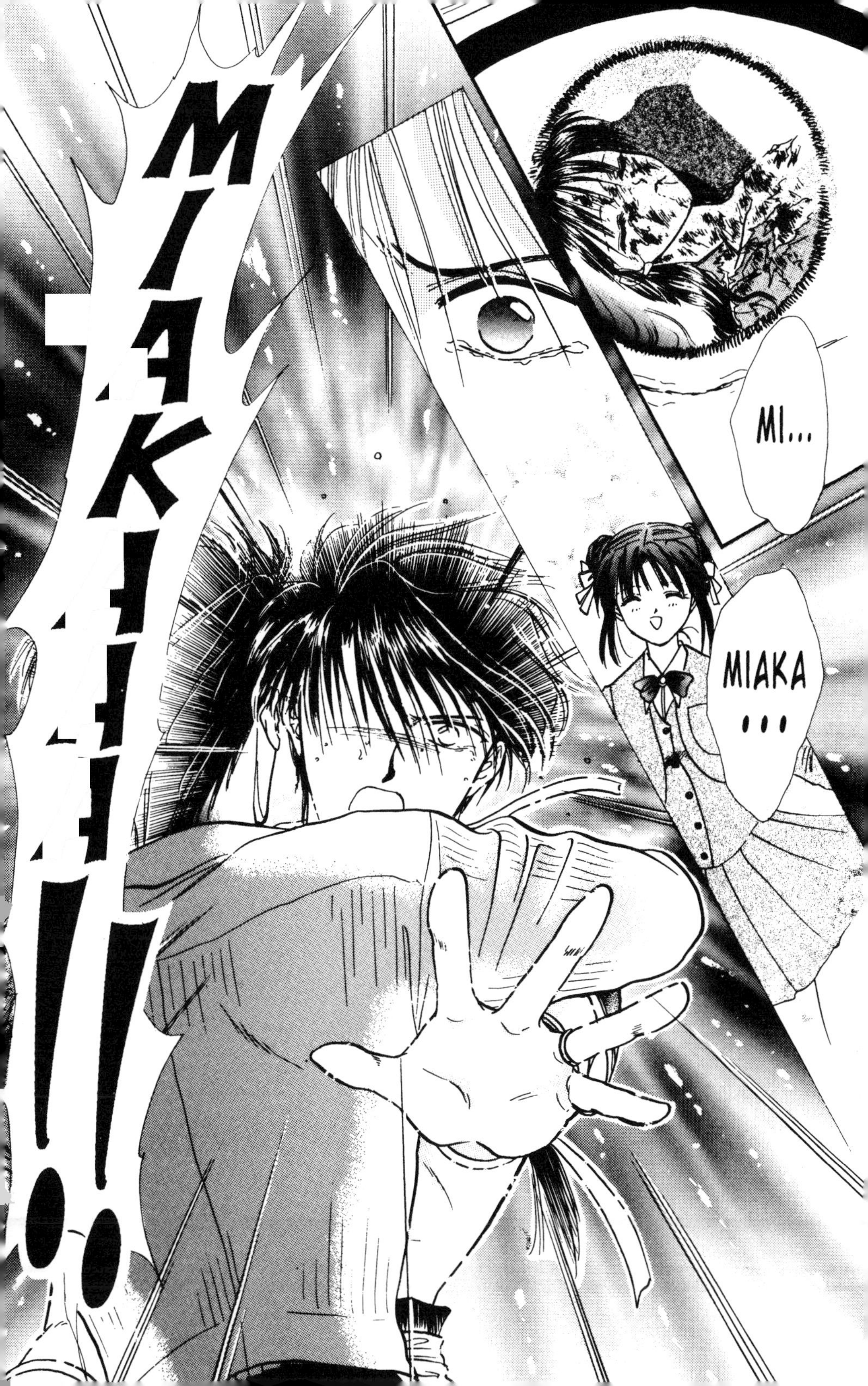
MI...
MIAKA...
MIAKAAA!!

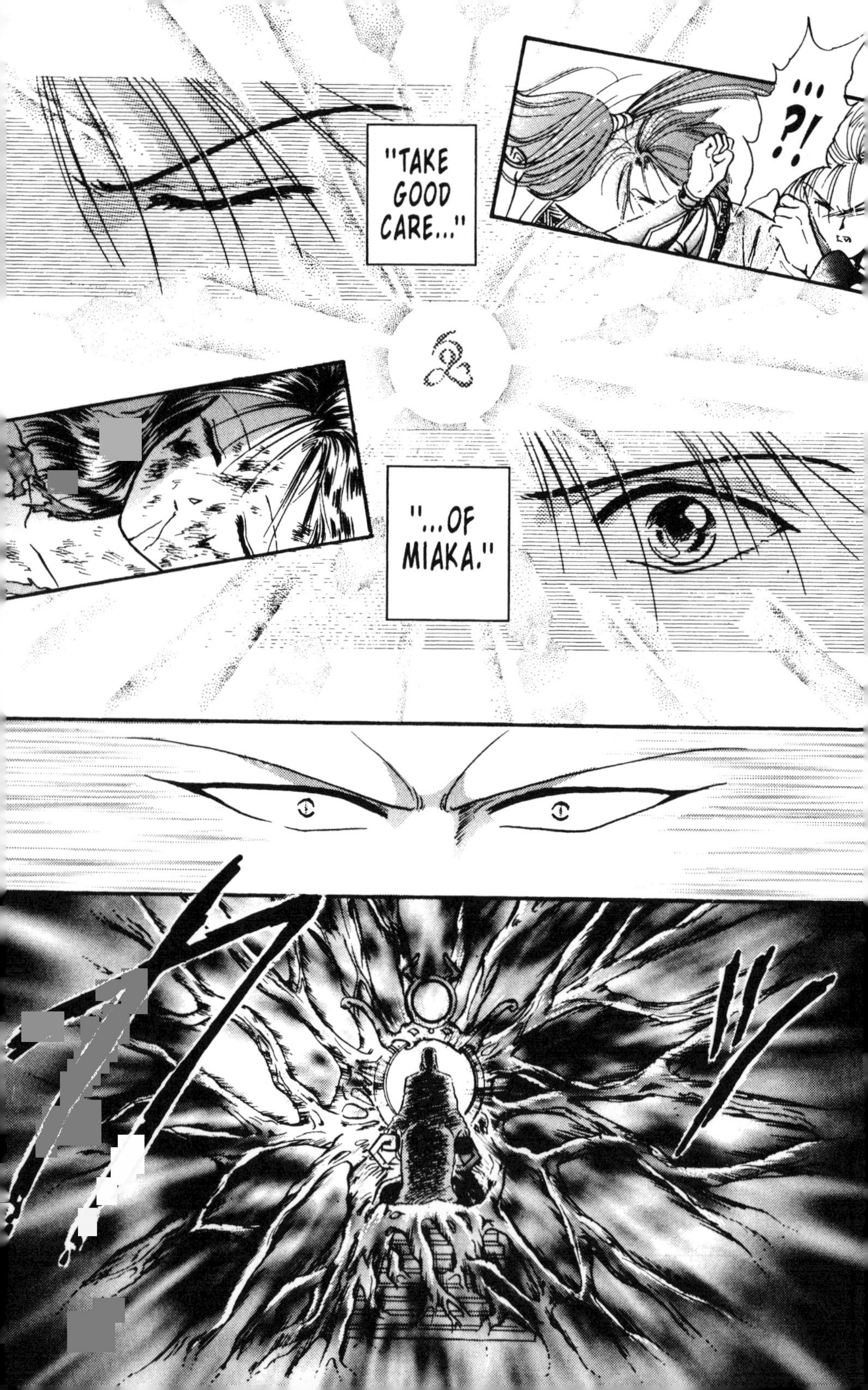
?!
"TAKE GOOD CARE..."
"...OF MIAKA."

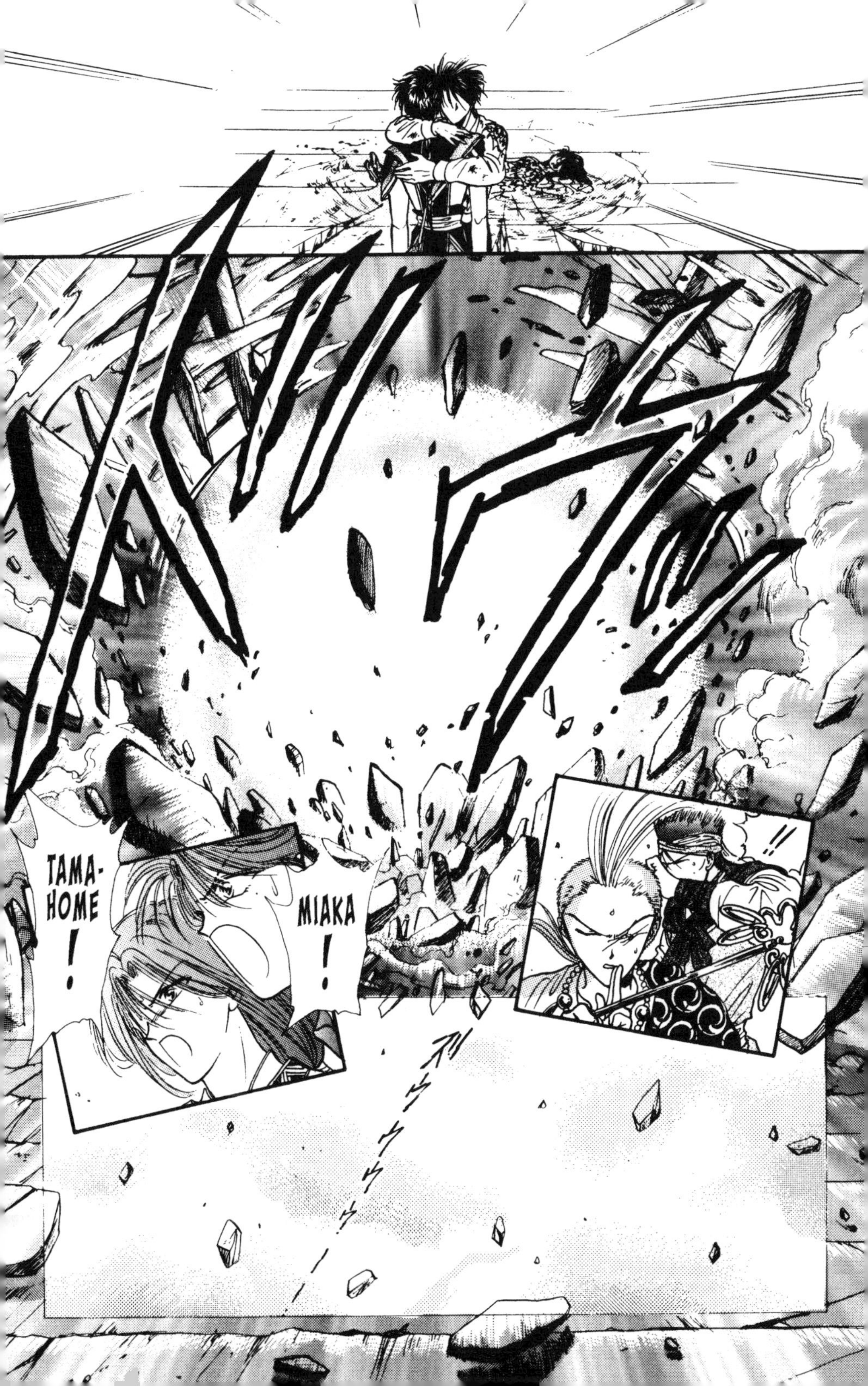
!!
MIAKA!
TAMA-HOME!

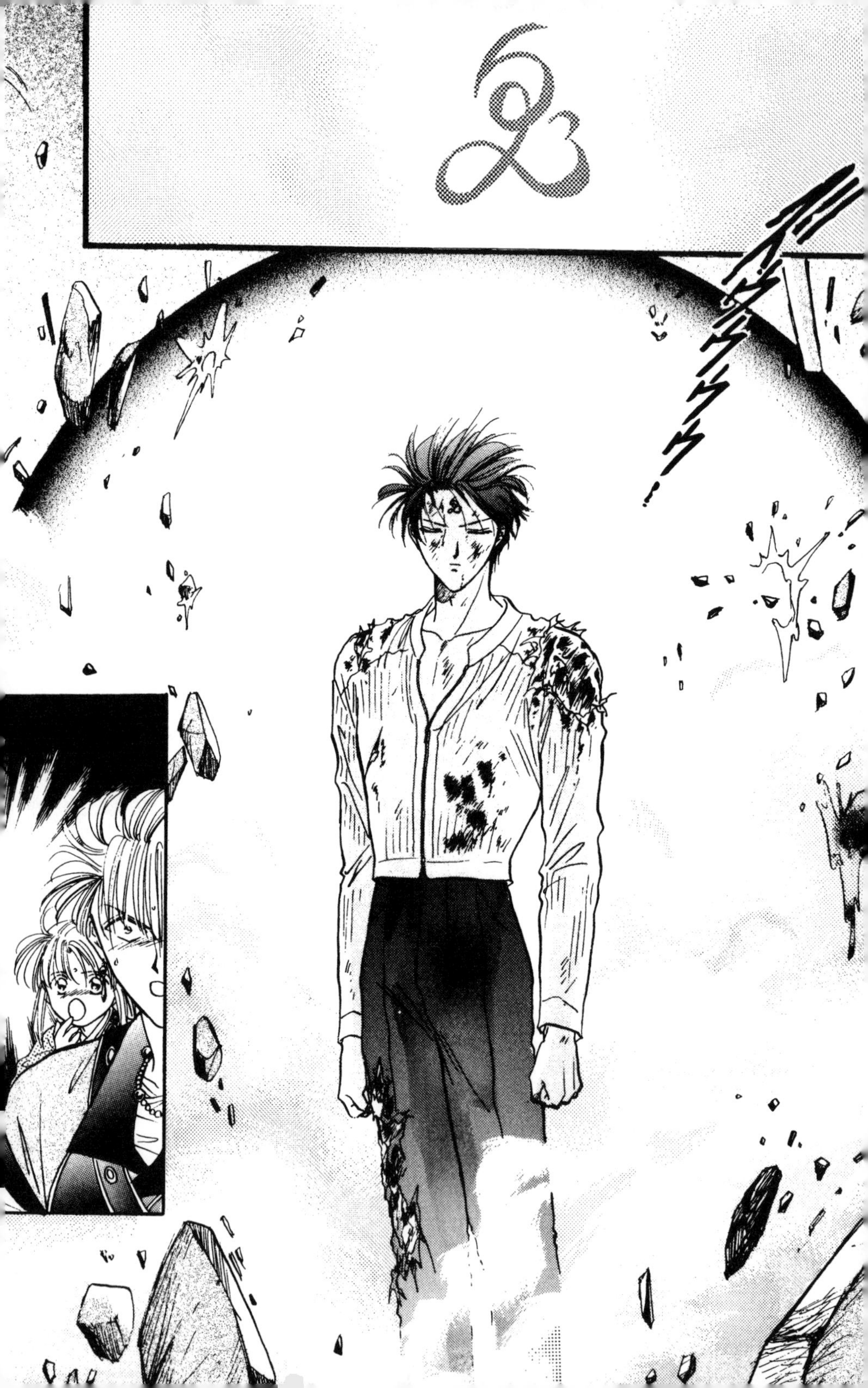

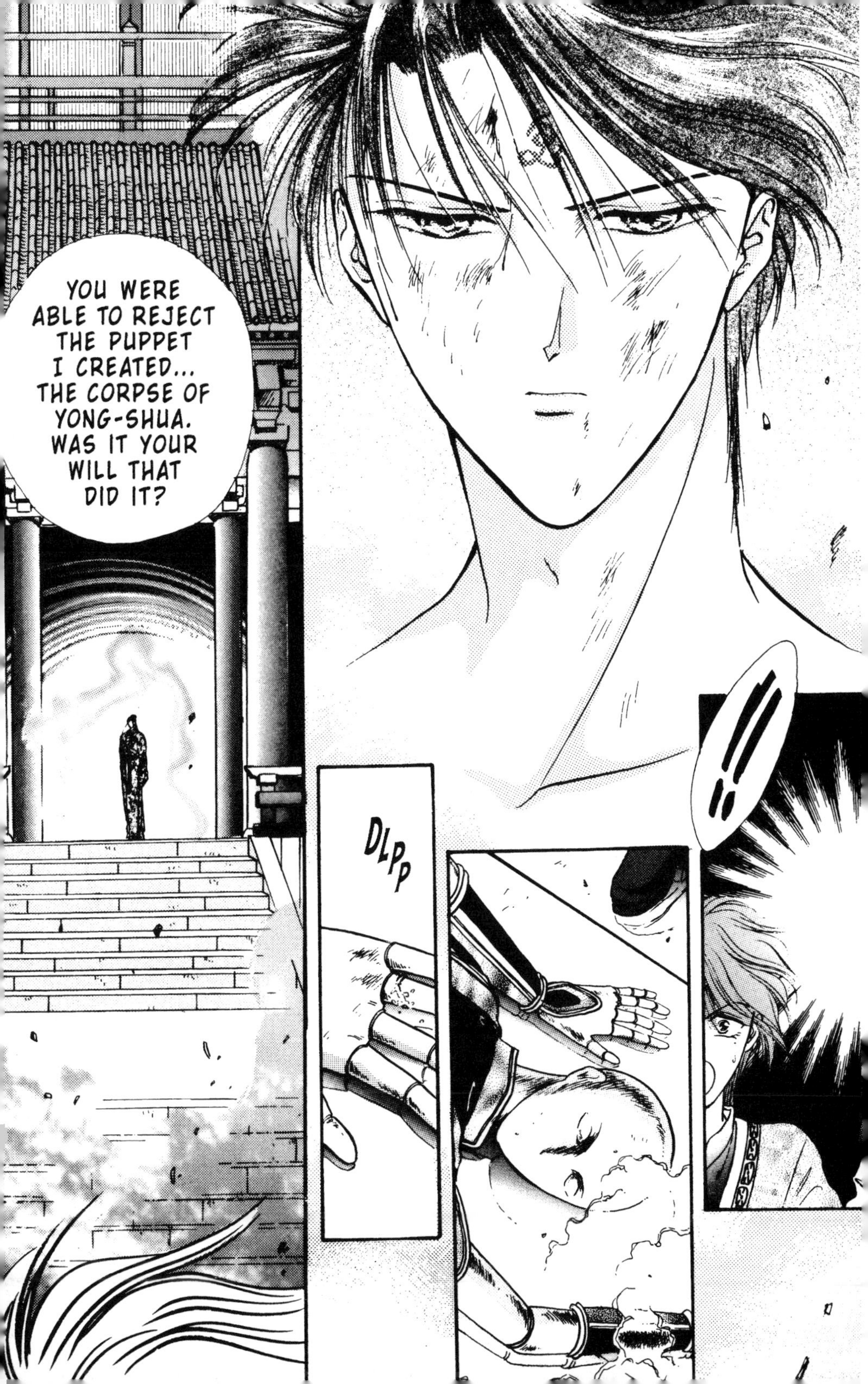
YOU WERE ABLE TO REJECT THE PUPPET I CREATED... THE CORPSE OF YONG-SHUA. WAS IT YOUR WILL THAT DID IT?
!!
DLPP

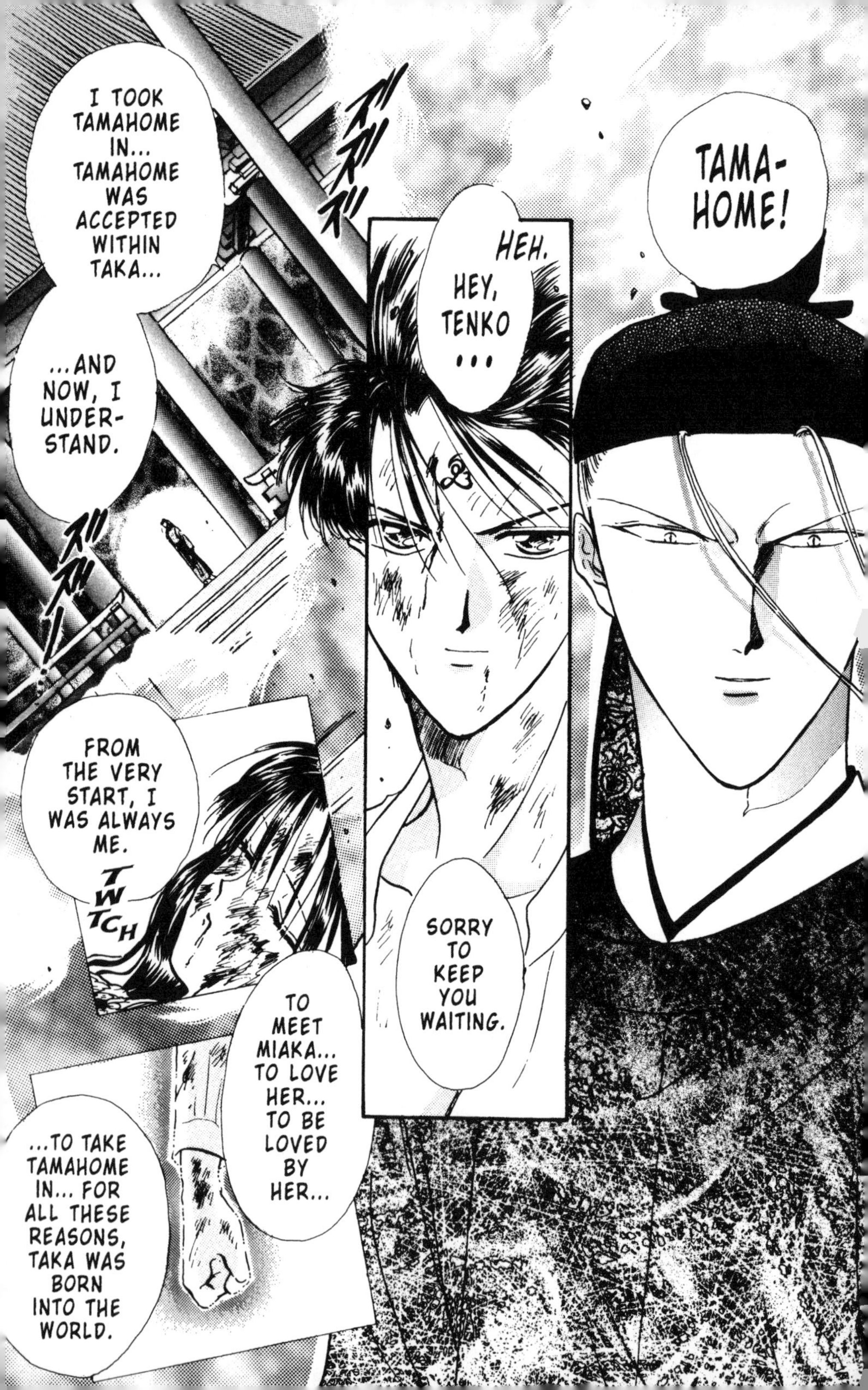
TAMA-HOME!
HEH.
HEY, TENKO...
SORRY TO KEEP YOU WAITING.
I TOOK TAMAHOME IN... TAMAHOME WAS ACCEPTED WITHIN TAKA...
...AND NOW, I UNDERSTAND.
FROM THE VERY START, I WAS ALWAYS ME.
TWTCH
TO MEET MIAKA... TO LOVE HER... TO BE LOVED BY HER...
...TO TAKE TAMAHOME IN... FOR ALL THESE REASONS, TAKA WAS BORN INTO THE WORLD.

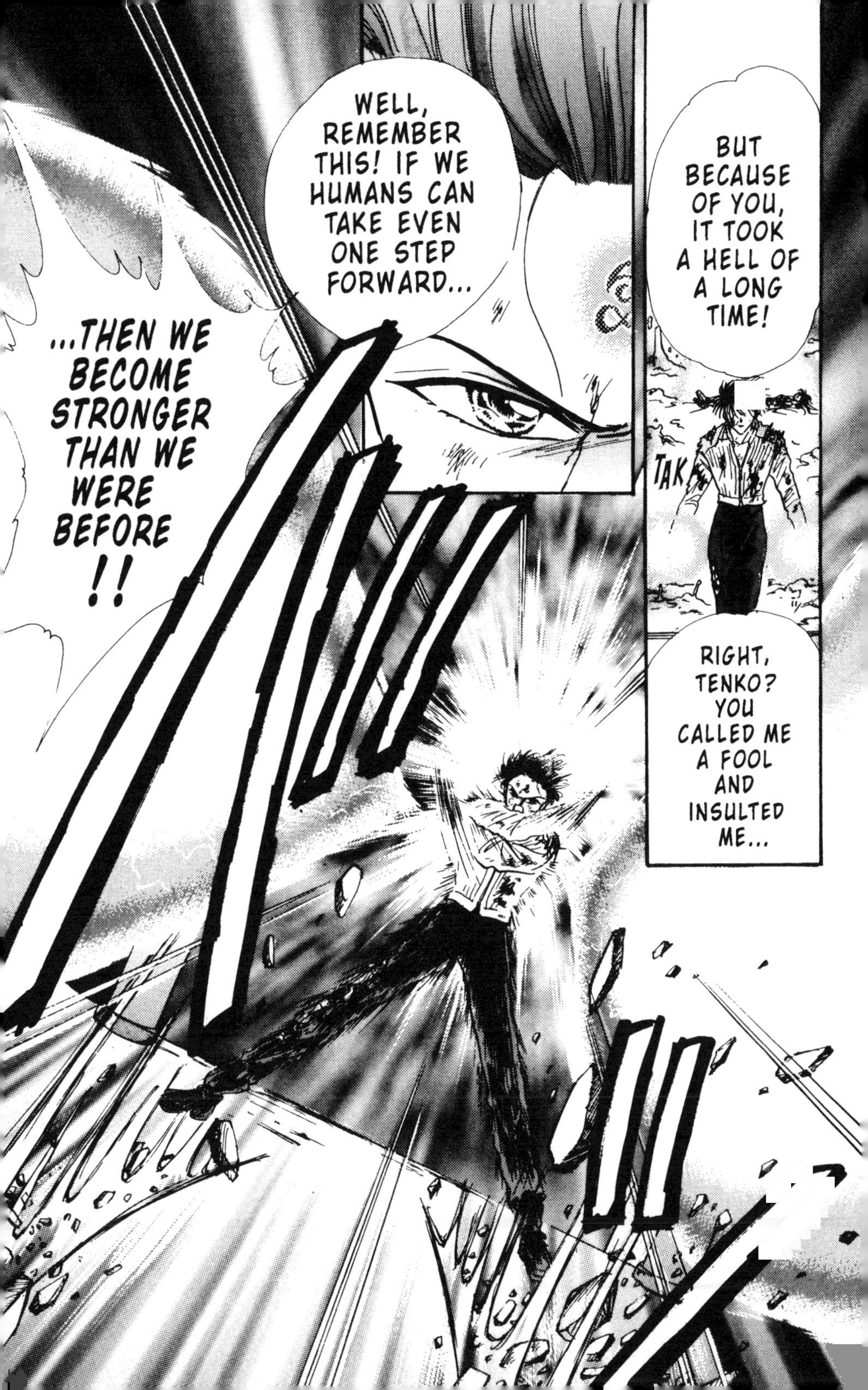
BUT BECAUSE OF YOU, IT TOOK A HELL OF A LONG TIME!
TAK
RIGHT, TENKO? YOU CALLED ME A FOOL AND INSULTED ME...
WELL, REMEMBER THIS! IF WE HUMANS CAN TAKE EVEN ONE STEP FORWARD...
...THEN WE BECOME STRONGER THAN WE WERE BEFORE!!

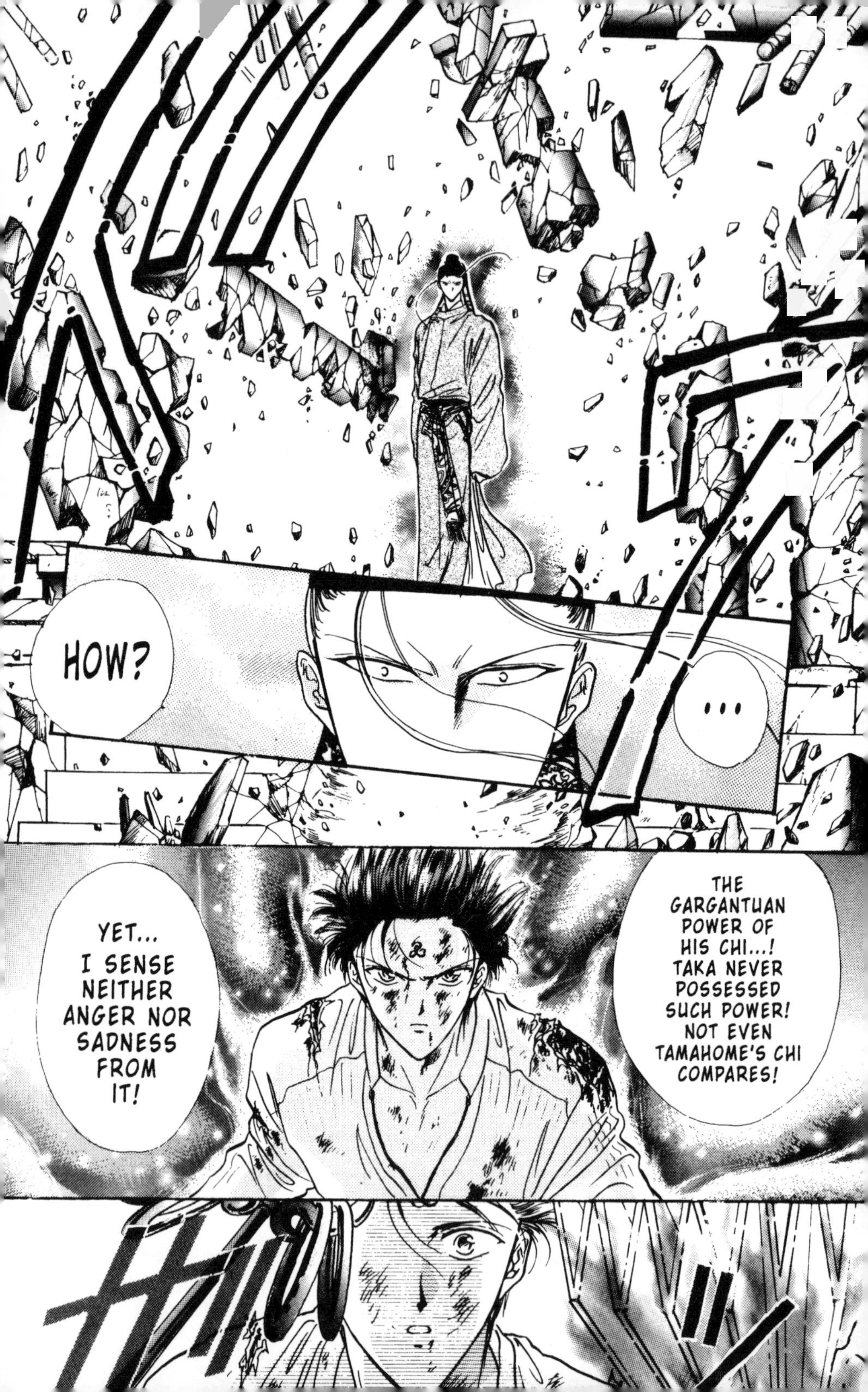
...
HOW?
THE GARGANTUAN POWER OF HIS CHI...! TAKA NEVER POSSESSED SUCH POWER! NOT EVEN TAMAHOME'S CHI COMPARES!
YET... I SENSE NEITHER ANGER NOR SADNESS FROM IT!

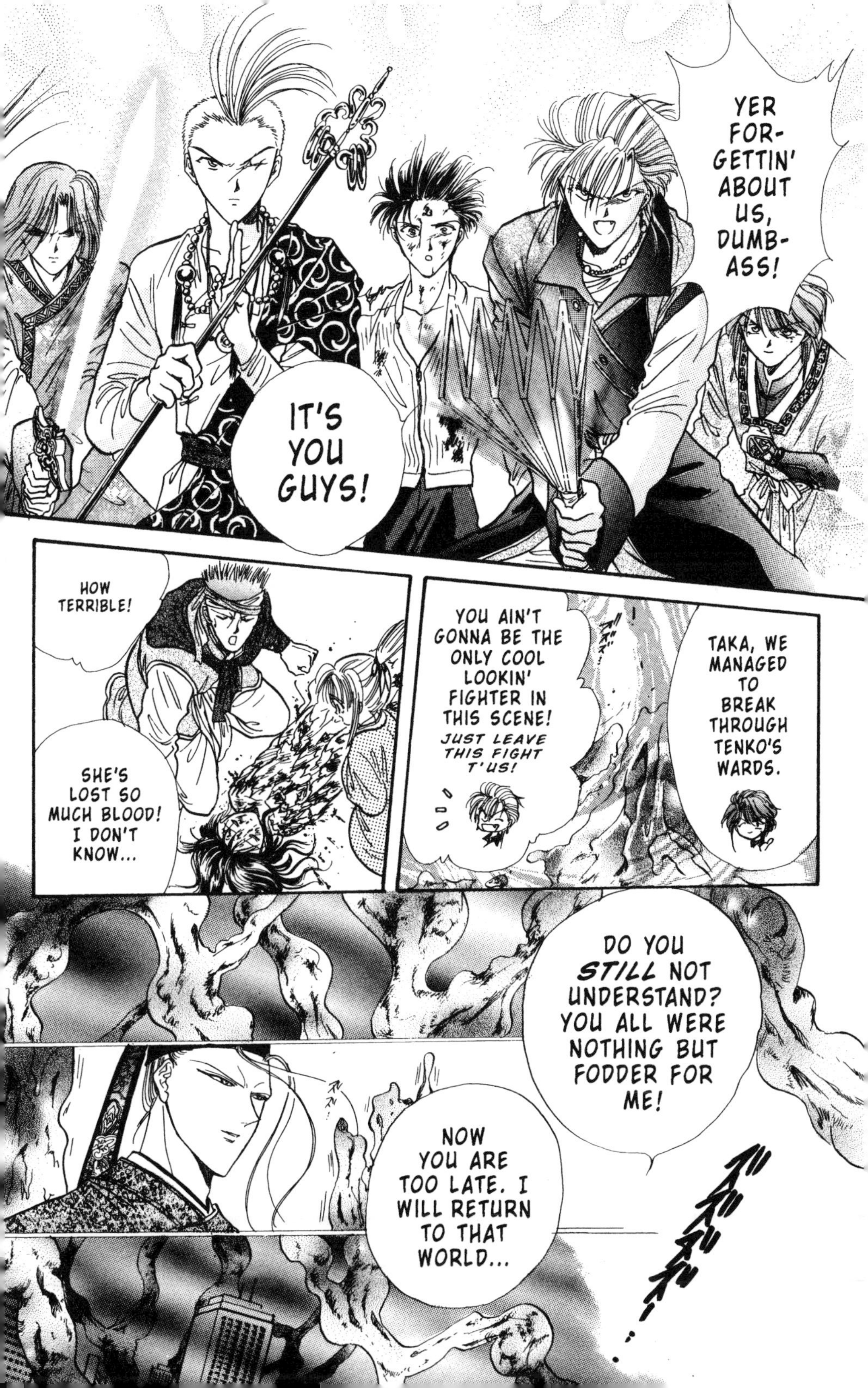
YER FOR-GETTIN' ABOUT US, DUMB-ASS!
IT'S YOU GUYS!
TAKA, WE MANAGED TO BREAK THROUGH TENKO'S WARDS.
YOU AIN'T GONNA BE THE ONLY COOL LOOKIN' FIGHTER IN THIS SCENE!
JUST LEAVE THIS FIGHT T'US!
HOW TERRIBLE!
SHE'S LOST SO MUCH BLOOD! I DON'T KNOW...
DO YOU STILL NOT UNDERSTAND? YOU ALL WERE NOTHING BUT FODDER FOR ME!
NOW YOU ARE TOO LATE. I WILL RETURN TO THAT WORLD...

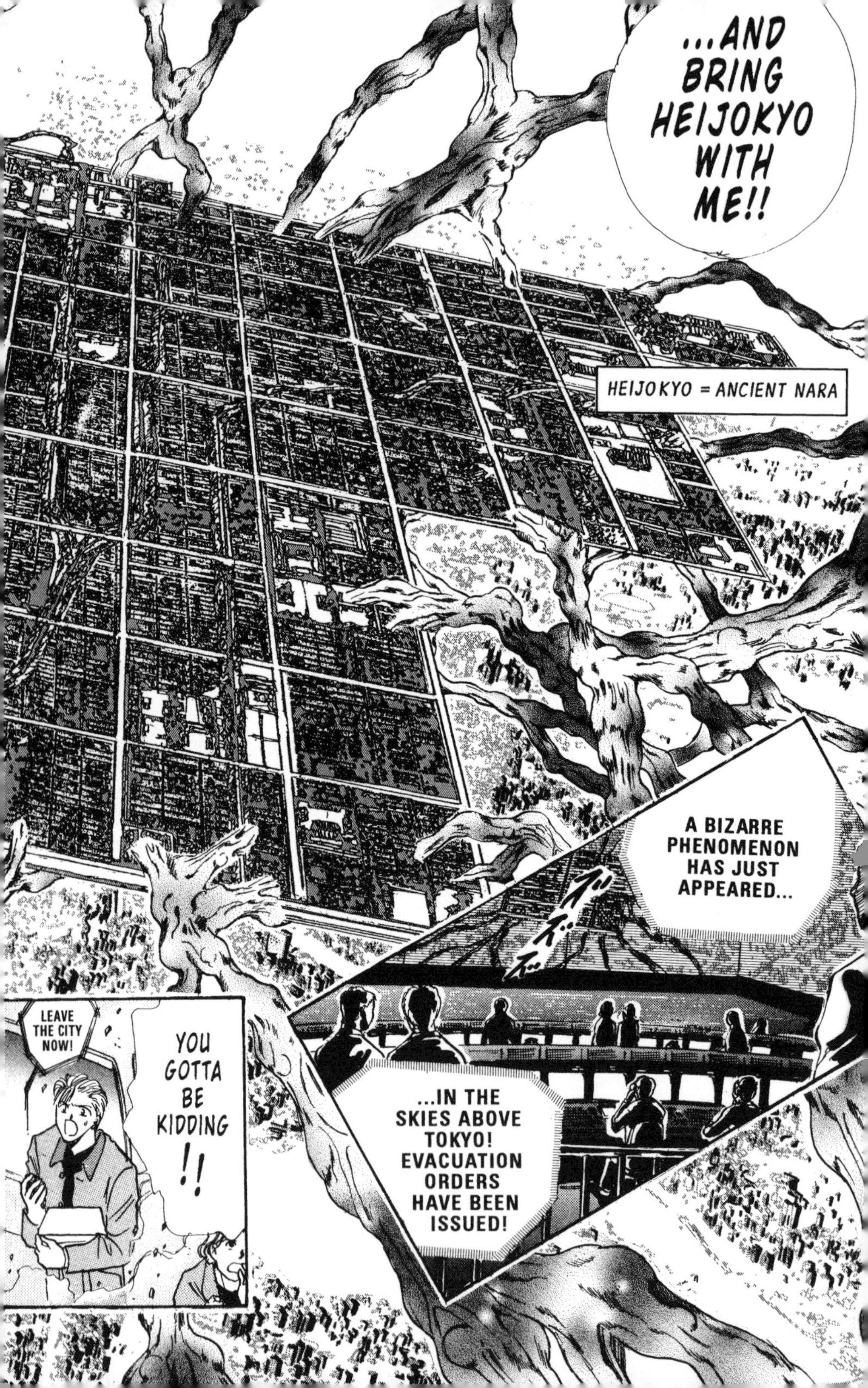
...AND BRING HEIJOKYO WITH ME!!
HEIJOKYO = ANCIENT NARA
A BIZARRE PHENOMENON HAS JUST APPEARED...
...IN THE SKIES ABOVE TOKYO! EVACUATION ORDERS HAVE BEEN ISSUED!
LEAVE THE CITY NOW!
YOU GOTTA BE KIDDING!!

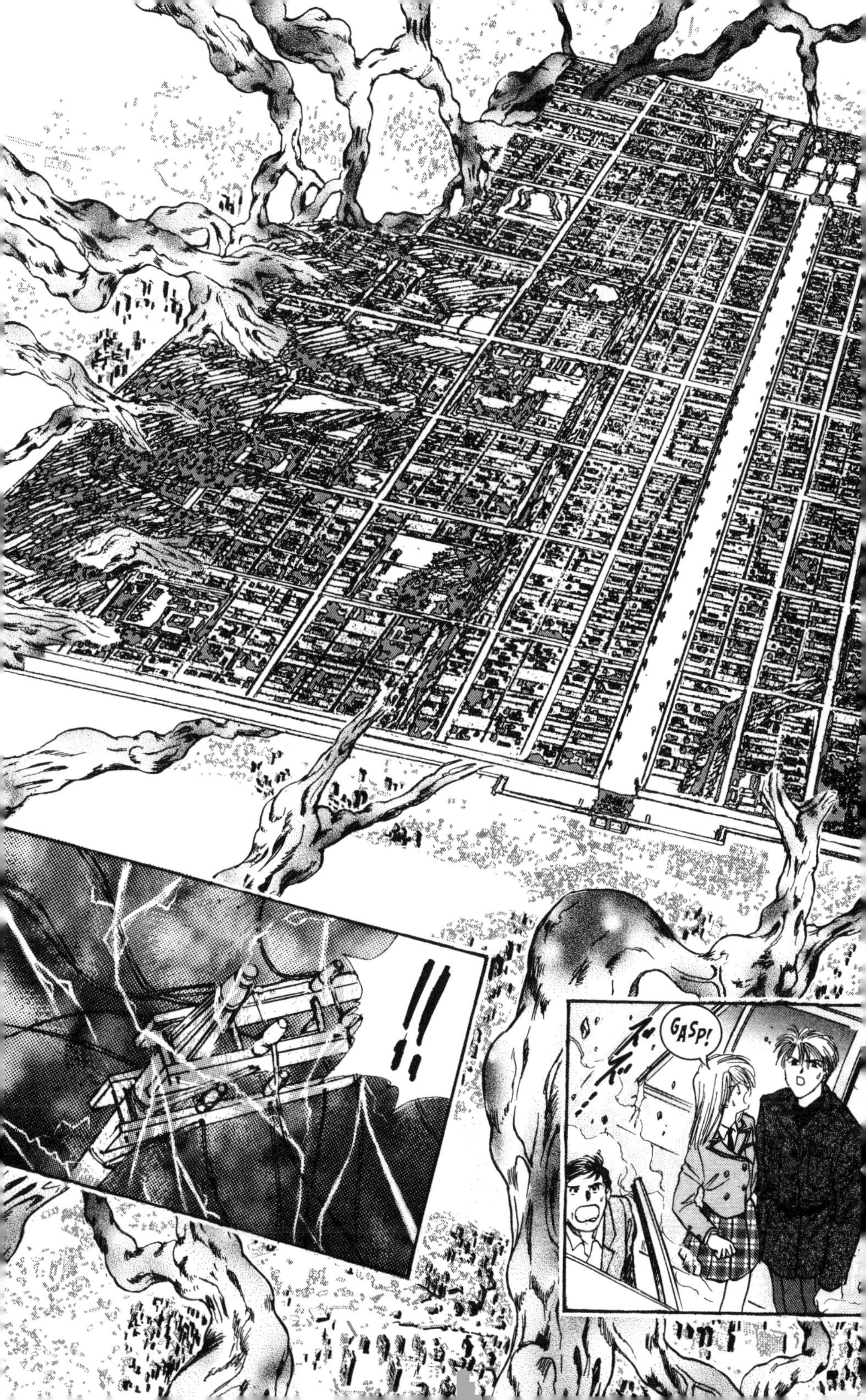
GASP!
!!

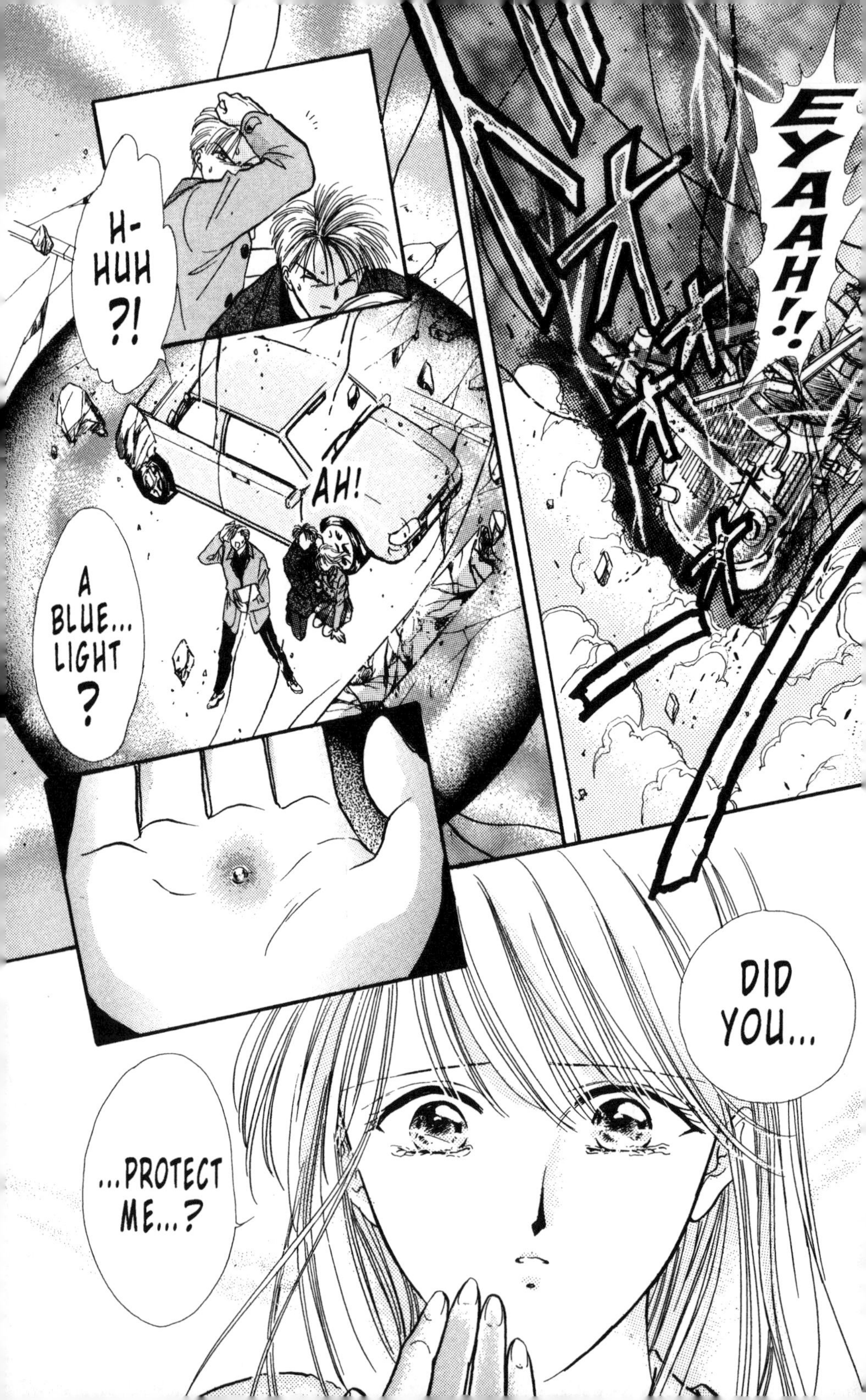
EYAAAH!!
H-HUH?!
AH!
A BLUE... LIGHT?
DID YOU...
...PROTECT ME...?

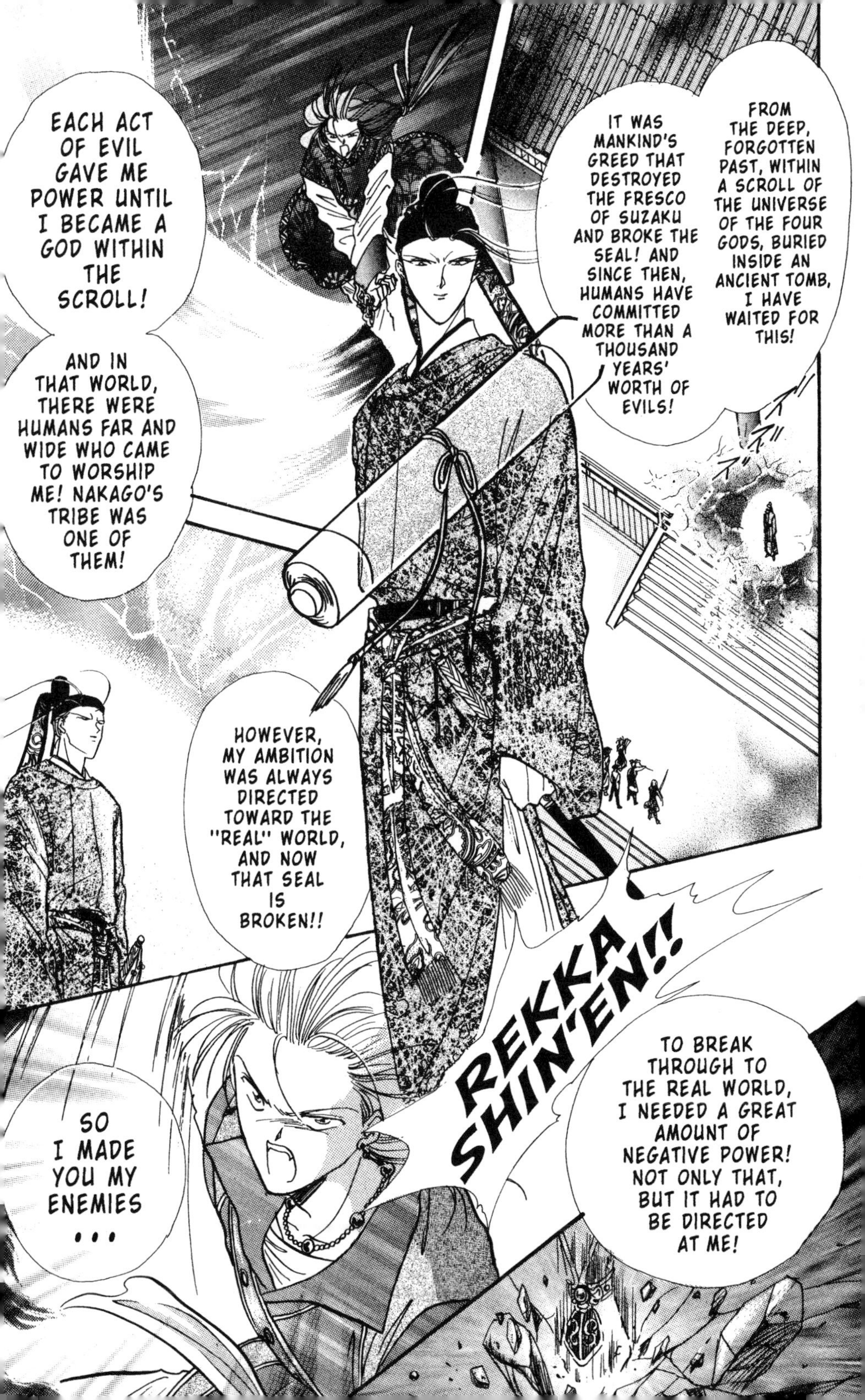
FROM THE DEEP, FORGOTTEN PAST, WITHIN A SCROLL OF THE UNIVERSE OF THE FOUR GODS, BURIED INSIDE AN ANCIENT TOMB, I HAVE WAITED FOR THIS!
IT WAS MANKIND'S GREED THAT DESTROYED THE FRESCO OF SUZAKU AND BROKE THE SEAL! AND SINCE THEN, HUMANS HAVE COMMITTED MORE THAN A THOUSAND YEARS' WORTH OF EVILS!
EACH ACT OF EVIL GAVE ME POWER UNTIL I BECAME A GOD WITHIN THE SCROLL!
AND IN THAT WORLD, THERE WERE HUMANS FAR AND WIDE WHO CAME TO WORSHIP ME! NAKAGO'S TRIBE WAS ONE OF THEM!
HOWEVER, MY AMBITION WAS ALWAYS DIRECTED TOWARD THE "REAL" WORLD, AND NOW THAT SEAL IS BROKEN!!
TO BREAK THROUGH TO THE REAL WORLD, I NEEDED A GREAT AMOUNT OF NEGATIVE POWER! NOT ONLY THAT, BUT IT HAD TO BE DIRECTED AT ME!
REKKA SHIN'EN!!
SO I MADE YOU MY ENEMIES...

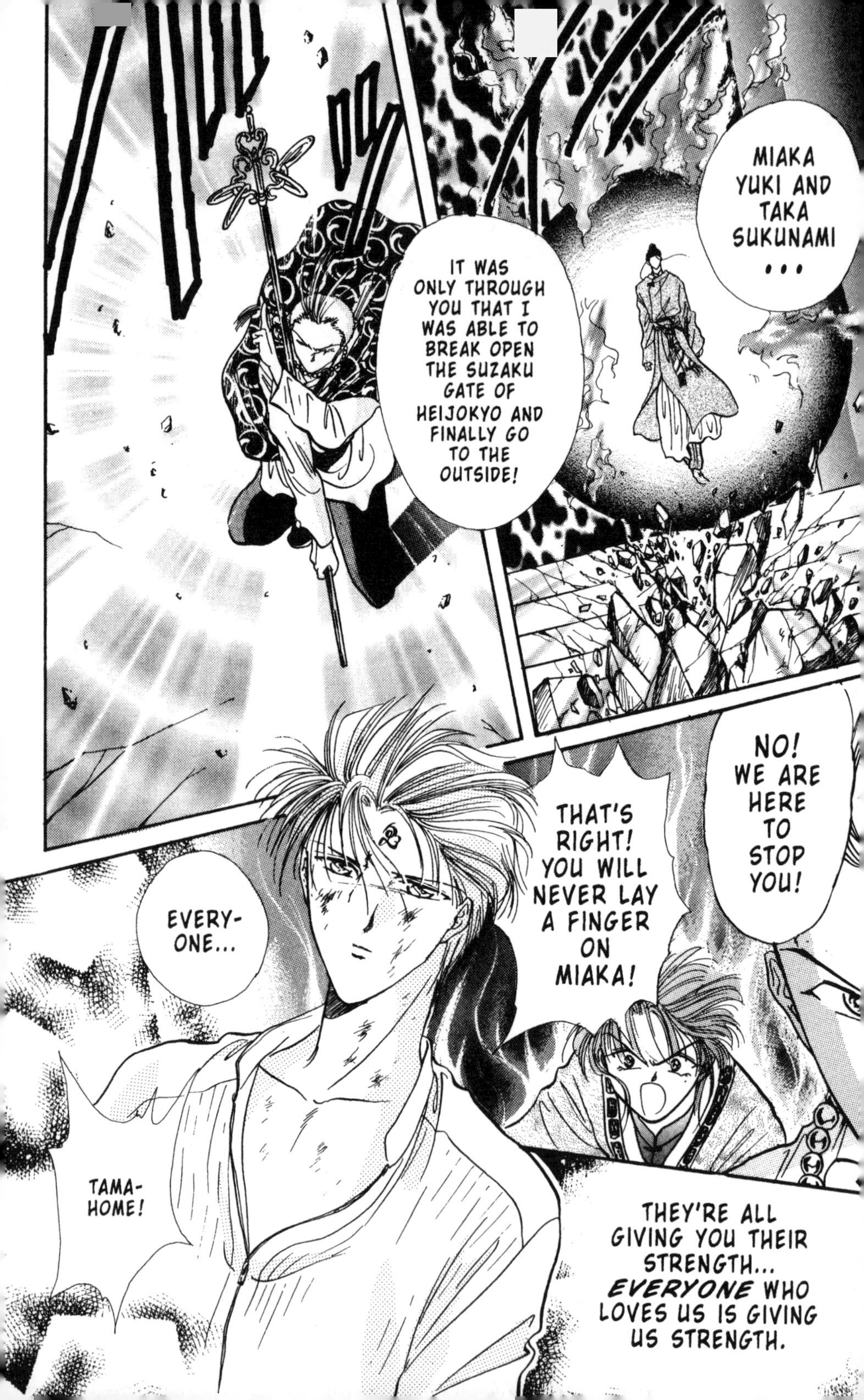

MIAKA YUKI AND TAKA SUKUNAMI...
IT WAS ONLY THROUGH YOU THAT I WAS ABLE TO BREAK OPEN THE SUZAKU GATE OF HEIJOKYO AND FINALLY GO TO THE OUTSIDE!
NO! WE ARE HERE TO STOP YOU!
THAT'S RIGHT! YOU WILL NEVER LAY A FINGER ON MIAKA!
EVERY-ONE...
TAMA-HOME!
THEY'RE ALL GIVING YOU THEIR STRENGTH... *EVERYONE* WHO LOVES US IS GIVING US STRENGTH.

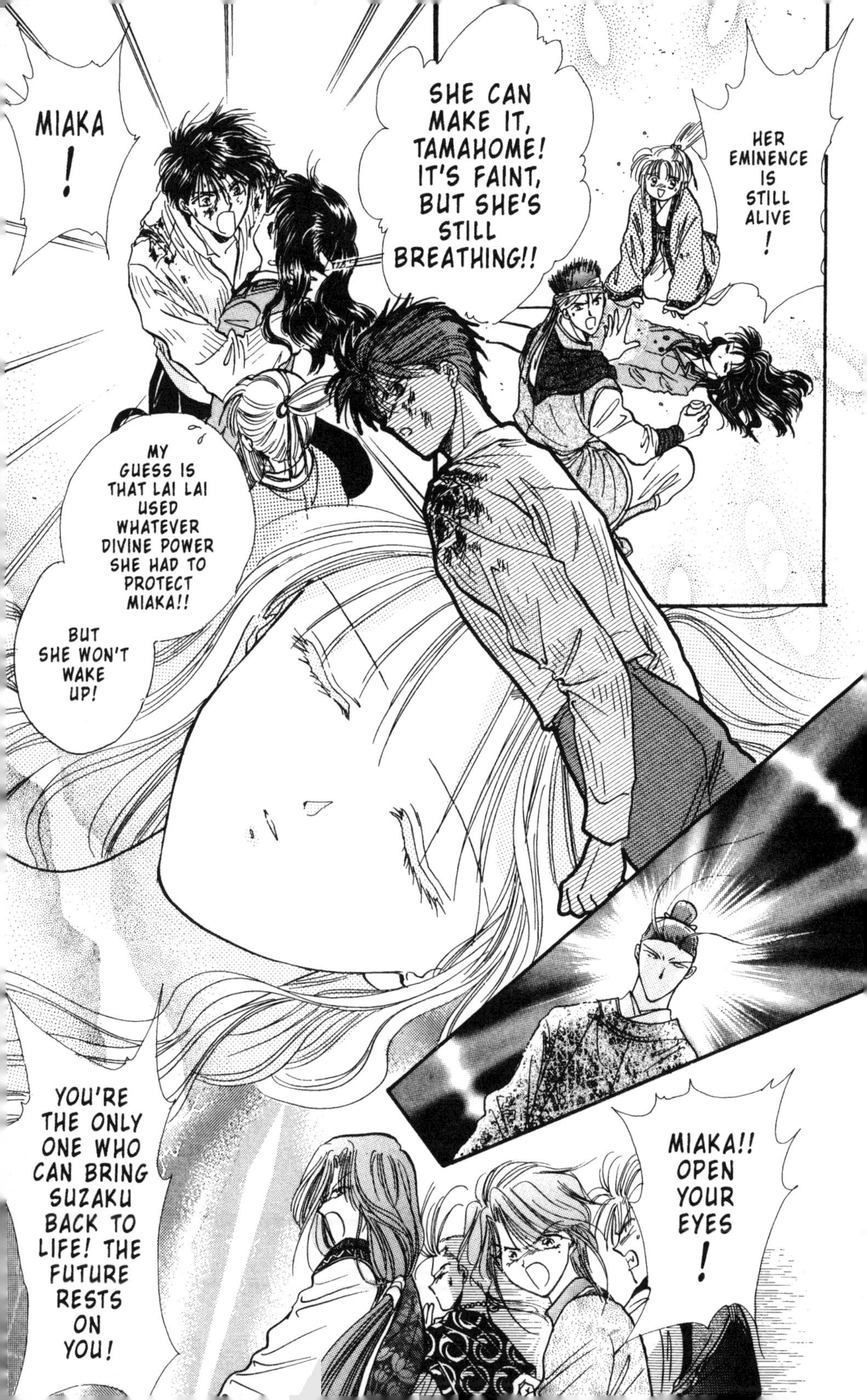
HER EMINENCE IS STILL ALIVE!
SHE CAN MAKE IT, TAMAHOME! IT'S FAINT, BUT SHE'S STILL BREATHING!!
MIAKA!
MY GUESS IS THAT LAI LAI USED WHATEVER DIVINE POWER SHE HAD TO PROTECT MIAKA!!
BUT SHE WON'T WAKE UP!
MIAKA!! OPEN YOUR EYES!
YOU'RE THE ONLY ONE WHO CAN BRING SUZAKU BACK TO LIFE! THE FUTURE RESTS ON YOU!

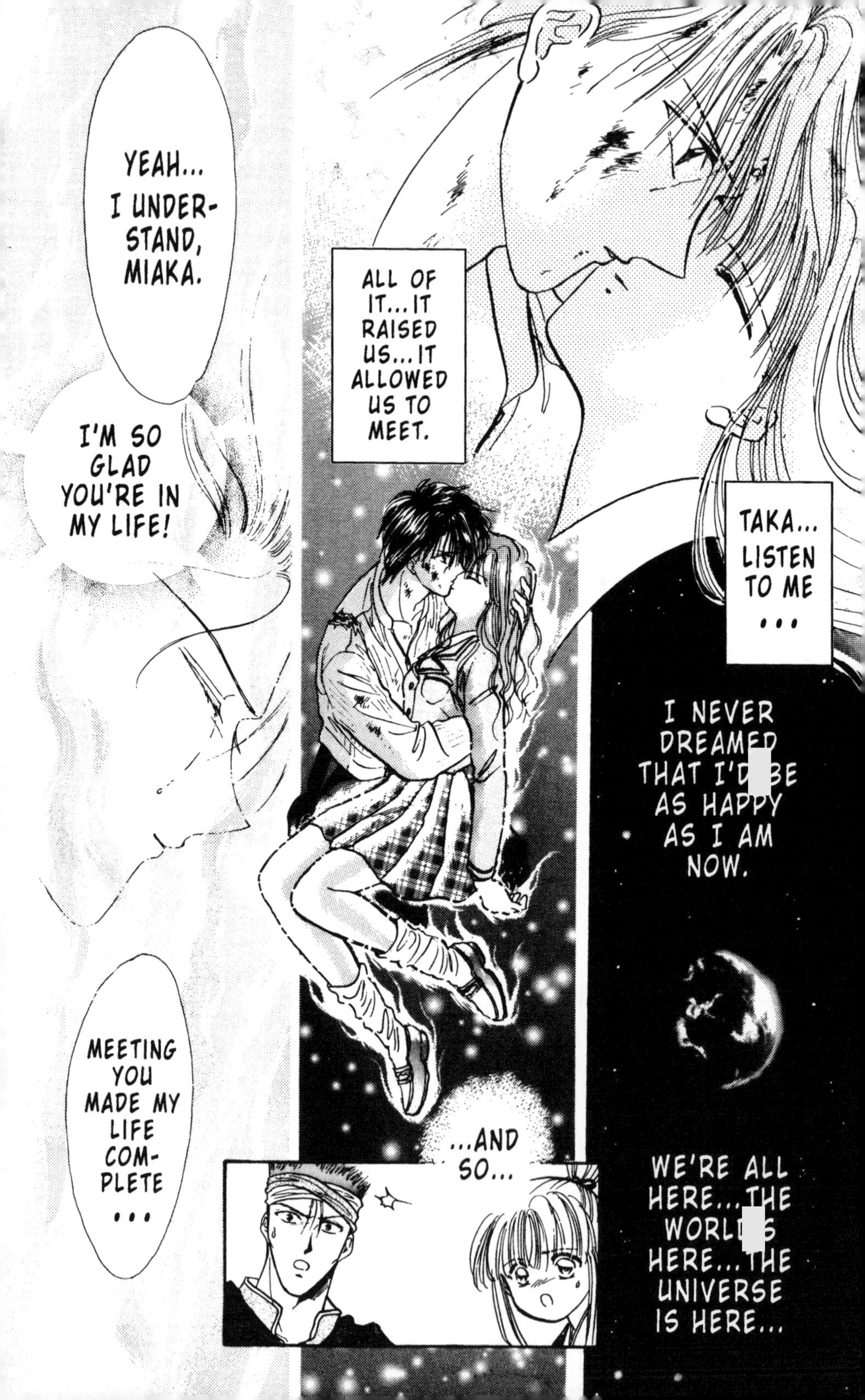
TAKA... LISTEN TO ME...
I NEVER DREAMED THAT I'D BE AS HAPPY AS I AM NOW.
ALL OF IT... IT RAISED US... IT ALLOWED US TO MEET.
YEAH... I UNDERSTAND, MIAKA.
I'M SO GLAD YOU'RE IN MY LIFE!
WE'RE ALL HERE... THE WORLD'S HERE... THE UNIVERSE IS HERE...
...AND SO...
MEETING YOU MADE MY LIFE COMPLETE...

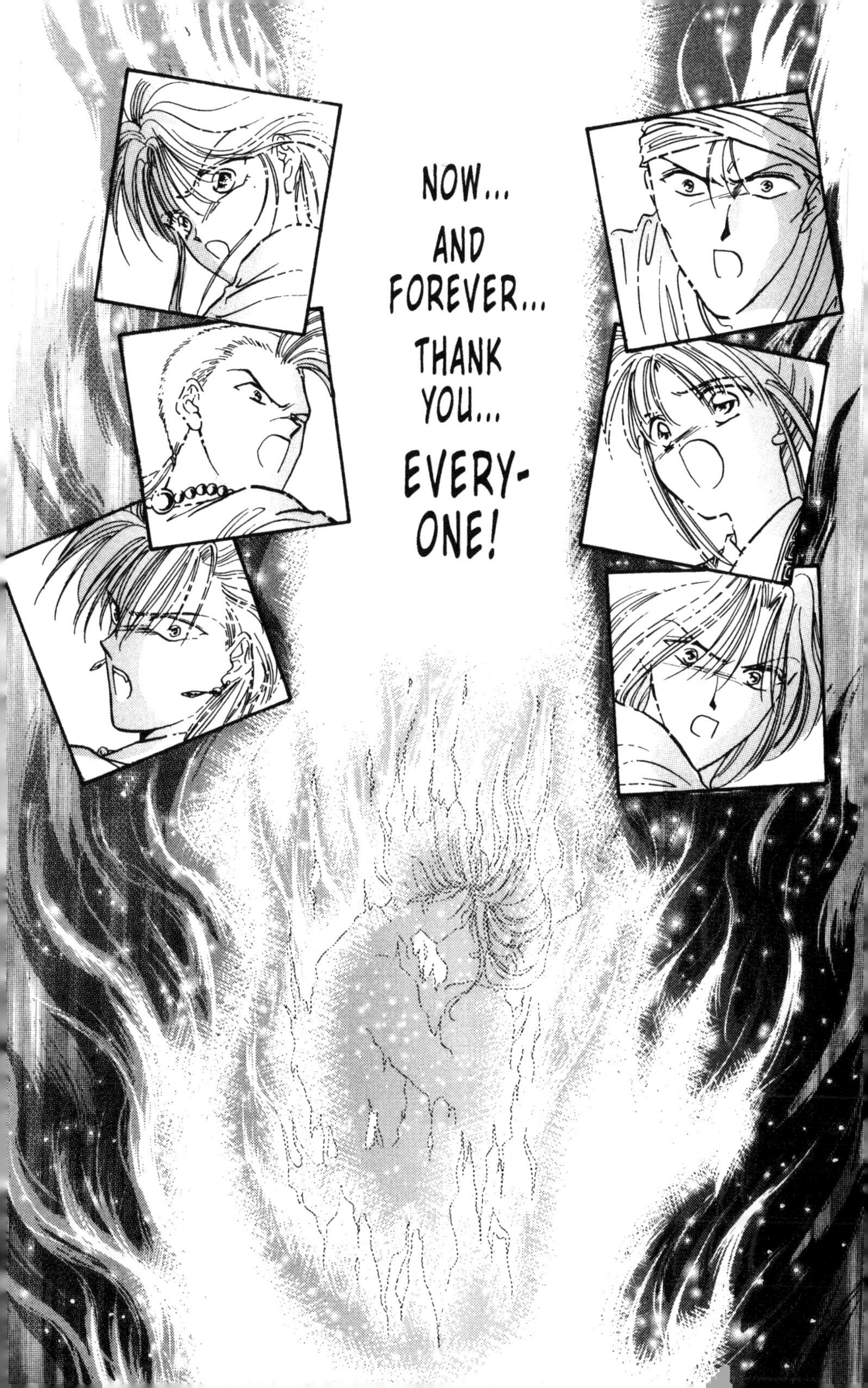
NOW... AND FOREVER... THANK YOU... EVERY-ONE!

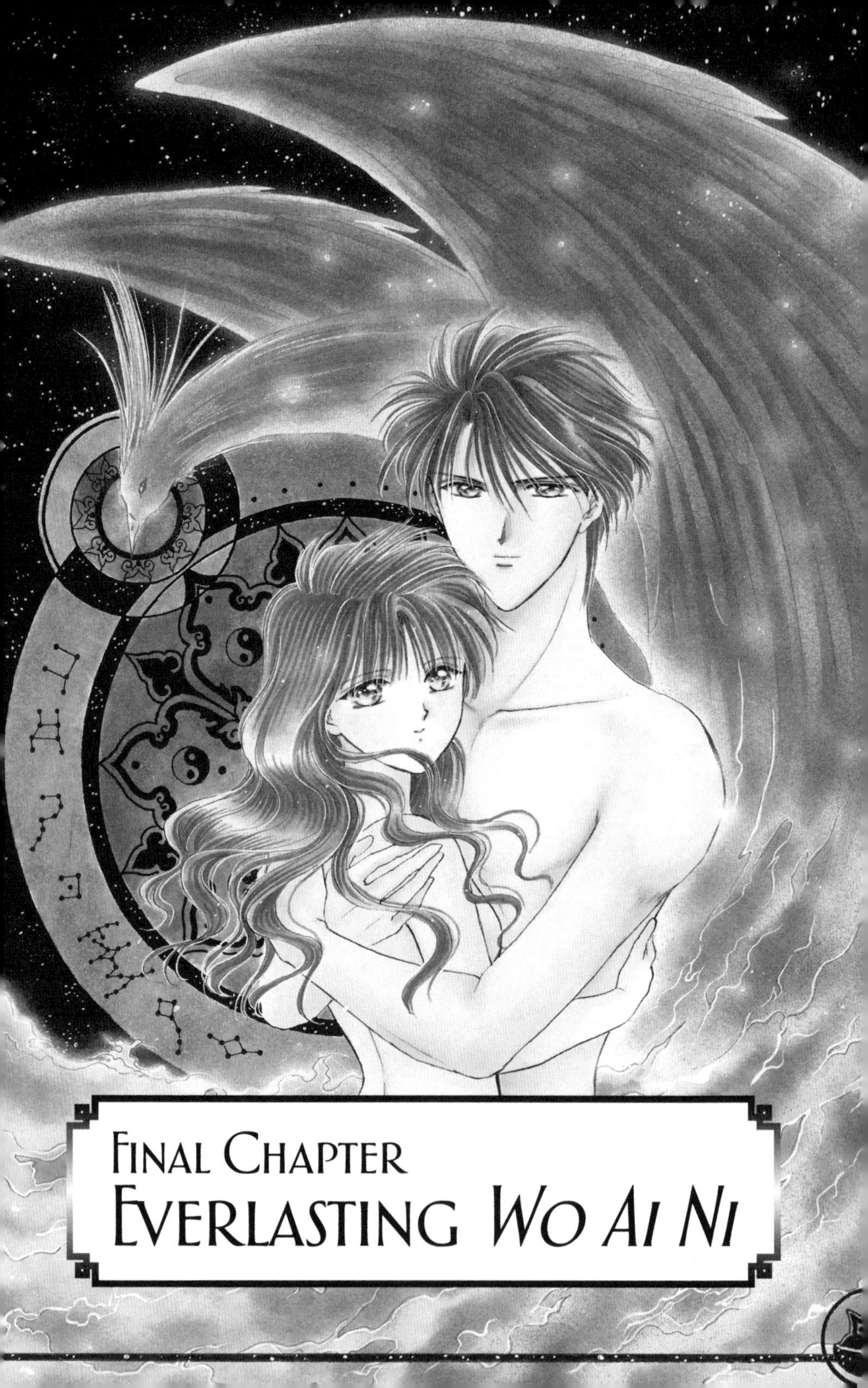
Final Chapter
Everlasting *Wo Ai Ni*

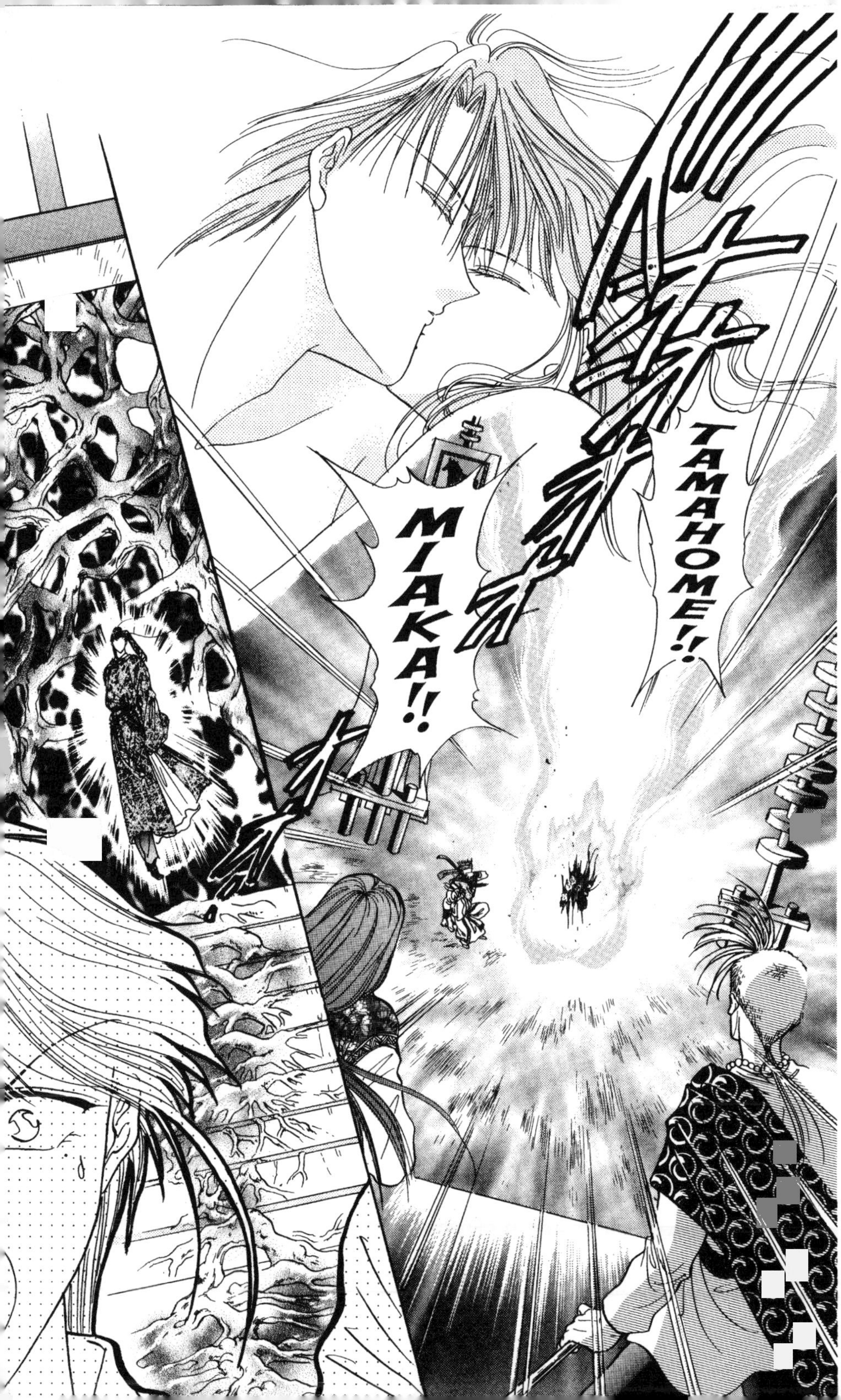
TAMAHOME!!
MIAKA!!

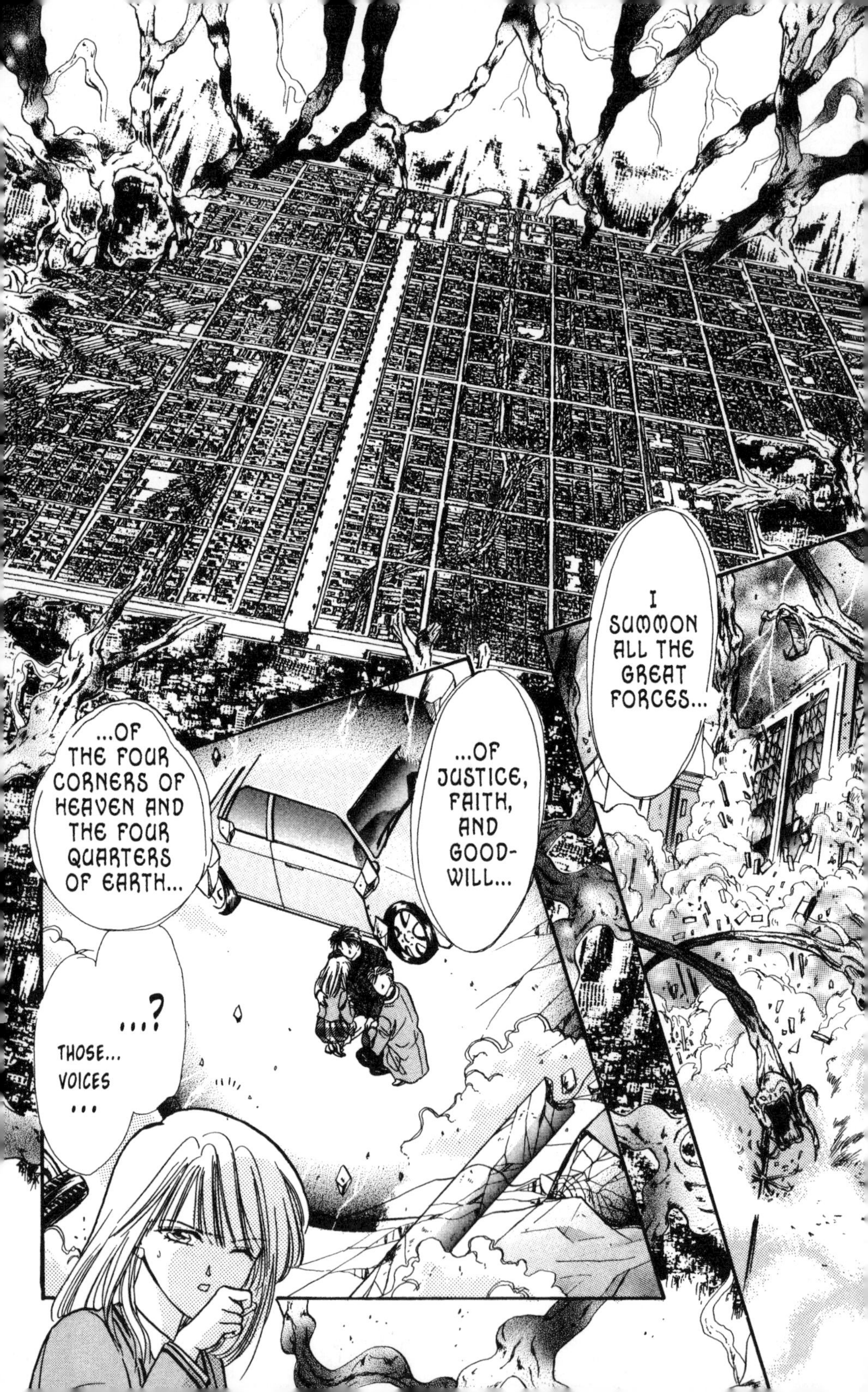
I SUMMON ALL THE GREAT FORCES...
...OF JUSTICE, FAITH, AND GOOD-WILL...
...OF THE FOUR CORNERS OF HEAVEN AND THE FOUR QUARTERS OF EARTH...
...?
THOSE... VOICES ...

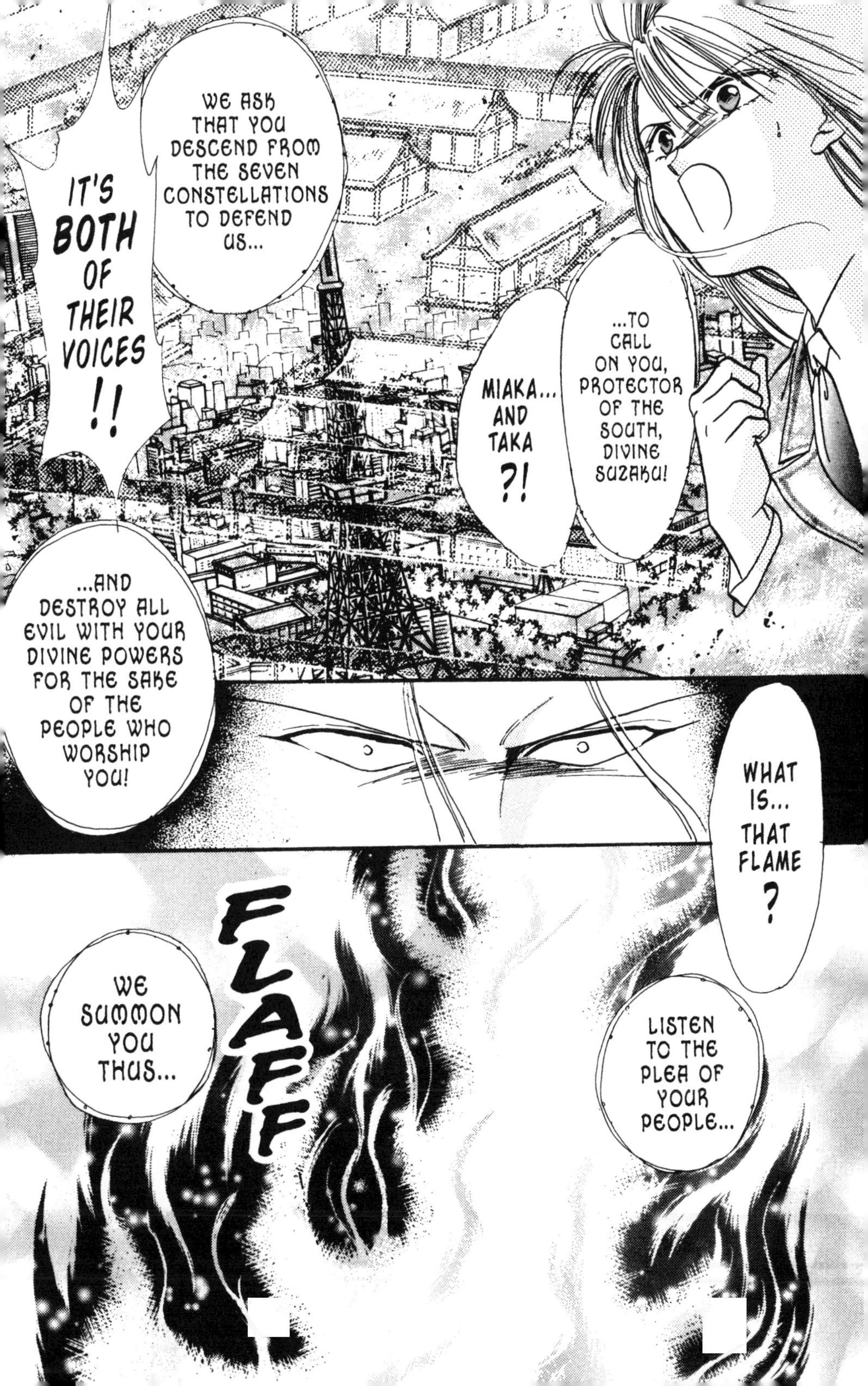
...TO CALL ON YOU, PROTECTOR OF THE SOUTH, DIVINE SUZAKU!
MIAKA... AND TAKA ?!
WE ASK THAT YOU DESCEND FROM THE SEVEN CONSTELLATIONS TO DEFEND US...
IT'S BOTH OF THEIR VOICES !!
...AND DESTROY ALL EVIL WITH YOUR DIVINE POWERS FOR THE SAKE OF THE PEOPLE WHO WORSHIP YOU!
WHAT IS... THAT FLAME ?
LISTEN TO THE PLEA OF YOUR PEOPLE...
FLAFF
WE SUMMON YOU THUS...

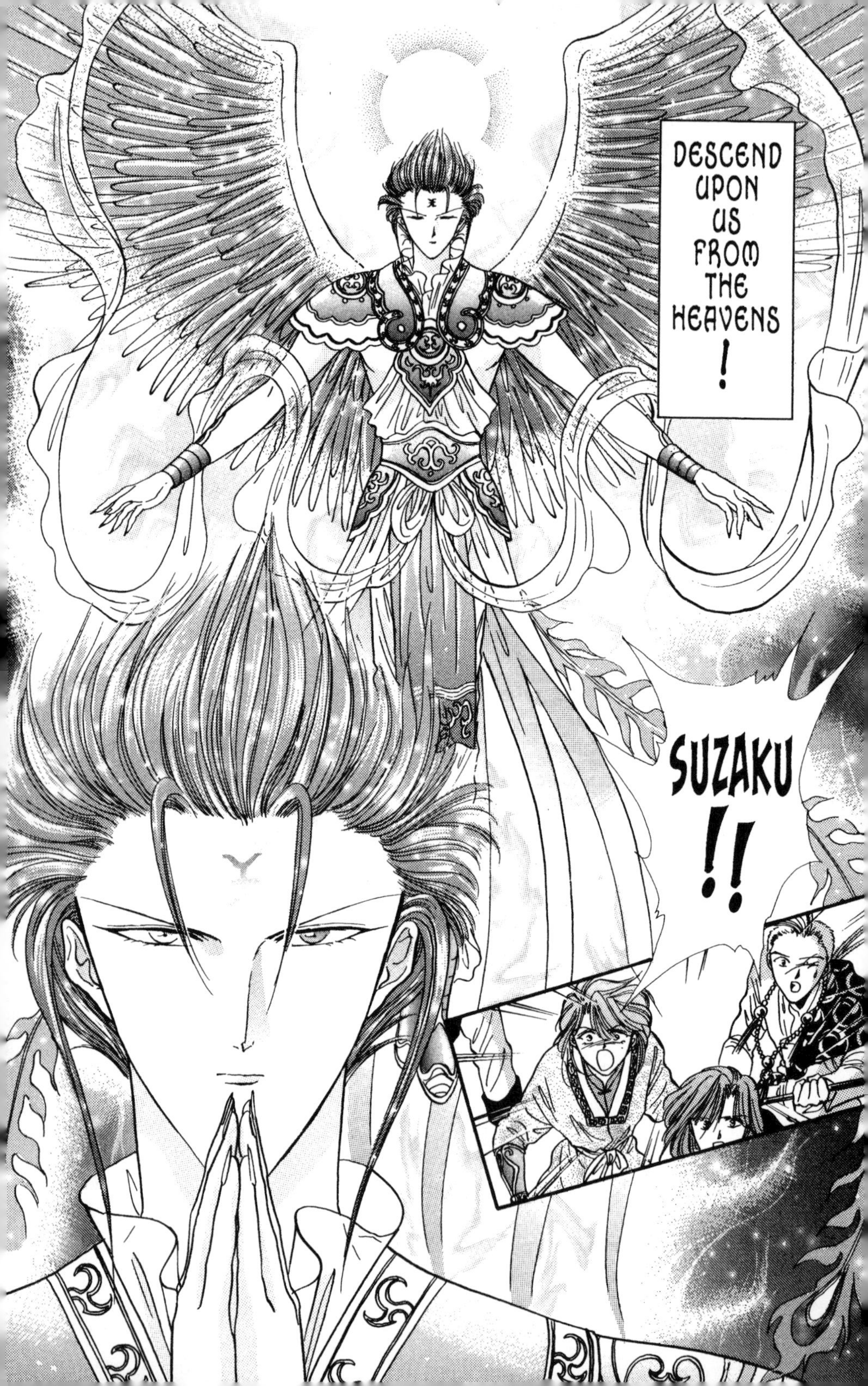
DESCEND UPON US FROM THE HEAVENS!
SUZAKU!!

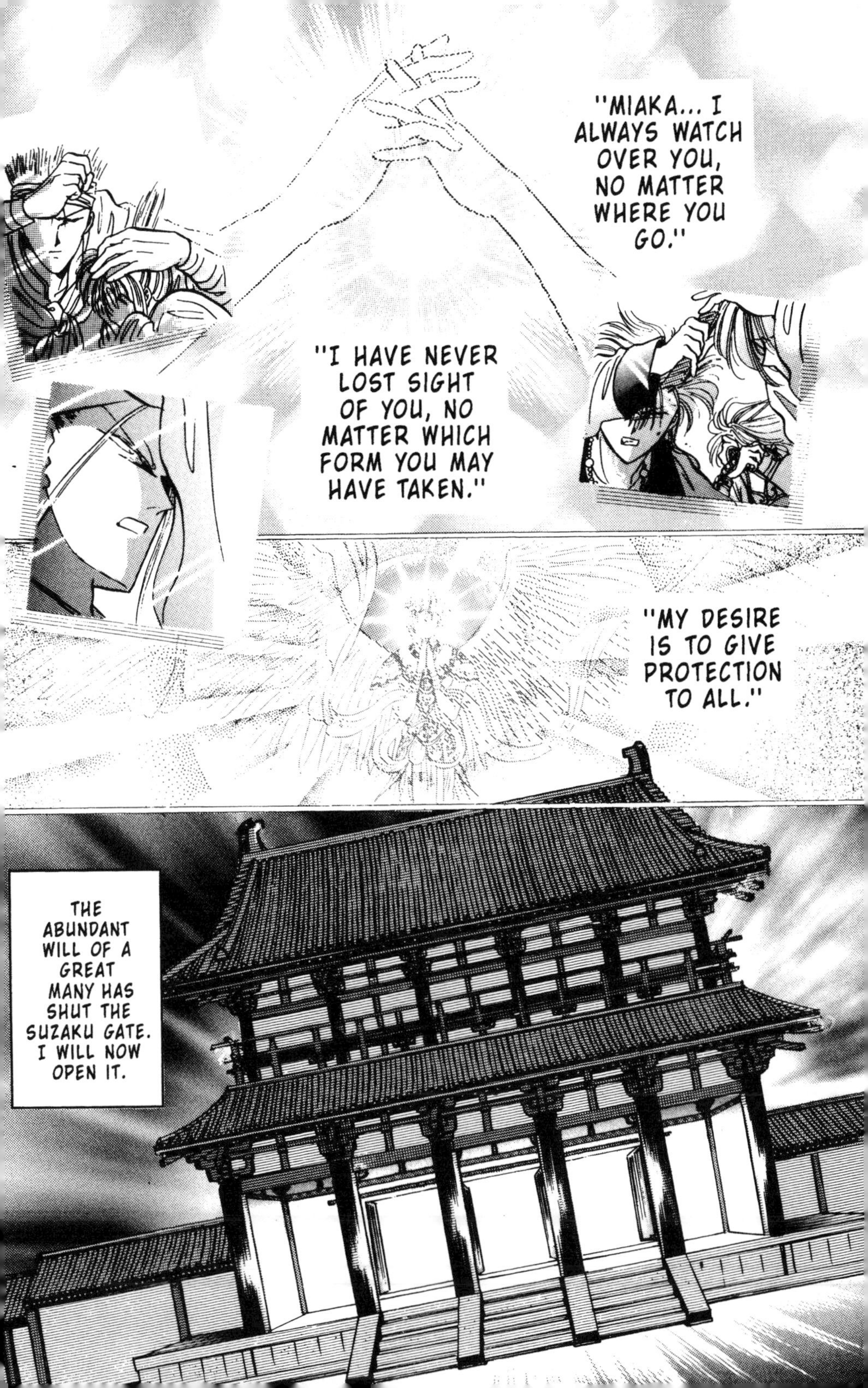
"MIAKA... I ALWAYS WATCH OVER YOU, NO MATTER WHERE YOU GO."
"I HAVE NEVER LOST SIGHT OF YOU, NO MATTER WHICH FORM YOU MAY HAVE TAKEN."
"MY DESIRE IS TO GIVE PROTECTION TO ALL."
THE ABUNDANT WILL OF A GREAT MANY HAS SHUT THE SUZAKU GATE. I WILL NOW OPEN IT.

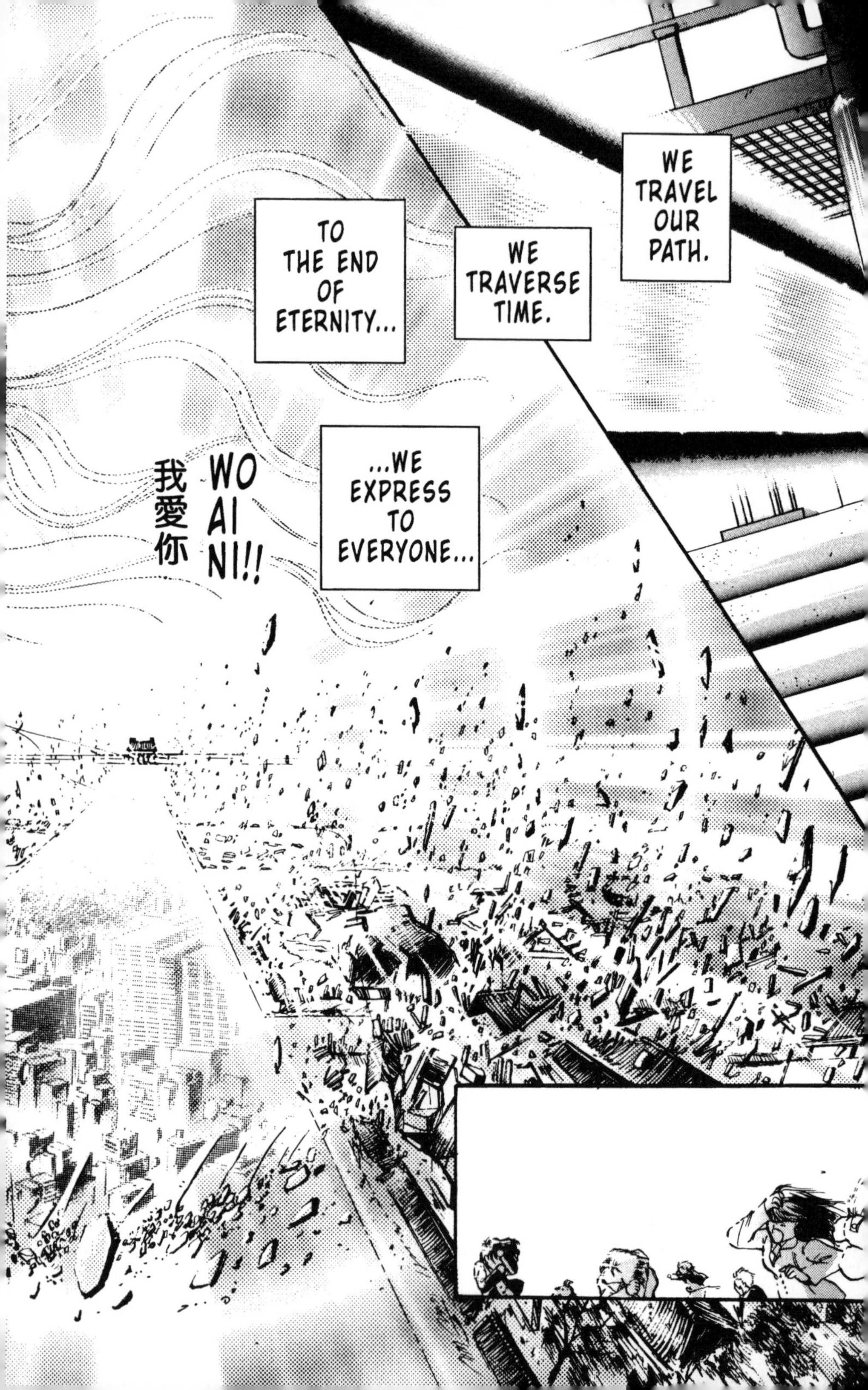
WE TRAVEL OUR PATH.
WE TRAVERSE TIME.
TO THE END OF ETERNITY...
...WE EXPRESS TO EVERYONE...
WO AI NI!!
我愛你

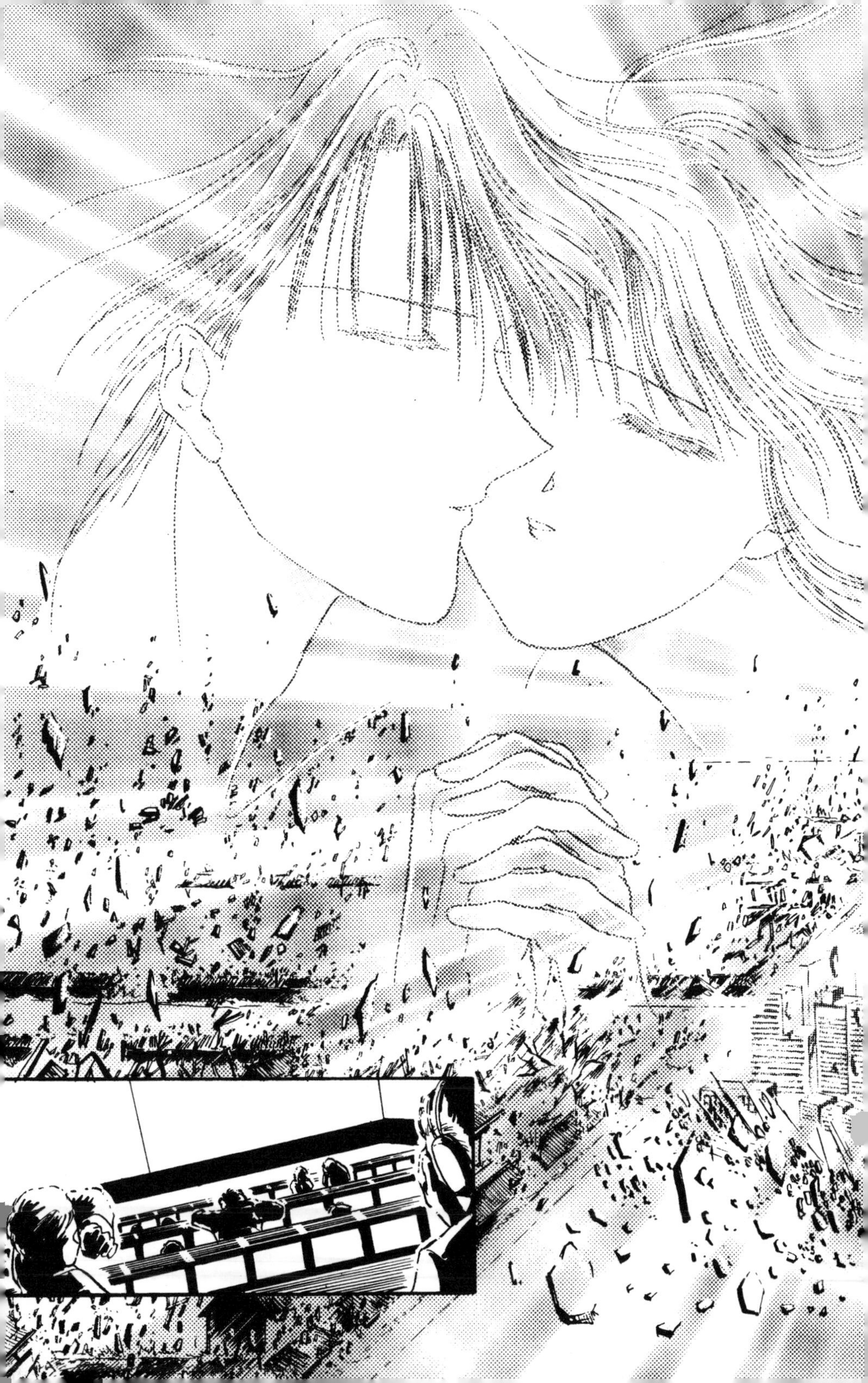

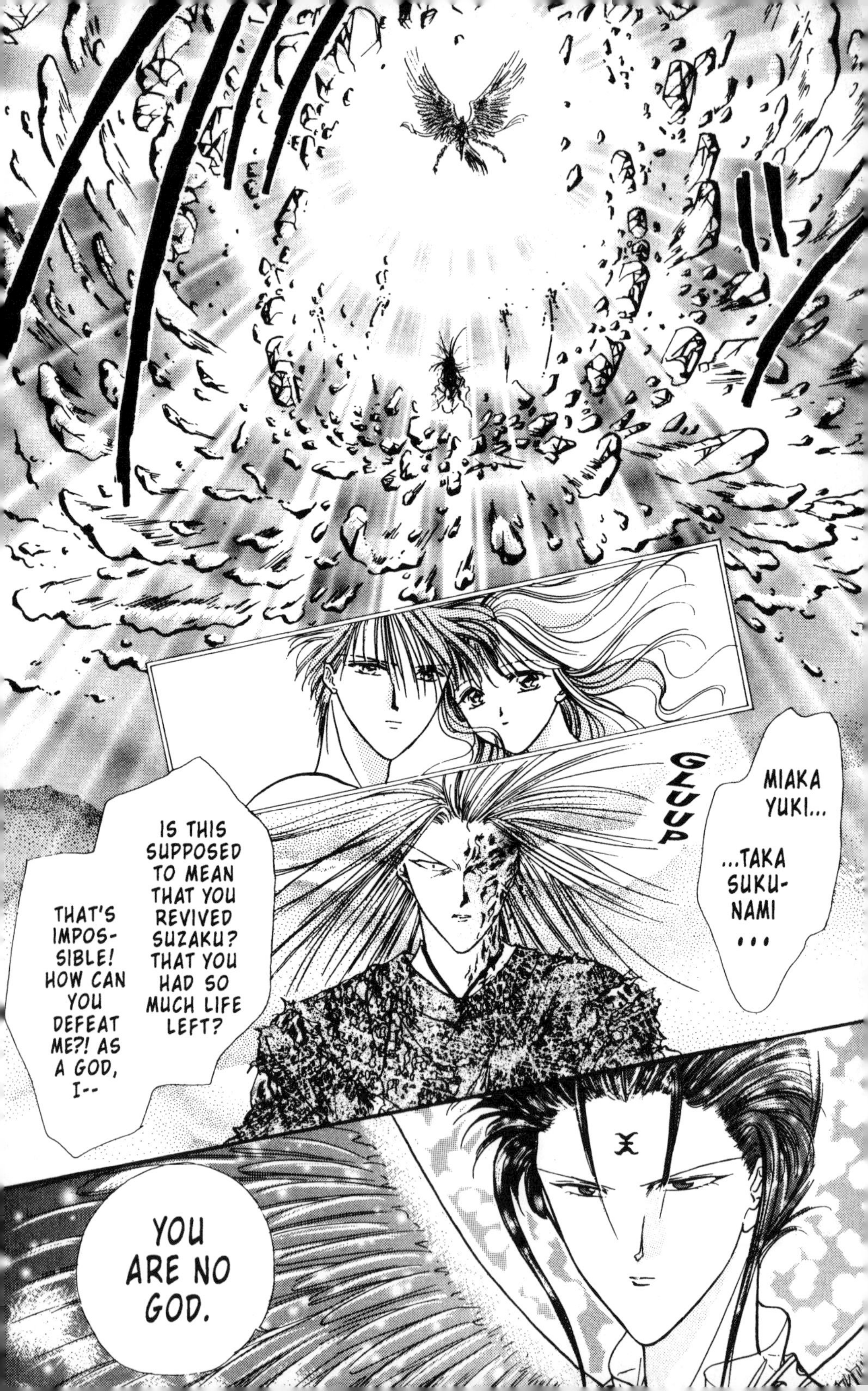
MIAKA YUKI...
...TAKA SUKU-NAMI...
GLUUUP
IS THIS SUPPOSED TO MEAN THAT YOU REVIVED SUZAKU? THAT YOU HAD SO MUCH LIFE LEFT?
THAT'S IMPOS-SIBLE! HOW CAN YOU DEFEAT ME?! AS A GOD, I--
YOU ARE NO GOD.

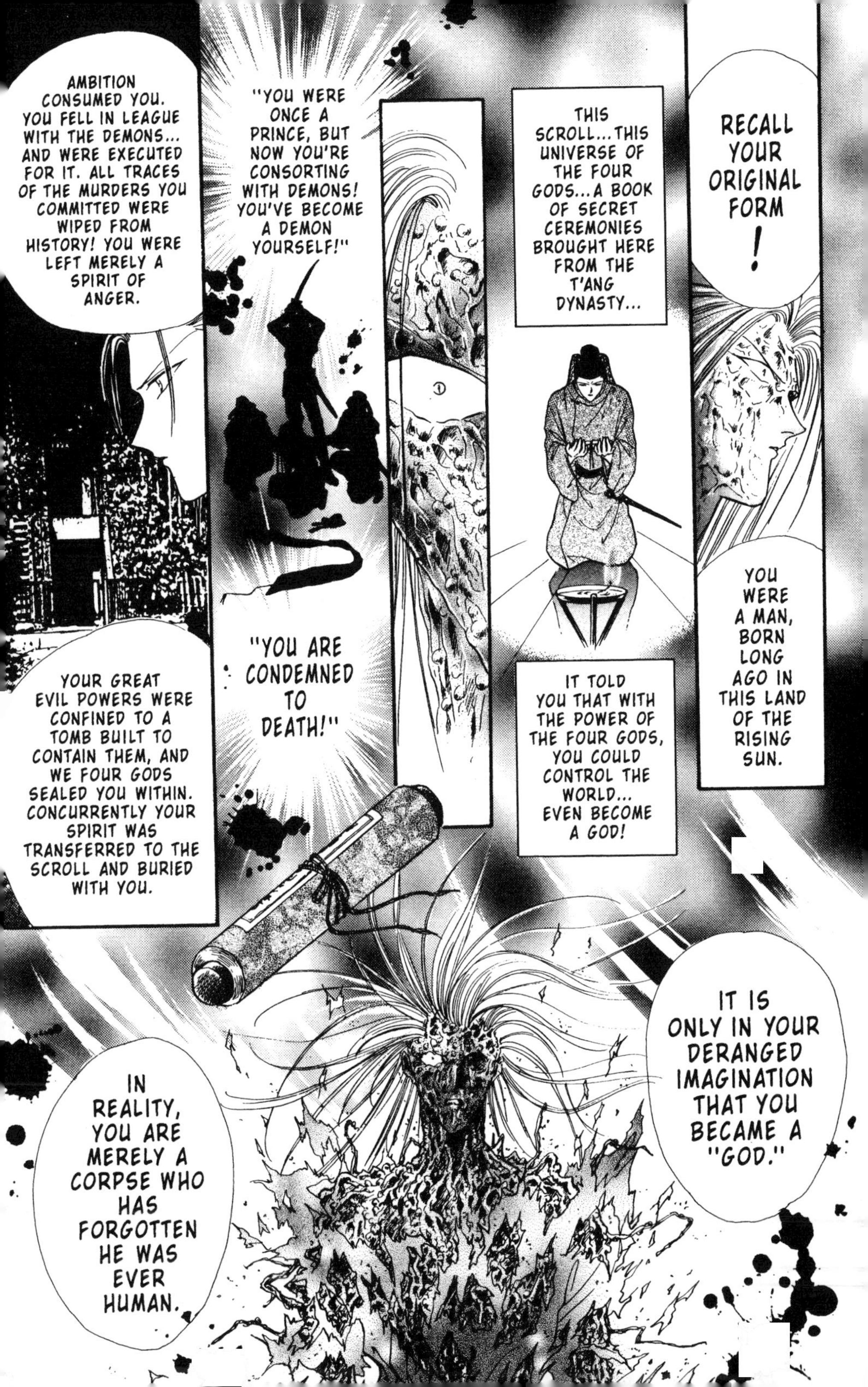
RECALL YOUR ORIGINAL FORM!
YOU WERE A MAN, BORN LONG AGO IN THIS LAND OF THE RISING SUN.
THIS SCROLL...THIS UNIVERSE OF THE FOUR GODS...A BOOK OF SECRET CEREMONIES BROUGHT HERE FROM THE T'ANG DYNASTY...
IT TOLD YOU THAT WITH THE POWER OF THE FOUR GODS, YOU COULD CONTROL THE WORLD... EVEN BECOME A GOD!
"YOU WERE ONCE A PRINCE, BUT NOW YOU'RE CONSORTING WITH DEMONS! YOU'VE BECOME A DEMON YOURSELF!"
"YOU ARE CONDEMNED TO DEATH!"
AMBITION CONSUMED YOU. YOU FELL IN LEAGUE WITH THE DEMONS... AND WERE EXECUTED FOR IT. ALL TRACES OF THE MURDERS YOU COMMITTED WERE WIPED FROM HISTORY! YOU WERE LEFT MERELY A SPIRIT OF ANGER.
YOUR GREAT EVIL POWERS WERE CONFINED TO A TOMB BUILT TO CONTAIN THEM, AND WE FOUR GODS SEALED YOU WITHIN. CONCURRENTLY YOUR SPIRIT WAS TRANSFERRED TO THE SCROLL AND BURIED WITH YOU.
IT IS ONLY IN YOUR DERANGED IMAGINATION THAT YOU BECAME A "GOD."
IN REALITY, YOU ARE MERELY A CORPSE WHO HAS FORGOTTEN HE WAS EVER HUMAN.

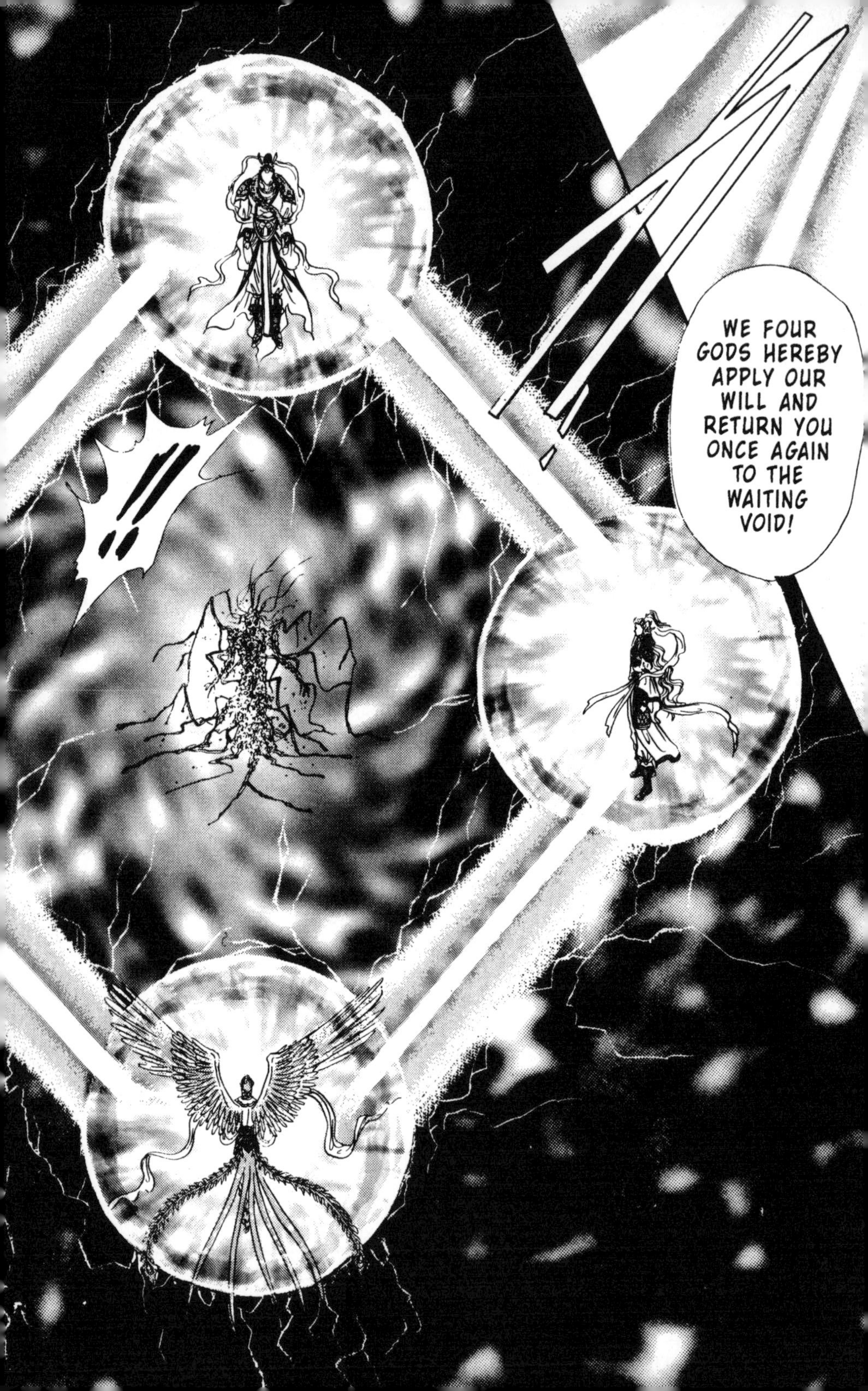
WE FOUR GODS HEREBY APPLY OUR WILL AND RETURN YOU ONCE AGAIN TO THE WAITING VOID!
!!

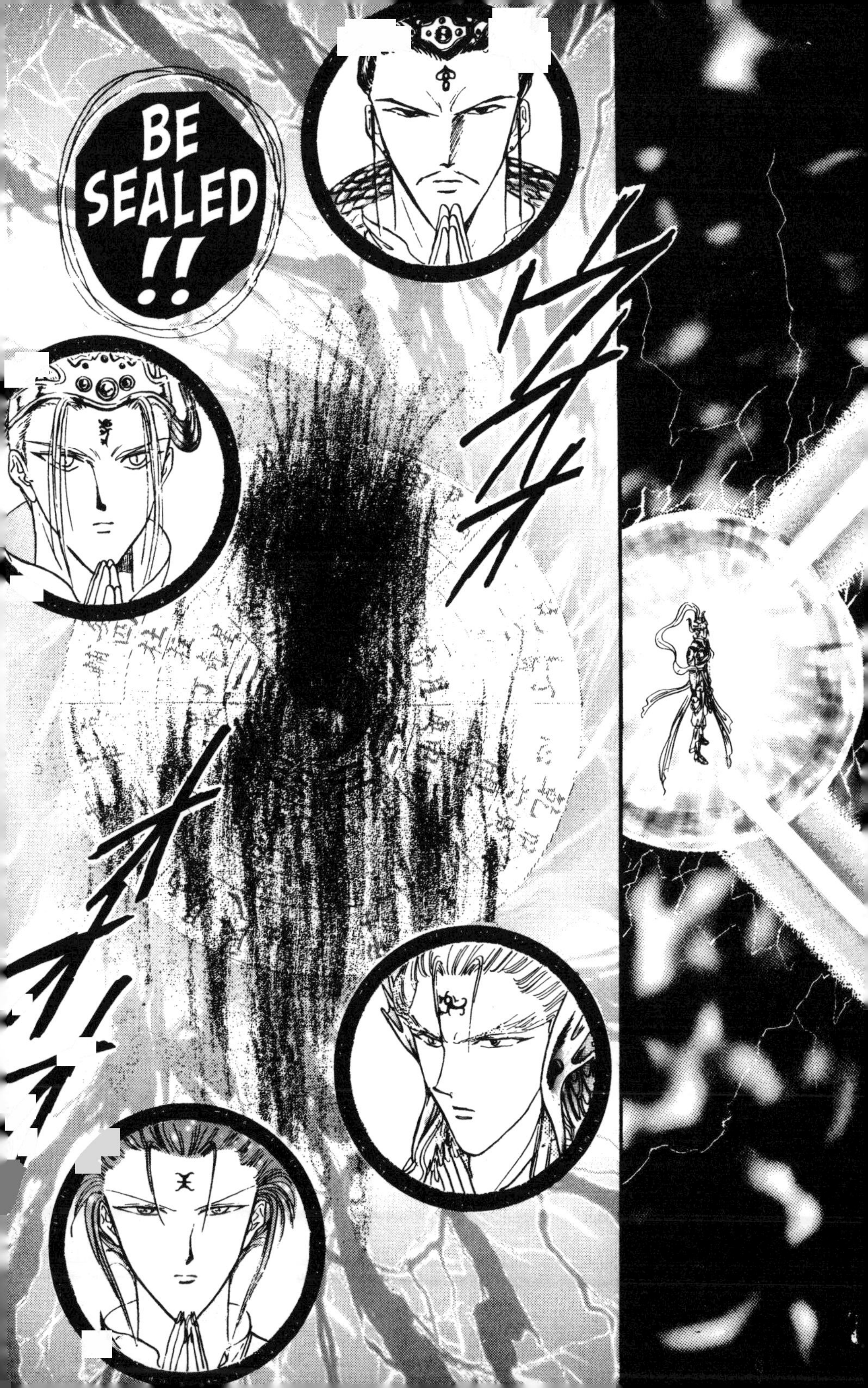
BE SEALED!!

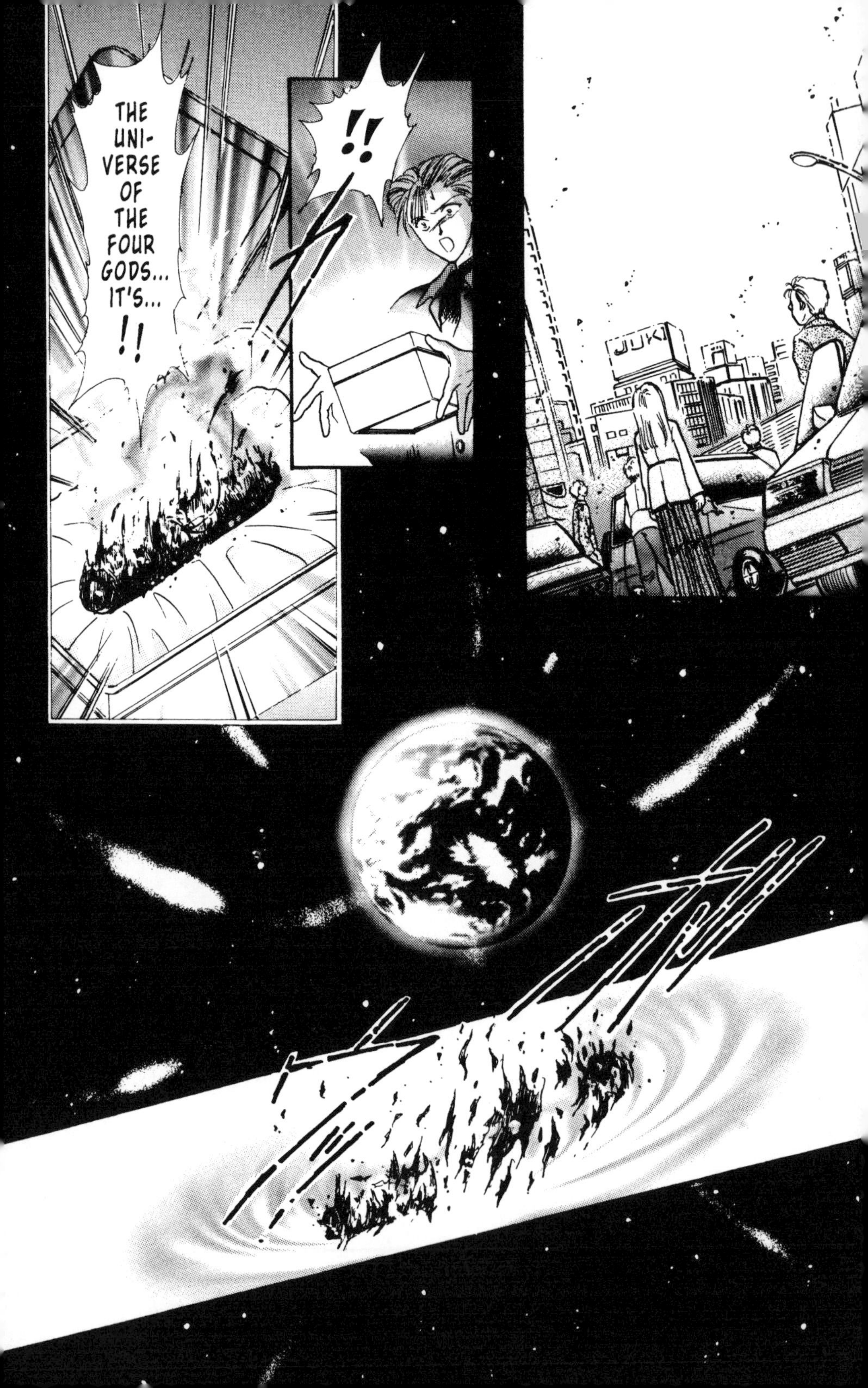
!!
THE UNIVERSE OF THE FOUR GODS... IT'S...!!
JUKI

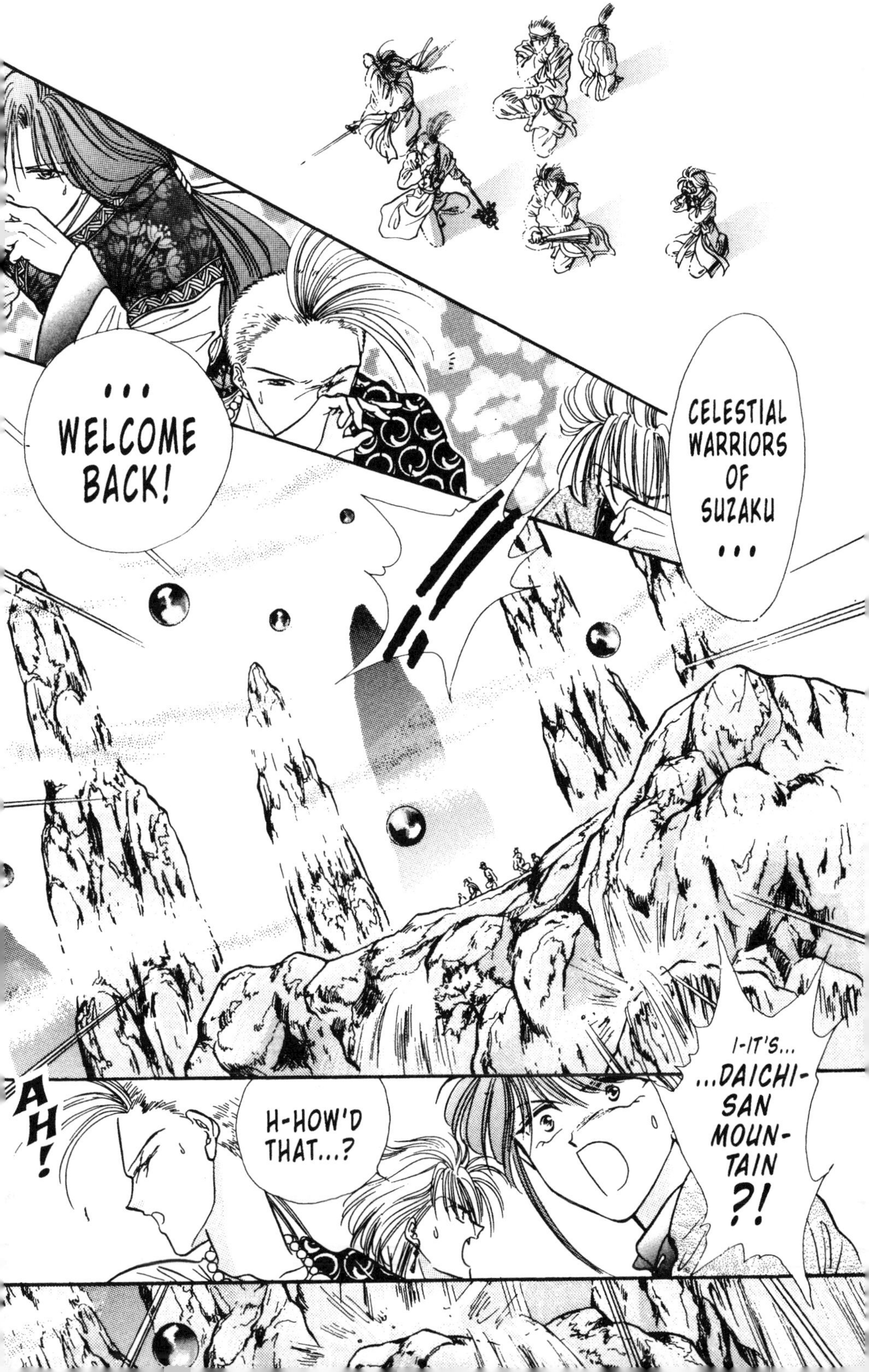
CELESTIAL WARRIORS OF SUZAKU...
...WELCOME BACK!
I-IT'S... ...DAICHI-SAN MOUNTAIN?!
H-HOW'D THAT...?
AH!

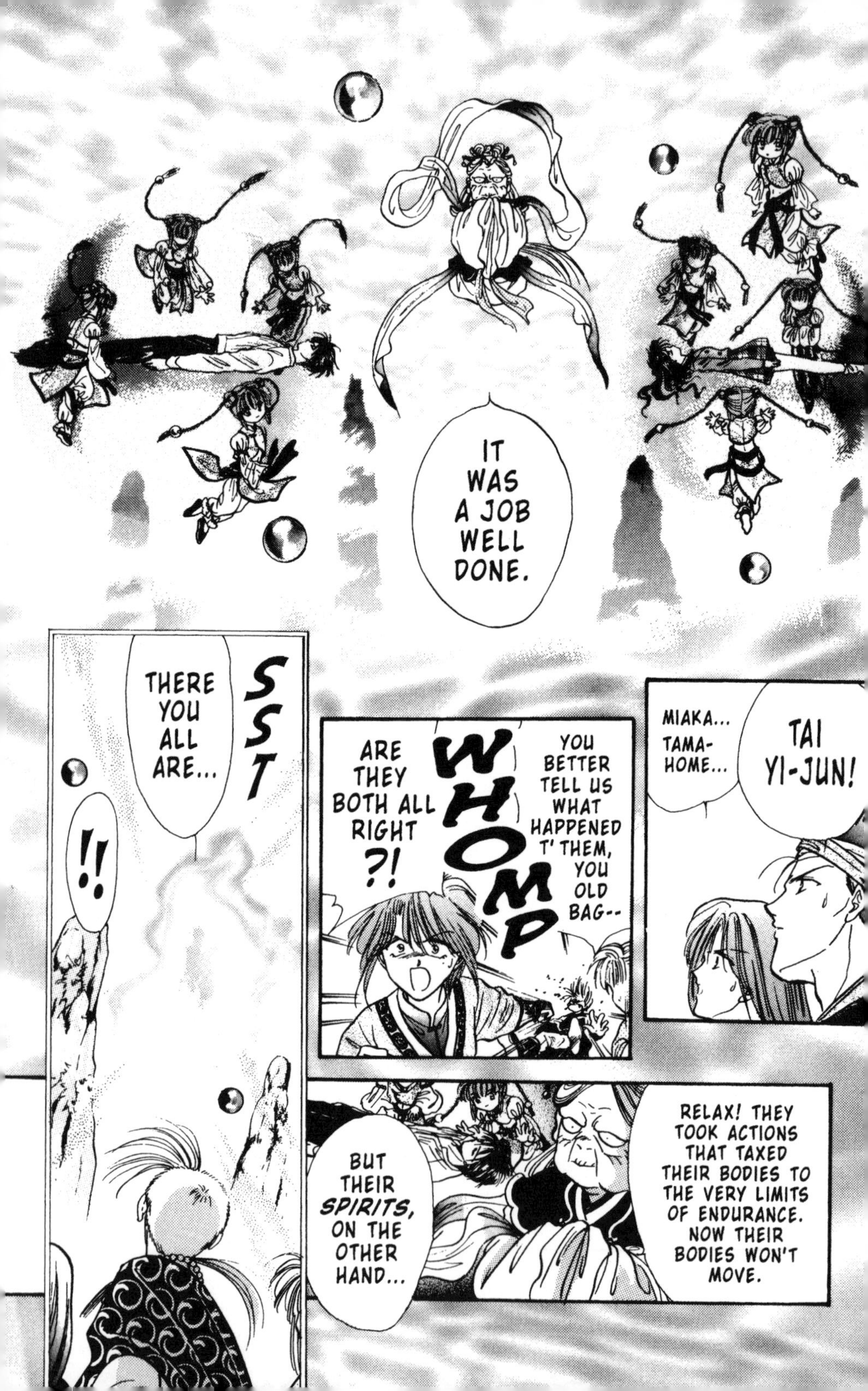
IT WAS A JOB WELL DONE.
TAI YI-JUN!
MIAKA... TAMA-HOME...
YOU BETTER TELL US WHAT HAPPENED T' THEM, YOU OLD BAG--
WHOMP
ARE THEY BOTH ALL RIGHT?!
RELAX! THEY TOOK ACTIONS THAT TAXED THEIR BODIES TO THE VERY LIMITS OF ENDURANCE. NOW THEIR BODIES WON'T MOVE.
BUT THEIR *SPIRITS*, ON THE OTHER HAND...
THERE YOU ALL ARE...
SST
!!

Now... Of all the deviations from the original story, the greatest one happened at the end of Part 1. And now I'm willing to tell you about it!
From the moment I started the series until there were only five or six chapters left, *I HAD PLANNED FOR MIAKA AND TAMAHOME TO SPLIT UP AT THE END.* My reasoning was, "Look, this is a story about how the main character views reality, and she could never wind up with such an ideal fiction of a man!" And for three years, the story was totally rooted in that concept. But...my editor at the time ♀ was dead set against it. And more than that, my own heart began to change... You remember, around chapter 70... I probably started to change my mind around the time Tamahome began to realize that he was a character out of a book and not a real human -- when that shock started to take hold. (The date they went on was supposed to be their last hurrah.) But I lost. I, the creator, tried to face down my own characters, Miaka and Tamahome, and lost.
Now I'm glad that I lost.
The way I see things, it's only natural for two lovers to see nobody but the one they love. They always want to be able to see the other's face...to hear the other's voice every day. When the other isn't around, it's lonely and painful. That's deep love -- the feeling that you'd like to become one with your lover. Those who don't understand that will just have to fall in love themselves, right? And when something like that happens, one feels grateful to the entire world for making it happen. That's how Miaka and Taka felt about it. But if you try to put their relationship from Part 1 in the context of reality, their love really is the "puppy love" of young men and women. Love is different from that. *Ha! A single woman saying all this!* In much the same way, all the Celestial Warriors, who are full of love themselves, ended up happy. I'm pretty sure of that. Even the ones who died will be just fine in the next life. Yeah! Considering that Part 2 is a manga with so many complications, it's interesting that I drew it with such an amazingly quiet heart. Yep! ☺

For volume 18's background music, any of these will do, so give them a try!

- Hiroko Taniyama: "Kyuka Ryoko" (Holiday Trip) & "Hitomi no Eien" (Eternal Eyes)
- PSY.S: Earth
- TMN: "Self Control" & "We Love the Earth"
- Daisuke Asakura: "D-Trick" & "1000-nen no Chikai" (1000 Year Vow)
- Akemi Sato: "Itoshii Hito no Tame Ni" Album Version (For the One I Love) From the CD Book.
- Yoko Ueno: "Sayonara wa Iranai" (There's no Need to Say Good Bye) & "Sennen no Chigiri" (Pledge of a Thousand Years)

I listened to this during vol. 13 too!

"Landing Time Machine." I've been listening to this ever since Part 1! *Especially Track 8!* Highly Recommended!

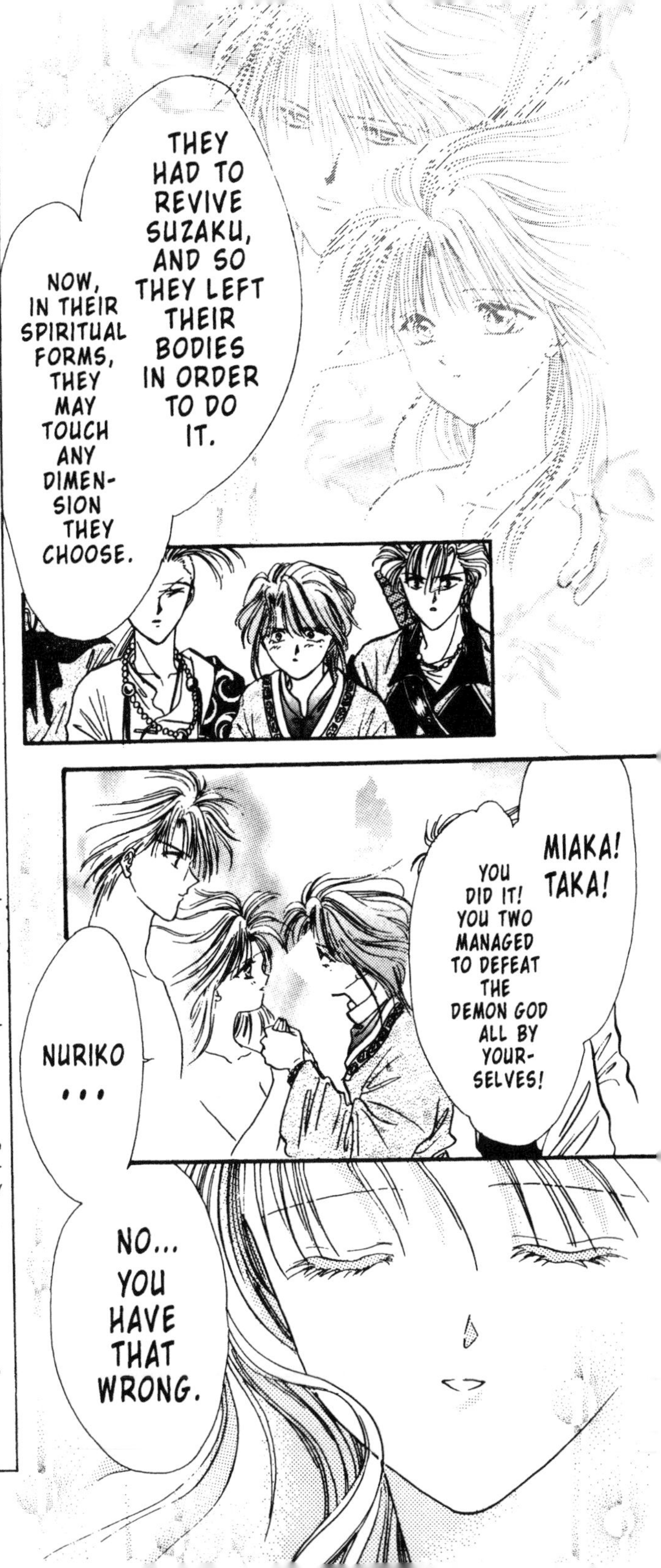
THEY HAD TO REVIVE SUZAKU, AND SO THEY LEFT THEIR BODIES IN ORDER TO DO IT.
NOW, IN THEIR SPIRITUAL FORMS, THEY MAY TOUCH ANY DIMENSION THEY CHOOSE.
MIAKA! TAKA!
YOU DID IT! YOU TWO MANAGED TO DEFEAT THE DEMON GOD ALL BY YOURSELVES!
NURIKO...
NO... YOU HAVE THAT WRONG.

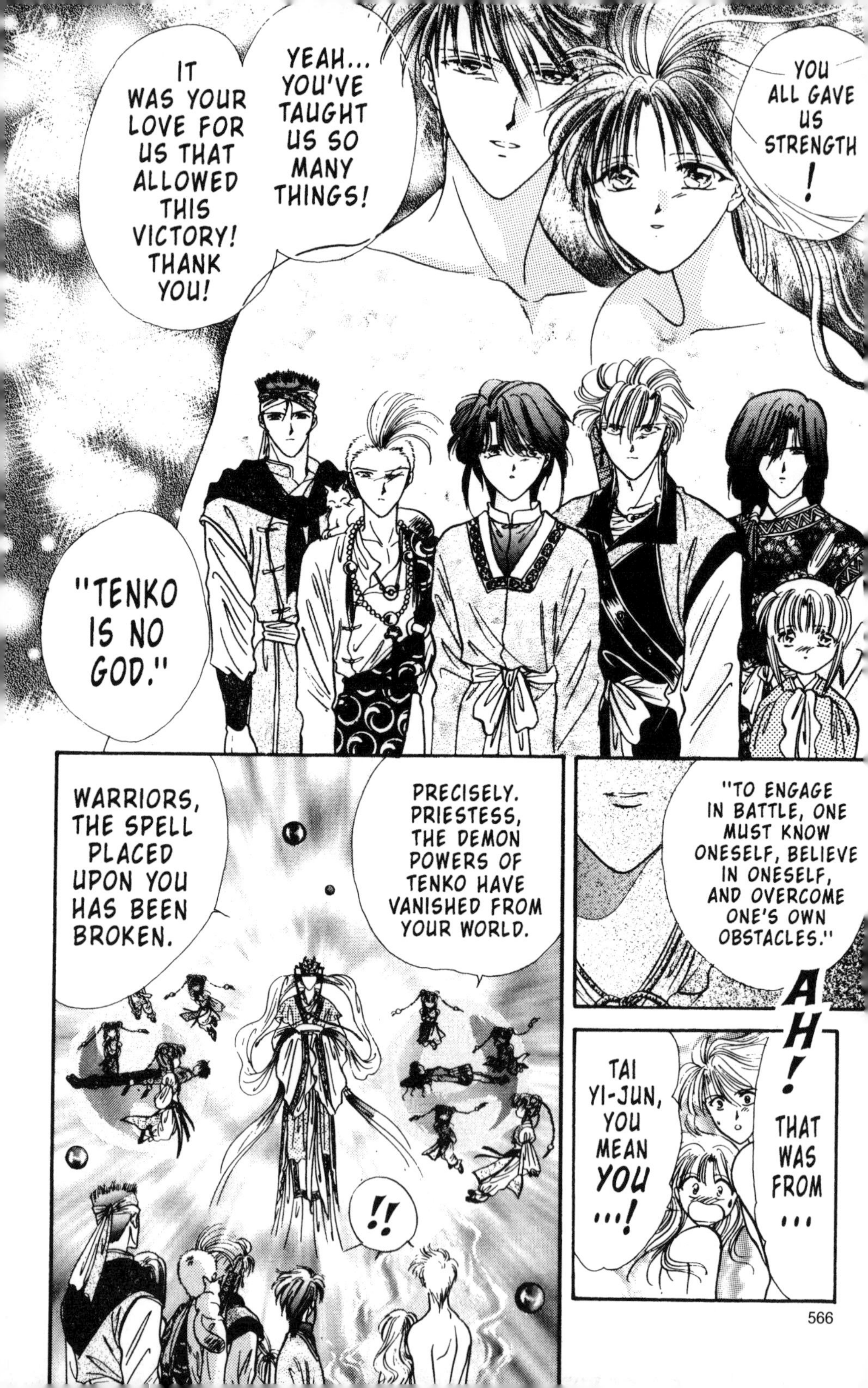
YOU ALL GAVE US STRENGTH!
YEAH... YOU'VE TAUGHT US SO MANY THINGS!
IT WAS YOUR LOVE FOR US THAT ALLOWED THIS VICTORY! THANK YOU!
"TENKO IS NO GOD."
"TO ENGAGE IN BATTLE, ONE MUST KNOW ONESELF, BELIEVE IN ONESELF, AND OVERCOME ONE'S OWN OBSTACLES."
AH!
THAT WAS FROM...
TAI YI-JUN, YOU MEAN YOU...!
PRECISELY. PRIESTESS, THE DEMON POWERS OF TENKO HAVE VANISHED FROM YOUR WORLD.
WARRIORS, THE SPELL PLACED UPON YOU HAS BEEN BROKEN.
!!

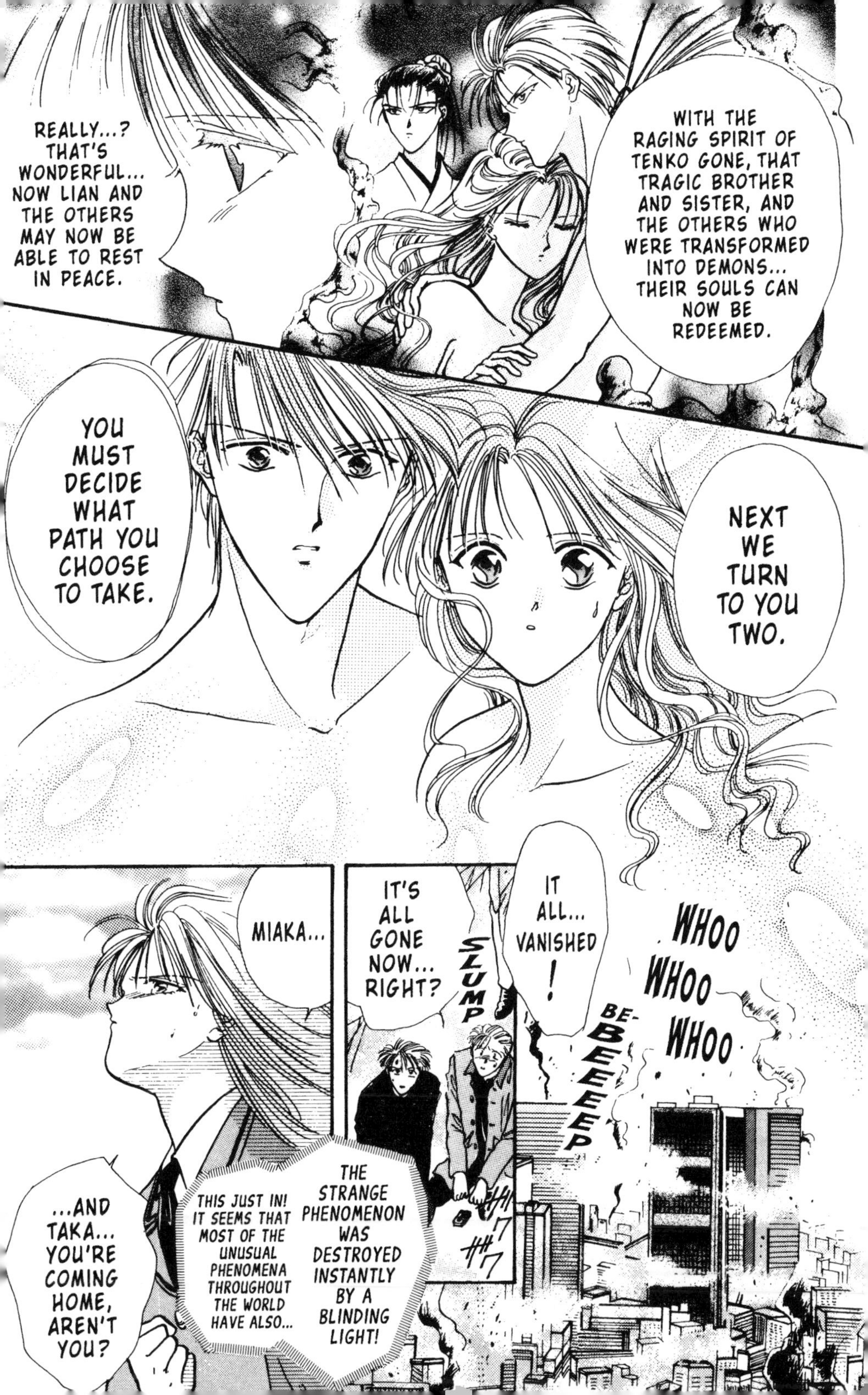
WITH THE RAGING SPIRIT OF TENKO GONE, THAT TRAGIC BROTHER AND SISTER, AND THE OTHERS WHO WERE TRANSFORMED INTO DEMONS... THEIR SOULS CAN NOW BE REDEEMED.
REALLY...? THAT'S WONDERFUL... NOW LIAN AND THE OTHERS MAY NOW BE ABLE TO REST IN PEACE.
NEXT WE TURN TO YOU TWO.
YOU MUST DECIDE WHAT PATH YOU CHOOSE TO TAKE.
WHOO WHOO WHOO
BE-BEEEEEP
IT ALL... VANISHED!
SLUMP
IT'S ALL GONE NOW... RIGHT?
THE STRANGE PHENOMENON WAS DESTROYED INSTANTLY BY A BLINDING LIGHT!
THIS JUST IN! IT SEEMS THAT MOST OF THE UNUSUAL PHENOMENA THROUGHOUT THE WORLD HAVE ALSO...
MIAKA...
...AND TAKA... YOU'RE COMING HOME, AREN'T YOU?

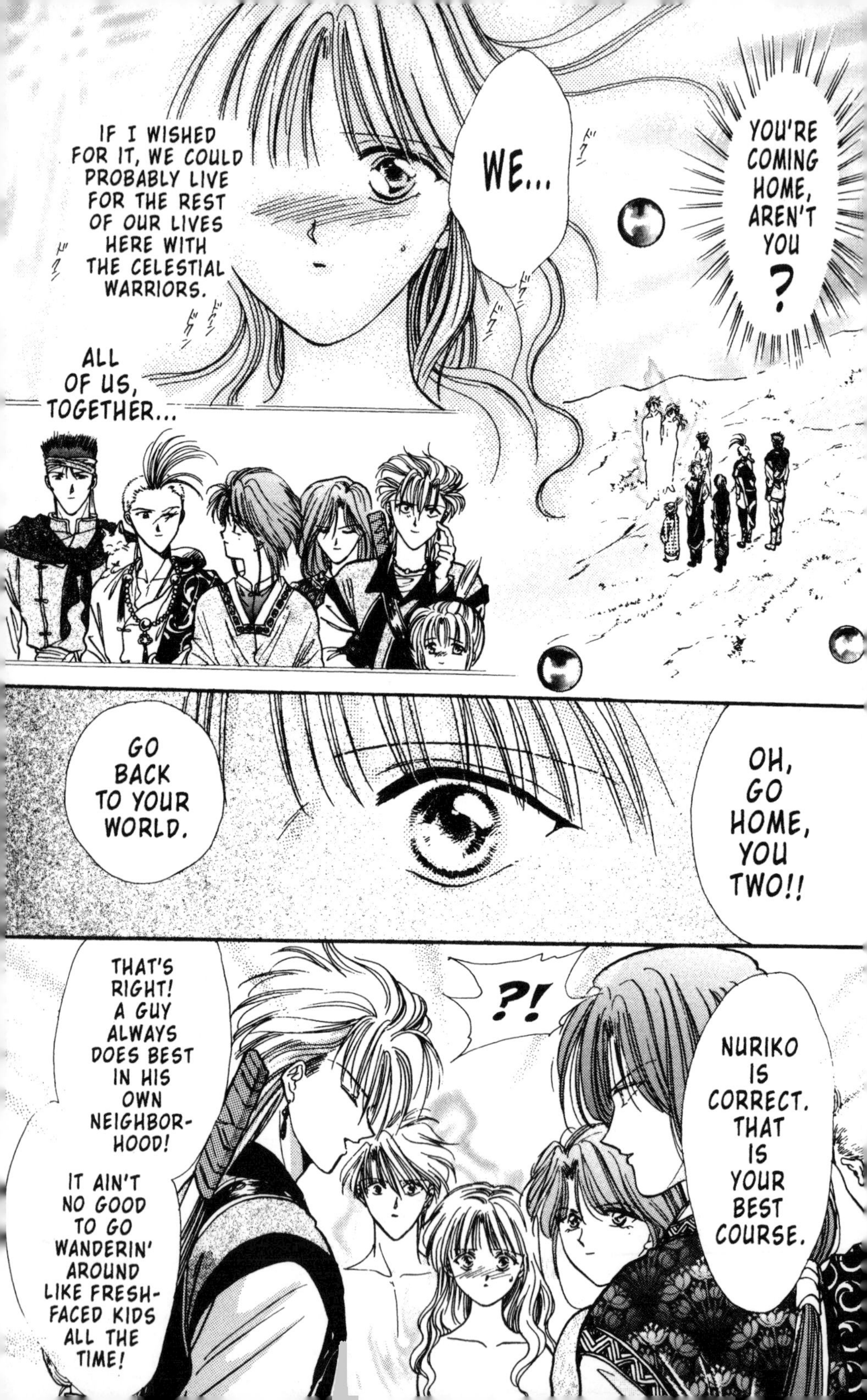
YOU'RE COMING HOME, AREN'T YOU?
WE...
IF I WISHED FOR IT, WE COULD PROBABLY LIVE FOR THE REST OF OUR LIVES HERE WITH THE CELESTIAL WARRIORS.
ALL OF US, TOGETHER...
OH, GO HOME, YOU TWO!!
GO BACK TO YOUR WORLD.
?!
NURIKO IS CORRECT. THAT IS YOUR BEST COURSE.
THAT'S RIGHT! A GUY ALWAYS DOES BEST IN HIS OWN NEIGHBOR-HOOD!
IT AIN'T NO GOOD TO GO WANDERIN' AROUND LIKE FRESH-FACED KIDS ALL THE TIME!

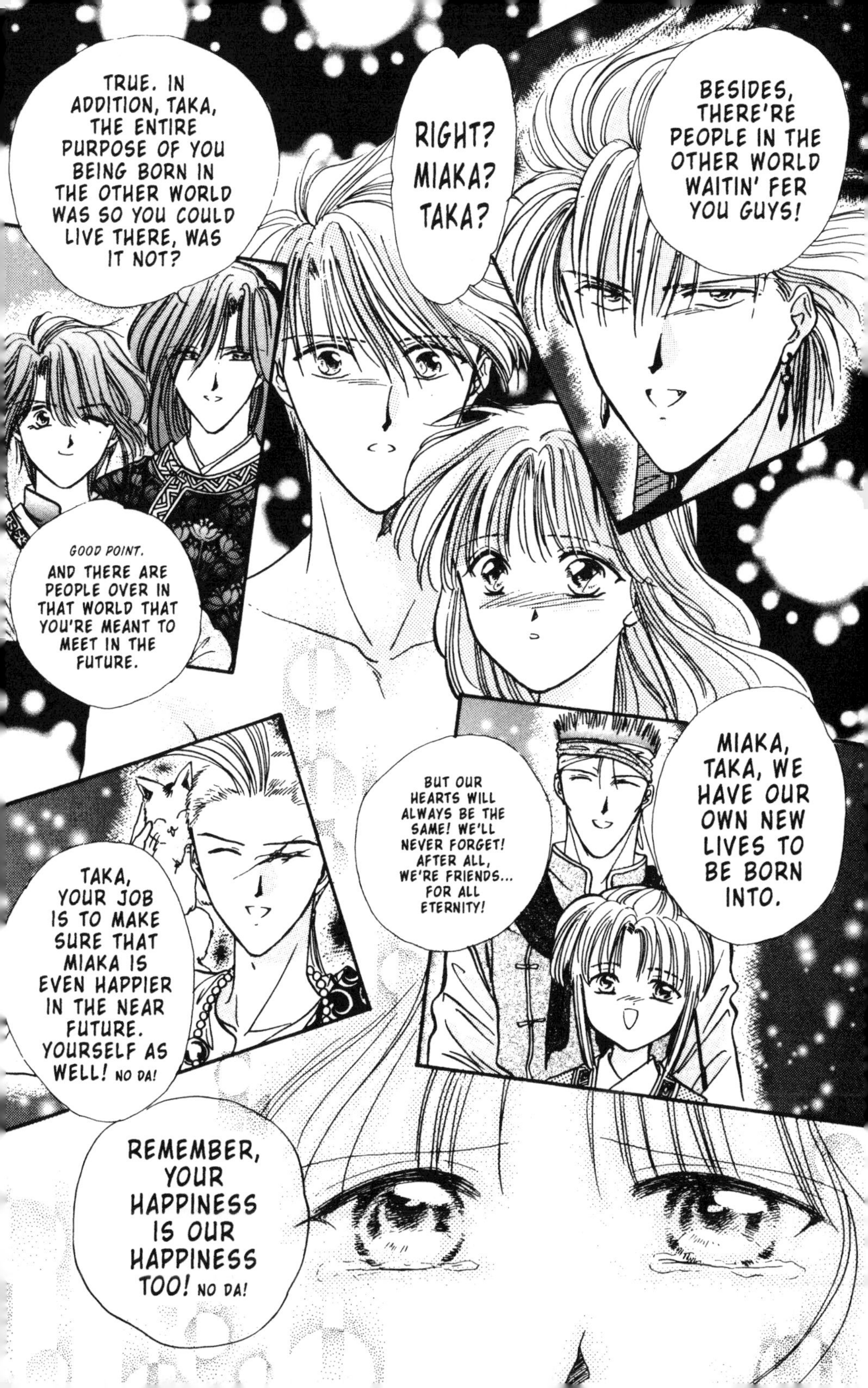
BESIDES, THERE'RE PEOPLE IN THE OTHER WORLD WAITIN' FER YOU GUYS!
RIGHT? MIAKA? TAKA?
TRUE. IN ADDITION, TAKA, THE ENTIRE PURPOSE OF YOU BEING BORN IN THE OTHER WORLD WAS SO YOU COULD LIVE THERE, WAS IT NOT?
GOOD POINT. AND THERE ARE PEOPLE OVER IN THAT WORLD THAT YOU'RE MEANT TO MEET IN THE FUTURE.
MIAKA, TAKA, WE HAVE OUR OWN NEW LIVES TO BE BORN INTO.
BUT OUR HEARTS WILL ALWAYS BE THE SAME! WE'LL NEVER FORGET! AFTER ALL, WE'RE FRIENDS... FOR ALL ETERNITY!
TAKA, YOUR JOB IS TO MAKE SURE THAT MIAKA IS EVEN HAPPIER IN THE NEAR FUTURE. YOURSELF AS WELL! NO DA!
REMEMBER, YOUR HAPPINESS IS OUR HAPPINESS TOO! NO DA!

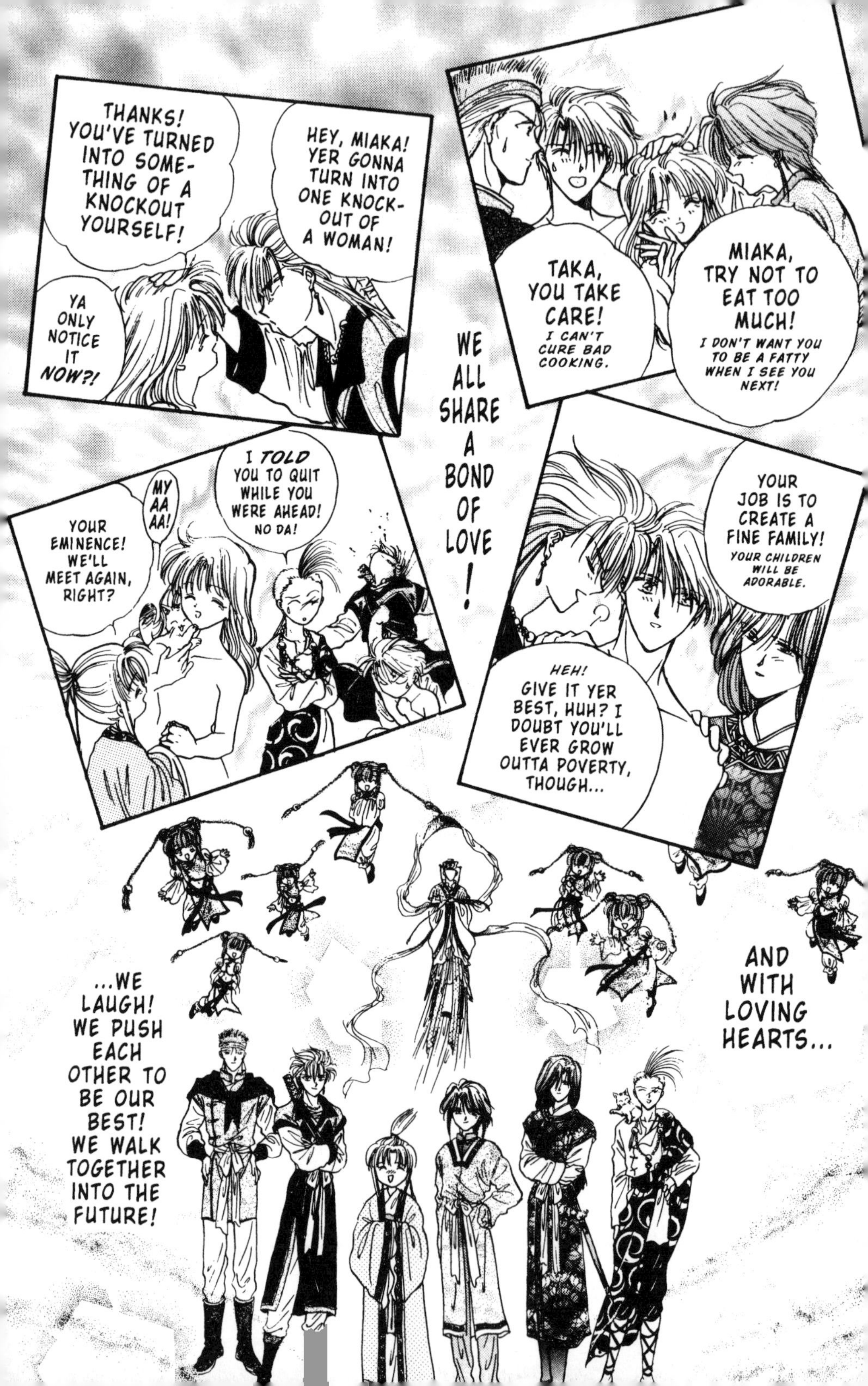
MIAKA, TRY NOT TO EAT TOO MUCH! I DON'T WANT YOU TO BE A FATTY WHEN I SEE YOU NEXT!
TAKA, YOU TAKE CARE! I CAN'T CURE BAD COOKING.
HEY, MIAKA! YER GONNA TURN INTO ONE KNOCK-OUT OF A WOMAN!
THANKS! YOU'VE TURNED INTO SOME-THING OF A KNOCKOUT YOURSELF!
YA ONLY NOTICE IT NOW?!
WE ALL SHARE A BOND OF LOVE!
YOUR JOB IS TO CREATE A FINE FAMILY! YOUR CHILDREN WILL BE ADORABLE.
HEH! GIVE IT YER BEST, HUH? I DOUBT YOU'LL EVER GROW OUTTA POVERTY, THOUGH...
I TOLD YOU TO QUIT WHILE YOU WERE AHEAD! NO DA!
MY AA AA!
YOUR EMINENCE! WE'LL MEET AGAIN, RIGHT?
AND WITH LOVING HEARTS...
...WE LAUGH! WE PUSH EACH OTHER TO BE OUR BEST! WE WALK TOGETHER INTO THE FUTURE!

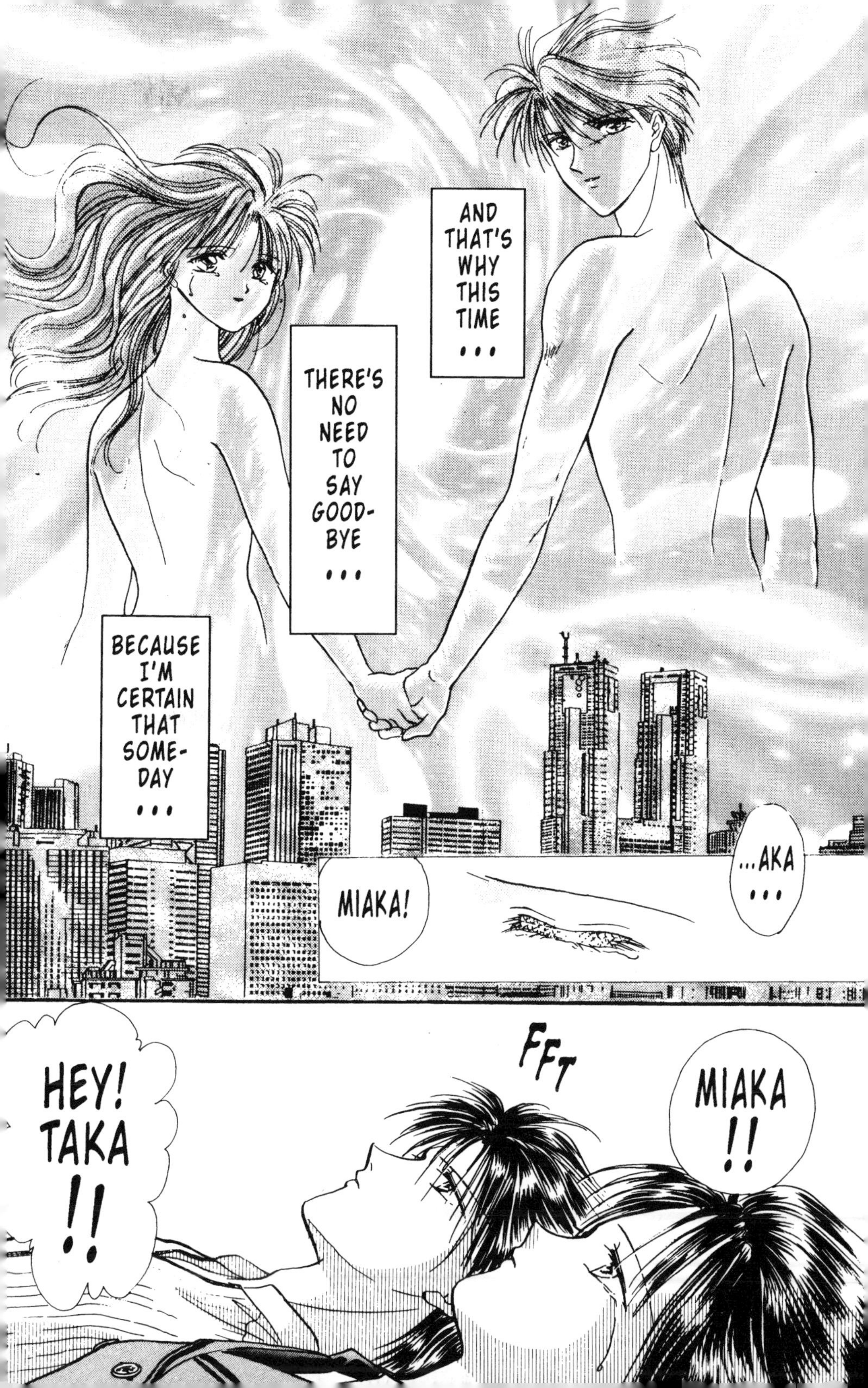
AND THAT'S WHY THIS TIME...
THERE'S NO NEED TO SAY GOOD-BYE...
BECAUSE I'M CERTAIN THAT SOME-DAY...
...AKA...
MIAKA!
MIAKA!!
FFT
HEY! TAKA!!

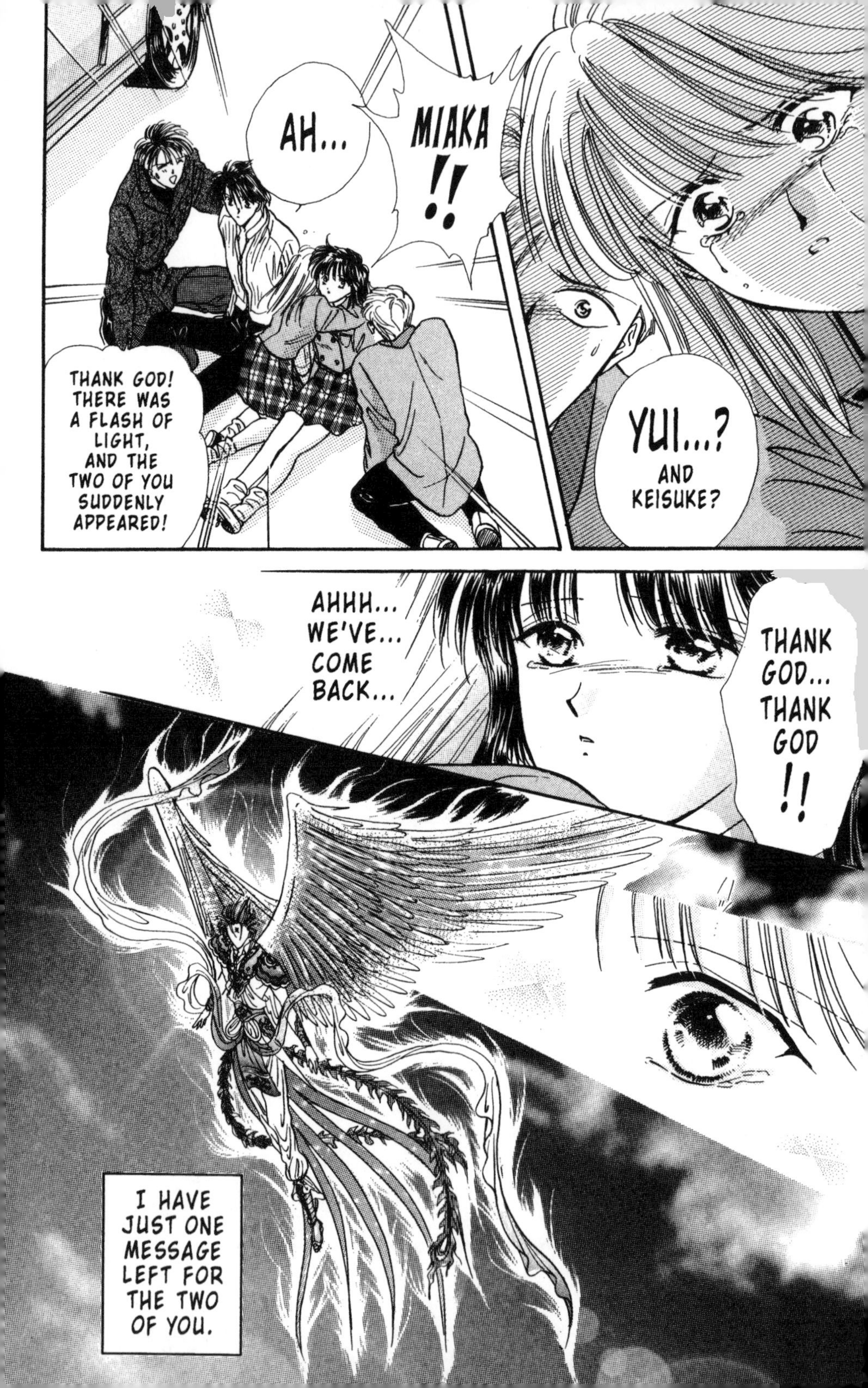
YUI...? AND KEISUKE?
MIAKA!!
AH...
THANK GOD! THERE WAS A FLASH OF LIGHT, AND THE TWO OF YOU SUDDENLY APPEARED!
THANK GOD... THANK GOD!!
AHHH... WE'VE... COME BACK...
I HAVE JUST ONE MESSAGE LEFT FOR THE TWO OF YOU.

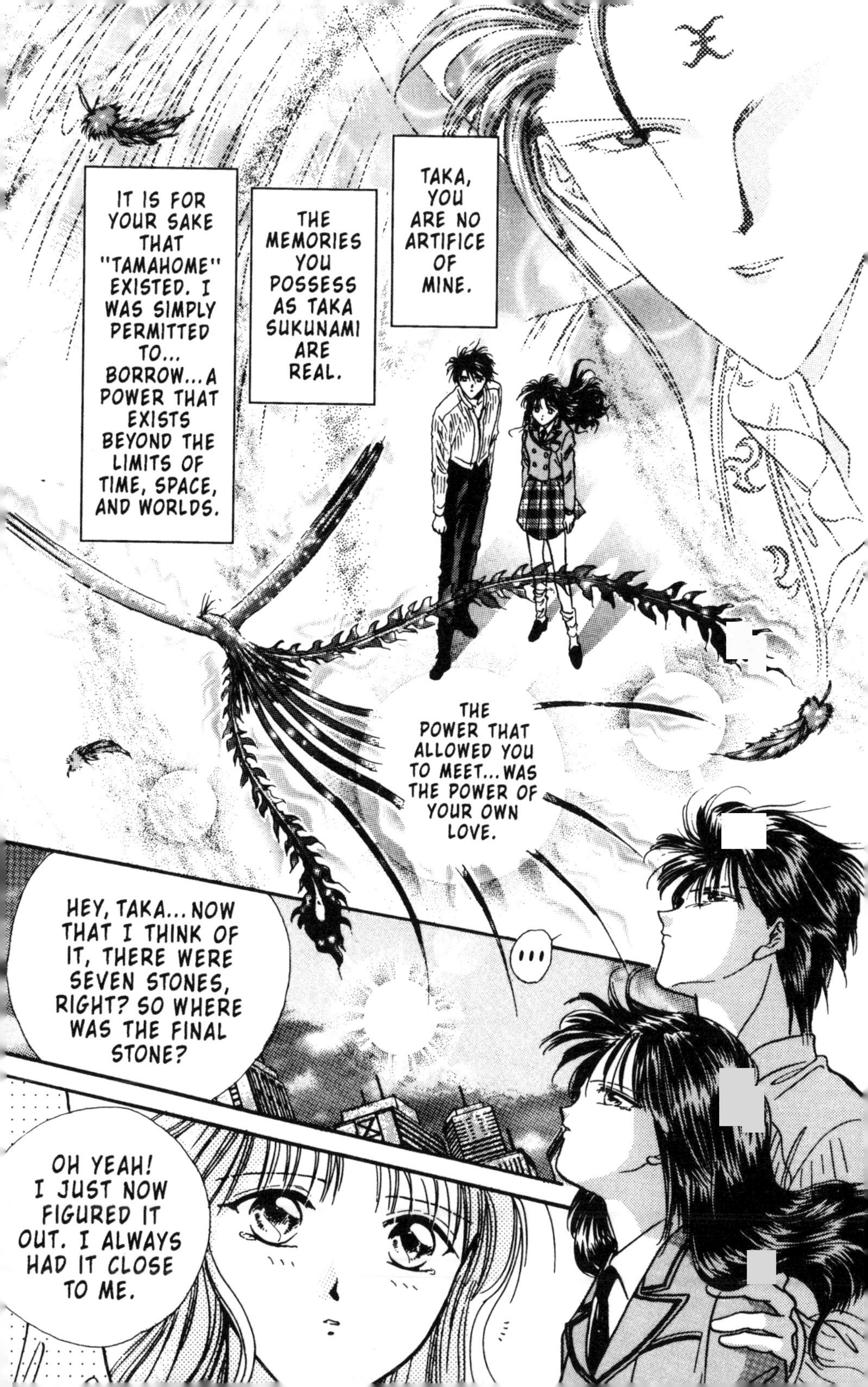
TAKA, YOU ARE NO ARTIFICE OF MINE.
THE MEMORIES YOU POSSESS AS TAKA SUKUNAMI ARE REAL.
IT IS FOR YOUR SAKE THAT "TAMAHOME" EXISTED. I WAS SIMPLY PERMITTED TO... BORROW... A POWER THAT EXISTS BEYOND THE LIMITS OF TIME, SPACE, AND WORLDS.
THE POWER THAT ALLOWED YOU TO MEET... WAS THE POWER OF YOUR OWN LOVE.
...
HEY, TAKA... NOW THAT I THINK OF IT, THERE WERE SEVEN STONES, RIGHT? SO WHERE WAS THE FINAL STONE?
OH YEAH! I JUST NOW FIGURED IT OUT. I ALWAYS HAD IT CLOSE TO ME.

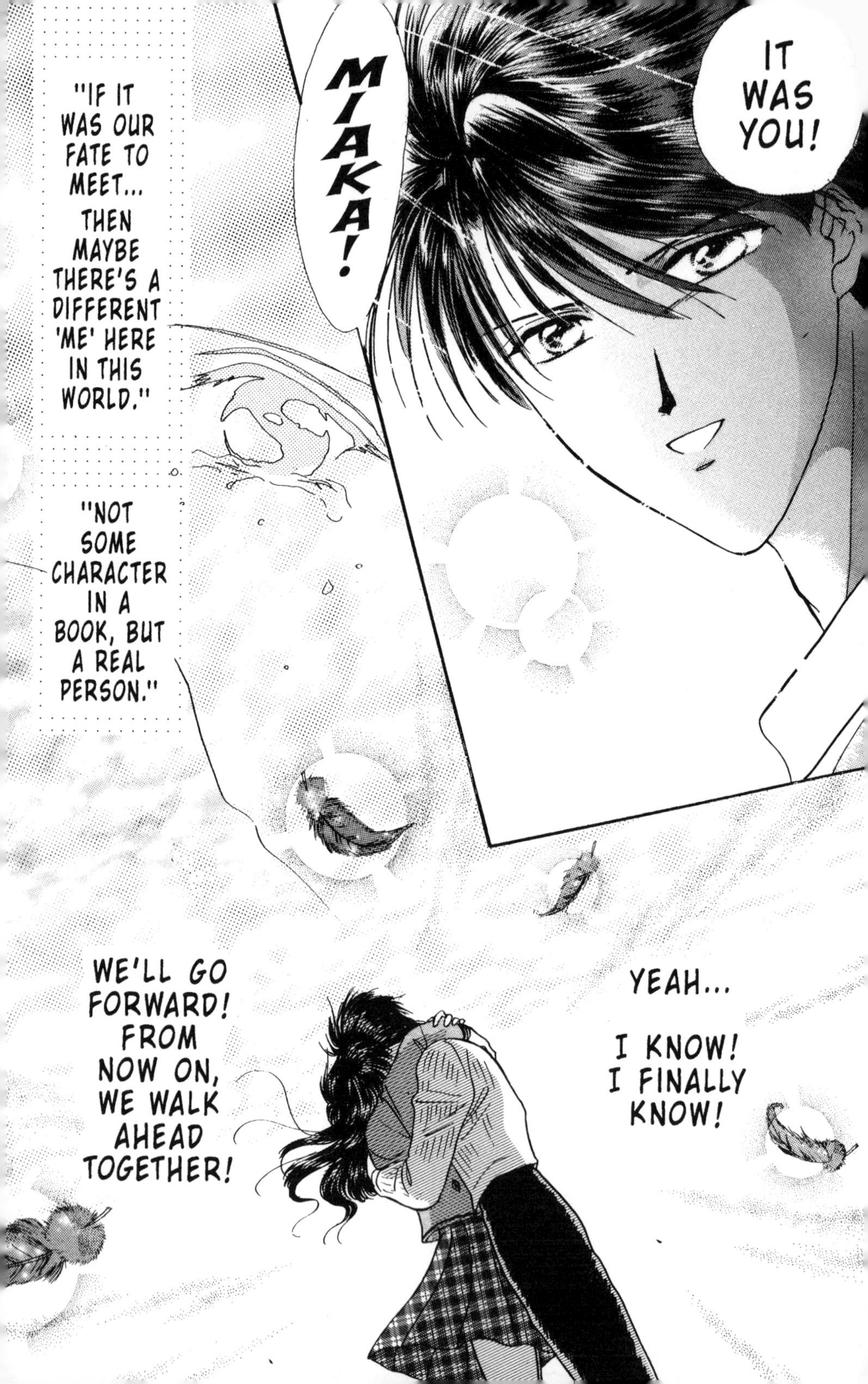
IT WAS YOU!
MIAKA!
"IF IT WAS OUR FATE TO MEET... THEN MAYBE THERE'S A DIFFERENT 'ME' HERE IN THIS WORLD."
"NOT SOME CHARACTER IN A BOOK, BUT A REAL PERSON."
YEAH...
I KNOW! I FINALLY KNOW!
WE'LL GO FORWARD! FROM NOW ON, WE WALK AHEAD TOGETHER!

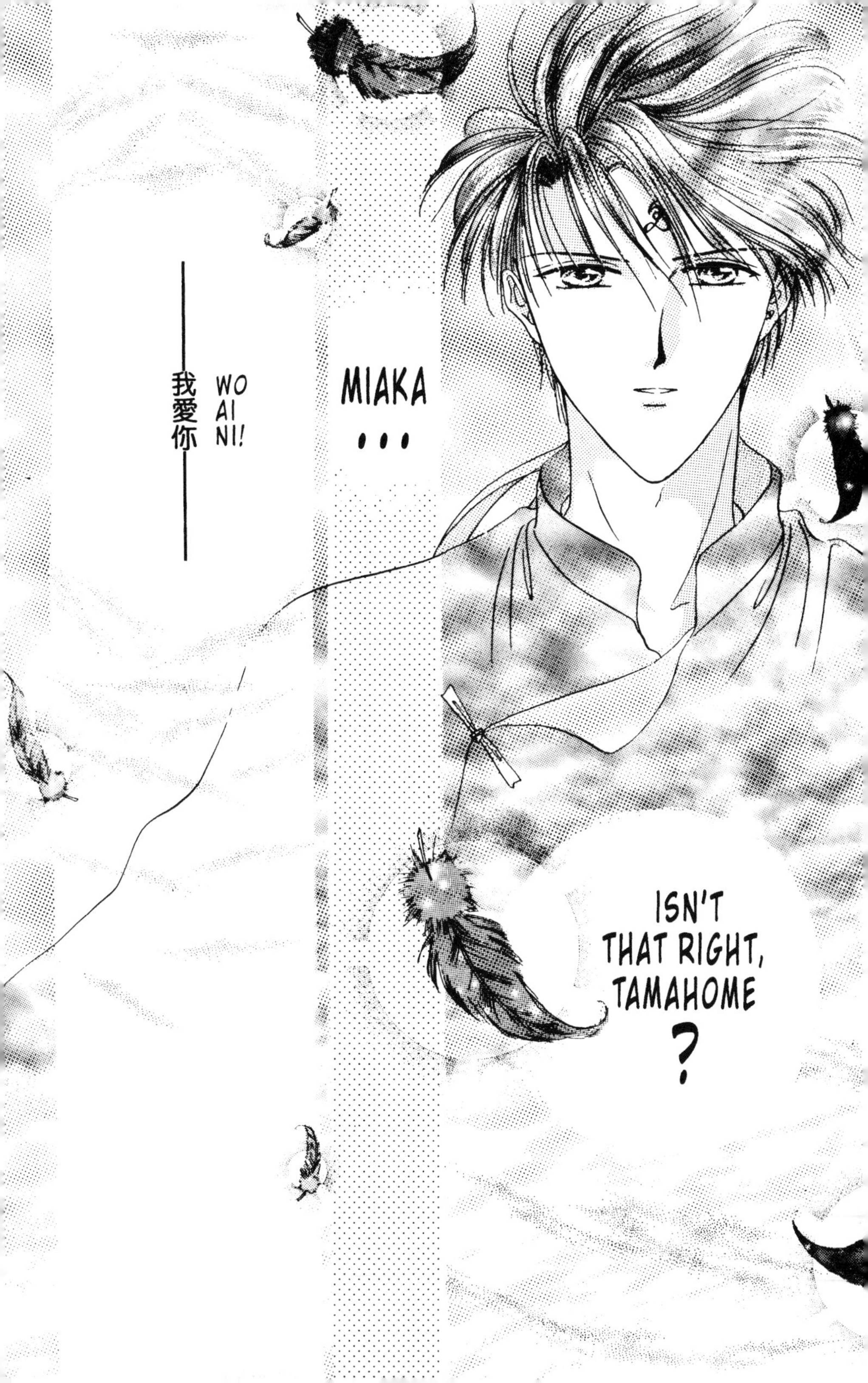
ISN'T THAT RIGHT, TAMAHOME ?
MIAKA ...
我愛你
WO AI NI!

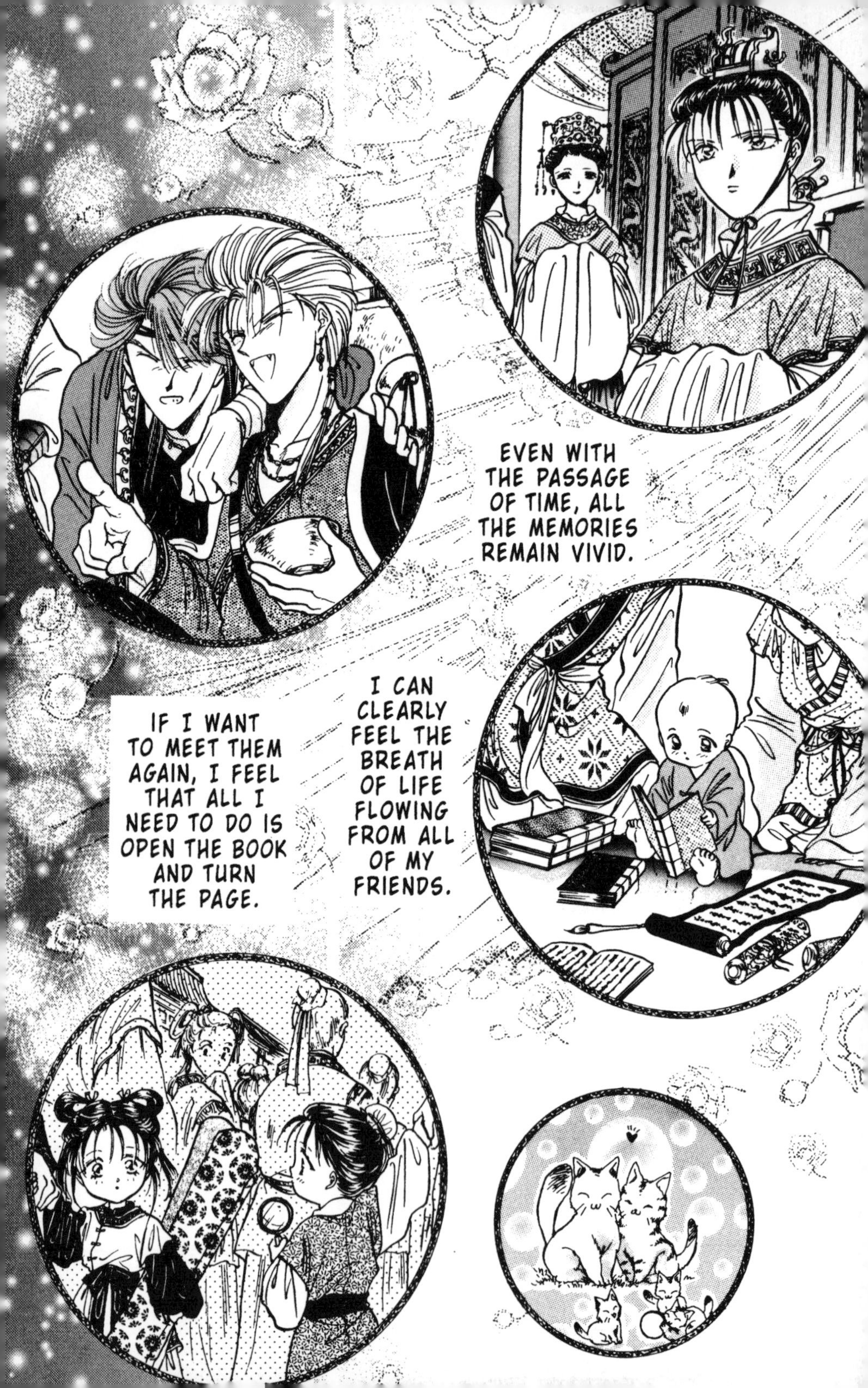
EVEN WITH THE PASSAGE OF TIME, ALL THE MEMORIES REMAIN VIVID.
I CAN CLEARLY FEEL THE BREATH OF LIFE FLOWING FROM ALL OF MY FRIENDS.
IF I WANT TO MEET THEM AGAIN, I FEEL THAT ALL I NEED TO DO IS OPEN THE BOOK AND TURN THE PAGE.

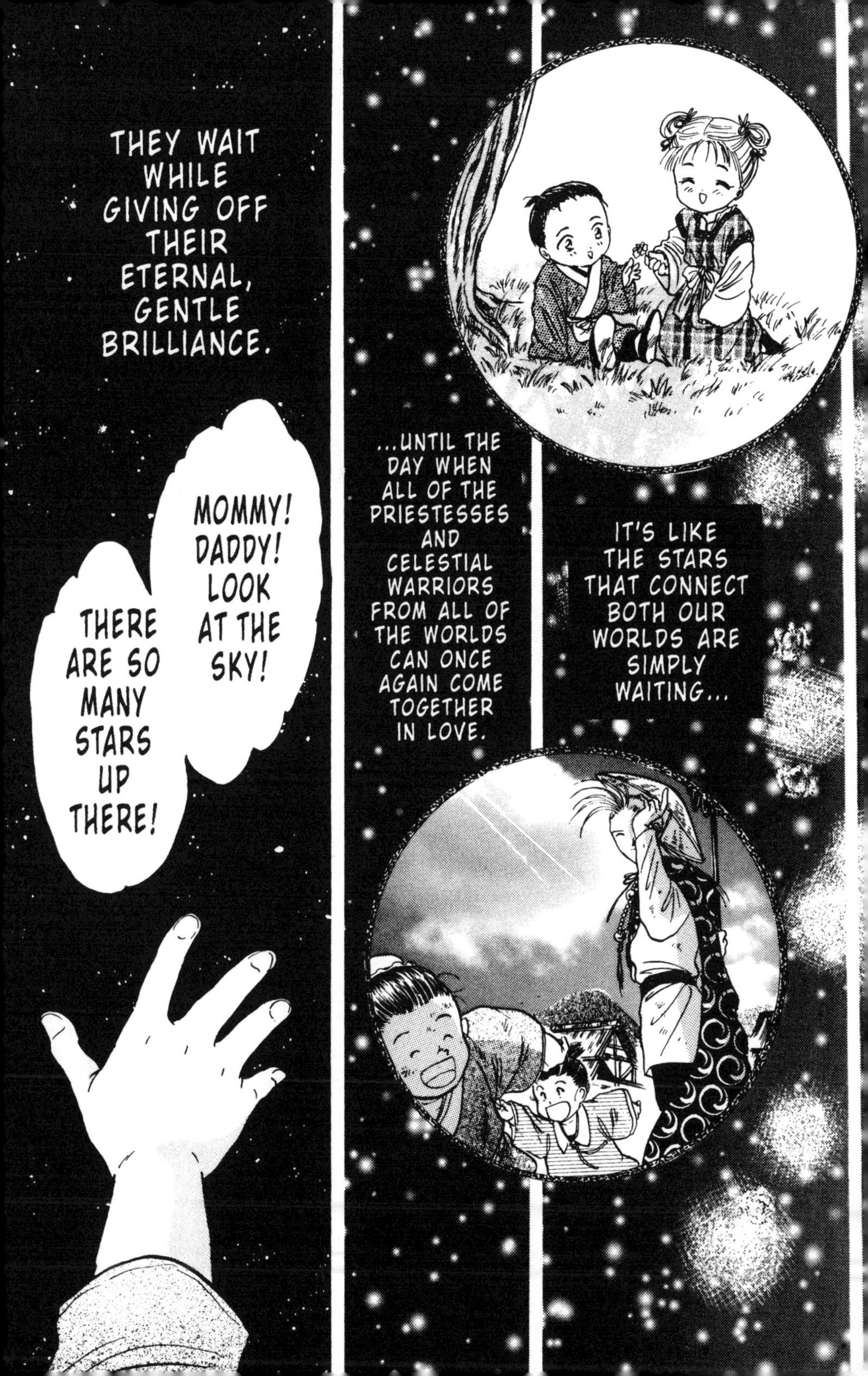
IT'S LIKE THE STARS THAT CONNECT BOTH OUR WORLDS ARE SIMPLY WAITING...
...UNTIL THE DAY WHEN ALL OF THE PRIESTESSES AND CELESTIAL WARRIORS FROM ALL OF THE WORLDS CAN ONCE AGAIN COME TOGETHER IN LOVE.
THEY WAIT WHILE GIVING OFF THEIR ETERNAL, GENTLE BRILLIANCE.
MOMMY! DADDY! LOOK AT THE SKY!
THERE ARE SO MANY STARS UP THERE!

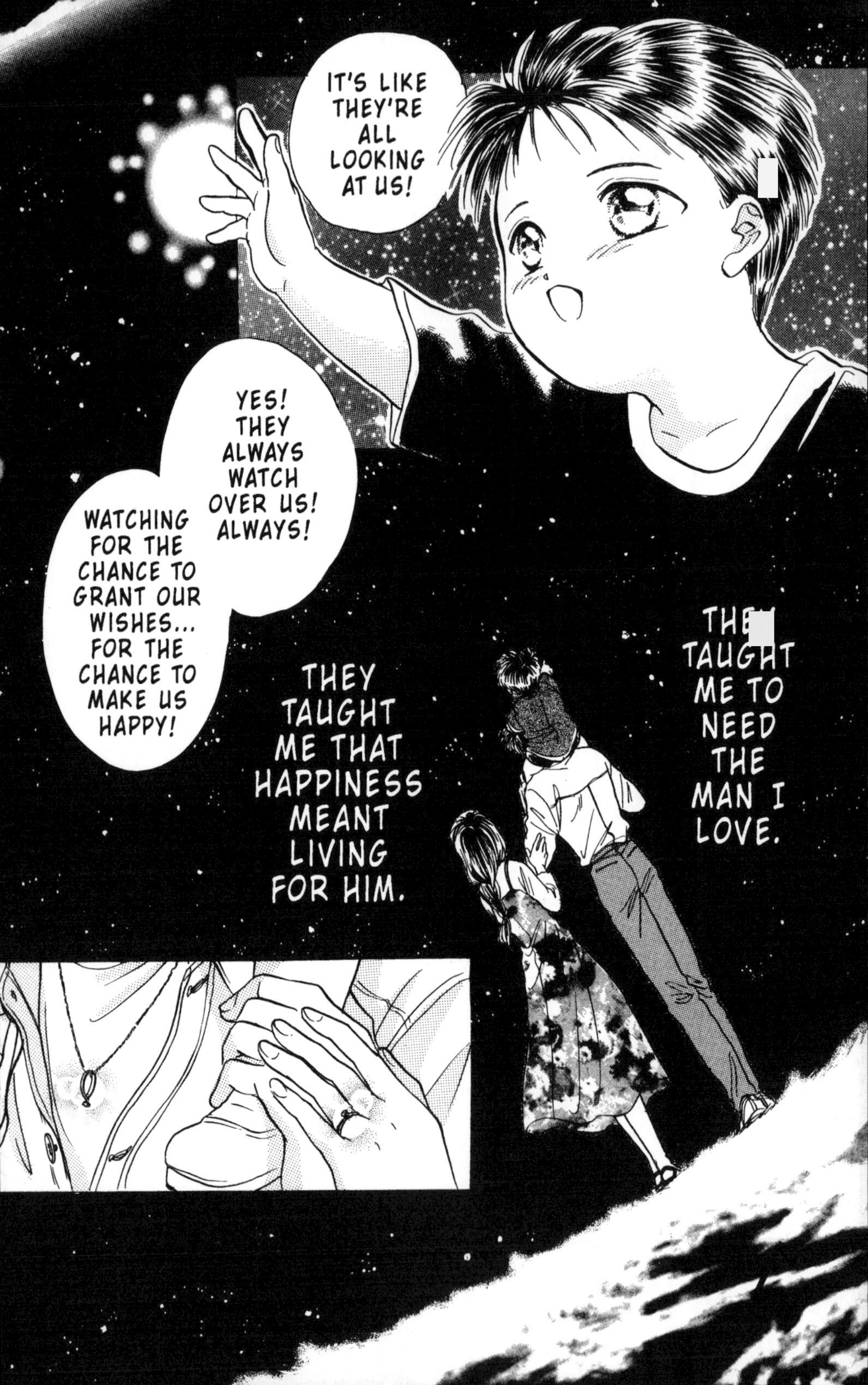
IT'S LIKE THEY'RE ALL LOOKING AT US!
YES! THEY ALWAYS WATCH OVER US! ALWAYS!
WATCHING FOR THE CHANCE TO GRANT OUR WISHES... FOR THE CHANCE TO MAKE US HAPPY!
THEY TAUGHT ME TO NEED THE MAN I LOVE.
THEY TAUGHT ME THAT HAPPINESS MEANT LIVING FOR HIM.

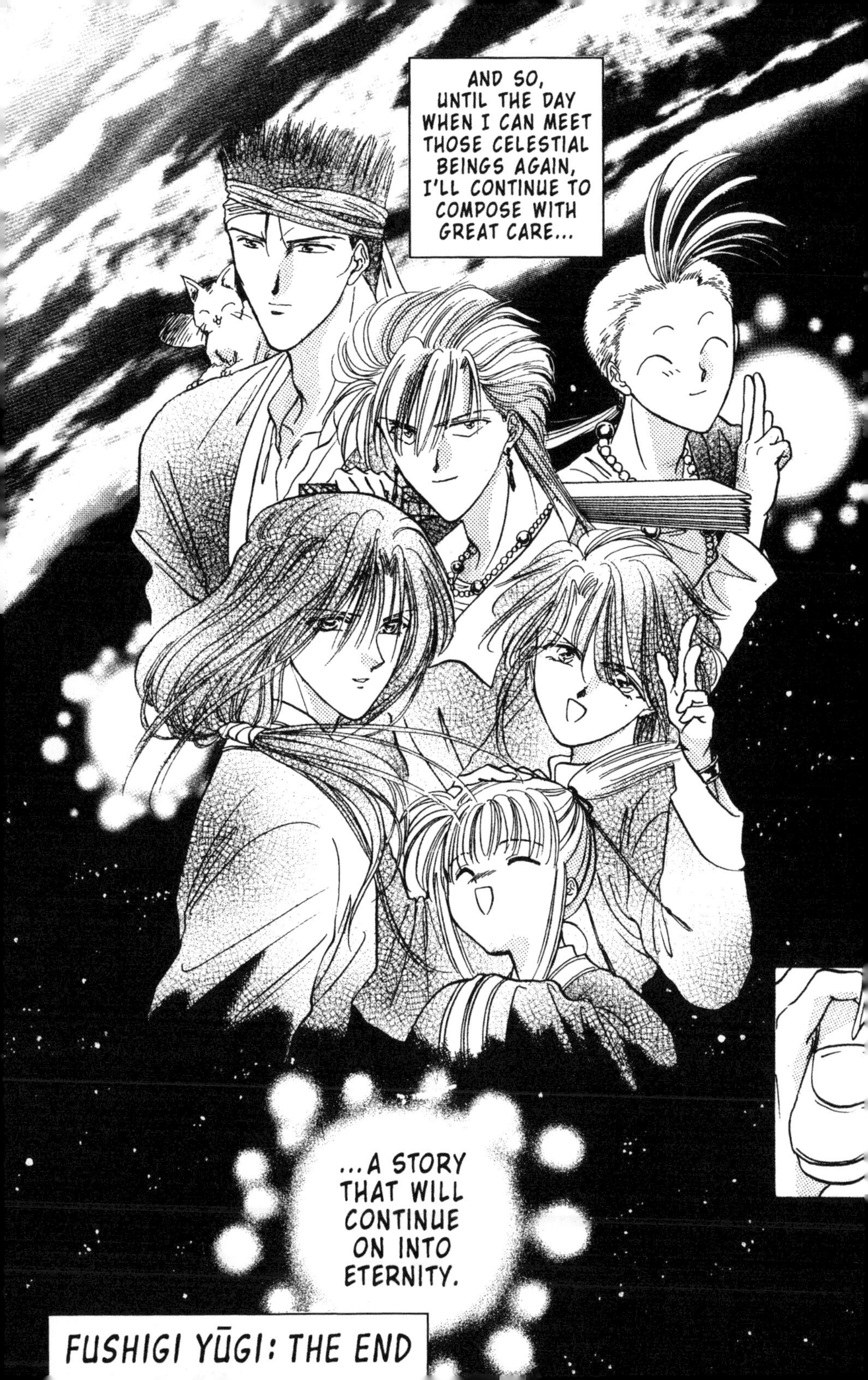
AND SO, UNTIL THE DAY WHEN I CAN MEET THOSE CELESTIAL BEINGS AGAIN, I'LL CONTINUE TO COMPOSE WITH GREAT CARE...
...A STORY THAT WILL CONTINUE ON INTO ETERNITY.
FUSHIGI YŪGI: THE END

THANK YOU SO MUCH!
…谢谢你

The day we begin our new journey... I suppose I can call it that. Rather than call it the ending of a continuing story, it's like everyone is leaving the nest. That's the feeling I get. I think that I've raised all of the Celestial Warriors... All of them have grown into fine, upstanding men (in their own ways). And the reason I was able to continue it this far is truly thanks to you readers. There were so many letters, and they constantly cheered us up when we were down. They made us cry...laugh...get angry...and there were those that really moved us. About the time when Part 1 ended, we got a letter from a student who was studying for her entrance exams, and she wrote, "I was anxious and scared, but I remembered Miaka's words. Miaka and Tamahome gave their very best, so I know I can take on this challenge with everything I've got!"

"I was filled with envy for Miaka. I mean, I was really jealous! But that inspired me to do my best to make myself into a girl that someone could love!"

"In the manga, when Nuriko wondered wistfully whether he were still alive... I had been contemplating suicide. But reading that made me want to hang on instead."

And there were more.

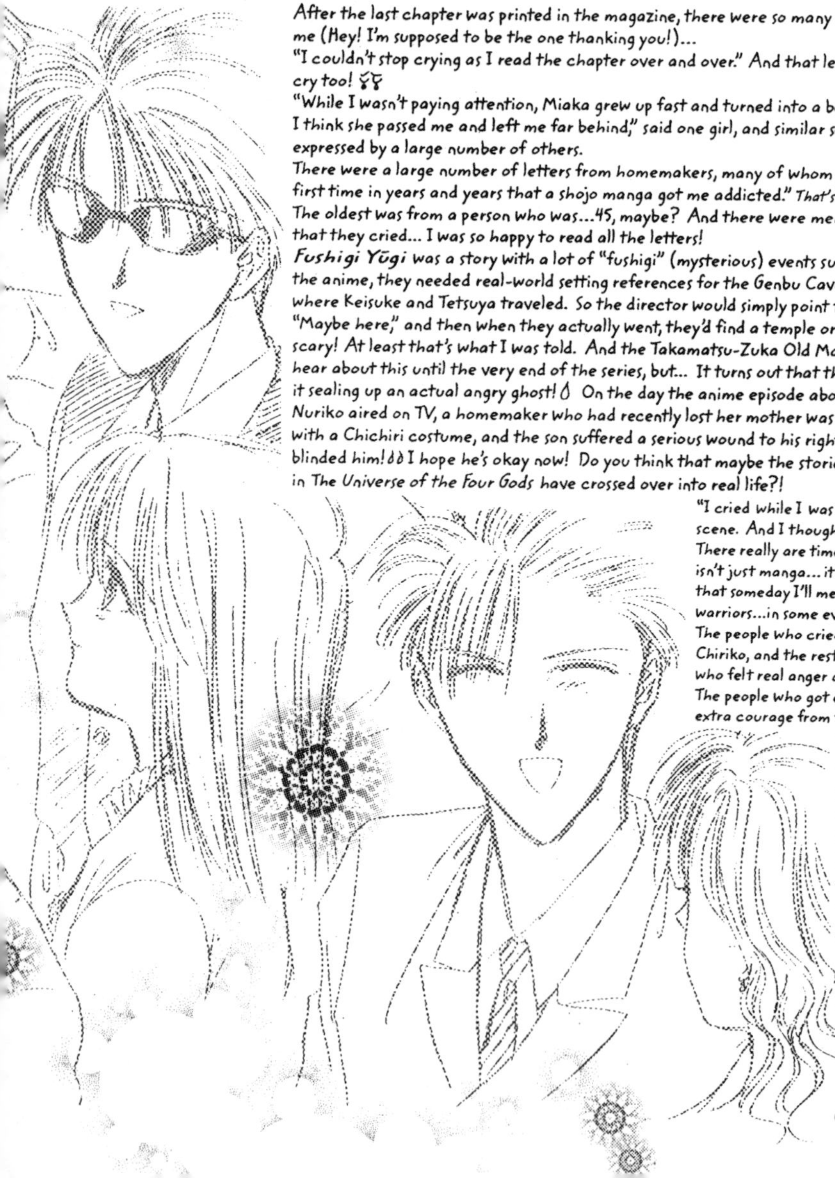

After the last chapter was printed in the magazine, there were so many letters thanking me (Hey! I'm supposed to be the one thanking you!)...

"I couldn't stop crying as I read the chapter over and over." And that letter made me cry too!

"While I wasn't paying attention, Miaka grew up fast and turned into a beautiful woman! I think she passed me and left me far behind," said one girl, and similar sentiments were expressed by a large number of others.

There were a large number of letters from homemakers, many of whom said, "This is the first time in years and years that a shojo manga got me addicted." That's interesting, isn't it...?

The oldest was from a person who was...45, maybe? And there were men who admitted that they cried... I was so happy to read all the letters!

Fushigi Yûgi was a story with a lot of "fushigi" (mysterious) events surrounding it. In the anime, they needed real-world setting references for the Genbu Cave and the place where Keisuke and Tetsuya traveled. So the director would simply point to a map and say, "Maybe here," and then when they actually went, they'd find a temple or graveyard. It was scary! At least that's what I was told. And the Takamatsu-Zuka Old Mound... I didn't hear about this until the very end of the series, but... It turns out that there's a legend of it sealing up an actual angry ghost! On the day the anime episode about the death of Nuriko aired on TV, a homemaker who had recently lost her mother was fitting her son with a Chichiri costume, and the son suffered a serious wound to his right eye that nearly blinded him! I hope he's okay now! Do you think that maybe the stories that appeared in *The Universe of the Four Gods* have crossed over into real life?!

"I cried while I was reading the last scene. And I thought, 'They're alive!' There really are times when a manga isn't just manga... it's reality! I'm sure that someday I'll meet Miaka and her warriors...in some even happier destiny."

The people who cried when Nuriko, Chiriko, and the rest died... The people who felt real anger at their enemies... The people who got even a little bit of extra courage from this story:

I wish for you to keep that precious feeling, and find a wonderful, happy destiny for yourselves! We'll meet again!

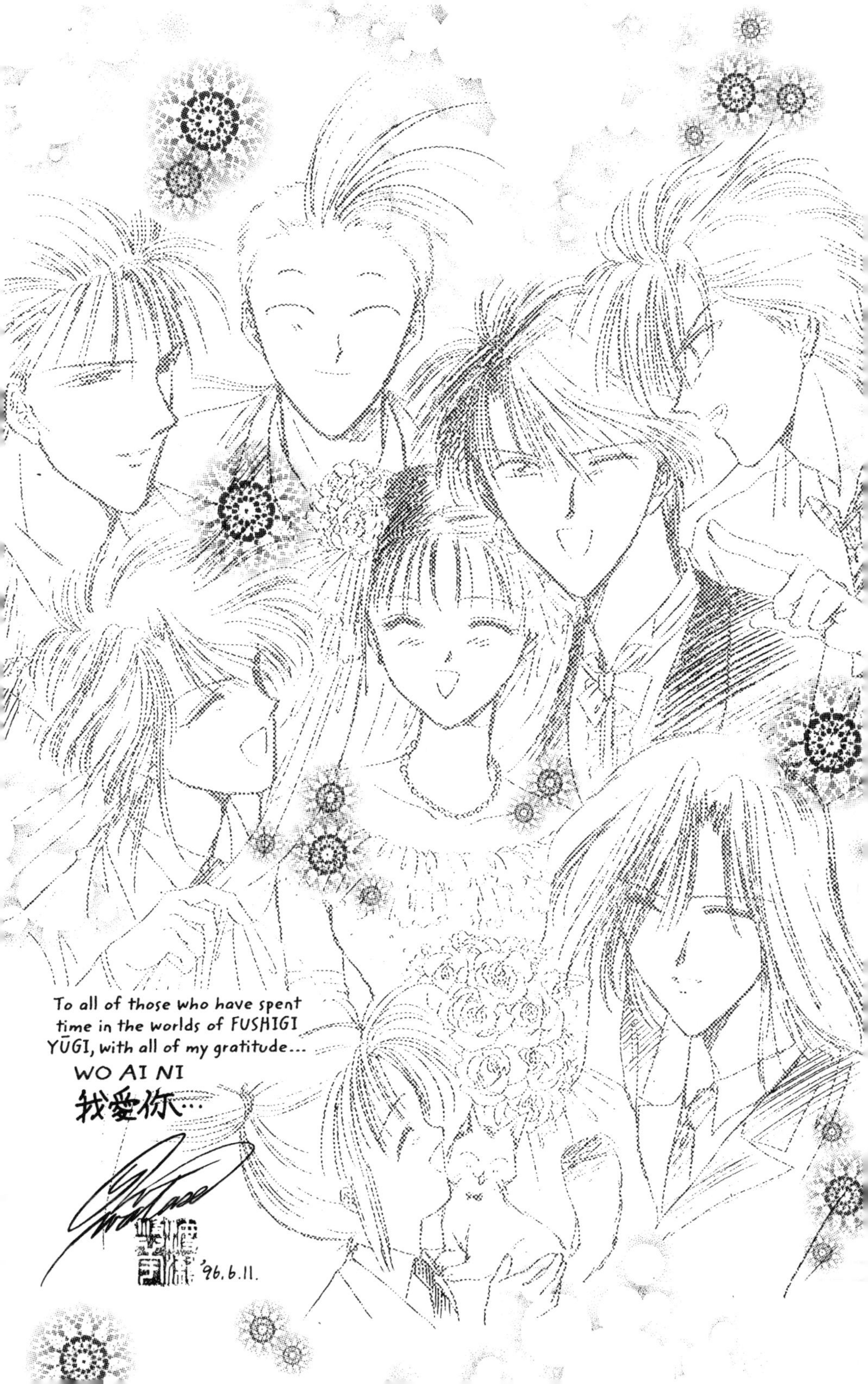
To all of those who have spent time in the worlds of FUSHIGI YŪGI, with all of my gratitude...
WO AI NI
我愛你…
'96.6.11.

Sound Effects Glossary

Many of the sound effects (FX) in *Fushigi Yûgi* are as Yuu Watase created them, in the original Japanese. This glossary lists the page number followed by the panel number (e.g., "13.1" is page 13, panel 1).

Chapter Eighty-Nine
The Crushed Passage

13.1 FX: KA [flash]
13.4 FX: SUUUU [build up of energy]
13.5 FX: KA [flash of light]

14.2 FX: KA [flash]

17.1 FX: NUUUUN [intense disapproving stare]

20.2 FX: ZAWA [background chatter]
20.3 FX: ZAWA [background chatter]
20.4 FX: ZAWA [background chatter]

25.3 FX: DA [running]
25.5 FX: BAN [opening the door]

26.2 FX: BAN [crashing through the door]

27.4 FX: HA [sudden realization]

28.5 FX: ZUDADA [falling]

29.2 FX: GUSHA [crunching sound]
29.3 FX: GA [pulling hair]

30.1 FX: ZA [stepping]
30.2 FX: DOKUN DOKUN DOKUN DOKUN [heavy heartbeats]
30.6 FX: SU [movement]

31.3 FX: TO [landing]
31.4 FX: SHARA [jingle]

32.1 FX: GRASHA [crunching]
32.2 FX: PARA [clatter]
32.4 FX: GUGU [grinding]

34.3 FX: KI [anger]

36.1 FX: DOKA [breaking in]
36.2 FX: DOSA [sudden movement]
36.3 FX: HA [breaking the spell]

37.3 FX: ZA ZA [stomping]
37.5 FX: MUKI [clothing being peeled away]

38.1 FX: JIIIIN [glaring]
38.5 FX: DAN [jumping]

39.4 FX: HYUUUUUU [wind]

40.2 FX: HA [sudden realization]
40.3 FX: SHULULULU [unrolling]

42.4 FX: ZAWA ZAWA [background chatter]

43.4 FX: HYUUU [wind]
43.6 FX: SUUU [disappearing]

44.1 FX: SUUU [disappearing]

46.1 FX: DOKUN [heavy heartbeat]
46.2 FX: GYU [holding tight]

Chapter Ninety
Miiru

53.3 FX: NIKO [grin]
53.6 FX: ZAAAA [shower sounds]

54.3 FX: BURU BURU BURU [shaking head]

55.1 FX: GISHI [drying with towel]
55.2 FX: PIKU PIKU [veins popping out]

59.2 FX: BASA [flap]
59.3 FX: FUU [vanishing]
59.4 FX: BASA [flap]

62.3 FX: BASA [flap]
62.4 FX: SU [vanishing]

63.1 FX: SHUWA SHUWA SHUWA

64.1 FX: HAA HAA [panting]
64.5 FX: PAMU [plopping into his hand]

65.1 FX: BURU BURU [trembling]

66.5 FX: SAWA [wind through his hair]
66.6 FX: SAWA SAWA [wind rustling]

69.4 FX: DOKI DOKI [heartbeats]

70.1 FX: ZAAA [unscrolling]

71.1 FX: GASHI [grabbing]

72.1 FX: DOSA [hitting the floor]

95.3	FX: NI [smile]		73.3	FX: TSU [sucking]

95.3 FX: NI [smile]
95.4 FX: SU [slight movement]
95.5 FX: KIII [door creaking]

97.1 FX: BASHI [a hit]

98.4 FX: BATAN [door slamming]

100.3 FX: SHARA [fidgeting]
100.5 FX: HA [sudden realization]

101.2 FX: GU [gripping]
101.4 FX: KA [flash of light]

102.4 FX: HA [sudden realization]

103.2 FX: KYU [clench]

106.1 FX: GI GI GI [electricity]

107.1 FX: PIN [stretching taught]

CHAPTER NINETY-TWO
THE BROKEN PLAN

112.4 FX: ZAWA ZAWA [background noise]

113.1 FX: SO [placing the stone]

114.2 FX: TON TON [footsteps on the stairs]
114.3 FX: KYU [tightning]
114.4 FX: DOKI [heartbeat]

115.2 FX: GAKUN [powerful flinch]

116.1 FX: HOO [shining]
116.3 FX: SU [appearing]

118.1 FX: NYA [smiling]
118.2 FX: KIII [door creaking open]

119.1 FX: DOOOO [dramatic appearance]
119.2 FX: DOKAN [falling down]

121.3 FX: DO [explosive movement]

122.2 FX: ZUBA [slashing]
122.3 FX: SHAAA [hissing]
122.4 FX: BATA BATA BATA [footsteps]

123.1 FX: SHU [fast movement]
123.2 FX: DO [sudden stop]

124.2 FX: GATA GATA [trembling]

125.4 FX: FOOOOON [howling]
125.4 FX: ON ON ON [howling]

73.3 FX: TSU [sucking]

74.2 FX: PASHA PASHA [splashing sounds]
74.3 FX: KACHA [door latch]

75.1 FX: KACHA [picking up receiver]
75.6 FX: DA [running]

76.3 FX: HAA HAA HAA [panting]

77.1 FX: YORO [wobble]
77.3 FX: TOSA [hitting the ground]
77.6 FX: BAN [pounding]

78.1 FX: KA [flash]
78.2 FX: SUUU [disappearing]
78.4 FX: NYA [smile]
78.5 FX: FU [vanished]

CHAPTER NINETY-ONE
THE MYSTIC FANG

80.1 FX: FU [vanishing]
80.3 FX: KAPPO KAPPO [hoof sounds]

81.2 FX: KAPPO KAPPO [hoof sounds]

82.4 FX: PACHI [blink]
82.5 FX: GABA [rising suddenly]

83.2 FX: ZAWA ZAWA [rustling]

85.3 FX: ZAWA ZAWA [wind rustling]
85.5 FX: BAN [slamming the table]

86.3 FX: SU [sudden appearance]
86.6 FX: BAN [slam]

87.2 FX: ZAWA ZAWA [crowd noises]

88.1 NOTE: Tasuki's joke was "A crab [kani] who apologizes gets forgiveness [kannin]." Not the best of puns.

90.2 Small Sign: Chao ["Cho" in Japanese. It means "ultra" but is most likely a family name]

90.2 Large Sign: Nanpandaichao ["Nanbandaicho" in Japanese. It means "south, platter, large, ultra" but is most likely just fortuitous Chinese kanji strung together to make a shop name.]

91.3 FX: FU [lit incense]
91.5 FX: SHIIIIIN [silence]

93.1 FX: KYAA KYAA [happy squeals]
93.3 FX: U U [sniffles]

126.5 FX: DA [running]

131.1 FX: ZAZA [violent rustling]
131.2 FX: SHA [hissing]

132.2 FX: HIHIIIN [whinnying]

134.2 FX: BA [gushing]

136.2 FX: GABA [pulling off]

138.4 NOTE: Tasuki's joke in Japanese was "The bedding [futon] flew away [futtonda]."

CHAPTER NINETY-THREE
THE GULF OF COURAGE

140.2 FX: YORO [wobble]

143.4 FX: PON [sweat appearing]

145.5 FX: KATA KATA [shivering]

146.2 FX: IRA IRA IRA [worry]

147.1 FX: KA [rushing]

148.3 FX: BAN [bang]

150.1 FX: BYUN [zooming past]

151.2 FX: GYU [gripping]
151.4 FX: BAN [bam]

152.5 FX: GUI [grabbing]

155.4 FX: MUKU [lifting his head]
155.5 FX: GU [holding]

156.1 FX: SU [movement]
156.2 FX: BIKU [surprise]
156.3 FX: GYU [clenching]

157.1 FX: BI-BIKU [flinching back]

158.2 FX: BIKU [flinch]
158.4 FX: HA [gasp]
158.2 FX: GIRIRI [grinding]

160.1 FX: GYU [holding tight]
160.3 FX: ZURU [something slurped in]

161.1 FX: SHAAA [rising up, taking shape]
161.2 FX: DOO [explosive movement]

165.4 FX: SU [movement]

167.4 FX: BOHYU [flames]

CHAPTER NINETY-FOUR
A DREAM DRAWN FOR YOU

169.2 FX: BOHYUU [flames]
169.4 FX: KAAAAA [light shining]

170.3 FX: PON [clap]

171.1 FX: HATA [sudden realization]

173.3 FX: KAAAAA [light]

174.3 FX: SUUU [vanishing]
174.4 FX: BISHUN [vanishing in light]

175.2 FX: KA [flash of light]

177.4 FX: GYU [gripping]

178.4 FX: GABA [hugging]

179.1 FX: GORON [twirl]

181.4 FX: KI [anger]
181.5 FX: PAN [a slap]

182.5 FX: UU UU [crying]

183.1 FX: KI [anger]

189.4 FX: HA [realization]

190.4 FX: ULULULULU [growling]

191.1 FX: ZUZU ZUZU ZU… [shape shifting]

193.5 FX: KA [concentration]

194.1 FX: BAN [bang]
194.2 FX: BARA BARA [breaking into pieces]
194.3 FX: SU [flowing]

196.3 FX: DOO [explosion]

197.1 FX: ZUUUU [burning]
197.2 FX: GOOOO [roaring fire]

CHAPTER NINTEY-FIVE
CAPTAIN OF RUIN

202.2 FX: UUUUUU [truck engine running]
202.3 FX: PIII POOO PIII POOO [siren]

203.2 FX: BIKU [surprised twitch]
203.3 FX: SHUUUUU [sizzling]

206.3 FX: HA [sudden realization]
206.6 FX: BA [rush of air]

208.2 FX: BASHA BASHA [splashing]

209.2 FX: ZAWA [rustling in the trees]
209.3 FX: KA [flash of light]
209.4 FX: DOSA [falling with a thud]
209.5 FX: SAPA [rushing out of water]

213.3 FX: BURU BURU [trembling]
213.5 FX: KA [sudden anger]

214.3 FX: ZUUUU [radiating energy]
214.5 FX: KA [sudden release]

215.1 FX: DO [hitting]

216.2 FX: DOKUN [heartbeat]
216.4 FX: DOKUN DOKUN [heartbeats]
216.5 FX: DOKUN DOKUN DOKUN [heartbeats]

217.5 FX: SHIKU SHIKU [sniffling]
217.6 FX: WAKU WAKU [excitement]

219.1 NOTE: What Lai Lai says means "Opening Wave."
219.1 FX: KA [flash of light]

220.1 FX: GAKUN [being released]

223.4 FX: YORO [wobble]

224.4 FX: DOOOOO [explosion]

225.2 FX: ZURU [slipping]

226.3 FX: KA [flash of light]
226.4 FX: DOUU [engulfed in flame]
226.6 FX: GOOOOOO [burning]

227.6 FX: BA [rush of air]

228.3 FX: KAAAAA [light]

CHAPTER NINETY-SIX
OVERFLOWING DOUBT

233.2 FX: DAN [slamming]

234.1 NOTE: Genbon is a book of ancient Chinese and Japanese documents. The Asuka period was between A.D. 600-710.

237.2 FX: GYAA [kaw]
237.3 FX: GYAA [kaw]

239.5 FX: SU [rising]

240.4 FX: BASA BASA BASA [flapping]
240.5 FX: BASA BASA [flapping]

241.2 FX: BYOOOOOO [whirlwind]
241.3 FX: ZAWA ZAWA [rustling]

242.5 FX: PO [frustration]

243.4 FX: BAKI [twigs snapping]

244.3 FX: DOKUN DOKUN [heavy heartbeats]
244.4 FX: DOKUN DOKUN DOKUN DOKUN [heavy heartbeats]

245.5 FX: JABABABABABA [swimming back]

246.1 FX: DOKI [heartbeat]

250.2 FX: SAWA [rustling]

254.4 FX: ZAKU ZAKU [walking]
254.5 FX: PITA [sudden stop]

255.5 FX: BA [explosion]

256.4 FX: BASHI [attack hitting]

258.1 FX: BUWA [high wind]

259.2 FX: BASA [wings flapping]

260.2 FX: ZAWA ZAWA [rustling]

266.2 FX: GAKU [slumping over]
266.3 FX: BO [flame]
266.4 FX: ZURU [slipping]

267.1 FX: DOKI [heartbeat]

268.3 FX: ZUUUU [radiating energy]

CHAPTER NINETY-SEVEN
THE NIGHT WANDERING

270.2 FX: SAWA SAWA [rustling]

271.1 FX: BYUN [fast movement]
271.2 FX: REEEE REEEE [crickets chirping]
271.6 FX: ZAKU ZAKU ZAKU [footsteps]

272.1 FX: ZAWA [rustling]
272.3 FX: ZAZA [wind]

273.3 FX: HA [realization]

273.4 FX: YORO [wobble]
273.5 FX: HA [realization]

276.4 FX: BO [burning]

280.3 FX: HA [realization]

282.4 FX: PAN [clap]

283.2 FX: YORO [wobble]
283.2 FX: DON [thud]

286.2 FX: JARA [chinking of beads]
286.3 FX: ZOKU [shock]
286.4 FX: GI [shifting weight]
286.5 FX: BA [sudden movement]

287.1-3 FX: DOKUN DOKUN DOKUN DOKUN DOKUN DOKUN [heavy heartbeats]

289.1-2 FX: ZA ZA ZA [running footsteps]

291.3 FX: BA [a rush]

293.5 FX: NYA [a grin]

296.2 FX: BOTA BOTA [dripping blood]
296.3 FX: ZURU [lifting himself]

CHAPTER NINETY-EIGHT
BLAZE OF CAMARADERIE

298.1 FX: GYAA GYAA [crows cawing]

299.4 FX: GATA GATA GATA [shaking]

300.1 FX: BASHA [splash]
300.2 FX: GATA GATA GATA GATA [shaking]
300.2 FX: BASA BASA [books falling]
300.4 FX: ZUZUZU [rumbling]
300.6 FX: ZUZUZU [rumbling]

301.1 FX: ZUZUZU [rumbling]
301.4 FX: ZUZUZU [rumbling]

302.2 FX: ZUZUZU [rumbling]

307.3 FX: KA [sudden anger]
307.4 FX: BA [quick movement]

308.1 FX: BAKI BAKI [things breaking]

313.2 FX: DOKUN [heavy heartbeat]
313.3 FX: DOKUN [heavy heartbeat]
313.4 FX: DOKUN [heavy heartbeat]
313.5 FX: DOKUN DOKUN [heavy heartbeats]
313.6 FX: DOKUN [heavy heartbeat]

314.2 FX: DAN [movement]
314.3 FX: HA [realization]

315.4 FX: DON [explosion]

316.1 FX: WAAA [shocked yells]
316.3 FX: BA [rushing]
316.4 FX: GARAN [clanking to the floor]

317.4 FX: KAAAA [light glowing]

318.4 FX: KAAAAA [light glowing]

324.2 NOTE: In Japanese, "Fei-gao" is pronounced "Hikô." Miaka says that he's splitting up friends...what airplane ["hikôki"] does that? And Tasuki corrects her that the name is "hikô," not "hikôki."
324.3 FX: PIKU [becoming aware]
324.5 FX: HA [realization]

325.1 FX: DOO [explosion]

CHAPTER NINETY-NINE
THE TRAGIC TRANSMIGRATION

327.4 FX: GUGU [tightening]
327.5 FX: SUPA [splash]

328.1 FX: BIKU [surprise]
328.2 FX: HA [realization]

330.4 FX: DOOO [rushing]

331.2 FX: ZURU [sliding down]
331.5 FX: ZUZUZU [sliding through]

333.1 FX: DOOOOOOOO [explosion]
333.3 FX: GOOO [roaring]
333.4 FX: KARA KARA [crackling]

334.3 FX: DOKUN DOKUN DOKUN [rhythmic beating]
334.5 FX: SUUU [movement]

336.1 FX: SHAAAA [rain]
336.3 FX: DOTA DOTA [rushing about]

338.5 FX: GYU [clench]

339.1 FX: ZAAAAA [rain]

341.2 FX: GISHI [rising]
341.4 FX: ZAAAAAA [rain]
341.5 FX: DOOOO [rushing water]

342.4 FX: BIKU [surprise]

343.3 FX: KI [anger]

344.2 NOTE: In Japanese, "Han-gui" is pronounced "Kanki." The Japanese word for "great joy" is also "kanki," but with different kanji. After Han-gui introduces himself, Miaka responds that there's nothing to be joyful about!

345.2 FX: GOOOO [thunder]

346.2 FX: ZAPA [water sounds]
346.3 FX: ZAAA [rushing water]

348.1 FX: BASHAA [exploding water]
348.3 FX: PASHA [splashing]

349.2 FX: SHAN [jangling of rings on staff]

351.3 FX: SHAN [jangling rings on staff]

352.2 FX: BA [explosion]
352.3 FX: SHAN [jangling rings on staff]

354.1 FX: GOOOO [fire]
354.5 FX: DOOOO [rushing water]

356.1 NOTE: The word that Chichiri shouts is the character for victory.
356.1 FX: DOO [explosion]

359.1 FX: BA [sudden movement]
359.2 FX: SHU [appearance]
359.3 FX: SHULULULU [wrapping]

CHAPTER ONE HUNDRED
THE EPHEMERAL REFLECTION IN THE WATER

361.1 FX: ZAAAA [rain]

364.4 FX: GYU [tight grip]

365.2 FX: DOON [explosive force]
365.4 FX: GOOO [flames]

366.3 FX: GOOOO [flames]

367.1 FX: ZUBU [rushing fist]
367.3 FX: ZAA [breaking through]

368.1 FX: DON [explosion]
368.4 FX: BA [sudden movement]

369.1 FX: BASHA [splashing water]

375.1 FX: SUKU [raising his head rapidly]

376.4 FX: HA [sudden realization]
376.5 FX: SU [appearance]

380.2 FX: ZA [shock]

382.2 FX: YORO [wobble]
382.5 FX: GYU [gripping tightly]

385.3 FX: BA [rushing]
385.6 FX: GYU [holding tight]

387.1 FX: DON [punching]

388.2 FX: BATA BATA BATA BATA [running]
388.5 FX: DA [heavy footstep]

389.1 FX: PATA PATA [footsteps]

CHAPTER ONE HUNDRED ONE
TAMAHOME'S SHADOW

394.1 FX: ZAWA ZAWA [leaves rustling]

397.2 FX: DOOON [dramatic music]
397.4 FX: DOGU DOGU [flowing blood]

399.4 FX: GASHI GASHI [scratching]

400.4 FX: BIKU [surprise]
400.5 FX: DOKUN [heavy heartbeat]

401.1 FX: DOKUN DOKUN [heavy heartbeats]

402.5 FX: GABA [pulling at clothes]

404.1 FX: DOU [explosion]
404.2 FX: HA [surprise]
404.5 FX: GYURURURURU [swirling threads]

405.4 FX: GIRI GIRI [electric-shock-like pain]
405.5 FX: GIRI GIRI [electric-shock-like pain]

406.1 FX: BA [massive power]
406.2 FX: DO [explosion]
406.2 FX: ZUGAZUZU [cracking rubble]

408.1 FX: ZAWA ZAWA [crowd noises]
408.2 FX: GYU [holding tight]
408.3 FX: HYUUUU [wind blowing]

412.5 FX: PON [placing a hand on shoulder]

413.4 FX: ZAWA ZAWA [wind in leaves]
413.6 FX: ZA ZA [footsteps in the grass]

414.3 FX: FU [light shining]

415.2 FX: KAAAA [light shining]

418.3 FX: DA [running footstep]

419.3 FX: GABA [getting up]

420.6 FX: DOKIN [heartbeat]

CHAPTER ONE HUNDRED TWO
SOULS SEEKING THEIR MATES

423.6 FX: GU GU [struggling]

424.2 FX: BAN [slam]

426.1 FX: BAN [explosion]

427.2 FX: BARI BARI BARI [breaking apart]
427.3 FX: GASHAN [exploding glass]

433.4 FX: FURU FURU [trembling]

434.2 FX: BURORORORO [engine racing]
434.6 FX: HYUUUUUU [wind blowing]

435.2 FX: HYOOOOOO [wind blowing]

436.3 FX: KYUN [heart pang]
436.6 FX: BA [sudden movement]

437.1 FX: HYUUUU [wind blowing]
437.2 FX: BYOOOO [wind blowing harder]

442.2 FX: BATAN [gate closing]
442.3 FX: FURU FURU [trembling]

443.4 FX: YORO [wobble]

444.1 FX: DOO [explosion]

445.2 FX: BA BA BA BA [sudden appearances]

447.1 FX: PATAN [door closing]

449.1 FX: GAKU GAKU [trembling]

CHAPTER ONE HUNDRED THREE
THE ETERNAL VOW

455.1 FX: BURORORO [car engine]

459.2 FX: SARA [fingers through hair]

460.2 FX: GYU [holding tight]

463.1 FX: ZAAN [waves]

464.3 FX: KA [sudden appearance]
464.4 FX: DOOON [explosion]

465.1 FX: BASA BASA BASA [flapping wings]
465.2 FX: WAN WAN [barking]
465.6 FX: KACHA [door latch opening]

466.4 FX: DOKUN DOKUN DOKUN
DOKUN DOKUN [heartbeats]
466.5 FX: KUSHA [hand in hair]

467.5 FX: BO [blush]

469.5 FX: GACHA [door opening]

470.1 FX: DOKUN DOKUN DOKUN
[throbbing sounds]
470.3 FX: GYU [clenching]
470.5 FX: DOKUN DOKUN [throbbing sounds]

474.4 FX: BOO [glowing]

478.1 FX: HYOOOO [wind blowing]
478.3 FX: KA [flash of light]

480.1 FX: HA [sudden realization]
480.2 FX: KAAA [flash of light]

483.4 FX: SHULULULULU [unrolling]

485.1 FX: HA [sudden realization]

486.4 FX: BA [dramatic movement]

487.1 FX: SHULU [throwing off the scroll]
487.2 FX: KA [flash of light]
487.3 FX: FUWA [flipping the bo staff]

489.1 FX: GYU [clenching]

490.3 Pictures: Huan-Lang
[Tasuki's Chinese name]

CHAPTER ONE HUNDRED FOUR
THE RED WAVE OF LOVE

494.6 FX: KA [blush]

496.1 FX: DOKIN [heartbeat]
496.5 FX: GUSHI [wiping away a tear]

497.5 FX: KOSO KOSO [sneaking]

498.4 FX: SHAN [rings jingling]
498.5 FX: PAA [sudden appearance]

499.3 FX: KA [lightning]
499.3 FX: BABA BABA [thunder]
499.4 FX: DO [explosion]

500.1 FX: JIJI [electrified harisen]
500.3 FX: PON [pop]

501.3 FX: DON [dramatic appearance]
501.5 FX: DOKUN DOKUN DOKUN DOKUN DOKUN [throbbing]

502.1 FX: SHAN [rings jingling]
502.1 FX: ZUZUZUZUZUZU [low rumbling]

503.2 FX: PAPPAAA PAAAA [car horns]
503.5 FX: PIKU [twitch]

505.4 FX: ZUZUZUZUZU [rumbling]

506.1 FX: KA [sudden appearance]

507.1 FX: DON [explosion]
507.4 FX: DOOOOON [explosion]

509.2 FX: KO [a footstep]
509.3 FX: DO [threads striking]

510.3 FX: KA KA [steps]

511.2 FX: ZA [fighting stance]
511.3 FX: ZUOOOOOO [blast of energy]

512.2 FX: BA [rushing air]
512.3 FX: DOGU [hitting]

513.1 FX: DOGAGA GAGA [multiple hits]
513.2 FX: DO BASH DO [more hits]

514.1-3 FX: DOSHAA [kick]
514.5 FX: KA [determination]

515.2 FX: KA [power surge]
515.2-4 FX: DOOOOO [explosive power]

CHAPTER ONE HUNDRED FIVE
THE FINAL BATTLE

522.1 FX: ZUZUZU [rumbling]
522.4 FX: DOOOON [explosion]

523.1 FX: ZUUUUN [smoke clearing]

524.2 FX: VOON [energy burst]

525.1 FX: VOON [energy burst]

531.1 FX: KA [flash]
531.2 FX: BA [explosion]

534.7 FX: KA [flash]

535.2 FX: DOO [explosion]
535.5 FX: ZUUUUU [clearing smoke]

536.2 FX: ZUUUUU [clearing smoke]

538.3 FX: ZUZUZU ZUZU [rumbling]

539.3 FX: BA [explosive energy]

540.1 FX: DOO [collapsing]
540.4 FX: ZA [sudden appearance]

541.2 FX: ZUZU [rumbling]
541.5 FX: ZUZU [rumbling]
541.6 FX: ZUZUZUZU [rumbling]

542.2 FX: ZUZUZU [rumbling]

543.2 FX: ZUZU [rumbling]

544.1 FX: DOOOON [crashing]

546.1 FX: DO [energy]
546.2 FX: BA [attack]

FINAL CHAPTER
EVERLASTING WO AI NI

551.1 FX: DOOOOO [fiery explosion]

558.1 FX: BA [explosion]

560.1 FX: KA [flash]

561.2 FX: UOOOOOO [great energy]

562.2 FX: KA [flash]
562.4 FX: BOO [burning]

567.4 FX: ZAWA ZAWA [crowd noise]

568.1 FX: DOKUN DOKUN DOKUN DOKUN DOKUN [heartbeats]

CHINESE-TO-JAPANESE GLOSSARY

The Universe of the Four Gods is based on ancient China, but Japanese pronunciation of Chinese names differs slightly from their Chinese equivalents.

Chinese	Japanese	Person, Place, or Object	Meaning
Xong Gui-Siu	Sô Kishuku	Tamahome	Demon Constellation
Hong-Nan	Konan	Southern Kingdom	Crimson South
Gong Wu	Kyûbu	Clue	Palace Strength
Tai Yi-Jun	Tai Itsukun	Oracle	Preeminent Person
Kang-Lin	Kôrin	Lady of Hong-Nan	Peaceful Jewel
Daichi-San	Daikyokuzan	Mountain	Greatest Mountain
Lai Lai	Nyan Nyan	Helper(s)	Daughters
Qu-Dong	Kûto	Eastern Kingdom	Gathered East
Zhong-Rong	Chûei	Second Son	Loyalty, Honor
Chun-Jing	Shunkei	Third Son	Spring, Respect
Yu-Lun	Gyokuran	Eldest Daughter	Jewel, Orchid
Jie-Lian	Yuiren	Youngest Daughter	Connection, Lotus
Shou-Shuang	Jusô	Province	Lasting Frost
Ligé-San	Reikakuzan	Mountain	Strength Tower
Knei-Gong	Kôji	Bandit	Young Victor
Rui-Nei	Eiken	Bandit	Imperial Likeness
Huan-Lang	Genrô	Bandit Leader	Phantom Wolf
Changhung	Chôkô	Northern Town	Expansive Place
Shao-Huan	Shôka	Mystical Person	Small Flower
Miao Nioh-An	Myo Ju-An	Hermit	Miracle Peaceful Life
Diedu	Kodoku	Potion	Seduction Potion
He-Yan	Waen	Palace Room	Eternal Peace
Bei-Jia	Hokkan	Northern Kingdom	Armored North
Wong Tao-Hui	Ôdokun	Chinese Name	King Bright Path

Chinese	Japanese	Person, Place, or Object	Meaning
K'o-Ju	Kakyo	Bureaucracy Exam	Departmental Trial
Hsing-Shin	Shôshi	Second Exam	Ministry Test
Shentso-Pao	Shinzahô	Treasure	God's Seat Jewel
Ming-Ho	Meiga	Canal	Signature Stream
Liu-Chuan	Ryûen	Nuriko's Given Name	Willowy Beauty
Nucheng-Kuo	Nyosei-koku	Island Kingdom	Woman Fort Country
Hua-Wan	Kaen	Woman	Flowery Grace
Dou	To	Tribe	A Measure
Tomolu	Tomoru	Elder	Earth Silent Duty
Teniao-Lan	Touran	City	Unique Crow Orchid
Xi-Lang	Sairô	Western Kingdom	West Tower
Feng-Qi	Hôki	Hotohori's Bride	Rare Phoenix
Shi-Hang Lian	Shigyo Ren	Transfer Student	Worship-Journey Collect
Shun-Yu	Jun'u	Tasuki	Handsome Home
Yang	Yô	Monster	Illness
Ai-Tong	Aidô	Tasuki's sister	Love Eyes
Mang-Chen	Bôshin	Crown Prince	Spreading Dawn
Po-Leiwu	Hakuraibu	Technique	Body Puppet Dance
Lian-Fang	Renhô	Yang Monster	Retreat, Virtue
Lu-Hou	Rokô	Nuriko's Brother	Backbone Lord
Mei-Song	Miisû	Monster	Collect Beauty
Rong-Yang	Eiyô	Capital	Glorious Heaven
Hang-gui Fei-gao	Kanki Hikô	Tenko's Servant	Drought Spirit Fly Shore
Jia-Pao	Kahô	Village	Add Cloak
Fang-Zhun	Hôjun	Chichiri's Name	Fragrant Accordance
Yong-Shua	Yôsui	Tenko's Servant	Evil Commander
Tao-Hui	Dôkun	Chiriko's Name	Bright Path

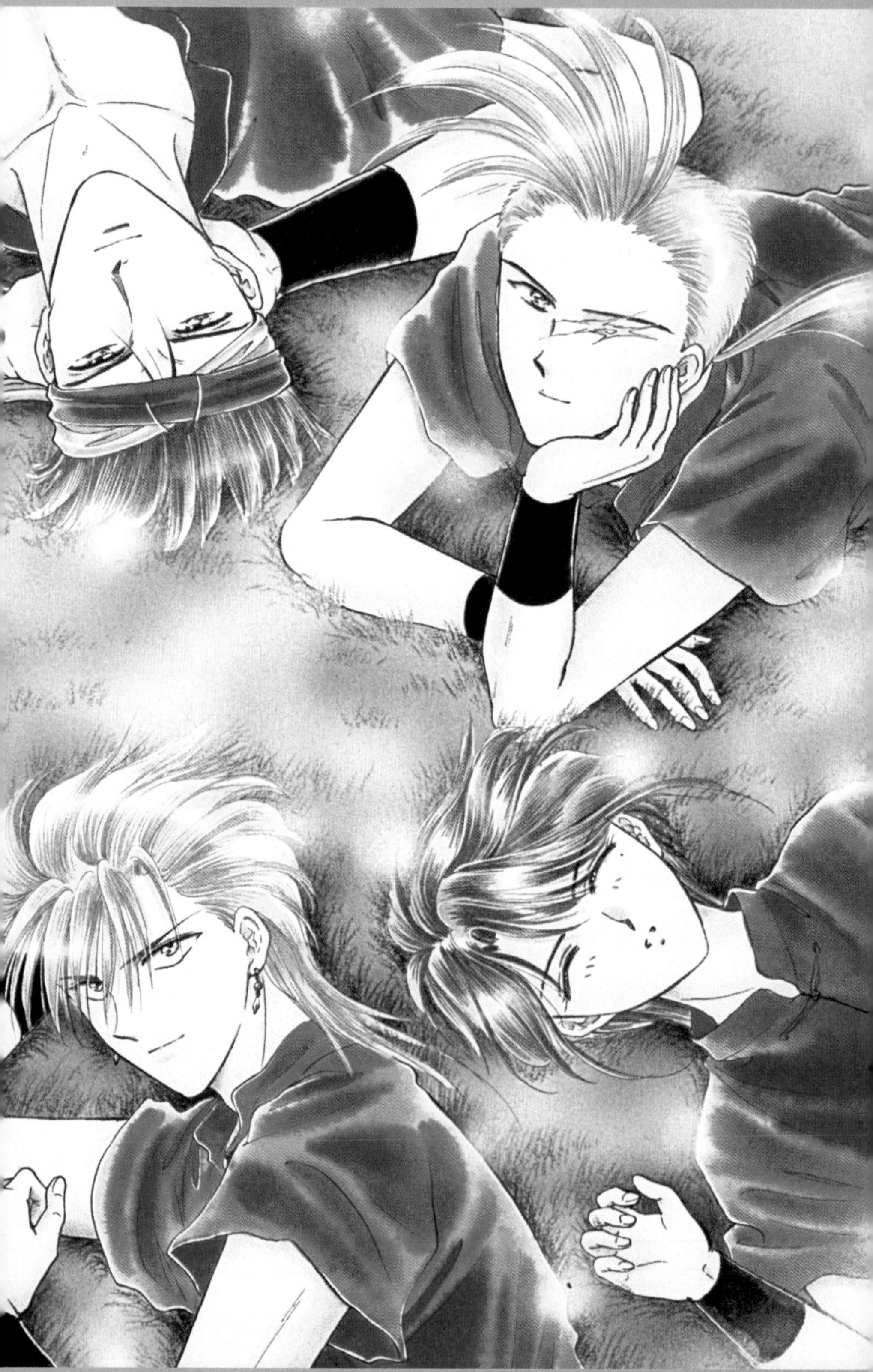

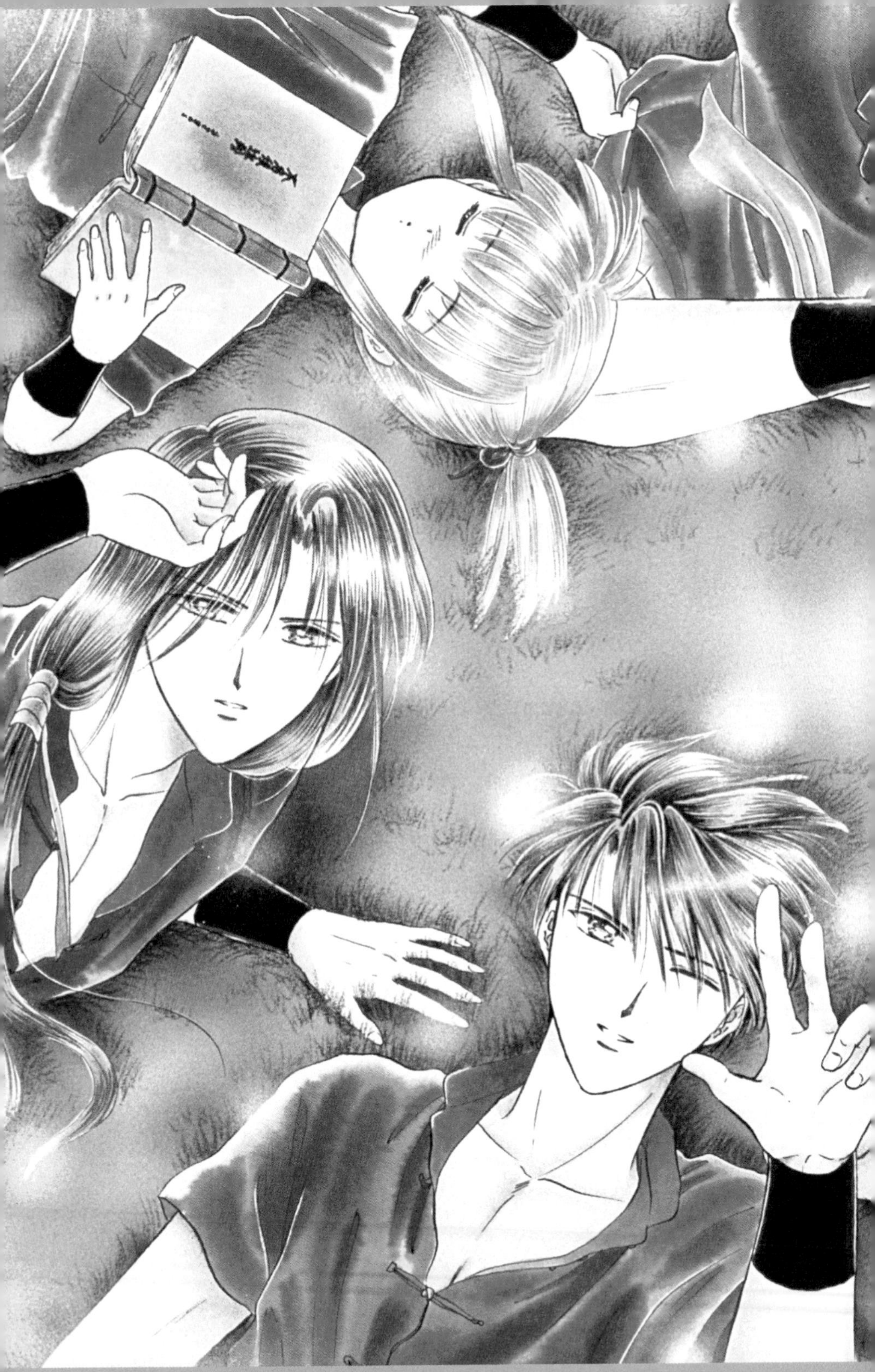

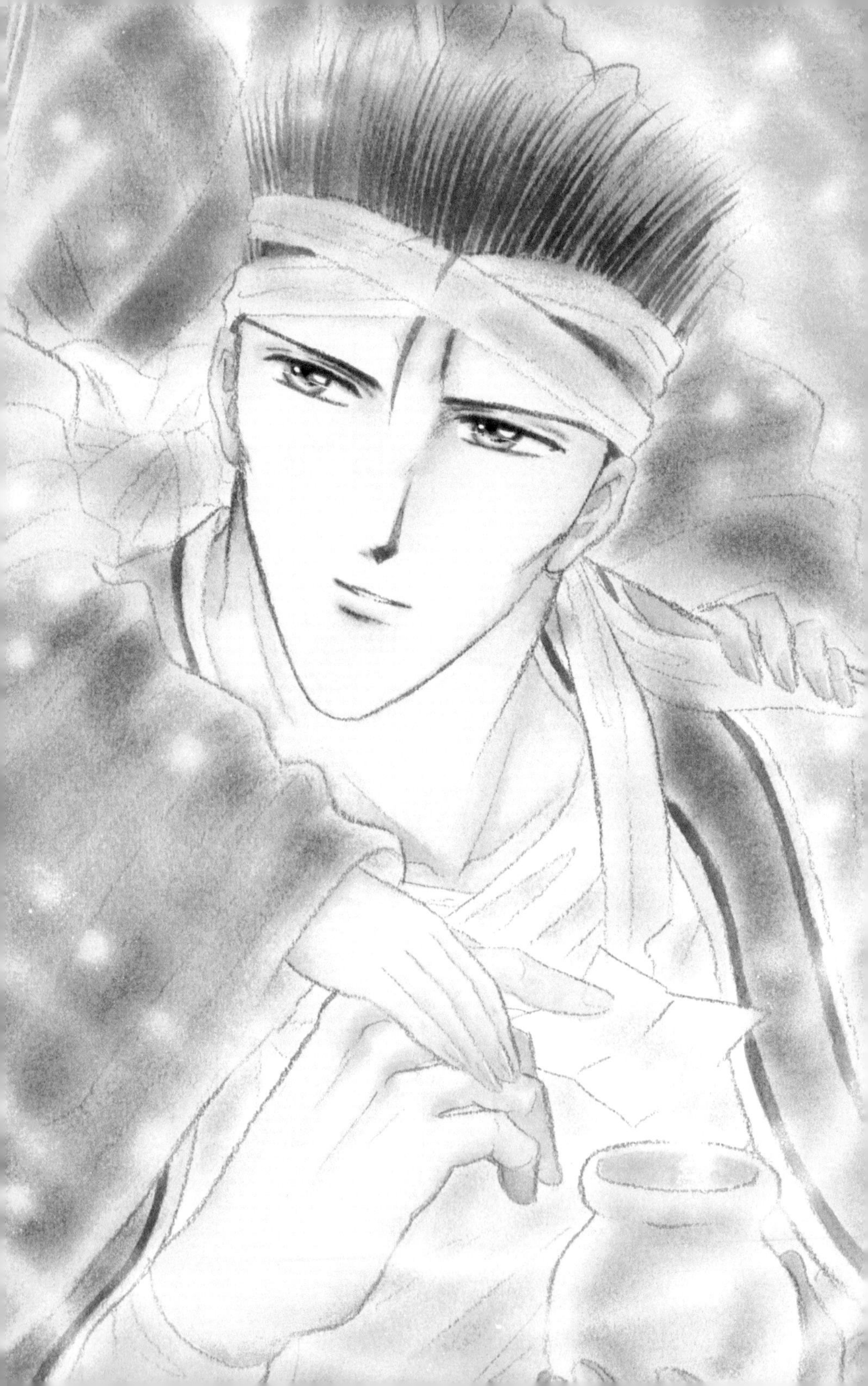

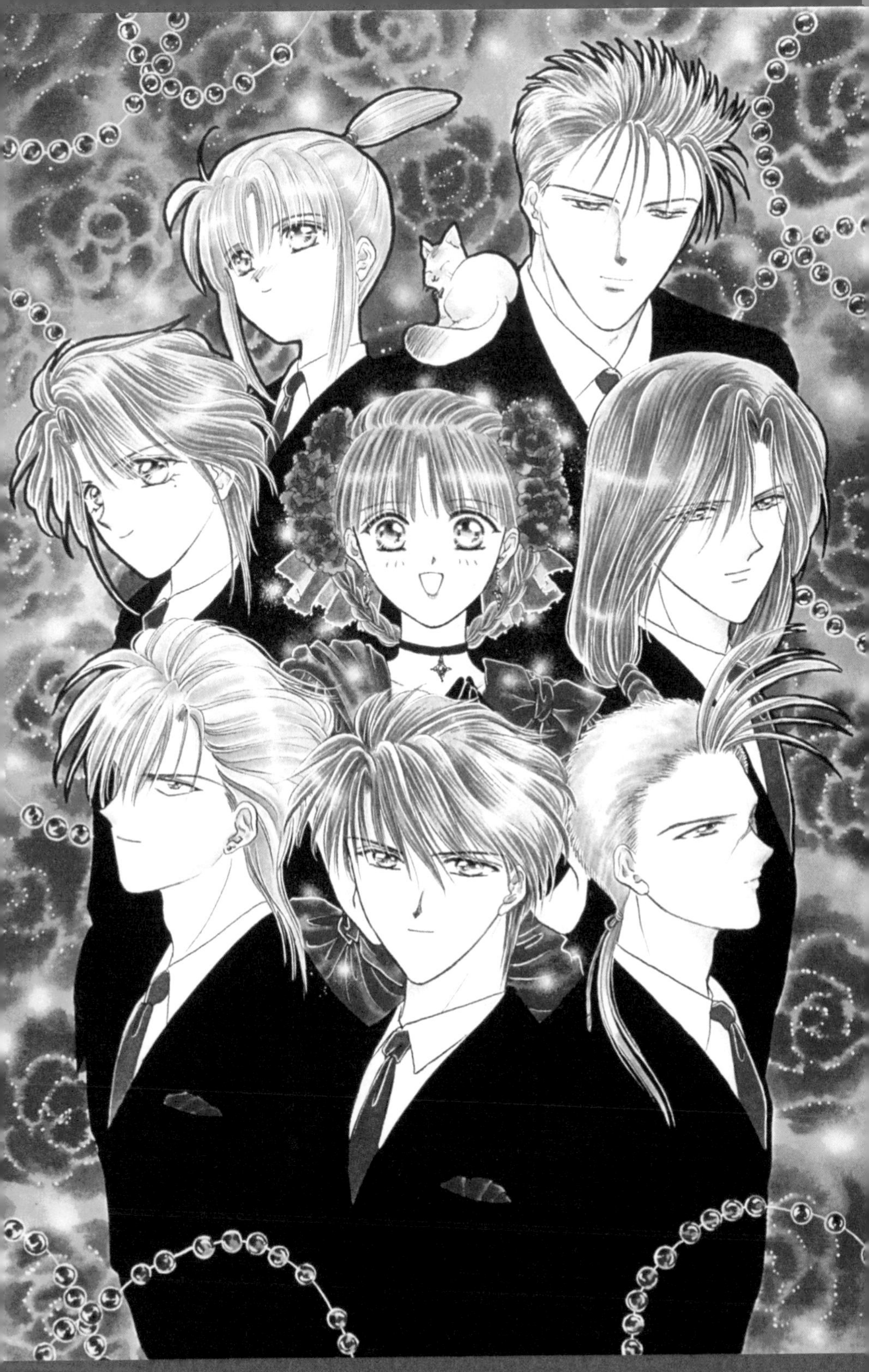

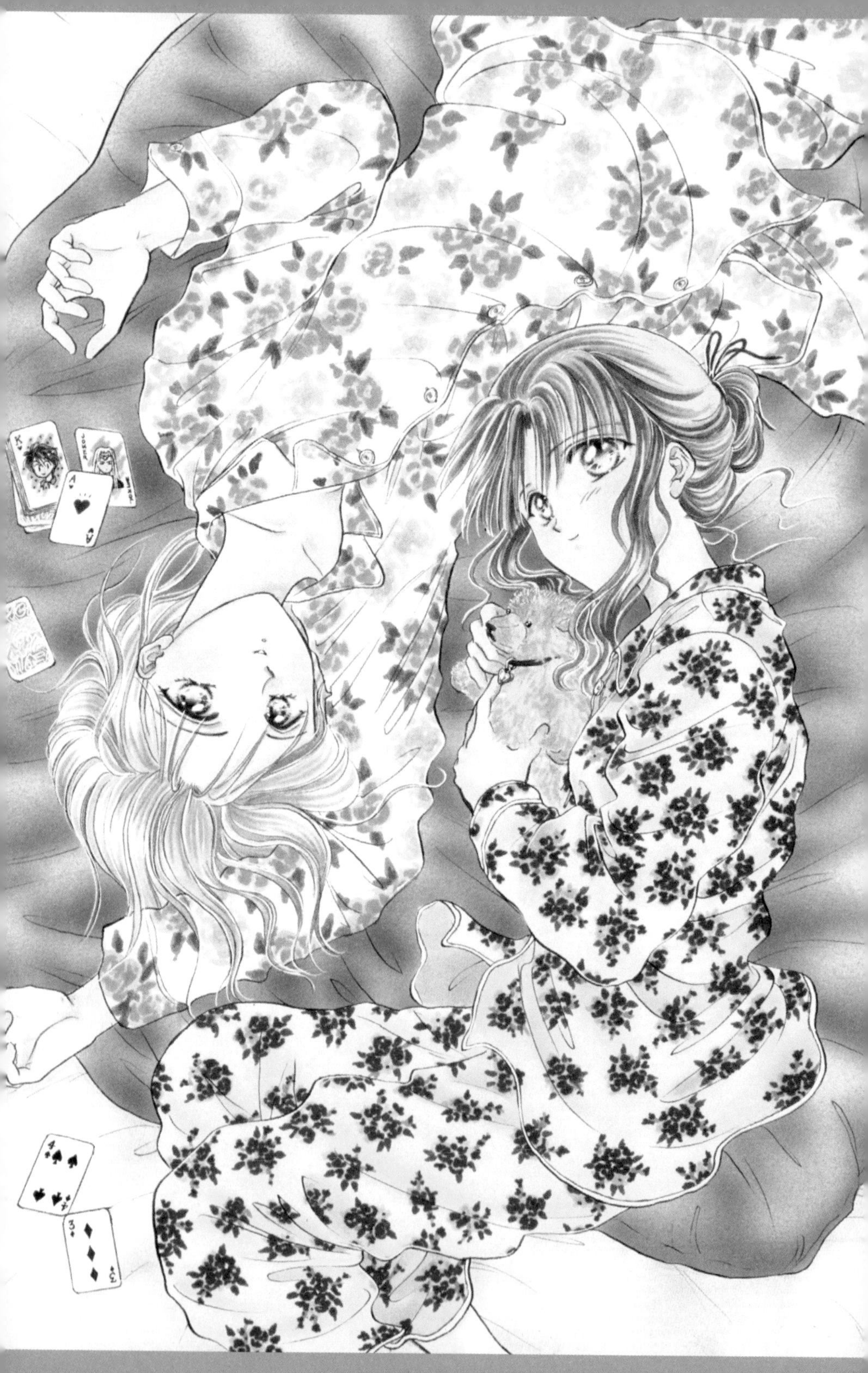

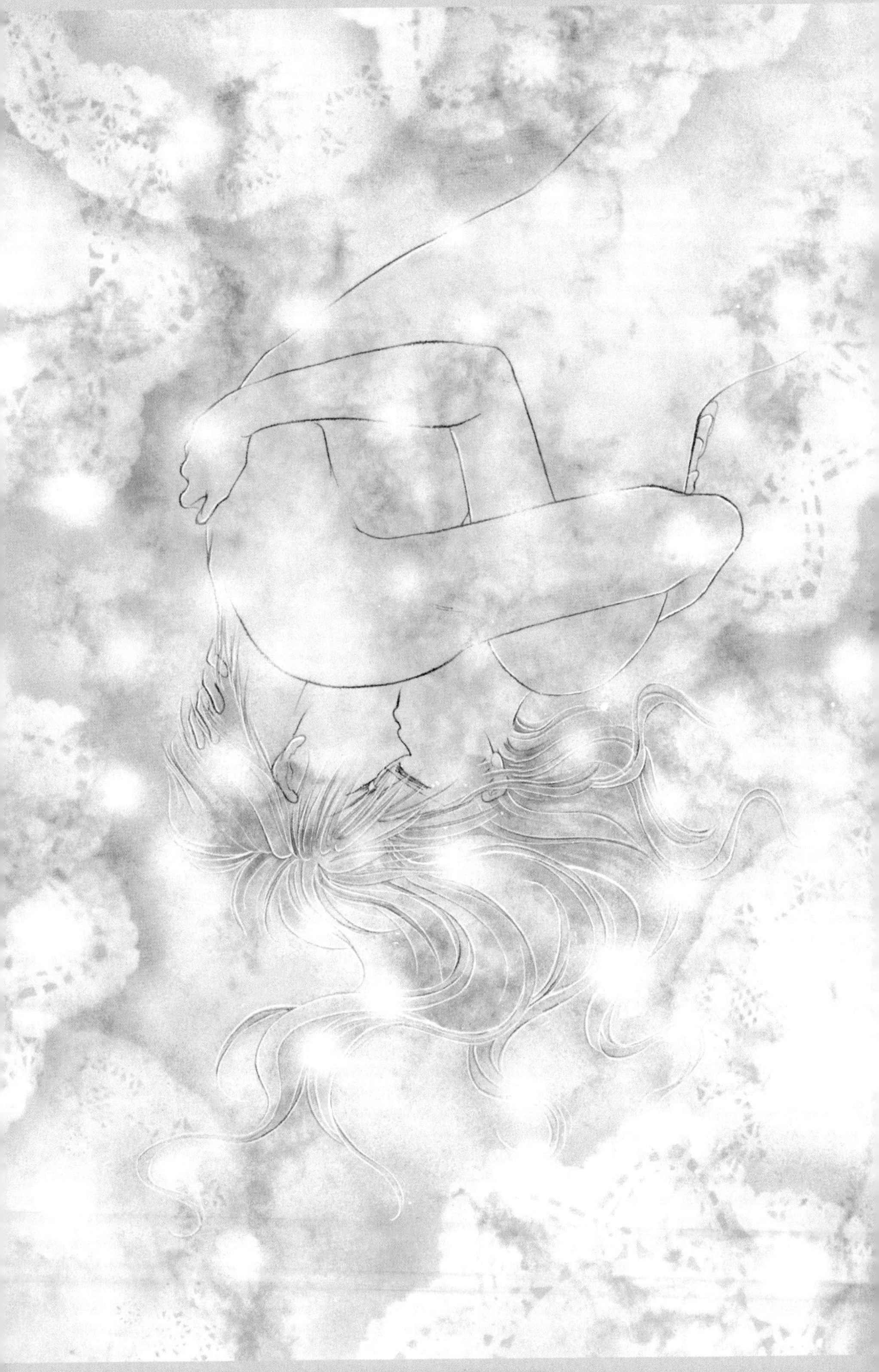

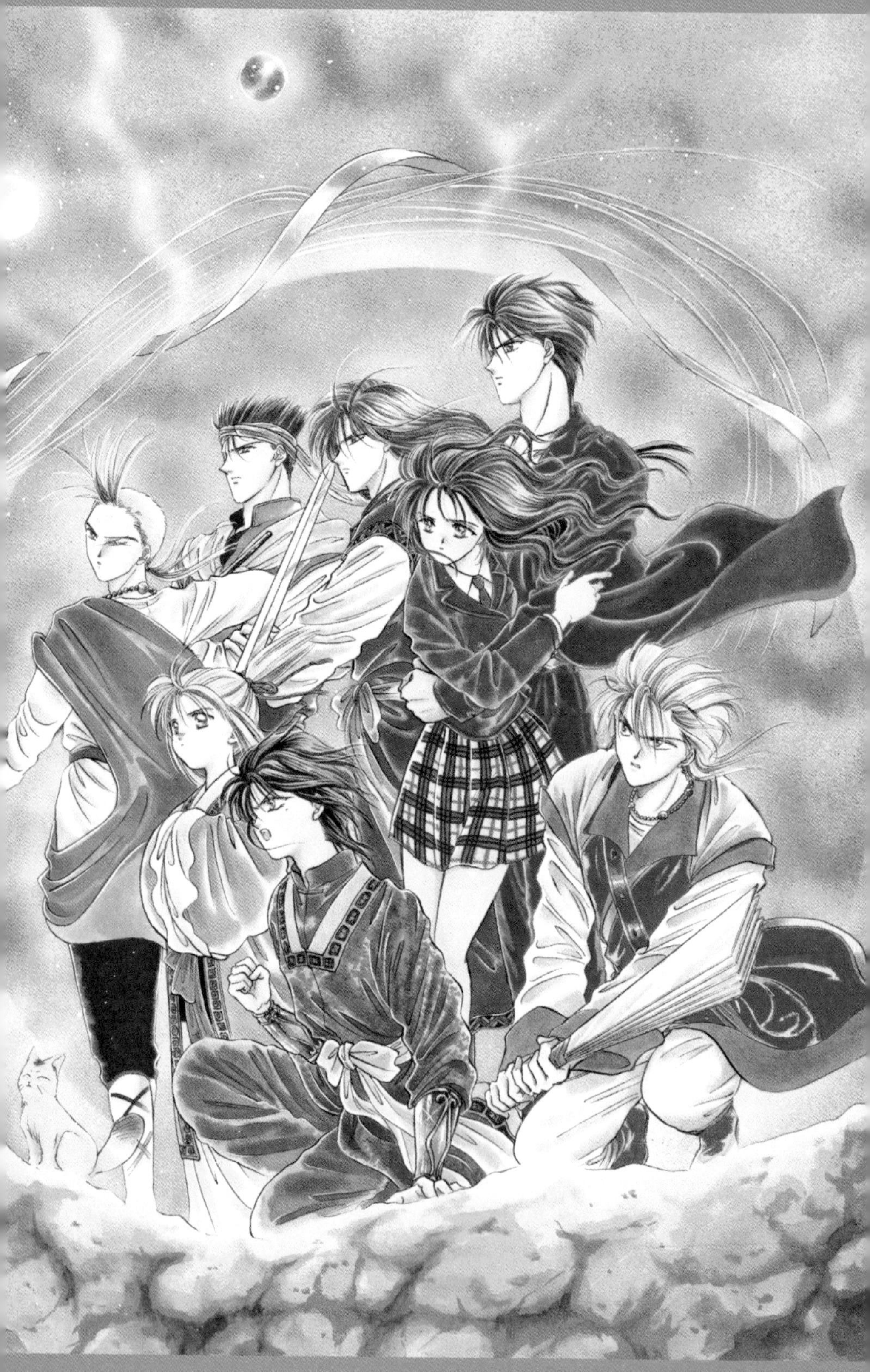

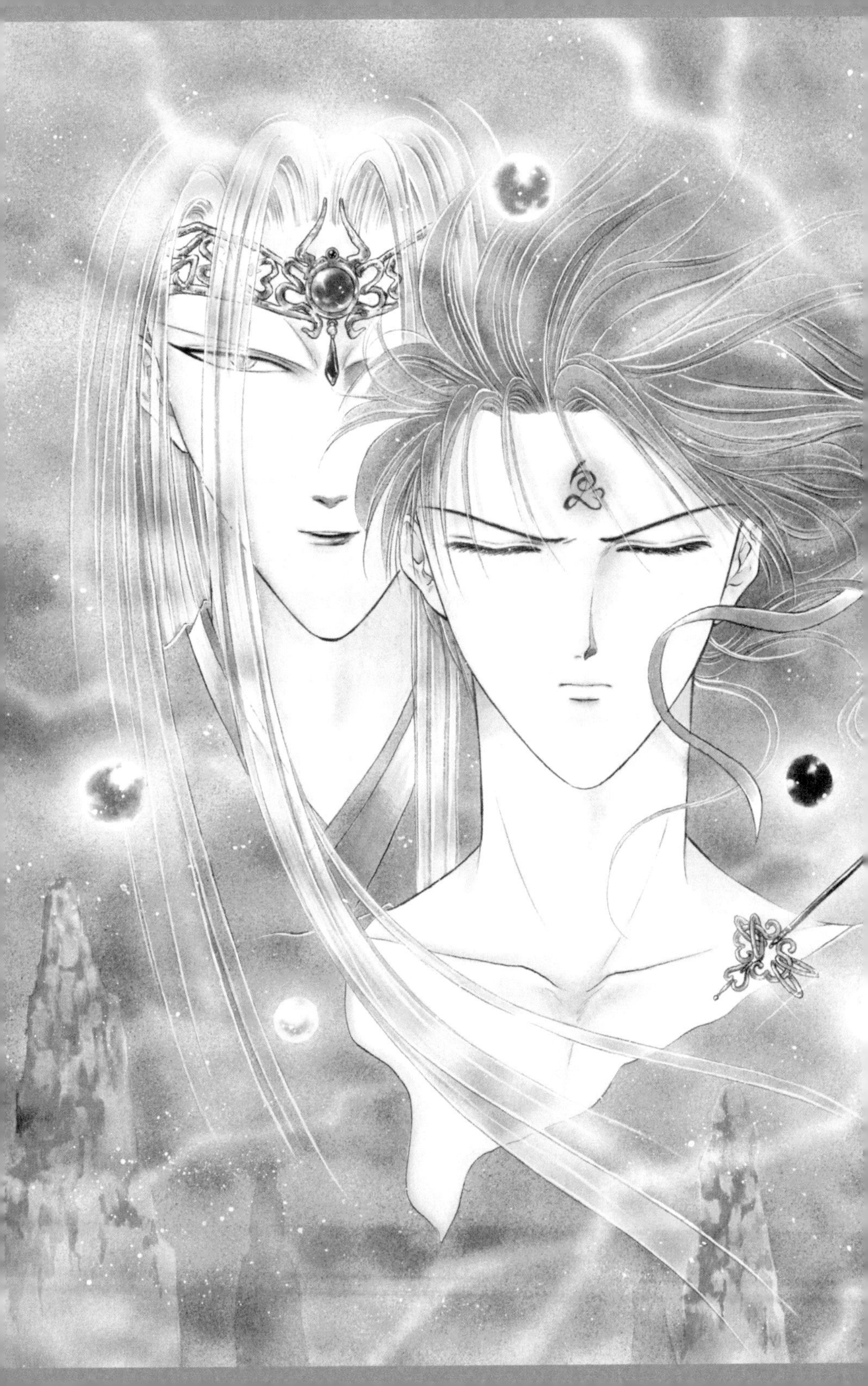

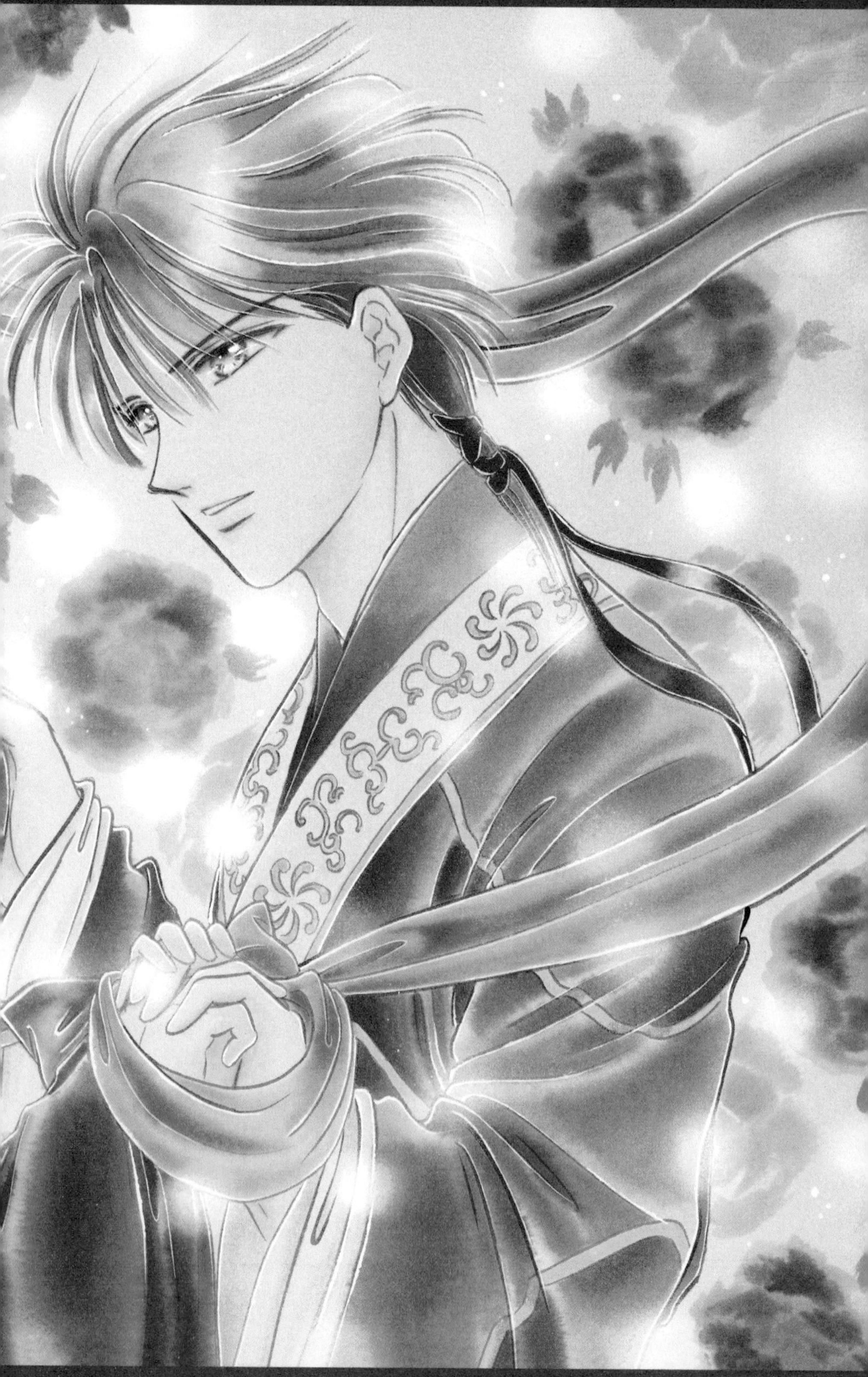

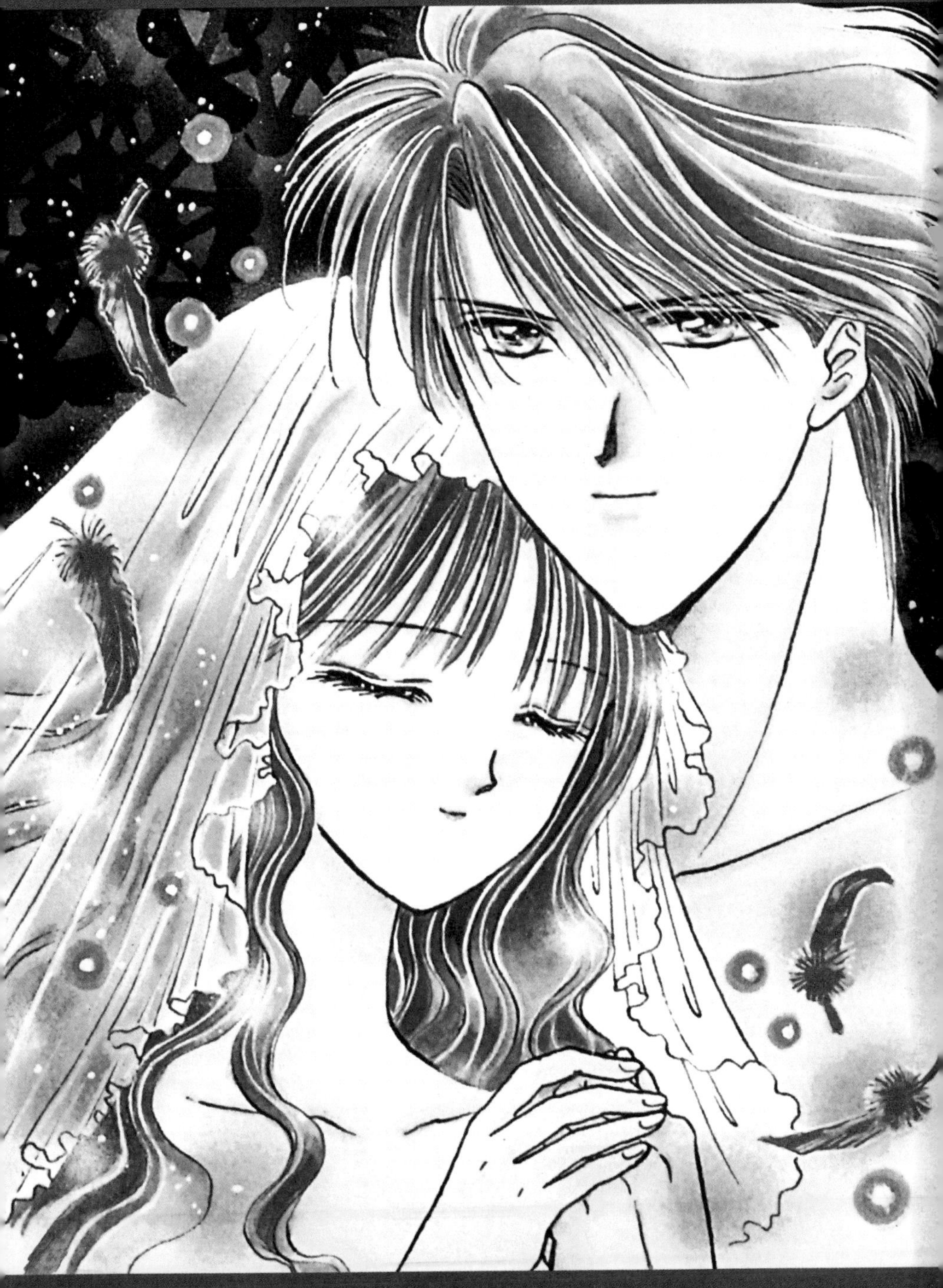

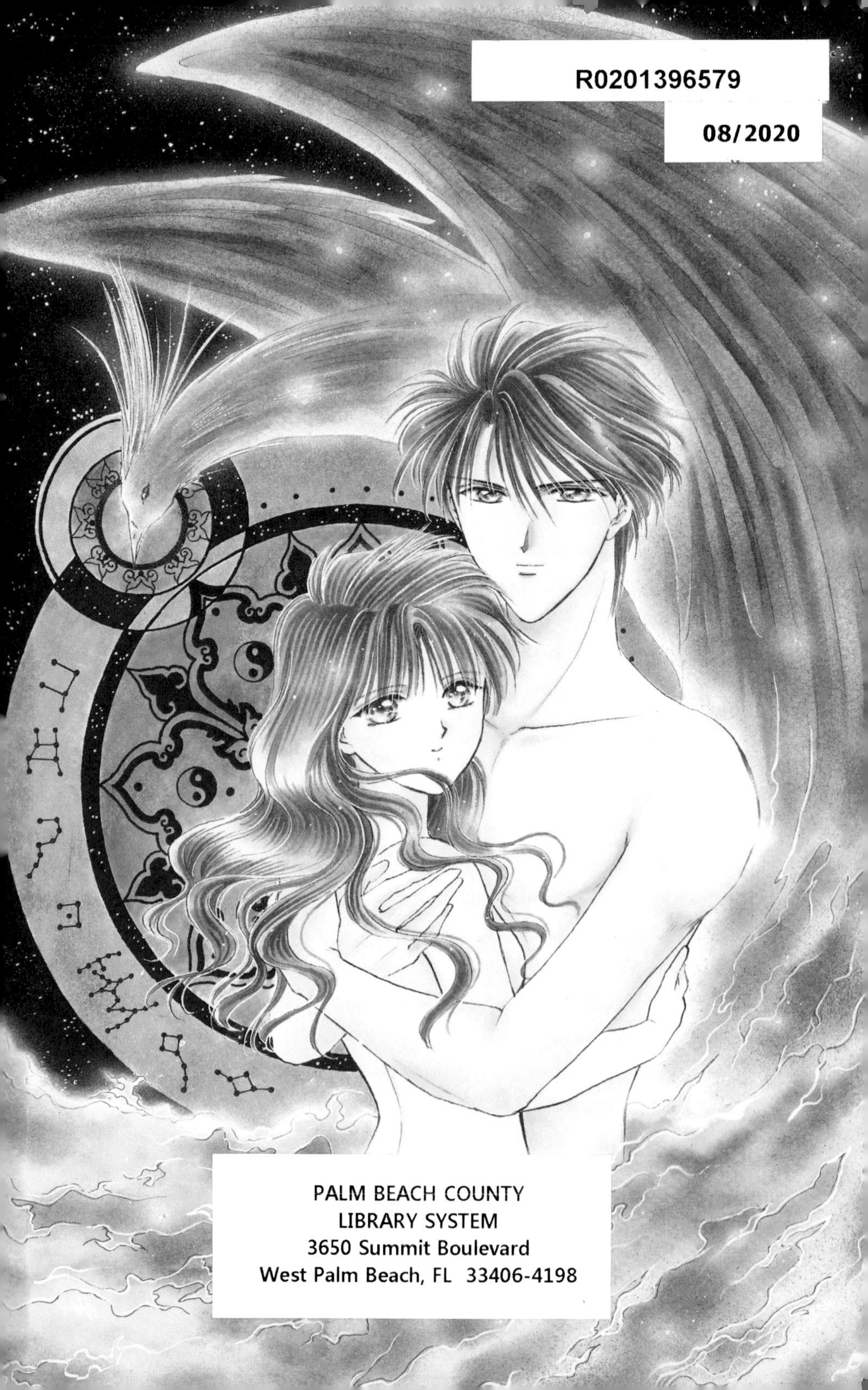